Japan

Guide Bleu

Japan

PRENTICE HALL

NEW YORK

Published by Prentice Hall Trade Division
A division of Simon & Schuster, Inc.
1 Gulf + Western Plaza
New York, New York 10023

Originally published in France by Hachette Guides Bleus 1984
Copyright © 1984 by Hachette Guides Bleus

Maps © Hachette 1989

English translation copyright © 1989 Harrap Books Ltd

Published in Great Britain by Harrap Books Ltd 1989

First American Edition 1989

Production by Book Production Consultants Ltd, Cambridge, UK

Phototypeset by Witwell Ltd, Southport, UK

Printed and bound in UK by Richard Clay & Co., Bungay, Suffolk.

While every care has been taken in the compilation of this guide,
the publishers cannot be held responsible for any changes to the
information listed.

Library of Congress Cataloguing-in-Publication Data
Modot, Jean.
  Japan.

  (Les Guides bleus)
  Translation of: Japon.
  Bibliography: p.800
  Includes index.
    1. Japan–Description and travel–1945   Guide books
  I. Pezeu-Massabuau, Jacques.   II. Daudé, Evelyne.
  III. Lannois, Philippe.   IV. Title.   V. Series.
DS805.2.M6313   1989   915.2'0448   86-527
ISBN 0-13-509027-X

Contents

Preface

Japan is best approached as a stranger whom you'd like to know better. It's vital to shed all your preconceptions, which in any case are often mistaken, so as to be receptive to all the surprises this new acquaintance has in store for you. On the other hand, the individual qualities of the Japanese, and their thirst for knowledge – especially among the young – make possible a direct mutual understanding across cultural barriers. It has been rightly said that Japanese civilization, which on first acquaintance seems chaotic and many-faceted – opposites attracting rather than repelling, and feelings themselves forming a complex harmony – is such that all opinions formed of it are neither wholly true nor wholly false.

Although we are aware that this guide can offer you only an incomplete and selective image of Japan – far different from the one you'll be bringing back from your travels – we have sought to make it as objective and as accessible as possible. In adopting an alphabetical structure, which we have found most suitable for the practical use of the Western traveller, we have had to make a choice of Japanese cities which in the opinion of the Japanese themselves offer the tourist either particular attractions or else a particularly representative view of the country's modern urbanization and socio-economic life. For each locality described, we have included information of practical value, placing the stress – in accordance with the policy of all the *Guides Bleus* – on cultural and artistic features. The main activities and industries of each region have also been briefly touched upon. Finally, we have tried our best to give some idea of the location of the various sites you might wish to visit by giving details of their distances apart (often considerable), their position in relation to the nearest station or other landmark, and lastly by suggesting how to get there.

The difficulties of finding your way in Japan (lack of street names, notices all in Japanese, the rapidly changing face of the city) led us to place a heavy reliance on maps, giving a number of street plans for the larger cities such as Tokyo, Osaka and Kyoto and including maps of Tohoku and Shikoku, places for which it might otherwise prove difficult to get information in English.

Under the title 'Getting to know Japan', we have assembled a concise portrait of some 30 pages which, we hope, will serve as an introduction to the Japanese world. If you encounter many names which look strange at first glance, they will be repeated often enough in the course of the book to allow you, we are sure, to feel at home with them before long. Finally, we hope that this second edition will allow you to enjoy even more, no matter what the length of your proposed stay, this Japanese world whose way of life – particularly on account of the language barrier – occasionally proves extremely confusing to the Western visitor. But once you have made the necessary effort, you will discover a country never less than amazing, a country whose magic will have a lingering effect long after you have left it.

MAPS AND PLANS

Maps

Plans

How to use this guide

The guide is divided into four parts:

Journey to Japan

Here you will find all general practical information needed to prepare for and plan your trip. The section is divided into several chapters:

YOUR JOURNEY - this gives information on the best times to go to Japan, the formalities involved, how to get there, what packages are available, transport in Japan (pp. 17–33);

YOUR STAY IN JAPAN — you will find everything you need to know about accommodation, restaurants, Japanese food, everyday life in Japan (currency, shopping, opening times, etc.) as well as a glossary of useful Japanese phrases (pp. 34–62);

THE TOURIST'S JAPAN — will help you plan your holiday with the help of maps of 'Natural resources', 'Places of Interest', as well as 'Suggested itineraries' (pp. 63–79)

Getting to know Japan

You will find on pp. 83–112 a series of introductions to various aspects of Japanese civilization.

Visiting Japan

This alphabetically ordered guide section, from pp. 113 to 679, describes towns, sites and monuments.

Useful information index

To locate a place name, choose a hotel or restaurant, find out about the main events and festivities where you are staying; you can turn to this alphabetical list of places referred to in the guide section (pp. 681–800).

Classification of places and items of interest
Sites, buildings, museums, works of art, documents

These are classified according to two criteria:
- Their place in a 'hierarchy of merit', drawn up as objectively as possible:

*noteworthy	***of exceptional interest
**of great interest	★remarkable, unusual, of outstanding interest

- The location, by means of symbols, of the most important places and items of interest along each route.

Symbols

A list of the symbols to be found in the margin of the text follows. The same ones are used in all the Guides in this series, so they do not all necessarily appear in this particular book.

They are extremely simple in design, and most of them are generally understood. They will enable the reader to locate at a glance the places and items of interest along any route or in any district. They can also help in planning stops or excursions to the places or buildings of the greatest interest.

The type of itinerary is clearly signposted. For example, a succession of black index fingers ☛ indicates the main itinerary and, by making it easier to read the corresponding text, enables the reader in a hurry to concentrate on information of interest to him in the description of the route he is going to follow.

Signposting of the itineraries

☛ Main itinerary

☞ Alternative or secondary itinerary

↦ Detour from a main or secondary itinerary to a place or building of special interest

Other symbols

� Panorama, viewpoint

▌ Place of great
▬ historic interest

☼	Site or building in exceptional setting	🏰	Castle, fortification, ramparts
👁	Unusual sight or feature	⁂	Ruin, archeological site
☐	Civic building of interest	☯	Tao monuments and shrines
◼	Museum	👫	Regular events, e.g. markets, religious and folk festivals
✎	Literary information or anecdote		
✗	Work of art or document of such exceptional interest that it alone makes the museum or building worth visiting	🔬	Arts and crafts
		⚕	Thermal spring
		≋	Seaside resort, beach
♪	Musical information or anecdote	🌲	Forest, park, wooded area
✝	Church, abbey	🌴	Palm grove, oasis
✙	Wayside cross	🥾	Walk
☪	Islamic mosque or monument	▲	Recommended mountain excursion
☸	Hindu monuments and shrines	Z	Winter sports resort
◉	Buddhist monuments and shrines	🦩	Zoological gardens, nature reserve
⛩	Shinto monuments and shrines	🐟	Fishing
			Hunting

Abbreviations

alt.	altitude	**Bd**	boulevard
ANA	All Nippon Airways	**bldg**	building
Apr.	April	**c.**	circa/century
approx.	approximately	**cm**	centimetre
arch.	architect	**cuis.**	cuisine
Aug.	August	**d.**	died
Ave	avenue	**Dec.**	December

E	East	**mm**	millimetre
Feb.	February	**min.**	minute
Fri.	Friday	**Mon.**	Monday
ft	feet	**N**	North
h.	hour/s	**Nov.**	November
ha	hectare/s	**Oct.**	October
hab.	inhabitants	**p./pp**	page/s
in.	inch/es	**Pl.**	place/plan
it.	itinerary	**pop.**	population
JAL	Japan Air Lines	**r.**	right
Jan.	January	**rm/s**	room/s
Jap.	Japanese	**S**	South
JNR	Japan National Railways	**Sat.**	Saturday
JNTO	Japan National Tourist Organization	**Sept.**	September
		sq. (ml/ft)	square (mile/foot)
JTB	Japan Travel Bureau	**Sun.**	Sunday
Ju.	June	**t**	ton
Jul.	July	**TDA**	Toa Domestic Airlines
kg	kilogram	**Thurs.**	Thursday
km	kilometre	**Tues.**	Tuesday
kWh	Kilowatt-hour	**V**	see
l.	left	**vol.**	volume
m	metre/s	**W**	West
Mar.	March	**Wed.**	Wednesday
ml/s	mile/s	**yd/s**	yard/s

Journey to Japan

Your journey

When to go?

There are many surprising aspects to Japan, not least of which is the fact that the best time to travel there is the 'late season'. In autumn and winter there is a clarity in the atmosphere which lends great brilliance to the lush vegetation, while the temperature remains mild – except for the first two months of the year – throughout most of the archipelago. The summer is never excessively hot, but the high degree of humidity in the air makes it hard to tolerate. In the 'rainy season' – mid-June to mid-July – the rains sweep up from the more southerly islands towards Hokkaido, closely followed by typhoons whose effect, worsened by the aftermath of Asian monsoons, can be felt until September: the vegetation in summer is a riot of the most vivid and various shades of green.

Nevertheless, you can visit Japan all year round, provided that you adapt to variations in climate and landscape. During the winter the islands rarely escape snowfall, especially frequent from December to March on the western half of Honshu, which faces the Sea of Japan. On the highest peaks of the main island the snow is abundant enough to allow winter sports. Tokyo registers an average of 38.7°F (3.7°C) in January, while Hokkaido may experience lows of some -4°F (-20°C) in Asahikawa. However, winter is soon beaten back by an early spring: in February, the first plum blossom is already appearing; until the end of April in some regions, the cherry trees flower. The traditional image of a Japan covered in spring flowers is attractive but fleeting: a flower report is issued at this time, indicating the main flowering sites and giving the dates on which the blooms are expected to be at their best.

From spring until the end of autumn the temperature is generally moderate to hot, depending on the latitude, permitting bathing in the sea all along the archipelago as far as the southern part of Hokkaido (especially in July and August). Just as the sun will occasionally break through in the rainy season, so the hottest months may be troubled with typhoons which sometimes cut all communication links with the most southerly islands (including the Ryukyus): but this is the best time to go to Hokkaido. And then the mild and sunny Japanese autumn returns.

NB: The Japanese are great travellers all year round, so make sure you book your tour in advance and try to avoid public holidays and school/university breaks (in March and July-August); during these times all the main tourist spots in the country are very crowded.

Major events. There are so many good reasons to go to Japan that you don't have to choose your dates solely according to weather conditions: once you're there, you may decide to go on a trip or pay a visit to a temple in order to see religious or cultural events. Hardly a day goes by without a festival taking place somewhere: processions of carts and litters, costumed parades, traditional rituals and fireworks bringing extra colour to the towns.

Certain festivals are celebrated on fixed dates throughout the Japanese world. These are as follows:

JANUARY 1: *New Year,* the festival *par excellence,* when people go to worship in shrines with family and friends.

FEBRUARY 3 OR 4: *Setsubun,* marking the end of winter on the lunar calendar.

MARCH 3: *Hina Matsuri,* festival of dolls: dressed in ancient costume, the dolls are given to little girls or used to decorate houses.

END OF MARCH: *Higan* week, prayers in the temples in memory of the departed.

APRIL 8: *Hana Matsuri,* festival of flowers, coinciding with the birthday of the Buddha.

MAY 5: *Shobu no Sekku,* festival of children, who receive gifts: kites, in the shape of multicoloured carp, are set up on long poles at the entrance to the houses.

JULY 7: *Tanabata,* festival of the stars (Vega and Altair, in the Milky Way), in the hope of a good harvest.

AUGUST 13—15: *O Bon Matsuri,* Buddhist festival in honour of the dead, in which the family home is made ready to receive them.

NOVEMBER 15: *Shichi-go-san* (7-5-3), in honour of children aged seven, five and three.

We should also mention the national festivals: January 1, New Year; January 15, festival of adults; February 11, day to commemorate the Creation of the Nation; March 21 or 22, Vernal Equinox; April 29, the Emperor's birthday; May 3, Constitution Day; May 5, Children's Day (these three days make up the golden week which is an almost universal public holiday); September 15, Day of Respect for Elders; September 23 or 24, Autumnal Equinox; October 10, Day of Health and Sport; November 3, Culture Day; November 23, festival of work.

We indicate, in the tables of general information on various localities and descriptions of temples and shrines, those festivals which take place in specific places.

NB: The Japanese write dates in Western style or, in place of the year AD, they put the year of the current imperial epoch. Hence 1987 corresponds to the year 62 of the current Showa period.

The following table is a list of the finest local festivals. It is a wise precaution, for festivals which attract large crowds, to reserve seats, unless you are happy just to follow some of the processions through the streets. You may obtain details in the Japanese tourist offices in Tokyo and Kyoto, including the exact dates of the events, which may vary from year to year.

Place	Date	Event
Tokyo	January 6	*Dezome Shiki*: firemen's parade at Ginza
Akita	January 17	*Bonten*: decorated poles (*bonten*) are carried to the shrine
Sapporo	end January–early February	*Snow Festival*
Tokyo	April	*Azuma Odori*: dance of the cherries at the Shimbashi Embu-jo theatre
Kyoto	April	*Miyako Odori*: dance of the cherries at the Pontocho Kaburen-jo theatre
Takayama	between April 14 and 17	*Sanno Matsuri*: at the Hie shrine: procession of floats
Kyoto	May 15	*Aoi Matsuri*: festival of the Shimogamo and Kamigamo shrines
Nikko	May 17–18	*Great Festival of Tosho-gu*: procession of a thousand people in costume
Kyoto	3rd Sunday in May	*Mifune Matsuri*: boat festival at Arashiyama
Morioka	June 15	*Chagu Chagu Umakko*: horse festival at the Sozen shrine
Fukuoka	July 1–15	*Hakata Yamagasa*: cart procession
Nachi-Katsuura	July 14	*Nachi Himatsuri*: festival of fire
Kyoto	July 16–17	*Gion Matsuri*: at the Yasaka shrine: procession of floats
Miyajima	mid-July	*Kagensaï*: festival of music, procession of sacred boats
Hirosaki	August 1–7	*Nebuta Matsuri*: night-time processions of huge papier-mâché effigies
Aomori	August 3–7	
Akita	August 5–7	*Kanto Matsuri*: tall poles hung with paper lanterns carried with great dexterity through the streets
Sendai	August 6–8	*Tanabata*: festival of stars, Sendai's finest
Tokushima	August 15–18	*Awa Odori*: procession of dancers and musicians

Okinawa	end of August	*Eisa*: local dance for the festival of Bon
Takayama	September 14–15	*Hachiman Matsuri*: procession of floats
Nagasaki	October 7–9	*Okunchi*: festival of Chinese origin, at the Suwa shrine
Himeji	October 14–15	*Kenka Matsuri*: festival of quarrels, procession of litters
Kyoto	October 22	*Jidai Matsuri*: parade in traditional costumes from all periods in history
Hakone	November 3	*Daimyo Gyoretsu*: procession of daimyo along the old Tokaido road

To this list may be added various other events such as the Sumo tournaments which are held in Tokyo, Osaka, Nagoya and Fukuoka in the course of the year, and various floral displays, especially those related to chrysanthemums, which take place in the autumn, etc.

How to get there

Some formalities

PASSPORTS. A valid passport is necessary for British and Commonwealth nationals as well as for US and Canadian citizens. No visa is required, except by US citizens, if the stay is to be less than ninety days.

NB: A visa is required for a trip of *any* duration which is not undertaken as a tourist.

A visitor wishing to extend his or her stay should apply to the Immigration Office in the nearest provincial capital at least ten days before the expiry of his permit. Such an extension is not automatically granted.

INFORMATION: Tokyo Immigration Office, 3-3-20, Konan, Minato-ku, Tokyo (*Tel.* 471–5111).

Osaka Immigration Office, 2-31, Tanimachi, Higashi-ku, Osaka (*Tel.* 941–0771).

VACCINATIONS. No vaccination is required at present, except for travellers arriving from infected areas.

Taking your dog or cat: the entry of domestic animals into Japan is subject to very strict controls. A certificate of anti-rabies vaccination (dated not more than a year and not less than a month previously) and a certificate of health (dated less than eight days previously) are necessary. On arrival in the country, an entry permit must be obtained from the veterinary service of the Ministry of Agriculture. This formality sometimes necessitates a period of quarantine (at the expense of the animal's owner).

The Ministry of Agriculture (2, Kasumigaseki 1-chome, Chiyoda-ku, Tokyo, *Tel.* 502-8111) has offices in the international airports at which the necessary steps can be taken on your arrival.

CUSTOMS. It is sufficient to make a verbal declaration at the Japanese border of personal effects, the value of which should not exceed 100,000 yen: you must make a written declaration if you enter at a port, or if you are importing unaccompanied luggage, which should arrive within 180 days of the arrival of the passenger. The entry of cars in transit poses no problem: you have only to obtain a 'transit voucher' validated by the Japan Automobile Federation (3-5-8, Shiba Park, Minato-ku, Tokyo, *Tel.* 501-1511), represented by Nippon Express in the ports of Yokohama and Kobe.

CURRENCY. The import and export of foreign currencies (or Japanese yen) are completely unrestricted. The export of more than 5 million yen must, however, be declared.

TOURIST INFORMATION

Japan National Tourist Organization (JNTO).
London: 167 Regent Street, W1 (*Tel.* (01) 734-9638).

New York: Rockefeller Plaza, 630 Fifth Avenue, NY 10111 (*Tel.* (212) 757-5640).

Tokyo: 6-6, Yuraku-cho 1-chome, J-100 (*Tel.* (03) 502-1461). Also in Chicago, Dallas, Honolulu, Los Angeles, San Francisco.

Travelling by plane

There are direct flights to the principal international Japanese airport of Tokyo-Narita (40mls/60km NE of the city centre) from London and other European airports as well as from N American airports. A frequent and regular international service is provided by 30 airlines operating from Narita airport: Air France, British Airways, Canadian Pacific Airways, Lufthansa German Airlines, United Airlines, Aeroflot Soviet Airlines, Air New Zealand, etc.

Japan Air Lines (JAL) also provides regular flights to and from Asian capital cities: Peking (Beijing), Seoul, Manila, Hong Kong, Bangkok, etc. Its sister company, Japan Asia Airways, also flies from Tokyo, Osaka and Naha (Okinawa) to the airports of Taipei and Kaohsiung (Taiwan) as well as Hong Kong.

INFORMATION AND BOOKINGS

Japan Air Lines (JAL).

International flights: Daini Tekko Bldg, 1-8-2, Marunouchi, Chiyo-daku, J-100 Tokyo (*Tel.* (03) 747-1111).

Domestic flights: 5-37-8, Shiba, Minato-ku, J-100 Tokyo (*Tel.* (03) 456-2111).

Offices in the United States

Los Angeles: 555 West Seventh St, CA 90014 (*Tel.* (213) 620-9580).

New York: JAL Bldg, 655 Fifth Ave, NY 10022 (*Tel.* (212) 838-4400).

San Francisco: Hotel Nikko San Francisco, 275 Ofarrell St 94102 (*Tel.* (415) 928-8141).

Washington: 1130 Connecticut Ave, NW, DC 20006 (*Tel.* (800) 525-3663).

Offices in the United Kingdom

London: 8 Hanover St, W1R ODR (*Tel.* (01) 408-1000), also in Birmingham, Glasgow, Manchester.

Japan Air Lines offer very economical plane + hotel packages.

NB: You will find addresses for other airlines in the Useful information section (pp. 681–800).

Travelling by boat

Air travel has almost eliminated sea crossings to Japan (they used to take more than a month). Now, apart from luxury cruises and a few cargo companies which accept the occasional passenger, there are only three ways of reaching Japan by sea, all from neighbouring countries:

FROM THE SOVIET UNION. Travel is in combination with the Trans-Siberian railway (see Travelling by train). Connections are operated between Nakhodka (east of Vladivostok) and Yokohama by the Soviet navigation company.

INFORMATION

From the Intourist bureau of your nearest major city or from Tokyo: Japan Soviet Tourist Bureau, Kamiyacho Bldg, 5-2-21, Toranomon, Minato-ku (*Tel.* 432-6161).

FROM SOUTH KOREA. There is a ferry service three times a week, from the Korean port of Pusan, which will get you to Shimono-seki in a few hours.

INFORMATION

Tokyo: Ginza Asahi Bldg, 3-8-10, Ginza, Chuo-ku (*Tel.* 567-0971).

FROM TAIWAN. There is now a regular link between Keelung (north of Taipei) and Naha (Okinawa), leaving Keelung every Sunday and Naha every Friday.

INFORMATION

Tokyo: Arimura Sangyo Co., Echo Kyobashi Bldg, 3-12-1, Kyobashi, Chuo-ku (*Tel.* 562-2091).

Travelling by train

This is a venture which is well within the bounds of possibility (simply go via Paris to Moscow, change to the Trans-Siberian Express, then take the boat from Nakhodka). But it is probably not the most economical or pleasant way to travel (crossing Siberia seems to take an age). The journey lasts about two weeks, but may be effectively shortened by taking a plane for certain stages of the Siberian section. Furthermore journey breaks in Moscow or Lake Baikal (in summer) certainly compensate for the monotonous stretches of this itinerary.

INFORMATION

You are best advised to seek details from Intourist.

Package holidays

Is the Far East really so inaccessible that the range of package holidays in Japan should be so restricted? Only a handful of travel agencies offer such trips, maximum two weeks, and even then often only as an extension of existing tours to Hong Kong or Bangkok. Admittedly, your travel budget for Japan will be considerable, and you should not expect a low-cost holiday even if you take advantage of cheaper charter flights. There's no sun worshipping, no Mediterranean-style lazing here. All too often Japan is a stopover point for a few brief hours in Tokyo or Kyoto, despite the delights to be found in the landscape, the culture and the Japanese people themselves. In such a situation there is little room for imagination; tour operators do their best, however, to offer the essentials in the shortest time possible, organizing guided tours and business trips to take advantage of principal fairs, conventions and events.

Among the various agencies offering tours, we recommend the following:

IN THE US

Maupintour, 408 E 50th St, New York, NY 10022.
American Express, American Express Plaza, New York, NY 10004.
Japan & Orient Tours, 250 E 1st St, Los Angeles, CA 90012.

IN THE UK

Bales Tours, Bales House, Barrington Rd, Dorking, Surrey.

Kuoni Travel Ltd, Kuoni House, Dorking, Surrey.

W.F. and R.K. Swan, 237 Tottenham Court Rd, London W1P OA1.

IN JAPAN

Organized trips might be the ideal solution for the businessman on a tight schedule, but they would not entirely suit the traveller with more time: Japanese tours are rigidly scheduled from start to finish and strictly run by charming uniformed guides who rely on the blasts of a whistle to organize coach manoeuvres and wave a coloured flag to reassemble their flocks: strictly for lovers of exotic behaviour patterns! Most tours are conducted in English, except in the smaller towns, where they may be in Japanese only.

Here are some of the main tour operators based in Tokyo:

Fuji Tours International, Ryuwa Bldg, 2-3-5, Yurakucho, Chiyoda-ku, Tokyo (*Tel.* 571-4811; telex J 26448).

Fujita Travel Service, 7-2-22, Ginza, Chuo-ku, Tokyo (*Tel.* 573-1011; telex J 22508).

Hankyu Express International, 3-3-9, Shimbashi, Minato-ku, Tokyo (*Tel.* 503-0211; telex 222-2565).

Japan Travel Bureau, 1-6-4, Marunouchi, Chiyoda-ku, Tokyo (*Tel.* 284-7026; telex J 24418).

Kinki Nippon Tourist Co., Kanda-Matsunagacho, Chiyoda-ku, Tokyo (*Tel.* 255-7111; telex 222-3131).

Meitetsu World Travel, Taiyo Bldg, 8-8-5, Ginza, Chuo-ku, Tokyo (*Tel.* 572-6371; telex 252-3952).

Mitsui Air & Sea Service, 1-16-4, Shimbashi, Minato-ku, Tokyo (*Tel.* 504-0271; telex J 28367).

Nippon Express, 3-12-9, Soto-Kanda, Chiyoda-ku, Tokyo (*Tel.* 253-1111; telex J 22610).

Nippon Travel Agency, Shimbashi-Ekimae Bldg, 2-20-15, Shimbashi, Minato-ku, Tokyo (*Tel.* 572-8181; telex 252-2355).

Seibu Travel, 1-16-15, Minami-Ikebukuro, Toshima-ku, Tokyo (*Tel.* 431-3745; telex J 26833).

Tobu Travel, Nichido-Yaesu Bldg, 3-4-12, Nihombashi, Chuo-ku, Tokyo (*Tel.* 272-1421; telex 222-4388).

Tokyo Tourist Corporation, Shibuya Chikatetsu Bldg, 1-16-14, Shibuya, Shibuya-ku, Tokyo (*Tel.* 407-0121; telex 222-4993).

Transport in Japan

It will only take you a few days in Japan to realize that, except for submarines, flying saucers and hot-air balloons, all imaginable kinds of public transport are in use. From tourist light aircraft to huge jets, from dinghies to ocean liners, from jolting streetcars to the Shinkansen trains, from litters (if you can find one still in use) to luxury coaches, not to mention funiculars and cablecars, all these services combine to bring regular daily transport to millions of people – over 15 million a day in the area covered by Tokyo's rail network alone.

Air links. Flights in the Japanese interior are run by three main companies: Japan Air Lines (JAL), All Nippon Airways (ANA), and TOA Domestic Airlines (TDA). Most international flights land at Narita, whereas internal flights tend to go from Haneda Airport, much closer to Tokyo. Nevertheless the Shinkansen remains the greatest rival to the airlines, avoiding the necessity to change planes and airports, and bringing the traveller right to the centre of town.

The aircraft used by the internal companies range from the Boeing 727 to the DC 10 and even the A-300 Airbus.

SOME TOWNS WITH AIR LINKS FROM TOKYO

Destination	Company	Flying time
Akita	TDA	1 h.
Fukuoka	JAL, ANA, TDA	1 h. 40
Hakodate	ANA, TDA	1 h. 25
Hiroshima	ANA	1 h. 25
Kagoshima	ANA, TDA	1 h. 45
Kumamoto	ANA, TDA	1 h. 40
Kushiro	ANA, TDA	1 h. 40
Matsuyama	ANA	1 h. 25
Misawa	TDA	1 h. 15
Miyazaki	ANA	1 h. 40
Nagasaki	ANA, TDA	1 h. 55
Nagoya	ANA	0 h. 50
Niigata	TDA	1 h. 40
Oita	ANA, TDA	1 h. 40
Okayama	ANA	2 h.
Okinawa	JAL, ANA	2 h. 30
Osaka	JAL, ANA	1 h.
Sapporo (Chitose)	JAL, ANA, TDA	1 h. 35
Sendai	ANA	0 h. 45
Takamatsu	ANA, TDA	2 h.

For all reservations and confirmations, contact in Tokyo: Japan Air Lines (*Tel.* 456–2111); All Nippon Airlines (*Tel.* 552–6311); TDA Domestic Airlines (*Tel.* 747–8111).

Sea links. Here again the ingenuity of island Japan is unrivalled: ocean liners, car ferries, hydroplanes, hovercraft – anything that can float and carry a few passengers is pressed into service, daily crossing the blue waters of the land of Madame Butterfly. An undersea tunnel links Kyushu with Honshu (and there are plans to do the same for Hokkaido and Honshu), but these islands, like Shikoku, already have permanent sea links with Honshu. So too do the minor islands, which often have additional links among themselves: even the most far-flung islands (the Ryukyu and Ogasawara groups) are included in the network. Passengers on these crossings often feel as if they are really on a cruise, and the sea, especially when whipped up by a summer typhoon, lends an air of realism to the fantasy. Sailing the sea route from Osaka to Kyushu is one of the most pleasing trips, covering the entire length of the Inland Sea. In addition to the services from ports listed in our alphabetical guide, please note the following daily crossings:

From Tokyo to Nachi Katsuura and Kochi, by Nippon Kosuku Ferry.
From Chiba to Tokushima, by Ocean Ferry.
            to Tomakomai, by Nippon Enkai Ferry.
From Kawasaki to Hyuga, by Nippon Car Ferry.
From Nagoya to Yokkaichi and Kitakyushu (Moji), by Meimon Car Ferry.

From Osaka and Kobe to Beppu, by Kansai Kisen Steamship Co.
From Kobe to Hyuga, by Nippon Car Ferry.
From Matsuyama to Kitakyushu (Kokura), by Kansai Kisen
    Steamship Co.
From Hiroshima to Hyuga, by Hankyu Ferry.
            to Beppu, by Hirobetsu Kisen.
From Kagoshima to Naha, by Shokoku Yusen.

Rail links. The railway is still without doubt the most convenient, as well as the cheapest, way to travel – whatever the length of your stay. See the inside back cover of this book for a map of the national railways (Japanese National Railways – JNR); it will give you an idea of how dense the rail network is. In the suburbs and between the major cities, rail traffic is so intense that you will have no problem during the daytime in finding several trains to a given destination. The railway lines push right up into isolated parts of the country, often following most picturesque routes in areas still inaccessible by road.

Of course the slowness of certain local services may prove at times frustrating; it stems from the difficulty of the terrain through which the train must weave and turn, or from the fact that on certain single-track routes priority has to be given to express trains, no matter which direction they are travelling. There are two classes of express train – specials (*tokkyu*) and ordinaries (*kyuko*) – ensuring that even the most distant town is less than 24 hours from Tokyo: on the longest routes there are night trains with couchettes.

Special mention must be made of the Shinkansen railway (with a total network of about 1,000mls/1,800km) whose trains average a speed of 130mls (210km) per hour, and thus rank alongside the High Speed Train (the French TGV) as among the fastest in the world. From Omiya (north of Tokyo) the *Joetsu* takes 2h. to Niigata, and the Tohoku takes 3h.45 to Morioka, while the Hikari ('the Light'), faster than the Kodama ('the Echo', which stops more frequently) goes from Tokyo to Fukuoka (Hakata) in 6h.40. Trains between Osaka and Tokyo (a three-hour journey) depart every ten minutes.

An extension of the line is planned towards Nagasaki and Kagoshima in the south, towards Sapporo in the north, and to Osaka via Toyama in the centre of the country.

PRIVATE RAILWAYS. There are 4,550mls (7,320km) of private track in Japan, mainly concentrated around the big cities and in the two great settlements of Kanto and Kansai, on the outskirts of Tokyo, and in links between Kobe, Osaka, Kyoto and Nagoya. Private railways also run express services on their main routes. We list the principal lines in the alphabetical section of this guide. The tickets of these private companies are sometimes valid on the national railways; for example you may switch to a JNR train to finish your journey, provided that you have paid the full amount for the entire journey.

TRAVELLING BY TRAIN IN JAPAN. Let us look at the difficulties (see also Urban transport), because if you don't know any Japanese, you might run into problems! You have learned one thing – that the names of all stations, or most of them, are displayed in romaji (roman script); beneath the station name are written, in smaller letters, the names of the stations before and after this one, together with an indication of the direction in which they lie. Generally the name of the station is announced before each stop over loudspeakers in the train, and in the station itself when the train halts. The name of your station will be hidden in a string of verbiage, but your ears will soon get used to untangling it. A further boon is that the railway staff have a smattering of English, and so can be of assistance to you. Do note, though, that Japanese trains have a reputation for absolute punctuality: if you are to catch the 10.12 train, don't go leaping onto the 10.10 departing from the same platform. Trust your watch.

If you take an express you will have to pay a supplement which may be as much as 50% of the price of the initial ticket: travelling first class (green car) will not mean you are exempt from paying this extra tariff. The Shinkansen also requires a special ticket. On the other hand, the JNR gives a reduction on certain return tickets, but in these cases it is not possible to break your journey. They have also introduced a season ticket for tourists, the 'Japan Rail Pass', allowing unrestricted travel on the whole of the national network. This pass, which makes travel very much easier and represents a considerable saving, must be purchased at overseas offices of Japan Air Lines (see Travelling by Plane), Japan Travel Bureau (see Tourist Information), and Nippon Ryoko.

TAKE OUR ADVICE: RESERVE YOUR SEAT. This will not be a problem. You make your reservation a week before you plan to travel, at station ticket offices with a green sign showing a person sitting in a chair, and at travel agencies. A remarkable electronic booking system is in operation throughout Japan: wherever you are you can reserve a seat anywhere on the national rail network, change or cancel a reservation, request a refund, etc. The reservation ticket, alone or combined with your travel ticket, lists the departure point and the destination, date and time of departure, the number of your carriage and of your seat or couchette. Get someone to explain all this information because, apart from the Arabic numerals, it will be written in Japanese. Look out for a similar system of reservation on certain private lines, too.

FURTHER ADVICE: REGISTER YOUR LUGGAGE. For a modest additional charge you will be able to have your cumbersome baggage delivered to you at the station of your destination – sometimes even to your accommodation address. Remember to despatch it 24 hours before you leave: that way you'll avoid having to haul it up staircases and so on, and your journey will be all the more enjoyable. You may find the occasional porter at the main stations, and there are automatic luggage-lockers everywhere. As a general rule, it is wise to provide yourself with several small, soft bags; it is impossible to travel with a suitcase in a train compartment.

Coaches. As well as the railways, Japan is crisscrossed by a regular road service: daily excursions that will take you to the main tourist attractions, express coach lines duplicating railway routes or filling in the gaps between them, and suburban bus links allowing you to travel between neighbouring areas or to explore the outlying districts of a town. However, the fares are higher than on the train. For example, the JNR offers a daily service from Tokyo (departing frequently from Yaesu Minami guchimae, a station in Tokyo), taking 5½ hours to Nagoya by the Tomei motorway, with the possibility of further travel to Kyoto, Osaka or Kobe by the Meishin motorway. There are some direct night services between Tokyo, Kyoto, Osaka and Kobe.

The bus stations in towns are generally situated close to the railway station.

TRAVELLING BY COACH IN JAPAN. Unless you've already bought your ticket in advance, or paid your cash directly to the driver, or boarded a single-tariff bus, you will have to trust the tender mercies of automation. As you get on board, a recorded voice, or the driver, will ask you to take from a machine a little ticket on which is printed your fare stage number. All through the journey, on an illuminated panel close to the driver, will be displayed running totals corresponding to the distance covered: as you alight you have merely to settle up by paying the sum corresponding to the number of the fare stage at which you got on. Another recorded voice announces the stop, so you won't miss your destination.

Urban transport. In view of the importance of the city to the Japanese way of life, urban transport plays a vital role, and you will find a wide range of choice when it comes to travel: there are the city services of the JNR, the private lines, the underground, the buses and, finally, a few remaining tramlines (streetcars).

If you don't speak Japanese and are unfamiliar with the routes, you may well experience difficulties finding your way round by bus. At bus stops there is often a table of the routes, but in the form of ideograms: the same goes for the front of the bus, and in the vehicle each stop is announced in recorded Japanese. So if you don't understand Kanji ideograms, you'd best avoid this form of transport – or ask at your hotel to have the precise details of your journey explained to you: where to catch the bus, the number of the line you want, and where to get off. (As an added precaution, make a note of the ideograms involved.)

The national and private railways, as well as the underground, work in the same way – except that the private lines tend to spread out towards the suburbs while the underground goes straight across town, and the national lines (JNR) do both at somewhat cheaper rates. In Tokyo, the city lines and the underground operate on the same principle as the London Underground system. Only Tokyo, Osaka, Nagoya and Sapporo are blessed with a complete underground network, Kyoto and Fukuoka having relatively few underground lines.

Certain towns (e.g., Kyoto and Nagasaki) run economical whole-day tickets. The system is continually expanding, so make enquiries as soon as you arrive in town.

TRAVELLING BY URBAN TRAIN OR UNDERGROUND IN JAPAN. Try first of all to procure from your hotel or a tourist information bureau a map in English. In Tokyo at least, the colours of the lines on the map are reproduced on the carriages. Inside the train you will find a diagram of the line you're on, but in Japanese script. Before getting into the maze that leads to the platforms, you'll have to negotiate the automatic machines. If you have no change, you may use one of the ticket windows, staffed by competent clerks. There are also automatic change-giving machines that take banknotes. Equipped with your personal map, check your present position and your destination against the station map, in ideograms, posted near the ticket machines. Once you've done this you will realize that the fare for your journey is listed against the destination. Armed with these pieces of information, get your ticket from a machine, not forgetting to pick up your change: the system is not unlike the one on the London Underground. There are few ticket-cancelling machines, however: tickets are collected by rail-staff as you pass through the exit. On the platform, the name of the station is written up in romaji, along with the names of the stops on either side of it. On the first carriage you can read the name of the terminus: connections and exits are marked in English, but stops and connections are announced over loudspeakers in Japanese.

Taxis. These are to be found everywhere, especially where crowds gather (stations, public buildings, shops, hotels): you can call them by phone (radio-taxis) or hail them in the street if you can't find a taxi-rank nearby. There are at least two classes of taxi – the ordinary and the express: there is a difference of a few dozen yen between them. It's up to you whether you travel in a simple taxi (automatic doors, radio, air-conditioning), or in real style (where the driver wears white gloves). You may also hire a self-drive car. Whichever you choose, never expect the driver to help you with your bags: once the automatic door is open, pile into the taxi and arrange your luggage around you – light luggage preferably, since there is not much space in the trunk for big cases. The driver will sit there, unmoving, looking a little impatient: he'll drive off without even waiting to hear where you want to go. On alighting, pay according to the meter: prices are on the high side but not unreasonable. There is no tipping.

FINDING YOUR WAY TO A TOKYO ADDRESS. This is one of the greatest difficulties in the capital! For the Japanese as for the *gaijin* or foreigner, finding a Tokyo address is a real adventure. You might think that the best thing is to place your trust in the reliable taxi-driver: You'd be wrong. He'll often be at least as much at sea as you are in the jumble of streets and alleys in the more chaotic areas of the capital.

Tokyo is divided into districts, vast areas called *ku*, which are further subdivided into *chome*, blocks or units of numbered houses. The *chome* are then divided into alleys flanked by houses with non-consecutive numbers. Each dwelling is given a number which has more to do with the date of its construction than with its geographical location. To get from *chome* no. 2 to no. 3 you might have to march through miles of pedestrian alleys, passing dozens of numbers before coming across no. 3 nestling between nos. 215 and 56! Such a quest will need a lot of patience, but there's no better way of meeting the local residents (always ready to give you directions), or the local police, on whose doorstep you may well find yourself after many defeats. But almost all hotels and restaurants give their customers matchbooks printed with the address and a detailed map, so your taxi will always be able to bring you safely back to base.

Japan by car. We're tempted to say, 'Forget it, go by train', especially since it's easy and agreeable to travel by rail, but difficult to adapt to driving on Japanese highways. Japan from behind the steering-wheel is, fortunately, more accessible than it used to be. Although *kamikaze* taxis still beset the roads at supersonic speed, the average Japanese citizen observes the severe rules of the highway code - driving is on the left, of course, and there is a speed limit of 60mls (100km) per hour on motorways, and 35mls (60km) everywhere else except in built-up areas, where 25mls (40km) is the rule. Add to that an exemplary strictness about drunken driving, and you will understand why the Japanese driver has become so cautious.

For a foreigner the main drawback lies in having to decipher road signs. Although international symbols are used, additional directions are all written in Japanese: only a few very important pieces of information in towns, and directions to public monuments, are transcribed in romaji. The names of streets, districts and towns are, of course, well marked, but not always in a useful manner - so you may find yourself facing two mysterious ideograms at a critical road junction. To drive in Japan you will need an international driver's licence and a road permit, or else a Japanese licence: but don't forget that if you're taking up residence, it will be very difficult to import your car (see Customs, p.21).

INFORMATION: Available from the Japanese Automobile Federation (JAF), 3-5-8, Shiba Park, Minato-ku, Tokyo (*Tel.* 436-2811).

Car hire. If you simply can't do without a car, there are car hire firms in the towns, at stations, ports, airports, and at travel agencies. You get your car, usually of Japanese manufacture, from a company and can leave it at one of its branches anywhere you wish. Some of the big names are Avis and Hertz, as always, and Mitsubishi, Nissan, and Toyota. Prices vary a little from one firm to another, but are in line with Western charges.

SOME ADDRESSES

In Tokyo:

ACU Rent-a-Car, 1-13-2, Hyakunin cho, Shinjuku-ku (*Tel*. 364-2211).

Aloha Rent-a-Car, 4-13-8 Minami Azabu, Minato-ku (*Tel*. 473-2411).

Isuzu Rent-a-Car, 3-16, Takaido Higashi, Suginami-ku (*Tel*. 334-2411).

Japaren, 2-12-7, Shijuku, Shinjuku-ku (*Tel*. 352-7635).

Mitsubishi Rent-a-Car, 1-11-8, Kyobashi, Chuo-ku (*Tel*. 563-5271).

Nippon Rent-a-Car (Hertz), Jinnan Bldg, 4-3, Udagawa cho, Shibuya-ku (*Tel*. 496-0919).

Nissan Rent-a-Car, 1-5-7, Azabu-dai, Minato-ku (*Tel*. 586-2301).

Toyota Rent-a-Lease, 1, Samban-cho, Chiyoda-ku (*Tel*. 264-2834).

In Osaka:

Japaren, 1-2-18, Nippombashi-Nishi, Naniwa-ku (*Tel*. 632-4881).

Mitsubishi Rent-a-Car, 1-5-23, Minami, Horie, Nishi-ku (*Tel*. 538-2428).

Nissan Rent-a-Car, 19-22, Chaya machi, Kita-ku (*Tel*. 372-0289).

Nippon Rent-a-Car, 1-1-3, Shibata-cho, Kita-ku (*Tel*. 373-2652).

Toyota Rent-a-Car, 3-74-3, Kawaraya machi, Minami-ku (*Tel*. 763-4471).

In Kyoto:

Japaren, 14-1 Kitanouchi cho, Nishi-kujo, Minami-ku (*Tel*. 681-7956).

Nippon Rent-a-Car, 42-13, Kitanouchi cho, Nishi-kujo, Minami-ku (*Tel*. 661-0311).

Nissan Rent-a-Car, 94-3, Ikenouchi cho, Nishi-kujo, Minami-ku (*Tel*. 661-2161).

Toyota Rent-a-Lease, Hachijo-Agaru, Nishioji, Shimogyo-ku (*Tel*. 661-2080).

Gasoline. Japan imports 100% of its petroleum, and the price at the pump is slightly higher than in Britain and the US. There are numerous service stations, selling a variety of brands, right across the country. Some Japanese brand names are: *Diamond, Kygnus, Maruzen, Stark.*

Japanese roads. The road network is altogether excellent: a glance at a road map will show you how very dense it is. The roads are under continual maintenance and extension. Motorways (with tolls) are progressively covering the whole of Japan. The Tomei and Meishin motorways link Tokyo with Osaka and Kyushu: an additional spur via Suwa-ko is in the process of being built. Other motorways are being built to Niigata and Morioka: there are some short stretches in Hokkaido, Kyushu, Shikoku, and Okinawa.

Numerous other toll roads allow you to cross valleys, follow the coastline, reach the highest peaks, and trace the ridges of mountains, enjoying the most magnificent panoramic views. Expressways forge their way through the towns, carelessly spawning rather unsightly viaducts in every direction, sometimes petering out alarmingly into space where they are incomplete. Be cautious, especially in the mountains, where climatic conditions and frequent movements of the earth (landslides, tremors) may cause difficulties. Even the very smallest island has its fair share of roads, but don't complain if some of them are still at the dirt-track stage – they'll be invaded by heavy traffic soon enough!

Choosing a map. There are a great many maps, of varying quality, covering the Japanese archipelago. The majority of them –including the very best – are in Japanese. We have therefore stuck to the Area Map series (available in all Japanese bookshops, published by Shobunsha, 2-6-5, Hongo, Bunkyo-ku Tokyo, *Tel.* 813-5981), covering the whole of Japan in eight maps scaled at 1/300,000 (Hokkaido at 1/600,000); headings are given in English and the main place-names are in romaji: each map comes with a little booklet (in Japanese) containing useful facts, route diagrams, and some town maps.

At scales between 1/25,000 and 1/3,000,000 you will find a series of maps and charts published, in Japanese, by the national geographical institute (*Kokudo chiri in*), and distributed by authorized retailers whose address in Tokyo is: Kanda Ogawa machi, 3-22, Chiyoda-ku (*Tel.* 291-0338).

You will also find numerous town maps in Japan from which we have singled out a series with the same name (Area Map): a guidebook with useful tourist information usually comes with these maps. The following maps are available in English:

Handy maps: street maps from the Japan Guide Maps collection (72, Tateno, Naka-ku, Yokohama).

Maps and charts by *Teikoku Shoin* (29, Kanda Jimbo cho, 3-chome, Chiyoda-ku, Tokyo).

Map of Japan, by *Bartholomew World Travel Maps*, scale 1/2,500,000.

Map of Japan, by *Recta/Foldex*, scale 1/3,000,000.

Road and rail maps by *Nippon Kokuseisha* (18-24, Kohinata, 1-chome, Bunkyo-ku, Tokyo).

Map of Japan, scale 1/2,000,000 by *Nichi Shuppan* (2-2-15, Nishi Kanda, Chiyoda-ku, Tokyo).

Finally, we recommend (though not for its street maps) the little book *Japan: the Pocket Atlas,* published by Heibonsha Ltd (1, Yonban cho, 4-chome, Chiyoda-ku, Tokyo, *Tel.* 265-0451), under the aegis of the JNTO (see Tourist information, p.21).

Japan by bike. Why not? This is a truly original way to explore the country. Tours are organized within the national parks or the areas most popular with tourists (around Mount Fuji, Kyoto and its environs, etc.) (see The tourist's Japan pp. 63–79).

Your stay in Japan

Where to stay

Hotels. There are two kinds of hotel in Japan: the *ryokans* and Western-style hotels.

NB: The electrical voltage is 110, and plugs are of the American type. You may need to take a manual razor or adaptor.

WESTERN-STYLE HOTELS. These will be familiar to you – they are international, with the same advantages and the same impersonality worldwide. Only the occasional detail will remind you that you're in Japan. In general, they are very large, with as many as a thousand rooms or more: they match first- or second-class hotels in the West for comfort. All have rooms (often very small), with private bath and WC, which are sometimes in the form of a prefabricated unit set into the corner of the room. Some additional comforts – air-conditioning, TV, the *yukata* (a kimono, not to be removed from the premises), slippers, a sterilized toothbrush, a cooler for drinks, newspapers (in English, with any luck) and so on – help to make your stay in these establishments even more pleasant. Finally, there are many extra services: a choice of restaurants (Japanese, Chinese, Western, some with fine views), bars, lounges, rooms for meetings and conferences, shopping facilities, gardens, Japanese and Turkish baths, sauna, massage, sports facilities (swimming pool, golf course, bowling green, running track), etc. The majority also offer Japanese-style rooms. We mention a large number of hotels for each town, but our list will be far from complete, because new ones are being opened each year. Charges are comparable to those in the West; breakfast (Japanese or Western) is substantial but expensive. Take the precaution of booking your room in advance: you'll stand a better chance if you do it through a travel agent.

The JNTO (Japan Travel Bureau in London, New York or San Francisco) runs a package deal for foreign tourists, the 'Sunrise Super Saver' (or SSS), which, with its particularly economical prices and reliable booking service, makes travel to Japan much easier.

Exchange vouchers (for one or two weeks) must be bought abroad.

INFORMATION: Japan Hotel Association, Shin-Otemachi Bldg, 221, Ote machi 2-chome, Chiyoda-ku (*Tel.* 279-2706).

BOOKING: This is not easy except for hotels of international class. For further information, apply to the JNTO (see Tourist information, p. 21).

RYOKAN. These traditional hotels prove most interesting to the traveller who wishes to delve more deeply into the Japanese mentality. There are large numbers of them throughout the islands, even in the remotest and least developed parts of the country. They are generally of modest capacity, around a dozen rooms or so. But there you will find a far warmer welcome, an engaging family intimacy, and the habits and customs practised by the Japanese themselves when they travel. On entering a *ryokan*, you will exchange your shoes for slippers; remember to leave them off when you enter the bedroom. The floor is covered in *tatami*, and the furniture is very sparse: a low table from which to eat your meals, and cupboards concealing the *futon* (mattress and eiderdown). There is a neat recess or *tokonoma*, a veranda that serves as a little sitting-room, with one or two armchairs and overlooking the street, the countryside, or an exquisite Japanese garden. Lastly, the inevitable TV set – never missing, though a wash-basin sometimes is!

The best of these *ryokan* have, in each room, a washroom and WC, Western-style or Japanese (containing bidet and steamroom). If your *ryokan* has communal facilities only, don't forget to exchange your own slippers for those provided for use in that particular area, if you don't want to be stared at in the corridor. In your room, a member of the household will offer you *o-cha* (green tea) with a biscuit, before ushering you to the bath.

Let us take this opportunity to say a word about the finer points of the Japanese bath (*ofuro*): do follow the instructions given by your host, which may also be written up in English in the bathroom itself. You will have to withstand very hot water (often above 100°F/40°C, to which the Japanese are quite accustomed): the baths are communal and not always segregated by sex), so your anatomy will hold no secrets for anyone – but it won't cross anyone's mind to give it the slightest attention. There are 'torture instruments' at your disposal, including a little seat to squat on, a tub to douse yourself from, a running-water tap, and sometimes the joy of a cold tap for Westerners. There is almost always a shower nearby for taking a 'first rinse' (obligatory before entering the bath, which is intended for enjoyment not ablution). Take care. Don't plunge straight into the hot bath or you could do yourself some damage: once you have had a good wash and rinse, then is the time to lower yourself slowly into the hot water, savouring all the benefits of a Japanese bath and participating, if the occasion arises, in the pleasures of conversation. You can repeat the whole process, staying in as long as you wish. To dry yourself, you will be presented with a tiny but nonetheless effective towel.

An evening meal, and breakfast, are often included in the price of the room. Dinner may be taken in your room or in the dining-room where the guests dine wearing the *yukata*.

NB: The prices charged by *ryokan* are similar to those of Western-style hotels.

INFORMATION: The Japanese Association of Ryokans, sponsored by the Japanese National Tourist Office (JNTO), publishes an annual guide which is distributed free in all the JNTO's information bureaux.

BUSINESS HOTELS. These hotels, originally designed for Japanese businessmen, offer a relatively cheap alternative. They manage to pack into a limited space all the Western-style comfort of hotels in a higher category, so they are the ideal solution for tourists who wish to spend their days out of doors. A list of these hotels may be found in the 'Useful information' section at the end of this book.

INFORMATION: Association of Japanese Business Hotels: c/o Hokke Club Tokyo-ten, 2-1-48, Ikenohata, Taito-ku, Tokyo (*Tel.* 823-0601).

'LADIES' HOTELS'. This is a label which is becoming increasingly widespread. This kind of hotel is, as the name indicates, reserved for ladies travelling alone or in parties. There is as yet no English-language guide to these hotels. If you are interested in learning more, apply to any JNTO office in the bigger Japanese towns.

Cheaper lodgings. Various more economical types of accommodation are also available.

FAMILY HOSTELS (*Minshuku*). Especially for you if you wish to make direct contact with a Japanese family by becoming its paying guest and sharing its way of life. These establishments are, indeed, rather like the *ryokan*, if somewhat more modest and in the midst of their intimate atmosphere you will be able to retain your independence. For information and bookings, contact the Japan Minshuku Association in Japan, New Pearl Bldg, 2-10-8, Hyakunincho, Shinjuku-ku, Tokyo (*Tel.* 367-0155); the Japan Minshuku Centre, Kotsu Kaikan, 2-10-1, Yuraku cho, Chiyoda-ku, Tokyo (*Tel.* 216-6556); or the Japan Minshuku Federation, Ginza Kikuchi Bldg, 7-3-15, Ginza, Chuo-ku, Tokyo (*Tel.* 543-7431).

In Kyoto: Kyoto Minshuku Centre, Kyoto Station (*Tel.* 661-5481).

National holiday villages (*Kokumin kyuka mura*). There are 21 of these in Japan, allowing you to enjoy a sporting holiday in a natural setting.

INFORMATION AND BOOKINGS: Corporation of National Vacation Villages, Tokyo Kostu Kaikan Bldg, 2-10-1, Yuraku cho, Chiyoda-ku, Tokyo (*Tel.* 216-2085), and at the JNR station at Umeda, Kita-ku, Osaka (*Tel.* 343-0131). It is also possible to make reservations through the Japan Travel Bureau (JNTO), 6-4, Marunouchi 1-chome, Chiyoda-ku, Tokyo (*Tel.* 211-2701).

Self-catering co-operatives (*Kokumin shukusha*). These offer popular holiday accommodation, and have been built by local collectives under government control: they are open to tourists. One of the most economical kinds of accommodation in Japan, they may well be booked up during the busiest Japanese holiday seasons: April-May, July-August, October-November. To be safe, book in advance through the JNTO (address above), directly at the Kotsu Kaikan Bldg, 1st floor, 2-10-1, Yurakucho, Chiyoda-ku, Tokyo (*Tel.* 216-2085).

Youth Hostels. There are about 600 in the whole of Japan. Some, built with public funds, are run by the local authorities, but the majority are privately run: they are open not only to members of the International Youth Hostel Association or its Japanese counterpart, but also to any traveller with a means of identification. Beautifully situated for the most part, they give you a very good insight into Japan and its way of life. Further details from Japan Youth Hostels Inc., 1-2, Ichigaya Sadohara cho (3rd floor, Hoken Kaikan Bldg), Shinjuku-ku Tokyo (*Tel.* 269-5831). A great number of these hostels, together with various branches of the YMCA and YWCA, are listed at the end of this guidebook.

Campsites. Camping is another possibility, of course, and you will find several purpose-built sites. A list of these is obtainable from the Japan Auto-camping Federation, Shin Ueno Bldg, 1-2-4, Yotsuya, Shinjuku-ku, Tokyo (*Tel.* 357-2851).

Staying in a Buddhist temple. This is a most interesting option for the male tourist with plenty of time and a desire to learn about the spiritual side of Japanese life.

To participate in monastic life is an unusual experience. You can adjust the rhythm of your day to match that of the monks: prayers at 06.00 in the temple (it is expected that you will attend the service in normal dress, and you should not on any account arrive wearing the *yukata* you dressed in for the previous evening's dinner). Anyone wishing to sleep on later than prayertime will find it impossible as at the first stroke of the gong announcing the service the whole monastery is awake. After prayers there is an entirely vegetarian Japanese breakfast – delightful to those already following a non-meat diet, but others may find it a little hard so early in the morning to swallow the bowlful of white rice accompanied by *tofu* (soya bean curd), *miso* soup with its soya base, and various kinds of seaweed, all washed down by the indispensable green tea, *o-cha*. The day of a Buddhist monk varies from one temple to another. Study is the main occupation of the monasteries, and each village is blessed with at least one temple, often inhabited by a single monk and his family. Once morning prayers are over, he will go to visit the families of the recently-deceased to chant *sutras*, commemorate the anniversary of the death of a believer with a ceremony in the temple, or take part in various celebrations and religious festivals in neighbouring temples. Added to these different functions are the teaching of Buddhist precepts and the life of Buddha, and the practice of calligraphy and its teaching to children and adolescents. It must be remembered that a monk relies for his living on gifts made to him by the faithful; that he may marry and raise a family; that he is not obliged to live the life of an ascetic; that he may drink *sake* and beer (sometimes in rather large quantities), and lives, all in all, a rather agreeable life. You may perhaps see it at first hand if you are lucky enough to find a welcome in a little country temple nestling in the ricefields where life is lived at the most peaceful pace imaginable.

The JNTO provides all the information necessary to make a booking in a temple *shukubo*, and is especially recommended for shrines 'in the heart of nature', such as the monastery of Koya-san.

Food and drink

Restaurants. You are unlikely to die of starvation in Japan – eating houses are plentiful and various. From simple kebab restaurants (*yakitori*) and establishments where you swallow your portion of *soba* without standing on ceremony, to luxurious restaurants complete with orchestra, all kinds of cuisine are on offer: Japanese, Chinese, Korean, French, and other Western varieties (though seldom Mediterranean or Near Eastern). Remember to dine before 20.30; after that you might experience difficulties in finding somewhere to serve you. In some towns there are whole blocks given over to nothing but restaurants, with a different speciality on each floor, and prices that increase with each storey: often the whole establishment is topped with a panoramic rotating room. Hotels and department stores frequently contain a dozen different types of restaurant. If you're eating out with friends, it is often the case that you'll have to agree among yourselves on the same kind of dish for everyone because a *sukiyaki* restaurant, for example, will not necessarily serve *sushi* or *tempura*. Similarly, the *yakitori*, which specialize in kebabs, will only serve chicken, liver, mushroom, pepper and other sorts of kebabs from a fixed menu, and that is *all* they will serve. It is not unusual for the Japanese to go to two or three different restaurants in the course of a single evening, beginning with *sushi*, then enjoying *tempura* somewhere else, and ending up in a restaurant devoted entirely to serving *shabu-shabu*. In nearly all restaurants there is a display of available dishes: don't be misled – they are plastic replicas, but the resemblance is realistic. They may save you many a disappointment if you can't read the menu: just point out the dish you want to the waitress. Self-service is unknown, but you sometimes have to obtain from the desk a ticket corresponding to your chosen dish, before sitting down to eat: fail to observe this little formality, and you may find yourself entirely ignored by the staff. In the humbler establishments prices will be written in Japanese only: learn them, or trust your waiter – you won't be cheated. Forget tipping: if you leave change on the table, it will be returned to you – be tactful, especially in the more select establishments. Our guide contains mainly this latter kind of restaurant: a more exhaustive list would be endless. It is advisable to book your table in these places.

INFORMATION: Japan Restaurant Association, Ozawa Bldg, 8-4-25, Ginza Nishi, Chuo-ku, Tokyo (*Tel.* 571-2438).

Japanese cuisine.

There are numerous Japanese restaurants these days in Western countries, and they may serve as a useful introduction to Japanese food; food which is, in a phrase, healthy and good. The Japanese cook rarely launches himself into complex preparations, which is the main difference between him and his Chinese counterpart, and he will use natural foodstuffs which you will quickly recognize in his cooking. Apart from soups, there are noodles (*soba*) with various seasonings, chicken kebabs (*yakitori*), a delicious dish based on eels (*unagi*), curried rice (*karri raisso*) eaten with a spoon and not very tasty, plus various other adaptations of economical dishes. However, a good Japanese meal will make a noticeable dent in your budget.

Whatever the menu, it is eaten with chopsticks, but you can always ask for Western cutlery, and for bread in place of the little bowl of rice which usually takes its place in Japan. Look around to see how others eat, so as to be less clumsy when it comes to picking up pieces of food and dipping them in the appropriate sauce (it's more embarrassing if, out of politeness, you are allowed to go first). If you're asked out to dine, don't forget to compliment your host or hostess on the presentation of the meal: it will look beautiful, always, and much trouble will have been taken behind the scenes.

A Japanese meal may include an assortment of raw and cooked fish, some hot and cold vegetables, sometimes a little meat, various condiments, and, as an accompaniment, a thin soup flavoured with fish and herbs.

There are special regional dishes, but you are unlikely to get the chance to taste these unless you are introduced to a Japanese family. Here, briefly, are a few dishes which have become nationally known, and which can sometimes constitute a meal in themselves.

Sashimi (raw fish) is frequently encountered: tuna, carp, sole, squid or octopus are cut into small pieces for dipping in *shoyu* sauce or *soya sauce* (rather stronger) seasoned with horseradish.

Sushi is a variant of *sashimi*: the raw fish is cut into fine strips and served on little rice canapés,

Tempura is of course a typical Japanese dish (though originally introduced by the Portuguese), and it seems to appeal to Western palates. Fish, prawns (*ebi*) and fried vegetables are often prepared as you watch, coated lightly in batter, and served up immediately. Soya and horseradish provide the seasoning. Certain authorized restaurants serve *fugu*, a poisonous globefish: eat at your own risk...

Sukiyaki, not actually an indigenous dish, has become for foreigners synonymous with Japanese food. Various vegetables and thin slices of beef, constantly replaced with new ones as you eat, simmer, at your table, in a broth containing, among other things, soya, sweet *sake*, and sugar. Before eating them, you dip into raw beaten egg the pieces you have chosen – or, at least, those you've managed to grip with your chopsticks. *Shabu-shabu*, a kind of Japanese hotpot, is also prepared at the table on a small burner.

Okariba-yaki or *Genghis Khan barbecue* is the latest in Japanese cooking, and is a trifle trendy. It derives partly from *sukiyaki*, cooked for you on a hotplate rather than being boiled: to avoid burning yourself during the meal, put on the protective apron provided and enjoy the procedure.

Japanese pastries, rarely eaten with a meal but available for consumption at all times of day, are very varied but seldom to Western taste.

Finally, a word about *o-bento*, which is not a restaurant dish but a traveller's snack. The Japanese traveller never fails to buy himself one of these 'meals in a basket', comprising rice, chopsticks and condiments. Look out for them especially at rail and bus stations, and in the train; buy one, and you get a little container of green tea as well.

Drinks. The traditional Japanese meal is accompanied by *sake*, which is rice wine, served cold or, preferably, slightly warm and in small but subtly intoxicating quantities. Abstainers will have to make do with green tea (*o-cha*), rather tasteless but freely drunk, without sugar, at the start and end of the meal, and whenever the opportunity arises: black tea (Indian) is called *ko cha*. The coffee (adapted from English as *kohi*) is rather tasteless. You will come across all manner of fruit juices and fizzy drinks (*saida*) under many brand names. Beers, mainly rice lagers of reasonable quality, are sold under the names Asahi, Kirin, Sapporo and Suntory.

Whisky is a great favourite with Japanese drinkers and as well as several imported brands, there are the local labels *Nikka* and *Suntory*. Wines are expensive, and are mainly imported from France, clarets being especially popular. There is however some Japanese wine production: *Suntory* have their Chateau Lion (red), *Mercian* is taking over the market, and *Mann*'s are producing very acceptable wines from French vines, such as their Cabernet (red) and Semillon (white). Sparkling wines and brandy are also now being produced locally. Finally, among the brands of mineral water we suggest *Nikka* and *Suntory*, as well as *Fuji*, which is rather like Évian water.

Daily life in Japan

Spending money. Japan has the reputation of being an expensive country. This is often justified, but though your budget should in any case be substantial, it will not be divided up in the same way as it would in Europe. For example, accommodation, transport (buses, underground, taxis, trains), admission to museums, temples and shrines, are costly. On the other hand, food - if you stick to certain dishes (*tempura*, curried rice, Chinese cooking) - can be very economical. Remember, tipping is - apart from one or two rare exceptions - non-existent in Japan: so you don't have to worry about adding that to the price in restaurants, taxis and bars. If you feel compelled to register your gratitude for a service rendered, do put your thankyou money in an envelope.

The Japanese currency, the yen (¥), is at present one of the strongest in the world. Its value fluctuates, of course, but it is always very high. There are coins to the value of 1, 5, 10, 50, 100 and 500 yen, and notes of 500, 1000, 5000 and 10,000 yen.

Though you may use your credit cards in Japan, they are still covered by the rules in force in the country of origin.

Travellers' cheques are readily accepted all over Japan. It is advisable to buy them in yen rather than in any other currency, to avoid punitive bank charges for commission. Foreign currencies (US dollar, pound sterling, etc.) are not accepted everywhere, but you'll have no trouble exchanging them for yen in the bigger towns. Banks are open from Monday to Friday, 09.00-15.00, and Saturdays 09.00-12.00. Some UK and US banks have branches in Tokyo or Osaka (e.g. American Express, Bank of America, Barclays Bank Int., Midland Bank, National Westminster Bank): their addresses are given in the 'Useful information' section of this guide.

Visiting monuments, gardens and museums. Temples, shrines and gardens generally have the same opening times as museums and private collections with admission to the public: from 08.00 or 09.00 (10.00 for museums) to 16.00 or 17.00, according to the season. Temples and shrines less famous than those of Kyoto or Nara are open every day from dawn to dusk, but may vary their timetable to take account of festivals or religious ceremonies. Museums and private collections stay shut on Mondays and on certain public holidays. For a complete list see the 'Your journey' section of this guide.

Admission charges are levied almost everywhere, and you frequently have to buy a supplementary ticket to see exceptional treasures belonging to the temple or shrine. A handy hint: when visiting a temple, shrine or palace take a pair of slip-on shoes rather than lace-ups, because you will often be required to remove them.

You will soon realize that the title 'museum' is occasionally used to dignify insignificant collections which will make very little impression on you. Nonetheless, the Shoso-in treasure in Nara, the national museums in Tokyo, Kyoto and Nara, and the Goto and Nezu museums in Tokyo are indeed richly endowed: there are also some magnificent private collections open to the public, chief among them the Yamato Bunkakan Museum in Nara, the Bridgestone Gallery in

Tokyo and the Ohara Gallery in Kurashiki. Finally, it should be remembered that many monasteries, temples and shrines contain remarkable treasures, and these are listed in the descriptive section of this guide.

A word of warning to visitors is in order here: museums and galleries rarely display their whole collection at one time, tending instead to arrange exhibitions centred around historical themes, maybe commemorating a particular anniversary. It is therefore not possible for us to give detailed descriptions of what is to be seen in all of these establishments, so we will restrict ourselves to indicating the major pieces stored in each collection.

NB: Artists, school and university students, etc., may make an appointment with the museum director to see any particular piece which especially interests them.

Additionally, the offices of the JNTO will furnish you with the details of the themes of exhibitions that will be on during your stay.

VISITING A JAPANESE TEMPLE. To visit a Japanese temple is to penetrate to the very heart of the culture of the country and, perhaps, to discover something of its soul. For here the authentic Japan is preserved, in the teeth of intensive and overwhelming modernization. The symbol of traditional Japan, its architecture, in accordance with religious and philosophical principles, is matched with the natural environment in an often perfect blend of calm and tranquility. This harmony with nature – this complementarity – makes Japanese architecture accessible to the aesthetic sense of the Western visitor even if he remains a stranger to the religious ideas of the country.

Everything, indeed, contributes to the harmony. The plan of the building is as simple as the natural space surrounding it. The roof-structure, although it may be immense (e.g. at Nishi Hongan-ji in Kyoto) or somewhat smaller (e.g., at the Lotus Hall of Todai-ji in Nara), strikes a fine balance with the proportions of the body of the building. Lastly, the widespread use of wood, that national product with symbolic resonances all its own, adds a note of natural colour.

But before you visit a Japanese temple, you must first of all know how to distinguish a Shinto shrine from a Buddhist temple. Also, you have to remember that many religious edifices are grouped together into large complexes – monasteries, convents, schools – which may sometimes, as at Koyasan, take on the importance of a small town. Other aspects may be brought into play, too: trees and water in Shinto shrines, the presence of animals (cockerels at Ise, deer at Nara), the 'dry gardens' conducive to Zen meditation (the one at the Ryoan ji in Kyoto is especially famed), or even teahouses. In short, everything – nature, man, art, aesthetics and daily life – combines to make a Japanese temple alive and approachable, to lend it a very human face.

Let us remind ourselves – somewhat cursorily – that Shintoism, the national 'religion', embodies the very root of the nation, whereas

Buddhism, imported long ago from India via China and Korea, has been able to find new expression here without losing sight of its origins. This brief distinction is confirmed by the architecture: Shinto shrines take their inspiration from the local context, while the Buddhist temples introduce into that context foreign elements which are then adapted to it.

The Shinto shrine, originally constructed on the model of wooden barns, is modest in size and is divided into two parts: the *Hon-den*, forbidden to laymen, in which is kept the Miama-shiro, the jewel symbolizing the spirit of the divinity (*Kami*); and the *Hai-den*, open to the public and connected to the Hon-den by a covered elevated corridor. At the entrance of the shrine is the *torii*, a kind of wooden portico originating from India and said to serve as a perch for the rooster crowing to the sun-goddess Amaterasu. The shrine contains a whole series of essential features: heavy cylindrical pillars visible at the front and back of the edifice and supporting the roof-ridge; billets placed crosswise in the double-sloping roof, and covered with thatch; and twin 'cupolas' of angled uprights (*chigi*), aligned with the line of slope and forming a large V at the ends of the roof.

Under the influence of Buddhism other styles appeared: these variants are called Taisha (temple of Uzumo), Nagare (Kamo temple in Kyoto), Kasuga (from the Kasuga shrine in Nara) or Hachiman (from the temple of Usa, near Beppu).

A particular feature is created by the members of the Shinto clergy, dressed in weighty white robes and black bonnets, moving silently along the cloisters or motionless in hieratic poses of meditation at the entrance to the temple.

The Buddhist temple, far more complex and stylistically more varied, is based on Chinese or Korean architecture (though originating from India) which, with the addition of numerous adapted local elements, has become an authentically Japanese style. Each great period of political or artistic change that the country has known has also made its mark, so that there is a world of difference between the temples in Nara and those in Nikko.

It was during the 6th century that Buddhism, coming from Korea, was introduced into Japan. It rapidly became the state religion and, with the establishment of the capital in Nara in the middle of the 7th century, it gave birth to a new kind of expression in art. During this prosperous era Japan maintained continuous relations with China, where the T'ang dynasty was at its height: hence the artistic influence. Nara itself is built on the model of X'ian (then the Chinese capital), just as Kyoto was later to be. The temples of the new cult drew their inspiration from similar sources (Horuy ji, then Todai ji), though the Chinese influence was often tempered by the Korean.

However, these basic elements were soon overlaid by the Japanese style. It is manifested, under the influence of Shinto, in a simplification of the line of the buildings, and especially in the widespread use of wood in their construction.

The Japanese Buddhist temple is just one of a vast grouping of buildings, including the temple itself, monastic buildings, gardens, domestic houses, etc., the whole surrounded by a wall punctuated with little doorways.

The temple, together with its direct outbuildings, takes up only a part of the whole space. Often preceded by one or two pagodas, it is surrounded by an enclosure (sometimes two) serving as a covered cloister with doors at each point of the compass (after which they are named). Within these doors stand huge statues of grimacing giants, to keep away evil spirits.

The temple proper, housing the Buddha's statue, is constructed to a very simple architectural concept. Its style is defined by its function. In fact, all elements of the basic structure, and of the structure of the roof, are exposed to view. It is therefore very easy to study, and to the pleasure of knowing and understanding the techniques used is added aesthetic pleasure, for each element represents a work of art in itself.

The statue of Buddha usually rests on a pedestal in the form of a lotus blossom and is surrounded by statues of the Buddhist Triad, the Kannons, or Bodhisattvas (*disciples*). Behind it there spreads a great sculpted halo.

In front of the temple stands a wooden construction with a bronze bell and a basin of fresh water, both necessary for the performance of religious rites. At the back, sometimes outside the temple enclosure, are grouped the monastery buildings, the reading room and the abbot's residence, often (in the case of a Zen temple) close to gardens of meditation.

Buddhism in Japan gave rise to numerous sects which, while remaining faithful to the general style described above, adapted it to fit their own particular rites, so creating new styles.

VISITING: Japanese temples, with very few exceptions, are still used for worship and are inhabited by monks and students of theology. Try to remember this, and do as little as possible to disturb their peace and meditative calm.

There is nearly always an entrance fee in the more 'historic' temples, and you must follow the route marked by arrows; certain parts remain strictly closed to the public.

Inside temples and monasteries you must always take off your shoes (special slippers are provided for visitors). At certain monasteries you may be able to buy green tea and little sweet cakes. During your visit, take note of the religious rites which, though they vary according to the sect and the divinity being worshipped, are generally similar. For example, in all cases the believer claps his hands or strikes a gong to attract the deity's attention. Incense is always burned, with deep devotion, while slips of paper attached to the bushes, especially in Shinto shrines, symbolize good intentions or penances.

The Japanese religious sense, which has achieved a sort of hybrid of Shintoism and Buddhism, of almost animist beliefs and a practical philosophy, has remained a vital part of Japanese daily life, and of those who live it.

Sport and leisure. In Japan you can practise any sport imaginable: however, except for the facilities offered by hotels - gyms, tennis courts, swimming pools, stables, skating rinks, golf courses, etc. - you need to belong to a club to enjoy its facilities. This is especially true of golf. There are a number of courses up to international standard (18 holes) in Japan, but more often than not the Japanese practise sport in enclosures with a high fence, crammed into the smallest possible space (often to be seen on the roof of a large building). Baseball is another imported game of which the Japanese have become very fond, and ten-pin bowling has gained so many devotees that there is an abundance of large bowling alleys. Mountaineering and simple mountain walking also have their share of fans: you may obtain information about these activities from the Japanese Mountaineering Association, 25, Kannami cho, Shibuya-ku, Tokyo (*Tel.* 467-3111, ext. 247), or from the Japanese Alpine Club, 23, 3-chome, Nishiki-cho, Chiyo-da-ku, Tokyo (*Tel.* 293-7441). We should mention, too, that there are routes suitable for cyclists, across country, well away from cars and pedestrians.

SAILING AND WATER SPORTS. These have recently been enjoying a wave of popularity, and you may hire a boat on the Abuzuri coast, near Miura, from: Abuzuri Kaigan, Hayama machi, Miura gun, Kanagawa ken (*Tel.* (0468) 75-2670). As for pleasure sailing, it too has its following; look out for entries elsewhere in this book. But for a foreigner, Japan's national sports perhaps offer the greatest attraction, as spectator or even as participant.

SUMO. It would be surprising if you could reach the weight for this; wrestlers participate in a tournament which takes place annually in six sessions of about two weeks each. There are sumo halls in Tokyo, Osaka, Nagoya and Fukuoka (see also alphabetical guide). Apart from certain philosophical and religious rituals, which are deeply rooted in the traditions of Japan, the rules of sumo are extremely simple: one of the two wrestlers has to unbalance the other and force him thereby to step outside a circle traced on the ground with the aid of a piece of string. The combat rarely lasts more than a minute or two.

JUDO. It is equally popular in Japan, and if you're already a black belt, or if you are tempted just to have a go, you may meet potential adversaries and take lessons at Judo Kodokan, 1-16-30, Kasuga cho, Bunkyo-ku, Tokyo (*Tel.* 811-7151).

KARATE. A Chinese import, karate has schools in Japan, too. You may become an associate member of the Nippon Karate Kyokai, 1-3, Koraku, Bunkyo-ku, Tokyo (*Tel.* 812-8340).

KENDO. Japanese fencing with bamboo swords, it is practised at the Metropolitan Police Board PR Center, 3-5, Kyobashi, Chuo-ku, Tokyo (*Tel.* 561-8251).

AIKIDO. This is another unarmed sport of military origin, its purpose being to increase physical suppleness: 102, Wakamatsu cho, Shinjuku-ku, Tokyo (*Tel.* 203-9236).

HUNTING. There is an enormous variety of game in Japan: birds - migratory or otherwise - stags, boars, hares, wild cats or squirrels. Golden pheasants and wild bears are highly prized, but to find these you'd have to search many square miles and we cannot recommend too strongly that you obtain a guide. Apply to local centres at the hunting grounds, or to the Japan Hunters' Association, 3-2-11, Kudan, Chiyoda-ku, Tokyo (*Tel.* 261-0818). The hunting season opens at the beginning of October (in Hokkaido) or November (in Honshu), and lasts until 15 February. Restrictions are imposed as to the number and kinds of animal you may bag - and for the protection of humans! A hunting licence, issued by the Security Commission, must be sought from the district (*ken*) office: it is valid for one district only and must be renewed if you wish to hunt elsewhere. To import weapons into Japan you will need to show a firearms licence, issued by the Security Commission. Good hunting! But we hope that the animals you encounter will move you to love them, as they have succeeded in doing for the Japanese, who have created several nature reserves for them.

FISHING. It would be very strange indeed to talk of Japan without touching on fishing: One of the most practical methods of providing food in Japan, it is rarely thought of as a pastime. There is, however, no need for you to forgo it, for there is an abundance of salt and freshwater fish everywhere. Particularly good is the trout, which may be fished in Nikko National Park and in Lake Ashino-ko (Hakone) from March until September. Fishing is strictly controlled and the season varies from region to region. It is wise, therefore, to make inquiries with the local authorities or to ask your travel agent to do it for you. You may also enlist the help of Japanese anglers, who have evolved tried-and-trusted methods for catching Japanese fish - fish which would, no doubt, treat Western techniques with contempt!

You may well wish to see cormorant fishing (*u-kai*), apparently Chinese in origin, and mentioned in the *Kojiki* (AD 712). It is practised in summer, from May to October, at night, by the light of lanterns placed in the bows of light craft usually rafts or houseboats: it is a great favourite with tourists. A dozen trained cormorants are released just at the right moment by their master (*usho*) so that they will snap up little trout (*ayu*). All the skill lies in preventing the bird from swallowing its prey; once the *ayu* is in its beak, a rapid tug on the string fetches it back, and its gullet than has to be squeezed in order to make it disgorge the fish. The two most famous cormorant fishing sites are on the Nagara gawa at Gifu, and on the Uji gawa around Kyoto. You are advised to book a place through your hotel or travel agent.

A typical Japanese day. Every day, early in the morning, Mr Taneda (*Taneda-san*) leaves his little house in a suburb of Tokyo. His wife walks with him to the gate at the end of their tiny garden, they say goodbye, and Taneda-san takes the train to Ueno Station. From Ueno he'll take the underground to get to his office in Shinjuku: the whole journey takes him 1½ hours. While he's travelling, Taneda-san will have a refreshing sleep, just like all his fellow-passengers, crammed together, jolting along from one station to the next, but all of them making up for the lack of sleep that characterizes the Japanese early morning. As for Taneda-san himself, he has a few hours' sleep to make up: last night, as is often the case, his working day was made longer by a business dinner, ending up in the bar he frequents with his office colleagues. Mariko, the friendly barmaid, was there as usual to listen to everyone's problems and to the office gossip while serving *sake* and getting people to sing the old songs. Today is a day like any other: after a morning's work, Taneda-san will grab a quick lunch in a little restaurant specializing in *scoba* (noodles); then he'll be back in the office until six in the evening. Tonight he will be home earlier, but still not before spending an hour at the *pachinko-ya* near his office. He's very fond of *pachinko*, is Taneda-san: despite the infernal row made by the steel balls as they roll along, he loves the game and sits riveted to his seat, his hand on the little handle which enables him to roll marbles down the right slot and win a few bits of cake, chocolate, rice, or other foodstuff. On leaving the *pachinko-ya*, perhaps he will go and have his horoscope read by the astrologer in the next street.

Back at home, Taneda-san will enjoy a bath before his evening meal; then, wrapped up in his *yukata*, he'll dine with his wife and children, sitting on *tatami*, while looking at the samurai serial on TV, which the whole family adores.

And what about Mrs Taneda? What has she been doing all day? She got up before anyone else, to prepare breakfast: rice, fish, seaweed, *miso* and *o-cha*, plus milk and cornflakes, the children's latest craze. With everyone out of the house, Mrs Taneda put the *futons* back into their built-in closets and did her housework, watching in between times a TV programme on cooking. Then she decided to do a spot of shopping in Ginza, stopping for lunch at one of the many restaurants situated on the top floor of a shopping block. From there Mrs Taneda went to give her class in *ikebana* (see p. 48), her speciality, which she teaches in a local school. Next she took her children to their private lessons: piano lessons for one, French for the other before going home to prepare the *ofuro* and the dinner.

Life and traditions

CHA NO YU. The tea ceremony has been handed down from several schools: one of the greatest of its adepts was Sen no Rikyu in the 16th century. A specially-made pavilion, proper ritual implements, among them a bowl (*cha wan*) and bamboo whisk (*cha sen*), are necessary for the preparation of this slightly frothy infusion of powdered green tea. The host keeps his guests waiting a while, then ushers them into the room where the tea is to be served. The slowness of the gestures, the offering of the bowl to the first guest, who contemplates it before passing it on with due ceremony to the next guest, all these things, together with the delights of unhurried conversation, make for a ritual which – though its leisurely pace comes hard to us – is highly pleasurable.

IKEBANA. The art of flower arranging also comes from several sources, and Sen no Rikyu achieved distinction in the field also. It is primarily through the striking simplicity of the compositions that *ikebana* excites admiration, but it is a simplicity which may take years of study and a real talent to achieve. Other forms which may be considered as floral art of a kind are *bonkei*, the creation of a miniature garden on a tray, and *bonsai*, the cultivation – sometimes over years or even whole generations – of dwarf trees.

KODO. The burning of incense, although it still boasts many practitioners, has passed rather out of favour: it recalls, in the skill it requires for research into and blending of fragrances, the philosophy which inspires the floral arts and the tea ceremony.

MEETING THE JAPANESE AT HOME. This is possible through the assistance of the Home Visit Program, which allows foreigners to visit families in a dozen or so towns. The visits are not in any way to be considered as leading on to accommodation, but they do allow you to get a close-up of daily life. Enquire at the local tourist office in the following towns: Kagoshima, Kobe, Kyoto, Nagoya, Osaka, Otsu, Sapporo, Tokyo, Yokohama.

Shows and nightlife

. We refer you first of all to the explanation elsewhere in this book of the various forms of traditional Japanese theatre. Quite apart from the language barrier, approaching the drama takes preparation – quite difficult preparation for those of us used to Western culture. Nevertheless, it may vouchsafe a glimpse of Japanese civilization.

The main Noh theatres are to be found in Tokyo, Kyoto and Osaka, while the principal *Kabuki* theatre is the Kabuki-za in Tokyo (Ginza) whose performances, almost all year round, start at 11.00 and 16.30, alternating with those of the National Theatre (17.00, weekdays only): in Kyoto, go to the Minami-za; in Osaka, to the Shin Kabuki-za. The extreme length of Kabuki plays, interrupted by little entertainments or *kyogens*, explains why you never stay for the whole event; rather, you leave for a quick bite to eat and then return to watch a little more, as and when you like. You may obtain a synopsis of the play in English, on request. Since the 17th century, all the roles, even the female parts, have been played by men. *Bunraku* shows are put on at the National Theatre in Tokyo, at the Gion Corner in Kyoto, and also at the Asahi-za in Osaka, the birthplace (along with the island of Awaji) of the puppet theatre. In addition to concerts of Japanese music, there are other kinds of Japanese art, of a seasonal character: the Azuma and

Myako Odori, during the spring blossom time in April, at the Shimbashi Embu-jo in Tokyo, and the Pontocho Kaburen-jo in Kyoto.

All forms of Western theatre are popular with the Japanese, too. Concerts, drama, ballet and opera performances abound. In addition to the Fujiwara, Nikkai and Kansai troupes, numerous foreign companies appear with great success. You'll also encounter all sorts of revues and cabaret acts, of which the best are the all-female troupe Takara-zuka (in Tokyo and Takarazuka) and Tokyo's Nichigeki theatre. As for the cinema, more than 300 films a year are released in Japan, not counting foreign productions, often shown in their original versions. Entertainments are concentrated in particular areas, especially in Tokyo, Osaka and Kyoto.

You may book seats through your hotel or through the 'play guide' theatre-booking agencies: for more information, consult the two free publications the *Tour Companion* and the *Japan Visitor's Guide*, obtainable from the JNTO (Tokyo and Kyoto) and elsewhere.

JAPANESE NIGHTLIFE. Restaurants with entertainments, cabaret clubs, bars, etc., open early in the evening and, in keeping with the Japanese image, are very well organized and regulated.

Let us begin with one of the things which symbolize Japan more than anything else for a Westerner: *geishas*. The generally-held view of them is false: there is no hint of vulgarity about them. The authentic *geisha* holds an honoured position: her role is to provide lively and rich entertainment in the evening, displaying her many skills as musician, singer, dancer, and conversationalist. Today, the profession is becoming a little less select, and in most cases you will be entertained by *maiko* (*geisha* apprentices). Travel agencies arrange *geisha* evenings, in which women tourists may also take part, but they are very much a modernized version, with only one *geisha* to several visitors. The individual attention of a real *geisha* is extremely costly.

In general, areas reserved for nightlife are contained within well-defined geographical limits (Shinjuku in Tokyo, for example, or, in lesser towns, around central railway stations). Whole areas of a town, then, and sometimes whole streets, are given over to certain specialized categories of entertainment (bars with or without hostesses, gay bars, etc.). These may include restaurants with floor-shows and cabarets, generally staying open until 23.30 (later only if specially licensed); discotheques, with closing time between midnight and 02.00; and bars without hostesses – that is, bars where the only women present are waitresses (often these are tantamount to drinking clubs, a fact borne out by the rows of whisky bottles labelled with the drinker's name). These bars, frequently very small, are not visited by unaccompanied ladies. However, a foreign woman, whose status is different from that of a Japanese woman, will not be shunned if she wishes to venture in. Even though these bars appear claustrophobic, you may rest assured that they are not at all dangerous. A feature common to many of them is that guests may sing all the latest songs, through a microphone, to taped accompaniment. This is called *karaoke*. If you like singing, feel free to have a go, since many of the bars have a small selection of songs in English. The greatest treat of all, though, is for a *gaijin* to sing a few bars in Japanese: this will be sure to amaze the whole audience and, no matter what, you will be assured of warm applause.

The unguarded tourist might occasionally find himself refused entry to a bar: he shouldn't be too surprised, for many are in fact private clubs patronized by particular firms or political parties. He shouldn't be too sorry, either, because the prices in such establishments can be inordinately high.

In the 'Useful Information' section of this guide we give a list of the major cabaret cubs, bars and night clubs in the more important towns of Japan.

Purchases and souvenirs. On this score, Japan may be thought of as a bottomless pit waiting to receive your money. Some of its goods have gained a worldwide reputation: porcelain, cultured pearls, photographic equipment, and anything electronic. For your shopping you will, like the Japanese, go to chain stores, shopping concourses at railway stations, the world of underground shops, commercial streets with arcades set aside for pedestrians, and the alleys leading to buildings of a religious significance, which overflow with little shops, veritable temple traders who are there for the pilgrim and tourist. We indicate in our tables of general information where the prime shopping areas are to be found.

With certain articles, you may be able to take advantage of discounts on export goods: look for the 'tax-free' sign. The following goods are likely to be exempt from tax under this arrangement: gems and precious metals, pearls, coral, amber and ivory, tortoiseshell articles, furs, sporting guns, televisions, hi-fi equipment, cameras and photographic accessories. To get a discount of between 5% and 40% you will need to show your passport and fill in a form to keep in your passport. When you leave Japan, Customs will check the form against your belongings: it is as well to pack such valuables in a carry-on bag, since the check may take place after your luggage has been checked.

Sale times in Japan, like those at home, are periods of frantic shopping. You may find real bargains in the big shops, especially at the end of spring and of summer.

GIFTS. Every occasion is an excuse for giving gifts – the Japanese wouldn't dream of coming home from a trip without something for their friends and relations. You will doubtless be called upon to give or receive a present before you leave Japan, so be ready. Great importance is attached to the wrapping, which will be carefully done by the shop assistant. On receiving a gift, you should protest your unworthiness, and praise the exquisite presentation of the object, the fine choice of ribbons and paper: but never open the package there and then – its contents should concern only you. Similarly, be discreet in your thanks – complete them at a later date. It's a good idea to find some well-turned little phrase for the occasion.

NB: Be aware that certain 'luxury' items (perfumes, haute couture, ready-to-ware garments, silk scarves, etc.) are less expensive in Japan.

SHOPPING HOURS. Generally speaking, big shops are open from 10.00 to 18.00, Monday to Saturday. They do not shut on Sundays but they do on public holidays and most shops shut one day a week. Reckon on (at least) an extra hour's opening at either end of the day for smaller businesses, which also often stay open on Sundays and certain holidays.

Some practical details

POST OFFICES. They are open to the public from 09.00 to 17.00, Monday to Friday, and from 09.00 to 12.30 on Saturdays. The main post office in every town stays open from 8.00 to 20.00 (except Sundays and public holidays, when it shuts at noon).

INTERNAL TELEGRAPHIC SERVICES. Telegrams may be submitted in romaji, and services are available at post offices, stations and airports, etc., as well as the reception desk of your hotel.

To send an overseas cable you have to go through the KDD (Kokusai Denshin Denwa), which is available 24 hours a day in larger towns (ask your hotel for details: they may also be able to arrange to have your telegram sent).

THE TELEPHONE. There are automatic exchanges throughout Japan. In the streets, in cafés, stations, shops – everywhere, in fact – you will find telephones, generally red in colour and taking 10-yen coins for all intercity calls: you pay in advance according to the length of your conversation, and unused coins are returned to you at the end of the call. The rate varies with distance: you may find it more convenient to look out for a callbox accepting 100-yen coins for a long-distance call. There is a code number for each town or prefecture: these are listed in the 'Useful information' section at the end of this book (e.g. (03) for Tokyo, (06) for Osaka). To phone abroad, dial (03) 211-4211 for Asia (except Hong Kong), and (03) 211-5511 for Hong Kong and the rest of the world. It is worth waiting to call the USA and Canada until Sunday, when a cheap rate is in operation. The 'Japan Travel Phone' service is a boon to tourists with language problems. It provides answers in English to questions that might be of concern to a tourist, and gives information about travel in Japan. Just dial 502-1461 in Tokyo or 371-56-49 in Kyoto. Elsewhere, dial 106 and ask for 'Collect call TIC' (Tourist Information Centre).

NEWS AND NEWSPAPERS: If the Japanese language holds no terrors for you, you may read one of the three great dailies: the *Asahi shimbun*, or the *Mainichi shimbun*, with a circulation of more than 10 million a day, the *Yomiuri shimbun,* or the *Mainichi shimbun*. The *Chubu*

Nippon shimbun (newspaper of central Japan) deals mainly with Nagoya: *Nishi Nippon* is popular in Fukuoka, the *Hokkaido shimbun* in Sapporo, and *Chugoku shimbun* in Sendai. If you wish to read about world events in English, take one of these dailies: *Japan Times, Asahi Evening News*, the *Daily Yomiuri, Mainichi Daily News, International Herald Tribune*.

Radio and TV news are broadcast by several private channels as well as the Japanese radio and TV service, Nippon Hoso Kyokai (NHK), 2-3, Uchisaiwai cho, 2-chome, Chiyoda-ku, Tokyo (*Tel.* 501-4111). The Far East Network of the American Armed Forces in Japan also broadcasts information in English. In addition some receiving sets pick up an English-language programme, among them those belonging to the big hotels in the capital.

HEALTH. Japanese medical care is excellent, and there are many doctors who speak English (as well as German and, occasionally, French). All Protestant and Catholic hospitals are run by bilingual staff. Don't forget to take out travel insurance: Japanese medical charges are as high as the standard of treatment. Some hospitals are: Hibiya Clinic, International Catholic Hospital, St Luke's Hospital and Clinic, Tokyo Medical and Surgical Clinic (all in Tokyo); Yodogawa Christian Hospital in Osaka; and Japan Baptist Hospital in Kyoto.

SECURITY. Tokyo is proud of its crime rate, one of the lowest in the world. Thefts are rare, and even rarer are those committed against foreigners. If your wallet goes missing, ask yourself first if you could have mislaid it: if you have, you stand a very good chance of recovering it – the Japanese are wonderfully honest. To find lost property, try first at the station, the underground, or reception at your hotel. If you have no luck, apply to the lost property offices which gather together all finds which are unclaimed after three to five days: Central Lost and Found Office, Metropolitan Police Board, 1-9-11, Koraku, Bunkyo-ku, Tokyo (*Tel.* 814-4151).

Further information

Some addresses: Japan National Tourist Organization (JNTO):

Kyoto, Kyoto Tower Bldg, Higashi-Shiokojicho, Shimogyo-ku.
London, 167 Regent St, W1, England.
Los Angeles, 624 South Grand Ave, CA 90017.
New York, 630 Fifth Ave, NY 10111.
Tokyo, Yurakucho 2-chome, Chiyoda-ku (Central Office), and 6-6, Yurakucho 1-chome, Chiyoda-ku (Information Centre (*Tel.* 502-14651, 502-1661). At Narita Airport (*Tel.* (0476) 32-8711).
There is also a Teletourist Service for all information concerning Tokyo: a taped voice will tell you what's going on and what you should look out for in town: *Tel.* 503-2911, in English.

The cultural service of your nearest Japanese Embassy, or Consulate, or an office of Japan Air Lines will also provide you with leaflets and information.

Useful words and phrases

A glossary of topographical, botanical, religious and architectural terms

The following is a list of the principal Japanese expressions which will be found throughout this guide and which we shall hereafter leave untranslated for the most part.

Amida: the Buddha of Mercy, Amitabha in Sanskrit
Ashura: Buddhist demon fond of battles
Bashi, hashi: bridge
Ben(zai)ten: god of music and song, Sarasvati in Sanskrit
Bosatsu: Bodhisattva, or Buddhist saint
Butsu: the Buddha (he who has attained supreme enlightenment)
Byobu: screen
Chashitsu: teahouse
Cho: Small town, district
Chu, naka: region
Dai: great
Daichi: plateau
Dake: mountain
Daki, taki: waterfall
Dani, tani: valley
Den, do: hall, temple building
Dera, ji: Buddhist temple
Do: hall; grotto; road
Dori: street
Eki: railway station
Emakimono: pointed scroll (horizontally-wound)
Enma: ruler of hell, Yama in Sanskrit
En, koen: garden
Fu: regional government, city prefecture
Fudo: fire-god, Acala in Sanskrit
Fudo-do: room housing the statue of Fudo

Fugen: bosatsu charged with the education of the Buddha, Samantabhadra in Sanskrit
Fuji: wistaria
Gata: lagoon, lake
Gawa, kawa: river
Geku: outside (shrine)
Gu: Shinto shrine
Gun: canton, district
Gunto: archipelago
Hachiman: god of war
Haiden: oratory
Hama: beach
Hanto: peninsula
Hara: field
Hashi: bridge
Hasu: lotus
Heiden: room in which the Shinto gohei is kept
Heiya: plain
Higashi or **Tō**: east
Hinoki: Japanese cypress
Ho: Dharma, religious law
Hōdō: treasure hall
Honden: main hall of a Shinto shrine
Hondo, kondo: main hall of a Buddhist temple
Ike: pond
In: branch of a great temple
Iwa: rock
Ji, in, do: temple
Jima, shima: island
Jinja, gu, sha: Shinto shrine
Jizo: bosatsu who protects children, Kshitigarbha in Sanskrit
Jo: castle
Kai: sea
Kaigan: coast, shore
Kaikyo: straits, sound
Kairo: walkway
Kakemono: painted scroll (vertically-wound)
Kami: superior, Shinto god
Kankiten: god of happiness
Kannon: *bosatsu*, goddess of mercy, Avalokitesvara in Sanskrit
Kannon-do: houses the statue of Kannon
Katsuogi: roof-tree
Kawa: river
Kei, kyo: gorge
Ken: rural prefecture, administrative district
Kiku: chrysanthemum
Kita: north
Ko: lake
Kodo: room for preaching or reading
Koen: garden

Kogen: plateau
Koke: moss
Kokubun-ji: temples founded in the 8th c. on the orders of the Emperor Shomu
Kondo: main temple building
Ku: district, ward (of a town)
Kusunoki: camphor tree
Kyō: gorge; capital
Kyōzo: hall *sutras*
Machi: town
Mandara: ritual magic calligraphy; religious painting
Mandara dō: hall housing a mandala
Matsuri: festival
Mikoshi: sacred litter or palanquin
Minami: south
Mine: peak, mountain
Miroku: *bosatsu* of the future, saviour of the world, Maitreya in Sanskrit
Misaki, mizaki: cape
Momiji: maple tree
Momo: peach blossom
Mon: temple gate
Monju: *bosatsu* of wisdom, Manjusri in Sanskrit
Mura: village
Nada: sea
Naikū: inner shrine, especially at the Ise shrine
Naka: district
Nio: guardian statues at the entrance of Buddhist temples
Nishi, sai: west
Numa: marsh
Nyorai: Tathagata, one of the six names of the Buddha
O: great, honourable
Oku: inside (shrine)
Onsen: thermal spring
Retto, shoto: archipelago
Sai: west
Saki, zaki: cape
Sakura: cherry tree
San, zan: peak, mountain
Sanchi: mountainous rock formation
Sanmayaku: mountain range
Seto: channel, fairway, straits
Sha: Shinto shrine
Shakuyaku: peony
Shi: town, city
Shichō: mayor
Shima: island
Shimo: lower (shrine)
Shin: new
Shobu: iris

Shoji: light sliding door
Shonyudo: natural grotto
Shoro: campanile, bell-tower
Shoto: archipelago
Shu: religious sect
Sugi: cryptomeria (tree)
Suido: channel
Taishakuten. god, ruler of the 32 lesser divinities, Sakra devanam Indra in Sanskrit
Take: mountain peak
Taki: waterfall
Tani: valley
Tatami: mat of plaited rice-straw (always 71in × 35in/180cm × 90cm)
Tenshu: castle keep
Tō: metropolis, capital
To: east, island; pagoda; lantern
Toge: mountain pass
Torii: portico (Shinto shrine)
Tokonoma: recess containing an arrangement of flowers, etc.
Tsubaki: camellia
Tsutsuji: azalea
Ume: plum tree
Umi: lake, sea
Ura: lake, shore, beach
Wan: bay, gulf
Yaki: porcelain
Yakushi: Buddha of healing, Bhaisajyaguru in Sanskrit
Yama: mountain
Yosui: irrigation canal
Za: theatre
Zaki: cape
Zan: peak, mountain
Zukuri: architectural style

Some common words and expressions

Here, as elsewhere in this Guide, the Hepburn method of transcription, known as the *Hebonshiki romaji*, has been used (see p. 109).

Numbers

One	ichi, hitotsu
Two	ni, futatsu
Three	san, mittsu
Four	shi, yon, yottsu
Five	go, itsutsu
Six	roku, muttsu
Seven	shichi nana, nanatsu
Eight	hachi, yattsu
Nine	ku, kyu, kokonotsu
Ten	ju, to
Eleven	ju ichi
Twelve	ju ni
Thirteen	ju san
Fourteen	ju shi
Fifteen	ju go
Sixteen	ju roku
Seventeen	ju shichi
Eighteen	ju hachi
Nineteen	ju ku
Twenty	ni ju
Twenty-one	ni ju ichi
Thirty	san ju
Forty	yon ju
Forty-four	yon ju shi
Fifty	go ju
Sixty	roku ju
Seventy	nana ju
Seventy-seven	nana ju nana
Eighty	hachi ju
Ninety	kyu ju
Ninety-nine	kyu ju ku
One hundred	hyaku
Two hundred	ni hyaku
Three hundred	san hyaku
Four hundred	yon hyaku
Five hundred	go hyaku
Six hundred	roppyaku
Seven hundred	nana hyaku
Eight hundred	happyaku
Nine hundred	kyu hyaku
One thousand	sen, issen
Two thousand	ni sen
Three thousand	sansen
Four thousand	yon sen
Five thousand	go sen
Six thousand	roku sen
Seven thousand	nana sen
Eight thousand	hassen
Nine thousand	kyu sen
Ten thousand	ichi man
Twenty thousand	ni man
A hundred thousand	ju man
Two hundred thousand	ni ju man
A million	hyaku man
First	ichi bamme, dai ichi bamme
Second	ni bamme, dai ni bamme
Third	san bamme
Fourth	yon bamme
Seventh	shichi bamme
Ninth	kyu bamme
Half, a half	han, han bun
A third	san bun no ichi
A quarter	yon bun no ichi
Three quarters	yon bun no san

Time of year/day

Year	nen, toshi
One year	ichinen
Two years	ni nen
New Year	shinnen
Last year	sakunen, kyonen
Next year	rainen
This year	kotoshi
Twenty years (old)	hatachi
Season	kisetsu
Seasons (the 4)	shiki
Spring	haru
Summer	natsu
Autumn	aki
Winter	fuyu
Month	tsuki
January	ichi gatsu
February	ni gatsu
March	san gatsu
April	shi gatsu
May	go gatsu
June	roku gatsi
July	shichi gatsu
August	hachi gatsu
September	ku gatsu
October	ju gatsu
November	juichi gatsu
December	juni gatsu

Week	shu
Day	hi
Monday	getsu yobi
Tuesday	ka yobi
Wednesday	sui yobi
Thursday	moku yobi
Friday	kin yobi
Saturday	do yobi
Sunday	nichi yobi
One day	ichi nichi
Two days	futsuka kan
Three days	mikka kan
Four days	yokka kan
Five days	itsuka kan
Six days	muika kan
Seven days	nanoka kan
Eight days	yoka kan
Nine days	kokonoka kan
Ten days	toka kan
Eleven days	ju ichi nichi kan
Twelve days	ju ni nichi kan
First day of the month	tsuitachi
Second day of the month	futsuka
Last day of the month	misoka
Last day of the year	o misoka
Morning	asa
This morning	kesa
Midday	o hiru
Afternoon	gogo
Evening	yugata
This evening	komban
Night	yoru
Tonight	konya
Today	kyo
The day before yesterday	ototoi, issaku jitsu
Tomorrow	ashita
The day after tomorrow	asatte, myogo nichi
Hour	jikan
Half-hour	han jikan
One hour	ji
Minute	fun
One minute	ippun
Two minutes	nifun
Three minutes	sanpun
Four minutes	yonpun
Five minutes	gofun
Six minutes	roppun
Seven minutes	shichifun nanafun
Eight minutes	hachifun
Nine minutes	kyufun
Ten minutes	juppun

Second	byo
10h. 10	ju ji juppun
10h. 15	ju ji jugofun
10h. 30	ju ji sanjuppun
Half-past ten	ju ji han
five to ten	ju ji gofun mae
What is the time?	ima nanji desu ka
It is	desu
What day (date) is it?	kyo wa nannichi desu ka
What day of the week is it?	nan yobi desu ka
What month is it?	nan gatsu desu ka

Common words and phrases

I	boku (masc.), watashi (wa) (fem.), watakushi (wa) masc. & fem.
You (informal)	kimi
He	kare, ano kata, ano hito
She	ano kata, kano jo
We	watashitachi, watakushitachi
You	anatagata, anatatachi
You (polite)	anata
They (masc.)	ano katatachi karera
They (fem.)	ano katatachi, ano kanojotachi
My	watashi no, watakushi no
Your (informal)	anato no
His	ano kata no
Their	(add 'tachi' in front of 'no')
I, you, he, she, we, you, they, am (...) is (...) are	(pronoun) wa... desu.
I, you, he, she, we, you, they, was (...) were	(pronoun) wa... deshita.
I, you, he, she, we, you, they, am, not (...) is not (...) are not	(pronoun) wa... de waarimasen.
I, you, he, she we, you, they, was not (...) were not	(pronoun) wa... de wa arimasen de deshita.
I, you, he, she, we, you, they,	... wo motte imasu,...ga

have (...) has	*imasu,...ga arimasu.*
I, you, he, she, we, you, they, had	*...wo motte imashita,...ga arimashita.*
I, you, he, she, we, you, they, didn't have	*...wo motte imasen deshita. ...ga arimasen deshita.*
Have you got, is there?	*arimasu ka.*
Yes, I've got some, there is some	*hai, arimasu.*
No, I haven't got any, there isn't any	*ile, arimasen.*
Do you have (someone, something)?	*...wo motte imasu ka.*
Yes, I've got	*hai, motte imasu.*
NB – Don't you have?	*anata wa... motte imasen ka.*
Yes, I have got	*hai, arimasu.*
No, I haven't got	*iie, arimasen.*
(question)?	*ka.*
Yes	*hai.*
No	*iie.*
How many? (no. of people)	*nannin*
How many children are there?	*nannin kodomo ga imasu ka.*
How much? (quantity)	*dono kurai.*
How much money do you need?	*dono kurai okane ga irimasu ka.*
How much? (price)	*ikura.*
What does this cost?	*kore wa ikura desu ka.*
How do you say this in Japanese?	*kore wo nihongo de nan to iimasu ka.*
How are you?	*gokigen ikaga desu ka, ogenki desu ka.*
I'm fine thanks	*arigato, genki desu.*
Which?	*dochira.*
Where?	*doko.*
Where is it?	*doko desu ka.*
It's there	*koku desu.*
Here	*koku.*

There	*asoko.*
Why?	*naze.*
When?	*itsu.*
Which?	*dono.*
Which...would you like?	*dono...hoshii desu ka.*
What?	*nani wo, nani ga.*
What does that mean?	*sore wa do iu imi desu ka.*
Who?	*donata, dare.*
Who is that man?	*ano kata wa donata (dare) desu ka.*
It's Mr, Mrs, Miss	*san, desu.*
Who are you?	*anata wa donata desu ka.*
I'm Mr N.	*N...desu.*
Do you speak English?	*Eigo o hanase-masu ka.*
I don't speak Japanese	*Nihongo o hana-semasen.*
Do you understand	*wakarimasu ka.*
I understand	*wakarimasu.*
I don't understand	*wakarimasen.*
Excuse me, sorry	*gomen kudasai, sumimasen, gomennasai.*
I'm sorry to disturb you	*ojama shite sumimasen.*
Please	*kudasai.*
Thank you	*arigato, arigato gozaimasu.*
Thank you very much	*domo arigato (gozaimasu).*
Wait a minute	*chotto matte. kudasai.*
Goodbye	*sayonara.*
Good	*yoi.*
Good morning	*o hayo, o hayo gozaimasu.*
Good afternoon	*konnichi wa.*
Good evening	*kon ban wa.*
Good night	*o yasumi nasai.*
Bad	*warui.*
Hot	*atsui.*
Cold (weather)	*tsumetai, samui.*
Big, large	*okii.*
Small, little	*chiisai.*
Smaller, less (size)	*motto chiisai.*
Less (quantity)	*motto sukunai.*
Little, a little, some	*sukoshi, shosho.*

Would you like some more .... *mo sukoshi ikaga desu ka.*
Only a little ...... *honno sukoshi itadakimasu.*
More .... *motto.*
Would you like some more? ... *motto ikaga desu ka.*
I'd like a lot more .... *motto takusan hoshii desu.*

Too much .... *amarini.*
That's too much.......... *amarini osugi masu.*

That's not enough, there isn't enough ... *amarini sukuna sugimasu.*
All .... *minna* (people), *zembu.*
Nothing .... *nanimo.*
Sometimes ...... *toki doki.*
Always .... *itsumo, itsu demo.*
Never .... *kesshite...nai.*
Often........... *tabi tabi, toki doki.*
Early, quickly, soon .... *hayaku, hayaka ni.*
Fast, quickly .... *hayaku.*
Slowly.......... *yukkuri.*
Slow .... *osoi.*
Far .... *toi.*
Near .... *chikai, chikakuni*
To want, wish for .... *nozomu.*
I would like ...... *hoshii desu.*
Really! .... *ah so desu ka, honto desu ka.*

White .... *shiroi.*
Blue............. *ao, buryu.*
Grey .... *nezumi iro.*
Yellow .... *kiiro.*
Black............ *kuro.*
Red .... *aka.*
Green .... *midori.*

Weather
Mist .... *kiri.*
Eruption (volcanic) ...... *funka.*
Damp .... *shikke.*
Snow............ *yuki.*
Cloud .... *kumo.*
Storm .... *arashi.*
Rain............. *ame.*
Sun .... *taiyo.*
Earthquake ...... *jishin.*
Typhoon......... *taifu.*
Wind .... *kaze.*
It's fine (of weather) ... *ii o tenki desu.*

It's warm (of weather) ... *atatakai desu.*
It's hot (of weather) ... *atsui desu*
It's cold (of weather) *samui desu.*
The weather's bad .... *warui o tenki desu.*
It's raining .... *ame ga futte imasu.*
It's windy .... *kaze ga huite imasu.*

Customs, administration
Spirits, alcohol ... *arukoru.*
Embassy .... *taishi kan.*
Consulate ...... *ryojoi kan.*
Customs .... *zeikan.*
Foreigner .... *gaikokujin.*
Export........... *yushutsu.*
Frontier .... *kokkyo.*
Passport......... *ryoken.*
Quarantine ...... *ken eki.*
Tobacco .... *tabako.*
Vaccination ...... *shuto.*
Anything to declare? *nani ka shinkoku suro mono ga arimasu ka.*

In the street
Bank .... *ginko.*
Library .... *tosho kan.*
Bicycle .... *jitensha.*
Shop, boutique... *mise.*
Information office .... *annaijo.*
Booking office, Reservations ..... *kippu uriba.*
Cinema.......... *eiga kan.*
Barber .... *tokoyasan.*
Hairdresser ...... *biyo-in.*
Station (railway)........ *eki.*
Town hall. Guildhall .... *shiyakusho.*
Museum......... *hakubutsu kan.*
Chemist .... *kusuriya, yakkyoku.*
Theatre.......... *shibai, gekijo.*
Police station .... *koban.*
Policeman .... *junsa.*
Police force ..... *keisatsu.*
Apartment block .... *tatemono, biru-dingu.*
Exhibition .... *tenjikai.*
Excursion (circuit) ...... *yuran, ryoko.*
Excursion (city rail) ...... *kembutsu, kanko.*
Park, gardens .... *niwa, koen.*

Bridge . . . . *hashi, bashi.*
Road,
  thoroughfare . . *dori.*
Beach . . . . *kaisuiyokujo.*
Entrance . . . . *iriguchi.*
Exit . . . . *deguchi.*
Please direct me . . . *wa doko desu*
to . . . . *ka.*
Where are *doko e irasshai-*
  you going? . . . . *masu ka.*
I'm going
to... *...e ikimasu, ... e*
I wish to
  go to . . . . *ikitai desu.*

By car, by taxi

Car . . . . *jidosha.*
Driver . . . . *untenshu.*
Petrol, gasoline. . . *gasorin.*
Garage . . . . *gareji.*
Petrol/gasoline
  station . . . . *gasorin-stando.*
Fare. . . . . *unchin.*
Taxi. . . . . *takushi.*
Please ring *denwa de takushi*
  for a taxi. . . . . . . *wo yonde kudasai.*
Please take me *koko e tsurete*
  here. . . . . *itte kudasai.*
Please take me *eki made tsurete*
  to the station . . *itte kudasai.*
Go straight
  ahead . . . . *massugu ni.*
On the right . . . . . *migi e.*
On the left . . . . *hidari e.*
Stop here, *koko de tomatte*
  please. . . . . *kudasai.*
Wait here, *koko de matte*
  please. . . . . *kudasai.*
I'll be back in . . . . *sugu ni kae-*
  a second . . . . . . *rimasu.*

Other forms of transport

Airport . . . . *kuko.*
Arrival. . . . . *tochaku.*
Bus . . . . *basu.*
Plane . . . . *hikoki.*
Luggage. . . . . *nimotsu.*
Boat . . . . *boto, fune, kisen.*
Ticket . . . . *kippu.*
Booking office . . . *shussatsu guchi.*
Change trains. . . . *kisha wo nori-*
  kaeru.
Train, railway . . . . *kisha.*
Class (1st, 2nd) . *to (itto, nito).*
Left luggage . . . . . *nimotsu azu-*
  karijo.

Couchette,
  sleeper . . . . *shindai.*
To disembark . . . . *joriku suru.*
Departure . . . . *shuppatsu.*
Destination *mokutekichi,*
  yukisaki.
To embark . . . . *josen suru.*
Ferry-boat . . . . *renrakusen, feri-*
  boto.
Station . . . . *eki.*
Underground,
  subway, metro . *chikatetsu.*
Passenger . . . . *jokyaku, sen-*
  kyaku (boat).
Seat. . . . . *seki.*
Reserved seat . . . . *yoyaku seki, shi-*
  tai seki.
Port . . . . *minato, ko.*
Porter . . . . *akabo.*
Platform
  (station) . . . . . . *homu.*
Platform No. 1 *ichiban-sen.*
Reservation . . . . . . *yoyaku.*
Train . . . . *kisha.*
Express (train) . . . *kyuko.*
Rapid (train) . . . . . *tokkyu*
Semi-express
  (train) . . . . *junkyu.*
Tram . . . . *densha.*
Sleeping-car . . . . . *shindaisha.*
Dining-car,
Restaurant-car . . *shokudosha.*
Journey . . . . *ryoko.*
Have a good *itte irasshai,*
  journey! . . . . *genki de.*
Where is the *shussatsu guchi*
  booking office? *wa doko desu ka.*
What day are *itsu odekake*
  you going? . . . *desu ka.*
I leave on... . . . . . . *ni dekake masu.*
When does the *...yuko no kisha*
  train for . . . . . . *wa nanji ni*
  ...leave? *demasu ka.*
When does the *kono kisha wa*
  train get to... ? *nan ji ni...e tsu*
  kimasu ka.
I'd like a *...yuki no itto o*
  first-class
  single to... . . . . *ichimai kudasai.*
I'd like a *...yuki no ofuku*
  second-class *no nito o nimai*
  return to . . . . *kudasai.*
Are there any *shindaisha ga*
  sleeping-cars? . *tsuite imasu ka.*
I'd like to *...made, shindai*
  reserve two *ken ni mai*
  sleepers for. . . . *kudasai.*
How much will *...made ikura*
  it cost to go
  to...? *desu ka.*
Which platform *...yuki wa nan*

does the...train *bansen kara*
leave from ..... *demasu ka.*
Platform No ....*ban desu.*

In the hotel, the restaurant

Air conditioned . *reidanbo.*
Bathroom .... *furoba, basu rumo.*
Bill.............. *kanjo.*
Beef .... *gyuniku.*
Bean .... *mame.*
Bed .... *nedoko (Jap.), betto (West.).*
Beer .... *biiru.*
Blanket, cover ... *kake buton, mofu.*
Bottle .... *bin.*
Bowl, cup .... *chawan, koppu.*
Bread .... *pan.*
Breakfast ....*choshoku.*
Butter .... *bata.*
Cafe .... *kissaten.*
Cake .... *o kashi (Jap.), keki (West.).*
Cancel .... *torikesu.*
Cashier.......... *suito gakari.*
Central heating . *danbo.*
Chambermaid ...*jochu,meido.*
Cheese..........*chiku.*
Cheque ....*kogitte.*
Cigar............*hamaki.*
Chicken ....*niwatori.*
Cigarette ....*makitabako.*
Clean (verb) .....*soji suru.*
Coffee ....*kohi.*
Cook (person) ...*ryori nin (Jap.), kokku (West.).*
Crab ....*kani.*
Dinner ....*yushoku.*
Dining room, restaurant (of hotel) ......*shokudo.*
Director ....*shihainin, maneja.*
Dish ....*o sara.*
Drink............*nomimono.*
Egg ....*tamago.*
Emergency ......*hijoji, kyuyo.*
Fish ....*sakana.*
Flannel ....*tenugui (Jap.), taoru (West.).*
Floor ....*kai (nikkai, sangai,...).*
(1st, 2nd,...)
Fork ....*hoku.*
Fruit ....*kudamono.*
Fruit juice ....*furutsu) jusu.*
Full (fully booked) . *man in desu.*
Glass ....*koppu.*

Ground floor.....*ikkai.*
Hall ....*robi.*
Hotel *ryokan (Jap.), hoteru (West.).*
Hot napkin ......*o shibori.*
Key ....*kagi.*
Knife ....*naifu.*
Lemon ....*remon.*
Lemonade ......*saida.*
Lunch ....*chushoku.*
Massage.........*amma, massaji.*
Meal ....*shokuji.*
Meat ....*niku.*
Menu ....*menyu.*
Milk ....*gyunyu.*
Omelet ....*omuretsu.*
Pepper ....*kosho.*
Pillow ....*makura.*
Potato..........*jagaimo, poteto.*
Radiator.........*sutobu.*
Raw.............*nama.*
Refrigerator .....*reizoko.*
Reservation......*yokaku.*
Restaurant.......*ryoriya (Jap.) resutoran (West.).*
Rice (cooked)....*gohan.*
Salt ....*shio.*
Sandwich........*sandoitchi.*
Sheets ....*shitsu.*
Shower..........*shawa.*
Shrimp ....*ebi.*
Spicy ....*togarashi.*
Spoon...........*supun.*
Sugar ....*sato.*
Table napkin .....*napkin.*
Tea ....*o cha (Jap.), ko cha (Ind.).*
Telephone ....*denwa.*
Television ......*terebijon.*
Toilet, WC ....*semmenjo, benjo.*
Tomato..........*tomato.*
Tuna ....*maguro.*
Vegetables.......*yasai.*
Waiter ....*boisan.*
Waitress ....*ojosan.*
Water ....*mizu.*
drinking water *nomi mizu.*
hot water ......*o yu.*
mineral water *mineraru uota.*
Wine *bodu shu.*
Do you have a *heya ga arimasu*
room? *ka.*
Please call the *jochu wo yonde*
chambermaid . *kudasai.*
This isn't clean ... *kore wa kirei de wa arimasen.*
May I sit here? ... *koko e kakete mo il desu ka.*

The tourist's Japan

What to see

There is no Chartres Cathedral, no Colorado River in Japan: but the maps of the main natural and manmade curiosities will give only the merest hint of the country's innumerable resources. We are almost tempted to catalogue what to avoid seeing in Japan. In their quest for domination over nature the Japanese have not refrained from disfiguring it: roads of various kinds (highway, coast road, motorway, etc.) have been built, cablecar lines and galleries are carved into the mountains, bridges and viaducts cut across valleys or overhang the sea, and children's playgrounds, observation platforms and billboards are plastered with garish advertising posters. Despite their usefulness, all these surely deserve to be denounced aesthetically. However, nature is essential to the Japanese conception of the world. Driven mercilessly back by the sprawling towns, it still dominates the rest of the island chain, so that only a few miles outside the great urban centres you can find yourself immersed in it. It influences all the traveller's moods, and has for all of time been intimately linked with the Japanese way of life. Traditional religious and secular buildings, using much carved wood in their construction, harmonize beautifully with their surroundings. The natural settings are further domesticated by the exquisite art of skilfully made gardens, and in the barest of rooms pride of place is given to *bonsai*s (miniature trees) and to the artistic floral arrangements of *ikebana*.

Natural parks. There are no fewer than 27 national parks in Japan, of which the most important is Daisetsuzan Park in Hokkaido; there are also protected areas and islands under the jurisdiction of the Ministry of Public Health and Social Affairs. We list later in alphabetical order all the parks of major interest to tourists. They are easily accessible, being admirably served by coaches, in co-ordination with the railways and daily excursions. To the list may be added a great number of semi-national parks, natural regions and reserves, which we include under the heading of their various locations.

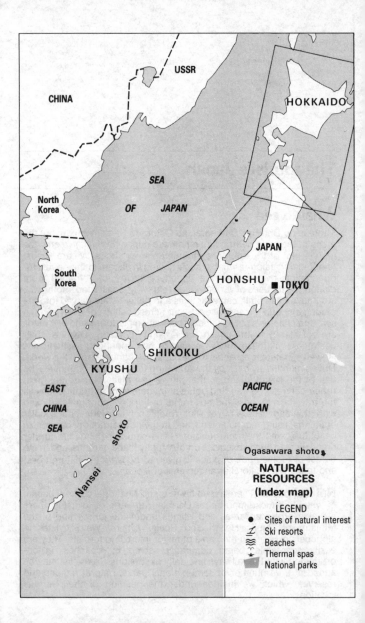

CHINA

USSR

HOKKAIDO

North
Korea

SEA

OF

JAPAN

South
Korea

JAPAN

HONSHU

■ TOKYO

SHIKOKU

KYUSHU

EAST

CHINA

SEA

shoto

Nansei

PACIFIC

OCEAN

Ogasawara shoto

**NATURAL
RESOURCES**
(Index map)

LEGEND
● Sites of natural interest
⅃ Ski resorts
≋ Beaches
⁓ Thermal spas
National parks

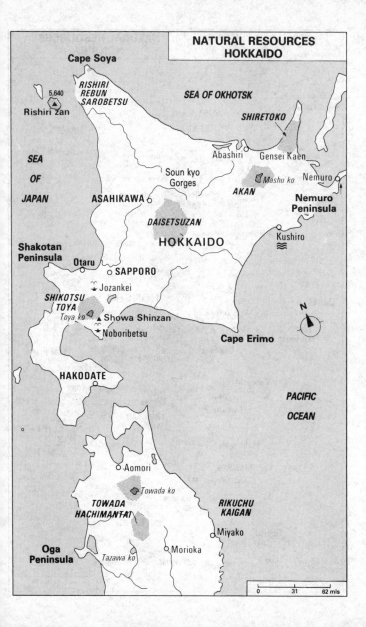

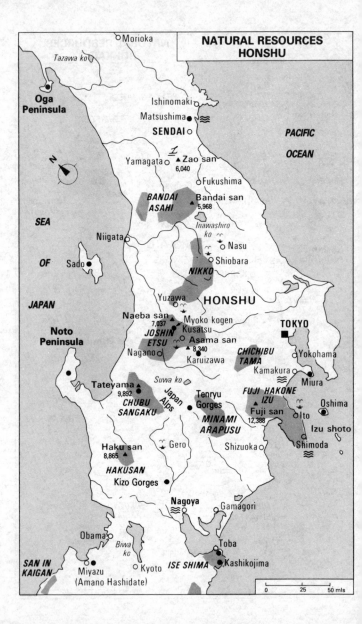

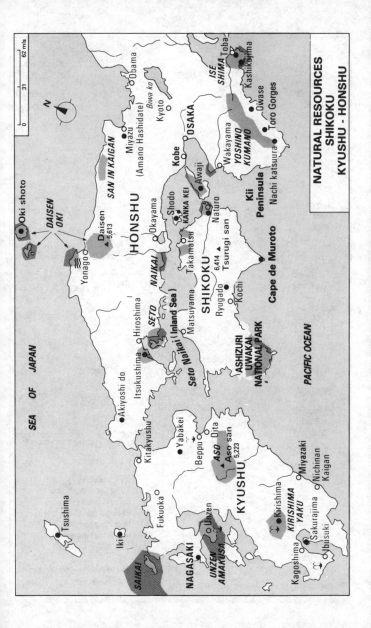

NATURAL RESOURCES
SHIKOKU
KYUSHU - HONSHU

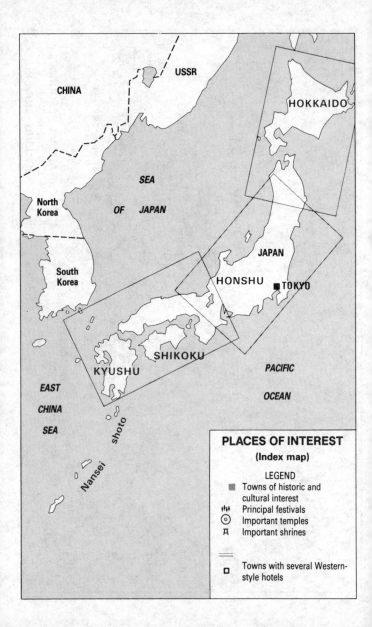

PLACES OF INTEREST
(Index map)

LEGEND

■ Towns of historic and cultural interest
♨ Principal festivals
⊙ Important temples
☗ Important shrines

▭ Towns with several Western-style hotels

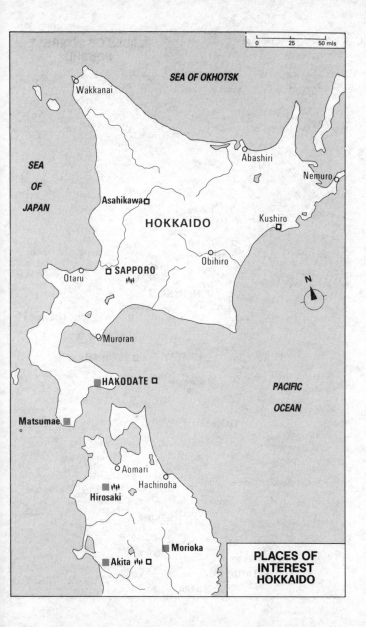

SEA OF OKHOTSK

SEA
OF
JAPAN

HOKKAIDO

Wakkanai

Abashiri

Nemuro

Asahikawa

Kushiro

Otaru

SAPPORO

Obihiro

Muroran

HAKODATE

PACIFIC

OCEAN

Matsumae

Aomari

Hachinoha

Hirosaki

Morioka

Akita

PLACES OF
INTEREST
HOKKAIDO

0   25   50 mis

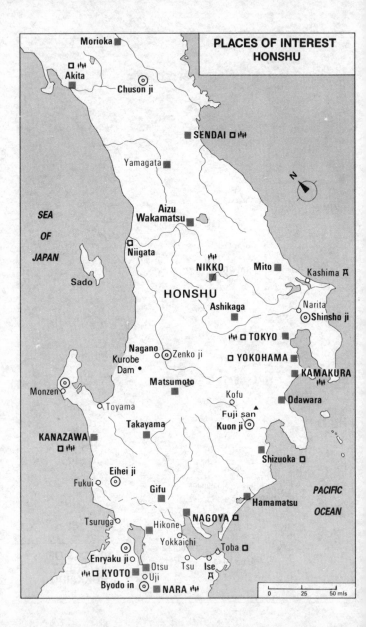

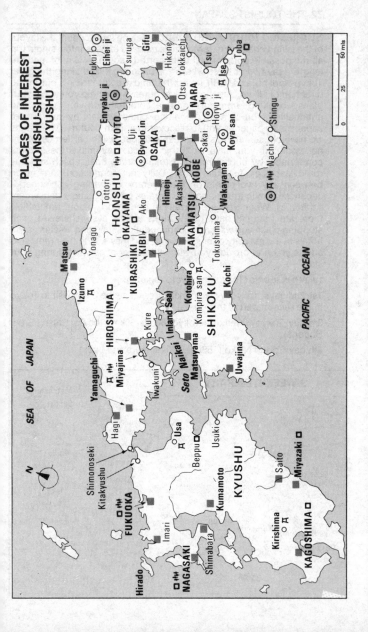

PLACES OF INTEREST
HONSHU-SHIKOKU
KYUSHU

Suggested tours of the islands. Taking into account the layout of the island chain, very few tourists manage to pack into a single trip all the possible ports of call from north to south. A stay of medium length – say two or three weeks – is often organized along the great Tokyo-Kyushu axis, with its northernmost point striking out in the direction of Nikko. Japanese travel bureaus will help you make your plans, booking transport and accommodation for you, and channelling you if need be along paths beaten by millions of Japanese as eager as you to discover their own country. The stages we have chosen are easily driveable by car, using car ferries where necessary: if you have no vehicle, you may make these tours comfortably by public transport (plane, train, boat, coach and bus route, cablecar, funicular, etc.). Daily rail connections are made between any two points on the itinerary; everything is planned – Japanese public transportation operates on surprisingly convenient schedules. When you are travelling, don't worry about timetables: there are frequent daily connections almost everywhere. At each stopping place you will find accommodation, including Western-style hotels in the majority of bigger towns, and they will do their utmost to advise you and provide you with all manner of services during your stay.

1 JAPAN IN 10 DAYS (Tokyo and Kyoto regions)

1st-2nd days: Tokyo; visits to main areas (see the 2-day visit to Tokyo in the second part of this guide).

3rd day: Tokyo-Kamakura-Tokyo (60mls/90km), the Dai Batsu (Great Buddha).

4th day: Trip to Nikko (168mls/270km there and back).

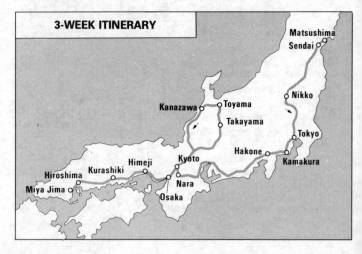

5th-7th days: Tokyo-Kyoto (304mls/489km) (see the 3-day visit to the city in the descriptive section of this guide).

8th-9th days: Kyoto-Nara (27mls/44km); visit the temples and shrines of Nara Park, together with surrounding area.
10th day: Nara-Tokyo (305mls/491km) return to the capital.

2 JAPAN IN THREE WEEKS (2,125mls/3,420km approx.)

1st-2nd days: Tokyo (see the 2-day visit in the descriptive section of this guide).
3rd day: Tokyo-Nikko (84mls/135km); visit Toshu gu, major shrine with a five-storey pagoda and the Yomei mon gate, not forgetting the beautiful national park with its celebrated waterfall.

4th day: Nikko-Sendai (121mls/194km); visit Matsushima, site of one of Japan's most beautiful temples, the Chuson-ji (via Ichinoseki); return to Sendai.

5th day: Sendai-Tokyo (232/374km).

6th day: Tokyo-Kamakura (28mls/45km).

7th day: Kamakura-Hakone (28mls/45km); walk by Lake Ashi to see Mount Fuji (fine weather only).

8th day: Hakone-Kyoto (267mls/430km); your first glimpse of Kyoto.

9th-11th days: Kyoto; visit the city and its environs (see the 3-day visit in the descriptive part of this guide).

12th day: Kyoto-Nara (27mls/44km); visit the Nara site and environs (Horyu-ji); return to Osaka in the evening.

13th day: Osaka-Koya-san (37mls/60km); visit the necropolis and the temples in this very holy Buddhist place; stay in monastery accommodation.

14th day: morning in Koya-san; travel back to Osaka and Kyoto (90mls/145km).

15th day: Kyoto-Nagoya-Takayama (194mls/312km); visit Takayama, a charming town nestling in the heart of the Japan Alps.

16th day: Takayama-Kanazawa (112mls/180km); very fine garden, Kenroku en.

17th day: Kanazawa-Kyoto (144mls/231km).

18th day: Kyoto-Himeji (78mls/125km); visit the most impressive castle in Japan.

19th day: Himeji-Hiroshima (155mls/250km); visit the town and the Park of Peace, with its museum; Hovercraft to Miyajima; night in a ryokan.

20th day: Miyajima; in early evening, Hovercraft back to Hiroshima, then Shinkansen as far as Kurashiki.

21st day: Visit Kurashiki, then go by Shinkansen to Tokyo (431mls/694km).

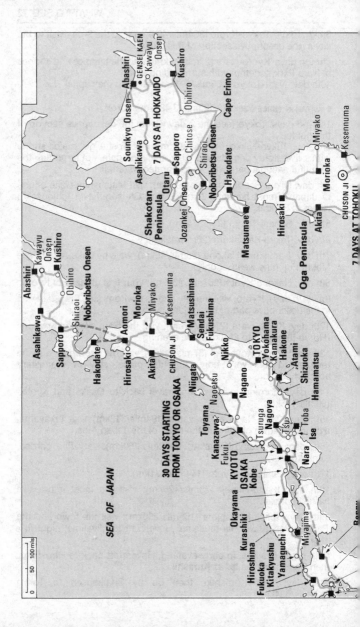

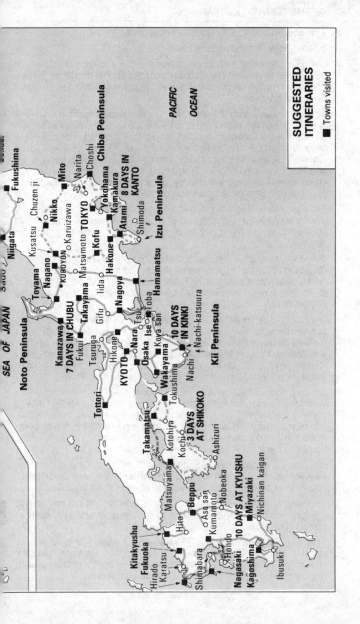

SEA OF JAPAN

Noto Peninsula

Fukushima

Niigata

Toyama

Kanazawa

7 DAYS IN CHUBU

Tottori

Kusatsu Chuzen ji
Nikkō
Nagano
Karuizawa
KUROYON
Matsumoto TOKYO

Takayama
Iida
Gifu
Fukui
Tsuruga
Hikone
Nara
Osaka
KYOTO
Tsu
Ise
Kōya san

Nagoya
Hamamatsu

Kōfu
Hakone
Atami
Shimoda
Izu Peninsula

Mito
Narita
Choshi
Chiba Peninsula
Yokohama
Kamakura
8 DAYS IN KANTO

PACIFIC
OCEAN

Wakayama
Tokushima
Nachi
10 DAYS IN KINKI
Nachi-katsuura
Kii Peninsula

Takamatsu
Kotohira
Kochi
Ashizuri
3 DAYS AT SHIKOKU

Kitakyushu
Fukuoka
Hirado
Karatsu
Shimabara
Nagasaki
Kagoshima
Ibusuki

Hita
Asa san
Kumamoto
Hondo
Nobeoka
Beppu
Miyazaki
Nichinan kaigan
10 DAYS AT KYUSHU

Matsuyama

SUGGESTED ITINERARIES

■ Towns visited

3 30 DAYS IN JAPAN (3,900mls/6,300km approx.)

1st-2nd days: Tokyo; visit the town.

3rd day: Excursion to Kamakura, seat of the ancient bakufu, where you will go to see the Dai Butsu (direct rail connection from Tokyo); you may stop off on the way back at Yokohama to visit the beautiful Sankeien gardens.

4th day: Tokyo-Atami (83mls/134km), the Hakone region. If you don't wish to go with an organized trip, take a JNR train from Tokyo station to Hakone via Odawara (castle), or go by Odakyu Electric Railway from Shinjuku. From Odawara, take the connection (Hakone Tozan Railway) to Gora, or go by coach. Next, a cablecar will take you to the shores of Lake Ashino-ko (Togendai) which you cross by boat to Hakone, and a coach will drive you via Hakone tôge to view Mount Fuji. Hakone Skyline will take you on to Atami.

5th day: Atami-Nagoya (153mls/247km); the quickest journey is by Shinkansen (JNR), stopping off at Shizuoka at least to visit Sengen jinja while you're there; set aside the later part of the afternoon for Nagoya.

6th day: Nagoya-Iseshima (81mls/131km); travel by JNR train, changing at Taki, or by Kintetsu Railway; visit the shrines of Geku and Naiku before continuing on to Toba, home of cultured pearls (but also of 'cultured pearl tourism'), which you may get to by Ise-shima Skyline coach.

7th day: Iseshima-Osaka (145mls/234km); a busy day, many connections to make. From Ise (Uji-Yamada), take the Kintetsu Railway as far as Sakurai, then JNR (Sakurai Line) to Yomato Takada, and Wakayama Line to Hashimoto; from here, go by coach or Nankai Railroad train to Koyasan, well worth a visit. In the late afternoon, take the Nankai Railroad back down to Namba station in Osaka.

8th day: Osaka-Okayama (99mls/160km); devote the morning to a swift look round Osaka (Shitenno-ji, castle), then take a train (JNR or private) from a station in Osaka or nearby Umeda, as far as Kobe, where you mustn't miss the chance to go up Rokko-san. From Shin-Kobe the Shinkansen will whisk you to Okayama via Himeji, where you'll see the most flamboyant castle in Japan.

9th day: Okayama-Miyajima (112mls/180km); see Kurashiki on the way, then by Shinkansen to Hiroshima; visit the memorial and Park of Peace, then by hovercraft to Miyajima, pearl of the Inland Sea.

10th day: Miyajima-Fukuoka (155mls/250km); spend the morning in Miyajima and leave in the afternoon for Hiroshima; Shinkansen to Hakata (Fukuoka).

11th day: Fukuoka-Nagasaki (88mls/142km); leave plenty of time to see the shrine at Daizafu (coach or Nishitetsu train from Fukuoka, changing at Futsukaichi). From Futsukaichi, JNR will take you to Nagasaki, where you'll spend most of the afternoon.

12th day: Nagasaki-Beppu (186mls/300km); Kamenoi Bus will relay you to Unzen, Shimabara, Kumamoto and Mount Aso.

13th day: Beppu-Osaka (250mls/400km); after a morning's stay in Beppu, a Toa Domestic Airlines (TDA) plane will take you back to Osaka.

14th day: Osaka-Kyoto (53mls/85km); catch a JNR train from Minatomachi or Tennoji stations to Horyuji, where there is one of the oldest and most magnificent temples in Japan. At lunchtime, take a bus to Nara, and spend a leisurely afternoon there. Kinki Nippon Railway will then take you directly from Nara-Kintetsu to Kyoto.

15th–16th days. Kyoto; treat yourself to taxi rides, and try to see as much as you can in two days.

17th day: Kyoto-Kanazawa (144mls/231km); leave early if you'd like to see the castle in Hikone on the way. Continue with JNR (Hokuriku Main Line) as far as Fukui, from where you can make a detour (by bus or Keikufu Railway) to the Eihei ji temple; make sure you arrive in Kanazawa early enough to visit the Kenroku en gardens.

18th day: Kanazawa-Nagano (121mls/195km); a long day in the Tateyama mountains. Take the Hokuriku Main Line (JNR) as far as Toyama, then the Toyama Chiho Railway to Tateyama station, from where (by funicular, coach and cablecar) you can reach the Kuroyon Dam, via Tate-yama (see Chubu Sangaku National Park). From Kuroyon, take a cablecar and coach back down to (Shinano) Omachi, and finally a bus to Nagano.

19th day: Nagano-Akita (290mls/467km); set aside the early morning for the Zenko ji, then let the JNR express service speed you to Akita, changing at Naoetsu or Niigata.

20th day: Akita-Asahikawa (334mls/537km); having spent the morning in Akita, fly TDA to Sapporo, whence you will have to take a train to Asahikawa.

21st day: Asahikawa-Abashiri (135mls/218km); travel as far as Rubeshibe by Dohoku Bus, going across Daisetsuzan National Park via Soun kyo. From Rubeshibe to Abashiri the JNR follows a beautiful scenic route, especially along the shores of Lake Abashiri.

22nd day: Abashiri-Kushiro (145mls/233km); train to Bihoro, then coach connection (Akan Bus) which will allow you to see Lakes Kussharo, Mashu and Akan: from there, you'll reach Kushiro by evening.

23rd day: Kushiro-Sapporo (245mls/395km); by JNR express or TDA flight, to spend the latter part of the afternoon in Sapporo.

24th day: Sapporo-Hakodate (203mls/327km); JNR will convey you from Sapporo to Noboribetsu, and from Toya station to Hakodate: make your connection between the two by Donan bus via Noboribetsu Onsen, Orofure toge, and Toya-ko.

25th day; Hakodate-Aomori (70mls/113km); devote the morning to Hakodate, then take a JNR ferry (4-hour crossing to Aomori).

26th day: Aomori-Morioka (141mls/227km); go by JNR train as far as Hirosaki; then take a coach to Nenokuchi, on the shores of Lake Towada, which you may cross by boat (to Yasumiya); a JNR bus will take you to Minami Towada station; then train to Morioka.

27th day: Morioka-Kesennuma (148mls/238km); JNR train as far as Miyako, from which point a boat trip is highly recommended. From Miyako to Kesennuma you'll follow the superb Rikucho coastline, via Kamaischi and Ofunato.

28th day: Kesennuma-Sendai (101mls/163km); using the Ofunato Line (JNR), travel as far as Ichinoseki, where a bus will take you to the Chüson ji, which attracts numerous pilgrims. Bus again to Ichinoseki, or train direct from Hiraizumu (JNR Tohoku Main Line), to reach Sendai.

29th day: Sendai-Fukushima (49mls/79km); after a swift look round Sendai, don't miss Matsushima, site of some of Japan's most interesting buildings (a 36-mls/58-km detour; JNR Ishinomaki line); from Sendai, proceed to Fukushima by Shinkansen.

30th day: Fukushima-Tokyo (212mls/341km); leave reasonably early, so you can devote as much of your time as possible to Nikko and its shrines; Shinkansen from Fukushima to Utsunomiya, then change trains for Nikko, from where you may travel direct to Tokyo by Tobu Railway, arriving at Asakusa station.

Beaches and seaside resorts. Several thousand islands, 17,000 miles (28,000km) of splendid coastline (of which, sadly, 60% is now under concrete), acres of silver sand, pine-trees – and yet there is no Japanese seaside tourism to speak of. The beaches, overcrowded during the season, are few in number: the coast, most of it made up of reefs, doesn't readily lend itself to tourist facilities. Industrialization and pollution have driven the would-be bather some distance from the towns, and yet it is the towns which provide the coast with its visitors. Among typical resorts we would cite Oarai, near Milto, the coastal strip of Kamakura as far as Eno shima, the Izu peninsula, especially around Shimoda, the coastal area of the Iseshima National Park, Shirahama on the Kii peninsula, Amanohashidate, and the extreme tip of the Yamaguchi province, towards the Sea of Japan. It is on Kyushu that you'll find the best beaches, but the Ryukus are the place where you feel as if you'd stepped into a dream world of deserted sands, a warm, crystal-clear sea, luxuriant vegetation and cloudless skies (except in the typhoon season).

Hot spas (*onsen*). These are to be found almost everywhere in Japan; formed as a result of volcanic activity, the waters of these famous hot springs (which reach temperatures of up to boiling point) are sent for sale, chilled, in bathing establishments and hotels. The properties of the different springs are credited with being effective against skin disorders, digestive problems and nervous pains. Some of the springs are very mildly radioactive.

However, the healing properties of the waters are not the main attraction of the spa towns: one's stay is generally brief – a weekend, or a short break – and generally motivated by the other activities on offer at the spa: walks, winter sports, bathing in the sea.

The major spas are: Jozankei and Noboribetsu on Hokkaido; Atami, Ito, Kusatsu, Shirahama, and Shiobara on Honshu; Beppu, Ibusuki and Unzen on Kyushu.

INFORMATION: Japanese Hot-Spring Association, Kokusai Kanko Kaikan Bldg, 1-8-3, Marunouchi 1-chome, Chiyoda-ku, Tokyo (*Tel.* 231-1640).

Winter sports.

There is no shortage of snow in winter and ski-slopes abound. Here again, things are very different from Europe. The ski resorts, almost all of them concentrated in the area of the 'Japan Alps' (Nagano and Niigata provinces), are very close to the great metropolitan centres of Tokyo, Nagoya and Osaka. Consequently the crowds that pour off trains and coaches in winter are enormous, and they swarm all over the ski lifts. A typical skiing jaunt rarely lasts for more than 48 hours but they are well-filled hours, for there are even floodlights for the benefit of nocturnal skiers. However, you will find good hotels if you do want to sleep. Zao and Naeba are among the best-known Japanese ski resorts.

Getting to know Japan

First impressions

by Dr Jacques Pezeu-Massabuau
D. Litt, course director at Tokyo University

Japanese society

The family: mainstay of society. To visit a Japanese house or, better still, to spend a few days there, is without doubt the finest introduction you can have to Japanese society. In its very construction you will find expressed in practice the essential principles which ensure the functioning of that society. The stress is laid on the impermanence of man and all his works. The house is a simple construction, with no foundations, made of lightweight materials - wood and paper (opaque for walls, translucent for windows) - and mats on the floor (thick *tatami* on which you walk barefoot). Partitions are light, moveable, and permeable to the slightest sound. The rooms all interconnect, so that each person's activities can be observed by everyone else. The individual is considered subordinate to the group as a whole. There is a hierarchy of rooms and functions: the entrance hall is floored with the same material as the street or lane outside, kitchen and corridors are wooden-floored, and only the rooms are provided with matting. At the top of the house is the *zashiki* (what we'd call the living-room), the principal room, distinguished by the 'tokonoma', a recess decorated with a bouquet of flowers and a painting, the aesthetic centre-piece of the house. There are regional variations in the pitch and building material of the roof, and sometimes in the layout of the house itself, but the essentials remain constant. Life is generally lived at ground-floor level, functions increasing with importance as you go up the house. In every home there are *tatami*, traditional throughout Japan, for sitting or lying on.

Rural families no longer adhere so strictly to their former structure, which was founded on Confucian ethical codes. The father is the absolute authority, a woman ruling over the household but subject first to her father, then to her husband, and finally to her eldest son. The primal drive is to perpetuate the line, if need be by adoption, which is still widely practised as, in the case of large families, is the subordination of the descendants of younger brothers to those of an older one. All this is supported by a system of protective relationships and obligations. In times gone by one or more of these extended families constituted a village. Whether the dwellings were scattered among the rice fields or gathered at the centre of the locality, community relations remained the same, fixed by custom and hierarchy: relationships based on mutual aid dictated by the material imperatives of life (harvesting, roof-making, the repair of roads and dykes), or by events in the family (at weddings and funerals particularly, when everyone's role was strictly prescribed, as were their duties). From the age of seven until they were sixteen, boys and girls lived in 'dormitories' where they served their apprenticeship for communal life and where, sometimes after several trial relationships, they would find the ideal spouse.

Since the Emperor Meiji, this strong continuity has been undermined by the migration of young men to the cities. Arriving alone, they marry women from other regions and maintain only sporadic relations with their 'home town'. The new city-dweller lives with his wife and children, increasingly reluctant to accept the presence in his house of their parents. Once a producer, he is now a consumer, often renting a flat (even though the *tatami* still finds its place in his bedroom). If he stays on in the village, he works part-time in town, and the old bond between man and the soil has ceased to be quite so vital.

Nevertheless, the cohesive force of the traditional family has not entirely lost its effect on the social groupings of modern life. In towns especially, since feudal times, the district has taken over from the rural community, but above all it is the firm for which a person works which has replaced old professional ties and even the bond between neighbours. From the largest corporations to modest workshops, a precise and complex network of relations between superior and subordinate embraces everyone and directs behaviour in all circumstances. Within smaller-scale companies, the old terms *oyabun* (father) and *kobun* (child) are still current, showing how deep-rooted is the family model in all relations between two or more individuals from different social strata.

Recently, it is true, the town-dwelling Japanese has become less willing to sacrifice his domestic happiness for the sake of his employers, and the rising cost of living has meant longer and more determined strikes about pay-claims at the start of each year. Class consciousness, though, in the classical sense, seems far from prevalent because of the rapid increases in the standard of living and the still firm grip of traditional bonds. The emergence in Japan of a movement such as socialism has always been thought of as unlikely, and it has taken many compromises with their own social system for the left-wing parties (socialist and communist) – coherent and committed though they are – to win a significant proportion of the electoral vote.

The remarkable persistence of the family model in human relations within a modern industrial society has conferred an uncommonly strong sense of collective identity. The integration of the individual into the group, the endurance (in the past) of the worst of living conditions, and the keen sense of each person's duties (negligence of which is punishable by expulsion, and is therefore 'unthinkable'), bestow a remarkable efficiency on all measures taken to ensure the continuing mastery of mankind over an environment whose hostility has already been described. Paradoxically, this sense of group identity has a great effect on aspects of life which we would consider as private areas subject to personal taste, for example religion, or even the sense of beauty.

The cult of beauty. This is without doubt invested with far more importance in Japan than in the West. It originates in the bond that has always existed between man and nature – the 'nature' of Japan herself, which moves her children by turns to love, worship and fear and kindles in them a patriotism which can at times seem oppressive. But those monstrous events, typhoons and earthquakes, which mark the cycle of the seasons with tragedy, have tinged the worship of nature with a sharp sense of the impermanence of things; a sense which Buddhism has no doubt accentuated. It is the very transience of their appearance which makes the beauty of the cherry blossoms so moving, and our enjoyment of them so precious. From the gentle days of spring and autumn, with their delicate range of colours, death is never far away and even the perfect outline of Mount Fuji, perhaps the very jewel of these islands, frames a volcano...

This sense of beauty, so deep, so different, and the subtle terms for the expression of aesthetic pleasure, are the fruits of centuries of collective education. Here in Japan, it is in groups that people admire flowers and gardens, mountains and waterfalls, as well as human works that record their beauty; this pleasure experienced communally, together with the search for the exact phrase to express it, reflects the yearning for solidarity that runs deep in the Japanese community. Shapes, delicate materials (the grain of wood or marble, the quiet colours of rushwork, the harmony of a garden arrangement), the identical image which is embodied in each traditional house in every part of the country, will repeat the same lesson in aesthetics to every inhabitant throughout his life, and so draw him or her still deeper into the group.

The sacred. It is sometimes said, as if it were a paradox, that the only thing the Japanese worship is Japan itself. Questioned about their beliefs, many men and women would declare themselves to be non-religious, and there is little in the appearance of their daily lives to invalidate this assertion. Japan seems to have devoted itself to the quest of the most materialistic of pleasures, and the signs of leisure are blazoned all over its cities. In this respect, a visit to the Shinjuku district of Tokyo constitutes an unforgettable experience: the hurrying crowds of people of all ages and conditions, hungry for all kinds of sensation, eccentric clothing, the brazen display of all manner of sensual delights, the noise of slot machines within the brightly-coloured neon fairyland... Where now are the mystic Orient, the ascetism of Zen, the patient search for that inner peace? They do still exist, and the traveller will see living proof of that fact in many places: in the great Shinto shrines of Izumo and Ise, thronged by pilgrims, in the calm retreats of Zen monasteries, such as the Eiheiji tucked away in a lonely valley not far from the Sea of Japan. But clearly it is in a more subtle and diffuse manner that those two great national religions, Shintoism and Buddhism, today find their way into the thought and the lives of the people.

SHINTOISM. This is Japan's oldest religion. It is an animistic, pantheistic belief which venerates the forces of nature, so much so that one might say 'the true Shinto shrine is nature'. It has neither theology (though it possesses millions of gods) nor metaphysics (though it is an idealist philosophy). The gods exist in the waters of springs or torrents, in grass and trees, in rocks and mountains and in the woods growing round the temples, those woods in which people walk as if indeed in a shrine and which are just as much as the modest buildings they protect, infused with the divine presence. Based on Japanese national mythology, Shintoism has always had the support of the State, even in the time of Shotoku Taishi, when Buddhism enjoyed its first flowering. It regained total favour under the Tokugawas, and especially after Meiji, when it became the spiritual base of the new regime by 'demonstrating' the divine origin of the Emperor. Today, though deprived of official support, it remains, in the heart of every Japanese, the very core and essence of a fierce patriotism.

BUDDHISM. Arriving from Korea in the 7th century, Buddhism was initially imposed by those in power, who saw in it, in addition to a moral discipline, a means of introducing Chinese culture into the islands. Its coming brought the discovery of a whole host of notions new to the Japanese: the cycles of death and rebirth, the moral interdict on giving oneself over entirely to pleasure, and the promise of divine grace made to the true believer. However, remaining faithful to their old tribalism, the Japanese rejected all parts of Buddhist doctrine that did not accord with their old beliefs, particularly metaphysical speculation, which had already lost much of its status through the earlier connection with China.

Above all, the Japanese grafted onto Buddhism their fundamental tendency towards sectarianism, the division into many small chapels in which, grouped around a venerable master, holy teaching was administered to them personally. There have been many Buddhist reformers in the country's religious history since the Heian era. Perhaps because of a national distaste for harsh monastic discipline and the intellectual speculations of the Lesser Vehicle, the vast majority of the Japanese adopted the Great Vehicle, whose simpler doctrine has a greater emotional appeal. All these sects (13 at the present day) have in common the wish to avoid philosophical complexities and to concentrate instead on practicalities, on the heart rather than the head. Like Shintoism and other religions, Buddhism today receives no State support and many temples are experiencing difficulties, despite the considerable revenue from tourism and investments (mainly in the form of real estate) into which some of them have unhesitatingly launched themselves. More than Shintoism, which is the very inner soul of Japan, Buddhism has left its mark on the whole of the national culture, e.g. in architecture. The traditional house, standing on its stilts, may derive largely from the earliest Shinto shrines, but it is to Buddhism that it owes the discreet harmony of its interior – the colour and building material of the walls, the natural, artless, almost unfinished look of its appearance, the arrangement of the reception room, which appears to be very closely based on a monastic chapel – and finally the symbolism behind the layout of the garden. Similarly, Japanese poetry, drama and all literary and artistic expressions owe far more to Buddhism than our own culture does to Christianity.

All the religions (including Confucianism – more of a discipline than a religion – and Christianity, though it has no more than 300,000 adherents) blend into a kind of syncretism in the Japanese soul, of which they are hardly even aware. Though the majority of the inhabitants do not practise a given religion, it marks their whole way of life, their houses, the most worldly of their preoccupations, their attitudes to life's problems, great and small, their language and their games. The spectacle of their gardens, their way of paying homage to nature – around the great temples where they gather in happy or reverently hushed groups and indeed anywhere else in the islands – innumerable gestures and remarks which have become habitual or, indeed, ritual are stamped with the seal of a religion from which thought and action have become inseparable.

Should we say, then, that the whole of life in Japan is essentially religious? Or that religion has so blended in with patterns of behaviour as to be indistinguishable from them? However we choose to put it, to declare that the Japanese have solved the religious question by ignoring it would be to take little account of the profundity of their civilization, including the stage it has reached in modern times. The innumerable temples, the great pilgrimages, the Shinto and Buddhist altars set up in almost every dwelling, are just external signs – often forgotten about by the Japanese themselves – of an attitude to life and to their own country which appears to be an essentially religious feeling.

A unique conception of space and matter: Japanese art

Architecture. That intimate communion between mankind and nature which we mentioned earlier is particularly noticeable in architecture, painting and sculpture. It produces characteristic solutions to the management of space, to the modelling of forms, to pictorial representation. Be it for a castle, a temple or a house, the architecture is first and foremost the art of using wood, an abundant building material that is easy to work, simple to repair after a fire or an earthquake by replacing damaged portions and whose richness of grain and colour has always been the pride of the Japanese carpenter to bring out. There is in Japanese architecture a great variety in style, matched by a great concern for durability: certain parts of the Horyuji in Nara have survived intact from the 6th century. It is, however, something of an exception, and all too often fire has necessitated several rebuildings of edifices; therefore, only the form, not the original structure, has lasted to the present day.

Construction has been standardized since the Middle Ages: even the *tatami* itself is of a constant size, as, within any one region, are the moveable (and therefore interchangeable) partitions. The structure should always be clearly visible. The regular frame of beams, lintels and pillars, standing out against the immaculate roughcast walls (looking rather like a Mondrian) and topped by the thin grey shell of the roof (of thatch or bark or, more frequently, of tiles) – this ensemble in turn contrasting with a dark backdrop of perpetually green foliage, the whole reflected in a pond – seems to be the aesthetic ideal of the Japanese for building a home. All of this was perfectly embodied in the 17th century by Kobori Enshu in the palace of Katsura, near Kyoto.

The garden, an integral part of the dwelling, is made up of elements highly charged with symbolic significance: bridges of various shapes, water (real, or represented by grey sand in which rakes are used to simulate waves), a few scattered rocky islets. Next comes stone which, though inanimate, is made into expressive objects, some polished, some roughly hewn. There are also lanterns, artfully arranged by the water's edge, pathways under the trees and cut into the moss, banks that lead down to the pond, and miniature reefs. Finally, there is the vegetation itself, planted in groups of varying shapes and densities, from moss creeping over the stones of the path to the great conifers framing the nearby mountain and extending the vista of the garden. Sometimes the garden is designed to be viewed from the veranda; in others you have to walk along an ingeniously contrived route to enjoy it to the full. In either case, art mimics nature, expressing its character with delicate subtlety.

Sculpture. Japanese sculpture is essentially religious, and its disappearance at the end of the 13th century was certainly due to a lack of spiritual nourishment. One may find, as early as in the *haniwa*, or funeral urns of the great tombs (4th-6th centuries), a remarkable talent for individual expression. It was, however, Buddhist statuary which, from the 6th to the 13th centuries, was to allow Japanese artists to show what they were capable of, following the example of Korean and Chinese sculptors who came over from the mainland to teach them the art. Working in groups in studios, using bronze and lacquered or painted wood, these sculptors were at their peak in the Nara and Kamakura periods. From the former, the marvellous Miroku Bosatsu (housed in the temple of Chuguji, near Nara) is perhaps the masterpiece of all Japanese sculptures and one of the greatest artefacts in the world. The great bronze statues of the Todaiji, in Nara (8th century) and of Kamakura (13th century) are exceptional by any standards, but it is rather in the finely chiselled woodcarvings, on a more human scale, that one can sense the virtuosity, sometimes indeed the depth of expression, in Japanese sculpture of the Middle Ages.

Painting. As with sculpture, the Japanese were taught painting by the Koreans and later by the Chinese, who travelled to Japan from the 6th century onwards. They brought with them paper, brushes (made of the tails of rabbits, badgers or deer), and a method of preparing colours from plants and minerals, water-soluble and applied without washing. But China ink remained the favourite medium of Japanese artists who, like other Orientals, never wholly separated painting from calligraphy. From the 14th to the 19th centuries, the colours employed in the decoration of the walls of temples and palaces became increasingly more vivid and, in the Muromachi period, entirely gilded backgrounds were used to make them stand out even more.

The first works of art were created well before the Middle Ages, notably the frescoes adorning the walls of the funeral chambers of aristocrats, in a style imitating Chinese or Korean tombs: but it was in Nara, with the frescoes of the Horyuji (destroyed by fire in 1949) that the great age of Japanese painting really began, essentially Buddhist and inspired by the Chinese. In the Heian period, this art was 'Japanized' and further technical advances were made: there were great religious compositions, *mandala*, and the first portraits, a genre which produced many masterpieces. To decorate houses, more secular themes were chosen, the four seasons for example, while long horizontally-wound scrolls (*emakimono*) were painted to illustrate the great novels of the time, such as the *Genji Monogatari*.

The Kamakura period was an age of portraits and of Zen-inspired ink-painting, executed on vertically-hung scrolls (*kakemono*) which graced the walls of chapels and the main room of the house. It was the Muromachi period which saw the birth and productive years of the greatest Japanese masters of this art form, Shubun, and especially Sesshu. A century later, the Kano School was depicting, with clean lines and brilliant colours, animals and landscapes which were used as decoration for the walls of the residences of lords and high priests. But it was the Momoyama period, and the early Edo period – the age of the sumptuous residences of Nobunaga and Hideyoshi, then of the Tokugawa – which saw the zenith of decorative painting: Kano Eitoku decorated the castle of Azuchi (no longer standing) and the palace at Kyoto. A fullness of composition, ingenious framing, vibrant colours and a delicacy of touch characterize the Kano school, and the works of Sotatsu and Korin who were the successors of the great Kano masters. Other schools and other brilliant painters brought renown to the Edo period, but a new form of art was developing, dedicated entirely to the representation of scenes from daily life, in works of more modest dimensions: this was Ukiyoe, the Japanese print of the 18th and 19th centuries.

While the great painters worked mainly for the ruling classes, the aristocracy, Ukiyoe was aimed at the bourgeois merchant class, first of Osaka, then of Edo: in it they saw reflected their world, their lifestyle – urban landscapes teeming with passersby, scenes from the brothel, the faces of famous actors and celebrated beauties. These were engraved on wood and printed on heavy paper, with delicate tints added one after another (as many as 78 separate printings, more often a dozen or so), making repeated prints until the original woodblock was worn out. Two exceptional artists, Hokusai and Hiroshige, assiduously portrayed their contemporaries and famous scenes in their country, such as Mount Fuji or the 53 stages of the journey along the Tokaido road.

Before them, Kiyonobu, Kiyomasu, Harunobu and Utamaro, among others, had already depicted with great delicacy romantic or sentimental scenes, and made beautiful drawings of young women draped in sumptuous kimonos, gossiping beneath the cherry trees or undressing with exquisite nonchalance. Following them, Kunisada, Kuniyoshi and numerous imitators heralded the decline of an art form which led the West, as soon as it discovered it, to believe it knew all there was to know about Japanese painting. The influence it had on Western painters, particularly the Impressionists, is well known.

After the Meiji Restoration, traditional painting and sculpture continued along their set path, all the while gathering inspiration from Western art and 'trading' to some degree with the Impressionists and Fauvists, adding a 'westernized' aspect to their own tradition. Very few names from the years 1868–1945 have survived, except Maeda Sesson and Yokoyama Taikan. It was not until after World War II that Japanese art, influenced by Surrealism and all the international art movements, was to rediscover, paradoxically enough, the great national predilection for simplicity and definition of form, the cult of the daring curve and the simple subject – in short, a taste for abstraction which was latent in the old ink paintings. For their part, Japanese pupils of the German Bauhaus learned to apply, in concrete, glass and steel, the lesson of Katsura.

Other arts and skills. Architecture, sculpture and painting by no means exhaust the whole range of Japanese art: there are some minor arts, such as textile, ceramics, metalwork, and lacquer, which have expanded their repertoire and increased their impact on everyday life. The aesthetic sense of this nation, essentially practical, and so to speak tactile, has perhaps found its greatest satisfaction in the countless objects - garments, mirrors, boxes of all kinds, pots and vases - which are handled daily. There is hardly a material that has not been worked and made to yield surprising creations - ivory, iron, gold, bronze, linen, hemp, silk, clay, wood, bamboo and paper. Never, in the case of fine-quality goods, is the nature of the material sacrificed to the sophistication of design or the emphasis of form. Furthermore, one might say that the talent of the artist has always been in the ability to bring out the very life of the material, its grain, its warmth, the subtle play of its colours in the light. All these objects are made to be touched as well as looked at, and need to be studied over a long period of time, contemplated and handled, before they divulge the full secret of their charm.

There are today some 40 villages and hamlets scattered throughout the archipelago in which tea bowls and other receptacles of all kinds are fired, according to centuries-old formulae. A pilgrimage to one of them, often to be reached only after a long and exciting trek through forest and mountains, is one of the 'tests' a foreigner must undergo in order to be 'initiated' into Japanese sensibility. The Japanese also still manufacture the beautiful paper with which window-frames are faced, or onto which a painter using China ink will apply delicate or powerfully sweeping brush strokes. Other kinds of paper, grainy and brightly coloured, are used to make dolls and masterpieces of skilful origami. Or take Nishijin, the silk-weavers quarter in Kyoto; there, in the silence of old dwellings backing onto tranquil gardens, generations of craftsmen have woven the world's richest brocades, with which are made the heavy sashes used to tie a kimono - or even the whole kimono, for the very wealthy. They may be further embellished by the use of dyes, and this is yet another old art that certain present-day masters, Serizawa for example, have perfected to a degree worthy of the ancients.

The treasure of the Shosoin, in Nara, includes lacquerwork inlaid with mother-of-pearl, statues made of lacquered wood, and other objects whose lacquer coating is splashed with gold. In later periods there was a preference for the use of single-colour lacquer in red or black, in which shape and lustre are what gives the object its quality. From the Muromachi period onwards, however, and especially in the Edo, virtuosity was increasingly prized; writing cases, toilet articles and combs, as well as cosmetic containers, were encrusted with decorative scenes, often rustic and with figures. These objects, technical masterpieces of great taste, do not, however, have quite the same appeal for us today as do the beautiful single-colour pieces such as the canisters, dishes and oblong boxes which are still being made to this day. The carving and painting or lacquering of wood are used in sometimes stunning combination in the art of making masks (especially in Noh theatre), dolls and certain kinds of furniture: sideboards, for example, and low tables, always very light and of supreme elegance.

The gestural arts. That beauty which the Japanese have been striving for centuries to incorporate into their daily lives is occasionally captured by the very carriage of their bodies, to which their traditional dress lends - for men as well as for women - an unquestionable nobility. Its ultimate expression is to be found in the *Noh* and *Kabuki* dramas; and dance, from the earliest Shinto rites, has always been the object of fervent dedication. In a more static form, the tea ceremony is, too, a gestural discipline: carried out within a strict framework of studied simplicity, with the help of utensils made of porcelain, metal or lacquer - works of art in themselves - it represents today the very purest, and the simplest expression of beauty in the Japanese style. The same may be said of the martial arts, including archery, which were also evolved under the influence of Zen; the moulded beauty of the poses displays a perfect state of balance between intention and effort.

On a more everyday level, the etiquette of gestures - the deep bow with which people greet each other, the dexterous and graceful use of chopsticks at table, the way a person sits on the *tatami*, legs tucked under and torso bolt upright - is a part of that general concern with the aesthetic which affects the whole of Japanese life. This discipline, practised with such grace and vigour by a whole people, seems, alas, to be in danger of being squeezed out by the modern age, and is restricted to certain traditional contexts.

Literary and musical forms of expression

Poetry and the novel. Japan possesses a rich and varied literature, of which the rest of the world has until recently been almost entirely ignorant, because of the difficulty of learning Japanese. Here again, the starting point is nature, whose beauty and violence have never ceased to enthrall the Japanese people. Steeped in emotion, they have forged a vocabulary that captures with perfect subtlety the finest shades of feeling, the agglutinative character of their native tongue permitting them to construct an infinite number of terms. It is a wilfully imprecise language, in which strict definition gives way to nuance, conceptual thinking to instinctual. It is also a language which lends itself readily to the most controlled writing as well as to the most dramatic oration. Lack of space here forbids even the most rudimentary exposition of the evolution of this literature. Its poets have produced the world's shortest pieces in the popular form of the *haiku*, whose 17 syllables strive to create in three lines a moment frozen as if painted in ink or on lacquer. The form, has had its masters, notably Basho, who lived in the 17th century; but every Japanese loves to try his hand at it, and poetry contests - at court or in the rice fields - have long been a favourite national pastime. Although Japan has neither an epic tradition nor great love poetry or poetic drama, true poetry is to be found elsewhere, in narrative and especially in plays.

The art of the novel in Japan began very early and was at first mostly in the hands of women. The masterpiece of Japanese literature,

Genji monogatari ('The Tale of Genji'), was written around AD 1000 by a woman at the Heian court, Murasaki Shikibu. This fictionalized biography of a scion of the Imperial family has remained the model for all Japanese writers. In a more abbreviated form, the art of the storyteller has produced gems which translations commissioned by UNESCO are at last happily bringing within the reach of everyone. Titles include: *Konjaku Monogatari* ('Stories that are now of the past') from the 11th century, *Ugetsu Monogatari* ('Stories of the rain and the moon') by Ueda Akinari (18th century) or, from the 20th century, the tales of Akutagawa Ryonosuke, among which perhaps the most famous is *Rashomon*. The novel proper blossomed with the rise of the bourgeoisie in Osaka (related by Ihara Saikaku in the 18th century), and again since Meiji, largely influenced by the great 19th century novelists of the West. The hopes and fears of modern Japan are dealt with in the works (mostly now available in translation) of Tanizaki, Oe, Dazai, Kawabata and Mishima.

Theatre. The Japanese are devoted enthusiasts for all kinds of theatrical performance, among them the three which have been the staples of their tradition: Noh, Kabuki and Bunraku (puppet theatre). Noh came into being around AD 1400 under the influence of the two Kanze, Kenami and his son Zeami, authors of the bulk of the present-day repertoire and – in the case of the latter – formulator of the rules of this complex art form. There is no 'plot' in the conventional sense of the term, but rather a 'moment' in a story expounded, analysed and illuminated in depth by means of a skilful commentary, extraordinary proliferation of gestures and poses, simple music and spectacular costumes.

Contrasting with this scholarly and aristocratic form of theatre, there were story-tellers who sometimes used puppets to enliven their recitals. The famous Bunraku, or puppet theatre, was founded in Osaka; ballads, and later, at the end of the 17th century, stories written by Chikamatsu Monzaemon were presented by marionettes operated by puppeteers dressed in black. The narrator, perched on a dais close by, declaimed the text while the puppeteers brought their charges to life with gestures synchronized exactly with the story. The plays either deal with moral questions or are historical dramas which revive for us the social and romantic conflicts of the aristocratic and bourgeois classes of society in the Edo period. Thanks to the poetic genius of Chikamatsu and the beauty of the puppets whose expressive faces are the work of great sculptors, as well as the talents of the narrators and the wonderful skills of the puppeteers, a good Bunraku show is perhaps the most striking performance that Japanese theatre today can offer a foreign spectator. Less exotic than the *Noh*, less ostentatious than Kabuki, Bunraku is one of the world's great dramatic forms.

Kabuki is, admittedly, more spectacular. Derived in about AD 1600 in Kyoto from dances with a dramatic theme, and accompanied by musical instruments, it nowadays appears relatively static, made up from a succession of moments rather than from a continuous action in progress. It has, as a theatrical form, always tended to work by conventions, in matters of the richness of its costumes, gestures deliberately held over-long in order to excite admiration for their elegance and harmony, poses struck during narration, the rich and varied (though never 'natural') tones of voice, the systematic organization of scenes into a few strict categories for which the informed spectator will be on the lookout (love scenes, quarrels, slaughters, discoveries of treachery, flight into the forest, etc.).

Here again, there are social and romantic dramas, often both at once, with conflicts of duty heavily emphasized, even after the increased drive towards realism in the Meiji period. In the service of this drama, a whole stagecraft was developed: revolving stages, extremely elaborate scenery with visible scene changes, a bridge running between the back of the hall and the stage, through the audience allowing them to admire from all sides the whirling dancers, and sometimes supporting part of the action. Never vulgar, occasionally grandiloquent, always magnificent, Kabuki remains the most lively of the ancient forms of Japanese theatre: numerous provincial theatres and two great halls in Tokyo (the Kabukiza and the National Theatre, which also stages Bunraku shows) keep alive the ancient rituals in daily performances.

Music. Whether in Noh, Bunraku or Kabuki theatre, music is an essential ingredient to the dramatic atmosphere. In addition to instruments of Chinese origin from the Heian court (such as the lutelike *biwa*, the flute, and the long zither or *koto*) which are still played by hordes of enthusiasts, and feature in very popular concerts, other instruments are used on the stage, including the *shamisen*, a sort of guitar with three strings (apparently imported from the Philippines and popular from the Edo period onwards), and drums of all sizes, hand-held or resting on stands. The human voice itself, especially in Noh, contributes to the feel of the drama, produced with a hoarse or very shrill timbre for which the Western ear is scarcely prepared, but which expresses shades of meaning vital to the drama.

Since Miji there have been numerous modern symphony orchestras: Tokyo boasts several which fully meet Western standards, while Japanese soloists are internationally renowned for their stage performances. Recently, though, young Japanese composers have been searching for musical forms and themes for sound that will not only appeal to the West but will also draw on the emotional resources of their traditional instruments. In this respect, the heart-rending modulations of the end-blown bamboo flute (*shakuhachi*), brought from India by the Chinese some 13 centuries ago, appeal strongly to our senses whether in a work of our own period or one that comes to us across the ages.

Cinema. Japanese cinema goes back to the start of the century: its beginnings show a heavy Kabuki influence and, even today, the heroic stories of the warriors of olden times constitute an important part of the country's film output. Later, militarism was to strengthen this historical interest, adding a strong tinge of nationalism. Since World War II, western influences of all kinds (Italian neo-realism, Hollywood comedies, and Westerns) have made themselves felt. Among the prodigious annual output some masterpieces appear, but the films most appreciated by westerners are not necessarily those the Japanese themselves like best. Apart from stories of feudal times, realistic family dramas (and sentimental ones) represent the bulk of the film industry's effort.

The setting up of numerous television channels dealt a crippling blow to the art of film making, and has partly replaced it: many films are produced for TV, and deal with stories of chivalry or problems of private life – now as ever the Japanese take pleasure in conflicts between love and duty or, better still, between two contradictory kinds of duty, forcing heart-breaking decisions on the protagonists. On this level the majority of films, no matter how bad they are, provide a rich insight into the Japanese way of living in society – and of living. Even the frenzied advertising which accompanies all broadcasting on the private TV channels gives, in its own way, an image of the Japanese people.

An historical survey

by Dr Jacques Pezeu-Massabuau
D. Litt, course director at Tokyo University

In relation to other Asian, or even western, countries, Japan is a 'young' country. The Neolithic age extended here right up to the start of our own era, and writing did not make its appearance until the 5th century. This imbalance – redressed from time to time by an injection of Chinese culture – became more pronounced during the Edo period, when the country was systematically cut off from all foreign influences. When Queen Victoria came to the throne, the islands were under the sway of feudalism and the steam engine was still unknown. This lagging behind the world's other great civilizations only shows to more remarkable effect the immense energy which the country has displayed, since 1868 (Meiji) and especially since 1945, to overtake other great nations.

From the 4th to the 7th centuries, Japan passed from prehistory into history. The great clans wore themselves out in struggles that lasted almost into the 17th century. Nevertheless, the court of Yamato (the Imperial clan) gradually asserted its pre-eminence, organizing itself along Chinese lines, thanks especially to the determination of Shotoku Taishi. Writing and Buddhism, together with the arts and sciences of the Asian continent, were received and absorbed enthusiastically, even though Japan still had no fixed capital city.

367: The first Korean envoy arrives in Japan, an emissary of the government of Kudara.

369: Creation in Korea of the Japanese state of Mimana.

c.400: The court of Yamato undertakes and partly achieves the unification of Japan.

c.430: Yamato province covered in great tombs.

538: Introduction of Buddhism.

592: Shotoku Taishi becomes regent.

604: He sets up a Constitution of seventeen articles.

607: He sends an ambassador to the court of the Sui in China. Building of the Horyuji.

630: Ambassador sent to the T'ang court.

645: Great reforms of Taika.

668–701: Great statutes (Omi, Asuka, Taiho) provide the regime with a framework in law.

The Nara period (710–94)

A fixed capital was established at Nara, modelled on the Chinese system. Buddhism became the official religion and Asian culture spread through all aspects of public life: writing, arts, sciences. Yamato power was spread further north in the islands by conquest, at the expense of the Ainu. The Yamato were warrior lords and great shrine-builders who amassed large domains which were later to provide a base for their resistance to Imperial domination. The imitation of Chinese civilization and the ambience of the Buddhist faith made these years the first golden age of Japanese art. The great Fujiwara family gained a lasting influence at court, while the Buddhist priesthood gained in power. The Emperor gradually lost effective power.

710: The capital established at Nara.

712: Official date of the Kojiki, the oldest Japanese chronicle.

718: The law of Yoro.

741: The Emperor decides to create in each administrative area a State Temple (*kokubunji*).

743: Land recently cleared is turned over to private ownership.

745: Construction work begins on the Great Buddha at the Todaiji temple in Nara, to be completed in 752.

766: The monk Dokyo, having become all-powerful at court, tries to usurp the throne. He fails, but his attempt sets off massive unrest. From this time on, the influence of the monks is to increase more and more.

790: Date of the first collection of Japanese poetry: the *Manyoshu*. The Emperor Konin decides to leave Nara.

The Heian period (794–1192)

Established in Heian, 30 miles (50 km) north of Nara, the court was dominated by the Fujiwara. At the end of the 9th century, relations with China were broken off and, for two centuries, Japan was to live off its own achievements: a national art and literature were born, producing the first authentically 'Japanese' masterpieces. The wars waged between the great Taira and Minamoto clans bathed the land in blood. In spite of several attempted coups (by Horikawa, Go-Shirakawa, etc.) these would-be emperors could not regain power and either gave up or were ousted. The court, refined and decadent, now exercised only literary and aesthetic power, while civil war raged unabated. It was halted by the naming of Minamoto Yoritomo as 'supreme general for the subjugation of the barbarians' (*sei-i-tai-shogun*) and the setting up of his seat of authority at Kamakura. The court was to remain, powerless but still officially respected, in Heian (Kyoto) until 1868.

794. The court transfers to Heian (Kyoto).

805-6: The monks Saicho and Kukai establish the Tendai and Shingon sects in Japan.

815: Tea is introduced to Japan.

841: The power of the Fujiwara becomes so absolute that the years 857-1160 are commonly known as the 'Fujiwara period' among historians.

861: Adoption of the Chinese calendar. Rise of the 'Yamato-e' school of painting.

866: Fujiwara Yoshifusa becomes regent.

894: Sugawara Michizane decides to break off diplomatic relations with China.

905: The *Kokinshu* poetry collection.

950-1000: The age of the great holy buildings in Heian: the hills of the 'Mountain of the East' (Higashiyama) and the slopes of Mount Hiei are covered with Buddhist shrines.

966-1027 Regency of Fujiwara Michinga.

1000: Publication of *Genji monogatari* ('The Tale of Genji'), the most famous Japanese novel.

1053: Construction of the Byodin at Uji, to the south of Heian.

1073-1156: Reign of the cloistered emperors.

1123-66: Violent struggle between the Taira and the Minamoto.

1156: War of the Imperial succession. Consolidation of the power of the Taira.

1160-85: The Taira period; a revolt against them by the Fujiwara and the Minamoto, in 1159, fails.

1180: Minamoto forces regroup and make Kamakura their base.

1185: Final destruction of the Taira clan at the battle of Dan-no-ura.

The Kamakura period (1192-1338)

Yoritomo established his military regime in Kamakura, far from the decadence of the court. The wise rule of the Hojo after him maintained peace in the country until about 1300. It was a great age of Buddhism: new sects were founded (worship of Amida Buddha, Nichiren), more popular than previous ones – except Zen, which was adopted by the military class. It was the last great age of Japanese sculpture. In painting, *yamato-e* continued, but *sumi-e* (China ink painting) produced its first masterpieces. In architecture, several new styles emerged: one of these, the 'Chinese style' (*Karayo*), was adopted for the great Zen shrines erected at Kamakura. From the year 1300 onwards, the military classes weakened and the Emperor at one stage tried to wrest power from the Hojo, but was unsuccessful. The Ashikaga family emerged triumphant from the ensuing struggles and took in its turn the title of Shogun. Kamakura was taken in 1333.

1192: Minamoto Yoritomo becomes *sei-i-tai-shogun*.

1199: Death of Yoritomo.

c.1200: Publication of *Hojoki* ('Notes from the ten-foot-square Cabin').

1219: End of the Minamoto: power passes to the Hojo (descendants of the Taira).

1229: Founding of the Seto potteries.

1232: Joei Shikimoku law, legal basis of the Kamakura government.

1250: *Ima Monogatari* ('Stories of the present day').

1252: Construction of the Great Buddha at Kamakura.

1253: Erection of the Kenchoji Temple at Kamakura.

1272: Construction of the Nishi-Honganji at Kyoto.

1274: First Mongol invasion, repelled at Tsushima.

1281: Second Mongol invasion.

1321: The Emperor Go-Daigo assumes power.

1324: *Tsurezure gusa* ('Occasional remarks') by Yoshida Kenko.

1331–2: Fall of Kamakura, captured by Yoshisada.

1336: Imperial schism: Emperor of the Ashikaga sets up in Kyoto, but the traditional line continues in the southern mountains. The split lasts until 1392.

The Muromachi period (1338–1573)

Remarkable contrasts characterize this era, during which the Ashikaga family held the office of Shogun. Their court, set in the Muromachi suburb of Heian, was sophisticated in the extreme: 'The fine arts, literature, architecture, painting in the grand manner, strange follies, debauches and short poems were all practised to perfection.' (P. Landy.) The country as a whole, though, was ravaged by lawlessness: there was fighting in the town and in the country, in the streets of the capital, around the monasteries and the castles. Even the court did not remain unaffected by the universal misery. Everywhere, raging civil war helped to hasten the fragmentation of the Empire, and some areas went so far as to declare independence.

1338: Ashikaga Takauji becomes *sei-i-tai-shogun*.

1356: The *Tsukubashu* collection: theoretical work on 'chain poems' (*renga*).

1368: Ashikaga Yoshimitu, third Shogun, defeats the other clans and further secures power for his house. Subsequently he abdicates, becomes a monk and builds the Kinkaku-ji (Pavilion of Gold). Rise of the *shoin-zukuri* style of architecture.

1370: The *Taiheiki* chronicles ('Story of the great peace').

1392: End of the dynastic schism.

1404: Ashikaga Yoshimitsu sends to the Ming court an embassy which begins trade relations with China.

Chinese poetry undergoes a renaissance at the Nanzen-ji temple in Kyoto.

1429: Peasant rebellion.

1467: Start of the Onin war between the great clans; fire in the Muromachi palace in Heian.

1473: Ashikaga Yoshimasa builds the Ginkaku-ji (Pavilion of Silver).

1477: End of the Onin war.

1485: Renewal of peasant rebellion.

1486: Death of Sesshu, the greatest Japanese painter of landscapes in China ink.

1495: Outbreak of lawlessness; local wars intensify; neither Emperor nor Shogun can wield effective power any longer.

1510: The first Japanese porcelain wares. Rise of the Kano school of painting.

1532: Revolt of the Honganji Temple against the Shogun.

1534: The Portuguese land in Tanegashima; Japan discovers firearms.

1549: Francis Xavier begins preaching in Japan.

1573: Oda Nobunaga deposes Ashikaga Yoshiaki; end of the Muromachi military government.

The Azuchi-Momoyama period (1573–1600)

This period, brief but of vital importance, saw the reunification of the country. Three men, great commanders and prudent administrators, Oda Nobunaga, Toyotomi Hideyoshi and Tokugawa Ieyasu, took it in turn to continue the task. Christians, who had increased considerably in number, were judged undesirable, but the weapons they had brought with them found favour. This was an age of sumptuous palaces, blazing with gold leaf, through which these brilliant upstarts sought to display their newly-won power. In the theatre, new forms emerged which were to become classical in subsequent eras: Bunraku (puppets) and Kabuki.

1576: Oda Nobunaga (1534–82) builds the castle of Azuchi.

1580: He puts an end to the military might of the monks, by razing the monasteries of Mount Hiei.

1582: Nobunaga is assassinated. Toyotomi Hideyoshi (1536–98) assumes power. He undertakes reforms aimed at stabilizing the existing structure of society.

1583: He builds the castle at Osaka.

1587: He forbids Christianity and expels the missionaries.

1588: He forbids the carrying of arms by the peasantry, reserving the privilege for the nobility.

1590: The whole of Japan is united under the iron rule of Hideyoshi.

1592: Hideyoshi fails in his attempt to invade Korea.

1594: He erects the castle of Momoyama to the south of Kyoto.

1597: Second attempt to invade Korea; defeated again. Second edict against Christians, of whom 26 are executed at Nagasaki.

1598: Death of Hideyoshi.

1600: His second-in-command, Tokugawa Ieyasu, is victorious at Sekigahara and thus becomes master of all Japan.

The Edo period (1600–1868)

For two and a half centuries, the Tokugawa kept a firm hold on the office of Shogun. Society was fixed and regulated, with the bourgeoisie occupying second from lowest place. Its power grew, though, thanks to commerce and – first in Osaka, then in Edo – encouraged the growth of a new culture, different from that of the court and the military aristocracy. Western science and technology were creeping in gradually, although the country was still rigorously closed to outsiders. Towards the end of the period, the wretched condition of the peasants led to uprisings, while the military classes became impoverished and frustrated. The bourgeoisie suffered because of the monopolies run by the trade guilds, and intellectuals felt the lack of stimulating contact with the outside world. All these factors led to the crumbling of the sociopolitical edifice raised by the Tokugawa when, in 1853–54 Westerners – that is, Americans – came to seek trade links with the country. The action of some of the more resolute clans paved the way for an Imperial restoration: the Meiji Revolution of 1868.

1603: Tokugawa Ieyasu becomes the *sei-i-tai-shogun*, and Edo (Tokyo) the administrative capital of Japan.

1609–13: Dutch and English traders arrive and settle in Hirado (Kyushu).

1616: Death of Ieyasu.

1622: Christians put to death in Nagasaki.

1636: Construction of the great mausoleum at Nikko.

1637-8: Revolt of Christians at Shimbara: all Japanese subjects forbidden to travel abroad, on pain of death.

1641: Dutch trade restricted to the area of Deshima (Nagasaki).

1642: Birth of the novelist Ihara Saikaku.

1643: Birth of the poet Basho.

1649: Laws defining the duties of the peasantry.

1650: Rise of porcelain made in Kutani, near Kanazawa.

1657: Great Fire of Edo (Tokyo).

1658: Start of the official publication of the *Great History of Japan* (until 1907).

1673: Decree forbidding the parcelling out of land.

1688-1703: Genroku period, artistic peak of the Edo period.

1703: Great earthquake of Edo.

1707: Last eruption of Mount Fuji.

1709: Arai Hakuseki, chief of police and reformer.

1720: Ban on foreign books lifted (except for religious works).

1721: Census (of all non-noble persons).

1728: Great famine at Shikoku.

1745: First Dutch-Chinese dictionary.

1776: *Stories of the Rain and the Moon* by Ueda Akinari.

1783: Great famine throughout the land; peasant uprisings.

1786: Great Fire of Edo.

1788: Great Fire of Kyoto.

1792: Catherine the Great endeavours to forge links with Japan.

1806: Death of Utamaro.

1807: Russia attempts to invade Ezo (Hokkaido).

1825: Orders given to destroy any foreign vessel approaching the coast of Japan.

1832: Great famine and rebellion.

1839: Punishment of intellectuals wishing to open the country to foreigners.

1849: Death of Hokusai.

1853: Perry's warships drop anchor at Uraga, in the Bay of Edo.

1854: Perry returns; treaty of Kanagawa, opening the ports of

Shimoda and Hakodate to American shipping.

1856: The first foreign consul (American) arrives in Japan.

1858: Trade agreements with the USA, Great Britain and France. Death of Hiroshige.

1861-2: Westerners murdered.

1863: Western ships, in reprisal, bombard Shimonoseki and Kagoshima.

1865: Civil war waged by the Choshu clan; the Emperor's supporters are victorious.

1866: Alliance of the Choshu and Satsuma (Kagoshima) clans against the Shogun.

1867: End of the military rule of the Tokugawa.

1868: The Emperor leaves Kyoto (where the court has been settled some 1075 years) and settles in Edo castle: the city is re-named Tokyo.

The Meiji period (1868-1912)

The Meiji era was the era of modernization in Japan, which passed in the space of 50 years from medieval feudalism to the political and economic system of a great contemporary state. The constitution of 1889 adopted a parliamentary regime modelled on that of Britain, but still keeping much of the power within the grasp of counsellors surrounding the sovereign. The foundation of the Press took place in 1868, and there were no fewer than a hundred periodicals in the country within five years. In literature, the 'discovery' of western writers brought about great changes. A wave of realism came first, accompanying – as in the West – the rise of science and industrialization: the main realist practitioners were Tsubouchi Shoyo, Futabatei Shimei and Mori Ogai, who developed a social literature heavily influenced by the Russians. From about 1905 onwards, a more idealist trend took over, with writers such as Natsume Soseki, Nagai Kafu and Tanizaki Junichiro. In the arts, western influences made a strong impression on painting, sculpture and architecture, making a return to tradition impossible, but without a harmonious balance having been established as yet. The Meiji period was thus a period of transformation in Japan and is marked by its first attempts to conquer the outside world, attempts crowned with a degree of success that astonished the world and taught it very quickly to treat this newcomer with respect.

1868: Abolition of the Shogunate. Edo becomes Tokyo. Foundation of the Press.

1869: End of the Tokugawa resistance at Hakodate (Hokkaido).

1871: Fiefs (*han*) are abolished and replaced by about 50 administrative districts.

Start of the colonization of Hokkaido, as a precaution against a Russian advance in the Far East.

1873: Introduction of conscription gives rise to peasant revolts. Adoption of the Gregorian calendar.

1874: Expedition to Formosa.
Rise of the 'Movement for the freedom and rights of the people' which, together with other factions, demands the creation of a national assembly under the leadership of Itagaki.

1876: First exhibition of Western painting in Tokyo.

1877: Satsuma uprising put down by the army. Arrival of Josiah Conder, western architecture professor.

1881: Creation by Itagaki of the Liberal party.

1884: Liberal party dissolved.

1885: *The Essence of the Novel* by Tsubouchi Shoyo.

1889: Promulgation of the Meiji Constitution.

1890: *Floating Cloud* by Futabatei Shimei.
First parliamentary meeting.

1894–5: First Sino-Japanese War. Treaty of Shimonoseki.

1902: Alliance with Britain.
The Flowers of Hell by Nagai Kafu.

1904–5: Russo-Japanese War; Japan victorious. Treaty of Portsmouth.

1905: *I am a Cat* by Natsume Soseki.

1906: *Botchan* by N. Soseki.

1910: Annexation of Korea.
The Heart by N. Soseki.

1911: *The Tattoo* by Tanizaki Junichiro.
Construction of the Palace of Akasaka, made of stone and in the style of classical western architecture.

1912: Death of Emperor Meiji.

The Taisho and Showa periods (1912–1945)

The history of these two periods is one of military and imperial ventures for Japan. Moves towards liberalism, after World War I, accompanied by social change and a wave of enthusiastic modernism, could not prevent the growth of militarism due notably to the efforts of small groups of officers anxious to restore to the country its traditional values – 'forgotten' in the new cult of all things western – and to end the country's political isolation (since it had left the League of Nations in 1933). Henceforth, the army and police were to exercise ever more stringent control over political and intellectual life. Literature, which had been open to all kinds of influences under

Taisho, was increasingly restricted by official propagandists and censors. Popular literature, which sprang up through various social and political upheavals, left a legacy of very few worthwhile pieces.

1914: World War I; Japan declares war on Germany.
Construction of Tokyo Station.

1915: The '21 demands' against China.

1918: Expedition to Siberia.

1919: The '21 demands' are refused but Japan receives compensation; it nevertheless sees itself as humiliated on the international scene.

1920: First May Day celebrations.

1921: The Crown Prince (the present Emperor) travels in Europe. Assassination of Hara Satoshi, followed by a long series of political assassinations lasting until 1940.
The Crown Prince becomes Regent on the illness of his father.
Washington Conference.

1922: Formation of the Japanese Communist party, outlawed the following year.
Death of Mori Ogai.

1925: A liberal cabinet passes a law of universal suffrage.
The Prostitute, popular novel by Hayama Yoshiki.

1926: Start of the Showa period, reign of the present Emperor. End of the 'liberal era' begins, with an upsurge in right-wing reaction until the outbreak of World War II.

1931: Manchurian incident.

1932: Assassination of Prime Minister Inukai, opposed to militarism.

1933: Japan withdraws from the League of Nations.

1936: Conspiracy by young officers in Tokyo fails.

1937: Start of Japanese aggression against China.

1940: Three-Power Pact with Germany and Italy.

1941: Occupation of Indo-China; the Americans respond with an embargo against Japan. Attack on Pearl Harbor.

1941-2: Period of Japanese advances, as far as Burma in the west and New Guinea in the south.

1942: Battle of Midway Island; start of the Japanese withdrawal.

1943: Creation of the Pan-Asian Ministry.

1944-5: Worsening defeats for Japan; Tokyo bombarded. The American capture Okinawa. Atomic bombs dropped on Hiroshima, then Nagasaki.
The USSR declares war on Japan. Imperial decree brings war to an end.
2 September, Japanese surrender.

The present age (since 1945)

From 1945 to 1952, Allied occupation (carried out, in fact, by the USA alone) attempted to remodel Japanese society and its way of life, in order to eliminate militarism and nationalism. The *zaibatsu* were dismantled, trade unions encouraged, and a new constitution drawn up that put an end to the (always theoretical) absolute power of the Emperor. Japan allowed itself to be 'democratized' without a murmur. Again in charge of its own destiny, it took advantage of the conflict in Korea to make good its post-war economic recovery. It elected a Conservative government which was to turn it into the Old World's greatest economic power. Left-wing opposition remained active and made its presence felt over certain issues (security pact with the USA, the return of Okinawa, relations with Peking, etc.). Agreements with China and the USSR ushered in a period of peace in the Far East. Japan was opened up more than ever to the scientific, intellectual and artistic influence of the West, and material prosperity brought with it a flowering of the arts, conjoining great international movements and trends (surrealism, abstract art, existentialism, structuralism, minimalist music, etc.) with traditional Japanese forms. Though it has never lost touch with itself, Japan now listens more than ever before to the rest of the world. On the international level, though, its political influence has lagged far behind its economic importance.

1946: The Emperor disclaims his divine ancestry.
Agrarian reforms divide the great estates.
New constitution.

1947: Universal suffrage extended to include both sexes.

1948: Eugenics laws passed, effectively allowing many women to have abortions.
Foundation of the Zengakuren, national union of student associations.

1951: San Francisco Peace Treaty.

1953: Start of Japanese television.
Armistice in Korea.
Japanese industry begins large-scale reconstruction.

1954: Creation of the defence force.

1956: Normalization of relations between Japan and Russia.

1960: Prime Minister Kishi resigns and is replaced by Ikeda, who promises to 'double the national revenue in ten years', a promise which is more than fulfilled.
Assassination of the socialist leader Asanuma.

1962: Semi-official agreement between Tokyo and Peking.

1964: Opening of the Tokaido super-express railway (called Shinkansen); the first motorway built from Tokyo to Nagoya.
The Eighteenth Olympic Games held in Tokyo.

1966: Cultural Revolution in China; Japanese Communist party breaks with its Chinese counterpart.

1968–70: Student unrest in Tokyo.
Kawabata Yasunari wins the Nobel Prize for literature.

1969: Agreement with the USSR over the development of land in Siberia.
Launching of the first Japanese atomic ship.

1970: Launching of the first Japanese satellite.
World Fair in Osaka.
Spectacular suicide of the writer Yukio Mishima, reproaching his country for forgetting its old ideals and for failing to rearm.

1972: Okinawa handed back to Japan.
Agreements signed by Chou-en-Lai and Tanaka.
Suicide of Nobel Prize winner Kawabata Yasunari.

1974: Miki takes over from Tanaka in a difficult period following the oil crisis.

1975: Visit by the Emperor Hirohito to the USA.
Expansion of trade with China but, correspondingly, cooling of relations with the USSR, especially over the question of the Kuril Islands.
Expo '75 in Osaka.

1976: Golden Jubilee of the Showa reign.
The Lockheed scandal rocks the Liberal-Democrats and leads to the arrest of former Prime Minister Tanaka and the fall of Miki, who is replaced by Fukuda.
Improving relations between Japan and the USSR take a turn for the worse after the interception of a MIG 25 at Hakodate.
Empire of the Senses, film by Nagisa Oshima.

1977: Elections in the summer show a reduced vote for the Liberal-Democrats, though they retain their majority. Fukuda is successful in considerably reducing inflation.
Difficulties in maintaining good relations with Moscow, and also with Peking; but ties are strengthened with ASEAN (Association of South East Asian Nations).
Left-wing riots at Narita.
The Shinkansen reaches as far as Morioka, in the north of Honshu.

1978: Treaty of peace and friendship signed with China.
Ohira succeeds Fukuda. Opening, despite numerous demonstrations of protest, of the international airport at Narita.

1979: Trial of Tanaka and other Liberal-Democrat leaders implicated in the scandals of 1976: the party just manages to hold on to its majority in new election.
Exchange of official visits between Ohira and President Carter.
Elsewhere, relations with China normalized, though disaffection with the USSR grows over its refusal to negotiate about the Kuril Islands.

1980: New elections in which the Liberal-Democratic party is returned with a more comfortable majority, allowing Suzuki to take office as Prime Minister.
The film *Kagemusha*, by Akira Kurosawa, wins first prize at Cannes.

1981: 1.2 million unemployed in Japan: economic austerity measures planned, but trade recovers thanks to intensive Japanese export drive; Western countries take a dim view of this.
Pope John Paul II visits Japan.

1982: Nakasone takes over from Suzuki, whose popularity has waned as a result of the austerity measures.

1983: Liberal-Democrats lose many seats through scandal involving former leader Tanaka.

1984: Yo Yamashita wins gold medal for judo at the Olympic Games in Los Angeles.

1986: Nakasone re-elected as Liberal-Democratic Prime Minister. Prince and Princess of Wales pay state visit to Japan. Japanese open Nissan car factory in Sunderland.

Some notes on the language

by **Fujimori Bunkichi**
Affiliated to the Institut National des Langues et Civilisation Orientales

It may seem unnecessary for you to know any Japanese in hotels and, generally speaking, in business circles, where English is fairly widespread. But you will be missing some of the most appealing sides of Japanese life. If you wish to leave the beaten track, knowing even a little of the language of the country will be of considerable aid in getting to know the inhabitants. The legendary hospitality of the Japanese will do the rest.

People often imagine that Japanese and Chinese are similar. It is mainly the written word, largely borrowed from classical Chinese, which is responsible for this impression. In fact the two spoken languages don't have a single fundamental feature in common, either in terms of pronunciation or, above all, of syntax.

Japanese is a language whose origins are somewhat obscure. Many experts have tried to find proof of relationships with either the Malayo-Polynesian or the so-called Ural-Altaic group of languages, which includes Mongol, Manchurian, numerous Siberian and Central Asian languages, as well as Turkish. However, as far as we know, only Korean can be considered to belong to the same family as Japanese.

PRONUNCIATION. Japanese is very easy to pronounce, especially for someone who can speak a Romance language and is therefore used to 'open syllables' ending in a vowel. A few basic precautions are all you will need to make yourself understood. The tourist who does not have a great deal of time to devote to language-learning would do well to get to know the ground rules of the so-called Hepburn system of transliteration, because it is the one most commonly used in Japan. It will be seen wherever the Japanese have endeavoured to save western visitors some trouble...

This Hepburn transliteration has the merit of being very simplistic: to put it in a nutshell, the vowels are transcribed more or less as in Italian, and the consonants, broadly speaking, in the English manner. Although that is a good rule of thumb, it doesn't mean that you actually have to speak the consonants as in English and the vowels as in Italian. To arrive at a tolerable Japanese pronunciation through the transliteration, you need to know at least a few essentials, of which the following is an outline:

VOWELS. There are five of these: A-I-U-E-O (to give them in the Japanese order).

U: pronounce it *oo* (as in *two*), and you'll be understood, but if you want to make a better job of it, you should do as follows: say a flat English *e* (as in *the*) and then close your lips tightly, repeating the same sound softly. At the same time, try to 'relax' your lips and tongue, so that there is no tension in them. Having done that, you'll be pronouncing the Japanese *U*, which is simply a flat closed vowel. Try to say *MUZU DESU* (it's hard).

The letter in heavy type shows where the stress falls. In Japanese, accentuation does not equate to vocal stress. You only have to raise the pitch of the voice a little and then revert to the lower tone.

Don't forget, while we're on the subject, that a *U* or *I* can be mute in the final position in a word if unstressed (thus, in the above example *DESU* becomes *dess*). This 'muting' also happens when *U* or *I* come between two mute consonants: *TAKUSHI* (taxi) is pronounced *tak'shi*, *ASHITA* (tomorrow) is spoken as *ash'ta*.

E: as in *then*, never as in *the*. As an example, try to pronounce *O-KANE* (money) (=*OH-KAHNEH*).

LONG VOWELS. These last twice as long as short vowels (for example, *A=AA*, *U=UU*, *O=OO*). On the other hand, two or more different vowels occurring together are pronounced separately, except for *EI=EE*: *KITE Kudasai* (come), *KIITE KUDASAI* (listen), *ISOIDE KUDASAI* (hurry up).

CONSONANTS. In general, a consonant is always followed by a vowel or possibly by *YA*, *YU*, *YO*. English speakers will only need to note the following:

CH: As in *church* not *loch*: *O-CHA* (tea).

F (only in *FU*): say a Japanese *U* and whistle at the same time (on no account actually pronounce an *f*): *FUNE* (boat).

G: *GE, GI* should be pronounced with a hard *g*, as in *get*, *give*. G is nasal when not at the start of a word: *KAGI* (key) = KA-NGI.

H: always pronounced, but be careful not to add one where it isn't needed: *HASHI* (bread sticks), *HASHI* (bridge): *ASHI* (legs or feet).

R: Rest the tip of your tongue lightly behind your teeth and say *l*; do not roll the *r*, or you won't be understood.

S: unvoiced, never like a z: *MISE* (shop).

W (only in *WA*): this is a combination of a Japanese *U* and *A*. It sounds much more like an English *wa* as in *water* than, say, a German one as in *Wagner*: *WATAKUSHI/WATASHI* (me, I).

WRITING. The Japanese system of writing is perhaps the most complex in the world. There are two series of specific signs, of a phonetic nature, called *KANA* (*KATAKANA* and *HIRAGANA*, 48 signs in each series), together with ideographic characters borrowed from the classical Chinese (*KANJI*, some 1,850 in number according to a very limited official list). These different signs are used as follows:

- The *KATAKANA* are used principally for the transliteration of foreign words.

- The *HIRAGANA* represent native elements and especially those of a grammatical kind.

- The *KANJI*, much the most common, are used to represent words of Chinese origin (in a dialect named *ON*, derived from imitations of ancient Chinese dialects), and also to transcribe words of purely Japanese origin. In the latter case there can be no phonetic equivalence between the Chinese characters and their 'readings' (*KUN*), which are simply translations of their meaning into Japanese. As a result, the same character may be 'read' in many different ways.

Efforts have been going on since 1946 to simplify the whole system, but radical solutions such as romanization have always been rejected. The argument usually cited is that most words necessary to modern life are made up of characters which often have the same sound, and that words would become unintelligible without their 'visual support'.

THE RENEWAL OF THE LANGUAGE. Since the modernization of Japan, the language has undergone a considerable enrichment in terms of its vocabulary. Western concepts have been translated into Japanese, in the form of words built up in Chinese fashion. Other terms transcribed have been without modification so that contemporary Japanese appears to be contaminated by many foreign words, particularly English ones.

However, closer examination reveals that a word of Western origin has often been incorporated into Japanese with a very particular usage: *start* (written as *SUTATO*) means start of athletes or of a motor; *avec* (from the French word for 'with' and written *ABEKKU*) refers to a *man and a woman* out walking together!

So every borrowed word, whether Chinese or Western, becomes an invariant Japanese word (usually a noun). In order to integrate it into a sentence, it is necessary to combine it with Japanese particles: *SUTATO-SURU* (*SURU* meaning 'to make') corresponds to 'to leave', and *ABEKKU-DE ARUKU* (*DE* being a particle indicating the state of, *ARUKU* 'to walk') means 'to go for a walk as a couple'.

As these examples show, the language has safeguarded its fundamental structure as a whole, in spite of a great many foreign imports and repeated neologisms.

The language evolves, but the basis of it remains unchanged. In much the same way, the specific steps of Japanese thought remain just as they used to be, cast in the image of the whole of the country and its civilization; the constants of the culture survive the progression of centuries, adapting perfectly to modernization; possibly the most rapidly-achieved modernization in the world.

This written language, with all its complexity, is relayed daily, just as it is, by a formidable array of telegraphic lines and computers, which deal with it in 'real time' without so much as a hiccup. The more we study the technology underlying this achievement, the more remarkable it appears.

Visiting Japan

Alphabetical guide to towns, monuments and places of interest

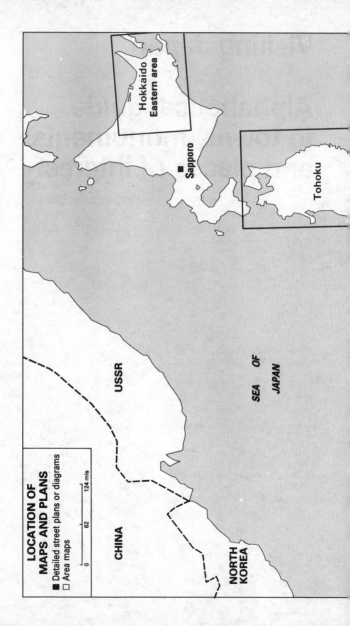

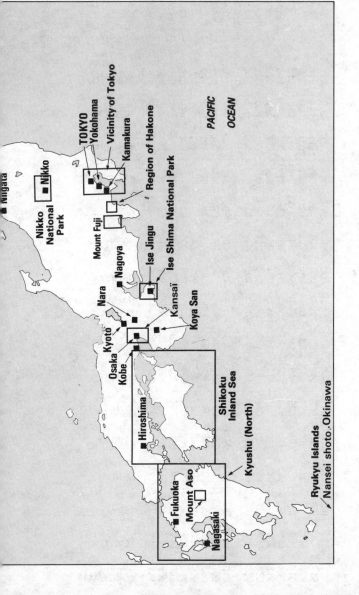

Table of distances (in miles) by the most direct routes.

	AOMORI	FUKUOKA	HIROSHIMA	KAGOSHIMA	KOBE	KYOTO	NAGOYA	NAHA (Okinawa) as the crow flies	NIIGATA	OKAYAMA	OSAKA	SAPPORO	SENDAI	TAKAMATSU	TOKYO
AOMORI															
FUKUOKA	1054														
HIROSHIMA	883	141													
KAGOSHIMA	1249	194	366												
KOBE	691	363	191	558											
KYOTO	644	410	241	605	47										
NAGOYA	544	494	322	688	130	83									
NAHA (Okinawa) as the crow flies	1331	566	666	417	765	804	864								
NIIGATA	279	776	604	970	412	365	263	1102							
OKAYAMA	780	274	102	469	89	136	219	725	501						
OSAKA	670	384	212	579	21	26	109	784	391	110					
SAPPORO	244	1298	1126	1494	935	888	786	1490	523	1024	914				
SENDAI	241	918	746	1113	555	508	425	1203	143	644	534	485			
TAKAMATSU	807	301	129	496	116	163	246	1204	528	27	137	1032	670		
TOKYO	445	714	543	909	351	304	220	1204	208	440	330	689	204	466	
YOKOHAMA	454	699	527	934	336	289	206	1013	223	425	315	704	219	458	15

■ Abashiri (Island of Hokkaido)

Map of Hokkaido, pp. 228–9.

Tokyo, 920mls (1,481km) – Asahikawa, 142mls (228km) – Kushiro, 103mls (165km) – Nemuro, 132mls (212km) – Obihiro, 122mls (197km) – Sapporo, 231mls (371km) – Wakkanai, 216mls (347km).

Hokkaido – pop: 44,777[1] – fishing port and fish canning.

Set on the coast of the Sea of Okhotsk, between Lake Abashiri and the bay, the town is an active fishing port despite being poorly sheltered and icebound in winter. The Abashiri gawa flows through Hokkaido, the most important town, dividing it in two. It faces the northernmost seas around Japan. For the tourist, Abashiri acts mainly as a base for exploring the surrounding area, with its lagoons and farmlands, forming the coastal Abashiri Park (92,447 acres/37,412 ha).

KATSURAOKA KOEN (½ml/1km SE of the station) contains a small local museum housing the results of the excavations at the Moyoro site (3mls/5km N); near a pile of shells (*kaizuka*) were discovered the remains of a Neolithic-style civilization, dating back about 1,000–1,500 years. The garden also has an aquarium and an interesting collection of tropical plants.

VICINITY

1 ABASHIRI KO AND TENTO ZAN (2½mls/4km S, coach as far as Tento zan). Lake Abashiri (13sq.mls/33km^2) freezes in winter, so that skating is possible; at other times, it is full of carp. There is a panoramic view of the whole lake from Tento zan (679ft/207m), from which you may also look out over the coastal Abashiri Park.

2 NOTORO MISAKI (approx. 7mls/12km N). This steep rocky headland to

---

[1]Population figures are taken from the statistical yearbook released by the Japanese Embassy in Paris.

the E of Notoro ko is distinguished by its twin rocks, Futatsu iwa (3mls/5km N of Abashiri).

3 'GENSEI KOEN (approx. 11mls/17km E; coach). Spread out between the Tofutsu ko and the sea, a vast multi-coloured carpet of flowers blooms between May and September drawing many visitors.

4 SAROMA KO (approx. 40mls/65km E; coach or train as far as Kami Yubetsu). 9mls (15km): Notoro ko, vast lagoon open to the sea through a narrow gully. Oysters.

22mls (35 km): Tokoro, from where you can travel back up the Tokoro gawa valley as far as Kitami.

5 AKAN, DAISETSUZAN, AND SHIRETOKO NATIONAL PARKS, see entries under these names.

40mls (65km): Saroma ko, largest outlying lagoon on the island of Hokkaido (58sq. mls/149km^2).

54mls (87km): Yubetsu, from where you may travel to Mombetsu (49mls/79km NW) and Rubeshibe (20mls/32km S).

■ Aioi (Island of Honshu)

Map of Shikoku (Inland Sea), pp. 536–7.

Tokyo, 386mls (621km) – Kobe, 45mls (73km) – Kyoto, 90mls (145km) – Ilayama, 43mls (55km) – Osaka, 66mls (106km) – Tottori, 81mls (131km).

Hyogo ken – pop: 40,657 – naval dockyards, saltworks.

Tucked away in a narrow bay whose seafront provides a delightful view of the national park of Seto Naikai, the town contains important dockyards belonging to the IHI company, second in the world only to those in Nagasaki. Specialists in giant petrol-tankers, IHI launched the *Idemitsu Maru* (209,000ft) in 1966, followed by the *Universe Ireland* (300,000ft) and the *Nisseki Maru* (372,000ft) and, in 1973, by the *Globtik Tokyo* (447,000ft), more than 1000ft (300m) in length. But since the oil crisis, the reopening of the Suez Canal and the upsurge of competition from Korea, the firm has had to introduce massive diversification programmes.

■ Aizu Wakamatsu (Island of Honshu)

Map of Places of Interest, p. 70.

Tokyo, 165mls (250km) – Fukushima, 78mls (125km) – Maebashi, 152mls (244km) – Niigata, 75mls (120km) – Sendai, 129mls (208km) –Utsunomiya, 91mls (146km) – Yamagata, 81mls (131km).

Fukushima ken – pop: 114,528 –718ft (219m) alt.

On the edge of a mountain valley dominated to the W by the Echigo mountain range, and rising to the E up the foothills which form the basin of Lake Inawashiro, the town has for many years past played a vital strategic role in northern Japan.

THE MEETING. This is the meaning of the name Aizu; it was here that in 88 BC, their mission accomplished, the two Shoguns Ohiko and Takenukawa wake met, having been ordered by the Emperor Sujin (149-130 BC) to pacify the north of the country. At the end of the 12th c., Suwara Yoshitsura, from the important Miura family, became feudal overlord of Aizu and his grandson took the name of Ashina. In 1384, Ashina Morinori built the castle then called Kurokawa. In 1583, Ashina Moritaka died without an heir and the castle passed into the possession of a son of Satake Yoshishige (1547-1612), an old enemy of the Ashina, whose power extended over a large part of the Tone basin. At the age of 12, the young Satake took the name Ashina Morishige, but those loyal to the Ashina clan allied themselves instead with Date Masamune who thereupon laid siege to the castle and captured it, in 1589. He vacated it, however, the following year at the demand of Toyotomi Hideyoshi.

THE LAST STAND. In 1500, Hideyoshi entrusted the castle to Gamo Ujisato (1557-96), to help him subdue the daimyo in the north of Japan. He rebuilt the castle of Kurokawa and gave it the name of Wakamatsu. In 1643, the castle was inherited by Hoshina Masayuki (1611-72), half-brother of the Shogun Iemitsu, and it remained in the charge of this branch of the Tokugawa family until the Meiji Restoration of 1868. Hoshina Katamori, a committed proponent of Shogunal power, put up a valiant fight against the forces of the Imperial army which seized the last bastion of resistance on the island of Honshu, in September 1868: the town and the castle were then razed.

TSURUGA JO (2mls/3km S of the Aizu-Wakamatsu station; bus). The old castle of Wakamatsu was the main one in Tohoku; the keep, recently reconstructed, is of stately appearance and houses a museum in which there are local works of art; from the top there is a view over the town and its surrounding area.

IIMORI SAN (2mls/3km E of the station; bus as far as the foot of the hill).

THE COMPANY OF WHITE TIGERS (Byakkol tai). In 1868, at the time of the siege of the castle, a group of boys, all under 17 years of age, fought fiercely against the Imperial troops. Seeing smoke rising from the castle, they wrongly interpreted it to mean the defeat of the occupants and committed suicide. Of the twenty youths, only one survived: there is a monument to the memory of the other nineteen who are all buried close by.

VICINITY

1 HIGASHIYAMA ONSEN (3mls/5km SE; bus). Surrounded by hills, this spa is known for its sulphurous salt waters, between 95° and 149°F (35° and 65°C), used in the treatment of rheumatism and nervous disorders. There are several hotels (*ryokans*); a funicular railway takes you to the top of Mount Seaburi (2,841ft/866m) from where you get a view of the Aizu basin on the one side and Lake Inawashiro on the other; ski slopes in winter.

2 YANAIZU ONSEN (14mls/23km W, coach; train as far as Aizu-Yanaizu station). This is a delightful resort, where you may visit the Enzo ji (550yds/500m SE of the station) which dominates the Tadami gawa.

The Enzoji or Yanaizu Kokuzo (Rinzai sect) was founded in 807; the imposing buildings to be seen today – notably Nio mon and Hon do – date back to the Edo period.

From Yanaizu, you may like to travel back up to the high route along the Tadami gawa (by train as far as Koide, 71mls/115km), distinguished by gorges and hydroelectric dams, of which the most important are at Tanokura and Oku Tadami.

3 INAWASHIRO, BANDAI ASAHI NATIONAL PARK see entries under these names.

■ Akan (National park; Island of Hokkaido)**

Map of Hokkaido (Eastern Area), pp. 228–9.

HOW TO GET THERE

– From Teshikaga, 2h. by train to Abashiri (60mls/96km NW) and 1h.20 to Kushiro (45mls/73km to the S), from where it is an easy coach ride to Kawayu Onsen, Akan Kohan, Bihoro and the major tourist areas.

– From Bihoro (17mls/28km S of Abashiri, 30 mins, by train), from where you may make a coach trip round the whole park as far as Akan Kohan via Teshikaga.

– From Akan Kohan (49mls/75km NW of Kushiro), in 1h.50 by Akan Bus, and then by a route in the opposite direction to the preceding one as far as Bihoro.

– Other coach services from Teshikaga and Akan Kohan, to Obihiro, Kitami or Sounkyo.

This is possibly the most beautiful – and mysterious – national park in Japan, where the volcanoes are mirrored in clear waters to give a breathtaking landscape symbolic of all Japan, with its blue drifting mists and colourful and unusual vegetation, in which even the pines seem to change colour with the seasons, adding their particular magic to this exciting place.

FROM AKAN KOHAN TO BIHORO (68mls/110km by the N241; Akan Bus runs a service in both directions. Akan Kohan is a thermal spring (140°F/60°C), situated S of *Lake Akan (46sq.mls/118km², 1,375ft/419m alt.), which lies at the foot of Mount Me-Akan (4,931ft/1,503m) to the W, and Mount O-Akan (4,498ft/1,371m) to the E, both extinct volcanoes which add to the grandeur of the scene.

The lake, 118ft (36m) deep, is full of red salmon and a special weed called marimo (*Aegagropila santeri*): shaped like small downy globes

2-6in (6-15cm) in diameter, they are to be found near the islets in the northern part of the lake, at depths of 3-10ft (1-3m). Similar weeds have been recorded in the Yamanaka ko near Mount Fuji, as well as in Switzerland and some North American lakes. There is a boat that makes trips round the lake. You can go up Me-Akan and O-Akan; from their summits* the view is magnificent. Marimo Festival is held on the lake by the Ainu on the first Saturday or Sunday in October.

8½mls (14km): *Soko dai, a position from which, after a winding journey round the S of the O-Akan dake, you can look out over a landscape of conifers, surrounding the delightful lakes of Penke and Panke, into which flows the Akan ko.

25mls (40km): Keshikaga, spa town (hot springs 82°-205°F/28°-96°C) and excursion base for the Akan National Park.

1ml (1.5km) SW, resort of Tobetsu Onsen, with springs 86°-158°F (30°-70°C).

30mls (49km): *Mashu Ko, 1,152ft (351m) alt.

Set in a crater, this lake is so clear that you can see to the bottom - some 130ft (40m) or more (a world record). It is 696ft (212m) at its deepest point. The lake's transparency is not immediately obvious, since its surface more often acts as a mirror, reflecting the typical volcanic cone of Kamui nupuri (2,812ft/857m). It is quite difficult to reach the lake, as there is no path leading up to its shores: the absence of all forms of animal life underlines its strange, mysterious appearance, giving it an atmosphere that has given rise to many legends. It changes in appearance according to the time of day and the season of the year. From the opposite bank, where the road doesn't go, the view is said to be even more unusual. For the Japanese the great discovery is to make out the islet in its centre that is often shrouded in mist. The Juhyo matsuri, or festival of frost-covered trees, takes place some time in mid-March.

(62km): Io san, the sulphur mountain, is a volcano (1,680ft/512m high) which emits burning hot sulphur fumes (io); it also has the name of Atosa nupuri. In July its base is smothered with the flowers of a species of white Alpine azalea (iso tsutsuji).

39mls (63km): In Kawayu Onsen there are several springs (104°-140°F/40°-60°C) whose waters flow into the Kussharo ko. From Kawayu, you will find it easy to get to this lake (a few miles to the NW), the largest on our route (30sq.mls/77.5km², 397ft/121m alt.). It flows south into the Kushiro gawa.

42mls (67km): Branch off to the r. towards the Wakoto promontory, a lone, rather insignificant rock spur jutting into the lake. From here you may board a boat which travels around the lake in summer. The hot alkaline spring Wakoto Onsen rises near the shore, below the surface of the lake.

51mls (82km): Bihoro toge (alt. 3,363ft/525m), up to which the road has been built in stages. From here you can see on one side the Kussharo ko reflecting the surrounding mountains, and on the other, a panorama which stretches away as far as Abashiri and the Sea of Okhotsk.

68 mls (110km): Bihoro, from where you may catch a train for Abashiri or Kitami.

■ Akashi (Island of Honshu)

Map of Shikoku (Inland Sea), pp. 536–7.

Tokyo, 354mls (570km) - Kobe, 14mls (22km) - Kyoto, 58mls (94km) -Okayama, 66mls (106km) - Osaka, 34mls (55km) - Tottori, 103mls (166km).

Hyogo ken - pop: 206,525 - industrial town.

The most recent addition to the vast Osaka-Kobe conurbation which encloses the Bay of Osaka on its north side, the town faces the island of Awaji and is linked with it by a frequent motorboat service (Bantan Renraku Kisen Co., as far as Iwaya).

THE FIRST MAN IN JAPAN. It was in the soil of Akashi that the most ancient skeleton in Japan was discovered: these venerable remains are those of a contemporary of the Pithecanthropus of Java: both point to the existence in Paleolithic times of 'a civilization distantly related to the Chinese and Siberian centres' (D. and V. Elisseeff – *La Civilisation japonaise*).

Akashi was the birthplace of the Confucian holy man Mikaye Shosai (1662-1741).

Akashi Park, to the N of Akashi Station (JNR), is on the site of the old castle built in 1618 of which there now remain only two turrets and the ramparts, and which was among other things the residence of the noble house of Matsudaira from 1693 to 1868; in autumn a famous exhibition of effigies made from chrysanthemums is held here.

Hitomaru yama, further to the E, is the site of the shrine dedicated to Kakinomoto, one of the authors of the *Manyoshu* anthology of poems (7th c.), and of the Gessho ji, through whose grounds passes the Akashi meridian (longitude 135° E), used to set official Japanese time. On the slopes of the hill there is a municipal astronomy museum and planetarium; from the summit there is a view over the island of Awaji.

VICINITY

1 BYOBUGA URA (2½mls/4km W; bus; Nishi Akashi JNR station or Sanyo ER). 'Windbreak bay' no doubt owes its name to the arrangement of the cliffs running along the coast for about a mile (2km).

2 MAILO (2½mls/4km E; bus; trains JNR and Sanyo ER). Beside the sea there is a pine-forest of 5.6 acres (2.3 ha), preserved since ancient times when it was celebrated by poets and painters, among them Hiroshige Ando (1797-1858).

 3 ZENKAI (6mls/10km NE; coach from Akashi Station). The Taisan ji

(Tendai sect) was founded in 716 by Fujiwara Umakai (694–737). Note particularly the Hon do, built in 1304, and the Nio mon with its Deva guards from the Muromachi period (15th c.). The Amida-do houses a seated statue of Amitabha and the important Lotus *sutra* (Hoke kyo), made up of 32 handwritten volumes; also a collection of ancient armour as well as one of Buddhist paintings, displayed on 25 June (lunar calendar), the date of the annual airing of the treasure. The temple is hidden away in a pretty forest setting, with several little waterfalls nearby.

4 AWAJI SHIMA, HIMEJI, KOBE, see entries under these names.

A | **Akita** (Island of Honshu)

Map of Tohoku, pp. 232–3.

Tokyo, 370mls (595km) - Aomori, 121mls (195km) - Morioka, 73mls (117km) - Sendai, 149mls (240km) - Yamagata, 133mls (214km).

Pop: 284,863 - capital of Akita ken (pop: 668,869) - industrial town: petrochemicals, sawmills, textiles - state and private universities.

Close to the delta of the Omono gawa, the former capital of the Ugo province owes its present-day vitality not only to its traditional activities (woodworking, silk-weaving) but also to the presence of deposits of oil and natural gas (Yabase and Saru kawa). In addition to its famous dog-breeding, the region abounds in pretty 'Obako' with complexions of snow, answering to the most exacting standards of Japanese female beauty.

SENSHU KOEN (½ml/1km NW of the station). Surrounded by ancient moats that run the entire length of the great avenue leading to it from the station, this park, famous for its cherry trees and azaleas, is set on a hillock and occupies the site of the former castle of Akita.

A first fortress was erected in 733 to hold back the Ebisu in the north; they rebelled in 878 and burned down the castle. In the 15th c. Ando Sanesue took the family name of Akita, and after 1602 the castle passed into the possession of the Satake, who held it until the Restoration of 1868.

The shrine of Akita Hachiman, situated in the park, is dedicated to Satake Yoshino (1570–1633), founder of the house of Akita.

Below the level of the park, close to the moats, a curious modern building houses the regional art gallery.

Approx. 1½ml (2km) from the castle stands the Tentoku ji and, behind it, Heiwa Koen (Park of Peace), a public area of some 50 acres (20 ha), with a memorial cemetery.

Approx. 2mls (3km) W of the station, beyond the administrative buildings (town hall, regional offices), lies the important sports centre of Yabase.

TSUCHIZUKI (5mls/8km NW; bus, train). Akita's prime industrial suburb is divided from the town by oilfields and drilling-sites. The bed of the Omano gawa has here been entirely canalized, as far as the busy port of Tsuchizaki; it is now one long string of industrial establishments, oil reservoirs and areas of land gradually reclaimed from the sea. Offshore, there are underwater drilling-sites.

VICINITY

1 **TAIHEIZAN** (14mls/22km NE: coach). The road, leading past the Miyoshi shrines where the Bonten festival takes place in winter, goes almost to the top of Mount Taihei (3,842ft/1,171m); skiing in winter. When the weather permits, it is said that one can see as far as the island of Sado; on the mountain slopes is the pretty forest park of Nibetsu.

2 **OGA PENINSULA, TOWADA HACHIMANTAI NATIONAL PARK,** see entries under these names.

■ Akkeshi (Island of Hokkaido)

Map of Hokkaido (Eastern Area), pp. 228–9.

Hokkaido - Tokyo, 926mls (1,491km) - Kushiro, 27mls (44km) - Sapporo, 237mls (381km).

The evocative name of Akkeshi, 'place of oysters' in the Ainu language, is a reminder that these shellfish are the pride and joy of the locality; its lagoon, covering 12sq.mls (32km²), ends to the S in a peninsula on whose point Honcho and Shinryu stand opposite each other, these two settlements, nowadays linked by a 1,500ft (450m) bridge, form the town of Akkeshi. The Bay of Akkeshi, spreading out to the W, is Hokkaido's last remaining herring-fishing ground.

Kontai ji (½ml/1km SW of Honcho), on the promontory overlooking the Bay of Akkeshi, is one of Hokkaido's three major temples; it was founded in 1802. Further S, the University of Hokkaido has set up a marine biology laboratory, complete with aquarium. Beside the lagoon there is the little shrine of Atsugishi Benten jima. The whole Akkeshi region, as far as Hamanaka, is an important nature reserve, classed as a regional park: the coast, from Akkeshi to Tobutsu misaki, is the most interesting region for the tourist.

■ Ako (Island of Honshu)

Map of Shikoku (Inland Sea), pp. 536–7.

Tokyo, 393mls (632km) - Kobe, 52mls (84km) - Kyoto, 96mls (154km) - Okayama, 35mls (56km) - Osaka, 73mls (117km) - Tottori, 88mls (142km).

Hyogo ken - pop: 45,942 - cement works, saltmarshes, station: Banshu Ako.

Set back a little from the shores of the Inland Sea, this town is associated with the memory of Asano Naganori, founder of Ako; he killed himself over a minor point of protocol and was avenged by Oishi Yoshio (see below; see also the Sengaku ji in Tokyo).

OISHI JINJA (660yds/600m SW of the station) stands on the site of the old castle of Ako. Built by Ukita Naoie in about 1575, this castle was taken over by the Ikeda in 1600, then by the Asano in 1645. Following the seppuku (ritual suicide) of Naganori (1701), the castle was confiscated and presented to the Nagai, who were then replaced by the Mori from 1706. The mighty walls of the castle are still standing, and the corner towers, doorway and attractive bridge over the moat have all been restored.

Close to the castle stood the house of Oishi Yoshio (1659–1703) who led the conspiracy designed to avenge his late master.

A little museum nearby is dedicated to him and to the 46 other *ronin* (*samurai* who have lost their master) who, after their act of vengeance, followed his lead and killed themselves. There were as many of them as there are provinces in Japan; and the same number of artists from all the regions have portrayed them. Anniversary celebration, 14 December.

KAGAKU JI (550yds/500m W of the station). This temple, belonging to the Soto sect, built in the 15th c., was the shrine of the Asano when they ruled in Ako. Here there is a cenotaph dedicated to the *ronin* who are buried in Tokyo.

A second museum exhibits objects and mementoes of the Asano family and their palace, including the sabre used by Naganori to commit suicide.

VICINITY

1 AKO MISAKI (2½mls/4km SE; bus). From here you can look out over the Inland Sea, and towards the W, the port of Sakoshi on the Chikusa gawa estuary. The road, following along the coast towards Aioi, hugs a shoreline of cliffs and rocks eaten away by the waves.

2 HIMEJI, OKAYAMA, SETO NAIKAI NATIONAL PARK, see entries under these names.

Alps, Japan (Island of Honshu)

Map of Natural Resources, p. 66.

We have included under this title the central mountain ranges of the main island. There are three distinct major chains: the Hida sanmyaku, in the NW, culminating in Hotaka dake (10,466ft/3,190m), with other well-known peaks including the famous Tate yama (9,892ft/3,015m); in the central region are the mountains of the Kiso sanmyaku, between the superb valleys of the Kiso gawa and the

Tenryu gawa (highest peak: Komaga take, 9,698ft/2,956m); and finally the southernmost chain, Akaishi sanmyaku, dominated by Shirane san (10,472ft/3,192m), the second highest mountain in Japan after Mount Fuji.

The fold formation of these young mountains, together with their resemblance to the landscapes of the great European range, earned them, from the end of the 19th c., the name of Japan Alps. The word is written as Arupusu, but you can say Alps as you would in English. Two national parks, containing natural formations of great beauty, have been created in these mountains: Chubu sangaku and Minami Arupusu (see under these names).

A Amami shoto (Nansei shoto)

Map of Nansei shoto, pp. 430–1.

Kagoshima ken – Tokyo, 833mls (1,340km) – Kagoshima, 249mls (400km) – Okinawa, Nansei shoto, 186mls (300km).

This archipelago, composed of five main islands – O shima (largest town is Naze), Kikai jima, Tokuno shima, Okino erabu jima, Yoron jima – is attached to the great arc of the Ryukus which stretches away SW in the direction of Taiwan. It also forms the southern part of that string of islands to the S of Kagoshimaken, still known by the name of Satsunan shoto. With a gently rising skyline (2,277ft/694m on Yuwan dake, island of Amami oshima), the islands fulfil everyone's dream of faraway places: subtropical climate, clear blue seas washing beaches of fine sand, coral reefs, and a lush growth of banana trees, papayas, pineapples, passionfruit, palm trees, etc. The coasts are lashed by the waves and have been carved into fantastic shapes; there are several grottoes to complete this enchanting setting. The inhabitants have their own customs and traditions, and speak a Japanese dialect interspersed with Korean and Chinese words.

AMAMI OSHIMA OR O SHIMA. This is the main island, about 40mls (60km) in length; its coast is very indented, especially in the south part, the Bay of Setouchi, facing the smaller island of Kakeroma jima; its many beaches are beautiful. It is in one of these sheltered coves that Naze, the island's main town, was established from where you may go exploring O shima or take a boat to other islands in the group. The island produces pineapples, bananas, oranges, papayas, sugar-cane and betel nuts.

KIKAI JIMA. It lies to the E of O shima, and also has lovely seascapes and a rich plantlife; in certain places you may notice paths enclosed between dry stone walls nearly 7ft (2m) high, marking the boundaries of private property.

TOKUNO SHIMA. SW of O shima, and second in importance to it, also attracts numerous visitors; pineapple and sugar-cane are grown and bullfights take place here.

OKINO ERABU JIMA. Further S and triangular in shape, it is perhaps the most interesting island of all. There is an airport in the NE of the island but access by sea is to the two ports of China and Wadomari. The cliffs of Tamina misaki, on the NW tip of the island, drop sheer into the sea. The erabu lily is specially cultivated here; its essence and even its flowers are exported to North America and Europe. There are several coral reefs surrounding the island. Look out for a local type of rice barn (*takagura*) with a thatch roof mounted on sturdy wooden piles. The *Shonyu do grotto, on the lower western slopes of the O yama (807ft/246m), ranks second in Japan after that at Akiyoshi do (Yamaguchi); with its magical stalactites, it reaches 7,200ft (2,200m) in length. Not far away is the Suiren do grotto, with an underground watercourse.

YORON JIMA. The southernmost and the smallest in the Amami shoto group, it is accessible only by boat; very flat, less than 330ft (100m) high at its highest point, it boasts a coral barrier reef. Although it is the least visited of the islands, it still has a lot to offer.

■ Anan (Island of Shikoku)

Map of Shikoku (Inland Sea), p. 536–7.

Tokyo, 511mls (823km) - Kochi, 106mls (170km) - Matsuyama, 185mls (298km) - Takamatsu, 65mls (104km) - Tokushima, 12mls (20km).

Tokushima ken - pop: 58,467 - industrial settlement.

Situated between the estuary of the Naka gawa and the Bay of Tachibana, the town is of interest only inasmuch as it forms the northern departure point for the very beautiful *coastal park of Muroto Anan.

VICINITY

KONOURA (44mls/71km SW by the N55; coach). This coastal park actually continues on into Kochi province and, having skirted the Muroto Cape, passes the town of Muroto (see entry under this name). Muroto Kaigan attracts many visitors, not only because of its remarkable coastal scenery (Minami Awa Sun Route), but also for its shrines.

1½mls (2km): Fork to the r., in the direction of Yahoko jinja (2mls/4km W), the shrine which overlooks Anan and the Bay of Tachibana, and houses two statues of gods from the Fujiwara period (10th–12th c.).

4mls (7km): Tachibana is justly famous for its bay, whose islets have earned it the title of Matsushima of Awa Province: sadly, their appearance has been badly spoiled by the industrial expansion of Anan. A boat does round trips of the bay; the islet of Benten jima is covered with tropical plants. Parts of the coast here are very rough, but the main road and the railway avoid Tsubakidomari village and Kamoda misaki.

19mls (31km): At Hiwasa you should visit the Yakuo ji, to the W of the town, with its curious modern domed shrine, housing the five golden statues of Amida Nyorai. To the NE there is a pleasant beach at Ohama kaigan; a boat travels from the port, hugging the steep coastal cliffs.

*Sembakai Heki lies to the SW of the town.

At Hiwasa, it pays to leave the motorway and to travel instead along the *Minami Awa Sun Route toll-road, which allows you to enjoy the panoramic sea view.

25mls (40km): Ebisu do, from where a funicular takes you to an observation platform.

29mls (47km): At Mugi rejoin the motorway, which now runs along the pretty Bay of Yasaka.

38mls (61km): Kaifu, at the mouth of the Kaifu gawa.

Approx. 16mls (25km) NW is the Karei valley, with a little shrine and a waterfall.

44mls (71km): Konoura (see below, and the continuation of the route towards Muroto).

Aomori (Island of Honshu)

Map of Tohoku, pp. 232–3.

Tokyo, 446mls (717km) – Akita, 121mls (195km) – Morioka, 130mls (210km).

Capital of Aomori ken (pop: 938,948) – pop: 287,594 – trading port – private university.

Spreading along the southern side of the vast Bay of Mutsu, and at the SE base of the Tsugaru peninsula, the town thrives thanks mainly to its port, opened in 1906, which is still today the main access point by sea to Hokkaido. It was on account of this vital function that it was bombed in 1945 since when it has been entirely rebuilt.

Aomori is relatively uninteresting to the tourist, apart from its importance as a transit point for Hokkaido and a good departure point for exploring the vicinity. We mention in passing the Uto shrine (½ml/1km from the station), built on what used to be marshland, and the Gappo-koen, or Aomori park, approx. 2mls (3.5km) E of the station.

VICINITY

1 NATSUDOMARI ZAKI (21mls/33km NE approx.; coach).

10mls (16km): Asamushi Onsen (train and hovercraft from Aomori), spa town with springs at 136°–174°F (58°–79°C). Further on, the seaside panoramas are quite remarkable.

21mls (33km): O shima is the northernmost part of the Natsudomari peninsula, projecting into the Bay of Mutsu. From there, you can reach Tsubaki yama, the hill of camellias, where the flowers bloom over an area of more than 50 acres (20ha). You may continue this route as far as Noheji, passing through the pretty Bay of Asadokoro on the E of the peninsula.

2 MINMAYA (42mls/67km NW, by the N280; train). The road goes along the E and N of the Tsugaru peninsula, in sight of the Bay of Mutsu, then along the Simokita peninsula.

27mls (44km): Beyond Tairadate the road turns progressively westwards; the coast becomes ever more picturesque.

32mls (52km): Takano zaki is the northern point of Horozuki kaigan, where the coast has several reefs, precipices and attractive but hazardous marine grottoes.

38mls (61km): Imabetsu; rejoin the railway here.

42mls (67km): Minmaya (Tsugaru Kankyo car ferry for Fukushima on Hokkaido) was an active port during the Edo period for traffic with Hokkaido.

3 HIROSAKI, TOWADA HACHIMAN NATIONAL PARK, see entries under these names.

■ Arida or Arita (Island of Honshu)

Map of Shikoku (Inland Sea), pp. 536–7.

Tokyo, 381mls (613km) – Nara, 81mls (130km) – Osaka, 61mls (98km) – Tsu, 121mls (194km) – Wakayama, 17mls (27km).

Wakayama ken – pop: 34,257.

To the E of the Kii peninsula and on the estuary of the Arida gawa, running down from the Koya mountains, the town is often filled with processions of pilgrims making their way to the shrines in the nearby regions.

VICINITY

1 SHIMOTSU (3mls/5km N; train). This port is established in a well-sheltered bay where nowadays the fumes of petroleum refineries rise; off the coast is the pleasant little island of Benten (boat trips).

2 YUASA (7mls/11km SE by the N 42 or coastal road; train). The coast between Arida and Yuasa is particularly interesting, and forms the regional park of Nishi Arida. Among the temples in the Yuasa area, we would draw your attention particularly to: Shoraku ji (550 yds/500 m E of the station), Choho ji (1½ml/2km E) and Semui ji (2mls/3km NW).

■ Asahikawa (Island of Hokkaido)

Railway map on inside front cover.

Tokyo, 779mls (1,253km) – Abashiri, 142mls (228km) – Obihiro, 115mls (185km) – Rumoi, 53mls (85km) – Sapporo, 89mls (143km) –Takikawa, 33 mls (53km) – Wakkanai, 160mls (258km).

Hokkaido – pop: 352,619; 371ft (113m) alt.; industrial town, cotton spinning, wood industry, brewing; private university.

The second most important town of the large island of Hokkaido, and undoubtedly its most progressive, Asahikawa is established in the Kamikawa basin, near the confluence of several watercourses flowing down from the mighty Daisetsuzan mountain range, which forms a boundary to the urban hinterland in the E.

Thus hemmed in the town has been set up like a chessboard, cut in two by the Kami kawa or Ishikari gawa, and with a concentration of business and administrative activities on the S bank. Nothing seems able to halt its sprawl, not even the harshness of the climate, which brings temperatures as low as –22°F (–30°C) in winter. Asahikawa may yet become the most northerly great city of Japan.

Tokiwa koen (1ml/1.5km N of the station; bus), on the r. bank of the Ishikari gawa, is a garden of 40 acres (16 ha) with the Chidoriga ike at its centre, flanked by a large sports complex and an astronomy observatory.

Kaguraoka koen (2mls/3km SE, bus) is a park set out on a wooded plateau bordered by the Chubetsu gawa, which dominates the whole town. Skiing is possible here in winter. Kamikawa jinja is a shrine sacred to the town's guardian deity.

VICINITY

1 **ARASHI YAMA** (5mls/8km NW; bus; Chikabumi station).

2½mls (4km): Chikabumi, home of an Ainu community (see Hokkaido), completely integrated with the Japanese population here. A little museum houses various utensils from everyday Ainu life: weapons for hunting and fishing, Ainu clothing and furniture, etc.

5mls (8km): Arashi yama is a wooded park containing Ainu huts, the traditional style of dwellings, built entirely without nails.

2 **KAMUIKOTAN** (12mls/20km W by the N12; coach). The road goes through gorges carved out by the Ishikari gawa through the Yubari mountains, between the Kamikawa and Ishikari basins. For about a mile the cliff face is riddled by grottoes that were once lived in by cavemen; primitive pottery, iron tools, etc., have been found here.

3 **NIMOSHIRI** (27mls/43km E, by the N39; coach; train as far as Kamikawa). This is another village whose inhabitants are of Ainu origin; on a square scattered with huts and a barn on stilts, there stands a small polygonal museum building; it includes models representing scenes from the lives of the first inhabitants.

4 **DAISETSUZAN NATIONAL PARK**, see entry under this name.

■ Ashikaga (Island of Honshu)

Map of Shikoku (Inland Sea), pp. 536-7.

Tokyo, 57mls (91km) - Fukushima, 140mls (226km) - Maebashi, 25mls (41km) - Mito, 65mls (104km) - Utsunomiya, 33mls (53km).

Tochigi ken - pop: 165,756 - silk industry - private university.

It is to the N, on the left bank of the Watarase gawa, tributary of the Tone, that this silk-manufacturing town has sprung up; after a decline in 1868, the industry has made a great recovery, bringing Ashikaga up to second place in the whole of Tochigi ken in terms of its population; in 1832 a cloth market was opened, in competition with that of the town of Kiryu which had until then had a monopoly. The name of Ashikaga also conjures up that of the Shogunal family who came from here and who ruled over the lives of the Japanese people from their stronghold in Kyoto during the Muromachi period (14th-15th c.). Here too is one of Japan's oldest academic institutions, still revered today by many scholars and intellectuals.

☐ **SHRINE DEDICATED TO CONFUCIUS** (660yds/600m N of the station). This shrine, built in 1668, together with its library of more recent date, is all that remains on the site of the old Ashikaga gakko.

A PRESTIGIOUS SCHOOL The creation of the Ashikaga school is attributed to the intellectual Ono no Takamura (801-852), who would seem in fact to have been one of the institution's 'patron saints', its actual founder being Ashikaga Yoshikane (1147-1196), former lieutenant of Minamoto Yoritomo. Open to all who wished to be educated, it was attended above all by many Buddhist priests, attracting students from all over the islands. From 1350 onwards, Ashikaga Motouji promoted the school, and it was transferred to these parts by Nagao Kagehisa in 1394. The school lost some of its initial impetus, but was restored in 1432 by Uesugi Norizane (1411-1466), who provided it with considerable funds and appointed the priest Kaigen as director; the latter imported rich manuscripts and books from China, preserved to this day in the library. Protected by the descendants of Norizane, the school saw its reputation grow until the 16th c. In 1601, however, Tokugawa Ieyasu removed one of its teachers, Sanyo, to found a new school in Fushimi (Kyoto), and other establishments were opened during the Edo period, bringing about the gradual decline of Ashikaga gakko until, in 1871, it closed down.

◎ Banna ji (½ml/1km N of the station). This temple, in olden times the neighbour of Ashikaga gakko, was also founded at the end of the 12th c. by Ashikaga Yoshikane, in the grounds of his house. The important Hon do contains a statue of Dainichi Nyorai; note the bell tower.

☞ **VICINITY**

GYODO SAN (5mls/8km N; coach to the foot of the hill). This walk is especially interesting in autumn; at the top, at approx. 1,300ft (400m), stands the Join ji belonging to the Rinzai sect.

■ Ashizuri Uwakai (National park; Island of Shikoku)**

Map of Shikoku (Inland Sea), pp. 536–7.

HOW TO GET THERE

- From Nakamura, 2h by train from Kochi (72mls/116km NE), from where you will find coach services with connections for Tosa Shimizu and Sukumo.

- From Umajima, 64mls (103km) S of Matsuyama, 2 h. 10 by train; from there, one of several coach services to Sukumo and Tosa Shimizu.

- From Tosa Shimizu: here you are at the centre of things, and you will find several coach and boat services which will take you to your destination.

This coastal park of 26,949 acres (10,906ha) occupies the southernmost part of the island of Shikoku; its remarkable seascapes stretch out from Tosa Shimizu towards Kochi in the NE and Uwajima in the NW.

FROM UWAJIMA TO NAKAMURA (102mls/164km by the N56 and N321; travel is possible in either direction, changing coaches at Sukumo and Tosa Shimizu; an overnight stay in one of these places is recommended). For the description of Uwajima and the bay, see entry under that name.

11mls (17km): Tsushima, set in a narrow inlet.

18mls (28km): Fork to the r. in the direction of the very jagged promontory of Yurano, which forms the northern boundary of *Uchi Bay.

30mls (48km): Once past Jonen, another road off to the r. goes to Nishiumi (7mls/11km W), at the foot of Gogan yama (1,611ft/491m), around which the road curves. You can explore the various inlets in the area by boat.

42mls (67km): Sukumo (pop: 25,028; boat to Utsuki: coral work). Little town on the Bay of Sukumo, from where you may take a trip to the island of Okino (see below).

On the mound of Sukumo (approx ½ml/1km W), fragments of pottery from the Jomon and Yayoi periods have been found.

*OKINO SHIMA (approx. 16mls/25km SW; by boat from the port of Kashima). It is worth a detour … You disembark at the little port of Okino, or at Hirose – even more charming – hidden away in a deep inlet; look out for the narrow cultivated terraces, as well as those on which stand the houses, built of big blocks of rough-hewn stone, but scrupulously cared for.

52mls (84km): A new fork to the r. leads towards **Odo kaigan; coaches generally make a detour to take in the park, where monkeys live in freedom; very fine view of the coast, carved by the sea into rocky spurs; lower down is the little island of Kushiwa, accessible by road and, in the distance, Okino shima.

59mls (95km): Here you reach the Pacific coast, at the southern tip of Shikoku; it is magnificent.

70mls (113km): Tatsukushi is an area of bizarrely shaped rocks, eroded into perpendicular shapes by the waves, so that they resemble huge bamboo canes. Nearby an underwater observation point has been installed. To the S you can see the outline of Senzin misaki, whose Minokoshi (access by boat) is comparable with Tatsukushi (see above).

80mls (128km): Tosa Shimizu (pop: 24,122), a fishing port.

➡ 7mls (11km) SE: *Ashizuri misaki (toll road along the ridge; coach) is the southernmost point on Shikoku. Here there are cliffs at the foot of which lie rocks smashed by the action of the waves. The Kongofuku ji, near the lighthouse, was created in 822 by Kobo Daishi in honour of Kannon of the thousand hands: the buildings date from 1662.

Cutting through the base of Cape Ashizuri, the motorway goes N to the lovely Bay of Oki matsubara, then continues in the direction of:

102mls (164km): Nakamura (pop: 33,573), former feudal seat of the Ichijo, on edge of the Shimanto gawa.

■ Aso (National mountain park; Island of Kyushu)**

Map of Kyushu (North), pp. 388–9.

HOW TO GET THERE

– From Beppu (60mls/97km to Aso station), by coach to the top of the mountain, then back to Beppu or on to Kumamoto and Nagasaki.

– From Kumamoto, by train to Aso station (JNR Hohi line, 31mls/50km in 1 h.) or to Aso Shirakawa station (Takamori line), then a coach; or from Kumamoto by coach all the way, taking a route in the reverse direction to the one above.

– From Oita by train as far as Aso (61mls/98km in 2 h.); coach.

The main attraction of this park of 180,602 acres (73,087 ha) is the magnificent Mount Aso, a place where nature runs wild and the air is acrid with the smell of sulphur: visitors make their pilgrimage by thousands to stand in awe before the largest active volcano in the world. It must be said that this sensation of standing 'on the edge of the abyss' is quite without equal, and all the stronger for the reminder provided by the shelters which are erected all round the crater that the volcano grows angry from time to time! But there is no danger at all in taking a stroll round; if there were, the authorities would not permit it. The park extends in a NE direction via Kuju san and the mountains that overlook the splendid bay of Beppu.

FROM BEPPU TO KUMAMOTO, VIA ASO SAN (91mls/147km by the Yamanami Highway and the N57; coaches; if you use a private vehicle you will have to drive up and back down the Aso Tozan Driveway from Aso machi). See entry for Beppu for a description. On leaving the station, you climb rapidly to the W on the slopes of the Tsurumi dake; don't forget to look behind you for beautiful views. If you choose to take one of the many organized tours of the area, avoid the bear park, which is in fact little more than a dismal zoo. Local tours of the Aso region may be the best way to cram the maximum amount of sightseeing into the minimum of time, including a compulsory stop to try milk produced locally. The whole trip is rounded off by a short song recital from the tour-guide, wearing traditional hat and gloves.

16mls (26km): Yufuin Onsen, to the r. of the road; hot springs at 108°-149°F (42°-65°C); and resort at the foot of the Yufu dake (5,197ft/1,584m), an extinct volcano - a beautiful mountain - which is quite difficult to climb (it takes 2h.); it well deserves its nickname of the Fuji of Bungo province; from the summit there are fine views, especially of the bay of Beppu.

21mls (33km): Mizuwake toge (2,349ft/716m alt.); from here, take the Yamanami Highway which heads S in the direction of *Kuju san.

The highest point on the island of Kyushu, Mount Kuju (5,866ft/1,788m) has several secondary peaks: Daisen, Hiji, Hosho and Minata. On the lower slopes is spread out the Kuju Kogen, rich with pasture lands, of which the best known is the Shuchikujo. The hot springs of Hokkein, Makinoto, Sujiya and Ukenokuchi provide the finishing touch to this verdant scene.

From there, or from Kuju, to the SE of the mountain, you may begin the ascent, which takes an average of 4h. walking. The very extensive *view from the summit allows you to take in at a glance the whole of Aso san and its vast crater, the bay of Beppu, then, to the W, the Unzen mountains and, still further S, the peaks of Kirishima.

45mls (72km): Road off to the r. towards Kuju Kogen, Kuju machi and (19mls/30km SE) Taketa (see entry under this name).

53mls (85km): Here we arrive on the outer lip of the immense crater of Mount Aso: 80mls (128km) in circumference, with a width of 14mls (23km) from N to S, containing an area of 98sq. mls (255km²) in all; the lower slopes are given over to cattle raising and crop-growing on terraces, while the floor of the basin is covered with rice-paddies. The *view is imposing and spectacular; the central part of Mount Aso is visible from here, looking - say the Japanese - like a great Buddha lying outstretched, the form of his body suggested by the mountain peaks.

In the centre of the island of Kyushu, **Mount Aso is made up of several cones, of which Naka dake is nowadays the most active. It has four other cones; from E to W they are: Neko dake (4,619ft/1,408m),

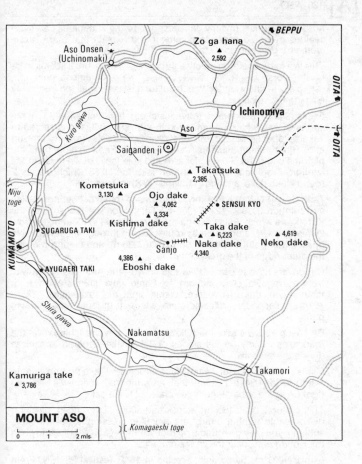

MOUNT ASO

```
0        1        2 mls
```

Taka dake (the highest, at 5,223ft/1,592m), Eboshi dake (4,386ft/ 1,337m) and Kishima dake (4,334ft/1,321m).

The outer rim of the crater looks as if it used to form the slopes of a far bigger mountain which exploded, leaving only these central cones. The first recorded eruption goes back as far as 553, but the most recent occurred as late as 1884 (when the ash fell on Kumamoto), 1889, 1929 and 1933. To the N and S of the central mountain ranges, the valleys of Aso and Nango join up and run W towards Kumamoto. It is very easy to go up this mountain using coach and funicular services, especially on the N face. The funicular which takes the hordes of tourists (mainly Japanese) up to the summit has an over-zealous guide so eager to comment and explain that there isn't a moment's peace to enjoy the view of the landscape!

This is a fairly common practice throughout Japan, but it seems to be at its worst just here! Nevertheless, we recommend this trip, especially in fine weather. Watch out for mists which all too frequently envelop the volcano.

58mls (94km): Ichinomiya (Miyagi station); here you should visit the shrine of Aso which was founded in the 1st c. BC, and is sacred to Takeiwatatsu no Mikoto, the local divinity; festivals: Tazukuri matsuri and Hiburi shinji matsuri, in mid-March. From Ichinomiya, the pilgrims begin the climb as far as Sanjo jinja (see below) close to the summit. From Ichinomiya you can take the N265 which travels E round Neko dake, arriving (14mls/23km S) in Takamori.

7mls (12km) NW of Ichinomiya: Aso Onsen (bus), hot springs, saline and sulphurous, 95°-122°F (35°-50°C); the spa is established on the Kuro kawa which drains Aso dani; you may travel to Kikuchi (approx. 25mls/40km W) along a pretty route passing through the remarkable observation point of Daikan bo (3,071ft/936m), and cutting through the outer ridge of the great crater.

Car drivers have to use – as we said above – the Aso Tozan Driveway from Kurogawa (Aso station) to Sanjo jinja (13mls/21km from Ichinomiya); this road passes within sight of *Takatsuka (2,385ft/727m), a secondary volcanic cone, with natural outlines of striking purity.

By coach you will take the following route: beyond Ichinomiya, the road rises rapidly up the slopes of Taka dake, covered in azaleas during the season.

63mls (101km): Sensui, near a stupa. From here, take the cable car to Narao dake (4,341ft/1,323m), then an 'armoured' coach will take you right up to the edge of the *main crater of Naka dake.

This crater, 2,000ft (600m) across and 500ft (160m) deep, gives off disagreeable sulphur fumes; the overall impression is, nevertheless, sublime; you may go round it on foot. Another cablecar goes down to the Hondo area, near the shrine of Sanjo.

64mls (103km): Sanjo jinja, erected in 1842; festival 28 July. From here carry on by coach to Kumamoto or go back to Beppu.

66mls (107km): On the r. the Aso Tozan Driveway branches off in the direction of Ichinomiya.

68mls (109km): Road off to the l. in the direction of Yunotani Onsen (½ml/1km S, 2,700ft/820m alt.); hot spring at 162°F (72°C) and a geyser capable of reaching 100ft (30m); this route extends in the direction of Tarutama Onsen and Jigoku, whose waters (140°-207°F/60°-97°C) contain sulphuric acid.

72mls (116km): Akamizu Shimono; rejoin the N57 and stay on it as far as Kumamoto.

75mls (121km): Tatano; 2mls (3km) E Toshita Onsen lies on the junction of the Kuro kawa and the Shira kawa, the latter running on westwards, as do the road and the railway, cutting through the outer edge of the crater of Mount Aso.

91mls (147km): Kumamoto, see entry under this name.

■ Atami (Island of Honshu)*

Map of the Region of Hakone, p. 161.

Tokyo, 59mls (95km) - Kofu, 80mls (128km) - Nagano, 185mls (297km) - Nagoya, 153mls (247km) - Shizuoka, 45mls (72km) - Yokohama, 43mls (70km).

Shizuoka ken - pop: 51,281 - hot springs.

Less than 60 miles from Tokyo, beautifully situated at the base of the Izu peninsula, Atami is one of the main tourist resorts in Japan.

The circle of hills enclosing the town is supposed to be the perimeter of an ancient crater, part of which collapsed into the ocean. Whatever the case, there are obvious signs of volcanic activity, including hot springs that often exceed a temperature of 194°F (90°C); Oyu, at 258°F (108°C), is the hottest in Japan and used to spout an average of 5,300 l/h until the earthquake of 1923 extinguished it.

■ **Atami Museum of Art** (Atami Bijutsu kan, open daily except Thursday from 09.30 to 16.00; 550yds/500m NW of the station). Access is by road from the station. Japanese Messianic church. Okada Makichi collection.

Among the works preserved here, note especially the double screen of *The Red Plum Tree and the White Plum Tree*, a masterpiece by the painter Ogata Korin (1658–1716); valuable calligraphic poems; various prints (*ukiyo-e*); the illustrated *sutra* of Cause and Effect (8th c.); and also Japanese, Chinese and Korean paintings, sculptures and bronzes, including some Egyptian, Indian and Iranian pieces; Noh theatre, teahouse, Japanese garden.

The shrine of Kinomiya, N of the station of the same name (1ml/1.5km SW of Atami), boasts one of the largest camphor trees in the whole of Japan.

Soshisha, 200yds (200m) S of the station, is the former abode of Shoyo Tsubouchi (1859-1935), author and Japanese adaptor of the works of Shakespeare. (It is possible to visit the house.)

Bai en, further W, with railway tunnels beneath it, is a park famous for the blossoming of its 1000 plum trees, from December to February.

Uomi zaki (2mls/3m S) forms the town's southern boundary; the shape of the two rocks that jut into the sea to form this cape resembles that of two kinds of antique military head-dress, hence their nicknames, Kabuto iwa and Eboshi iwa. Above the headland, the castle (recently restored; access by cablecar) occupies the site of the old local fortress.

☞ **VICINITY**

1 *NISHIKIGA URA* (approx. 3mls/5km S; coach). An interesting coastal ride takes you S of the cape of Uomi, to Atami Tropical Park where nearly 200 species of fish and 1000 plants flourish.

2 KURO DAKE (2,621ft/799m alt.; coach; access by cablecar). From here you overlook the whole of Atami; nearby is the Izu skyline (see entry under Fuji-Hakone-Izu National Park).

3 YUGAWARA ONSEN (4mls/7km N; coach; 1½mls/2km W of Yugawara station). 1½mls (2km); Izusan, hot spa (salt springs); at the top of the Izu hill (to the NW, difficult climb) is the shrine of Izusan, founded at the beginning of the 9th c.

4mls (7km): Yugawara Onsen, in a pretty mountain setting that opens out on to the sea; springs at 100°-198°F (38°-92°C); nearby are the waterfalls of Fudo and Godan.

4 HATSU SHIMA (6mls/10km SE; boat). This island off the coast of the Izu peninsula is a favourite holiday site for campers; abundant jonquils and camellias.

A Awaji shima

Map of Shikoku (Inland Sea), pp. 536–7.

Hyogo ken - Tokyo, 373mls (600km) - Kobe, 32mls (52km) - Tokushima, 25mls (40km).

Closing off the Bay of Osaka to the W, this island, roughly triangular in shape, is separated from Honshu to the N by the straits of Akashi and from Shikoku by the busy fairway of Naruto. The entire western side of Awaji is washed by the Inland Sea (Seto Naikai); in fact it is the largest island in those waters. Rich in arable land, it is also the most densely populated, with up to 1,550 inhabitants per sq. ml (600 per km²).

IN THE VERY BEGINNING: IZANAGI AND IZANAMI. The Host (Izanagi) and the Hostess (Izanami) not only produced by their union the myriads of kami (gods and godesses) which issued from the various parts of their bodies and are the source of all natural things, but they are also noted above all for having settled on the island of Onogoro, created on their descent from heaven, where they gave birth to the Japanese archipelago. Several islands, especially those around Awaji, lay claim to having once been Onogoro shima, but there is no doubt at all in Japanese mythology that Awaji shima was the firstborn of the divine couple. Close to the province of Yamato, the crucible of Japanese history, Awaji was naturally used as an area for exile. The Emperor Jonin (732-65) died here, strangled on the orders of the Empress

Koken, who had ceded power to him but then took it back, at the urging of the monk Dokyo, under the name of Empress Shotoku. From the 17th to the 19th c., the island was in the hands of the noble lords of Awa who ruled in Tokushima (Shikoku).

BUNRAKU Awaji shima may be thought of as the birthplace of these Japanese puppets, which gained their great reputation in Osaka thanks to the dramas of Chikamatsu Monzaemon (1653-1724), one of Japan's greatest playwrights; indeed, one of the world's great literary figures. The puppets are superbly articulated dolls, often dressed in sumptuous costumes, and generally manipulated by three assistants camouflaged in black hoods; the life and feeling these puppet-masters put into a performance focuses the audience's attention on the story and on the 'actors'.

Sumoto (pop: 44,499), the main town of Awaji, and the most common landing site for visitors to the island, is in fact little more than a big village with a small port attached to it.

Mikuma yama, a hill ½ml (1km) S of the town, is crowned by the castle of Sumoto (rebuilt) which, during the 16th and 17th centuries, was successively occupied by the Wakizaka, the Ikeda and the Hachisuka; a fine observation-point.

Yura (7mls/11km SE; coach); from here, enjoy a view of Awaji hashidate; although not quite up to the standard of the beach of Amano (see Miyazu), this spit of sand nevertheless calls to mind the floating 'bridge of heaven' over which the two divine creators came down to earth (see above, In the very beginning).

Sen zan (4mls/6km NW approx., to the foot of the hill); at the summit (1,470ft/448m) stands the Senko ji (Shingon sect), the most interesting temple on the island, sacred to Kannon of the thousand hands; the treasure includes several objects from the Muromachi period (15th-16th c.), including a kind of gong (*waniguchi*); the bronze bell in the belfry dates from 1283; view over the whole of the island and the straits dividing it from Shikoku and the Kii peninsula.

FROM SUMOTO TO FUKURA VIA IWAYA (63mls/102km; special coach along the E coast or by the N28 direct from Sumoto to Fukura). The winding road snakes around the whole island along the coast.

16mls (26km): Ura; approx. 3mls (5km) SW, Myoken zan (1,690ft/515m), with the Joryu ji on its summit.

21mls (33km): Iwaya, beyond the tiny holy island of E-shima.

22mls (36km): Northernmost point of the island, facing Akashi.

36mls (58km): Ichinomiya; approx. 1½ml (2km) to the S is Izangi jingu, dedicated to Izanagi, the creator of Japan (see p. 138).

43mls (69km): Goshiki; beyond it, Goshiki hama, with its pine-grove, is the island's most beautiful beach.

50mls (80km): Minato, the point at which you drive away from the coast to pick up the toll road again, leading to the promontory of:

57mls (91km): *Minami Awaji, from where you can look down on Naruto kaikyo (see Naruto). The road follows the length of the pretty Bay of Fukura (or Nandan).

63mls (102km): Fukura; area in which narcissi are cultivated.

→ 7mls (12km) SE: Nada, at the foot of Yururuha yama (1,995ft/608m), highest point on Awaji, opposite the little island of Nu; nearby, monument and esplanade of the Youth of Omi yama.

◼ Bandai Asahi (National park; Island of Honshu)**

Map of Natural Resources, p. 66.

HOW TO GET THERE

- From Tsuruoka, Yamagata, Yonezawa; see under these names.

- From Fukushima, coach service (Aizu Bus) for Inawashiro and Aizu Wakamatsu via the Azuma Skyline and Bandai Gold Aizu Line.

- From Aizu Wakamatsu (78mls/126km SE of Niigata, 2h. 10 by train) or Inawashiro (23mls/37km NW of Koriyama, 40 mins. by train) by Aizu Bus on the Fukushima or Yonezawa lines.

Three volcanic areas (the Echigo range and the Iide san, the twin chains of Asahi dake and Dewa, and the peaks of Azuma and Bandai san), with Lake Inawashiro, make up this mountain park of 468,662 acres (189,661 ha), created in 1950, which is the oldest on Honshu.

To find our more about the Iide san, see Yonezawa; for the Asahi dake, see Yamagata; Gassan (Dewa san zan) is included under the entry for Tsuruoka; Inawashiro-ko is listed under its own name.

FROM AIZU WAKAMATSU (OR INAWASHIRO) TO FUKUSHIMA (61mls/98km NE; coach services run in both directions). For a full description of Aizu Wakamatsu and Inawashiro, see entries under those names.

7mls (11km): Travel up the Bandai Gold Line, a toll road which takes a winding route with many hairpin bends up the western slopes of Bandai san (look out for waterfalls), giving a fine view over the whole of Inawashiro-ko; lower down towards the W is the basin of Aizu Wakamatsu.

*Bandai san (5,968ft/1,819m), nicknamed Aizu Fuji, is a violent volcano, as was shown by its last eruption in 1888 which blew the top off the mountain, ravaged the valleys for miles around, sweeping away the lakes and basins on the plateau of Urabandai, and engulfed several villages, taking some 460 lives.

14mls (23km): The landscape changes completely: the road begins its gentle descent to the *plateau of Urabandai, entirely remodelled by the eruption of last century, which created a chaotic jumble of a hundred lakes or more, all of different sizes. To the human eye, they are far more appealing than the slopes of Inawashiro on the opposite side.

18mls (29km): Hibara ko, the largest of these lakes, is scattered with many islets; a boat will take you round it. From here, you can make the ascent of Bandai and wander round Goshikinuma (1½ml/2km; 'the many-coloured ponds'), with their five or six little lakes with strangely-coloured waters.

↦ 9mls (14km) SE, direct route to Inawashiro.

↦ 30mls (48km) N, Yonezawa (coach), by another toll road which goes part of the way along Hibara ko and skirts W round Nishi Azuma san (6,640ft/2,024m).

▰ 19mls (31km): Dividing of the Bandai Azuma Lakeline, running between Lakes Onogawa and Akimoto.

30mls (49km): Take the N115 for a time, as a link between Inawashiro and Fukushima.

35mls (57km): Fork to the l. of the **Azuma Skyline, without doubt the most beautiful stretch of road on this itinerary, not least for the superb views it offers: you will lose count of the hairpin bends!

44mls (71km): Pass close to the summit of Azuma Kofuji (5,594ft/1,705m); easily reachable crater-ridge; vast panorama; signposted trails through the mountains. Winding even more, the road leads back down to Fukushima.

53mls (85km): Takayu Onsen, at an altitude of 2,460ft (750km), overlooking the whole of the Fukushima region.

61mls (98km): Fukushima: see entry under this name.

B Beppu (Island of Kyushu)

Map of Kyushu (North), pp. 388–9.

Tokyo, 780mls (1,255km) - Fukuoka, 101mls (162km) - Kumamoto, 93mls (149km) - Miyazaki, 132mls (213km) - Oita, 7mls (12km).

Oita ken - pop: 123,786 - hot springs - private university.

It is, surely, ill-advised to make comparisons, but Beppu, set in a delightful bay against a backdrop of lush green mountains - among them Takasaki yama - with palm-trees lazily waving by the sides of avenues, brightly coloured street-scenes and carefree young people will remind you irresistibly of some Mediterranean resort. However, the clothes that people wear are very obviously not Mediterranean, nor are the neon signs with their huge Japanese characters, or the throngs of patients wearing the *yukata* who make their way to take the waters of the 'Springs of Hell' famous throughout the land.

Beppu has two distinct aspects: the town proper, crowded around the station, with the port acting as its boundary to the E and the Sakai gawa to the N; and the spa with its hot springs stretching away into green and rocky country.

HEAVEN OR HELL? 'Jigoku', hell, is the name given to the springs of Beppu, despite their pretty setting. No fewer than 3,000 have been counted, each giving an average daily yield of 2¾ million cu.ft (78,000m³), and each with its own peculiarities of colour, smell, temperature, force and frequency of eruption. Whether it is a boiling pool or a sulphur spring, the springs and the 'smoke' issuing from the mountain make this area seem like the netherworld. The best springs have been put to good use: their temperatures range between 99° and 201°F (37° and 94°C) and their waters contain sulphur, carbon dioxide and alkali. A physical sciences laboratory and the Institute for the Study of Hot Springs at the University of Kyoto are conducting research into these springs.

Given the considerable distances between some of the springs, you are advised to ask your hotel to book you a taxi for your visit.

The most interesting **springs may be easily reached from the station in Kamegawa, 3mls (5km) N of Beppu. Particular ones to note, going W from the station, are as follows.

Tatsumaki jigoku, a geyser which discharges at fixed 17-minute intervals for 3 mins. at a time; *Chino ike jigoku (203°F/95°C), blood-red because of underwater oxidation; it is said to reach a depth of 541ft (165m); next come Kamado jigoku and Shibaseki Onsen (iron carbonate). The same road leads to Kannawa Onsen (2mls/3km from Kamegawa), with steam baths at 192°F (89°C): one of Beppu's most famous springs. Close at hand there are Kinryu jigoku, Shiraike jigoku and Oniyama jigoku (with alligator pools by the side of the springs). Further W, *Umi jigoku, the colour of the sea and without doubt the most beautiful spring of all, and Bozu jigoku, one of the weirdest, with its heaving grey mud in which bubbles rise up like bald heads. From a hill topped by an imitation castle, you can get a view over the whole area, with jets of steam indicating the position of the hot springs.

If you cross the Yamanami Highway and head towards Beppu, you will come to the botanical gardens of Fujita kanko, with their greenhouses full of tropical plants. From there, catch a bus to the Daibutsu (½ml/1km NW of Beppu station), a recent statue 79ft (24m) high. Close to the port, the Beppu Tower, all too conspicuous, reaches a rather ostentatious 330ft (100m).

VICINITY

1 TAKASKAI YAMA (2,060ft/628m alt.; 2½mls/4km SE; bus). Its fine outline

separates Oita from Beppu; a popular place for visitors on account of the large colony of monkeys living there. Near the coast, Marine Palace, with sizeable aquarium.

2 *KIJIMA KOGEN (7mls/12km SW; coach). It is situated between the extinct volcanic peaks of Tsurumi (4,511ft/1,375m; access by cablecar) overlooking Beppu and its bay, and Yufu dake. Nearby is the little Lake Shidaka, much visited (pink flamingoes).

3 OITA, USA, USUKI, ASO NATIONAL PARK, see entries under these names.

Chiba (Island of Honshu)

Map of the Vicinity of Tokyo, p. 565.

Tokyo, 23mls (37km) – Mito, 83mls (133km) – Urawa, 38mls (61km).

Capital of Chiba ken (pop: 3,923,911) – pop: 746,430 – industrial town – state and private universities.

Lying across from Tokyo, with which it is linked by fast roads and frequent rail services, Chiba is undergoing a considerable industrial expansion. In the course of the development of Tokyo Bay, land reclaimed from the sea has been invaded by heavy industry (steelworks, a massive thermal power-station), and Chiba, former capital of the daimyo of that name, has doubled its population in ten years.

Chiba dera (880yds/800m SE of Hon-Chiba station) is said to have been founded in 709 by the Korean priest Gyoki.

In Kasori (3mls/5km E) you will find the Kasori kaizuka ('heap of shells'; 1ml/1.5km N of Kasori), which gives evidence of a settlement in the area as early as the Jomon period.

VICINITY

NARITA, TOKYO, see entries under these names.

Chichibu (Island of Honshu)

Tokyo, 53mls (86km) – Chiba, 76mls (123km) – Kofu, 49mls (79km) – Maebashi, 34mls (54km) – Mito, 107mls (172km) – Nagano, 100mls (161km) – Urawa, 50mls (80km) – Utsunomiya, 83mls (133km).

Saitama ken - pop: 60,867; cement works, factories, silk industry.

Set high up in the Ara kawa, which runs down to Tokyo Bay, Chichibu can be thought of as a good place (along with Ome, see entry under this name) from which to begin a visit to Chichibu Tama National Park. Chichibu jinja, next to the station (Chichibu Railway and Seibu

ER), is an ancient shrine where sacred dances (*kagura*) are still practised, especially during the festival of 3 December.

☞ **VICINITY**

1 **NAGATORO** (7mls/12km N; Chichibu Railway; coach). Popular with visitors on account of its spring flowers, its rich colouring in the autumn, and its *gorges, with their steep rocky walls, stretching for about ½ml (1km) along the Ara gawa. Mount Hodo (1,631ft/497m, access by cablecar) rises to the W; observation platform at the summit.

2 **CHICHIBU TAMA NATIONAL PARK**, see entry under this name.

■ Chichibu Tama (National park; Island of Honshu)

Map of Natural Resources, p. 66.

HOW TO GET THERE

- From Chichibu, which you can reach from Tokyo (Ikebukuro) by Seibu ER, via Higashi-Hanno; or else by Chichibu Railway from Kumagaya (JNR station, from Tokyo-Ueno).

- From Kofu or Enzan, bus going to Ome.

- From Ome or Hiwaka, which you can reach from Tokyo (Shinjuku) via Tachikawa or Hajima.

Created in 1950, this national park (299,000 acres/121,000ha), the closest of all to the capital, is part of the 'great green belt' in the Tokyo area. Mountainous, cut through by superb valleys, covered with forests that are a blaze of colour in the autumn, and studded with natural grottoes, this park makes an excellent place to walk, climb, pitch your tent or fish.

1 **FROM CHICHIBU TO KOFU** (49mls/79km SW). The road that climbs back up through the charming Ara gawa valley.

8mls (13km): Mitsumine guchi, terminus of the Chichibu Railway.

12mls (19km): Owa, where you can take the cablecar to the shrine of Mitsumine (see below, Mitsumine jinja).

16mls (26km): Futase Dam, holding back the man-made Chichibu lake, in the upper reaches of the Ara kawa.

3½mls (6km) S (access by coach), by a picturesque winding road rising above the Ara valley, you come to Mitsumine jinja, clinging on to Mitsumine san (4,370ft/1,332m); founded in the 2nd c. AD, this shrine, visited by many pilgrims, contains important carvings. From here, you may ascend Mount Mitsumine (shrine at the summit) and, much further S, Kumotori yama (6,621ft/2,018m).

25mls (41km): Karisaka toge (6,831ft/2,082m), high ridge on the crest of the main peaks of the national park which are called, from W to E: Kimpu san (8,514ft/2,595m), Kokushiga take (8,504ft/2,592m),

Karumatsuo yama (6,919ft/2,109m) and Kumotori yama (6,621ft/2,018m).

35mls (57km): Little spa of Kawaura, in the upper reaches of the Fuefuki gawa.

42mls (67km): Yamanashi; see separate entry.

49mls (79km): Kofu; see separate entry.

2 FROM OME TO KOFU (60mls/97km W; coach; JNR train to Hikawa). (For a description of Ome, see entry under that name).

6mls (9km): Sawai, from Kanzan ji, near Sawai station, you get a fine view of the beautiful *Shazan gorge, through which both road and railway wind.

7mls (11km): Mitake, road off to the r. in the direction of Mitake san, access by cablecar.

14mls (22km): Hikawa, rail terminus; coach service to Itsukaichi (35mls/56km), see below, 22mls (35km).

4mls (7km) SE (coach): Mitake jinja, near Bushu Mitake (3,084ft/940m); the main shrine and the chapel are built in the *shimmei* style. The treasure house contains numerous antique mirrors, armour, weapons and ancient documents. Surrounded by splendid cherry trees, azaleas, maples, and an avenue of Japanese cypresses.

9mls (15km) NW (coach): Nippara shonyu do: there are eight natural grottoes along this route; the largest, at Shingu, is 550yds (500m) long and is open to visitors.

17mls (28km): Ogochi dam (1957) and the reservoir of Oku Tama, supplying mainly Tokyo.

22mls (35km): A panoramic toll road makes a loop to the r., rejoining the route at Itsukaichi (27mls/43km SE); coach service between this town and Hikawa (see above, 14mls/22km).

28mls (45km): Tabayama, in a pretty valley where the Oku Tama is little more than a mountain stream.

37mls (59km): Yanagisawa toge (4,829ft/1,472m); the road leads back down to the Kofu basin.

50mls (80km): Enzan.

54mls (87km): Kofu, see entry under this name.

◼ Chino (Island of Honshu)

Tokyo, 122mls (197km) - Gifu, 139mls (224km) - Kofu, 39mls (62km) - Maebashi, 91mls (147km) - Nagoya, 139mls (224km) - Niigata, 189mls (304km) - Shizuoka, 89mls (144km) - Toyama, 146mls (235km) - Urawa, 140mls (225km).

Nagano ken - pop: 36,200 - alt. 2,585ft (788m).

As far as the tourist is concerned, Chino is first and foremost the entry point to the Tateshina plateau (with the Shirakaba man-made lake).

◼ In Chino itself, the little Togariishi archeological museum houses the finds from digs – Jomon pottery, notably – from sites in Togariishi (Chino) and from Tokuri and Fujimi.

☞ **VICINITY**

SHIRAKABA KO (21mls/33km N by the Tateshina toll road; coach).

9mls (15km): Tateshina Onsen, in the centre of the Tateshina plateau and close to a small lake, makes for a pleasant stopover in summer (skating and skiing in winter); it is overlooked to the N by the very beautiful *mountain of Tateshina (8,301ft/2,530m). A marked trail leads to the Shirakaba ko (see below, 21mls/33km) and from there on to Kiriga-mine (approx. 16mls/25km).

↔ 3mls (5km) SE: Shibu, another spa, bounded to the E by the Yatsuga take mountain chain, comprising eight peaks of which Aka dake (9,511ft/2,899m) is the biggest.

13mls (21km): Turn l. for the cablecar up to one of the peaks in the Yatsuga chain, from which there is a wide panoramic view.

21mls (33km): Shirakaba ko, a little reservoir in the heart of the nature park of Yatsugatake-Chushin kogen, at an altitude of roughly 4,590ft (1,400m) whose shores are thronged by tourists; the lake freezes over in winter, allowing skating; in summer, boats sail across it.

↔ 14mls (22km) NW: the Wada ridge (5,023ft/1,531m alt.), on the road from Suwa to Saku, accessible via the *plateau of Kiriga-mine (7mls 11km; coach); from here, a **most extensive view of the whole of the Japan Alps, with Asama yama to the NE and Mount Fuji to the S. Beyond Waga toge, the road strikes out for Matsumoto; a coach link between this town and Shirakaba ko is coming soon.

2 **MATSUMOTO, SUWA-KO,** see entries under these names.

◼ Chofu (Island of Honshu)

Map of the Vicinity of Tokyo, p. 565.

Tokyo; 15mls (24km) – Chiba, 38mls (61km) – Kofu, 75mls (120km) –Urawa, 30mls (48km) – Yokohama, 27mls (44km).

Tokyo to – pop: 180,548.

This suburb of Tokyo is linked to Shinjuku station by the Keio Teito ER.

✺ **JINDAI JI** (1½ml/2km NE of the Chofu-Keio-Teito ER station; bus). This temple belonging to the Tendai sect, situated in a wooded area of 7 acres (3 ha), was founded in 733 by the priest Manku; but the Hon do dates only from 1919; inside it sits the gilded bronze statue of Sakyamuni, from the Nara (8th c.).

 Since 1962, there has been a hexagonal tower (crematorium)

adjoining the temple, large enough to take the ashes of 180,000 animals.

To the N of the temple, Jindai botanical gardens (Jindai Shokubutsu koen; 7 acres (3 ha) are planted on what used to be Musashi Plain.

S of Chofu station are the Daiei and Nikkatsu film studios, the gardens of Keio Hyakka (Keio-Tamagawa station), in flower all year round, and, on the banks of the Tama, the Keio kaku velodrome.

■ Choshi (Island of Honshu)

Railway Map on inside front cover.

Tokyo, 71mls (115km) – Chiba, 50mls (80km) – Mito, 55mls (88km) – Urawa, 87mls (140km).

Chiba ken – pop: 89,416 – fishing port.

Facing the Pacific Ocean, raised up to the E and S on a rocky peninsula through which the Tone gawa, Japan's longest river (200mls/322km) runs down to the sea, the town has turned its position to account, and has become one of Japan's main fishing ports. Nowadays, trading with the Ibaraki district to the N is made easier by the bridge (1,590ft/1,450m long) linking the town with Hasaki. Don't miss the morning activity in the busy port and fish market.

The author Kunikida Doppo (1871–1908) was born in Choshi.

The Empuku ji (1ml/1.5km E of the station; Shingon sect), built on the model of the Kannon ji of Asakusa (Tokyo), houses a statue of Kannon of the eleven heads.

⌐ VICINITY

1 IIOKA (12mls/19km SW; Choshi ER train as far as Tokiwa, then coach).

Travel across Choshi eastwards, parallel with the Tone gawa.

1½mls (2.5km): Kawaguchi Myojin or Hakushi Daimyojin; the nearby mound of Sennin zaka ('mound of the thousand'), which dominates the estuary of the Tone gawa, was erected in 1614 to the memory of those lost at sea.

3½mls (6km): Inubo saki (access point) is topped by a lighthouse (1874) with a range of 23mls (37km). To the N of the headland lies the lovely beach at Kurobae, with the isles of Ashika just off the coast; they are called the sea lions, because they were formerly inhabited by such creatures.

5mls (8km): Tokawa; the starting point of *Byobuga Ura, a stretch of coast where the white cliffs of Dover wouldn't look out of place; a toll road runs along the edge.

≈ 12mls (19km): Iioka, where the immense Kujukuri hama beach begins.

2 SAWARA, see entry under this name, in summer, motorboats ride along the Tone as far as here.

3 KASHIMA, NARITA, MITO, see entries under these names. **SUIGO-TSUKUBA NATURE PARK**, see Tsuchiura.

■ Chubu Sangaku (National park; Island of Honshu)**

Maps of Natural Resources, pp. 64–7.

HOW TO GET THERE

– From Matsumoto or Shimashima (9mls/15km W of Matsumoto, by private railway), from where you catch a coach service in the direction of Kamikochi and Takayama.

– From Takayama, from where you can catch a coach to the area around Norikura dake or Hotaka dake and Matsumoto.

– From Omachi, take the JNR Oito line to Shinano Omachi station (22mls/35km from Matsumoto); from there, follow the route for Toyama via Tate yama.

– From Toyama as far as Omachi, following the route above in reverse.

In the very heart of Japan, this mountainous park (419,506 acres/169,768ha) encompasses the highest peaks of the Hida mountain chain, topped by Hotaka dake (10,466ft/3,190m). This volcanic range, with an average altitude of 8,860ft (2,700m), is worthy of comparison with the European Alps for its superb mountaintops, its valleys and its scenery: so many imposing locations, as different as possible from urbanized Japan, yet all within easy reach thanks to the spread of roads and communication networks. The main axis of the mountain range runs N–S, but two great radial lines bisect it, one between Omachi and Toyama, passing through the Kuroyon dam, the other between Matsumoto and Takayama, via the high peaks of Hida.

1 FROM MATSUMOTO TO TAKAYAMA (60mls/97km by the N158; coach services in both directions). The road climbs the Azusa gawa valley and passes by the Nagawado dam.

28mls (45km): Nakanoyu Onsen, where the river Azusa rises, and flows from the N, in the direction of Matsumoto.

4mls (7km) N (coach): Kamikochi, very pleasant summer resort, with hot spa, alt. 5,000ft (1,500m) approx. To get there, you first have to go past the pool at Taisho, created in 1915 by an eruption of the Yake dake. From Kamikochi, you can scale the highest peaks, such as the Hotaka dake (10,466ft/3,190m), highest point of Hida sanmyaku, and Yake dake (8,054ft/2,455m).

6mls (9km) S (toll road; coach direct from Matsumoto): Shirahone Onsen, a little hot spa overlooking the Norikura dake (9,928ft/3,026m), which you may also care to climb.

30mls (49km): Abo toge, at an alt. of 5,945ft (1,812m), between the districts of Nagano and Gifu.

36mls (58km): Hirayu Onsen, at the northern foot of Norikura dake, a spring discovered by Takeda Shingen (1521-1573), Hirayu Rotemburo is an open-air pool acting as a reservoir to a hot spring; tropical fish are kept in its alkaline waters of 126°-190°F (52°-88°C). The resort also functions as a winter sports centre.

Yakushi do houses some Buddhist statuettes by the monk Enku, who travelled through the land in the 17th c.: he is said to have left behind him several hundred thousand similar naïve but expressive pieces. Near the spa is a little village museum (minzu kukan), with reconstructions of houses with tall thatched roofs, characteristic of the upper Hida valleys.

1½ml (2km) S: Hirayu no taki, 150ft (45m) high pretty waterfall, access by footpath.

11mls (18km) N (coach): Shin Hotaka, hot spa and winter resort: reached via Shin Hirayu Onsen (4mls/6km) where the Zentsu ji also has a figurine by Enku, then 7mls (11km) along a road which pulls away l. from the valley of the Takahara gawa (see Takayama), passing by the springs of Gamada and Yarimi. Some springs rise in the very bed of the Kamata gawa; you can bathe in them. Cable-car to the top of the Nishi Hotaka ski slopes.

Hotaka dake (10,466ft/3,190m) or Oku Hotaka has its highest point further N; it is made up of three lesser peaks: Mae Hotaka, Nishi Hotaka and Kita Hotaka; Oku Hotaka is the third highest peak in Japan, after Mount Fuji (12,388ft/3,776m) and Mount Shirane (10,472ft/3,192m). It is possible to climb up it from Shin Hotaka or Kamikochi. Further N rises Yari dake (10,433ft/3,180m), with the characteristic spur; it is a difficult mountain to climb.

42mls (68km): Hirayu toge (5,525ft/1,684m alt.); here the *Norikura Skyline route branches off. It is the highest, most 'aerial' toll road in Japan; superb panoramas in all directions.

10mls (16km) S along this road (coach from Hirayu, Kamikochi or Takayama): shelter at the foot of Norikura dake (9,928ft/3,026m), a large conical volcano to the south of the Chuba Sangaku National Park, situated between the two great mountain ranges of Hotaka in the N and On take in the S.

60mls (97km): Takayama: see entry under this name.

2 FROM OMACHI TO TOYAMA (53mls/86km; frequent connections, various forms of transport; buy a direct ticket from either end of the route). It is not possible to do this journey in a private car, but you will have no trouble if you follow the route in either direction.

4mls (7km): Omachi Onsen, which you may reach by coach from the JNR station of Shinano Omachi.

5mls (8km) SW: Kuzu Onsen, beyond which the gorges of Takase keikolu begin.

11mls (18km): Ogisawa, from where a trolleybus goes through an underground tunnel of 5,900 yds (5,400m) cut through the side of Jiiga take (8,760ft/2,670m).

15mls (24km): *Kuroyon dam, at an altitude of 4,774ft (1,455m); this structure, completed in 1963, 610ft (186m) high and 1,614ft (492m) at its widest, creating a reservoir of 200 million t of water, is one of the world's largest dams; it can supply electric power of 258,000 kW to the industrial zone of Kansai. The hydroelectric power station has been housed 500ft (150m) below ground in order to cause minimum damage to the picturesque gorges of the Kurobe gawa, which join up with the Kurobe machi downstream (see entry under that name).

In summer, a boat makes trips around the artificial lake, which extends into the Kumano taira gorges in the south.

The top of the dam has to be crossed on foot to reach Kurobe eki (½m/1km), before you can begin the ascent of Tate yama.

16mls (25km): Kurobe eki; from here the funicular will take you up into the mountains as far as Kurobe Daira; then a cable-car will carry you out over the lake, the dam, and the surroundings.

17 mls (27km): Daika mine (alt. 7,598ft/2,316m), from where a coach takes the 4,000yd (3,600m) tunnel through Tate yama.

Tate yama is, along with Fuji san and Haku san, one of Japan's three sacred mountains. It is in fact a chain made up of several peaks that form the NW tip of the Japan Alps; from N to S they are Tsurugi dake (9,836ft/2,998m), Bessan (9,449ft/2,880m), Onanji (9,892ft/3,015m), O yama (9,816ft/2,992m), Jodo dake (9,423ft/2,872m) and Yakushi dake (9,600ft/2,926m). Snow covers the whole area all year round.

19mls (31km): Murodo, plateau (8,005ft/2,440m) below Mount Jodo and Mount O yama; there are several sulphur springs dotted round it, including one called O jigoku. From there, you can go up O yama (3mls/5km), to the very top if you wish, where there is a shrine said to have been founded in 703.

Now take a coach back down towards Toyama via Midaga hara (alt. 6,200ft/1,900m), famous for its display of alpine flowers in late July. Further on down the route, in a deep valley, is the spectacular *Shomyo waterfall, at 1,150ft (350m) one of the highest falls in Japan.

34mls (54km): Bijodaira; funicular to Tateyama (Senjuga hara); finally, take the train (Toyama Chiho Railway) to:

53mls (86km): Toyama, see entry under this name.

■ Daisen Oki (National park; Island of Honshu)

Map of Natural Resources, p. 67.

HOW TO GET THERE

- Direct from Kurayoshi by coach, or else by rail with a connection in Yamamori (11mls/18km SW), then on to Daisen.

- From Yonago, easy coach journey to Daisen.

- From Yubara Onsen, S of the park to which coaches run (13mls/21km) from the station at Chugoku Katsuyama (JNR: on the Kishin line) between Niimi and Tsuyama (22mls/36km in all, in 50min); or direct by coach from Okayama (62mls/100km S).

As its name indicates, this park comprises the huge mass of Dai sen, nicknamed the Fuji of Hoki and, offshore, in the Sea of Japan, the Oki archipelago (see entry under this name); further W, the park also includes the coastal fringe of the Shimane peninsula, north of Izumo and Matsue (please see the separate entries for these names). The whole area covers 78,893 acres (31,927 ha).

FROM YUBARA TO YONAGO (47mls/76km; coach services via Hiruzen kogen and Daisen).

Yubara Onsen, lying in a mountain valley, has springs at 113°-122°F (45° to 50°C).

→ ½ml (1km) N, very beautiful Yubara reservoir, on the upper course of the Asahi gawa, at an altitude of 1,319ft (402m). The whole region is inhabited by a protected species of giant salamander.

12mls (19km): Yatsuka; leave the N313 to head W to the Asahi gawa; Kofun period tomb in this area, worth a visit.

16mls (26km): Kawakami, from where a road leads up in the direction of the Hiruzen plateau.

17mls (28km): Hiruzen kogen, a plateau of green pastures clinging to the southern slopes of Kami hira yama (3,937ft/1,200m), providing ski slopes in winter. From here, a toll road branches off in the direction of Mount Giboshi.

22mls (36km): Giboshi yama (3,560ft/1,085m) which you may climb, descending to the SW, in the direction of Kofu.

27mls (43km): Mizuku, junction with the Daisen kogen line, a toll road which circles Dai sen to the south.

*Dai sen (5,620ft/1,713m); this 'great mountain', seen from a distance, and especially when it is covered with snow, is reminiscent of the lovely Fuji. It stands in the centre of a former volcanic field, nowadays contained within the Daisen National Park and surrounded by lush vegetation from temperate climes, which autumn turns to a blaze of colour.

35mls (57km): Daisen, starting place for the ascent of Dai sen, which takes approx. 2 h. (3½mls/5.5km), has become the main winter sports centre in Chugoku, with its 14 ski-lifts and its slopes lit up at night; skiing takes place here from the end of December until the end of March.

Daisen ji, belonging to the Tendai sect and founded in 718, once knew great prosperity; but a series of fires has reduced it in size, though it has been reconstructed on the same principles and using the original beams; among the surviving buildings, the Hon do and the Amida do are the most interesting.

In the temple are preserved a statue of Kannon of the eleven heads in gilt copper, three other representations of Kannon, and a wooden statue of Amida, all of them registered treasures. The position of the temple - high in the mountains, surrounded by gigantic trees - makes it a very impressive place: when the wind rises, the forces of nature remind even the *gaijin* that the gods of Japan are never far away! The whole location breathes an air of mysticism rarely found in Japanese temples. The ascent as far as the temple is a very pleasant walk, offering an enjoyable vista over Dai sen (in fine weather only).

14mls (22km) N: Akasaki, on the shore of the Sea of Japan, in an area where silkworms are cultivated. You can get there via Senjo san (2,012ft/616m), the mountain where in 1333, under the protection of Nawa Nagatoshi, the Emperor Go Daigo (1288-1339) fled after escaping from the Oki archipelago (see entry under that name).

47mls (76km): Yonago, see entry under this name.

Daisetsuzan (National park; Island of Hokkaido)**

Map of Hokkaido (Eastern Area), pp. 228-9.

HOW TO GET THERE

- From Asahikawa or Kamikawa (30mls/49km in 50 min. by train between these two towns), with a coach link to Sounkyo.

- From Obihiro or Tokachi Mitsumata (50mls/80km N of Obihiro in 1h. 40 on the train), again with coach link to Sounkyo.

- From Rubeshibe, 14mls (23km) W of Kitami, 20 min. by train, taking a coach to Sounkyo via Onneyu Onsen and Obako.

To get to Obihiro from Asahikawa, you have a choice between two itineraries (see A and B below) which meet up again at the junction of motorways N39 and 273 (A: 51mls/82km, B: 65mls/104km).

Occupying the middle of the great northern island, Japan's largest national park – nicknamed the 'roof of Hokkaido' – with an area of 573,109 acres (231,929 ha), is a remarkable collection of peaks around 6,500ft (2,000m) high, of which Asahi dake is the crown at 7,513ft (2,290m). Lava-flows, hot springs, fumaroles and sulphur springs all indicate volcanic activity; while breathtaking gorges, impressive waterfalls, primeval forests and natural and man-made lakes add even more to the grandeur of Daisetsuzan.

A FROM ASAHIKAWA TO OBIHIRO VIA SOUN KYO (150mls/241km by the N39 and N273, then departmental roads; plentiful coach links via Soun kyo, Nukabira ko and Shikaribetsu ko). From Asahikawa to Kamikawa (30mls/49km), see Asahikawa and surrounding area, p. 130.

Beyond Asahikawa (30mls/49km), leave the N273 and head in the direction of Mombetsu. The Kami kawa valley becomes narrower and winds in and out between the **Soun gorges, whose high walls and basaltic cliffs seem to hang like great curtains.

43mls (69km): Soun kyo, hot spa in the midst of the gorges, with springs at temperatures between 115°F and 199°F (46° and 93°C). Access by cablecar to Kuro dake (6,509ft/1,984m), from where you can look out over the whole gorge area. From here, you may undertake the ascent of Asahi dake.

45mls (72km): Near to each other, the *waterfalls of Ryusei no taki and Ginga no taki, the finest in Daisetsuzan, are separated by vertical rocks about 520ft (160m) high.

47mls (75km): Kobako, then Obako, the 'little box' and the 'big box', names which allude to the sheer rocky walls which surround reservoirs in these areas.

51mls (82km): Junction of highways N39 and N273.

32mls (51km): NE: Onneyu Onsen, reached via the Sekihoku ridge (3,445ft/1,050m); beautiful scenery.

From the junction, the N273 turns south, cuts through Mikuni yama (5,056ft/1,541m) to the NE of Ishikari dake (6,473ft/1,962m), before entering the valley of the Otofuke gawa not far from its source.

71mls (115km): Tokachi Mitsumata, terminus of the JNR. From here you can travel directly to Obihiro.

84mls (135km): Nukabira Onsen (springs at 140°F/60°C) to the SW of a reservoir of about 2,000 acres/800ha formed by the hydroelectric dam of Nukabira. A boat does round trips of the reservoir, leaving from the spa.

From Nukabira Onsen we recommend a detour by coach via Shikaribetsu ko.

 94mls (152km): Yamada Onsen and, further on, *Shikaribetsu ko.

98mls (157km): Shikaribetsu Onsen, to the SW of a pretty lake (853 acres/345ha) whose waters reflect the forests and mountains round its shores.

99mls (160km): Ridge with a view over Shikaribetsu ko.

118mls (190km): Road to the l. in the direction of Obihiro (25mls/41km SE); continue along this road to cross the Tokachi gawa.

119mls (192km): Road to the r. in the direction of Tomuraushi.

→ 32mls (51km) N: Tomuraushi Onsen (coach from Shintoku; see below), on the upper course of the Tokachi gawa, in the heart of a wild area from where you may scale Tokachi dake and cross the Goshikiga hara (see below, itinerary B, at 19mls/31km).

123mls (198km): Shintoku, where you rejoin the railway and the N38 between Furano and Obihiro.

150mls (241km): Obihiro, see entry under this name.

 B FROM ASAHIKAWA TO OBIHIRO VIA TENNINKYO ONSEN, YUKOMAMBETSU ONSEN AND ASAHI DAKE (163mls/263km; by a route far hillier for the first 65mls/104km; coach as far as Yumogawa or Tenninkyo).

– Leave Asahikawa and head in the direction of Higashikawa (SE).

19mls (31km): Turning to the r. for Tenninkyo.

→ 5mls (8km) E (coach); Tenninkyo Onsen, on the upper course of the Chubetsu gawa, whose springs reach a temperature of 127°F (53°C). Upriver from the spa is the pretty waterfall of Hagoromo ('feather gowns'), which is composed of a series of five successive falls, then the falls of Shikishima. The upper course of the Chubetsu also encompasses the *Tennin gorges, which are narrow, with high walls of basalt carved like organ pipes.

From Tenninkyo, you can scale Asahi dake and Chubetsu dake, or tour the Goshiki plateau (Goshikiga hara), lying between the highest peaks in Daisetsuzan, and covered in flowers during the summer; information is available regarding the whereabouts of shelters.

 26mls (42km): Yukomambetsu Onsen, at an alt. of 3,445ft (1,050m), on the slopes of Mount Asahi, ski resort (2 ski-lifts, skiing from October to the end of June) and spa, springs at 140°F (60°C).

*Asahi dake or Daisetsu zan (7,513ft/2,290m), 4mls (6km) as the crow flies to the E of the spa, is the highest point on Hokkaido; along with Tokachi dake (6,814ft/2,077m) further S, it is one of the two most impressive peaks in the park; from here the major rivers of the island

(Tokachi Ishikari) flow in different directions; Asahi has also been volcanically active in recent times, and its slopes are carpeted in summer with lovely alpine flowers.

Beyond Yukomambetsu, a tortuous road weaves between the high peaks of Daisetsuzan, swings N round Asahi dake, then sweeps high over the valley of the Kami kawa; superb views; some coach services – make enquiries.

65mls (104km): Crossroads of the N39 and the N273. From here to Obihiro is 99mls (159km); see above, itinerary A, from 51mls (82km) to 150mls (241km).

163mls (263km): Obihiro, see entry under this name.

Ena (Island of Honshu)

Tokyo, 242mls (390km) – Fukui, 140mls (225km) – Gifu, 52mls (84km) – Kanazawa, 171mls (276km) – Nagano, 121mls (194km) – Nagoya, 42mls (67km) ≈ Otsu, 114mls (184km) – Toyama, 133mls (214km) – Tsu, 108mls (174km).

Gifu ken – pop: 31,488 – alt. 890ft (270 m).

At the foot of Ena san (7,185ft/2,190m), which towers above it to the E, this town is interesting above all for the gorges in the vicinity of the Kiso gawa.

VICINITY

1 *ENA KYO (2½mls/4km N; coach from the station to the Oi dam). From March to December a boat sails regularly about 3½mls (6km) along these picturesque gorges, upstream and downstream.

2 MIMO KAMO (gorges of the Hida and Kiso gawa). See entry under this name.

Esashi (Island of Hokkaido)

Railway map on inside front cover.

Tokyo, 567mls (913km) – Hakodate, 52mls (83km) – Sapporo, 185mls (298km).

On the W of the Oshima peninsula, this port is sheltered by an islet nowadays linked to the mainland by a causeway. Formerly the main herring-fishing port for the island of Hokkaido, its population had already reached 30,000 by the time of the Edo period. It now trades with the island of Okushiri.

VICINITY

OKUSHIRI TO (37mls/59km NW of the Esashi; 3h. by boat). Off the coast of the Oshima peninsula, this island of 56 sq.mls (144km²) seems to have been formed by the upthrust of coastal terraces, as is indicated by traces of the sea's erosion of the island's highest point, Kamui yama (1,919ft/585m). The inhabitants are simultaneously fishermen and farmers; they live in the little ports of Aonae and Okushiri on the E side of the island, where they are well sheltered in the winter. There is a frequent coach service between the two places, as well as one in the direction of Inaho misaki, in the N of the island.

■ Fuchu (Island of Honshu)

Map of the Vicinity of Tokyo, p. 565.

Tokyo, 21mls (33km) – Chiba, 44mls (71km) – Kofu, 70mls (112km) –Urawa, 22mls (35km) – Yokohama, 24mls (38km).

Tokyo to – pop: 192,198.

Once the capital of Musashi, gateway to the N of Honshu for travellers coming from Kamakura, the town was eclipsed by the great metropolis of Tokyo, eventually becoming just one of its crowded suburbs.

Okunitama jinja or Rokusho jinja (330yds/300m E of Fuchu-Honmachi station, JNR train from Kawasaki; or close to the one at Fuchukeibajo-Seimonmae, Keio Teito ER, from Tokyo-Shinjuku), is said to have been founded in AD 113 though the buildings themselves are no older than the 17th c. The magnificent keyaki (zelkowas) surrounding it are said to have been planted by Minamoto Yoriyoshi; it seems more likely that those you see today are attributable to Tokugawa Ieyasu (16th c.).

Further S from the shrine is the large Tokyo race course.

Approx. 2½mls (4km) N of Fuchu-Honmachi station, near the station of Tamabochimae (Keio Teito ER), is the Tama cemetery (250 acres/100ha), created at the beginning of the 20th c., in which many famous people are buried, such as Admiral Togo Heihachiro (1847-1934) and Dr Nitobe Inazo (1862-1933). It looks more like a park than a cemetery.

To the W of Fuchu, Bubaigawara station recalls the victory of Nitta Yoshisada (1301-1338), supporter of the Imperial restoration, against the Hojo who were then in power, a victory that played a decisive role in the fall of the *bakufu* of Kamakura.

Fuji-Hakone-Izu (National park; Island of Honshu)***

Map of Natural Resources in Japan, p. 66 – maps of Mount Fuji, p. 163 and the Hakone region, below.

HOW TO GET THERE

– From Atami (Shinkansen station) there are several coach services to Hakone, as well as coaches and trains crossing the length and breadth of the Izu peninsula.

– From Fuji and Fujinomiya; the two towns – 7mls (12km) apart – are linked by train. Fujinomiya is the departure point for one of the routes

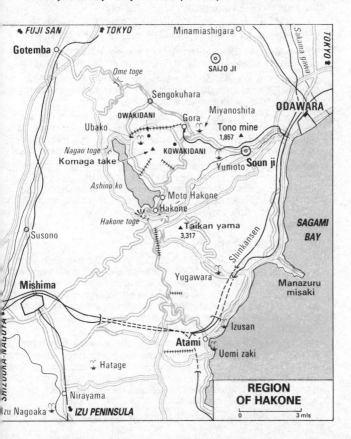

up Fuji san; there is a bus link from Kofu. Fuji (Yoshiwara) is linked by a car-ferry to Toi, on the western coast of the Izu peninsula.

- From Fuji Yoshida, one of the best places from which to start your ascent of Fuji (track and coach route); there is a good view over its lakes. The town has a rail connection with Kawaguchiko and Otsuki (Fuji Kyuko Railway; direct JNR trains from Tokyo-Shinjuku; motorway from Tokyo by coach).

- From Gotemba, on the Gotemba line (JNR) between Kozu and Numazu, where you can easily find a coach to take you to Fuji Yoshida and Kofu, to the mountain peaks of Hakone, or to Atami and Odaware. Coach rides and footpath to Mount Fuji.

- From Ito, 11mls (17km) S of Atami (JNR train), then easy journey to Shimoda by coach or train (Izu-Kyuko Railway).

- From Kofu, 83mls (134km) from Tokyo-Shinjuku in 1h. 50 by JNR train; coaches for Fujinomiya and Gotemba via Fuji Yoshida.

- From Mishima (Shinkansen station) and Numazu, from where you can travel to Atami, Gotemba or Fuji, or else across the Izu peninsula.

- From Odawara, 45 min. by train from Tokyo (52mls/84km), or Odakyu ER from Shinjuku; there is a link from the town to Atami; it is a gateway to the whole Hakone region.

- From Tokyo you can travel independently to any of the towns mentioned above, or take an excursion (Fujita Travel service and JTB, with English-speaking guides) lasting one or two days, calling at Fuji, Hakone, and Atami via Kamakura, possibly extending as far as Kyoto.

Easy to reach from Tokyo, this park of 302,226 acres (122,309ha) comprises the splendid Mount Fuji (12,388ft/3,776m), Japan's highest point and a veritable Nipponese Olympus, the mountains of Hakone rising all round Lake Ashino, the Izu peninsula which divides the bays of Sagami and Suruga, and finally the Izu archipelago.

A ***Mount Fuji

When first you set eyes on Mount Fuji, you will experience such a moment of peace and fulfilment that sight and feeling will blend into one harmonious sensation. You will come to appreciate its whole mystique, born of its purity of line and its majestic isolation. For 'in addition to its sacred character it possesses an unequalled aesthetic value which has inspired many poems and paintings' (D. and V. Elisseeff, *La civilisation japonaise*).

THE GODDESS OF FIRE. The etymology of the word Fuji remains uncertain; but it is known to be a Japanese adaptation of an Ainu term. The meaning is not entirely clear from its transcription into ideograms, and seems to be purely phonetic. 'In Ainu, though, Fuchi is the name of the goddess of fire and the hearth, which suits a volcano perfectly' (Fosco Maraini).

We know little more about the precise geological origins of the

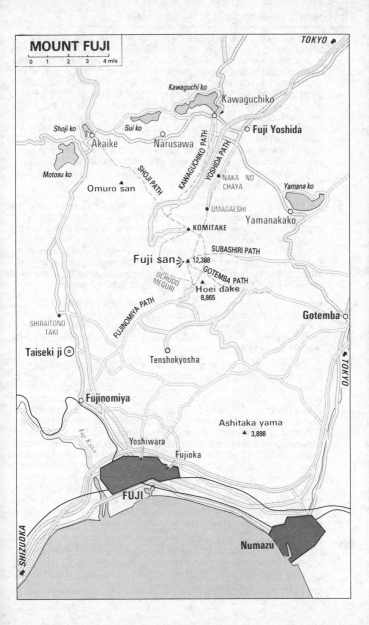

mountain. Of 'recent' formation, it apparently goes back to the beginning of the !ce Age; about 600,000 years ago, two mountains appeared one after another; a little later (approx. 300,000 years), they were covered in lava, which gave the mountain its final shape, with a diameter of almost 25mls (40km) at its base. Fuji san is part of the great volcanic axis that runs through the Mariana Islands, the Bonin archipelago, and the islands and the peninsula of Izu. Some people link the formation of Fuji with the depression of Lake Biwa in the Kyoto region. A mere 18 eruptions have been recorded in history; the most recent, in 1707, was sufficiently violent to cover Edo (Tokyo), 60 miles (100km) away, with ash; since then, the volcano has stopped smoking. The vegetation growing all over the slopes of Mount Fuji is very varied; no fewer than 1,200 species have been counted throughout the forest, subalpine and alpine areas.

NB: You should not, when in Japan, talk of Fuji yama; rather, use the expression Fuji san, in accordance with the sound of the Sino-Japanese ideogram signifying the mountain. The term *san* is used in speech as an honorific for a man or woman, placed after the family name. It is, moreover, consecrated to a female divinity; Konohana Sakuya hime. It is also a mistake to be in too much of a hurry to find out all about Fuji san. It often hides its face coquettishly behind veils of mist, only rarely deigning to reveal itself fully. Be patient!

ASCENT. Until the Meiji Restoration, women were forbidden to ascend Mount Fuji, but they have made up for it since. The average yearly number of pilgrims is estimated at 300,000. The first foreigner to undertake the climb, in 1860, was the British Ambassador, Sir Rutherford Alcock.

The ascent of Fuji is possible from 1 July to 31 August; the staging posts which offer food and shelter remain shut outside this period. Even so, during the season you should take the usual precautions for mountain-walking. Towards the summit, you will come across slopes with a gradient of between 23° and 34°, and the winds can be fierce. There are six main signposted access routes: from Gotemba, Subashiri, Fuji Yoshida, Kawaguchiko, Shoji and Fujinomiya, each between 9 and 16 miles (15 and 25km) in length, and divided into ten irregular sections, each with a staging-post. It takes from 5 to 9 hours to get to the top and, with the help of loose ash, from 3 to 5 to slither down. These days, coaches can drive up roads as far as the fifth and sixth levels, which are themselves connected by a half-way path; from there, you go on foot up to the seventh or eighth level, where you spend the night in order to reach the summit before dawn, so as to enjoy the *sunrise.

FROM GOTEMBA TO FUJI YOSHIDA, GOING ROUND FUJI ON THE N SIDE (57mls/92km by the N138 and N139; coach trips in both directions, with views of the lakes). From Gotemba (see entry under this name) the road turns NW in the direction of Lake Yamanaka.

6mls (10km): Subashiri, a little shrine which is the starting point for the trail bearing this name (coach as far as the second stage, journey time 4½ h.).

10mls (16km): Kagosaka toge (3,622ft/1,104m alt.), gives a fine view of Yamanaka ko.

12mls (19km): Asahigaoka, on the shores of Yamanaka ko, which is the biggest and highest of Fuji's five lakes (1,596 acres/646ha; alt 3,222ft/982m); freezes in winter, allowing skating to take place, as well as fishing (*wakasagi*) through holes in the ice. Boat trips in summer.

A road goes all round the edge of the lake, giving delightful views of Fuji san; to the N, hot springs at Oshino Hakkai. Festival of the lake, 1 August.

19mls (31km): Fuji Yoshida (pop: 50,046; textile industry). It is the main point of access for those travelling from Tokyo to Mount Fuji and the five lakes at its base. From here, it is easy to join up with the Kawaguchi road.

The festival of Sengen, 26 August, marks the end of the season for ascending Fuji san.

The Yoshida trail (12¾mls/20.5km) is accessible to coaches as far as Umageshi (6mls/9.5km); it takes a further 10h. on foot to reach the top.

22mls (35km): Kawaguchiko, by the shore of lake Kawaguchi (1,502 acres/608ha; 2,726ft/831m alt.).

Festival 5 August; boats sail on the lake in summer.

½ml (1km) N of Kuwaguchiko station, near the edge of the lake is the little museum of the Fuji National Park, with exhibits of specimens of the local flora and fauna, minerals and fossils, plus many objects of archaeological interest.

1½ml (2km) E of the station, cable-car up to Tenjo san (3,543ft/1,080m), where you will find a marvellous *view of Mount Fuji, the lake and its wooded island of Uno with its shrine dedicated to Benten.

19mls (30km) S (coach from April to November): Komitake, at an altitude of 7,562ft (2,305m), accessible by *Fuji Subaru line, and toll road with numerous observation points over the lakes, the Japan Alps and the bay of Suruga. This road passes within sight of the *Osawa gorge.

From Komitake, 5th stage of the Kawaguchiko trail, it takes a further 4½ h. on foot to reach the edge of the crater.

The **crater of Mount Fuji, or Nai in (shrine), circular in shape, is 1,600-2,000ft (500 to 600m) in diameter and 260ft (80m) deep. Eight peaks mark the outline of the ridge; Kenga mine, Hakusan dake (or Shaka dake), Kusushi dake, Dainichi dake (or Asahi dake), Izu dake, Joju dake (or Seishda dake), Komaga take and Mishima dake. The Kenga mine, in the SW, the highest at 12,388ft (3,776m), has a meteorological observatory with radar. The *sunrise is an amazing sight from the summit. The **view is endless, stretching away in the direction of the Japan Alps, the Tokyo region and the Pacific.

Two trails circle the crater, one inside (2mls/3km) and the other outside, and the two provide links between the major peaks. The Ochudo meguri trail, level with Komitake and the fifth or sixth stages – average altitude 8,000ft (2,500m) – circles round Fuji halfway up; it takes from 8 to 10 hours to walk its 12mls (20km); it is nicknamed 'the boundary between heaven and earth'.

The N139 heads W away from the Kawaguchi lake.

26mls (42km): Volcanic cave at Narusawa; inhabited by bats whose heads, bearing a crest of hair, resemble chrysanthemums.

🌲🌲 28mls (45km): Koyodai (ascent takes 30 min.), a hill covered in maples, with a view of the lakes Sai (the closest), Kawaguchi (in the E), and Shoji (in the W), as well as Jukai ('sea of trees'), dense forests including the Aokigahara forest, where hundreds of people go each year to end their lives.

To the SW of Koyodai there is a lava grotto Fugaku Fuketsu ('of the wind'), with stalactite formations.

➡ 2½mls (4km) NE (access road): Sai ko (568 acres/230 ha; 2,966ft/904m alt.) with inhospitable shores, far less popular with visitors than the aforementioned lakes; so far no one has discovered how it was formed. There are several grottoes throughout the area, formed by volcanic lava; some of them are permanently frozen.

35mls (57km): Shoji ko, the smallest of Fuji's five lakes (215 acres/87 ha), surrounded by mountains and by woods on three sides, is open to Mount Fuji on its SE shore.

The Shoji trail (7¾mls/12½km) winds from Akaike (on the shores of the lake) through the forest of Aokigahara, passing through Omuro san (4,747ft/1,447m) via a lava tunnel called Fuji Feketsu.

➡ 16mls (26km) N: Kofu: see entry under this name.

39mls (62km): Motosu, on the eastern shore of *Lake Motosu (1,203 acres/487ha; 2,959ft/902m alt.), the only one which doesn't freeze in winter, because of its great depth (453ft/138m). It is famous for its intensely blue waters; trout fishing.

High up on Eboshi dake (4,124ft/1,257m; 1h.30 to reach the summit), between Lakes Motosu and Shoji, pretty view of Fuji and Jukai.

Beyond Motosu, the N139 turns S and forms the Fuji Sanroku Highway (toll road) between Fuji and the mountain chain that runs N–S, dividing the volcano from the Fuji gawa.

➡ 45mls (72km): Asagiri kogen, a lovely view point, leaving the N139 to the r.

➡ 3mls (5km) S: Small artificial lake of Tanuki (coach from Fujinomiya, see below, 57mls/92km), at the foot of Fuji san. South of the lake is a garden with around 2,000 varieties of flowers and several species of birds.

50mls (80km): *Shiraito no taki, the 'silver thread waterfall', a veritable curtain measuring 85ft (26m) from top to bottom and 427ft (130m) across. Close by is the Otodome waterfall. In these parts you will also find the tombs of the Soga brothers and of Kudo Suketsune.

A DRAMATIC TALE. After the murder of their father, the two children Sukenari and Tokimune (who had been adopted by Soga Sukenobu and had taken his name), decided to avenge him; it took them 18 long years of patience but they achieved it with the help of Toragozen, mistress of the elder brother. In the course of a hunt in which the murderer, one Kudo Suketsune, was taking part, they attacked and killed him. Sukenari was captured and executed immediately, and Tokimune was condemned to death; this was in 1193. The legend has been the subject of many works of Japanese literature, in which the two Soga brothers are known by the names of Juro and Goro.

57mls (92km): Fujinomiya, see entry under this name.

B **The Hakone mountains

The Hakone region, between Mount Fuji and the sea, lies on the site of an extinct volcano whose crater is thought to have reached 25mls (40km) in circumference; its main peaks are Kami yama (4,718ft/1,438m), Komaga take (4,354ft/1,327m), and Futago yama (3,579ft/1,091m). Crossed by the Tokai do, the area owed its strategic importance to the Hakone tariff-wall, to the battle in 1335 in which Ashikaga Takauji defeated Nitta Yoshisada, and to the town of Odawara, its gateway and its checkpoint.

FROM ODAWARA TO ATAMI VIA HAKONE (27mls/44km using our itinerary and suggested means of transport; but the whole region is crisscrossed with roads and covered by a dense network of coach services. Moreover, you can go up as far as Gora - see below, 9mls/14km - by coach from Odawara, or by private railway, via Ohidarai, Hakone Tozan Railway; from Gora, by funicular, cablecar, and boat, you can get to Hakone). Departure from Odawara, see entry under this name.

1½mls (2km): The Hakone Turnpike Driveway branches off l., in the direction of Kurakake yama (9mls/15km SW), via Shirogane yama (3,258ft/993 m) and Taikan Yama (3,317ft/1,011m); views.

3mls (5km): The Hakone Bypass Road branches off l., toll road leading back up the Sukumo gawa towards Hakone toge (9mls/14km SW).

4mls (6km): ½ml (1km) off to the l., by the road, is the Soun ji, founded by Hojo Soun (1432-1519), ancestor of the junior branch of the Odawara.

The buildings were burned during the Odawara siege in 1569, but the temple was rebuilt by Hojo Ujimasa and became the largest in Kanto. In 1509, Toyotomi Hideyoshi made it his headquarters after a second siege which brought about the downfall of the Hojo and the ruin of the temple. The present buildings, far fewer in number, were restored by Tokugawa Iemitsu in the mid-17th c.

The temple houses a statue of Hojo Soun and portraits of five other clan chiefs, as well as two paintings attributed to Kano Motonobu.

4mls (7km): Yumoto Onsen is at an altitude of 394ft (120m), where the river Haya meets the Sukumo, with springs at temperatures between 77° and 165°F (25° and 74°C).

½ml (1km) N on the slopes of Tono mine (1,857ft/566m) stands the Amida ji, founded in the 17th c.; fine view.

5mls (8km): Tonosawa Onsen, springs (111°-153°F/44°-67°C) recommended for rheumatism, nervous illnesses and skin complaints.

Festival (beginning of November) of the *Procession of the daimyo, along the old Tokai do road, between Yumoto and Tonosawa.

6mls (9km): Ohidarai, another hot spa, with salt springs at 167°F (75°C).

7mls (12km): Miyanoshita, at an altitude of 1,480ft (451m), is the busiest spa in Hakone, along with the nearby springs of Dogashima (with the little pine-grove of Matsugaoka) and Sokokura (550yds/500m SW), visited in the 16th c. by Toyotomi Hideyoshi.

1h. 30 on foot to the N, via Dogashima, is Myojoga take (3,031ft/924m), where the Daimonji yaki matsuri takes place on 16 August.

1 hour's walk to the S, Sengen yama (2,631ft/802m), which offers an extensive view of the whole area.

ALTERNATIVE ROUTE FROM MIYANOSHITA TO HAKONE MACHI, ALONG THE TOKAI DO ROAD (6mls/9km S, as opposed to 9mls/14km using the main itinerary coach). Take the road for Sokokura (½ml/0.5km SW; see above, 7mls/12km).

1½mls (2km): Kowakidani, the 'little valley of bubbling waters' whose name alludes, like that of Owakidani mentioned later, to nearby sulphur springs. Close at hand, Hosai en, garden of azaleas and cherry trees.

½ml (1km) N, next to the station of Chokoku no Mori, *Hakone open-air museum (Ninotaira, Hakone machi); opened in 1969, it covers an area of 7 acres/3ha (open daily from 09.00 to 17.00).

'The spaces given over to the display of artworks under an open sky were designed by the sculptor Inoue Bukichi; they include a pond, used as a setting for pieces by the French artist Marta Pan; a soundtrack of electronic music provides a sonorous background. In the middle of the park, a little covered museum traces the major developments in modern sculpture, from Rodin to Maillol' (D. and V. Elisseeff, *La civilisation japonaise*). There are also works by Archipenko, Bourdelle, Giacometti, Moore and Zadkin.

½ml (1km) S: Chisujiga waterfall ('of a thousand threads').

3mls (5km): Ashinoyu Onsen, with sulphurous spring waters.

550yds (500m) S: Shogen ji, within whose walls there are three monuments, to the memory of the Soga brothers (Sukenari and Tokimune) and Toragozen.

1½mls (2km) W: Departure point of the funicular to Komaga take (see below), which you reach by going through the spa of Yunohanazawa (springs at 162°F/72°C).

3½mls (6km): Little volcanic lake of Shojin, devoid of animal life. To the E stands Futayo yama (3,579ft/1,019m).

4mls (7km): Moto Hakone, spa on the eastern tip of Lake Ashi.

550yds (500m) W: Hakone jinja, in a delightful woodland setting, with its *torii* planted in the waters of the lake.

In this shrine, founded in 757, Minamoto Yoritomo took refuge after his defeat near Odawara during his campaign against the Taira (1180).

The shrine houses a wooden statue of its founder, the priest Mangan, a painted scroll tracing the historical origins of the shrine, and the sword used in the vengeance of Soga Tokimune (see above), etc. Festival 31 July.

2mls (3km) NW: Hakone en (campsite, pleasure resort, amusement park). From here, you may take a cable-car to Komaga take (4,442ft/1,354m). View from the summit over Mount Fuji, Ashi no ko and the Izu peninsula. Further N is Kami yama (4,718ft/1,438m), highest point in the Hakone region, still emitting sulphurous fumes to this day.

6mls (9km): Hakone machi, see below (16mls/26km).

From Miyanoshita, the N138 and railways head towards Gora.

8mls (13km): Kiga, springs at temperatures of 99°-138°F (37°-59°C); the resort was visited by General Lebon (1845-1923), French military adviser to Japan at the end of the 19th c.

9mls (14km): Gora, at an altitude of 2,585ft/788m, terminus of the Odawara line of the Hakone Tozan Railway.

The Hakone art museum, west of the Gora town hall, is open daily from 09.00 to 16.00, April to November, and contains exhibits of paintings and porcelain from ancient China and Japan.

FROM GORA TO GOTEMBA (12mls/19km NW by the N138; coach). The road climbs steadily up the Haya kawa, as far as the outskirts of Sengokuhara.

3½mls (6km): Sengokuhara, marshy plateau where the springs of Hyoseki, Motoyu, Owakudani, Sengoku, Shitayu, Urawa, have been reclaimed; temperatures vary between 68° and 167°F (20° and 75°C).

5mls (8km): Road off to the l. in the direction of Nagao toge (2mls/3km SW, alt. 2,963ft/903m), from where you can either travel back to Gotemba or carry on southwards in the direction of the Ashinoko Skyline. The N138 passes through a tunnel under the

Otome ridge (3,278ft/999m alt.), situated between Kintoki yama (3,980ft/1,213m) and Maru dake (3,786ft/1,154m), which form the edge of the former crater of what is now Hakone.

12mls (19km): Gotemba, see entry under this name.

☞ From Gora, you could take a coach direct to Togendai and Hakone machi; but we would recommend that you follow our itinerary, using funicular, cablecar and boat.

☛ In Gora, take the funicular to Sounzan.

9mls (15km): Sounzan, where a cablecar will take you on to Togendai, via Owakidani and Ubako.

From the summit of Soun zan (3,730ft/1,137m) there is an extensive panoramic view.

 11mls (17km): Owakidani, 'the great valley of bubbling waters', which also goes by the name of O jigoku ('the great hell'), is an old crater of Kami yama which still exhibits some signs of volcanic activity: hot springs, fumaroles, and sulphur springs.

11mls (18km): Ubako, at an altitude of 3,000ft (900m) and with springs at temperature of 97°F (36°C), is recommended for the treatment of disorders of the eye and brain.

12mls (19km): Togendai, N of the *Ashi no ko.

Lake Ashi, 'lake of reeds', at an altitude of 2,372ft (723m), occupies part of the bottom of a vast crater; it flows out in the N into the Haya kawa, which crosses the whole of the Hakone region to join the sea S of Odawara.

Boat service on the lake between Tosendai, Kojiri, Moto Hakone and Hakone machi.

➜ 7mls (12km) S: coach service via Kojiri toge (2,904ft/885m) along the toll road *Ashinoko Skyline to Hakone toge; views over the lake, Suruga bay, and Fuji san.

From Togendai, you board ship for Hakone machi, on the southern shore of the lake.

16mls (26km): Hakone machi. To the N of the town, a column marks the site of the old Hakone Gate, built in 1618 and reconstructed in modern times.

A small museum contains further mementoes: daimyo seals, ancient maps and coins, passports, etc., conjuring up memories of the Tokai do.

THE TOKAI DO. It was mainly in the Kamakura period that the great highways were built out from the Shogunal capital. The most important of these linked Kamakura with the Imperial capital of Kyoto; it was the Tokai do which crossed the eastern region bordering on the ocean. It was much used in the Edo period, when it was further extended to the town which is now Tokyo; several toll gates were set up along its length, including the Hakone Gate.

The painter Ando Hiroshige (1786-1858) represented the 55 stages of the Tokai do in a famous series of prints (in the Tokyo National Museum). In literature the humorous writer, Jippensha Ikku (1765-1831) wrote *Dōchū hizakurge*, 'the most entertaining book in the Japanese language'; Asa Ryoi published a 'tourist' guide in 1658, accompanied by maps and explanatory captions.

Today, the Tokai do corresponds to the N1, between Tokyo and Osaka, cutting across Hakone; it ends in a motorway and a series of railways, among them the Shinkansen, which do not, however, touch Hakone. We should add that some 855mls (1,376km) has also been established along this route, passing through several regional and national parks and with picnic areas marked out, as well as campsites and reception centres; enquire at JNTO offices in Tokyo or Kyoto (see Useful information).

North of the old toll gate, Hakone Park, on the site of a former Imperial town and bordering on Lake Ashi, gives a fine view of Fuji, reflected in the lake water.

From Hakone machi there are coach routes to: Odawara, Yugawara, Mishima, Numazu, Ito, and Atami; we opted for the last of these possibilities.

17mls (28km): Hakone toge (2,785ft/849m alt.), at the crossing of several roads, is a place where, on a clear day, you get a *splendid view of Fuji san. Follow the Hakone Skyline in the direction of Atami.

20mls (32km): Cable-car to Kurakake yama (3,294ft/1,004m), from which the view is even finer.

23mls (37km): Cable-car to Jukkoku toge (2,539ft/774m). Equally good *view of Fuji san and of Atami.

24mls (38km): Atami toge, from where several roads fan out, including the Izu skyline (see below, 4mls/6km) to the S and a road towards Atami, which we will follow.

27mls (44km): Atami, see entry under this name.

C**The Izu peninsula

This peninsula is also volcanic in origin; numerous hot springs point to this fact, and the name Izu, which means 'to spring,' used to be prefixed by the term *yu* ('hot water'). The peninsula carries the Hakone mountains further south, and offers a jagged and picturesque coastline; in numerous places there are good views to be had of Fuji san. Winter here is far milder than in Tokyo.

1 FROM ATAMI (OR ITO) TO SHIMODA (58mls/94km from Atami by the Izu Skyline and Higashi Izu Road, both toll roads; coach; JNR and Izu Kyuko Railway, via Ito). From Atami (see separate entry), you follow the **Izu Skyline, a road which runs along a ridge at a height of 1,650-2,300ft (500-700m), with views over Sagami Bay, the island of

O shima on the one side, and on the other the whole of the peninsula, against which, if the light conditions are right, Fuji san is silhouetted.

10mls (16km): Kemeishi toge (1,480ft/415m alt.). A road drops down on the l., in the direction of Usami; further on, another forks r. towards Ohito.

25mls (40km): The road branches off to the r. in the direction of the Amagi range, whose highest point is Amagi san (or Manzaburo, 4,616ft/1,407m).

The Amagi chain is a former volcanic range, crowning the centre of the Izu peninsula; it is covered with a dense forest full of game. Wild boar hunts are organized from November to February (see 2 below, 15 and 16mls/24 and 26km). Coaches drive up as far as Amagi kogen, at the foot of Togasa yama (3,927ft/1,197m).

The Izu Skyline heads once more for the coast.

30mls (48km): Tropical cactus garden on the western slopes of Omuro yama (1,906ft/581m).

31mls (50km): Take the N135 (on the r.) as it comes from Atami and Ito via the coast.

35mls (57km): Take the *Higashi Izu Road off to the l.; it now continues as a coast road all the way to Shimoda.

42mls (67km): Atagawa Onsen, one of the most attractive coastal resorts. Near the station (Izu Kyuko Railway), the springs feed a garden of tropical plants (many banana trees); crocodiles are also kept here.

45mls (72km): Inatori, resort in use since 1956, to the S of the Inatori headland, which divides it from Higashi Izu.

47mls (75km): Imaihama Onsen is a bathing resort as well as a spa, with a pine forest running along the edge of its fine sandy beach.

49mls (79km): Kawazu Onsen, on the mouth of the Kawazu gawa.

½ml (1km) NW: Yatsu Onsen has three springs between 108° and 212°F (43° and 100°C). Further up river, a gigantic camphor tree grows in the shrine dedicated to Sugihokowake no Mikoto.

The road carries on in the direction of Mine Onsen and Amagi Yugashima: see below, 2.

58mls (94km): Shimoda (terminus of the Izu Kyuto Railway; daily or weekly boats for Kozu shima, Miyake jima, Nii jima, O shima and Tokyo) is a little port tucked away in a pretty bay and surrounded by beaches and rocky coastal stretches. Imperial villa.

AMERICAN DIPLOMACY. The sight of Commodore Matthew Galbraith Perry's (1794-1858) 'black ships' appearing in Shimoda in 1854, on the occasion of the Treaty of Kanagawa, must have been an impressive one (see Yokohama). In Shimoda, a mutual trade agreement was worked out with the Shogun's envoy. In 1856-57, the first American delegation, under Townsend Harris (1804-78), was established in this port, but when it proved an inadequate site, Harris requested and was granted permission to set up in Edo (Tokyo); the port of Yokohama then outstripped Shimoda. In addition, a treaty was signed in Shimoda in 1855 (implemented in 1875) by which the Japanese ceded the island of Sakhalin in exchange for the Kuril islands.

Kurofune matsuri (festival of the black ships) in mid May.

Ryosen ji, W of the locality, where negotiations with Commodore Perry took place in 1854.

Benten jima, in the Bay of Shimoda, is the islet from which Yoshida Shoin (1831-60) wanted to sail in order to find out about Western civilization, though he was fiercely opposed to foreign intervention in Japan. He narrowly missed a Russian vessel, moored in Nagasaki when, the following year (1854), Commodore Perry refused to let him on board his ship. The tale was retold by Robert Louis Stevenson.

➤ 4mls (7km) SE (via Kakisaki, 1½ml/2km): Suzaki. In this village, the Gyokusen ji was the residence of Townsend Harris while he was settled in Shimoda. The temple was restored in 1927 by the America-Japan Association. Several reminders of that American foundation are kept there, along with a portrait of Consul Harris. In the temple grounds are several graves of Russian and American nationals who died in Shimoda, and a memorial to the vessel of the Russian Admiral Putiatin, which sank in Shimoda in December 1854.

➤ **2 FROM MISHIMA TO SHIMODA VIA THE VALLEY OF KANO GAWA** (40mls/ 65km; coach service; Izu-Hakone Railway train from Mishima to Shunzenji). After Mishima (see entry under this name), the N136 meets up in the S with the Kano gawa valley, where the river emerges from the Amagi mountains and flows into the sea at Suruga.

5mls (8km): Nirayama Onsen. This spa town is ½ml (1km) E of the station. To the S, the ruins of the castle of Nirayama are still standing (moat and ramparts).

A ROMEO IN EXILE. It was in Hirugakojima, now known as Nirayama, that Minamoto Yoritomo (1147-99) was exiled in 1160, on the orders of the Taira. Placed under the surveillance of Ito Sukechika and Hojo Tokimasa, he had a love affair with Sukechika's daughter; the furious father wanted to kill him, so he fled to Tokimasa's household , where he seduced Masako, Tokimasa's daughter, and married her. In 1180, Yoritomo formed an alliance with Prince Mochihito o against the Taira; it was the start of a climb to power which was to take him eventually to the rank of Shogun in Kamakura.

THE HOJO ESTATE. In the 12th c., the powerful Hojo family owned an estate in this area. In 1457, Ashikaga Yoshimasa established his brother Masatomo (1436-91) there to rule over Kanto; two years later he was killed by his son Chacha maru who wished to inherit his father's power; the son was defeated in turn two years later by Ise Nagauji (1432-1519), who married a Hojo heiress, took the name Hojo Soun and recaptured the province of Izu. He had a fortress built in Nirayama and died there. In 1590, Hojo Ujinori was beseiged in this castle by Hideyoshi's generals, Oda Nobuo and Fukushima Masanori; the castle then fell into the hands of Tokugawa Ieyasu.

To the E of the village of Nirayama stands the old residence of Egawa Tarozaemon (1801-55), a *samurai* and distinguished citizen of Nirayama who introduced Western military tactics into Japan. The house, which is open to visitors, is one of the oldest in Japan, going back to the 13th c.

7mls (11km): Izu Nagaoka Onsen, on the l. bank of the Kano gawa, with springs recommended for rheumatism and nervous illnesses. Cable-car to Katsugari yama (1,450ft/452m); fine view over the bay of Suruga and Fuji san.

1½mls (2km) E: reverberating furnace, built in the last century by Egawa Tarozaemon (see below).

10mls (15km): Ohito, another hot spa, with views of Fuji.

11mls (17km): Yokose-Shuzenji, terminus of the Izu-Hakone Railway.

2mls (3km) SW (coach): Shuzenji, on the edge of the Katsura gawa, is one of the three principal spas in Izu, along with Atami and Ito. Salt springs between 140° and 162° (60° and 72°C), effective against gastric trouble and skin ailments, known since the 9th c.; the Tokkonoyu spring rises from the very bed of the river.

Shuzen ji, on a hill in the centre of the locality, is said to have been founded in the early 9th c. by Kobo Daishi. It was in this temple that Minamoto Yoritomo confined his younger brother Noriyori, whom he killed in 1193 for failing to support the new Shogun against their brother Yoshitsune. It was also in this temple that Hojo Tokimasa (1138-1215) had his grandson Yoriie (1182-1204), son of Yoritomo and Masako (see above, Nirayama Onsen 5mls/8km), executed, to secure his power over Kamakura. Near the tomb of Yoriie stands the Shigetsu den, founded by Masako after the death of her son.

3mls (5km) W: The grotto of Shogaku-in (or Okuno-in), in which Kobo Daishi is said to have defeated the devil; it has been consecrated as a temple.

12mls (19km): Asahi waterfall, which flows into the Kano gawa; behind it is the Shiro (or Shuzenji) hill, covered with cherry and plum trees. Good view of the surrounding area.

15mls (24km): Aobane, where a road branches off in the direction of Toi (see 3 below, 31mls/50km).

1½ml (2km) SW: Funabara Onsen, salt springs and pleasant resort to the N of Amagi san (see 1 above, 25mls/40km; and below, 16 and 22mls/26 and 36km); wild boar hunts are organized from here.

16mls (25km): Yoshina Onsen; off to the r. of the road, said to be the oldest known spa in Izu. The road becomes hillier and more picturesque.

16mls (26km): Amagi Yugashima, close to the springs of Yugashima,

Yoshina, Tsukigase and Sagasawa, from any of which you may begin the ascent of the Amagi mountains (see 1 above, 25mls/40km).

18mls (29km): *Joren taki, an 82-ft (25-m) waterfall, in front of a basalt grotto which you may enter.

22mls (36km): Amagi toge, from where you can climb to the Amagi peaks or take a 2h. walk to the little Hatcho pool, at an altitude of 3,937ft (1,200m). A modern road bypasses this ridge through a tunnel.

24mls (39km): the *Seven waterfalls of Kawazu, on the upper course of the Kawazu gawa, of which the Odaru falls are the highest at 89ft (27m).

27mls (43km): Yugano Onsen, salt springs at 93°-115°F (34°-46°C). The road carries on towards Kawazu on the coast; we turn r. towards Shimoda.

29mls (46km): Mine Onsen, whose springs feed green houses and iris-fields; note the giant fern (*sotetsu*) said to be 800 years old.

39mls (62km): Rendaiji (station), very old springs whose waters are mainly diverted to the spa at Shimoda.

40mls (65km): Shimoda (see 1 above, 58mls/94km).

3 FROM NUMAZU TO SHIMODA BY THE W COAST OF THE IZU PENIN-SULA (78mls/125km; coaches passing generally through Shuzenji and Toi). From Numazu (see entry under this name) the road follows the coast, sweeping round the lovely Bay of Mito.

6mls (10km): Mito hama; pearl culture. Famous *view of Fuji san (one of the finest), standing out against the background of the Bay of Suruga.

A cablecar goes out over the sea to the isle of Awa. A glass-bottomed boat sails back and forth from Numazu. Aquarium in the SW of the locality.

From Mito onwards, the coast becomes much more rugged.

11mls (18km): Kou, where a road branches off for the Heda ridge (6mls/9km; 2,411ft/735m alt.) and Shuzenji (see above, 11mls/17km).

1½ml (2km) S of the ridge, via a toll road, the Daruma yama (3,222ft/982m) provides a wonderful *view of Fuji, Heda and the Bay of Suruga.

16mls (26km): Oze zaki, on the NW tip of the Izu peninsula, from where the view is also quite remarkable. The road now turns S.

21mls (34km): Heda has a little fishing port tucked away in a pretty inlet. The inhabitants occupy themselves with agricultural work.

31mls (50km): Toi (boat for Yoshiwara), hot spa on the W coast of the Izu peninsula; beautiful beach. Since the 16th c. gold has been mined in the area.

From here, the route continues on by the N136, which is very winding.

46mls (74km): Dogashima, an *area of rocks and natural grottoes hollowed out by the sea's erosion; they are thought to have been inhabited by cavemen in prehistoric times.

48mls (78km): Matsuzaki, seaside bathing resort, to the SW of the Izu peninsula. The route continues along the coastal road; view of *Hagachi kaigan.

56mls (90km): Turn r. towards Hagachi zaki (1½ml/2km SW); from this cape you have a view of the coast, with its 800-1600ft (250-500m) high cliffs. Large numbers of monkeys live in the area.

67mls (108km): Nagatsuro; the road branches off to the S in the direction of Cape Iro.

➡ 1ml (1.5km) S: *Iro zaki, on the southernmost point of the Izu peninsula. Exceptionally fine rock formations, view of the Izu archipelago. Close to the cliff-wall (160ft/50m high) stands the shrine of Iro Gongen, visited by many sailors.

73mls (117km): Rejoin the N136.

➡ 2mls (3km) W: hot spa of Shimokamo (springs between 140° and 212°F/60° and 100°C).

➡ 78mls (125km): Shimoda (see 1 above, 58mls/94km).

D Izu Shoto, see entry under this name.

■ Fujiidera (Island of Honshu)

Map of Kansai, pp. 500-1.

Tokyo, 333mls (536km) - Kobe, 32mls (52km) - Kyoto, 38mls (61km) - Nara, 22mls (36km) - Osaka, 12mls (20km) - Wakayama, 49mls (79km).

Osaka fu - pop: 50, 414.

Fuji dera, NE of the station in the town of Fujidera (Kintetsu ER from Osaka Tennoji), is a temple founded in 725 by Gyoki Bosatsu (670-749). It houses a *statue of the bodhisattva of the thousand hands, thought to date from the end of the 7th c.

Approx. 880yds (800m) S of the station, is the Yachuji with its remarkable bronze Miroku Bosatsu, made in AD 666.

☞ **VICINITY**

1 TAKAWASHI (1½ml/2km W; Kintetsu ER); visit the Yoshimur farm, a traditional house dating from the 17th c.

2 HABIKINO, OSAKA, see entries under these names.

■ Fujinomiya (Island of Honshu)

Map of Mount Fuji, p. 163.

Tokyo, 91mls (146km) - Kofu, 55mls (88km) - Nagano, 150mls

(242km) – Nagoya, 144mls (232km) – Shizuoka, 29mls (46km) – Yoko-hama, 73mls (118km).

Shizuoka ken – pop: 88,880.

The Sengen shrine (½ml/1km N of the station) is the most important of a group named after Fuji; it is sacred to Konohana Sakuya hime, guardian goddess of the volcano. Festival of the opening of the ascent of Fuji san, 1 July.

The shrine is the starting-point of the Fujinomiya trail (coach as far as Shin go gome, then 3h. 30 on foot), formerly the principal access route to the top of Fuji san; views over the Izu peninsula and Suruga bay.

VICINITY

1 TAISEKI JI (5mls/8km N; coach from Fujinomiya), built by the Buddhist priest (*bonze*) Nikkan (1246-1333), follower of Nichiren. This temple was the seat of the Nichiren sho sect founded by Nikkan and known since 1930 under the name of Soka Gakkai. The present buildings, dating from 1958, are an interesting and successful blend of reinforced concrete and traditional Japanese architectural concepts (arch.: Yokoyama Kimio).

The Soka Gakkai is in fact a secularized version of the Nichiren sho shu, with the aim of bringing to everyone his or her daily quota of happiness through participation in the politicized activity of this 'great family' of between 5 and 15 million members, recruited mainly from socialist opponents of the establishment. It represents to some extent 'the present-day renaissance of the old fighting nationalist Buddhism of Nichiren' (D. and V. Elisseeff).

2 FUJI-HAKONE-IZU NATIONAL PARK, see entry under this name.

■ Fujisawa (Island of Honshu)

Map of the Vicinity of Tokyo, p. 565.

Tokyo, 35mls (57km) – Kofu, 86mls (139km) – Shizuoka, 76mls (122km) – Yokohama, 144mls (23km).

Kanagawa ken – pop: 228,978.

Although some 40mls (60km) from the heart of the capital, Fujisawa makes a pleasant break from the bustle of Tokyo: during the high season, the access roads are packed solid and the beaches crowded with people. Lying to the S of the agricultural plain of Sagami, the town gives access to a stretch of coast suitable for bathing, at the head of which is the little isle of Eno.

Shojoko ji or Yugyo (½ml/1km N of Fujisawa station), set up in 1325, became the stronghold of the itinerant priests (*yugyo*) of the Ji sect. In the temple hangs a portrait on silk of the Emperor Go Daigo. The bell in the belfry dates from 1356.

Ensho Daishi, known during his lifetime (1239-89) as Ippen Shonin, educated in the schools of Tendai, Jodo and Nembutsu sects, founded a new sect: the Ji sect, whose monks were to travel the country preaching and doing good works. Up to 13 branches were established, most of them in Kyoto.

Festival on 21 September.

In the temple grounds there stands a monument to the memory of the victims (men and animals) of the battles between the Uesugi and the Ashikaga from 1416 to 1417.

Behind the temple, in the Chosei in (or Oguri do), are the tombs of the lovers Teruta Hima and Oguri Hangan.

FEMALE VIRTUES. Oguri Hangan (1398–1464), whose real name was Sukeshige, was defeated by the Shogun Ashikaga and forced to leave his estate with a handful of servants. In 1426, he met Yokoyama Daisen who was supposed to kill him, having first got him drunk on sake. Alerted to the plot, Teruta Hime, niece of Daisen, saved Hanagan just in time and fled with him on a wild horse to Fujisawa. Later, Hangan's enemies successfully tricked him into taking a poisoned bath, as a result of which he contracted leprosy. Immediately, his faithful lover took him on a sort of barrow to the health-giving Yunomine springs, in the Kii peninsula; once more she saved his life. On his recovery, Hangan became a monk at the Shokoku ji in Kyoto, and it is said that Teruta founded the Chosei in, where the pair of them now lie in peace. Japanese literature has, naturally, made much of the legend.

VICINITY

1 KATASE (2mls/3km S; bus: Odakyu ER or Enoshima Kamakura Kanko ER train). Near the Katase-Enoshima station, Katase beach (Marine Land and Enoshima aquarium) extends W into the Shonan kaigan and E beyond the Katase gawa into Shichiriga hama. In good light conditions, you may glimpse Fuji san.

220yds (200m) E of the station of Enoshima (Enoshima Kamakura Kanko ER) stands the Ryuko ji (Oeshiki festival 12 September), built at the end of the 13th c. by followers of Nichiren.

THE EXECUTION OF NICHIREN. A little monument marks the spot where the priest Nichiren (1222–82) is thought to have been beheaded for his strong opposition to the recognized Buddhist sects and for his politics. The sword used to execute him mysteriously broke in two.

2 ENO SHIMA (2½mls/4km S; bus from the station in Fujisawa or Katase Enoshima). No more than 1½mls (2.5km) round and 200ft (60m) high, this little island of 44 acres (18ha), covered with pine trees, has lost much of its charm since the days when Thomas Raucat's 'Honourable country party' took place here. It has undergone several 'improvements': a 200ft (600m) double bridge linking it to the mainland, the erection of an observation tower surmounted by a lighthouse, the creation of an amusement park with botanical gardens, the construction of a marina for the 1964 Olympic Games, and even the installation of escalators between the island's different levels. In the middle of Eno shima, the shrine bearing that name was originally consecrated (in 1182 by the priest Mongaku) as a Buddhist temple (Kogan ji), at the request of Minamoto Yoritomo. Erosion by the sea has attacked the S coast of the island, hollowing out several grottoes, including the Benten or dragon grotto, open to visitors. Many sellers of rare shells.

3 KAMAKURA, ODAWARA, see entries under these names.

Fukui (Island of Honshu)

Railway map on inside front cover.

Tokyo, 324mls (522km) – Gifu, 109mls (175km) – Kanazawa, 49mls (79km) – Kyoto, 99mls (159km) – Otsu, 91mls (147km).

Capital of Fukui ken (pop: 480,221) – pop: 200,509 – silk industry – state and private universities.

Entirely rebuilt since the earthquake of 28 June 1948, which claimed 3,895 lives, the town has expanded continuously, given over mainly to its traditional activity of silk production. It is also the place through which pass the many pilgrims and tourists on their way to the Eihi ji or to explore the surrounding area.

THE SILK INDUSTRY. As a result of influences from mainland Asia (China and Korea) the manufacture of silk goods has occupied Fukui since the 10th c. This activity was already highly successful when in the 17th c., the daimyo Matsudaira came to power and did even more to make it prosper. What might have remained a huge cottage industry became a real one with the appearance in 1871 of habutae-style factories, copies of those in Kyoto; then, in more recent years up-to-date processes for making rayon and other synthetic fibres were introduced.

Fukuie jo, about 110yds (100m) N of the station, still preserves its circuit of moats and ramparts, within which the regional government of Fukui was established.

Shibata Katsuie (1530–83) built a castle here, from which he organized his conquest of the Noto region in 1582. In the following year he fought against Toyotomi Hideyoshi and was beseiged in the castle. Katsuie, unable to maintain a defence, killed himself together with his wife and 30 or more servants. In the 17th c., the town was given the name of Fukui and the castle remained in the hands of the Matsudaira family until the Restoration of 1868.

½ml (1km) N of the station, the Okajima Art Gallery (Kenri tsu Okajima Bijutsu kaikan 3 Hoei cho), situated near a former *samurai* villa, houses collections gathered in New York by Okajima Tatsugoro: statues, swords, copper and silver ware, smokers' articles, etc.

☀ Jenkei ji, ½ml (1km) SW of the station, houses the tomb of Hashimoto Sanai, ill-fated supporter of the Emperor, executed on the orders of the Shogun in 1859.

☀ Asuwa yama, behind the temple, is a hill covered with cherry trees, with a view of the town and the Haku san mountain.

⛩ Asuwa jinja, to the N of that wooded hill, is dedicated to the Emperor Keitai (449–531), who is thought to have lived in the Fukui region and canalized parts of the Hino, Asuha and Kuzuryu rivers.

Fujishima jinja, further S, is dedicated to Nitta Yoshisada (1301–38), supporter of the Emperor Go Daigo and of Yoshino's court, who was murdered in Tomyoji, in the Fukui region, where until 1901 the shrine stood in his memory.

The Asuwa park also contains a botanical garden and a museum of local interest.

👉 **VICINITY**

☀ 1 *EIHEI JI (12mls/20km E; coach; Keikufu ER train, via Higashi Furuichi). In a delightfully green and cool setting (cedar forest of 74 acres/30 ha), it is one of the main centres of the Zen sect of Soto. You may stay as a visitor, in the Eihei ji, and share the monastic way of life (Tel. (077) 663-3102; English spoken).

The temple founded in 1244 by Dogen Zenji – or Shoyo (Joyo) Daishi (1200–53) – a Buddhist priest and poet who, on his return from China, introduced Zen into Japan (see Kamakura). There is a total of about seventy buildings making up the whole temple, including seven main ones called Shichido garan: the bonzes dedicated themselves as a group to the practice of their religion. There are several modern buildings which can accommodate pilgrims and visitors.

There are also group visits with monks as guides.

The first stage is Kichijo kaku, a huge modern edifice for receiving pilgrims, complete with rooms for reading and meditation, with sleeping quarters, kitchens and bathrooms. Among the main buildings, the *San mon (1749) is the oldest edifice of the Eihei ji; the top floor houses the statue of Buddha Sakyamuni, preaching the Kegon *sutra* and accompanied by his five hundred disciples (*rakan*). From the San mon, corridors lead W to the Sodo, the main Zen meditation room, and E to the Dai Kuin, a vast kitchen building; next comes the Butsu den or Kakuo hoden, in the centre of the Shichido garan, rebuilt in 1902 in the Chinese Song style. Behind, the Hatto or Hall of Dharma, rebuilt in Song style in 1833, can hold up to a thousand people. To the S of it is a stairway and gate (Itte mon) to the Joyo den (1881), which houses the founder's mausoleum.

The Shobokaku (treasure), next to the Kichijo kaku, contains the temple bell, from 1327, mementoes of the priest Dogen, and a painting by the hand of the founder himself.

🏯 2 MARUOKA (8mls/13km N; coach; train to Hon-Maruoka station 1½mls/2.5km W of the castle). The castle of Maruoka was built in

1575 by Shibata Katsuie; the residence of the Arima from 1695 to 1868, it is one of the oldest castles still standing in Japan. Open to visitors.

3 AWARA (12mls/19km N; coach, Keifuku ER train; JNR as far as Kanazu). Popular hot spa; salt springs.

6mls (9km) W (coach from Awara or Mikuni-Keifuku station): *Tojimbo, formed of high basalt columns 230–300ft (70–90m) tall, plunges sheer into the sea. Further N, off the tip of the Anto cape, lies the isle of Ojima with its little shrine.

7mls (11km) NW (coach), hot spa of Yoshizaki, in use from the 15th c. Remember to visit the Nishi Hongan ji while you are there; the narrow Kitagata ko, hugged by the road, meets the sea on a level with this resort.

4 ECHIZEN (25mls/41km SW; coach). Leaving the Fukui to the W, you come to:

15mls (24km): Omi, with its little nearby temple of Houn ji. From here, the road goes through the *coastal park of Echizen-kaga, very rugged and studded with numerous rocky islets.

23mls (37km): Echizen misaki, a location which typifies this park; from here, a toll road runs as far as:

25mls (41km): Echizen.

5 HAKUSAN NATIONAL PARK, see entry under this name.

F | Fukuoka (Island of Kyushu)*

Map of Kyushu (North), pp. 388–9; street plan, pp. 182–3.

Tokyo, 715mls (1,150km) – Kumamoto, 70mls (112km) – Oita, 108mls (174km) – Saga, 33mls (53km).

Capital of Fukuoka ken (pop: 2,807,584) – pop: 1,089,000 – industrial town: heavy industry, chemicals, textiles, foods, and seaport harbour, regional and private universities.

Fukuoka, today the economic and industrial capital of the great northern island, was formerly separated from Hakata by the Naka gawa.

Today the two form a single entity, served by a rapid Shinkansen connection to Tokyo (7h.), and by an international airport. These attractions go far to explain the agreeable character of this town, a veritable 'southern' city; in Fukuoka, you will come across those open-air stalls where you can taste noodles and local specialities; there, too, in the Nakasu quarter, you will find the greatest concentration of bars, clubs and night-spots in the whole of Kyushu: not to be missed! In the suburbs of Fukuoka, let us mention the

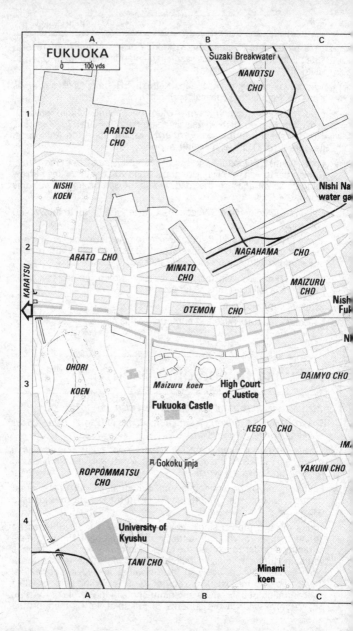

FUKUOKA

0   100 yds

Suzaki Breakwater

NANOTSU CHO

ARATSU CHO

NISHI KOEN

Nishi Na water ga

KARATSU

ARATO CHO

MINATO CHO

NAGAHAMA CHO

MAIZURU CHO

Nish Fuk

OTEMON CHO

NI

DAIMYO CHO

OHORI KOEN

Maizuru koen

High Court of Justice

Fukuoka Castle

KEGO CHO

IMA

ROPPOMMATSU CHO

ㅉ Gokoku jinja

YAKUIN CHO

University of Kyushu

TANI CHO

Minami koen

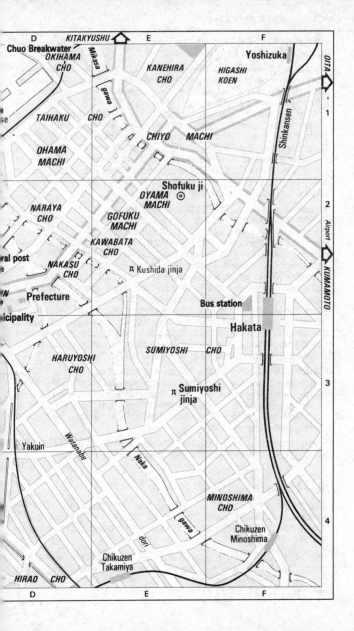

coastal park of Genkai and the Dazaifu shrine, whose name was formerly that of the whole province.

HISTORICAL ORIGINS Within easy reach of Korea by sea (thanks to the intermediate ports of call at Iki shima and Tsu shima), Fukuoka was certainly one of the first points of contact with China. The area was inhabited from the end of the Stone Age (300 BC), and the first encounters with the Chinese go back to the start of our own era. The presence of several tombs (of the Kofun variety) indicate the flourishing of an indigenous civilization, established before the Nara period and persisting until the Heian. In the 9th c., Chinese merchants settled in Nanotsu (the ancient name of Hakata) and brought with them the civilization of the mainland, introducing to the court in Kyoto rich goods produced in China, and making their fortune by exporting Japanese minerals.

ATTEMPTED INVASIONS. The barbarian tribe of the Djutchet, natives of the Asian continent, having seized the islands of Iki and Tsu at the start of the 11th c., tried to land in Fukuoka; the Imperial court seemed not to be aware, and it was left to Futiwara Takaie (979-1044), governor of Dazaifu, to liberate the two islands in 1019. The threat became more serious in the 13th c. when, having first sent an emissary, Kublai Khan landed an army in Fukuoka Bay in 1274; but a storm forced the invaders to take to their ships again. Learning by experience, the Japanese set up a coastal wall along Hakata Bay, while the Mongols prepared a second sizeable expeditionary force, which they sent across in 1281. Some 100,000 men massed to storm the wall but were swept away by a providential typhoon christened 'breath of the gods' (*kami kaze*). These failed landings were the only attempts to invade Japan until World War II.

FUKUOKA. In 1601 Tokugawa Ieyasu established his servant Kuroda Nagamasa in Najima. There he built a castle and changed the name of the town to Fukuoka. The two settlements of Hakata and Fukuoka became one in 1889; the latter more oriented to trade and business, and the former, more industrialized, gained from having a fishing and trading port close at hand.

The philosopher and botanist Kaibara Ekiken (1630-1714) and Marshal Oku Yasukata (1845-1930) were both born in Fukuoka.

A—Hakata

Surrounding the station of Hakata (plan: F2-F3), terminus of the Shinkansen (JNR) lines, the whole district is crammed with skyscrapers, offices, shops, restaurants, and shopping centres built in a great tangle.

 Sumiyoshi jinja (plan: E3), on a little rise 550yds (500m) SW of the station, is said to be one of the oldest shrines in Chikuzen (former province of Fukuoka), restored in 1623. There are cedars and a huge camphor tree in the shrine's grounds.

🔴 Kushida jinja (plan: E2), 550yds (500m) W of the station, is the shrine in which the festival of Yamagasa takes place in July.

Further on, between Hakata and Fukuoka, the island of Nakasu (plan: D2), lying on the Naka gawa, is an entertainment centre crowded with theatres, cinemas and clubs.

🔆 Shofuku ji (plan: E2), 550yds (500m) N of the station, was founded in 1195 by the priest Eisai (1141–1215), who on his return from China introduced tea planting to the province of Echizen. In the temple there is a collection of *haniwa* statues said to be from the tomb of Iwai, a governor of Echizen province in the 6th c.

To the N of the Mikasa gawa you will find:

🌲 HIGASHI KOEN (plan: F1), to the W of Yoshizuka station (1½mls/2km N of Hakata station); it is a wooded garden of 79 acres (32ha); you will see a monument commemorating the invasions of 1274 and 1281, a statue of the Emperor Kameyama (1249–1304) who was alive at the time of the invasions, and a 30ft (10m) statue of the priest Nichiren, who predicted the Mongol landing.

To the W of the park is the Faculty of Medicine of the University of Kyushu, together with a University hospital.

🔴 Hakozaki or Hakozaki Hachiman gu (W of Hakozaki station; JNR, 2mls/3km N of Hakata station), one of the most famous *hachiman* shrines, sacred to the *kami* of war, founded in 923. The present buildings date back to the 16th c., and the gate, built without the use of nails, was erected in 1594 thanks to donations by Kobayakawa Takakage.

🎎 FESTIVALS: Tamaseseri, festival of ball games, 3 January; Hojo-e between 12 and 18 September, with archery contests for horsemen.

B—Fukuoka

To the W of the Naka gawa, Fukuoka spreads out around Tenjin and Daimyo, a complex of administrative and commercial buildings which then give way to a succession of gardens.

🌲 Maizuru koen (plan: B3; ½ml/km W of Nishitetsu-Fukuoka, 2mls/ 3km W of Hakata station) containing, in addition to the sports facilities of Heiwadai, the ruins of the old castle of Fukuoka (a gate and a turret).

🌲 Ohori koen (plan: A3), set among the moats of Fukuoka Castle, forming an extension to the W of Maizuru park; with its vast pool and string of islets in the centre, it is Fukuoka's busiest park.

🌲 Nishi koen (plan: A2), occupying Asato hill, former small island now connected to the shore, is situated approx. ½ml/1km N of Ohori Park.

Kinryu ji, in Nishi machi (½ml/1km W of Ohori koen and 3mls/5km W of Hakata); Kaibara Ekiken, philosopher and botanist, born in Fukuoka, lies buried here.

To the N of Meinohama station (JNR; 6mls/10km W of Hakata), near the sea, stand the remains of ramparts, erected to repel the Mongol invasions.

VICINITY

1 *DAZAIFU (10mls/16km SE; coach; Nishitetsu train via Futsukaichi, where you have to change trains).

9mls (14km): Futsukaichi Onsen (JNR and Nishitetsu stations) has hot radioactive springs (100°–104°F/38°–40°C); it is the smart resort of Fukuoka. To the SW towers Tempai zan (846ft/258m), where Michizane prayed for the Emperor Daigo who had sent him into exile.

10mls (16km): Dazaifu, one of the best known shrines in Japan, sacred to the memory of Sugawara Michizane.

A GOVERNMENT FOR EXILES. In the beginning, the province of Chikuzen was a small kingdom, enjoying commercial relations with China; it came under purely Japanese control after the defeat of its governor Iwai in 528. The government of Dazaifu then became the centre of power for the whole of the north of Kyushu; from there, the conquest of South Korea was organized, and the Japanese bases were not recaptured by the Koreans until Mimana fell in 663. Dazaifu came under control of the Fujiwara, the Taira, and then a bakufu envoy from Kamakura. Among the many governors are numbered Imperial princes who would sometimes delegate rule to a vice-governor (*nagon*) or a minister in exile, as was the case with Sugawara Michizane (845–903), Fujiwara Korechika (974–1010), rival in love of the ex-Emperor Kazan, and Fujiwara Takaie (979–1044), who drove back the Djurtchet invasion. Persecuted by the Minamoto, Taira Munemori, holding as hostage the young Emperor Antoku, sought refuge for a time in Dazaifu in 1183; he was chased out by the revolt of Ogata Koreyoshi and the supporters of the Emperor Go Shirakawa.

SUGAWARA MICHIZANE (845–903). Having gained much influence with the Emperors Uda and then Daigo, Michizane discharged the highest offices of state in Kyoto, at the expense of the Fujiwara and other ministers who together plotted his downfall. Falsely accused of wishing to overthrow the Emperor Daigo, he was ousted and sent to govern Dazaifu in 901, and died there two years later. Learned and cultured, Michizane was rehabilitated and sanctified under the name of Tenjih or Kanko, and made the patron of letters and calligraphy.

*Dazaifu Temman gu or Sugawara jinja stands 850yds (800m) NE of the station (Nishitetsu); it was founded by Ajisaka Yasuyuki, disciple of Sugawara Michizane, who kept watch over his master's tomb and had a shrine built on this site in honour of Kanko, between 905 and 919. After a series of fires, the shrine was rebuilt in 1595, with funds from Toyotomi Hideyoshi. The great gate to the shrine was rebuilt in 1914, and the whole collection of buildings restored in 1951.

The vermilion colour of the buildings contrasts with the greenness of their surroundings: a plum orchard that flowers in February and March, an iris pond which is at its best in June. In front of the main building of the shrine, the 'flying plum tree' (*tobi ume*) is said to have been brought by the wind from Michizane's garden in Kyoto. Next to it is a giant camphor tree, protected by government ordinance. The treasure room (1928) contains paintings, calligraphy and other items associated with Michizane; in the Bunsho kan (1902) and the Kanko Rekishikan, there are further documents and mementoes connected with him.

Kanzeon ji (Tendai sect), 1½mls (2km) SW of the Dazaifu shrine, was once west Japan's largest temple. Built in 746, the only remaining parts date from the 17th c. In the Hon do there is a *statue of Kannon, in camphor wood, from the Fujiwara period (12th c.). The museum attached to the temple houses *sculptures from the Heian and Fujiwara periods, from the 11th to the 13th c.

Tofuro, approx. 1½mls (2km) N of the Dazaifu shrine, used in former times to the Dazaifu government's seat of power; some traces remain.

Homan zan (2,851ft/869m), approx. 3mls (5km) NE, with a tomb of the Kofun era complete with traces of murals; open to visitors.

2 *COASTAL PARK OF GENKAI (coaches run to and from the park to the E and W of Fukuoka; JNR train as far as Saitozaki, Maebaru or Fukuma; Nishetetsu train from Kaizuka to Tsuyazaki; boat from Hakata to Shikano shima). Covering an area of 23,993 acres (9,710ha), this park stretches out through much of Fukuoka, over approx. 56mls (90km); its seaward edge offers a series of beaches and pine forests, a rocky coast and eroded islets, even in places the remnants of the 'Mongol ramparts'.

Kashii gu, 5mls (8km) NE of Fukuoka, near Kashii station, is dedicated to the Emperor Chuai and his wife Jingu, who is said to have boarded ship from the nearby beach. Monument built in 1801.

A TIMELY BIRTH. The Emperor Chuai died prematurely and it was his wife Jingu who, as regent, directed an invasion of Korea, conquest of which, according to divine revelation, would allow the subjugation of the rebellious province of Echizen. Jingu, who was pregnant, slid a stone under her girdle and directed operations with brilliance. When a storm broke out, the very fish of the sea upheld the regent's vessel. Back in Japan, she gave birth to the Emperor Ojin. According to Japanese dates these events go back to the year AD 200, but Korean documents put them at something closer to 346.

Shikano shima (6mls/10km NW of Fukuoka, 16mls/25km by road) is a pleasant place to relax, in the Bay of Fukuoka. The island is connected by a bridge to the spit of sand which stretches out to it.

*Keyano oto (22mls/35km W; coach from Fukuoka or Maebaru) is an area of basalt rock columns plunging into the sea; the whole coast of the Itoshina peninsula, and the surrounding area, is equally fascinating.

3 KARATSU, KITAKYUSHU, see entries under these names.

■ Fukushima (Island of Honshu)

Railway map on inside front cover.

Tokyo, 168mls (270km) – Maebashi, 198mls (318km) – Mito, 114mls (184km) – Niigata, 124mls (199km) – Sendai, 52mls (83km) – Utsunomiya, 101mls (163km) – Yamagata, 58mls (93km).

Capital of Fukushima ken (pop: 1,261,764) – pop: 262,837 – alt. 217ft (66m) – textile industry – state and regional universities.

The production of yarn and fabrics in silk and rayon forms the basis of the flourishing economy of Fukushima, one of the most important towns in northern Japan. It services several spa towns in the surrounding area, and constitutes the main gateway to the national park of Bandai Asahi.

In about 1180, Sugitsuma Yukinobu built a castle called Sugitsuma jo, where he and his descendants were to live. Later on the castle was taken over by the Gamo (1590-1600), then by the Uesugi, until the Shogun confiscated it in 1601. From 1679 to 1868 it was owned in turn by the Honda, Hotta and Itakura families.

The view from the streets of this town is blocked to the W by the tall Azuma mountains, which are more visible from the park of Shinobu yama and especially from the hill of the same name (896ft/273m) which it adjoins, about a mile (1.5km) NE of the station.

VICINITY

1 **KANNON JI** (3mls/5km NW; coach) is famous for its stone *shinobu mojizuri*, 11ft (3.5m) tall but buried for the most part in the earth; people would rub spring leaves against it to make their lover's face appear.

2 **IIZAKA ONSEN** (6mls/10km N; coach; private railway) is situated with its neighbour Yuno Onsen on either side of the Surikami gawa; these springs are among the most important in Tohoku along with those of Onahara and Tennoji, further upriver.

3 **RYO ZEN** (12mls/20km E; coach as far as the shrine) is a mountain (2,641ft/805m) of typical Japanese outline; from its sumit you may see the sea as far as Kinka zan. The Ryo zen shrine (1882) is sacred to Kitabatake Chikafusa and his son Akiie (1318-38), who built a temporary castle here in order to offer resistance to the Ashikaga.

4 **SENDAI, BANDAI ASAHI NATIONAL PARK** see entries under these names.

■ Fukuyama (Island of Honshu)

Map of Shikoku (Inland Sea), pp. 536-7.

Tokyo, 460mls (741km) – Hiroshima, 68mls (110km) – Matsue, 118mls (190km) – Okayama, 40mls (65km) – Tottori, 126mls (202km) – Yamaguchi, 154mls (248km).

Hiroshima ken – pop: 255,086 – heavy industry.

Near to the estuary of the Ashida gawa, Fukuyama is the second largest town in the province of Hiroshima; it owes much of its prosperity to industrial expansion.

Fukuyama Castle, to the N of the station, stands proud with its elegant keep, reconstructed after the war; the interior houses several antiques. From the top is a view of the Inland Sea.

Fukuyama jo was erected between 1619 and 1622 by Tadamasa Katsushige (1564-1651), one of Hideyoshi's generals and a cousin of Tokugawa Ieyasu, and hence a very powerful lord. The castle remained secure in the possession of his descendants until 1698, then passed on to the Okudaira and the Abe, who held it until the Restoration in 1868.

VICINITY

1 INDUSTRIAL ZONE (4mls/7km SE; coach); to visit the steelworks, ask in advance to book a place: Nippon Kohan Kabushiki Kaisah, 1-3, Ote machi, 1-chome, Chiyoda ku, Tokyo, Tel. (03) 212-7111.

2 *TOMO (8½mls/14km S; coach). This little port used to receive ambassadors to the Yamato court, and is now a bathing resort in a pretty inlet sheltered by the isle of Sensui. *Homei shu*, a speciality of Tomo, is the rice wine given as a gift by Abe lords to both Emperor and Shogun.

2½mls (4km) SW (coach): Abuto promontory, with the little Kannon ji at the top, where Korean sailors used to leave offerings. View of the Inland Sea. From Abuto guchi (15 min. walk from the temple), where coaches stop, you can go back to Fukuyama by road along the ridge with fine *viewpoints over the many islands of the Inland Sea.

3 YAMANO ONSEN (15mls/24km N; coach). A hot spa close to the Emmei gorges, especially interesting in autumn.

4 KURASHIKI, ONOMICHI, SETO NAIKAI NATIONAL PARK, see entries under these names.

Furukawa (Island of Honshu)

Map of Tohoku, pp. 232-3.

Tokyo, 231mls (372km) - Akita, 120mls (193km) - Fukushima, 78mls (126km) - Morioka, 88mls (142km) - Sendai, 27mls (43km) - Yamagata, 66mls (106km).

Miyagi ken - pop: 57,060.

Furukawa has spread out to meet the great Tohoku highroad and the Arao gawa. About 25mls (40km), no more, to the N of Sendai, it is within easy reach of the group of spas and winter resorts of Naruko, thanks to the Shinkansen station built there.

VICINITY

1 NARUKO ONSEN (19mls/31km NW; JNR train; coach). This is a whole group of spas along the Arao gawa, enclosed to the W by Arao dake

(3,264ft/995m), and along some of its tributaries. The entire area merges further N with the national park of Mount Kurikoma (see Ichinoseki Vicinity).

These springs, with temperatures ranging from 122° to 176°F (50° to 80°C) were known as early as 835 when – so it is said – after rumbling underground they suddenly gushed out of the side of the mountain. Nowadays, Naruko is popular chiefly as a summer holiday and winter skiing resort. The University of Tohoku has set up a Thermal Institute there.

Naruko station is the main centre from which to tour the spas. Higashi Naruko station also gives easy access to the springs there, and Nakayama daira station is close to the plateau bearing the same name: a fine place for walking, at an altitude of approx. 1,000ft (300m).

1½ml (2km) from Naruko is the Narugo dam on the Arao gawa, at an alt. of 833ft (254m); and upstream from the reservoir, 8mls (13km) from Naruko (coach) is the Onikobe spa, with the Fukiage zawa and Megama geysers.

2 MATSUSHIMA. see Shiogama.

■ **Gamagori** (Island of Honshu)

Map of Natural Resources, p. 66.

Tokyo, 183mls (294km) - Gifu, 57mls (92km) - Nagano, 186mls (299km) - Nagoya, 34mls (55km) - Shizuoka, 79mls (127km) - Tsu, 76mls (123km).

Aichi ken - pop: 82,868 - bathing resort.

In the Bay of Mikawa, encroached upon little by little by the industrial expansion of Toyohashi to the E, and by that of the outlying districts of Nagoya to the NW, the Gamagori region, with its beautiful hinterland, is one of the finest sights to be seen in this bay, so popular with summer holidaymakers.

Gamagori has a pretty beach on the Bay of Mikawa, bounded to the E by the spa of Miya, where there is also an experimental fishing ground. Offshore are the little islands of O shima and Take shima: the latter, the nearer of the two, is connected to the coast by a bridge and has a small shrine.

VICINITY

1 NISHIURA ONSEN (6mls/10km SW; coach) is another spa and seaside resort, on the tip of a peninsula; beyond it Rabbit and Monkey islands (Usagi and Saru jima) can be seen.

2 HAZU (7mls/12km SW; coach; Meitetsu train). You would be best advised to drive to this seaside resort along the toll road which rises up to Sangane san (1,073ft/327m), giving you interesting *views of the Bay of Mikawa along the way, as well as of the peninsulas which frame it, the Japan Alps, and Mount Fuji; half-way up Sangane san there is a temple, founded in the 7th c., and sacred to Kannon.

3 TOYOHASHI (24mls/39km SE; JNR train; coach). Another panoramic toll road circles the Gamagori area; it offers views over Mikawa wan in one direction and the mountainous hinterland in the other, including Mount Fuji

4 NAGOYA, TOYOHASHI, see entries under these names.

■ Gero (Island of Honshu)

Map of Natural Resources, p. 66.

Tokyo, 256mls (412km) - Gifu, 65mls (105km) - Mino Kamo, 45mls (73km) - Takayama, 34mls (55km).

Gifu ken.

Gero is a spa in the Mashita valley, on the upper reaches of the Hida gawa, whose springs (113°-167°F/45°-75°C) used once to enjoy a reputation as good as any in Japan for their healing virtues.

Mori Hachiman gu, on the left bank of the Mashita gawa, contains a dozen or so statues of Shinto gods. Festival: 14 February.

In Gero Park you may see a house built in the *gassho* style, from the district of Shirakawa go (see Takayama).

VICINITY

1 **HAGIWARA** (6mls/10km N; JNR train; coach) is the site of the Kuza Hachiman gu, the foundation of which is attributed to Minamoto Yoshihira who, in 1159, fled to the Hida region.

2 **MINO KAMO** (45mls/73km S; JNR train; coach). This most interesting journey descends the **Hida gawa valley, which often cuts a path across the gorges, and is closely followed by both road and railway. Among the most remarkable places en route, note: *Nakayama shichiri (approx. 10mls/15km), Fujikura kyo (approx. 20mls/30km) and Hisui kyo (approx. 30mls/50km). The Hida gawa meets the Kiso gawa upriver from Mino Kamo (see entry under this name).

3 **TAKAYAMA**, see entry under this name; **ONTAKE SAN**, see under Kiso Fukushima.

■ Gifu (Island of Honshu)

Railway map on inside front cover.

Tokyo, 236mls (379km) - Fukui, 109mls (175km) - Kanazawa, 140mls (226km) - Nagano, 175mls (282km) - Nagoya, 23mls (37km) - Otsu, 53mls (85km) - Tsu, 65mls (104km).

Capital of Gifu ken (pop: 1,056,617) - pop: 385,725 - industrial town: (weaving, paper-making, cutlery), some commerce - state, regional and private universities.

Gifu was a trading stop on the old Nakasen do, which used to run from Kyoto to Edo (Tokyo) across the 'Central Mountains'. To the S of the Nagara gawa, the town is now the intellectual capital and major satellite town in the Nagoya region. It is, moreover one of the busiest centres on the Nobi plain, which stretches away to the S. Tourists come to Gifu to see the cormorant fishing which takes place at night. The town was entirely rebuilt after the 1891 earthquake, and again following World War II.

 Gifu Park (or Gifu koen; 2mls/3.5km N of the station; bus or tram all the way to Gifu koen). The park represents the main tourist attraction, along with the Kinka zan which dominates the scene.

It was set up in 1888 at the foot of a group of hills bordered to the N by the Nagara gawa. The area includes the Inaba shrine, founded in 114 AD and transferred here in 1539, the district library, a large aquarium and the Entomological Institute, founded in 1896 by Professor Nawa Yasushi (1857–1926) and specializing in the study of harmful insects; it has a collection of several thousand specimens.

There is a three-storey pagoda, near which a cablecar goes up to the top of Kinka zan or Inaba yama (1,112ft/339m), where there is a reconstruction of the Gifu jo, the ancient Gifu castle; extensive view out to the Hakusan mountain and the high peaks of Hida.

Gifu jo was built in 1203 at the top of the Inaba yama by a vassal of the Shogun of Kamakura. In 1564, Oda Nobunaga (1534–82) expelled the Saito from this castle; he ceded it in 1576 to his son Nobutada and moved to Azuchi. Hidenobu (1581–1602), son of Nobutada, was only one year old when his father and illustrious grandfather died. He was sent to Kiyosu until Toyotomi Hideyoshi brought him back in 1585. In 1600, having mounted opposition to Tokugawa Ieyasu, he was besieged in his castle by Fukushima Masanori and Kuroda Nagamasa; he was forced to surrender. Ieyasu exiled him to Koya san, where he lived until his death; the castle was left empty and abandoned.

From Gifu koen a road – suitable for driving, if rather winding – runs across the hilly region of Kinka zan.

Shoho ji (Obaku sect), approx. 1km (½ml) SW of Gifu koen and close to steps leadings to the Inaba jinja, was founded in 1683; inside there is a great seated Buddha, made of lacquered paper over a willow frame, and looking just like a solid sculpture (17th c).

VICINITY

1 TANIGUMI (15mls/24km NW; Meitetsu train from Tetsumeicho or Chusetsu) is a hill at the top of which stands the Kegon ji (founded in 798), one of the 33 temples sacred to Kannon in the western provinces. The buildings, erected far more recently, are in a pleasant setting of cherry and maple trees. Look out for the statue of Kannon of the eleven heads.

2 YOKOYAMA DAM (26mls/42km NW; coach; Meitetsu train to Ibigawa) is on the upper course of the Ibigawa; you must first pass through the Ibi gorges to reach it, approx. 16mls (26km) from Gifu.

3 INUYAMA, MINO KAMO, NAGOYA, OGAKI, see entries under these names.

Gotemba (Island of Honshu)

Map of the Region of Hakone, p. 161.

Tokyo, 67mls (108km) – Kofu, 45mls (72km) – Shizuoka, 49mls (79km) – Yokohama, 53mls (86km).

Shizuoka ken – pop: 55,997.

Gotemba occupies a particularly good position at the foot of Mount Fuji, very close to the Hakone mountains and to the N of the Izu peninsula, making it an invaluable base for the tourist who wishes to make excursions into the Fuji-Hakone-Izu National Park.

Gotemba marks the start of the path up to the top of Mount Fuji (coach for 8mls/13km as far as the second level, then 5h. 30 on foot).

VICINITY

1 MOUNT FUJI (17mls/28km W; by coach to the fifth stage on the S face of the crater). Splendid views from the road.

 8mls (13km): Second level, from which the Gotemba trail continues.

11mls (18km): Road to the l., towards the *Jurigi observation point, on the slopes of Ashitaka yama, to the NE of Echizen dake (4,938ft/1,505m).

12mls (20km): Omotefujii Road continues for another 14mls (22km) towards Fujinomiya. Fujisan Highway takes the opposite direction, towards Fuji.

17mls (28km): Gogome, fifth level of the ascent of Fuji, to the SW of Hoei zan (8,865ft/2,702m), formed by the eruption of 1707. For the summit of Fuji, see p. 165.

2 FUJI-HAKONE-IZU NATIONAL PARK. see entry under this name.

■ Goto retto*

Map of Kyushu (North), pp. 388–9.

Tokyo, 901mls (1,450km) - Fukuoka, 186mls (300km) - Nagasaki, 55mls (88km).

Nagasaki ken.

This island chain, off the shore of Kyushu, and belonging to the province of Nagasaki, comprises a veritable swarm of some 150 islands whose coastlines, fractured and eroded, will capture the imagination of any tourist. Fukue, Hisaka, Naru, Wakamatsu, Nakadori, Ojika and Uku are the main islands in the group, which is one of the richest elements in the Saikai National Park. Despite the gentle subtropical climate, the islands are exposed to occasional typhoons.

Goto retto was the place where some of the vanquished Taira fled after their defeat at Danno ura (Shimonoseki, 1185), and served as a haven from the 17th c. onwards for many Christians who sought – often in vain – to escape from the persecutions of the Edo government.

There are several sea links between the various inhabited islands.

FUKUE (pop: 33,442; boat headed for Nakadori shima and Nagasaki; plane bound for Omura; coaches round the island). This little fishing port is the economic capital of the archipelago. The town stands on an island bearing the same name, of which Tetega take (1,512ft/461m) is the highest point.

Ishida jo, close to the sea, was the residence of a daimyo who, taking the name of Goto, held the castle until the Meiji Restoration. Burned down in 1614, it was rebuilt in 1849 by Goto Moriakira.

To the N of Fukue, the Dozaki church was built in 1909 by Father Marmande, a Frenchman, using materials brought from Italy.

13mls (21km) W (coach): Arakawa is a spa facing the island of Shimayama; a lovely area.

25mls (40km) SW (coach): *Ose zaki, a magnificent promontory crowned by a lighthouse.

NAKADORI SHIMA (boats from Narao to Fukue and Nagasaki; from Arikawa to Ojika shima, Uki jima and Sasebo; coach between Arikawa and Narao). The second most important island in the group, to the NE of Fukue jima, it has an even more complex topography than the latter. Tsuwa zaki point (coach as far as Tatekushi) is at the very N of the island, at the very end of a long rocky ridge.

■ Habikino (Island of Honshu)

Map of Kansai, pp. 500–1.

Tokyo, 318mls (512km) – Kobe, 33mls (53km) – Kyoto, 38mls (61km) – Nara, 19mls (31km) – Osaka, 15mls (24km) – Wakayama, 46mls (74km).

Osaka fu – pp: 77,134.

∴ Approx. ½ml (1km) N of Furuichi-Habikino station (Kintetsu ER from Osaka-Tennoji) stands the giant tumulus of the Emperor Ojin (Ojin tenno ryo). Its dimensions (max. length, 2,297ft/700m, 1,375ft/419m for the tumulus proper, 118ft/36m high) make it the second largest of its kind after that at Nintoku, near Sakai (see entry under this name).

This tumulus, dating back probably to the end of the 5th c., in a so-called 'keyhole' shape and surrounded by moats, marks the height of the Kofun period; it forms part of the twin group of Furuichi and Konda which contain, among other things, the more modest tombs of the Emperors Chuai and Inkyo.

Homuda (201-310 according to the Nihongi) or Ojin tenno, son of the Emperor Chuai and his wife Jingu, relinquished power to his mother for 69 years. He fostered relations with Korea, had many favourites and several children. He has been assimilated in Shinto beliefs with the god of war, and was the patron saint of the Minamoto.

🕱 Close by stands the Konda Hachiman gu, one of the oldest shrines in Japan (5th c.), sacred to the Emperor Ojin.

■ Hachinohe (Island of Honshu)

Map of Tohoku, pp. 232–3.

Tokyo, 398mls (640km) – Akita, 140mls (225km) – Aomori, 69mls (111km) – Morioka, 78mls (126km).

Aomori ken – pop: 238,179 – industrial town, fishing port.

The second most important town in Aomori province, Hachinohe syphons off a great deal of the economic activity of northern Japan. Because of its high productivity, Hachinohe's fishing port is second only to Kushiro (on Hokkaido) in the whole of Japan. A mineral port is connected with it, and the town is surrounded by an industrial belt (food and chemical industries); there are also proven coal and petroleum deposits off-shore.

VICINITY

1 **TANESASHI KAIGAN** (9mls/14km E; JNR train; coach). This seaside summer resort is near a fine rocky coast.

2 **RIKUCHU KAIGAN AND TOWADA HACHIMANTAI NATIONAL PARKS**, see entries under these names.

■ Hachioji (Island of Honshu)

Map of the Vicinity of Tokyo, p. 565.

Tokyo, 30mls (49km) – Chiba, 53mls (86km) – Kofu, 60mls (96km) – Urawa, 37mls (59km) – Yokohama, 27mls (44km).

Tokyo to – pop: 387,178 – textile factories, food industry.

Hachioji, on the western edge of the Musashi plain and at the junction of railway lines coming from Tokyo and Yokohama, acts as a dormitory town to those two metropolitan centres.

VICINITY

1 **TAKAO SAN** (5mls/8km SW by the N20; coach from Hachioji or the JNR station in Takao; Keio Teito train from Tokyo-Shinjuku; then funicular).

This wooded hill at an altitude of 2,000ft (600m) is famous for its maples in autumn, a pleasant walking place in the very suburbs of Tokyo.

2½mls (4km): Road to the r. to the Tama mausoleum (660yds/600m). Two hillocks paved in granite slabs house the tombs of the Emperor Taisho (1879– 1926), son of Meiji tenno, and his wife Teimei (1884– 1951), the parents of the present sovereign, Hiro Hito.

3½mls (7km): Kiyotaki; take a funicular from here up to Takao san. Small Natural History museum, close to the station.

5mls (8km): Takao san.

Approx. 880yds/800m SW: Yakuo in, dedicated to Yakushi Nyora; its foundation is attributed to the priest Gyoky. A little higher up, there is an observation post.

2 **TOKYO, YOKOHAMA, CHICHIBU TAMA NATIONAL PARK**, see entries under these names.

Hagi (Island of Honshu)

Map of Places of Interest, p. 71.

Tokyo, 681mls (1,098km) - Hiroshima, 140mls (225km) - Matsue, 152mls (245km) - Yamaguchi, 29mls (47km).

Yamaguchi ken - pop 53,000 - fishing port, orange growing.

Facing the Sea of Japan, this town is set in an elegant bay which stands at the end of the delta of the Abu gawa. Hagi is one of those localities, rare in Japan, which have been spared the depersonalized modernization of so many other towns and have managed to preserve the old world atmosphere of the Edo period. It presents one of the most romantic reminders of the Japan of old. The potter's art, sometimes drawing on centuries-old traditions, also helps to keep the past alive here.

THE MORI RESIDENCE. After their defeat at Sekigahara, the Mori, who had dared to oppose Tokugawa Ieyasu, were dispossessed of their vast domains (of which Hiroshima was the capital). Restricted to the provinces of Nagato and Siwa, the present-day Yamaguchi area, they settled in Hagi, where Hidenari built a new castle. His successors stayed there until 1863, then established themselves in Yamaguchi, bringing prosperity to the little town.

REVOLUTIONARY FERVOUR. Hagi is the proud birthplace of certain politicians who took part in the restoration of Imperial power. Foremost among them, Mori Motonori, head of the Choshu clan, exercised a nationalist influence on the Emperor and was an active architect of the overthrow of the Shogun. After the Restoration, Motonori turned over the whole of his land and revenue to the Emperor Meiji. In 1876, Maebara Issei, who had also favoured the Imperial restoration but was disillusioned with subsequent political developments, took advantage of an uprising in Kumamoto to organize a rebellion in Hagi; he was defeated, captured while trying to escape by sea, and beheaded in Yamaguchi.

FAMOUS SONS OF HAGI. Sugimori Nobunori, known as Chikamatsu Monzaemon (1653-1724), Japan's greatest playwright; Mori Motonori (1839-96), mentioned above; Marshal Yamagata Aritomo (1838-1922), who was Prime Minister; Yamada Akiyoshi (1844-92) and Katsura Taro (1847-1913), who also took part in the Restoration and were members of the first Meiji government.

Hagi jo (3mls/4.5km W of the Higashi-Hagi station, 1ml/1.5km NW of Tamae station; bus) lies at the foot of Shizuki yama, surrounded by the sea and with little more than the memory of its keep (demolished in 1873), strong ramparts and moats. There are other ruins at the top of the hill and a little shrine at its foot.

A first fortress had been built in the 13th c. by Hojo Naomoto. The Mori established themselves in the area at the beginning of the 17th c. and erected a castle, completed in 1608 and abandoned in 1862.

Edo ga yoko cho, running parallel with the great modern street which goes past the castle and ends up at the Higashi-Hagi station, is the most atmospheric of all the town's ancient arterial roads. At the end of it, if you turn to the l. (NW), you come to the main road mentioned above and, close by, the folk museum (collections of local crafts), in a house that dates from 1768; if on the other hand you were to turn to the r. (SE), you would soon come to the neighbouring houses of Takasugi Shinsaku and Kido Takamasa.

Takasugi (1839–67) was a valiant *samurai* of the Choshu clan, opposed to the Shogun and to all alliances with foreigners. Kido Takamasa or Koin (1834–77) also acted in the interest of the Imperial cause, and was responsible for the replacement of the former provinces by new administrative districts.

Approx. 1½mls/2km SE (make enquiries), close to the Abu gawa, stands the house where Marshal Yamagata Aritomo was born.

Shoka Sonjuku (1ml/1.5km SE of the Higashi-Hagi station) is the little school where Yoshida Shoin (1831–60) taught; a supporter of the Emperor and a xenophobic nationalist, he was nevertheless curious about Western learning (see Shimoda, p. 172). The nearby shrine is dedicated to him.

Toko ji, further NE, in a lush green setting, used to be the Mori family temple and it houses their remains.

VICINITY

1 KASA YAMA (3½mls/6km N; coach) is one of the fine promontories of volcanic origin (367ft/112m) in the Bay of Hagi; wide *view over the coastal park of Kita Nagato. Not far away is the sheltered little inlet of Myojin.

2 AI SHIMA (8mls/13km NW; boat) is a small island with rugged coastline and cliffs.

3 *MI SHIMA (28mls/45km NW; boat) has an even more extraordinary coastline and rocky promontories which have earned it the nickname of the 'Sea Alps'.

4 SUSA WAN (24mls/38km NE; coach; JNR train) is among the most beautiful inlets in Kita Nagato kaigan, between Hagi and Susa.

5 NAGATO, YAMAGUCHI, see entries under these names; AKIYOSHI DAI, CHOMON KYO, see Yamaguchi.

H | Hakodate (Island of Hokkaido)

Railway map on inside front cover.

Tokyo, 516mls (830km) - Aomori, 70mls (113km) - Esashi, 45mls (72km) - Otaru, 156mls (251km) - Sapporo, 165mls (265km) - Tomakomai, 157mls (252km).

Hokkaido - pop: 320,154 - fishing and trading port - private university.

The third most important town on Hokkaido, Hakodate is the principal landing place for the island. The town, lying at the foot of the hill on which the Goryokaku fortress was built, occupies a narrow isthmus attached to Hakodate yama, jutting out into the sea like a Japanese rock of Gibraltar. The forthcoming opening of an undersea tunnel between Honshu and Hokkaido is bound to increase the town's importance.

In 1855 Hakodate was, along with Shimoda, one of the first Japanese ports opened up to foreign trade, following the Treaty of Kanagawa (1854; see Yokohama). In 1869, vice-admiral Enomoto Takeaki (1836-1908), one of the Shogun's last supporters, withdrew his fleet into the Bay of Hakodate and set up a short-lived republic in the Goryokaku fortress; he held out for six months against the Imperial forces, under the command of General Kuroda Kiyotaka (1840-1900). The same year (1869) saw the creation in Hakodate of the Colonial Commission (*kaitakushi*), it was transferred in 1871 to Sapporo.

In the narrowest part of the Hakodate isthmus, at the crossing of two broad arterial roads, stands the Municipality (550yds/500m S of the station). One of the two roads runs SW of Hakodate yama. If you turn r. at the end it, you come to the cable-car for Hakodate yama; to the l. you are heading for Hakodate koen.

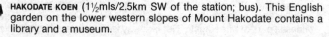

HAKODATE KOEN (1½mls/2.5km SW of the station; bus). This English garden on the lower western slopes of Mount Hakodate contains a library and a museum.

Hakodate Museum, the oldest regional museum in Japan, now displays its collections in a modern building; but it was first opened in 1879 on the initiative of the American adviser Horace Capron (1804-85). It houses archaeological collections from local digs, notably some articles of Jomon pottery; an ethnological department devoted to the Ainu and Gilyak civilizations (from the islands of Hokkaido and Sakhalin); mementoes and manuscripts of the poet Takuboku Ishikawa (1886-1912). The natural history and fishing exhibits have remained in the original old building, which is constructed in Western style, of wood.

550yds (500m) SW of Hakodate koen stands the Hachiman shrine, the most important one in Hakodate (festivals 29 July and 15 August).

North of the cablecar for Mount Hakodate stands the Greek Orthodox Church of the Resurrection, rebuilt after a fire, founded in 1861 by the Russian prelate Ivan Nikolai Kasatkin (1936-1912), who was responsible for the introduction of the religion into Japan.

*HAKODATE YAMA (2½mls/4km SW of the station; bus; cable-car to the top). It reaches its peak at 1,099ft (335m) with Goten yama. An exposed extinct volcanic cone, it falls away into sheer 300-500ft (100-150m) cliffs that plunge into the sea. From the summit, which is crowned by radio and telecommunications aerials, you can see out over the Strait of Tsugaru as far as the Sea of Japan, and the whole town can be seen spread out at the foot of the mountain.

Close to the top there is a monument to the memory of the Englishman Thomas Wright Blakiston (1832–91), a merchant who settled in Hakodate, and who gave his name to the Blakiston Zoographical Line (Strait of Tsugaru), having observed that the birds living on either side of the strait were of different species. In the Mount Hakodate observatory there is a bust of Tadataka Ino (1745–1818), the Japanese scientist who made his first topographical observations here, which were used in his *Atlas of Japan*.

Goryokaku Fortress (2mls/3km NE of the station; bus) owes its name (Five-pointed star) to its pentagonal shape; it was built, between 1855 and 1864, by Takeda Hisaburo on his return from the Netherlands and was the first of its kind in Japan.

Goryokaku was under the direct control of the Tokugawa and it was here that Enomoto Takeaki established himself in 1869. Today the fortress stands in a state-managed public park where there is a small museum commemorating the battles of 1869. From the nearby observation tower, there is a view of the town and its surroundings.

VICINITY

1 TRAPPIST MONASTERY (15½mls/26km S by the N228; 1¼mls/2km W of Tobetsu station) founded in 1895 by Fukie Okada, born in France; open to male visitors only.

2 'ONUMA KOEN (17mls/28km N by the N5; coach, train). This nature park of 234,152 acres (94,760ha) is dominated by the spur of Komaga take (3,717ft/1,133m; see below), at the foot of which lie three shallow pools called O numa, Ko numa and Junsai numa; there is skating on the lakes in winter, and in summer a boat sails on the largest, O numa (2 sq. mls/5km$_2$), lying NW of the other two; you may fish for *funa* (little carp). From the top of Konuma yama, between Ko numa and Junsai numa, there is a lovely view over the whole group.

Komaga take (3,717ft/1,133m) or Oshima Fuji is an active volcano whose crater is in the form of a horseshoe. You can go up it from Komagatake station (4mls/6km) in 3h.30.

11mls (17km) NE (coach): Shikabe Onsen, at the foot of Komaga take, with springs between 126° and 214° (52° and 101°C). The Tsurunoya geyser, the only one on Hokkaido, is the spa's main attraction; it spouts every ten minutes, reaching heights of up to 16ft (5m), at a temperature of 212°F (100°C).

3 E SAN (29mls/46km E by the N278; coach). Drive E along the coast from Hakodate; views of the Shimokita peninsula.

3½mls (6km): Yunokawa Onsen, discovered in the 17th c., is the oldest known hot spring on Hokkaido and is to the day the most frequented in the S of the island; water temperature between 88° and 153°F (31° and 67°C).

✝ 2mls/3km E (coach): Trappist nunnery, founded in 1898 by a French mission. Today there are about 100 sisters living there, with a thriving output of butter and cheese (entry forbidden to men).

13mls (21km): Shiokubi misaki.

20mls (32km): Shirikishinai; a road turns off to the r. and skirts E san to the S.

25mls (41km): Todohokke, where a Neolithic Jomon site was discovered. From here, the road to Esan misaki branches off.

29mls (46km): *Ekan misaki is an active volcano which, on the eastern tip of E san (2,028ft/618m), falls away into cliffs; you can climb it in an hour; extensive view.

■ Hakui (Island of Honshu)

Tokyo, 321mls (517km) – Fukui, 76mls (123km) – Gifu, 168mls (270km) – Kanazawa, 27mls (44km) – Toyama, 52mls (83km).

Ishikawa ken - pop: 28,530 - industrial centre.

There is a wide network of roads running in all directions over the Noto peninsula; Hakui makes a good place to base yourself while you explore.

↦ **VICINITY**

1 TOGI (18mls/29km N by the N249 coach). If you are travelling by car it is better to follow the coast road.

🛆 2½mls (4km): Keta shrine, facing the sea, against a backdrop of forests, is dedicated to Okuninushi no Mikoto, descendant of Susano o no Mikoto (see Izumo).

☼ 5mls (8km): Myojo ji (Nichiren sect) is one of the most important temples in the area; note especially the Hon do, Kaisan do and Kigan do, as well as a listed five-storey pagoda.

14mls (22km): A road turns off to the l., in the direction of *Noto kongo (approx. 2½mls/4km W), revealing one of the finest sights on the coast including the Gammon natural arch and the high Takanosu (falcon's nest) rock, its top so high that only those birds can reach it. Motor-boat trips in summer.

↦ 7mls (11km) NW (coach excursions), the rocky Sekino kaigan may well remind you of parts of the Mediterranean.

≋ 2 KANAZAWA (see entry under this name; 27mls/44km S; coach; JNR train), reachable by toll road running along the shore of the Sea of Japan with its many beaches. The one at Chiri hama, S of Hakui, is among the most interesting. From Nanatsuka (approx 15mls/24km) the road, which is being extended towards Kanaiwa, sweeps round the Kahoku lagoon, mainly on land reclaimed from the sea.

3 NANANO, WAJIMA, see entries under these names.

■ **Hakusan** (National park; Island of Honshu)

Map of Natural Resources, p. 66.

HOW TO GET THERE

– From Kanazawa 22mls (36km) as far as Hakusanshita, using the Hokuriku Railway or a coach to the hot spas of Iwama or Hakusan.

– From Katsuyama (19mls/30km E of Fukui, by Keifuku ER or coach), heading for Hakusan or Kanazawa.

– From Komatsu (24mls/38km SW of Kanazawa and 48mls (77km) NE of Fukui, with JNR rail links to both these towns), coach bound for Hakusanshita.

FROM KANAZAWA TO KATSUYAMA VIA HAKU SAN (60mls/96km; make enquiries as to the passability of the access route to Haku san; coach route direct from one town to the other or to Hakusan Onsen; Hokuriku Railway train to Hakusanshita). Leave Kanazawa and head SW by the N8.

3½mls (6km): Nonoichi; the N157 turns off l., quickly rising up along the Tedori gawa, parallel with the railway line.

16mls (26km): Tedori Onsen, downriver from the pretty Tedori gorges, which you will cross.

22mls (35km): Hakusanshita, rail terminus.

23mls (37km): To the l., road off to Iwama Onsen.

32mls (51km): Iwama Onsen; beyond this point, you will have to make your own enquiries about the condition of the road which continues up, close to Haku san. Beautiful mountain scenery.

37mls (60km): Murodo (alt. 8,054ft/2,455m); from here, begin the ascent of Gozen mine (see below).

**Haku san is, along with Mounts Fuji and Tate, one of Japan's sacred mountains and also one of the most spectacular. There are five main peaks around it: Gozen mine (8,865ft/2,702m) is the highest; Onan ji (8,681ft/2,646m) and Tsurugiga mine (8,714ft/2,656m) are to the W, and Bessan (7,871ft/2,399m) and Sanno mine (6,955ft/2,120m) further S. There is a little shrine standing on the top of Gozen mine from which there is a *remarkable view out towards Tate yama and On take.

37mls (60km): Hakusan Onsen, at an altitude of 3,166ft (965m), at the foot of Sanno mine.

46mls (74km): Shiramine, where you rejoin the N157 heading for Katsuyama.

51mls (82km): The road passes through a tunnel under the Tani ridge, then descends the valley of Kuzuryu gawa.

60mls (96km): Katsuyama (pop: 32,691); textile industry.

■ Hamada (Island of Honshu)

Railway map on inside front cover.

Tokyo, 614mls (988km) – Hiroshima, 71mls (115km) – Matsue, 78mls (126km) – Tottori, 162mls (260km) – Yamaguchi, 75mls (121km).

Shimane ken – pop: 49,407 – fishing port.

The economy of this town depends on the Sea of Japan. An active fishing port, it holds an important fish market every morning; the fish, processed and packed, are exported to the countries of Southeast Asia. The manufacture of ceramics and tiles known as Iwami also represents a traditional speciality of the area.

Kame yama is a public park, approx. 1ml (1.5km) W of the station, and is the site of the ancient Hamada castle which, under the Tokugawa, was the residence of the Furata, the Matsui, the Honda and the Matsudaira.

The coastline around Hamada boasts many beautiful seaside spots, such as Tono ura and Tatamiga ura.

■ Hamamatsu (Island of Honshu)*

Railway map on inside front cover.

Tokyo, 149mls (239km) – Kofu, 112mls (181km) – Nagano, 181mls (291km) – Nagoya, 67mls (108km) – Shizuoka, 45mls (72km) – Yokohama, 132mls (213km).

Shizuoka ken – pop: 432,221 – industrial town: cotton and synthetic textiles, chemicals, motorbikes, musical instruments.

Hamamatsu occupies a key position, centred round a castle built on the junction of the road running from Kyoto to Edo (the Tokai do) and the Shinano do, coming from the N. Today, Hamamatsu has become the main town in the Shizuoka district; it was here that Mr Honda began to build his financial empire (the majority of Japanese motorbikes are still made in Hamamatsu). In addition, the pianos made in the town are exported all over the world, and have gained an international reputation.

As the discoveries of Shimi zuka indicate, Hamamatsu was the site of a Neolithic settlement; but it is not until the 14th c. that mention is made of the castle of Hikuma – the town's original name – built by the Miyoshi. In about 1505, Okochi Sadatsuna commissioned a new castle, in which Tokugawa Ieyasu established himself in 1570, directing the battle of Mikatahara from there in 1572; then, ceding it to Honda Shigetsugu, he forced him to rebuild it. In 1590, Horio Yoshiharu acquired the castle and, during the Tokugawa era, it had many different owners.

The author Kamono Mabuchi (1687–1769) and the film director Kinoshita Keisuke (b. 1912) were born in Hamamatsu.

Hamamatsu jo koen (½ml/1km W of the station), on the site of

Hamamatsu castle, is a public park in which some ramparts and earthworks still survive. The 14th c. keep, with three storeys, was abandoned during the Meiji period and rebuilt in 1958; it houses an exhibition of items of archaeological and local historical interest. Little zoo nearby.

Shijimi zuka (1½mls/2.5km W, bus), close to the Sanaru pool, is a heap of shells, excavated in 1889 close to the site of a Neolithic settlement (Jomon) from about 3,000 years ago. As in Toro (see Shizuoka), five primitive huts have been reconstructed.

VICINITY

1 NAKATA JIMA SAND DUNES (3mls/5km S; coach); spread over 2½mls (4km) along the Pacific shore. In May, there are kite competitions here.

2 *HAMANA KO (round trip of 45mls/72km if you follow this itinerary; coach excursions leave from Hamamatsu; boat services run back and forth across the lagoon). On the probable site of an extinct volcanic crater, the Hamana lagoon (28sq. mls/73km^2, 78mls/126km of coastline) was once separated from the ocean by a spit of sand, removed in 1498; all that now remains of it is the little island of Benten. Shallow and encircled by low hills, the lagoon is nonetheless delightful; little eels and edible seaweed are farmed in it. There are numerous pleasure grounds around its edge. Go N along the N257 from Hamamatsu.

5mls (8km): Mikatahara, site of a battle in 1572, where Takeda Shingen (1524-73) met Tokugawa Ieyasu (1542-1616), who was being besieged in Hamamatsu Castle. The conflict, first turning to the advantage of Shingen, was won in the end by Ieyasu, who made a sudden and decisive attack.

9mls (15km): Turn l. for Hosoe and Hamana ko.

4mls (7km) NW: Oku yama, on whose wooded slopes stands the Hoko ji (Rinzai sect), founded in the 14th c. by the priest Mumon (1323-90), son of the Emperor Go Daigo. Open to visitors.

17mls (27km): Road off r. to Mikkadi, N of the pretty Inohana creek. A toll road divides it from Hamana ko, running along the Ozaki peninsula.

20mls (32km): Seto; quay from which you may take a boat to Washizu (see below) to the SW of the lagoon.

24mls (38km): Kosai; the little Washizu promontory is topped by the *Honko ji, whose Hon do (1552) still preserves the murals painted by Tani Buncho (1765-1842), of the Nanga school; the Japanese garden was designed by the master of the tea ceremony, Kobori Enshu (1579-1647).

25mls (41km): Arai used once to be the key to the Imagiri pass, between the western shore of the lagoon and Benten jima. The town hall, standing on the site of the old toll gate, contains a display of some memorabilia connected with it.

☐ 29mls (46km): Benten jima is the old islet which blocked access to Hamana ko from the ocean; these days, it is mainly noted for its 'luna park', crossed by road and rail viaducts. One of them, Hamanako ohashi, is a toll bridge, curving over 5,250ft (1,600m), and cutting through the N of the lagoon. Follow it towards Kanzanji.

☼ 35mls (57km): Kanzanji Onsen is another entertainment area on the western coast of Hamana ko; a cable-car goes from the resort to the Ogusa yama (367ft/112m) observation point. The founding of the Kanzan ji, on the tip of the Muragushi peninsula, is attributed to Kobo Daishi (in the 9th c.); lovely view.

Return to Hamamatsu via the floral gardens of the same name (huge tropical greenhouses).

45mls (72km): Hamamatsu.

3 TENRYU GAWA VALLEY, see Iida and Tenryu.

■ Hanamaki (Island of Honshu)

Map of Tohoku, pp. 232-3.

Tokyo, 296mls (476km) - Akita, 98mls (158km) - Aomori, 157mls (252km) - Morioka, 24mls (38km) - Sendai, 91mls (147km).

Iwate ken - pop: 68,873.

On the great Tohoku line, between Tokyo and Aomori, Hanamaki is a large industrial borough, serving several nearby spas and, with its airport, the town of Morioka.

Hanamaki is the birthplace of the poet Kenji Miyuzawa (1896-1933).

1ml (1.5km) S of the station, near the Kitakami gawa, stands the site of Toya jo, the former name of Hanamaki. Castle built in the 11th c. by Abe Yoritoki.

☞ **VICINITY**

♨ 1 HANAMAKI ONSEN (6mls/9km NW; coach), set in the valley of the Dai gawa, it catches the waters of Dai Onsen. An area of waterfalls.

♨ 2 NAMARI ONSEN (11mls/18km NW; coach) is in a pretty valley (look for the maples in autumn), along which flow both the Osawa and Shidotaira brooks.

↦ 2mls (3km) upstream are the Toyosawa dam and reservoir.

3 MORIOKA, RIKUCHU KAIGAN NATIONAL PARK, see entries under these names.

■ Handa (Island of Honshu)

Tokyo 210mls (338km) - Gifu, 50mls (81 km) - Nagano, 192mls (309km) - Nagoya, 27mls (44km) - Shizuoka, 106mls (171km) - Tsu, 68mls (110km).

Aichi ken - pop: 80,663.

At the mouth of the Sakai gawa, NW of Mikawa Bay, the town of Handa, and the town of Hekinan which faces it, are among the industrial satellites clustered around Nagoya. The two towns are linked by a tunnel under the sea (coach). Handa, specializing in cotton textiles, also produces vinegar, soy sauce and *sake*. Kariyado Park, on a hill to the W of the town, is well worth a visit.

⌐ **VICINITY**

·CHITA PENINSULA (round trip of 35mls/57km from Handa to Tokoname; coach between those two towns and Morozaki, or from Nagoya; JNR train to Taketoyo, Meitetsu train to Mihama; boat from Handa to Mihama and Morozaki). This lovely route circles the peninsula which is bounded to the W by Mikawa Bay and to the E by Ise Bay; the southern coast, more eroded, is the more interesting; seaside resorts.

3mls (5km): Taketoyo, little industrial town and port, terminus of the JNR railway.

9mls (14km): Mihama, terminus of the Meitetsu Railway, beyond which the coast, protected as a nature reserve, offers strikingly beautiful sights.

16mls (25km): Morozaki (boat for Irako misaki), little tourist spot, popular with swimmers, S of which is Cape Hazu, the most southerly point of the Chita peninsula. From here, you may return directly to Nagoya (32mls/52km N) on a *toll road along a ridge, with stunning views of the two bays of Mikawa and Ise.

→ 3mls (5km) SE (boat): Shino jima, little pine-covered island at the entry to Mikawa Bay, between the Chita and Atsumi peninsulas.

→ 18mls (29km): Toyohama, small port set in a creek.

23mls (37km): Utsumi or Minami Chita, seaside resort close to which stands the Iwajiri temple, open to visitors.

26mls (42km): Noma, and nearby Omi do temple.

29mls (47km): Kasugaya.

→ 2mls (3km) E: Uno ike, 'lake of the cormorants', inhabited by those birds and also by herons.

⌐ 35mls (57km): Tokoname; from here, travel directly back to Nagoya by coach or train (Meitetsu line).

▌ Haramachi (Island of Honshu)

Tokyo, 178mls (286km) - Fukushima, 47mls (75km) - Maebashi, 202mls (325km) - Mito, 112mls (181km) - Niigata, 176mls (283km) - Sendai, 48mls (78km) - Utsunomiya, 140mls (226km) - Yamagata, 97mls (156km).

Fukushima ken - pop: 46,052.

Whatever you do, don't forget to go to Haramachi in July, to watch the Nomaoi festival of Soma, which takes place on the heath of Hibarino, E of the town.

👥 Riders come in from the surrounding villages, mounted on wild horses, dressed in traditional costumes and carrying huge banners, the subject of great rivalry. The festival, held regularly since the 17th c. at the behest of local lords as a military exercise, is supposed to evoke a battle which took place in the 10th c.

👉 **VICINITY**

FUTABA (18mls/29km S; JNR train).

6mls (10km): Otaka, where the ruins of old castle are still to be seen.

18mls (29km): Futaba; to the S of the locality the Kiyotosako burial ground was discovered in 1967; open to visitors.

■ Hikone (Island of Honshu)

Map of Places of Interest, p. 71.

Tokyo, 258mls (415km) – Fukui, 66mls (107km) – Gifu, 19mls (31km) –Kyoto, 40mls (64km) – Otsu, 32mls (52km) – Tsu, 60mls (97km).

Shiga ken – pop: 78,753 – textile factories, synthetic fibres.

On the western shores of Lake Biwa, Hikone has grown up around its castle, one of the most representative of feudal Japan, which increases the tourist's interest in this little-known locality.

The master of the tea-ceremony, and landscape gardener, Kobori Enshu (1579-1647), and the politician Ii Naosuke (1815-60) were both born in Hikone.

🏰 HIKONE CASTLE (½ml/1km W of the station). It stands on a mound surrounded by earthworks and ramparts, today made into a park.

THE RESIDENCE OF THE II. This family achieved pre-eminence from the 17th c. on with Ii Naomasa (1561-1602) who, after the victory of Sekigahara seized the castle of Sawayama, set on a hill to the NE of the present town. His son Naokatsu established himself in 1603 on the site of the castle but, having refused to take part in the seige of Osaka (1615), was dispossessed by the Shogun Hidetada in favour of his brother Naotaka (1590-1659). The latter finished building Hikone Castle in 1623 and his descendants held it until the Restoration, keeping the title of Kamon no kami, attached to the Imperial Household. In 1845, Ii Naosuke (1815-60) was the last inheritor of the castle, on the death of his elder brother; in 1858 he achieved the rank of *tairo* (Prime Minister) under the Shogun Iesada, at whose death he set the young Iemochi (1846-66) on the throne; he signed on his own authority several treaties allying him with foreign powers (the USA, Great Britain and France). Though it marked a great turning point in Japanese history, this move was highly unpopular at the time and

Naosuke was assassinated two years later as he was leaving the palace in Edo (Tokyo).

Winding through a maze of enclosures, you come to a terrace overlooking Lake Biwa; above your head towers the keep with its three storeys; inside it there are memorabilia of the Ii family

N of the castle wall lie the gardens of the lords of Hikone. Rakuraku-en is dependent nowadays for its upkeep on a restaurant in the grounds: Hakkei en is a Japanese garden, skilfully planned by Kobori Enshu and featuring, in miniature, the eight wonders of the Omi lake (see Otsu).

☞ **VICINITY**

1 TAGA SHRINE (4mls/7km SE; Omi Railway train), sacred to the divine creators Izanagi and Izanami (see Awaji), one of the best-known shrines in the area.

2 AZUCHI, see Omi Hachiman; BIWA KO, see Otsu; IBUKI YAMA, see Ogaki.

▌ Himeji (Island of Honshu)

Railway map on inside front cover.

Tokyo, 373mls (601km) – Kobe, 33mls (53km) – Kyoto, 78mls (125km) – Okayama, 47mls (75km) – Osaka, 53mls (86km) – Tottori, 82mls (132km).

Hyogo ken – pop: 450,000 – industrial town: steelworks, rubber, textiles, leather – regional university.

One of the 'musts' of your journey, the Himeji fortress is far and away the finest and most authentic in Japan; if there is one castle you simply mustn't miss, it is this! It is in April, when the cherry trees are blossoming, that the fortress looks its most striking. But all year round, you cannot but admire the splendour of Himeji jo, often compared to an egret or white heron, on account of its graceful outlines. The 'personality' of the fortress is further underlined by the contrast it makes with the world around it: an urban sprawl made up of anonymous office-blocks, factories and gleaming TV transmitters. The town and its suburban port of Shikama also hum with industrial activity: altogether, it is a vast urban regional development.

Owing to its key strategic position overlooking the Sanyo do, vital gateway to the provinces in the west, Himeji at the height of its powers had to have a castle. Akamatsu Sadanori built the first in about 1350, named Himeyama with the Kodera in charge; the latter, having thrown off the shackles of vassaldom, stayed in the castle until 1577, when Toyotomi Hideyoshi (1536-98) seized it; he extended it and made it his seat, controlling from it the whole of central Japan between 1581 and 1585. Hideyoshi then yielded his place to his brother-in-law Kinoshita Iesada (1543-1608) who, after Sekigahara, was forced to leave the castle to Ikeda Terumasa (1594-1613), son-in-law of Tokugawa Ieyasu (1542-1616). Terumasa built the castle that we see today, but the Tokugawa family continued to keep a close watch over the succession of families who came to occupy Himeji until 1868: the Honda, the Matsudaira, the Sakaikibara and the Sakai.

**Himeji jo (880yds/800m N of the station) is today the most complete Japanese castle in existence. There is a tall keep in the centre, overlooking a complex of enclosures, courtyards and moats, making an impressive defence system.

JAPANESE FORTRESSES. Occupying strategic positions, the first Japanese fortresses, *yama shiro*, were perched on the tops of hills; later, for reasons of convenience, they were built on simple mounds in the middle of open countryside (*hirayama shiro*). Water was diverted or channelled round them (from a river, lake, or arm of the sea), to provide stronger defence; Himeji is such a fortress. A system of enclosures, one inside another, walls plummeting straight down into trenches, surmounted by battlements with loopholes, etc., divided one part of the castle from another; gates with passages over them opened in zigzag paths between the courtyards in which were located the armouries, wells, stores of ammunition and supplies. Palace living quarters (*nimonaru and sannomaru*) occupied the second and third courts respectively, and were inhabited by the family and household of the lord; he himself lived in the main palace (*honmaru*), generally placed next to the keep. The keep was a symbol of his power; made up of several storeys, it dominated the whole castle and was usually uninhabited; in times of war it would become the last bastion of resistance into which the lord and his dependants would withdraw, ready to set it on fire and die when 'all was lost, save honour'. Besides the castle, the lord usually owned a summer villa with a Japanese garden; his vassals (*daimyo* or *samurai*) also had their dwellings in the immediate vicinity of the castle.

The whole of the Himeji Castle area (see Historical survey) was restored and strengthened carefully between 1956 and 1963.

Crossing the vast courtyard of the *sannomaru*, you come to the Nishinomaru (western palace) on the l., with a defensive corridor nearly 330yds (300m) long down one side of it. Then, you pass through the little courts surrounding the keep, to enter the latter. Flanked to the W by two smaller keeps, it also contains further courts and fortified corridors. From the top of its five storeys, at a height of some 200ft/60m, you can see over the surrounding district as far as the Inland Sea. Below, you can lose yourself in the many courtyards, containing the *honmaru* and other buildings.

After your visit to the castle, stroll in its grounds, along the immense avenue leading to the station. Here and there, shaded shopping centres offer interesting merchandise to the visitor.

Nagoyama (1ml/1.5km W of the castle, 1½mls/2km NW of the station) is as much a park as a cemetery. A large modern *stupa* (1960) in the shape of a pagoda enshrines some of the ashes of Gautama Buddha, a gift of Pandit Jawaharlal Nehru of India (1889–1964).

Tegara yama (1½ml/2km SW of the station; bus) is a vast public park, nicknamed Central Park, and equipped with several sports centres; a municipal library and Himeji art gallery are here, too (temporary exhibitions and local collections).

卍 Matsubara Hachiman gu (3½mls/6km SE of Himeji station; bus; Sanyo ER train to Shirahamanomiya); standing 220yds (200m) S of Shirahamanomiya, this shrine is famous for its lively *Kenka matsuri*, in which there are contests between litter-bearers; it takes place on 14 and 15 October.

⌐ **VICINITY**

1 HIROMINE YAMA (2½mls/4km N; bus: A hill covered in plum trees which blossom early in the year; at the top is a shrine, founded in the 8th c., and sacred to Susano o no Mikoto and his son Itakeru no Mikoto. Festivals: 3 and 4 February; 17 and 18 April.

2 *SHOSHA ZAN (5mls/8km NW; coach up to the summit, or on foot as far as the cablecar station). The Enkyo ji was built in a setting of forest and rock: this temple, once upon a time among the most revered in the western provinces, together with the one on Mount Hiei near Kyoto and the Daisen ji on the mountain of the same name (province of Tottori), was founded in 966 by the priest Shoku (910–1007).

➥ 4mls (7km) N, the little spa of Shioda.

3 IESHIMA SHOTO (13mls/21km SW; boat from Shikama) is a group of islets between Himeji and Shodo shima; Ie shima is the biggest, Nishi jima – rising to 906ft (276km) – the most picturesque.

4 AKASHI, AKO, TATSUNO, SETO NAIKAI NATIONAL PARK, see entries under these names.

■ Hirado shima*

Map of Kyushu (North), pp. 388–9.

Tokyo, 791mls (1,273km) – Fukuoka, 76mls (123km) – Nagasaki, 70mls (113km).

Nagasaki ken – 17km².

Most Europeans have heard of Hirado, the peaceful island which welcomed the 'Barbarians out of the South' and whose natural beauty led to its inclusion within the boundaries of the national park of Saikai.

THE PORTUGUESE AND THE SPANISH. In 1549, the Portuguese appeared in Hirado; but it was not until 1584, following the example of the Spanish, that they began a trading house, which allowed commerce between China and Japan, keeping a monopoly until 1641. In 1550 St Francis Xavier, expelled from Kagoshima, landed to a warm welcome in Hirado; from this island he set out for Kyoto on foot, to preach his message there – but he failed; Father Cosme de Torrès, who stayed on the island, was more successful. Shortly afterwards, the missionaries were deemed to be a harmful influence and banished from Japan (1597).

THE DUTCH AND THE ENGLISH. In 1609, with the consent of Tokugawa Ieyasu, a Dutch trade mission was set up in Hirado by Abraham Van den Broek. Richard Cocks and other Englishmen arrived in 1613 and it was on his arrival in Hirado that William Adams, the first Briton to settle in Japan (see Yokosuka) died in 1620. The arrival of these new Europeans offset, in the view of Ieyasu, the Portuguese influence; but he still went on in 1616 to restrict foreign establishments to Hirado and Nagasaki. Persecution of Christians also made life difficult for Europeans in Hirado; the Matsuura, rulers of the island, were converted for a while but then repressed Western beliefs: in 1640, the Dutch warehouses were destroyed and all houses bearing a date in years AD were demolished.

Things were not especially easy between the Europeans either, since their respective countries were often at war with one another. So it was that the English trade mission was besieged in 1618 by the Dutch, requiring Japanese intervention to restore law and order! The English were forced to leave the island in 1621, and took no further interest in Japan, preferring to turn their attention to India. As for the Dutch, in 1629 their trade mission came under the direction of François Caron, member of a French Calvinist family that had fled to the Netherlands. In 1641, he handed it over to M. Lemaire, who had to transfer the organization to Deshima (see Nagasaki), the only European base in Japan that remained open until the 19th c.: Caron offered his services to Colbert in India and died at sea off Lisbon on his way to France. He had published, in Dutch, a descriptive account of Japan as it was at that time. Nowadays, very little remains to remind us of those European traders, especially as the town was burned down in 1906.

The island is joined to the main island of Kyushu by a bridge that links it with the town of Hiradoguchi.

HIRADO (pop: 32,865), the capital of the island, lies sheltered in an inlet.

Miyuki bashi, S of the port, is an old stone bridge built in 1702; the Dutch and English establishments once stood nearby. To the E of this site, and dominating the whole S side of the harbour, is Kameoka Hill: attempts have been made to make a modern reconstruction of the Hirado Castle (keep with three storeys); nearby is a little shrine and, further down the hill, towards the port, the recently-built International House.

To the W and N, other hills are crowned with various monuments which you reach via enclosed paths and staircases, said to have been the work of the Dutch. One such path leads W to Chinese temples and a 19th-c. Catholic church.

■ The former residence of the Matsuura, who governed the island from the 11th to the 19th c., is nowadays a museum, with a collection of historical objects tracing the island's history and that of its rulers: Japanese, Chinese and European everyday objects and scientific, military, religious or purely artistic items; and in the garden a little teahouse, *kanun tei*.

Lastly, in the N there stands a monument to the memory of St Francis Xavier, who landed on the island in 1550.

The remainder of the island, with Yasuman dake (1,755ft/535m) as its highest point, may be crossed by coach as far as Cape Shijiki, right in the S (27mls/43km), from where you can look out over the Goto archipelago. We recommend, if you are going by car, driving back along the W coast, with its fine landscapes, more attractive than those facing the great island of Kyushu.

The island of Ikitsuki, to the NW of Hirado shima (boat from Nirado to Itsuki, 11mls/18km), is well worth a visit.

▰ Hiratsuka (Island of Honshu)

Map of the Vicinity of Tokyo, p. 565.

Tokyo, 34mls (55km) – Kofu, 76mls (122km) – Shizuoka, 81mls (130km) – Yokohama, 19mls (31km).

Kanagawa ken – pop: 163,671 – rubber industry, electrical goods, tobacco factories.

To the W of the estuary of the Sagami gawa, Hiratsuka is an industrial centre, facing Sagami Bay, along whose shores it is more usual to find tourist resorts. We think you will still find it an interesting area to visit.

VICINITY

1 OISO (2½mls/4km SW; coach: JNR train), a sizeable holiday and residential town which is reminiscent of Kamakura. You can still see the Shigitatsuan hermitage, where the famous poet and archer Saigyo Hoshi (1118–90) used to live; closer to our own time, Oiso is also the location of the villa, with a remarkable garden, where the post-war Prime Minister Yoshida Shigeru (1878–1967) lived and died.

½ml (1km) N: Shonandaira lookout (alt. 594ft/181m), with its view of Mount Hakone and Fuji san to the W, Sagami Bay to the S, and O yama to the N.

2 'TANZAWA OYAMA REGIONAL PARK (12mls/20km NW as far as O yama; coach from Hiratsuka or the Odakyu ER station in Isehara; then by funicular). This park of 65,098 acres (26,345ha), lying between the national parks of Fuji-Hakone-Izu and Chichibu-Tama, rises up to the peaks of Mounts Hiro (5,489ft/1,673m) and Tanzawa (5,141ft/1,567m); in it, the Sagami gawa begins. To the SE of the park, the O yama soars to 4,108ft (1,252m); the funicular will take you up to the major shrine of Afuri; the summit, where there is another subsidiary shrine, is a 1½ml (2km) walk further on.

◼ Hirosaki (Island of Honshu)*

Map of Tohoku, pp. 232-3.

Tokyo, 428mls (688km) - Akita, 96mls (155km) - Aomori, 25mls (40km) - Morioka, 108mls (17km).

Aomori ken - pop: 175,330 - alt. 131ft (40m) - state university.

At one end of the Tsugaru agricultural plain (rice and fruit trees), Hirosaki has grown up around a mighty feudal castle and is today one of the main economic centres of the Aomori province. To the NW stands Iwaki san, attracting numerous skiers and walkers.

The *Nebuta matsuri, similar to the one at Aomori, takes place between 1 and 7 August and is one of the most entertaining festivals in Japan.

It was not until the end of the 16th c. that the Oura family had asserted complete control over the Tsugaru region and received the name from Hideyoshi, with whom they had formed an alliance. In the early 17th c., Tsugaru Nobuhira (1586-1631) had the castle of Hirosaki built, in which his descendants were to live until the Meiji Restoration. Nobuhira had also adopted the Christian faith and in 1614 welcomed several Christians to Hirosaki, when the persecutions against their religion first began.

*Oyo koen (1½mls/2km NW of the station; bus) is on the site of the old castle, of which the moats, ramparts, and five gates still survive. The present keep was built in 1810, SE of the courtyard in which the previous one had stood (completed in 1611 and burned down in the early 19th c.); it now houses historical curiosities. Hirosaki jo, formerly one of Japan's major castles, is still famous today, but mainly on account of the blossoming of its remarkable cherry trees, at the end of April.

Among the various temples and shrines scattered throughout the town, we would draw your attention especially to the following:

Hirosaki hachiman gu (1½mls/2km N of the station);

Saisho in (1ml/1.5km W of the station), whose pagoda - 102ft (31m) high, with five storeys - was erected in 1648;

Chosho ji (2mls/3km W of the station) which was commissioned by the Tsugaru in 1629, and its tiered gate which contains the statues of the gohyaku Rakan (500).

VICINITY

1 OWANI ONSEN (8mls/13km SE by the N7; coach; JNR train; private railway from Chuo Hirosaki station). It is a hot spa famous for its apple orchards and a winter ski resort with ski slopes on Mount Araja (2,326ft/709m) which stands to the SE.

2 *IWAKI SAN (20mls/32km NW; coach). This extinct volcano, standing

at 5,331ft (1,625m), towers above the surrounding peaks; its conical shape has earned it the nickname of Tsugaru Fuji or Oku Fuji.

3½mls (6km): Oura; on the r. stands the site of the one-time castle of the Oura lords, who established themselves in Hirosaki and changed their name to Tsugaru.

7mls (12km): Road off r. in the direction of Takateru jinja, sacred to the first ancestor of the Tsugaru and three other deities; the front beams of the main building carry unique decorations.

9mls (15km): Hyakusawa Onsen; visit the sumptuous Iwakiyama shrine, founded in the 9th c. but bearing decorations added in the 17th, which have earned it the nickname of the Nikko of northern Honshu.

16mls (20km): Date Onsen, another spa at the foot of Iwaki san, which you ascend from this point; many possible walks in the surrounding area.

► 7mls (12km) S: Meya reservoir, at an alt. of 600ft (183m), in the midst of a forest zone, and downstream from the Ammon waterfall.

14mls (22km): The road carries on towards Nakamura gawa and meets the Sea of Japan at Ajigasawa (16mls/25km N), but we turn r. here along the Tsugaru-Iwaki toll road in order to make the ascent of the mountain (many hairpin bends).

20mls (32km): End of the road; a chair-lift leads to the top of Iwaki, where the little Okuyama shrine stands.

3 **JUNI KO** (59mls/95km W, partly by the N101; JNR train to Matsukami station, long route; coaches in summer). Travelling by car, you leave Hirosaki to the NW, keeping Iwaki san on the left.

20mls (32km): Ajigasawa, a little fishing port typical of those on Sea of Japan. Both road and rail hug the rocky coast from this point onwards; note the ledge on which stand Odose zaki and Todo jima.

43mls (69km): Fukaura used to be a good anchorage for the Sea of Japan. The N101 carries straight on along the Nakayama ridge; you are advised to follow the coast with its collection of reefs, sea caves and cliffs; you will pass the capes of Nyumae and Henashi, among others.

52mls (83km): Iwasaki, where we rejoin the N101.

55mls (89km): Matsukami, from where we take the road leading E to Juni ko.

↘ 59mls (95km): Juni ko (the 12 lakes); there are in fact more than 30, spread over the plateau and at an average altitude of between 500 and 800ft (150 and 250m). The Nippon Canyon, one of Japan's natural phenomena, is a part of the whole scene.

4 TOWADA HACHIMANTAI NATIONAL PARK, see entry under this name.

Hiroshima (Island of Honshu)**

Map of Shikoku (Inland Sea), pp. 536-7; street plan, p. 218.

Tokyo, 542mls (873km) - Matsue, 119mls (191km) - Okayama, 103mls (165km) - Yamaguchi, 88mls (141km).

Capital of Hiroshima ken - pop: 902,725 - industrial town: metallurgy, chemicals, textiles, foodstuffs, and port - state, regional and private universities offering all disciplines - cathedral town.

'The phoenix reborn from its ashes' is an expression which fits Hiroshima perfectly, a city immortalized by an attempt to destroy it, but a living, developing, daily growing city which astonishes you with its energy. No effort seems to have been spared to erase, in approximately 40 years, all the material signs of devastation. A traveller who comes here finds a town just like any other, except that the Park of Peace in the heart of the city acts as a reminder of that terrible morning in August 1945 which marked the beginning of a whole new age in the history of mankind. For the first time, a new kind of energy was used for military ends against a civilian population, with consequences for mankind and the environment which are not fully understood even today.

As you go round the museum, you may wish to reflect that the Hiroshima bomb was less powerful by a factor of several thousand than those in present-day arsenals.

The history of the town

RI JO. Between 1589 and 1593, Mori Terumoto (1553-1625), head of one of the most powerful families in the western provinces of Japan, built the so-called castle of the carp (Ri jo) on the big island (Hiro shima) in the estuary of the Ota gawa. But having fought at Sekigahara against the Tokugawa faction, Terumoto was unsuccessful in his bid to be pardoned by Ieyasu and had to become a monk; his son handed over Hiroshima Castle to Fukushima Masanori (1561-1624) and withdrew to Hagi Castle. In 1619, Asano Nagaakira (1582-1632) took control of Hiroshima and his family held it until 1868. The castle became the administrative headquarters of the Province of Hiroshima, and was eventually turned into administrative, and then military, offices when, during the Sino-Japanese War of 1894 and the Russo-Japanese War of 1904-05, Hiroshima, close to the naval base of Kure, became Japan's prime military base.

6 AUGUST 1945, 08h.15. The American aeroplane *Enola Gay* flew across Hiroshima and released an atom bomb above the town. The explosion annihilated everything over a radius of 2mls (3.5km) from the epicentre. It produced a thermal wave at 3,632°F (2,000°C); the sudden destruction of all life-forms; dreadful suffering; the growth afterwards of fearful keloids; a continual search for healing, thirst-

quenching water; crazed flight from the hell-hole that had been a city; the undreamt-of effects of radiation. Aid poured in to this nightmare world of beings so horribly mutilated that it was at first scarcely possible to tell the living from the dead. The appalling casualty figures, which it is only possible to guess at, added up to something like 200,000 deaths on and around 6 August. The figure has since risen to 300,000, for hundreds of people are continuing to die each year as a direct result of the bombing. The town suffered 92% damage, and 40% total destruction. The bomb which was dropped on Hiroshima, closely followed by the one that ravaged Nagasaki, played a decisive role in Japan's surrender in 1945.

The Americans made a large contribution to the initial disaster relief and, from 1949 onwards, to the reconstruction of the two cities, under the direction of the Japanese architect Tange Kenzo. Although the town now has a population larger than the pre-war figure and has once more become the most important metropolis in south-west Honshu (Chugoku), the terrible imprint remains and 'Japan bears on its body and in its soul the atomic scar; it is a wound which has never completely healed.' (Robert Guillain)

The dress designer Issey Miyake was born in Hiroshima in 1938.

Visiting the town

TWELVE HOURS IN HIROSHIMA. The delta of Ota gawa divides the town into several islands which are strung out towards the Bay of Hiroshima; they have been extended to the S by industrial zones and harbours, gradually reclaimed from the sea; there are also little age-old islets which today are public parkland. Tourist agencies rarely give over more than half a day to visiting the town; they will show you the Shukkei en, give you a glimpse of the castle, whisk you up Hiji yama for a view of the town, then back down along the Peace Boulevard to the Peace Memorial Park, whose museum represents the last sad port of call.

A WALK THROUGH THE TOWN. Hiroshima is one of those rare Japanese towns which you can cover on foot without getting too tired; its centres of interest are gathered around Peace Bd and the Hon dori quarter, to the N of which you may visit the Cathedral of Peace, the Shukkei en and the castle. To the W, wander across the Peace Memorial Park and go to the museum. It is a harrowing but compelling demonstration of the horror and stupidity of war in its most atrocious form; don't miss it. Finally, you can walk along Peace Bd to Hiji yama.

If you like Japanese gardens, do go to the Shukkei en, one of the most beautiful in all of Japan.

'SHUKKEI EN (plan: B1; 770yds/700m W of the station; address: Kami Nobori cho; open daily from 09.00 to 18.00, April to September, and from 09.00 to 17.00, October to March; closed from 29 December to 3 January). Lying to the S of the Kanda gawa, this garden of 48,000 sq. yds (40,000 m²), planted in 1620, was the isolated dwelling-place of

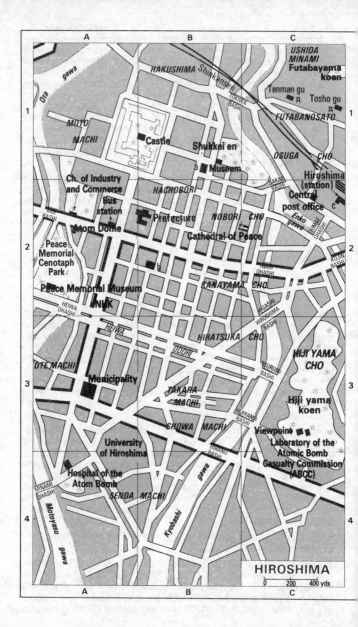

HIROSHIMA

Asano Nagaakira; his family donated it to the municipality in 1940.

Destroyed in 1945, it was opened again in 1951, and has regained its former splendour, with its lake dotted with islands, its Chinese-style hump-back bridge of Koko kyo, and its teahouses, including the Seifu pavilion. The miniature landscape-garden (*shukkei*) is in the shape of the 'western lake', Si Huon, which used to lie on the W of the former Song capital of China, Hangzhou.

▣ To the W of the garden, practically opposite the Hiroshima Town Hall, stands the regional Art Gallery (880yds/800m W of the station; Kami Nobori cho, 2-22; open daily from 09.00 to 17.00 except Wednesdays); this modern museum building (1968) has a wealth of permanent exhibits: calligraphy, porcelain, sculpture, contemporary Japanese painting (works by Maruki Suma, Kodama Kibo, Satomi Umrei) and some Western painting; frequent visiting exhibitions are also held there.

✝ Approx 330yds (300)m SE of the Shukkei stands the Memorial Cathedral of Peace (plan: C2), built in 1954 by the Japanese architect Murano Togo with the help of international funds and on the initiative of the German priest Hugo Lassalle; the organ pipes were a gift of the city of Cologne, the bells from Bochum.

▟ **HIROSHIMA JO** (plan: B1; 1ml/1.5km W of the station; open daily from 09.00 to 17.30 from April to September, and to 16.30 from October to March; closed from 29 December to 2 January). The castle, built by Mori Terumoto in the late 16th c. (see The history of the town), was annihilated by the bomb and restored to its original state in 1958.

The five-storey keep is typical of its original period; nowadays it houses a museum of Hiroshima and district. You will note various art objects, ancient pottery, armour, maps, manuscripts, botanical and mineral collections, etc. From the top there is a good view of the town and its surrounding area.

PEACE MEMORIAL PARK (plan: A2, 1½mls/2km SW of the station; bus). At the northernmost point of Nakajima, between the Hon and Motoyasu rivers, this park occupies a site that was once the town centre of Hiroshima, completely devastated by the atomic explosion. Along an axis stretching away from the Atom Dome stands a line of monuments comprising the Peace Flame, the Cenotaph, the Peace Memorial Museum, the Prayer Fountain and the statue of the Mother and Child in the Storm. Other monuments, some of them very moving, are scattered throughout the park.

The Atom Dome is in fact the skeleton of what used to be the Chamber of Industry and Commerce, the only building even partially to withstand the force of the explosion, preserved as a testimony to events.

The Cenotaph, and behind it the monument of the Peace Flame, were designed by Tange Kenzo in 1952. A brief inscription, 'Rest in peace, that the same mistake never be made again', has been cut into the Cenotaph, which also lists the names of the known victims, the number of whom rises anually.

■ The Peace Memorial Museum (plan: A2; 1–3, Nakajima cho; open daily from 09.00 to 16.30 except between 29 December and 2 January; talking guidebooks available in English). Also built by Tange it is raised up on stout piles. We leave you to ponder the meaning of this visit which is a most distressing evocation; it ends with a film shown in a separate building close to the museum.

To the S of the Peace Memorial Park, the 2ml (3km) Peace Bd goes right through the town centre.

HIJI YAMA (plan: C3; 1ml/1.5km S of the station; bus). This hill rises to the E of the Kyobashi gawa, at the far end of the Peace Bd. From a height of 233ft (71m) it overlooks the whole town, with a view stretching away as far as the docks and the islands of the Inland Sea.

On this hill stand the buildings of the Atomic Bomb Casualty Commission (ABCC); it offers specialist care and research.

☞ VICINITY

1···ITSUKU-SHIMA (14mls/22km SW by the N2 or expressway; coach; JNR or Hiroshima ER train to Miyajimaguchi, then ferry; boat from the port of Ujina; half-day excursion from Hiroshima, with an English-speaking guide). An unforgettable area, one of the most beautiful sights Japan has to offer, Itsuku-shima or Miya jima's main attraction is its 'floating' shrine, supported on stilts, which is cut off from land at high tide; out to sea there is a wooden *torii*, making a composition typical of the Far East and one of the best known of Japan's romantic faces. The island of Itsuku, with an area of approx. 12sq. mls (30km²), far from industrial Japan and a favourite place of the nature-loving Japanese, is among the three greatest such locations in the land, along with Amano Hashidate and Matsushima.

Leave Hiroshima and head SW.

12mls (19km): Miyajimaguchi; from here, board the boat for the island of Itsuku.

➜ 9mls (14km) SW: vast industrial complex (petrochemicals) and harbour of Otaki-Iwakuni.

14mls (22km): Miyajima. The Great Shrine of Itsuku-shima stands approx. 330yds (300m) W of the landing-stage.

AN ISLAND OF PURITY. There is no cemetery on Itsuku-shima, the dead being buried in Ono on the opposite shore. Until the Meiji Restoration, it was forbidden for anyone at all to be born or to die on the sacred island: 'The remnant of a very old Japanese superstition which has subsequently disappeared, according to which death, the consummation of a marriage, and childbirth were considered impure events' (Fosco Maraini).

Dogs, too, are banished from the island, but numerous deer live there in the wild. They are extraordinarily greedy, and calmly gobble up everything that tourists leave in litter-bins. It must be said that in summer Miyajima loses something of its tranquillity as a result of the influx of travellers on ferries and hovercraft. But at nightfall, there remain only a few lucky visitors to the isolated *ryokans* on the island. After dinner, they walk in their *yukata* to the illuminated *torii*, following a path marked out by glowing stone lanterns. At this time of the day, serenity returns to the temple grounds, where all that can be heard is the splashing of the waves against the wooden pilings. It is worth staying at least one night in Miyajima, in order to taste the magic of the place when quiet returns to it.

Once you have passed the great *torii* (1875), which emerges from the water at low tide, you come to the **Great Shrine, set in a little bay; the various parts which make up the whole are interconnected by covered walkways set on pilings.

In the centre stands the main shrine, comprising the traditional rooms for prayer (Hai den), offerings (Hei den), and the main hall (Hon den); in an open space stands the platform on which sacred Shinto dances (*bugaku and kagura*) sometimes take place; along the same axis, out to sea, stands the *torii*.

To the NE of the Great Shrine is the Marodo shrine, set out in the same fashion, and where the first ceremonies take place. To the S are buildings in which Noh dramas are staged; built in 1568, but reconstructed during the Edo period, they constitute the oldest Noh theatre still in existence in Japan. Further back, note the Sori bashi, with many arches.

*Kangen sai, the festival of music, takes place yearly around mid-July in the shrine; with its night-time parade of boats on the water and the lighting of countless lanterns in the shrine, it is one of the most highly-regarded of such events in Japan.

Coming back SW onto dry land, and crossing the river Mitarashi, you leave behind you on the r. the Daigan ji (founded in 802), and come to the treasure house (or museum) built in 1934. It contains, among other items, rich *sutras (Heike no kyo) presented by the Taira (Heike), rare examples of painted scrolls from the Heian period (12th c.) – the decoration of the case containing them is attributed to Tawaraya Sotatsu – and there is also on show a small portable Buddhist reliquary, and 400 other articles (fans, armour, porcelain, Noh masks, religious objects, lacquerware, etc.). Behind the museum stands the Tahoto (pagoda).

Going round to the SE of the shrine, you can climb the hill which rises in the N to the *Senjo kaku ('hall of a thousand tatami'), a fine wooden building, said to have been made in its entirety from a single camphor tree; it was endowed by Toyotomi Hideyoshi in 1587 for the shrine of Itsuku shima. Next to it, a five-storey pagoda, built in 1407, maintains a collection of interesting paintings.

The rest of the island is covered in rocks and forests in which around 1,400 different species of plants grow. Mount Misen (1,736ft/529m) overlooks the whole area. You may reach the top in 50 min. by the cable-car from just behind the Momijidani park. Anyone prone to vertigo is bound to suffer somewhat during the ascent, but the view from the cars swaying high above the valley full of maples is worth a little nervousness; it is quite astonishing. Once at the top, you will be able to enjoy an extraordinary panoramic view of the island itself and of the Bay of Hiroshima. It is possible to walk back down to where you set off, but keep an eye open for the monkeys that live hereabouts: generally grouped together near the mountain top, they are expert thieves, with a particular penchant for glasses and cameras. On your way down, stop off at the Gumonji-do, founded in the 9th c. by Kobo Daishi on his return from China.

Another pleasing feature of the island is the beaches, of which there are several very pleasant ones, strikingly clean (which is not always the case on the Inland Sea).

2 KURE (19mls/30km SE; JNR train; coach; boat). A toll road along the coast links Hiroshima with Kure, complete with lovely views, especially of Eta jima.

19mls (30km): Kure, see entry under this name.

3 NISHI CHUGOKU SANCHI NATURE PARK (50mls/81km NW to Sandankyo, by the N54 and N191; coach; JNR train to Sandankyo).

Set in the Chugoku mountains (highest peaks Juppo zan, at 4,327ft/1,319m and Kammuri yama at 4,393ft/1,339m), this park makes a pretty destination for a walk from Hiroshima.

The road, and also the railway, follow the Ota gawa almost the whole way.

28mls (45km): road off r., 7mls (11km) SW to the little spa of Yuki.

40 mls (64km): The N186 branches off l., heading for Yoshiwa (11mls/18km SW), where you may begin the ascent of Kammuri kogen.

50mls (81km): Sandankyo; giving access to the *Sandan gorges (3mls/5km NW), via the upper course of the Ota gawa.

➜ 16mls (26km) NW by the N181 (coach), further upstream is the Tarutoko dam; the road follows the shores of this artificial lake; the source of the Ota gawa is only a few miles away.

4 IWAKUNI NATIONAL PARK OF SETO NAIKAI, see entries under these names.

■ Hita (Island of Kyushu)

Map of Kyushu (North), pp. 388–9.

Tokyo, 736mls (1,185km) – Fukuoka, 52mls (83km) – Kumamoto, 72mls (116km) – Miyazaki, 190mls (306km) – Oita, 57mls (91km).

Oita ken – pop: 64,866 – woodworking.

On the upper course of the Mikuma gawa, Hita is an old market town with narrow streets lined by ancient houses. It will appeal especially to anyone wishing to explore the regional park of Yaba-Hita-Hikosan.

From Hita, you will enjoy a trip (in summer, from June to October) down the rapids of the Mikuma gawa as far as Arase (8mls/13km NW downriver); it takes about 2 hours to do the journey on foot.

VICINITY

1 TSUETATE ONSEN (21mls/33km S by the N212; coach). A small spa, which you reach by travelling along the extremely pretty course of the Oyama gawa.

2 *YABA-HITA-HIKOSAN REGIONAL PARK (50mls/81km round trip, following the itinerary suggested; coaches all the way: JNR train from Kusa to Hita; coach trips to Hiko san from Fukuoka or Kitakyushu, and to Yabakei from Beppu). This park, with an area of 268,867 acres (108,809ha), is notable for its valley gorges, with their extraordinary rock formations and lush vegetation.

From Hita, drive along the N212 NE towards Nakatsu.

11mls (18km): Morizane Onsen; from here, the road leads down the gorges of the Yamakuni gawa.

14mls (22km) NW: Kaneno torii (by coach from the JNR station in Hikosan) stands 2½mls (4km) away from the Hiko-san shrine at the top of the extinct volcanic peak (3,937ft/1,200m), founded at the end of the 7th c. by En no Ozanu, and one of the oldest on Kyushu; it was a major centre for Buddhist pilgrims from the 16th c. onwards, but Shintoism took over again from 1868.

20mls (32km): Yabakei, in the middle of the *Yamakuni gawa gorges, which were immortalized by the poet Sanyo Rai (1780-1832).

6mls (10km) NE: Hon Yabakei, downriver from the gorges; the road goes through a tunnel close to a mountain path, supposedly dug in 30 years by the Buddhist monk Zenkai. From this point, one of the valleys of the Yaba kei group leads off to the SE, where we find the little temple of Rakan ji (chair-lift for access), founded in 645 and clinging to the rock-face.

From Yabakei, the *Shin Yaba kei valley rises to the SE; it is one of the prettiest in the region; note especially the beauties of Hitome Hakkei and Utsukushi dani.

25mls (41km); Shigina Onsen, at the top of the valley.

34mls (55km): Minami Yaba kei, another group of gorges facing the slopes of the Mikuma gawa.

36mls (58km): Kusa, where we rejoin the N210 and the railway, running parallel with the upper valley of the Mikuma gawa.

43mls (69km): Amagase Onsen, a pleasant resort upriver from Hita.

50mls (81km): Hita.

3 ASO NATIONAL PARK, see entry under this name.

Hitachi (Island of Honshu)

Tokyo, 93mls (150km) – Chiba, 94mls (151km) – Fukushima, 112mls (180km) – Mito, 24mls (39km) – Urawa, 109mls (176km) – Utsunomiya, 70mls (112km).

Ibaraki ken – pop: 204,596 – copper mines and processing plants, cement works, petrochemicals.

Set on the Pacific coast, the town is the birthplace and main centre of operations for the big metal company that bears its name. The copper mines in the area supply the main manufacturers in Japan. The Tokai nuclear power station is also close by.

The poet Okubo Shibutsu (1767–1837) was born in Hitachi.

VICINITY

TOKAI (12mls/20km S; coach; not open to visitors) is the location, close to the sea, of the Japanese Institute of Atomic Energy Research, occupying some 855 acres (346ha). A laboratory was set up here in 1956, despite protests, and the first American atomic reactor, using raw uranium and heavy water, was brought into service in 1957. Since 1965, a Calder Hall type of reactor has been in use, with a maximum power of 166,000 kW. Tokai is still Japan's main centre of nuclear energy.

Hitoyoshi (Island of Kyushu)

Railway map on inside front cover.

Tokyo, 846mls (1,361km) – Fukuoka, 131mls (211km) – Kagoshima, 70mls (113km) – Kumamoto, 62mls (99km) – Miyazaki, 79mls (127km) – Oita, 183mls (294).

Kumamoto ken – pop: 42,196.

On the upper course of the Kuma gawa, Hitoyoshi proudly calls itself the Kyoto of the Island of Kyushu. It is also a spa, whose alkaline springs, with temperatures between 109° and 118°F (43° and 48°C), are prized for their beneficial healing and anti-rheumatic properties. Places to visit:

The shrine of Aoi Aso (550yds/500m S of the station), which was built in 1611.

 Hitoyoshi Castle (1ml/1.5km SE of the station; bus). There remain now only ruins standing in the middle of a park. From the 13th to the 19th c., it was the residence of the Sagara daimyo, descendants of the Fujiwara.

☞ **VICINITY**

1 'SHOOTING THE KUMA GAWA RAPIDS (from April to October; boarding-stage close to Hitoyoshi Castle; return by train or coach). The journey takes about 2h.30, covering a distance of 11mls (18km) as far as Osakama and is, thanks to its difficult passes, one of the most famous in all Japan. On the way you pass the Konose grotto.

2 YUYAMA ONSEN (24mls/39km NE; JNR train to Yunomae station). Little spa town near the Ichifusa reservoir (well upstream on the Kuma gawa), overlooked to the E by Ichifusa yama (5,650ft/1,722m) and, further N, by Eshiro yama (5,272ft/1,607m).

3 KIRISHIMA-YAKU NATIONAL PARK: see entry under this name.

Hokkaido (Island of)

30,317sq. mls (78,521km²) - pop: 5,576,000.

Hokkaido became world-famous when its capital, Sapporo, hosted the Winter Olympics in 1972. Although industrialization has begun to make itself felt (in Sapporo, for example, and Hakodate or Asahikawa), the island has remained a paradise for winter sports. But the beauty of its scenery and the coolness of its climate when everywhere else is scorched by the heat of summer, mean that its summer season, too, looks set to enjoy a boom, especially since the famous rail tunnel (1984) linking it with Honshu brings the Shinkansen to Sapporo.

Your journey to Hokkaido

HOW TO GET THERE. Japan Airlines runs a frequent service to Sapporo, departing from Tokyo (a dozen flights a day) or from Osaka. The domestic company TDA also operates from Tokyo to Sapporo, Hakodate, Memanbetsu, Obihiro, Kushiro and Asahikawa. The domestic airline ANA flies to Sapporo from Tokyo, Sendai, Nagoya, Niigata, Komatsu and Osaka; to Hakodate from Tokyo and Nagoya; and to Kushiro from Tokyo. The journey by rail is long - about 13 hours by 'express' - despite the extension of the Shinkansen as far as Morioka; so it's advisable to travel at night in a sleeper or couchette. Nevertheless, crossing from Aomori to Hakodate is still an experience.

TRANSPORT ON HOKKAIDO. To travel around the island, we would recommend the use of railways (your Japan Rail Pass is valid everywhere), making connections, especially across national parks, by bus (Akan Bus, for example). Possibly you will have time enough to enjoy long bicycle treks (you can hire a bike from the Akan Bus company); if, on the contrary, you're pressed for time, the domestic flights operated by TDA between Sapporo and Asahikawa, Kushiro, Obihiro and Memanbetsu might suit your better, or indeed a flight with the local company, Nihon Kinkyori-Koku, which serves the islands of Okushiri, Rishiri and Rebun as well as Wakkanai and Nakashibetsu.

Hokkaido for the tourist

WHAT TO SEE ON HOKKAIDO. There are not very many sites of historical and artistic interest on Hokkaido. Still, you may find the castles of Matsumae and Hakodate (Goryokaku) fascinating places; even more so the Ainu villages, of which the most compelling is Shiraoi (14mls/22km from Tomakomai).

On the other hand, the national parks will not fail to impress you with the almost untouched beauty of their scenery, their floral life, their volcanoes (sometimes barely projecting above ground, like Showa Shinzan), and the habitat they provide for wildlife, especially birds.

Finally, if you are in Japan during the winter, you may be able to see the sea frozen over, to the N of the island, just off Abashiri, for example; and don't miss the snow festival in Sapporo.

SUGGESTED ROUTE FOR A ROUND TRIP. Three days, five days, seven? It all depends on your interest in nature, because that is what is mainly on offer on Hokkaido.

SEVEN-DAY PROGRAMME (1,027mls/1,652km; stopover points widely spaced).

1st day: Hakodate-Matsumae (58mls/93km); explore Hakodate in the morning, then take a train to Matsumae (visit the castle).

2nd day: Matsumae-Noboribetsu (191mls/308km); cross the Oshima peninsula by bus via Esashi, travelling as far as Onuma or Onuma koen, set in pretty lakeland; then continue by rail to Noboribetsu (bus to the spa).

3rd day: Noboribetsu-Sapporo (153mls/246km); tricky stage of the journey; train or bus to the town of Tomakomai, with a stop at the Ainu village of Shiraoi; then catch a series of coaches that will take you as far as Yoichi or Otaru, via Shikotsu-ko, Kutchan, Iwanai, Furubira and the remarkable Shakotan peninsula; lastly, a train will take you on to Sapporo, and you may wish to make a detour via the spa town of Jozankei.

4th day: Sapporo-Soun-kyo (129mls/207km); devote your morning to Sapporo, then take a train to Asahikawa, where you should catch a bus for Soun-kyo.

5th day: Soun-kyo-Abashiri (134mls/215km); a bus will take you via the superb Soun-kyo pass to Rubeshibe; from there, take a bus or train to Yubetsu; then another train, skirting the shores of the Saroma and Notoro lagoons, finally reaching lake Abashiri and the town of the same name.

6th day: Abashiri-Kushiro (145mls/233km); by train to Bihoro, then a coach connection (Akan Bus) which will carry you past the Kussharo, Mashu and Akan lakes, arriving in Kushiro in the evening.

7th day: Kushiro-Sapporo (281mls/452km); the longest stage of the journey; catch an early train and change at Obihiro for Hiroo; from there, a coach will take you to Samani station via Cape Erimo. Finally, on to Tomakomai and then Sapporo.

Getting to know Hokkaido

GEOGRAPHICAL FEATURES. The great northern island of Japan is divided from Honshu only by the Strait of Tsugaru; it is surrounded by the Pacific Ocean, the Sea of Japan and the Sea of Okhotsk. To the S, the mountains of Honshu are broken up by the Oshima peninsula; two more parallel mountain ranges run from the N of the island to the S, crossing the volcanic region of Chishima in the centre of the island; an archipelago of the same name extends NE off shore. The Daisetsuzan Mountains form the spine of the island, with their highest point right in the middle (Asahi dake, 7,513ft/2,290m). Between the mountains lie river plains: the one through which the Ishikari gawa (river 267mls/430km long) runs is the biggest in Japan.

Here you will find, as throughout the country, a patchwork of paddyfields but, unique to Hokkaido, vegetable and cereal crops are also grown on dry land: mechanization has been a great help to farmers, and they have even begun to raise livestock in the fields. Still, some 75% of the island is covered with woodland (mainly deciduous trees in the S and conifers in the N) where brown bears live, as well as sables and Asian pheasants, etc.

Weather conditions are on the whole harsh; although the island lies on similar latitudes to the south of France, snow persists from September to May, and Siberian winds keep the temperature in the Asahikawa basin as low as -22° F (-30° C). It is for this reason that the population of Hokkaido, the last of the Japanese islands to be inhabited, is less dense than anywhere else in Japan (183 inhabitants per sq. ml/71per km^2); young and energetic, this population is concentrated mainly in and around the industrial and shipping centres. Fishing occupies a very important place in the economy of Hokkaido; the island can claim the four busiest fishing ports in Japan. As for industry, it is supplied by a subsoil rich in minerals, especially in the W part of the island (coal and petroleum). Hokkaido looks set to enjoy a rich future, with the rail link under the sea to Honshu and the expansion of the industrial ports of Muroran and Tomakomai, not to mention the urban development of Sapporo, the island's capital, or of Asahikawa, the most northerly of Japan's big trade centres.

THE AINU. Hokkaido used to be inhabited by a native population, the Ainu, racially different from the rest of the Japanese, who called them Ebisu or Ezo. Possessing a language and customs of their own, they divided their time between fishing and agriculture, which they doubtless inherited from the Jomon period. Once also settled in the northern part of Honshu, they were gradually pushed out and, confined to Hokkaido, they slowly died out. There are no more than about 10,000 of their descendants alive today, and they have been assimilated into Japanese society. A few of them struggle to maintain the traditions and crafts which distinguish their inherited culture.

THE HISTORY OF HOKKAIDO. The first mention of Hokkaido goes back to the 7th c., when Abe Hirafu defeated the Ainu on their own island and set up trading posts there. Later, the island became the home of the

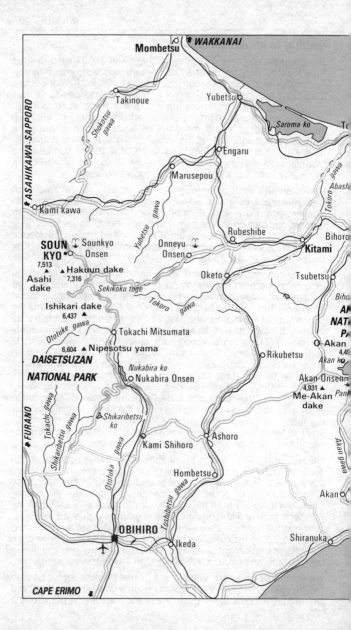

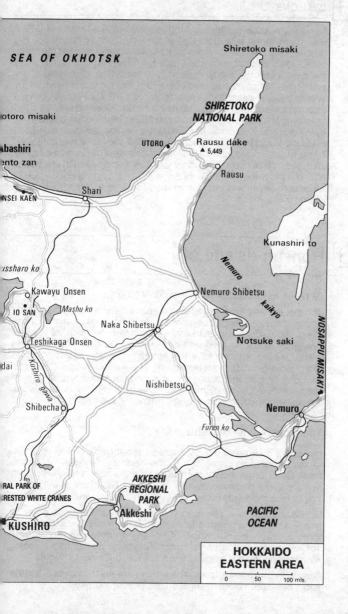

SEA OF OKHOTSK

Shiretoko misaki

SHIRETOKO
NATIONAL PARK

otoro misaki

UTORO ● Rausu dake
▲ 5,449

Abashiri

ento zan

Rausu

NSEI KAEN

Shari

Kunashiri to

ussharo ko

Kawayu Onsen

Nemuro Shibetsu

Nemuro kaikyo

IO SAN Mashu ko

Naka Shibetsu

Notsuke saki

Teshikaga Onsen

dai Kushiro gawa

Nishibetsu

NOSAPPU MISAKI

Shibecha

Nemuro

Furen ko

RAL PARK OF
RESTED WHITE CRANES

AKKESHI
REGIONAL
PARK

KUSHIRO

Akkeshi

PACIFIC
OCEAN

**HOKKAIDO
EASTERN AREA**

0   50   100 mls

fallen Fujiwara, and after the Ainu rebellion of Koshamain (1457), it was once more subjugated, this time by Takeda Nobuhiro. His descendants built their residence in Matsumae and adopted the name of the town as their own; they took the Ainu into their service and there were several revolts, especially in the 18th c. It was also at the end of the 18th c., and the start of the 19th, that the island received the first of several visits from Westerners. In 1787 La Pérouse passed through the strait which now bears his name, between Hokkaido and Sakhalin; after several Russian expeditions had landed in Nemuro, Hakodate and Kunashiri, the Tokugawa regime decided in 1812 to place the island under its direct rule. In 1855, the island was colonized by the armed forces, and in 1869 its former name of Ezo was officially changed to Hokkaido. The same year saw the creation in Hakodate, after the short-lived republic of Enomoto, of a colonial commision or *kaitakushi*, which was transferred two years later to Sapporo, the new capital of the island.

H Honshu (Island of)

89,120sq. mls (230,822km²) - pop: 93,247,000.

Honshu, the very heart of Japan, the spot where its history began and where its most prestigious achievements have taken place, today offers its visitors the starkest of contrasts between an almost Orwellian industrial modernization in endless and often faceless towns, and the majesty of the holy Mount Fuji, some perfect examples of the temple-builder's art (especially in Nara and Kyoto), the gentle harmony of gardens as orderly as a musical score, and scenes as beautiful as Ise or as painful and moving as Hiroshima. In a word, Japan, with all its traditions and learning, is summed up in this one island.

Your journey to Honshu

TRANSPORT ON HONSHU. For information about travel on Honshu, turn to the appropriate paragraph in the 'Your journey' section of this book. Don't forget that there are 30 or so airports, served by JAL or the two Japanese domestic airlines (ANA and TDA), which will enable you to take short cuts on some of the routes if you wish.

Similarly, there is a very dense network of railway lines covering nearly all of the suggested itineraries. The famous Shinkansen runs through practically the whole of Honshu, from Morioka in the N to Tokyo-Omiya, and then on from Tokyo to Shimonoseki, facing Kyushu, and there is also the line from Tokyo-Omiya to Niigata.

Finally, in those few places where there are no trains, you'll always find a bus to complete the final stages of your journey.

Honshu for the tourist

WHAT TO SEE ON HONSHU. It's tempting simply to say 'everything', because here you will find the whole of Japan, ancient and modern. The Island of Honshu by itself makes your trip to Japan worthwhile: you could almost say the same even of some of its individual provinces (Kinki, for example). At any rate, you really need at least three weeks to see it properly – more if you're intending to combine your stay with visits to the adjacent islands. Whatever you decide, there can be little doubt that central Japan will occupy most of your time and attention, for it is the very birthplace of Japanese life.

SUGGESTED ROUND TRIPS. A complete voyage of Honshu could be divided along the lines of the four itineraries suggested below, each of them containing the major places of interest in the four great provinces: Tohoku, Kanto, Chubu and Kinki (see the maps, pp. 74–5).

1 SEVEN-DAY PROGRAMME IN TOHOKU (943mls/1,517km)

1st day: Sendai-Fukushima (112mls/180km); take a train to Yamagata (JNR, Senzai line), then go by coach via the Zao Echo line to Fukushima; a very interesting journey, especially in winter.

2nd day: Fukushima-Niigata (157mls/252km); very enjoyable coach trip as far as Inawashiro or Aizu-Wakamatsu (castle) through the Bandai National Park, via Azuma yama, Azuma Skyline and Bandai Gold line; finally, proceed by train to Niigata.

3rd day: Niigata-Akita (160mls/257km); direct train link (JNR) via Tsuruoka, from which point you may take a detour to the foot of Mount Gassan (50mls/80km there and back).

4th day: Akita-Hirosaki (99mls/159km) by train; you might like to include a detour to the Oga peninsula, but it's quite tricky to fit in unless you have half a day available.

5th and 6th days: Hirosaki-Kesennuma (289mls/465km) via Morioka, following the route indicated in the 30-day programme (see pp. 77–8), 26th and 27th days, from Hirosaki.

7th day: Kesennuma-Matsushima (121mls/194km); follow the 30-day programme as above, 28th day to the Chuson ji. From Ichinoseki you can take a coach to Ishinomaki and from there continue by train to Matsushima, and finally back to Sendai.

2 EIGHT-DAY PROGRAMME IN KANTO (819mls/1,318km)

1st day: Tokyo-Choshi (186mls/300km); if you take a trip round the Boso peninsula, take a JNR train from Tokyo by the Uchibo and Sotobo lines.

2nd day: Choshi-Mito (95mls/153km); the best idea is to make a detour via Narita, to visit the Shinsho ji there; then take the train again as far as Sawara (Katori jingu), and cross the Tone-gawa by bus to get to Kashima-jingu. Next go through the Suigo region to Mito, where you should visit the Kairaku-en gardens.

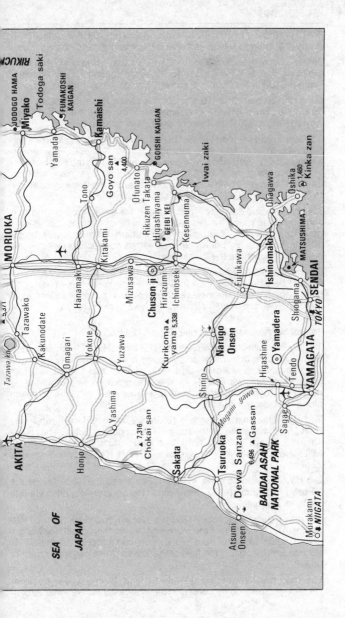

3rd day: Mito-Nikko (65mls/105km); catch a bus to Utsunomiya, then go by JNR train to Nikko, and spend the afternoon looking round.

4th day: Nikko-Kusatsu (80mls/128km); an interesting coach trip from the Nikko National Park to the Joshin-Etsu-Kogen Park, via Numata. From the spa in Kusatsu, you can slip down to the Shiga-Kogen.

5th day: Kusatsu-Kofu (99mls/160km); coach to Onioshidashi, with its jumble of lava-flows from Asama yama; the on to the high-altitude spot of Karuizawa, then Komoro and finally to Kofu by train.

6th day: Kofu-Hakone (116mls/187km); this stage of the journey will take you round Fuji san but not to the summit. First go to Kawaguchiko, from where you can go round four of the Fuji lakes on the N face, then the W face by coach to Fujinomiya; next, take the train to Gotemba, another coach to Gora, and from there by cablecar to Togendai and finally cross Ashino-ko by boat.

7th day: Hakone-Atami (107mls/172km); we would recommend that you take a trip round the Izu peninsula as far as Shimoda, or at least go by coach across its Amagi mountain chain. From Shimoda, take a train to Ito, then continue your trek with a connection to Atami, or else take a coach via the Izu skyline.

8th day: Atami-Kamakura (70mls/113km); go straight to Odawara (castle) by Shinkansen, then to Shin-Yokohama (Sankei-en garden), before going back to Kamakura where you will spend the latter part of the day; there are frequent trains from here back to Tokyo.

3 SEVEN-DAY PROGRAMME IN CHUBU (895mls/1,440km)

1st day: Nagoya-Hamamatsu (97mls/156km); take a Meitetsu train as far as Mihama, then carry on by coach (or go all the way by coach from Nagoya) to Morozaki on the tip of the Chita peninsula. From here, cross Mikawa Bay by boat to Irako misaki and continue by coach to Toyohashi; from there to Hamamatsu by JNR or coach along the Hamana lagoon.

2nd day: Hamamatsu-Nagano (219mls/352km); a long journey by train (JNR), travelling up the superb Tenryu gorges (Iida line) as far as Tatsuno, where you will have to change trains before you get to Matsumoto and its fascinating castle. While in Nagano, don't miss the Zenko ji.

3rd day: Nagano-Toyama (81mls/135km); see the 18th day of the 30-day programme (p. 73), travelling in the opposite direction via Tate yama to Toyama.

4th day: Toyama-Kanazawa (203mls/326km); round trip of the Noto peninsula; take a train in the morning to Himi, then coach for Nanao; coach again to Suzu from where you can proceed to Hakui via Wajima, still by cocah; the final stage to Kanazawa can be by train or coach.

5th day: Kanazawa-Fukui (63mls/101km); having seen the Ken-rokuen, you may go by coach to Katsuyama via the National Park of

Hakusan; then use the Keifuku Railway as far as Fukui, with a detour via Eihei-ji.

6th day: Fukui-Takayama (112mls/180km); coach trip via Ono, the Hida mountains, and the Shiragawago area.

7th day: Takayama-Nagoya (118mls/190km); after quickly looking round Takayama, go by JNR (Takayama line) to Gifu; you may leave the train at Mino Ota in order to follow the Kiso gawa rapids down as far as Inuyama, then pick it up again for Gifu and finally catch another train to Nagoya.

4 TEN-DAY PROGRAMME IN KINKI (746mls/1,202km)

1st day: Osaka-Kyoto (53mls/85km).

2nd and 3rd days; Kyoto; give it as much time as you can spare and see if you can't also fit in a visit to Hiei-zan.

4th day: Kyoto-Tottori (129mls/207km); go by JNR to Fukuchiyama (San In main line) or Wadayama, continuing by coach to Tottori.

5th day: Tottori-Hikone (211mls/340km); the longest stage of the journey, by train via Amano Hashidate; change at Toyooka and Tsuruga.

6th day: Hikone-Iseshima (101mls/162km); Omi railway to Kibukawa, then JNR to Ise, where there are shrines well worth the visit. Afternoon in Toba.

7th day: Iseshima-Nachi Katsuura (104mls/168km); change trains at Taki; enjoy a trip round Doro Hatcho from Shingu.

8th day: Nachi Katsuura-Wakayama (117/189km); devote the morning to Nachi, with its waterfall, the Kumano shrine and the Seiganto-ji; in the afternoon, try a trip to the Shirahama spa.

9th day: Wakayama-Koya san (41mls/66km); Wakayama Castle in the morning; remember to change trains at Hashimoto for Koya san, if you wish to spend the night there, or else go back to Osaka.

10th day: Koya san-Osaka (40mls/65km); take the Nankai Railroad back to Osaka; spend the rest of the day there, or make a stop in Sakai on the way.

Getting to know Honshu

GEOGRAPHICAL FEATURES. Honshu, or Hondo, the largest of the Japanese islands, stretches for over 870mls (1,400km) between the Sea of Japan and the Pacific Ocean, as if to form a bridge between the islands of Hokkaido in the north and Kyushu in the south. Two mountainous volcanic regions – Hakusan to the SW and Chokai to the NE – run from one tip of the island to the other. In the widest part of Honshu (186mls/300km as the crow flies) these volcanic regions lie opposite the Fossa Magna which runs up from the Bonin archipelago (Ogasawara) and raises along a N-S axis the main central caps of the Japan Alps (see entry under this name) whose highest peaks are here, including Fuji san, the highest of all at 12,388ft (3,776m). Some narrow river basins also feature in the landscape, as do coastal plains; of these, the Kanto (Tokyo area) and Nobi (Nagoya) are the principal ones; rice-growing is of paramount importance on the island, and apart from fruit-farming and a few other rare exceptions, the rice crop covers the whole of the island up to the lower mountain slopes. Forests are still widespread and provide abundant resources. Natural conditions are generally hard on Honshu, with earthquake, volcano and climate all threatening the production of crops and the safety of the people; the mountain ranges of the centre have pushed much of the population into the coastal areas, where shoals of fish are constantly on the move thanks to the Kuro-shio (warm current) coming from the S and the Oya-shio (cold current) flowing from the Arctic.

These currents also contribute to the weather conditions on the side of Japan facing the Sea of Japan (heavy snowfall in winter) and the Pacific Ocean (dry in winter, very wet in summer). Nonetheless, more than these natural factors, it has been the historical development of the land which has progressively brought about the remarkable imbalance in population densities between the two coasts, concentrating the bulk of the people on the Pacific side of Japan; thus 'the coastal region, stretching 311mls (500km) from Tokyo to Osaka, is overpopulated. The whole of this part of Japan is, in fact, a giant conurbation with centres encroaching on each other, to the point where it is now predicted that Tokyo and Osaka will merge into one huge megalopolis with 50 million inhabitants' (Office of Franco-Japanese Economic Study). Population density is nearly 1,046 per sq.ml (404 per km^2), and between them the administrative districts of Tokyo and Kanagawa (Yokohama) contain one-sixth of Japan's total population.

Faced by so enormous a human and economic imbalance, the Japanese are trying to develop new industrial centres in order to relieve congestion in the big cities and stabilize things between the economic pivots of Honshu which are, from N to S: Tohoku (capital Sendai), formerly a poor hinterland but now starting to open up to industries, which are imported from Kanto into a few places such as Sendai, Akita, Hachinohe and Kamaishi; Kanto, all of whose activity is directed at Tokyo; Chubu, the central area, with its two halves, Tokai in the SE, dominated by Nagoya, and Hokuriku in the NW, with Niigata and Kanazawa as the only two towns on the Sea of Japan with more than 300,000 residents; Kinki, the crucible of Japanese history (Kyoto, Nara), with Osaka, Japan's second city; and finally Chugoku, comprising San in, rural in character and facing the Sea of Japan, and San yo on the Inland Sea, with its industrial and urban areas, Hiroshima and Okayama.

THE HISTORY OF HONSHU. This island was the cradle of Japan's most ancient civilizations; their evolution, relatively fast, indicates just how remarkably adaptable the Japanese are: a quality they have retained well into the present day, though without ever turning their backs on the past. First of all there was the Jomon civilization, a mixture of

Siberian and Chinese elements but with some additions from Southeast Asia; next came the Yayoi (Bronze Age) civilization, this time arriving from South Asia. The Iron Age (a period of tombs, *kofun*) coincides roughly with the dawn of Japanese history, in the first century BC.

The reign of the Emperor Jimmu marks the arrival of politics in Kansai (Nara and Osaka regions). The shifting Imperial capitals came and went until the flowering, with the introduction of Buddhism (6th-7th c.), of a fully-formed civilization which settled first in Nara then in Kyoto, turning these places into cultural centres of the first order, until the 12th c. At the same time, the Ebisu were being pushed progressively further N. After the defeat at Danno ura (1185), the bakufu or Kamakura set up a centre of political life in the NE. Kyoto and its hinterland resumed their importance in the Ashikaga and Momoyama periods, only to lose it again (17th c.) to the Edo of the Tokugawa; however, Osaka largely retained its economic role. In 1869 the Imperial capital was established in Edo which, under the name of Tokyo, was to become the gigantic metropolis we know today.

■ Hyuga (Island of Kyushu)

Map of Kyushu (North), pp. 388-9.

Tokyo, 852mls (1,371km) - Fukuoka, 183mls (295km) - Kagoshima, 120mls (193km) - Kumamoto, 122mls (197km) - Miyazaki, 42mls (67km) - Oita, 83mls (134km) - boat services to Hiroshima, Kawasaki, Kobe and Osaka.

Myazaki ken - pop: 47,420.

Lying on the W side of Kyushu, this industrial town is used as a landing point by a proportion of the island's visitors; its name is the same as that of the historical province of Hyuga, the place where the earthly descendants of the goddess Amaterasu lived, and from where the Emperor Jimmu set sail to win first the Yamato region, then all of Japan.

The coastline around Hyuga contains some marvellous sights, such as the bay and island of Oto in the N, and Isega beach in the S.

VICINITY

SHIIBA (52mls/84km W; coach), delightful area downriver from the Kami Shiiba dam, which you reach by going up the winding course of the Mimi gawa with its succession of dams, including those of Tsukabaru and Iwayado.

■ Ibusuki (Island of Kyushu)

Map of Natural Resources, p. 67.

Tokyo, 935mls (1,504km) - Fukuoka, 221mls (355km) - Kagoshima, 30mls (49km) - Kumamoto, 152mls (244km) - Miyazaki, 110mls (177km).

Kagoshima ken - pop: 31,472 - seaside resort and spa.

The position of Ibusuki, at the entrance to the bay of Kagoshima, is enhanced by the cliffs and inlets that make up its jagged coastline, with the cone of Kaimon dake rising sheer above it. The town, basking in a subtropical climate, is famous for its salt springs, with carbonated waters containing iron salts, at temperatures between 68° and 163°F (20° and 73°C); the Surigahama spring, which rises close to the sea, allows sand baths to be given. One of Japan's most famous 'tropical baths' (jungle-buro) is here, too.

☞ **VICINITY**

1 KAIMON DAKE (30mls/48km there and back; coach); an interesting trip in the shadow of Kaimon dake, passing through a part of the *Kirishima-Yaku National Park (see entry under this name).

The N226 goes S from Ibusuki and skirts the bay of Yamagawa.

3mls (5km): Road branches off to the little port of Yamagawa (1½mls/2km).

6mls (10km): Turn l. for Kaimon Onsen.

👁 9mls (14km): Road off l. to *Nagasaki bana (1ml/1.5km), a rocky cape eroded by the sea, with good views (weather permitting) of the Io, Kuro and Take islands. Interesting botanical and zoological garden nearby.

9mls (15km): Kaimon Onsen, with a pretty view of Kaimon dake; lush vegetation all along the coast.

12mls (20km): There is a road round Kaimon dake, an extinct volcano whose shape has earned it the nickname Satsuma Fuji.

16mls (25km): Kaimon, at which point you cross the N226 and continue N.

20mls (32km): Ikeda ko, an old crater lake, SW of which stands Kaimon dake; at an alt. of 217ft (66m), this crystal-clear lake reaches a depth of 764ft (233m). To the N a toll road offers beautiful views out over the bay of Kagoshima (coaches).

25mls (40km): Iwamoto, back on the coast again; further S, the N226 brings you to:

30mls (48km): Ibusuki.

2 KAGOSHIMA, OSUMI SHOTO, see entries under these names.

◼ Ichikawa (Island of Honshu)

Map of the Vicinity of Tokyo, p. 565.

Toyko, 11mls (17km) – Chiba, 15mls (24km) – Mito, 66 mls (107 km) – Urawa, 25mls (41km).

Chiba ken – pop: 364,244.

This town, which functions as both industrial and residential centre, is divided from the capital by the Edo gawa, which flows into the bay of Tokyo further S.

Guho ji (550yds/500m NE of the Konodai station (Keisei ER); ½ml (1km) from the JNR station in Ichikawa). This temple, dedicated to the great monk Kobo Daishi (774-835), standing on a wooded hill, was often referred to in ancient poetry; its gate of several storeys (Nio mon) houses statues of the Deva kings, attributed to the sculptor Unkei (13th c.).

Kono dai (1ml/1.5km N of the Konodai station, Keisei ER; 1½mls/2km NW of the JNR station in the Ichikawa; bus) is a wooded area on the site of the former capital of the former government of the Shimosa province; it was here that the Hojo vanquished Ashikaga Yoshiaki (1538), and then Satomi Yoshihiro (1564).

Hokekyo ji (N of the Keisei ER station of Onikoshi; 550yds/500m N of the Shimosa-Nakayama JNR station). Founded by Nichiren in 1260, this temple occupies an area of 8 acres (3.2ha) and still has in its possession some manuscripts of its famous founder priest.

◼ Ichinomiya (Island of Honshu)

Railway map on inside front cover.

Tokyo, 246mls (396km) - Gifu, 12mls (19km) - Nagano, 162mls (261km) - Nagoya, 12mls (19km) - Tsu, 53mls (85km).

Aichi ken - pop: 219,274 - textile factories.

Lying half-way between Nagoya and Gifu, Ichinomiya is thus economically dependent, like much of the neighbouring district, on the former town. In 1564, Tokugawa Ieyasu built a castle here.

MASUMIDA JINJ (½ml/1km NE of the Ichinomiya JNR station), in the midst of greenery, has been sacred since 628 to Kunitokodachi no Mikoto, a diety from the first of the seven heavenly generations in Shinto mythology; sacred masks are kept here, to be worn by bugaku dancers.

MYOKI JI (E of Myokoji station, Meitetsu ER: ½ml/1km S of the JNR Ichinomiya station) posesses several catalogued ancient paintings.

■ Ichinoseki (Island of Honshu)

Map of Tohoku, pp. 232–3.

Tokyo, 260mls (418km) – Akita, 116mls (186km) – Aomori, 193mls (310km) – Sendai, 55mls (89km).

Iwate ken – pop: 60,214 – alt. 72ft (22m) – silk production.

An important borough in the Kitakami gawa valley, lying on the great Tohoku highroad, Ichinoseki makes a good starting point for visiting the natural sights around the Chuson ji, one of the most celebrated places of pilgrimage in northern Japan.

ICHINOSEKI CASTLE (½ml/1km S of the station); set on a mound and now a public park, the surviving ruins come from the castle of Date Munekatsu, son of Masamune: in 1695 the property passed into the possession of the Tamura, junior branch of the Date family.

In 1701 Asana Nagamori fled to the castle and committed suicide after the affront to Kira Yoshinoka; he was avenged by the 47 *ronin*: see under the Sengaku ji in Tokyo.

VICINITY

1''**CHUSON JI** (6mls/10km N by the N4; JNR train to Hiraizumi; coach from Ichinoseki or Hiraizumi stations). Leave Ichinoseki on the N side. 5mls (8km): Hiraizumi, giving access to the Chuson ji. Fujiwara festival from 1 to 5 May.

550yds (500m) W: Motsu ji, founded in 850 by Jikaku Daishi, as was the Chuson ji, and completely rebuilt in the 12th c. by Fujiwara Motohira, it is one of the finest temples in the area. Today, apart from the Jyogyo do and Hokke do, only the bases of the columns of the old buildings (the rest was destroyed by fire) and a romantic Heian style garden remain.

3mls (5km) W by the same road (coach): Takkoku no Iwaya, where Sakanoe Tamuramaro (758–811), who drove the Ebisu back to this area, dedicated a little shrine to the war deity Bishamon. A wooden structure clinging to the side of a nearby mountain wall, it houses a plain but impressive statue of Dainichi Nyorai, thought to be from the late 11th c.

6mls (10km): Little square with an avenue of cryptomeria pines leading up to the various buildings of the Chuson ji.

UNDER THE PROTECTION OF THE FUJIWARA. Like the Motsu ji, this temple was founded in 850 by the priest Ennin or Jikaku Daishi (794–864). In 1094, Fujiwara Kiyohira (d. 1126) settled in Hiraizumi, where he built a castle in which his descendants were to live after him. From 1105 to 1108, the Fujiwara endowed the Chuson ji with considerable riches, and built their tombs close by. But the grandeur of the Mutsu Fujiwara offended Minamoto Yoritomo. Moreover, Yoshitsune (1159–89), fleeing from his brother's jealously, looked to Fujiwara Hidehira for protection, but died shortly afterwards at the hands of Fujiwara Yasuhira, son of the latter, in the Koromo gawa, N of the Chuson ji. According to an unsubstantiated story, Yoshitsune escaped death in 1189 and went into exile on Hokkaido, eventually ending up in Mongolia as the famous Genghis Khan. In spite of Yasuhira's support for him, Yoritomo had the Chuson ji destroyed almost immediately. The temple was rebuilt and destroyed a second time by fire in 1337. Of the 40 original buildings, only the Konjiki do and the Kyo zo still survive to this day.

If you follow the avenue of pines for about 220yds (200m), you pass the Benkei do on your l. (1826) which houses several mementoes and relics associated with Yoshitsune and his inseparable companion Benkei; there is a statue attributed to him (although it is certainly from the Edo period). Further up, on the r., after passing under the Omoto mon (1659) you will reach the Hon do, nowadays the main temple building; it was erected in 1908 and contains a statue of Amida Nyorai (Muromachi period).

On the r. you will pass the Mine no Yakushi do (1684) and the belfry (*shoro*), rebuilt in 1343, then on to the most holy of the buildings.

Konjiki do or **Hikari do ('sparkling room'), at the top of a flight of steps, is located today within a modern pavilion (1968); small but sumptuous, covered in gold-leaf, it contains a triple platform whose pedestal and canopy are encrusted with images of gods and animals in mother-of-pearl from Okinawa. On the main altar, spared by Yoritomo, which was used as a mausoleum for Fujiwara Kiyohira and two of his descendants, is displayed a group of eleven statues from the Fujiwara period, attributed to the sculptor Jocho: Amida is enthroned in the centre, surrounded by six Jizo, in front of whom stand two menacing Devas; note the rose of gilt bronze, finely worked, suspended over the whole edifice.

The **Kyozo**, behind the Konjiki do, is the old *sutra* pavilion; built in 1108, it is the oldest surviving part of the Chuson ji; fire ravaged one floor in 1216. Of the 2,379 *sutras* presented by the Fujiwara which used to be kept here, a large number have since been taken to Koya san; others are still kept in the temple museum; on an octagonal altar, its plinth decorated with incised bronze plaques, you can see the Monju Bosatsu seated on a lion, with a group of his followers.

The old Konjiki do, built in 1288, is not far from here.

*Sanko zo (1955), below the Konjiki do, is the treasure house of the temple, containing displays of works from various periods including the Fujiwara and Kamakura. The main room houses the sarcophagi of Kiyohira Motohira and Hidehira Fujiwara, who used to rest beneath the Konjiki do; there are also various objects on view, including rich garments retrieved from the coffins, the box which contained the head of Yasuhira, presented to Yoritomo, *sutras* and their case from the Kyozo, a scroll from the Muromachi period, tracing the history of Yoshitsune, some *keman* (finely worked plaques in bronze gilt) which used to decorate the Konjiki do, a statue of Dainichi Nyorai in cherry wood, from the Heian period, etc. In a small adjoining room there is a wooden sculpture of Ichiji Kirin, attributed to Kokei (12th c.); it has eyes of crystal. The little museum contains a statue of Amida Nyorai, a Kannon of the thousand hands, and two of Yakushi Nyorai from the Fujiwara period, as well as a Dainichi Nyorai from the Kamakura period. Also in the Chuson ji you may see, to the E, a Noh stage (1853) where plays still sometimes take place, in May and October. Close to the square from which the Chuson ji cryptomeria avenue begins, stands the tomb of Benkei.

BENKEI. He was born in the province of Kii and became a monk against his will. Strong as an ox, he clashed with Yoshitsune on a bridge in Kyoto and was defeated by him; he became the faithful companion of the unfortunate brother of Yoritomo, helped him in his campaigns against the Taira and died by his side in the battle of Koromo gawa (1189). He has been immortalized in literature and legend.

On the other side of the N4 stands the Hiraizumi Museum, in which there is a display of dioramas making up a historical panorama, some painting, and archaeological objects of great beauty.

→ 880yds (800m) SE of the Chuson ji, on the far side of the railway and dominating the valley of the Kitakami gawa, stands the Yoshitsune do, dedicated to the brother of Yoritomo, on the very site of his home.

👁 2 ˙GEIBI KEI (16mls/26km NE; JNR train to Matsukawa, then coach; coach direct from Ichinoseki). This gorge, with superb sheer cliffs down to the Satetsu gawa, is passable in part by flat-bottomed boat.

3 KURIKOMA YAMA (29mls/46km W; coach). The road out of Ichinoseki rises W along the Iwai gawa.

4mls (7km): ˙Gembi kei, where the river bed is edged with rocks of all shapes and sizes, to the l., below the level of the road.

♨ 29mls (46km): Sukawa Onsen, high-altitude spa (3,694ft/1,126m) to the NW of Mount Kurikoma, which it takes 1½ hrs to ascend over a distance of 2½mls (4km). This extinct volcano is remarkable for its plant-life, the views from its summit, and its position at the meeting point of three administrative regions; its name varies between these regions: in Miyagi ken, it is known as Kurikoma yama, in Iwate ken as Sukawa dake, and in Akita ken as Dainichi dake.

▮ Iida (Island of Honshu)

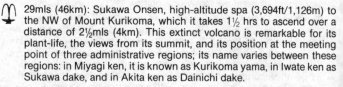

Tokyo, 189mls (304km) - Gifu, 104mls (167km) - Kofu, 105mls

(169km) - Maebashi, 155mls (250km) - Nagano, 105mls (169km) - Nagoya, 93mls (150km) - Niigata, 227mls (365km) - Shizuoka, 127mls (204km) - Toyama, 168mls (270km) - Urawa, 206mls (332km).

Nagano ken - pop: 77,261 - alt. 512ft (156m).

Situated in the middle course of the Tenryu gawa, which rises from Lake Suwa, Iida makes a good base for a visitor to the river gorges.

There used to be a castle in Iida, built in 1195 by Kondo Kaneie; it came into the possession of a succession of owners, including the Hori family between 1672 and 1868.

VICINITY

"THE TENRYU GORGES. The boat ride down the Tenryu rapids is perhaps one of the most spectacular and enjoyable of all such trips in all Japan. The journey, which you may make in summer and autumn, covers about 12mls (20km) in approx. 1h.30, going from Ichida (4mls/7km upriver from Iida JNR train station) to *Tenryu kyo (10mls/16km downriver; station). Indeed, the most attractive areas in the gorges are further downstream; we strongly recommend that you travel down them from Iida, despite the numerous tunnels, going by JNR train towards Tenryu. The walls of the gorges are formed by mountains covered in pine forest; the river winds between 300ft (100m) precipices, with more or less plentiful flows of water, crossed by the Yasuoka, Hiraoka, Saruma and Akiha dams. The loveliest stretches are those at Tenryu and Nangu.

■ **Iiyama** (Island of Honshu)

Tokyo, 163mls (263km) - Gifu, 197mls (317km) - Kofu, 117mls (188km) - Maebashi, 100mls (161km) - Nagano, 22mls (35km) - Nagoya, 186mls (300km) - Niigata, 94mls (152km) - Shizuoka, 176mls (284km) - Toyama, 104mls (168km) - Urawa, 149mls (239km).

Nagano ken - pop: 32,159.

On the upper course of the Shinano gawa, known at this point as the Chikuma gawa, Iiyama gives access to the skiing resorts of Madarao and Nozawa.

Ruins of Iiyama Castle, close to the Chikuma gawa. This castle, built in 1577 by Uesugi Kagetora (1552–79), became the property of Mori Tadamachi in 1584; under the Tokugawa there was a succession of noble occupants, among them the Honda family from 1717 to 1868.

VICINITY

1 MADARAO KOGEN (3½mls/6km W; coach); on the slopes of Madarao yama (4,534ft/1,382m), skiing resort from which in summer you may take a pleasant walk.

2 NOZAWA ONSEN (9mls/14km NE; coach from the station in Iiyama or Kijima). A spa and, more particularly, winter sports resort, on the NW slopes of Kenashi yama (5,413ft/1,650m): 27 ski-lifts; night-time skiing; season from early December to mid-April.

MYOKO KOGEN, NAGANO, JOSIN ETSU KOGEN NATIONAL PARK, see entries under these names.

■ Iizuka (Island of Kyushu)

Map of Kyushu (North), pp. 388–9.

Tokyo, 705mls (1,134km) – Fukuoka, 20mls (32k) – Kumamoto, 76mls (122km) – Oita, 93mls (150km) – Saga, 40ml: (64km).

Fukuoka ken – pop: 75,643.

Iizuka is part of the cluster of industrial and mining towns in the N of Kyushu, and lies in the Chikuho coal belt.

☞ **VICINITY**

THE GREAT TOMB OF OTSUKA (5mls/8km S; JNR train). This tumulus from the Kofun period, NE of the Keisen station, is one of the most representative of its kind; it comprises a richly decorated burial chamber, with its entrance guarded by two horses, painted black; apply for a permit to visit.

■ Ikaruga (Island of Honshu)**

Map of Kansai, pp. 500–1 – plan on opposite page.

Tokyo, 306mls (493km) – Nara, 7mls (11km) – Yamato Koriyama, 4mls (6km).

Nara ken.

Ikaruga is the name of the village in which the Horyu ji was set up; from the village its many buildings can be seen in the distance, merging with the vivid green of the surrounding countryside. The whole scene is restful to the eye, with the harmonious balance of roofs and walls, each complementing the other, and the softened contours of wood and tiles which draw the eye up to the heavens; such are the first feelings of tranquillity you will experience as you approach the Horyuji. A detailed visit to the temple can easily take up a whole day.

A The ***Horyu ji

Access: 1ml (1.5km) N of the JNR Horyu ji station; train from Osaka-Minatomachi, then bus; coach from Nara and Yamato-Koriyama. The temple is open to visitors daily from 08.00 to 16.00.

The Horyu ji, one of the oldest wooden buildings in the world, is also Japan's oldest temple; it is the most complete, and the most perfect from the point of view of the architecture, sculpture and painting of the Asuka period; it now comprises 40 or so buildings divided into two main groups: those in the W (Sai in) and those in the E (To in);

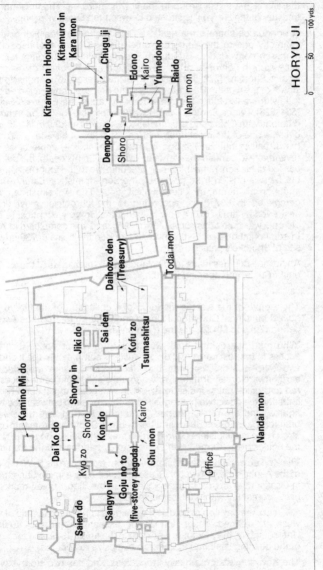

HORYU JI

0   50   100 yds.

Kitamuro in Hondo
Kitamuro in
Kara mon
Chugu ji
Edono
Kairo
Yumedono
Raido
Nam mon
Dempo do
Shoro
Daihozo den (Treasury)
Todai mon
Sai den
Jiki do
Kofu zo
Tsumashitsu
Kamino Mi do
Shoryo in
Dai Ko do
Shoro
Kyo zo
Kon do
Kairo
Sangyo in
Goju no to (five-storey pagoda)
Chu mon
Saien do
Office
Nandai mon

there is also a lesser group in the N (Kitamuro in). The museum or treasury of the Horyu ji is situated between the E and W groups.

IN HONOUR OF BUDDHA THE HEALER. The creation of the Horyu ji is indirectly due to the Emperor Yomei (540–587), the first Japanese monarch converted to Buddhism. Having fallen ill shortly after his accession, he embraced the new religion at the behest of his son, Prince Shotoku (572–621), whom he then asked to commission a statue of the healing Buddha Yakushi; the Emperor, however, died the following year. Under the regency of his aunt, the Empress Suiko (554–628), Prince Shotoku – who was responsible for the opening of relations with China and the official adoption of Buddhism in Japan – became one of the most important personalities of his age: In 601 he had a palace built in Ikaruga, with the Wakakusa temple close by (eventually to contain the statue of Yakushi). On his death, the palace passed to his son Yamashiro, heir presumptive to the Empress Suiko; but he was ousted from power by the Soga ministers. Later, under attack in his home, he killed himself (643). The Wakakusa temple, completed in 607, was, according to the chronicle of Nihongi, destroyed by fire in 670; a new building, the Horyu ji, identical to the old one, was then constructed further NW, and was completed in 708. In addition, the priest Gyoshin Sozu founded the E site in 739 on the site of Shotoku's palace.

An avenue of pines leads to the Nandai mon (great gate of the south) built in 1439, and opening into the W site.

"SAI IN

The temple of the west is made up of a collection of the Horyu ji's holiest buildings: Chu mon, Kon do and Goju no to, from the Asuka period (7th and 8th c.), are the main ones.

*Chu mon, the central gate, with a suite of rooms above it, gives access to the vast courtyard of the western 'complex'. To the l. and r., two *Nio guards, the oldest in Japan (711), were moulded in earthenware on an armature of wood; they still retain some traces of red and black paint, indications that they represent respectively the light and the dark; two passages rather than one run between the two figures, and are rarely opened. According to tradition, they were built for the Empress Suiko and her nephew Shotoku. From this gate stretch the two cloisters (*kairo*) which meet the Dai Ko do to the N. In the enclosure so formed stand a five-storey pagoda and the Kon do.

The Kon do and pagoda are situated on an axis that runs E–W, typical of the Asuka style, and not N–S, as was still the case in the Shitenno ji in Osaka; they are, though, very similar to the Sino-Korean model in being contained within the same enclosure.

**Kon do, the pavilion of gold, is the main building of the temple of the west; its refined decoration is of exceptional artistic quality. Unfortunately, the paintings were lost in the fire of 1949, and the shell of the building itself had to undergo extensive restoration.

The Kon do rests on a heavy stone base, and has two storeys with tiled roofs with twin gables of the *irimoya* type. The upper roof is supported in the Chinese manner by four slender wooden pillars around which carved dragons are coiled. The secco paintings which used to adorn the interior walls were considered to be one of the masterpieces of Japanese art, and were of a style related to contemporary Asian works (Ajanta); painted in all probability in or around 710, they represented the four Buddhist heavens of Amida, Miroku, Shaka and Yakushi; only a few fragments still remain – now in the museum – plus some fine photographs, fortunately taken before the fire of 1949.

Inside the Kon do, which is unfortunately very dark, there are several surviving statues: Yakushi Nyorai, the Buddha of Medicine, a sculpture said to have been completed in 607 by the sculptor Tori, at the time the temple was founded; the *Shaka trinity (historical Buddha), more impressive, on a pedestal, bears the signature of Tori on its back and is dated 623; it is said to have been carved as a votive offering in the likeness of Prince Shotoku, in order that he might regain his health. These statues all show a direct Chinese influence. Overhead there is a suspended wooden platform, carved and painted. Making a pair with the statue of Yakushi, there is another statue of Amida, Buddha of the western heaven. The four divine guardians (Shi tenno) of the cardinal points of Buddhism, which accompany the whole display, are the oldest known representations of the four deities in the whole of Japan; their wooden figures, each with its own particular attributes, used once to be painted in colours symbolic of their function.

*Goju no to, the five-storey pagoda (107ft/32.5m tall), stands on a granite block; very elegantly proportioned, it was dismantled during the war and has been rebuilt since.

On the ground floor, on the four sides of the pillar which supports the whole structure, there are high-relief and terracotta miniatures of (from E to S): the conversation between Yuima and Monju; the Heaven of Miroku; the cremation of the remains of the Buddha Sakyamuni (Shaka); the *entry of Buddha into Nirvana. Some of the figures are of a powerful realism, if somewhat difficult to see in the dim lighting conditions.

Dai Ko do, or hall of preaching, stands to the N of the enclosure formed by the Kairo. The present-day building, in Fujiwara style, was transferred from Kyoto in 990 to replace the original one which was burned down in 925. It houses a group of three statues from the same period, representing Yakushi Nyorai flanked by Nikko and Gakko Bosatsu, the bodhisattvas of the sun and moon. In the Ko do there are also several models of the Horyu ji on display, including a cross-section of the Kon do showing where the paintings were before they were destroyed by fire.

In various parts of the Dai Ko do there are: to the W, the Kyo zo (repository of the *sutras*), built in the 8th c., and to the E the 9th c. *shoro* (belfry).

Outside the courtyard, and behind the Ko do, stands the Kamino Mi do, or upper temple, and further W the octagonal pavilion of the Saien do, dedicated to the princess Tachibana, wife of Shotoku Taishi; it contains a statue of Yakushi dating back to the 8th c.

Shoryo in, the first building to the E of the enclosure formed by the Kairo, is sacred to the memory of Prince Shotoku and occupies the southern portion of the old eastern sleeping quarters (Higashi muro); it is matched on the other side of the enclosure by the Sangyo in and western sleeping quarters (Nishi muro). This 12th c. building contains statues including that of Prince Shotoku, his sons, and the priest Eji.

To the E of the Shoryo in stand the Tsumashitsu and the little building of the Kofu zo; the latter used once to contain the Emperor's gifts to the temple. Then, behind the Sai den, is the Jiki do (old refectory).

■ 'DAIHEZO DEN. The treasure-museum of the Horyu ji, further W, is a double building in modern (1941) concrete style, containing exhibits of the finest works of art in the Horyu ji, coming notably from the Kofu zo. A large number of the treasures from this temple are to be found in the Tokyo National Museum, in a purpose-built gallery. We will not list every item in the series of rooms in this museum, as there are rather too many, but the following deserve special mention.

**Tamamushi no zushi, reliquary of the golden scarab, a reminder of the 9,000 'tamamushi' scarab wing-cases (*Chrysochroa elegans*) which used to glisten beneath the edging of the pedestal and columns of bronze. The architecture of this tabernacle, said to have belonged to the Empress Suiko, is in keeping with the stylistic precepts of the Asuka period, and hence is contemporary with the oldest parts of the Horyu ji. The upper part has three sets of double doors that open (note the detail of the '1,000' little Buddhas) to reveal a niche nowadays containing a figure of Kannon.

The *external paintings on the reliquary, rare examples from the 7th c., are of a unique variety, on lacquered wood and in a mixture of oil and lead oxide. On the outer surface of the side doors are depicted four bodhisattvas; and two elegant divine kings guard the front doors. The rear panel of the niche is said to bear the image of Mount Ryoju, where Sakyamuni preached the Lotus *sutra*. The four inner flaps show the veneration of the remains of the Buddha, set against the background of Mount Sumeru, pillar of the universe according to Buddhist cosmogony; the side paintings are of two episodes from the former life of the Buddha: his meeting with Indra and, better known, his self-sacrifice to a starving tigress. The whole artifact is influenced by the Chinese Wei style.

The reliquary of the Lady Tachibana, more modest than the above, exemplifies a transitional style between the Asuka and Nara (8th c.) periods; it contains a little Amida trinity in bronze gilt, very typical of its time (Hakuho period).

*Kudara Kannon is a statue in camphor wood of Avalokitesvara, which is reputed to be Korean in origin (Kudara), but was almost certainly created by a Japanese artist following Chinese rules; from the Asuka period (7th c.), the statue is from another hand than those in the Kon do, and is distinguished by the graceful elongation of the body with its close careful draperies; there are still traces of lacquer and coloured paintwork on the statue, which is more than 6½ft (2m) high.

Yumechigai or Yumetagai Kannon is an elegant piece in bronze, of the Nara period, credited with the power of moderating bad dreams. The museum contains other works of the Asuka period, such as the little Boshinen Shaka trinity (628), made for the Minister Soga Iname; the six statues of bodhisattvas (though once there were eight) from the late 7th c; the statue of Kannon of the nine heads, imported in 718; plaques of carved wood which were used to print the so-called Shotoku codex; some rare paintings saved from the fire in the Kon do; and so on.

To the S of the museum buildings, the Todai mon, great gate of the east gives access to the east site.

**TO IN

An avenue leads from the Todai mon to the eastern temple; various buildings have been arranged around the Yumedono, to be reached by passing into the courtyard enclosed by the Kairo.

*Yumedono, the pavilion of dreams, is the oldest octagonal religious building in Japan. From the Nara period (8th c.), this monument stands, like those of the preceding period, on a double stone plinth.

It was here that Prince Shotoku received in the form of dreams the solutions to his political and philosophical problems.

**Guze Kannon, a statue from the time of Shotoku, got its nickname of Saviour of the World during the Heian period. It is worked in camphor wood, covered in gold leaf, with a crown of engraved bronze, and of a style which links it to the statues by Tori in the Kon do of the Sai in; it does, however, possess a feminine grace all of its own, which it doesn't share with Tori's work. Protected and hidden away until the 19th c., the statue is remarkably well preserved.

The Yumedono also contains a statue in dry lacquer (*kanshitsu*) of the priest and founder Gyoshin Sozu, and another in clay of the priest Dosen Risshi; they date back to the Nara and early Heian periods.

Edono, N of the Yumedono, is a building from the Kamakura period (1219), where once was painted the story of Shotoku Taishi (the painter was Hata Chitei); the present paintings are copies from the Edo period. This building, divided into the E den and Shari den, has a corridor running through it to the Dempo do, or Buddhist teaching room, similar to the Ko do of the Sai in, and built in 739 by another princess, Tachibana, mother of the Empress Komyo.

It contains some 20 statues from the Nara and Heian periods, including one of Amida in dry lacquer, standing in the middle.

Following to the N the outside west wall of the Kairo, you will pass the Shoro of the To in, a bell tower from the Kamakura period, with even older bells, taken originally from the Chugu ji. Next, passing the Dempo do, you will come to the entrance to the Chugu ji.

 CHUGU JI

This temple, founded by Prince Shotoku in honour of his mother, was moved in the 15th c. to its present site, and was placed under the administration of an abbess of Imperial blood. The main pavilion, a modern building surrounded by water, contains some treasures from the Asuka period (7th c.).

**Nyorin Kannon Bosatsu, Buddha of Mercy, is in fact a Miroku Bosatsu, a Buddha of the Future, seated in a pose of meditation, his right leg resting on his left and his right hand held up near his face. This statue, along with the one in the Koryu ji in Kyoto, almost identical and also made of wood, is a masterpiece of sculpture, Japanese or worldwide.

*The Tenjukoku Mandara embroidery was made in 622; its unique character and its age make this a most original work of which only a few fragments remain; it is known as the Tenjukoko or 'Celestial Kingdom of Immortality', and was once made up of two large panels embroidered by the ladies of the court on the orders of Tachibana no Oiratsume, wife of Prince Shotoku, for the repose of his soul after his death. Shotoku is shown as being in the Buddhist heaven, where there are imaginary creatures and buildings; the colours and design betray a Sino-Korean influence.

B Vicinity

1 HORIN JI (1½mls/2km NE of the Horyu ji; access on foot or by coach to the Hokki ji) was founded in 621 by Yamashiro, eldest son of Prince Shotoku. The three-storey pagoda, of the Asuka period, was destroyed by lightning in 1944. In the Kon do are several statues, including one of *Yakushi Nyorai seated (12th c.), in the style of Tori, and Heian period figures of Kichijo ten, Bishamon ten and Sho Kannon. In the Kodo, you will note, too, a large, fine statue of Kannon of the eleven heads (Fujiwara period), as well as wooden carvings of Jizo and Kokuzo Bosatsu; the latter is actually of Kannon and comes from the Nara period.

550yds (500m) E of the Horin ji, stands the Hokki ji, created in 638 at the behest of Prince Shotoku by the priest Fukuryo. The three-storey pagoda, 79ft (24m) high, is said to have been built in 685. Several statues are kept there, among them one of Kannon, in bronze gilt of the Asuka period, a wooden Jizo Bosatsu from the Heian period, and a Kamakura period Buddha.

2 NARA, KONGO-IKOMA NATURE PARK, see entry under Nara.

◾ Ikeda (Island of Shikoku)

Map of Shikoku (Inland Sea), pp. 536–7.

Tokyo, 487 mls (784km) - Takamatsu, 40mls (65km) - Tokushima, 47mls (75km).

Tokushima ken – Awa-Ikeda station.

Ikeda lies on the middle reaches of the Yoshino gawa, the longest river on the island of Shikoku (121mls/194km), just below the point where it bends towards Tokushima.

VICINITY

TSURUGI SAN (38mls/61km SE; coach to Minokoshi; or JNR train to Sammyo, then coach). Drive W out of Ikeda by the N32 and N192.

2mls (3km): Having crossed the Yoshino gawa, leave the N192 (which rejoins the coast at Kawanoe) to follow the N32 up along the *Yoshino gawa gorges.

5mls (8km): Iyaguchi, at which point you leave the Yoshino valley and climb up the Iya gawa valley instead.

3½mls (6km) S: Koboke; from here, and for a distane of 4mls (7km) to Oboke, the railway runs parallel with the very interesting *Yoshino gawa gorges.

The road, climbing the Iya valley, soon crosses *Iya kei, gorges which are lined by cliffs, cut through like those of Yoshino in the mountain range of Shikoku; the colour of the maples in the autumn adds much to the splendour of the scene.

16mls (25km): Nishi Iyayama; on the r., a new toll road (4mls/7km; coach) meets the Yoshino gawa again at Sammyo.

17mls (27km): Zentoku, close to the Iya no Kazura bashi, a rope bridge 52ft (16m) above the torrential river, which used to be the means by which the inhabitants of these high valleys crossed the water. It is one of very few bridges of this type remaining in Japan, and a valuable reminder of a past way of life.

34mls (54km): Nagoro, from where a toll road stretches away to the wooded slopes of Tsurugi san; pretty views.

38mls (61km): Minokoshi, at an altitude of 4,593ft (1,400m), the lower station of a cablecar up to Mount Tsurugi: see Tokushima and vicinity.

◾ Iki and Tsu shima*

Map of Natural Resources, p. 67.

Tokyo, 757mls/1,218km (Iki), 792mls/1,274km (Tsu) - Fukuoka, 42mls/68km (Iki), 77mls/124km (Tsu) - Nagasaki, 96mls/154km (Iki), 130mls/210km (Tsu).

Nagasaki ken

Separated by a distance of about 43mls (70km), these two islands, vastly different from each other, have been incorporated into a single nature park. There are several *ryokan* on the site.

STRATEGIC POSITION. Legend says that these islands were among the first created by Izanagi and Izanami (see Awa jima); no one knows if the gods had been planning to make them ports of call between Korea and Japan, but their half-way position between Kyushu and the Korean peninsula and China has meant that since prehistoric times sailors – merchant and military – have used them as they sought to establish links between the two countries. The islands, not spared the Mongol invasions (see Fukuoka), served as a haunt of pirates plundering along the coast of western China, and were used as a military base by Toyotomi Hideyoshi during his Korean campaign of 1592. It was at this time that Iki was taken over by the Matsuura, lords of Hirado, while Tsu remained in the hands of the So, who had come to power there during an uprising of the inhabitants in 1246. In more recent times, the Strait of Tsushima which divides the two islands was the scene of the crushing defeat inflicted during the Russo-Japanese War by the fleet of Admiral Togo on the ships of Rodzhestvensky, which had sailed from the Baltic and were passing through the strait on their way to Vladivostok (May 1905).

IKI SHIMA (plane: ANA flights from Ishida Airport, 6mls/10km E of Gonoura, to Fukuoka; sea links from Gonoura to Fukuoka and Tsu shima; from Ashibe via Seto to Fukuoka; from Ishida via Intsuji to Yobuko; from Katsumoto to Tsu shima; coach trips round the island). This island, with an area of 53sq. mls (138km²), is rather flat and has a neat, attractive landscape; the coastline is formed of numerous inlets and islets, and is more rugged to the N. Gonoura, where boats between Fukuoka and Tsu shima put in, is the main settlement on the island. Toyotomi Hideyoshi built a castle there during his Korean campaign in 1592. The town is also a spa. Several of the islets off shore are accessible by boat.

➧ 1½mls (2km) SE: the Takeno tsuji observation point (699ft/213m), highest point of the island.

☞ **ROUND TRIP OF THE ISLAND** (32mls/51km; coach), leaving Gonoura to the N.

1½mls (2km) or 6mls (10km): The road bears left towards Yunomoto, the main spa on the island; there are pearl oyster beds in the next bay, and the Monkey Rock (Saru iwa) 2½mls (4km) NW.

12mls (20km): Katsumoto, a little port to the N of the island, was formerly the capital of Iki shima, and the home of a junior branch of the Matsudaira between 1689 and 1868.

➧ 2mls (3km) NW off shore (boat) lies the islet of Tatsuno, with the stunning *Ebiga tani fault line.

☞ 18mls (29km): Seto, on the W coast; the road skirts round the Ashibe Bay.

22mls (35km): Ashibe, S of the bay.

➥ 3½mls (6km) SE: Yahata Point and the pretty, rocky coast of Sakyo bana.

☞ 27mls (44km): Ishida, from where you may get to the airport at Iki, the little port of Intsuji, or travel W back to Gonoura.

➥ 3mls (5km) E: Tsutsukiga hama inlet.

☞ 32mls (51km): Gonoura.

'TSU SHIMA (sea links from Izuhara to Iki shima and Fukuoka, and from Kami-Tsushima via Hidakatsu to Kitakyushu; coaches between Izuhara and Kami-Tsushima). Larger, more mountainous and with a still more indented coastline than the previous island, Tsu shima is in fact made up of two islands (263sq. mls/682km^2 in total), linked by a narrow isthmus, said to have been cut through in the 16th c. to allow the passage of the fleet of Hideyoshi; they are called Kamino shima (the more northerly of the pair) and Shimono shima (the more southerly). Izuhara, the capital, is a little port tucked away deep in an inlet, where Hideyoshi had the Mori build a castle during the expedition to Korea. In 1666, So Yoshizane, ruler of the island, took up residence there. In the town, you should see the ruins of the old Kanaishi Castle and the little Bansho temple.

➥ 6mls (9km) N (taxi); Kami zaka is an observation point overlooking the extraordinary ****Aso Bay**, formed from a myriad of islets and promontories of complex design, between the two main islands of Tsu shima.

➥ 11mls (18km) W: Komoda, on the W side of the island; in this area, look out for barns build with a unique kind of roof, made of broad, flat stone tiles.

➥ 16mls (25km) S: Tsutsu, to the S of the island, reached by a road most often running along a coastal ledge above the sea.

☞ **KAMI-TSUSHIMA** (57mls/91km N; coach). A road travels the entire length of the island and gives good views of its prettiest aspects.

6mls (9km): Mitsushima; in summer, you may board a boat here for trips round Aso Bay.

8mls (13km): Bridge across the strait that divides Shimono from Kaminoshima.

30mls (49km): Mine.

➥ 2½mls (4km) W: Kisaka Kaijin jinja, sacred to the god of the sea in Shinto mythology.

➥ 57mls (91km): Kami-Tsushima, with the little fishing port of Hidakatsu.

■ Imabari (Island of Shikoku)

Map of Shikoku (Inland Sea), pp. 536–7.

Tokyo, 518mls (834km) – Kochi, 91mls (146km) – Matsuyama, 28mls (45km) – Takamatsu, 71mls (115km) – Tokushima, 112mls (181km) – sea links to Beppu, Osaka, Hiroshima and Onomichi.

Ehime ken - pop: 111,125.

A fishing, trading and transit port, Imabari is also an important industrial town on the Inland Sea, devoted mainly to the weaving of cotton, and accounting for 40% of Japanese production.

The contemporary architect Tange Kenzo was born in Imabari in 1913.

Fukiage Park (1ml/1.5km E of the station; bus), situated on the ruins of the old Imabari Castle, was a subsidiary of the one at Matsuyama, which was built in the early part of the 17th c. and belonged between 1635 and 1868 to the Hisamatsu, related to the Tokugawa.

☞ **VICINITY**

 1 CHIKAMI YAMA (3mls/5km NW: bus) is a wooded park on the edge of the town; it rises to a height of 801ft (244m), where an observation point allows you to look out over the Strait of Kurushima and the islands in the Inland Sea.

2 HASHIHAMA (3½mls/6km N; JNR train). Half a mile (1km) N of the station there is a headland which offers one of the best views of the Kurushima kaikyo, a narrow passage between Shikoku and O shima; the fluctuating tides can set up fierce currents and whirlpools, but boats frequently go by this route nonetheless.

3 NIBUKAWA ONSEN (7mls/11km SW; coach). This spa, in a mountainous area with cherry and maple woods, can be reached via the Tamagawa dam.

4 OMI SHIMA (15mls/24km N; boat from Imabari or Hashihama to Miyaura). It is one of the countless islands in the Inland Sea; visit the Oyamazumi shrine (E of Miyaura), one of Japan's oldest, rebuilt in the 15th c.: it contains some very fine armour and other items, presented in olden times by illustrious imperial and military visitors.

5 MATSUYAMA, ISHIZUCH SAN, See Matsuyama.

■ Imaichi (Island of Honshu)

Map of Nikko National Park, p. 464.

Tokyo, 83mls (134km) – Fukushima, 147mls (237km) – Maebashi, 63mls (101km) – Mito, 63mls (101km) – Urawa, 71mls (115km) – Utsunomiya, 17mls (28km).

Tochigi ken - pop: 50,423.

Imaichi is a gateway to the Nikko National Park; we would refer you to the separate entry under that name. From there roads head variously for Nikko, with its sumptuous shrines, and the hot spas of Kawaji and Shiobara.

Close to Imaichi stands the superb *avenue of cryptomerias, planted in the 17th c. along the path to the Nikko shrines, as a gift to the Tosho gu from Okochi (Matsudaira) Masatsuna (1576-1648). There is a total of about 13,000 trees along a stretch of 24mls (38km).

VICINITY

1 SHIOBARA ONSEN (32mls/52km NE; coach via Kinugawa Onsen; Tobu Railway to Kinugawa kogen). The road (N121) climbs the pretty valley of the Kinu gawa up as far as the level of the Fujiwara.

8mls (13km): Kinugawa Onsen, spa frequented by pilgrims to Nikko, with waters at temperatures between 59° and 135°F (15°F and 57°C). Upstream, the river forms gorges known by the name of Ryuo kyo.

11mls (18km): Kawaji Onsenguchi, where the toll road *Nichi en Highway branches off (fine views of the mountains of the Nikko National Park) and sweeps round to the NW of Takahara yama with its twin peaks Sakaga dake (5,889ft/1,795m) and Keicho san (5,794ft/1,766m).

3mls (5km) N by the N121 (coach): Kawaji Onsen, another hot spring close to the Ikari reservoir and dam (the road passes close by).

27mls (43km): Arayu Onsen, first of the Shiobara group of spas, and the highest, at an alt. of 3,084ft (940m). From here you may climb Takahara yama.

32mls (52km): Furumachi, more easily accessible by coach from the Nishi-Nasuno JNR station (Tohoku line), is the administrative centre of *Shiobara Onsen. There are seven main hot spas along the Hoki gawa, which flows from Takahara yama and winds down between that mountain to the SW and Nasu dake to the NE.

The name Shiobara, 'field of salt', was apparently derived from the many salt concretions deposited by the springs. According to tradition, it was the priest Kobo Daishi (744-835) who discovered these springs, which gained a great reputation during the last century thanks to the governor of Tochigi ken, Mishima Michitsune (1835-88). The temperature of these sulphur-bearing alkaline springs varies between 102° and 167°F (39° and 75°F); they are effective against rheumatism, neuralgia and skin diseases.

550yds (500m) S: Monzen, divided from Furumachi by the Hoki gawa, is one of the most popular places in Shiobara. Visit the Myoun ji, founded in the 12th c. by the nun Myoun, a relation of Taira.

1½ml (2km) E: Fukuwata. Two strange rocks stand in the vicinity of the river here: Tengu, covered in pines, near the roadside, and Nodachi, lying in the actual river bed.

2½mls (4km) E: Oami, with a spring that issues from a crevice in a rock,

N of the Hoki gawa. Close by is the Chigogafuchi pool, reputed to be bottomless; note the swirling of the waters.

2 NIKKO NATIONAL PARK, see entry under this name.

■ Imari (Island of Kyushu)

Map of Kyushu (North), pp. 388–9.

Tokyo, 764mls (1,229km) – Fukuoka, 49mls (79km) – Nagasaki, 52mls (84km) – Saga, 38mls (61km).

Saga ken – pop: 61,561.

A small industrial town and export centre for the Arita potteries, Imari has gained worldwide renown thanks to its porcelain ware, better known by the name of Imari Yaki.

Ton-ten-ton Festival, from 22 to 24 October, features competitions between litter-bearers.

☞ VICINITY

1 ARITA (10mls/16km S; JNR train; coach). Visit the Arita Porcelain Museum; housed in the offices of the Chamber of Commerce and Industry, it has some remarkable items on display.

This pottery is said to have been introduced to Arita in 1592 by a Korean craftsman from Nagasaki; considerable deposits of fine clay nearby played an important part, but it was Japanese potters, Goroshichi and the Kakiemons, who established its reputation in the 17th c.; there were at that time nearly 300 pottery kilns in Arita. Highly prized by the Dutch inhabitants of Dejima (Nagasaki), numerous pieces were exported to the Netherlands and had a great influence on the potters of Delft, and in fact on the whole of Europe. The name of Kakiemon is often linked with Arita porcelain. There are two kinds of 'Kakiemon': one, the so-called 'brocade style' is decorated on top of the glaze with patterns in red, blue and green; the other, called 'glazed brocade' is characterized by the use of cobalt oxide. The designs of the young Kakiemon – rocks, flowers, and birds – take their inspiration fairly directly from painting, whereas those by his uncle cover the sides of vases or the bottom of great dishes with brilliant patterns taken from textiles. For some people, it is the Nabeshima potteries which produce Arita's finest porcelain ware.

The pottery market takes place from 1 to 5 May, a wonderful opportunity to barter and haggle, during which huge quantities of porcelain goods of all descriptions are sold.

You can enjoy some beautiful walks in the area around Kurokami yama, which rises to a height of 1,700ft (518km) in the N.

2 KARATSU, TAKEO, see entries under these names.

Inawashiro (Island of Honshu)

Map of Natural Resources, p. 66.

Tokyo, 173mls (297km) - Aizu Wakamatsu, 18mls (29km) - Fukushima, 36mls (58km).

Fukushima ken.

Situated at the foot of Mount Bandai and to the north of Lake Inawashiro, this town is an ideal starting point for exploring either of these two places.

Inawashiro Park (1½mls/2km N of the station) stands on the former site of Kamego jo, which belonged to the lords of Inawashiro.

VICINITY

1 INAWASHIRO KO (2mls/3km S; ½ml/1km S of station; bus). This lake is the fourth largest in Japan (40sq. mls/105km^2). Lying at an altitude of 1,686ft (514m), tradition has it that the lake was created in 806 following an eruption of Bandai san; it seems to have come into being when a dam of lava from Mounts Bandai and Nekoma was formed. In summer there are boat trips, lasting approximately three hours.

2 OKINAJIMA (3mls/5km W; JNR train; coach). Small spa town and summer resort which was the home of the bacteriologist Noguchi Hideyo (1876-1928), to whom we owe the yellow-fever vaccine. It is possible to visit the house where he was born (traditional interior of the last century and a few artifacts).

3 AIZU WAKAMATSU, BANDAI ASAHI NATIONAL PARK, see entries under these names.

Inuyama (Island of Honshu)

Tokyo, 247mls (397km) - Gifu, 15mls (25km) - Nagano, 166mls (267km) - Nagoya, 15mls (24km) - Shizuoka, 143mls (230km) - Tsu, 60mls (97km).

Aichi ken - Pop: 50,594 - textile industries.

As it has efficient connections with Nagoya, this town is a natural outlet for the great metropolis of central Japan. The surrounding area seems specifically planned to receive the pleasure-hungry urban population. Note here the landing stage for the flat-bottomed boats which go down the Kiso gawa that flows to the N of the town (see Mino-Kamo).

Inuyama Castle (550yds/500m W of the Inuyama-Yuen Meitetsu station) stands on the summit of a small hill overlooking the Kiso gawa. The little keep of Inuyama is one of the oldest in Japan; it has recently been restored.

Known as the White Castle, Inuyama jo was built in the 15th c. by Shiba Yoshitake, who entrusted it to the Oda family in 1435. In 1584, Ikeda Nobuteru was in the process of seizing it, but died that same

year in the battle of Nagakute, defeated by Tokugawa Ieyasu. In the
17th c., the Tokugawa gave the castle over to the Naruse family who
built the present keep in 1600 and stayed there until the Restoration.

The Japanese garden Uraku en is spread out at the foot of the hill on
which the castle stands. Of particular interest are the pavilions of Jo
an and Kyu Shodenin Shoin.

To the E of the railway, a group of hills along the Kiso gawa has been
partly laid out as a public amusement park; it houses a zoo and a
centre for studying the behaviour of monkeys (access by monorail).

VICINITY

1 MEIJI MURA (5mls/9km SE; Meitetsu train to Meijimuraguchi; coach
from Inuyama and Nagoya). 2mls (3.5km) E of the small station
(access by bus), is a site on the shores of the Iruke ike, to which
several buildings have been brought with a view to reconstructing a
model village of the Meiji period (1868-1912). These buildings come
from all parts of the country and bear witness to Western influence in
the methods of construction with wood or brick. Amongst them are
the homes of several famous figures of the Meiji Restoration; Saint
John's church dates from 1908. The village is open daily from 10.00 to
17.00.

2 IWAZAKI (6mls/10km S; Meitetsu train). Of interest here are the fertility
festivals (15 March) of the Tagata shrine (phallic cult processions).

3 GIFU, NAGOYA, see entries under these names; KISO GAWA RAPIDS, see
Mino-Kamo.

■ Ise Shima (National Park of; Island of Honshu)**

*Map of Natural Resources p. 66 – map of Ise shima National Park,
opposite page.*

HOW TO GET THERE

– From Ise or Toba, the two principal towns of the National Park; they
are about 10mls (16km) apart, and are linked by JNR trains and by the
Kinki Nippon ER (Kintetsu), which extends as far as Kashikoijima.
The main coach and excursion services also operate from these two
towns.

– From Kyoto or Osaka, Ise is accessible by direct train, JNR or
Kintetsu (Namba station at Osaka), taking approx. 1h. 50 from these
two towns, which are 87mls (140km) and 99mls (160km) away. From
Osaka (Tennoji) there is also a JNR service: 5h. approx. changing at
Taki. Coach services from these two towns.

– From Nagoya (87mls/140km from Ise), JNR train, direct or via Taki
or Kintetsu trains in 1h.10 approx. Ferry services between Nagoya
and Toba, with the Kinki Nippon Tourist Company or Shima Katsuura
Kanko Steamship Co. Coach services.

- From Shingu, 95mls (153km) SW of Ise, in 2h.40 by JNR train via Taki.

- From Tsu, 22mls (36km) NW of Ise; JNR and Kintetsu trains in 40min. approx. Coaches.

This park (128,584 acres/52,036ha) covers the Ise peninsula, which forms the southern side of Ise Bay, to the E of the Kii peninsula. It is one of the most popular parks in Japan, ranking with Fuji-Hakone-Izu and Nikko, and is a major centre of pilgrimage, owing to the double

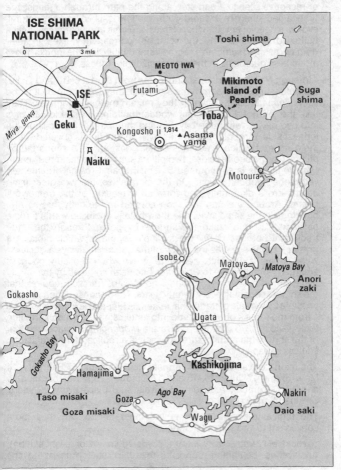

shrine at Ise. This rugged coastal region was, along with Toba, the birthplace of the cultured pearl.

1 ''ISE (pop: 103,576; see plans of the shrines, p. 261).

The two shrines of Ise (Naiku and Geku) are amongst the most venerable in Japan and attract more than 2 million visitors every year. There are about 120 lesser shrines, affiliated to the two main ones; they are collectively known as Ise jingu: the Grand Shrine of Ise. It is appropriate to behave with a certain formality here; a formality born of receptive silence. Each step along the path through a landscape first tamed, then re-ordered with sublime skill to remain natural, evokes a special emotion: here, trees, streams and pilgrims all fulfil a hallowed function. And the temples, permanently fixed in their domain, seem to symbolize sacred immutability, like the monks, those motionless guardians in their starched, white robes.

Although Naiku, the inner shrine, dates from the 1st c. BC and Geku, the outer shrine, dates from the 5th c. AD, they were both built in the same *shimmei* style, of which they remain the best examples. They take the form of a rectangular wooden building divided lengthways into two naves, with three bays cutting them; the entrance is on the longest side, through the central bay. The building is covered with a thatched roof which overhangs on all sides, and it is supported by pillars. On the shorter sides, two pillars support the main roof-beam (*katsuogi*); this is surmounted by small beams (*chigi*) ornamented with sober wooden inlays. On the extremities, the two great main beams cross diagonally and form an extension of the framework beams. Around the Sho den, consecrated to the deity, are several buildings in the same style, and the whole is enclosed within a triple palisade. You can reach the shrines by going through the three traditional porticos (*torii*), the symbolic origin of which remains a mystery. Some see it as the perch of the cockerel (always associated with Amaterasu) which began to crow when the sun goddess emerged from the cave to which she had been confined by the unruly behaviour of her brother Susano o no Mikoto. Tradition requires that the shrines be rebuilt every twenty years. This reconstruction is made possible by the sale of traditional materials (Japanese cypress – *hinoki* – from the forests of Kiso) made into amulets; the last reconstruction took place in 1973. The alternative site (*kodenchi*) is adjacent to that of the shrine, the architecture of which is a replica of the prehistoric edifices of Japan.

The main festivals of the Ise shrines occur on 4 and 17 February, 14 May, 15 and 17 June, 14, 15 and 17 October, 23 November, and 15 and 17 December; rebuilding festivals take place every 20 years: Shikinen Sengu or Sengusai.

The logical place to begin is the inner shrine, but it is more convenient to visit the outer shrine first.

TOYOUKE DAI JINGU or **GEKU JINGU** (770yds/700m SW of Iseshi station). An avenue beginning opposite the JNR station leads to the

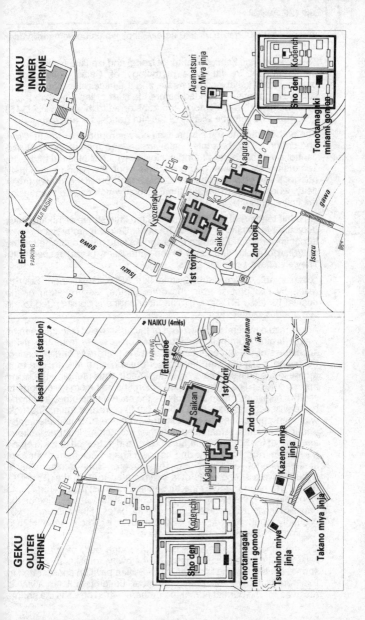

GEKU OUTER SHRINE

Iseshima eki (station)

NAIKU (4mls)

PARKING

Entrance

Saikan

1st torii

Kagura den

2nd torii

Magatama ike

Sho den

Kodenchi

Tonotamagaki minami gomon

Tsuchino miya jinja

Kazeno miya jinja

Takano miya jinja

NAIKU INNER SHRINE

Entrance

PARKING

UJI BASHI

Isuzu gawa

Kyozensho

Saikan

1st torii

2nd torii

Isuzu gawa

Kagura den

Aramatsuri no Miya jinja

Sho den

Kodenchi

Tonotamagaki minami gomon

magnificent wooded park 220 acres/89ha) which contains the outer shrine.

Toyouke bime no kami, daughter of Izangi and Izanami (see Awaji), is the equivalent in Japanese mythology of Ceres, venerated as patroness of the harvest, the home, and the necessities of living. Her shrine was probably founded before the start of the Christian era to the N of the Kyoto prefecture, and transferred to this place in AD 478 in compliance with the wishes of the sun goddess Amaterasu.

The path leading to the shrine itself curves round after the first *torii* and continues to the triple enclosure beyond the second *torii*. You cannot go through the second enclosure which is blocked off by the Tomotamagaki minami gomon: at this door the pilgrims cast their offerings and clap their hands to make their presence known to the deity, whose spirit resides in the Sho den which can be seen inside the first enclosure.

On a hill to the S of the shrine stands the little shrine of Takano miya dedicated to the living spirit of Toyouke. Below it are two shrines of lesser importance, Tsuchino miya and Kazeno miya, dedicated to the guardian of Geku jingu and to the wind Kami (Kaze) respectively. They also have *kodenchi* areas.

KOTAI JINGU or **NAIKU JINGU** (2½mls/4km SE of Geku jingu; easy to reach by bus or taxi from the outer shrine, Iseshi station or the nearest Kintetsu ER station). The inner shrine is consecrated to the sun goddess Amaterasu.

Amaterasu o mikami was born out of the right eye of Izanagi when he was returning from hell; the Japanese consider her to be the divine ancestress of the Imperial Family, and the patroness of their nation. Following a dispute with her brother Susano o no Mikoto, she took refuge in the heavenly cave on Mount Kagu, thus plunging the world into darkness. The light returned when she re-emerged, curious to see the festivities organized outside the cave by the other gods who had devised this stratagem to induce her to come out again. Susano o was then condemned to settle in the province of Izumo (see entry under his name). Amaterasu sent her grandson Ninigi no Mikoto, ancestor of the Emperor Jimmu, to earth and entrusted to his keeping a sacred mirror which reflected her own image. The mirror was kept in the Imperial residence until the Emperor Sujin decided that it should have a shrine of its own consecrated to it. In the 1st c. BC, during the reign of the Emperor Suinin, Princess Yamato hime, into whose keeping the mirror had fallen, chose a site for the shrine on the banks of the Isuzu gawa. According to the dates of the *Nihongi*, it was probably founded in the year 4 BC. However, it is more reasonable to assume that it was founded in the 4th c. AD.

On the other side of the Uji bashi (a bridge built of cypress and zelkowa across the Isuzu gawa), a pathway turns r. towards the shrine. On the l. of the first *torii* is the Saikan pavilion consecrated to the purification of the priests: another building not far away is reserved for the purification of the Emperor when he visits the shrine.

Between the first and second *torii*, you can go down on the r. to the Mitarashi, the pilgrims' place of purification, on the banks of the Isuzu gawa.

Some choose to see this sacred river as the one into which Isanagi dived after he had escaped from hell and was fleeing the evil spirits sent to pursue him by his wife Izanami, who was furious at being discovered in a state of discomposure. It was in wiping his eye that he gave birth to Amaterasu. Others prefer to believe that Izanagi's purification took place on Kyushu.

After the second *torii* the route continues past the sacred cowshed (Miumaya) on to Kagura den where sacred dances are performed. This is followed by Gojo den and Misaka dono, another purification room where barrels of offerings, alcohol and rice are stored. Behind these stand Mike den, the room given over to daily offerings of food, and Gehei den, the former treasury.

Imibiya den is the holy kitchen where the food offered to the deity is prepared; the rice used for this purpose is kept in the Mishine no Mikura. The shrine itself is at the top of a flight of steps and, like the adjacent Kodenchi, it occupies an area 413ft by 174ft (126m by 53m). It is similar to the Geku, in that it is positioned facing N to S.

This is where the sacred mirror Yata no kagami is kept. It is one of the three sacred insignia of the Empire, along with the sword Murakumo no tsurugi, which is in the Atsuta jingu in Nagoya, and the magatama jewels in the Imperial Palace in Tokyo.

The bronze mirror is undoubtedly of a type commonly produced in the Kofun period, before the 5th c. AD. Of either Sino-Korean or native origin, this type of mirror is believed to share the powers of its owner, and a great many were found in the tumuli of this period, which is also the time when the Japanese Imperial dynasty was founded.

Several other shrines are dependent on this one, notably Aramatsuri situated behind the main one, where the living spirit of Amaterasu is venerated.

At Ise, in Kuratayama Park (550yds/500m E of the Kintetsu station, Uji Yamada), are Jingu Chokokan, a historical museum housing a collection of artifacts relating to the shrine, and Jingu Nogyokan, an agricultural museum.

→ 10mls (16km) SE of Ise (coach): Isobe (see below) which can be reached by the toll road *Ise Highway.-

— 2 FROM ISE TO TOBA, via Ise shima Skyline (13mls/21km E; coach from Iseshi station or the shrine of Naiku). Beyond Naiku jingu, the toll road *Ise shima Skyline becomes a coast road rising up onto the slopes of Asama yama (1,814ft/553m); the scenery is not unlike that of the Mediterranean.

⟩ 8mls (13km): Kongosho ji (Rinzai sect), built on this mountain, was founded by Kobo Daishi in 830. The buildings, reconstructed in the

15th c., house a statue of Kokuzo, attributed to Kukai (Kobo Daishi), a sword which belonged to Minamoto Yoshitomo (12th c.), a portrait of Kuki Yoshitaka (16th c.), the chess set which belonged to Tokugawa Ieyasu (17th c.), etc.

10mls (16km): *Belvedere with a view over Toba Bay and its countless islets.

13mls (21km): Toba, see below.

 ALTERNATIVE ROUTE FROM ISE TO TOBA BY THE N167 (10mls/16km E; JNR and Kintetsu trains; bus). Head NE out of Ise.

4mls (7km): Futami, small summer resort. Off the nearby Futamiga ura coast, note the famous 'wedded' rocks: Myoto iwa. The Japanese associate these rocks with the original couple of the creation, Izanagi and Izanami. The 'inviting male' (29ft/9m high), surmounted by a small *torii*, is linked to the 'inviting female' (13feet/4m high) by a rope of plaited straw, which, if broken, would signify a bad omen; it is ceremoniously changed every year, on 5 January, a time when the sunrise seen between the rocks is particularly beautiful.

10mls (16km): Toba

TOBA (pop: 29,462; ferry services to Gamagori, Irako, Nagoya, Nishiura). The cultured pearl has invaded all and conquered all in Toba; you will find it hard to leave the place without taking one with you in one form or another ... The marine site of Toba has been forgotten and allowed to deteriorate because of it. Opposite the Mikimoto jetty (aquarium nearby), near to the station, is the island of pearls, a piece of Mikimoto Company publicity, of limited interest to the tourist.

It was around this island that Mikimoto Kokichi (1858–1954) succeeded in creating artificial pearls in 1893. The formation of a pearl normally takes about seven years. The young oysters, fed by artificial means, are submerged in crates and kept enclosed there for three years. Then women divers or *ama* introduce a small speck of nacre into each one, around which the pearl will be secreted. The process continues for several more years, during which time the oysters are cleaned out and re-immersed. The Mie and Nagasaki regions are the foremost pearl producers in Japan. The Toba region suffered a typhoon in 1959 which destroyed 75% of the cultures, but nowadays there is an annual harvest of 80 million pearls, or 41t, more than half the national production.

A small pearl museum is situated on the island. Note the pagoda, nearly 4ft (1.2m) high, composed entirely of pearls, more than 10,000 of them.

Motor launches link Toba with the various offshore islands, including:

3mls (5km) NW: Hyuga jima or Iruka jima (Dolphin Island), with an oceanographic and science museum; in addition to the dolphin pool mentioned above, the island is an amusement park and houses other animals, peacocks, fallow deer, monkeys, etc. Demonstrations of pearl fishing.

➜ 3½mls (6km) NE: Suga jima or Shinju to (Pearl Island) rises to 777ft (237m) at its highest point and is also a centre for the culture of pearl oysters, with its traditional women divers or *ama*.

➜ 12mls (20km) NE: Kami jima, another pearl culture island, was celebrated by the contemporary novelist Yukio Mishima (1925-70).

➤ **3 FROM TOBA TO KASHIKOJIMA** (23mls/37km S, via Pearl Road and the N 167; Kintetsu ER train; coach). Heading SE out of Toba you will soon rejoin the coast to cross one of the numerous inlets between Imaura and Motoura.

⤳ 4mls (7km): Motoura; *Pearl Road (a toll road) runs from here, providing a new of the Ise peninsula coast, and quickly coming within sight of the attractive Bay of Matoya.

15mls (25km): Matoya; the Bay of Matoya is extended westwards by Izona ura creek, famous for its oysters and sea eels.

18mls (29km): Isobe, where you can rejoin the N167. It is possible to visit the Izono miya shrine, which is part of Ise Jingu (550yds/500m W of the Shima Isobe, Kintetsu station).

➜ 7mls (12km) E (coach): Anori zaki; you will pass Kokubun ji temple to get there. Situated to the S of the Bay of Matoya, *the view from here is very beautiful; puppet theatre in the small village nearby.

➜ 8mls (13km) SW (coach): Gokasho ura is at the head of the bay of this name, which can be crossed by boat to Hazama or Tasoura. Satsuma orange growing.

➤ 21mls (34km): Ugata, where the N167 and N260 diverge and head towards Kashikojima and Goza.

➜ 6½mls (11km) SW (coach): Hamajima (boat to Goza and Kashikojima) lies in Ago Bay opposite Goza.

➤ **FROM UGATA TO GOZA BY ROAD** (15mls/25km SW; coach). The N260 goes E out of Ugata and runs the whole length of the Saki shima peninsula.

6mls (10km): Daio, a busy little fishing port near to Cape Daio, juts out to the SE of the Ise shima National Park and is a favourite haunt of artists.

12mls (19km): Wagu, a small village facing the Pacific Ocean with one foot in Ago Bay. Pearl oyster culture.

15mls (25km); Goza (boat to Hamajima and Kashikojima), at the tip of the Saki shima peninsula. Note here the statue of a recumbent Buddha, half under water.

➤ 23mls (37km): Kashikojima (boat to Goza and Hamajima) stands on one of the numerous peninsulas which jut out all around the extremely attractive *Ago Bay. Pearl culture occupies the entire bay, which is strewn with many pine-covered islets. The National Pearl

Research Laboratory was set up at Kashikojima in 1955; it has several collections of interest in this field.

Ishinomaki (Island of Honshu)

Map of Tohoku, pp. 232–3.

Tokyo, 250mls (403km) – Akita, 142mls (228km) – Fukushima, 83mls (133km) – Morioka, 110mls (178km) – Sendai, 33mls (54km) – Yamagata, 91mls (147km).

Miyagi ken – pop: 120,699.

Situated in Sendai Bay, at the mouth of the Kitakami gawa, the longest river in Tohoku (151mls/243km), this town was once an ideal loading port for the rice harvests of northern Honshu. When the railways arrived, this business was diverted from Ishinomaki, which is now becoming one of the most important fishing ports in Japan.

Hiyori yama (1½ml/2km S of the station; bus) towers high above the mouth of the Kitakami gawa; this hill, covered with cherry trees, affords attractive views over the coast and the surrounding area. There is a Japanese garden worth seeing on the lower slopes.

☞ VICINITY

1 *KINKA ZAN (35mls/57km SE by the itinerary shown; coach to Ayukawa; boat from Ishinomaki and Ayukawa). On the way out of Ishinomaki, a toll road runs beneath Maki Yama, which has been landscaped into a lovely public park, and then rejoins the JNR railway from Onagawa.

4mls (7km): Turn off on the r. for a road which runs part way along the rocky coast to Oshika.

7mls (12km) SE (coach); small inlet of Tsukino ura, where Hasekura Tsunenaga embarked for the courts of Madrid and Rome in October 1613, commissioned by Date Masamune, Lord of Sendai.

9mls (15km): A toll road to Oshika branches off on the r.

½ml (1km) E (coach; JNR train from Ishinomaki): Onagawa, a small fishing port (whalers), and point of embarkation for Kinka zan. Tohoku University (Sendai) has a marine laboratory here.

The toll road runs all the way along the Oshika peninsula, which reaches a height of 1,460ft (445m) at Dairokuten zan and provides beautiful *views on both sides over the Pacific Ocean and Sendai Bay, and over the island of Kinka zan further on.

28mls (45km): At the very end of the scenic route, cut across Cape Kuro before reaching Oshika.

31mls (50km): Oshika, and Ayukawa port, where you can embark for Kinka zan, once again skirting Kuro saki. Small whaling museum at Oshika.

35mls (57km): *Kinka zan; this little island measures no more than

3mls (5km) from any one point to another, and rises to a height of 1,460ft (445m) at Kogane yama. Its name 'golden flower' almost certainly originates from the nature of the granitic rock which has patches of mica gleaming on its surface. Any visitor to the island will be particulary delighted by the rich and varied vegetation, and by the monkeys and a great many fallow deer. A number of pathways cut across the island, providing pleasant walks around the island, or directly to the summit. The Shinto deities Kanayama hiko and Kanayama hime no Mikoto, children of Izanami, are venerated here.

2 MATSUSHIMA, see Shiogama.

◼ Ito (Island of Honshu)

Map of Natural Resources, p. 66.

Tokyo, 73mls (117km) - Kofu, 93mls (150km) - Nagano, 198mls (319km) - Nagoya, 167mls (269km) - Shizuoka, 58mls 694km) - Yokohama, 57mls (92km).

Shizuoka ken - pop: 63,003 - spa town and summer resort.

Ito and Atami are the main tourist resorts on the Izu peninsula. Like Atami, Ito was built on the E side of the peninsula, and is a good point of departure for exploring this area. Ito possesses about 800 thermal springs in all, the waters of which may be pumped up from a depth of several hundred feet; their temperature varies from 77°F to 158°F (25°C to 70°C).

Ito, like Hirugakojima (see Nirayama Onsen), sheltered the exiled Minamoto Yoritomo between 1160 and 1180, and also the priest, Nichiren, a century later.

Masuyu and Moto Shishido are the two main springs at Ito. The first of these has been known since the 16th c., and the second is renowned for its antirheumatic and healing powers.

Jono ike (1ml/1.5km S of the station) is a pool fed by a lukewarm spring and stocked with fish of African and Indian origin.

On a hill to the E of this pool stands the Butsugen ji containing a painting of the Buddhist Paradise attributed to the priest Nichiren (12th c.), who spent some time in exile here. The buildings date from the 18th c.

Monument to William Adams (1ml/1.5km SE of the station): a monument to William Adams (1564-1620) was erected close to the O kawa estuary. He was the first Briton to settle in Japan and was entrusted, about the year 1605, with the construction of a Western-style ship which was launched at Ito. An annual festival takes place in his honour, on 10 August (see also Yokosuka).

▷ VICINITY

1 KAWANA (3mls/5km SE; Izu Kyuku Railway train; coach). This bay, with Amagi san (4,616ft/1,407m) in the background, is one of the most beautiful places in the Ito area. Further S is Ippeki pool, an agreeable centre for relaxation and recreation.

2 ATAMI, FUJI-HAKONE-IZU NATIONAL PARK, see entries under these names.

Itoigawa (Island of Honshu)

Railway map on inside front cover.

Tokyo, 220mls (354km) - Fukushima, 219mls (352km) Maebashi, 146mls (235km) - Nagano, 80mls (129km) - Niigata, 105mls (169km) - Toyama, 49mls (79km) - Yamagata, 211mls (339km).

Niigata ken - pop: 38,395 - chemical industries.

Sandwiched between the outermost foothills of the Japan Alps and the Sea of Japan, on the narrow coastal strip of the Hime kawa estuary, Itoigawa is at the junction of the great Hokuriku railway line and that of Oïta, which serves the Matsumoto basin.

☞ **VICINITY**

1 OYASHIRAZU AND KOSHIRAZU (7mls/12km W; coach). These two rocky passes on the way to Hokuriku were once particularly difficult to cross and are known respectively as the Father and the Abandoned Child. The mountain drops sheer into the sea at this point, and the names refer to the risk one was forced to take in crossing it. The only way to be sure of a safe passage was to adopt the attitude 'every man for himself'...

2 HAKUBA (11mls/18km S; JNR train; coach). This is the overall name given to several spa towns (Gamawara, Himekawa, Kajiyama), which are scattered along the Hime kawa and its tributaries.

3 CHUBU SANGAKU AND JOSHIN ETSU KOGEN NATIONAL PARKS, see entries under these names.

Iwaki (Island of Honshu)

Railway map on inside front cover.

Tokyo, 130mls (209km) - Fukushima, 74mls (120km) - Maebashi, 152mls (245km) - Mito, 61mls (98km) - Niigata, 158mls (255km) - Sendai, 100mls (161km) - Utsunomiya, 106mls (171km) - Yamagata, 132mls (213km).

Fukushima ken - pop: 342,074 - industrial town.

At the foot of the Joban Mountains, E of Fukushima region, Iwaki brings together seven industrial towns (Taira, Uchigo, Joban Izumi, Onahama, Ueda, Nakoso), which stretch for 19 miles (30km) along the Joban coal basin, the most important in Honshu. In spite of a drop in coal production, Iwaki has been chosen for a special development programme: it is hoped that the Iwaki-Koriyama region will become an area of importance to the balance of the economy. The port of Ena at Onahama is Iwaki's outlet to the sea.

Taira is the principal town of the urban area of Iwaki. Note the ruins of Iwaki jo (770yds/700m NW of Taira station): this castle, built in the 16th c., has belonged successively to the Kitabatake, the Iwaki, the Torii, the Naito, the Inoue, and the Ando, who kept it until the Restoration in 1868.

Yumoto (3½mls/6km SW of Taira; station), which stands at the heart of the Joban coalfield, is also a spa town with springs containing saline hydrogen sulphide.

Nakoso (15mls/25km SW of Taira; station) was once a fortified town responsible for keeping up the Ebisu threat to the N; a toll-post was later set up on the Joban road between the provinces of Hitachi and Iwaki.

VICINITY

1 KOFUN DE NAKATA (approx. 3½mls/6km E of Taira). This tumulus, next to the road, was excavated from 1969 onwards. The inside has been restored and made safe for the public; some traces of mural paintings are visible.

2 AKAI DAKE (approx. 6½mls/11km NW of Taira). It is possible to begin the ascent of this mountain (alt. 1,985ft/605m) from Akaidake station, 3mls (5km) NW of Taira station. The Jofuku ji, dedicated to Yakushi Nyorai and founded in 806, is near the summit.

3 NATSUIGAWA GORGES (5-15mls/8-24km NW of Taira). These gorges cut deep into the Joban massif and stretch for about 9mls (15km) between Ogawa and Kawamae stations; the railway is built into the side of the gorge.

Iwakuni (Island of Honshu)

Map of Shikoku (Inland Sea), pp. 536-7.

Tokyo, 566mls (911km) - Hiroshima, 24mls (38km) - Matsue, 142mls (229km) - Yamaguchi, 64mls (103km).

Yamaguchi ken - pop: 113,000 - industrial town: synthetic fibres, petrochemicals.

At the mouth of the Nishiki gawa a feudal town was once built on a bend of the river. Nowadays, Iwakuni has become one of the main economic centres of Yamaguchi ken. It extends towards the N and the town of Otake (in the Hiroshima prefecture) on an important industrial area of land reclaimed from the sea.

'KINTAI BASHI (1ml/1.5km W of Nishi-Iwakuni station or 1ml/1.5km NW of Kawanishi station; bus from Iwakuni station). This sharply humped bridge across the Nishiki gawa was built in 1673 by Kikkawa Hiroyoshi, Lord of Iwakuni.

633ft long by 16ft wide (193m by 5m), the bridge reaches a maximum height of 39ft (12m) and has five arches. It was destroyed by a typhoon in 1950 and rebuilt in 1953. It is nicknamed Soroban Bashi, or abacus bridge, because the shape is suggestive of the traditional

Japanese abacus. Upstream from this bridge, the river narrows into a series of gorges; there are several teahouses along the shore.

 Opposite the bridge, a little cablecar goes up to Iwakuni Castle, where the Nishimura Museum houses several collections relating to the history of Iwakuni and the Kikkawa.

This castle was built between 1603 and 1608 by Kikkawa Hiromasa, who had received the land from the Mori, but Tokugawa Iemitsu had it demolished shortly afterwards; a building inspired by those of southern Europe was built on the same site in 1962.

Izu shoto**

Map of Natural Resources, p. 66.

Tokyo, 207mls (334km, Hachijo jima), 73mls (117km, O shima).

Tokyo to.

This archipelago is made up of seven main islands (Izu shichito: O, To, Nii, Kozu, Miyake, Mikura, Hachijo) which are dotted around the S of Sagami Bay, linking Honshu to the distant Ogasawara islands. These islands form part of the great Bonin volcanic arc, which ends in central Japan with the Izu peninsula and the mountains to the N of Fuji san. Although administratively governed by the Tokyo prefecture, the islands are included in the Fuji-Hakone-Izu National Park (see entry under this name).

Like many of the minor islands surrounding Japan, they have been used as places of exile and refuge throughout history. Notable figures who have passed through them include Minamoto Tametomo (1139-70), uncle of Yoritomo, who was a semi-legendary hero. when he was banished to O shima by the Taira, he settled here and succeeded in conquering the other islands of the archipelago. In the 17th c. Urika Hideie, following his defeat at Sekigahara, was exiled on the orders of Tokugawa Ieyasu, to Hachijo jima where he became a Buddhist monk.

ˈO SHIMA. This is the nearest and largest of these islands. Lying in the Sagami Sea, off the Izu peninsula, its highest point is Mihara yama (2,487ft/758m), a volcano which is still active. Readily accessible from Tokyo, the island is particularly attractive for its mild climate and luxuriant vegetation (camellia cultivation); the native people maintain their own traditional way of life. Oshima (Motomachi) to the W and Okada to the N are the two points of access to the island.

→ MIHARA YAMA (7mls/12km E of Motomachi and S of Okada; coach). A road affording beautiful *views over the island and Izu Bay in the distance winds rapidly upwards to the edge of the outer crater; the small spa town of Yuba lies en route.

→ SENZU (5½mls/9km SE of Okada; coach). You can go to Oshima

Prefectural Park (296 acres/120ha) from here, with its tropical and subtropical vegetation, zoo and campsite. A religious figure, attributed to a Buddhist ascetic of the 8th c., is carved into the rocks of Gyoja Cave (in the S of the park) which opens onto the sea. Above the park, on the slopes of Mihara yama, towards the W, stands a giant cherry tree (Sakura kabu) which is 10ft (3m) tall and extremely beautiful when it flowers in spring.

→ **HABUMINATO** (9mls/15km SE of Motomachi; coach). This is a small man-made port, constructed in 1751 inside the actual crater of a volcano; it may be reached from the western side of the island, which is indented by cliffs beyond Nomashi. A site of the Jomon period was discovered at Tatsunokuchi, near Nomashi.

TO SHIMA (17mls/27km S of O shima; boat). Situated between O shima and Kozu shima, this is the smallest inhabited island of the Izu archipelago. It towers to a height of over 1,650ft (500m) and has a steep, sheer coastline.

NII JIMA, SHIKINE JIMA AND KOZU SHIMA. These three form a line of islands to the S of the preceding islands. They are linked to each other and are accessible from O shima or Shimoda. There are two thermal springs: Mamage and Jinata Ashitsuki.

MIYAKE JIMA (45mls/73km S of O shima). It is a round island above which rises the volcano O yama (2,671ft/814m). It last erupted in 1983.

'HACHIJO JIMA (65mls/105km S of Miyake jima; 109mls/175km S of O shima). This is the second most important island of Izu shichito, and the most frequently visited after O shima; although it is further from the capital, there are regular flights to it. It is a very attractive spot, overlooked by two volcanos: Nishi or Hachijo Fuji to the NW (2,802ft/854m alt.) and Higashi or Mihara (2,300ft/701m) to the SE, which can be climbed. To the NE of this island is the seismic epicentre which causes tremors felt as far away as Tokyo. The island is a paradise for fishermen and lovers of exotic fruits and seascapes.

Izumo (Island of Honshu)

Map of Places of Interest, p. 71.

Tokyo, 556mls (895km) – Hiroshima, 114mls (184km) – Matsue, 21mls (34km) – Okayama, 131mls (211km) – Tottori, 104mls (167km) – Yamaguchi, 129mls (207km).

Airport: TDA flights to Oki shoto and Osaka.

Shimane ken – pop: 69,078.

Izumo is a small town some distance from the Sea of Japan and Lake Shinji. A number of visitors and pilgrims pass through it to reach the shrine of Izumo, which is undoubtedly the oldest and most venerated in Japan after Ise. Many young girls go to Izumo-Taisha since pilgrimages to this shrine are renowned for fulfilling one's desires for marriage.

VICINITY

1 **IZUMO TAISHA** (5½mls/9km NW: JNR train to Taisha; coach; Ichibata ER train from Matsue). The shrine, which has an avenue of pine trees leading to it, is ½ml (1km) N of the station.

DIVINE HERITAGE. The unruly prince Susano o no Mikoto, born out of the nose of Izanagi, was sent to earth by the assembly of the gods for having forced Amaterasu to retire from the world (see Ise); it was the land of Izumo to which he came. There he met an old couple who ruled over the country, and who were in despair at the havoc being wrought by a dragon with eight heads and eight tails, Yamata no orochi. To make matters worse, they were to hand over to the dragon their youngest daughter, Princess Inada. Fortunately, Susano o devised a plan: he had the beast served with eight large bowls of *sake* so that each of the monster's eight heads became inebriated; it was then quite easy to cut them off and, the legend adds, to pull out the sacred sword, Murakumo no tsurugi, now kept in the Atsuta jingu in Nagoya. Then Susano o married Inada hime, and their descendant Okuninushi became ruler of the land of Izumo. Amaterasu, the sister of Susano o, laid claim to the kingdom for her grandson Ninigi no Mikoto, and Okuninushi had to give way and settled on the site of the Izumo shrine which is dedicated to him. Modern historians seem to interpret the mythological rivalry between Susano o and Amaterasu as symbolic of a struggle between two rival clans who, around the 3rd c. AD, were contesting governmental supremacy. This finally fell to the sovereigns of Yamato, founders of the Imperial dynasty.

OYUSHIRO ZUKURI. The architectural style of the Izumo shrine is regarded as the oldest in Japan; it differs considerably from that of Ise. Several rectangular enclosures surround the principal shrine, or Hon den. This is built on a square plan and surmounted by a high roof of cypress bark (hinoki) supported by a central pillar; at the corners and sides, eight secondary pillars divide each side into two. A covered staircase, jutting out to the r. of the centre of the front wall, leads to this raised shrine. Two *chigi*, sparsely ornamented flat wooden beams, cross over each other on the roof.

The main festivals of Izumo shrine take place between 14 and 16 May.

Pilgrims flock there in October in particular, as this is when the Kami are supposed to meet at Izumo, abandoning all the other shrines in Japan for this period.

The main opening on the perimeter of the shrine is a huge *torii*, 75ft (23m) high, which leads into a vast courtyard containing the Izumo taisha buildings. These were last rebuilt in 1874, and stand at the foot of Hanakata sen (1,758ft/536m) which forms a background of vivid greenery. The Hon den itself, in the centre of the enclosure, was rebuilt in the 18th c. West of the great courtyard is a modern building by Kiyonori Kikutake, which houses the treasury: *objets d'art,* religious furniture and finds from excavations undertaken within the shrine enclosure.

→ 6mls (10km) NW (coach): Hino Point, which marks the tip of Hanakata sen, at the W end of the Shimane peninsula. Former shrine; lighthouse. All this area, along with the shrine at Izumo, is part of Daisen Oki National Park (see entry under this name).

2 *TACHIKUE KYO (7mls/12km S; coach). These rocky gorges stretch for half a mile along the Kando gawa.

3 MATSUE, ODA, see entries under these names.

■ Joshin Etsu Kogen (National park; Island of Honshu)**

HOW TO GET THERE

- From Karuizawa, this place is 14mls (22km) E of Komoro and 25mls (41km) W of Takasaki; it is linked by JNR train and coach to these two towns. Direct trains go from Tokyo to Karuizawa (2h. from Ueno), and from Omiya to Takasaki. Coach services from Karuizawa Onsen to Shirane san.

- From Komoro (JNR station), 104mls (168km) NW of Tokyo (2¼h. by train) and 32mls (52km) SE of Nagano (45 min. by train): direct trains from these two towns; coach from Komoro to Shin Kazawa Onsen.

- From Nagano or Nakano, you can take the train (Nagano ER) to Yudanaka station (19mls/30km in 1h.10 from Nagano), where coaches leave for Shiga kogen and Kusatsu Onsen; direct coaches from Nagano.

- From Shibukawa, JNR train to Manza-Kazawa guchi station (35mls/56km W in 1h. approx.; direct trains from Tokyo-Ueno); from this station, coaches operate to Karuizawa, Shin Kazawa, Kusatsu and Shirane san.

This mountain park (466,818 acres/188,915ha) is made up of two distinct areas, one focusing on Myoko san (8,090ft/2,466m), and the other between the Plateau of Shiga and Asama yama (8,340ft/2,542m). These regions, situated in central Japan, are separated by the Nagano basin. The famous spa town Kusatsu is in this park, and Karuizawa, a fashionable mountain resort frequented by the people of Tokyo, lies to the SE of Asama yama. With regard to this part of the national park, we would recommend a visit to Myoko kogen.

➤ **1 FROM KARUIZAWA TO KUSATSU** (30mls/49km N; coach, direct or changing at Manza Kazawa guchi station). Karuizawa, at an altitude of 3,081ft (939m), is mainly a summer resort, appreciated for its coolness (average 68°F/20°C in August) and popular with inhabitants of Tokyo fleeing from the humid heat of the capital. Since the end of the 19th c. it has been a favourite place for foreigners. Karuizawa is a peaceful spot with a large number of detached houses scattered across a huge forest park, and its population quadruples during July and August.

3mls (5km) NE: Kumano shrine, above the Usui pass (3,136ft/956m), which can be crossed by the N18 road or the railway, and which leads from Kanto to the higher regions of Shinano. Observation platform near the shrine.

From Karuizawa, one can go directly to Onioshidashi (via Hoshino Onsen) using a toll road (coach). It is more usual to take the coach from Karuizawa station or from Naka-Karuizawa.

Head W out of Karuizawa on the N18.

3mls (5km): Naka Karuizawa; take the N146 to the N of here.

5mls (8km): Senga taki, where Karuizawa ice rink is situated. Walks in the surrounding area on the slopes of Asama yama. The N146 continues up the sides of Asama yama, and crosses some beautiful forests.

9mls (14km): At this junction, take the attractive forest toll road towards Onioshidashi; the N146 continues towards Kusatsu.

13mls (21m): *Onioshidashi; a strange conglomeration of basalt, formed by the lava from Mount Asama when it erupted in 1783.

*Asama yama (8,340ft/2,542m), which rises up to the S, is one of the most famous active volcanos and one of the highest mountains in the country. The ascent of this mountain is best undertaken on its south face, and can be attempted from Komoro or from the crossroads 9mls (14km) away, mentioned above. The walk around the crater (½ml/1km approx.) is most impressive, but beware of vertigo; view over a wide area on all sides.

19mls (31km): Manza Kazawa guchi station, where you can rejoin the N146 (toll road) and reach Kusatsu, or continue N (13mls/21km; toll road; coach) towards Manza Onsen, see 2 below.

6 mls (10km) SW: Shin Kazawa Onsen, spa and winter sports resort at an altitude of 4,101ft (1,250m); also accessible from Komoro.

30mls (49km): *Kusatsu Onsen (direct coach from Naganohara), at an altitude of approx. 5,000ft (1,500m), is overlooked to the NW by the Shirane san. This spa town is one of the most popular in Japan. Its springs containing sulphur, iron, arsenic and alum are thought to be effective against skin diseases, rheumatism and circulation problems. The water gushes forth at temperatures of between 109°F and 147°F (43°C and 64°C). Although they have been known since antiquity, the springs were made fashionable in the 12th c. by Minamoto Yoritomo.

The great attraction of Kusatsu is its hot open-air bath (Netsu-noy), situated at Yabatake; after running through a series of pools, the water, which is very hot, is brought down to the (still unbearable) temperature of 120°F (50°C). The bath, which is quite spectacular (about 50 people per session), has a 'bathing master' who beats time, and lasts just over three minutes; the whole treatment is repeated three times a day over a seven-week period, at the end of which the bathers go to regenerate their skin in the springs of Sawatari or Shibu.

There are some pleasant walks around Kusatsu: the wooded hill Kakomi yama, the sulphur springs of Saino Kawara, the rocks of Sesshogawara (on the slopes of Shirane san), the frozen valley of Kori, the Osen waterfall, etc. There are also winter sports in Kusatsu from December to March.

2 FROM KUSATSU TO YUDANAKA (22mls/36km NW by the N292 toll road; coach via Shiga kogen). The **Shiga Kusatsu driveway, going out of Kusatsu, follows the slopes of Shirane san through the *rocky valley of Sesshogawara (cable-car; ski runs).

8mls (13km): Path to *Shirane san (7,054ft/2,150m), also known as Kusatsu Shirane to distinguish it from two other peaks of the same name. This volcano consists of three craters, and the middle one, Yugama (hot water cauldron), throws up thick steam (geysers).

1½ml (2km) W (coach): Manza Onsen is a spa town and winter sports resort (cable-car and ski-lift) between the mountains of Shirane, Moto Shirane (7,139ft/2,176m) and Manza (6,542ft/1,994m).

11mls (18km): Shibu toge, alt. 7,126ft (2,172m). A chair-lift goes from here to the neighbouring peak, Mount Yokote (7,559ft/2,304m). The return route is over the high valleys of Shiga.

14mls (22km): Kumanoyu Onsen is the main spa town of *Shiga kogen, a plateau with an average altitude of 5,000ft (1,500m). Lakes, forests and hot springs make it an excellent place for walks, most of which are signposted. There are many winter sports resorts in the surrounding area. The spa towns of Shiga kogen, along with those of Yudanaka, are known collectively by the name Yamanouchi.

15mls (25km): Maruike Onsen, at the heart of Shiga kogen and Joshin Etsu National Park. A cable-car goes from near this resort (with a change at Happo Onsen), to the summit of Higashi Tate-yama (6,600ft/2,030m; viewpoint); from there one can head NE on foot to Iwasuge yama (7,529ft/2,295m).

22mls (36km); Yudanaka Onsen belongs to the Yamanouchi thermal group. Amongst the Yudanaka springs are Andai and Shibu to the SE, which are the most popular.

2mls (4km) E: Kambayashi Onsen, where you can walk to the *valley of Jigoku (1ml/2km on foot towards the N), famous for its verdant setting and hot springs; geysers; monkeys.

From Yudanaka station, the Nagano ER can take you to Nagano.

Kaga (Island of Honshu)

Tokyo, 345mls (556km) – Fukui, 21mls (34km) – Gifu, 130mls (209km) – Kanazawa, 28mls (45km) – Toyama, 68mls (110km).

Ishikawa ken – pop: 56,514 – textile industries.

Kaga, in the S of the Ishikawa region, is near the Sea of Japan and is overlooked to the E by the massif of Hakusan. Easy access from the town to the neighbouring spa resorts.

The scholar, Hayashi Doshun, or Razan (1583-1657), was born in Kaga.

DAISHOJI CASTLE RUINS (1¼mls/2km W; bus). The castle is in a park at the western limit of the town, near the Daishoji gawa.

The castle, which bears the old name of the town of Kaga, was erected in the 15th c. by the Tsuba daimyo. It had several owners until the 1868 Restoration, including the Maeda clan from 1600.

½ml (1km) approx. to the S is the shrine of Enuma, with a teahouse, Choryu tei, built by the master Kobori Enshu (1579-1647).

VICINITY

1 KATAYAMAZU ONSEN (6mls/10km NE; coach; or JNR train to Ibarihashi, then coach). This is a resort situated on the shores of Shibayama lagoon, which has saline springs (154°F/68°C). There is fishing and boating on the lake.

2 YAMANAKA ONSEN (6mls/10km SE; coach). Head E out of Kaga on the N305 which joins the N8, and go straight on up the Daishoji gawa valley.

3mls (5km): Turning for the spa town of Yamashiro.

½ml (1km) NE (coach from Kaga): Yamashiro Onsen (saline springs of 126°-153°F/52°-67°C) near the little village of Kutani, famous for its brightly coloured china; small museum at the spa town.

KUTANI YAKI. The presence of kaolin, discovered in Kutani in the 17th c., drew several potters from Arita (see Imari) to this village; they set up their ceramic workshops which rapidly prospered. The decoration is often a mixture of basic geometric themes and bold naturalistic ones, which on a rather crude and heavy object gives an impression of strength and assurance, combined with a daring sense of design.

➡ 4mls (7km) NE by the same route (coach from Yamashiro Onsen): *Nata dera (Shingon sect); this temple, built on the side of a hill, was founded in 717. Amongst the buildings, reconstructed in 1644, the most noteworthy are the Saihin kaku (main hall), the three-storey pagoda, the belfry, the Goma do and the Sho in. Pretty garden.

♨ 6mls (10km): Yamanaka Onsen, a resort with saline and sulphur springs (91°-124°F/33°-51°C), situated between attractive hills (the maples are especially beautiful in autumn). You can visit the Io ji. Cable-car up Minashi yama (1,148ft/350m) which has a fine view. Boat trips up the beautiful *Kuro dani gorge between the bridges of Korogi and Kurodani.

3 FUKUI, KANAZAWA, HAKUSAN NATIONAL PARK, see entries under these names.

K Kagoshima (Island of Kyushu)**

Map of Natural Resources p. 66, and Places of Interest p. 71

Tokyo, 910mls (1,463km) - Kukuoka, 194mls (313km) - Kumamoto, 120mls (194km) - Miyazaki, 79mls (127km).

Capital of Kagoshima ken (pop: 878,290) - pop: 403,340 - centre of industry and commerce - national and private universities.

Numerous towns have tried to resemble Venice; Kagoshima is comparable with Naples, and the menacing volcano Sakurajima, which confronts the Italian city's twin, serves only to underline this resemblance. The place really does captivate the visitor with its harmonious shapes, gentle climate (average temperatures 43.9°F/6.6°C in January, 80.8°F/27.1°C in August), subtropical fragrances, and 'exotic' vegetation. Kagoshima also channels the economic and intellectual activity of southern Kyushu, and constitutes one of the main ports of access to the archipelago of Nansei.

SAINT FRANCIS XAVIER IN JAPAN. Kagoshima only plays a significant part in history from the 16th c. onwards, when the Portuguese were welcomed by the Shimazu daimyo who were trying to establish trade links with them. On 15 August 1549 Francis Xavier (1506-52) came from Malacca and disembarked at Kagoshima, where he was received by Shimazu Takahisa (1514-71). The latter, noticing that the Portuguese preferred the anchorage at Hirado (see entry under this name), blamed this change of mind on the missionary, who was forced to go to Hirado in 1550.

THE SHIMAZU OF SATSUMA. By the end of the 12th c. the private kingdom of Satsuma had come back into the hands of Shimazu Tadehisa, the illegitimate son of Minamoto Yoritomo, and it remained in this family until the Imperial Restoration of 1868. The Shimazu of Kagoshima organized pirate raids to the Ryuku islands and eastern China. From the 16th c. onwards they tried to expand their influence to the S of Kyushu, but their efforts were checked by Toyotomi Hideyoshi. In 1609 Tadatsune (1576-1638) turned his attention to the Ryuku islands, which he placed under his sovereignty. By the 19th c. the Satsuma clan had become one of the most powerful in Japan. They were in favour of an Imperial return to power, but against the idea of opening up the country to foreigners. Following an incident of honour, in which an English merchant was killed by the men of Satsuma, the British Admiral Kuper took reprisals by bombarding the town of Kagoshima in 1863.

THE SATSUMA REVOLT. Saigo Takamori (1826-77) was a native of Kagoshima who had distinguished himself as a partisan of the Imperial Restoration, acquired the title of marshal and took a part in the new government. However, he disapproved of the westernization of the country, and withdrew to Kagoshima. There he formed an 'anti-establishment' school, which caused offence to the government. This was how the Satsuma rebellion began. Saigo seized Kagoshima in 1877 and then Kumamoto, but was defeated at Hyugu, and fell back on Kagoshima where he put up fierce resistance to the Imperial troops. He finally committed suicide at Shiro yama, along with his partisans. The town was then set on fire and the toll of victims was high. Saigo's good reputation was restored in 1890.

FAMOUS PEOPLE BORN IN KAGOSHIMA. Several famous men born in this town were contemporaries: Marshal Saigo Takamori (1826-77); General Kuroki Tamesada (1844-1923); Admirals Ito Sukeyuki (1843-1914) and Togo Heihachiro (1847-1934); the politicians Mori Arinori (1847-89), Okubo Toshimichi (1832-78) and Sakomizu Hisatsune; the industrialist and collector Matsukata Kojiro (1865-1950); and the producer Yamamoto Satsuo, born in 1910.

*SHIRO YAMA (1½ml/2km NE of Nishi-Kagoshima eki; 1ml/2km SW of Kagoshima eki; bus from the latter). Standing between the stations of Kagoshima and Nishi-Kagoshima, this wooded hill (approx. 600 different species of plants; alt. 351ft/107m) acts as a natural *vantage point in the town centre, with a view over the town, which is bounded to the E by the sea, and beyond to the volcano of Sakurajima belching thick smoke. The main historical monuments of the town are spread out at the foot of the hill.

Behind Shiro yama is the cave where Saigo Takamori killed himself (see Historical survey).

Izuro dori starts at Nishi-Kagoshima station and forms one of the main arterial roads of the modern town; before reaching the port it joins the Noya dori, which leads N to Kagoshima station.

Just after Nishi-Kagoshima station, Izuro dori crosses the Kotsuki gawa, which runs through the town.

Nishida bashi is the first bridge upstream on this river and was constructed in 1839. For a long time it was one of the few stone bridges in Japan.

A monument dedicated to Saint Francis Xavier (1ml/1.5km NE of Nishi-Kagoshima eki), the first Christian missionary to set foot in Japan (see Historical survey), consists of a sculpted arcade and a bust (about 110yds/100m to the N of the bus stop or Takami Baba tram stop).

Close by, a memorial church was built in 1949 for the 400th anniversary of the arrival of Saint Francis Xavier.

Between this church and the monument, a road forming a continuation of Nishida bashi (see above) crosses Tenmonkan dori to the NE; this street leads l. to Terukuni shrine.

A **TERUKUNI JINJA** (1½ml/2km NE of Nishi-Kagoshima eki; bus to Tenmonkan dori). Built at the end of the 19th c., this shrine is dedicated to Shimazu Nariakira (1809-58), a partisan of the Emperor who opened his country to western technology; behind the shrine, a flight of steps goes up to Shiro yama. Close by, there is a large statue of Saigo Takamori.

A road going past the *torii* of this shrine, and continuing NE along the foot of Shiro yama, provides a good vantage point for the following.

■ **PERFECTURAL MUSEUM OF FINE ARTS** (1½ml/2km NE of Nishi Kagoshima eki; open daily from 09.00 to 17.00). Several temporary exhibitions are held here, and the museum's collections include some ancient paintings, Satsuma pottery, mementoes of Saigo Takamori, a paleontological collection, etc.

▙▟ **RUNS OF TSURUMARU JO** (1½ml/2km NE of Nishi-Kagoshima eki; ½ml/1km SW of Kagoshima eki). Only a series of ramparts bordered by moats remains. The site is occupied by the Medical School of Kagoshima.

A castle was first built on this site by the Ueyama, who were succeeded by the Kimotsuki, who were themselves dispossessed in 1341 by Shimazu Sadahisa. Iehisa, a descendant of the latter, rebuilt Tsurumaru Castle on this site in the 16th c., and the Shimazu remained there until the Restoration. Converted into a barracks, the castle burnt down in 1874.

SATSUMA GISHI. This is a monument at the foot of Shiro yama, which can be reached by skirting the castle to the NW. Built in 1920, the monument is dedicated to the memory of the supporters of the Satsuma clan who, under the direction of Yukie Hirata, attempted to build a dam on the Kiso gawa in the 18th c., at the request of shogun Tokugawa. Faced with failure and the ruinous expense incurred, about 40 of them committed suicide.

▲ •ISO KOEN (2mls/3km) NE of Kagoshima eki; 3½mls/6km NE of Nishi-Kagoshima eki; bus). This park was designed in the 17th c. at the request of Shimazu Mitsuhisa. It is a typical Japanese garden, and boasts an ornamental lake, well-kept vegetation and a graceful detached house, where the present-day Japanese flag was designed.

◼ Shoko shusei kan, situated to the S of the park, was built in 1855 under the aegis of Shimazu Nariakisa, and used to be a factory making munitions, glassware and pottery. It employed up to 1,200 workers and is now arranged as a history museum with exhibits relating to the Shimazu family and the Satsuma clan.

At Ijin kan, next to the park, some English engineers set up a cotton weaving centre under the protection of the Shimazu.

A cable-car goes up Iso yama (554ft/169m), which rises behind the park, and provides a view over Sakurajima from the summit. The *coast beyond Iso koen is very beautiful and, recalling the comparison with the Naples region, it is reminiscent of the Amalfi coast.

KAMOIKE PARK (2mls/3km SE of Nishi Kagoshima eki; bus). This is a huge leisure complex containing a sports ground, the Marine Tower, a tropical botanical garden, etc.

⌐ VICINITY

1 ••SAKURAJIMA (2mls/3km E; ferry from Sakurajima jetty; mornings only, coach trips round the mountain). This active volcano is made up of several peaks, namely, from N to S: Kita dake (3,668ft/1,118m), Naka dake (3,642ft/1,110m), and Minami dake (3,478ft/1,060m), the most active of the three. This former island was joined to the land again by the 1914 eruption. Apart from the barren areas where the lava was scattered, the fertile mountain earth produces fruit: melons, lemons, citrus fruit, miniature oranges (an inch, or 3cm, in diameter) and giant radishes (daikon) which grow to a circumference of 4½ft (1.4m)! Access to the spa town of Furusato to the S (waters at 118°F/48°C), and to the viewpoints of Yunohira and Arimura.

2 IJUIN (11mls/18km NW; JNR train). This is the birthplace of Satsuma pottery; this porcelain, with its crackled appearance, is very popular for its richly coloured floral motifs which stand out against a cream or gold background. Festival at Tokushige shrine 20–21 October.

3 IBUSUKI, KIRISHIMA YAKU NATIONAL PARK, see entries under these names.

K **Kamakura** (Island of Honshu)**

Map of the Vicinity of Tokyo, p. 565; street plan of Kamakura, pp. 282–3.

Tokyo, 28mls (45km) – Kofu, 93mls (150km) – Shizuoka, 83mls (133km) – Yokohama, 13mls (21km).

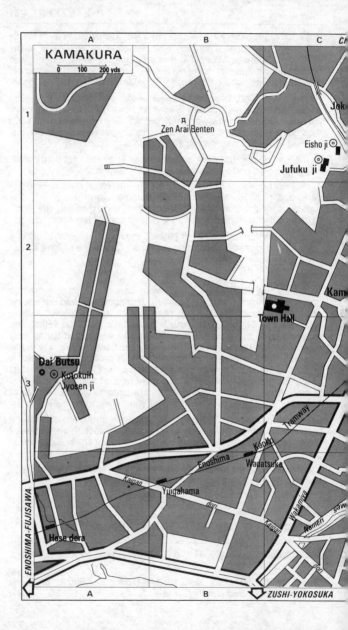

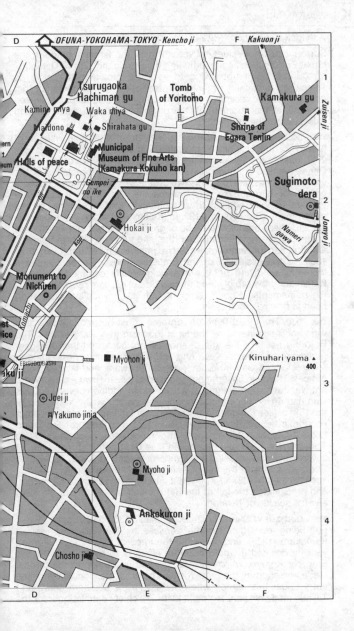

OFUNA-YOKOHAMA-TOKYO · Kencho ji   F   Kakuon ji

Tsurugaoka Hachiman gu

Kamino miya   Waka miya

Maidono   Shirahata gu

Municipal Museum of Fine Arts (Kamakura Kokuho kan)

Halls of peace

Gempei no ike

Koji

Hokai ji

Komachi

Monument to Nichiren

st ice

aku ji

EBISUDO BASHI

Myohon ji

Joei ji

Yakumo jinja

Myoho ji

Ankokuron ji

Chosho ji

Tomb of Yoritomo

Kamakura gu

Shrine of Egara Tenjin

Sugimoto dera

Zuisen ji

Jomyo ji

Nameri gawa

Kinuhari yama ▲
400

D   E   F

1   2   3   4

Kanagawa ken - pop: 139,249 - seaside resort.

Surrounded on all sides by verdant hills, the famous image of the Great Buddha has been meditating here since the 12th c. The influx of tourists, no doubt owing to its close proximity to Tokyo, is somewhat inimical to poetic contemplation, which demands that one's senses be receptive. One should ignore distractions however, because, at that moment, in the presence of the Buddha, nothing exists except the moment itself.

1192: THE BAFUKA OF KAMAKURA. It was from the little village of Kamakura, to which he had retreated, that Minamoto Yoritomo (1147–99) harassed the Taira, masters of Kyoto, until they were defeated at Danno ura (see Shimonoseki). Yoritomo was a remarkable character, who did not hesitate to kill his two brothers in order to gain complete power for himself. He was granted the title of Sei i Taishogun (general-in-chief against the Barbarians), and set up his official government (Bafuka) in 1192 in Kamakura, which he made his capital. These events were to be of great importance in the history of Japan since they established the shogun line whose hold on authoritarian government was to continue almost unbroken until 1868, to the exclusion of the Emperor. The latter represented a hierarchy of divine right, and was generally confined to Kyoto. Kamakura grew rapidly, and martial discipline, as a reaction against the refinements of court, brought with it a 'masculine' civilization open to new religious sects.

THE HOJO. The direct heirs of Yoritomo could not retain power and were soon eliminated by the Hojo to whom they were related. The Hojo did not take the title of shogun, but bestowed that of regent (*shikken*) on themselves, and organized a powerless shogun succession, chosen from amongst the Fujiwara, and later, Imperial princes. The Hojo government imposed its rule for over a century, but not without showing signs of weakness. In addition several knights who had driven back the Mongol invasions of Kyushu at the end of the 13th c. (see Fukuoka) vainly hoped for land in recompense; other economic factors gave rise to discontent. The Emperor Go Daigo (1288-1339) saw his chance, and rallied new supporters. Hojo Takatori (1303-33) had him exiled (see Oki Shoto), stripped him of sovereignty and installed the Emperor Kogen in Kyoto. Go Daigo returned, and with the aid of Ashikaga Takauji, seized Kyoto. Nitta Yoshisada (1301-38) also played a part by laying siege to Kamakura, and precipitated the fall of the Bafuka with the capture of the town and the suicide of Takatori.

THE KANRYO OF KAMAKURA. Ashikaga Takauji (1305-58), disappointed at not being rewarded for the services he had rendered, seized Kamakura (1335), and drove out the Imperial forces. The following year he decided it would be more effective to settle in Kyoto; the Emperor Komyo, whom he had assisted in his rise to the throne, made him shogun, the Emperor Go Daigo fell back on Yoshino (see entry under this name), where he set up the southern court, and Takauji made his son, Motouji (1340-67) 'chief commissioner for the

Kanto region' (Kanto Kanryo) in 1349. Motouji's successors retained power in Kamakura more or less successfully, trying in vain to take the title of shogun, and contesting that of Kanryo with their Uesugi ministers. One of these, Noritada (1433-54), was assassinated in 1454; this caused an uprising of his supporters, the devastation of Kamakura and the flight of Ashikaga Shigeuji to Koga. The Uesugi stayed in Kamakura, where the rivalry which began between two branches of this family led to their ruin and considerably weakened Kamakura. Hojo Soun (1432-1519) and his line took advantage of the situation, and secured for themselves the government of the province of Kanto, at Odawara. Their successors, the Tokugawa, settled in Edo (Tokyo), making this town a new centre of government. This terminated the political role of Kamakura once and for all.

ZEN. In some respects, Kamakura is the home of Zen in Japan. Zen, derived from the Chinese Ch'an sect and ultimately from India, was introduced by the priest Eisai (see Jufuku ji p. 291, but was principally taught by his disciple Dogen (1200-53). 'Zen states that no doctrine can teach the true spirit of Buddha, and declares that the Supreme Being can only be known through silent and instantaneous communication (Satori), being established between the Higher Principle and men ... Consequently, everyday activities of life must not be considered as an end in themselves, but rather as the normal expression of the spirit. A strict training, physical as well as spiritual, is absolutely necessary' (Louis Frédéric, *Japon*). This spirit, which is more philosophical than religious, must have suited the martial character of the new masters of Kamakura. The Engaku ji, Jochi ji, Jomyo ji, Jufuku ji and Kencho ji were once considered the five great Zen temples of Kamakura.

NB: If you are short of time, we recommend using a taxi to explore Kamakura. The streets are steep, and some of the monuments are several miles apart. There are signposted routes, with directions in English; note also that you must pay to enter most of the temples and shrines.

To the E of Kamakura station, and quite near it, is Wakamiya Oji which runs right across the town. This long avenue (1,500yds/1,400m) has three *torii* and leads NE to the shrine of Tsurugaoka. A terrace stands between the first and second *torii*, and is planted with azaleas and cherry trees. It reminds one of the size of the original path, made in the 12th c. on the order of Minamoto Yoritomo.

TSURUGAOKA HACHIMAN GU (plan: D1; ½ml/1km N of Kamakura station; bus). One of the finest shrines in Kamakura, it stands on a hill in the centre of a huge park containing other buildings of interest.

This shrine was founded in 1063 by Minamoto Yoriyoshi, an ancestor of Yoritomo, and dedicated to the Emperor Ojin. Yoritomo had the shrine transferred to this site, and its buildings were reconstructed in the Momoyama period (16th c.) and again in 1823.

After crossing the Aka bashi, which spans the lotus-covered pool of Gempei, Wakamiya Oji comes to an end (at the foot of the stairway to the main shrine) in front of Maidono, or dance pavilion.

On the r. is the Waka miya, a lesser shrine dedicated to the Emperor Nintoku, son of Ojin tenno. It was rebuilt in 1628.

It was in front of this shrine that Shizuka, Minamoto Yoshitsune's mistress, performed a dance, still famous in Japanese history, at the request of Yoritomo, who was trying to lure his brother from his hiding place.

To the l. of the staircase indicated above, a giant ginkgo tree has been planted on the site of the one behind which Kugyo, the great priest of Hachiman gu, hid in 1219 after making an attempt on the life of his uncle, the shogun Minamoto Sanetomo, of whom he was jealous.

Shirahata gu, a little further to the r. in relation to the Waka miya, is dedicated to Yoritomo and his son Sanetomo, and owes its name to Yoritomo's white standard.

*Kamino miya, the upper shrine at the top of the steps mentioned above, is made up of the Hon den, an oratory, and a public gallery, and its door is of special interest; the whole, although rebuilt in the last century, is richly decorated in the Azuchi-Momoyama style.

The shrine houses an important collection of treasures on display in a section of the public corridor; you can see a sword, a coffered writing case with inlaid mother-of-pearl and a wooden statue of Benzai Ten (1225), which is dressed in different clothes according to the circumstances. This statue is sometimes exhibited at the Museum of Fine Arts. Notice also the *mikoshi* (small portable shrines) which are paraded in the streets for annual processions.

FESTIVALS: The New year celebration between 1 and 3 January; the flowering of the cherry trees between 1 and 10 April; the festival of Kamakura 7 to 14 April; the lantern festival 7 to 9 August; Yasubame on 16 September.

Within the grounds of the shrine are the Modern Art Museum and the Municipal Museum of Fine Arts.

The Modern Art Museum near Gempei no ike, was built in 1951 by the architect Sakakura Junzo, a pupil of Le Corbusier. The building fits in well with its environment; part of the edifice rests on fine metal pillars plunging deep into the lake. Temporary exhibitions only.

*KAMAKURA KOKUHO KAN (plan: D1-E1; 1½ml/2km N of Kamakura station; address; 2-1-1 Yukinoshita; open daily except Mondays and national holidays from 09.00 to 16.00). The Municipal Museum of Fine Art is a reinforced concrete building (1928) in the *azekura* style (old wooden constructions built without nails, like the Shoso in, Nara). The exhibits in the museum come either from shrines or from private collections. They include some masterpieces which belong to periods covering four centuries including the Kamakura (1192-1333) and the Muromachi (1333-1573). The collections were unfortunately depleted by the 1923 earthquake.

Sculptures. The finest examples of Kamakura sculpture are in Kyoto and Nara. Japanese sculpture, which here achieves a kind of fulfilment, is manifestly an extension of Heian sculpture, even a return to the Nara canons of art. Nonetheless, Kamakura also shows the influence of the Unkei school which marked this period with its strength and realism.

The statue of Shoko o (one of the two judges in Hell), sculpted in wood (1250), belongs to the Enno ji temple, and is the best specimen of the power and virility of Kamakura art. The statue is signed by Koyu. The statues of Fudo (belonging to the temple of Kakuon ji) and of Jizo (which is attributed to Unkei and comes from Jochi ji) are in the same style. The statue of Suigetsu Kannon (belonging to Tokei ji) is, in contrast, a masterpiece of grace and refinement, noticeably influenced by the Sung Dynasty of China. That of *Uesugi Shigefusa belongs to Meigetsu in (p. 286).

A triad of Yakushi Nyorai (a Buddhist healer) of the Heian period is roughly hewn, and seems to have been deliberately left unfinished. Note finally a statue of Minamoto Yoriyoshi, founder of the Tsurugaoka shrine. Dating from the Muromachi period (14th-15th c.), it is sculpted in wood and was originally painted.

Paintings. The museum also contains a precious collection of *emakimono* (horizontal paintings). These occupy a very important place in Japanese art, and their themes are often drawn from everyday life.

The *Taema mandara no Engi*, belonging to Komyo ji, consists of two long scrolls which tell the story of a young nun who received as a reward for her exemplary piety a tapestry of miraculous origins.

The scrolls on which this legend is depicted are respectively 25ft 5in (7.75m) and 22ft 6in (6.88m) long by 1ft 6in (0.48m) wide, which makes them quite exceptional. The colours, which have worn away in many places, show the solid design of the compositions. Certain details were painted in silver, the mandara itself is gilded, and appears three times on the second scroll. Although the authors are unknown, these works are so natural and realistic as to suggest that they date from the middle of the Kamakura period.

A scroll from Kosoku ji also relates an event in the life of the sculptor Unkei: a female customer slapped the artist because she thought him too slow at his work.

Amongst the minor *objets d'art*, we would draw attention to lacquered wooden writing cases and an elegantly shaped bronze bell, from Joraku ji, dated 1248.

At approximately 550yds (500m) E of Tsurugaoka Hachiman gu park are the grounds of the Yokohama University Faculties of Education and Fine Arts. They stand on the very site of Minamoto Yoritomo's Governmental Palace, or Okura Bakufu:

The modest tomb of Yoritomo (plan: E1), to the N of this complex, consists of several large stones placed one on top of the other to form a little pagoda. Festival 13 April. 110yds (100m) to the E are the tombs of Shimazu Tadahisa (1179-1227), founder of the Satsuma clan and

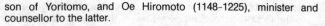

son of Yoritomo, and Oe Hiromoto (1148–1225), minister and counsellor to the latter.

From Hachiman gu park, a road heading E passes to the S of Okura Bakufu, and another road heading NE to Kamakura shrine branches off it at an oblique angle. A pathway to Egara shrine branches l. off this second road.

½ml (1km) E of Tsurugaoka Hachiman gu (plan: F1; bus from Kamakura eki): Ega Tenjin, dedicated to Sugawara Michizane (see Dazaifu).

KAMAKURA GU (plan: F1; 1½ml/2km NE of Kamanura eki; bus). This shrine was erected in 1869 in honour of Prince Morinaga (1308–35), son of the Emperor Go Daigo, who was imprisoned in this place by Ashikaga Takauji following an attempt at the restoration of his father. Festival 20 August.

Behind the shrine is the cave where Prince Morinaga was imprisoned and then killed after seven years of captivity. The prince's tomb is situated on the hill of Richiko, 220yds (200m) E of the Shrine.

770yds (700m) N by a path leading off on the l. from Kamakura shrine: Kakuon ji (plan: just off F1), founded in 1218 by Hojo Yoshitoki. This temple houses an important triad of Yakushi Nyorai, the work of Unkei (12th–13th c.), along with the venerated statue of a Jizo Bosatsu (guardian against fires), made of wood and known as black Jizo (Kuro Jizo). Painted ceiling above the Unkei statues. Festival 6–9 August. Behind this temple are a number of caves, collectively called *yagura*; judging from the tombstones and bones found there, they must have been used as a cemetery.

½ml (1km) E by a road running along the r. side of Kamakura gu, then across a tributary of the Nameri gawa: *Zuisen ji (plan: just off F1), founded in 1327 by the Zen priest Soseki (posthumous name Muso Kokushi, 1271–1346). This temple contains a wooden statue of Soseki, seated, with a serene and expressive face. It is a fine example of sculpture of the early Muromachi period (14th c.). The garden which we owe to the founder monk has suffered much since its creation, but it still partly shows the artistry of Soseki, who had a special gift for adapting gardens to the surrounding countryside. At the summit of Kimpei san, which overlooks this garden, the Ichiran tei pavilion provides a view over the Hakone region and Mount Fuji.

1ml (1.5km) NE, to the N of Zuisen ji: Kamakura ten en (Paradise of Kamakura), a wooded park which includes the hills around Mount Tendai 462ft (141m). Extensive views over the Miura peninsula, and the bays of Tokyo and Sagami.

From Kamakura shrine, you can join a road to the S which goes E along the Nameri gawa; this road, which is part of the bus route, comes from the fork which, if you are coming from Hachiman shrine, also has a turning NE to Kamakura gu (see above); it passes close to the Sugimoto and Jomyo temples.

SUGIMOTO DERA or **SAMPON JI** (plan: F2; 770yds/700m S of Kamakura gu; 1ml/2km NE of Kamakura eki; bus). The foundation of this temple is attributed to the priest Gyoki (734), making it the oldest temple in Kamakura. The present edifice, rebuilt in 1678, houses three statues of Kannon of the eleven heads; two of them are thought to be of the Kamakura period. The middle statue was sculpted by Ennin Jikaku; the one on the l. was the work of Genshin; the third, of archaic style, was created by Gyoki (7th c.). This temple, which receives most of its visitors at the time of the Kanto pilgrimages, is also called Okura no Kannon.

JOMYOJI (plan: just off F2; 440yds/400m E of Sampon ji; 1½mls/2.5km NE of Kamakura eki; bus). Founded in 1188 by Ashikaga Yoshikane, this was the fifth of the great temples of Kamakura. The only remaining building (1756) houses a wooden statue of the Zen priest Taiko. Three members of the Ashikaga family, including the founder, are buried in the garden of this temple.

The residence of the Ashikaga of Kamakura once stood at a point further E of Jomyo ji, before the road crosses the Nameri gawa.

The road running along the S side of Gempei no ike (see Tsurugaoka Hachiman gu) ends up opposite Hokai ji at:

KOMACHI KOJI (plan: D2). Parallel to Wakamiya Oji and the Nameri gawa, which it crosses to the S, this road was once the main artery of the town, with *samurai* houses and small businesses all along it.

HOKAI JI (plan: E2; 330yds/300m E of Tsurugaoka Hachiman gu; 880yds/800m NE of Kamakura eki). This temple occupies the site of the Hojo residence. It contains statues of Jizo Bosatsu and Kanki ten.

Kofuji hill behind this temple and on the other side of the Nameri gawa was once the site of Tosho ji, where Hojo Takatori and his followers committed suicide (1333) when Kamakura was captured by Nitta Yoshisada. The seat of the regency was further to the SW on the other side of Komachi koji.

Coming S down Komachi koji, you will pass a monument dedicated to the priest Nichiren, at the spot where he used to teach his doctrine.

NICHIREN (1222-82). He was born in the little village of Kominato (see Kamogawa), and received his religious education at the monasteries of Mount Hiei, near Kyoto; there he formulated a new doctrine, which he began to preach from 1253 onwards. He set up a hermitage on the hill of Matsuba ga yatsu, near Kamakura, and came to teach the Myohorenge kyo (*sutra* of the True Law; see Minobu) at Komachi koji. He attracted new disciples, but also the wrath of the government which Nichiren criticized in no uncertain terms. The first time he was exiled to Ito, and then, on being condemned to execution in 1271, he miraculously escaped death (see Fujisawa). Banished once again, he went into exile on the island of Sado. He died at Ikegami, on the present site of the Hommon ji in Tokyo, and his ashes were brought to Minobu san.

HONGAKU JI (plan: D3; 300yds/300m SE of Kamakura eki). To the S of Komachi koji, just before it crosses the Nameri gawa, this temple was built (1436) on the site of Ebisu do, where Nichiren lived on returning from Sado. Some of the ashes of the great preacher were transferred there in the 15th c., which earned this temple the name of Minobu san of the East.

The famous blacksmith Okazaki Masamune (1264-1344) is buried within the precincts of this temple.

MYOHON JI (plan: E3; 550yds/500m E of Hongaku ji; 770yds/700m E of Kamakura eki). Cross the Nameri gawa by the Ebisudo bashi and proceed E. You will soon reach this temple founded in 1274 by Hiki Daigakusaburo, a disciple of Nichiren. The Shoshi do, hall of the patriarchs, houses a holy statue of Nichiren (13th c.). Festival 12 May.

Komachi koji, beyond the Ebisudo bashi, joins to the S a major road which crosses Kamakura from E to W; heading E along this road, you will arrive at the O machi quarter, where a narrower road branches off, just before you cross a tributary of the Nameri gawa. You are now on the hill of Matsuba ga yatsu. The road leads to:

ANKOKURON JI (plan: E4; ½ml/1km SE of Kamakura eki; bus to O machi). This temple was built in the 8th c. on the orders of the Tokugawa, on the site of Nichiren's first hermitage.

In the cave that can be seen on the right of the main portal, Nichiren wrote his first treatise *On Justice and Public Peace* (Rissho Ankokuron), which was to serve as advice to the Regent Hojo Tokiyori (1227-63). A copy of it, which we owe to the priest Nichiro, one of his main disciples, belongs to the treasury. Nichiro is buried within the temple enclosure. Festival of 27 September.

KOMYO JI (just off plan: E4; ½ml/1km S of Ankokuron ji; 1½ml/2km S of Kamakura eki; bus). This temple (Jodo sect), situated to the S of the railway on a hill overlooking Zaimokuza beach, was founded in 1243 by Hojo Tsunetoki (1224-46). It contains several paintings on silk, including those of the Eighteen Arhats, and possesses the Taema mandara, which is usually exhibited at the Museum of Fine Arts (see above). Festival 13-14 October.

Wakamiya Oji (p. 285) ends, near the mouth of the Nameri gawa to the S, at the Shonan Highway (toll road and part of the bus route). The latter links Fujisawa to Yokosuka, and runs along the beautiful beaches of Zaimokuza and Yuiga hama between Cape Iijima and Inamuraga Point (approx. 2½mls/4km to the W). This was a military port, and it was from this coast that Nitta Yoshisada invaded the town of Kamakura (1333). To the NW of the Yuigahama quarter is the Hase quarter where you can visit the Dai Butsu.

KOTOKUIN JYOSEN JI plan: A3; 1½ml/2km SW of Kamakura eki; 440yds/400m N of Hase station, Eoshima Kamakura Kanko ER; bus). Here you can marvel at the great bronze statue of ***Dai Butsu.

The Great Buddha of Kamakura, a copy of the Todai ji statue in Nara, was erected by the wife of Minamoto Yoritomo, Masako. The original wooden statue was replaced in 1252 by this bronze statue (37ft 5in/ 11.4m high, 124ft), and its creation (by fitting together flat horizontal plates) is attributed to the bronze founder Ono Goroemon. It is undeniably one of the finest examples of this art, far superior to the one at Nara, although it is smaller. The statue represents Amida (Amitabha, in Sanskrit), Buddha of Eternal Light, sitting in the traditional meditating pose: the expression of face, with the eyes half closed, is wonderfully serene; the hands are joined, with the palms upturned towards the sky, and the thumbs meet in a symbol of profound faith.

It is possible to climb up inside the statue. It was, at one time, protected by a strong wooden housing, which was destroyed by a tidal wave in 1495, so that only the foundations remain.

HASE DERA (plan: A4; 220yds/200m NW of Hase station). If you head S again from Dai Butsu, and go up to the r. towards Kannon yama, you will reach this temple which houses a revered statue of Kannon of the eleven heads, 29ft 6in (9m) high. This gilded wooden statue is a mediocre reproduction of the Edo period.

According to the legend, the original statue was sculpted in 721 from part of a camphor tree by the priest Tokudo Shonin, at the same time as the one from the temple of the same name, near Nara. The Kamakura statue was washed up in Sagami Bay, and an original temple was built to house it on the orders of the Emperor Shomu. The bronze bell dates from 1264.

Gorei sha or Mitami jinja, to the S of Hase dera, is a shrine dedicated to Gongoro Kagemasa, a heroic knight of the 11th c. who was a native of the Kamakura region.

GOKURAKU JI (770yds/700m SW of Hase dera; to the N of Gokurakuji station, Enoshima Kamakura Kanko ER). The temple was set up in 1259 on this site by Hojo Shigetoki, who entrusted its running to the priest Ninsho (1217-1303). After being destroyed several times, it was rebuilt on a much more modest scale. A number of statues from this temple are on show in the Museum of Fine Art; a standing statue of Sakyamuni (12th c.) is venerated here.

THE NAGAO MUSEUM (approx. ½ml/1km NW from Gokuraku ji). The museum occupies a house which came from the Takayama region (information about opening times can be obtained from the tourist office at Kamakura station). It houses paintings which include *The Bird on a Withered Branch*, by Miyamoto Niten, and the *Imaginary Portrait of Kanzan*, by the priest Kao; sculptures, objects cast in bronze, pottery, clothes, materials, swords and examples of ancient Chinese and Japanese calligraphy.

Follow a long road N up from Wadazuka station (Enoshima Kamakura Kanko ER), or rejoin this road to the W near the town hall, from Kamakura station, to get to:

JUFUKI JI (plan: C1; 880yds/800m N of Kamakura eki). Founded in 1200 by Masako (1156-1225), wife of Minamoto Yoritomo, and placed under the direction of the priest Yosai or Eisai (1141-1215), it was the third of the great temples of Kamakura.

This temple holds a wooden statue of Jizo with eyes of jade (Kamakura period), and the *statue of the priest Eisai, who introduced Zen Buddhism and tea growing; this wooden statue of the Kamakura period is sometimes exhibited in the Museum of Fine Arts. In the temple gardens two little caves shelter tombs alleged to be those of Masako and his son the shogun Sanetomo.

EISHO JI (plan: C1). To the N of the above, near the railway, this temple was erected in 1636 by Dame Eisho, concubine of Tokugawa Ieyasu and descendant of Ota Dokan (1432-86).

In the garden is the tomb of the nun Abutsu (13th c.), authoress of the *Izayoi Nikki* (Journal of the sixteenth day of the moon).

JOKOMY JI (plan: C1; 220yds/220m NE of Eisho ji). This temple, which stands on the other side of the railway line, was erected (1251) by Hojo Nagatoki; it is one of the oldest in Kamakura.

The temple is the depository of the *Izayoi Nikki* by Abutsu, and of three seated statues of Amida of the Kamakura period. The Ashikaga, the Yoshikane, the Motouji and the Ujimitsu lie buried in the garden.

After a short walk following the railway, you will soon reach the steep slope of Kamegatsu (path for walkers), which meets the slope of Kobukuro. This is more suitable for vehicles and leads up to Choju ji (880yds/800m N of Jokomyo ji). If, however, you cross this railway line and head NW, you will arrive at Kaizo ji (550yds/500m from Jokomyo ji) a temple founded in 1394, which has a cave in which are 16 legendary wells. You might also go to Zeniarai Benten (880yds/800m from Jokomyo ji; bus from Kamakura station) which is a popular shrine: whatever sum of money you choose to dip in the stream of a nearby cave, on days of the serpent (Chinese zodiac), you are sure one day to gain double or triple the amount of your 'stake', according to legend.

Running along the W side of the park of Tsurugaoka Hachiman shrine (p. 285), a road goes up the slope of Kobukuro and then down to Kita Kamakura station; road on the r. to:

*KENCHO JI** (plan: just of D1; 1ml/1.5km SE of Kita Kamakura eki; 1½ml/2km N of Kamakura eki; bus). This remains the most important of the five great shrines of Kamakura. It was founded in 1253 by Hojo Tokiyori (1227-63), and entrusted to the Chinese priest Daigaku Zanji. The temple, which burnt to the ground in 1415, was rebuilt by the priest Takuan (1573-1645) at the beginning of the Edo period. It stands enveloped in dense vegetation including a great many Japanese cedars. Kara mon (Chinese gate) and the Hon do were erected in 1646.

The Hon do has a coffered ceiling painted by Kano Motonobu, and contains, amongst other things, the wooden statue of *Hojo Tokiyori, a masterpiece of the Kamakura period, a portrait of silk of Daigaku Zenji, and eight other paintings of the Sixteen Arhats (disciples of

Buddha), by the priest Mincho. The bronze bell was cast in 1255.

→ 550yds (500m) NE: Hanzo bo which is past the tomb of the Japanese physician Zuiken Kawamura (1618-1700). Beyond that is the wooded area of Ten en.

→ 550yds (500m) S: Enno ji or Arai Emma do, near Kobukuro zaka (see above), erected in 1250, holds a statue of the same period of Emma, governor of Hell. The statue of Jizo is in the Museum of Fine Arts.

→ 770yds (700m) NW: Meigetsu in; take the path which branches off to the N of Kobukuro zaka. This temple, founded in the 14th c. by Uesugi Noritaka, houses the wooden statue of *Uesugi Shigefusa, one of the most remarkable of the Kamakura period (13th. c.). The statue still shows traces of having once been multicoloured. It is pyramid-shaped, and sculpted from a single block of wood, which gives it a characteristic stability and balance. It is often on display at the Museum of Fine Arts.

JOCHI JI (550yds/500m S of Kita Kamakura eki; 770yds/700m NW of Kencho ji). You can get to this temple by crossing the railway in the direction of Kita Kamakura station. It was founded in 1283 by Hojo Morotoki, and placed under the Chinese priest Funei (1197-1277). The statue of Jizo, attributed to Unkei, was sent to the Kamakura Museum of Fine Arts after the 1923 earthquake which destroyed this temple.

TOKEI JI (330yds/300m S of Kita Kamakura eki). Immediately to the N of Jochi ji, this temple was founded in 1285 by Kakusan, the widow of Hojo Tokimune.

It is popularly known as Enkri dera, the temple of divorce, because until the Meiji Restoration, women who were unhappily married could withdraw there under the protection of religion. It includes the important Matsugaoka Buddhist Library, and a wooden statue of Kannon (14th c.). In the lovely garden are the tombs of the foundress, Kakusan, and of several philosophers of the Meiji period.

*ENGAKU JI (immediately to the E of Kita Kamakura eki; 1½mls/2.5km N of Kamakura eki; bus). Founded in 1282 by Hojo Tokimune (1251-84), it was one of the five great Zen temples of Kamakura; it was badly damaged in the 1923 earthquake. The main buildings are laid out on a S-W-N-E axis from the wide San mon, which marks the main entrance. Only that part of the temple which is furthest from this gate, around the Shari den, is positioned facing N to S.

To the SE of the San mon, at the top of a staircase is a bell-tower where hangs a bronze bell (1301), the biggest in Kamakura.

*Shari den, a pavilion of relics, contains a tooth of Gautama Buddha, brought from China. The edifice, which was rebuilt after the 1923 earthquake, was originally constructed in 1285 by Hojo Sadatoki, the son of Tokimune. It is one of the best examples of Zen art in Kamakura, and one of the only two monuments in the *kara yo* style (in the Chinese fashion) of this period still surviving in Japan. Since its restoration, the high thatched roof has lost some of its bold, upward-curving sweep.

The tooth is kept inside a quartz tabernacle. Behind this is the Tokimune mausoleum.

☞ **VICINITY**

1 SHICHIRIGA HAMA (2½mls/4km S coach; Enoshima Kamakura Kanko ER train). This coast stretches for about 3mls (5km) between Inamuraga saki and Katase, and the Shonan Highway runs along it, providing beautiful views over the island of Eno shima (see Fujisawa).

2 OFUNA (3½mls/6km N; JNR train; coach). This is a railway junction and small town where the Shochiku Company Film Studios are situated. To the N of the station, on Mugaro san, is a giant bust (82ft/25m high) of Kannon, which is made of reinforced concrete and is most unsightly.

↦ 1ml (1.5km) SW (bus): Ofuna botanical garden. This floral park (17 acres/7ha) was created in 1962, and flower shows are organized here. It is famous for the flowering of its peonies in April and May.

↦ 1½mls (2.5km) NW (JNR train to Taya; bus): The caves of Taya. On a hill behind Josen ji, these caves were hollowed out of the rock in the 13th c. to hold the treasures of the Hojo family. Shingon monks, in the Edo period, sculpted numerous Buddhist figures here. In places the caves are 4mls (6km) deep and it is possible to visit part of them.

3 FUJISAWA, MIURA, YOKOHAMA, YOKOSUKA, ZUSHI, see entries under these names.

■ Kameoka (Island of Honshu)

Tokyo, 307mls (495km) - Fukui, 110mls (178km) - Kobe, 56mls (91km) - Kyoto 12mls (19km) - Nara, 39mls (63km) - Osaka, 46mls (74km) - Otsu, 19mls (31km) - Tsu, 66mls (107km).

Kyoto fu - pop: 47,151 - alt. 325ft (99m).

👁 The principal attraction of Kameoka, in the suburbs of Kyoto, is that it forms an ideal starting point for going down the *Hozu gawa rapids, which penetrate deep into the Tamba range and form a series of famous gorges.

To the N of Kameoka station (JNR) are the bridge over the Hozu gawa and Hozuno hama landing stage (direct coaches from Kyoto). The trip, lasting 1h. 30 approx to Arashi yama, is by flat-bottomed boat. Trips are possible from April to mid-December; departures are frequent and can be booked from Kyoto. The most beautiful passes are those of Kanaga ga taki, Takase daki and Shishigakuchi (the lion's mouth, the most difficult). Of particular note are the azaleas at Gakuga te, Byobu iwa (the screen rock), several waterfalls, etc.

■ Kameyama (Island of Honshu)

Tokyo, 252mls (406km) - Gifu, 59mls (95km) - Kyoto, 48mls (78km) - Nagoya, 40mls (64km) - Nara, 52mls (84km) - Otsu, 41mls (66km) - Tsu, 12mls (20km) - Wakayama, 111mls (179km).

Mie Ken - pop: 30,623.

Situated on the middle stretch of the Suzuka gawa, the town of Kameyama stands on the route between the region of Nagoya and those of Kyoto, Nara and Osaka.

RUINS OF KAMEYAMA CASTLE (½ml/1km N of the station). The ruins are now covered by a garden to the N of the locality.

The castle, built in the 16th c. by Seki Munekazu, was entrusted by Oda Nobunaga to Gamo Ujisato. It came back to the Seki clan for a while, then passed on to several other clans, including the Ishikawa, between 1744 and 1868.

NOBONO SHRINE (½ml/1km NW of the station). Behind the shrine is Nobono go ryo, tomb of the legendary prince Yamato Takeru (81-113).

Son of the Emperor Keiko, this prince distinguished himself by his exploits of cunning and bravery. Once he had subjugated the Kumaso on Kyushu, he immediately turned on the Ebisu in the NE of Honshu, and was consequently regarded as the man who unified Japan. On returning from his second expedition, he fell victim to a malignant fever. After his death, a white dove rose into the air, and his tomb was given the name Shirahata no Sanryo. The shrine which is dedicated to him was erected in 1879.

■ Kamogawa (Island of Honshu)

Map of the Vicinity of Tokyo, p. 565.

Tokyo, 75mls (121km) - Chiba, 52mls (84km) - Mito, 130mls (209km) - Urawa, 90mls (145km).

Chiba ken - pop: 31,680.

Lying to the SE of the Boso peninsula, Kamogawa is one of several pleasant places, either ports of seaside resorts, which line the S coast of the Boso peninsula. The whole of this gently rolling coastal section, with its beaches and rocky cliffs, forms part of the Minami Boso Regional Park. Several offshore islets make this place the Matsushima of Kamogawa.

Kyonin ji (1ml/1.5km N of Awa Kamogawa eki; bus) was founded in 1281 by Nichiryu, a disciple of Nichiren.

VICINITY

1 FUTOMI (2mls/3km S; JNR train; coach). Note the islet of Niemon, offshore from Futomi, where Minamoto Yoritomo sought refuge for a while in the 12th c.

2 KAMEYAMA ONSEN (13mls/21km N; coach). This is a small spa town on the upper stretches of the Obitsu gawa, which can be reached by toll road through the wooded hills of the Boso peninsula.

3 KOMINATO (7mls/12km E, on the N 128; JNR train; coach). The road and the railway both run along the lovely *Minami Boso coast.

4mls (6km): Awa Amatsu: station.

➡ 3mls (5km) N (coach): Kiyosumi yama (alt. 1,256ft/383m), on the slopes of which stands Seicho ji or Kiyosumi dera, a temple founded in 771. In 1253 the priest Nichiren preached his first sermons here; a statue was erected to him. The Hon do, consecrated to Kokuzo Bosatsu, is an edifice of the Edo period. The temple's treasury holds several Buddhist paintings and a statue of Kannon. Kiyosumi hill is a 5,560-acre (2,250ha) forestry zone, where the Tokyo University of Agriculture observes experimental plantations. The road goes past Kiyosumi yama (15mls/24km N) and rejoins the Yoro gawa valley upstream from the gorge of Yoro Keikoku.

7mls (12km): Kominato, meaning 'little port', was the home town of the famous priest Nichiren (1222-82, see Kamakura). The Tanjo ji, (1½ml/2km) E of the station (bus), was erected in 1276 by his disciples; however, the present buildings date from the beginning of the 19th c. This temple contains a statue of Nichiren, attributed to Jakunichibo Nikka (12th c.), and the holy symbol of the Nichiren sect, given by Tokugawa Mitsukuni, Lord of Mito, in the 17th c.; festival on 16 February. In the nearby Taino ura Bay, the sacred gilthead fish live in safety, protected by a ban which Nichiren imposed. Anyone who offended by trying to catch them would lose his sight.

➡ 3mls (5km) E (JNR train): Namegawa, amusement park near the ocean, with a bird sanctuary which is worth seeing.

K Kanazawa (Island of Honshu)**

Railway map on inside front cover.

Tokyo, 324mls (522km) - Fukui, 49mls (79km) - Gifu, 140mls (226km) - Toyama, 40mls (64km).

Principal town of Ishikawa ken (pop: 652,838) - pop: 404,000 - textile industries - national, regional and private universities.

☀ Built between two water courses, at the foot of the massif of Hakusan and 6mls (10km) from the Sea of Japan, Kanazawa is the second town of Hokuriku after Niigata. It is a real metropolis with intellectual and artistic traditions, and has retained its old appearance, having been spared the bombings of 1944-45. The Kenroku is regarded as one of the three most famous gardens in Japan, and the area around Kanazawa offers many pleasant excursions.

BUDDHIST PRINCIPALITY. In 1471, the priest Rennyo Shonin (1415-99), leader of the Jodo sect of Buddhism, was driven out of the Hongan ji in Kyoto and chose to settle on a little hill in Yamazaki village, on the present site of Kanazawa Castle. He had a new Hongan ji built there, but it was razed in 1475. Nevertheless, Rennyo's disciples fortified their new temple, which was known as Oyama Gobo. From there they established their domination of the area, at the expense of the Togashi lords, whom they overthrew in 1488. The monks managed to maintain this situation for almost a century by developing the economic resources of the region. They were expelled in 1580 by Sakuma Morimasa, who became the new master of Oyama.

ONE MILLION KOKUS. In 1583, Maeda Toshie (1538-99) received the province of Kaga from Toyotomi Hideyoshi and drove Morimasa out so that he could settle in the town, which he renamed Kanazawa. His son Toshinaga (1562-1614), who was related to Tokugawa Ieyasu, managed to remain in power there, as did his descendants throughout the Edo period. The powerful Maeda received the largest annual income of all the Japanese daimyo, that is to say, over 1 million *kokus* (a *koku* is a measure of rice which equals 39.7 gals/180.4l). They rebuilt the castle and expanded the town. They also assured its economic prosperity which came from textile industries, Kutani porcelain (see Kaga), and the commercial port of Kanaiwa. A number of artists and men of letters received their education in Kanazawa, which was also the centre of a Noh theatre school. Although the town suffered at the time of the Meiji Restoration, it has since returned to the prosperity for which it is known.

FAMOUS PEOPLE BORN IN KANAZAWA. The painter Ganku (1749-1838), the philosopher Nishida Kitaro (1870-1945) and the chemist Takamine Jokichi (1857-1922), who succeeded in synthesizing adrenalin, were all native to Kanazawa.

Opposite Kanazawa station, a wide road branches off and heads S. At a crossing, another major road meets a busy junction on its E side and the Korimbo dori runs S from here. Korimbo dori is the town's main arterial road, leading to the Kata machi business quarter in the S, before crossing the Sai gawa. It passes the entrance to the Oyama shrine en route.

OYAMA JINJA (1½mls/2km S of the station; bus). The shrine is dedicated to Maeda Toshiie, founder of the Kaga clan, and stands on the site of the villa which belonged to him.

This shrine is particularly notable for its gate (1875), the upper part of which has stained-glass windowpanes, and once acted like a lighthouse, guiding sailors on the Sea of Japan. The shrine's treasury has a few mementos of Toshiie. Festival, Oyama matsuri, on 14-15 June.

KANAZAWA JO (1½mls/2.5km SE of the station). The Maeda's castle rests on a hill behind Oyama jinja. It was destroyed by fire in 1881 and nothing is left now except the Ishikawa gate, made of neatly bonded stones, which was built in 1788. Sanjukken Nagaya, inside the castle area, is a small museum displaying weapons and other objects related to the castle. Kanazawa University occupies most of the grounds.

To the N of the castle you can visit Ozaki shrine, founded in 1643 by Maeda Mitsutaka in honour of Tokugawa Ieyasu. The shrine was reconstructed here in 1878 and is an imitation of Tosho gu in Nikko.

'KENROKU EN (2mls/3km SE of Kamakura eki; bus). The garden is separated from Kanazawa Castle by Hyakkenbori dori, and is regarded as one of the greatest and most famous gardens in Japan. Others include the Kairaku en in Mito, the Koraku en in Okayama, and the Ritsurin in Takamtasu.

This 25-acre (10-ha) park was originally designed in 1676 as the outdoor garden of Kanazawa Castle. It was expanded in 1774, constructed in its present fom in 1822, and was opened to the public in 1875. The name Kenroku evokes the 'combination of six harmonies', which corresponds to the themes of ideal beauty in this art; spaciousness, solemnity, reverence, artificiality, decorative beauty, and coolness and abundance of water.

A number of man-made hills, and two ornamental lakes, Kasumi and Hisaga, are the main features of this park. On the shores of Kasumi you can see a stone lantern, Kotoji toro, and the teahouse Uchibashi. Near Hisaga is Yugao tei, built by the master Kobori Enshu (1579-1647). The *kiku-zakura* (a cherry tree chrysanthemum) is another of this garden's famous sights.

In the S corner of the park is the shrine of Kanazawa. A wall nearby runs round the little garden of Hikakutei, which contains the Seison kaku and the Museum of Fine Arts.

Seison kaku is a house built in 1863 by Maeda Nariyasu for his mother Shinryu in.

The Museum of Fine Arts (1ml/1.5km, Kenroku machi; open daily from 09.00 to 16.00, except Mondays and public holidays) was opened in 1959; it houses, amongst other things, an incense burner made by Ninsei, and some very fine Kutani china (see p. 271).

Gyokusen en, to the E of Kenroku en, was once the Nishida family's garden. It was planned in the 17th c. by Naotaka Wakida for the wife of Maeda Toshinga, the second lord of Kanazawa.

½ml (1km) SE of Kenroku en (bus) is Tentoku in, built in 1623 by Maeda Toshitsune in honour of his dead wife. It has a very beautiful gate (end of 17th c.) which was influenced by the style of the Zen Obaku sect, and is attributed to the Chinese priest Kosen.

Hyakkenbori dori, which runs in a hollow between the park and the castle, finishes at the W end of Kenroku en. There is a junction here, with a turnoff S to Sakura bashi. Approx. 330yds (300m) S of this junction, you can visit the garden which once belonged to the Honda family, and also the adjoining Nakamura Museum (arts and crafts). The collections were brought together by Nakamura Eishun.

A road heading W from this junctions runs between the Prefecture of Kanazawa and the town hall of that name, and joins Korimbo dori.

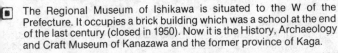 The Regional Museum of Ishikawa is situated to the W of the Prefecture. It occupies a brick building which was a school at the end of the last century (closed in 1950). Now it is the History, Archaeology and Craft Museum of Kanazawa and the former province of Kaga.

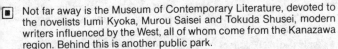 Not far away is the Museum of Contemporary Literature, devoted to the novelists Iumi Kyoka, Murou Saisei and Tokuda Shusei, modern writers influenced by the West, all of whom come from the Kanazawa region. Behind this is another public park.

Korimbo dori becomes Saigawa Ohashi, and then joins Tera machi (2mls/3km S of Kamakura eki), which runs parallel to the Sai gawa and has former temples and traditional-style dwellings along it, reminiscent of Kanazawa as it used to be.

Among these temples the following are of special interest: Myoritsu ji, famous for its maze of corridors and secret rooms, and Fushimi ji, which houses a statue of Amida believed to be of the Heian period.

Further, S, 3½mls (6km) S of Kanazawa eki (bus) on the slopes of Teraji yama, stands Daijo ji (Soto sect), founded in 1263. Daiyu den, the main hall, is a fine example of the Edo period. There is a wooded park of pines and Japanese cedars around the temple.

From here you can go on to Noda yama, where the family cemetery of the Kaga daimyo was set up on the orders of Maeda Toshinaga (1562-1614). The tombs are spread out in the middle of a 17-acre (7-ha) pinewood.

VICINITY

1 **UTATSU YAMA** (2mls/3km SE, coach). This mountainous wooded park (123 acres/50ha) has been turned into recreation areas, a zoo, an aquarium, etc. It rises to a height of 462ft (141m), and there is a view over the massif of Hakusan and the Sea of Japan. Uesugi Kenshin (1530–78) built a fortress, which was soon destroyed, on this hill (1577).

2 **KANAIWA** (4mls/7km NW; coach). This town near the Sai gawa estuary was once the commercial port serving Kanazawa. Profitable links with Korea were set up from here, in spite of the Tokugawa government's prohibition.

Zeniya Gohei (1773-1852), who was a native of Kanaiwa, advised the Maeda, following a famine, to re-establish trade with the mainland of Asia, thus reviving the prosperity of the province and his own fortunes. His success aroused jealousy, and he was accused of putting poison in the Kahoku lagoon, which lies further N. The Maeda seized this opportunity to put him in prison, where he died claiming that he had helped renew trade links with the outside world. A small museum is dedicated to him.

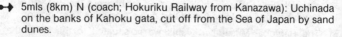

➼ 5mls (8km) N (coach; Hokuriku Railway from Kanazawa): Uchinada on the banks of Kahoku gata, cut off from the Sea of Japan by sand dunes.

♨ **3 YUWAKU ONSEN** (9mls/14km SE; coach). This is a spa town in a pleasant mountain setting. Of particular interest here is the *Edo village, which is a collection of different buildings of this period, spread out over an area of 39 acres (16 ha): they include inns, peasant dwellings and masters' residences, with carefully reconstructed interiors.

➼ 3mls (5km) NE (direct coach from Kanazawa): Io zen (3,081ft/939m), a mountain once considered sacred because of its medicinal plants. About 50 temples stood on the slopes of the mountain at that time. View over Tate yama (p. 152) and Haku san; skiing in winter.

4 FUKUI, KAGA, KOMATSU, HAKUSAN NATIONAL PARK, see entries under these names; **NOTO PENINSULA,** see Hakui, Nanao, Wajima.

■ Kannonji (Island of Shikoku)

Map of Shikoku (Inland Sea), pp. 536–7.

Tokyo, 480mls (773km) – Kochi, 79mls (128km) – Matsuyama, 68mls (109km) – Takamatsu, 33mls (54km) – Tokushima, 78mls (125km).

Kagawa ken – pop: 143,162.

This is a small town in the N of Shikoku, near the Inland Sea. The visitor will find plenty to satisfy his curiosity in Kannonji.

KOTOHIKI PARK (1ml/1.5km NW of the station; bus). The park is spread out on a hill overlooking Ariake beach. Round the beach is a famous pinewood, with trees which seem to stand on their roots as if on tiptoe. In the park is the shrine of Kotohiki Hachiman which houses a Buddhist painting of the Kamakura period, representing Buddha Amida's descent from heaven.

⊚ **KANNON JI,** at the foot of the hill, also has a painting on silk of the Kamakura period, representing the temple, and a wooden statue of a recumbent Buddha, of the Fujiwara period.

 The summit of Kotohiki affords the best view of the rather curious *Zenigata, a giant imprint of a Kan ei coin (17th c.) which was hollowed into the ground by the natives, to remind their lord that they would not tolerate money being squandered.

■ Kanoya (Island of Kyushu)

Tokyo, 965mls (1,553km) – Kagoshima, 61mls (98km) – Kumamoto, 150mls (242km) – Miyazaki, 69mls (112km).

Kagoshima ken – pop: 66,995.

Kanoya is a railway stopping point on the banks of the Kimotsuki gawa, which cuts across the base of the Osumi peninsula and forms a good point of departure for exploring the peninsula.

VICINITY

1 UCHINOURA (28mls/45km SE; JNR train to Koyama, then coach). Head E out of Kanoya on the N220 to:

5mls (8km): Turn off on the r. before Kushira; the road heads S along the railway.

9mls (15km): Koyama; head E following the Kimotsuki gawa.

14mls (23km): Mouth of the Kimotsuki gawa, on the very beautiful *Shibushi Bay; the bay probably covers the site of a former crater, of which Biro Island could have been one of the central cones.

28mls (45km): Uchinoura, a little fishing port in a natural harbour, protected by the Cape of Hi.

→ 3mls (5km): Kagoshima Space Centre, attached to Tokyo University, where the first Japanese satellite (Osumi) was launched in 1970.

2 SATA MISAKI (43mls/70km S, on the N269.

5mls (9km): Takasu, on the edge of Kagoshima Bay, which the road follows to the S.

15mls (24km): O Nejime; boat to Ibusuki (see entry under this name).

18mls (29km): Nejime (boat to Yamagawa), at the place where Kagoshima Bay narrows before opening out on the East China Sea. The coast becomes much more fully hilly and attractive here.

30mls (48km): Sata (boat to Yamagawa). A road goes S towards the point from here.

38mls (61km): Turnoff for a toll road along the coast looking down on the W and E sides of the point.

43mls (70km): *Sata misaki, on the extreme southern tip of Kyushu island. At lat. 31°N is Agadir Point where a small shrine was built on the promontory. The island's lighthouse down below it is the oldest in Japan.

3 SAKURAJIMA, see Kagoshima.

Karatsu (Island of Kyushu)

Map of Kyushu (North), pp. 388–9.

Tokyo, 747mls (1,202km) – Fukoka, 32mls (52km) – Nagasaki, 69mls (112km) – Saga, 33mls (53km).

Saga ken – pop: 74,233 – fishing port.

Situated in an attractive bay on the Matsuura gawa estuary, Karatsu makes a pleasant holiday resort in the north of Kyushu Island. There are some interesting walks to Genkai National Park.

The name Karatsu means 'the port from which ships set sail to Kara' (Korea). This explains the capital of this place, from which contact with Korea was once initiated. Toyotomi Hideyoshi took advantage of this activity. At the end of the 16th c., the time of his expedition (see below, Vicinity 2), he had a castle built which he entrusted to Terazawa Hirotaka, and which remained in the latter's family until 1647. Several lords succeeded them, including the Ogasawara, 1817–68. Karatsu is still an important fishing port. In addition, Hideyoshi brought craftsmen back from Korea, and they settled in Karatsu, where there were many pottery kilns at the start of the 17th c. Karatsu pottery is plain and utilitarian, but full of strength and character.

The town is split into two parts by the wide Matsuura gawa estuary, which is narrowed by an excess of sand at the actual mouth of the river. A bridge provides a direct link between Higashi Karatsu and the town of Karatsu itself.

⊙ Konsho ji (660yds/600m NW of Karatsu eki) had the honour of providing the religious education of Chikamatsu Monzaemon (1653–1724); he preferred to settle in Osaka, however, where he became known as the greatest Japanese dramatist.

MAIZURU PARK (½ml/1km NE of Karatsu eki; ½ml/1km W of Higashi Karatsu eki). The keep of the former castle of the Ogasawara has been rebuilt here. It was once known as Bukaku jo, the castle of the flying stork, because that was what it looked like, with its two great pine-fringed beaches spread out on either side like wings. A museum houses archeological collections of local and Chinese origin; pottery.

*Nijino Matsubara is a superb pine forest, which curves elegantly round Karatsu Bay for nearly 3½mls (6km) to the E of Higashi Karatsu. Access from Higashi Karatsu or Nijino Matsubara station.

☞ **VICINITY**

1 **KAGAMI YAMA** (3mls/5km SE; coach). A winding road goes up this hill which is 932ft (284m) high, with a very fine view over Nijino Matsubara and Karatsu Bay. There is a little shrine dedicated to Benten, in memory of Matsuura Sayohime.

WAVE OF FAREWELL. Hirefuri yama (hill of the waving scarf) is the name given to this hill, which Sayohime climbed to wave to her lover Otomo no Sadehiko until he disappeared from view as he sailed to Korea; the unhappy girl could not wrench herself from the place, and was petrified on the spot.

2 **NAGOYA** (13mls/21km NW on the N204; coach). The road skirts the Matsuura peninsula to the N and follows its jagged coastline.

9mls (14km): Turn-off on the r. (1ml/1.5km N) to Nanatsu gama, 'the cavern of the severn ovens', made up of seven caves hollowed into the cliff. You can get a much better view of them from the sea (motor launches from Yobuko).

11mls (18km): Yobuko (boat to Iki shima) is a small port built at the bottom of an inlet protected by several islets.

↔ 1½ml (2km) N (boat): Kabe shima, which is bordered by rocky cliffs of basalt, and has a little shrine dedicated to Sayohime (see above).

13mls (21km): Nagoya, which you cant get to by crossing the Nagoya Ohashi toll bridge, has the ruins of the castle erected by Toyotomi Hideyoshi (1536-98).

THE KOREA EXPEDITION. Hideyoshi wanted to subjugate Korea and launched an expedition in 1592. With the help of China, the Koreans managed to free themselves from the grip of the Japanese, but Hideyoshi felt that their peace proposals were unacceptable, and decided to attempt another conquest (1596), which he abandoned when he sensed his own death drawing near.

2½mls (4km) NW (coach): Hado misaki, on the northern tip of the Matsuura peninsula.

3 FUKUOKA, IMARI, see entries under these names.

Kasama (Island of Honshu)

Railway map on inside front cover.

Tokyo, 83mls (133km) - Chiba, 81mls (130km) - Fukushima, 127mls (204km) - Mito, 14mls (22km) - Urawa, 71mls (114km) - Utsunomiya, 49mls (79km).

Ibaraki ken - pop: 31,225.

Kasama is an old feudal town, the first place of any importance in the hills to the W of Mito. It has a castle (ruins 1ml/2km NE of the station) which was erected by the Kasama lords, descendants of the Taira. The Makino lived there from 1747 to 1868.

Kasama inari (1ml/1.5km N of the station; bus) is dedicated to Ukanomitama no kami or Toyouke bime no kami, sister of Amaterasu and patroness of the harvest. Her main shrine is at Ise (see entry under this name). The Kasama shrine draws over a million pilgrims each year. Display of chrysanthemums in November.

VICINITY

1 INADA (2½mls/4km SW, JNR coach). Here you can visit Sainen ji or Inada Gobo (1ml/1.5km W of the station), built on the site of the hermitage of the priest Shinran (1173-1262), founder of the Jodo Shin Shu sect. This is where he wrote the *Kyogo shinsho* (1217-24), an exposition of the principles of his doctrine.

2 KATANIWA (3mls/5km NW; coach). This is where Ryogon ji stands. It has a venerated statue of Kannon of the thousand hands; the main door of the temple is also of special interest. The other speciality of this place is the breeding of a particular kind of cicada, the *hime haruzemi*.

Kashihara (Island of Honshu)

Map of Osaka and vicinity, pp. 500-1.

Tokyo, 320mls (515km) - Kyoto, 40mls (65km) - Nara, 13mls (21km) -

Osaka, 24mls (39km) - Tsu, 53mls (85km) - Wakayama, 51mls (83km) - Unebi JNR station.

Nara ken - pop: 75,508.

Situated to the S of the Nara basin and Yamato, this place was the first historical capital of Japan where the Emperor Jimmu settled. The nearby site of Asuka was also chosen as the capital in the 7th c. AD. The Yamato Rekishikan Museum has a number of mementos.

GOING BACK TO THE ORIGINS OF HISTORY. The ancient chronicles of the Kojiki or the Nihongi report that in 660 BC, Jimmu tenno, descendant of Amaterasu (see Ise), set up his capital at the foot of Mount Unebi on a plain of oak trees (Kashiwara hara, or Kashihara). He had made himself master of Yamato, having defeated the semi-legendary prince Nagasune hiko, following his odyssey across the Inland Sea and his campaigns on the Kii peninsula. He had himself crowned in Kashihara, built his palace, and died in 585 BC. As the place was then considered impure, Jimmu's successors, until the Nara period, set up their offical seat in a new capital at the time of each Imperial accession.

However, it was N of Kashihara that the Emperor Sujin had a shrine built in 92 BC, independent of the Imperial Palace, to house the mirror of Amaterasu, later transferred to Ise (see entry under this name). Modern historians have cast doubt on the dates given in the official chronicles: owing to archeological evidence and Chinese and Korean archives, it it thought that the Emperor Jimmu lived from 62 to 1 BC, which would place the creation of the shrine at Ise in the 4th c. AD.

Prince Shotoku (574-622; see Ikaruga, Horyu ji) was born in Kashihara.

KASHIHARA JINGU (770yds/700m NW of Kashihara jingu station, Kintetsu ER). It was built in 1889, on the supposed site of the Emperor Jimmu's palace.

This shrine, the beams of which came from the old Imperial Palace of Kyoto, was restored and expanded in 1939; it is dedicated to Jimmu tenno and his wife Himetatara isuzu Hime. Festivals on 11 February and 3 April.

Unebi yama (653ft/199m alt.) towers up behind the shrine. To the N of this hill, note the tumulus surrounded by ditches and in the shape of a keyhole, traditionally believed to be the tomb of Emperor Jimmu.

YAMATO REKISHIKAN (open daily from 09.00 to 16.00). The History Museum of Yamato is near Kashihara shrine. This museum possesses a noteworthy collection of finds from several excavations carried out at Kashihara and in the region: prehistoric objects, pottery, etc. all help to evoke the past of a protohistoric Japan, midway between the neolithic age of Yayoi and the earliest times of the legendary Nippon chronicle.

Amongst the collections on display are: pottery of the Yayoi period (from 4th c. BC to 4th c. AD), which came from digs at the Karako site at Tawaramoto (3mls/5km N of Kashihara); terracotta sarcophagi from the Nara basin, *haniwa* figures, with cylindrical bodies; and clay models of the earliest times which were left in the tumuli (Kofin period).

VICINITY

1 *ASUKA (2½mls/4km SE; coaches from Unebi JNR station, or from Kashiharajingu Kintetsu station). The town stands on the group of hills to the SE of Kashihara, and was once the centre of an Imperial capital which gave its name to a chronological period of Japanese history.

The Empress Suiko (554–628), on her accession in 593, established her capital in Asuka. Although the government had been practically assured by her nephew, Prince Shotoku (574–622), it was under her reign that the Code of Seventeen Articles was promulgated. This was notable for its recognition of Imperial authority and protection of the Buddhist religion. It was a period of economic and artistic prosperity, and the Horyu ji (see Ikaruga) remains excellent proof of this.

Asuka dera or Ango in is all that remains of Hoko ji), founded at the end of the 6th c. by Soga Umako, brother of the Empress Suiko. It was one of the first temples set up in Japan, and the site was excavated from 1956 to 1957. Ango in now houses the Great Buddha of Asuka, a bronze statue attributed to the sculptor Tori and created in 606 at the command of the Empress Suiko, Prince Shotoku and Soga Umako. This statue, typical of the Asuka period, is possibly the oldest in Japan, and represents Buddha Sakyamuni sitting in meditation. It has been restored several times.

Oka dera or Ryugai ji (approx ½ml/1km SE of the temple mentioned above) was placed under the direction of the priest Gien in 663, and then restored at the beginning of the 9th c. by Kobo Daishi. Note here a sitting statue in lacquered wood of Gien (Nara period) and a standing statue of Nyorin Kannon (early Heian, clay). To the S of Oka dera is the tumulus of Ishibutai; it is traditionally attributed to Soga Umako (above), whose residence was nearby. The only remains of this *kofun* tomb (7th c.) are marks left by the ditches which surrounded it. The tumulus itself has been removed in order to reveal the vault which is supported by huge blocks of stone.

½ml (1km) W of Oka dera: Tachibana ji; the founding of this temple is attributed to Prince Shotoku, who was probably born on this site (574). The buildings themselves have been destroyed so only the Kon do can be seen, rebuilt in 1864. It contains a statue of the Muromachi period, which represents Shotoku taishi.

Near Asuka (you will need to inquire about the exact situation, and when this tomb is open to the public) is the tumulus of *Takamatsu zuka. This remarkable sepulchre, discovered in 1972, still has mural paintings of the 7th or 8th c. They are richly coloured and represent elegant figures who were doubtless friends and family of the deceased. Apart from the human figures, there are symbols and mythical animals, an early reference to Confucianism. Although Chinese influence is evident, these paintings reflect a purely Japanese mode of expression, heralding *yamato e*.

2 NARA, SAKURAI, YOSHINO, see entries under these names.

Kashima (Island of Honshu)

Map of Places of Interest, p. 70.

Tokyo, 66mls (107km) - Mito, 33mls (54km) - Tsuchiura, 37mls (59km).

Ibaraki ken.

Kashima once attracted crowds to its shrine, one of the oldest in Japan, but now it is an industrial town centred on the new harbour created artificially on the Pacific Ocean to help relieve the overcrowding of ships in Tokyo Bay.

 *KASHIMA JINGU (SE of the station of the same name). This is a shrine which, according to legend, was founded in 660 BC by the Emperor Jimmu (see Kashihara). The present buildings, of which the most notable are the Ro mon and the Hon den, were built between 1604 and 1619.

It is dedicated to Takemikazuchi no Mikoto and Futsunushi no Kami, who were sent by Ninigi no Mikoto, the first earthly descendant of Amaterasu, to conquer the province of Izumo. The shrine was placed under the direction of Onokatomi, and traditionally rebuilt every 21 years.

Vast wooded gardens of pines and Japanese cedars spread out behind the shrine. Here you will find the mysterious pool of Mitara, whose water never rises above the chest of anyone who chooses to bathe in it, whatever their size and stature. You will also find the equally legendary Kaname ishi, the stone surmounting the pillar of the Japanese world to which the subterranean catfish is attached. The moods of this catfish cause the country's earthquakes which, however, spare the region of Kashima.

The site of Kashima Castle is 2mls (4km) SE of Kashimajingu eki. It was built in the 12th c. by Kashima Munemoto, and was captured in 1590 by Satake Yoshishige.

The industrial port of Kashima (6mls/10km S of Kashimajingu eki; bus; private train from Kita-Kashima eki), which was completed in 1975, has two jetties 1,150yds (1,050m) and 5,000yds (4,500m) in length; it receives oil and minerals, and can take ships of 200,000 t.

☞ VICINITY

1 SHIMOTSU KAIGAN (2mls/3km E). This is Kashima beach, which stretches out along the Pacific Ocean.

2 KITA URA (½ml/1km W). This narrow lagoon extends nearly 19mls (30km) from N to S and is immediately W of Kashima; the most

picturesque views of the lagoon are to the S, not far from the confluence of Katsumiga ura and Tone gawa. A toll road (coach) runs across this region.

3 ITAKO (5mls/8km W; coach; JRN train). Lying between the lagoons of Kita and Kasumi, it is particularly famous for its irises which flower in June.

4 CHOSHI, MITO, SAWARA, see entries under these names; SUIGO TSUKUBA REGIONAL PARK, see Tsuchiura.

Kashima (Island of Kyushu)

Map of Kyushu (North), pp. 388–9.

Tokyo, 772mls (1,243km) - Fukuoka, 52mls (84km) - Nagasaki, 48mls (77km) - Saga, 19mls (31km).

Saga ken - pop: 35,475.

Situated near the estuary of the Shiota gawa, which flows into the Gulf of Ariake, this town was once the residence of the Nabeshima. The castle ruins can still be seen, about 1ml (1.5km) SW of the station.

VICINITY

YUTOKU INARI JINJA (3mls/5km S; coach). It was founded in 1687 by Yutoku in, wife of Nabeshima Naotomo, and is one of the most famous shrines in Inari. Its ornamentation has earned it the name of Nikko of Chinzei.

Kawachi Nagano (Island of Honshu)

Map of Kansai, pp. 500–1.

Tokyo, 335mls (539km) - Kobe, 38mls (62km) - Kyoto, 47mls (76km) - Nara, 30mls (49km) - Osaka, 18 mls (29km) - Wakayama, 42mls (67km) - Kawachi Nagano station, Kintetsu and Nankai ER.

Osaka fu - pop: 5,994.

This town on the road from Osaka to Koya san (see Koya) is overlooked by the mountain range of Kii to the S.

VICINITY

1 AMANO SAN (4mls/7km SW; coach). On the slopes of this hill stands Kongo ji, which you can visit. Its foundation is attributed to the priest Gyoki (668-749). The temple was partly reconstructed in 1171 and again in the Kamakura period. It served as a place of refuge in the 14th c. for the Emperors Go Daigo and Go Murakami, sovereigns of the Yoshino court (see entry under this name). Amongst the treasures here are the *Nichi getsu sansu screens, with landscapes beneath the sun and moonlight. They are anonymous works from the end of the 16th c.

2 KONGO ZAN (7mls/12km SE, coach then cable-car). Head SE out of Kawachi Nagano on the N310.

 2mls (3km): Kanshin ji, founded in the 7th c., then restored by Kobo Daishi in the 9th c. The Kondo was rebuilt by Kusunoki Masashige, and houses a venerable statue of *Nyorin Kannon in multicoloured wood (9th c.). It is rarely on display.

4mls (7km): Take a small road on the l. towards:

5½mls (9km): Chihaya, where there are ruins of a castle built by Kusunoki Masashige (1294-1336). Continue r. towards the SE.

 7mls (12km): Cable-car up Kongo zan (3,648ft/1,112m), which makes the ascent much easier. A belvedere with a remarkable view of Kongo Ikoma Regional Park (38,610 acres/15,625 ha; see vicinity of Nara) forms the actual peak.

■ Kawagoe (Island of Honshu)

Map of the Vicinity of Tokyo, p. 565.

Tokyo, 26mls (42km) - Chiba, 50mls (80km) - Kofu, 86mls (138km) - Maebashi, 65mls (105km) - Mito, 88ml (142km) - Nagano, 125mls (202km) - Urawa, 12mls (20km) - Utsunomiya, 64mls (103km).

Principal town of Saitama ken (pop: 4,497,202) - pop: 259,314.

Kawagoe is an important town in the great suburbs of Tokyo, situated to the N of Musashi plain.

The famous engraver Utamaro Kitagawa (1753-1806) was born in Kawagoe.

 KITA IN (1ml/1.5km N of Kawagoe eki, JNR from Omiya; or Tobu ER from Tokyo Ikebukuro; 550yds/500m E of Hon Kawagoe eki, Seibu ER from Tokyo Seibu-Shinjuku). The temple was founded in 830 by the priest Ennin or Jikaku Daishi (794-864). The present buildings have for the most part been rebuilt using elements of what used to be Tokugawa castle in Edo (Tokyo); note the caricatured representation of the *Five Hundred Disciples of Buddha* (Gohyaku Rakan).

Further S is the shrine of Tosho gu, built at the beginning of the 17th c. in honour of Tokugawa Ieyasu. The buildings are painted in vermilion.

Site of Kawagoe Castle, approx. 550yds (500m) NE of Kita in.

The main street is lined by a series of rough clay houses with richly ornamented roofs, built during the 19th century by the town's merchants. They are now the town's chief point of interest.

■ Kawasaki (Island of Honshu)

Map of the Vicinity of Tokyo, p. 565

Tokyo, 13mls (21km) - Chiba, 37mls (59km) - Kofu, 96mls (154km)

- Shizuoka, 79mls (127km) - Yokohama, 9mls (15km).

Kanagawa ken - pop: 973,486 - industrial town - private university.

Except for the crossings over the Tama gawa and the Tsurumi gawa, which forms the town's limits to the N and S, and in spite of its 1 million inhabitants, Kawaski usually goes unnoticed by anyone travelling from Tokyo to Yokohama. These three cities, which are linked to each other, form a monotonous and characterless urban landscape.

HEIGEN JI OR **KAWASAKI DAISHI** (220yds/200m SE of Kawasaki-Daishi station, Keihin Kyuko ER from Keihin-Kawasaki; 2mls/3km E of Kawasaki JNR station; bus). This temple dedicated to Kobo Daishi, was founded in 1128; reduced to ashes in 1945, the principal buildings (main gate, belfry, Fudo do) were re-erected in 1964. Festivals on 3 or 4 February, also on 21st of months of January, March, April, May, September, December.

VICINITY

1 **KUJI** (9mls/15km NW; JNR train). You should go to the banks of the Tama gawa (770yds/700m N) in spring, to admire the flowering plum trees, peach trees and pear trees.

2 **NOBORITO** (11mls/18km NW; JNR train), where you can head W on the Odakyu ER to Yomiurirandomae station, near Yomiuri Land Amusement Park, or to Kakio station, near the Ozenji Atomic Research Centre.

3 **TOKYO, YOKOHAMA**, see entries under these names.

Kirishima Yaku (National park; Island of Kyushu)**

Map of Natural Resources, p. 67.

HOW TO GET THERE

- From Kagoshima or Kokubu; JNR train to Kirishima station (33mls/53km from Kagoshima, 1h. approx.), where you can take the coach to the shrine or the spa town of Kirishima; direct coaches from Kagoshima to Kirishima Onsen.

- From Miyazaki, where you can go via Miyakonojo to Kobayashi station (53mls/86km in 2h. 10 approx. by JNR train), and from there by coach, to Kirishima Onsen; direct coaches from Miyazaki to Kirishima Onsen.

This park of 136,479 acres (55,231ha) offers various attractions: the coast to the N of Kagoshima and Sakurajima (see Kagoshima), the Ibusuki and Kaimon dake region (see Ibusuki), Sata Point (see Sata), Yaku shima (see Osumi shoto), and the volcanic range of Kirishima, see below.

FROM KOBAYASHI TO KIRISHIMA (30mls/49km by a forest toll road; coach).

Head SW out of Kobayashi on a road which rises up onto the slopes of the Kirishima massif.

7mls (12km): Tamakino, at the entrance to the National Park. The toll road continues past here, and affords beautiful views over the peaks of the Kirishima range and over more distant horizons, such as Kagoshima Bay and the volcano of Sakurajima.

The **Kirishima volcanic range, a group of mountains typical of southern Kyushu, covering 53,276 acres (21,560ha) and made up of about 20 peaks, the most important being Takachihono mine (5,164ft/1,574m) and Karakuni dake (5,577ft/1,700m). There are ten crater lakes, thermal springs which are the highest in Japan, and dense, thriving vegetation.

15mls (25km): *Ebino kogen, at an altitude of about 4,000ft (1,200m), is one of the most famous places in this park. The plateau is overlooked to the SE by Karakuni dake or Nishi-Kirishima (alt. 5,577ft/1,700m).

The crater lakes, Rokukannon, Fudo and Byakushi are nearby. Further S is a lake reflecting the volcano Onami. You can climb the latter from the resort Eno o (below), 4mls (6.5km) SW of the summit, which you can walk to via Onami in about 4 hs. *View over a wide area including Takachihono mine, Sakurajima (p. 281), and Mount Aso (see entry under this name).

19mls (31km): Shin yu, in the middle of the Kirishima thermal springs, of which there are over a dozen. They include:

➡ Eno o, 1½ml (2km) W, once frequented by the Shimazu, daimyos of Kagoshima. Hayashida, 3mls (5km) W, is the most famous and its waters contain iron, sulphur and carbon (104°-140°F/40°-60°C). Iodani and Myoban, further S, possess sulphur springs between 104°F and 207°F (40°C and 97°C).

➡ The toll road continues E and comes rapidly within sight of Takachihono mine, with its remarkable contours.

23mls (37km): Junction; on the r. leave the road to Kirishima shrine, and go on to Takachiho gawara, at the foot of Takachi-hono mine.

*Takachihono mine, or Higashi Kirishima (5,164ft/1,574m), is the legendary mountain where Ninigi no Mikoto is supposed to have landed, sent by his grandmother Amaterasu. You can climb to the summit in 1h. 30 (1½mls/2.5km E). The nearby crater, which is active, is 656ft (200m) in circumference and 223ft (68m) deep. A breathtakingly high path runs round it, offering a view over a wide area. Note also a large hole, made by Amaterasu's two-edged sword which was kept in a wooden shelter near the summit.

➡ Approx 6mls (10km) NE of Takachiho gawara (track): Sanu miya (accessible by road from Takaharu) marks the site of the Emperor Jimmu's birthplace (711-585 BC, see Kashihara).

At the junction mentioned above, go back down towards:

27mls (43km): Kirishima jingu; built in a very fine forest of Japanese cypresses, this shrine, which was reconstructed in the 19th c., is dedicated to Ninigi no Mikoto. Festival 19 September.

30mls (49km): Kirishimajingu eki, station where you can take the JNR train to Kagoshima or Miyazaki. There are direct coach links from Kirishima shrine to Kagoshima.

Kisarazu (Island of Honshu)

Map of the Vicinity of Tokyo, p. 565.

Tokyo, 45mls (73km) – Chiba, 22mls (36km) – Mito, 104mls (169km) –Urawa, 60mls (97km).

Chiba ken - pop: 110,711 industrial town.

Kisarazu and Kimitsu, which is further S, mark the southern limit of the Tokyo Bay industrial development. In fact, from Yokohama, through Tokyo, Chiba and Ichihra, the entire perimeter of the bay has been completely reclaimed by the polderization of industrial zones, which totally alter the original appearance of the landscape.

VICINITY

KANO ZAN (15mls/24km S; coach) is a wooded hill with a *remarkable view from the summit on fine days over the Boso peninsula to Mount Fuji in the W, or to the Nikko mountains in the N. Near the summit is Kano ji or Jinyu ji, reputedly founded by Prince Shotoku (see Ikaruga). The numerous buildings, reconstructed in the 16th c. and 18th c., house several Buddhist statues including one of Shotoku taishi. Hanayome matsuri, the festival of brides and grooms, is on 28 April. There is also a little shrine on this mountain dedicated to Prince Yamato Takeru (see Kameyama).

Kiso Fukushima (Island of Honshu)

Tokyo, 170mls (273km) - Nagano, 81mls (130km) - Shiojiri, 27mls (44km).

Nagano ken.

Standing half-way between Tokyo and Kyoto, by the Nakasen do (inland road), is Kiso Fukushima, once an important toll post. The forests, which are the chief glory of this region, are apparently inexhaustible. They once belonged to the Tokugawa and are now state property. The development of over 350 sq.mls (1,000km²) of forest provides the whole of Japan with wood. Particular uses of it are in the reconstruction of certain shrines, such as Ise (see entry under this name).

Horse breeding, and fairs in July and September.

VICINITY

1 AGEMATSU (3½mls/6km S on the N19; JNR train; coach). The road and the railway to Agematsu run along the superb *gorges of the Kiso gawa. Very fine views of them stretch for about 12mls (20km) from Kiso Fukushima to Suhara. These gorges, like those on the Tenryu gawa and the Hida gawa, are amongst the loveliest in Japan.

1½ml (2km) S of Agematsu: *Nezamino toko is such a beautiful place that, as the name suggests, anyone contemplating it is mesmerized by it. Note the curiously shaped rocks, which have been given animal names. Further S is the Ono waterfall which plunges about 100ft (30m).

2 'ONTAKE SAN (18mls/29km W; coach to Mikasa yama). Head S out of Kiso Fukushima on the Agematsu road (N19).

1½ml (2km): Confluence of the Kiso gawa and the Otaki gawa. Follow the course of the latter, which has several dams across it (Makio, Miure).

10mls (17km): Otaki, where you can go N on a toll road.

18mls (29km): Mikasa yama (7,401ft/2,256m). You will have to walk from here (2½mls/4km in 5h. approx.) to the summit of Ontake san (10,049ft/3,063m). Pilgrims flock here in summer. On the summit is a little shrine dedicated to the deity of this extinct volcano, which is the southernmost of the great Chuba Sangaku chain.

3 MATSUMOTO, CHUBU SANGAKU NATIONAL PARK, see entries under these names; **KOMGAG TAKE,** see Komagane.

K Kitakyushu (Island of Kyushu)

Map of Kyushu (North), pp. 388-9.

Tokyo, 677mls (1,089km) - Fukuoka, 41mls (66km) - Kumamoto, 100mls (160km) - Oita, 78mls (125km) - Saga, 64mls (103km).

Fukuoka ken - pop: 1,042,321 - industrial town - regional university.

This huge city lying opposite Shimonoseki, to the S of the Kammon Strait, was formed in 1963 by the merging of Moji, Kokura, Tobata, Yahata and Wakamatsu, which together make up the seventh city of Japan (180sq.mls/465km²), situated in the N of Kyushu. Kitakyushu, which leads the world in iron and steel production, stands on Dokai Bay and is linked to Honshu (Shimonoseki) by several railway and road tunnels, and by the Kammon suspension bridge.

Each of the towns which make up Kitakyushu has its own historical importance. In the 3rd c. Moji was the disembarkation port for Korean envoys who came to pay their tribute to Japan. The Taira retreated there in the 12th c. before their final defeat at Danno ura. During the Edo period Moji was an ordinary little fishing port, administered by the lords of Kokura. They were the Ogasawara clan between 1632 and 1868. The group of towns finally prospered as a result of the railways and the industrial boom which has taken place since the end of the 19th century. The Yawata Steel Co., which was set up in 1901, profited from the Chikuho coal basin. This company joined with Fuji Iron Steel in 1970 to form Shin Nippon Shitetsu (Nippon Steel Corporation). Although it now imports almost all its raw materials, this company has an annual iron and steel production of 1.7 million t.

Kokura Ku

Stations at Kokura (JNR) and Uomachi (Nishitetsu).

Kokura is the commercial and administrative centre of this vast urban conglomeration. It opens out to the N opposite Shimonoseki, and has become busier since a Shinkansen station was opened.

Kokura Castle (½ml/1km W of Kokura JNR station; 330yds/300m SE of Daimon Nishitetsu stop) offers the visitor its old donjon lovingly restored in 1959. It stands in the middle of gardens surrounded by moats and ramparts. The shrine of Yasaka is also here. (Festival 10-12 July.)

The original castle, built in 1442 by Reizei Takasuke, was reconstructed in 1596 by Mori Katsunaga, but burned down in 1866.

Moji Ku

Moji and Mojiko JNR stations.

Moji, to the NE of Kokura, lies close beside the sea on the Kiku peninsula, which rises to 1,962ft (598m) with Adachi san to the S. The following routes from Shimonoseki terminate in Moji: the railway tunnel, 1,420yds (1,300m) long, dug in 1942; the road tunnel with pedestrian footpath, 3,780yds (3,460m), of which 850yds/780m are under the sea, completed in 1958; the Shinkansen railway tunnel (1975), 10mls (16km) long, of which 830yds (760m) are under the sea; and finally *Kamon Ohashi, a road suspension bridge, opened in 1973 (1,168yds/1,068m long; 779yds/712m of this is between the two main supports).

MEKARI PARK (to the N of Moji; Moji Nishitetsu station; or 1½mls/2.5km N of Mojiko, JNR; bus). The park completely covers Cape Mekari and overlooks the bridge and the Kammon Strait.

Mekari jinga, which is in this park, was founded by the Empress Jingu following her conquest of Korea (N of Kyushu) in 202. To the E on the slopes of Mount Kojo is a Pagoda of Peace, a gift from Burma in 1958.

Tobata Ku and Yahata Ku

Tobata, Edamitsu, Yahata, Kurosaki JNR stations; stops: Tobata, Makiyama, Chuonachi, Kurosaki and Sadamoto (Nishitetsu).

Tobata and Yahata lie to the W of Kokura and S of Dokai Bay, where the Nippon Steel Corporation's industrial units stretch for over 2½mls (4km), occupy 468sq.mls (1,211km²) and form rather a strange sight. Yahata station houses a small science museum.

Hobashira yama (1½ml/2km S of Yahata JNR station; bus to Ogurakoen funicular railway stop). This wooded park reaches its highest point at Sarakura yama (2,041ft/622m), which provides an interesting view over Kitakyushu and Dokai Bay.

*Wakato Ihashi (Tobata Nishitetsu stop) hangs over Dokai wan, and links Tobata to Wakamatsu. This suspension bridge was opened in 1962. Its total length is 2,262yds (2,068m), with 744yds (680m) between its two main supports. It is possible to cross beneath; view over Yahata industrial area.

Wakamatsu Ku

Wakamatsu JNR station.

Wakamatsu lies to the NW of Dokai Bay, and is the port which the Chikuho coalmines traditionally use to export their coal.

Takato yama (770yds/700m NW of Wakamatsu eki; access by bus and cable-car) is another wooded hill with a view over the whole of Kammon kyo, Dokai wan and the Kitakyushu suspension bridges.

K Kobe (Island of Honshu)

Map of Kansai, pp. 500–1; street plan pp. 316–317.

Tokyo, 351mls (565km) – Kyoto, 47mls (76km) – Okayama, 89mls (143km) – Osaka, 21mls (34km) – Tottori, 120mls (193km).

Principal town of Hyogo ken (pop: 3,879,116) – pop: 1,367,000 – trading port, industrial town – national, regional and private universities.

Kobe is the greatest port in Japan, and indeed in the whole of the East. It provides a sight which is characteristic of maritime Japan and of modern-day Japan in general. Built on the narrow coastal strip, bounded immediately to the N by the Rokko san range, the town spreads W as far as the island of Awaji, the perimeter of the Osaka development and its suburban districts. But Kobe is especially a town synonymous with bursting vitality all the more in evidence for the way that civil works are bringing together the town and its port. Each has truly become a part of the other. Vast projects are in hand for levelling the nearby hills, and filling in the sea; housing is built on the resultant landfill. An artificial island (Port Island) was created between 1966 and

1981 to expand the port installations and house over 20,000 people. A second one, Rokko Island, is currently being created. The most striking thing about these spectacular achievements is the extremely 'modernistic' aspect of today's Japan which seems to rest on the conviction that the future will belong primarily to technology. And a hint of anxiety soon creeps into our undeniable admiration, at the thought of all those mechanized, dehumanized tomorrows ...

AT THE GODS' COMMAND As a small fishing port whose people were dedicated to creating a hereditary guild (*be*) to the deity of Ikuta shrine, Kobe in the 4th c. was still only an insignificant haven, through which precious elements of Chinese and Korean culture were already passing.

THE PORT OF HYOGO. In 1157, Taira Kiyomori (1118–81) had Fukuhara Castle built, and founded the trading port of Kobe. When he was confronted with a difficulty in building dykes, it was decided that about 30 people should be walled in alive. They only escaped this gruesome ceremony, which existed in numerous countries, through the self-sacrifice of a servant of Kiyomori. When the Taira fell at the hands of the Minamoto, Taira Menemori left his castle (1183) and Kobe disappeared from history, to re-emerge with the battle of Minatogawa, when Ashikaga Takauji defeated the supporters of the Emperor Go Daigo (1136). The port of Hyogo continued to prosper until the Edo period when it was surpassed, following the Imperial Restoration, by the port of Kobe.

THE DEVELOPMENT OF KOBE. In 1867, Kobe was still only a simple fishing village, where a naval college was set up. From 1868 onwards the port expanded considerably. The foreign concession was established W of the Ikuta gawa, and thanks to the governor of Hyogo ken, Ito Kirobumi (1841–1909), Kobe became a major port, even busier than Hyogo. In 1874 the railway came to Kobe, and the wars against China (1894–95) and Russia (1904–5) increased the business of the port, which was completely rebuilt during 1902. After the 1923 earthquake, Kobe attracted the silk trade and industry which had been the mainstay of Yokohama. The town and port were two-thirds destroyed in 1945, but have since been reconstructed and have revived their industry and commerce: metallurgy, shipyards, manufacture of railway materials, light industries and rubber, etc.

THE PORT. This includes: to the SW, the domestic trade port, to the NE, the international trade port, and offshore the massive artificial Port Island (1,075 acres/435ha), completed in 1981. The port handles an average traffic of 11.6 million t per annum which represent 23.3% of Japanese exports and 11.6% of imports. The imports (raw materials, cereals, cotton) come mainly from the United States, Australia, Malaysia and West Germany. The exports are mostly cotton weaves, synthetic fibres, porcelain, manufactured products and electric appliances, etc., and are sent to a number of countries, the United States being the most important. In addition to this, Kobe is the world's leading port in container traffic. It is going to be linked to the port of Osaka at some time in the future, by the development of the

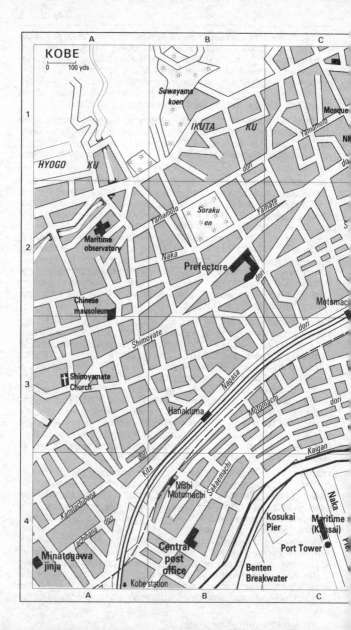

Hanshin industrial zone which runs for 20mls (30km) along Osaka Bay.

Visiting the town

A HALF DAY IN KOBE. If you have an afternoon free in Kobe, we recommend that you spend it as follows. Take a boat trip round the port (departures from Naka pier), then take a taxi through the business quarter which lies to the S of Sannomiya and Motomachi stations, to visit Ikuta shrine (plan: D1), or head directly to the Namban Art Museum. Towards the end of the afternoon go up Rokko san, either by taxi or by the itinerary given below. The view over Kobe and Osaka is particularly striking at night and early in the morning.

THE TOWN ON FOOT. Kobe is far too extensive to be suitable for long walks, and we can't recommend public transport strongly enough. A stroll along the shopping streets of Motomachi, Sannomiya or Santica ton would not, however, be too strenuous.

A Ikuta ku

Sannomiya, Motomachi and Kobe JNR stations.

The central district of Ikuta is spread out on either side of the national and private railways, between Futatabi and the sea. Towards the S, in the direction of the port, there are busy shopping and business areas, hotels, administration buildings and banks around the Kaigan dori, Sakaemachi dori and Motomachi dori. A wide arterial road, Hamabe dori, branches off S of Sannomiya station and crosses the lively district of Santica ton (underground passage). This road then runs past the town hall of Kobe (plan: E2), to the N of which is a totem pole presented by the American city of Seattle in 1961. Past the town hall is a public garden within which is the Consulate General of the United States (arch. Yamasaki Minoru), at the southern end. Hamabe dori passes under the Hanshin express road and comes to an end past the Customs Building, at the port of Kobe.

The shopping streets Sannomiya and Motomachi radiate out from Santica and run parallel to the railways.

THE PORT OF KOBE (plan: C4-F4, see pp. 316–17). The vast port gives the impression of being striped with a great many jetties which jut out like the irregular teeth of a comb. There is only a simple numbering system to distinguish them. Kobe Ohashi bridge links jetty No 4 to Port Island, which is entirely reclaimed from the sea. The only piers which have names are Naka and Meriken (American's).

Naka Pier (plan: C4; 550yds/500m E Of Kobe eki; ½ml/1km S of Motomachi eki) is the point of departure for various ferry services, and motor launches which provide trips round the port between 11.00 and 16.00 (lasting approx. 50 min.). On this pier stands the Port Tower (338ft/103m high), erected in 1963 by Nikken Sekkei Komu; marine and port museum in the Kansai Kisen building.

IKUTA JINJA (plan: D1, 330yds/300m W of Sannomiya eki). This shrine, which stands to the NW of the railway lines, on the other side of a district with a lively night-life, is the most interesting in the town.

Although it was reconstructed after 1945, in the style of the Kasuga shrine at Nara, Ikuta jinja was probably founded in the 3rd c. by the Empress Jingu. It is dedicated to Wakahirume no Mikoto, goddess patroness of Kobe, whose official guild (*kami be*) gave its name to the town. There is a little wood of cedars and camphor trees behind this shrine. Festivals 15-16 April, and 19-23 September.

To the N of the Ikuta jinja domain runs a wide avenue which forks towards the SW, and goes to either side of the Prefecture of Hyogo ken.

On the fifth floor of the Zentan Building (Shimoyate dori 4-chome), is the local ceramic museum of Hyogo. This entire district (Shimoyate, Yamamoto) is also full of religious buildings, Christian, Jewish and Muslim.

Soraku en (plan: B2; 550yds/500m NW of Motomachi eki), to the N of the Prefecture, is a lovely Japanese garden which is particularly beautiful when the azaleas are in flower.

Further N of this garden, on the slopes of Ikari yama, is Suwayama Park, where the French astronomer Jules Janssen (1824-1907) settled in 1874 to observe the transit of Venus; commemorative plaque.

SHRINE OF MINATOGAWA OR **NANKO** (plan: A4; 330yds/300m NW of Kobe station; 1½mls/2.5km SW of Sannomiya eki). The shrine is near to the spot where Masashige Kusunoki (1294-1336) committed suicide following the battle of Minatogawa (see Historical survey section) which he fought unsuccessfully against Ashikaga Takauji.

The shrine, built in his memory in 1871, was burnt down in 1945 and has since been re-erected. The tomb of Kusunoki was set up in 1692 by Tokugawa Mitsukuni, lord of Mito. Festival 25 May.

B Fukiai ku

Shin Kobe, Sannomiya and Nada JNR stations; Kasuganomichi private stations (Hanshin and Hankyu).

Fukiai ku lies to the E of Ikuta ku, and the N side of it leans towards the Futatabi and Maya san. The southern part of this district forms an extension of the central business quarters. The tall modern tower of Kobe Shoko Boeki Center (Centre of Trade and Industry; arch. Nikken Sekkei Komu) stands in this area.

*NAMBAN MUNICIPAL ART MUSEUM (Shiritsu Namban Bijutsukan; 650yds/600m E of Shin Kobe eki; 1ml/1.5km NE of Sannomiya eki; 770yds/700m N of Hankyu Kasuganomichi; address: 4-35-3 Kumochi cho 1-chome, Fukiai ku; open daily from 09.30 to 16.30, except

Mondays). This museum presents a panorama of Japanese art created at the school of European missionaries of the Counter-Reformation. They were known as the 'Barbarians from the South' (*Namban*) and the expression came to refer to this pictorial method. You will observe a collection of *screens: Namban byobu. 'They use a purely Japanese technique to deal with the colourful scenes of a Portuguese ship coming in to harbour, (...) the arrival of the priests and the celebration of the mass. These Namban screens are the work of genre painters of the Kano school.' (D. and V. Elisseeff, *La Civilisation Japonaise*.)

Among the screens, note also a map of the world, on which the contours of western Europe and Africa are correctly drawn, whilst those of Japan are somewhat exaggerated. The museum also displays objects in current use which show the influence of Namban art.

***FUTATABI SAN.** This vast wooded park stretches to the N of Shin Kobe station, on the slopes of Mount Futatabi (1,535ft/468m), which has a scenic toll road running through it (coach).

This hill, which is part of the Rokko range, probably owes its name 'twice visited' to the fact that the priest Kukai (Kobo Daishi) stopped there both before and after his trip to China, in 804 and 806.

Futatabi is a lovely spot for the people of Kobe to walk to, as they can visit the following: near Shin Kobe eki are the twin waterfalls of Nunobiki, known as Odaki (male and female); near the summit is the Dairyu ji, founded in 768 by Wake Kiyomaro, which houses a statue of Nyorin Kannon, of the Nara period (8th c.); NW of the summit is the pool of Shiogara (5 acres/2ha), which has an amusement park; adjacent to it is the Municipal Botanical Garden 1ml/1.5km N of Futabai san), which has a 250-acre (100-ha) arboretum with 1,300 varieties from all over the world. There is also the foreigners' cemetery, where the tombs are laid out according to the different religions.

C Nada ku

Nada and Rokkomichi JNR stations; Nishinada and Rokko Hankyu ER stations.

The ascent of Mounts Maya and Rokko is the main attraction of this district, which forms an extension of Fukiai ku to the NE.

To the W of Kankyu-Nishinada eki is Oki Park, which has a zoo and sports grounds.

To the S of the park is the Hyogo Modern Art Museum (8-30 Harada dori 3-chome, Nada ku), built in 1970, which has several contemporary Japanese paintings, and organizes exhibitions.

***MAYA SAN.** You can go up on the funicular railway, and then take the cable car from the Takao stop ¾ml/1.2km N of Kankyu-Nishinada station; 2mls/3.5km NE of Sannomiya JNR station; No 18 bus from the latter). From the summit (2,293ft/699m) there is a panorama over Kobe and the surrounding area (particularly spectacular at night).

The slopes of Maya san are wooded with cedars, and a flight of 398 steps leads up amongst them to Toritenjo ji, founded in 646 by the Indian priest Hodo. It contains a statue of Kannon of the eleven heads and another of Maya Bunin, the mother of Buddha Gautama.

**ROKKO SAN (coaches from Sannomiya). The Dobashi funicular railway stop (Rokkosan cableway) can be reached from Hankyu-Rokko station, by No 16 bus. Rokko san (3,058ft/932m) is part of Seto Naikai National Park (see entry under this name). In addition to the view over Kobe, this mountain provides a veritable 'gold mine' of walks.

The visitor will find the following provided for his enjoyment: a viewpoint with a rotating platform, a golf course, a garden full of alpine plants, a model pasture, etc. From the top of the funicular railway, a cable-car goes in three stages up to the spa resort of Arima (see below, Vicinity 1).

D Hyogo ku

Hyogo JNR station; Shinkaichi private station.

This district to the W of Ikuta ku is spread over a wide area from N to S between the lower hills of the Rokko range and the sea. Worth visiting are:

Minatogawa Park (Shintetsu-Minatogawa station), on the site of the battle of Minatogawa (1336), which took place along the river of that name (the course of which was altered in 1892). Statue dedicated to Masashige Kusunoki (see p. 319). One of the town's liveliest districts for night-life is Shinkaichi to the S of this park.

Nofuku ji (550yds/500m E of Hyogo JNR station) has a designated statue of Kannon of the eleven heads, of the Heian period (9th c.).

E Suma ku

Takatori and Suma JNR stations.

This district, which has been joined to Kobe, extends the town to the SW, and is about 6mls (9km) from Sannomiya station. Zensho ji (1ml/1.5km N of Sanyo-Itayado station) is situated at the foot of Mount Takatori (1,053ft/321m), surrounded by maple woods and close to Myohoji gawa. This temple was founded in the 14th c. in honour of Kannon; the 17th-c. door is designated.

Fukusho ji or Suma dera (880yds/800m N of Suma JNR station or 660yds/600m NW Of Suma Sanyo ER station) was built in 886, at the request of the Emperor Koko. This temple contains two statues of Kannon, of the Muromachi period; there are beautiful cherry trees in April.

SUMANO URA (near to Sumanoura koen, Sanyo ER station). This park stretches for several miles between the mouth of Myohoji gawa and the lower hills of Mount Hachibuse, and then extends even further in the form of Maiko beach; it is famous for its pinewood.

Sumano ura was once a natural pass, where the Rokko range drops sharply to the sea. In 1184, the Minamoto confronted the Taira there.

The aquarium on the E beach is one of the most interesting in Japan. There are about 4,000 different species of sea and freshwater fish.

From Sumanoura koen station, you can take the cablecar and then the chairlift up to the summit of Mount Hachibuse; view over Awaji Island.

Beyond Suma ku is the district of Tarumi, where you can visit Taisan ji (Muromachi period) and the shrine of Wadatsumi, patron of sailors and fishermen.

F Vicinity

1 **ARIMA ONSEN** (15mls/24km N; Shintetsu ER train from Shinkaichi station; coach from Sannomiya eki or from Rokko san; cablecar from Rokko san, see pp. 312-3. This spa town, altitude 1,191ft (363m), is a standard place to walk to from Kobe. Its saline springs containing iron and carbon are amongst the oldest known springs in Japan.

2 **AKASHI, AWAJI SHIMA, OSAKA, TAKARAZUKA, SETO NAIKAI NATIONAL PARK**, see entries under these names.

■ Kochi (Island of Shikoku)

Map of Shikoku (Inland Sea), pp. 536-7.

Tokyo, 542mls (873km) - Matsuyama, 79mls (127km) - Takamatsu, 96mls (154km) - Tokushima, 121mls (194km).

Principal town of Kochi ken (pop: 240,481) - industrial town and port - national and regional universities.

Situated at the end of Urado Bay and in the S of Shikoku, Kochi is one of the liveliest towns on the island. Although it was once traditionally devoted to fishing and sea products, Kochi has now taken on an industrial role and has partly succeeded in redressing the balance of Shikoku's southern economy, which was disrupted by the attraction of the shores of the Inland Sea.

Although this site has been occupied since the Jomon and Yayoi periods, Kochi only really plays a part in history from the 17th c. onwards, when Yamanouchi Kazutoyo (1546-1605) received the province of Tosa, and built Kochi Castle, which remained in the possession of his family until the Meiji Restoration. In 1874, Itagaki Taisuke (1837-1919), who was from a Samurai family native to Kochi, set up the Public Patriots Party (Aikokutoko), in the hope of bringing a greater degree of democracy to the new government. He did not, however, form an alliance with the opposition clans, the Choshu and the Satsuma, as he wished to keep his own independence. He later founded the first Japanese Liberal Party.

KOCHI CASTLE (1ml/1.5km SW of the station). Situated on a small hill in the town centre, there are still some traces of its ramparts, a few entrance gates and the little keep, erected in 1748 following the fire of 1727. The original castle was built in 1603 by Yamanouchi Kazutoyo.

The keep contains a local archaeology museum (Neolithic pottery), *kagura* (sacred dance) masks, Tosa sabres and other artifacts and documents relating to the castle and the province of Tosa. There is a view from the summit over the town and the surrounding area.

VICINITY

1 *GODAI SAN (3mls/5km SE; coach from the station; access by cable-car). This hill, which is 469ft (143m) above sea level, affords an exceptional overall view of Kochi and Urado Bay. Near the peak is *Chikurin ji, founded in 724 by the priest Gyoki, where Kobo Daishi stayed for a while. The garden, originally designed by Soseki (1271–1346), is worth a visit, and so is the Monju do or Hon do, which house several Buddhist statues of the Fujiwara and Kamakura periods. There are some more interesting statues in the modern treasure house. At the foot of the steps leading to the temple, you will find a botanical garden with greenhouses full of tropical plants, and a small museum dedicated to the botanist Makino Tomitaro (1862–1957), who came from this region.

2 **KATSURA HAMA** (36mls/11km S; coach). This is a promontory which encloses Urado Bay to the S, and extends along Tosa Bay (Pacific Ocean) with inlets of white sand and pinewoods.

3 MUROTO, NANKOKU, TOSA, see entries under these names; YOSHINO GAWA GORGES, see Ikeda.

Kofu (Island of Honshu)

Railway map on inside front cover.

Tokyo, 90mls (145km) – Nagano, 93mls (150km) – Shizuoka, 66mls (107km) – Urawa, 97mls (156km) – Yokohama, 87mls (140km).

Principal town of Yamanashi ken (pop: 383,404) – pop: 182,689 – crystal works, silk weaving, vineyards.

Kofu is situated in the fertile Kai basin, at the foot of the Chichibu mountains, which tower up to the N. Towards the S the skyline is dominated by the noble shape of Mount Fuji, which is skirted to the W by Fuji kawa. This is formed by the confluence of several rivers of the Kofu plain. There are a number of thermal springs in the town and close by, such as the one at Yumara (2mls/3km NW).

Kofu was originally called Fuchu, and was the residence of the Ichijo during the Kamakura period. In 1582, Oda Nobunaga took this town from the Takeda who lived there at that time. Hideyoshi placed one of his companions in power there, and from 1600 onwards the town came under the domain of the Tokugawa Shogunate. They retained more or less direct control of it until the 1868 Restoration.

JAPANESE WINES. The fertility and the exposed position of the Kofu region's hillsides have made viticulture possible from earliest times. The vine was imported from China in the 6th c. It is uniformly in vine arbours (6½ft/2m above ground level), under which you can walk. The traditional types of vine have been supplemented with plants which come from Languedoc and from the Caspian Sea. The wines have a 13° to 14° alcohol content, and while the reds are similar to Bordeaux, the whites are like Moselle. Annual production is more than 1 million gals (4,800 kl) of wine and 16,000 t of table grapes.

Maizuru Park lies to the SE of the station, behind the Prefecture, on the former site of the castle, with a view over the whole town.

Otamachi Park (1ml/1.5km SE of the station) once belonged to Ichiren ji. It is famous for its plum trees, lilacs and bamboo forests.

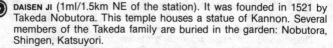

DAISEN JI (1ml/1.5km NE of the station). It was founded in 1521 by Takeda Nobutora. This temple houses a statue of Kannon. Several members of the Takeda family are buried in the garden: Nobutora, Shingen, Katsuyori.

SITE OF TAKEDA CASTLE (1½mls/2.5km N of the station). The Takeda were lords of Kofu. Apart from the marks left by moats and ramparts, you can also see the shrine dedicated to Takeda Shingen (1521–73), son of Nobutora. Festival 12 April.

ZENKO JI (1½ml/2km E of the station). It was founded in the 16th c. by Takeda Shingen, to house a statue which came from the temple of the same name in Nagano. The buildings have been reconstructed since.

☞ **VICINITY**

1 MITAKE (11mls/17km N on the toll road; coach). It is possible to head N to the Ara kawa valley which is hemmed in by the narrow *Shosen pass, lined with rocky cliffs for 2mls (4km); one of the finest sites of the Chichibu Tama Natural Park.

7mls (12km): Kanasakura shrine, which stands in a wooded park, is very pleasant in autumn.

11mls (17km): Mitake, at the foot of Kayaga take (5,591ft/1,704m).

2 *MINOBU SAN (29mls/46km S on the N52; coach JNR train to Minobu station 1ml/2km from Kuon ji; bus). Head S out of Kofu to rejoin the N52 which you will reach after crossing the Fuji kawa, 12mls (20km) downstream from Kajikazawa. From this point onwards the N52 follows the river. It is possible to go part way down the rapids in summer.

24mls (39km): The N300 branches off to the l. and after crossing the Fuji kawa once again, reaches the spa town of Shimobe (1ml/2km E) which has springs at a temperature of 86°F (30°C).

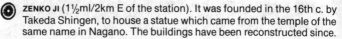

29mls (46km): Minobu, at the foot of Minobu san (3,766ft/1,148m), is famous as the place to which Nichiren retired. It has become a veritable Mecca for the disciples of this priest who built numerous temples over a total area of 2,500 acres (1,000ha).

It was in 1274 that Nichiren (1222-82; see Kamakura) chose to set up a hermitage on the slopes of Minobu san, where he built the main temple of Kuon ji in 1281. His ashes were scattered there, but it is only since the 15th c. that this site has really been developed. The buildings suffered several fires (notably in 1887) which meant that most of them had to be partly or totally rebuilt.

Nichiren shu or Hokke shu, the sect of Nichiren, rests on the doctrine of the Myohorenge kyo (*sutra* of the Lotus of the True Law), drawn from the last teaching of Buddha. This sect had a great many schools and drew millions of followers. Certain disciples with nationalist leanings went on to form the Sakka gakkai (see Fujinomiya, vicinity).

If you carry on through the village of Minobu you will reach the main buildings of Kuon ji, which are scattered at the foot of an interminable flight of steps. These buildings are: Soshi do, the founder's hall; Shinkotsu do, the hall of the true relics; and Ikaï do, the hall of posthumous inscriptions. Note also the *shoro* (the belfry), the Hojo kan, which houses the ashes of Nichiren, and the Nokotsu do, which contains those of the pious daimyo.

Approx. 1ml (1.5km) W of here is Nishiga dani, where Nichiren set up his first hermitage; pagoda and octagonal pavilion.

From Kuon ji, a cable-car goes to the summit of Minobu san, where Okuno in stands. This is the 'Holy of Holies' of the entire complex; nearby are two temples dedicated to Nichiren and Tokugawa Ieyasu. There is a view over the Fuji kawa valley, and to the N over the Kofu basin.

3 CHICHIBU TAMA, FUJI HAKONE IZU AND MINAMI ARAPUSU NATIONAL PARKS, see entries under these names.

■ Komatsu (Island of Honshu)

Railway map on inside front cover.

Tokyo, 359mls (577km) - Fukui, 35mls (57km) - Gifu, 140mls (226km) - Kanazawa, 17mls (28km) - Toyama, 58mls (93km).

Ishikawa ken - Pop: 95,684 - trade centre, synthetic fibres

Komatsu is the second most important town of the Ishikawa region and like Kaga and Kanazawa it is overlooked to the E by the massif of Hakusan. To the W a series of lagoons separates it from the Sea of Japan.

VICINITY

1 AKATA (3mls/5km W; coach). This place was once the site of a famous toll post. The exact spot where it stood is now submerged by

the Sea of Japan. Taira Kiyomori and the followers of Minamoto confronted each other here in 1183; some years later, Minamoto Yoshitsune, fleeing from the wrath of his brother Yoritomo, stopped here.

2 AWAZU ONSEN (6mls/10km S; coach). Spa town which has been known since 717; sulphur springs renowned for their dermatological properties.

3 KAGA, KANAZAWA, HAKUSAN NATIONAL PARK, see entries under these names.

Komoro (Island of Honshu)

Tokyo, 108mls (174km) - Gifu, 219mls (352km) - Kofu, 62mls (100km) - Maebashi, 48mls (77km) - Nagano, 34mls (55km) - Nagoya 170mls (273km) - Niigata, 161mls (259km) - Shizuoka, 114mls (183km) - Toyama, 168mls (270km) - Urawa, 93 mls (150km).

Nagano ken - pop: 39,093 - 2,218ft (676m) alt.

At the foot of Asama yama (8,340ft/2,542m), Komoro is a historical town situated on the upper reaches of the Chikuma gawa. From here you can visit Joshin Etsu Kogen National Park, or the Regional Parks of Yatsugatake Chusin Kogen and Myogi Arafune Saku kogen.

KOMORO CASTLE (330yds/300m SW of the station). Two fine gates still remain and also the ramparts which provide a setting for the Kaiko en public park, which stretches as far as the Chikuma gawa. Some sports grounds and a small zoo have been set up there.

The castle, built in the 15th c. by Oi Iga no kami, was overrun in 1553 by Takeda Shingen (1521-73) who entrusted it to Oyamada Bitchu. It was confiscated once again by Toyotomi Hideyoshi and passed into the keeping of Sengoku Hidehisa (1551-1614) in 1590. Several daimyo followed in succession throughout the Tokugawa period, including the Makino from 1702 to 1868.

You can still see the gates, San mon (1766) at the entrance to the Kaiko en, and the beautiful Omote mon, built in 1613, and now standing to the N of the railway lines.

☞ VICINITY

1 KAZAWA ONSEN (13mls/21km N on the toll road; inquire about an eventual road link-up. Head N out of Komoro to get onto the toll road which rises up onto the slopes of the Asama yama. Beautiful views all along the route.

5½mls (9km): Kurumazaki toge (6,457ft/1,968m alt.), at the foot of Takamine (6,906ft/2,105m).

7mls (11km): Thermal spring of Takamine.

11mls (18km): Jizo toge, (5,686ft/1,733m alt.), where the toll road comes to an end.

13mls (21km): Kazawa Onsen, another spa and winter sports resort, which is also accessible from Shin Kazawa Onsen.

2 JOSHIN ETSU KOGEN NATIONAL PARK, see entry under this name; YATSUGA-TAKE CHUSIN KOGEN REGIONAL PARK, see Chino; MYOGI SAN, see Tomioka.

■ Koriyama (Island of Honshu)

Railway map on the inside front cover.

Tokyo, 145mls (233km) - Fukushima, 30mls (49km) – Maebashi, 135mls (217km) - Mito, 84mls (135km) - Niigata, 112mls (181km) – Sendai, 82mls (132km) – Utsunomiya, 73mls (117km) – Yamagata, 88mls (141km).

Fukushima ken - pop: 286,451 - 751ft (229m) alt. - industrial town.

Koriyama, which is a railway junction, is also one of the most important towns of the Fukushima region. Its industrial activity is connected with that of Iwaki and the Joban mining basin. Although the town itself is of little interest to the tourist, it is near Lake Inawashiro and Mount Bandai, so you could seek accommodation there.

VICINITY

1 BANDAI ATAMI ONSEN (11mls/17km NW on the N49; JNR train; coach). Head W out of Koriyama to get onto the N49.

2mls (3km): You can rejoin this road near Kaisei zan, which is a pleasant public park, famous for its cherry trees. You can visit an ornithological museum.

11mls (17km): Bandai Atami Onsen, on the slopes of Otaki san (4,495ft/1,370m). The springs are recommended for the treatment of nervous ailments. Skiing in winter.

2 OGOE (19mls/31km E, to Sugaya station). Here you can visit (1ml/2km E of the station) the cave of Irimizu. It is possible to go up Otakine yama (3,914ft/1,193m), 4mls (7km) E.

3 INAWASHIRO, BANDAI ASAHI NATIONAL PARK, see entries under these names.

■ Kotohira (Island of Shikoku)*

Map of Shikoku (Inland Sea), pp. 536-7.

Tokyo, 461mls (743km) - Takamatsu, 15mls (24km) - Zentsuji, 4mls (6km).

Kagawa ken.

Kotohira's major point of interest is the shrine of Kompira san, which is one of the most frequently visited of all the great Japanese centres of pilgrimage.

*KOTOHIRA GO OR KOMPIRA SAN (880yds/800m SW of the JNR station at the foot of the entrance steps). The road leading to the shrine branches off to the W of the N319, which runs through the locality.

This shrine, built on the slopes of Zozu san (1,709ft/521m alt.) is dedicated to Okuninushi no Mikoto, descendant of Susano o no Mikoto (see Izumo), and to Sotoku tenno. Familiarly referred to as Kompira san, it is particularly venerated by travellers and sailors, who come under its protection. It is probable that people also pray to Kompira san in Hawaii, the South Seas, and even Brazil.

Most of the present buildings, which are richly ornamented with sculpture, go back to the beginning of the 19th c.; you can reach them gradually by climbing up an exhausting series of steps approx. 1 mile (1½km) long which leads to the sanctuary. Annual festival 9–11 October. The ball game *Kemari* is practised here in ancient costumes, and there are also sacred dances.

The first flight of steps leads to the Dai mon, from which you can continue to the Sho in; note the covered gallery running along the steps as you climb. The Sho in, or parlour, was built in 1659 and is decorated with Okyo Maruyama paintings (1733-95). The nearby treasure house has several paintings of Chinese origin, ancient *emakimono* and Buddhist statues which include Jizo Bosatsu, the guardians of the Buddhist Paradise, and a Kannon of the Fujiwara period.

Opposite the Sho in another flight of steps goes up to the Chado koro, or tea pavilion; another series of steps goes up from there to the Asahi sha, or hall of the rising sun, which has sculpted wooden beams (early 19th c.) famous for the realistic nature of the human and animal figures carved into them.

It is almost half an hour's walk, through a very thick wood of pines, cedars and camphor trees, to the Okuno in. There is a view from the summit as far as the Inland Sea.

☞ **VICINITY**

1 MANNO IKE (3½mls/6km SE; JNR train to Shiori station, 1ml/1.5km SE of the lake). It is thought to be one of the oldest reservoirs in Japan. It is believed to have been dug between 701 and 704 to irrigate the surrounding countryside.

2 ZENTSUJI, see entry under this name.

■ Koya (Island of Honshu)**

Map of Kansai, pp. 500–1 - street plan on p. 329.

Tokyo, 360mls (580km) - Hashimoto, 18mls (29km) - Wakayama, 41mls (66km).

Wakayama ken.

The energy which the founders of the Koya san monastery demand of visitors is still clearly evident, in spite of the installation of a rack-railway. In order to climb up gradually from the plain through the changing vegetation, to arrive at the convent-village where everything

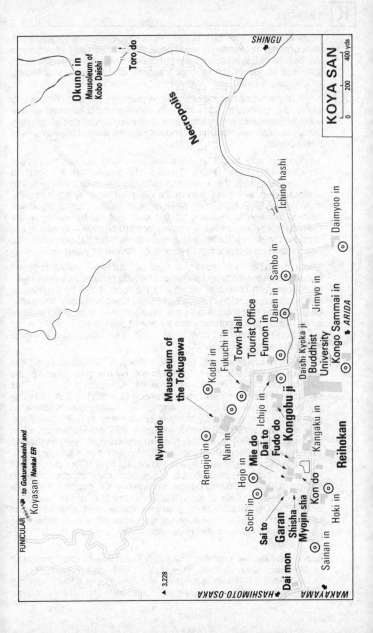

KOYA SAN

FUNICULAR to Gokurakubashi and Koyasan Nankai ER

Okuno in
Mausoleum of
Kobo Daishi

Toro do

SHINGU

Necropolis

Ichino hashi

Daimyoo in

Santo in

Daien in   Jimyo in
Fumon in
Kongo Sammai in

Tourist Office   ARIDA
Town Hall

Fukuchi in
Kodai in   Daishi Kyoka ji
Buddhist
University

Mausoleum of
the Tokugawa

Nyonindo

Rengjio in   Nan in
Ichijo in
Kongobu ji

Hojo in   Mie do   Dai to
Fudo do   Kangaku in
Reihokan

Sochi in   Kon do   Hoki in

Sai to
Garan   Shisha
Myojin sha

Dai mon

Sainan in

▲ 3,228

WAKAYAMA   HASHIMOTO·OSAKA

0   200   400 yds

suggests a search for the inner self, does require a certain preparation, although not necessarily a pilgrimage. A high degree of sensitivity to the beauty of the place and the temples, to silence and to prayer, is sufficient to justify the journey up there and to leave you feeling emotionally fulfilled.

Koya is the official name of the spot (average alt. of 3,000ft/900m) where the illustrious Koya san monasteries stand perched on the crest of venerable mountain peaks. They constitute one of the holy places of Japanese Buddhism, and are centred around the memory of Kobo Daishi.

The easiest way to get to Koya san is to take the private Nankai Railroad train from Osaka (Namba station) to the terminus at Gokurabashi; from there you can take the funicular railway to the Koyasan stop, which is linked to the village of Koya by a bus service. If you go by JNR train from Wakayama or Osaka (Tennoji) you will have to change at Hashimoto, and continue by Nankai Railroad. Coming from Kyoto or Nara, you will need to change at Osaka or Oji, to rejoin the Nankai Railroad line from Osaka (Namba) or Hashimoto. Coach services operate from Hashimoto, Osaka or Wakayama.

There are no hotels or *ryokans* at Koya san but many monasteries will accommodate visitors and pilgrims. The lodgings are Japanese style, of course, with collective *ofuro*, and the food is strictly vegetarian. Although an excursion to Koya san can be fitted into a day, it can also be enriching to participate in the experience of monastic life for a while. A stay in a monastery can be one of the high points of the trip for anyone in search of traditional Japan. Few places can compete with Koya san in this respect.

AN INFLUENTIAL MONASTERY. The priest Kukai (774–835) selected this site at Koya san, which was given to him by the government of the day, to found the first monastery there, Kongobu ji, in 816. This became the centre of the esoteric Shingon Buddhist sect. Assisted by the protection of the Emperor and of rich daimyo, he became so prosperous that eventually there were as many as 1,500 buildings, occupied by over 90,000 monks. Although they were rather cut off on their mountain, they nonetheless led an active life, in open opposition to the monks of Hiei zan, of the rival Tendai sect, and even went so far as to organize a punitive militia in the capital Kyoto. The buildings of Koya san have suffered a number of fires, and the monasteries had to submit in 1581 to Oda no bunga, who unified the country. Koya san has also been a place of exile, notably at the time of the Tokugawa accession, after which a decline began. Women were allowed access to Koya san in 1873. They soon set up a convent of nuns there. The present buildings were nearly all reconstructed during the 19th and 20th centuries.

KOBO DAISHI AND THE SHINGON. The monk Kukai was born on the island of Shikoku, near Zentsuji (see entry under this name). Having completed his religious education in China (from 804 to 806), he withdrew to Koya san where he laid the foundations of his doctrine.

Kukai, to whom we owe the phonetic script known as *hira gana*, is better known under the posthumous name of Kobo Daishi. The Shingon doctrine invites one to seek supreme illumination, through the experience of an ascetic life, leading to a greater knowledge of the self. Although this doctrine was only available to the initiated who venerated the Dai Nichi Nyorai (Buddha Vairocana), the sect enjoyed a certain prosperity by the time of the Heian period.

Koya san is now the seat of a religious university. One of the students will be pleased to act as your guide.

From the stop at Koyasan, you can take a bus to the centre of Koya village (2mls/3km E of the stop), where you can head W on foot to Kongobu ji.

*KONGOBU JI. Set up by Kukai (816), it became the main temple and the headquarters of the Shingon sect. The present building, of the Edo period, is the residence of the chief priest of Koya san.

On the inside, the rooms are carpeted with *tatami*, and alternate with little traditional gardens; note the vast hall of the kitchens.

* GARAN (220yds/200m W of Kongobu ji). It is the holy enclosure where the most venerated buildings stand, overlooked by an imposing pagoda (Dai to; 1937) dedicated to Dai Nichi Nyorai, the great Buddha of Shingon esotericism.

The Kon do (1929) to the SW of this pagoda was also founded by Kobo Daishi.

The Fudo do, to the SE of the Dai to, was probably founded in 1197 by the priest Gyosho. It houses statues of Fudo (late 12th c.), the hunter of demons and protector against fires, and of eight other divine guardians.

The Mie do, to the W of Dai to, is built on the site of Kobo Daishi's residence. It contains a statue of the latter. Further W note the western pagoda (Sai to), the oldest building of the Garan (887), which has a revered statue of Dai Nichi Nyorai.

Shisha myojin sha, to the S of Sai to, is a group of four small Shinto shrines dedicated, amongst others, to Nyumyojin, patroness of Koya san, and to her son Koya Myojin.

To the N of Garan are several monasteries, including the following which you can visit: Myoo in, which has a famous painting of the *Aka Fudo (the red Fudo), of the early Heian period (9th c.). This Fudo, endowed here with his characteristic rope and sabre, is one representation of this deity, sometimes assimilated with Dai Nichi Nyorai.

To the S of Garan, you can rejoin a road running beneath the Kon do, which leads (to the E) to the Koya san museum.

THE REIHOKAN (open daily from 09.00 to 16.00 except public holidays). In spite of its outdated method of presentation, this museum possesses invaluable treasures, including no less than 29,000 coins, which come from different monasteries of Koya san, and are presented in rotation. The works which are regularly on display include the following.

Paintings. There are numerous painted scrolls (a great many of which are of Korean origin); that of the *Death of Buddha*, or Buddha's entry to Nirvana, which belongs to Kongobu ji, is dated 1086 and depicts a dramatic contrast between the serenity of the bodhisattvas and the unrestrained grief of the other disciples; a long creation depicting *Amida's Descent from Heaven*, escorted by 30 bodhisattva musicians or bearers of offerings. This scroll, painted on silk, and attributed to the priest Genshin (942-1017), was probably a work of the early 12th c.

Sculpture. There are several representations of Buddha, notably in the guise of Amida or of Dai Nichi Nyorai, as well as other characters of the Buddhist world. These works are mostly from between the 12th and the 17th centuries. Note, however, a wooden Fudo of the early Heian period (9th c.). Note also the offerings left by visitors at the foot of certain statues. In addition to these, the museum has objects of Buddhist worship, lacquered *sutra* caskets, calligraphy, china, etc.

880yds (800m) W on the road in front of the museum is the * Dai mon (1705), which saw numerous pilgrims going up to Koya san until the railway was opened. Through the magnificent cedars, which rise up on all sides, you can make out the island of Awaji in the distance.

If you go back to the centre of Koya and then head E (1ml/1.2km) you will reach the Ichino hashi Museum, on the furthest inhabited edge of Koya.

In the village itself you can visit various monasteries, such as:

the Fumon in, with its landscape garden of the Edo period, created by Kobori Enshu;

the Kongo Sammai in, which has a pagoda erected in 1222, at the request of Masako (1157-1225), the wife of Minamoto Yoritomo;

the Mausoleum of the Tokugawa, dedicated to Ieyasu (1542-1616) and his son Hidetada (1579-1632). The decor is reminiscent of the Tosho gu of Nikko.

 From Ichino bridge - a nearby monument to the dead of World War II - a paved footpath wends its way through the *great necropolis of Koya san.

Anyone walking through here would never believe it was a cemetery, as you go through a superb wood of Japanese cedars, with thousands of monuments at their feet. These were erected from the Kamakura period onwards, and particularly during the Edo period, to the memory of the greatest Japanese families who wished to be near Kobo Daishi; amongst them you will find the famous names of Asano, Date, Mori, Shimazu, Tokugawa, etc.

NB: Beware of the ferocious mosquitos which abound in the necropolis. Use some kind of protection (especially in summer).

1ml (2km) E of the Ichino hashi, you will arrive at the Toro do (hall of lamps) where hundreds of moving votive offerings hang in honour of Kobo Daishi. Behind this is the mausoleum of Kobo Daishi, or Okuno in, the holiest of the Koya san buildings, where the spirit of the great monk is supposed to be meditating still, whilst awaiting Miroku, the Buddha of the future. The nearby Nokotsu do holds the ashes of those who wished to rest near the venerable Kukai.

From Okuno in, you can take a detour S to get to the bus stop, which will take you back to the centre of Koya or to the funicular railway stop.

VICINITY

1 RYUJIN ONSEN (35mls/56km S; coach). A beautiful forest road goes through the *Koya Ryujin Regional Park which is overlooked by the Gomada zan (4,495ft/1,370m alt.). There are some very attractive landscapes on the peaks in the centre of the Kii peninsula.

35mls (56km): Ryujin Onsen on the upper reaches of the Hidaka gawa; alkaline springs at 117°F (47°C). You can continue past Tanabe (32mls/52km; coach).

2 YOSHIMO KUMANO NATIONAL PARK, see entry under this name.

Ⓚ Kumamoto (Island of Kyushu)*

Map of Kyushu (North), pp. 388–9.

Tokyo, 784mls (1,261km) – Fukuoka, 70mls (112km) – Kagoshima, 121mls (195km) – Miyazaki, 123mls (198km).

Principal town of Kumamoto ken – pop: 440,020 – industrial town – national, regional and private universities.

Kumamoto is traversed by the Shira kawa, which flows from the crater of Mount Aso, and is the third most important town on the island of Kyushu. It has grown up on the centre of a plain which opens out to Shimabara Bay. It is an excellent starting point for trips to Mount Aso or Unzen Amakusa National Park and the town itself draws tourists to the castle and to Suizenji Park.

The history of Kumamoto starts with that of the castle, erected by Ideta Hidenobu, in the 15th c. In 1588, Toyotomi Hideyoshi ceded it to Kato Kiyomasa (1526-1611), who decided to rebuild it on a larger scale in 1599. The Kato were dispossessed in 1632, in favour of the Hosokawa who kept it until the Meiji Restoration. Eight years later (1876) a mutiny against the new regime erupted in the castle. It was rapidly suppressed and the castle was placed under a military garrison. The following year, however, Colonel Tani Tateki was to lay siege to it for two months in the campaign against the Satsuma rebellion, led by Saigo Takamori (see Kagoshima). The town was delivered only by the intervention of General Kuroda Kiyotaka, in April 1877.

 *KUMAMOTO JO (1½mls/2.5km) NE of the station; bus; tramway). Built in the centre of the town on the Chausu yama, this castle is one of the most important in Japan with regard to its size, but not its authenticity, as the present castle has been entirely rebuilt.

Before entering the castle itself note the long wall (Nagabei) which has the Tsuboi running along it. After crossing the maze of ramparts you will come to the first courtyard with its double keep, which was destroyed in the siege of 1877 and rebuilt in 1960 with a concrete framework. An historical museum (weapons, manuscripts, paintings, various antiques) relating to the Kato and Hosokawa daimyo has been set up there. There is a view from the summit over the surrounding area, and as far as the massif of Mount Aso. There is a shrine dedicated to Kato Kiyomasa in the grounds spreading westwards. Note finally a stone bridge, a trophy brought back from the 1598 Korea expedition, led by Kiyomasa.

½ml (1km) NE of the castle (550yds/500m E of the Fujisaki Kumamoto ER station; bus from Kumamoto eki), near the Shira kawa, is the shrine of Hachiman of Fujisaki, dedicated to the Emperor Ojin and his mother the Empress Jingu. The Boshita matsuri takes place on 15 September.

**SUIZENJI KOEN (2½mls/4km E of Kumamoto eki; JNR; ½ml/1km SE of Suizenji eki, JNR; tramway from the first station, passing 330yds/300m from the second one). Although not as famous as those at Kanazawa, Mito, Okayama or Takamatsu, the landscape garden of Kumamoto can compete with the finest in Japan. As everywhere else, tourists crowd around the central pond to feed the enormous, multicoloured carp with which it teems.

In 1632, Hosokawa Tadatoshi allowed Gentaku, a monk from Kyoto, to settle there, and he founded the Suizen ji. This temple was later removed and replaced by a pleasure park of 1,502 acres (608ha) built around a tea pavilion called Joju en, which is also the name of the park. There are artificial hills, pools and plantations which are a miniature evocation of the 53 stages of the Tokai do. Mount Fuji is one of the most impressive sights. To the W of the garden is the shrine of Izumi consecrated in 1879 to the Hosokawa family.

Around the Suizenji koen there are dozen of stalls all competing to sell souvenirs to tourists, and a few restaurants where you can taste the local speciality, *sakura*, thin strips of raw horse meat dipped in soya sauce.

660yds (600m) S of Suizenji koen is the pool of Ezu, fed by a cool spring flowing from the park; small zoo nearby.

Tatsuda yama (3½mls/6km NE of Kumamoto eki, JNR; ½ml/1km E of Kitakumamoto eki, Kumamoto ER; bus from the first station) is a hill with Tatsuda Park lying at its foot, around the Taisho ji (1646). This contains the tombs of Hosokawa Tadaoki (1564–1645) and his son

Tadatoshi (1586-1641), who became the lord of Kumamoto. Note also the Kosho ken tea pavilion.

Further E near to the N57 is the little Museum of Popular Arts.

VICINITY

1 KIMPO ZAN (6mls/10km W; coach). On the slopes of this hill (2,182ft/665m alt.) to the W of Kumamoto are the little statues of the Five Hundred Disciples of Buddha (Gohyaku Rakan) sculpted by a monk called Ryozen. From the summit, there is a view over Shimabara Bay and the massif of Unzen.

2 ASO and **UNZEN AMAKUSA NATIONAL PARKS,** see entries under these names.

K | Kurashiki (Island of Honshu)**

Map of Shikoku (Inland Sea), pp. 536–7.

Tokyo, 431mls (694km) - Hiroshima, 93mls (150km) - Kobe, 91mls (146km) - Okayama, 11mls (17km) - Tottori, 96mls (155km).

Okayama ken - pop; 404,000 - iron, steel and textile industries.

Kurashiki presents in miniature the most characteristic image of Japan. Here the satellite towns of Kojima, Mizushima and Tamashima, isolated on the shores of the Inland Sea, in the smog of rapidly expanding industry, meet and contrast with the traditional world and the old town. In Kurashiki you will feel as if you are, in effect, living on the outer fringe of the modern world. The old houses, the charming bridges across the Kurashiki gawa and the little alleyways, remnants of a former time, make this place one of the absolute 'musts' of the trip, even though it is rather tourist-oriented.

THE RICE TRADE. Kurashiki is an abbreviation of Funakurayashiki. This name is evocative of the lofts and warehouses where the rice and *sake* were stored before being sent down the Kurashiki gawa. This trade was very prosperous during the Edo period, and was placed under the direct control of the Shogun Tokugawa. They protected and favoured the business of the Kurashiki tradesmen, who adopted the style of the rich Osaka and Edo (Tokyo) merchants, and built opulent homes near to their warehouses.

A Kurashiki

Opposite Kurashiki station, follow the Motomachi dori to the SE, for approx. 550yds (500m), as far as Kurashiki gawa.

There is a group of old houses and warehouses, of the Tokugawa and Meiji eras, now occupied by museums, so that it could be aptly named the **museums district. It stretches along the Kurashiki gawa, which is canalized and curves round to the S, towards Maigami bashi.

■ **'OHARA MUSEUM OF WESTERN ART** (address: 1 Chuo; open daily from 09.00 to 16.00, except Mondays and from 28 December to 1 January). The museum bears the name of its founder, Ohara Magosaburo, who was largely responsible for the development of Kurashiki, as well as for the restoration of the former warehouses and rice lofts, which now house some of the collections.

The rather surprising main building is in Greek revival style (1930) and exhibits Western paintings. Behind that is a new edifice (1961) containing Eastern art and archeology collections, and contemporary Japanese paintings. In actual warehouses are pottery, lesser *objets d'art* and crafts.

The **collections of Western paintings are quite surprisingly rich for this provincial Japanese town. The best French and Western contemporary schools are represented. Apart from an *Annunciation* by El Greco (1541–1614), painted in 1600, which is the oldest picture in the museum, you will also see the names of Monet (*Water Lilies*), Gauguin (*The Scented Garden*, 1892), Segantini (*Midday in the Alps*, 1893), Utrillo (*Street in a Paris Suburb*, 1910), Renoir (*Young Woman at her Toilet*, 1914), Picasso (*The Cage*, 1925), Miró (*Women at Night*, 1946), Pollock (*Cut Out*, 1949), Cézanne, Chagall, Matisse, Pissarro, Puvis de Chavannes, Rouault, etc. Post-classical sculpture is represented by Rodin (*The Man Walking, St John, A Burger of Calais*) and Bourdelle (*Aged Bacchante, Beethoven*). The modern gallery houses works by Japanese artists influenced by contemporary Western painting, notably German realism. These painters include: Kishida Ryusei (1891–1929): *Still Life* (1920) and *Young Dancer* (1924); Yasui Shotaro (1888–1955): *Two Workmen* (1923), *Red Landscape* (1925), *Portrait of a Little Girl* (1950), *The Studio* (1951); Umehara Ryusaburo: *The Sunrise* (1945–47); Koide (1887–1931): *The N. Family* (1919), *Woman on a Chinese Divan* (1930); Sakamoto Shigeshiro (1882–1969): *Young Girl Washing Her Hair* (1917), *Bay Horse* (1930) and Fujita Tsuguji (1886–1968): *Before the Ball* (1925).

The Near Eastern archaeology section (in the new gallery) presents a vast panorama: Egyptian antiquity, Mesopotamia, Hellenic art, Rome, Persia (12th- to 16th-century pottery). These collections are completed by a section of Asiatic art notably Chinese art.

The pottery gallery has contemporary works from Japan and even from abroad, by Hamada Shoji, Kawai Kanjiro, Tomimoto Kenkichi, Bernard Leach, etc.

The printed cloth and wood carvings room exhibits the artistic works of Munakata Shiko and Keizuke Serizawa.

To the E of the Ohara Museum, at the canal bend, is the former town hall of Kurashiki (Meiji period) which now houses a little local history museum. Next to this is a new museum exhibiting pottery, statues and 19thc. Western bronzes. The present town hall was built by Tange Kenzo, on the Motomachi dori, to the SW of the museum district.

⊡ ***MUSEUM OF POPULAR ARTS** (address: 1 Chuo; open daily from 09.00 to 16.00, except Mondays and from 30 December until 1 January). To the S of the former town hall, this museum, which was set up in 1949, also occupies old warehouses restored for the purpose. There is a large collection of Japanese crafts (wood, pottery, textiles), a re-creation of a traditional interior, etc.

To the S of the Museum of Popular Arts is the Toy Museum (open daily from 08.00 to 17.00), with over 5,000 toys from all over the world, although most are from Japan. A shop attached to the museum sells new, brightly-coloured specimens.

⊡ **ARCHAEOLOGY MUSEUM** (address: 1 Chuo; open daily from 09.00 to 16.00 except Mondays; closed 29 April). The museum lies to the N of the canal, opposite the bridge which crosses the canal in front of the old town hall. It has been set up in an old rice loft.

This museum, which was opened in 1950, has assembled the finds from excavations carried out in the Kurashiki region, and in the Kibi (see Okayama, Vicinity): artefacts, weapons, utensils and pottery of the Paleolithic, Neolithic (Jomon, Yayoi, and Kofun), and Protohistoric periods. It also possesses several finds of Chinese, Korean, Persian and even Inca archaeology.

Past the archaeology museum to the W, on the same bank and opposite the Ohara Museum, is the former home of Ohara Magosaburo, who donated the museum which bears his name.

Ivy Square, which stands opposite the museums, on the other side of the river, is the heart of old Kurashiki, and the meeting place of the local youth. Shops and restaurants.

B Kojima

Kojima extends the Kurashiki area to the S as far as the headland of Washu zan. You can visit the little fishing port of Shimotsui.

*WASHU ZAN (2mls/3km SE of Shimotsui; bus; 16mls/26km S of Kurashiki; coach). The most pleasant route to this promontory, from Kurashiki, is by the toll road, Washuzan Skyline. Washu zan, 436ft (133m) above sea-level, is one of the most renowned and beautiful viewpoints of the Inland Sea.

↦ 2mls (3km) off Shimotsui (boat): The little island of Mukuchi, famous for its rock, is known as the elephant, and was shaped by marine erosion.

↦ 6mls (10km) NE of Shimotsui (coach); Yuga san jinja, on a wooded hill, dedicated to Yuga Daigongen, the deity protecting travellers at sea. At the nearby Rendai ji, you can still see the rooms of the Ikeda lords of Okayama.

↦ 7mls (12km) E of Shimotsui (coach): Ojiga dake is a rocky promontory, where the blocks of granite seem to have been placed one on top of the other like the blocks of a building set. A chair-lift goes up to the summit, where there is also a view over the Inland Sea.

C Mizushima

Mizushima is the actual industrial zone of Kurashiki, set up on the Takahashi gawa estuary. The petrochemical and iron and steel complex, built almost entirely on land reclaimed from the sea, is the fifth largest in Japan. It is on the way to becoming one of the most important of its kind in the world. Apart from its steel foundries, there are car factories, shipyards and refineries which process 58,100kl (about 400,000 barrels) of crude oil per day. Oil tankers of over 100,000t can dock here. This complex is also renowned in a more negative sense, since the pollution levels reach dizzy heights. On certain days the air is practically unbreathable. It is worth noting that the new road linking Honshu to the Island of Shikoku passes through Mizushima.

D Tamashima

To the SW of the former site of Kurashiki, Tamashima stands opposite the Mizushima industrial zone and has spread out to the E of the Takahashi gawa estuary.

 Entsu ji (2mls/3km SW of the Shin Kurashiki JNR station) is where Ryokan, the Zen priest, poet and calligrapher, was educated. There is a pretty garden around the temple, and a view over the Inland Sea from the summit.

 6mls (9km) SW of the Tamashima eki: Popular beach at Sami.

VICINITY

OKAYAMA, SETO NAIKAI NATIONAL PARK, see entries under these names: KIBI REGION, see Okayama.

▦ Kurayoshi (Island of Honshu)

Tokyo, 460mls (740km) – Hiroshima, 176mls (284km) – Kobe, 150mls (242km) – Matsue, 58mls (94km) – Okayama, 81mls (130km) – Tottori, 33mls (53km).

Tottori ken – pop: 49,629.

At the foot of Dai sen, on the E side, Kurayoshi is traversed by the Tenjin gawa, which flows into the Sea of Japan, a little further N. The chief attractions of the town are the spa resorts which lie on the outskirts, and the Daisen National Park.

☞ VICINITY

1 ASOZU ONSEN (5½mls/9km NE; coach) is a small spa town, opposite Togo, on a lagoon of the same name, and chiefly known for its eel breeding.

2 MISASA ONSEN (6mls/10km SE; coach) possesses Japan's most important radioactive source station. A Radioactivity Research Institute attached to Okayama University has been set up here. There is a bust in honour of Madame Curie.

→ 4mls (7km) E (coach): Sambutsu ji, a temple founded in the 8th c. on the slopes of Mitoku san (2,935ft/900m alt.).

→ 7mls (11km) SE (toll road; coach): the picturesque gorge of Osaka.

3 SEKIGANE ONSEN (8mls/13km SW; JNR train; coach). This is Japan's second most important radioactivity centre after Misasa. There is a view from a nearby hill over the Dai sen and several peaks of the Chugoku range.

4 DAISEN OKI NATIONAL PARK, see entry under this name.

■ Kure (Island of Honshu)

Map of Shikoku (Inland Sea), pp. 536-7.

Tokyo, 525mls (845km) - Hiroshima, 18mls (29km) - Matsue, 137mls (220km) - Okayama, 104mls (168km) - Tottori, 190mls (305km) - Yamaguchi, 106mls (170km).

Hiroshima ken - pop: 235,193 - iron and steel industries and shipyards.

Kure owes its prosperity to its well-chosen position, sheltered by the Eta Islands and Kurahashi, which made it the leading naval base of the Far East. The Japanese fleets were directed from here in the Pacific war. Nowadays Kure has turned to building giant oil tankers and has become, along with Eta jima, the headquarters of the national naval security forces.

Of interest to the tourist are the town hall, one of the great monuments of modern Japanese architecture, by Sakakura, and the Japanese Navy Museum (which is partly a memorial to Admiral Togo, the 'father of the Japanese Navy'), at Eta jima.

⌐ **VICINITY**

1 NIKO KYO (2mls/3km N; coach). This is a pleasant walk, immediately N of the town.

2 NORO SAN (16mls/26km E, on the N185 and a toll road; coach). Head E out of Kure.

(4mls/7km): Horo.

→ 3½mls (6km) N: the Nikyu gorge, hemmed in at the base of the Nikyu dam, built on the Hironishio kawa.

10mls (16km): Kawajiri, where the toll road up Noro san branches off.

16mls (26km): Noro san (2,753ft/839m alt.). The road stops below the summit, and forms a belvedere over the Inland Sea.

3 ONDO (4mls/7km S; coach). Head S out of Kure.

☐ 3½mls (6km): Ondo Ohashi. The bridge has a double hairpin bend in the road leading to it, and links the island of Kurashashi to Honshu. It was opened in 1961.

The Ondo bridge across the Ondo no Seto Strait, is 77yds (70m) wide, and tradition claims that it was opened by Taira Kiyomori (1118-81). It is even believed that the sun slowed its course so that the work could be finished.

➡ 3mls (5km) N (coach): Yasumi yama (1,644ft/501m), which affords a view over the whole of Kure and the neighbouring islands.

4mls (7km): Ondo at the entrance to Kurahashi island.

➡ 11mls (18km) S: Kurahashi, at the southern tip of this rugged island, which rises to a mere 1,640ft (500m) alt.

▣ 4 ETA JIMA (4mls/7km W; boat). The centre of Eta jima village is ½ml (1km) W of the landing stage, and opens, on the W side, onto a beautifully sheltered bay. You can visit the Japanese Naval History Museum. A monument has been erected to Admiral Togo Heihachiro (1847-1934).

5 HIROSHIMA, SETO NAIKAI NATIONAL PARK, see entries under these names.

■ Kuroiso (Island of Honshu)

Map of Natural Resources, p. 66.

Tokyo, 107mls (173km) - Fukushima, 68mls (109km) - Maebashi, 97mls (156km) - Mito, 79mls (127km) - Utsunomiya, 39mls (63km).

Tochigi ken - pop: 46,574.

Kuroiso, to the S of the Naka gawa, is the point of access to the thermal springs and winter sports of Nasu, which are some of the features of Nikko National Park.

☞ VICINITY

1 NASU YUMOTO ONSEN (10mls/16km N; coach). Standing at an altitude of 2,800ft (850m), Yumoto is the first of a group of sulphur springs which are effective against rheumatism and nervous illness. The others are at Benten, Daimaru (or Omura), Kita, Sandogoya and Takaomata; the whole group is overlooked by the volcanic massif of Nasu. The Shikano yu ('Deer') spring is the most famous at Nasu Yumoto.

This spring, which has powers comparable to the Kusatsu springs (p. 275), is said to have been discovered by a hunter who had shot a doe (hence the name), and found the spring near the wounded animal.

Near to Nasu Yumoto is the Yuzen shrine dedicated to Okuninushi, son of Susano o no Mikoto and his acolyte Sukuna bikona who helped him to conquer the province of Izumo. This shrine is famous for the 'stone of death' (*sesshoseki*). The sulphurous vapours emitted nearby cause the deaths of many animals. The barren spot where it stands bears the name given to the banks of the river of hell: Saino Kawara.

➡ 6mls (9km) NW: *Chausu yama or Nake dake, which you can reach by taking the toll road (coach) as far as Omaru, and then by cable-car from Kakkodaira and Tenguhama. There are two great craters in the summit and also sulphurous springs and steam. The principal peaks of the Nasu volcanic range are Chausu (6,289ft/1,917m), Nagetsu (5,827ft/1,776m), Kurooya (5,194ft/1,583m), Asahi (6,243ft/1,903m) and Sambonyari (6,283ft/1,915m).

→ 13mls (21km) W (coach): the spa town of Itamuro, in the upper valley of the Naka gawa; springs at 99°F (37°C); an attractive toll road between Nasu and Itamuro.

2 SHIOBARA, see Imaichi; NIKKO NATIONAL PARK, see entry under this name.

■ Kurume (Island of Kyushu)

Map of Kyushu (North), pp. 388-9.

Tokyo, 738mls (1,187km) - Fukuoka, 23mls (37km) - Kumamoto, 46mls (74km) - Oita, 86mls (138km) - Saga, 15mls (24km).

Fukuoka ken - pop: 194,178 - cotton weaving, rubber industry - private university.

This important industrial town in the N of Kyushu has grown up in the middle of the plain of Tsukumi, through which flows the Chikugo gawa. The main activity of Kurume is the rubber industry; it is one of the world's leading producers.

◉ Suiten gu (330yds/300m W of the station). Near the Chikugo gawa, this shrine was founded at the end of the 12th c., dedicated to the Emperor Antoku (1178-85). Part of it was transferred to Edo (Tokyo) in 1818, by the Arima lords who were governing the region at that time.

▥ Kurume Castle (550yds/500m N of the station), occupies the former site of the Arima's residence with its ramparts and surrounding gardens. The Ishibashi Cultural Centre (2mls/4km E; bus) boasts a public park, an exhibition gallery and a concert hall by Kikutake Kiyonori, etc.

⌐ VICINITY

HARAZURU ONSEN (19mls/30km E on the N210; coach; JNR train to Ukiha, then coach). The road and the railway head E out of Kurume and go up the Chikugo valley.

16mls (25km): Yoshii, where you can head directly to Harazuru Onsen. Several tumuli in the area (including those of Hino oka or Mezurashi) have been excavated and found to possess burial chambers covered with symbolic paintings.

19mls (30km): Harazuru Onsen, to the N of Chikugo gawa, where cormorant fishing takes place in summer.

■ **Kushiro** (Island of Hokkaido)

Map of Hokkaido Eastern Area, pp. 228–9.

Tokyo, 897mls (1,443km) – Abashiri, 103mls (165km) – Nemuro, 78mls (125km) – Obihiro, 76mls (123km) – Sapporo, 207mls (333km).

Hokkaido – Pop: 214,694 – fishing port and industrial town.

Kushiro with its marshy hinterland is situated to the S of Hokkaido, on the Pacific Ocean, and is Japan's foremost fishing port. It is fortunate in being free of ice in winter. The recent industrial expansion of the town, founded on fishing and dairy products, wood and fertilizers, makes Kushiro the busiest place in eastern Hokkaido. In addition to this, there is an estimated 2 million t of coal reserves, some of it in deposits beneath the sea.

Harutori ko (1ml/2km SE of the station; bus) is a little pool inhabited by a special kind of carp; skating in winter. A fort stands on a small hill to the NW, with a view over the whole of the town.

☞ **VICINITY**

1 AKAN (21mls/33km NW on the N240; coach). Head W out of Kushiro on the N38.

9mls (14km): Otanoshike, where the N240 branches off to the NW.

15mls (24km): Tancho zuru is a gathering place for red-crested white cranes. Several specimens of these birds are kept in enclosures not far from the road. They come to seek refuge, between May and November, on the many stretches of marshland in the area (approx. 10sqmls/27km²). and are rarely sighted anywhere else.

21mls (33km): Akan where you can visit the Transport and Mining Museum, which specializes in local railway and mining developments.

2 NEMURO, AKAN NATIONAL PARK, see entries under these names.

K **Kyoto** (Island of Honshu)***

Map of Places of Interest, p. 70 – plans: general, p. 343, the town centre, pp. 348–9; Higashiyama, pp. 356–7.

Tokyo, 304mls (489m) – Fukui, 99mls (159km) – Kobe, 47mls (76km) – Nara, 27mls (44km) – Osaka, 26mls (42km) – Otsu, 7mls (12km) – Tsu, 61mls (98km).

Principal town of Kyoto fu (pop: 1,799,468) – pop: 1,473,000 alt. 160ft (50m) – industrial town, silk weaving – national, regional and private universities – congress town.

Kyoto, the town of the plain, or the 'Capital City' was built in the Chinese 'chessboard' fashion. This impression of horizontality is given by the vast temple roofs challenged by the skyline of gently rolling

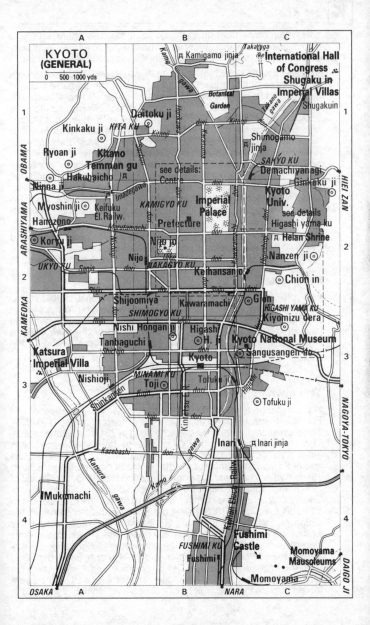

hills which come right up to the gates of the city, where, against a backdrop of green, in districts which have retained all their legendary character, rise some of the loveliest buildings of the eternal Japan.

Spared from the bombings of World War II, Kyoto still presents, both on the outer limits and in the very heart of the spreading city, a near-perfect image of the old Japan: that of temples hovering over a landscape which seems to have come straight from a painted silk scroll, dreamy gardens and pavilions, monks in hieratic attitudes, and, perhaps more than anywhere else, an affection for the ways of times past. The many kimonos blend their shades with the colours of the streets. Although Kyoto did not suffer in the war, it is still very much a developing town and it is a surprise to find on arrival at the central station little but skyscrapers, television towers, huge neon advertisements and dense traffic. This evolution has been taking place in the town since the beginning of the Meiji era, and it is scattered with startling edifices of the 'Japanese emended Victorian' style...

However, 'the charm of Kyoto works slowly and imperceptibly', and the town 'finally emerges as one of the most enchanting places in the world' (Fosco Maraini). Its hold on you is insidious, and urges you to explore it further every day. The subject of Kyoto and its vicinity is inexhaustible.

In Kyoto, the town 'where one lives well', traditional craftsmanship has remained alive. The silk is still woven according to the ancient methods which came from China and Korea, and embroidery and lacquerwork are still thriving too. This aspect of the town really is worth staying a while for, so that you can develop a feeling for the atmosphere. Kyoto is twinned with Paris and Florence.

The town in history

THE CAPITAL OF PEACE. Faced with the increasing influence of the Buddhist monasteries set up in Nara, the Emperor Kammu (736–805), under pressure from the Fujiwara, decided in 784 to move the capital. The site of Nagaoka, to the SW of present-day Kyoto, was chosen initially, but circumstances – the assassination of Fujiwara Tanetsuga and of Sawara, the Emperor's brother – made Kammu tenno settle in 794 in Kyoto. The town was originally called Heiankyo, the Capital of Peace, then took the name Miyako, Imperial City, and finally Kyoto, Capital City. The name continues to be used, but the town ceased to fulfil this function in 1868. It was designed on the same lines as the Chinese capitals, and is positioned facing N to S, according to the axis of the Kamo gawa, and forms a quadrilateral with 2½ml (4km) sides; the main avenues inside the town cross at right angles. They are numbered from one to ten (Ichijo dori, Nijo dori, Sanjo dori, etc.) from the Imperial Palace (Dai Dairi, to the N of the enclosure) to the Rasho mon gate in the S of the town. The temples and shrines were forced outside the city, which did not prevent Enryaku ji, founded in

788, from becoming a powerful religious domain and a threat to the capital.

THE FUJIWARA PERIOD. The power of the Fujiwara reached its height between the 9th and 11th centuries. Members of the family occupied the most elevated positions of *sessho* (regent) or *kampaku* (principal secretary) in the government, and became members of the Imperial Family by marriage. They limited the luxury and licentiousness of the court and occasionally removed men who had become too influential, such as Sugawa Michizane (845-903). Fujiwara Michinaga (966-1027) was the most outstanding member of the family, but a decline set in after he died. The Emperor Go Sanjo (1034-73) blamed the failings of the government on the Fujiwara and took up the reins of power once again.

HEIKE AGAINST GENJI. The Emperor Shirakawa (1053-1129) continued the administration of his predecessor Go Sanjo, but retired after 1086 in favour of his son Horikawa (1078-1107), and then his grandson Toba (1103-56). He nonetheless continued to wield power surreptitiously. This new *in sei* system, peculiar to Japan, brought about the rivalry of the Minamoto and Taira families (Genji and Heike), the Imperial ascendancy and civil wars which the Fujiwara could do nothing to avoid and which also exacerbated the animosity between the monks of the great temples around Kyoto. When Toba tenno died there was more conflict (1156-60) which led to the accession to power of Taira Kiyomori (1118-81), who was appointed Daijo daijin (Prime Minister), and to the exile of Minamoto Yoritomo (1147-99). The fighting was intensified from 1181 onwards, threatening the Taira's safety in Kyoto. They fled from both sides of the Inland Sea, and the final debacle came at Danno ura in 1185. This was followed by the accession to power of Yoritomo, who began the seige of the bakufu in Kamakura (see entry under this name).

THE MUROMACHI PERIOD (1333-1573). The Hojo, the successors of Minamoto Yoritomo in Kamakura, also imposed their control on the Imperial capital. They set up their Kyoto residence on the former site of the Imperial Palace and supervised the nomination of the Emperors. One of these, Go Daigo (1287-1338), attempted to escape their tutelage and was exiled to Oki in 1331. Go Daigo returned under the protection of several partisans, including Kusunoki Massashige (1294-1336) and his cause was upheld by Ashikaga Takauji (1305-58), who had initially come to fight him (1333). Ashikaga was dissatisfied at not being made Shogun and seized Kyoto. After the battle of Minatogawa (1336, see Kobe), he became master of Kyoto, drove out the Emperor Go Daigo (see Yoshino) and enthroned the Emperor Komyo (1321-80) in his place. In 1392 the dynasties of the N and S (the Kyoto and Yoshino courts) merged, but the power remained in the hands of the Ashikaga Shoguns who held a dazzling court. Luxury and the arts (Higashiyama period, 1443-89) co-existed, however, with internal plots and rivalry which reached a climax under the government of Ashikaga Yoshimasa (1443-96), who cared little for public affairs. His succession brought about the Onin Civil War

(1467-77) of which the Hosokawa family took advantage but which completely devastated the town of Kyoto. When Yoshimasa died, total anarchy reigned. The economic situation was catastrophic and Kyoto was pillaged a number of times. This chaos lasted almost a century, until the town was captured in 1568 by Oda Nobunaga (1534-82) and the Ashikaga shogunate was abolished in 1573.

AZUCHI, MOMOYAMA AND EDO. Having almost succeeded in unifying the country, Nobunaga was assassinated in Kyoto by one of his generals, Akechi Mitsuhide (1526-82). Toyotomi Hideyoshi (1536-98) took power. He revived the arts and the economy of Kyoto and restored the Enryaku and Hongan ji temples which Nobunaga had destroyed. In 1603 the Tokugawa transferred the seat of the shogunal government to Edo (Tokyo), but Kyoto nonetheless remained the Imperial capital and a significant commercial and religious town. During this period it suffered a terrible fire (1788) which destroyed the centre of the town. The situation changed rapidly during the 19th c. when the Emperor Komei (1831-67) died; the Shogun Keiki was led to abdicate and the restoration of Imperial power was promulgated in Kyoto. The new Emperor Mutsuhito (Meiji tenno, 1852-1912) decided in 1869 to establish the capital in Tokyo. The Imperial coronation still takes place in Kyoto. Kyoto was spared the bombings of World War II thanks to the intervention of several distinguished oriental scholars, including the Frenchman Serge Elisseeff.

FAMOUS PEOPLE BORN IN KYOTO. Numerous emperors were born in the former capital of Japan, including the Emperor Meiji (1852-1912) who transferred the capital to Tokyo. The following were also native to Kyoto: the man of letters and politician Sugawara Michizane (845-913); the famous Minamoto Yoritomo (1147-99), founder of the Kamakura bakufu; the poet Kamo no Chomei (1154-1216), author of the *Hokoji*; the priest Shinran (1174-1268), founder of the new Jodo sect; the painters Tosa Mitsunobu (1435-1525), Kano Eitoku (1543-90), Kano Tanyu (1602-74), Sumiyoshi Gukei (1631-1705), Tosa Mitsunari (1646-1710), Ogata Korin (1658-1716), Uemura Shoen (1875-1949) and Domoto Isao (born in 1927); the writer Kamo Mabuchi (1697-1769); the politician Iwakura Tomoyoshi (1835-83); and the poetess Kujo Takeho (1887-1928).

PORCELAIN AND SILK. The silk industry has been a tradition in Kyoto since the town was founded at the end of the 8th c. There was a particularly noticeable boom when Chinese and Korean processes were introduced, during the Tokugawa period and after the country was reopened to foreigners. Printed and hand-painted cloth, embroidery and other textile arts also come under this category. Porcelain, which is abundant, is also well known, especially since the 17th c., with the Kiyomizu and Awata products. Nowadays the town manufactures looms, electrical appliances, precision tools and medical instruments. Fushimi *sake*, chemical and pharmaceutical products and copper metallurgy complete the list of the town's industries.

JAPANESE GARDENS. It is in Kyoto that you will feel most at leisure to admire Japanese gardens. They are an art form in themselves and bring together, usually in a small surface area, refinement, tranquillity and the disciplining of a miniaturized landscape. They may excite surprise at the sudden change in perspective or induce contemplative meditation. As in other fields the inspiration came from China and Korea and was quickly remodelled by Japanese genius. The Heiankyo palace followed Nara in being embellished with landscaped gardens (hills, lakes, artificial woods), to conform to the Zen disciplines during the Kamakura period. Hence these gardens of profound symbolic significance expressed by the layout of the sand and rocks (dry gardens: *kare sansui*). The Daisen in at Daitoku ji and the Ryoan ji are the most famous examples. During the Azuchi, Momoyama and Edo periods these gardens sprang up everywhere as did the innumerable villas of the Emperors and daimyo. Masters such as Soami (1472-1523), Senno Rikyu (1520-91) and Kobori Enshu (1579-1647) stood out in this field. The garden around a villa is the fundamental element which co-ordinates the arrangement of the edifices (the buildings of the villa or the tea pavilions) which provide the best vantage point for admiring the landscape which has been disciplined this way. The Katsura Detached Palace (17th c.) is the most perfect example of this. In the monasteries, notably Zen, the dry garden invites meditation. Each plant, each carefully chosen stone, each mark left by the rake conjures up the free imagination of the person in contemplation of it. Japanese gardens require constant, painstaking care to control the growth of the vegetation, and keep the ordered but 'natural' look of the garden.

Visiting the town

TWO DAYS IN KYOTO. This is really very little and we would advise you to stay at least five days to take a good look round the town and the surrounding area. If you have only two days we would recommend that on the first day you use the tourist services of an agency (Fujita Travel Service, JTB in English; departures from the main hotels). The morning and afternoon routes will include: Higashi Hongan ji, Nijo jo, Kinkaku ji, the Imperial Palace, the Heian shrine, Sanjusangen do and Kiyomizu dera. In the evening you could go to a performance in the Noh, Kabuki, Miyako or Kamogawa Odori traditions (in April, May and October), or in summer go on an organized tour to take part in the Yasaka Hall (Gion Corner) spectacles, or go on a cormorant fishing trip. On the second day, if this system suits you, you could join a trip (certain mornings in the summer) to some of the classic gardens (Koke dera, Ninna ji, Ryoan ji) and end the afternoon on Mount Hiei. Otherwise you could go to the Imperial Household Agency (see Useful information, Imperial Household Agency), to visit the villas at Katsura or Shugaku in (or at least visit the garden of Daisen in, and the Ryoan ji), and continue as far as Demachiyanagi station (Keifuku FR) to go to Mount Hiei for the end of the afternoon. (Visiting Katsura or Shugaku in requires written permission from the

Imperial Household Agency which should be applied for at least one month before the proposed visit.) From Shugaku in, you can go directly to Mount Hiei, taking the private train to Shugakuin station. Do spare some time to visit the Ryoan ji. If you prefer to stay in Kyoto, you will find plenty to interest you at Higashiyama, which is close to the Ginkaku ji, the Chion in, the Tofuku ji, or the National Museum.

ONE DAY IN KYOTO. With so little time to spare, we would advise you to take part in an organized tour of the town (as above), or engage the services of an English-speaking taxi driver, through your hotel. Then you can either trust your guide to choose an itinerary or discuss one with him. Try to visit Higashi or Nishi (visits at certain times only), Hongan ji, Nijo jo, Daitoku ji, Ryoan ji, Kinkaku ji, Ginkaku ji, Heian jingu, Chion in, and Sanjusangen do, and end the afternoon at the Kiyomizu dera, watching the sunset.

THE TOWN ON FOOT. You will soon realize that to explore Kyoto on foot is an impossibility; the principal monuments are too far apart. The only reasonable walk would be around the temples and shrines of Higashiyama, to the E of the Kamo gawa, from Ginkaku ji to Tofuku ji; that would be quite enough for one day. Simply taking a detailed trip round a temple like the Daitoku ji could easily occupy more than half a day. We therefore recommend that you use the taxi services or public transport. Inquire at your hotel or at the JNTO about the bus and tram lines, and at which stops to get off. In Kyoto, there are books of public transport tickets valid for a full day which can be obtained at the Urban Transport Office, next to the exit from the central station. Finally, while you are walking around, beware of the bicycles which tend to use the sidewalks. You have to pay to enter the principal shrines and temples.

IF YOU LIKE ...

Shrines and temples. Kyoto boasts 253 Shinto shrines and 1,598 Buddhist temples– enough to exceed all your expectations. Obviously, you will have to be selective. Amongst the shrines, note: Heian jingu, Kitano Temman gu, Kamigamo and Shimogamo jinja, Inari jinga; the most remarkable of the temples are: Higashi and Nishi Hongan ji, Daitoku ji, Myoshin ji, Ninna ji, Nanzen ji, Chion in, Kiyomizu dera, Tofuku ji, To ji, and in the immediate vicinity of Kyoto, Enryaku ji (Mount Hiei) and Daigo ji.

Japanese gardens. Most of the temples and shrines have gardens round them which are meant to induce meditation. The most famous are at: Daitoku ji, Ninna ji, Saiho ji (Koke dera), Ryoan ji, Kinkaku ji, Ginkaku ji, Nanzen ji, Tofuku ji and Heian jingu. The remarkable gardens of the Katsura and Shugaku in Imperial villas should be added to this list.

Old Japanese palaces. Visit the Imperial Palace, Nijo jo and Fushimi jo, the architecture of which dates from the Momoyama, Edo and pseudo-Heian periods.

Japanese sculpture. Kyoto is distinguished in this field and most of its great temples are interesting from this point of view. We would draw particular attention to the thousand statues of Sanjusangen do, the 'unique' statue (Miroku Bosatsu) at Koryu ji, the works in the To ji, and we would certainly recommend a visit to the Kyoto National Museum.

Japanese painting. Go to the National Museum, but also visit some of the temples: Nishi Hongan ji, Daitoku ji and Myoshin ji.

A Shimogyo ku

Kyoto and Tambaguchi JNR stations.

This central district of Kyoto is what you will see when you come out of the station. You will doubtless be struck by the ungainly Kyoto tower (panoramic view from the top: 430ft/131m), and the characterless commercial buildings and wide avenues. You will, however, find a visit to Higashi Hongan ji and Nishi Hongan ji interesting. This district is bounded to the N by the Shijo dori, a shopping street with banks and large stores along it.

"NISHI HONGAN JI (general plan: B3; 1,000yds/900m NW of Kyoto eki and 660yds/600m E of Tanbaguchi eki, JNR; No 9 bus from Kyoto station; open from 10.00 to 16.30; tours of the inside at 10.00, 11.00, 13.30 and 14.30, except Saturday afternoons). This temple stands immediately to the N of Kosho ji, along Horikawa dori, and is one of the most revered in Japan, the seat of the new Jodo sect. The buildings are amongst the most complete and perfect examples of Buddhist architecture in Japan. Ho onko festival 9-16 January.

Founded in 1224 at Higashiyama by the priest Shinran (1174-1268), the seat of the Jodo shinshu sect was transferred here in 1591. Hideyoshi made the priest Kocho the superior here, as he was displeased with his brother Koju. The latter had the opportunity in 1602 to found a separate branch of the temple, hence the distinction between the western and eastern temples: Nishi and Higashi Hongan ji. Nishi Hongan ji is also known by the name Monzeki. Derived from the Jodo sect and taught by Honen in the 12th c., the new Jodo sect (Jodo shin shu) holds that salvation can only be obtained through the grace of Amida, who should be invoked with deep sincerity, free of all superstition and all false practices. 'Simplicity in life-style and purity in heart earned the Shin shu a popularity which, even today, can not be denied.' (D. and V. Elisseef, *La civilisation japonaise.*)

The Hon do (main hall, 1760) and the Daishi do (founder's hall, 1637) to the S of it, both open to the main courtyard, opposite the Sei mon entrance (1645).

In the Hon do are statues of Amida, Prince Shotoku (see Ikaruga) and the priest Honen. The sliding doors, with phoenix and peacock decorations, were created by artists of the Kano school. Daishi do houses a sitting statue of the founder priest Shinran (1174-1268), and a self-portrait which he created at the age of seventy-one. The statue is believed to be lacquered with a mixture containing the ashes of the priest himself.

To the S of these buildings is the part of the temple which you can visit with a monk as your guide, at the times indicated above. You will see the **abbey rooms, which is a collection of old apartments from Fushimi Casle which were decorated by the great masters of the period, the Kano painters (Eitoku, Hidenobu, Koi, Ryokei, Ryotaku and Tanyu) and the Maruyama painters (Okyo and Ozui).

THE KANO SCHOOL. 'Kano Masanobu (1434–1530), founder of the school, was born into a small warrior family in the eastern region, in a village called Kano in Izu province. He came to Kyoto and worked in the service of the shogun. With Shubun or Sotan, he perfected his craft which he seems, in all probability, to have learnt from his father Kagenobu. His talent was appreciated and ensured his acceptance as Sotan's successor in the shogunal academy. He soon became the first secular painter to use the wash technique, which had previously been the monopoly of the monk-painters from the Zen tradition. His works were already showing the basic characteristics of the Kano school: lightness of expression, clarity of line and balanced composition, whilst they dealt with traditional Chinese-inspired subjects. Free from symbolism or Zen mysticism, this secular painting appealed more directly to the tastes of the military class' (Akiyama Terukazu, *Japanese Painting*). The painters Eitoku, Sanraku, Sansetsu, Kaihoku. Yusho, Koi and Tanyu were also great masters of this school.

Daisho in, Kono ma (chamber of the storks), where the priest gives audience, is the most important of the rooms. It was once Hideyoshi's council chamber and was decorated by Kano Ryokei, Tanyu and Maruyama Okyo. The carved wooden parts are the work of Hidari Jingoro. Shirosho in or Shimei no ma was also an important hall in Fushimi jo and was ornamented by Kaiho Yusetsu, Kano Koi and Kano Ryotaku. Kurosho in has several sliding doors created by Kano Eitoku. There are two Noh theatre scenes on either side of Daisho in. The northern one, which comes from Fushimi Castle, is one of the oldest in Japan. To the E of Daisho in is a little dry garden of rocks and sand: Kokei niwa. The whole of the western part of the temple is occupied by an even bigger landscaped garden: Hyakka en. In the SE corner of Nishi Hongan ji is the *Hiun kaku (1587) pavilion, which was once part of the Hideyoshi apartments, and which has been partially decorated by Kano Eitoku, Kano Sanraku and Kano Tanyo. On the upper storey is a painting of Mount Fuji by Kano Motonobu (1476-1554).

HONKOKU JI. This temple of the Nichiren sect, to the N of Nishi Hongan ji, was transferred here from Kamakura in 1345. The *sutra* library rebuilt in 1607, has a manuscript copy of the *Rissho Ankokuron*, written by Nichiren. The shrine of Seishoko, in the centre of this temple's enclosure, is dedicated to Kato Kiyomasa (1562-1611).

*HIGASHI HONGAN JI (general plan: B3; 550yds/500m E of Nishi Hongan ji; 550yds/500m N of Kyoto eki; open from 9.00 to 16.30). This temple to the E of Nishi Hongan ji, which opens onto Karasuma dori, is the seat of the dissident Jodo Shin shu sect. It is one of the largest in Kyoto, and indeed in the whole of Japan. It has been reconstructed several times following a number of fires. The Daisho do (founder's hall) has the largest wooden roof in the world. It houses a statue of Shinran, attributed to the priest himself. In the Hon do, to the S of the enclosure, note a thick, *plaited rope of female hair. It was presented by the faithful of the temple and was used to pull up the wooden beams, when this room was reconstructed in 1895.

The temple has six volumes of the *Kyogyo shinsho*, in which the foundations of the Shinran doctrine were transcribed by the priest himself.

SHOSEI EN (330yds/300m E of the Higashi Hongan ji; 660yds/600m NE of the station). This temple is situated between Kamizuzuyamachi and Shimozuzuyamachi streets which lead E from Higashi Hongan ji. It is better known by the name Kikoku tei, and was once the house of the Higashi Hongan ji priests.

These lands on the site of a former Minamoto Toru residence (822–95) were given by the Shogun Iemitsu to the priest Sennyo in 1631. The *garden was originally designed by Ishikawa Jozan (1583-1672) and Kobori Enshu (1579-1647).

B Nakagyo ku

Nijo JNR station.

This central district to the N of Shimogyo ku is the liveliest in the town, and stands where the heart of the old Heiankyo district used to be. The main hotels, the Kyoto government buildings and the shopping and amusement centres are here. The wide tree-lined Oike dori runs E to W through this district. Kawaramachi, Shin Kyogoku and Pontocho, to the SE of Nakagyo ku, are the shopping and entertainment quarters. Nijo Castle is one of the town's best-known monuments.

··NIJO JO (plan of Kyoto centre: A4; 880yds/800m NE of Nijo eki and 2mls/3km N of Kyoto eki, JNR; No 9 bus from the latter station; open from 08.45 to 16.00). It is on a level with Nijo dori (the second street). This palace, bounded to the E by Horikawa dori, was once the official Kyoto residence of the Tokugawa.

The castle, built from 1603 onwards at the order of Tokugawa Ieyasu, was extended between 1624 and 1626. The finest artists of the period, under the direction of Kobori Enshu (1579-1647), decorated the apartments of the Nino maru and uncovered some fine items from Fushimi Castle. Nijo jo was, however, abandoned. Following the abdication of the last Keiki shogun, which was proclaimed here in 1867, the castle became the seat of the Imperial government in 1868. It then became the seat of Kyoto Prefecture from 1871 to 1884 , and was a separate residence of the Imperial Palace. The Imperial

Household handed it over to the town in 1893.

The castle is bounded by moats and an enclosure, which contains the various buildings, courtyards and gardens. If you go through the eastern gate (Higashi Otemon), and then the Chinese gate (Kara mon), you can get to the courtyard of the *Nino maru. The entrance to the apartments is through a porch with a richly sculpted pediment The state rooms are set a little apart from each other, bordered to the SW by the gardens and linked to each other by corridors with floorboards of *hinoki* word (Japanese cypress) known as 'nightingale floors'. They were laid, by a technique now lost, so that they 'sing' c creak slightly to indicate the presence of intruders. The rooms, with coffered ceilings, have alcoves, sliding doors and other surface painted by Kano Tanyu (1602–74) and his school. Wax models i historical costume have been placed in two of the rooms ('The visit t the shogun').

A second moat surrounds the square enclosure of the Hon maru which was burnt down in the 18th c., and where the Katsura no miya Palace was brought in 1893. It was part of the Imperial domain.

☞ Shinsen en (plan of Kyoto centre: A5). This lake to the S of Nijo jo i all that remains of the old Imperial Palace of Heiankyo, which wa erected at the end of the 8th c., burnt down several times, and finall abandoned in 1177.

Nijo jinya, the former hostelry of a trader who was Oda Nobunaga' companion-at-arms, stands to the S of Shinsen en and opens ont Omiya dori. (Visit by appointment. Enquire at the JNTO.) The house built in the 17th c., has a series of entrenchments and secre passages. It escaped a serious fire in 1788, as a result of its specia safety measures.

Head S along the Horikawa dori, which runs along the E side of th moats of Nijo jo. The third road after Oike dori is Rokkaku dori which leads E to Rokkaku do just after it crosses Karasuma dori. It is als possible to follow Oike dori to the E, then take Karasuma dori to th S, where the third road to the E is Rokkaku dori.

⊚ CHOBOJI or ROKKAKU DO (plan of Kyoto centre: C5; 1½mls/2½km N o Kyoto eki, JNR; 440yds/400m N of Shijo Karasuma eki, Hankyu EF buses Nos 2, 25 and 26 from these two stations to Karasuma Sanjo) This hexagonal temple was founded in 587 by Prince Shotoku; it wa venerated in the early 13th c. by the priest Shinran (see Nishi Hongan ji), who made a daily pilgrimage there for 100 days, on foot fror Mount Hiei. The present building dates from 1876 and houses severa statues, including one of Shotoku Taishi aged two, and another c Shinran with his pilgrim's staff, both sculpted posthumously.

Behind the Chobo ji the Ikenobo house is famous for its school c flower arranging (*ikebana*) which was set up in the 15th c. by Ikenob Senkei, priest of the temple.

Honno ji, which was once the Kyoto residence of Oda Nobunag (1534–82), lies to the S of Rokkaku do. It was here that the brav warrior was attacked by Akechi Mitsuhide (1526-82), who actually waited five years to exact personal vengeance. Having been mortally wounded by arrows, Nobunaga had just time to fire the temple and slit the throats of his wife and children, before committing seppuku.

To the N of Rokkaku do, Karasuma dori is intersected by Sanjo dori which leads (to the E, past a post office) to the Heian History Museum.

HEIAN MUSEUM (plan of Kyoto centre: C5; address: Sanjo Takakura dori, Nakagyo ku; 220yds/200m NE of Rokkaku do; ¾ml/1.2km SE of Nijo jo; 1½mls/2.5km N of Kyoto eki; buses Nos 2, 25 and 26 to Karasuma Sanjo; open daily from 09.00 to 16.00 except Mondays). This Kyoto museum is little known, but interesting, recalling the historical past of the old capital Heiankyo.

The brick building of the Meiji period is situated on the former site of some of the town's historical dwellings. The museum has a collection of artifacts, discovered in Kyoto and the vicinity, dating from both historic and prehistoric periods. Also on display are various documents, maps and explanatory photographs, along with a reconstruction of court life at Seiryo den (or palace of the Imperial court) during the Heian period. A room is dedicated to Lady Murasaki Shikibu, authoress (10th c.) of the famous tale of Genji (*Genji Monogatari*).

If you go E along Sanjo dori, then turn l. into Teramachi dori and then r. into Anekoji dori, you will get to Honno ji, just before Kawaramachi dori:

HONNO JI (plan of Kyoto centre: D5, 660yds/600m E of the Heian Museum: 1ml/1.6km SE of Nijo jo; 1½mls/2.5km NE of Kyoto eki; No 5 bus from the latter station to Kawaramachi Sanjo). Following a number of fires, this temple now stands on the site of the temple referred to above, which was near Rokkaku do. A statue dedicated to Oda Nobunaga has been erected in the courtyard.

Pontocho, to the SE of Honno ji, between Sanjo dori and Shijo dori, on the banks of the river Kamo (plan of Kyoto centre: D5-D6), is the centre of Kyoto nightlife, so that is where to go at nightfall. There are bars, restaurants, nightclubs, and geisha houses all along the quay sides, which have retained something of their old-world charm. You will see more kimonos here than anywhere else and the quick glimpse of geisha girls disappearing behind the sliding panels will delight the foreigner who is looking for authenticity.

C Kamigyo ku

Kamigyo ku, situated to the N of the districts above, was also the northern part of the old capital Heiankyo. This was where the old Imperial Palace Dai Dairi once stood. The present palace occupies what was probably the NE corner of the town. This district, along with Nishijin, is the centre of the Kyoto silk textile industry. It is worth visiting the Imperial Palace and Kitano Temman gu.

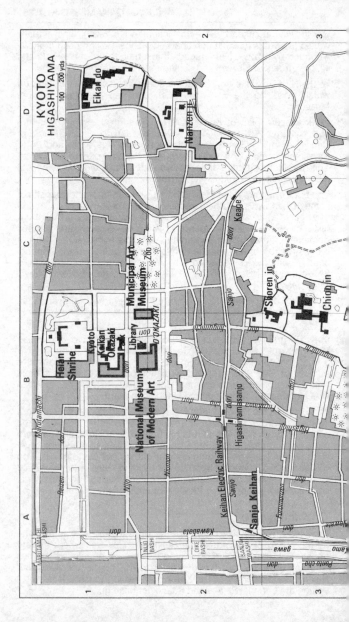

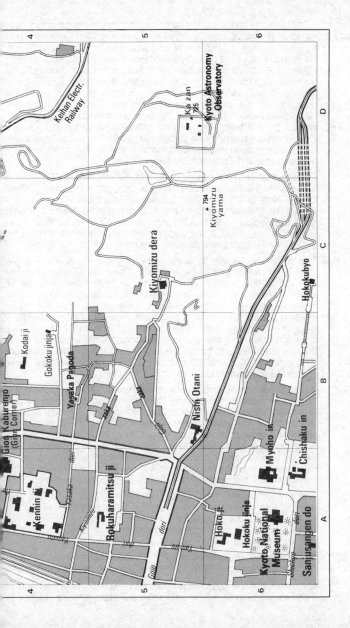

*IMPERIAL PALACE OF GOSHO (plan of Kyoto centre: C2; 2½mls/4km N of Kyoto eki, JNR; 1½ml/2km N of Karasuma or Kawaramachi eki, Hankyu ER; bus No 2 or 36 from Kyoto station, Nos 30, 32 or 47 from either of the other two to Karasuma Nakatachiuri or Kawaramachi Marutamachi; tours daily except Saturday afternoons, Sundays and public holidays; closed 25 December – 5 January. You can obtain a pass to visit on presentation of your passport, at the Imperial Household Agency to the W of Seisho mon, the entrance gate to the palace; guided tour). The present palace is surrounded by a vast English-style garden, Kyoto Gyoen (208 acres/84ha), bounded to the N and S by Imadegawa and Marutamachi streets, and to the W and E by Karasuma and Teramachi streets.

The Imperial Palace of Heiankyo built in 794 was further W in relation to the present palace, and occupied a rectangular plot approx. 950yds by 1,200yds (870m by 1,100m), between Ichijo and Nijo dori. This palace has been destroyed and rebuilt several times. It was only after the fire of Kyoto in 1788 that the present site of the Gosho Palace was chosen. It was rebuilt in the original Heian style, burned down again in 1854, and rebuilt in the form with which we are familiar today.

The visitor will be able to see the main rooms which make up the palace, but not actually to enter them. They are: Shodaibu no ma (the dignitaries' room), behind which is Seiryo den, the hall of ceremonies, decorated by painters of the Tosa school; Shishi den, the principal hall, where the coronation ceremonies take place, and which is preceded by covered galleries surrounding a vast courtyard; Kogo sho and Ogakumon jo, which open onto an inner garden Oike niwa; and Otsune Gote, the Imperial apartments, which are richly ornamented. To the N, inside the Gosho enclosure, is the Empress's Palace, which is similar to the Emperor's but on a more modest scale. (Tours are not permitted.)

To the SE of the Imperial Palace, in the Kyoto Gyoen enclosure, are the former palaces of Sento and Omiya which share a common wall and a very pleasant Japanese garden. Nowadays they are used only by guests of the government visiting Kyoto, so the public is not admitted. Sento gosho was, from the 17th c. onwards, the residence of emperors who had retired according to the *in sei* system (see section on The town in history). Omiya gosho was the residence of the dowager empresses, and rebuilt in 1867 for the Empress Eisho, the widow of Komei tenno, the last sovereign to reign in Kyoto.

To the W of the Imperial Palace, outside the enclosure, is Goo jinja (plan of Kyoto centre: B2), dedicated to Wake Kiyomaro (733-799), who dissuaded the Empress Shotoku from marrying the scheming monk Dokyo (see Usa), and was one of the great 'town planners' of the new capital Heiankyo.

To the N of the Imperial Palace is the important Doshisha Christian University, founded in 1873. To the N of this, you can visit **SHOKOKU JI**.

SHOKOKU JI (plan of Kyoto centre: C1; 1000yds/900m N of the Imperial Palace; 3mls/5km N of Kyoto eki; from this station take a No 4 or 14 bus to Karasuma Kamitachiuri, or No 65 bus to Doshishamae). This temple of the Rinzai sect was erected in 1392 by Ashikaga Yoshimitsu (1358-1408), at the request of the Emperor Go Kameyama (1347-1424). Having been devastated in the 15th c., the temple was rebuilt in the early 17th c. by Toyotomi Hideyori, then Tokugawa Ieyasu. The Ko do (reading room, 1605) is the only important manifestation of this period and houses a statue of Sakyamuni. The shogun, Ashikaga Yoshimasu (1435-90), the intellectual Fujiwara Seika (1561-1619) and others are buried in the gardens here.

Imadagawa dori passes between the Imperial Palace and Doshisha University and heads W to the Nishijin weavers' quarter.

The silk craftsmen traditionally supplied the Imperial Palace and the Court, which assured most of their income. The Onin Civil War (1467-77) caused them to flee in great numbers. They settled in Sakai or Yamaguchi and learned new Chinese techniques. When peace returned they went back to Kyoto and settled in the devastated Nishijin area (part of the western military camp), which enjoyed considerable prosperity during the Edo period. In spite of a slight decline when the capital was transferred to Tokyo, the silk industry has experienced a boom once again since new Jacquard techniques were imported from France and modern automation was introduced.

NISHIJIN MUSEUM (plan of Kyoto centre: A1; Imadagawa Omiya dori, Kamigyo ku; 1ml/1.5km NW of the Imperial Palace; 3mls/5km from Kyoto eki; No 59 bus from Karasuma dori, past the Imperial Palace; to Imadagawa Omiya; open daily from 09.00 to 17.00). This 'museum', which occupies a 1925 building (second block of houses after the junction where Imadagawa dori meets Horikawa dori), is in fact an exhibition and sales centre of silk products made in the Nishijin area; kimono display.

Imadagawa dori extends W and goes to the shrine of Kitano.

*KITANO TEMMAN GU (general plan of Kyoto: A1; 1ml/1.5km W of the Nishijin Museum; 1½mls/2.5km W of the Imperial Palace; 3½mls/5.5km NW of Kyoto eki, NR; 550yds/500m NE of Kitano Hakubaicho eki. Keifuku ER; No 50 bus from Kyoto station to Kitano; open from 06.00 to 17.00). This important shrine was founded in 974 in honour of Sugawara Michizane (845-903, see Dazaifu, p. 186), patron of men of letters and students who throng here just before their exams. The main buildings were reconstructed in 1607 and the plans inspired those of Tosho gu at Nikko.

Festival of the flowering of the plum trees (Michizane's favourite tree) 25 February. Ochatsubo Hokensai festival 26 November, in remembrance of the tea ceremony held in this shrine by Toyotomi Hideyoshi in 1587.

The treasure house of the shrine (open only on the 25th of each month, from 10.00 to 16.00) has several paintings of the Kamakura, Muromachi and Edo periods, including the painted scrolls of *Kitano Tenji Engi (early 13th c.) which trace the life of Michizane. These paintings, of purely Shinto influence, are completely free of any Buddhist constraint. 'The style of these scrolls is unique. Each scene unfolds with a dramatic sense of the facts being recounted, and all the characters are wittily brought to life. The faces and gestures are realistic, although at times exaggerated to the point of comedy. The colours are very bright but never lose their harmonious charm' (Akiyama Terukazu, *Japanese Painting*.)

➤➤ 440yds (400m) NE of the Kitano shrine, facing onto Shichihonmachi dori, is Daihoon ji or Senbon Shaka do, which possesses one of the oldest buildings in Kyoto, erected in the 13th c., and houses statues of the Terukazu period.

➤➤ 1ml (1.5km) SE of Kitano Temman gu, to the N of Marutamachi dori, between Sembon dori to the E and Rokkenmachi dori to the W, is the site of Daigoku den, where a stone marks the spot on which the hall of the Dai Dairi Palace of Heiankyo stood. There were plans in the 9th c. to build a new edifice in the Heian style there, but in the end the shrine of Okazaki park (see below, Heian jingu) was created here.

Higashiyama ku

Tofukuji and Yamashina JNR stations.

This district, along with Sakyo ku, which extends it towards the N, is one of the most important in Kyoto, and is particularly worth taking some time to visit. The large number of temples which stand on the slopes of the hills to the E of Kyoto remain a source of admiration, and used to serve as an artistic model for other towns, which followed the fashion of the capital, by possessing their own Higashi yama.

➤ *TOFUKU JI (general plan: C3; 1ml/1.5km SE of Kyoto eki and 450yds/400m SE of Tofukuji eki, JNR and Keikan ER; No 207 bus from Karasuma Shijo to Tofukuji; open from 09.00 to 16.00). The name of this temple (Rinzai sect) is a contraction of Todai ji and Kofuku ji, the names of two temples in Nara.

◉ Tofuku ji was founded in 1236 by the monk Ben en. Its successive embellishments by Ashikaga Yoshimochi (1386-1428), Toyotomi Hideyoshi (1536-98) and Tokugawa Ieyasu (1542-1616), have made it one of the loveliest in Kyoto. Unfortunately, the main buildings were burnt down in 1881. They were rebuilt between 1911 and 1927.

The main buildings of the temple, positioned broadly on a N-S axis, open southwards with the *San mon (14th c.), the oldest existing gate of its kind in Japan.

On the upper storey is a row of Buddhist statues by the priest Jocho (11th c.), with a sitting statue of Buddha, by the monk Koei (16th c.), in the centre. The ceiling was painted by Cho Densu, a monk at the temple, and his pupil Kan Densu.

To the N of San mon stands the Hon do, rebuilt in 1932 and decorated with a painted ceiling by Domoto Insho.

The temple treasure house has a precious work by Cho Densu (1352–1431):*Buddha Sakyamuni's Entry into Nirvana*. This large painting (39ft by 59ft/12m by 18m) is exhibited in the Hon do, at the time of the festivals on 15 March.

Past the Hon do are the priests' apartments, Hojo reconstructed in 1890, which open onto a rock garden, redesigned in 1938 by Shigemori Mire. The artist managed to create a modern composition influenced by the spirit of Zen.

A covered bridge, on high supporting piers, spans a dramatic ravine, and leads to the hall of the founder, which houses a statue of the priest Ben en. There is also another beautiful garden here.

From Tofuku ji, you can rejoin Higashioji to the N. It is a wide arterial road, which crosses the railway line and then, to the N, meets Shichijo dori, near the National Museum. Sanjusangen do opens onto Shichijo dori, 220yds/200m along it, on the l.

RENGE O IN or SANJUSANGEN DO (plan of Higashi yama: A6; 1ml/1.5km N of Tofuku ji; ¾ml/1.2km E of Kyoto eki, JNR; 450yds/400m E of Shicijo eki, Keihan ER; bus No 208 from Tofukuji or Shijo Karasuma to Higashiyama Sichijo; open from 08.00 to 17.00) is one of Kyoto's famous monuments.

Founded in 1164, at the request of the Emperor Go Shirakawa (1127–92), this temple was burnt down in 1249, and rebuilt in 1266. It has a vast hall, 390ft (119m) long, divided into 33 (*san ju san*) bays. This figure evokes the number of incarnations undergone by the goddess of compassion Kannon Bosatsu (Avalokitesvara). In the centre is a *statue of Kannon with eleven heads (10ft/3m high), made of cypress wood, covered in gold-leaf and carved by the artist Tankei (1254). The *thousand and one statues of Kannon, sculpted by Unkei, Tankei Kozyo and their pupils stand in graded rows on either side. Although each is endowed with the same attributes, all are different. Behind these are most of the **twenty-eight statues (Nijuhachi Bushu) of the retinue of the goddess Kannon. They are realistic works of Japanese sculpture, of the Kamakura period or later. They include: Mawaranyo, old woman at prayer; the gods Gobujo and Kongo Yasha, Karura o Basu Sennin, Fujin, the god of wind, Rajin, the god of thunder, etc.

Archery festival (Toshiya) on 15 January.

NATIONAL MUSEUM (plan of Higashi yama: A6; address: Yamato Oji Shichijo Kita, Higashiyama ku; opposite Sanjusangen do; No 206 or 208 bus from the station; open daily from 09.00 to 16.30 except Mondays). The Kyoto Museum, one of the richest in Japan, has a number of significant works which cannot all be exhibited at once. The collections are therefore displayed in rotation, as is habitual in Japan, and they are complemented by special exhibitions.

Founded in 1875 like the Imperial Museum, it was inaugurated in 1897 in the 'neo-Renaissance' brick building, originally exhibiting the Imperial collections from Kyoto shrines and temples. This museum was handed over to the town in 1924, and became national property in 1952. A new building by the architect Keiichi Morita was opened in 1966.

The museum's two buildings contain departments of archaeology, sculpture, painting, calligraphy and lesser arts, along with a research and photographic laboratory. A great many works which belong to the shrines and temples of Kyoto are stored and displayed in this museum.

Archaeology. The collections are the result of excavations and discoveries from a cross-section of prehistoric and protohistoric ages: Jomon, Yayoi, Kofun. Note the tools made of bone and horn, the Jomon and Yayoi period pottery, the Yayoi and Kofun bronze objects, such as the 'bells' (*dotaku*), the mirrors and swords, and the clay *haniwa* figurines found in tumuli. There are also some objects from the earliest Buddhist times, such as a reliquary vase of the Nara period from the Wakayama region.

◯ *Sculptures. The museum offers a wide collection of works of the
✗ Nara, Heian and Kamakura periods. These were the high points in Japanese sculpture. They produced outstanding masterpieces, which the Western world often does not even know exist. During the Heian period Japanese sculpture achieved a purely national mode of expression. The themes generally selected belong to Buddhist iconography, but were also descended from works influenced by the syncretism between Buddhism and Shintoism (*ryobu-shinto*). The materials used vary: bronze, terracotta and especially wood, but very rarely stone.

Amongst the works regularly on display, it is worth noting: a statue of Nyorin Kannon (8th c.), in gilded bronze, which comes from Oka dera (Asuka); statues of the Heian period: Kannon of the thousand hands, Kichijo ten (from Koryu ji) of the early Heian period (9th c.), and a statue of Shinto divinity of the same period, from a shrine in Kyoto; statues of Jizo Bosatsu and Amida, in the Jocho style (11th c.); statues of Jikoku ten, from Rokuharamitsu ji, and from Tamon ten, celestial guardians of the late Heian period; and a *wooden statue of the monk Hoshi (12th c.), with a broken face revealing that of Juichimen Kannon inside, whose reincarnation this priest was supposed to be: 'a very curious work, unique and remarkably executed' (Louis Frédéric, *Japon*). There is another wooden statue of Jizo Bosatsu, of the 13th c., attributed to Chosei.

◯ **Paintings. The Kyoto National Museum's art collection provides a
✗ complete panorama, from the Heian period to the Edo period, bearing witness to Japanese genius in this mode of artistic expression.

Whether influenced by China or purely Japanese, painting since the Heian period has been inspired by Buddhism or by mythological and romanticized subjects which were popular at court, and in the temples, and shrines. Realist painting dominated the art of portraiture. Narrative and traditionalist painting was confined to the national art of the *yamato e*. Abstract painting acquired a high degree of confidence in the use of Chinese inks (*sumi e*). Finally, it became purely decorative with the advent of the Kano school, and found a new outlet in the creation of engravings (a trend inadequately represented in the Kyoto Museum).

We would draw attention to the following: *Naki Fudo Engi*, a 13th c. scroll, relating the miracles of Fudo, the hunter of evil spirits; *Painting of Nirvana* (*kakemono* on silk, 14th c.), from the Zenrin ji; *kakemono*, attributed to Mincho (1352-1431), representing the Five Hundred Rakans (disciples of Buddha); painting by Sesshu Toyo (1420-1506), depicting *Amano Hashidate, where the painter manages 'neatly to capture the intensity of a famous place and without losing its concrete solidity, succeeds in reviving the traditional lyricism of Japanese landscape painters' (Akiyama Terukazu, *Japanese Painting*); works of Soami (1472-1523): *Ducks and Country Scene*; *Pictures of Flowers and Birds* (*sumi e*) by Unkoku Toeki (1591-1644); double *screen of *The Gods of the Wind and Thunder*, by the painter Sotatsu (17th c.), who 'succeeded in harmonizing decorative effect and the energy of movement' (Akiyama Terukazu).

Specialists will admire several pieces of *calligraphy. Some are Japanese, of the Nara, Heian, Kamakura and Muromachi periods, and others are Chinese of the Song (or Sung), Yuan and Ming periods.

The minor arts are well represented: *pottery and ceramics from the Nara to the Edo periods, arranged next to a collection of Chinese porcelain of co-eval periods, from the Han through to the Ming dynasties in China; and lacquered objects, wrought metal work, cloth and clothing, toys and Japanese dolls.

To the N of the museum, looking out onto Yamato oji dori, is Hokoku jinja or Tokyokuni shrine, dedicated to Toyotomi Hideyoshi (1536-98). This shrine was founded in 1598 and rebuilt in the 19th c. The fine gate, Kara mon, comes from what was Fushimi Castle.

Immediately to the N of this shrine you can visit Hoko ji. This temple was built by Hideyoshi, who had a great Buddha (62ft/19m high) erected there. The bronze statue was put up in 1801, but disappeared in a fire in 1973. Note a monumental bronze bell, a gift from Toyotomi Hideyori, son of Hideyoshi, on which Tokugawa Ieyasu claimed to see the transcription of his name engraved.

CHISHAKU IN (plan of Higashi yama; A6; 220yds/200m E of the National Museum; 1ml/1.5km E of Kyoto eki; No 16 bus from Shijo Karasuma; open from 09.00 to 16.00). This temple of the Shingon sect stands on Higashioji dori, to the E of the National Museum and Sanjusangen do, and was built between 1598 and 1601 at the request of Tokugawa Ieyasu. Its reconstruction is now finally completed, following a serious fire in 1947 which unfortunately destroyed many of the temple's treasures. Amongst these were several sliding doors (*fusuma*), painted in the 16th c. by Kano Eitoku and Kano Sanraku.

A small, modern building now holds several *paintings (*Maple Tree in Autumn Grass, Maples and Cherry Trees, Pines and Plum Trees, Pines and Autumnal Plants*) which escaped the disaster, and which are mounted on screens. They are tentatively attributed to the painters Hasegawa Tohaku and Hasegawa Kyuzo, who lived at the end of the 16th c., and are excellent examples of the Momoyama period. The *temple garden is a remarkable creation by Senno Rikyu, and was probably inspired by Mount Rozan in China.

 MYOHO IN (plan of Higashi yama: A6); to the N of Chishaku in, this temple was originally set up on Mount Hiei. It contains some interesting paintings (*Plum Tree Room: ume no ma*), works by Kano Shoei (1519–92) and Kano Eitoku (1543–90).

Between Chishaku in and Myoho in is a long hill leading E to Amidaga mine (½ml/1km E of Higashioji dori), at the summit of which is Hokokubyo, the tomb of Toyotomi Hideyoshi (1536–98). A five-storey pagoda was erected there in his memory in 1897.

Higashioji dori extends N, passes under the beginning of the express route Higashiyama Bypass and then meets a path, on the r., by Gojo dori, leading to the Nishi Otani temple.

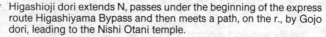 NISHI OTANI (plan of Higashi yama: B5; 440yds/400m N of Myoho in; 1ml/2km NE of Kyoto eki, JNR; 1,000yds/900m E of Gojo eki, Keihan ER; No 6, 16 or 44 bus from Shijo Karasuma to Gojozaka). The present buildings of the temple (1870) are in front of the Toribeyama cemetery, where the priests of Nishi Hongan ji (p. 351) are buried, including Shinran, the founder of the new Jodo sect.

If you go across this cemetery, or go up Gojo zaka from the crossroads where Gojo dori meets Higashioji dori, you will reach the temple of Kiyomizu. On Gojo zaka, you can visit the house of the master potter Kawai Kanjiro (open daily from 10.00 to 17.00 except Mondays), which exhibits pottery and ancient Japanese furniture. This road joins Kiyomizu zaka, or Teapot Lane, as the English have nicknamed it, because of the large number of pottery displays in the Kiyomizu quarter.

**KIYOMIZU DERA (plan of Higashi yama: C5; 770yds/700m NE of Nishi Otani; 1½mls/2½km NE of Kyoto eki; bus No 207 or 206 from Shijo Karasuma station to Kiyomizumichi or Gojozaka; open until sunset). This temple (Hosso sect) is one of the most popular in Kyoto, especially at dusk, and it is particularly famous for the strong wooden framework which supports the Hon do.

Kiyomizu dera or Seisui ji was founded in 798, at the request of the priest Enchin, by Sakanoe Tamuramaro (758–811), the conqueror of the Ebisu; the temple is dedicated to Kannon Bosatsu and enriched itself by acquiring the Shishin den, from the old Imperial Palace in Nagaoka. Most of the present buildings were erected in 1633, on the orders of Tokugawa Iemitsu.

You can go through the main entrance gate, Nio mon (15th c.), and then carry on to the *shoro* or belfry dating from 1607 (with a bell from 1478), and to the Sai mon, or west gate; behind that is the three-storey pagoda which houses a statue of Dai Nichi Nyorai. Beyond that, note the hall of the *sutras* (Kyo zo), the founder's hall (Tamura do), the

Asakura hall, originally built in 1510, and the Hon do.

The Hon do has a *terrace in front of it, which was created for religious ceremonies, and rests on a large framework of skilfully jointed supports. View over Kyoto.

Further E the Shaka do, the Amida do and the Okuno in stand in a row, on the spot where the Priest Enchin's hermitage probably was. It was here that the triple waterfall of Otowa sprang up and pilgrims sometimes stand under it to pray to Fudo Myo o.

The temple treasury possesses a statue of Kannon of the eleven heads, exhibited only once every 33 years, which is believed to be the work of the monk Enchin (8th c.), or at least a reproduction of it (according to the Mosher Governor, *Kyoto: A Contemplative Guide*).

To the N of the Hon do is the little shrine of Jishu Gongen, which is also supposed to have been founded in 798 and rebuilt in 1633. Further N is the priests' residence which surrounds a *delightful garden, attributed to Kobori Enshu (1579-1647).

If you come down Kiyomizu zaka and follow Matsubara dori past Higashioji dori, you can get to the temple of Rokuharamitsu by a road which leads off on the l. before Yamato oji dori.

ROKUHARAMITSU JI (plan of Higashi yama: A5; ½ml/1km W of Kiyomizu dera; 1ml/2km NE of Kyoto eki; No 102 bus from Shijo Karasuma to Yamotooji Gojo). Founded in 963 by the priest Kuya (903-72), this temple was reconstructed in 1463, and is particularly interesting for the *statues it contains.

Amongst the statues (of the 12th and 13th c.), are works by Unkei: a self-portrait, and the four guardians of the Buddhist Paradise. Other works are attributed to his descendants: a statue of Taira Kiyomori reading a *sutra* (late 12th c.); a presumed self-portrait of the sculptor Tankei (1254); a statue of the priest Kuya Shonin calling on the name of Amida Butsu, who is represented by little figurines coming out of the mouth (12th c.).

Heading N from Rokuharamitsu ji, you will arrive at the grounds of:

KENNIN JI (plan of Higashi yama: A4; 440yds/400m N of Rokuharamitsu ji; 1½mls/2.2km NE of Kyoto eki; No 16 bus from Shijo Karasuma to Gion; open daily from 09.00 to 16.00). Founded in 1202 by the priest Eisai (1141-1215), it was the oldest Zen temple in Japan. All that remains from this period is the gate of the Imperial Messenger (Chokushi mon). The main hall was reconstructed in 1763, whilst the priests' apartments come from a temple built in the 14th c. by Ashikaga Takauji, in the province of Aki (Hiroshima). The priest Eisai is buried in the temple.

Kanzen ji has several paintings and screens which are notably the work of Kaihoku Yusho (1533-1615). The famous screen of Sotatsu (*The Gods of Wind and Thunder*) is now displayed in the National Museum. Do visit the garden of Ryosoku which belongs to this temple.

Yasaka dori runs to the S of the Kennin ji enclosure, and the Yasakano to stands in line with it. This five-storey pagoda (128ft/39m high) was built in 1440 by Ashikaga Yoshinori. To the NE of it are the grounds of Kodai ji.

KODAI JI (plan of Higashi yama; B4; 660yds/600m E of Kennin ji; 1¾mls/2.8km NE of Kyoto eki; 1,000yds/900m SE of Shijo eki, Keihan ER; No 16 bus from Shijo Karasuma or Shijo eki to Higashiyama Yasui; open 09.00 to 16.00). This temple was founded in 1606 by Yodogimi (1569–1615), the widow of Toyotomi Hideyoshi, in memory of her husband.

*Kaisan do, one of the main buildings of this temple, was spared the fires and decorated at the beginning of the 17th c. by artists of the Tosa and Kano schools. The mortuary chapel, to the E of this building, is famous for its three-dimensional lacquerwork (*tatamaki e*). The two pavilions behind this chapel come from the old palace of Fushimi. The *temple garden is the work of Kobori Enshu.

To the S of this temple stands Ryozen Kannon, a cement statue, 79ft (24m) high, which represents this deity.

→ 330yds (300m) N of Kodai ji is Higashi Otani where, as at Nishi Otani (see above), the priests of the Higashi Hongan ji (p. 352) have been buried since 1671; a chapel is dedicated to the priest and founder Shinran.

On either side of the Shijo dori, to the N of Kennin ji and to the W of Yasaka jinja, is the 'pleasure-seeker's quarter', Gion, where you will find a 'traditional' atmosphere, luxurious kimonos and geishas. A great many antique dealers and craftsmen are to be found there. Immediately to the E of the junction of Higashi oji dori and Shijo dori, are the grounds of the Yasaka shrine.

YASAKA JINJA (plan of Higashi yama: B3; 440yds/400m NW of Kodai ji; 1½mls/2½km NE of Kyoto eki, JNR; 660yds/600m E of Shijo eki, Keihan ER; No 16 or 31 bus from Shijo Karasuma). This shrine, rebuilt in 1654, was dedicated to Susano o no Mikoto, his wife Inadahime and their children. The Shinto Ryobu made it into the Gion ji, which became the most famous temple in Kyoto. It returned to the pure Shintoism, however, after the Imperial Restoration. The Gion matsuri, on 16 July, is connected with this shrine.

A great stone *torii* forms the entrance, from Shijo dori, to the main building which gave its name to the Gion style of architecture. The treasure house has two wooden statues of Koma inu (mythological dog-lion), attributed to Unkei (13th c.).

Maruyama Park is spread over an area of about 25 acres (10ha) and clings to the slopes of Higashi yama, to the E of Yasaka shrine. Visitors are attracted by the lovely cherry trees. To the N of this park is Chion in.

CHION IN (plan of Higashi yama: B3–C3; 550yds/500m NE of Yasaka jinja; 2mls/3km NE of Kyoto eki, JNR ½ml/1km SE of Keihan Sanjo eki; Keihan ER; No 203 or 206 bus from the station to Chionmae; open from 09.00 to 16.00). This temple, one of the foremost in Kyoto, is the seat of the Jodo sect of Buddhism. Most of the buildings have been reconstructed since the 17th c.

Festival in honour of Honen Shonin, 19–25 April.

This temple was erected in 1234 by the priest Genchi, around the mausoleum of Genku or Honen Shonin (1133–1212), near the spot where the latter set up a hermitage. It was rebuilt several times as the result of a series of fires which occurred up until 1633. The shogun Tokugawa Hidetaka then had most of the buildings which you can still see today rebuilt, and they were completed in 1639. The superior of this temple always came from the Imperial Family, until the Meiji Restoration.

The priest Honen, also known by the posthumous name of Enko Daishi, established the fundamental precepts of the Jodo sect. This sect sees salvation only in the supreme grace of Buddha Amida, whose universal glory must be extolled so that one may be reborn in the Western Paradise of the Pure Land (Jodo). The words of the nembutsu (Namu, Amida Butsu: save me Buddha redeemer) must be continually recited in his praise.

The main entrance to the temple is to the SW, by the great gate *San mon (1619), surmounted by an upper storey and which is the most perfect of its kind in Japan.

In the great courtyard of the temple to the N stands the imposing Mie do or Hon do, which is linked by a gallery to the E to the Amida do. To the S of this building is the pagoda Re to, which dates from 1959. To the E of this is the Kyo do, hall of the *sutra* - the temple has over 5,600 of these - and to the S is the Taihei tei (1958), a long pavilion, reserved for tea ceremonies.

Further SE, after climbing a short path with steps, you will see the *shoro* or belfry, which has a 74-t bell cast in bronze in the 17th c.

*Mie do, the most important building in the temple, is dedicated to Honen Shonin. It has a statue which is believed to be a self-portrait of the founder. It is surrounded by an altar with a richly decorated canopy, but it is usually hidden from the sight of visitors. There are other statues in this hall, including those of Amida, the monk Genchi, Tokugawa Ieyasu, etc. Amida do, reconstructed in 1910, houses a large statue of Amida, the venerable Buddha of the Jodo sect.

Behind Mie do is a covered galley leading to Shue do and the priests' apartments. The corridors with their sonorous wooden floors, which produce a sound like the cry of the *uguisu* (nightingale), were the work of the carpenter Hidari Jingoro.

Shue do, known as the hall of the thousand *tatami* (there are in fact 360), is used when major ceremonies take place, as an assembly hall for the priests, before they proceed to Mie do. To the E of Shue do are the two hosts' rooms, Ohojo and Kohojo (large and small), built in 1639, and which open onto the *garden designed by Kobori Enshu in 1644.

The Hojo rooms contain *paintings of the Kano school. The chambers worth seeing are the Cranes chamber (Tsuru no ma), attributed to Kano Naonobu (1607–50) and, in the Kohojo, the rooms known as Sansui no ma (landscape covered with snow), Rakan no ma (disciples), and Kacho no ma (flowers and birds). Note also the painting on wood of the *Cat Staring in Three Directions*, the chambers of the chrysanthemums (Kiku no ma), the flight of the sparrows (Nuke suzume), the heron (Sagi no ma) and the willow (Yanagi no ma).

If you head E up the hill from Mie do, you will arrive at Seishi do, situated on the spot where Honen Shonin had his hermitage. This building, erected in 1530, is structurally the oldest of Chion in (it was however, rebuilt in 1639). Above this is mausoleum of the founder, originally set up in 1234, then rebuilt at the end of the 16th c.

In the great courtyard is the modern treasure house which has several artefacts and documents relating to the history and the life of Chion in.

If you head NW out of Chion in you will immediately arrive to the N of here at:

Shoren in (Higashi yama plan: B3-C3; 330yds/300m N of Chion in; 2mls/3km NE of Kyoto eki; 550 yds/500m SE of the Higashi yama Sanjo-Keihan ER stop; No 39 bus from Shijo Karasuma or No 104 from Kyoto eki to Jigu dori; open from 09.00 to 17.00). This temple was once the residence of priests of the Tendai sect. In spite of a fire which made it necessary to restore most of the buildings after 1893, there are still several paintings of the Kano and Tosa schools to be appreciated. The Ao Fudo is now in the National Museum of Nara. Magnificent *gardens created by the greatest masters of this art: Soami and Kobori Enshu.

Behind the Higashi yama, a toll road (Higashiyama Driveway) leads to the *belvedere of shogun zuka (Higashi yama plan: C4; 4mls/7km NE of Kyoto eki; No 102 bus from Shijo Karasuma, No 103 from Kyoto eki), which affords a view over the whole of Kyoto and especially over the temples of Higashi yama beneath it. It was here that, at the time of the foundation of Heiankyo, the statue of an armed giant was buried to ensure the protection of the town. This was probably the tomb of Tamuramaro, founder of the Kiyomizu dera (p. 364).

½ml (1km) SE of the shogun zuka is Mount Kazan (725ft/221m alt.), where an astromony observatory, connected with Kyoto University, has been set up.

E Sakyo ku

Keihan Sanjo Keihan ER station and Demachiyanagi Keifuku ER station.

This district abuts on Higashiyama to the N. The area between the shrine of Heian and the villas of Shugaku in, is endowed with many interesting edifices, including Ginkaku ji. The National University of Kyoto has its headquarters here.

Jingu dori goes from Shoren in, crosses Sanjo dori to the N and meets Niomon dori, opposite Okazaki Park. You can get to Nanzen ji by continuing E along the Shirakawa canal which borders the S side of this park.

NANZEN JI (Higashi yama plan: D2; ½ml/1km NE of Chion in; ½ml/1km SE of Heian Jingu; 2½mls/4km NE of Kyoto eki, JNR; 440yds/400m NE of the Keage, Keihan ER stop; No 103 bus from Kyoto eki or No 39 from Shijo Karasuma to Keage; open from 09.00 to 16.30). This temple, of the Rinzai sect, is regarded as one of Kyoto's greatest monasteries.

The creation of Nanzen ji began in 1291, when the Emperor Kameyama (1259-1305) donated a large house which he had had built on this site. The buildings were reconstructed after several fires and the oldest of them go back to the Tokugawa Ieyasu period (17th c.).

To the W is the great gate *San mon (1628), the upper tier of which is rarely visible and houses the statues of Buddha and his disciples. It also has a painted ceiling by artists of the Kano and Tosa schools.

To the E of San mon is Hon do, the main building of which was rebuilt after the fire of 1895.

To the E of Hon do, you may be interested in visiting the *Dai Hojo or priests' apartments which come from Seiryo den (the Imperial Palace), transferred here in 1611, and from the old castle of Fushimi. These buildings house a statue of Kannon, of the Heian period, but more noteworthy still are the **paintings on sliding doors (*fusuma*), by Kano Motonobu (1476-1559), Kano Eitoku (1543-90) and Kano Tanyu (1602-74). Near the latter, note also *Tigers in Bamboo Forest*; the carved beams are the work of Hidari Jingoro (1591-1634); the 17th-c. garden is deservedly famous.

Amongst the temples attached to Nanzen ji (but usually closed to the public) are:

to the SW of the Hojo, Nanzen in, on the site of the Emperor Kameyama's residence, which is endowed with a landscape garden designed in the 14th c.;

immediately to the S of the San mon, the Tenju an stands in the enclosure where the poet Gen. Hosokawa Yusai (1534-1610) is buried;

finally, the furthest to the W is the Konchi in, the garden of which is attributed to Kobori Enshu (1632).

If you take a Shishigatani dori, you will reach the Eikan do, towards the N, past a school.

Zenrin ji or Eikan do (Higashi yama plan: D1; 550yd/500m N of Nanzen ji; ¾ml/1.2km E of Heian jingu; 2¾mls/4.5km NE of Kyoto eki;

No 5 bus from Kyoto eki to Tennocho; open from 09.00 to 17.00). This temple was founded by a disciple of Kobo Daishi, rebuilt in the 15th c., and is surrounded by beautiful gardens.

There is a statue of Amida, named Mikaeri no Amida (looking back), because she turned towards the priest Eikan, who was addressing his prayers to her, and called her by name. This legend explains the position of the statue's head.

Behind this temple the Daimonji yama or Nyoiga dake (1,529ft/466m) rises up to the E. On the 16 August for the Bon festival, fires are lit on its slopes in the shape of the ideogram Dai (large) and these are visible from the town. The origin of this tradition is the fire lit by the priest Kukai (Kobo Daishi) which was intended to rid Kyoto of an epidemic and a famine from which it was suffering.

If you go W again from this temple, you will reach:

OKAZAKI PARK (Higashi yama plan: B1). The Shira kawa canal runs along it, and it is a center of contemporary culture.

To the S, on either side of the huge *torii*, you will see on the l. (W) the Regional Library (1872) and the National Museum of Modern Art (Okazaki Enshoji cho, Sakyo ku; open daily except Mondays from 10.00 to 17.00), which chiefly exhibits works from the Tokyo Modern Art Museum, and has a fund of pictures by Japanese painters of the 20th c., china and other contemporary works of craftsmanship. To the E stands the Municipal Art Museum (Okazaki, Enshoji cho, Sakyo ku; open daily from 09.00 to 16.30), which also organizes exhibitions, and has several paintings and sculptures from the Meiji period to the present day. To the E, behind this museum is the town's zoological park. To the N of the Modern Art Museum, note the Kyoto Kaikan (arch. Maekawa Kunio, 1962), which has congress and exhibition halls, and an auditorium which seats 2,500.

The N part of the park is occupied by the Heian shrine.

ꞌHEIAN JINGU (Higashi yama plan: B1; ¾ml/1.2km N of the Chion in; 2½mls/4km NE of Kyoto eki, JNR; 850yds/800m NE of the Higashi yama Sanjo, Keihan ER stop. No 5 or 203 bus from Kyoto eki; open from 08.30 to 17.00). This shrine was built in 1895, in commemoration of the 1,100th anniversary of the creation of Heiankyo by the Emperor Kammu.

Built in the Heian style, in imitation of the Imperial Palace of that time, the brightly coloured shrine is dedicated to the Emperors Kammu (736–805) and Komei (1831–67), who were the first and last sovereigns to reside in Kyoto.

Festivals: *Takagi Noh, a Noh play, performed by torch light (1 and 2 June), and *Jidai matsuri, a historical procession (22 October).

The shrine's treasure house has many mementoes and documents relating to the Emperors Komei and Meiji.

Some very beautiful *gardens are laid out behind the treasury, and are admired, according to the season of the year, for their cherry trees, irises and autumn maples. In these gardens you can see the Shobi kan, which comes from the former Imperial Palace (*fusuma* painted by Mochizuki Gyokukei in the 19th c.), and an elegant covered bridge, surmounted by a phoenix.

½ml (1km) N of the Heian jingu is the Yoshida yama (335ft/102m). The Yoshida jinga stands on the flanks of this hill and is particularly popular with students from Kyoto University, which lies to the W. Imadegawa dori passes to the N of the University and Yoshida yama, and meets Higashioji dori to the W.

Near to the crossroads is Chion ji (650yds/600m NW of Yoshida jinja), founded by Honen Shonin, which has been called Hyakumanben, in memory of the nembutsu (see Chion in p. 366) which was repeated a million times during an epidemic in 1331.

Imadegawa dori meets Shirakawa dori to the E, then continues in the form of a narrower road, which rises up towards the Silver Pavilion.

**JISHO JI or GINKAKU JI (general plan: C2, 1ml/1.8km NE of the Heian jingu; 4mls/6km NE of Kyoto eki; No 203 bus from Shijo Karasuma; open from 09.00 to 16.30). This is one of the most delightful spots in Kyoto, in spite of its relative simplicity.

Ashikaga Yoshimasa (1435–90) had the Higashi yama country house (p. 375) built, between 1479 and 1482, in imitation of the Kinkaku ji, at the foot of the hills to the E of Kyoto; it was converted into a Zen temple after his death.

The elegant Silver Pavilion (*ginkaku*), the main attraction of this temple, was to be clad in silver, but this was never actually done. It has an upper storey and houses a statue by Jizo Bosatsu.

To the N of the pavilion, note the Hon do (17th c.) and Togu do (1487), which contains a wooden statue of Ashikaga Yoshimasa, and two other statues of Buddha by Jocho (11th c.) and Kannon by Unkei (13th c.). The **garden, attributed to Soami, is one of the finest in Kyoto. It evokes a west Chinese landscape and is of two parts, one which is classical and has a lake, the other of sand and stones which is specially set up so as to symbolize the sea and mountains.

*SHISEN DO 1½ml/2km N of Ginkaku ji; 2mls/3km NE of Heian jingu; 4mls/7km NE of Kyoto eki; No 5 bus from the latter, or Shijo Karasuma to Ichijoji; open from 09.00 to 17.00). This temple was founded in 1631 by Ishikawa Jozan (1588-1672). The 36 portraits of Chinese poets, attributed to the painter Kano Tankyu, hang in one of the rooms. The *temple garden is a model of its kind.

Shirakawa dori continues N; road leading to Shugaku in house (770yds/700m on the r.) branches off near Shugakuin station (Keifuku ER).

**SHUGAKU IN RIKYU (general plan: C1; 1ml/1.5km N of Shisen do; 3mls/4.5km NE of the Heian jingu; 6mls/9km NE of Kyoto eki; No 5, 36 or 65 bus from this station, or No 31 from Shijo Karasuma, to Shugakuinmichi; Keifuku ER train from Demachiyanagi to Shugakuin; tours: morning or afternoon by appointment; ask at least 24 hours in advance at the Imperial Household Agency, Tel. 211-1211, or at the Imperial Palace, where you will have to obtain a pass to attend; closed Saturday afternoons, Sundays and public holidays, also 21 December and 5 January). The three imperial villas of Shugaku in (69 acres/28 ha) standing on the foothills of Mount Hiei, to the NE of Kyoto, leave visitors with a captivating memory.

Situated on the site of the Shugaku temple, which disappeared in the 15th century, these villas, or tea pavilions, were set up at the request of the Shogun Tokugawa, for the retired Emperor Go Mizuno o (1596-1680) who frequently went to stay there. The upper villas (Kami no chaya) and the lower one (Shimo no chaya) were completed in 1659. The middle villa (Naka no chaya) had been built for this Emperor's daughter. Although it later became the Rinkyu temple, part of it was reconverted (1885) to form the present house.

Visitors will be guided successively through the gardens of the lower, middle and upper villas. The middle villa has paintings attributed to Gukei Sumiyoshi (1631-1705); the *upper villa, which also has the Rinun tei and Kyusei tei pavilions, is the most important and the finest of the three. There is a view looking out over a verdant garden which frames a lake, and extends as far as Kyoto and the neighbouring hills.

750yds/700m S of Shugaku in is Manju in, which possesses its own garden and tea pavilion.

If you go W from Shugaku in to meet the railway line (Keifuku ER), and cross the Takano gawa, you will come to Lake Takaraga, ½ml (1km) W of Takaragaike Keifuku ER station.

TAKARAGA IKE KOEN (general plan: C1; 1½ml (2km) W of Sugaku in; 3 mls (5km) N of Heian jingu; 6mls (9km) N of Kyoto eki; No 17 bus from Keihan Sanjo eki, or No 72 from Shijo Karasuma to Takaragaike koen). This pool has an amusement park along its shores and also the huge International Hall of Congress (Kokuritsu Kyoto Kokusai Kaikan; arch. Otani Yukio, 1966), which has over 70 conference rooms and an auditorium which seats 2,000.

1ml (1.5km) NW (½ml/1km SW of Konomachi eki, Keifuku ER) is Entsu ji (open from 10.00 to 16.00), which was built as an Imperial residence in the 17th c., whilst Shugaku in was being completed; the garden was competently restored after World War II, in the manner of the original by Kobori Enshu; a statue of Kannon, kept in the temple, is attributed to Jocho (11th c.).

To get to Shimogamo jinja take the No 17 or 72 bus from Takaragaike koen to Shimogamojinjamae, or the train (Keifuku ER) from Takaragaike to Demachiyanagi, across the Takano gawa and to the N of the shrine's gardens.

*SHIMOGAMO JINJA (general plan: C1; 1½mls/2.5m S of Takaraga Ike; 1½mls/2.5km N of Heian jingu; 3½mls/6km N of Kyoto eki, JNR; ½ml/1km N of Demachiyanagi eki, Keifuku ER; No 4 or 14 bus from Kyoto eki, or No 72 from Shijo Karasuma to Shimogamojinjamae;

open from 9.00 to 17.00). This shrine, along with its twin, Kamigamo (below) is one of the most famous in Kyoto. Festival: Aoi matsuri, 15 May, established in the 6th c.

Founded by the Emperor Kimmei (510-571), this shrine is dedicated to Hono Ikatsuchi no Mikoto, god of the mountains, and his wife, the goddess of the rivers, both of whom are patrons of the province of Yamashiro, which surrounds Kyoto. Rebuilt in 1628 and 1863.

Head NW along the Kamo gawa to:

 KYOTO BOTANICAL GARDEN (general plan: B1; 1ml/1.5km NW of Shimogamo jinja; 3mls/4.5km NW of the Heian jingu; 4mls/7km N of Kyoto eki; No 36 bus from the latter or from Shijo Karasuma to Shokubutsuen). This garden was opened in 1923, to commemorate the coronation of the Emperor Taisho (1879-1926). There are a number of greenhouses and a commemorative hall. To the E of the park is the Municipal Library, which houses a small museum.

F Kita ku

Situated to the W of Sakyo ku and N of Kamigyo ku, this district covers some of the hills to the N of Kyoto. If you have to be selective in your visit to Kita ku, we would recommend the Daitoku ji, and the Kinkaku ji or the Gold Pavilion.

Continue along the Kamo gawa from the botanical garden to get to:

*KAMIGAMO JINJA (general plan: B1; 2mls/3km NW of Shimogamo jinja; 1½ml/2km NE of Daitoku ji; 5mls/8km N of Kyoto eki; No 6, 16 or 46 bus from Shijo Karasuma; always open). Kamigamo has connections with Shimogamo jinja, and is dedicated to the god of thunder, who was born of the union of the deities protecting the Shimogamo shrine.

To the W of Kamigamo jinja is the field used for the ritual races. On 5 May, ten horses compete and all are winners, because the kami do not like losers ...

After crossing the Kamo gawa to the S of the shrine, you will come to Horikawa dori which meets Kitaoji dori, much further down, to the S. Kitaoji dori will take you rapidly W to Daitoku ji.

*DAITOKU JI (general plan: B1; 2mls/3km N of Nijo jo; 4mls/6.5km N of Kyoto eki; No 206 bus from Kyoto eki to Daitokujimae; most of the monasteries open from 09.00 to 17.00). This group of monasteries forms a vital part of any visit to Kyoto. It has, in addition to the main buildings, twenty-three temples, seven of which can be visited. These include Daisen in, which is the most famous.

This temple of the Rinzai sect was erected, between 1319 and 1324, by the priest Daito Kokushi (1282-1337), at the request of the Emperor Go Daigo (1287-1338). It immediately became renowned for its fine buildings. These were burnt down in 1453, and again in 1468, and then rebuilt under the direction of the priest Ikkyu (1394-1481) at a later date (1479). Since the 16th c., in particular, numerous secondary temples have been added. They possess invaluable treasures which are usually exhibited in October.

From Kitaoji dori, a path goes right through the monasteries and leads up to the Chokushi mon. A little road runs E along this temple, providing access to a car park where you will also find direct access to the temple.

Chokushi mon (1599), the gate of the Imperial messenger, rises up to the S of the main buildings of the Daitoku ji. This gate comes from the old Imperial Palace, and was transferred here in 1640.

*San mon, behind the above-mentioned gate, was completed in 1589 by Senno Rikyu; on the upper storey are several Buddhist statues, including those of the sixteen disciples (Rakan) brought from Korea by Kato Kiyomasa, and given to this temple. The ceiling was painted by Hasegawa Tohaku (1539-1610).

The Butsu den or Daiyu den, the main temple building, to the N of the San mon, was built in 1664. It is characteristic of Zen architecture; note the statues of Buddha Sakyamuni, his disciples Anan and Kayo, and the founder priest Daito Kokushi. Hatto, the preaching hall, stands still further N and was erected in 1636. The painted ceiling is by Kano Tanyu.

To the N of Hatto is the Honbo or *Hojo (apartment of the superior of Daitoku ji), also rebuilt in 1636.

The *removable screens (*fusuma*) were decorated in the *sumi* e style (monochrome ink), by Kano Tanyu. Those depicting the egrets and the monkeys are particularly famous; gardens attributed to Tenyu Joka (1586-1666) and Kobori Enshu (1579-1647).

To the E of the Hojo is *Kara mon, or Higashuri mon, a gate which originally came from the old castle of Fushimi, and is ornamentated with delicate carvings by Hidari Jingoro (1594-1634).

You will arrive at *Daisen in, one of the most frequently visited monasteries of Daitoku ji, by skirting the Honbo to the W.

This temple was created in 1509 by Kogaku Shuko (1465-1548). The most noteworthy features are the Hon do or Hojo, which has *fusuma* (sliding doors) painted by Soami (1472-1523: *Landscape in the Four Seasons*), by Kano Motonobu (1476-1559: *Flowers and Birds of the Four Seasons*), and by Kano Yukinobu (1513-1575: *Agricultural Labours.*) This building is surrounded by three **gardens in the *kare sansui* style, sometimes attributed to Soami, and sometimes to the founder Kogaku Shuko (which is more probable). The garden, which is laid out NE to E, is particularly striking. It is divided into two by an observation platform; in the NE corner is the symbolic Mount Horai, which has an equally symbolic waterfall flowing down it; this plunges into the 'stream' – a sandy track – representing the current of life, which surrounds the islands of the tortoise and the crane (the limits of human knowledge); it flows to the W, towards the 'Inland Sea', and towards the S it crosses a dam and becomes a river (the widening of the mind) on which the ship of human understanding floats. Another little tortoise tries in vain to swim against the current (the past). To the S of the Hon do lies the ocean of eternity.

The other temples of Daitoku ji are also worth visiting (though some of them are closed to the public). They usually have several fine gardens. We would recommend:

immediately to the l. (E), coming out of Daisen in, is Shinju an, which was the residence of the priest Ikkyu and which has paintings by Hasegawa Tohaku, Soami and members of the Kano school.

Hoshun in, which opens out to the W of Daisen in, was founded in 1608 by the wife of Maeda Toshie. There is a pleasant *garden, attributed to Kobori Enshu, with an elegant pavilion, Donko kaku (1617), at its centre. The tombs of the Maeda family are in the temple enclosure.

Immediately to the S of the Hoshun in, opposite the Honbo of Daitoku ji, is the Juko in; where the tea master Senno Rikyu (1520-91) committed suicide. It houses *paintings by Kano Eitoku. Soken in is adjacent to this temple and Toyotomi Hideyoshi held the funeral of Oda Nobunaga, who was assassinated in Kyoto in 1582.

Past this point is a junction of several paths, to the SW of which you can visit the Koto in, founded in 1601 by Hosokawa Tadooki (1563-1645), one time companion-at-arms of Hideyoshi and Nobunaga. The garden is famous for its maples.

A little further W is the Kobo an, which you can also visit and which has a **garden by Kobori Enshu.

Once you are back on the main path which leads past the principal buildings of Daitoku ji, you can go into the following temples:

Sangen in, the first building opposite the Hatto, was founded in 1589 by Ishida Mitsunari and possesses some *fusuma (the tiger and monkeys are particularly famous) painted by Hara Zaichu.

Further S are the Shoju in, the Korin in, with its tea pavilion (Kankyo tei) and garden without rocks, and the Zuiho in, which has a *modern abstract garden by Shigemori Mirei (1961).

If you follow the pathway opposite the Chokushi mon, you will arrive at Ryogen in, on the r. and to the S: Ryogen in has a garden of moss and rocks, and another very small inner garden. This temple has the chessboard on which Toyotomi Hideyoshi and Tokugawa Ieyasu are said to have played, and also a 'tanegashima' gun, one of the oldest known models in Japan, an imitation of European weaponry.

From Daitoku ji, Kitaoji dori continues W and curves round to the S after Senbon dori. The road then becomes Nishioji dori. Another road very soon branches off it towards the W and leads to Kinkaku ji.

'ROKUON JI or KINKAKU JI (general plan: A1; 1ml/1.5km W of Daitoku ji; 4mls/7km NW of Kyoto eki; No 12 bus from Shijo Karasuma or the Daitoku ji, to Kinkaku ji; open from 09.00 to 17.30). The Gold Pavilion (Kinkaku ji) is one of the most popular monuments in Kyoto and famous throughout Japan.

Kinkaku ji, at the foot of Mount Kinugasa (656ft/200m alt.), was originally a country house belonging to Saionji Kintsune (1171–1244), who was related to Minamoto Yoritomo and the Emperors Go Saga and Go Fukakusa. The outstanding Shogun Ashikaga Yoshimitsu (1358–1408) ceded power to his son Yoshimochi and chose this spot to retire to. He had the Gold Pavilion built in 1394 and the garden around it designed. All this was turned into a Rokuon temple after his death. Most of the buildings disappeared at that time, and the pavilion was burnt down in 1950, when a young monk of the temple committed suicide. The one which you can see today was reconstructed, identical to its predecessor in 1955.

The Rokuon ji buildings contain several Buddhist statues, including one of Kannon, attributed to the priest Jocho (11th c.), and one of the Shogun Yoshimitsu. The decorations on the removable panels are the work of the Mincho and Kano schools. The Gold Pavilion (covered with gold-leaf) stands by a lovely pool. It is surmounted by two storeys, with a bronze phoenix on the very top. In the *gardens is the 17th-c. Sekka tei tea pavilion, built by the Emperor Gomizuno o. Near the exit from here there is a little temple, dedicated to Fudo Myo o.

G Ukyo ku

Hanazono and Saga JNR stations.

This huge district in the W of Kyoto is spread out on either side of the Hozu gawa, which is spanned, near Arashiyama, by the famous Togetsukyo bridge. There are also a great many temples in Ukyo ku. Note especially Myoshin ji and Ninna ji. The gardens of Ryoan ji, Koke dera and Katsura Rikyu, rank amongst the loveliest in Kyoto.

Kitsuji dori runs along the S side of Mount Kinugasa, linking the temples of Kinkaku ji, Ryoan ji and Ninna ji.

RYOAN JI (general map, A1; 1ml/1.5km SW of Kinkaku ji; 1ml/1.5km N of Myoshin ji; 3mls/4.5km NE of Arashiyama; 4mls/6.5km NW of Kyoto eki, JNR; 880yds/800km N of Ryoanjimichi station, Keifuku ER; No 52 bus from Kyoto eki and Shijo Karasuma Ryoan ji; open from 08.00 to 17.00). This temple has one of the most admired Zen dry gardens (*kare sansui*), but has unfortunately lost much of its value through excessive commercial development, inhibiting the meditation which the garden is supposed to induce.

The temple was created in 1473 by Hosokawa Katsumoto (1430–73), one of the greatest lords of his age, on ground which had belonged to the Tokudaiji. It was rebuilt in 1499 after the Onin Civil War (1467–77), then again in 1797 after a fire.

The **rock and sand garden, attributed to the master Soami (1472–1523), is 98ft by 33ft (30m by 10m). It is bounded by a wall, which is a very significant feature in the composition of a Zen garden.

Fifteen rocks, of different shapes and sizes, a little moss growing on them, are laid out in five groups; a sea of sand is spread out around them, and carefully raked over every day. Wherever you stand to contemplate them, you will never see more than fourteen stones at once. Each of the Zen schools interprets this in its own symbolic way.

Behind this temple are the tombs of several members of the Hosokawa family, and behind these are the tombs of the Emperor Go Shujaku (1009–45) and his sons the Emperors Go Reizei (1025–68) and Go Sanjo (1034–76).

To the S of the dry garden, you can walk through the remarkable *landscape garden which has been set up around Lake Oshidori, which Tokudaiji Sanesada caused to be dug out in the 12th c. In this park, note the Zoroku tei tea pavilion.

From Ryoan, Kitsuji dori begins to bend round towards the S before reaching the S entrance of:

*NINNA JI (general plan: A1; 880yds/800m SW of the Ryoan ji; 880yds/800m NW of Myoshin ji; 2mls/3.5km NE of Arashiyama; 3½mls/6km NW of Kyoto JNR; 220yds/200m N of Omuro Keifuku ER station; No 59 bus from Keihan Sanjo to Ninna ji; open from 09.00 to 16.00). This is one of the great Kyoto temples, although it does not attract many visitors.

It was originally a palace, commenced in 886 by the Emperor Koko (830–87) and completed by his son Uda tenno (867–931) who later retired there as high priest. Until the Meiji Restoration, the priests of this temple were chosen from amongst the princes of the Imperial Family. Owing to a series of fires, the buildings have been reconstructed several times, and the oldest amongst them date from the 17th c.

To the N of the San mon, on the r. is the Omuro Gosho, which stands on the former site of the Imperial Residence, and was rebuilt at the beginning of the 20th c. in the Momoyama style. At the far end, past the Chu mon, are the main temple buildings. These include the Kon do, which houses a wooden statue of Amida, the five-tier pagoda (108ft/33m high) and the Kyo zo (hall of the *sutra*); to the W is the Miei do. The temple has a *lovely garden which contains the Ryokaku tei tea pavilion; Ninna ji is particularly popular during the second fortnight in April, when its famous cherry trees are in flower.

Ichijo dori branches off to the SE from Ninna ji, crosses the private Keifuku ER railway lines, and goes along the northern wall of Myoshin ji enclosure.

**MYOSHIN JI (general plan: A2; 880yds/800m SE of Ninna ji; 2½mls/4km NE of Arashiyama; 3mls/5.5km NW of Kyoto eki and 650yds/600m NE of Hanazono eki, JNR; 330yds/300m SE of Myoshin ji Keifuku ER station; No 26 bus from Kyoto eki; open from 09.00 to 16.00). Myoshin ji is also a zen temple of the Rinzai sect, comparable in importance to Daitoku ji.

This temple was erected, between 1337 and 1342, on the site of a villa which belonged to the Emperor Hanazono (1297–1348). The buildings were destroyed by various fires and rebuilt in the

Momoyama and Edo periods, between the 16th and 18th c. The numerous lesser temples of which this huge monastery is comprised have been embellished with gardens and enriched with paintings, notably of the Kano school.

The temple may be entered on the S side by the beautiful San mon gate (1599), behind which are the Butsu den (housing a statue of Sakyamuni), followed by the Hatto, which has a decorated ceiling by Kano Tanyu (1602-74). To the W of the Hatto, note the *shoro* (belfry) which contains the oldest known bell in Japan, cast in 698.

The following lesser temples are worth seeing;

Tenkyu in (1635): near to the N gate of Myoshin ji enclosure, it possesses some *fusuma* (sliding doors) painted by Kano Sanraku (1559-1635).

*Reuin in: to the NW of the Hatto, to the W and opposite the Hojo, it has many **paintings, which are now mounted on *kakemono*, and are the work of Kano Motonobu (1476-1559). They are principally landscapes, some ornamented with flowering trees and birds, whilst others portray characters from Chinese history.

Taizo in: to the W of the Butsu den, it holds several Josetsu ink drawings including *Man with a Calabash Fishing for a Catfish* (*Hyonen zu*).

Ryusen an: it lies to the E of the San mon; here you can stand and admire the lively monkeys painted by Hasegawa Tohaku (late 16th c.).

Opposite the S entrance of Myoshin ji a road branches off towards the SW, and after crossing the JNR railway line, it goes to Uzumasa Keifuku ER station. Koryu ji stands to the N of this. You can get to this temple by taking the Keifuku ER train, to the NW of Myoshin ji, from Myoshin ji to Katabiranotsuji. You can change trains here, to head back E to Uzumasa.

*KORYU JI (general plan: A2; 1ml/1.8km SW of Myoshin ji; 1½mls/2.5km E of Arashi yama; 3mls/5.5km NW of Kyoto eki JNR; 110yds/100m NW of Uzumasa Keifuku ER station; No 11 bus from Shijo Karasuma, or No 28 bus from Kyoto eki to Uzumasa; open from 09.00 to 17.00). Also known by the name of Uzumasa dera, this temple was founded in 622 by Hata Kawatsu, in honour of Prince Shotoku (572-621). Ushi matsuri festival 12 November.

The Ko do, or preaching hall (1165), is one of the oldest edifices in Kyoto. It houses a statue of Buddha and two others of Kannon. The Taishi do (1720), behind the Ko do, is dedicated to Shotoku taishi, and has a statue which is probably a self-portrait of the prince. To the NW of the temple is the octagonal pavilion, *Keigu in or Hakkaku do (1251), which contains another statue of Shotoku, a statue of Nyorin Kannon, which came from Korea, and a statue of Amida.

Finally, there is the temple treasury (Reiho kan), behind the Taishi do, which has other Buddhist statues of the Heian period, and the famous **Miroku Bosatsu of the Asuka period.

This statue is thought to have been a gift from the Korean kingdom of Silla in 623, or it may have been created at the request of Prince Shotoku. Whatever its origins, Korean influence is evident and the statue is very similar to that in Chugu ji (see Ikaruga). It was sculpted from a single piece of wood, has been restored several times and has lost some of the adornments it once had. This Buddha of the future has his gaze 'turned inwards, towards a universe of gentleness and spiritually, with exceptional modesty and timidity' (Peter C. Swann, *Japan*).

Past Koryu ji you can take the bus or train (Keifuku ER) from Uzumasa station to the Arashiyama district, on the banks of the Hozu gawa, where the people of Kyoto flock to enjoy the cool air and to relax. The boats which go down the Hozu gawa rapids end the trip here (see Kameoka). Cormorant fishing on the river in summer. Book at the hotels or the JNTO.

TENRYU JI (2mls/3km W of Koryu ji; 5mls/8.5km NW of Kyoto eki, and 880yds/800m SW of Saga eki, JNR; 440yds/400m W of Arashiyama Keifuku ER station; No 11 bus from Shijo Karasuma, or No 28 bus from Kyoto eki to Arashiyama; open from 09.00 to 17.00). This temple was founded in 1339 by Ashikaga Takauji in honour of the Emperor Go Daigo (1287-1338). It was rebuilt after 1900, but its *garden is attributed to Soseki (or Muro Kokushi, 1271-1346), a temple superior.

Behind this is the Kamayama Park, where the Emperor of this name planted the cherry trees (13th c.), which came from Yoshino (see entry under this name). This park is still famous for its vegetation, and it flowers in spring.

From Arashiyama, you can take the No 28 bus towards the N:

†DAIKAKU JI (1ml/1.5km N of Arashiyama; 5mls/8.5km NW of Kyoto eki or ¾ml/1.2km N of Saga eki, JNR; No 28 bus from Kyoto eki; open from 09.00 to 16.30). This temple was created by the Emperor Junna (786-840) on the site of a villa which belonged to his brother the Emperor Saga (785-842) and lay W of the pool of Osawa.

It houses five Buddhist statues, traditionally attributed to Kobo Daishi (774-835), and it also possesses some paintings of the Kano school (Motonobu Eitoku, Sanraku, Tanyu; 16th-17th c.) and by Ogata Korin (1691-1716).

8mls (13km) N of Arashiyama, on the toll road *Arashiyama Takao Parkway (views over Kyoto and the surrounding area; No 104 bus), you can get to Takao, at the foot of Atago yama (3,045ft/928m), in the Kiyotaki gawa valley. The surrounding slopes are famous for the blazing colours of the maple trees in autumn.

In Takao it is worth visiting *Jingo ji, founded in 806, which has a number of *statues of the Heian period. Note also the paintings of *Sakyamuni in a Red Robe (12th c.); *Portraits of Fujiwara Mitsuyoshi, Taira Shigemori and Minamoto Yoritomo, by Fujiwara Takanobu 1142-1205).

Upstream from Takao, at Makino o and Togano o, are the temples of

Saimyo ji (1699) and Kozan ji. The latter once possessed several famous paintings which are now in the National Museum in Tokyo. Direct bus (No 8) from Takao to the centre of Kyoto.

The Hozu gawa is spanned at Arashiyama by the beautiful Togetsukyo bridge. Arashi yama (1,230ft/375m) stands to the SW of the bridge and Iwade yama Park covers its slopes. Monkeys are allowed to roam freely here. At the foot of this hill is Horin ji (1,968ft/600m S of Arashiyama Keifuku ER station; 440yds/400m W of Arashiyama Hankyu ER station), founded in 713; The Jusan Mairi festival for children aged thirteen takes place on 13 April.

You can take a direct coach from Arashiyama (N bank of the Hozu gawa) to the Koke dera.

SAIHO JI (1½mls/2.5km S of Arashiyama; 4mls/6.5km W of Kyoto eki; No 29 bus from Shijo Karasuma; open from 09.00 to 17.00; book beforehand). This temple has one of the most famous moss gardens in Kyoto, which is why it is often called the temple of mosses: Koke dera.

Saiho ji was probably founded in 731 by the priest Gyoki (670-749), on the site of a house which belonged to Prince Shotoku. It was rebuilt in 1339 by the priest Soseki (1271-1346), to whom the **garden is also attributed. This is carpeted with moss (about 20 different species) which give the park a particular charm. We would suggest that you go there after a shower of rain. The lake, which lies alongside a tea pavilion (Shonan tei), is shaped like the Chinese ideogram *kokoro*: heart, mind.

The No 29 bus from Koke dera goes to Kami Katsura station (Hankyu ER), where you take a train to Katsura station, which is 850yds (800m) SW of the Katsura villa. (Note restrictions mentioned on p. 347.)

KATSURA RIKYU (general plan: A3; 1½mls/2.5km SE of Koke dera; 2½mls/4.5km SE of Arashiyama; 3mls/5km W of Kyoto eki, JNR; 880yds/800m NE of Katsura eki, Hankyu ER; Hankyu ER train from Arishiyama or Kawaramachi to Katsura; tour, see Shugaku in Rikyu, p. 371). Here we have yet another of Kyoto's finest gardens. Like those of Shugaku in, they come under the supervision of the Imperial Household and require special permission to view which must be obtained one month in advance

This house was built on the banks of the Katsura or Hozu gawa, at the start of the 16th c., for Prince Toshihito Hachijo (1579-1629), the brother of the Emperor Go Yozei (1571-1617). The plans are said to have been entrusted to Kobori Enshu (1579-1647), and some work was done between 1620 and 1624. The extension of the house was commenced in 1642 by Prince Toshitada, but followed the same sober style, typfied by the buildings round the pool in the centre.

The garden is worth observing in every respect, for its effect of perspective, its plants, the unexpected details at each bend in the path, the harmony of the whole creation, the arrangement of the tea pavilions, and the main building (Shoin), which has an observation platform so that you can enjoy a nocturnal view of the garden on moonlit evenings. The tea pavilions (Shoka teik, Shokin tei and Gepparo) all have their own individual features. The Shoin was decorated by painters of the Kano school.

H Minami ku

Kyoto and Nishioji JNR stations.

This essentially popular district of Kyoto is spread out to the S of the railway lines (the Shinkansen line), at the junction where the Kamo gawa to the E meets the Katsura gawa to the W. The To ji is worth visiting.

KYO OGOKOKU JI or **TO JI (plan: centre B3; ½ml/1km SW of Kyoto eki, JNR; 440yds/400m W of To ji eki, Kintetsu ER; No 208 bus from Kyoto eki, or No 207 from Shijo Karasuma to Tojimae; open from 09.00 to 16.00). This temple of the Shingon sect has several interesting buildings and a collection of **noteworthy sculptures. The entrance is to the NE of the enclosure.

To ji, the E temple as opposed to Sai ji which once stood to the W of the southern (Rasho mon) entrance to Heiankyo, was founded in 796 by the Emperor Kammu, and in 823 was placed under the direction of the priest Kukai or Kobo Daishi (774–835). Most of the buildings were destroyed during the civil wars of the 15th c., and later rebuilt from the 18th c. onwards.

Amongst these buildings note:

Minami Dai mon, in the far S of the temple enclosure, was built in the 16th c., and came originally from the Sanjusangen do.

The *Five-storey pagoda (180ft/55m high), which towers up in the SE corner is the highest in Japan. It was rebuilt in 1644.

Three buildings stand to the N of Minami Dai mon.

To the S is Kon do, the principal hall of the temple, which was rebuilt on the command of Toyotomi Hideyori, between 1599 and 1606.

This building houses the triad of the Buddhist healer: *Yakushi Nyorai, with the two deities of the moon and the sun on either side: Gakko and Nikko Bosatsu. Note beneath the central statue, the 12 celestial guardians, which are thought to have been the work of the priest Kocho.

The Ko do, or preaching hall, which stands in the middle, was also rebuilt at the beginning of the 17th c.

Inside the building there are 21 **statues arranged round the Dai Nichi Nyorai, according to the precepts of the mandara of Mikkyo which are described in the principal *sutra* of the esoteric Shingon sects (see Koya san). Six statues were restored in the early 17th c. at the request of Toyotomi Hideyori, and the other fifteen are the work of the priest Kukai (about 825). The entire group of statues may date from the Heian period.

The Jiki do, or refectory (to the N), was rebuilt in 1930 in the original Muromachi style (14th to 16th c.).

Finally, to the NW of this group is the *Hozo, or treasury, constructed in the Kamakura period (1197), in the *azekura* style, without using nails.

The temple also has a number of religious paintings of the Heian period: mandara of the Diamond, Screen of Landscapes, etc.

I Fushimi ku

Inari and Momoyama JNR stations.

This district has merged with Kyoto and is almost its southern suburb, hemmed in by the Uji gawa to the S and the Meishin motorway to the N. The name Fushimi evokes the splendid Momoyama residence, which gave its name to the 16th c. period of art. The shrine of Inari and Daigo ji are also worth a visit.

**FUSHIMI INARI JINJA (general plan: C3; 1ml/1.5km S of Tofuku ji; 2mls/3km SE of Kyoto eki and 400yds/380m E of Inari eki, JNR; 440yds/400m E of Fushimi Inari Keihan ER station). This shrine is one of the most famous in Japan and its chief tourist attraction is its large number of wooden *torii* – over 10,000 of them – which have been presented as gifts throughout the ages and which bear the names of the donors.

The shrine was consecrated in 711 and is dedicated to Ukanomitama no Mikoto (or Inari), who is none other than Toyouke bime no kami, the daughter of Izanagi and Izanami. She is venerated at Ise (see entry under this name), as the patroness of food and of rice in particular. In the Inari shrines, the statues of foxes – an animal with divine attributes – are supposed to ensure protection of the rice. The shrine was rebuilt in 1499 in the Momoyama style.

From Inari you can take the JNR train to the next stop, which is Momoyama.

FUSHIMI JO or MOMOYAMA JO (general plan: C4; 2mls/3km S of Fushimi Inari jinja; 3mls/5km SE of Kyoto eki and ½ml/1km NE of Momoyama eki, JNR; ½ml/1km E of Tanbabashi, Keihan and Kintetsu ER; No 56 bus from Shijo Karasuma and Momoyama eki). Momoyama is a hill famous for its flowering peach trees, as its name suggests. It was chosen in the 16th c. by Toyotomi Hideyoshi as the site for a castle which he wanted to build as a symbol of his power.

TOYOTOMI HIDEYOSHI (1536–98). Hiyoshi was born in Nagoya, and later fled from monastic life to take up a military career. He enlisted in the service of Oda Nobunaga, and from 1562 onwards adopted the name Hideyoshi. Nobunaga made him responsible for subjugating the W provinces, and he directed operations from Himeji (see entry under this name). When Nobunaga was assassinated in 1582, he killed the murderer of his former master and then reinforced his own total power by removing the Oda. Hideyoshi first settled in Osaka, and then had two palaces built in Kyoto. From here he led two expeditions against Korea in 1592 and 1596, and even had designs on China, Toyotomi died at Fushimi jo in 1598 and was one of the three great Japanese figures of the late 16th c., as he brought peace and unity to Japan after the turmoil of the preceding centuries.

FUSHIMI CASTLE. In 1593, on returning from his first Korean expedition, Hideyoshi had a mighty castle built in the S of Kyoto and left Juraku tai, in the town. The greatest artists of the period worked at Fushimi and completed what was probably the most luxurious castle ever to exist in Japan. Unfortunately it was abandoned after the death of its owner in 1598 and the Tokugawa who took control of it had it entirely demolished from 1623 onwards. The main components of it were reused in the construction of many temples and palaces in Kyoto. The site was subsequently damaged by the violent clashes which took place in 1868 between the Imperial troops and the supporters of the Shogun. Momoyama jo has now been rebuilt, and does give some idea of what the splendid Hideyoshi residence was like.

The present *donjon* (1964), which is strengthened with reinforced concrete and covered with wood, in the old style, stands in the middle of Momoyama Park. It houses several documents and mementoes, relating to Hideyoshi and his glorious past.

To the W of Momoyama Park is the mausoleum of the Emperor Kammu (736-805), the founder of Heiankyo.

To the S of Momoyama Park, the mausoleums of the Emperor Meiji (1852-1912) and his wife the Empress Shoken stand next to each other (½ml/1km E of Momoyama eki, JNR; 660yds/600m N of Momoyama Minamiguchi, Keihan ER).

To the SW of these monuments (330yds/300m E of Momoyama eki, JNR), note Nogi jinja, built in 1916 in memory of General Mogi Maresuke (1849-1912) who committed suicide, according to the *seppuku* rite, when the Emperor Meiji died. In the garden of the shrine is a building which Nogi Maresuke used as a headquarters during the siege of Port Arthur (Russo-Japanese War 1904-5). It contains some artifacts relating to this episode.

Near the Momoyama-Minamiguchi Keihan ER station, you can take the No 26 bus to get to Daigo ji. From Tanbabashi Keihan ER station you can go by private train to Chujojima station then to Rokujizo. The No 26 bus goes from one of these stations to what was the village of Yamashima gawa valley and is now part of Kyoto.

**DAIGO JI (general plan: off C4; 2½mls/4km NE of Momoyama jo; 4mls/7km SE of Kyoto eki, JNR; 2mls/3km NE of Rokujizo eki, Keihan ER; No 26 bus from Chujojima and Rokojizo eki, or No 39, 40 and 41 bus from Shijo Karasuma to Daigo; open from 09.00 to 16.00). This temple is divided into an upper temple and a lower temple (Kami and Shimo Daigo), and is one of the oldest foundations in Kyoto.

The Daigo ji, of the Shingon sect, was created in 874 by the priest Shobo or Rigen Daishi (832-909). The upper and lower temple continued to expand until the 13th c., when most of the buildings were destroyed by fire. Only the Shimo Daigo pagoda was left unscathed by the Onin Civil Wars (15th c.), and it was not until the time of Toyotomi Hideyoshi that a decision was taken to restore the Daigo ji in full and rebuild the Sambo in. Many of the new buildings came from a ruined temple on the Kii peninsula.

Shimo Daigo. Past the Nio mon, of the Kamakura period (13th to 14th c.), you will see the Kon do, which dates from the same period. Both were transported from the Kii peninsula in the 16th c. The Kon do houses a triad of Yakushi Nyorai (12th c.), with the statues of the celestial guardians.

To the S of the Kon do is a five-tier *pagoda (936–951) which is one of the oldest existing monuments in Kyoto. It contains some *paintings on wood which illustrate two mandara of the Shingon sect (Heian period; usually closed to the public).

To the W of the pagoda is the little Shinto shrine of Seiryugu, founded in 1097, and rebuilt in 1517.

To the NW of the Nio mon stands the *Sambo in (the entrance is to the NW), a secondary monastery founded in 1115 and rebuilt between 1598 and 1601, at the command of Toyotomi Hideyoshi.

The apartments were decorated by Hasegawa Tohaku (1539–1610) and Kano Sanraku (1559–1635). The Hon do has a statue of Miroku Bosatsu by Kaikei (12th to 13th c.). There is a very lovely *garden in the Momoyama style, and also a tea pavilion, Chinryu tei, and a dry garden, which is rather more modest. Near the entrance is an old cherry tree which is greatly admired when it flowers in spring.

To the SW of the Nio mon is the Reiho kan or treasury (open in April, May, October and November) which has numerous statues and Buddhist paintings of the Heian, Kamakura and Muromachi periods (8th to 16th c.), and a rich collection of *sutra* and calligraphy.

Kami Daigo. This part of the shrine is scattered over the wooded heights which you can get to SE of the Shimo Daigo, beyond the little river which flows behind the latter.

You will see another Seiryu Shinto shrine (1434) and the Yakushi do (1211) which has a statue of Yakushi Nyorai, of the early 10th c. Further on is the Kyo zo, hall of the *sutra* (1198), and near the summit are the Nyorin do (11th-c. statue of Kannon) and the Miei (or Kazan do), rebuilt in 1608.

➡ 1½ml (2km) S of the Daigo ji (taxi or No 26 bus to Ishida, 770yds/700m NW of the Hokai ji): Hino, where you can visit the Hokai ji. The Amida do here (1057) houses a *statue of Amida of the same period, attributed to the priest Jocho. There are traces of mural paintings. Hadaka Odori festival 14 January.

J Vicinity

☞ 1 **HIEIZAN** (14mls/22km NE on the toll road, Hiei Driveway; No 101 bus from Kyoto eki; Keifuku ER from Demachiyanagi eki to Yase-Yuen, the funicular railway and cablecar from there to Hiei zan). Near the Hiei zan cablecar terminus, the *Mount Hiei belvedere (2,782ft/848m alt.) has been set up. In the amusement park there is a rotating platform which provides a view over the area round Kyoto and Lake Biwa. You can take a bus from there to get to the **Enryaku ji** (1ml/1.5km) to the S and further down (direct access from Otsu, on the funicular railway from Sakamoto to Eizanchudo).

The Enryaku ji was founded in 788 by the priest Saicho, or Dengyo Daishi (767-822), who spread the Tendai sect, demanding perfection in the practice of Buddhism from everyone. It soon became one of the most important temples in the Kyoto area.

It became involved in conflict with temples of other sects, notably that of Koya san (see entry under Koya). Armed conflict sometimes took place in the capital and brought about the destruction of the temple on a number of occasions. Finally, Oda Nobunaga reduced the number of unruly monks at Mount Hiei in the 16th c., and destroyed the buildings again. They were reconstructed with the help of Toyotomi Hideyoshi, and extended by Tokugawa Iemitsu (17th c.). Priests as famous as Genku (1133-1212), Shinran (1174-1268) and Nichiren (1222-82) received their education at Mount Hiei.

The temple buildings are divided into three main groups, the E (To to), the W (Sai to) and the furthest N, Yokawa.

From the bus stop near the E temple or the Eizanchudo funicular railway stop, you can go NE to the Daiko do (reconstructed in 1963), near to which you can see Kaidan in to the W (1604) and the belfry to the E. From there you can go down towards the *Kompon chu do, the main building of the Enryaku ji, originally built by the priest Saicho, then rebuilt in 1642. It houses the triad of Yakushi Nyorai, accompanied by Gakko and Nikko Bosatsu. The original statue of Yakushi by Saicho cannot be seen.

Above the Kompon chu do is the Monju ro, which dates from the same period.

From the Daiko do, you can go up towards the SW to the Amida do (1937), from which you can head NW on foot to the W enclosure (bus link). You can continue on foot past the Sanno in and the Jodo in, which has Dengyo Daishi's tomb behind it.

You will have to approach Sai to through the buildings next to it, the Jogyo do and the Hokke do, which were reconstructed in 1559. Past these buildings stands the *Shaka do, the main W building, erected in the 13th c. and rebuilt on Mount Hiei, at the request of Toyotomi Hideyoshi. The statue of Sakyamuni by Saicho is not usually exhibited. You can see a copy of it surrounded by the four guardians of heaven. To the NW is the Sorin to pagoda, originally built in 820.

3mls (5km) N of the Sai to, by the *Oku Hiei Driveway (coach): Yokawa, which has the Nyoho do and Chu do buildings, founded in 848, but rebuilt in the 17th and 20th c. You can continue by coach from there to Ogoto Onsen and Katada, on the banks of the Biwa ko (Lake Biwa). You can take the coach back to Kyoto from here, via Otsu, or direct JNR train (you will need to inquire when this line will come into operation).

☞ 2 OHARA (11mls/18km NE; coach from Demachiyanagi or Yase-Yuen; Keifuku ER train between the two stations). Ohara stands in the Takano gawa valley and is a pleasant village, joined on to the vast Kyoto conglomeration. You can visit a number of temples from here.

↦ 550yds (500m) E: *Sanzen in, founded in the 9th century by the priest Saicho. The main hall has a ceiling shaped like the inverted hull of a ship. It was built in 985 by the priest Eshin (942-1017) and decorated by him. The 25 Bosatsu on the ceiling have been effaced, however, and the illustrations on the walls of the mandara, Kongo kai and Taizo kai, are barely visible; statues of Amida by Eshin. Garden of the Edo period. Behind this temple are the tombs of the Emperors Go Toba (1179-1239) and Juntoku (1197-1242).

↦ 880yds (800m) NW: Jakko in, a convent to which the Empress Kenreimon in, mother of the Emperor Antoku, retired in the 12th c.

☞ 3 KURAMA YAMA (9½mls/15km N; Keifuku ER train from Demachiyanagi to Kurama, then funicular railway). On the slopes of this hill (1,870ft/570m) stands the Kurama dera which was founded in 770 by the priest Kantei. The temple was rebuilt after 1945 and is famous for its bamboo carving festival (20 June) and for the great Kurama fire festival (22 October).

☞ 4 YAWATA (9mls/14km SW, part of the way on the N1; Keihan ER train from Keihan Sanjo to Yawatacho). Head S out of Kyoto.

5mls (8km): Otetsuji, to the l. in the Fushimi direction; take a road on the r. heading SW.

7mls (11km): Yodo; the Kyoto hippodrome. A castle belonging to the Hosekawa once stood on this site, and Toyotomi Hideyoshi presented it to his wife. The Inaba lived there (1723-1868).

◉ 9mls (14km): Yawata. It is worth visiting Jobon Rendai ji, which has the *Illustrated Sutra of the Causes and Effects of the Past and Present* (Einga kyo), an early example of an illuminated scroll or *emakimono*, a style which blossomed during the Heian and Kamakura periods in particular. This Chinese-influenced style of *painting dates from the 8th c.

A funicular railway goes up to Iwashimuzu Hachiman gu. This shrine on the slopes of Otoko yama (469ft/143m) was founded in 859; richly ornamented Hon do. Festival 15 September.

☞ 5 KAMEOKA, NARA, OSAKA, OTSU, UJI, see entries under these names; BIWA KO, see Otsu.

◀ Kyushu (Island of)

16,228sq. mls (42,030km²); pop: 12,965,00

Kyushu, the southern island, was the first door of Japan to be thrown open to the West in the 19th c., and also the first image which the West received of Japan. It attracts few tourists, however, which is a great pity. No doubt its distance in relation to the other traditional centres of interest, Tokyo and Kyoto, is the reason for this, although the development of air services and the Shinkansen railway's arrival in Hakata make it easily accessible.

Kyushu may not be able to compete with Kyoto and Nara in wealth of monuments, but it does have some very fine temples and some touching 'places of remembrance'. You will be particularly attracted by the majestic beauty of its very 'Mediterranean' landscapes, as well as by its atmosphere, which is much more open and relaxed than in the N of the archipelago.

Your trip to Kyushu

HOW TO GET THERE. There are numerous daily air links between Kyushu (main airports at Nagasaki, Fukuoka, Kumamoto, Kagoshima and Miyazaki) and the large Japanese towns served by the domestic companies (All Nippon Airways: ANA, and Toa Domestic Airlines: TDA), as well as by Japan Airlines to Fukuoka. It is equally easy to get to Kyushu by Shinkansen train (regular rail links from Tokyo, Kyoto and Osaka) to Hakata-Fukuoka. You can then be sure of a connection to any main destination.

There are also ferry services - if you have time to spare - which depart from Tokyo, Osaka and Kobe to Kokura (Kitakyushu) and Oita (Beppu).

TRANSPORT IN KYUSHU. The rail services are well organized and frequent, though rather slow, but the itineraries below are feasible. They are aided or complemented by bus services. They will be cheaper, of course, if you have a Japan Rail Pass.

Tourist Kyushu

WHAT TO SEE IN KYUSHU. Here we list only the main places of interest on the island, grouped according to category. If you wish to know more, refer to the description in the alphabetical section of this guide. Historic and artistic sites: Dazaifu shrine (near to Fukuoka), the town of Nagasaki (for its temples, shrines, churches and Christian mementoes, the Dejima quarter and the 'Dutch district', the Park of Peace...), the town of Kumamoto (the castle and especially the Suizenji garden), the little town of Usuki (worth seeing in its own right, and for the river-bank site of Usuki Sekibutsu), Usa shrine.

Natural sites: Hirado island, Aso Bay at Tsushima, Omura Bay, the

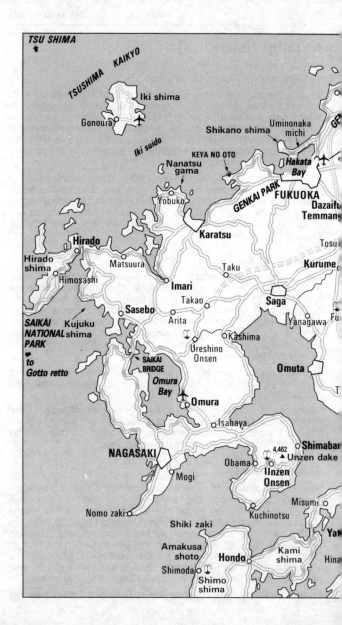

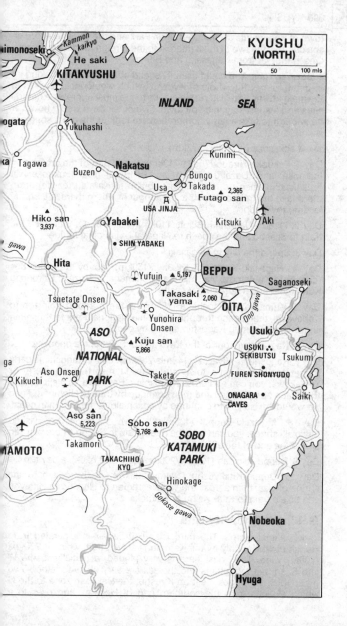

town of Kagoshima, Nichinan-Kaigan Park and the volcano Aso. The spa centres: the two of most interest to the foreign tourist are Unzen-Onsen (not far from Nagasaki) and Beppu.

SUGGESTED TOUR. You could usefully spend about ten days making an in-depth tour of the whole of Kyushu, which would include visits to the main artistic and historic sites, trips to the most impressive natural sites and a short stay in a spa town. Five or six days would however be enough to take a fairly comprehensive look at the great southern island.

10-DAY SCHEDULE (980mls/1,577km).

Day 1: Fukuoka-Hirado (70mls/113km); spend part of the morning in Fukuoka and Dazaifu (Nishitetsu Railroad from Fukuoka via Futsukaichi), then go from Hakata station to Karatsu (castle); from there take the train or coach to Hiradoguchi where there is a bridge leading to Hirado.

Day 2: Hirado-Nagasaki (68mls/110km); visit Hirado, then take the train to Sasebo and the coach to Nagasaki, via Saikai bridge.

Day 3: Spend the day in Nagasaki.

Day 4: Nagasaki-Kumamoto (93mls/150km); go by Kamenoi bus (coach) to Kumamoto via Unzen and Shimabara. Suizenji Garden in Kumamoto and a noteworthy castle.

Day 5: Kumamoto-Kagoshima (156mls/251km); a long train trip to Kobayashi, then coach through Kirishima National Park to Kirishima jingu. Then go on to Kagoshima, also by coach.

Day 6: Kagoshima; tour of the town and of Sakurajima opposite.

Day 7: Kagoshima-Miyazaki (148mls/238km). Leave Kagoshima early to get to Ibusuki (spa town and seaside resort). From here, or Yamakawa, you can go across Kagoshima Bay towards Nejime; take the coach up to Takasu and then continue by train to Nichinan. Then we would advise you to continue by coach along the Nichinan coast.

Day 8: Miyazaki-Beppu (136mls/219km). When you've visited Miyazaki shrine, you can take the direct train to Beppu where you can spend the end of the afternoon.

Day 9: Beppu-Aso san (124mls/200km there and back); a day trip.

Day 10: Beppu-Kitakyushu (184mls/296km); go by coach to the shrine of Usa, then across the Yabakei region to Hita. From Hita you can take a train to Kitakyushu or Fukuoka.

Getting to know Kyushu

GEOGRAPHICAL SIGHTS. The third island of Japan is separated from Honshu in the N only by the Kammon kaikyo strait, which is 770yds (700m) wide. The coast here is very jagged, especially to the W and S, so that mountains and the sea are very close together. Two great volcanic ranges meet on Kyushu: the Hakusan zone to the N which extends from the southern part of Honshu, and rises to a distinctive peak with the massif of Unzen (4,462ft/1,360m); and the Kirishima range to the S, which stretches beyond Kagoshima Bay with the Nansei archipelago; Sakurajima (3,668ft/1,118m) and Kirishima yama (5,577ft/1,700m) are the highest peaks. Where these two areas interlock, you will see the magnificent Mount Aso (5,223ft/1,592m), one of the most beautiful volcanoes in Japan. The island is situated on a much more southerly latitude than the rest of the country – between the 31st and 34th parallels of latitude N – and this is reflected in its climate and vegetation. Because of tropical currents which bathe the whole of the south coast, it is warm and rainy and suffers yearly typhoons. The population (798 people per sq. ml/308 per km^2) live principally on the plains and along the coasts, but also inhabit the lowest mountain slopes with their terraced rice paddies bordering the forestry zones. The N of the island, with its underground mineral wealth, has a large proportion of the population and the industry. Fukuoka and Kitakyushu are the two largest urban conglomerations.

KYUSHU IN HISTORY. Legend has it that Ninigi no Mikoto, sent by his grandmother Amaterasu, settled on the massif of Kirishima and it was from Kyushu that Jimmu, his descendant, departed to conquer Japan. However that may be, the island, facing China and Korea to the N, felt the continental influence very early, in this area where an important civilization grew up during the Yayoi period. It was also from the N that the Japanese government took control of the island, and that the Empress Jingu organized her expedition to Korea (3rd century). The island later became the base of operations for pirates who were sometimes in the pay of the Taira. Their main target was Chinese trade, and they prospered in the 16th c. in particular. During this period Toyotomi Hideyoshi profited from a dispute between the leading lords of the island and imposed his authority on it (1587).

He also led expeditions to Korea from Kyushu in 1592 and 1596. It was also in Kyushu that the Portuguese, who came up from the S, began to appear from the 16th c. onwards. They were welcomed by the Shimazu of Kagoshima (1549) and left the south of the island to settle in Hirado. They were gradually ousted, however, by the Spanish, the English and then the Dutch. With the arrival of the Europeans, numerous conversions to Christianity (Saint Francis Xavier) were made on Kyushu, but rivalry between the various trading posts and their subsequent disrepute in the eyes of Hideyoshi and the Tokugawa led to religious persecution. After the Shimabara revolt (1637) the Dutch were confined to Nagasaki, which remained the only Japanese port in contact with the West until the 19th c. Following the Imperial Restoration, the south of Kyushu remained hostile to the idea of opening the country to the outside world, which was one of the reasons behind the Satsuma revolt, led by Saigo Takamori in 1877. It should be remembered that the second atom bomb was exploded over Nagasaki on 9 August 1945.

M

■ Maebashi (Island of Honshu)

Tokyo, 81mls (130km) - Fukushima 198mls (318km) - Nagano, 80mls (128km) - Niigata, 151mls (243km) - Urawa, 62mls (100km) - Utsunomiya, 65mls (104km).

Shinkansen station at Takasaki (7mls/11km SW).

Principal town of Gumma ken (pop: 1,157,925) - pop: 265,169 - 351ft (107m) alt. - textile industries (silk).

Maebashi, on the upper Tone gawa valley, is an old feudal stronghold which has grown up, like the neighbouring towns of Isesaki and Kiryu, as a result of the silk industry.

The town used to be known as Umayabashi, and belonged to the family of this name who were vassals of the Uesugi. From the 16th c. onwards the Hojo, the Takeda and the Hojo again followed in succession. In 1590, Tokugawa Ieyasu ceded the town to Hiraiwa Chikayoshi who was replaced by the Sakai in 1601 and then the Matsudaira in 1749.

☞ **VICINITY**

*AKAGI SAN (15mls/24km N on the toll road; coach). This mountain rises up to the N of Maebashi and is made up of several peaks: Kurobi san (5,997ft/1,828m), Komaga take (5,541ft/1,689m) and Jizo take (5,492ft/1,674m). The road goes as far as the little lake of Omo which is surrounded by these various mountain peaks; the lake which stands at an alt. of 4,331ft (1,320m) is popular with skaters in winter and campers in summer. To the SE of the lake is Daido, with Akagi shrine, where you can go up some of the peaks, chair-lift and cable-car from Daido. Skiing in winter.

■ Masuda (Island of Honshu)

Tokyo, 616mls (991km) - Hiroshima, 73mls (118km) - Matsue, 104mls (168km) - Tottori, 187mls (301km) - Yamaguchi, 51mls (82km).

Shimane ken - pop: 50,071.

Although traditionally a producer of agricultural products and timber, the northern town of Chugoku on the Japan Sea has recently discovered an industrial outlet: wood derivatives and synthetic fibres.

It was in Taikian ji (1½ml/2km NE of the station; bus) that the painter Sesshu retired and died (1420-1507). He was one of the greatest artists of his age and raised ink painting (*sumi e*) to a greater art than ever before.

The temple gardens of Mampuku ji and Iko ji (1ml/2km E of the station) are attributed to him.

Takatsune yama (1½ml/2km W of the station; bus) is a hill at the foot of which stands Kakinomoto shrine dedicated to the poet Kakinomoto Hitomaro (8th c.). He is thought to have lived in a little house within the shrine enclosure, going back to the year 720; festival 15 April.

880yds (800m) N of the shrine: Fukiage pinwood, on the shore of the Japan Sea, where you can see the two pine trees known as Takatsu Renri no Matsu, which are joined to each other 13ft (4m) above ground.

VICINITY

HIKIMI (27mls/44km SE; coach). Upstream from here are the beautiful *gorges which the Hikimi gawa has hollowed into the Chugoku mountains. They are remarkable for the variously shaped rocks which you will find there. Monkeys roam freely in the wooded heights around here. The Hikimi gorges are part of the Nishi Chugoku Sanchi Regional Park (see vicinity of Hiroshima).

Matsue (Island of Honshu)*

Map of Places of Interest, pp. 68-71.

Tokyo, 510mls (820km) - Hiroshima, 119mls (191km) - Tottori, 83mls (133km) - Yamaguchi, 155mls (250km).

Principal town of Shimane ken (pop: 415,000) - pop: 132,000.

Although foreigners rarely come here, Matsue, the city of water, is certainly worth a visit. Situated where the Nakaumi lagoon meets Lake Shinji, this town has plenty of charming features for you. Its canals and old houses, its castle and temples cause a shadow of the past, unhurried by the present, to hover over Matsue.

SHIROYAMA PARK (1ml/1.6km NW of Matsue eki, JNR; bus). This is a wooded hill, at the top of which you will find Chidori jo or *Matsue Castle.

The domain of Matsue returned to the hands of Horio Yoshiharu (1543-1611) after the battle of Sekigahara and he had a castle built there. After the death of his grandson Tadaharu (1599-1633), the castle became the property of the Tokugawa, who entrusted it to the Kyogoku, then to the Matsudaira from 1638 onwards.

The three-storey *donjon* was erected in 1642. It is now one of the best preserved in Japan and is notable for its old wooden framework. On the inside there are some documents, models and photographs recalling the past of Matsue. There is a view from the summit over the town and surrounding area.

In Shiroyama Park is the Matsue Kyodo kan, a wooden edifice of the Meiji period which houses a museum of local interest (kitchen utensils, cloth, books and school exercise books, dolls, etc.).

To the N of Shiroyama Park, near to the moats which surround it, is the old daimyo's house where Lafcadio Hearn once lived; address; Okutani cho, 322.

LAFCADIO HEARN (1850-1904) was born on one of the Greek islands, of a Greek mother and an Irish father. After studying in France, he spent some time in the United States as a journalist and then settled as an English teacher in Japan. He lived in Matsue (from 1890 to 1891), settled in Kumamoto and finally taught at Waseda University in Tokyo where he ended his days. Lafcadio, who had married a Japanese woman, adopted the pseudonym Yakumo Koizumi. With twelve works such as *Glimpses of Unfamiliar Japan, Kokoro or Kaidan*, he was one of the first Western writers to interpret Japanese civilization.

Behind the Lafcadio Hearn museum, to the NE, is an attractive tea pavilion, Meimei-an, which dates from the Edo period and is built in the *Irimoya-zukuri* style. It can be extremely pleasant to taste the *o-cha* with cake made from red bean paste flavoured with green tea. The place is peaceful, especially in the morning, and you can enjoy a view of the castle from the terrace, not far from the tea pavilion.

To the S of Shiroyama Park is the Prefecture of Shimane. Near to this is the Regional Library (architect, Kikutake Kiyonori) which houses a museum with a collection of old musical instruments, including the Emperor Saga's lute (785-842).

½ml (1km) W of the Prefecture is Gessho ji, a peaceful park which has the funeral monuments of the Matsudaira, the former lords of Matsue.

VICINITY

1 YAEGAKI JINJA (2½mls/4km S; coach). This shrine, whose deity looks favourably on romantic trysts, is supposed to stand on the very site where Susano o no Mikoto slew the dragon which was devastating the province of Izumo (see entry under this name).

2 TAMATSUKURI ONSEN (6mls/9km SW on the N9; coach). Head SW out of Matsue on the N9 which runs along Lake Shinji, where the sunsets were much praised by Lafcadio Hearn. The little island of Yomega, which has a *torii*, lies offshore.

4mls (7km): Tamayu; go S up a small valley towards:

6mls (9km): Tamatsukuri Onsen, a famous resort in the Shimane region, in an attractive wooded setting.

3 KAGA (11mls/17km N; coach). It is one of the loveliest inlets of the Shimane peninsula, where you can take a boat to the sea cave of Kake do.

4 MIHONOSEKI (19mls/31km NE; coach). Head N out of Matsue. 6mls (10km): A toll road branches off on the l. (coach) and goes up to Makuragi san (1,496ft/456m). There is a view from here over the entire *Shimane peninsula which is highly indented on the coastal border of the Japan Sea, and forms part of the Daisen Oki National Park.

14mls (23km): A new bridge on the r. provides access to Sakaiminato.

19mls (31km): Mihonoseki is a beautiful little port tucked away at the bottom of an inlet in the Shimane peninsula. The nearby Miho shrine is dedicated to Kotoshironushino Mikoto, son of Okuninushi (see Izumo), and patron of sea travellers. Chairlift up to the Gohon matsui pine trees, view of Oki shoto and Dai sen.

→ 2mls (3km) E: Jizo zaki is the western tip of this peninsula.

5 DAIKON JIMA (8mls/13km E; boat to Yatsuka). This island in the middle of the Naka lagoon is volcanic in origin. On the SE coast is the 'wind hole': a tunnel made by lava, which descends to a depth of 305ft (93m) below the sea. There are plans to link this island to the N coast of the lagoon, by building levées.

6 IZUMO, OKI SHOTO, YONAGO, DAISEN OKI NATIONAL PARK, see entries under these names.

Matsumae (Island of Hokkaido)

Map of Places of Interest, p. 69.

Tokyo, 574mls (924km) - Hakodate, 58mls (94km) - Sapporo, 259mls (417km).

Hokkaido - fishing port.

Matsumae is the southernmost place on Hokkaido and the nearest to Honshu. As a result of this, it was one of the first towns on Hokkaido to attract Japanese settlers.

Matsumae Castle (¾ml/1.2km) W of the station, the donjon of which was rebuilt in 1961, stands in a park which is famous for its flowering cherry trees (early May).

Takeda Yoshihiro (1550-1618) had the castle of Fukuyama built in 1599 and took the name of Matsumae. His private kingdom became the foremost economic and political centre of Hokkaido. The castle was destroyed by fire in 1606 and reconstructed in 1854 by the Tokugawa who assumed direct control of it. In 1869 it was attacked by Admiral Enomoto Takeaki, the founder of the Republic of Hakodate (see entry under this name). In 1949 the donjon suffered another fire.

Matsumoto (Island of Honshu)*

Map of Places of Interest, p. 70.

Tokyo, 157mls (252km) - Gifu, 170mls (273km) - Kofu, 65mls (105km) - Maebashi, 94mls (152km) - Nagano, 45mls (72km) -Nagoya, 120mls (193km) - Niigata, 160mls (258km) - Shizuoka, 117mls (188km) - Toyama, 117mls (189km) - Urawa, 135mls (218km).

Nagano ken - pop: 162,931 - 1,942ft (592km) alt. - food and textile industries; silkworm breeding.

Matsumoto is situated at an important crossroads in the heart of Chubu and is one of the highest towns in Japan with the superb mountains known as the Japan Alps in the background. They make up the Yatsugatake Chushin kogen Regional Park to the E and the Chubu Sangaku National Park to the W. They also provide a setting of lofty peaks for Matsumoto Castle.

*MATSUMOTO CASTLE (½ml/1km NE of the station). The moats are fed by a little river nearby which has been harnessed for the purpose and they surround the superb keep, the last remaining vestige of a *hijo shiro* style of raised castle, which once stood there.

There was a fortress at Matsumoto before the 16th c., and Shimadate Sadanaga had it rebuilt in 1504. The castle became the residence of Ogasawara Nagatoki (1519-83), and was taken in 1549 by Takeda Shingen (1521-73), who entrusted it to the Masatoki. Then Oda Nobunaga (1534-82) and Uesugi Kagekatsu (1555-1623) followed in succession. Toyotomi Hideyoshi placed Ishikawa Yasumasa there in 1590 and finally the Toda held power between 1725 and 1868.

The present keep, erected in 1597 by the Ishikawa, is one of the oldest in Japan. It has six storeys and a smaller keep inside it housing a collection of historic souvenirs of Matsumoto.

VICINITY

1 NAKAYAMA (3mls/5km SE), a mound at the foot of Hachibuse yama (6,32ft/1,929m), where a prehistoric site of the Jomon period was discovered. On the slopes of Mount Hachibuse is the Gofuku ji (access by path), which has several Buddhist statues of the Heian and Kamakura periods.

2 UTSUKUSHIGAHARA ONSEN (3mls/5km E; coach). You can get here by a road which runs in front of the Matsumoto Museum of Popular Art (address: Satoyamabe; open daily from April to November, except the 3rd, 13th and 23rd of each month, from 10.00 to 16.00). This little museum was set up by Mr Maruyama in an old warehouse and takes a particular interest in wood crafts. From the spa town there is a view over all the neighbouring mountains.

3 *UTSUKUSHIGA HARA (17mls/28km E on the toll road; coach). Head N out of Matsumoto on the N254.

3mls (5km): Asama Onsen, springs renowned for their medicinal qualities. The Utsukushigahara toll road begins just beyond here.

7mls (12km): Misuzu ko, a small lake (skating in winter) on the W flank of the Utsukushi plateau.

17mls (28km): Utsukushiga hara; a mountainous plateau, very popular for walking and relaxation and a view over the Hida range of mountains. It is part of the Yatsugatake Chushin National Park.

4 CHUBU SANGAKU NATIONAL PARK, see entry under this name.

Matsuyama (Island of Shikoku)

Map of Shikoku (Inland Sea), pp. 536-7.

Tokyo, 547mls (880km) – Kochin, 79mls (127km) – Takamatsu, 101mls (162km) – Tokushima, 124mls (199km).

Principal town of Ehime ken - pop: 396,000 - private university.

Matsuyama, which lies in the W of Shikoku, is the most important urban development on this island. Mitsuhama is the main industrial suburb and a trading port. It is the old feudal town of the Matsudaira, and still attracts visitors to the thermal springs of Dogo. It is also possible to plan a trip to Ishizuchi san, the highest point on Shikoku Island, from Matsuyama.

The town of Matsuyama was placed in the hands of Kato Yoshiaki (1563-1631) by Tokugawa Ieyasu. In 1627 Gamo Tadatamo (1605-34) settled in Matsuyama, and gave Yoshiaki the domain of Aizu, to which his family was entitled. The Matsudaira, of the Hisamatsu branch of the family, succeeded Tadamoto and remained there until the Imperial Restoration.

The poet, Shiki Massaoka (1867-1902), was born in Matsuyama.

KATSU YAMA or SHIRO YAMA (1ml/1.5km E of Matsuyama eki, JNR; ½ml/1km N of Matsuyamashi eki, Iyo Railway; bus and tram from these two stations, cable-car and chair-lift). On this hill, in the town centre, stands *Matsuyama Castle.

The castle was originally built in 1601 by Kato Yoshiaki, and was rebuilt after fires in 1624 and 1784. The present keep, re-erected in 1854, has been set up as a museum (weapons, palanquins and other mementoes of the Matsudaira, the former lords of Matsuyama). The lower part of the castle gardens is occupied by a number of administrative buildings including the Hall of Congress, built by Tange Kenzo. You can enjoy an excellent view of the town and the vicinity from the castle, but the view provided by the chair-lift to the top of the hill is even more interesting.

DOGO (2½mls/4km NE of Matsuyama eki; bus and tram). On the E edge of Matsuyama, it is a centre for relaxation with the easy-going atmosphere typical of a spa town. Those who come to take the waters stroll around the hotels, bath houses and souvenir shops.

According to legend, the Dogo springs are some of the oldest known in Japan, since the divine Okuninushi himself frequented them. Since then, the springs have been visited by several emperors and eminent historical figures. The alkaline waters (108°F/42°C) are reputed to help the digestive and respiratory tracts and the nervous system. Festival 19 to 21 March.

Dogo Park, famous for its flowering cherry trees, stands on the former site of a castle built in 1335 by Doi Michihara and destroyed by Kato Yoshiaki who built Matsuyama Castle.

To pass Dogo without stopping to bathe in the waters is tantamount to a crime! How could anyone resist the pleasure of the *o-furo* in this three-storey wooden building which is the oldest public bath in the town? If you do take the time to relax here for a while, note that the establishment charges various rates, but the highest of these includes the cost of a massage followed by tea and cake, which you should try, wrapped in a splendid *yukata* (a cotton kimono, often decorated in indigo blue, worn in the evening.)

½ml (1km) E (bus): Ishite ji is an interesting little temple, built during the Kamakura period (between 1318 and 1333). The gate, surmounted by an upper storey, the belfry, the pagoda and the Goma do are the most noteworthy features.

2½mls (4km) NE (coach): Oku Dogo is a well equipped resort in a spot surrounded by wooded hills.

VICINITY

*ISHIZUCHI REGIONAL PARK (45mls/72km E on the N11 and a toll road; coach). Head SE out of Matsuyama on the N11.

12mls (20km): take a winding road on the r. which rises right up to a pass (3,542ft/1,074m alt.) then comes down again over the Omogo dam.

28mls (45km): Omogo, a little town, after which you can take a road on the l. which goes up the Niyoda gawa valley.

34mls (55km): exit from the Ishizuchi san toll road, and turn off to the N, for a little road leading to:

2mls (3km) N: *Omogo kei, one of those characteristic gorges where forests, rocks and running water combine to make a wild and delightful landscape. They are overlooked to the N by *Ishizuchi san (6,499ft/1,981m), the highest point on the island of Shikoku. The ascent of this mountain is possible from Omogo, but is usually undertaken – as a religious pilgrimage on 1 July – from Saijo, to the NE of the mountain. A road (coach 15mls/24km) and cable-car shorten this distance considerably. At the summit there is a little shrine and a view over the island of Shikoku, the Inland Sea and the Bungo Suido Strait, between Kyushu and Shikoku.

45mls (72km): end of the toll road. This road crosses part of Ishizuchi Regional Park which is overlooked by the mountain. It ends up below Kamega Mori (6,224ft/1,897m) which can be climbed.

■ Minakami (Island of Honshu)

Tokyo, 119mls (192km) – Maebashi, 39mls (62km) – Numata, 12mls (20km).

Gumma ken.

This large spa town stands at the heart of the Mikuni range, which has the great Joetsu routes to Niigata cutting through it to the N of

Minakami. It is very popular with winter-sports lovers and is also at the centre of a region of springs, which is part of the Joshin Etsu Kogen National Park.

VICINITY

1 DOAI (6½mls/11km N on the N291; JNR train; coach). Past the spa town of Yubiso, the railway line (JNR) enters a spiral tunnel which leads to Doai station. Past this station is the long Shimizu tunnel (6mls/9.7km), which pierces the Tanigawa dake (6,440ft/1,963m) and meets the slopes of the Uono gawa in the direction of Niigata. There is often a striking contrast in climate between these two regions, separated by the Mikuni range, and it is not unusual in spring to see snow on the sides of the Hokuriku, whilst the Kanto cherry trees are already in flower. From Doai, you can take the cable-car to the ski resort of Tenjin daira, on the slopes of the Tanigawa dake, at an alt. of 4,600 ft (1,400m).

2 UENOHARA KOGEN (12mls/19km NE). Head N on the N291.
2½mls (4km): Yubiso, where you can take a road on the r. up the upper Tone gawa valley, which is tranversed by the Fujiwara and Sudagi dams at this point.

12mls (19km): Uenohara kogen; this natural panoramic platform, to the N of the Hotoka yama (7,080ft/2,158m), is a good observation point for the Mikuni mountains.

3 YUZAWA, JOSHIN ETSU KOGEN NATIONAL PARK, see entries under these names.

Minami Arupusu (National Park; Island of Honshu)*

Maps of Natural Resources in Japan, pp. 64–7.

HOW TO GET THERE. The towns of Iida, Komagane, Ina, Okaya, Suwa, Chino, Nirasaki and Kofu surround the park. A road linking Kofu to Ina via the Yashajin pass and the Mibukawa gorge goes across the N part of the mountain range.

Situated to the S of the Chubu, this National Park of the South Japan Alps (*Arupusu* is a Japanese phonetic rendering of the English 'Alps'), an area of 88,457 acres (35,798ha), covers the Akaishi mountain range, which stretches between the regions of Nagano and Shizuoka, and spills over slightly into Yamanashi. The principal peaks are nearly 10,000ft (3,000m) in altitude. The most significant are Komaga take (9,731ft/2,966m), Hoo zan (9,321ft/2,841m), Shiomi dake (9,997ft/3,047m), Akaishi dake (10,236ft/3,120m), Arakawa dake (10,321ft/3,146m) and Shirane san (10,472ft/3,192m), the second highest mountain in Japan after Fuji san (12,388ft/3,776m). Granite cliffs, steep-sided gorges, waterfalls, dense forests and alpine flora are the main attractions of this mountain, which is quite difficult to reach. Only experienced climbers should attempt the ascent. There are several mountain hostels and huts providing refuge for travellers (*kokumin shukusuka,* see p. 37) scattered along the road mentioned above.

■ Mino Kamo (Island of Honshu)

Tokyo, 209mls (336km) – Fukui, 109mls (176km) – Gifu, 20mls (32km) – Kanazawa, 142mls (228km) – Nagano, 160mls (258km) – Nagoya, 25mls (41km) – Otsu, 70mls (113km) – Toyama, 134mls (216km) – Tsu, 74mls (119km).

Mino Ota JNR station.

Gifu ken – pop: 35,075.

As it stands at the meeting of the Hida and Kiso rivers, Mino Kamo is a good point of departure, either for going down the rapids of the Kiso gawa (the 'Japanese Rhine'), or to go up one of these two valleys which make up the Hida-Kisogawa Regional Park.

Tsubouchi Shoyo (1859–1935), novelist, dramatist, critic and translator of Shakespeare into Japanese, was born in Mino Kamo.

 *KISO GAWA RAPIDS. They rank with the most famous in Japan. Departures to the N of the Ota bridge, 1ml (1.5km) SE of Mino Ota JNR station (bus) or 550yds (500m) N of Imawatari Meitetsu ER station.

The whole trip (8mls/13km) as far as Inuyama (see entry under this name) takes about 1h. 15. There are departures every hour between 09.30 and 15.00. A reduced service operates from December to March. The most beautiful passes are those of Nishinoho and Fuji, where variously shaped rocks, including the 'lion', rise out of the water. The *Hida and Kiso gawa valleys are, in fact, much more interesting upstream from Mino Kamo and in the Gero or Ena directions (see under these names). The first of these rivers has the JNR railway running along it and the second has a bus service.

■ Mishima (Island of Honshu)

Tokyo, 69mls (111km) – Kofu, 65mls (105km) – Nagano, 158mls (255km) – Nagoya, 144mls (231km) – Shizuoka, 35mls (56km) – Yokohama, 53mls (86km).

Shizuoka ken – pop: 78,141 – industrial town.

Standing at the foot of Fuji sa, the Hakone mountains and the Izu peninsula, Mishima and its industrial development intrude darkly on the beautiful natural site of the National Park. You will probably find the juxtaposition of these two deplorable even though (or especially because) the powerful Kawasaki steelworks in Mishima possesses one of the largest blast furnaces in the world, with a volume of 116,540cu. ft ($3,300m^3$).

In the town you can visit the Mishima shrine, $\frac{1}{2}$ml (1km) SE of the station (JNR), and the Rakuju en, near the station of the same name

(Izu Hakone Railway), which once belonged to the Korean Royal Family.

VICINITY

1 HATAGE ONSEN (6mls/9km SE; coach), near the Kano valley, with an interesting view over Mount Fuji.

2 ATAMI, NUMAZU, FUJI HAKONE IZU NATIONAL PARKS, see entries under these names.

Mito (Island of Honshu)

Maps of Places of Interest, p. 70.

Tokyo, 71mls (114km) – Chiba, 77mls (124km) – Fukushima, 114mls (183km) – Urawa, 87 mls (140km) – Utsunomiya, 47mls (76km).

Principal town of Ibaraki ken (pop: 1,247,058) – pop: 215,566.

Mito, near the mouth of the Naka gawa to the S of the Joban, is an important road and rail junction. The Kairaku en in Mito is one of the most famous landscape gardens in Japan.

The town of Mito had already been the residence of Hitachi Daijo, then of Edo Michifusa in the 15th c., and in 1590 it passed into the hands of the powerful Satake, who were in control of the entire N of Kanto. But after the battle of Sekigahara, Tokugawa Ieyasu (1542–1616) placed his sons, Nobuyoshi, Yorinobu and finally Yorifusa (1603–61), over the province of Hitachi. Yorifusa was the founding father of the Mito branch of the Tokugawa, who had the right of succession to the title of Shogun. Tokugawa Mitsukuni (1628–1700) and Tokugawa Nariaki (1800–60) were the most outstanding members of this family. The son of Nariake, Tokugawa Yoshinobu or Keiki, was the last Shogun (1866–68).

Mito Park (330yds/300m NE of the station) is on the former site of Mito castle, which was almost entirely destroyed at the time of the Meiji Restoration (1868), then by air raids in 1945.

The park itself stretches out to the W in front of the Prefecture of Ibaraki. Behind this are two small shrines dedicated to Confucius and to the divine patroness of Kashima (see entry under this name).

'KAIRAKU EN or TOKIWA KOEN (1½ml/2km W of Mito station; bus; 220yds/200m NW of Kairaku en station). This garden was designed and completed in 1842. In the Kobun tei tea pavilion, which has been rebuilt, Noriaki used to entertain men of letters and he himself liked to write poems there. The park is famous for its plum trees (over a thousand in total), which flower between the end of February and mid-March.

To the E of the park is the shrine of Tokiwa, built in 1874 and dedicated to Tokugawa Mitsukuni and Tokugawa Nariaki, venerated here under the names of Giko and Rekko.

1ml (1.5km) N of Kairaku en and 1½mls (2.5km) NW of the station is

Yahata shrine, which came from Kuji and was rebuilt between 1596 and 1614 at the request of Satake Yoshinobu. The park has some fine trees, many of which are 100 years old.

550yds (500m) N of this shrine is Taninaka Chugan ji which has a very pleasant *landscape garden.

☞ **VICINITY**

1 OARAI (7mls/12km SE; coach), Mito's seaside resort, to the S of Cape Oarai. Apart from Oarai Isezaki jinja and Ganyu ji, you can visit the Meiji Museum dedicated to the Emperor Mutsuhito (1852–1912); a number of personal mementoes of the Emperor, his wife and the Imperial Family.

➺ 3mls (5km) SW of Oarai is the Hi lagoon, which covers an area of 3.6sq. mls (9.40km^2).

2 SUIGO-TSUKUBA REGIONAL PARK, see Tsuchiura.

◼ Miura (Island of Honshu)

Map of the Vicinity of Tokyo, p. 565.

Tokyo, 43mls (70km) – Kofu, 112mls (181km) – Shizuoka, 102mls (164km) – Yokohama, 29mls (46km).

Coaches from Yokosuka and Zushi to Misaki.

Kanagawa ken – pop: 45,532.

This town, on the southernmost tip of the Miura peninsula, is very pleasant for excursions near Tokyo, Yokohama and Kamakura. The fishing port of Misaki, the urban centre of Miura, is sheltered by the island of Joga, which is now linked by a bridge (1,880ft/575m long) to the peninsula.

*Joga shima (specializes in pottery), about 2mls (4km) in circumference, is surmounted by a lighthouse which throws its beam 18mls (29km). Above the cliffs on the S side of this island is the lighthouse museum which displays, notably, an 1893 sundial and the oldest mercury barometer in Japan, which was imported from England (1870).

➺ 3mls (5km) NW of Misaki is the lovely *Aburatsubo creek (coach; motor launch trips from Misaki harbour). The bay, which has been made into a harbour for pleasure boats, is bounded to the N by a garden of tropical plants, with a marine biology laboratory attached to the University of Tokyo.

4mls (7km) N of Misaki (coach; Keihin Kyuko ER train from Tokyo), the lovely beach of Shita stretches for about 6mls (10km).

■ Miyako shoto (Nansei shoto)

Map of Nansei shoto, pp. 430–1.

Tokyo, 1,213mls (1,952km) - Kagoshima, 606mls (975km) - Okinawa, 188mls (303km).

Okinawa.

To the SW of the island of Okinawa, between the east China Sea and the Pacific Ocean, this part of the Nansei archipelago comprises three main islands: Miyako, Irabu and Tarama.

MIKAYO SHIMA (*Swal* flights to Ishigaki and Okinawa; ferry services to Ishigaki, Okinwara and Tarama). The main island of this archipelago is triangular in shape and rather flat (358ft/109m at Noboru dake); sugar-cane production. Miyako is the only one of the Ryukyu islands not inhabited by the snake *habu*. The capital Hirara (pop: 29,721), to the W of the island, is a small port and a town full of light, reminiscent of the large, cheery villages of the Greek islands.

On the way out of Hiara on the Karimata road, the Poll Tax Stone recalls the difficult periods of the 17th and 18th c., when those islanders whose height exceeded that of the Stone paid heavy taxes to China or to the Japanese Satsuma clan. On this same road, which runs along the NE coast, is the lovely Sand Dune beach on Sunayama Bay.

→ 2½mls (4km) E of Hirara (taxi), you can visit the botanical garden of tropical and semi-tropical plants.

6mls (9km) S of Hirara, the road runs along the beautiful beach of Yonahamae where there are plans to build a huge tourist complex. Nearby at Hisamatsu is the monument built in 1966 to the memory of the five Japanese fishermen who spotted the Russian Baltic fleet heading N, at the time of the Russo-Japanese war. The Japanese fleet, thus warned in time, was able to position itself at Tsu shima and win its famous victory of that name in 1905. On the same road you will see the monument to philanthropy erected in 1878 by the Emperor Wilhelm I in homage to the people of Miyako who, during a typhoon, rescued the sailors from a German ship and then gave them another vessel in which to sail home.

In the S of the island, the high cliffs of Cape Mizaki look down on the reefs.

IRABU JIMA (5mls/8km NW of Miyako jima; boat from Hirara to Sarahama). This island is even lower than Miyako shima. It is barely separated from Shimoji (3mls/5km W of Sarahama), and you can walk across from one island to the other. As a result of the construction of the Air School Training Base on Shimoji, Japan Air Lines has managed to give a boost to the two islands, which were rapidly being drained of their population.

TARAMA JIMA (42mls/67km SW of Mikayo jima; boat to Miyako and Ishigaki): This island, which rises to a maximum height of 108ft (33m), only just emerges from the sea and is surrounded by a coral atoll.

■ Miyazaki (Island of Kyushu)

Railway map on inside front cover.

Tokyo, 924mls (1,487km) – Fukuoka, 217mls (349km) – Kagoshima, 79mls (127km) – Kumamoto, 123mls (198km) – Oita, 125mls (201km).

Principal town of Miyazaki ken – pop: 202,862 – national university.

Miyazaki, near the mouth of the Oyodo gawa, is a spacious town (parks and wide avenues), rebuilt after the war, which attracts a large proportion of the southern population of the island owing to its activity.

To the N of the Nichinan coastal park, the town and the region receive many summer holidaymakers.

Tachibana koen (½ml/1km S of the station) is a promenade lined with exotic trees, which stretches along the Oyodo gawa.

Ħ Miyazaki jingu (2mls/3km NW of Miyazaki eki; 660yds/600m W of Miyazaki jingu eki); this shrine, dedicated to the semi-legendary Emperor Jimmu (see Kashihara), stands in the middle of a superb park.

The Chokokan Museum, to the N of the park, is a modern edifice: ethnographical and archeological collections (Saito excavations, see entry under this name).

▲▲ HEIWADAI (1ml/1.5km NW of Miyazaki jingu; 3mls/5km NW of Miyazaki eki; bus). This is a huge wooded park, containing the unsightly Tower of Peace (121ft/37m high) built in 1940 by the Imperialist Japan of that period.

Reproductions of about 400 clay figurines (*haniwa*) have been amassed in this park.

These *haniwa*, placed around tombs, first of all took the form of simple annulated cylinders. From the 4th c. onwards they began to represent specific objects, animals and human beings. Their number and diversity provide valuable documentation on customs of dress, armour, weaponry, hairstyles, musical instruments, etc., used by people of this period (4th–7th c.). Some Japanese chronicles attribute the origins of these *haniwa* to Hajibe potters who came from Izumo at the request of the Emperor Suinin. He is believed to have introduced their use as a substitute for human sacrifices. This is actually only supposition, as no proof has yet emerged of funeral massacres being held during this period in Japan. It is more likely that these *haniwa* were thought to possess magic powers of protection.

☞ **VICINITY**

1 NICHINAN (34mls/55km S on the N220; JNR train; coach). The railway departs from the beautiful coast of the *Nichinan Regional Park about halfway along, but the road continues to run close to it.

10mls (16km): **Ao shima; this little 'blue island', about ¾ml (1.2km) in circumference, is completely covered by nearly 3,000 *biro* (betel palm trees). At low tide, an extraordinary rocky platform emerges around the island, striped with parallel rays which seem to have been combed into it by the sea. A little shrine stands at the centre on the Kyushu coast; pleasure garden and botanical park with greenhouses of tropical plants.

16mls (26km): Saboten, a cactus garden on the sea shore, where there are nearly a million cactus plants.

27mls (43km): Udo jinja, a small shrine built in the crevices of a cliff, hollowed out by the erosion of the sea.

34mls (55km): Nichinan, see entry under this name.

2 **NICHINAN, SAITO, KIRISHIMA YAKU NATIONAL PARK,** see entries under these names.

Miyazu (Island of Honshu)

Map of Natural Resources in Japan, pp. 64–7.

Tokyo, 349mls (561km) – Fukui 116mls (186km) – Kobe, 106mls (171km) – Kyoto, 76mls (122km) – Nara, 103mls (166km) – Osaka, 99mls (159km) – Otsu, 83mls (134km) – Tsu, 137mls (220km).

Kyoto fu – pop: 31,603.

Miyazu may well have remained unknown if the Japanese had not discovered a page of their mythological genesis nearby at Amano Hashidate. They made it one of the three high places (*san kei*) of the Nippon archipelago's coastal landscapes.

'**AMANO HASHIDATE** (Amanohashidate JNR station; 2mls/4km N of Miyazu station; bus). It is the long strip of pine-covered sand which blocks off the Aso lagoon to the E and stretches for more than 2mls (3km) between Ichinomiya and Monju. A swing-bridge, which lets boats go through from Miyazu to Ichinomiya, links it to the Monju shore.

This natural peninsula (110yds/100.58m wide) is often likened to the 'Heavenly Bridge' (Amanouki hashi) where Izanagi and Izanami settled when they drew the first islands of the Japanese archipelago out of the void (see Awaji shima).

Painters and poets have often been inspired by this legend and the Japanese attach great importance to this famous spot, which is indeed not without charm, although its development as a seaside resort, bringing thousands of bathers in summer, does detract a little from it.

At Monju, near the Aso lagoon, is Chion ji, most of whose buildings (Bonshu do, San mon, Taho to) date from the 16th and 18th c. A chair-lift, from Urashima to Otohime, goes up to the overlook and amusement park, where there is a lovely view over Amano Hashidate. You can walk along the Amano Hashidate strip of sand to Ichinomiya or take a boat trip. Near Kano shrine, a funicular railway or another chair-lift goes up to the *belvedere of Kasamatsu. The view from here is in the opposite direction. If you bend down and look between your legs at the 'celestial bridge', it really does seem to float between sea and sky: but then everything begins to float in that position ...

→ 2mls (3km) past Kasamatsu (coach), you can go to Nariai ji, one of the 33 temples of the western provinces.

→ ½ml (1km) SW of Ichinomiya, visit the Tango Folk Museum in Mizoshiri: historical and ethnographic artefacts relating to this former province. You can also see the site of a national temple, Kokubun ji, in this area.

■ Morioka (Island of Honshu)

Map of Tohoku, pp. 232–3.

Tokyo, 319mls (513km) - Akita, 73mls (117km) - Aomori, 130mls (210km) - Sendai, 114mls (184km).

Principal town of Iwate ken (pop: 800,321) - pop: 229,114 - 413ft (126m) alt. - horse fair in September and October - national and private universities.

Morioka, where Iwate san (6,696ft/2,041m) blocks the horizon to the NW, was once the capital of Nambu province and has now become one of Tohoku's busiest towns. The arrival, in 1982, of the Shinkansen railway, which is to be extended towards Aomori and Hokkaido, can only be a boost to the town.

Iwate koen (½ml/1km E of the station); this public park beside the Nakatsu gawa was laid out on the former site of the castle, of which a few ramparts still remain. Sakurayama shrine.

To the NW of this park, near the Law Courts, note the famous Ishiwari zakura, standing in a small garden; this cherry has its roots thrust into a block of granite.

Gohyaku en or Shimin kaikan (½ml/1km NE of Iwate koen), to the N of the Nakatsu gawa, is a landscape garden and also a botanical garden with medicinal plants, set up in the 17th c.

Josyu ji (450yds/400m W of the Gohyaku en), one of Morioka's many temples, possesses statues of Kublai Khan, Marco Polo and Erasmus, in addition to its Gohyaku Rakan (500 disciples of Buddha) sculpted between 1732 and 1736.

Takumatsu no ike (½ml/1km N of Kita Morioka eki; 1ml/1.5km N of Morioka eki; bus), a huge lake with attractive walks around its shores and skating in winter.

► **VICINITY**

1 AMIHARI ONSEN (22mls/35km NW, on the N46 and a toll road; coach). Head W out of Morioka on the N46.

6mls (10km): Turn off on the r. towards Takizawa.

➜ 2mls (3km) N: Takizawa where you can visit Sozen jinja: 15 June, festival of Chagu Chagu Umakko. The children and peasants of the neighbourhood bring their richly caparisoned horses to receive a blessing for a long life.

9mls (15km): Take the toll road on the r. to Iwate san.

➜ 1½ml (2km) S: Small spa town of Tsunagi.

22mls (35km): Amihari Onsen, spa and winter sports town (at an alt. of 2,461ft/750m), on the slopes of Iwate san (6,696ft/2,041m), which can be climbed. The ski resort is equipped with several mechanical ski-lifts. Season: beginning of December to mid-May.

*Iwate san, an extinct volcano which is very distinctive and easy to spot, is the highest point in Tohoku (northern Japan). It is nicknamed the Fuji of Nambu. It takes 4h. 30 mins to climb this mountain from Amihari.

2 RIKUCHU KAIGAN AND TOWADA HACHIMANTAI NATIONAL PARKS, see entries under these names; TAZAWA KO, see Omagari.

Muroran (Island of Hokkaido)

Railway map on inside front cover.

Tokyo, 638mls (1,026km) - Asahikawa, 157mls (252km) - Hakodate, 122mls (196km) - Otaru, 122mls (197km) - Sapporo, 174mls (158km) - Tomakomai, 43mls (69km).

Hokkaido - pop: 150,199 - industrial town - national university.

Situated at the E end of Uchiura Bay, Muroran occupies a favoured position in a natural harbour, enclosed to the S by the Cape of Etomo. The port thus formed has the second largest surface area after that of Yokohama. Muroran preceded Tomakomai as the first industrialized town of Hokkaido. It was bombed in 1945. Nowadays, iron and steel works (set up from 1909 onwards), chemical and petrochemical industries, cement works, shipyards, etc., have taken up all available land. The port exports coal, wood and sulphur, and imports nearly all its raw materials (iron ore is mined locally). It is also an active fishing port.

Mount Sokuryo (½ml/1km W of Muroran eki, JNR bus); on this hill (about 656ft/200m high) is a *belvedere, which overlooks the Etomo peninsula, with its cliffs forming a sheer drop 330ft (100m) into the sea. To the E is the outline of Charatsunai beach with its marine algae laboratory and Cape Chikiu, lined with reddish-coloured cliffs. To the N you can make out Yotei zan on the horizon (p. 539).

⌦ VICINITY

1 ETOMO MISAKI (2½mls/4km W; coach): on the tip of the peninsula of this name. The nearby aquarium (open from April to November) houses nearby 250 species of sea and freshwater fish.

2 TOMAKOMAI, SHIKOTSU TOYA NATIONAL PARK, see entries under these names.

Muroto (Island of Shikoku)

Map of Shikoku (Inland Sea), pp. 536-7.

Tokyo, 592mls (953km) - Kochi, 50mls (80km) - Matsuyama, 129mls (207km) - Takamatsu, 145mls (234km) - Tokushima, 88mls (141km).

Kochi ken - pop: 27,445 - fishing port.

The port of Muroto, which opens onto Tosa Bay, is only a short distance from Muroto misaki, which juts out into the Pacific Ocean to the S. The coastal park of Muroto Anan is spread out on either side of this cape.

☞ **VICINITY**

KANNOURA (29mls/46km NE on the N55; coach).

Head S out of Muroto.

3½mls (6km): *Muroto misaki plunges into the Pacific Ocean, shattering into a multitude of rocks. Near the lighthouse is the Hotsumisaki ji founded in 807 by the priest Kobo Daishi, which has several ancient Buddhist statues.

↦ 2½mls (4km) N (coach): *Muroto misaki summer-house, at 846ft (258m) altitude with a view over the whole of the cape and the seas around it.

Past Muroto misaki, the coast road clings to the cliffs along the edge of the *coastal park of Muroto Anan.

16mls (25km): Sakihama, where you can visit Kongocho ji. This temple, which has recently been rebuilt, accommodated the monk Kukai (Kobo Daishi) when he was leaving for China in 804. The treasury has several paintings and sculptures of the Heian and Kamakura periods. Festival 21 March.

29mls (46km): Kannoura (boat to Kochi and Osaka) is a little port at the bottom of an inlet which opens onto the Pacific, from here you can continue on towards Anan (see entry under this name).

Mutsu (Island of Honshu)

Map of Tohoku, pp. 232-3.

Tokyo, 459mls (738km) - Akita, 185mls (297km) - Aomori, 63mls (101km) - Morioka, 140mls (225km).

Aomori ken - pop: 47,610.

To the N of Mutsu Bay, where the Shimokita peninsula narrows considerably, the harbour town of Mutsu has grown up. It is in fact a combination of the former towns of Ominato, Shimokia and Tanabu.

☞ **VICINITY**

1 OSORE ZAN (6mls/10km W; coach). Osore or Usori zan, the Mount Terrible, is an old volcano, the crater of which is now filled by a lake

(4mls/6km in circumference). Entsu ji, to the N of this lake, was founded by the priest Ennin (Jikaku Daishi, 794-864). When the temples' festivals take place at the end of July, people come to communicate with the dead through the medium of seers who are well known in the area.

2 OMA (34mls/55km N on the N279; coach; JNR train to Ohata). Head N out of Mutsu to get to the Pacific coast.

9mls (15km): Ohata, a small fishing port to the N of the Shimokita peninsula, which opens onto the Pacific opposite Hokkaido.

6mls (10km) W (coach): Yagen Onsen, a small spa town tucked away in a valley of maples, at the foot of Asahina dake 2,867ft (874m).

34mls (55km): Oma (boats to Hakodate and Muroran), 1ml (2km) S Of Oma zaki and Benten jima, which mark the N tip of Honshu.

20mls (32km) S (coach in summer via Sai; ferry service along the W coast of Shimokita hanto to Wakinosawa): *Hatokega ura is a section of coastal cliff, spectacularly eroded by encroachments of the sea. This rocky sea front, Osore zan and Yagen Onsen all belong to the *Shimokita Hanto Regional Park.

■ Myoko Kogen (Island of Honshu)

Map of Natural Resources, pp. 64-7.

Tokyo, 173mls (278km) - Arai, 11mls (18km) - Niigata, 101 (162km).

Niigata ken.

Immediately to the N of Nagano are Mount Hiuchu (8,077ft/2,462m) and Mount Myoko (8,025ft/2,446m) only 12mls (20km) from the Sea of Japan, Myogo Kogen is a winter sports centre which can also offer a number of thermal springs and is part of the Joshin Etsu Kogen National Park (see entry under this name).

Akakura (3½mls/6km NW of Taguchi station; coach). At an altitude of 2,460ft (750m), it is the central resort around which the others, Ikenotaira, Seki, Tsubame, etc., revolve. They too have thermal springs and have been equipped as winter sports resorts. From the spa town of Akakura, the view stretches to the N over the Ara gawa basin as far as Naoetsu and the Sea of Japan.

Although Myoko san (8,025ft/2,446m) is difficult to climb, the ascent can be undertaken from Akakura and takes about six hours. Two routes through the valleys of Kita Jigoku or Minami Jigoku meet up 1ml (2km) below the summit. The view from the top sometimes extends as far as the island of Sado.

N

■ Nagahama (Island of Honshu)

Tokyo, 258mls (415km) – Fukui, 62mls (100km) – Gifu, 35mls (56km) – Kyoto, 47mls (75km) – Otsu, 39mls (63km).

Shiga ken – pop: 51,027 – 289ft (88m) alt. – industrial town.

This old feudal town on the shores of Lake Biwa has now become industrialized and is notable for processing polyethylene derivates.

In 1510 Uesaka Yasusada built Imahama Castle which Nobunaga ceded to Toyotomi Hideyoshi in 1573. He rebuilt it and bestowed the new name of Nagaham upon it. He made it his first operations base and began his rise to political power. The Tokugawa gave the castle to the Naito who left it after 1628.

 A public park to the E of the station occupies the former site of Hideyoshi Castle. Nearby is Daitsu ji (or Nagahama Betsu in). Some of the structural elements used in building this came from the Fushimi residence in Kyoto. The landscape garden of this temple was inspired by those of the Momoyama period (16th c.).

☞ **VICINITY**

1 SHIZUGA TAKE (12mls/19km NW; coach; JNR train to Kinomoto), is one of the eight famous sites of Lake Biwa (see Otsu), near to which Toyotomi Hideyoshi won an important victory over the armies of Shibata Katsuie in 1583. A cable-car goes up to the summit (1,388ft/423m), where there is a view over Lake Yogo to the N, Biwa ko to the SW and Ibuki yama to the SE.

2 ˙CHIKUBU JIMA (7mls/12km NW; boat). This island lies in the middle of the northern half of Lake Biwa. It is wooded with bamboo and Japanese cedar, and you can visit: Hogan ji, founded in the 8th c. by the priest Gyoki; and the little shrine of Tsukubusuma, rebuilt at the beginning of the 17th c. with parts of Fushimi Castle. This shrine houses several paintings by Kano Eitoku (1543–90).

3 HIKONE, see entry under this name; **BIWA KO**, see Otsu; **IBUKI YAMA**, see Ogaki.

N Nagano (Island of Honshu)*

Map of Places of Interest, p. 70.

Tokyo, 163mls (263km) - Gifu, 214mls (345km) - Kofu, 93mls (150km) - Maebashi, 80mls (128km) - Nagoya, 165mls (265km) - Niigata, 116mls (186km) - Shizuoka, 145mls (233km) - Toyama, 162mls (261km) - Urawa, 128mls (206km).

Principal town of Nagano ken - pop: 285,355 - 1,188ft (362m) alt. - textile and food industries.

Nagano, the main town of the inner Chikuma gawa basin (Shinano gawa), grew up around the great temple of Zenko ji, and has become the capital of the former province of Shinano. It still draws crowds of pilgrims to visit the shrine, whose name the town once bore.

*ZENKO JI (1ml/1.8km N of Nagano eki, JNR; bus; 660yds/600m W of Zenkojishita eki, Nagano ER). A long avenue runs from near the station right across the town centre (from N to S) and up a gentle hill towards the temple, one of the most revered in Japan.

FIRST BUDDHIST STATUES. The temple is devoted to Amida Nyorai, Kannon and Seishi, and the gilded bronze statues of them were probably a gift from the sovereign of the Korean kingdom of Paektche to the Japanese Emperor Kimmei (510-71). The latter had a temple built for them, but following an epidemic, Buddhism, which was already unpopular, was censured even further and the statues were thrown into a canal in Naiwa (now Osaka). Honda Yoshimitsu or Zenko (another version of the name) recovered the statues and brought them back to his native village, where he had an oratory built for them in 602. Some years later in 670 Zenko ji was founded. The statues were restored to the temple in 1598, and most of the buildings were re-erected from the 17th c. onwards. Festivals on 14 March and 31 July.

Before the first entrance gate, Nio mon, you can see on the I. (W) the monastery of Dai Hongan, one of the foremost Buddhist monasteries in Japan.

To the N of the Nio mon (19th c. statues), you will go past the pathway of the 'temple merchants' and through the beautiful San mon gate, built in 1750. To the W of this gate stands the Dai Kanshin which is the residence of the priest of Zenko ji, and is bordered by a moat.

The vast *Hon do, built in 1707, is the second largest wooden building in Japan, after the Todai ji in Nara. It houses some venerable statues, which are kept inside a 14th-c. reliquary. Note also the elegant Kei zo (1759) to the W of the Hon do.

The Joyama public park stretches to the NE of the temple grounds.

880yds (800m) N of Zenko ji is the Nihonchiryo den, built in 1970 to the memory of war victims.

Behind this building you can take the cable-car up to the Jitsuke belvedere, which provides a view over Zenko ji and the town of Nagano.

☞ **VICINITY**

1 MATSUSHIRO (6mls/10km S; coach; Nagano ER train via Suzaka). Head S out of Nagano on the N 18.

1½mls (2km): On the l. take the Matsushiro road which leads S.

2mls (4km): At Kawanaka jima, near the junction of the Sai and the Chikuma gawa, Takeda Shingen (1521-72) and Uesugi Kenshin (1530-78), the two great military figures of their day, confronted each other on several occasions (between 1553 and 1563). There is a monument dedicated to them.

6mls (10km): Matsushiro, a small spa town where you can see the ruins of Kaizu jo, rebuilt in 1537 by Takeda Shingen and given to Mori Nagakazu by Oda Nobunaga. The Tokugawa entrusted it to the Saneda from 1662 onwards. The nationalist poet Sakuma Shozan (1811-64) originally came from Matsushiro.

2 SHINANO (16mls/25km N; coach; JNR train to Kashiwabara station). Head N out of Nagano past Zenko ji.

16mls (25km): Kashiwabara is the centre of the Shinano area, where you can visit the house of the poet Kobayashi Issa (1763-1827), author of a number of *haiku* (see p. 92). Kurohime yama towers up to the NW (6,735ft/2,053m).

➡ 2½mls (4km) NE (coach): Nojiri ko, situated at an altitude of 2,146ft (654m), at the foot of Mounts Myoko and Kurohime. This lake attracts large numbers of visitors for fishing, camping, skating and boating. Motor launches on the lake in summer.

3 IIYAMA, MATSUMOTO, MYOKO KOGEN, CHUBU SANGAKU AND JOSHIN ETSU KOGEN NATIONAL PARKS, see entries under these names.

Nagasaki (Island of Kyushu)**

Map of Kyushu (North), pp. 388-9; street plan, p. 414.

Tokyo, 810mls (1,303km) - Fukuoka, 96mls (154km) - Saga, 68mls (110km).

Principal town of Nagasaki ken (pop: 927,394) - pop: 442,000 - heavy industries, fishing port - national, regional and private universities – archbishopric.

Tucked away at the end of a narrow fiord-like inlet, surrounded by greenery and fed by the Urakami gawa, Nagasaki gives the impression of being built to live alongside the sea and to live off it. It was, in fact, through distant outposts such as this one that Japan remained in contact for many years with the outside world. As the ultimate and unique meeting point between widely different world philosophies, Nagasaki was able to create controversial and often contrasting images out of the creative conflicts caused by its unique position. These very conflicts made the town into one of the most pleasant in Japan; a town where, in some respects, the Orient reflects our own image back to us, reviewed and corrected.

BEFORE THE EUROPEANS. At the end of the 12th c. this little fishing port, known as Fukaenoura or Tamanoura, was entrusted by Minamoto Yoritomo to Nagasaki Kotaro who gave it its present name. The latter's descendants remained there until the 16th c. when Omura Sumitada, the new ruling power in the locality, decided in 1568 to open the port of Nagasaki to foreign trading posts.

CHRISTIANITY AND PERSECUTION. The Portuguese, the Spanish, the Dutch and the Chinese gave the town its true economic impetus. The Japanese traded with China, Korea, India, Southeast Asia, the Philippines and the South Pacific. In 1587 Toyotomi Hideyoshi made Nagasaki his base of operations for subjugating the island of Kyushu. The Europeans introduced Christianity and the Jesuits made numerous conversions. They had too much success, however, and incurred the hostility of the Japanese authorities. The situation deteriorated and led to persecutions. In 1597 26 Christians were crucified on the orders of Hideyoshi. Subsequently throughout the 17th c. Spanish, Italian and Portuguese priests were burned, crucified, buried alive or thrown into wells. A few converts continued to practise their faith in secret and concealed a church which was intellectual, independent and out of step with the development of the Roman church. It did not re-emerge until the Oura Church was founded at the end of the 19th c.

DEJIMA: 'A DOOR LEFT AJAR ONTO THE OUTSIDE WORLD' (J. Pezeu-Massabuau). Dutch traders of Protestant faith saw the situation gradually developing in their favour. Like the Portuguese before them, who were confined to Dejima (1639) following the revolt at Shimabara, the Dutch were restricted to this island (1641). They remained the only Europeans to possess an official trading post in Japan. The town, placed under the direct authority of a governor sent from Edo (Tokyo), remained in contact with the outside world through this medium alone. Japan, retiring within itself, was cut off from the rest of the world, except for the port of Nagasaki, through which occasional ideas from the outside would slowly filter with difficulty. A certain relaxation of this situation was visible, however, from the 18th c. onwards. The Shogun encouraged the study of Western culture and in 1745 the first Dutch-Japanese dictionary appeared. Several scholars went to Nagasaki and, along with official interpreters, they set about studying this new civilization.

IRREVERSIBLE EVOLUTION. From the end of the 18th c. foreign ships began to reappear, with varying degrees of success, in Nagasaki harbour, sometimes flying a Dutch flag, as the Americans did in 1797. The French showed up in 1846 with the vessels *Cléopâtre*, *Sabine* and *Victorieuse* but failed to pursue negotiations. It took another ten

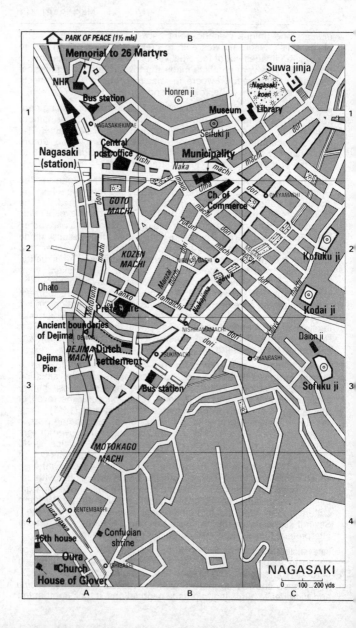

PARK OF PEACE (1½ mls)

Memorial to 26 Martyrs

NHK

Bus station

Honren ji

Suwa jinja

Nagasaki koen

Museum

Library

NAGASAKIEKIMAE

Seifuku ji

Nagasaki (station)

Central post office

Nishi

Naka

machi

machi

Municipality

Imauo

Uma

Ch. of Commerce

dori

OKEYAMACHI

GOTO MACHI

Fukuro

machi

machi

KOZEN MACHI

Manzai

machi

dori

MEGANE BASHI

gawa

dori

Kofuku ji

NIGIWAI BASHI

Hamaichi

Nakajima

dori

Kodai ji

Ohato

Motofuna

Kanko

Prefecture

Daion ji

Ancient boundaries of Dejima

DEJIMA

Dutch settlement

DEJIMA MACHI

NISHIHAMAMACHI

dori

gawa

Dejima Pier

SUKIMACHI

SHIANBASHI

Sofuku ji

Bus station

MOTOKAGO MACHI

BENTEMBASHI

Oura gawa

Confucian shrine

16th house

SHIRASHI

Oura Church

House of Glover

NAGASAKI

0   100   200 yds

years and the Treaty of Kanagawa before Nagasaki and other ports opened to the West and industrialization took hold of the town. By 1861 the ship-repair yards had been set up, and were taken in hand in 1887 by the Mitsubishi naval shipyards. The Yamate hills were soon covered with Western-style homes, and a new Catholic community was established. Economic development continued until 9 August 1945, when the second atom bomb (known as 'Fat Boy') was exploded over the town and took an official toll of 23,753 victims. Nowadays, the town has redoubled its former activity, but has preserved those historic areas which gave it its particular charm.

FAMOUS MEN BORN IN NAGASAKI: The Jesuit and martyr Francisco Marquez (1611-43); the painter Morio Sosen (1747-1821); Ueno Hikoma (1838-1904), who brought photography to Japan; the sculptor Kitamura Seibo (born in 1884).

THE PORT AND INDUSTRIES. Industrial activity in Nagasaki is dominated by the Mitsubishi shipyards, equipped to build giant oil tankers and cargo ships of over 100,000 t. The Koyagi dock, the largest in the world, is 3,250ft (990m) long and 330ft (100m) deep. Railway materials, printworks, pharmaceutical products and photographic workshops complete the list of industries. The port imports raw materials (oil, copper and nickel), and also electrical appliances, and barley. It exports coal, fertilizers, machine tools, glass and ceramics, food products and Satsuma oranges. In addition to this it is the foremost fishing port on the island of Kyushu, with a production of 275,000 t in 1981.

NB: Several bus and tram services run across the town of Nagasaki, linking the main centres of interest which are at some distance apart. It is worth knowing that there is a town transport ticket valid for one day at a very reasonable price (it can be brought at the Tourist Office - JNTO - at Nagasaki station).

NISHI ZAKA (plan: A1; 330yds/300m N of Nagasaki eki, JNR; tram stops: Nagasaki Ekimae or Mifune machi). Immediately behind Radio House (NHK), is a park laid out in 1949 to the memory of the 26 martyrs of Nagasaki. The monument museum and commemorative chapel were built in 1962. Pilgrimage 5 February.

THE FIRST JAPANESE MARTYRS. The first Jesuits who settled in Nagasaki brought about several conversions to Catholicism but were denounced to Toyotomi Hideyoshi as the precursors of a Spanish plot to conquer Japan. Hideyoshi was not slow to react. Six Western priests and twenty Japanese converts were crucified on this hill on 5 February 1597. They included Pedro Bautista (1545-97), the Spanish Ambassador to Japan, and Luis Ibaraki, at twelve years old the youngest of them all. Several days later miracles occurred and the martyrs were canonized in 1862. These holy places of Japanese Christianity were visited by Pope John Paul II in February 1981.

The monument dedicated to the Nagasaki saints is a large bronze cross with the 26 martyrs sculpted in relief on it by A. Funakoshi. Behind this is the museum (arch. Imai) which is covered with vast coloured mosaics depicting Faith, Hope and Charity. It retraces the martyrdom of the Jesuits and the history of the Christian religion in Japan: relics of martyrs, paintings and religious sculpture, a letter from Saint Francis Xavier to Juan III of Portugal. Note the statue of Saint Paul Miki on the cross by Masahiro Sawada. Saint Philip's Church, by the architect Imai Kenji, symbolizes with its two towers the union of God and man.

NAGASAKI KOEN (plan: C1; 990yds/900m E of Nagasaki eki; bus). It was once connected with the Suwa shrine. In this park, which is now public, note monuments erected to the memory of foreign intellectuals who lived in Nagasaki and introduced European science and technology to Japan: The Swede, Carl Peter Thunberg (1743–1822), the director of the Dutch trading post at Dejima, the Germans Engelbert Kaempfer (1651–1716) and Franz von Siebold (1796–1886). Kaempfer published *A Natural, Civil and Ecclesiastical History of the Japanese Empire*, and Siebold, a doctor and surgeon, is the author of the book, *Nippon*.

A banyan tree (*Ficus indica*) was planted in this park in 1879 by the American President Ulysses S. Grant. In the SW corner of the park is the Regional Library, which has records of the history of the town and its port. Immediately next to this museum you will find the Prefectural Art Museum, where annual exhibitions are organized.

'SUWA JINJA (plan: C1; NE of Nagasaki koen; ¾ml/1.2km E of Nagasaki eki; Suwajinjamae tram stop). It is preceded by a long flight of steps ornamented by *torii*, the first of which is probably the highest in Japan. This shrine, which was brought here in 1550, is thought to have come from the homonyous Suwa shrines (see entry under this name). It is especially famous for the Okunchi festival (7–9 October), in which, since the 17th c., all the districts of Nagasaki have taken it in turn to perform their folk dances.

From Suwa jinja you can go S to Nikajima gawa, spanned by several stone bridges including the popular Megane bashi, bridge of spectacles. It was built in 1634 by a Chinese priest from Kofuku ji.

It can be very pleasant to walk through the Kojiya, Furukawa and Kajiya districts to the E of the Nakajima gawa. It is one of the most attractive parts of Nagasaki and evokes the past. Potters and antique dealers have set up here, and the lower slopes of Kazagashira yama have several temples which are worth visiting.

'KOFUKU JI (plan: C2; 770yds/700m S of Suwa jinja; 1ml/1.5km SE of Nagasaki eki; 440yds/400m SE of Okeya machi tram stop). Founded in 1623, this was the temple of the Nankin Chinese. One of its priests, Itsune (1601–68), brought the art of Chinese painting to Nagasaki. Note the entrance gate, San mon, the Hon do (rebuilt in 1883) and the elegant belfry, Shokoro. Most of the buildings were restored after 1945 in the original Chinese style. The highly curved roofs are characteristic.

KODAI JI (plan: C2; 440yds/400m S of Kofuku ji; 1ml/1.5km SE of

Nagasaki eki; 440yds/400m E of Nigiwai bashi tram stop). In this third temple to the S of Kofuku ji there is a statue of Buddha 23ft (7m) high. It is also the burial place of Takashima Shuhan (1798-1866), who introduced Western logic to Japan, and of Ueno Hikoma (1838-1904), who set up the first Japanese photographic studio in Nagasaki.

As an interesting historical anecdote, note that the first photograph developed here caused the death of its subject, a *samurai* who committed *seppuku* at the sight of his own portrait.

'SOFUKU JI (plan: C3; 550yds/500m S of Kodai ji, 1ml/1.6km SE of Nagasaki eki; Shian bashi tram stop). This temple which is reached by skirting Daion ji to the W and continuing beyond Daiko ji, was also built by the Nagasaki Chinese community in 1629. The original entrance gate (Ryugu mon) was rebuilt in 1849.

A huge bronze cauldron used during the 1682 famine is kept in this temple. It is worth noting the elegent set of roofs of which you get an overall view by climbing a few steps behind this temple. Most of the buildings date from the 17th and 18th c.

DEJIMA or **DE SHIMA** (plan: A3; ½ml (1km) W of Sofuku ji; ½ml (1km) S of Nagasaki eki; Dejima or Tsukimachi tram stops). There remains only one real memento of the Dutch settlement which once occupied the land at the mouth of the Nakajima gawa. In 1958 some old Dutch warehouses were restored and are now incorporated into a museum which is bordered by a little garden.

CONFUCIAN SHRINE (plan: A4; ½ml/1km S of Dejima; 1ml/2km S of Nagasaki eki; Ishibashi tram stop). This shrine to the N of the Oura gawa was founded in 1893 in honour of Confucius by the Chinese traders of Nagasaki, and was completely rebuilt in 1967. As it is brilliantly coloured and ornamented it looks strange in Japan, but would be quite normal in Southern China.

The Tojin kan, attached to this shrine, is an exhibition centre for Chinese art. Chinese national dances are sometimes performed here.

Behind this shrine is Higashi Yamate, where you can see some of the former residences of the first Westerners to live in Nagasaki, outside the confines of Dejima.

'MINAMI YAMATE OR OURA (plan: A4; 440yds/400km S of the Confucian shrine; 1½mls/2km S of Nagasaki eki; Bentembashi tram stop). This quarter, which clings to the eastern hills which rise up to the S of the Oura gawa, was open to foreign concessions from 1859. Some interesting dwellings are still standing in a district which has now been transformed, not surprisingly, into a 'little Holland'.

If you climb one of these Dutch Hills (Oranda zaka) and go past the Miyogyo ji, you will arrive at the *Oura Catholic church.

This church, consecrated to the 26 martyrs of Nagasaki, was founded in 1864 by Bernard Petitjean (1829-84), a missionary who came from

Saône-et-Loire, in whom the Urakami Japanese Christians, who had concealed their religion up until then, placed their trust (see Historical survey). This wooden church was the first neo-Gothic building in Japan and was restored in 1945. It is known as Furansu dera, the temple of the French. The residence of the Bishop of Nagasaki still stands nearby.

Above the Oura Church, you can visit the residences of Ault, Ringer and Glover (plan: A4).

Thomas Blake Glover, British adventurer and industrialist, settled in Nagasaki in 1859 and built this house. The Ault and Ringer houses were also inhabited by various British citizens during the Meiji period.

These houses (with interiors furnished in the European style) are surrounded by a beautiful garden, with a view over Nagasaki Bay and out to sea. The Japanese like to see these heights as the spot where *Madame Butterfly* waited in despair.

Opposite the entrance to the park of the Glover residence, Juroku Bankan, house No 16, has a number of souvenirs relating to the foreigners who stayed in Nagasaki, along with the paper dragon and the whale which are the main attraction of the Okunchi festival at Suwa jinja (p. 416).

THE PARK OF PEACE (plan: A1; 3mls/4.5km N of Oura; 1½mls/2.5km NW of Nagasaki eki; Matsuyamamachi tram stop).

This park commemorates the atomic explosion which occurred on 9 August 1945 at 11 o'clock in the morning. It was designed in 1955. The tall Statue of Peace (32ft/9.7m high) was the work of the sculptor Kitamura Seibo, a native of Nagasaki. A sign marks the epicentre of the explosion. The park is ornamented with a fountain. Some remaining vestiges of Urakami Cathedral have been left here. The park contains monuments, some of which are very beautiful, presented by various countries.

To the SE of the park is the International House of Culture (address, 2, Tateyama machi; open daily from 09.00 to 16.00). The dramatic events of 1945 are evoked here with historical evidence as disturbing as that in the Hiroshima museum.

The building also contains an auditorium for conferences.

440yds (400m) E of the Statue of Peace stands the new Urakami Cathedral. The original Church had been built (between 1895 and 1925) according to the plans of the French missionary Fraineau. It was large enough to hold 6,000 people.

The church was completely destroyed during the war and was rebuilt on a more modest scale in 1958. Some statues from the old cathedral have been placed in the gardens which surround the new one.

*Inasa yama (1½ml/2km W of the station; bus as far as the cable-car). This belvedere, which has television aerials on the top of it, affords a view over the whole town and the surrounding area. The view at night is worth seeing.

VICINITY

1 MOGI (5mls/8km SE; coach), a small fishing port on Tachibana Bay. You can go to Reihoku on the island of Shimo (Amakusa shoto) from here. The region specializes in the growing of satsuma oranges.

2 OMURA, SASEBO, UNZEN AMAKUSA NATIONAL PARK, see entries under these names.

Nagato (Island of Honshu)

Tokyo, 699mls (1,125km) - Hiroshima, 157mls (252km) - Matsue, 169mls (272km) - Yamaguchi, 46mls (74km).

Yamaguchi ken - pop: 27,815 - fishing port.

Nagato, which faces the Sea of Japan, is a pleasant place, all the more so for having the very beautiful Kita Nagato Coastal Park in the area. Nearby you will also find the spa town of Yumuoto and Akiyoshidai Regional Park.

VICINITY

1 YUMOTO ONSEN (3mls/5km S; JNR train; coach). This spring at the foot of Mount Zuiun has been known for a very long time and is reputed to be effective against neuralgia, rheumatism and skin diseases. The waters vary in temperature from 79°F to 108°F (26°C to 42°C).

2 'OMI SHIMA (3mls/5km NE; coach). This island to the N of Nagato is 7 sq. mls (18km²) in area and separates Nagato Bay from Senzaki Bay. On the W coast note the strip of land called Namino Hashidate. The N coast, edged with cliffs, is made up of a number of sea caves and rocky needles, etc; the extremely beautiful Senzaki Bay is to the E of the island. At Ohibi on the E coast you can visit Saien ji and at the E point is Seigetsuan ji, where there has been a *cemetery for whales since 1692. This island is part of *Kita Nagato Coastal Park, which covers an area of 19,842 acres (8,030ha) and extends beyond Hagi.

3 HAGI, see entry under this name; AKIYOSHIDAI REGIONAL PARK, see Yamaguchi.

Nagoya (Island of Honshu)*

Railway map, inside front cover - plan, pp. 420-1.

Tokyo, 213mls (342km) - Gifu, 24mls (39km) - Nagano, 165mls (265km) - Shizuoka, 109mls (175km) - Tsu, 46mls (74km).

Capital of Aichi ken (pop: 4,390,914) - pop: 2,088,000 - trading port and industrial town: car and textile manufacturing, industrial machinery, chemical products, pottery, toys - national, regional and private universities - bishopric.

Nagoya, the third town of Japan, is also one of the most bustling in the country. It is 2h. by train from Tokyo and only 1h. from Osaka, and is the balancing factor in metropolitan central Japan. Its industrial activity drains off the population from the high mountain valleys of the Chubu. Built on the Bay of Ise, this former capital of the province of Owari has gradually extended across the vast alluvial basin of Nobi plain. This was possible only at the expense of the paddyfields which have been overrun by urbanization and industrialization. Although it might seem rather unwelcoming at first, this city does ultimately reveal its personality and you will discover, some way from the centre, districts where a tourist can enjoy wandering about.

A RECENTLY CREATED TOWN. The founding of Nagoya only goes back to the Tokugawa period, when Ieyasu (1542-1616) transferred the seat of the Owari government to Nagoya. He had a castle built there for his son Yoshinaɔ (1600-50) who settled there in 1610 and whose dynasty remained in power until the Restoration (1868). From this period onwards Nagoya experienced its real economic and industrial expansion. The population of the town at that time was only 70,000. By 1880 trading companies were interested in Nagoya and six years later the first railway line was opened. The Sino-Japanese War (1894-95) gave a new impetus to the industrial activity of the town which was growing on all sides until it reached the port, completed in 1907. World War II was to benefit Nagoya's industrial plant even further, but 50% of the town was destroyed by bombing in 1945. Now it has been rebuilt according to a huge urban development plan and has recovered all the prosperity and dynamism which make it one of the leading cities of the Japanese archipelago.

FAMOUS MEN BORN IN NAGOYA: Toyotomi Hideyoshi (1536-98), one of the greatest men of the nation, and his generals Kato Kiyomasa (1562-1611) and Koide Masahide (1539-1604); the politician Kato Takaakira (1859-1926).

PORT AND INDUSTRIES. The port of Nagoya has a surface area of about 24,700 acres (10,000ha), much of which has been reclaimed from the sea, and it is the third port of Japan after Kobe and Yokohama. Sheltered off-shore by a 5-ml (8-km) embankment, it can take ships of considerable tonnage and can handle 950,000t of crude oil. Nagoya is still developing its traditional industries – bicycles, sewing machines and textiles (85% of Japanese woollen textile produce) – its food and wood industries and Noritake porcelain (92% of all Japanese pottery exported), but it is also operating in new fields: chemical industries, aircraft and car (Toyota) manufacturing.

ᐧATSUTA JINGU (3½mls/5.5km SE of Nagoya eki, JNR; 330yds/300m SW of Atsuta eki, JNR; Jingumae Meitetsu ER station; Jingumae underground station). Along with those of Ise and Izumo, the shrine of Atsuta is one of the most venerated in Japan. It is dedicated to the goddess Amaterasu, and stands in the heart of a thickly wooded park (pines, cryptomeria, camphor trees), where cockerels live in freedom. It is worth making this the first place you visit when you come to Nagoya.

Festivals at the beginning of the year, the Bugaku dance on 1 May, Shinyo Togyo Shinji on 5 May and the Great Festival on 5 June.

According to ancient chronicles, the shrine was founded in AD 86 to house the sacred sword of Kusanagi no tsurugi. This sword is one of the three jewels of the Japanese Empire and was given by the goddess Amaterasu to the prince who unified Japan, Yamato Takeru (see Ise and Kameyama). He was attacked by a group of rebels but managed to escape by using his sword to cut through the grass around him which his enemies had set on fire. The present shrine, which is very similar in its architecture to those at Ise, was rebuilt in 1955 in the *shimmei* style. It is also devoted to Yamato Takeru, his wife Miyasu hime, his brother Take inadane and to Susano o Mikoto, Amaterasu's brother (see Izumo). Early in its history this shrine was visited by emperors who further embellished it.

The main shrine, Hon gu, stands in the N section of the park and is preceded by a secondary shrine which has a sacred enclosure, Nakanoe, around it. The faithful are not allowed to pass through this, so they come up only to the Hai den, the entrance porch of the enclosure.

There are more than 40 lesser shrines scattered about the park. They vary in size and appearance but are all associated with the main shrine. To the S of this, around Magatama pool, are several tea pavilions including that of Matabei, which is reminiscent of rural buildings of the Hida region. Note also a giant camphor tree, planted in the 9th c. by Kobo Daishi. To the E of this garden is the Bunka den, a modern building in the *azekura* style where the shrine's treasures are on display. Amongst them are ancient and modern paintings (*sutra* of the *yushutsu bon*), and calligraphy, mirrors and ancient jewels, *bugaku masks, clothes, some pottery and several blades and swords.

➤ 660yds (600m) NW of Atsuta jingu: the Shiratori no Misasagi, the mound of the white bird, probably contains the remains of Prince Yamato Takeru who died at Nobono (see Kameyama and above).

➤ Higashi Hongan ji (2mls/3km SE of Nagoya eki; 220yds/200m NW Of Higashi Betsuin underground station). This temple, founded in 1692 and rebuilt after 1945, occupies the site of Furuwatari Castle, built in 1535 by the Oda Nobuhide, the father of Nobunide.

◉ Tsuruma koen (2½mls/4km SE of Nagoya eki; SE of Tsurumai JNR station; ¾ml/1.2km E of Kamimaezu underground station), a 56-acre (23-ha) park with sports facilities, a library, an auditorium and an open-air concert hall.

▣ Shirakawa koen (plan: D4; 1ml/1.8km SE of Nagoya eki; 880yds/800m W of Yabacho underground station; 550yds/500m S of Fushimi underground station). In this garden, which is more modest than that mentioned above, is the Nagoya Science and Technology Museum (open daily except Mondays from 09.00 to 17.00); planetarium.

➤ 550yds (500m) S of Shirakawa koen, via Fushimi dori is Shimpuku ji, known as Osu Kannon ji, which was built on this spot in 1612 by Tokugawa Ieyasu. It is famous for its library which has numerous records.

To the S of this temple is Chofuku ji (or Nanatsu dera) founded in 735 and transferred here in 1611. It was damaged in 1945 but still houses statues of Amida, Kannon and Seishi (Fujiwara period).

Hisaya Odori is a wide arterial road with some of the main edifices of the modern town along it. It leads N from Yabacho underground station.

This route is intersected near Sakae by Nishiki dori and and Hirokoji dori, which are also two of Nagoya's major roads leading from the station. An underground commercial quarter has grown up in the vicinity of Sakae, where the two underground lines cross. To the N of Sakae is Nagoya Tower (591ft/180m high), which has an observation platform overlooking, notably, the Japan Alps.

*NAGOYA CASTLE (plan: C1–D1; 1½ml/2km NE of Nagoya eki; 880yds/800m NW of Horikawa Meitetsu ER station; NW of Shiyakusho underground station; open daily from 09.00 to 16.30). Once the glory of Nagoya and one of the finest castles in Japan, Nagoya jo was demolished in the bombing of 1945. It was rebuilt with a reinforced concrete framework in 1959.

The Oda possessed a fortress on this site, which was totally rebuilt by Tokugawa Ieyasu for his son Yoshinao. Ieyasu thus secured control of the province of Owari for himself, and the surrender of the Toyotomis' last supporters. Until 1867 the castle remained in the possession of the Owari branch of the Tokugawa. Nagoya Castle became a military garrison from 1872, and was then used as a residence separate from the Imperial demesne. It was handed over to the town council in 1930 and opened to the public.

In the inner courtyard can still be seen the foundations of the Hon maru bombed in 1945, but of which some remains are on display in the present keep. This five-storey tower (157ft/48m high) has been laid out as a museum exhibiting models of the old castle, original fragments and the re-creation of the golden dolphins on the ridge of the roof, sliding door paintings from the Hon maru (a sleeping tiger, a cart full of flowers, a waterfall, etc.), and a collection of sabres. The view from the top storey extends over the town and surrounding area.

The dolphins which crown the roofs of many Japanese castles are supposed to protect them against fire. Those of Nagoya, however, are blamed for causing the 1959 tidal wave.

To the E of the Hon maru is the garden of Nino maru, an interesting re-creation of an old feudal garden. To the NW, in another garden, you will see some old warehouses and a funeral vault of the Kofun period, brought here in 1949 from the Shimane region.

660yds (600m) S of the castle, on Fushimi dori, is the shrine of Aichi, reconstructed in 1952 and dedicated to the victims of the war.

Further S across the private railway line, you can visit the Tosho gu, founded in 1619 in honour of Tokugawa Ieyasu (rebuilt in 1952; festival 16 and 17 April), and the shrine of Nagoya, to the E of the above, originally founded by the Emperor Daigo (festival 15 and 16 July). Not far from here is the shrine of Tagata, centre of the Japanese phallic cults.

'TOKUGAWA ART MUSEUM (Address: 27, 2-chome, Tokugawa cho, Higashi ku; 3mls/5km NE of Nagoya eki; 770yds/700m SW of Ozone JNR station; ½ml/1km S of Ozone Meitetsu ER and underground stations; open daily except Mondays from 10.00 to 16.00; closed 25 December to 1 January). This museum, which has been open since 1935, possesses more than 12,000 works and has recovered all the ancestral collections of the Owari Tokugawa. Amongst the most famous works sometimes on display, note the following:

The ****** *Genji Monogatari emakimono*, an illustration of the famous tale of the lady Murasaki Shikibu, attributed to Fujiwara Takayoshi (12th c.). The museum possesses a set of 13 scenes. Six other fragments are kept in the Goto Museum in Tokyo.

'This important series must originally (...) have been composed of ten scrolls which contained a total of eighty to ninety scenes illustrating the fifty-four chapters of this saga (...). The illustrations have been carefully executed on sheets of paper of the same size ([9 in] 22 cm long by [19 in] 48 cm or [14 in] 36 cm wide). They each represent some outstanding episode of the novel, and are preceded by an extract from the text beautifully written in cursive script on richly decorated paper. The choice of subjects indicates that the artist, rather than striving to capture the actions of his characters, has attempted to express, in a plastic form, the lyricism and the sentimentality which animate the novel.

'All the scenes, in principle, conform to one particular effect of perspective, which is very different from Western traditions. They are viewed at an oblique angle, from top to bottom and from right to left, in accordance with the natural movement of the eye when the scroll is unfolded from right to left. Making use of another convention, the artist does away with the roofs of the houses so that the interiors are completely visible' (Akiyama Terikazu, *Japanese Painting*).

Also attributed to Takayoshi is the *Murasaki Shikibu ekotobu* which illustrates the private notes of this lady of the Heian court. In addition to these you can also see several *kakemono* and calligraphy of the Kamakura period, screens of the Edo period, a portrait of Tokugawa Ieyasu, ancient swords and armour, pottery, etc.

Nittai ji (4mls/7km E of Nagoya eki; 550yds/500m N of Kakuozan underground station). This temple, dedicated to Nippon-Thai friendship, was built in 1904 to house a gilded statue of Buddha, given in 1900 by the King of Siam, Rama V. In the gardens there is a monument to those who died in the Russo-Japanese War (1904–05).

Nearby is an edifice which contains little statues of the Five Hundred

Disciples of Buddha (Gohyaku Rakan). Sculpted in the 18th c., some of them are the work of Kita Tametaka.

 Heiwa koen (5mls/8km E of Nagoya eki; ½ml/1km N of Higashiyama koen underground station). This Park of Peace is in fact a huge cemetery with about 200,000 tombs, recovered after the war from the old town of Nagoya. Amongst them is the tomb of Oda Nobunaga (1534–82), the unifier of Japan and a native of Owari province. In 1964 a Pagoda of Peace was erected, to house a statue of Kannon presented by China.

Higashiyama koen (5mls/8km SE of Nagoya eki; 550yds/500m S of Higashiyama koen underground station). This 230-acre (82-ha) park covers the wooded heights which, along with Heiwa koen and Yagoto yama, rise up to the E of Nagoya.

In the shade of this park are the zoological and botanical gardens of Nagoya, the astronomy observatory and the cultural centre of the town. Nagoya University (arch. Maki Fumihiko) lies to the W.

Yagoto yama (5mls/8km SE of Nagoya eki; bus). These are hills which extend Higashi yama, where Kosho ji is situated, towards the S; five-storey pagoda; festival of the Thousand Lanterns in summer.

Odaka Park (8mls/13km SE of Nagoya eki; 1ml/1.5km SE of Odaka eki, JNR). This public park with its amusement areas lies on the S edge of the town.

To the S of Odaka station are the ruins of the castle of this name, which belonged for some time to Tokugawa Ieyasu.

Nakamura koen (2mls/3km W of Nagoya eki; to the W of Nakamura koen underground station). This park was created on the site of the farm where the famous Toyotomi Hideyoshi was born (1536–98: see Fushimi Castle in Kyoto). A shrine dedicated to him was built in 1897.

VICINITY

1 JIMOKU JI (4mls/7km NW; Meitetsu ER train from Nagoya eki to Jimokuji station). Situated 550yds/500m SE of the station, this temple was founded in the 7th c., in honour of a statue of Kannon salvaged from the sea by Jimoku Tatsumaro. The statues of the Deva kings on the Nio mon gate date from the 13th c. The temple also has a statue of Fudo and a painting of Nirvana.

2 KIYOSU JO (5mls/8km NW; JNR train to Kiyosu station). To the SE of the station are the ruins of the castle built at the beginning of the 15th century by Shiba Yoshishige, and entrusted to the Oda. In 1553 Nobunaga seized it and ousted his cousin Nobutomo. Hideyoshi established his adopted son Hidetsugu there, then Ieyasu placed his sons Tadayoshi and Yoshinao in power there.

3 GAMAGORI, GIFU, HANDA, INUYAMA, SETO, YOKKAICHI, ISE SHIMA NATIONAL PARK, see entries under these names.

■ Nanao (Island of Honshu)

Tokyo, 318mls (511km) – Fukui, 92mls (148km) – Gifu, 175mls (281km) – Kanazawa, 43mls (69km) – Toyama, 43mls (70km).

Ishikawa ken – pop: 47,855.

Nanao is the principal town on the Noto peninsula and is open to Nanao Bay. It was once the naval base of the Maeda, the lords of Kanazawa. The shipyards built by this family were taken over by Kawasaki Heavy Industries. The Maeda also founded a famous school which produced Takamine Jokichi (1845-1922) to whom we owe the discovery of adrenalin.

Ikutamahiko jinga (½ml/1km W of the station) was probably founded under the Emperor Kogen who lived, according to the Nihongi, from 273 to 158 BC. This shrine, dedicated to Okuninushi no Mikoto (see Izumo), was venerated by numerous Japanese warriors including Minamoto Yoritomo in the 12th c.

VICINITY

1 SITE OF NANAO CASTLE (3mls/5km SE; coach). This castle on a wooded hill was erected in 1398 by Hatakeyama Mitsunori. Uesugi Kenshin captured it in 1577, and then Maeda Toshie (1538-99), but the latter abandoned it in 1583 in favour of Kanazawa (see under this name).

2 WAKURA ONSEN (4mls/7km NW; coach; or JNR train and bus). These thermal springs, which gush forth from the ground at Cape Benten at a temperature of 185°F (85°C), are appreciated for their healing and anti-rheumatic qualities.

3 NOTO SHIMA (3½mls/6km N; boat). This island occupies almost the whole of Nanao Bay and reaches a maximum altitude of 656ft (200m). Several small fishing ports, including Notojima, stand along its outer edge. Its eastern front is lined with cliffs which have earned it the nickname 'screen island'.

4 HAKUI, WAJIMA, see entries under these names.

■ Nankoku (Island of Shikoku)

Map of Shikoku (Inland Sea), pp. 536-7.

Tokyo, 549mls (883km) – Kochi, 6mls (10km) – Matsuyama, 85mls (137km) – Takamatsu, 102mls (164km) – Tokushima 114mls (184km) – Gomen station.

Kochi ken – pop: 41,096.

Nankoku, a little distance from Kochi, is one of the more important places of the former province of Tosa, to the N of which is the Shikoku mountain range. There are interesting rambles around here.

VICINITY

1 KOKUBUN JI (2mls/3km N; coach). This national temple was founded by the priest Gyoki (670-749). The main hall, rebuilt in 1558, houses a statue of Yakushi Nyorai.

2 'RYUGA DO (9mls/15km NE on the N55 and a toll road; coach). These caves, discovered in 1931, rank amongst the most famous in Japan. The trip takes 1h. to 2h. approx. Traces of a Yayoi-period civilization have been found here. Near the entrance is a little museum relating to the caves. It also exhibits several *cockerels (*onaga dori*) which are characteristic of the Tosa region and sometimes have plumes 10ft (3m) long.

3 MONOBE (18mls/29km NE on the N195; coach). A road leads to this village and sticks closer to the Monobe gawa valley than the 'A' road. It runs past the spa town of Inono, Oku Monobe gorge and Nagase dam.

4 OTAGUCHI (23mls/37km NE; JNR train). If you are going by road, you will need to rejoin the N32 to the N.

9mls (15km): Wakamiya Onsen; sulphur springs at 61°F (16°C).

19mls (30km): Osugi, where, 550yds (500m) SW of the station, you can visit the shrine of Yasaka. Two giant cedar trees grow inside the shrine's enclosure. One of them reaches a height of 223ft (68m) and is the largest in Japan. These trees are probably about a thousand years old.

23mls (37km): Otaguchi. You can go from here to Buraku ji (½ml/1km N of the station) where you will see the Yakushi do, dating from 1150. This temple contains several ancient statues of Amida, Gautama and Yakushi Nyorai.

5 KOCHI, see entry under this name.

■ Nansei shoto (Archipelago of)

866sq. mls (2,244km²) - pop: 969,000.

GEOGRAPHICAL SIGHTS. Stretched out over 600mls (1,000km) between the island of Kyushu and Taiwan, this archipelago separates the East China Sea from the Pacific Ocean. It is, in fact, made up of two major areas. To the N is Satsunan shoto (region of Kagoshima), with the lesser archipelagos of Amami shoto and Osumi shoto (see under those names). To the S is Ryukyu retto (region of Okinawara), a name commonly given to the whole group, which includes Okinawa shoto, Miyako shoto and Yaeyama shoto (see under these names). Off shore of this archipelago are the Ryukyu deeps, descending to over 25,600ft (7,800m). The sea takes on fascinating shades of colour and the waters are exceptionally clear. Some of the islands are surrounded by coral reefs (Tarama jima). Owing to its subtropical latitude (between the 24th and 31st parallels N), Nansei shoto enjoys a sunny and particularly pleasant climate year-round (average at Naha: 61.3°F/16.3°C in January, 95°F/35°C in August). The typhoon period, from April to October is, however, fearsome. The vegetation matches the climate. There is an abundance of subtropical plants and specialized cultivation such as pineapple and sugar cane. Though the people in the archipelago live primarily by agriculture the harvests are sometimes damaged by typhoons and tidal waves. An industrial scheme has brought, to Okinawa in particular, a new form of economic activity, since the archipelago has, until recently, remained in an underdeveloped state. Petrochemical industries and machine and electronic equipment factories are now being set up in the southern region. Oil fields have been found to the N of Senkaku retto (to the W of Okinawa). There is, however, a serious lack of drinking water. In spite of this, everything possible is being done to make up for lost time, and the position of Okinawa, exposed as it is to the ocean, has also contributed to the economic expansion of the archipelago. The tourist trade, made up mostly of Japanese, is also an increasingly important economic resource for the Ryukyu Islands.

NANSEI SHOTO IN HISTORY. The people of Ryukyu claim to be born of a son of the sun, who gave birth to the male and female divinities who created the archipelago. This appreciably different version of the Japanese cosmogony remains in an Asian context which reveals the Chinese, Korean and even Malay origins of the population of these islands. Here you will recognize an ethnic group which is much closer to the Pacific or Southeast Asian peoples than to the Japanese themselves. The Nansei archipelago was known to Chinese sailors by the 3rd century BC; it has, throughout history, maintained trade links with the continent, and in 1372 formally submitted to the Middle Kingdom. In 1187, however, Shunten the King of the Ryukyu (Liu Ch'iu to the Chinese) succeeded to power. According to the Japanese version he was the son of Minamoto Tametomo, who sought refuge on this island in the 12th c. Some modern historians prefer to see the Sho sovereigns as the descendants of the Taira defeated at the battle of Danno ura (see Shimonoseki). From 1451 onwards, in addition to their allegiance to China, the Ryukyu kingdom sent an annual embassy to Kyoto. In 1609, however, when this gesture of obeisance was omitted, Shimazu Iehisa, the lord of Kagoshima, seized Shuri (Okinawa) and placed the archipelago of Amami under his own direct authority. He left what is now the prefecture of Okinawa in a state of semi-dependence and controlled the silk trade to Osaka. From the 19th century onwards, European missionaries began to put in there and to settle at Naha (see Okinawa). In 1879, the Ryukyu archipelago was united with Japan and its last sovereign, Sho Tai (1843-1901), received the title of Marquis in recompense. In spite of protests from the Chinese, this situation was confirmed by the Treaty of Shimonoseki (1895), after the Sino-Japanese War. During the Pacific War, after heroically resisting the American forces in 1945, the archipelago of Okinawa, along with that of Ogasawara (see under these names), was used as an operations base for the bombing of Japan. In 1952 the exact status of the Ryukyu was left undetermined, and it was not until 1972 that the archipelago became a part of Japan again. Nonetheless, the island of Okinawa continues to be the United States' main Pacific

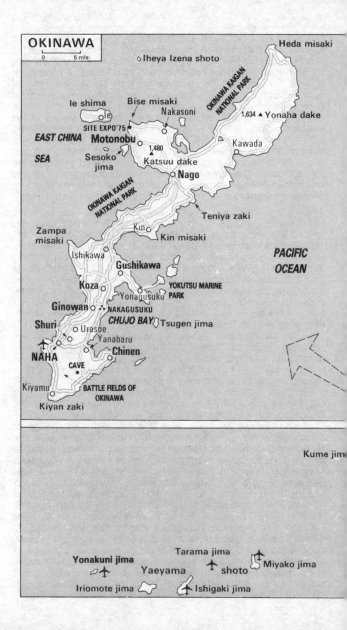

OKINAWA

0   5 mls

Heda misaki

○ Iheya Izena shoto

OKINAWA KAIGAN NATIONAL PARK

Ie shima   Bise misaki
Ie   Nakasoni
SITE EXPO'75   1,634 ▲ Yonaha dake
EAST CHINA **Motonobu**
                                Kawada
SEA   Sesoko   1,480
            jima   Katsuu dake
                    Nago

OKINAWA KAIGAN NATIONAL PARK

                    Teniya zaki

Zampa   Kin ○
misaki   ○ Kin misaki
    Ishikawa   **PACIFIC**
        Gushikawa   **OCEAN**

    Koza   YOKUTSU MARINE
        Yonagusuku   PARK
Ginowan ○ NAKAGUSUKU
Shuri   **CHUJO BAY** Tsugen jima
        Urasoe
            Yanabaru
NAHA   ○ **Chinen**
    CAVE
Kiyamu   BATTLE FIELDS OF
            OKINAWA
    Kiyan zaki

Kume jim

                Tarama jima
Yonakuni jima   ✈ Miyako jima
    ✈   Yaeyama   ✈ shoto
Iriomote jima   Ishigaki jima

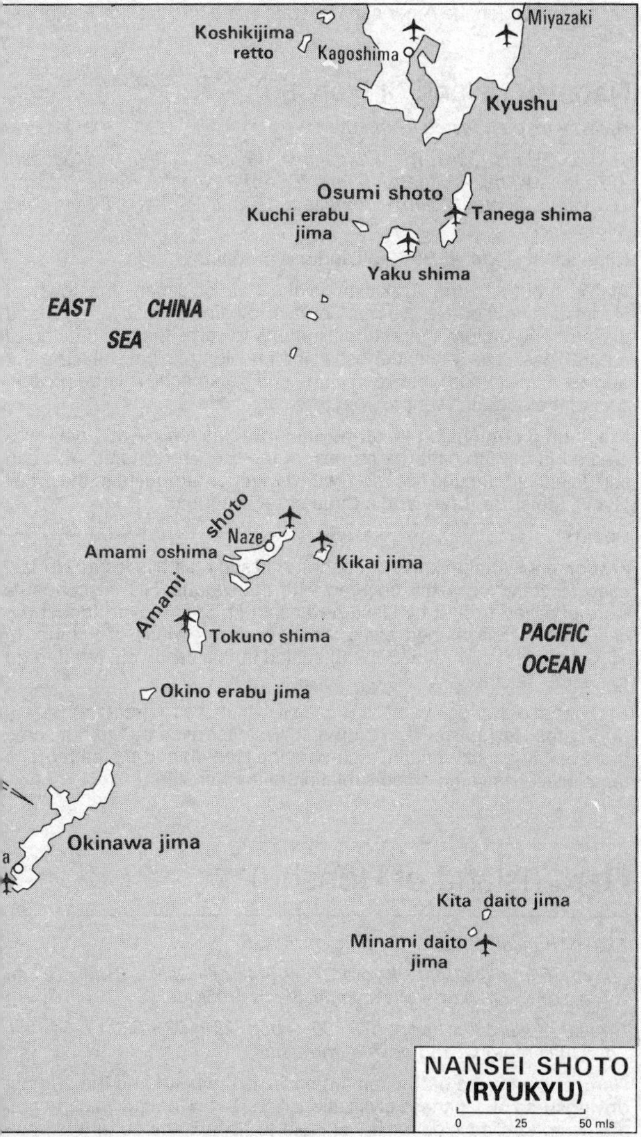

Miyazaki

Koshikijima
retto
Kagoshima

Kyushu

Osumi shoto
Kuchi erabu
jima
Tanega shima

Yaku shima

EAST CHINA

SEA

Amami oshima
shoto
Naze

Amami

Kikai jima

Tokuno shima

PACIFIC
OCEAN

Okino erabu jima

Okinawa jima

a

Kita daito jima

Minami daito
jima

**NANSEI SHOTO
(RYUKYU)**

0   25   50 mls

base, from which the Americans operate in the direction of Southeast Asia.

■ Naoetsu (Island of Honshu)

Railway map on inside front cover.

Tokyo, 190mls (306km) – Fukushima, 192mls (309km) – Maebashi 127mls (204km) – Nagano, 53mls (86km) – Niigata, 78mls (126km) – Toyama, 76mls (123km) – Yamagata, 184mls (296km) – ferry service to Sado.

Niigata ken – pop: 45,357 – oil and gas production.

At the mouth of the Arakawa on the Sea of Japan, the town of Naoetsu is now one of the main ports providing access to the island of Sato. The region is directing its efforts towards the exploitation of natural gas. The main deposits stretch along a coastal strip for approx. 6mls (10km), between Kuroi and Katamachi. A large proportion of the output is sent to Tokyo.

⊙ Kokubun ji (1ml/1.5km W of the station). This temple at Gochi was created in the 8th c. at the request of the Emperor Shomu. You can still go and admire the Nio mon, with its statues attributed to the priest Gyoki, the *sutra* library and a three-storey pagoda.

☞ **VICINITY**

KASUGA YAMA (3mls/5km SW; coach). A castle built by Uesugi Noriaki used to stand on a hill covered with pinewoods. His descendants were expelled from it by Uesugi Kenshin (1530-78), who rebuilt the castle and strengthened his power over the province of Echigo. In 1596, Hori Hideharu (1575-1606) settled in this castle but left it to go to nearby Takada.

At the foot of Kasuga yama is Rinsen ji, which was a great monastery during the Uesugi Kenshin period. It was destroyed by fire but some of its buildings still remain, including the Hon do and the belfry. The temple still has some objects relating to the Kenshin.

N Nara (Island of Honshu)***

Map of Kansai, pp. 500-1 – plan, pp. 434-5.

Tokyo, 305mls (491km) – Kyoto, 27mls (44km) – Osaka, 21mls (33km) – Tsu, 65mls (104km) – Wakayama, 66mls (106km).

Capital of Nara ken (pop: 573,530) – pop: 281,693 – 322ft (98m) alt. – national, regional and private universities.

Nara, at the centre of the Yamato basin, is the heart and the original driving force of Japanese civilization. Here, in this unique melting pot, a new culture developed. It was able to absorb the cultural stimuli offered by China and Korea, naturalise them, and transmute them into specifically Japanese modes of creativity.

It is here that all trips to Japan should begin so that you can be inspired by the very spirit of the country, made all the more accessible by the natural setting in which its finest jewels have been kept. The presence of sacred deer – which are also tame – makes the atmosphere even more tangible and brings the gods closer.

HEIJOKYO. It was probably due to the influence of Fujiwara Fuhito (659–720) that the Emperor Gemmei or Gemmyo (662–722) transferred the site of the Imperial capital from Fujiwara to Nara. Thus Heijokyo, the capital of peace, was created in 710, and it was to retain this function, made permanent for the first time, until the capital was transferred to Nagaoka and then to Kyoto in 784. The town, 'inscribed in a perfect square, measuring just over 2mls (4km) on each side, was crisscrossed by a network of perpendicular streets. Temples and palaces were crammed close together, rivalling each other in richness, each trying to achieve the best expression of the splendour of the times.' (D. and V. Elisseeff, *La civilisation japonaise*.)

A MONK WHO WAS TOO INFLUENTIAL. Seven emperors followed in succession in Nara which, during the Tempyo era (722–748), experienced one of Japan's most dazzling periods of art. The two great chronicles of myth and history, the *Kojiki* and the *Nihongi*, were written during this period, and the poetry anthology of Manyoshu (*Collection of the Ten Thousand Folios*) was also published at that time. Artists and craftsmen helped to produce masterpieces which are still proudly preserved today by the great temples. Most of these artists, were educated in the monasteries, of which there were a great many in the town. They increased in importance and meddled in politics. One of the priests, Dokyo, grew very influential at court and became the lover of the Empress Koken or Shotoku (718–770), in whose name he soon began to wield power. He did not, however, succeed in marrying her, as the Imperial lineage was supposed to be of divine origin. He was exiled after the death of the Empress by the new sovereign Konin tenno. Konin was succeeded by the Emperor Kammu (736–805), who decided to transfer the capital once more. Heijokyo was thenceforth known as Nara. The town lost its political importance and from then on felt only the repercussions of historical events. A fire in 1180 destroyed most of the temples at the time of the rivalry between the Taira and the Minamoto.

NB: A great many of Nara's principal monuments are scattered across Nara Park (1,305 acres/528ha), where there are many deer roaming freely. Sanjo dori, which runs from Nara eki (JNR), and Noborioji dori, which runs from Kintetsu-Nara, both go to the E of this park. It is quite possible to take a trip round it in half a day. A more inclusive visit to Nara would need more than a day. Some of the temples and the Yamato Bunkakan Museum, situated on the outer edge of Nara, will be referred to in the second part of our itinerary. Most of the temples are open from 09.00 to 16.00. Some have an entrance fee.

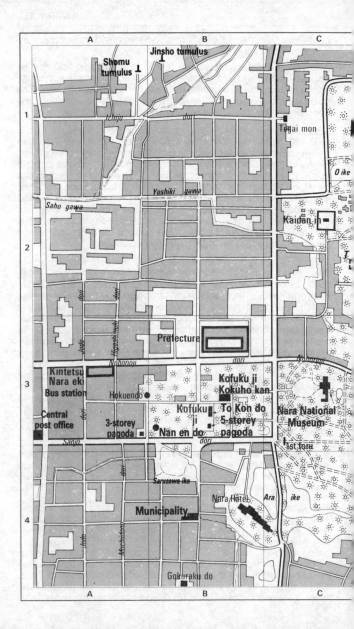

MIKASA ONSEN

Toll road to Kasuga Okuyama

Jukkokudai

Wakakusa yama 1,122

...an

Kaisando

Nigatsu do

butsu
...en

Belfry

Sangatsu do

Tamukeyama
Hachiman gu

Kagami ike

Nandai mon

Yoshiki gawa

Toll road to
Kasuga Okuyama

Mizuya gawa

Kasuga yama 928

Manyo Botanical
Garden

PARKING

Kasuga
taisha

2nd torii

Kasuga
Wakamiya
jinja

NARA PARK

0   100 yds

D   E   Shin Yakushi ji   F

A Nara Park (Nara koen)

"KOFUKU JI (plan: B3; 330yds/300m SE of Kintetsu-Nara eki; ½ml/1km E of Nara eki JNR; bus from the latter as far as the Prefecture, to the N of the temple). This is one of Nara's main temples and along with Yakushi ji (p. 445) it is the seat of the Hosso sect, founded in 654 by the monk Dosho.

This temple was founded in 669 at Yamashina, near Kyoto, in honour of Fujiwara Kamatari (614–669), the forefather of the dynasty of great ministers which ruled Japan from the 8th to the 12th c. Before the founding of Heijokyo, the temple was transferred here by Fujiwara Fuhito, the son of Fujiwara Kamatari, and by the emperors Gensho and Shomu. It was laid out over an area of over 10 acres (4ha), and during the Tempyo period it became one of the seven great temples of Nara. The decline soon came, however, and it was destroyed in 1180 by the Taira. It was rebuilt by Minamoto Yoritomo, but was still to suffer in the civil wars (14th and 15th c.) and numerous fires, including one in 1717, which left only the buildings which can still be seen today.

Festivals: Tsuina Shiki, the demon hunt on 13 March; fan-throwing festival to exorcize evil spirits on 19 May.

To the S of Sanjo dori, note the pool of Sarusawa in which the temple's five-storey pagoda is reflected. The night-time view in the autumn moonlight is a particular favourite of the Japanese. A few steps lead to the site of the Nandai mon, where the S gate once stood.

"Gojuno to (plan: B3), the five-storey pagoda, stands to the E. It is the second tallest in Japan (180ft/55m high), after that of To ji in Kyoto.

It was erected in 730 and rebuilt in 1426 in the Muromachi style. The Shaka, Amida, Yakushi and Miroku Buddhas are represented inside.

To Kon do, the eastern gold pavilion, immediately to the N of the great pagoda, was built in 726 in honour of the Empress Gensho and rebuilt in 1415. It houses a triad of Yakushi Nyorai attended by Nikko and Gakko Bosatsu.

To the W stood the western gold pavilion, Sai Kon do, and to the N was the central pavilion or Chu Kon do rebuilt in 1819 (12th c.; statue of Shaka Nyorai).

The Nan en do, to the W, opposite the great pagoda, is an octagonal edifice which was founded in 813 by Fujiwara Fuyutsugu and rebuilt in 1741.

The statue of Fukukenjaku Kannon (1189), attributed to Kokei, is venerated here.

Behind this is a *three-storey pagoda, built in 1143 and rebuilt at the end of the 12th c.; the interior decorations depict the Thousand Buddhas. To the N of this pagoda is the Hokuen do, another octagonal pavilion, founded in 721 and rebuilt in 1208.

"KOKUHO KAN (plan: B3; open daily from 09.00 to 17.00). To the NE of the Gojuno to and the To Kon do, the Kofuku ji treasure museum stands on the former site of the refectory. This recent building exhibits a large proportion of the works owned by the temple.

This museum, and Nara in general, posess a sufficiently large number of works of the Unkei school to warrant a few words on the subject here. Unkei (1148–1223), the son of Kokei and descendant of Jocho, is the most famous of a whole dynasty of artists which continued with his sons Tankei and Koen, and his grandson Kogen. 'Buddhist sculptors of this school continue in the Heian style but add to it a realism which shows a distinct return to the Nara traditions. The new style is full of vigour and has an inner strength which the statues of the Heian period seemed rather to lack. The pictures of monks, treated in a realistic manner, are remarkably lifelike. Nature is viewed here from very close quarters, as in a portrait.' (Louis Frédéric, *Japon*.)

Amongst the works usually on show, we would mention the following:

A *head of Buddha, of the Hakuho period (7th c.), which is probably that of Yakushi Nyorai, perhaps created under the direction of the Chinese masters (according to Louis Frédéric).

'The Eight Guardians of Shaka Nyorai' (Tempyo period: you will in fact see only four and a bust). The *Ashura is the most representative of them. These statues 'represented the Hachibu shu or the eight classes of supernatural beings referred to in the *Sutra of the Lotus* (*Hokekyo*). They were created in dry lacquer (734?). Ashura is the king of hunger and anger. He is not often portrayed. Here he is standing and has six arms with two of the hands joined in prayer. He has three faces, the expressions of which are truly most beautiful' (Louis Frédéric).

The three *great disciples of Buddha (Furuna, Kazenen and Ragora) date from the 8th century, and the four celestial guardians (Tamon, Komoku, Jikoku and Zocho ten) from the 9th c.

The statues of the *Patriarchs of the Hosso sect including those of Gyoga, Mujaku and Seshin. These statues, of the Kamakura period, were sculpted in the 12th and 13th c., under the direction of Kokei with the help of his son Unkei.

*Statues of Ryutoki and Tentoki, demons bearing lanterns, sculpted by Koben in 1215.

Other statues of the Kamakura period, such as *Kongo Rikishi (attributed to Jokei), Bonten, Senju Kannon and Amida date from the 12th c.

Amongst the paintings, note a portrait on silk of the priest Jion (11th c.).

NARA NATIONAL MUSEUM (plan: C3; address: 50, Noborioji dori cho; 550yds/500m E of Kofuku ji; 1ml/1.7km E of Nara eki JNR; open daily from 09.00 to 16.00 from November to February, and from 08.00 to

16.30 from March to October; closed on the third Monday of each month, and from 26 December to 3 January). This museum, founded as an Imperial museum in 1895, is made up of two separate buildings, standing at right-angles. To the W is a European-style building, erected at the end of the 19th c., and to the S is a modern building which evokes the style of the Shoso in.

The first building houses the archaeological collections of Nara Museum, but their presentation is rather outdated. The second building, conceived on modern museographical lines, displays a considerable number of works of art (mainly paintings and sculptures), most of which are kept at Nara Museum and come from numerous temples in the town and the surrounding area. As is the case everywhere, do not expect to find a complete display of the collections. What you will see is a temporary selection of works. A large number of them, in the possession of Shoso in (see below), are likewise displayed in rotation in this museum. It is a pity that the explanatory inscriptions in English are so limited.

Sculptures. Asuka and Hakuho periods (552–710): several *statuettes including Kannon, which came from Hokki ji, Miroku Bosatsu from Kono dera, Sho Kannon from Kakurin ji and Miroku (?) Bosatsu from Horyu ji. An *embossed bronze plaque from the Hase dera probably dates from the Asuka period. It represents a *mandara* imitated from a Chinese model.

– Tempyo period (710–794): a statue of Miroku Bosatsu (dried lacquer work) and a statuette of *Tanjo Butsu, which stands in the middle of a pond.

– Heian period (794–1192): a very expressive sitting statue of *Gien in dried lacquer (early Heian period), and a late Heian statue of Binzuru Sonja, Statue of *Yakushi Nyorai, from Ganko ji. 'The whole gives an impression of imposing grandeur, lightened by the rhythm and life of the sculpture' (Peter C. Swann). There are other statues of Juichimen Kannon, with very long arms: of Senju Kannon, Shaka Nyorai, Daichi Nyorai and Amida Nyorai, and of Kichijo ten. *Shinto statuettes in painted cypress wood, from Yakushi ji. *Wooden plaques in *bas relief* which, without doubt, depict the twelve guardians of Yakushi Nyorai. These figurines, which are full of vitality, are attributed to Gencho (according to Louis Frédéric).

– Kamakura period (1192–1333): several statues including one of a reclining Buddha, Bato Kannon and Aizen Myo o, 'the deity symbolizing love, in spite of his awesome appearance' (Louis Frédéric).

– Muromachi period (14th to 15 c.): a lovely wooden statue of *Shaka Bosatsu coming down from the mountain after his period of asceticism (15th c.).

Paintings. Amongst the paintings kept in the museum, we would draw your attention to the following. The depictions of Bon ten and Juni ten, of the 13th c. The *emakimono* of Honen Shonin Eden, which trace in 48 scrolls the life of the priest Honen (they were painted between 1307 and 1317 and belong to the Chion in in Kyoto). Painting of *Nirvana*, of the Fujiwara period, from Shin Yakushiji, and comparable to the one in the Koya san museum (see entry under this name). Painting of *Ao Fudo* (Blue Fudo), believed to date from the mid-11th c., originally from the Shoren in in Kyoto; this richly coloured painting 'conforms with the usual iconography of this deity; her body is blue and she is sitting on a rock, flanked by two attendants, Kongara (Kinkarah) and Seitaka (Cetakah), who look like two young boys. The triangular arrangement of the figures gives a classic stability to the composition, and the sublime power of the deity is expressed in the movement of the flames, which evoke the symbolic shapes of the Karula (Garuda), the mythical bird' (Akiyama Terukazu, *Japanese Painting*). Three painted scrolls of the *Descent of Amida* (early 11th c.). 'In the central scroll, Amida is sitting on a red lotus flower and looking at the person who is looking at the painting. The colours are simple and the robe has no decoration other than the scarcely visible motif of swastikas drawn in dark red' (Akiyama Terukazu). These paintings come from Hokke ji.

Objets d'art. These are numerous and varied: *bugaku* and *gagaku* masks; objects of worship and religious furniture; perfume vases: a beautiful bronze bell from the Kofuku ji; *keman* (a carved, bronze pendentive to ornament a temple) representing mermaid-birds; a small *reliquary (1249) in carved gilt bronze from Saidai ji, etc.

In the old building of Nara National Museum you will see several finds from excavations; pottery and ancient utensils; *haniwa* figurines and sarcophagi of the Kofun period; beautiful tiles from the dripstones of vanished temples; jewels and *magatama*; swords; etc.

To the E of the National Museum you will soon reach Hi Oji, which meets the great southern gate of Todai ji, to the N.

***Todai ji (plan: D2; 550yds/500m NE of the National Museum. 1½ml/2km NE of Nara eki, JNR; bus to Kasugano cho). This temple, one of the greatest monuments in Japan, possesses the largest wooden edifice in the world. The treasure house, Shoso in, which stands behind it, could be regarded as the oldest museum in the world. Todai ji is the seat of the Kegon sect, based on the last teachings of Buddha Sakyamuni, which was introduced to Japan in 735 by the Chinese priest Dosen.

Following certain misfortunes which marked the beginning of his reign, the Emperor Shomu (718-758) founded Todai ji to house the colossal statue of Buddha. Built 'for the protection and prosperity of the nation', this temple was one of the loveliest monuments of the 8th c. It was destroyed in the 12th c., rebuilt, ruined again by a fire in 1567 and then reconstructed on a much more modest scale.

*Nandai mon (plan: D3). This gate (1199) surmounted by a tier is 95ft (29m) high and has the two statues of the *Nio or Deva kings. These statues, which are much admired, appear 'one with the mouth closed, symbolizing power contained, and the other with the mouth wide open, in an expression of power turned outward' (D. and V. Elisseeff). They are attributed to Unkei and Taikei.

'Whilst respecting the curious conventions of anatomical fantasy, the artists have been superbly successful in giving the impression of a monstrous force which corresponds to the sudden explosion of anger. This effect is all the more extraordinary for the fact that they had to master such rigid, unmanageable material' (Fosco Maraini). Behind these statues are two lion dogs (*koma-inu*), attributed to the Chinese sculptor Chinnakei (1196).

Opposite the Nandai mon a path leads to the Chu mon which is linked by corridors with the Daibutsu den. The upper part of this is reflected in the Mirror Pond (Kagami ike). On either side of this pond you will notice the sites of the east and west pagodas, which were seven storeys high.

Daibutsu den or Kon do (plan: D2), with a façade 187ft (57m) long and 159ft (48.5m) high, is the largest wooden building in the world. It houses the great bronze statue of *Buddha Vairocana or Birushana Bosatsu. The roof is surmounted by two enormous *kutsugata*, in imitation of Chinese buildings, which are supposed to protect the temple against fires. There is a superb octagonal bronze lantern of the Nara period in front of the entrance; restored in 1974.

This building was erected between 747 and 751, at the same time as the statue was created by the Korean Kimimaro. The grandiose inauguration of the temple took place in the presence of the Emperor Shomu, his entire court and about 10,000 monks. An earthquake first damaged the statue in 885. The head and right hand were melted in the fire of 1180 which also destroyed the Kon do. The whole structure was restored on the orders of Minamoto Yoritomo, between 1185 and 1195, by the priest Chogen, but suffered again in the fire of 1567. The present building was rebuilt in 1708 and in fact only represents about three-fifths of the original edifice.

The statue of Buddha is still interesting today for its exceptional dimensions, which exceed its artistic merit, the quality of which has dwindled with repeated restorations. Only the lower part and the sculpted plinth still remain to bear witness to the original. Its total height of 53ft/16.2m (the length of one ear is 8ft/2.5m) makes it the largest bronze statue in the world. It is taller than the Buddha at Kamakura which is, however, without question, aesthetically far superior. The darkness of the hall and the lack of space in which to stand back make it difficult to observe properly. Note also the statues of Nyorin Kannon and Kokuzo Bosatsu in gilded wood of the 17th c., and behind the Dai Butsu the statues of the celestial guardians, Komoku ten and Tamon ten. There is a model of the Todai ji, as it was, in the Kond do, where one of the columns is partly hollowed out and brings wealth to anyone who can get through it.

Kaiden in (plan: C2) stands on a small hill 330yds (300m) W of the Daibutsu den. The mound was made in 754 of earth which came from Mount Wa Tai Shan in China, and here the priest Ganjin (688–763) ordained numerous monks from Todai ji.

This temple was rebuilt in 1731 and houses statues of Sakyamuni and Taho Nyorai. They are surrounded by four *celestial guardians, which are remarkable works of the Tempyo period.

The Kon do or preaching hall once stood to the N of the Daibutsu den. To the NW of here you will reach:

■ ***Shoso in (plan: D1; 330yds/300m from the Daibutsu den; open only on certain days in April and October). This venerable building was once the treasure house of Todai ji and is now administered by the Imperial Household Agency. Some of its collections are usually on display at the National Museum in Nara (see above).

The *building, which rests on strong piers, was constructed in the *azekura* style (without nails), after the fashion of Yayoi period rice-lofts. As the wood expands or contracts according to whether the season is wet or dry, the building provides an ingenious air-conditioning system which has made it possible to preserve an exceptional collection of objects up until the present day. They were assembled in the 8th century by the Emperor Shomu and were used at the inauguration of Todai ji in 752.

Some of these thousands of objects given to the temple treasury by the sovereign's widow, came originally from countries as far apart as China, Korea, India, Persia, Greece and the Byzantine Empire. They testify to the trade links which Japan maintained them, and to the eclectic taste of the Japanese, which their art, blossoming at that time, was able to put to good use.

The best-known pieces are: *the screen of the *Beauties beneath the tree*, a unique work of Japanese painting, of the Nara period, which has unfortunately been damaged; Buddhist line and ink drawings on hemp; a series of musical instruments ornamented with leather patches with miniature scenes painted on them ('Musicians on the back of a white elephant'); *bugaku* and *gagaku* masks; weapons; cloth and garments; ceramics and pottery from various sources; an infinite number of decorative artifacts; and religious and secular furniture. Most of the objects date from the 8th c.

330yds (300m) W of the Shoso in, near the Nara Kaido road, is the Tegai mon, one of the oldest structures of Todai ji still in existence (8th c.).

Flights of steps, to the E of the Daibutsu den, lead to the Shoro or belfry (1207-10), which holds a huge bell, cast in 1239, and 9ft (2.8m) in diameter. Nearby is the Shunjo do, which houses a statue of Chogen. If you continue up the slopes of Wakakusa yama, towards the E, you will arrive at the Nigatsu do and the Sangatsu do.

● Nigatsu do (plan: E2; 440yds/400m E of the Daibutsu den), is the more northerly of the two buildings, the 'temple of the second month', founded in 752 and rebuilt in 1669. Onizutori festival on 12 March.

This building, constructed on a wooden terrace supported by a great many pillars, contains two statues of Kannon, hidden from the public view. Their size is not known. The smaller of them, found in Osaka Bay by the priest Jichu, is supposed to still feel warm to the touch.

*Sangatsu do (plan: E2), the 'temple of the third month'. The Hokke do here was completed in 747 and is now the oldest existing building of Todai ji. It has some remarkable *statues of the Tempyo period.

In the centre stands Fukukenjaku Kannon, surrounded by 14 other dry lacquer statues. The main one is well proportioned; 'its head, which is serene and has a third eye in the middle of its forehead in addition to the Byakugo (tuft of white hair between the eyebrows, symbolized by a jewel), is crowned with a diadem of silver filigree. A statuette of Amida Nyorai, which occupied the tip of this crown, was stolen and never replaced. The halo around the statue, which is of a unique type , is composed of a large number of rays held in place by concentric bars' (Louis Frédéric, *Japon*). Kannon is attended by Nikko and Gakko Bosatsu, the bodhisatvas of the moon and sun, and by four celestial guardians. Amongst the other statues, note a beautiful Jizo Bosatsu of the Kamakura period.

From Sangatsu do you can go SW to the Nandai mon of Todai ji, and from there S to Sanjo dori. This road actually becomes a pedestrian footpath, which runs E to the shrine of Kasuga, after passing Manyo Botanical Garden. Past the second *torii* of this shrine, the path is lined with numerous stone lanterns.

It is possible to go directly to the Kasuga taishi, by heading S, past the shrine of Tamukeyama Hachiman. It was founded in 749 and rebuilt in 1691. Note two small structures in the *azekura* style.

****KASUGA TAISHA** (plan: F4; ¾ml/1.2km SE of Todai ji; 1½ml/2.5km E of Nara eki; bus). On the lower slopes of Wakakusa yama, to the E of Nara Park, this Shinto shrine is the most important in the town and surrounding area. The bright red painted buildings contrast strongly with the deep greens of the park vegetation.

Lantern festival, 3–4 February, and on 15 August; Kasuga matsuri on 13 March; *gagaku* dances on 3 November; On matsuri at the Kasuga Wakamiya on 7 December.

This shrine was founded by Fujiwara Nagate (714–771). The temple was greatly enriched by the Fujiwara family and has several works of art which go back to the Heian period. The numerous deer in Nara park are regarded as messengers of the gods and venerated as such.

The shrine is surrounded by about 10,000 lanterns made of iron, bronze, wood and stone. The oldest probably go back to the 8th c., and some of them date from 1323. When they are lit, twice a year, they are an extremely beautiful sight. The Nandai mon gate (1179), to the S opens onto the main courtyard; then you can go through the Chu mon (1179), to the second courtyard where the four small Kasuga-style shrines stand in a row. They were erected when the Kasuga taishi was founded, and have periodically been rebuilt. In the main courtyard note the *yadogine tree onto which a number of indigenous plants such as lilacs, maples, camellias and cherry blossoms have been grafted.

Opposite the S entrance a pathway leads (for about 110yds/100m) to the lesser shrine of Wakamiya, which was consecrated in the 12th c.

To the W of the main shrine you can visit the treasury which is housed in a modern building; there are several *kakemono*, some fine ritual dance masks, some ancient arms and armour, a lacquered wooden koto board of the Heian period, etc.

Kasuga yama, which rises up to the E of the shrine, was once regarded as the home of the gods. Near the summit there are some small *bas reliefs* representing Buddha, sculpted on the walls of various rocky shelters. They seem to be of the Heian period.

550yds (500m) S of the Kasuga taisha: Shin Yakushi (plan: off F4), is a temple founded by the Empress Komyo (701–760), when her husband, the Emperor Shomu, was ill. Of the old buildings you can still see the Hon do, erected at the end of the Nara period, which houses a remarkable set of *statues: Yakushi Nyorai, the Buddha of medicine, carved from one piece of wood (9th c.), is surrounded by a dozen celestial guardians (*Juni Shinsho). 'These statues, 5ft (1.60m) high, are made from earth covered with *gofun* (lime carbonate), and painted or covered with gold-leaf. The colouring has now almost completely disappeared (...). The eyes of the warriors are inlaid with obsidian. Tempyo period (710–94) or late Hakuho' (Louis Frédéric). This temple also possesses a painting of Nirvana, which is kept in the National Museum.

To the E of Nara Park are the hills of Wakakura, which rise to a maximum height of 1,122ft (342m) and are traversed by some attractive forest toll-roads including the Kasuga Okuyama Driveway (coach from Nara eki and Kintetsu nara eki). This itinerary also provides an opportunity to go to Jukkokudani belvedere, and the small spa town of Mikasa (1ml/2km NE of Todai ji).

You can also see ...

GOKURAKU DO (plan: B4; at Chuin cho; 880yds/800m SE of Kintetsu Nara eki; ½ml/1km SE of Nara eki, JNR). This building, reconstructed during the Kamakura period, is all that remains of the former Ganko ji, which was one of the principal temples of Nara in its day.

MAUSOLEUM OF EMPEROR KAIKA (plan: B4; 330yds/300m SW of Kintetsu Nara eki; 550yds/500m NE of Nara eki JNR). This *kofun* to the S of Nororioji dori is believed to be that of the semi-legendary ninth Emperor of Japan, who was supposed to have lived for 110 years (208–98 BC). Historical examinations show, however, that mausoleums such as this one did not exist before the 4th c. AD.

The mausoleum of the Emperor Shomu (718–758) stands ½ml (1km) N of Kintetsu Nara eki. Behind it is the mound of Tamon, which was once occupied by a castle built in 1567 by Matsunaga Hisahide.

½ml (1km) NE of here, by way of Nara Kaido: Hannya hi, which has a fine wooden statue of Monju Bosatsu on a lion (1324). Note the 13-storey stone pagoda (height 49ft/15m, of the Kamakura period) of this temple.

B Western sector of Nara

Opposite the Tegai mon of Todai ji (p. 439), Ichijo dori leads W as far as Kairyuo ji (a fine five-tier pagoda; Hon do and Kyo zo of the 12th c.), to the NW of which is:

HOKKE JI (2mls/3km W of Todai ji; 880yds/800m N of Kintetsu-Shinomiya eki; 1½mls/2.5km NW of Nara eki, JNR; bus). This temple was founded in the 8th c., as was Kairuo ji, by the Empress Komyo on grounds which belonged to her father Fujiwara Fuhito (659–720). This was once an important convent.

The Hon do, rebuilt in 1601, houses a statue of *Kannon of the eleven heads, in sandalwood, which was probably created as a likeness of the Empress Komyo. Note the disproportionately long arms, which are nonetheless very elegant. The three painted scrolls of the *Descent of Amida* are now kept in the National Museum of Nara.

½ml (1km) approx. W of Hokke ji: the site of the Imperial Palace of Heijokyo. The Dai Dairi, the foundations of which have been discovered, once stood to the N of the capital and occupied an area of 264 acres (107ha). This palace was abandoned by the Emperor Kammu in 784. Now children come to fly their kites there, which makes the place very romantic.

After skirting Kairuo ji and Hokke ji, Ichijo dori continues and finishes to the W, at Saidai ji (map of the Vicinity of Osaka, pp. 500–1, the junction of the Kintetsu private railway lines.

SAIDAI JI (220yds/200m SW of Kintetsu Saidaiji station; 2mls/4km NW of Nara eki, JNR; bus). Unlike Todai ji, which rises up to the E of the old capital, the great western temple has lost much of its former glory. Ochamori festival on the second Saturday and Sunday in April; tea is drunk from a gigantic bowl.

This temple was built in 780 at the command of the Empress Shotoku and became one of the seven leading temples of the capital. It was destroyed several times and only partly reconstructed after 1752.

The Shaka do, the main building, houses a statue of Sakyamuni attributed to Eison (1201-1290), one of the greatest reforming monks of this temple during the Kamakura period.

The Shio do, reconstructed in 1771, contains statues of Juichimen Kannon and four celestial guardians, of the Heian period.

In the Kon do are statues of Monju and Miroku Bosatsu, of the Kamakura period. The Kon do was once luxuriously ornamented in the Chinese fashion and was one of the finest temples in Nara. In front of the present building (18th c.), note the quadrangular base of the eastern pagoda. The western pagoda stood about 110yds (100m) to the W. These five-tier pagodas were originally octagonal in shape.

The building of Aizen do is thought to be from Kyoto: it has a statue of Aizen Myo of the Kamakura period.

The temple also holds a very beautiful *statue of Eison by Zenshun (1280), and a series of 12 scrolls representing the celestial guardians (Juni ten).

▶ ½ml (1km) N of Saidai ji: Akishino dera was founded in 780 and only the *Ko do escaped the fire of 1135. This building is now the main hall and houses statues which include the *Gigei ten, 'one of the most sensitive works which Nara's art has produced (...). Gigei ten is believed to represent the deity who presides over the arts and dance. It is the only such representation known in Japan' (Louis Frédéric). The dry-lacquerwork head is all that remains from the Nara period. The wooden body was sculpted by Unkei at the beginning of the 13th c.

▶ ½ml/1km NE of Saidai ji, to the SE of Heijo station (Kintetsu ER) are the tombs of the Emperor Semiu (83-190, according to the Nihongi) and the Empress Koken, or Shotoku (718-770).

▶ 1ml (1.5km) S of Saidai ji, near Amagatsuji Station (Kintetsu ER): the mausoleum of the Emperor Sainin, who is thought to have lived from 70 BC to 70 AD (in fact it was the 4th c. AD), and in whose reign the shrine of Ise was founded.

*YAKUSHI JI (2mls/3km S of Saidai ji; 110yds/100m SE of the Kintetsu-Nishinokyo station, the second one to the S after Saidaiji). Here is yet another very interesting temple of old Nara. It is, along with Kofuku ji, one of the seats of the Hosso sect of Buddhism. This temple was founded in 680 and almost totally reconstructed from the 13th century onwards.

The Ko do, the first building that is encountered to the N, was rebuilt in 1858 and houses a beautiful sculpted triad by Yakushi Nyorai (Kamakura period), but it is of less interest than the one contained in the Kon do.

In the Kon do (1600-35) is the very fine group of *Yakushi Nyorai, the Buddhist healer, accompanied by Nikko and Gakko Bosatsu, in gilded bronze. These statues of the Hakuho period (late 7th c. or early 8th c.) show the direct influence of T'ang art.

To the SE of the Kon do stands the To to or *East Pagoda (680-729). It is 115ft (35m) high and has three storeys, but appears to have six, owing to the canopies (*mokoshi*) at the centre of each level. It is surmounted by an elegant bronze *sorin*, the *suien* (or uppermost part) which is finely worked and ornamented with angel musicians. The base of the west pagoda (Sai to) can still be seen to the W of here.

To the N of the eastern pagoda is a modern belfry which has a bell of Korean origin.

The Toin do (1285), to the E of the To to, contains the bronze statue of

*Sho Kannon. It is comparable to those in the Kon do and is known by the name of Kadura Kannon. There are other statues (Jikoku ten, Tamon ten, celestial guardians) of the Heian or Muromachi periods.

In the Bussoku do, to the S of the base of the Sai to, you can see a stone imprinted with a mark, said to be the 'footprint of Buddha', which dates from 753.

The temple also contains several ancient paintings, including the famous *Kichijo ten (8th c.), which is exhibited in spring and autumn. 'The portrait with its human echoes, its voluptuous body and its heavily painted face, has a distinctly profane aspect, and illustrates just how far the Nara period was influenced by the glamour of the T'ang civilization' (Peter C. Swann, *Japan*). There is also the *portrait of *Jion Daishi* (632–682), founder of the Hosso sect; 'this portrait, the composition of which is based, in all likelihood, on a Chinese original, expresses very well the spiritual vigour of the great monk, whose pose suggests that he is taking part in a theological discussion. His lavish patriarchal dress, the treatment of the body standing out in pink relief, and the finely decorated inkwell which is by his side, are details which reflect the true tradition of the T'ang. At the same time, the effect of the light and harmonious colours point rather to Japanese taste of the 11th c.' (Akiyama Terukazu). The 9th c. Shinto statues which belong to this temple are now stored in the National Museum.

➡ 1½mls (2.5km) E of Yakushi ji, via Rokujo dori: Daian ji was once one of the most magnificent temples in Nara. The places where the Kon do, the Ko do, Naka mon and Nandai mon once stood have been discovered on land which is now private, and the sites of the temple's two pagodas have also been found further S. The statue of Sakyamuni, which was venerated in this temple, was considered to be one of the finest in Nara.

➡ **TOSHO DAI JI** (770yds/700m N of Yakushi ji and the Kintetsu-Nishinokyo station) is also worthy of interest. It was set up in 759 by the Chinese priest Kien Tchen or Ganjin (688–763), the blind founder of the Risshu sect, of which this temple is the seat. It is now the foremost Buddhist seminary in Japan.

⊚ The Kon do, opposite the Nandai mon, is an elegant building of the Nara period and is influenced by Chinese architecture. Inside you can see the statue of *Birushana Butsu (Buddha Vairocana), which has a halo bearing about 1,000 little Buddhas, and is attributed to the priests T'an Ching and Szu T'o, disciples of Ganjin: painted and gilded dry lacquerwork.

The walls of the hall were once covered with 2,000 other painted representations of Buddha, but these are now almost totally effaced; beautiful painted coffered ceiling. Birushana is flanked by two *statues: one of Kannon of the thousand arms and one of Yakushi Nyorai, created in dry lacquer, in the 8th c. In front are the smaller statues of Bon ten, Taishaku ten and four celestial guardians.

The *Ko do (748), behind the Kon do, was once part of the Imperial

Palace of Nara. It was put here in 760 and then reassembled in the 17th c. It is now the only known edifice of the Dai Dairi in Nara. Inside there are several statues including Miroku Bosatsu, which is thought to be the work of Chun Fa Li.

Between the Kon do and the Ko do, note to the E the extremely attractive *Koro (1240), or drum hall. Behind this is the Sobo or Higashimuro (the priests' residence), which opens to the S through the Raido (1202). To the E of this building note, finally, the Kyo zo, a little *sutra* hall, in the *azekura* style.

To the NE of the Ko do is the Miei do or founder's hall, which houses a multicoloured dry lacquer statue of *Ganjin (763), which you can see only on 6 June each year.

'According to legend, it was a pupil of Ganjin who created this portrait on the last day of Ganjin's life, having been warned by a prophetic dream of the master's forthcoming death. The master is sitting unostentatiously but radiating serenity and strength. He seems to have his eyes closed to capture the thread of his inner meditation better. In fact this expression indicates blindness. Ganjin, who only managed to reach Japan on his sixth attempt at making the crossing, was said to have lost his sight through the continual shipwrecks and the numerous troubles which he suffered on his travels. This statue is the oldest known lacquered effigy' (D. and V. Elisseeff).

Note finally the former Shin den of Kofuku ji, a building of the Edo period (1650), with reception halls, which was transferred to Toshodai ji in 1964, along with the modern monument, presented by the People's Government of China in 1981.

YAMATO BUNKAKAN (address: 1-11-6, Gakuen minami, Sagawara cho; 330yds/300m SE of Kintetsu-Gakuenmae, the 2nd station to the W from Saidaiji; open daily except Mondays from 10.00 to 17.00; closed 28 December to 4 January). This museum, which stands on a small hill to the W of the Ayame pond, was opened in 1960 (architect Isoya Yoshida). It is one of the most interesting private museums in Japan, and offers a constantly changing selection of oriental works of art.

Amongst the **paintings kept here you can see: the *emakimono of the Yamai zoshi*, or the scrolls of the ailments (late 12th c.), which show a gift for observation full of subtlety and humour; the *emakimono of the Ise Monogatari* (13th c.) which bear a Sanskrit transcription of a *sutra*; the *Sanjuroku Kasen Emaki*, attributed to Fujiwara Nobuzane (1177–1265), describing the life of the ancient poets; a Chinese ink portrait of Yuima by Bunsei (1475), 'very different from conventional Zen portraits, because of its strength and freedom of expression. Its animation and vigour are typically Japanese' (Peter C. Swann); *Self-portrait of Sesson* (1504–89) and *Portrait of Ryodhin*, also of the 16th c.; *Landscape*, mounted on a screen, by Shubun (16th c.) and *Torrent*, in *sumi e* by Kano Motonobu (same period); *Matsuura Screen* (17th c.); scenes of domestic life, anonymous painting with coloured figures standing out against a gold background; *Portrait of Fujin*, by Miyagawa Choshun (1682–1752).

The museum also has a tray painted by Ogata Korin (1658-1716) exquisite calligraphy; ceramics and pottery; bronze and metal objects from China and Japan.

☞ C Vicinity of Nara

1 ***KONGO IKOMA REGIONAL PARK** (27mls/44km W as far as Chogosonshi ji, via Hanna Road and Shigi-Ikoma Skyline; coach from Hozan ji) The simplest approach is to take the Kintetsu ER train (Osaka line) from Nara to Ikoma station.

11mls (18km): Ikoma, where you can take the funicular railway to Hozan ji.

12mls (20km): Hozan ji, on the slopes of Ikoma yama, which has a funicular railway up to the summit (2,106ft/642m alt.: belvedere and astronomy observatory). From Hozan ji you can continue by coach on the *Shigi Ikoma Skyline, which runs along the wooded hills separating the Yamato basin (Nara) from Osaka Plain. There is a striking contrast between the eastern side, still immersed in a bygone age, and the huge urban built-up area which stretches out westwards as far as the sea.

26mls (42km): Shigi san funicular railway station where you return to Shigisanguchi (Kintetsu) station to get back to Osaka.

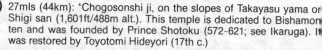 27mls (44km): *Chogosonshi ji, on the slopes of Takayasu yama or Shigi san (1,601ft/488m alt.). This temple is dedicated to Bishamon ten and was founded by Prince Shotoku (572-621; see Ikaruga). It was restored by Toyotomi Hideyori (17th c.)

***Shigisan Engi emaki*, which is in the possession of this temple, ranks amongst the finest *yamato* e style scrolls of all Japanese painting. Far from inspiring solemnity as religion should, these three scrolls are a humorous, moving evocation of the miracles of the priest Myoren: the magic bowl of rice, the cure of the Emperor Daigo, the pilgrimage of the priest's sister to search for her brother. 'This *emaki*, by an anonymous author of the 12th c., forms a strange contrast with the Genji scrolls [see Tokugawa Museum in Nagoya and Goto Museum in Tokyo], not only in its choice of subject, but more especially by the use made of colour, which is here very light, and flows through the ink drawing, giving evidence of a mobility and a surprising skill.' (Théo Lésoualc'h, *Japanese Painting.*)

Temple festivals take place on the 1st, 3rd and 15th of each month, the most important on 3 July.

From the temple you can take the funicular railway down towards Oji and then the train (JNR) from there to Nara.

☞ 2 KASHIHARA, KYOTO, OSAKA, SAKURAI, TENRI, UJI, YAMATO, KORIYAMA, YAMATO TAKADA, YOSHINO, see entries under these names: HORYUJI, see Ikaruga.

N Narita (Island of Honshu)

Map of Places of Interest, p. 70.

Tokyo, 37mls (60km) - Chiba 19mls (30km) - Mito, 63mls (101km) - Urawa, 52mls (84km) - Tokyo International Airport and Shinkansen (JNR) train. See Useful information/Tokyo.

Chiba ken - pop: 68,418.

The new Tokyo International Airport has been built near Narita. In spite of the rather futuristic aspect presented by the airport, Narita remains, for the pilgrim and the tourist, the town of the Shinsho ji, one of Japan's most venerated temples.

'SHINSHO JI (880yds/800m N of Narita JNR, and Keisei ER stations; bus) is the most popular of the temples dedicated to Fudo Myo o, who drives out passions from the soul; it is also known by the name of Narita san. With the park around it, it occupies an area of 42 acres (17ha). A visit to the temple and park makes a very pleasant excursion from Tokyo.

Principal festivals on 1 January (New Year); 3 or 4 February (Setsubun). Throughout the year the temple attracts about 7 million visitors.

In 940, the Fujiwara launched an expedition with a view to quelling Taira Masakado, a rebel who ruled the whole of Kanto and intended to usurp the title of emperor. The soldiers were accompanied by the priest Kancho, who had armed himself with a statue of Fudo and the sacred sword Amakuni no tsurugi. When the victory had been won, the statue did not return to Kyoto: a temple was built for it at Kozu, near Narita, where it was left. In 1705 it was transferred to Narita.

In the first courtyard, the Nio mon (1831) stands at the top of some steps; on the l. is the vast Korinkaku (1974), built to accommodate visitors. At the foot of this is the Doshigaido, a well for ablutions, where pilgrims come to sprinkle themselves with cold water. Past the Nio mon, a flight of steps leads to a vast terrace, where the new Dai Hon do (arch. Yoshida Isohachi), built in 1968, stands in place of the old Hon do of 1857.

A broad canopy and other gilded metal ornaments hang in the huge hall. The sacred statue of Fudo, which comes from Jingo ji, is venerated here. It is accompanied by the statues of the two assistants Kongara and Seitaka, which could be the work of Kobo Daishi.

On the r. is the three-storey pagoda (1803) and behind that is the belfry (1706). Nearby stands the Issaikyo do (1809) which contains the *sutra* in a library of revolving compartments. Behind the Dai Hon do is the Okuno in, a cave which houses a statue of Dainichi Nyorai.

To the W of the temple you can see the Shaka do (1858) and on another terrace, slightly set back, is the Komyo do (1701) where a statue of Dainichi Nyorai and several votive paintings are kept.

The temple treasures include the sword Amakuni no tsurugi (see above) forged in the reign of the Emperor Mommu (8th c.) by the blacksmith Amakuni; a statue of Namikiri Fudo, carved by Kobo Daishi from a piece of the boat which took him to China; and a wooden plaque sculpted in *bas relief* by Matsumoto Ryozan based on a sketch of the five hundred disciples of Buddha (Gohyaku Rakan) by Kano Kazunobu (19th c.).

The *park is partly of Japanese design, partly English and even partly French, with flowerbeds, rocks and a pond. It is one of the loveliest features of the temple and was created in 1928.

☞ **VICINITY**

1 **NARITA INTERNATIONAL AIRPORT** (4mls/6km E). It is the largest airport in Japan.

2 **CHIBA, CHOSHI, KASHIMA, SAWARA, TOKYO**, see entries under these names.

■ Naruto (Island of Shikoku)

Map of Shikoku (Inland Sea), pp. 536–7.

Tokyo, 492mls (792km) – Kochi, 130mls (210km) – Matsuyama, 134mls (215km) – Takamatsu, 45mls (73km) – Tokushima, 10mls (16km).

Tokushima ken – pop: 60,634 – fishing port; saltpans.

The Naruto channel is less than 1ml (1.3km) wide and separates the island of Shikoku from Awaji shima. In this narrow corridor there are violent whirlpools, for which Naruto is famous. 660yds (600m) E of the station Okazaki Castle has been restored and houses a local archaeology collection.

☞ **VICINITY**

👁 1 ***NARUTO KAIKYO** (7mls/12km N; coach). You can reach the island of Oge by crossing the Konaruto suspension bridge. A public garden, laid out as a terrace, has been created above the strait, where the waters of the Inland Sea and the Pacific Ocean meet. A difference in levels of about 4½ft (1.40m) produces whirlpools, in particular at high tide, which are 50ft (15m) in diameter. They have earned the place the name of Awa no Naruto, or the Roaring Pass of Awa. From Oge jima or Naruto a ferry service operates to Awaji shima (Fukura), and boats go as close as possible to the whirlpools.

➡ 5mls (8km) W: the wooded park of Konaruto can be reached by coach along Naruto Skyline which joins Oge jima and Shimada jima to the Shikoku coast.

2 **BANDO** (7mls/11km W; JNR train via Ikenotani; coach); ½ml (1km) to the N of the station, you can visit the attractive Ryozan ji, the founding of which is attributed to the priest Gyoki (8th c.).

3 AWAJI SHIMA, TOKUSHIMA, SETO NAIKAI NATIONAL PARK, see entries under these names.

Nemuro (Island of Hokkaido)

Map of Hokkaido, pp. 228–9.

Tokyo, 974mls (1,568km) – Abashiri, 132mls (212km) – Kushiro, 78mls (125km) – Sapporo, 285mls (458km).

Hokkaido – pop: 45,381 – fishing port; fish canning factories.

Nemuro lies to the S of the bay of the same name, on the eastern appendage of Hokkaido which juts out into the sea to form the Habomai archipelago.

VICINITY

1 NOSAPPU MISAKI (12mls/20km E; coach) is on the tip of the Nemuro peninsula, which is carved out by cliffs. Beyond Goyomai Strait you can see the Habomai islands.

2 SHIBETSU (67mls/108km NW to Nemuro-Shibetsu; JNR train via Attoko and Naka-Shibetsu). Nemuro Bay and the surrounding area make up the Notsuke Furen Regional Park. Head SW out of Nemuro on the N44.

21mls (33km): Attoko, where you can take the N243 northwards.

27mls (44km): Okuyukiusu, station approx. 2mls (4km) W of Furen lagoon which stretches over an area of 20 acres (52km^2). Between October and March it gives shelter to about 10,000 white swans, which are fantastic to see.

35mls (56km): Nishibetsu. The N243 curves round to the W. Another road and the railway continue N in the direction of 49mls (79km): Naka-Shibetsu, where you can get on the N272 leading NE to:

61mls (98km): Shibetsu, which is open to the Nemuro Strait between Hokkaido and Kunashiri.

7mls (12km) SE (coach): Odaito, is a small fishing village on the strip of land which stretches as far as the Cape of Notsuke (access by motor launch in summer). You will notice a strange forest here, which is dead and semi-petrified. As at Furen ko, a great many swans spend the winter in the lagoon formed by the cape.

3 HABOMAI SHOTO (124mls/200km NE as far as Shikotan to). This archipelago extends Nemuro peninsula to the NE. The main islands are Suisho, Akiyuri, Yuri Shibotsu, Taraku and Shikotan (98sq. mls/ 255km^2), the last being the largest.

4 CHISHIMA RETTO (Kunashiri is 124mls/200km N of Nemuro and Etorofu is 249mls/400km to the NE). This is another archipelago 1,800sq. mls (4,640km^2) in area, of which Kunashiri to and Etorofu to are the two main islands. It is extended to the N by the Kurile islands, which link Japan to the Kamchatka peninsula (USSR). They are very mountainous, reaching their highest point at Chacha dake

(5,978ft/1,822m on Kunashiri Island) and form part of the long Chishima volcanic range. They are now under the control of the Soviet Union, although Japan has been laying claim to them since the end of World War II. It is consequently impossible to visit them from Hokkaido.

■ Nichinan (Island of Kyushu)

Map of Natural Resources, p. 67.

Tokyo, 958mls (1,542km) – Fukuoka, 251mls (404km) – Kagoshima, 81mls (131km) – Kumamoto, 15mls (24km) – Miyazaki, 34mls (55km) – Oita, 159mls (256km).

Miyazaki ken – pop: 53,288 – fishing port; wood and paper mills.

This town, situated in the S of the Miyazaki region, is noteworthy for the coastal border of Nichinan Kaigan Regional Park, which spreads out over 115,255 acres (46,643ha) on either side of the Hiroto gawa estuary.

 VICINITY

TOI MISAKI (29mls/46km S; coach; JNR train to Nango). Head S out of Nichinan on the N222, then the N220.

2mls (3km): Aburatsu, Nichinan's small port, near the Umega hama coast which is made up of bizarre rocky ridges.

7mls (12km): Nango; O shima, off-shore from here, is endowed with an underwater park inhabited by tropical fish. Past Nango, leave the N220 and continue by a coastal road which stays with the coast along *Nichinan kaigan for nearly all the rest of the route.

16mls (26km): Ichiki, and off shore Ko jima, where monkeys roam freely.

25mls (40km): Toi, where you can take the cape road to the S.

29mls (46km): *Toi misaki encloses Shibushi Bay to the E. A stud farm has been set up on the tip of this cape which is crowned by a lighthouse.

N Niigata (Island of Honshu)

Railway map on inside front cover – plan on p. 454.

Tokyo, 208mls (335km) – Fukushima, 124mls (199km) – Maebashi, 151mls (243km) – Nagano, 116mls (186km) – Toyama, 155mls (249km) – Yamagata, 106mls (170km).

Capital of Niigata ken (pop: 1,395,545) – pop: 383,919 – Trading port; industrial town (crude oil); flower growing – national university.

At the mouth of the Shinano gawa – the longest river in the country 229mls (369km) – which drains a large part of central Japan, Niigata is also the point where the great cross-country Joetsu railway, linking Tokyo to the Japan Sea, comes to an end. This doubly important position meant that by 1869 it was open as a trading port to foreign merchants and it became, owing to its industrial activity, the main town of Hokuriku, linked from then on to Tokyo-Omiya by the Shinkansen.

Niigata is separated from the open sea by a string of dunes which help to protect the town from the cold winter climate. It is spread out on either side of the Shinano gawa, is traversed by, amongst others, the Bandai Ohashi, and crisscrossed by wide arterial roads lined with modern commercial blocks. All in all, Niigata has little of interest to offer the tourist.

Bandai City (880yds/800m NW of Niigata eki; bus) is one of the liveliest commercial districts (large stores, amusement centre) in the town. It is overlooked by the Rainbow Tower (330ft/100m) which has a revolving observation platform.

Hakusan Park (1½mls/2.5km NW of Niigata eki; bus), in the centre of the town, stretches to the banks of the Shinano gawa. You can visit the little shrine of Hakusan there. A zoological garden, the Prefecture, Niigata University and sports facilities are all situated near this park.

Hiyori yama (2mls/3km NW of the station; bus), by the Sea of Japan, is the highest dune on the Niigata sea front. It has been laid out as a public park and terrace, with a view over the island of Sado.

VICINITY

1 YOKOGOSHI (10mls/16km SE; coach) stands on the banks of the Agano gawa, which is linked by a number of canals to the Shinano gawa before the mouth of these two rivers. You can visit the Hoppo Bunka Hakubutsukan here. This ancient Japanese house surrounded by a garden has been converted into an archaeological, historical and ethnographic museum about northern Japan.

2 YAHIKO REGIONAL PARK (23mls/37km SW; JNR train to Yahiko station, via Yoshida). Head SW out of Niigata on the N116.

5mls (8km): Takeo, where there is a botanical garden and the Niigata tree nurseries. Numerous flowers are grown from bulbs here: tulips, hyacinths, narcissi, etc.

6mls (10km): Uchino, where you leave the N116 to continue along the foot of the Yahiko range, on the eastern side.

22mls (35km): Yahiko shrine, surrounded by beautiful Japanese cedars. Lantern festival (Tanabata) on 25 and 26 July. Behind this shrine is a cable-car which goes up to the summit of Yahiko yama (2,093ft/638m). View in the direction of Sado Island.

23mls (37km): Yahiko and, nearby, the small spa town of Kannonji. A toll road (coach from Yahiko station) follows the crest of the *Yahiko Mountains for 9mls (14km).

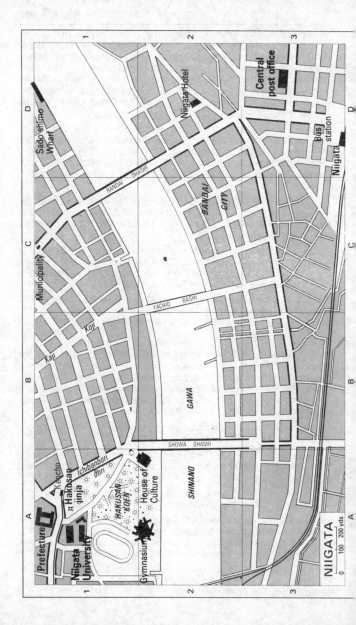

NIIGATA

0   100   200 yds

A

Prefecture

Niigata University

Hakusan jinja

Kecho

Ichibandori dori

Kaji

Koji

Municipality

Sado shumo Wharf

B

Gymnasium

House of Culture

HAKUSAN KOEN

SHINANO

GAWA

SHOWA OHASHI

YACHIO BASHI

BANDAI OHASHI

BANDAI CITY

Niigata Hotel

C

D

Central post office

Bus station

Niigata

1

2

3

➡ 11mls (17km) N (coach): Kakuda misaki can be reached by a toll road which follows the coast of the Sea of Japan.

■ Nikko (National Park of; Island of Honshu)**

Maps of Natural Resources – Places of Interest p. 70 – map of Nikko National Park, pp. 464 – map of Nikko, pp. 456-7.

HOW TO GET THERE?

– From Numata, 55mls (89km) SW of Nikko, by Tobu Railway Bus coaches. The service may be suspended for part of the year. (You will need to inquire.)

– From Tokyo, the simplest way is to take the direct express train (Tobu Railway) from Asakusa station, which links Tokyo to Nikko (84mls/135km) and takes 1h.05. By national railway (JNR) from Ueno station, you will usually have to change at Utsunomiya. This itinerary, though longer than the one above, is certainly the quicker of the two since the Shinkansen line between Tokyo-Omiya and Utsunomiya was opened. If you have only one or two days to spare, place yourself in the hands of the JTB who organize daily excursions which depart from the main hotels of the capital.

– From Utsunomiya; see above for the rail links.

If you have some time to spare in Tokyo, go on a trip (one or two days) to Nikko. This magnificent shrine is world-famous. It shows an architectural side of Japan which is quite different from anything you will see elsewhere in the country (Kyoto, Nara). Here, art has achieved a baroque mode of expression in which everything seems pushed to an extreme. There are some who would criticize Toshu gu for betraying the traditional ideals of the Japanese mind. But in spite of, or perhaps because of, their lavishness, the shrines of Nikko make a wonderful effect. You will need a few extra days to see Nikko National Park as well, and further to the NE the spa towns of Shiobara (see Imaichi) and Nasu (see Kuroiso). The whole ensemble covers an area of 347,665 acres (140,698ha.).

A Nikko: temples and shrines

◉ An in-depth visit to Nikko (pop: 23,885) and its shrines will easily take up a day. Tosho gu, mentioned above, is dedicated to Tokugawa Ieyasu and is the most famous of them all. By the 17th c. it had revived the religious fervour of this little place on the banks of the Daiya gawa. Opinions about Tosho gu vary considerably. A Japanese proverb states 'Nikko wo minai uchi wa kekko to iu na', which translates as: 'You do not know Excellence if you do not know Nikko'. Fosco Maraini, on the contrary, writes: 'Nikko is exhausted, old, spiritless and full of false aestheticism trying to redeem itself with gold, with that which is grandiose, fantastical, amazing and excessive.'

BEFORE IEYASU. The first temple founded at Nikko was the Shihonryu ji,

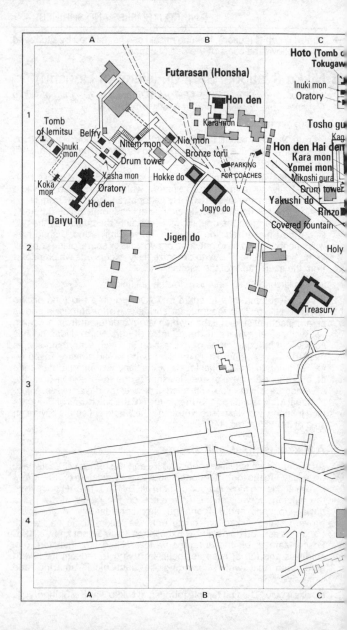

NIKKO

0   50 yds

shita mon

cred markets

mon

rey pagoda

Gohoten do

Sorin to

atsu do

dori

Rinno ji   **Hon bo**

Inari   gawa

Site of
Shihonryu ji

3-storey pagoda

Hon den

Hai den

Hon gu

Shinkyu
(Sacred bridge)

Daiya   gawa

created by the priest Shodo Shonin (735-817). In 808 Tachibana Toshito rebuilt this temple, which was known from then on as Futarasan. Two years later the priest Kyobin, a disciple of Shodo, began to build the Mangan ji (Rinno ji). The place was called Futara yama (or Nikko san in Chinese: the sunlight). It was visited at the time by Kobo Daishi (774-835). In 850 Jikaku Daishi (794-864) started to erect three new temples at Nikko. These were followed by about 30 subsidiary temples. Emperors and other important figures made numerous gifts to Nikko. Its prosperity was considerable until 1590, when Toyotomi Hideyoshi (1536-98) imposed his power on the religious town, leaving only nine temples. Nikko regained its splendour in 1617, when the ashes of Tokugawa Ieyasu were brought here.

TOKUGAWA IEYASU (1542-1616). He was a native of Okazaki and rapidly took control of central Japan. In spite of several ineffectual confrontations with Oda Nobunaga and then with Toyotomi Hideyoshi, he proved sufficiently diplomatic not to compromise his safety and to secure for himself, at the first opportunity, the succession to Hideyoshi. The battle of Sekigahara (1600) reinforced his power, and in 1603, for the benefit of his family, he reinstated the title of shogun, which the Tokugawa kept until the 19th c. Although he officially abdicated in 1605 in favour of his son Hidetada, he continued to meddle in public affairs. He instigated the siege of Osaka which eliminated the Toyotomi heirs, thus ensuring the power of his family. He also enclosed Japan in the type of society which was to be its own for nearly two centuries. Ieyasu died at Shizuoka and was provisionally buried at Kano zan (see Shizuoka), before being laid to rest at Tosho gu in Nikko.

AFTER IEYASU. The building of Tosho gu was finally begun in 1634, by Ieyasu's grandson Iemitsu (who is also buried at Nikko). At this time the Emperor Go Komyo (1633-54) elevated Ieyasu to the posthumous title of Tosho Daigongen, and it was decided that an Imperial prince would be president of the monument, a custom which was upheld until the fall of the shogunate in 1868. At the time of the Meiji Restoration, the shrine, regarded as a national treasure, narrowly escaped destruction, since some Tokugawa partisans who took over the buildings were determined to stay there. Fortunately the statesman Itagaki Taisuke (1837-1919) intervened and persuaded them to leave the shrine.

FESTIVALS: 13 April, Yayoi matsuri at the Futarasan shrine; 2 May, Gohan shiki, rice ceremony at Rinno ji; 17 and 18 May, the Spring Festival at Tosho gu, with a procession of a thousand people in ancient costume (*Sennin Gyoretsu); 7 August, Waraku Odori; 17 October, Autumn Festival. The temples and shrines are open from 08.00 to 16.00 in winter, and until 17.00 in summer (April to October). You will need an entrance pass.

 A long road, starting from the station, leads W to the Daiya gawa, which you can cross near the Sacred Bridge (plan: F4; 1ml/1.5km W of the Nikko JNR and Tobu stations), rebuilt in 1907 on the same lines as the 1636 original.

Legend has it that the priest Shodo wanted to cross the river at this point and used two huge snakes as a bridge. The existing 'divine bridge' (Shin kyo or Mihashi) is 17mls (28km) long and opened only for important ceremonies.

Further on, notice a little monument dedicated to Matsudaira Masatsuna, who planted (1628) the superb pathway of cryptomerias, 25mls (40km) long which leads to the Nikko shrines (see Imaichi).

➤ 220yds (200m) to the N is the Hon gu, with its red lacquered buildings, and to the N of that is the site of Shihonryu ji (plan: F3), founded in 766 by the priest Shodo. These shrines were partly reconstructed in the 17th c. In the second, a statue of Kannon with a thousand arms is venerated. It is attributed to Shodo and flanked by statues of Godaison and Shodo. The three-tier pagoda was a gift from Minamoto Sanetomo (1191-1219).

To the l. of the sacred bridge a path leads up to *Rinno ji (plan: D3). This temple of the Tendai sect lies to the E of Ote dori, which leads N to Tosho gu.

It was once known by the name of Mangan ji, and became the principal temple of Nikko. Its abbots were nominated by the Emperor and were often members of his family. It was rebuilt in the 17th c., when it took its present name and lost much of its greatness.

FESTIVAL: 2 May, Gohanshiki, in the Sambutsu do.

The Hon bo (abbots' residence) opens onto Ote dori, to the r. of the entrance. In the eastern part of the Hon bo you can visit the religious building (ask for a permit at the temple offices, on the other side of Ote dori). The stelae of the superiors, who belonged to the Imperial family and followed in succession of Nikko, are kept there; there is a luxurious lacquered altar embellished with gold-leaf. The garden is one of the loveliest features of this temple.

The American President Ulysses Grant stayed in the Hon bo in 1879 when he came to visit Nikko.

Sambutsu do (plan: D3), to the N of the Hon bo, is Nikko's largest edifice. It was erected in 1648, and was probably originally constructed by the priest Ennin or Jikaku Daishi (794-864), on Mount Hiei near Kyoto.

The temple houses three enormous statues of Buddha, each over 26ft (8m) high. Amida is flanked by Juichimen Kannon and Kannon Bato, who has a horse's head. This deity is venerated as the patroness of animals. Note also the portraits of the priests Ryogen (912-85) and Tenkai (1536-1643).

To the NW of the Sambutsu do is the Sorin to, a copper column put up in 1643 by the priest Tenkai. It is comparable to the one in Enryaku ji on Mount Hiei. The Gohoten do, to the N of the Sambutsu do, contains the statues of Daikoku, Bishamon and Benzai ten. Note also an old cherry tree, known as *kongo zakura*.

··TOSHO GU (plan: C1) is now the main shrine at Nikko. You can get there, to the N of Ote dori, by the Sennin ishidan, 'stone stairway of the thousand Men'; the lower classes, who were forbidden to enter the temple, used to gather here on feast days. At the top of the steps is the granite *torii*, 26ft (8m) high.

On the l. of the *torii* is the five-tier pagoda (105ft/32m high), built in 1659, burnt down, and rebuilt in 1815. The architrave on the first floor is decorated with the signs of the zodiac. On every floor there are black lacquered doors set in each wall. Note the Tokugawa coat of arms.

After climbing a stone staircase, you will go in through the Omote mon or Nio mon gate, which is the main portal. On the pediment and pillars are sculptures representing peonies, chrysanthemums and lions' heads. The gigantic statues of the Deva kings have been replaced. You will find that you are standing in the first courtyard.

No effort has been spared to ensure that there are as many monuments as possible. The state invested almost unlimited sums. The finest workmen, mostly from Kyoto and Nara, rivalled each other in trying to make their work worthy of its dedication. The Momoyama style was adopted, since the Edo style had not yet made its mark on the country. The influence of Chinese Ming art is also manifest. The buildings have remained continually under repair. Tradition demanded that they be restored every 20 years. As it took 10 years to gather the materials and as long again to carry out the task, the building sites were never closed.

To the r. of the courtyard are three sacred stone warehouses, the last of which is decorated in painted-and-gilt high relief depicting elephants, based on drawings by Kano Tanyu (1602-74). On the l. is the holy stable, the only building of the whole group which is not lacquered.

On the second panel starting from the l. are the famous three wise monkeys.

At the end of the courtyard, near the pool designed for purification is the Rinzo, the sacred library which contains 7,000 volumes of Buddhist *sutra*.

If you mount another staircase, you will reach a terrace, at the foot of the Yomei mon, where there are a large candelabra and two bronze lanterns, gifts from the Dutch in 1636, presented through the intermediary, François Caron (see Hirado). A bronze bell comes from Korea.

On the l. behind the drum tower is the Yakushi do or Honji do, dedicated to Yakushi Nyorai. It was devastated by fire in 1961 and was rebuilt between 1967 and 1974. Its ceiling was decorated with a famous 'Weeping dragon' (Naki ryu), painted by Kano Yasunobu

(1616–85), replaced by another by the contemporary painter Nampu Katayama.

**Yomei mon (plan: C2), the 'portal of the sunlight', stands at the top of another flight of steps. It is the most famous monument of Tosho gu. The *samurai* of lower rank had to stop there. The great *samurai* could go further in, but had to leave their swords at the gate.

This portal is renowned for its matchless beauty and is supposed to hold the admiring gaze of the observer until the evening, hence its name the Twilight porch. It is surmounted by an upper storey and ornamented with a profusion of fantastic white and gilded sculptures. A complex corbelled structure supports the upper level balcony. The 12 columns supporting the portico are made of *keyaki* wood (*zelkowa*), painted white; on the medallions, birds, animals and flowers are sculpted in *bas relief*. On a central column note two sculpted tigers. The grain of the wood has been skilfully used to represent the fur of these animals which are known, for that reason, as *mokumeno tora* (tigers in wood). On another column called Sakasa bashira (inverted column), the motifs are sculpted upside down to ward off ill fortune.

The Yomei mon gate is extended by galleries running from E to W. On the outer panels are carvings of pines, bamboo plants, plum trees and birds.

When you have gone through Yomei mon you enter into a courtyard which is separated to the N from the main shrine by another enclosure. On the l. is the Mikoshi gura, a building in which the sacred palanquins are kept. They contain relics and are used for processions and annual festivals.

On the ceiling of the building, notice some large *tennin* (Buddhist angels), painted by Kano Ryotaku.

Opposite Mikoshi gura is the Kagura den (for the performance of sacred dances). On one wall is a sculpted basket, based on a drawing by Kano Korenobu (1753–1808) and showing Western influence. It is the only such example at Nikko.

*Kara mon, to the N of this courtyard, provides access to the Hon den. This gate is richly decorated. The pillars and door panels are inlaid with carved wooden dragons and flowers. A spirit playing the harp adorns the ceiling.

You will have to remove your shoes before going through the *tamagaki* on the r., the sacred fence surrounding the Hai den and the Hon den. This collection of buildings makes up the most important part of the whole shrine.

The *Hai den or oratory, which is, in some respects an antechamber of the Hons den, is divided into three halls with lacquered pillars enclosed in metal frames.

Above the lintels of the doors to the central hall are friezes depicting plants and birds, and portraits of the Thirty-six Poets, painted by Tosa

Mitsuoki (1617-91). There is a coffered ceiling adorned with dragons. At the end is the sacred mirror (2½ft/0.80m in diameter) which represents the holy spirit of the deity. The eastern hall was once reserved for the shoguns of the three Tokugawa houses of Owari (Nagyoya), Kii (Wakayama) and Hitachi (Mito). The western hall was intended for the superior of Rinno ji, who belonged to the Imperial family. The panels of these two rooms are inlaid with paulownia flowers and phoenixes.

The Hon den is reached by the passage called Ishino ma, a name which comes from the *tatami* resting on stone paving.

The *Hon den is made up of three parts: the *heiden*, where the golden *gohei* (golden paper) are kept; the *naijin* (inner hall); and the *nai-naijin*. In this last hall, surrounded by some of the greatest works of art, is the dazzling, gilt-lacquered shrine (the Holy Palace), where the three deified heroes Ieyasu, Hideyoshi and Yoritomo are worshipped. The inner halls are not open to the public.

On a gate which leads from the courtyard between Yomei mon and Kara mon is the famous *Nemuri neko, the 'sleeping cat', carved by the great sculptor Hidari Jingoro (1594-1634). When you have passed through this gate, you will come to the richly decorated Sakashita mon, past which is a stairway leading up to the Ieyasu Mausoleum, preceded by the Inuki mon and an oratory. This bronze monument, shaped like a small pagoda, was recreated in 1683 after an earthquake.

☛ If you come back to Ote dori, to the foot of the steps leading to the great *torii* and the five-storey pagoda (p. 460), you can go along an avenue which leads NW to the shrine of Futarasan.

This path goes past Koyo en on the l. where the Treasury Museum (plan: C2) was set up in 1915: there are a great many works of art from the temples and shrines of Nikko. Continue in this direction and you will come to a *torii* on your r. which opens onto a flight of steps going up to:

🏛 FUTARASAN SHRINE (plan: B1). Situated to the W of Tosho gu, this shrine was founded in honour of Okuninushi no Mikoto (see Izumo) and rebuilt in 1610. Sacred dances 13 to 17 April.

In front of the Hon den, note an old bronze lantern, called Bake doro, the 'lantern of the Spectre' (1293). The legend goes that in the glow from this lantern a number of ghosts appeared and gave battle. The traces of sword marks on it can still be seen.

↦ 220yds (200m) SW of the shrine is *Tokugawa Iemitsu's Mausoleum (1603-61), which is much less ornate; it is called Daiyu in (plan: A1-A2) or Daiyu byo. This tomb was built in a year, whilst the building of Tosho gu took thirteen. The Hai den was decorated by Kano Tanyu and Kano Yasunobu.

↦ 3mls (5km) N of Nikko (coach): Kirifuri Falls (cascade of mist) on Itana gawa, is a double waterfall 230ft (70m) high. On the way (from the Sacred Bridge) you will pass by Ritsu in, famous for its flowering plum trees. Past the waterfall is a new toll road which goes as far as the Kirifuri plateau (skiing in January to March).

B From Nikko to Numata

55mls (89km) SW on the N120; coach.

➤ Past Nikko Bridge, which runs beside the Sacred Bridge, the road goes past the grounds of the Nikko shrines.

1½ml (2km): Tamozawa bashi.

➤ 550yds (500m) S: Nikko Botanical Garden attached to Tokyo University, has several thousand plants, notably alpines. The old Imperial villa of Tamozawa, which is part of this park, houses the Nikko Museum, which has been given to the National Park: geology, flora, fauna, history, etc.

Behind this park is the Gammanga fuchi, where subsidence produces a waterfall in the Daiya. Note nearby the numerous statues of Jizo Bosatsu, which are said to be bewitched as no one can determine exactly how many there are. If you continue upwards and to the S you will come to Somen daki.

➤ 2mls (3km) NW: Jakko or Nunobiki Falls, on the Tamozawa gawa.

➤ 4mls (7km): Kiyotaki, where you can visit the shrine and temple of this name. Turn off on the l. to leave the N122 heading 38mls (61km) SW towards Kiryu.

6mls (9km): Umagaeshi, where *Irohazaka begins. This very windy road goes up as far as Lake Chuzenji.

There are in fact two similar roads (tolls), on either side of Kegon gorge. The more southerly one, or Daini (the second one), is better for going up and the other one, Daichi, for coming down.

10mls (16km): Akechidaira, terrace overlooking the Daiya gawa valley. A cable-car goes up from there to Tembo dai 4,478ft (1,365m).

From the summit there is a magnificent *panorama over Mount Nantai, Lake Chuzenji, the Kegon Falls, and in the other direction, over the plain of Kanto.

11mls (18km): Chugushi, on the eastern edge of *Chuzenji ko (4,170ft/1,271m alt.; boats on the lake in summer, cable-car from Mount Chanoki Daira).

This lake is 4.5sq. mls (11.6km^2) in area and volcanic in origin. It forms the southern part of a vast crater, the central cone of which would have been about where Nantai san stands. It is particularly popular in summer and autumn. There are many sports and leisure facilities. Lantern festivals from 31 July to 2 August.

➤ From Chugushi a lift goes down to the foot of the *Kegon Falls 315ft (96m), which flow from the lake. It is undoubtedly the most famous in Japan, but it is also, unfortunately, the chosen venue of many couples attempting suicide. Shirakumo taki, the Cascade of the white cloud, along with a dozen other smaller waterfalls, is nearby.

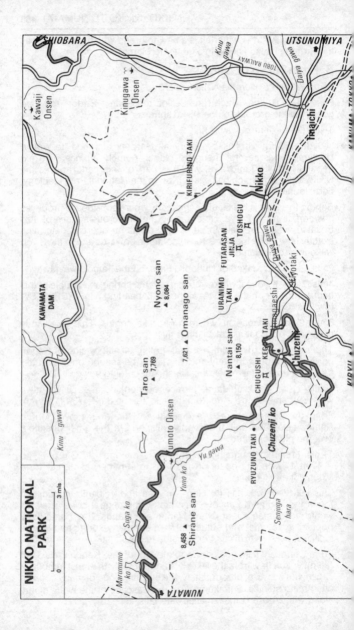

To the W, on the shores of the Chuzenji, stands Futarasan Chugushi (the Middle shrine), and from there you can go up Nantai san (8,150ft/2,484m), which takes approx. 5h. At the summit is Oku miya (Upper shrine). The Tohai matsuri takes place between 1 and 7 August. About 10,000 people make the climb, wearing the white pilgrim dress; it is an imposing sight.

➡ ½ml (1km) S of Chugushi, on the eastern shores of the lake; Chuzen ji or Tachiki Kannon, created in 784 by Shodo Shonin. This temple houses a statue of Kannon with a thousand hands, attributed to the priest Shodo.

➡ 4mls (7km) S (toll road; coach): Hangetsu toge, on the slopes of Hangetsu zan (5,751ft/1,753m), with a view of Chuzenji ko.

➡ 12mls (20km): Oku Nikko Musuem. Past Futarasan Chugushi is a small natural history museum where an axe is on view, which supposedly belonged to the priest Shodo. The N120 continues along Chuzen ji.

15mls (24km): Jigokuchaya. The Dragon's Head Falls, Ryuzuno taki, cut across the course of the Jigoku gawa, which flows into Chuzenji ko.

16mls (26km): marshy plain of Senjoga hara traversed by the Yu gawa. This river is an outlet to the N of the little Lake Yuno (4,849ft/1,478m alt.), which breaks into the Yu daki waterfall.

20mls (32km): Yumoto, spa town (waters from 133° to 154°F/56° to 68°C) surrounded by the high Oku Nikko Mountains. From Yumoto, the *Konsei toge toll road runs through a tunnel under the Konsei pass (6,699ft/2,042m), between Mounts Konsei (7,356ft/2,242m) and Yuzenga (7,654ft/2,333m), which separates the regions of Tochigi and Gumma.

Hikers could go from Konsei toge to Nikko via Kaneda toge (6,119ft/1,865m), Orokura san (6,627ft/2,020m), Sannoboshi zan (6,840ft/2,085m), Taro san (7,769ft/2,368m), Fujimi toge (6,670ft/2,033m), the Ara gawa valley and Jikanno taki. This trip takes about two days and is a pleasant excursion (inquire about it in Nikko).

25mls (40km): Suge numa (5,640ft/1,719m alt.), a lake formed by a dam of lava from Nantai san. The western slopes of the mountain are even wilder than those mentioned above. It is a grandiose spot and the water from the lake pours down Hatcho Falls into Lake Maru below.

36mls (58km): Katashina, see Numata (vicinity).

55mls (89km): Numata, see entry under this name.

■ Nobeoka (Island of Kyushu)

Map of Kyushu (North), pp. 388–9.

Tokyo, 838mls (1,349km) – Fukuoka, 152mls (244km) – Kagoshima, 134mls (216km) – Kumamoto, 90mls (145km) – Miyazaki, 55mls

(89km) – Oita, 70mls (112km).

Miyazaki ken - pop: 128,292 - fishing port; textile industries.

Nobeoka, on the eastern side of the island of Kyushu, is the best point of access to the Takachiho gorges.

The site of Nobeoka Castle (1ml/1.5km SW of Nobeoka eki) is on an island formed by the Gokase gawa, which is now occupied by a public park. Between 1587 and 1868 the castle was successively the residence of the Takahashi, the Arima, the Miura, the Makino and the Naito.

☞ **VICINITY**

1 KITAURA (22mls/36km NE; coach), a small fishing port at the bottom of a cove which opens to the N of the very lovely coastal region studded with little islands and named Hyuga Matsushima by analogy with the famous place in the Sendai region (see Shiogama).

2 TAKACHIHO (35mls/56km NW on the N218; JNR train; coach). From Nobeoka, the road and the railway go up the Gokase gawa valley.

3½mls (6km): on the r. a path branches off towards (4mls/6km NW) Mukabaki yama (2,726ft/831m alt.), a wooded mountain with the Munobiki Falls cascading down it. There is no form of transport to take you there.

24mls (39km): Hinokage. Past this point the valley narrows and becomes more picturesque.

35mls (56km): Takachiho, on the banks of the Gokase gawa, where you can go for pleasant walks in the surrounding area. Certain local traditions still survive.

➡ ½ml (1km) S: ** Takachiho kyo is one of the most spectacular gorges in Japan. This steep rocky site, formed by lava from Mount Aso, has waterfalls tumbling down it and has given rise to many legends.

➡ 11mls (17km) N: the boundary of the Miyazakai and Oita regions (coaches to Taketa). The whole mountainous area around here is known as the *Sobo Katamuki Regional Park (54,000 acres /22,000 ha), and includes Sobo san (5,768ft/1,758m) and Katamuki yama (5,266ft/1,605m), which are the main peaks. It is famous for its forests and wild animals (deer, antelope, bears).

3 HYUGA, MOUNT ASO NATIONAL PARK, see entries under these names.

■ Numata (Island of Honshu)

Tokyo, 106mls (171km) – Fukushima, 186mls (299km) – Maebashi, 25mls (41km) – Nagano, 75mls (120km) – Niigata, 126mls (202km) – Urawa, 88mls (141km) – Utsunomiya, 78mls (125km).

Gumma ken - pop: 47,150.

Numata is situated on a plateau where lies the confluence of the Usune and the Katashina with the Tone gawa; it is a suitable base from which to visit Nikko National Park (see entry under this name) and especially the peaks of Oku Nikko.

All that remains of Numata Castle (850yds/800m N of the station), originally built in 1153 by Numata Kagetoki, is the ruins. Tokugawa Ieyasu entrusted it to the Sanada who were dispossessed. The castle was rebuilt in 1703 and became the residence of the Honda, then of the Kuroda until 1868.

VICINITY

1 OZE NUMA (34mls/55km) NE: coach to Oshimizu). The entire area which lies to the W of Oze numa is known as Ozega hara. This region is accessible only to hikers, who will find some mountain huts there. It is all part of Nikko National Park. Head E out of Numata on the N120 which goes up the Katashina Valley.

19mls (31km): Katashina. Leave the N120 which goes towards Nikko (the itinerary in reverse is described on p. 465). Winter sports resort on the eastern slopes of Hotaka san (7,080ft/2,158m).

23mls (37km): Tokura.

3mls (5km): Fujimishita, where you can set off on a tour of Ozega hara.

32mls (51km): Oshimizu, where the coaches stop. You will have to continue on foot.

34mls (54km): Sampei toge (5,781ft/1,762m) with a view over Oze nume and Hiuchiga take.

34mls (55km): *Oze numa, a little lake (0.64sq. mls/1.67km^2 in area) which is rich in aquatic plants. To the N is Hiuchiga take (7,697ft/2,346m), an extinct volcano. There is a view from the summit over the entire region. Oze numa is the eastern part of the vast marshy plateau of Oze, which stands at an alt. of approx. 4,600ft (1,400m). It boasts several waterfalls and is scattered with a carpet of rare flowers in season, which attracts hikers and botanists. There is a signposted route which makes it possible to walk from Oshimizu to Tokura via *Ozega hara in two days.

2 YUZAWA (38mls/61km NW on the N17; coach). Head N out of Numata.

4mls (7km): Tsukinoyu. Past here, turn off on the r. to leave the N291 for Minakami (see under this name).

14mls (22km): Sarugakyo, a small spa town upstream from Akaya reservoir.

17mls (27km): the road goes through a tunnel under the Mikuni pass (4,081ft/1,244m) which the Mikuni kaido once used. There are some attractive landscapes beyond here.

21mls (33km): the Naeba winter sports resort at the foot of Naeba san (7,037ft/2,145m alt.). This is one of the best ski resorts in Japan (international competitions).

38mls (61km): Yuzawa, a spa and winter sports resort, at the end of the Shimizu railway tunnel, in the Uono gawa valley.

3 JOSHIN ETSU KOGEN AND NIKKO NATIONAL PARKS, see entries under these names.

Numazu (Island of Honshu)

Tokyo, 73mls (117km) – Kofu, 62mls (99km) – Nagano, 155mls (249km) – Nagoya, 140mls (225km) – Shizuoka, 31mls (50km) – Yokohama, 57mls (92km).

Shizuoka ken – pop: 189,038 – industrial town and port.

Although it has been taken over by industrial expansion, this town, which opens onto Suruga Bay at the mouth of the Kano gawa, is still a pleasant holiday resort and you can visit the Fuji-Hakone-izu National Park from here. The town was the residence of Mizuno until the 19th c. Now the Imperial family has a villa nearby.

Sembon Matsubara (1ml/1.5km SW of the station; bus), the lovely 'thousand pinetrees' beach, lies to the N of the Kano gawa estuary; aquarium.

Kanuki yama (1½ml/2km SE) rises to a height of 633ft/193m and provides a famous view over Suruga Bay and Mount Fuji.

VICINITY

FUJI-HAKONE-IZU NATIONAL PARK, see entry under this name.

Obama (Island of Honshu)

Map of Natural Resources, p. 66.

Tokyo, 320mls (515km) - Fukui, 71mls (114km) - Gifu, 83mls (134km) - Kanazawa, 120mls (193km) - Kyoto, 67mls (108km) - Otsu, 57mls (92km).

Fukui ken - pop: 33,702 - fishing port.

At the bottom of the attractive bay of the same name, Obama is a starting point for a trip round the coastal park of Wakasan wan.

Near the sea (1ml/1.5km N of the station) there are still some ruins of Obama Castle. The Kinoshita, the Kyogoku and the Sakai lived there between 1585 and 1868.

VICINITY

1 ONYU (2½mls/4km SE; JNR train); 2mls (3km) S of the station you can visit Jingu ji where the Hon do and Nio mon are of interest. Myoraku ji (2mls/4km SE by another road) is remarkable for its Yakushi do and five-storey pagoda. There are other temples around Obama which contain interesting Buddhist statues. (You will need to inquire locally.)

2 KUSUYAGA TAKE (9mls/15km N; coach). Take a winding toll road to get to the summit (2,031ft/619m) of the rocky peninsula which bounds Obama Bay to the N. View over the surrounding area and many natural curiosities in the vicinity.

3 *WAKASA SOTOMO (6mls/9km N; boat). An extraordinary group of inlets, natural arches and marine caves, which can be reached only from the sea.

4 TAKAHAMA (12mls/20km W; JNR train). In summer you can go from here (by boat; 4mls/7km NW) to the superb *Otomi cliffs, which are bounded by Cape Tai.

5 MIYAZU, TSURUGA, see entries under these names.

6 BIWA KO, see Otsu.

■ Obihiro (Island of Hokkaido)

Map of Hokkaido (Eastern Area), pp. 228–9.

Tokyo, 820mls (1,320km) – Abashiri, 122mls (197km) – Asahikawa, 115mls (185km) – Kushiro, 76mls (123km) – Sapporo, 130mls (210km).

Hokkaido – pop: 153,861 – sugar refineries – national university.

Obihiro has grown up at the point where several rivers meet: Otofuke, Shikaribetsu Satsunai and Tokachi. It is situated in the heart of the fertile Tokachi Plain which is dominated to the N by the mountain range of Daisetsuzan and to the W by the Hidaka range. Its recent industrial development makes it the seventh town of Hokkaido. Obihiro is a suitable starting point for a trip round Akan and Daisetsuzan National Parks.

Midorigaoka Park (1½ml/2km SW of the station; bus) is a group of wooded hills which covers an area of 104 acres (42ha) and has sports facilities.

☞ **VICINITY**

1 TOKACHIGAWA ONSEN (7mls/11km E; coach). Thermal springs which emerge from the bed of the Tokachi gawa at temperatures between 106° and 115°F (41° and 46°C).

2 HIDAKA (55mls/88km W on the N38 and 274; coach). From Obihiro, the N38 goes W up the Tokachi gawa valley.

21mls (33km): Shimizu, where you can take the N274 which crosses the Hidaka mountain range through a tunnel under the Nissho pass; it is a very pleasant *trip. This mountainous barrier, which is a continuation of the Daisetsuzan, finishes up in the sea at Erimo misaki and reaches its highest point at Horoshiri dake (6,732ft/2,052m).

55mls (88km): Hidaka, on the upper Saru gawa valley. From Hidaka you can take the train down the Saru and Mu kawa valleys.

3 AKAN AND DAISETSUZAN NATIONAL PARKS, see entries under these names.

4 ERIMO MISAKI, see Samani.

■ Oda (Island of Honshu)

Tokyo, 550mls (885km) – Hiroshima, 101mls (163km) – Matsue, 40mls (65km) – Tottori, 123mls (198km) – Yamaguchi, 115mls (185km).

Shimane ken – pop: 36,192.

Oda, along with its suburbs Kute and Torii, is an important trade centre on the Chugoku side, facing the Sea of Japan.

☞ **VICINITY**

SAMBE ONSEN (12mls/19km SE; coach). Springs at 108°F (42°C). This spa is situated on the S side and at the foot of *Sambe san

(3,694ft/1,126m), which has a toll road running round it (approx. 10mls/16km round trip; coach). Caves, sulphur springs, the flow of lava and the little lake of Ukinu testify to the former existence of a volcano named Fuji Iwami.

Odawara (Island of Honshu)

Map of the Region of Hakone, p. 161.

Tokyo, 48mls (77km) – Kofu, 65mls (104km) – Shizuoka, 57mls (91km) – Yokohama, 32mls (52km).

Kanagawa ken – pop: 156,654.

Odawara, at the mouth of the Sakawa gawa, in Sagami Bay, is the main point of access to the Hakone mountains. It was in the past a strategic point on the Tokai do. It is now a tourist town. From there you can head towards the Ashino ko or the Izu peninsula.

Odawara Castle (220yds/200m S of the station) stands in the middle of an attractive public garden. The four-storey keep, re-erected in 1960, houses souvenirs and documents concerning Odawara's historic past.

THE PRIVATE KINGDOM OF THE HOJO In 1494 Hojo Nagauji, better known as Hojo Soun (1432-1519), took over the castle of Omori Yoriaki and made it his residence. His son Ujitsuna and his grandson Ujiyasu progressively overcame the whole Kanto region and ousted the declining Uesugi who were theoretically in power. Uesugi Kenshin laid siege in vain to the castle in 1561. In 1578 Oda Nobunaga recognized Hojo Ujimasa's authority over Kanto, but the latter refused to submit to Toyotomi Hideyoshi and was besieged at Odawara, where he committed suicide. The castle then passed into the hands of the Okubo, and the government of Kanto was entrusted to Tokugawa Ieyasu. The Abe and then the Inaba succeeded the Okubo who took possession of Odawara again in 1686.

Near the castle is the shrine of Hotoku Ninomiya, dedicated to the botanist Sontoku Ninomiya (1787-1856), a native of Odawara.

VICINITY

1 MINAMI ASHIGARA (7mls/11km NW; Izu Hakone Railway train to the terminus at Daiyuzan). You can visit Saijo ji or Doryoson, 2mls (3km) SW of the station (bus). This temple, built in the 15th c. on the northern slopes of Myojinga take (3,835ft/1,169m), houses a statue of Kannon with eleven heads, and statues of the priest Doryoson and of Tengu (demon with the long nose), which is probably the posthumous metamorphosis of the founder priest. Festival 27th and 28th of each month.

2 MANAZURU (9mls/14.5km S; JNR train; coach). 2mls (3km) SE of the station (coach), the attractive rocky cape of Manazuru juts out and provides a view of the Atami and Odawara regions. Aquarium nearby.

3 ATAMI, GOTEMBIA, ITO, KAMAKURA, FUJI-HAKONE-IZU NATIONAL PARK, see entries under these names.

■ Oga (Island of Honshu)

Map of Tohoku, pp. 232–3.

Tokyo, 388mls (625km) – Akita, 19mls (30km) – Aomori, 119mls (192km) – Morioka, 91mls (147km) – Sendai, 168mls (270km) – Yamagata, 152mls (244km).

Akita ken – pop: 38,940.

Oga and its peninsula, like a spur on the western edge of Tohoku, is one of the pleasantest spots to visit from the town of Akita, in the north of Honshu. To the E is the former Hachiro lagoon, which has now been developed.

☞ **VICINITY**

1 HACHIRO GATA (7½mls/12km NE approx.). 80% of this former lagoon, 86sq. mls (223km²) in area, was improved between 1958 and 1968. Model co-operative farms, with intensive mechanization, have been set up with a view to increasing the rice yield. This lake was once the second largest in Japan after Biwa ko.

2 *TOUR OF THE OGA PENINSULA (44mls/71km, according to the itinerary given below; there are day trips by Oga bus; various alternative routes leave from Oga and Akita stations). Head NE out of Oga towards Akita.

5mls (8km): take a road to the N leading to the Panorama Line toll road which goes to:

8mls (13km): Kampu zan (1,165ft/355m alt.), the belvedere of Oga with a view over both sides of the peninsula and Hachiro gata.

15mls (25km): Kitaura, a small fishing port to the N of the Oga peninsula. Past this point, take *Hachibo Highline, which passes within sight of Toga creek, between Ichinome gata and Ninome gata.

24mls (38km): Nyudo zaki, on the NW tip of the peninsula. This rocky cape is crowned with a lighthouse. Go E along the northern coast.

27mls (44km): Oga Onsen, where you may be able to spend the night. You can reach Toga Bay to the S by crossing Hachibo Highline.

29mls (47km): Toga, a little fishing bay which opens to the W onto the Sea of Japan. Boat to Oga via Monzen and to Kitaura via Nyudo misaki.

30mls (49km): the Sannome gata basin, beyond which a cliff road (toll) branches off and runs along the *western coast of the Oga peninsula. This is one of the best parts of the trip: reef formations, natural arches and other irregularities in the contours. The coast is overlooked here by Hon zan (2,349ft/716m alt.). Note that you will pass within sight of the Daisankyo (access by boat) and the Kojakuno iwaya.

39mls (62km): Monzen, at the end of the toll road, where you can visit the little adjacent shrines of Gosha do.

44mls (71km): Oga.

3 **AKITA**, see entry under this name.

Ogaki (Island of Honshu)

Tokyo, 234mls (377km) – Fukui, 97mls (156km) – Gifu, 10mls (16km) – Kanazawa, 150mls (242km) –Nagano, 185mls (298km) – Nagoya, 33mls (53km) – Otsu, 43mls (69km) – Toyama, 175mls (282km) – Tsu, 52mls (84km).

Gifu ken – pop: 134,942 – industries: textiles, chemical and food products; industrial machinery.

Ogaki, to the W of the Ibu gawa which flows into Ise Bay, owes its prosperity to the textile industry (spinning and cotton weaving). The town has now become the second most important in the Gifu region, with a very varied range of industries.

Ogaki Castle (550yds/500m S of the station). The reconstructed keep stands in the middle of Ogaki Park and houses a local history museum.

This castle was built in 1535 by Miyagawa Yasusada, at the command of the shogun Ashikaga Yoshiharu. In 1546, Oda Nobuhide, the father of Nobunaga, seized it. The castle was the residence of the Toda from 1634 to 1868.

VICINITY

1 **YORO** (7½mls/12km SW; Kintetsu ER train.). ½ml (1km) SW of the station (coach) are the attractive wooded hills which are famous for the legend of the woodcutter Yoro (8th c.). He is supposed to have discovered a spring of sake which enabled him to help his sick father. A shrine is dedicated to him. The park is particularly noteworthy for its rich vegetation, which changes picturesquely with the seasons. The Yoro Falls, beyond the shrine, plunge to a depth of 105ft (32m).

2 **IBUK YAMA** (20mls/32km NW; coach; JNR train to Sekigahara). Head W out of Ogaki on the N21.

9mls (15km): Sekigahara, where you leave the 'A' road. A monument (1ml/1.5km W of the station) marks the spot where a tariff barrier once stood. Sekigahara is much more famous, however, for the battle of that name, which secured the power of the Tokugawa from 1600 to 1868.

IEYASU TRIUMPHS. It was at Sekigahara (21 October 1600) that the united forces of Toyotomi Hideyori, the successor of Hideyoshi, and legitimate claimant to government, confronted those of Tokugawa Ieyasu, who was aspiring to absolute power. Almost all the Japanese nobility were present at Sekigahara. The enemies of Tokugawa placed themselves under the command of Ishida Kazushige, who brought about the conflict. Some, such as Kobayakawa Hideaki, observed the progress of the battle before siding with the winners. Others, such as Mori Terumoto, when faced with defeat, tried vainly to throw themselves on the mercy of Ieyasu. The death toll was nearly 30,000. This great battle in Japanese history brought about the downfall of the defeated and a complete redistribution of feudal holdings in favour of the victors' supporters. It also led to the forming of the Tokugawa government which took direct control over the fate of the daimyo.

11mls (17km): a winding toll road branches off on the r. and leads to Ibuki yama.

20mls (32km): *Ibuki yama (4,518ft/1,377m alt.); a major winter sports resort and an extensive botanical reserve where over 230 different species of medicinal herbs are listed. The view stretches over Lake Biwa, Haku san and the Japan Alps.

It was on Mount Ibuki that the legendary hero Yamato Takeru was stricken with a malignant fever, caused by the spirit of the mountain. Some time later he died of it at Nobono (see Kameyama).

3 GIFU, NAGOYA, see entries under these names.

4 BIWA KO, see Otsu.

■ Ogasawara shoto (National Park of)

Tokyo, 606mls (975km).

HOW TO GET THERE

– From Tokyo, via Ogasawara Kisen, a weekly service to Chichi jima (Omura); 38-hour journey. Departures may be suspended owing to weather conditions.

– A local link operates from Chichi jima to Haha jima. There is no regular line to Io jima.

The Ogasawara archipelago, or the Bonin, is made up of about 97 islands, scattered between the 20th and 35th parallels N. Of these, two main groups, Ogasawara gunto and Io retto, stand out. Their average altitude is quite low, the highest point being Minami Io jima (3,012ft/918m). They are part of the Fuji volcanic range and are constantly shaken by orogenic movements. To the E is the Izu Ogasawara deep, which ranks amongst the deepest in the world (35,039ft/10,680m, off Tori shima). The archipelago is a long way from the capital and links are still poor. Nowadays it pursues a double vocation: fishing and tourism. The national park set up in 1972 covers an area of 15,898 acres (6,434 ha).

THE UNINHABITED ISLANDS. The archipelago got its name from Ogasawara Sadayori, a native of the province of Shinano who discovered it in 1593. These desert islands were also known by the term *munin* (hence Bonin), which means uninhabited. They were sighted by the Dutch navigator Mathieu Quast in 1639 and explored at the request of the shogun Tokugawa Ietsuna from 1675 onwards. In the 19th c., after a European attempt at occupation, the Japanese government settled fishermen from Hachijo jima there (see Izu shoto). The islands were recognized as Japanese in 1875 and placed under the authority of Tokyo in 1880. During World War II the island of Io was used as a military air base. After a terrible battle in February 1945 the island surrendered to the Americans and was used when the Japanese archipelago was bombed until the surrender in August 1945. The Ogasawara archipelago was given back to Japan by the United States in 1968.

We would draw your attention to the following islands of the archipelago, from N to S:

TORI JIMA, half-way between the Izu and Ogasawara archipelagos where a hundred albatross hunters were killed in 1902 when a volcano suddenly erupted.

NISHINO SHIMA, to the S of which a new volcano appeared in May 1973. Its evolution is being closely observed by experts.

CHICHI JIMA, the most important and active island of the archipelago. Its mountainous contours rise no higher than 1,047ft (319m) at Chuo zan. Note the attractive Futami bay, where Ogasawara or Omura is situated.

To the S of this island is Minami jima which looks rather Saharan, although it is surrounded by the ocean.

HAHA JIMA, where a small group of people live and grow lemons, pineapples, bananas and sugar cane.

IO JIMA, the largest of the Retto islands, where the terrible battle took place in 1945 (see above), with a toll of 4,000 dead; commemorative monuments.

OKINO TORI SHIMA, approx. 2,346ft (715m) SW of Io jima, is the southernmost island of the whole Japanese archipelago. It lies at latitude 20° 25' N, on a level with Nubia (Egypt) and Guadalajara in Mexico.

Oita (Island of Kyushu)

Map of the Kyushu (North), pp. 388-9.

Tokyo, 768mls (1,236km) - Fukuoka, 109mls (175km) - Kumamoto, 85mls (137km) - Miyazaki, 125mls (201km).

Capital of Oita ken (pop: 756,579) - pop: 260,584 - industrial town and port - national and private universities.

Oita, which is separated from Beppu by the Takasaki yama, spreads out at the mouth of the Ono gawa - a suburb of Tsurusaki - and has reclaimed land from the sea which it needed to develop its port and industries. Steelworks, petrochemical industries and oil refineries have been set up.

Funai, the old name of Oita, was the residence of the Otomo in the 16th c. The town was the capital of the province of Bungo. It established trade relations with the Portuguese and was visited in 1551 by Saint Francis Xavier.

🏰 The site of Oita Castle (½ml/1km NE of the station) has now been made into a public garden surrounded by huge moats.

☞ **VICINITY**

1 SAGANOSEKI (18½mls/30km E on the N197; coach). From this little spot which opens to the S onto Usuki Bay, you can walk (2½mls/4km NE) to Cape Seki which is opposite Taka shima and Sada misaki, the outermost tip of Shikoku island, on the other side of the Hoyo Strait. To the N a little inlet shelters a fishing port (ferry service to Misaki).

♨ **2 YUNOHIRA ONSEN** (20mls/32km W on the N210; JNR train; coach). This spa town (2mls/4km W of the station; coach) in an attractive situation (2,000ft/600m alt.) is traversed by the Hanano gawa; springs from 138° to 183°F (59° to 84°C). Festival 7 to 9 May.

3 BEPPU, USUKI, MOUNT ASO NATIONAL PARK, see entries under these names.

O **Okayama** (Island of Honshu)

Map of Shikoku (Inland Sea), pp. 536–7.

Tokyo, 440mls (708km) – Hiroshima, 101mls (163km) – Kobe, 89mls (143km) – Tottori, 85mls (137km).

Capital of Okayama ken (pop: 1,057,247) – pop: 546,000 – industrial town: rubber; chemical products; machinery – national and private universities.

Okayama is 4h.10 from Tokyo by super-express and offers travellers a view of a modern, industrial town. It is the political, cultural and economic centre of the district of the same name, but it is not really a new town. It was once the capital of Bizen province, and is renowned for Bizen yaki porcelain which has a tradition going back 1,200 years. Although you may find this pottery in the shops of Okayama, it belongs by right to the town of Imbe, which is a 45-min. train ride from the capital of San yo. It is worth a visit. Other reasons to stay in Okayama are the castle, the Korakuen garden and the surrounding area (the Kibi region).

The painter Kuniyoshi Yasuo (1893–1953) was born at Okayama.

🌲 ****KORAKUEN** (1ml/1.5km E of Okayama eki) is the main tourist attraction of the town of Okayama. The gardens rank with those of Kanazawa, Mito and Takamatsu as the most famous in Japan. That of Okayama (28½ acres/11.5 ha) stands on an island in the Asahi gawa, to the N of the old castle of the Ikeda.

This park was created in 1700 at the request of Ikeda Tsunamasa, under the direction of Nagata Tsuda. It is a landscape garden and in a relatively confined space displays a natural landscape tamed by art: a combination of rocks, ponds, artificial waterfalls, verdant mounds (Keshigo yama and Misao yama), a teahouse (Kokumei kan), tea plants, etc. which correspond to the teachings of the great master Kobori Enshu (1579–1647). The garden was donated to the town by the Ikeda family in 1884.

To the N of Koraku en, you can visit the Okayama Art Museum (open from 09.00 to 18.00), set up partly with the donations of the collector Ichiro Hayashibara: works of art, mementoes of the Ikeda (armour, swords), and artifacts of interest in the Okayama region; old Bizen pottery.

Okayama Castle, to the S of Koraku en, is linked to the latter by a footbridge. The keep, which seems to be an imitation of that at Azuchi (see Omi Hachiman), was destroyed in the bombing of 1945 and rebuilt in 1966. You can visit it.

UJO, the Castle of the Crow, is the name given to this 'black castle', as opposed to the 'white castle', or the Castle of the Heron, Himeji (see entry under this name). Okayama jo was built by Ukita Naoie (1530–82). His son Hideie was dispossessed of it after the battle of Sekigahara, then exiled to the island of Hachijo jima. The castle then passed into the hands of the Kobayakawa, and to the Ikeda from 1603 onwards.

SAIDAI JI (or Kannon in; ½ml/1km S of Saidaiji station; 7mls/11km E of Okayama; bus). It is famous mainly for the Eyo or Hadaka festival which takes place at midnight on the third Saturday in February. Ten thousand naked young males jostle each other in the darkness to try and get hold of a *singi*, a magic stick which is supposed to bring them happiness for the year. It is a very lively occasion! This temple, which has the Yoshii gawa running alongside it, was founded in the 8th c. in honour of Kannon of the thousand hands.

The former town of Saidaiji is now joined to the urban sprawl of Okayama which is about 6mls (10km) away.

VICINITY

1 'KONAN DAI (10mls/16km S; coach). Head SE out of Okayama towards the port.

6mls (9km): Kojima dyke (1ml/1.6km long), which has divided Kojima Bay since 1956 and holds back an irrigation lake to the W. This has meant that 24,710 acres (10,000 ha) of newly reclaimed land can now be cultivated, and mechanized farming is being greatly encouraged here. Past the dyke the road winds up Konan dai.

10mls (16km): Kinko zan (1,322ft/403m alt.), a peak with a view over the town of Okayama, Kojima wan and to the S the Inland Sea with its numerous islands.

2 SOJA (13mls/23km W on the N180; trip to Kibi by Chutetsu Bus on Sundays from Okayama station; coach and JNR train to Soja). At the point where the former provinces of Bizen and Bitchu meet is the

**Kibi region, which is enclosed in a triangle formed by the peaks of Kurashiki, Okayama and Soja. It has a rich historical past: tumuli of the Kofun period and ancient temples and shrines testify to this. Head W out of Okayama on the N180.

5mls (8km): Ichinomiya (station), where you can visit Kibitsu hiko jinja. This shrine was founded in 1563 at the foot of Kibi Hill and completed at the end of the 17th c. by Ikeda Mitsumasa. It is famous for its garden and its two great stone lanterns near the entrance. The treasury has several ancient paintings and swords.

6mls (10km): Kibi, where you can visit (550yds/500m S of the station), **Kibitsu jinja on the slopes of Kibino Nakayama, which was founded in the 4th c. in honour of the semi-legendary prince Kibitsu hiko, who pacified the provinces in the W in the 2nd c. BC. He is said to have lived for two hundred years... The shrine which is dedicated to him was rebuilt in 1425 and is typical of the Kibitsu style; it has roofs with double gables on the sides. Above the oratory (hai den), there is a second roof which is perpendicular to those covering the holy of holies (hon den). The oratory here is without partitions and to the r. of it you will see a very lovely covered gallery (1578; note the curved roof, 1,181ft/360m long) which goes down as far as the Kama dono, the cauldron room. This cauldron is famous for the prophecies it makes at the time of the Narukama ritual.

7mls (11km): road on the l. to Kiyone, which passes within sight of several tumuli including (on the r.) that of Tsukuriyama, which is one of the largest in Japan (1,150ft/350m long).

4mls (6km) W on this road is Bitchu Kokubun ji, where you can see the five-storey pagoda. This temple, founded in the 8th c. when the Emperor Shomu was founding institutions, was burned in the 14th c. and rebuilt on its present site, in 1707. You can get permission to see the original site approx. 550yds (500m) E. Half-way there is the little wooded *kofun* of Komori zaka, with a sepulchral chamber which you can visit.

8mls (13km): Takamatsu; Bitchu-Takamatsu station.

880yds (800m) N: the site of Takamatsu Castle, which Toyotomi Hideyoshi took over in 1582.

REVERSAL OF THE SITUATION. Shimizu Munehara was defending this castle in the name of Mori Terumoto who was engaged in combat with Hideyoshi at that time. The latter encountered problems in laying siege to the castle and appealed to Oda Nobunaga who sent reinforcements in the form of Akechi Mitsuhide. Mitsuhide actually took advantage of this situation to assassinate Nobunaga in Kyoto, and became master of the town. Hideyoshi, meanwhile, had had the course of the river altered so as to flood the area round the castle, and thus won the siege. He made peace with Terumoto and immediately defeated Mitsuhide.

2mls (3km) N (coach): Myokyo ji, which is particularly famous for the neighbouring shrine of Saijo Inari, which was founded in the 8th c.

and was once known as Mogami Inari. It is one of the principal Japanese shrines dedicated to the goddess Toyouke hime (see Ise and Inari jinja in Kyoto). There is a curious stone gate with cupolas of the Deva kings (1958). Behind this is Ryuo san, which has a small temple dedicated to Nichiren.

9mls (15km): Ashimori, which was once the residence of the Kinoshita (from 1600 to 1868).

→ 2mls (3km) N: Omizu koen is a charming garden of the Edo period, in the style of Kobori Enshu and designed at the request of the Ashimori lords.

13mls (23km): Soja (pop: 37,371), the home of the great master Sesshu (15th century); the attractive Gokei gorge.

3 KURASHIKI, TSUYAMA, SHODO SHIMA, SETO NAIKAI NATIONAL PARK, see entries under these names.

Okazaki (Island of Honshu)

Railway map on inside front cover.

Tokyo, 189mls (304km) – Gifu, 45mls (72km) – Nagano, 180mls (290km) – Nagoya, 22mls (35km) – Shizuoka, 85mls (137km).

Aichi ken – pop: 210,515 – textile industries – national university.

Okazaki is bounded to the W by the Yahagi gawa, and nowadays it merges into the great industrial outskirts of Nagoya. The town is heavily involved in the textile industry and there are nearly 500 factories along the river, which produce 80% of the cloth made in Japan.

Okazaki is the home town of the famous Tokugawa Ieyasu (1524–1616).

OKAZAKI CASTLE (2mls/3km N of the JNR station; bus). The keep has been rebuilt recently in the centre of a public park which is marked out by the moats of the former castle. Ieyasu has the place of honour inside the keep.

The castle was acquired by Tokugawa Kiyoyasu (1511–36), the grandfather of Ieyasu who was born there. Having entrusted the government of Kanto to Ieyasu, Toyotomi Hideyoshi placed Tanaka Yoshimasa in Okazaki.

Oki shoto*

Map of Natural Resources, p. 67.

Tokyo, 565mls (910km) – Matsue, 56mls (90km).

Shimane ken.

Two main units, Dogo and Dozen (Nishino, Nakano and Chiburi jima), and nearly 180 islets make up this archipelago of volcanic origin (8,650 acres/3,500 ha). Its contours are almost imperceptible as the promontories, capes, cliffs, creeks and other irregularities of the coastline which form its main attraction, are so numerous. This archipelago is also part of the Daisen Oki National Park (see entry under this name).

IMPERIAL EXILES. As with several of the lesser islands of the Japanese archipelago, the Oki islands were used as places of political exile. The Hojo sent two emperors there. The first was Go Toba who tried to regain power from the shikken of Kamakura and was exiled in 1221 to Ama (Nakano shima), where he died. Then in 1331, the Emperor Go Daigo was banished to Chiburi jima for similar reasons. The latter escaped, however, in 1333, and disembarked at Hoki. Nawa Nagatoshi accompanied him to Kyoto, where Ashikaga Takauji, who had come to fight them, ended up siding with the Emperor (see Kyoto).

DOGO (ferry services from Saigo to Nakano shima, Nishino shima, Shichirui, Sakaiminato; TDA flights to Izumo and Yonago). This island, which is circular in shape, is the largest of the archipelago and opens to the S at Saigo Bay. You can go touring from here (coach). The coast, which is very irregular, presents a wide variety of landscapes.

FROM SAIGO TO FUSE (22mls/35km N; coach via Goka). Head NW out of Saigo.

2½mls (4km): on the r. you will see the site of a Kokubun ji temple, near to which a palace was erected for the Emperor Go Daigo.

4½mls (6km): road on the l. towards Tsuma, (6mls/10km SW), at the bottom of a lovely inlet.

9mls (15km): the attractive Mizuwakasu shrine, which is similar in style to the one at Izumo. Festival on 3 May.

2½mls (4km) W: Goka, where you can visit a little folk museum in a wooden house (Meiji period).

15mls (24km): *Shirashima kaigan, the northern coast of the island which you can follow to the SE.

22mls (35km): Fuse, where you can either go E to the beautiful site of Jodoga ura, or climb Daimanji san (1,995ft/608m), which is the island's highest point and rises up to the SE.

DOZEN (18½mls/30km SW of Dogo). This group is also roughly circular in shape; the sea has separated its highest elevations into different islands.

NAKANO SHIMA (ferry services from Ama to Dogo, Nishino shima and Sakaiminato). 2½mls (4km) SE of the port (coach) you can visit the shrine of Oki, built in 1939 in honour of the Emperor Go Toba, whose tomb is nearby.

NISHINO SHIMA (1½mls/2.5km NW of Nakano shima; ferry services from Beppu or Nishinoshima to Chiburi jima, Dogo, Nakanoshima and Sakaiminato). **Kuniga kaigan, which occupies the entire 'outer'

(NW) coast of this island is the most interesting part: Cape Maten, which has a sheer drop of 1,000ft (300m), the Tsuten natural arch, Bibi ura, etc. The coast is 8mls (13km) W of Beppu (coach). Horse and cattle breeding.

CHIBURI JIMA (6mls/10km S of Nishino shima; ferry services to the other islands and Sakaiminato). This was the land of exile of the Emperor Go Daigo. You can walk (5mls/8km SW of the port of Chibu) to the Chibu Sekiheki, a rocky barrier which ranges from 330 to 600ft (100 to 180m) in height.

Okinawa shoto (Nansei shoto)

Maps of Nansei shoto and Ikonawa, pp. 430–1.

Tokyo, 1,025mls (1,649km).

These remote islands of the archipelago were ceded back to Japan in 1972 and are popular for the change of scenery they provide. They bask in a mild subtropical climate and their vegetation and atmosphere are quite different. The best time to visit Okinawa is from October to April (there are terrifying typhoons the rest of the year). The island of Okinawa itself does not always correspond to its popular idyllic image, particularly in the S where there is a long string of overpopulated towns and numerous American air bases. Nowadays Okinawa is trying to become industrialized to catch up with the dynamic impulse of the rest of Japan. There is something Mediterranean in the easy-going ways of the people, the liveliness of the streets and the human warmth. The traditional society has remained matriarchal in nature and women play a major role in popular beliefs. The priestess of each shrine usually acts as shaman. Other customs such as funeral rites, legends of the sea, languages, etc. also characterize the island.

A   Okinawa jima

The main island of Okinawa shoto stretches for approx. 75mls (120km) in length but is only 3 to 12mls (5 to 20km) wide. The N of the island is more mountainous and contrasts with the S which is urbanized and specializes in farming.

NAHA (pop: 276,380) is the capital of the island, and also the capital of Okinawa prefecture, half the population (575,323) of which lives here. Naha, between the old royal town of Shuri and the port of Tomari, became the administrative centre of the island from 1879 onwards. In this town, which was entirely rebuilt after the bombings of 1944, there are districts where the houses have low, tiled roofs with a traditional look, which contrasts with the lively centre where buildings of all sizes and functions spring up haphazardly.

Naha is traversed from E to W by the long Kokusai Chuo dori International Road (1ml/1.5km), which was laid after the war, across what used to be rice-paddies. It has numerous shops along it.

Heiwa dori, the centre of a picturesque market, intersects Kokusai at a right-angle and goes directly to the Tsuboya district (see below).

Kokusai dori ends to the NE at Sogen ji dori, where you can go W to the port of Tomari. This new road runs in front of Sogen ji, which is preceded by a mighty wall with stone arches. The former sovereigns of the Ryukyu have been lain to rest behind it. Note the curious tombs, with their 'tortoiseshell' roofs, where the bones of the dead were deposited. This type of tomb is found all over the Okinawa archipelago.

Tomari, to the N of the town, is the old port of Shuri (ferry services to the Ryukyu). A complete replanning has expanded and modified its facilities. It is a trade and passenger port which now occupies the entire seafront of Naha and extends S as far as the mouth of the Kokuba gawa, known as the Port of Naha.

Towards the middle of the 19th c. several foreign vessels attempted to approach Japan by putting in at Naha. Contract was then made with the King of the Ryukyu, with a view to establishing trade agreements.

½ml (1km) SW of Tomari is the old shrine of Naminoue which is still the most popular in Okinawa. It was rebuilt after the war.

To the SW of this shrine is the former Tsuji red-light area, where bars and gambling dens have grown up. On the 20th day of the first lunar month (December or January), the procession of the geisha (Juri uma) takes place here. The geisha are dressed in their most beautiful clothes, which are particularly colourful in Okinawa.

1ml (1.5km) SE of Kokusai dori, you will reach Yogi koen public park, if you go along Kainan dori past Himeribashi dori.

To the SE of this park is the Tsuboya pottery district. Many companies now use modern manufacturing processes, but there are still traditional craftsmen, some of whom use a firing kiln which is actually hollowed out of the rock face of the nearby hills. We would recommend a trip to a lacquerware factory (Bembo Lacquerware, 2-21-8 Matsuyama) and a batik workshop, the bingata (Natoyama Industrial Arts, 4-79-3 Shuri Gibo-cho).

☞ VICINITY

1 SHURI (4½mls/6km E; bus). This suburb of Naha overlooks the modern town. It was once the residence of the sovereigns of Okinawa. The University of the Ryukyu was built in 1950 on the former site of the royal palace of Shuri, which was destroyed in the bombings of 1944. Only the nearby church is still standing.

The castle was erected at the start of the 15th c. by Hashi, the lord of Sashiki, who dethroned the dynasty which was reigning in Okinawa at that time. He crowned his father, and then succeeded him in 1421, bequeathing the crown to his descendants. They were overthrown in

1470 by a new sovereign, Sho En, whose son, Sho Shin, managed to impose his power over the entire island. His heirs continued to rule there until Okinawa was reunited with Japan in 1879.

All that remains of the old castle is the Shurei no mon, the Gate of Courtesy, which is the most famous monument in Okinawa. It was originally built in 1527. The Benzaiten do, the old *sutra* pavilion, was rebuilt in the centre of the little pool of Ekan.

PREFECTORAL MUSEUM OF OKINAWA (Onaka cho, Shuri; open daily from 09.00 to 17.00, except Mondays and public holidays; closed from 28 December to 4 January). To the N of the pool of Ryutan, it was opened in 1972, and managed to gather together some of the collections once displayed in Shuri Castle; *objets d'art* of local interest, sculptures, paintings, calligraphy, textiles, the jewels of former sovereigns, a model of the courtroom of Shuri palace, etc.

2 OKINAWA SENSEKI (the battle fields of Okinawa; 37mls/60km round trip; coach; excursions). The violent Okinawa battles took place across the whole southern part of the island.

THE BATTLE OF OKINAWA. After preliminary bombing in October 1944, the Americans landed at Toguchi (Motobu) on 1 April in 1945. The battle which continued until 21 June, especially in the southern part of the island, was one of the most ferocious of World War II: 12,000 were killed on the American side, and 90,000 Japanese, not counting the innumerable injured and the civilian victims, nor the mass suicides of the Okinawa women, who leapt off the rocks into the sea with their children in their arms. The island was devastated. After the war, the United States assisted in the economic revival of Okinawa until 1972.

Head S out of Naha on the N331.

7mls (11km): Itoman, where you can visit the Armed Forces Museum of Fort Buckner; the various episodes of the Battle of Okinawa are retraced with photographs, maps and documents. At Itoman you will also see the monuments of Kochibara Monchu and General Simon Bolivar Buckner, the Commander of the American Tenth Army. There are boat races at Itoman in summer.

11mls (18km): Komesu. There are several commemorative monuments not far from here, such as the Himeyuri, dedicated to the memory of the pupils and teachers of the regional secondary school and the teacher training college of Okinawa, and the monument on the hill, dedicated to the memory of Lieutenant-General Mitsuru Ushijima, who committed suicide here.

17mls (28km): Minatogawa, where you can get to:

1¼mls (2km) NW (direct coach from Naha): **Gyokusen do, one of the largest natural caves in the East, was discovered in 1967. It has 900,000 stalactites and is 3mls (5km) long, of which 880yds (800m) has been open to the public since 1972. Nearby is a large centre where research on the *habu* snake is carried out (vaccine manufacture; battles between *habu* and mongooses).

▰▰ 25mls (40km): Chinen, where you can see the ruins of one of Okinawa's many castles. The sovereigns of this island used to stop here, when they were going on pilgrimage to the island of Kudaka.

➡ 4mls (7km) off shore (boat from Sashiki): Kudaka jima, the legendary island where the first divine couple of Ryukyu mythology settled. He gave birth to five children who organized the traditional society of the southern archipelago. One of these was Tenteishi, the first legendary king of Okinawa.

29mls (46km): Sashiki, a little port to the S of Nakagusuku Bay. You can go from here to Kudaka jima (see above).

32mls (51km): Yonabara, where you can head W on the N329 to get back to:

37mls (60km): Naha.

3 *OKINAWA KAIGAN NATIONAL PARK (177mls/285km round trip, which uses the N58 and N329 part of the way; coach; hovercraft from Naha to the site of Expo '75). In spite of the relatively short distances involved, an almost complete round trip of the island takes at least a day. The more popular and frequently congested roads make travelling very difficult, especially on the E side of the island, even though a motorway runs for 17mls (28km) between Nakadomari and Kyoda. Head N out of Nara on the N58.

4mls (7km): turn off on the r. towards.

➡ 1¼mls (2km) E: Urasoe (pop: 41,768), the ancient feudal town of Okinawa near to which are the tombs of Yodore, of the first Okinawa dynasty. Note also the mausoleum of Prince Sho Nei, imprisoned in 1609 by the Shimazu in Kagoshima.

7½mls (12km): Isa, one of the districts of Ginowan (pop: 39,390), of which Futenma (1ml/2km E) is the main centre.

18½mls (30km): Yamada, where you will reach the shores of the East China Sea again. All this part of the coast as far as Nago belongs to Okinawa Kaigan National Park, set up in 1972. Near Yamada is the *habu* snake research centre (where there are numerous poisonous snakes including 2,000 *habu*).

20mls (33km): Nakadomari. You can head SE from here to the new motorway which makes Nago easier to reach. At Nakadomari there is an interesting shell museum with specimens from Okinawa and all over the world.

21mls (34km): the famous seaside resort of Moon Beach.

35mls (56km): Imbu, where you can go N to Bushina misaki: underwater observation tower. A leisure centre has been built on the large neighbouring beach.

39mls (62km): Yofuke, where the N329 comes to an end.

➡ 2mls (3km) S (on foot): the beautiful Todoroki Falls.

40mls (64km): Nago (pop: 39,799) is a recently developed urban centre. It could be interesting to make detour via Motonobu. Leave the N58 to get on the coast road, or route 116, which goes N round Katsuu dake (1,365ft/416m).

50mls (81km): Toguchi, the port of Motonobu, where the Tenth American Army Fleet landed on 1 April 1945.

→ 6mls (10km) NW (boat): Ie shima, where Gusuku yama rises to a height of 564ft (172m); very beautiful beach. Note the monument to the American journalist Ernie Pyle, who died in the landing at Okinawa.

→ 28mls (45km) N (boat): the Iheya-Izena shoto archipelago. The names of the two main islands make up this double name.

52mls (83km): Urasaki, where route 114 goes W to Bise misaki through:

53mls (85km): the site of Expo '75 (hovercraft from Naha). This was the first world oceanographical exhibition, held in Okinawa between 1975 and 1976, on the theme of 'Man and the Sea'. The highlight of this exhibition was the Aquapolis (engineers: Hoshino Mamoru and Kokino Akira), a floating maritime city (107,640sq. ft/10,000m²) which is moveable and linked by a bridge 440yds (400m) long to the coast. It is endowed with a solar generator and a desalination plant, and was assembled near Hiroshima. Nowadays the installations have a neglected air. The main sections of the exhibition (Boats, Science and Technology, History and Ethnic Groups, Marine Zoo) are linked to each other by little remote-controlled vehicles operated by computer. The harbour lies to the S of here and the beach to the N. After the exhibition the whole complex (250 acres/100 ha and 2½mls/4km long) was converted into a seaside resort.

58mls (93km): Oyadomari, where you can head S to the ruins of Nakijin Castle. These ruins, firmly planted on a cliff overlooking the sea, are the largest in Okinawa.

68mls (109km): Nakaoshi, where you return to the N58 and the *Okinawa kaigan Regional Park, some of the finest sights of which can be seen from here onwards. The northern part of the island is much hillier, a beautiful contrast with the sea, which has dream-like shades of colour and crystal clearness.

75mls (120km): Shioya ohashi, a modern bridge across the mouth of a little estuary.

96mls (154km): *Hedo misaki, on the northern tip of the island with a view over Yoron jima (p. 127) on a fine day.

99mls (159km): Oku, where the N58 comes to an end in the N of Okinawa. You will need to inquire about the state of the road from here onwards, and about the possibility of a coach service. Otherwise you will have to return along the N58 to get to Futami or Ishikawa. Past Oku the road is much more winding and runs along the E side of Okinawa which is bounded by the Pacific Ocean.

106mls (170km): Aha, where you can go up the Aha gawa valley towards Yonaka dake (1,634ft/498m), the highest point on the island of Okinawa.

119mls (192km): Higashi, where the little Bay of Taira opens to the E.

130mls (210km): Futami, where you meet the N329 and follow it SE.

152mls (245km): Ishikawa (pop: 15,761), which is bordered to the E by the Kin Gulf and enclosed to the N by Kin misaki and to the E by Ikei jima. The attractive Nankai beach is 4mls (7km) NE of Ishikawa.

155mls (250km): Yenobi. A road on the l. goes towards Gushikawa (pop: 37,292) and its arena where there are bullfights every Sunday. The road continues along Cape Katsuren, which separates Kin Bay from Chujo Bay (Nakagusuku).

➡ 6mls (10km) SE (on this road): Yonagusuku, where you can head for the islands which enclose Kin Bay to the E. There are plans to link them to the land with a 500-acre (200-ha) platform which will hold the biggest oil terminal in Japan. An aluminium plant is to be built on Ikei jima, the most northerly of these islands.

160mls (257km): Koza (pop: 58,658), the second town of Okinawa, which owes its development to the proximity of the American air bases. The pleasure districts of this town enjoy a high reputation with United States citizens who live on Okinawa.

165mls (265km): Nakagusuku, where a castle was built in the 15th c. to defend the one at Shuri. We recommend a visit to the *Nakamura house at the foot of the castle. It is a magnificent residence built in 1700 in the style typical of Okinawa houses.

172mls (276km): Yonabaru, where the N329 heads W back to:

177mls (285km): Naha.

4 KERAMA RETTO (22mls/35km W; boat to Tokashiki and Zamami shima). This is a group of several islands of which Tokashiki and Zamami are the main ones. The Americans landed here in March 1945. These islands now attract a great many tourists, campers and divers.

B Kume jima

Ferry service and SWAL flights to Okinawa; some ryokan.

This island is situated in the East China Sea approx. 90mls (150km) W of Okinawa. Its highest point is 1,188ft (362m) above sea level. It is surrounded by coral reefs. Gushikawa airport is 6mls (10km) W of Nakazato, the island's main town.

On the little island of Sai Ojima (1½ml/2km SE of the port of Nakazato; boat), there is a curious causeway of solidified lava, known as Tatami ishi.

◼ Omagari (Island of Honshu)

Map of Tohoku, pp. 232–3.

Tokyo, 337mls (542km) – Akita, 31mls (50km) – Aomori, 147mls (236km) – Morioka, 57mls (92km) – Sendai, 115mls (185km) – Yamagata, 104mls (167km).

Akita ken – pop: 41,764.

Omagari stands at the confluence of the Omono gawa and the Tama gawa and is also an important railway junction where the Ou line forks. One route heads NW to Akita, and the other NE to Morioka.

VICINITY

1 TAZAWA KO (27mls/44km NE on the N105 and N46; JNR train to Tazawako station, then coach). Head NE out of Omagari on the N105 which goes up the Tama gawa valley.

12mls (20km): Kakunodate, the old feudal town which came under the Tozawa in the 16th c. and the Satake a century later. You can still see some former *samurai* houses which give the town a certain character. One of the streets is lined with cherry trees and attracts crowds of people in spring. Continue E on the N46.

17mls (28km): Jindai, where you can head for:

2mls (3km) SE: *Dakigaeri keikoku, a very attractive mountain ravine sheltering a little shrine, and further upstream, 5mls (8km) from Jindai (coach), the spa town of Natsuse.

24mls (38km): Tazawako, the nearest station to the lake of this name. The railway continues E towards Morioka and goes up some very lovely gorges before going through a tunnel under the Sengan Pass (2,933ft/894m alt.). Leave the N46 and continue N up the Tama valley.

26mls (42km): cross the Tama gawa, which continues N past Yoroibata dam, to get to:

27mls (44km): *Tazawa ko. This lake is 10sq. mls (26km²) in area, lies at an alt. of 820ft (250m), and reaches a record depth of 1,394ft (425m). It is famous for the lapis lazuli colour of its waters and their incomparable clarity. A *toll road goes round it for 9mls (15km) (coach) and there are ferry services across it. It is overlooked to the E by Komaga take (5,317ft/1,637m), which can be climbed (coach to the eighth stop, from Tazawako station). Pilgrimage from 15 July to 20 August.

2 AKITA, YOKOTE, TOWADA HACHIMANTAI NATIONAL PARK, see entries under these names.

Omi Hachiman (Island of Honshu)

Tokyo, 273mls (439km) – Fukui, 95mls (153km) – Gifu, 60mls (96km) – Kyoto, 29mls (47km) – Otsu, 22mls (35km) – Tsu, 55mls (88km).

Shiga ken – pop: 43,832.

Omi Hachiman is slightly set back from Lake Biwa, and stands to the E of it. It is the nearest town to the famous Azuchi ruins.

VICINITY

1 **CHOMEI JI** (4mls/7km NW; coach). Attributed to Prince Shotoku, it was rebuilt in the 16th c. The neighbouring village is regarded as one of the wonders of Lake Biwa.

2 **AZUCHI** (3mls/5km NE: JNR). The former site of Azuchi Castle is 1ml (1.5km) N of the station.

FORTRESS-PALACE OF ODA NOBUNAGA. Azuchi was, in its day, one of the mightiest castles in Japan. It was built by Oda Nobunaga (1534–82), who was the first ruler to unify a Japan devastated by civil war. He deposed the last Ashikaga shogun, and made himself master of Azuchi, where he established the seat of his power. He was assassinated in Kyoto by Akechi Mitsuhide, who immediately destroyed the shortlived castle.

Nobunaga had placed the direction of the work on Azuchi in the hands of the daimyo, Niwa Nagahide. The greatest artists, including Kano Eitoku (1543–90) contributed to its sumptuous decoration. The six-storey keep must have been 118ft (36m) high, surpassing the one at Himeji. As it was painted in bright colours, the castle could be seen from a long way off and was reflected in the waters of the ponds which defended the approaches to it. You will be able to make out the different enclosures, and at the Hon maru you can see a monument dedicated to Nobunaga. Soken ji also possesses a statue and some rare mementoes of the great man.

3 **BIWAKO**, see Otsu.

Omura (Island of Kyushu)

Map of Kyushu (North), pp. 388–9.

Tokyo, 794mls (1,277km) – Fukuoka, 79mls (127km) – Nagasaki, 24mls (38km) – Saga, 46mls (74km).

ANA flights to Fukue jima, Kagoshima, Osaka and Tokyo.

Nagasaki ken - pop: 56,538 - pearl oyster culture.

This town on the shore of the vast Bay of Omura, which is almost closed off to the N, is overlooked by Kyoga dake (3,530ft/1,076m), which can be climbed.

The physician Nagaoka Hantaro (1865-1947) was born in Omura.

Omura Park (1½ml/2km S of the JNR station) is on the site of the castle which once crowned a promontory jutting out into the bay.

From the 12th c. onwards the castle was the residence of the descendants of Fujiwara Sumitomo, who took the name of Omura. The authority of this powerful family extended as far as Nagasaki and it was Omura Sumitada (1532-87) who opened this port to foreigners. Sumitada was also the first Japanese daimyo to be baptized, with the name Bartholomew. His son Sumiyori was also baptized but later denied the Christian faith which set off a wave of persecution. As a result, his family remained secure in this castle until the Restoration of 1868. The Dutchman Peter Nuyts, the governor of the Taiwan trading post, was imprisoned at Omura. He was freed through the intervention of François Caron (see Hirado).

Onomichi (Island of Honshu)

Map of Shikoku (Inland Sea), pp. 536–7.

Tokyo, 533mls (858km) - Hiroshima, 55mls (89km) - Matsue, 108mls (173km) - Okayama, 51mls (82km) - Tottori, 136mls (219km) - Yamaguchi, 137mls (220km).

Hiroshima ken - pop: 101,363 - fishing port.

Onomichi, a port on the Inland Sea, is separated only by a narrow canal from the island of Mukai opposite. This confrontation between sea and mountain gives Onomichi remarkable natural charm, which attracts many artists with whom this town is a favourite. If we are to believe the aesthetes, the view over the harbour on a moonlit night is unforgettable.

Senko ji (½ml/1km NE of the station). This temple was founded in 806, and is surrounded by a park with splendid views, from which you can see the Geiyo islands to the S of Onomichi.

Saikoku ji (2mls/3km NE of the station). At this temple, a pair of sandals made of plaited rice straw is offered to the giant, Nio sama, every year to win his protection.

VICINITY

1 MUKAI JIMA (4mls/7km S over a toll bridge; coach). This is the nearest of the islands in the Geiyo archipelago which stretch out as far as the island of Shikoku. Flower cultivation, especially chrysanthemums.

2 FUKUYAMA, INNO SHIMA, SETO NAIKAI NATIONAL PARK, see entries under these names.

Osaka (Island of Honshu)*

Map of the vicinity of Osaka, pp. 500–1 – plans, pp. 490, 491 and 495.

Tokyo, 320mls (515km) - Kobe, 21mls (33km) - Kyoto, 24mls (39km) - Nara, 20mls (33km) - Wakayama, 42mls (68km).

Capital of Osaka fu (pop: 7,405,747) - pop: 2,648,000 - industrial and commercial town and port - national, regional and private universities - congress town.

The second city of Japan has grown up at the mouth of the Yodo gawa, on Osaka Bay. In terms of population, surface area, industry and economy it is a second capital which has made its influence felt in the whole western part of the country. The town is a huge urban

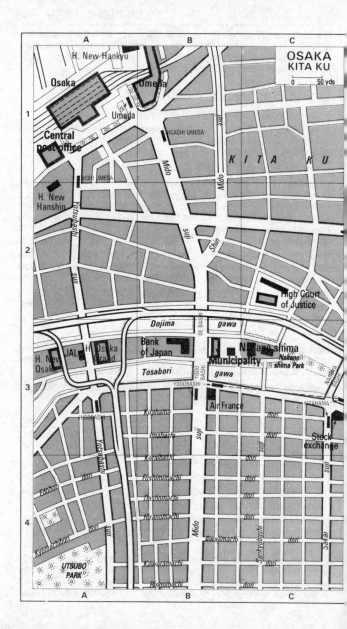

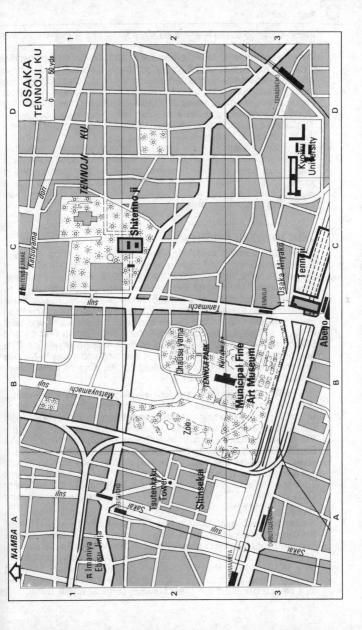

mass, bounded to the N and E by mountains, and scarcely checked by the sea from which large sections of the port have been reclaimed. It is of less interest to tourists than Tokyo and is surpassed by nearby Kyoto in this respect too. If Kyoto is cultural, Osaka is the business city *par excellence*. It has motorways running across it, winding among standardized buildings. The town is crisscrossed with wide, characterless avenues, a hive of activity with dense crowds swarming along the shopping arcades, and it can seem very unprepossessing. The fact is that Osaka only reveals its pleasant side at nightfall, when the nocturnal districts give this business city its rather sprightly air; after work, relaxation! Huge pleasure districts shine out with their neon lights billing, in Kanji characters, the names of bars, restaurants and nightclubs which attract a broadminded clientele always ready to strike up conversation with a foreigner. But Osaka also has a magnificent castle, temples and gardens, and it is the gateway to an interesting surrounding area.

The town in history

NANIWA. According to the Nipponese chronicle, it was at the mouth of the Yodo gawa that the Emperor Jimmu disembarked (7th c. BC), at the beginning of his odyssey on the Inland Sea. Because of the 'fast-flowing waves' (*naniwa*) of the river, the Emperor gave this name to the place. It was not until the 4th c. AD, however, that the Emperor Nintoku chose to make Naniwa his capital. He made use of the Yodo gawa delta to build the first canals and drain the site which was later to become Osaka. The Emperors Kotoku and Temmu (7th c.) and Shomu (8th c.) also chose Naniwa as their Imperial residence. The port had trade relations with Korea at that time and it was in Naniwa that the first statues of Buddha sent by the king of Korea, were received in 553 (see Nagano).

HIDEYOSHI LAUNCHES THE COMMERCIAL PROSPERITY OF OSAKA. It was not until the 16th c. that Osaka really began to supplant the port of Sakai, when Toyotomi Hideyoshi forced tradesmen to move here from Sakai. Hideyoshi himself chose to have a mighty castle built on the site of the Hongan ji temple at Ishiyama mido (see below, Osaka Castle), which stood up to the attacks of Oda Nobunaga for several years. This castle was deserted in favour of the one at Fushimi and became Toyotomi Hideyori's last bastion of resistance against Tokugawa Ieyasu. The latter had his son, Hidetada, lead the siege of Osaka (summer 1615) thus completely eliminating the Toyotomi and confirming the supreme power of the Tokugawa.

THE CENTURY OF OSAKA. Although the Tokugawa preferred Edo (Tokyo) to Osaka, they nonetheless placed a governor (*jodai*) in Osaka Castle. The merchant class was independent of the daimyo. As the *samurai* were in debt and the merchants enjoyed the shogun's protection, they profited from this to establish a trade monopoly covering virtually the entire Japanese archipelago. The merchants thus acted as a central bank and the great families, some of whom still survive today, first came into being. The merchants also supported a whole generation of artists, who bloomed in literature and in painting (novels, Kabuki theatre and engravings), and proved very talented at expressing the dissolute and violent habits of the period.

RANKED SECOND. From the 18th c. onwards, however, the commercial prosperity of Osaka was surpassed by that of Edo (Tokyo), the seat of the shogunal government, and from then on it was of secondary importance. The ossified, inward-looking nature of Japanese society brought about an economic crisis and popular uprisings. In Osaka in 1837 Oshio Heihachiro led one of the most significant riots of this period. At the end of the 19th c. the opening of the port to foreign trade and the industrialization of the city made it prosperous once again. The town was rebuilt after World War II and symbolizes better than anywhere else the image of Japan's economic miracle. The first International Exhibition in the East was held there in 1970.

FAMOUS PEOPLE BORN IN OSAKA. These include the novelist Ihara Saikaku (1641-93); the painter Hanabusa Itcho (1652-1724); the engraver Tachibana Morikuni (1679-1748); the painter and famous *haiku* writer Taniguchi Yosa Buson (1716-83); the woodcut artist Nakajima Tetsujiro or Hokusai (1760-1849); Fukuzawa Yukichi (1834-1901), the founder of Keio University in Tokyo; Kawabata Yasunari (1899-1972), who won a Nobel Prize for Literature; the philanthropist Sasagawa Ryoichi (born in 1899); the composer Matsushita Shin Ishi, born in 1922; and the film actress Kyo Machiko, born in 1924.

The *Asahi* and the *Mainichi shimbun*, two of the largest Japanese daily newspapers, also originated in Osaka.

PORT OF OSAKA. The present port, opened to international trade in 1868, has grown up around the mouth of the Yodo gawa and now includes the old port of Ajikawa. A large part of it has been regained from the sea, and it vies with Nagoya for the position of Japan's third trading port. It deals with 40% of Japanese exports and even aims to take business from Kobe. With its extension S towards Sakai and W to meet Kobe, it will eventually form, around Osaka Bay, the vast port of Hanshin which is currently being built. Festival 15 July.

Visiting the town

ONE DAY IN OSAKA. You can get a brief idea of what the town is like in one day. We would recommend that you visit Osaka Castle and Shitenno ji first of all. Some distance from these is Tennoji Park which contains the Municipal Art Museum. You could spend the afternoon at the shrine of Sumiyoshi or at the site of Expo '70. You can end the day in the shopping arcades of the subterranean city. You will find plenty to do in the evening in Dotombori.

THE TOWN ON FOOT. The main tourist attractions are too far apart to be toured on foot. Only some of the shopping districts are really suitable for strolling round. Apart from taxis, the underground and circle line railways make it easy to get about.

A Kita ku

Stations: JNR: Osaka, Temma; Hankyu and Hanshin ER: Umeda station; underground: Umeda, Higashi Umeda, Nishi Umeda, Minami Morimachi, Ogimachi, Tenjin Bashisuji. Plan p. 490.

This is one of the liveliest districts of Osaka, centred around the main stations of Osaka (JNR) and Umeda (underground and private lines). It is bounded to the S and E by an arm of the Yodo gawa, which surrounds the island of Nakanoshima. Some public buildings (the main Post Office, the Chamber of Industry and Commerce, the Town Hall, the Courts, and the Mint) are in Kita ku. Large stores, the shopping street Tenjinbashi, the subterranean shopping arcades of Umeda, theatres and cabarets complete the list. You can also visit Temma gu.

TEMMA GU (plan of Kita ku: off C2; 1ml/1.6km SE of Minami Morimachi underground station). This shrine was founded in 949 in honour of the scholar, Sugawara Michizane (845–903; see Dazaifu, Vicinity of Fukuoka). The present buildings were restored in 1901.

Tenjin matsuri, on 24 and 25 July, is the most famous festival of this shrine and in Osaka. There is a procession of boats, bearing the *mikoshi* (reliquaries) along the Dojima gawa.

NAKANOSHIMA (plan of Kita ku: A3–C3; ½ml/1km S of Osaka eki; to the N of the Keihan ER stations and underground stops of Kitahama and Yodoyabashi). This narrow island is hemmed in by the Dojima gawa to the N and the Tosabori gawa to the S. It now has expressways built on strong piers, running across and along it. Even Nakanoshima Park (1891), which lies to the E, has not been spared.

THE MINT (1½mls/2.3km SE of Osaka eki and 450yds/400m S of Sakuranomiya eki, JNR; 440yds/400m E of Minami Morimachi underground stop). This building on the banks of the Yodo gawa has the monopoly of minting Japanese coins. The river is thickly lined with cherry trees at this point.

B Higashi and Nishi ku

Morinomiya JNR stations; Keihan ER stations and underground stops: Yodoyabashi, Kitahama, Temmabashi; other underground stops: Awaza, Honmachi, Kujo, Nishi Nagahori, Sakaisuji Honmachi, Tanimachi Yon (4) chome, Yotsubashi.

These are the central districts of Osaka, bordered to the N by the Yodo gawa. The wide avenue, Mido suji (one way, N to S) runs across them and links the JNR station square to the big Dotombori commercial district. Banks, airline companies and office blocks have grown up on either side of this road, which is the most attractive in Osaka. It is the business centre of the town and the Osaka Stock Exchange is here. The main point of interest to tourists is the castle.

OSAKA CASTLE (plan opposite; 2mls/3km SE of Osaka-Umeda eki and ½ml/1km NW of Morinomiya eki, JNR; 880yds/800m SE of

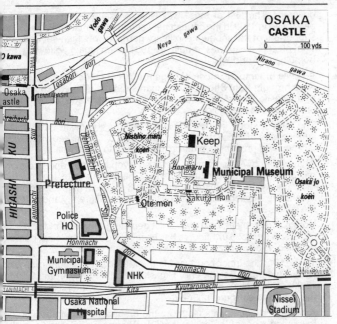

Temmabashi Keihan and underground station). You can get to the
castle to the E of Tanimachi suji. The vast grounds with wide moats
around them are now much smaller than the original ones. On the S
and W sides are Nissei Stadium, the Radio Company (NHK), the
Central Town Gymnasium, Osaka Prefecture and the Police
Headquarters. There is a bridge on a level with the last of these so that
you can cross the moats and go inside the enclosure.

A MIGHTY FORTRESS In the 16th c. the Hongan ji or Ishiyama mido stood
on this site. It became the seat of the Jodo sect following a fire at the
great temple in Kyoto. A formidable series of defences was set up
around this temple which was besieged by Oda Nobunaga in 1574.
He only made himself master of it six years later. In 1583 Toyotomi
Hideyoshi chose the site of Ishiyama mido to have a castle built as a
reflection of his arrogant power. Nearly 100,000 workmen helped to
build it and the great daimyo lent financial assistance. In 1598 Yodo
gimi, the widow of Hideyoshi, and her son Hideyori, who was five
years old, entrenched themselves here in the hope of upholding the
power of the Toyotomi. After one unsuccessful attempt, Tokugawa
Hidetada managed to capture the castle in the siege of 1615. Ieyasu
died of an injury he received in this battle. The castle was restored by
the Tokugawa and from 1619 onwards was placed in the hands of a

governor. The first of these was Naito Masanobu. The castle was destroyed in 1868 in the conflict between the Imperial armies and the supporters of the shogun. A military garrison was then set up here. The present keep was rebuilt in 1931, then again following the bombing of World War II.

A series of ramparts made of huge rough cut stones, most of which were brought from Shodo shima, marks out the different courtyards of the castle. Only four turrets are still standing, of the twenty which once crowned the enclosure.

The largest stone in the ramparts, near the Kyobashi gate, has a surface area of 860sq. ft (80m^2) and weighs 520t. It is known as *higo ishi* and was probably a gift from General Kato Kiyomasa.

The garden of Nishino maru, between Kyobashi mon and Ote mon, has been recreated. Sakura mon, the Cherry Tree Gate, leads to the inner courtyard, Hon maru, where the 138-ft (42-m) high keep stands. It contains a collection of weapons, armour, calligraphy and maps of the castle, etc.

Note a screen by an unknown artist depicting the siege of the castle in 1615. A total of 5,071 figures has been found in it. There is a portrait on silk of Hideyoshi and also a wooden statue of him.

▣ To the E of the inner courtyard is the Municipal Museum of Osaka Castle (address: Bamba cho, Higashi ku; open daily from 09.00 to 17.00), which traces the historical, economic and cultural evolution of the town and surrounding area.

Articles and documents testify to the prehistoric occupation of the town, and recount the commercial development of Osaka up to the present day; finds from archaeological digs; a model of the old Imperial Palace of Naniwa; and souvenirs of the great Konoike family of bankers who were powerful during the 16th c. Amongst the paintings are several screens of the Momoyama period (16th c.) including some, known as *Namban byobu*, which depict the life of the Portuguese in Japan. There are collections of armour and ancient swords and some very pretty bunraku theatre puppets; crafts.

Hokoku shrine, to the S of the Hon maru, has been rebuilt. It was founded in 1880 in honour of Toyotomi Hideyoshi and his two sons.

To the E of the castle, the former courtyard of Sanno maru has been laid out as Osaka jo Public Park, also called Central Park.

➤ 880yds (800m) approx. to the S of the castle, the former site of Naniwa Palace has been located and is now protected.

➤ ½ml (1km) W of Osaka Castle, note Osaka Merchandise Building which has 22 storeys, making it the highest commercial building in the city (256ft/78m). There is a panoramic restaurant at the top.

☛ UTSUBO KOEN (plan of Kita ku: A4; 440yds/400m NW of Honmachi underground stop) is one of the public parks which provides clean air for the city. To the S, on the corner of Naniwa suji, is the Municipal Natural Science Museum (2-27, Utsubo, Nishi ku; open daily from

09.00 to 17.00 except Mondays and public holidays), which specializes in regional botany and fauna.

ELECTRICAL SCIENCE MUSEUM (address: 1-6 Nishi Nagabori, Kita dori, Nishi ku; Yotsuyabashi underground stop; open daily from 09.30 to 16.30 except Mondays). This museum, set up in 1937, has become the best of its kind in Japan. It is centred around electrical technology and its application in the industrial and private sectors. It also deals with the problems of radio and telecommunications, as well as those connected with nuclear energy.

C Minami ku

Namba Nankai and Kintetsu ER station; Nagahori bashi, Namba, Nippon bashi, Shinsaibashi, Tanimachi Kyu (9) chome, Tanimachi Roku (6) chome underground stops.

Minami ku, to the S of the districts above, is also one of the central quarters of the town.

The whole sybaritic element of Osaka seems to be concentrated here and the name Dotombori has, since the 17th c., conjured up the red-light area of Osaka, which was once patronized by the middle-class tradesmen of the town. A great many bars, restaurants, cabarets and theatres (Shin Kabuki za – architect Murano Togo – and Asahi za for classical shows) spread as far as Namba station. Large stores, 'subterranean cities' and the 'arcade' of Shinsaibashi suji, which is parallel to Mido suji, are some of the additional pleasures to be enjoyed here.

D Tennoji ku

Momodani, Tennoji, Teradacho and Tsuruhashi JNR stations; Abenobashi, Tsuruhashi and Uehonmachi Kintetsu ER stations; Shitennojimae, Tsuruhasi, Tennoji, Tanimachi Kyu (9) chome underground stops. Plan, p. 491.

The mere mention of Shiteno ji should be enough to bring you to Osaka. Although it has been rebuilt since the war, this shrine is probably the oldest Buddhist foundation still existing in Japan today. Not far from Tennoji eki, one of Osaka's main stations, you can visit the park of this name where the Fine Art Museum is situated.

*SHITENNO JI (plan of Tennoji ku: C2; 880yds/800m N of Tennoji eki; 440yds/400m SE of Shitennojimae underground stop). The chronicle attributes the founding of this temple to Prince Shotoku, in 592, that is to say before the creation of Horyu ji (see Ikaruga). The layout of the main buildings, on a N-S axis, shows direct Sino-Korean influence. The whole group was bombed in 1945 and rebuilt in 1960.

Festivals: Doyadoya, the naked pilgrims' festival on 14 January; ceremonies on the equinox days; bugaku dance on 22 April.

Chu mon leads to the main courtyard, in the centre of which stands the five-storey pagoda. To the N of this is the Kon do. The Ko do, the preaching hall, is on the N side of this courtyard.

To the N of this enclosure is the Rokuji do, preceded by the Odera no ike which has a ritual bugaku dance platform across it. The temple treasury, behind the Eisie do, houses several noteworthy objects including a reliquary box covered in rare cloth of the Heian period, swords thought to have belonged to Prince Shotoku, and extracts from the *Hoke kyo*, the *sutra* of the True Law, transcribed onto a hundred fans (12th c.).

1ml (1.5km) N of Shitenno ji, along Uehonmachi suji, you will come to Homyo ji where the greatest Japanese dramatist Chikamatsu Monzaemon (1653-1724) is buried.

TENNOJI PARK (plan of Tennoji ku: B2; 440yds/400m NW of Tennoji eki). This huge public garden possesses a number of interesting features. The *Municipal Fine Art Museum (Tennoji koen, Tennoji ku; open daily from 09.00 to 17.00) exhibits archaeology and art collections from prehistory to the present day.

Amongst the objects of the Neolithic period, note a strange dogu statuette (Jomon period) which came from the N of Honshu. Amongst the paintings we would draw your attention to an illustration of the *Genji monogatari* from the Heian period (13th c.) attributed to the priest Denko, and several works by the painter Ogata Korin (1661-1716).

To the E of the museum is the lovely Keitaku garden, which was given to the town by Baron Sumitomo in 1926.

To the N of Tennoji Park, on the little hill of Chausu yama, 92ft (28m) alt., Tokugawa Ieyasu pitched camp for the siege of Osaka in 1614. A prehistoric burial place has also been excavated here. The western part of Tennoji Park contains Osaka Zoo.

E Naniwa ku

JNR stations: Ashiharabashi, Imamiya, Minatomachi and Shinimamiya Nankai ER stations: Ebisucho, Imamiyaebisu, Shinimamiya and Shiomibashi; underground stations: Daikokucho, Dobutsuenmae, Ebisucho and Sakuragawa.

This district, the name of which recalls that of the old capital Naniwa, lies to the W of Tennoji ku and S of Minami ku, which extends around the lively Namba district.

Tsutenkaku Tower (plan of Tennoji ku: A2; 330yds/300m SE of Ebisucho). This panoramic metal tower is 338ft (103m) high and stands to the W of Tennoji Park (above). Shinsekai, a particularly busy district at night, lies at the foot of it.

Imamiya Ebisu Shrine (plan of Tennoji ku: A2; 330yds/300m NW of Ebisucho; to the E of Imamiya ebisu station). It is dedicated to Amaterasu no mikoto, amongst others.

This shrine, rebuilt in 1956, is famous for the Taka Ebisu festival (9 and 10 January) which is held in honour of this goddess of good fortune.

Japanese Craft Museum (address: 3-168 Shankawa Naniwa ku: 330yds/300m SW of Namba; open daily except Mondays from 10.00 to 17.00). It is situated to the SW of the town gymnasium and houses some interesting folk and craft collections.

F You can also see...

FUJITA MUSEUM (Ajima cho, Miyakojima ku; 1½mls/2.5km E of Osaka-Umeda eki; 440yds/400m NW of Katamachi JNR and Keihan ER stations; open in spring and autumn daily except Mondays from 10.00 to 15.00). It occupies the former residence of Fujita Densaburo and houses a sizeable collection of *objets d'art*.

The works kept here include some interesting tea ceremony pottery and a portrait of the Emperor Saga (785–842) created in the 13th c. on paper inlaid with fragments of gold and silver which is a work of art in itself. The garden is also noteworthy.

To the W of this museum is Sakuranomiya Park which lines the eastern bank of the Yodo gawa, opposite the Mint (p. 494).

OSAKA TOWER (near Fukushima JNR station). It is the highest in the town (525ft/160m) and is used as a radio broadcasting station. It has an observation platform at 334ft (102m).

TRANSPORT SCIENCE MUSEUM (Benten cho, Minato ku; 3mls/5km SW of Osaka-Umeda eki; to the E of Bentencho JNR station; closed Mondays). It was set up in 1962 by the Japan Travel Bureau; historic and scientific panorama.

*SUMIYOSHI SHRINE (map of the vicinity of Osaka; 5½mls/9km S of Osaka-Umeda; 330yds/300m SE of Sumiyoshikoen station; Nankai ER from Namba). This temple is dedicated to the Empress Jingu (170–269, according to the *Nihongi*) and to the sea gods who protected her Korean expedition. It is supposed to have been founded in 202 (more likely the 4th c.). The present buildings in the Sumiyoshi style were rebuilt in 1810.

Note the numerous stone lanterns, gifts from sailors and shipowners, and Sori hashi, a highly arched bridge (recently rebuilt), for which the wife of Hideyoshi was responsible.

Rice-planting festival, Otaue matsuri, on 14 June and shrine festival on 31 July and 1 August.

To the W of Sumiyoshikoen station is Sumiyoshi Park where there are some very fine pines and camphor trees.

G Vicinity of Osaka

1 HIRAOKA (9mls/15km E; Kintetsu ER train from Namba). You can visit the shrine of this name, at the foot of Mount Ikoma. Behind it is a park of apricot trees (view of Osaka).

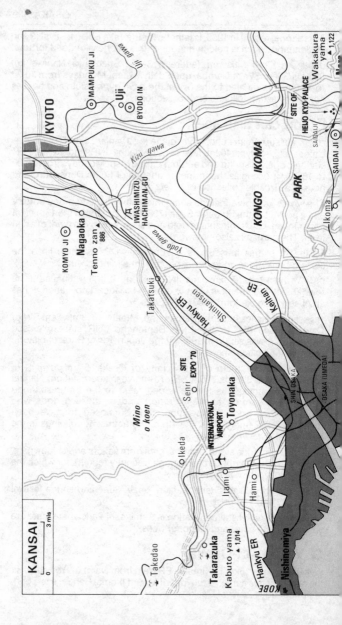

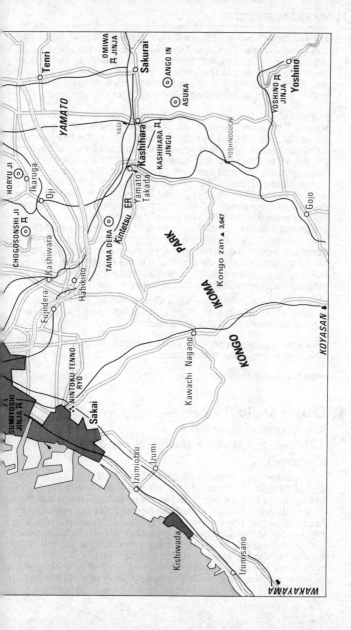

☞ **2 *HATTORI RYOKUCHI PARK** (7½mls/12km N; Hankyu ER train, Takarazuka line as far as Sone, then bus). Several houses from the Shirakawago region have been transported here (see Takayama); a rice-loft from Dojima, and a loft standing on stilts, from the Amami islands, have also been uprooted and brought to this huge natural park. The collection forms an interesting folk museum (closed on Mondays).

☞ **3 SENRI** (12mls/20km N; Hankyu ER train from Tenjinbashisuji to Minami Tenri. Coach from Osaka, Shin Osaka and Ibaraki stations to the site of Expo '70). It is possible to visit the site of the International Exhibition, which took place between March and November 1970 on the theme of 'Progress and harmony in aid of the human race'. Seventy-seven countries were represented there. The architect Tange Kenzo helped to create the 'symbolic area'. The Sun Tower is the work of the sculptor Okamoto Taro. This exhibition coincided with the peak of Japanese economic expansion, which placed this country third in the world in 1970. The site of the exhibition has now been made into a public amusement park and a university has recently been set up there. A beautiful landscape garden has also been designed there. The Ethnological Museum (Minzokugaku Hakubutsukan) stands on the site of the 1970 World Fair in a very attractive building by Kurokaura Kusho. There are some very fine collections, especially those devoted to music of the world.

How to get there: from Shin-Osaka, Umeda Namba, the Midosuji line to Senri-chuo then bus to Ekipso Lando. The new town of Senri spreads out over the neighbouring hills.

☞ **4 AWAJI SHIMA, KOBE, KYOTO, NARA, SAKAI, WAKAYAMA, SETO NAIKAI NATIONAL PARK,** see entries under these names.

5 HORYU JI, see Ikaruga.

■ Osumi shoto (Nansei shoto)

Map of Nansei shoto, pp. 430–1.

Tokyo, 969mls (1,560km) - Kagoshima, 62mls (100km).

Kagoshima ken.

This archipelago, which is attached to the Satsunan archipelago, comes between the great island of Kyushu to the N and the Amami islands to the S. It is made up of two main islands: Tanega and Yaku shima. Although they are quite close together they are very different from each other. The first of them is approx. 35mls (55km) long and barely rises above the waves. The second, circular in shape, is an extinct volcano with irregular, imposing contours. Its summit is the highest point in the whole of southern Japan. Yaku shima is covered with extraordinary vegetation (banyans, cryptomeria and other primitive conifers, etc.), and has extremely heavy rainfall (360 days of rain per year).

TANEGA SHIMA

The little port of Nishinoomote (pop: 26,222) is the main town of the Osumi archipelago. You can go from there 9mls (15km) N to the shrine of Misaki, near the cape of this name, where the first Europeans landed in 1542. A monument was erected to them in 1927.

Having been driven back from the Ryukyu by storms, the Portuguese Fernão Mendez Pinto and his men were classified as 'barbarians from the south', the Nambanjin. They brought with them the first firearms which the Japanese copied and called *tanegashima*. The way was open to new trading arrangements between Japan and Southeast Asia.

☞ **SHIMAMA** (32mls/52km SW; coach). The road heads S along the W coast of the island in the centre of which it rejoins:

16mls (25km): Nakatone. Another road branches off from here and goes via the E coast (the lovely Shotoin Bay) to Kukinaga near Cape Take and Tanegashima Space Centre.

24mls (39km): Shimotane. At nearby Hirota a prehistoric dwelling of the Yayoi period has been excavated. Ornamental carved shells (Chinese influence) have been found there.

32mls (52km): Shimama, where a boat goes to Yaku shima, which is visible from Cape Shimama.

*YAKU SHIMA

Yaku shima is by far the more attractive of the two islands. It is possible to take a look at it by touring along the coast, from the little ports of Miyanoura to the N and Ambo to the E.

☞ From Ambo you can take a taxi 10mls (16km) to the site of *kosugi dani. A path has been made between the mountain slopes, above a waterfall and across an ancient forest where a few exceptional trees are 2-3,000 years old. Walkers can get to Kurio to the SW by going round Miyanoura dake (6,348ft/1,935m), the highest point on the island. Deer and monkeys live in the wild here.

☞ Onoaida (9mls/15km SW of Ambo) is overlooked by the superb Mochomu dake (3,097ft/944m).

■ Otaru (Island of Hokkaido)

Railway map on inside front cover.

Tokyo, 672mls (1,081km) - Hakodate, 156mls (251km) - Sapporo, 24mls (39km) - Tomakomai, 66mls (106km).

Hokkaido - pop: 180,728 - fishing port - national university.

Otaru provides an outlet to the sea for Sapporo and the Ishikara basin and has the advantage of not freezing up in winter. The present town has grown up around an Ainu fishing village, built in 1850 by the lords of Matsumae. Its expansion, which made it the third town of Hokkaido (after Sapporo and Hakodate), has been at a standstill for several years and it has now been overtaken by more dynamic towns such as Asahikawa and Kushiro. Otaru is a useful base for touring the Shakotan peninsula.

The film director Kobayashi Masaki was born in Otaru in 1916.

☞ VICINITY

1 ASARIGAWA ONSEN (5½mls/9km SE; coach). This is a spa town and winter sports resort. Waters at 95°F (35°C).

2 TENGU YAMA (4mls/7km S; coach and cable-car). From this hill (1,754ft/532m high) there is a view over Otaru and Ishikari Bay. It is a good winter skiing resort.

3 IWANAI (61mls/98km SW on the N5 and N229; coach: JNR train via Kozawa). Head NW out of Otaru.

½ml (1km): turn off on the r. towards:

➡ 1¼mls (2km) N: Temiya. Opposite the station of this suburb is a statue to the memory of Joseph U. Crawford, an American who built Hokkaido's first railway between Sapporo and Temiya in 1880. Further N is Temiya Park where a cave was discovered in 1865 with inscriptions carved in the rock. Their origin is uncertain, although they are possibly prehistoric. This road runs as far as Cape Takashima.

3½mls (6km): road on the r. (½ml/1km N) towards the attractive rocky coast of Otamoi. View over the Shakotan peninsula.

8mls (13km): Oshoro; a road tunnel, before which a little road branches off on the r. towards the delightful Bay of *Oshoro. Past the tunnel another road on the l. leads to (you will need to enquire):

➡ 1ml (1.5km) SE: the megalithic circle of Oshoro, where a number of standing stones form an ellipse of 92ft (28m) in diameter at its widest point. The exact date of this pre- or protohistoric group is uncertain but it is very characteristic of Japan.

8½mls (14km): Ranshima. ½ml (1km) W of the small station the Fugoppe cave was discovered in 1950. It has incised carvings of human figures and animals, comparable to those at Temiya (see above). Comparison with similar discoveries made in Asia has led experts to believe that these inscriptions are evidence of human occupation during the late Paleolithic era.

12mls (20km): Yoichi. You can visit the Nikka whisky distilleries which are rather curious stone buildings with a European appearance. Nearby there is an experimental station concerned with orchards attached to Hokkaido University. Past Yoichi the N229 goes through several tunnels and along the superb **Shakotan peninsula. The coast is lined with cliffs, promontories and rocky points.

24mls (38km): Furubira, where the N229 cuts across the Shakotan peninsula to the S.

➡ 17mls (27km) NW: *Kamui misaki (coach from Yoichi), which you can reach via Bikoku and Yobetsu. The second of these places is situated between the beautiful Kamui and Shakotan headlands. The northern part of the peninsula is crowned by Shakotan dake (4,117ft/1,255m) and Yobetsu dake (4,258ft/1,298m), which remain covered in snow nearly all year round.

43mls (69km): Kamoenai, on the W coast of the Shakotan peninsula.

61mls (98km): Iwanai, a little port situated between the Shakotan peninsula and the remarkable Raiden coast which plunges down a series of sheer drops into the sea. *Raiden kaigan is where the Niseko mountains meet the sea, dropping as cliffs from an altitude of 3,300ft (1,000m). Some of these mountain peaks have been made into ski-resorts and the Japanese compare them with Saint-Moritz.

■ Otsu (Island of Honshu)

Map of Places of Interest, p. 70.

Tokyo, 290mls (467km) - Fukui, 94mls (152km) - Gifu, 67mls (108km) - Kyoto, 7½mls (12km) - Tsu, 54mls (86km).
Capital of Shiga ken (pop: 456,844) - pop: 171,777

Otsu, to the S of Lake Biwa (see below, Vicinity), is of interest to tourists, as there are several noteworthy temples here and it is a good starting point for visiting Biwa ko.

The town of Otsu was chosen in the 8th c. as Imperial capital. It was here that the assassination attempt on the Tsarevitch, the future Nicholas II, took place in May 1891.

The priest Saicho or Dengyo Daishi (767–822), the founder of Enryaku ji, was born in Otsu.

↗ VICINITY

1 *BIWA KO (ferry services on the lake). It is 260sq. mls (674km^2) in area and 146mls (235km) in circumference, and is therefore the largest lake in Japan. It lies in a rift or fault which is probably connected with the upthrust of Mount Fuji (p. 164). It is 315ft (96m) deep and its name comes from the shape of the lute or *biwa* which its outline makes. It flows out towards the S at 279ft (85m) alt. by the Uji gawa.

The natural beauties of this lake have earned it another name, Omi Hakkei, the eight wonders of Omi. 'The eight beauties of Lake Biwa, listed by Japanese poets, are as follows: the snow on Mount Hira at sunset; the flight of the wild ducks at Katata; the night rainfall at Karasaki; the sound of Mii temple bell at twilight; the sun and the breeze at Awazu; the last light of day at Seta; the autumn moon at Ishiyama; the return of the boats at Yabase' (Fosco Maraini).

Nowadays, most of them have lost much of their original charm. Lake Biwa has been enclosed in a regional park of 249,570 acres (101,000 ha), where eight new wonders have been found with a greater appeal to tourists: the great view of Shizuga take; the granite cliffs of Kaizu Osaki; the view in calm weather of Chikubu island; the old castle of Hikone; the white beach of Omatsuzaki; the coastal villages of Azuchi Hachiman; the dense foliage of Mount Hiei; and the calm waves of Seta-Ishiyama.

2 ISHIYAMA (5mls/8km SE; Keihan ER train to Ishiyamadera). Head SE out of Otsu on the N1 or a road closer to the lake.

1¼mls (2km): Zeze. Near Ishiba station (Keihan ER), you can visit Gichu ji (1550), in the enclosure of which Matsuo Munefusa, or Basho (1644–94), the greatest Japanese writer of *haiku* poems (p. 92) lies buried. Baisenkutsu, famous for its plantations of dwarf plum trees, is also at Zeze.

4½mls (6km): Ishiyama, where you go down the Uji gawa towards the S. The river is spanned by the double bridge of Seta, which is regarded as one of the splendours of Omi. Two railway bridges, a road bridge and a toll road, have unfortunately spoilt the original site.

5mls (8km): Ishiyama dera (550yds/500m S of the station of this name) owes its name to the surrounding rock formations. The temple, founded in the 8th c. by the priest Roben, was rebuilt in the 16th c. Worth noting are the E gate, Todai mon, of the Kamakura period; the Tohotoba pagoda, which is crowned like a stupa; and Genjino ma, a pavilion rebuilt on the site of the one where the lady Murasaki Shikibu (975–1031) is said to have written the famous *Genji Monogatari*. The review over Lake Biwa from this pavillion in the autumn moonlight is one of the wonders of Omi (see above). The temple treasury houses several works of art, including a statue of Kannon of the Hakuho period (8th c.), a Nyorin Kannon of the Kamakura period, and an *emakimono* relating the history of the temple.

3 IMAZU (35mls/56km N on the N161; coach; JNR train from Shiga, and Keihan ER from Hama Otsu to Sakamoto). Head N out of Otsu on the N161.

½ml (1km): *Onjo ji, better known as Mii dera (550yds/500m W of Miidera Keihan ER stop), owes this second name to the three wells from which the water was taken for the first baths of the Emperors Tenchi and Temmu and the Empress Jito (7th c.).

This temple was founded in 674 in honour of the Emperor Kobun and was one of the most important of the Tendai sect. It frequently engaged in rivalry with Enryaku ji and was nearly destroyed on several occasions by the monks from Mount Hiei. Out of the 859 buildings which it boasted at one time, only about 60 are standing today.

Amongst the buildings of this temple, note the Kon do, where a statue of Miroku Bosatsu attributed to Unkei is kept; Issaikyo zo, a revolving octagonal library, where the *sutra* are arranged in rows (1601); and Kannon do or Shoho ji, the most venerated building of Mii dera, with a lovely view over Lake Biwa. The temple has two famous bronze bells. One of them (1602) is renowned for its sonorous tone and the other, the older is thought to have been hung by Benkei, the companion of Minamoto Yoshitsune (see Chuson ji, p. 240). At Mii dera you can buy some reproductions of prints in the *otsu e* style, inspired by Iwasa

Matabei, a painter of the Tosa school (17th c.).

At the Homyo in, near Mii dera, is the tomb of Ernest Francisco Fenollosa (1853-1909), the American art critic who taught at the Imperial University of Tokyo and was converted to Buddhism.

2mls (3km): Omi shrine (440yds/400m W of Omijingumae Keihan ER station), dedicated in 1938 to the Emperor Tenchi (7th c.) who established his Imperial residence in this area; view over Lake Biwa. On the shores of the lake (Karasaki) is a famous pine tree, now dead, but which lived for a thousand years. Its spread is quite exceptional (161ft/48m) and makes it one of the 'sights of Omi'. It inspired the woodcut artist Hiroshige. A 'new Karasaki pine' has been planted at Hietsuji (1ml/2km further N) from a cutting off the old tree.

5½mls (9km): Sakamoto, where you can visit Hiyoshi shrine (330yds/300m W of the station; Keihan ER terminus). Past there you will come to the funicular railway which goes to Eizanchudo, near Enryaku ji (p. 385).

Hiyoshi taisha or Hie jinja contains the seven divine patronesses of Mount Hiei. The buildings were reconstructed after 1586. Sanno matsuri festival on 13 and 14 April. Near this shrine is Saikyo ji, one of the numberous Tendai sect temples in Sakamoto, founded in the 7th c. It was rebuilt during the Momoyama period (16th c.) and has several *objets d'art* of this period.

Sakamoto came under the Ashikaga during the 15th and 16th c. The members of this family who were opposed to the shogun in Kyoto, established themselves here. The shogun, Yoshihara himself, was driven from the capital by Hosokawa Harumoto and took refuge here in 1547. Oda Nobunaga placed Mori Yoshinari there, and, later, his future assassin, Akechi Mitsuhide. The latter's cousin, Akechi Mitsuharu, entrenched himself here after the murder of Nobunaga. He was attacked by Hideyoshi and killed himself and his entire family.

7mls (11km): Ogoto, a spa town with alkaline waters.

10mls (16km): Katata, where Lake Biwa narrows and is spanned by the Biwako ohashi (4,429ft/1,350m long), which will take you to Moriyama and Kusatsu on the other shore (coach). Katata is also one of the high spots of Lake Biwa. You can see the 'floating pavilion', the Uki mido or Mangetsu ji (Momoyama period, 16th c.), built on piles beside the lake.

15mls (24km): there is a small road on the l. to the cable-car up Mount Hira (3,852ft/1,174m) to take you up to the summit. There is a panoramic view over Lake Biwa and Mount Hiei. Skiing in winter. The beach of Omi Maiko or Omatsuzaki stretches out along the shores of the lake.

35mls (56km): Imazu, where you can go by coach to Obama or train to Tsuruga.

4 HIKON, KYOTO, OMI HACHIMAN, UJI, see entries under these names.

5 HIEI ZAN, see Kyoto.

■ Rikuchu Kaigan (National Park of; Island of Honshu)**

Map of Tohoku, pp. 232–3.

HOW TO GET THERE

- From Ishinoseki (58mls/93km N of Sendai, 1h. by JNR train). From here it will take 1h. 20 to get to Kesennuma on the Ofunato line (JNR); coach direct (31mls/50km) on the N284.

- From Morioka (114mls/184km N of Sendai in 2h. by train; 127mls/204km S of Aomori in 2h. 20). You can get to Miyako from here in 2h. 20 on the Yamada line (JNR); coach to Miyako (69mls/111km on the N106); coach also to Kuji (70mls/113km on the N4 and 281, in 3h.).

- From Kuji, Miyako or Kesennuma. These towns are linked to each other, in either direction, by a number of coach services which makes it necessary to change several times on the journey. The N45 and the railway remain, for the most part, fairly set back from the coast. You will find several coach and ferry services which will take you to the most interesting places.

The E coast of Tohoku is protected for 21,285 acres (8,614 ha) and presents the Pacific Ocean with an extraordinary facade of rugged contours forged by the constant erosion of the sea. Cliffs, promontories, inlets, rocks and isolated islets, natural caves and waterfalls are the main elements in this sublime orchestration and form one of the most beautiful Japanese images of wild, rebellious nature. Between Kuji and Kesennuma is Miyako, the main town, where we would recommend that you stop off when you visit the national park.

FROM KUJI TO KESENNUMA (158mls/254km S on the N45; coaches via Omoto, Miyako, Kamaishi, Rikuzen Takata. JNR train from Miyako to Kesennuma).

Kuji (pop: 39,013. JNR train to Hachinohe). Trading town on the Kuji gawa, where you would take the N45 towards the S.

→ 5½mls (9km) SE (coach): Kosode hama, one of the inlets of *Kuji kaigan which has a number of rocky cliffs and marine caves, and stretches as far as Misaki.

8mls (13km): Noda, where the wide Noda Tamagawa Bay spreads out as far as the mouth of the Akka gawa.

19mls (30km): Fudai, where you can go to a toll road, on the l. (direct coach between Kuji and Omoto), overlooking one of the loveliest sections of the Rikuchi coast over a distance of 9mls (15km). Cliffs 650-1,000ft (2-300m) high, natural arches, etc. stand on either side of the **Kitayama zaki.

29mls (47km): Tanohata, where you can go to:

→ 3mls (5km): the little port of Shimanokoshi. You could take a boat trip from here along the coast mentioned above, as far as Kitayama zaki, or you could go S to Miyako.

40mls (65km): Omoto, near the mouth of the Omoto gawa and another interesting stretch of the Rikuchi coast.

ALTERNATIVE ROUTE FROM KUJI TO OMOTO (on the inland road, 42mls/67km S; coach via Iwaizumi). Head SW out of Kuji up a tributary of the Kuji gawa.

5½mls (9km): Osanai keiryu, a steep-sided, wooded valley, beyond which the road skirts the eastern slopes of Toshima yama (4,140ft/1,262m), one of the peaks of the Rikuchi range.

19mls (30km): bridge on the Akka gawa. A little further upstream you can visit the natural cave, Akka do.

29mls (47km): *Ryusen do, the loveliest known natural cave in the region.

30mls (49km): Iwaizumi, where you can head E down the Omoto gawa.

42mls (67km): Omoto, see above.

The N45 continues, becomes very winding, and is occasionally intersected by tunnels.

54mls (87km): Taro, where you can go NE to Ma saki. Boat to Miyako.

60mls (96km): Miyako (pop: 62,478), a former fishing port on a long narrow bay. You can go back to Morioka from here (train, coach). Motor launches go on trips from Miyako along the Rikuchi coast and make a number of stops. Gassan (1,503ft/458m) stands facing the town and rises to a peak in the N, at Cape Hei.

→ 2½mls (4km) NE (coach; boat): the rather unusual rocks of *Jodoga hama, one of the most famous spots in the national park.

Past Miyako, the coast becomes much more jagged and takes the form of a series of promontories of varying sizes deeply indented by creeks and inlets.

75mls (120km): Yamada, at the bottom of the attractive bay of this name, where it could be interesting to take a boat trip round Konega saki and the *Funakoshi peninsula, to get to *Funakoshi Bay.

77mls (124km): road on the l. (2mls/3km) towards SE Funakoshi.

93mls (150km): Kamaishi (pop: 65,250), the main town on the Rikuchu coast. This port and industrial town (iron ore nearby) was equipped in 1874 with the first blast furnace in Japan.

A boat trip from Kamaishi goes around Ryoishi Bay as far as the little island of Sangan.

Past Kamaishi, the N45 cuts across the base of the promontories which jut out into the ocean in the form of multiple headlands.

95mls (153km): on your l. you will come to Kamaishi dai Kannon, a gigantic statue of Kannon Bosatsu (157ft/48m high) with access to its interior.

109mls (176km): Sanriku opens onto Okkirai Bay which is bounded to the N and S by Cape Kobe and Cape Sune.

130mls (209km): Ofunato (pop: 40,023), at the bottom of the narrow bay of this name. This old fishing port is now turning towards industry.

→ 2mls (3km) NW is Choan ji, founded at the beginning of the 19th c. and built in the Momoyama style. It is richly decorated.

☛ 134mls (215km): take a turning on the l. which continues for 2½mls (4km).

135mls (217km): on the l. you will arrive at the lovely triple arch of *Goishi misaki, which juts out to the S of Ofunato wan (3mls/5km SE; coach from Ofunato).

144mls (232km): Rikuzen Takata (pop: 29,356) looks onto Hirota Bay which is enclosed to the E by the *Hirota peninsula. You can visit Fumon ji, which was founded in the 13th c. (beautiful three-storey pagoda).

158mls (254km): Kesennuma (pop: 68,551), a pleasant fishing port opening onto the attractive *bay of this name where the island of *O shima is situated.

If you take a boat around Cape Osaki you will reach Karakuwa or the island of O shima which you can tour by coach. A chairlift goes to Kame yama (771ft/235m), which affords a view over the whole island and Kesennuma Bay.

→ 6mls (10km) SE (coach): Iwai saki, where a curious phenomenon of the sea tides produces a column of water, known as *Shio fuki, which leaps up between the rocks.

From Kesennuma, you can take a train to Ichinoseki or a coach to Ishinomaki (see entries under these names).

Rishiri – Rebun – Sarobetsu (National Park of; Island of Hokkaido)

HOW TO GET THERE

Coach services from Wakkanai go (4mls/7km W) to the coastal plain of Sarobetsu, and a ferry service operates to Rishiri (25mls/40km NW) and Rebun (30mls/50km). Other services exist between the two islands and coach services operate on each of them. You should be able to find accommodation.

This park is made up of Sarobetsu plain, famous for its wild flowers, and the two islands of Rebun and Rishiri, which are only about 6mls (10km) apart but completely different in their shape and relief. There are some charming fishing villages worth visiting on both islands.

The *marshy plain of Sarobetsu is a beautiful carpet of flowers in summer. Off-shore to the W you can see Rishiri zan.

*REBUN

This island, spread out over 12mls (20km), is famous for its bird life and its seawrack harvest. It is made up of a series of cliffs and headlands which plunge deep into the sea. Its highest point, Rebun dake, is only 1,608ft (490m) in altitude, however.

Kabuka, in the SE, is the island's main point of access. From there you can take a coach N to the Hamanaka lagoon, where you can go along the lovely W coast (Jizo iwa rock).

*RISHIRI

This island is circular in shape and is dominated by the magnificent Rishiri zan (5,640ft/1,719m), an active volcano nicknamed Fuji of Rishiri.

Oshidomari, in the N of the island, is the principal point of access. You can take a trip round it (coach) and see the little lakes of Hime numa and Numaura ko, in which Rishiri zan is reflected. To the S, note the solidified lava streams which jut out into the sea.

S Sado (Island of)*

Map of Natural Resources, p. 66.

Tokyo, 242mls (390km) - Niigata, 34mls (55km).

Niigata ken.

The island of Sado, off the Hokuriku coast is 338sq. mls (875km^2) in area. It is the largest island in the Sea of Japan and the fifth largest of the Japanese archipelago. Two parallel mountain ranges, which extend the contours of the Noto peninsula into the sea, determine its general geomorphology. Between these mountains is a plain which, like them, is positioned NE-SW, and links Ryotsu Bay to Mano Bay. Rice paddies have developed there and along with fishing and tourism they provide the main economic resources of the island. As the island is warmed by the Tsushima current, the climate here is less severe than on the coast of Honshu which lies opposite. Sometimes in winter boats have to dock at the port of Ryotsu when they are unable to put in at Niigata. Sado offers the tourist a pleasant collection of mountainous and coastal landscapes, especially on the W side of the island.

LAND OF EXILE. Sado seems naturally designed to welcome political exiles from the land of Nippon. These include the Emperor Juntoku (1197-1242), who had tried to overthrow the Hojo regents and the priest Nichiren (1222-82), the Great Buddhist reformer whose ideas were considered subversive by the government of the day. Yuzaki Motokiyo Zeami (1363-1443), who wrote the *Treatises on Noh* and was one of the main authors of the Noh theatre, was also exiled to Sado during the Ashikaga period (1434).

Ryotsu (pop: 23,483) is the principal town on the island, and lies to the N of the depression which separates Sado's two mountain ranges. To the S of Ryotsu is the vast lagoon, which has a circumference of 10mls (16km).

→ 19mls (30km) N (coach): Washisaki, the small port where you can set off on a boat trip round *Hajiki saki, and along *Soto kaifu kaigan to Ogura. The N tip of the island presents all the finest features of the coastline.

1 AIKAWA (22mls/35km SW; coach). Head SW out of Ryotsu on the Sawata road.

5½mls (9km): Izumi, where you can see the site of Kuroki Gosho, which was the residence of the Emperor Juntoki during his exile in the 13th c.

8½mls (14km): the road to Myosho ji (1ml/2km N) branches off on the r. Myosho ji was built on the site of the second residence of the priest Nichiren, who was also exiled to Sado.

9mls (15km): Sawata, where you can go to Mano Bay which you can follow W skirting Daino hana and passing Nanaura kaigan, before reaching Aikawa. From Sawane a road crosses the mountain and goes directly to:

22mls (35km): Aikawa, one of the main points of interest to tourists, which stands on the 'coast' edge of the island (Soto kaifu). A speciality here is *mumyoi yaki,* pottery with an ochre clay base, which is extracted from the nearby goldmines.

4mls (7km) N (coach): Tassha, where you can take a boat trip to see the *rocky coast and remarkable sites of Senjo jiki and Senkaku wan. You can go by coach to Ogura, then continue by boat to Washisaki and Ryotsu (see above).

From Aikawa it is possible to go back to Ryotsu via the very attractive **peak road (coach) which goes up to the island's main summits, the highest of which is Kimpoku zan (3,848ft/1,173m). This road affords some very pleasant vistas on either side and runs, not far from Aikawa, via the Sado goldmine, which has been worked since 1601 (silver and copper are also mined here). A museum has been set up in what used to be the mining galleries.

2 OGI (27mls/43km S; coach via Mano). Head out of Ryotsu by going E along Kamo ko.

5½mls (9km): Niibo, where you can visit Kompon ji. Nearby there is a re-creation of the hut where the priest Nichiren is supposed to have lived for six months. Some rare *toki* birds are protected in this area.

7½mls (12km): Hatano.

9mls (15km) SE: Tada. You will pass the temple of Hase dera (2mls/4km) to get to Tada. The temple has several *fusuma* in the Kano style. To the N of Tada is the coastal region of Konose Bana which is overlooked by Ochi yama (2,119ft/646m), the highest point on the E side of the island.

8½mls (14km): turn off on the l. to Myosen ji (17th c. buildings including a lovely five-storey pagoda), where Hino Saketomo, a supporter of the Emperor Go Daigo, lies buried. He was exiled to Sado by the Hojo and assassinated on their orders (1332).

½ml (1km): from here you can see the Kokubun ji of Sado island.

11mls (17km): Mano, which opens onto the bay of that name. To the S of here is the shrine of Mano, near to which the Emperor Juntoku is buried. He died on Sado after 20 years in exile. Sado Museum (to the N) houses objects of interest regarding all aspects of the island; natural science and mineral collections; reconstruction of the interior of an Edo period peasant dwelling, etc.

17mls (27km): Nishi Mikawa, a small place after which the road moves away from So hama cove and goes across the southern tip of Sado. The landscape of these hills is not unlike the English Downs.

24mls (39km): the little temple of Rengeho or Kobirei, some way to the l. of the road, the founding of which is attributed to the Emperor Saga (9th c.).

27mls (43km): Ogi is a little port divided into two basins by a promontory. From there you can take a boat trip as far as Sawasaki bana, passing within sight of the rocky coast of *Nansen kyo.

Saga (Island of Kyushu)

Map of Kyushu (North), pp. 388–9.

Tokyo, 748mls (1,203km) – Fukuoka, 33mls (53km) – Nagasaki, 68mls (110km).

Capital of Saga ken (pop: 424,254) – pop: 143,454 – textile industries – national and private universities.

A Western visitor in a hurry would generally pass through Saga without noticing it. In 1873, Eto Shimpei organized a short-lived revolt in this town against the Meiji government, which he opposed.

The politician Okuma Shigenobu (1838–1922) was born in Saga.

The town of Saga is crossed from E to W by the long avenue of Ginko which is lined with the moats of the old castle of the Nabeshima who once reigned in Hizen province. Part of the land is now occupied by the Prefecture. There are some fine camphor trees.

VICINITY

MITSUZE (13mls/21km N on the N263; coach). Head N out of Saga.

4mls (7km): Yamato, a small place past which the Kase gawa crosses the Kawakami kyo; spa town.

5mls (8km): the N323 branches off on the l. and after crossing the Kase gawa it continues up this valley towards the spa town of Kamanokawa and Hakuzan dam.

13mls (21km): Mitsuze, where you can go to Hakuzan dam, at an alt. of 1,138ft (347m). This reservoir which supplies Fukuoka and the Saga plain has also been equipped with facilities to attract tourists to its shores.

■ Saikai (National Park of; Island of Kyushu)*

Maps of Natural Resources in Japan, p.67.

HOW TO GET THERE

– From Imari and Karatsu you can get to Hiradoguchi by coach. A JNR train service links Karatsu to Sasebo via Hiradoguchi.

– From Sasebo. Train, coach and ferry services (from Kashimae) link Sasebo to Hirado.

– From Nagasaki you will have to go directly to Sasebo by coach via the Saikai Bridge (46mls/74km) or by rail (JNR).

A fragmented coastline, preceded by an explosion of little islets (Kujuku shima) characterizes this park which occupies the western tip of the island of Kyushu. Hirado shima and the Goto archipelago (see entries under these names) have also been absorbed into Saikai Park, which covers 60,105 acres (24,324 ha) in all.

FROM SASEBO TO HIRADOGUCHI (34mls/55km NW partly on the N204; JNR train; coach). Head W out of Sasebo (see entry under this name) towards:

2mls (3km): Kashimae. It could be interesting to take a boat trip to Hirado from here, to get a better view of the coast from the sea, and to take a look at the *Kujuku shima group of islets (over 170 of them) which are all different in shape and size, and covered in subtropical vegetation.

4mls (7km): return to the N204 and follow it l.

8mls (13km): Saza, where you will leave the 'A' road and rejoin the coast towards the SW.

3½mls (6km) NE on the N204 (coach: JNR train): Yoshii, where prehistoric pottery, thought to be pre-Jomon period (approx. 7500 BC) was discovered at Fukui.

16mls (25km): Ka Saza, where you will have a good view over the whole of the Kujuku archipelago.

28mls (45km): Emukae; the N204 leads directly to:

34mls (55km): Hiradoguchi, the bridge to Hirado (see entry under this name).

■ Saito (Island of Kyushu)

Maps of Places of Interest, pp. 68–71.

Tokyo, 905mls (1,456km) – Fukuoka, 201mls (324km) – Kagoshima, 94mls (152km) – Kumamoto, 140mls (226km) – Miyazaki, 16mls (25km) – Oita, 185mls (298km).

Miyazaki ken – pop: 38,509.

Saito baru (2½mls/4km NW; coach from Tsuma station) is the main curiosity of the Saito area. There is a strange collection of about 380 tumuli (Kofun period, 5th to 6th c. AD), in circular and quadrangular arrangements, or like 'keyholes' (a combination of circle and quadrangle).

The burial places of Osaho zuka and Mesaho zuka (which are 718ft/219m and 348/106m long respectively) are the largest of the group. Most of the finds from excavations in 1912, 1913 and 1936 are displayed in the museum nearby. This site of princely tombs confirms the legendary tales which place the historical origin of the Japanese Imperial dynasty in the province of Hyuga.

➡ From Saito you can go (4mls/6km NW) to Sugiyasu station (JNR railway terminus). Upstream from here are the Sugiyasu gorges on the Hitotsuse gawa.

◼ Sakai (Island of Honshu)

Map of Kansai, pp. 500–1.

Tokyo, 326mls (526km) – Kobe, 27mls (44km) – Kyoto, 31mls (50km) – Nara, 27mls (44km) – Osaka, 7mls (11km) – Wakayama, 35mls (57km).

Osaka fu – pop: 810,000 – industrial town and port.

Sakai merges into the immense urban sprawl of Osaka, which it extends to the S. The town is bordered by an industrial zone, reclaimed from the sea, and a residential conglomeration which is indistinguishable from the great western metropolis of Japan, and seems intent on forgetting a past which did, nonetheless, shine with its own particular glory.

Several Imperial tombs (see Nintoku tenno ryo, below) gave an historic importance to the region of Sakai as early as the 3rd and 4th c. AD. It was above all as a trading port that the town retained, up until the 17th c., its profitable activity and the advantages of genuine political autonomy. Sakai had obtained fiscal and administrative immunity at the end of the 14th c. After the Onin War it attracted artists from Kyoto as well as the bulk of Chinese trade, as the route which led to Hyogo (Kobe) was under threat from pirates. The daimyo from the neighbouring provinces, Hongan ji and Koya san, entrusted the merchants of Sakai with the transportation of their revenues from the provinces. In the 16th c. Sakai was the country's leading trade port. The Portuguese set up a trading post and the Jesuit, Gaspard Vilela, established a Christian community here under the protection of Oda Nobunaga. The latter, however, placed the town under the responsibility of a governor from 1577. The decline set in at that point, and was hastened by the rise of Osaka, which Toyotomi Hideyoshi favoured. In 1635 foreign trade was suspended and in 1703 the course of the Yamato gawa, which flowed through the town, was diverted towards the N.

Senno Rikyu (1520-91), master of *ikebana* and the tea ceremony, painter and creator of Japanese gardens, was born in Sakai.

Myokoku ji (550yds/500m SE of Myokokujimae station, Nankei ER from Osaka Namba). This temple is particularly famous for its giant fern (*Cycas revoluta*) which is 20ft (6m) high and thought to be about 450 years old.

SEPPUKU FRENCH STYLE. In 1868 some French sailors, caught plotting a survey of the nearby coast by *samurai* of the Tosa clan, were taken away and killed. The new Meiji government forced the 20 or so Japanese involved in the affair to commit seppuku inside the enclosure of Myokoku ji in the presence of French officers. The French were extremely shocked and disturbed by this and asked for mercy after the death of the ninth *samurai*. The nine victims lie buried in the temple.

NINTOKU TENNO RYO (to the W of Mozu JNR and Mikunigaoka Nankai ER stops). This tomb, traditionally recognized as that of the Emperor Nintoku (290–399, according to the *Nihongi*), is part of the Mozu group and appears to date from the 4th c. AD.

In terms of sheer size it is the largest mausoleum in Japan, even in the world. Its total length is 3,290ft (1,00m), and it has a triple moat surrounding a tumulus 1,594ft (486m) long, 1,000ft (305m) wide and 115ft (35m) high. It covers a surface area of 111 acres (45 ha). An aerial view gives a striking impression of this tomb, shaped like a 'keyhole', which marks the peak of the Kofun era, at a time when great lords were buried, before the introduction of Buddhism which practises cremation. The tomb was certainly erected by thousands of slaves and prisoners of mainland origin.

Many iron objects and some terracotta *haniwa* pottery were found inside (see Miyazaki). Other burial places, of lesser importance, are in the immediate vicinity.

Sakata (Island of Honshu)

Map of Tohoku, pp. 232–3.

Tokyo, 308mls (495km) – Akita, 62mls (100km) – Fukushima, 121mls (194km) – Niigata, 103mls (165km) – Sendai, 96mls (155km) – Yamagata, 65mls (104km).

Yamagata ken - pop: 102,600 - industrial town.

Sakata, at the mouth of the Mogami gawa on the Sea of Japan, has developed as a fishing and trading port. It was here that the rice was loaded during the Edo period, and rice-lofts were built for this purpose. New industries (chemical products) now make Sakata the second town of the region.

In the town you can visit Hiyoriyama Park (1ml/1.5km W of the station; bus), which stands on a hill overlooking the Sea of Japan. In this park you will find the shrine of Hie, an important library, and the Homma Folk Museum.

☞ VICINITY

1 CHOKAI SAN (23mls/37km NE; JNR train to Fukura, then coach). Get on the N7, to the N of Sakata, which runs along some distance from the Sea of Japan and its row of beaches.

12mls (20km): Fukura, where a road branches off and partially ascends Mount Chokai. There are a great many bends in the road. It passes within 4½mls (6km) of the main summit (2h. walk), near to which there is a shelter for spending the night. Skiing in winter.

·CHOKAI SAN (7,339ft/2,237m). It is considered to be the most beautiful mountain in Tohoku and is affectionately called the Fuji of Dewa. It is the highest peak in the Chokai range, which towers up on the boundary between the Akita and Yamagata regions. In fine weather you can see as far as the island of Sado to the SW and the Oga peninsula to the NE. Connoisseurs of beauty will particularly appreciate the sight of the shadow cast by the mountain over the Sea of Japan when there is a clear sunrise.

➡ To the NW of the mountain, you can go down towards the little town of Kisakata (14mls/23km), where you can take a (JNR) train to Akita or back to Sakata.

2 MOGAMI GAWA RAPIDS (24mls/38km SE, JNR train). You can descend for 5mls (8km) – 1h. 30 – from April to October, between Furakuchi (station) and Kusanagi Onsen; coach from there to Kiyokawa station.

3 TOBI SHIMA (25mls/40km NW: boat to Katsuura). This is a group of islets of which Tobi is the largest. The rocky cave formations are caused by marine erosion.

■ Sakurai (Island of Honshu)

Map of Kansai, pp. 500–1.

Tokyo, 309mls (497km) – Kyoto, 42mls (67km) – Nara, 16mls (26km) – Osaka, 29mls (47km) – Tsu, 50mls (80km) – Wakayama, 55mls (89km).

Nara ken – pop: 52,081.

Sakurai, to the S of the Yamato basin, stands close by the mountain ranges of the Kii peninsula. It is a good base for touring the area. There are several places of interest including Muro ji, which is one of the most noteworthy features.

☞ VICINITY

1 OMIWA JINJA (1¼mls/2km N; JNR train). This shrine 550yds (500m) NE of Miwa station is also known as Miwa Myojin, and lies at the foot of Mount Miwa (1,532ft/467m). It is dedicated to Okuninushi no Mikoto and is one of the oldest in Japan. On 1 January pilgrims come to take some of the sacred fire from here to light up their homes for the first meal of the new year.

2 DANZAN (3½mls/6km S; coach). Here you can visit the shrine of this name. The shrine was founded on the slopes of Tono mine (2,031ft/619m) by the priest Joe, the son of Kamatari (7th c.) and is dedicated to the latter, who was the forefather of the Fujiwara. The buildings were reconstructed in 1850 and are richly decorated in the Momoyama style. Note especially a 13-storey pagoda, orginally built in 1532. At the summit of Mount Tono, which stands to the N, is the tomb of Kamatari.

3 MURO (15mls/24km E to Muro ji; Kintetsu ER train to Muroguchi station, then coach). Head E out of Sakurai on the N165.

1¼mls (2km): continue E on the N165, which crosses the railway on the l.

3½mls (6km): *Hase dera (880yrds/800m N of Hasedera station). This temple is very pleasantly situated and was founded in 686. The Kannon do, the main building, was rebuilt in 1650. It houses a statue of Kannon made from camphor wood (39ft/12m) high. The slopes of Hase san, which rise up behind the temple buildings, are covered with pines and cherry trees. They afford a view over the temple roofs and the little valleys round about. There is a garden of peonies which flower in April and May.

11mls (18km): Muro, downstream from Muro dam which was built across the Uda gawa. A road from Muro goes SE up a tributary of this river. Before you get to Muro ji you will suddenly see, hollowed out of the rock face of your l., a large niche where artists of the 13th c. have placed the pensive image of Maitreya (Miroku), the Buddha of the future.

15mls (24km): **Muro ji, the buildings of which are preceded by a wood of Japanese cedars.

'At some vague time before the first written texts, people on the mountains of Muro were already venerating a *kami*, a patron of the springs which gush forth in this region and fertilize the little valleys of Yamato (...). He was identified with (...) Ryuketsu Jin ("Divine dragon which lives in the cave") and acquired tremendous renown. His power seemed so great that his miraculous favour was expected not only to make the rain fall but to grant all kinds of benefits to man. It was thus that, between 770 and 780, when the heir to the Empire (the future Kammu tenno) fell seriously ill, five priests spent several days in prayer and solitude on Mount Muro' (Fosco Maraini). One of these priests, Kenkei, is thought to have founded Muro ji, which is also sometimes attributed to Kobo Daishi. The latter was certainly responsible for renovating it.

Amongst the numerous buildings making up this temple you will notice the harmonious *Gojuno to (9th c.), the smallest five-storey pagoda in Japan (52ft/16m high). The *Kon do, of the 9th c., was refurbished in the 17th c. On the inside are traces of mural paintings and several statues of the Heian and Kamakura periods. The Hon do, or Kancho do, of the Kamakura period stands beyond the Kon do and houses a wooden statue of Nyorin Kannon of the Heian period. The

Miroku do has a lovely wooden statue of Shaka Nyorai (9th c.). Behind the pagoda, you can get to Okuno in Miei do, which is consecrated to Kobo Daishi, whose statue is inside. In the temple treasury are several statues, one of which is attributed to Unkei, and also a sandalwood Miroku Bosatsu which seems to be a Chinese work of the T'ang period.

4 KASHIHARA, NARA, YOSHINO, see entries under these names.

■ Samani (Island of Hokkaido)

Map of Hokkaido, pp. 228–9.

Tokyo, 733mls (1,179km) – Sapporo, 103mls (165km) – Urakawa, 11mls (17km).

Hokkaido.

Samani, at the end of the Hidaka main line (JNR), is a suitable starting point for a trip to Cape Erimo.

Toju in, 1ml (1.5km) NW of the station, was regarded during the 19th c. as one of the three main temples of Ezo (Hokkaido).

VICINITY

HIROO (51mls/82km NE; coach). Head E out of Samani on the N236.

3½mls (6km): Fuyushima, where you climb Mount Apoi to the NE. This mountain is covered with very interesting alpine flora and overlooks the rocky site of *Hidaka Yaba kei, alongside which the road runs before reaching:

6½mls (11km): the Horoman gawa estuary.

16mls (25km): Horoizumi. Past here, go l. off the N236 which runs along the foot of Toyoni dake (3,625ft/1,105m), before reaching:

22mls (35km): *Erimo misaki, at the very tip of the Hidaka range, plunges into the Pacific Ocean in the form of cliffs and a jumble of rocks jutting out into the sea for some distance. A lighthouse was erected here in 1889. Past Cape Erimo the road runs along the Hyakunin coast.

48mls (78km): note on the l. the Fumbe Falls.

51mls (82km): Hiroo, where you can take a train to Obihiro (see entry under this name).

■ San in Kaigan (National Park of; Island of Honshu)*

Map of Natural Resources p. 67.

HOW TO GET THERE

– From Tottori and Toyooka: 144mls (232km) and 93mls (150km) from Kyoto. You can get to these towns on the Sanin main line (JNR) in 4h.

and 2h. 45 respectively. They are linked to each other by this railway line and by coach services. Tottori is also linked to Okayama and Himeji, and Toyooka is linked to Himeji.

This national park between Tottori and Toyooka comprises 22,227 acres (8,995ha) of the coastline from Chugoku towards the Sea of Japan, collectively known as the San in coast.

FROM TOTTORI TO TOYOOKA (68mls/109km; JNR train; coach). On the way out of Tottori take the N9 to the NE.

5mls (8km): *Tottori sand dune (Tottori Sakyie), which stretches for about 9mls (15km) on either side of the estuary of the Sendai gawa, the river of Tottori. This dune formation, 1½ml (2km) wide, is the largest in Japan and one of the country's most remarkable natural phenomena (unspoilt in spite of its development as a tourist attraction).

8½mls (14km): leave the N9 and take the N178 on the l.

5mls (8km) E (coach): the small spa town of Iwai which has a number of springs.

10mls (16km): a road branches off on the l. (coach) and goes to the *Uradome coast, which is made up of inlets, cliffs, rocks and pine-covered islets.

24mls (38km): Hamasaka, where you can go to:

4mls (7km) NE (coach): Tajima Mihonoura, within sight of the rocky Cape of Amarube.

5mls (8km) S (coach): Yumura Onsen; springs from 135° to 208°F (57° to 98°C) with a reputation as being effective against rheumatism and digestive problems.

35mls (57km): Kasumi, a small fishing port with the beautiful *coastal scenery of San in National Park on either side of it. Motor launch trips in summer.

1½ml (2km) S (coach): Daijo ji or Okyo ji, in a wooded site near the Yada gawa. This temple was founded by the priest Gyoki (8th c.), almost totally rebuilt in the 18th c. and ornamented by Maruyama Okyo: beautiful *sliding doors (*fusuma*).

42mls (67km): a coastal toll road branches off on the l. and runs along the very pretty *Kinosaki coast. We would recommend this detour which the coaches use. This road skirts the Hiyori yama and Tsui yama viewpoints to the N.

57mls (92km): Kinsaki: A spa town on the banks of the Maruyama gawa; springs from 118° to 136°F (48° to 58°C) which have been known since the 7th c. Cable-car to Daishi yama (1,860ft/567m), on the slopes of which you will find Onsen ji.

60mls (97km): Gembu do, 1,640ft (500m) E on the r. bank of the Maruyama gawa; there are three adjoining caves and their name comes from the inscription *gem bu do*, which was carved into the rock in the 18th c. by the priest Shibano Ritsuzan.

63mls (102km): Toyooka (pop: 44,094), in the centre of a marshy, agricultural region where the only flocks of storks still to be seen in Japan may be found.

S Sapporo (Island of Hokkaido)

Railway map on inside front cover – plan, pp. 524–5 – map of Hokkaido, pp. 228–9.

Tokyo, 690mls (1,110km) – Asahikawa, 89mls (143km) – Otaru, 24mls (39km) – Rumoi, 85mls (137km) – Tomakomai, 42mls (67km).

Capital of Hokkaido (pop: 3,982,676) – pop: 1,401,757 – industrial town: agricultural machinery, textiles, paper, food industries (brewing) – national, regional and private universities – congress city.

Situated on the same latitude as Marseille, this huge city where a third of the population of Hokkaido lives, suffers a harsh continental climate subject to Siberian influences (average: January, 42°F/5.5°C; August, 71°F/21.7°C). Don't expect to find the last remains of the Ainu race in Sapporo. Although these people were once native to Hokkaido, they have now been absorbed into the population of cordial, lively, young Japanese. Sapporo has been designed on a grid plan, American style, and it is rather characterless. It had grown up by 1871 in the centre of the fertile plain of Ishikari, in the place called Sato poro petsu ('great dry river'). The Colonization Board was transferred here from Hakodata in 1869 and later became the Government of Hokkaido. The 1972 Winter Olympics were held in Sapporo.

550yrds (500m) S of Sapporo station (underground: Odori), is the superb O dori (344ft/105m wide and almost 1ml/1.3km long). It is ornamented with lawns, monuments, fountains and statues and in winter it provides the setting for the Sapporo Snow Festival.

The town is neatly laid out on either side of it. The main avenues run parallel and go in numerical order across to the N (Kita) or the S (Minami). The city is divided E to W (Higashi and Nishi) by the Ishikara kaido. The Sosei gawa runs along it in the form of a canal cutting across the eastern end of O dori. Not far from the point where they cross is the television tower (482ft/147m high; observation platform). In front of it is the attractive Sapporo Town Hall building. The Municipal Library occupies the old military training hall of Sapporo Agricultural College. The clock tower, which surmounts this wooden building (1881), has in many respects become symbolic of the town.

The western end of O dori is bounded by the Hokkaido Kosei Nenkin Kaikan, the Sapporo Hall of Congress, completed in 1971 and endowed with an auditorium which seats 2,300.

O dori is intersected by Nishi san chome, the liveliest street in

Sapporo. The underground railway follows it and a subterranean shopping arcade runs part of the way along it. It is lined by some of the town's finest shops.

This road leads S to Nakajima koen (plan: F4, 1½ml/2km S of Sapporo eki; between Nakajima and Horohirabashi underground stops). This public park (54 acres/22 ha) is near the Toyohira gawa where there are several sports and amusements facilities and an artificial lake, etc.

To the W of Sapporoekimae dori, which extends Nishi san chome, you will come across the former headquarters of the Hokkaido Prefectural Government (plan: E2; 550yds/500m SW of Sapporo eki) and the garden in front of it. It contains some mementoes of Hokkaido's colonization period in the 19th c. The new Prefecture stands nearby.

If you continue W you will reach the *Botanical Garden (plan: D2-E2; 770yds/700m SW of Sapporo eki; 550yrds/500m N of O dori and Nishi Jui chome underground stop; open daily from May to October and on Wednesdays, Saturdays and Sundays in April and November). This very fine English-style park, bounded to the N by Klita Gojo and to the W by Nishi Jui chome, covers an area of 32 acres (13 ha) in which 6,000 different species of flowers from all over the world are grown and tended by Hokkaido University, which is responsible for this garden.

Note a famous alpine garden in this park. You can also visit the Ainu Museum, dedicated to the Briton, John Batchelor (1854-1944), who studied this civilization (see Hokkaido): artefacts of the craft and everyday life of the ancient Ainu and Gilyak peoples, natural science collections (Hokkaido flora and fauna: collection of birds gathered together by Thomas Wright Blackiston), etc.

Hokkaido University (plan: D1-E1; 770yds/700m NW of the Sapporo eki; 330yds/300m W of the Kita Juni jo underground stop) spreads over an area of 173 acres (70 ha). It is one of the oldest national universities in Japan, and was built up around the old agricultural college, transferred from Tokyo in 1875, and directed at that time by the American Commissioner William S. Clark. A wide variety of subjects is now taught. Bust of Dr Clark. His farewell words to his pupils are engraved on the monument: 'Boys, be ambitious!' To the N is the university's model farm, intersected by a beautiful avenue of Lombardy poplars.

Between O dori and the botanical garden, Kita Ichijo dori comes to an end to the W at Maruyama Park (plan: A3; 2½mls/4km SW of Sapporo eki; bus; W of Maruyama koen underground stop). This park covers part of the hills which rise up to the W of the town. There are a number of sports facilities. You can visit the shrine of Hokkaido there, founded in 1869 and completed in 1915 (festival 14 and 15 June). Zoological park.

A great many cherry trees, which flower in May, grow in the vicinity. Further SE is Maru yama (741ft/226m), covered with first-growth forest vegetation, the species of which are protected.

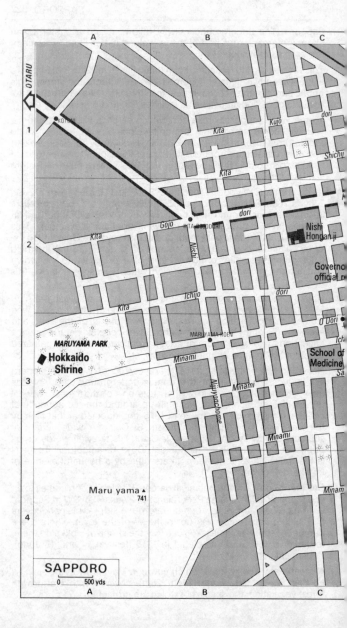

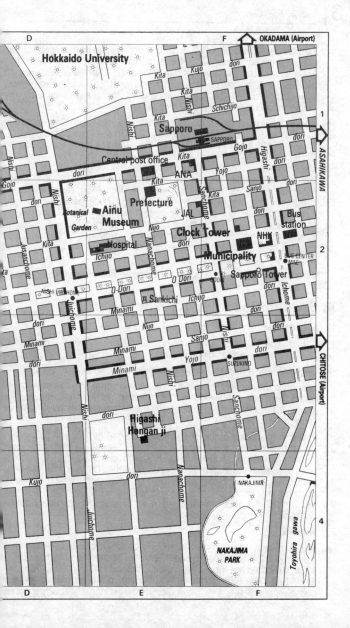

☞ **VICINITY**

1 MOIWA YAMA (5mls/8km SW; coach; Minami Ichijo tramway to Minami Jukujo, then cable-car). The slopes of this majestic hill (1,742ft/531m) are also covered with ancient natural forests. There are ski slopes on the E side. A toll road goes up to the summit with a view from there over Sapporo and the surrounding area; the plain of Ishikari, the Daisetsuzan massif and the Sea of Japan.

▪ **2 NOPPORO FOREST PREFECTURAL PARK** (Doritsu Nopporo Shinrin Koen; 8½mls/14km E; coach from Sapporo eki.) On the edge of the primitive forest of Nopporo is the Park of the Centenary of the Hokkaido Prefectural Government (1968). You can visit the Hokkaido Development Commemorative Museum (Hokkaido Kaitaku Kinen Kaikan; open daily except Mondays, from 09.30 to 16.30), which exhibits souvenirs and documents on the Ainu race, industrial progress, the life of the Nordic peoples and the contemporary development of the island. The care that has been taken in presenting the exhibits makes it one of the most interesting of its kind in Japan. The commemorative tower nearby is an unusual shape and was erected in 1970. There is a view from the top over the entire Ishikari basin.

3 OTARU, SHIKOTSU TOYA NATIONAL PARK, see entries under these names.

▪ Sasebo (Island of Kyushu)

Map of Kyushu (North), pp. 388–9.

Tokyo, 784mls (1,261km) - Fukuoka, 69mls (111km) - Nagasaki, 46mls (74km) - Saga, 43mls (69km).

Nagasaki ken - pop: 247,898 - industrial town; shipyards.

Sasebo is the second town of the Nagasaki region and has developed at the base of a sheltered bay. Since World War II it has become an important naval shipyard and one of the defence bases for Japanese security forces.

In the immediate vicinity of the town you can get to Yumihari yama (1¼mls/2km NW: coach), a hill (1,214ft/370m alt.) which acts as a belvedere with a view as far as the Kujuku archipelago (p. 515). At the base of this hill (2mls/3km N of Sasebo) on the N side you can see the curious natural archway, like a pair of spectacles, which is called Megane iwa. To the SW of Sasebo is Ishi dake (627ft/191m), with the beautiful Sasebo Botanical Garden at the foot of it; greenhouses containing tropical plants; zoo.

☞ **VICINITY**

1 SAKAI BASHI (13mls/21km S; coach; motor launch trips). This metal bridge (1,040ft/317m long, and 112ft/34m above the sea) has, since 1955, straddled the Inoura Pass which separates Omura Bay from the Goto Sea. The strong sea currents which build up in this narrow passage make this site particularly interesting. The bridge much improves the connection between Sasebo and Nagaski.

2 HIRADO, IMARI, NAGASAKI, OMURA, SAIKAI NATIONAL PARK, see entries under these names.

Sawara (Island of Honshu)

Maps of Places of Interest, pp. 63–6.

Tokyo, 51mls (82km) – Chiba, 33mls (53km) – Mito, 47mls (75km) – Urawa, 65mls (104km).

Chiba ken – pop: 49,200.

This area on the banks of the Tone gawa is furrowed with canals on which flat-bottomed boats pass to and fro. It is a possible starting point for touring the Suigo Regional Park (boats in summer to Choshi). Near the town is Katori shrine, one of the most venerated in the region.

½ml (1km) SE of the station (JNR) you can visit the house where Ino Tadayoshi (1730–1807) was born. He was an astronomer and geographer who made the first Japanese atlas; measuring instruments and personal memorabilia.

VICINITY

1 *KATORI JINGU (2½mls/4km SE; coach). One of the oldest shrines in Japan, it was founded in the 3rd c. during the reign of the Empress Jingu. It is dedicated to Futsunushi no kami, the companion of Takemikazuchi no kami, who is venerated at Kashima (see entry under this name). The buildings are in the middle of a wood of Japanese cedars. Note the Chokushi mon and Ro mon (1701) gates. The Shin den, the main building, was rebuilt in 1914. Festivals on 14 and 15 April. Behind the shrine is a hill, covered with cherry trees, which provides a view beyond the Tone gawa as far as Kashima. Kampuku ji has a statue of Kannon of the eleven heads, thought to date from the 9th c.

2 SUISHEI SHOKOBUTSU EN (3mls/5km N; coach). This garden is particularly pleasant in spring and summer. It occupies a marshy site (37 acres/15 ha) and is adorned with a great many aquatic plants (irises, lotuses, water lilies). Flat-bottomed boats sail here in summer.

3 CHOSHI, KASHIMA, NARITA, TSUCHIURA, see entries under these names.

Sendai (Island of Honshu)

Map of Tohoku, pp. 232–3 – plan, p. 528.

Tokyo, 204mls (329km) – Akita, 149mls (240km) – Fukushima, 52mls (83km) – Morioka, 114mls (184km) – Yamagata, 39mls (63km).

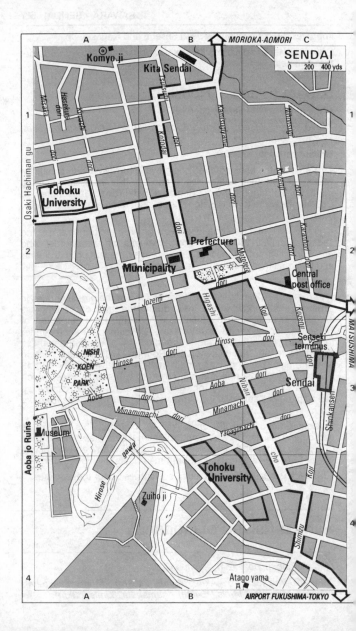

Capital of Miyagi ken (pop: 1,280,650) - pop: 664,868 - industrial town - national and private universities.

Sendai is the great metropolis of Tohoku. The name of this town seems to be derived from the Ainu word, *Sebunai* ('the great river'); that is, the Hirose gawa, on the banks of which the town developed when Date Masamune (17th c.) made it his capital. The present town, rebuilt and expanded after World War II, is also notable as an important railway junction and as a base for tourists en route to Matsushima, in particular. In addition to this, the new port zone of Sendai was opened in 1971 to take in new industrial installations which had been lacking up until then.

The scientist Shiga Kiyoshi (1870-1957), who identified the dysentery bacillus, was born in Sendai.

The town, which lies mainly to the E of the Hirose gawa, is served by wide arterial roads. One of the main ones, Higashi Niban cho, goes right across the centre of Sendai from the NW to the SE. It is intersected by the wide and attractive Aoba dori, which leads from the station to the Hirose gawa. Higashi Niban cho is extended to the N past Jozenji dori, by Koto dai dori, which runs between the Prefecture and the Town Hall (architect: Yamashita Toshiro). Before ending up at O hashi, Aoba dori goes along the S side of Sakuragaoka Park or Nishi koen (plan: A3; 1ml/1.8km W of Sendai eki; bus) which was once part of the private land of the Date. Municipal auditorium, astronomical observatory and Sakuragaoka jinja or Dai jingu.

Part of the Hirose gawa is lined with chalky cliffs which cut sharply across the hills to the W. Sendai Castle once stood on Aoba yama, which is one of these hills.

Past O hashi, note a turret, one of the few remnants of this castle, near to which a winding road leading to Aoba jo begins.

The Sendai Municipal Museum (plan: A3; address: Sannomaru ato, Kawauchi; 1½mls/2.3km W of Sendai eki; open daily except Mondays and the last day of the month, from 09.00 to 16.00) is a little way to the E of this road.

This museum has been set up in a modern building. It has collections and souvenirs of the Date family.

AOBA JO (plan: off A3; 2mls/3km W of Sendai eki; taxi). It was once the sumptuous residence of Date Masamune. Nothing but its memory and a few traces of ramparts still remain.

DATE MASAMUNE (1566-1636). He was one of the most powerful lords of his age. He fought in the service of Toyotomi Hideyoshi, then Tokugawa Ieyasu, and conquered the Uesugi in the name of the latter. He had Sendai Castle built, and his family stayed there until the Restoration of 1868. The castle burnt down shortly after.

On what used to be the castle terrace, from which you have a view over the town of Sendai, you will see the shrine of Shokon sha, dedicated to the war victims, and the bronze equestrian statue of

Masamune, inspired by a statue at Zuigani ji in Matsushima.

To the SW of this terrace the road crosses the Yatsugi gawa, a little tributary of the Hirose, by a bridge high above (262ft/80m) the ravine hollowed out by the river. Beyond that is Yatsugi yama public park.

➡ 880yds (800m) E of Aoba jo, the Hirose gawa skirts Kyoga mine, where Zuiho ji stands. In the vicinity of this temple are the tombs of Date Masamune, with 20 of his followers who committed suicide when he died, and members of his family. There is a monument to the victims of the Meiji Revolution.

⛩ *Osaki Hachiman gu (plan: off A2; 2mls/3km NW of Sendai eki; 1½mls/2.5km N of Aoba jo; near the terminus for the Hachiman-jinjamae tramway coming from the station). This shrine stands on top of a hill, to the N of Hachiman machi dori which runs in front of the old Tohoku University buildings. It was erected between 1604 and 1607 at the command of Date Masamune. The main building is a fine example of the Momoyama period, lacquered in black. The brightly-painted, sculpted cornice has been restored. Dondo matsuri festival on 14 January.

◉ KOMYO JI (plan: A1; 1½ml/2km NE of Osaki Hachiman gu; 330yds/300m NW of Kita Sendai eki and 2mls/3km N of Sendai eki; bus connecting these two stations). Within the temple enclosure are the mausoleums of Hasekura Tsunenaga (1571–1622) and the Jesuit missionary Luis Sotelo (1574–1624), who were protected by Date Masamune and sent by him to Spain and Rome, where they met Pope Paul V.

⛩ A little further to the W of this temple on the slopes of Kita yama is Aoba jinja, which is dedicated to Date Masamune. Festival 24 and 25 May, with a procession of men in ancient costume.

◉ Even further W is Rinno ji which has a lovely landscape garden, designed in the 14th c. by Date Mochimune.

➡ 1ml (1.5km) E of Kita Sendai eki, you can visit Tosho gu, a shrine erected in 1654 by Date Tadamune in honour of Tokugawa Ieyasu.

🌿 Tsutsujigaoka Park (1ml/1.5km E of Sendai eki; to the NW of Tsutsujigaoka station). This park once belonged to the Date domain and is famous for its azaleas and cherry trees. Further E you will see the Institute of Industrial Arts, and to the SE of this the Miyaginohara sports grounds.

☞ **VICINITY**

1 AKIU ONSEN (13mls/21km SW; coach). Spa town (springs from 113° to 158°F/45° to 70°C) on the Natori gawa valley, upstream from the Rairai kyo gorges. Further upstream still (8½mls/14km W) are the Akiu O taki Falls (180ft/55m high and 148ft/45m wide).

2 SAKUNAMI ONSEN (17mls/28km NW on the N48; coach; JNR train to the station of this name, then coach). Head W out of Sendai up the Hirose gawa.

7mls (11km): road on the r. towards Okura dam (889ft/271m alt.) and:

➤➤ 9mls (15km) NW: the spa town of Jogi (saline waters at 95°F/35°C) on the slopes of Ushiro Shirokami. Unmarried people and sterile women go to pray at the nearby temple, Jogi Nyorai.

17mls (28km): Sakunami Onsen in an attractive wooded site on the upper reaches of the Hirose gawa. The springs from 105° to 151°F (57° to 66°C) are well known for easing nervous ailments. They gush out of the banks of the river where you can bathe. There are ski slopes nearby. The N48 becomes very winding and continues via the Sekiyama Pass (1,949ft/594m), to get to Tendo and Yamagata (see entry under this name).

3 KINKAZAN, see Ishinomaki; MATSUSHIMA, see Shiogama; NARUKO, see Furukawa.

Seto (Island of Honshu)

Map of Places of Interest, p. 71.

Tokyo, 240mls (386km) - Gifu, 31mls (50km) - Nagona, 155mls (249km) - Nagoya, 18mls (29km) - Shizuoka, 136mls (219km) - Tsu, 64mls (103km).

Aichi ken - pop: 92,681 - ceramics production.

Seto is a large conglomeration in the suburbs of Nagoya and could be regarded as the capital of Japanese ceramics, known as *seto mono*. The first factories were set up here in the 13th c. There are now over a thousand of them, and 65% of their produce is exported. There is a ceramics experimental centre.

SETO MONO. The first kilns were opened in 1227 by Kato Toshiro who, on returning from China, found good-quality clay in this area. 'The pottery, fired at a high temperature, owed the individual look of its glazing to the ashes which were used as part of the process. The decoration was carved directly into the bare surface of the pottery which was then levelled on the wheel. This technique produced vases which were imperfect in shape with stylized linear decoration. This was particularly suited to the spirit of strength and austerity which made the Kamakura age great' (D. and V. Elisseeff, *La Civilisation japonaise*). Seto and the Mino region experienced a sudden boom with the fashion for the tea ceremony. Potters of Korean origin, who had first settled in Karatsu, exerted an influence over the Seto workshops at the end of the 16th c. Those of Shino and Oribe rank amongst the most famous, along with those producing the *raku* style bowls.

The Suehiko shrine in this town is dedicated to Kato Toshiro. A statue has been erected to him in Seto Park and the pottery lion dogs (*koma inu*) in Fukagawa shrine are attributed to him.

Seto Naikai (National Park of)**

Map of Shikoku (Inland Sea), pp. 536–7.

HOW TO GET THERE

– From Beppu, Kobe, Osaka, Takamatsu. These are the main ports of call for the Kansai Kisen company which runs daily across Seto Naikai between Osaka and Beppu, both ways. There are numerous other services linking the coastal towns, and various islands which are scattered everywhere. Reference is made to a great many of them in this guide.

The Inland Sea is the name commonly given to this extraordinary marine basin, which stretches for nearly 273mls (440km) between the Kii peninsula to the E and the island of Kyushu to the W. It is bounded to the N by the Chugoku, the western tip of the island of Honshu, and to the S by the island of Shikoku. Six hundred islands and islets of very different shapes and sizes enhance this remarkable marine park. Nowadays the finest sights of the Inland Sea come under the protection of a national park, 162,861 acres (65,909 ha).

This sea is like a shallow gulf caused by subsidence and it constitutes a natural 'point of contact' between the main islands around it. As early as the dawning of Japanese civilization, men were using this advantageous route. Rich in wonderful legends and glorious memories, the Inland Sea soaked up the contributions of Chinese, Korean and even European civilizations, which either infiltrated Japan or clashed with it. The number and variety of fish here has, for many years, delighted the fishermen who sail these waters. Economic expansion is also one of the main characteristics of this area, which has huge industrial complexes crowding its banks and sizeable urban conglomerations which are literally draining people from a hinterland which is being depopulated.

FROM OSAKA TO BEPPU (242mls/390km in approx. 14h. by daily Kansai Kisen service, direct; it would be best to take a daytime service; departures around 07.00 from Osaka, 08.30 from Kobe, or 08.00 – in the other direction – from Beppu; some ferries take cars). Embark at Osaka ko (see Osaka, Useful information).

13mls (21km) 1h. 20: Kobe (see entry under this name). The boat then passes between Akashi and *Awaji shima (see entries under these names), and sails into the Harima Sea.

63mls (102km) 4h. 10: you will be off Sakate, to the S of Shodo island (see entry under this name) where you can see the gap of Kanka kei.

82mls (132km) 5h.: to the N of Takamatsu (see entry under this name). This is one of the loveliest sections of the journey. There are countless pine-covered islands on all sides. Note that of Yo (which is cone-shaped). Honshu and Shikoku are near neighbours at this point. Washu zan (see Kurashiki) soon comes into view to the N.

145mls (234km) 8h. 20: the narrow *Kurushima Pass, between O shima and Imabari (see entry under this name), which separates the Seas of Hiuchi and Aki.

173mls (279km) 10h.: the boat goes between the islands of Gogo and Muzuki, off Matsuyama (see entry under this name). You will now be in the vast Iyo Sea. The coast of Shikoku is outlined to the S and stretches as far as the very tip of Sada misaki (see Yawatahama).

242mls (390km) 14h.: Beppu (see entry under this name). You will see Takasaki yama before coming to the attractive Beppu Bay.

■ Shibukawa (Island of Honshu)

Maps of Natural Resources, pp. 64–7.

Tokyo, 94mls (151km) – Fukushima, 198mls (319km) – Maebashi, 13mls (21km) – Nagano, 87mls (140km) – Niigata, 150mls (242km) – Urawa, 75mls (121km) – Utsunomiya, 78mls (125km).

Gumma ken – pop: 47,035.

Shibukawa, to the S of the confluence of the Agatsuma gawa and the Tone gawa, is a good base for trips to the mountains nearby (Joshin Etsu Kogen National Park) and to several spa towns.

VICINITY

1 HARUNA KO (13mls/21km W; toll road; coach).

5½mls (9km): Ikaho Onsen, a major spa town built on a terrace, 2,461ft (750m) alt. on the NE slopes of Mount Haruna: iron and sulphur springs (122°F/50°C). The spa is busy the whole year round and especially in summer when the mountains are covered with flowers. View from Ikaho shrine to the S.

13mls (21km): *Haruna ko, a crater lake, 3,556ft (1,084m) alt., overlooked by the peaks of Haruna san which stands facing Akagi san (see Maebashi). Amongst the main peaks note, to the E, Haruna Fuji (4,564ft/1,391m; access by cable-car), to the N, Eboshi dake (4,478ft/1,365m) and to the W, Kamon dake (4,751ft/1,448m). Skiing and skating in winter and fishing through the ice on the lake which flows out through the Benten Falls.

2mls (3km) SW (coach): Haruna shrine is in a setting of Japanese cedars and fantastic rocks which give it considerable appeal. Note also some fine pieces of sculpted wood.

2 KAWARAYU ONSEN (24mls/39km NW; JNR train). Head N out of Shibukawa on the N17.

2mls (3km): take a road on the l. which goes up the Agatsuma gawa. The railway runs along beside it, and it goes to:

14mls (22km): Nakanoji, where you follow the N145 to the W.

16mls (26km): Agatsuma, where you can go N to a pleasant spot called Shima Onsen, and S to the village of Haruna.

24mls (39km): Kawarayu Onsen, upstream from the Agatsuma gorges which are lined by beautiful ochre-coloured cliffs.

3 MAEBASHI, NUMATA, JOSHIN ETSU KOGEN NATIONAL PARK, see entries under these names.

Shikoku (Island)

7,252sq. mls (18,782km²) - pop: 4,163,000.

Shikoku is situated between the Inland Sea and the Pacific Ocean, and it attracts more pilgrims, who come to visit its 88 temples, than tourists. Although it is an island of contrasts between an industrialized N, which is almost integrated into the great economic centre of Osaka-Kobe situated opposite, and a rural and agricultural S, it offers some lovely landscapes, especially in the S. It has been able to preserve great individuality, which is nowhere more evident than in the welcome of its people, its cooking and its numerous religious and folk festivals.

Your trip to Shikoku

HOW TO GET THERE. The two internal airline companies (ANA and TDA) provide regular flights from Tokyo and Osaka to Takamatsu, and more irregularly to Kochi. There are also occasional flights to the same destinations from Nagoya, Okayama, Fukuoka and Kagoshima. There are boat services from Tokyo, Osaka, Kobe, the Kii peninsula and Kyushu, but the simplest way is to take the train to Okayama where a shuttle goes to the Uno ferry. The crossing to Takamatsu takes about 25 min., and the journey from Osaka takes less than 4 hours.

Note that a bridge, 8mls (13km) long, is being built between Kojima (SW of Okayama) and Sakaide in the NE of Shikoku.

TRANSPORT IN SHIKOKU. The rail services are fairly comprehensive and regular but rather slow. It is, however, possible to tour almost all the island by rail. Coach services are more frequent and rapid, but also more difficult for tourists to use if they do not speak or read Japanese. If you are travelling in small groups take a taxi for the day, or go on trips from Dochu or Kotohira-gu.

The tourist in Shikoku

WHAT TO SEE IN SHIKOKU. Although it is the least visited of the larger Japanese islands, Shikoku has a number of interesting tourist spots.

Historic and artistic sites: the shrine of Kotohira-gu and the shrine of Kotohiki Hachiman (both of which are near to Takamatsu), and Matsuyama Castle.

Natural sites: the whole southern coast of the island, the little island of Okino shima, Ashizuri Uwakai National Park, Ishizuchi Regional Park, the site of Dochu (the Fairy Chimneys), etc.

RECOMMENDED TRIP. So long as you do not follow the tradition and go on a pilgrimage to all 88 of the island's main temples (which would take between 45 and 60 days on foot), four full days should be enough time to visit Shikoku, though five days would enable you to make a more comprehensive tour.

FOUR-DAY PROGRAMME (430mls/690km).

Day 1: From Takamatsu (125mls/200km approx.) go to Tokushima (JNR train). There are some old castle ruins in an attractive park. Go from there to Awa Ikeda via Dochu (Fairy Chimneys), by coach. On the way back to Takamatsu stop at Kotohira (Kompira San shrine).

Day 2: Takamatsu-Matsuyama (Dogo; 125mls/200km). Cross the N of Shikoku by JNR train (3-h. journey) or by boat (cruise organized by the Kansai Kinsen company). In Matsuyama, visit the castle and Dogo public baths (2½mls/4km from Matsuyama). Accommodation in a *ryokan* in Dogo.

Day 3: (Dogo) Matsuyama – Kochi (80mls/130km). Take a coach across the island to Kochi, via Ashizuri coastal park. Visit Kochi and stay overnight there.

Day 4: Kochi-Takamatsu (100mls/160km) by JNR train. See the town (Ritsurin garden). Go back to Honshu by boat.

Getting to know Shikoku

GEOGRAPHICAL ASPECTS. Shikoku is the fourth island of Japan in terms of size and is separated from Honshu by the Inland Sea. It is cut off from the Kii peninsula (island of Honshu) by the Kii Channel and from the island of Kyushu by the Bungo suido. To the S the island is bordered by the Pacific Ocean, into which Capes Ashizuri and Muroto protrude on either side of Tosa Bay. The island is essentially mountainous and is traversed by the Shikoku range of which Ishizuchi san (6,499ft/1,981m) is the highest peak. Its economy depends mainly on fishing and farming. There is not much land available for the latter, although some of it is very fertile (the Kochi regions) and yields two rice harvests a year. Forests cover almost the entire island. The population (on average 572 inhabitants per sq. ml/221 per km^2) emigrates to the principal economic centres, particularly to the N, on the shores of the Inland Sea, where the main industrial zones have grown up: Takamatsu, Sakaide, Imabari and Matsuyama. In the S only Kochi has a sufficiently healthy economy to keep its population stable.

SHIKOKU IN HISTORY. Awa, Iyo, Sanuki and Tosa are the names of the 'four countries' (*Shi koku*) which once shared this island. They now correspond to the regions of Tokushima, Ehime, Kagawa and Kochi. According to the chronicle of the *Kojiki*, Shikoku was the third of the islands created by Izanagi and Izanami (see Awaji shima). After the fall of the Taira (1185), Minamoto Yoritomo entrusted it to four of his vassals. From 1334 onwards, the Hosokawa made themselves masters of the whole of Shikoku. They were succeeded by the Chosokabe whom Hideyoshi confined to the province of Tosa, giving the rest of the land to new families. This situation remained until the Meiji Restoration.

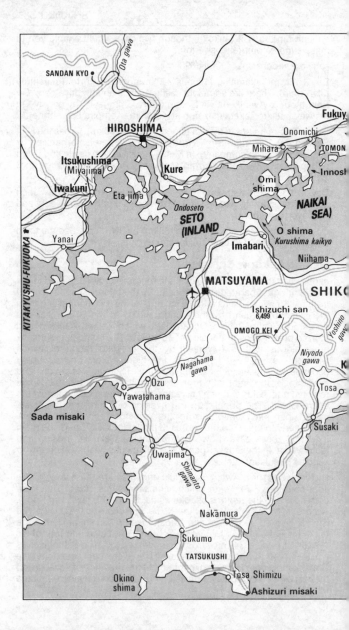

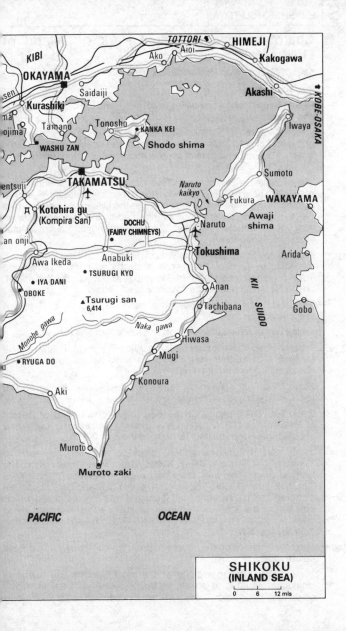

SHIKOKU
(INLAND SEA)

0   6   12 mls

Shikotsu Toya (National Park of; Island of Hokkaido)**

Map of Natural Resources in Japan, p. 65.

HOW TO GET THERE

- From Sapporo; coach services to Jozankei and the lakes of Shikotsu and Toya.

- From Muroran or Tomakomai; these two towns are linked to each other, and also to Sapporo, by JNR train and coach. You can take a coach from either of them to the spa town of Noboribetsu and continue on to Toya ko.

The two lakes of Shikotsu and Toya make up this mountainous park of 243,789 acres (98,660 ha) which is especially pleasant to visit in summer. This entire area, which includes the Oshima peninsula to the SW, is an active volcanic zone as indicated by the presence of some very young mountains (Showa Shinzan) and numerous hot springs (Jozankei, Noboribetsu).

FROM SAPPORO TO NOBORIBETSU (98mls/157km by the itinerary given, on the N230 to Toyako Onsen; coach all the way via Jozankei and Toyako Onsen). Head S out of Sapporo (see entry under this name), on the N8 which rejoins the Toyohira gawa valley.

5mls (8km): the toll road of Moiwa yama (see Vicinity of Sapporo) branches off on the r.

7mls (11km): a road branches off and leads S to Shikotsu ko.

FROM SAPPORO TO SHIKOTSU KO (24mls/39km S; coach). Follow the N8 for 7mls (11km), then take the road mentioned above to the S. It continues along a mountainous route.

20mls (32km): Ito. The road reaches Shikotsu ko, and continues as a toll road which goes along the northern shore of the lake.

2mls (3km) S: Marukoma Onsen (boat to Shikotsu kohan), at the foot of Eniwa dake (4,331ft/1,320m: a 3-h. climb), which has a lovely view over Mounts Fuppushi and Tarumae to the S of the lake.

24mls (39km): Shikotsu kohan (boats on the lake), to the E of *Shikotsu ko (29sq. mls/76km^2: 814ft/248 alt.) which flows out into the Chitose gawa. This lake does not freeze in winter. To the SW is Tarumae san (3,360ft/1,024m), an active volcano which can be climbed. The 1909 eruption left it capped with a dome of lava which now blocks the actual crater. From Shikotsu kohan it is possible to take a coach to Chitose (15mls/24km E) and Tomakomai (15mls/24km SW).

The N8 continues up the Toyohira gawa, which narrows into gorges before reaching:

18ml (29km): Jozankei, one of the most famous spa towns in Hokkaido, situated at an alt. of 980ft (300m) with saline waters containing boric acid. These springs have been used for a very long time and were given their name by the priest Jozan who had the spa linked by road to Sapporo in 1871.

30mls (49km): Nakayama toge (2,743ft/836m alt.). The road climbs through the maple woods from Jozankei up to here. There is a very pretty view over Yotei zan.

43mls (70km): Kimobetsu, on the upper Shibetsu gawa valley, which skirts Yotei zan and flows NW into the Sea of Japan.

➤ 16mls (26km) NW (JNR train): Kutchan, at the foot of the Niseko mountains, which end beneath the sea off the Raiden coast (see Vicinity of Otaru), and Yotei zan, which can be climbed.

◢ *Yotei zan (6,211ft/1,893m) is a beautiful mountain known as Ezo Fuji. Its lower slopes are covered with thick deciduous forests: higher up there are conifers, and the summit is still crowned with lava. Three craters occupy the summit, known respectively as the Father, the Mother and the Little Cauldron. The largest of them, the 'Father', has a circumference of about a mile (2km).

56mls (90km): road on the l. which goes down to Mukai Toya (3mls/5km) on the northern shore of Lake Toya, where you can take a boat to the island in the centre and to Toyako Onsen. The N8 continues and provides a view to the W of the lake.

65mls (105km): Toyako Onsen. It is worth spending the night here to break the journey; very popular resort; springs from 118° to 127°F (48° to 53°C).

From Toyako Onsen you can get to Toya JNR station 4mls (7km) W; coach.

*Toya ko (27sq. mls/70km²; 272ft/83m alt.) is one of the loveliest lakes in Hokkaido. It has a circular crater lake with the wooded island of Nakano and two smaller islets in the middle. It is overlooked to the S by Usu zan, and the snow-covered cone of Yotei zan is outlined to the N (see above).

68mls (110km): Sobetsu Onsen, another spa town to the S of Toya kon (boat to Toyako Onsen, Mukai Toya and Nakano shima).

➤ 1½ml (2km) S (coach): cable-car to Usu zan (2,385ft/727m), an active volcano which erupts particularly violently. The 1910 eruption created Meiji Shinzan (the new mountain of Meiji) on the N side, and the 1944–45 eruption formed *Showa Shinzan. The latter suddenly reached its present height (1,339ft/408m) in September 1945. There is a small museum which traces the history of its formation.

From Sobetsu you can go SE to the valley of the Osaru gawa, and continue up it for 4mls (7km) before climbing onto the slopes of Orofure zan (4,039ft/1,231m).

86mls (138km): *Orofure toge, a lovely belvedere with a view over the Toya ko region on one side and the Noboribetsu region on the other. The road winds back down towards this resort.

92mls (148km): Karurusu Onsen, at an altitude of 1,093ft (333m). Its name is a Japanese adaptation of Karlsbad (now Karlovy Vary in Czechoslovakia). Springs from 131° to 114°F (55° to 62°C).

98mls (157km): Noboribetsu Onsen (pop: 56,503), the most famous spa resort in Hokkaido, pleasantly situated in the Noboribetsu gawa valley, at an alt. of 650ft (200m) at the foot of Hiyori yama.

The springs (from 83° to 198°F/45° to 92°C) contain iron, radium and various salts and have been known for a very long time. They were visited in the 16th c. by the priest Enku who brought Buddhism to Hokkaido. The spa resort was set up in 1858. Hokkaido University has a Thermal Research Institute here.

To the N of the town you can see *Jigoku dani (the valley of hell), a barren place with sulphur formations emitting steam and hot springs. A cable-car goes to *Shirorei (1,837ft/560m alt.) which separates Noboribetsu from Kuttara ko (843ft/257m alt.): coach from Noboribetsu to this lake, 2½mls (4km) E. There is a pit of brown bears, a species which is peculiar to Hokkaido, Sakhalin and the Kuril islands.

■ Shimada (Island of Honshu)

Railway map on inside front cover.

Tokyo, 121mls (195km) – Kofu, 84mls (135km) – Nagano, 162mls (216km) – Nagoya, 97mls (156km) – Shizuoka, 17mls (28km) – Yokohama, 106mls (170km).

Shizuoka ken – pop: 66,489.

Shimada is a traditional centre for the wood trade on the lower reaches of the Oi gawa and was once an important stop on the Tokai do (pp. 170–1), which crossed the wide river flowing from the Akaishi mountains at this point (see Minami Arupusu National Park). The crossing, depicted in one of the famous prints of Hiroshige, was made at that time by palanquin or on the back of a hired porter.

☞ VICINITY

1 OMAE ZAKI (29mls/47km S; coach). The N1 crosses the Oi gawa to the W.

3½mls (6km): Kanaya. A road runs S from here across the Makino hara plateau.

6mls (10km): experimental tea station, where different species of green and black tea are grown. The plantations, which stretch for 51,650 acres (20,900 ha), constitute one of the main agricultural products of the Shizuoka area. The rows of rounded bushes which wind across the undulating slopes of the region are a distinctive feature of the landscape. The tiny leaves are harvested at the start of the summer.

16mls (25km): Sagara, where you will come to the coast and the N150 which you can follow S.

23mls (37km): Jitogata. Leave the N150 here and continue SE towards:

29mls (47km): Omae zaki, which encloses Suruga Bay to the SW.

2 IKAWA (46mls/74km N; Oigawa Railway train from Kanaya station; no road between Hon Kawane and Ikawa). Take the JNR train to:

3½mls (6km): Kanaya (see above), where you can take the private railway line which goes up the very attractive *Oi gawa.

34mls (55km): Senzu, the resort of Hon Kawane, where you can take the coach to:

➜ 7mls (11km) N: Sumatakyo Onsen, in a little steep-sided valley where the *Sumata gorges have formed; a small reservoir, wooden suspension bridges, deer and monkeys. This region is overlooked by Kuroboshi dake (6,781ft/2,067m) to the SW and Daimuken zan (7,641ft/2,329m) to the NE.

39mls (62km):*Sesso kyo, more superb gorges with the railway line running alongside them.

46mls (74km): Ikawa, where you can go by coach to *Ikawa reservoir, which is overlooked by the high peaks of the Akaishi mountains: hydroelectric dam 330ft (100m) high. You can take a coach from there to the spa town of Akaishi (11mls/17km N) or go back down by the peaks of Ikawa (view over Fuji), towards Shizuoka (37mls/59km SE).

Shimizu (Island of Honshu)

Tokyo, 98mls (157km) - Kofu, 60mls (97km) - Nagano, 139mls (223km) - Nagoya, 115mls (185km) - Shizuoka, 6mls (10km) - Yokohama, 82mls (132km).

Shizuoka ken - pop: 234,966 - farming products: green tea, mandarin oranges and food industries - shipyards - fishing port.

This port is sheltered to the S by the Mihono sand strip and affords a magnificent view of Mount Fuji which towers up to the NE. Nowadays Shimizu has become one of the main industrial towns of the Shizuoka region.

On the hills which rise up to the W of the town you can visit Ryuge ji (3mls/5km SW; bus) which provides a view over Suruga Bay, Fuji san and Mihono Matsubara.

➾ VICINITY

1 MIHONO MATSUBARA (3½mls/6km E; coach). This strip of sand stretches for 2mls (3km) to the S of the port of Shimizu. Industry has taken over the W side of it, but the beaches on the ocean side are bordered by a pinewood. There is a famous view looking towards Mount Fuji.

2 OKITSU (3½mls/6km NE; JNR train; coach). It was once a stopping point on the Tokai do. At that time, the daimyo would break the journey at the Minakuchiya inn, which is still standing today and has

been converted into a *ryokan*. A horticultural research centre has been set up near here.

➡ ½ml (1km) W of the station you can visit Seiken ji (founded in 572). This temple has a landscape garden of the Edo period. On the slopes of the hill which stands behind it are statues of the Five Hundred Disciples of Buddha (Gohyaku Rakan).

3 FUJI-HAKONE-IZU NATIONAL PARK, see entry under this name: **NIHON DAIRA,** see Shizuoka.

S Shimonoseki (Island of Honshu)

Map of Kyushu (North), pp. 388–9.

Tokyo, 670mls (1,078km) – Hiroshima, 127mls (205km) – Matsue, 200mls (322km) – Yamaguchi, 45mls (72km).

Yamaguchi ken – pop: 262,000 – industrial town – fishing and trading port – regional university.

The major town of Shimonoseki stands on the western tip of the island of Honshu, occupying a highly strategic position. Along with Kitakyushu which lies opposite, it controls the narrow passage of Kammon between the Sea of Japan and the Inland Sea. It is easy to cross this strait (less than ½ml/1km wide) using the roads and railways (see Kitakyushu) which make Shimonoseki the beachhead for crossings to Kyushu island.

DANNO URA, A WATERSHED IN JAPANESE HISTORY. Shimonoseki once came under the province of Nagato (the western part of the Yamaguchi region), of which Chofu was the capital. This site had been chosen for the Imperial residence by the Emperor Chuai (2nd c.) during a campaign against Kyushu. It was on the beach of Danno ura, between Chofu and Shimonoseki, that the resounding defeat of the Taira took place in 1185. They were pursued for several years across Shikoku and the Inland Sea and were finally driven to the edge of the Kammon Strait. Their fleet was wiped out by that of Minamoto Yoshitsune. Faced with defeat, the widow of the Taira Kiyomori threw himself into the sea taking her grandson, the young Emperor Antoku (1178–85), with her. The fall of the Taira began the era of Minamoto Yoritomo who was to establish his government in Kamakura (see entry under this name).

INTRIGUES AND DIPLOMACY. Shimonoseki played a major role in Japanese history again in the 19th c. The country had just opened its doors to the West when Mori Motonori, lord of the province of Nagato (or Choshu), gave orders (July 1863) to fire on the American, Dutch and French vessels which were using the Kammon kaikyo. The following year, under the orders of Admiral Jaurès, the French Fleet bombarded Shimonoseki. The town was chosen in 1895 as the venue where the Peace Treaty between Ito Hirobumi and Li Hung Chang would be signed following the Sino-Japanese War. The Chinese recognized the rights of the Japanese over the Ryuku and Taiwan.

There are several hills in the town, surrounded by the different districts of Shimonoseki. The port lies to the SE, opposite Moji (Kitakyushu) and the land joining it to Hiko shima has been reclaimed from the sea. This former island now juts out from Shimonoseki, and the underwater railway tunnel (built in 1942) runs beneath it.

1½mls (2.5km) NE of the station is the mound of Kame crowned by Kameyama Hachiman gu, dedicated to the Emperors Chuai, Ojin, and Nintoku, and the Empress Jingu, who was related to them. There is a lovely view over the Kammon kyo.

550yds (500m) NE of here is Benishi yama, where you can visit Akama gu, dedicated to the Emperor Antoku tenno. The young monarch and seven members of the Taira family lie buried within the temple enclosure. Festival from 23 to 25 April. Attractive view.

Nearby is the inn of Shumpan ro where the treaty of Shimonoseki was signed in 1895 (see Historical survey).

The coast of Danno ura, which is further down, is now spanned by the motorway bridge of Kammon Ohashi, which links Shimonoseki to Kitakyushu (see entry under this name).

To the NE of this motorway is Nino yama (93ft/286m alt.; 2½mls/4km NE of Shimonoseki eki; 3mls/5km S of Shin Shimonoseki eki; coach; toll road and cable-car). This hill acts as a viewpoint over the strait and the Kammon suspension bridge. The view extends over the Inland Sea and Kitakyushu and W as far as the Sea of Japan.

The N9 continues NE past Hino yama towards Chofu station (7½mls/12km NE of Shimonoseki station; 3mls/5km E of Shin Shimonoseki eki). You can visit the shrine of Imino (1¼mls/2km) before this station. It stands on the former site of the palace which Chuai had built at Chofu (see Historical survey). The nearby shrine of Nogi is dedicated to General Nogi Maresuke, the hero of Port Arthur during the Russo-Japanese War (1904–05).

Shiogama (Island of Honshu)*

Map of Natural Resources, pp. 64–7.

Tokyo, 215mls (346km) – Akita, 160mls (257km) – Fukushima, 62mls (100km) – Morioka, 125mls (201km) – Sendai, 11mls (17km) – Yamagata, 50mls (80km).

Miyagi ken – pop: 61,040 – fishing port.

The town of Shiogama opens onto Matsushima Bay, the principal attraction of this area. It is economically dependent on the large neighbouring town of Sendai and its new manmade port, to the S of Shiogama.

On a hill ½ml (1km) NW of Hon Shiogama station is the shrine of Shiogama (late 17th c.; tours permitted).

This shrine, which stands in a wooded setting overlooking the town, is venerated by travellers at sea and pregnant women; 12th c. bronze lantern, sundial with Roman numerals and a 400-year-old cherry tree. Behind this shrine is Okama jinja which is dedicated to the *kami* who first produced salt. You can see four receptacles which are copies of those used in the first crystallization process.

1½ml (2km) W of Shiogama station are the ruins of Taga Castle, which was originally built in the 8th c. To the S of here note the monument, said to come from Tagajo, which is a sort of 'signpost', erected in 762, giving the distances from this point to Hitachi, Kyoto, Shimotsuke, the land of Ezo and ... Manchuria.

VICINITY

1 ***MATSUSHIMA (to the NE of Shiogama; boat trips; trains and coaches along the coast). Matsushima, along with Itsuku shima and Amano Hashidate, is one of the three great sties (*san kei*) which are traditionally considered by the Japanese to be the loveliest in the archipelago. Matsushima is made up of a group of approx. 260 islets, of various shapes and sizes, and most of them are uninhabited. They are eroded by the sea, pierced by marine caves, lined with beaches and covered with pine trees, but they are also, unfortunately, a prey to all sorts of pollution.

If you head N out of Shiogama on the N45 you will come to:

4mls (7km): a toll road which climbs the slopes of Ogidani for 2mls (3km) (coach). There is a beautiful *view over Matsushima wan from here.

6mls (10km): Matsushima kaigan, where you can go to the delightful islet of Godaido and visit the little shrine of this name (1610: Momoyama style). It houses statues of the five Buddhist guardians, of the Heian period.

Not far from Matsushima Park Hotel, which stands facing the islet, you can still see the Kanran tei pavilion, which came from Fushimi Castle (Kyoto). Inside there are some traces of paintings attributed to Kano Sanraku (1559-1635). In Matsushima Museum there is a painting depicting the baptism of Hasekura Tsunenaga (1561-1622; see Sendai).

Finally, to the NE of Matsushima-Kaigan JNR station you can see the *Zuigan ji, founded in 828 by the priest Jikaku Daishi and rebuilt in the early 17th c. Most of the buildings are fine examples of Momoyama style. The *fusuma* (removable doors) of the Hon do are adorned with *paintings by artists of the Kano school. In the peacock hall which is the most notable of them, there is a wooden statue of Date Masamune in his armour, and candelabra presented by Pope Paul V to Hasekura Tsunenaga. The temple is preceded by an avenue of cryptomeria, along which you will notice several cavities hollowed into the rock. Travelling priests used to stop and sit in them to meditate.

11mls (17km); Tomi yama (384ft/117m alt.), which is skirted to the N by the N45 and which you can begin to climb from Rikuzen Tomiyama station. There is a beautiful view from the summit, and the Daigyo temple stands on its slopes.

14mls (22km): Kawakudari, on the banks of the Naruse gawa. You can follow this river down as far as Suzaki beach and:

19mls (31km): Miyato shima, the largest island of the archipelago which encloses Matsushima wan to the E. Overall view from the summit of Otaka mori (348ft/106m). It is possible to take a boat to Matsushima kaigan or Shiogama.

2 ISHINOMAKI, SENDAI, see entries under these names.

Shirahama (Island of Honshu)*

Maps of Natural Resources, pp. 64–7.

Tokyo, 421mls (678km) – Tanabe, 10mls (16km) – Wakayama, 73mls (117km).

Wakayama ken.

The twin spa towns of Shiraham and Yuzaki are situated on an interesting site, formed by the southern spur of the wide Kii peninsula. The climate is such that it is pleasant to visit this area at any time of year, and there are some lovely walks in the area. Shirahama (alkaline springs) traditionally attracts young couples on their honeymoon. There are a number of luxury ryokan here.

Shirahama and Yuzaki are separated by the little promontory of Seto. The former faces E to the small port of Shirahama and the latter faces W to the attractive Kanayama Bay, which is lined by Shirara Beach.

Yuzaki springs are some of the oldest known in Japan. Seven of them have been regularly visited by emperors.

From Shirara Oka, to the E of Yuzaki, a cable-car goes to Heisogen yama (430ft/131m), the highest point on the Shirahama peninsula, with a fine view. There is a golf course nearby.

2mls (3km) NW (coach from Shirahama and Yuzaki): *Seto zaki, a rocky, indented headland where you can visit the aquarium at the Experimental Marine Laboratory of Kyoto University, and also the Banshoyama Tropical Plants Garden. You can also visit a pirates' hideout, the 'San-Danheki', or 'Three stairways', and also, further on, a natural phenomenon called the '100 tatamis'. To the S is the double islet of Engetsu to, linked by a natural archway caused by the erosion of the sea.

VICINITY

1 TSUBAKI ONSEN (11mls/18km SE; coach from Shirahama and Yuzaki). A toll road leads to it from Yuzaki, for part of the way along the beautiful *southern coast of the Shirahama peninsula (remarkable rock sites such as Sandampeki).

Tsubaki is another spa town, with a view over the rugged coast of the Kii peninsula.

2 YOSHINO KUMANO NATIONAL PARK, see entry under this name.

■ Shiretoko (National Park of; Island of Hokkaido)*

Map of Hokkaido, pp. 228–9.

HOW TO GET THERE

– From Abashiri: JNR train (23mls/37km in 50 min.) to Shari where you can take the coach (23mls/37km further on) to Utoro.

– From Kushiro: take the train to Shari (82mls/132km N in 2h. 20) or to Nemuro Shibetsu (71mls/114km NE in 2h.) From there you can take a coach to Rausu (32mls/51km N of Shibetsu).

This national park (102,238 acres/41,375 ha) envelops the beautiful Shiretoko peninsula, which juts out to the NE of Hokkaido, into the Okhotsk Sea. It is virgin territory, as yet rarely visited by man. The Shiretoko mountain ridge reaches its highest point at Rausu dake (5,449ft/1,661m), and beyond this to the N are Mounts Io (5,128ft/1,563m) and Shiretoko (4,114ft/1,254m) which are always covered with snow. The lower slopes of these mountains are clothed in forests and form sheer drops into the sea, which freezes in winter. In summer you can take a boat round the peninsula from Rausu to Utoro.

The boats linking Rausu to Utoro (6h. either way) provide a view of the lovely coastal cliffs, which sometimes have a waterfall (*Kashunyu no taki) tumbling down them. The boats sail round Cape Shiretoko.

A toll road goes from the attractive port of Utoro for part of the way along the W coast. A turn-off leads to the five little lakes of Shiretoko. From Rausu, and off the E coast, there is a view over Kunashiri island.

S Shizuoka (Island of Honshu)

Maps of Places of Interest, p. 70.

Tokyo, 104mls (167km) - Kofu, 66mls (107km) - Nagano, 145mls (233km) - Nagoya, 109mls (175km) - Yokohama, 88mls (142km).

Capital of Shizuoka ken (pop: 2,266,982) - pop: 416,378 - centre of the green tea trade; farming region (livestock-breeding, citrus fruit growing) - national and regional universities.

Shizuoka is situated on the Tokai do between Tokyo and Nagoya and was once chosen as Tokugawa Ieyasu's place of retirement. He died there. The town is a lively place and is more interesting to visit than people usually realize.

The comic author Shigeta Sadakazu, known as Jippensha Ikku (1765–1831), was born in Shizuoka.

At the site of Shizuoka Castle (660yds/600m NW of Shizuoka JNR station), a double enclosure of moats and the remains of the ramparts mark out the castle of Sumpu (Shizuoka's old name) in the centre of the town. A municipal park, the Prefecture and other public buildings (library, gymnasium) now stand on the former site of the castle.

It was in 1582 that Tokugawa Ieyasu took over the domain of Sumpu from Toyotomi Hideyoshi. He retired there having ceded the shogunate to his son Hidetada, and ended his days there. The last shogun, Tokugawa Keiki, also spent his retirement in Sumpu (from 1889 to 1897). The castle was destroyed in the bombings of 1945.

Sengen shrines (880yds/800m NW of the castle; 1ml/1.5km NW of the station; bus). Several shrines were built at the foot of Shizuhata yama on the S side. Three of them (Kambe, Asama, Otoshimioya) are collectively known as Sengen, which is also the name of Asama jinja, the most important of the three.

These shrines, rebuilt in 1804, are regarded as the protectors of the city and were restored between the two World Wars. Festival from 1 to 4 April.

Behind them is a chairlift to Shizuhata yama, the slopes of which are covered with cherry trees, flowering in early April.

½ml (1km) N of the Sengen shrines (bus) you can visit Rinzai ji, which clings to the slopes of Shizuhata yama. This temple (16th c.) is decorated with *fusuma* painted by Kano Tanyu (1602–74) and has a pretty *garden of the same period. Near here is the tomb of Imagawa Yoshimoto (1519–60), the former lord of Shizuoka.

TORO (1½mls/2.5km SE of the station; bus). This is one of the leading prehistoric sites in Japan and is now shown off to advantage by the restoration of Yayoi period dwellings and the presence of a museum.

The site was discovered in 1943. The men of Toro had settled on the banks of the Abe gawa, which borders Shizuoka, and at the foot of the Kuno an to the SE. Their farming economy depended mainly on rice-growing.

Some oval and circular huts, on a raised bit of ground, and a loft mounted on stilts, have been faithfully reconstructed.

The museum, the architecture of which is inspired by the Toro dwellings, has gathered together some pottery, jewels and various objects found in excavations; photographs, texts and drawings, etc., explain the excavation operation and the way of life in Toro during the Yayoi period.

VICINITY

SHIMIZU (11mls/17km NE on the toll road from Nihondaira; coach). Go E of Shizuoka, past the Tomei motorway and the zoo, to get onto the toll road which winds through the *Nihon daira. The hills are of average height and covered with green tea and orange plantations. The view extends over the coast, overlooked by the cliffs, the town of Shimizu and Mount Fuji.

6mls (10km): cable-car to Kuno zan (886ft/270m alt.) to the S of Mount Udo (1,010ft/308m), where you can visit *Toshogu Daigongen, dedicated to Tokugawa Ieyasu.

In 1636 the shrine of Kuno jinja was renamed Toshu gu, when the venerable remains of Ieyasu were transferred here from Nikko (see entry under this name).

11mls (17km): Shimizu; see entry under this name.

■ Shodo shima*

Map of Shikoku (Inland Sea), pp. 536–7.

Tokyo, 414mls (666km) – Takamatsu, 11mls (18km).

Kagawa ken.

Shodo shima is the second largest island of the Inland Sea, after Awaji, in terms of surface area (60sq. mls/155km²). It has a Mediterranean aspect and is worth visiting if only for the imposing spectacle of Kanka kei.

Tonosho, to the W, is the main point of access to Shodo shima. You can travel from there to see the sights of the island.

☞ TOUR OF THE ISLAND (58mls/93km; trip by Shodoshima Bus, in 5h. approx.). Head E out of Tonosho towards Ikeda.

3mls (5km): on the r. is the way to Kujaku en which is a promontory laid out as a public park (peacocks roaming freely).

9mls (15km): the little port of Kusambe, where the road from Kanka kei, below, comes to an end. Near here are the only commercial olive groves in Japan.

10mls (16km): the centre of Uchinami (soya sauce and olive oil production), where you can go S to the port of Sakate (2mls/3km). Continue along the road, and you soon come in sight of the E coast, one of the loveliest stretches of coast on the island. It is overlooked by Hoshigajo (2,680ft/817m).

19mls (31km): Fukuda, an attractive inlet via which you can also get to Shodo shima. The winding road continues beyond Fujiga saki, and runs past the famous stone quarries of Shodo island; the huge blocks used in Osaka Castle fortifications (p. 495) came from here.

27mls (43km): the little loading port of Obe. Past here you will come to a creek where Toyotomi Hideyoshi fitted out his ships for the Korean expedition in 1592 and, further on, to the place where the blocks of stone from Shodo shima quarries were loaded.

31mls (50km): leave the coast road and take a road to the S which rapidly climbs the mountains in the centre of the island.

32mls (52km): head away from Tonosho and take a road on the l. which goes up the *Choshi kei gorges. There is a very attractive view towards Tonosho. You can visit a nature reserve (monkeys living in the wild).

39mls (63km): **Kanka kei. The most beautiful place on Shodo shima and one of the most imposing in Japan, with towering ridges of fantastically shaped rocks. The vegetation and the views towards Uchinami Bay highlight this place, part of which is overhung by cable-cars. A toll road, skirting Hoshigajo to the E, winds sharply back down towards the port of:

48mls (78km): Kusambe, where you can embark for Takamatsu or go back to:

58mls (93km): Tonosho.

Suwa (Island of Honshu)

Maps of Natural Resources, pp. 64–7.

Tokyo, 127mls (204km) – Gifu, 135mls (217km) – Kofu, 43mls (69km) – Maebashi, 87mls (140km) – Nagano, 68mls (110km) – Nagoya, 146mls (235km) – Niigata, 185mls (297km) – Shizuoka, 94mls (151km) – Toyama, 142mls (228km) – Urawa, 144mls (232km).

Nagano ken – pop: 48,125 – spa town – precision industries (optics, watchmaking).

This town on the shores of Lake Suwa is one of the highest in Japan. High mountains form the natural setting of Suwa, which attracts summer holiday makers and winter sports lovers and also people who come to take the waters (Suwa springs) and pilgrims who frequent the shrines of Shimo and Kami Suwa.

To the S of the town, the site of Takashima Castle, the former residence of the lords of Suwa, is occupied by a public garden. You can visit the keep.

VICINITY

1 SUWA SHRINES (Kami sha and Shimo sha) are the main attractions of Suwa and receive a large number of pilgrims, especially during the festival, which takes place every seven years in May.

Kami sha or Ichino miya, the upper shrine, 4mls (6km) S of Kami suwa (coach) is sheltered in a pretty forest setting which sets off the bright scarlet of its buildings. Shimo sha, the lower shrine, near to Shimo Suwa station (2½mls/4km NW; JNR train) actually comprises two separate shrines, which were erected on the slopes of Shimo Suwa hill.

2 SUWA KO (6½sq. mls/14.5km^2; 2,490ft/759m alt.). This shallow lake (4mls/7km maximum) flows out towards the W, to the S of Okada (textile manufacture) by the Tenryu gawa which has very famous gorges (see Iida). Several hot springs spurt out of the ground near the shores of the lake, which has a beautiful mountain setting. Skating on the lake in winter.

3 MATSHUMOTO, see entry under this name.

4 YATSUGATAKE CHUSSHIN KOGEN REGIONAL PARK, see Chino.

5 TENRYU GAWA GORGES, see Iida.

T

■ Tajimi (Island of Honshu)

Railway map on inside front cover.

Tokyo, 250mls (403km) – Fukui, 63mls (192km) – Gifu, 29mls (47km) – Kanazawa, 145mls (233km) – Nagano, 144mls (232km) – Nagoya, 21mls (34km) – Otsu, 100mls (161km) – Toyama, 146mls (235km) – Tsu, 67mls (108 km).

Gifu ken – pop: 63,522 – porcelain factories.

The Toki gawa flows through Tajimi which – together with neighbouring Seto and Toki – is one of the great centres producing Japanese porcelain (see Seto). An interesting visit can be made to the exhibition hall of the Prefectural Institute of Ceramics with its display of ancient pottery.

→ 1½mls (2km) NE of the station you can visit Eiho ji, on the slopes of Kokei zan, beautifully situated near a loop of the Toki gawa as it passes between steep banks. This temple was founded at the beginning of the 14th c. by the priest Soseki or Muso Kokushi. Kannon do, and Kaisan do – the founder's hall – are the two most outstanding buildings, of which there were about thirty at one time. There is an interesting painting of *Kannon of the Thousand Hands*.

↗ **VICINITY**

JOKO JI (6mls/10km S; coach). A toll road runs towards the lower end of the beautiful Toki gawa valley, one of whose gorges is the *Koko kei.

5½mls (9km): junction with a small road leading E to:

◉ 6mls (10km): Joko ji, ancient temple venerated by the Tokugawa of Nagoya.

■ Takahagi (Island of Honshu)

Railway map on inside front cover.

Tokyo, 101mls (162km) – Chiba, 106mls (170km) – Fukushima, 102mls (164km) – Mito, 33mls (54km) – Urawa, 117mls (189km) – Utsunomiya, 83mls (133km).

Ibaraki ken – Pop: 32,436.

Takahagi is a large village situated on the east coast of the ancient province of Hitachi.

About 1½mls (2km) SW of the station is the Space Communications Research Centre of ITT (International Telephone & Telegraph) which picked up the first television pictures transmitted on the Relay 1 satellite from California in 1963.

☞ **VICINITY**

1 HOUSE IN WHICH THE BOTANIST MATSUMURA JINZO WAS BORN (approx. 3mls/5km N; coach).

2 HANANUKI KEIKOKU (9mls/15km W). A pretty wooded valley (waterfalls) on the slopes of Tateware san (2,158ft/658m); the Hananuki hydroelectric dam, capable of holding 101,706cu. ft (2,880 million m³) of water, was completed in 1972.

T Takamatsu (Island of Shikoku)*

Map of Shikoku (Inland Sea), pp. 536–7.

Tokyo, 467mls (751km) – Kochi, 96mls (154km) – Matsuyama, 124mls (199km) – Tokushima, 47mls (75km).

Principal town of Kagawa ken (pop: 476,144) – pop: 309,000 – light industry.

Looking out over the Inland Sea, Takamatsu is the main port serving Shikoku and is one of the busiest towns on the island, although economically speaking it cannot match Matsuyama. Surrounded by beautiful hills which extend along the islands of the Inland Sea, the town is a tourist centre and is famous for Ritsurin Park.

TAMAMO KOEN (330yds/300m E of Takamatsu eki). Bounded to the N by the port of Takamatsu, this garden, in which three turrets and an ancient porchway still stand, is on the site of the former castle of

Takamatsu, built in the 16th c. by Ikoma Chikamasa and owned by the great Matsudaira clan between 1642 and 1868.

**RITSURIN KOEN (1½mls/2.5km S of Takamatsu eki, along the broad Chuo dori; bus). S of the town, this beautiful garden nestling against the east flank of Mount Shiun is classed among the most famous gardens of Japan. Other famous gardens are those at Kanazawa, Mito and Okayama.

Ritsurin Park (185 acres/75 ha) used to belong to the estate of the Matsudaira who designed it in the 18th c. It is said that it took a hundred years to complete. The landscape garden *par excellence*, it is nature tamed in accordance with the Japanese idea of beauty, with little slopes and hollows, artificial lakes and islands, and trees which flower in spring and are a blaze of colour in autumn. Kikugetsu tei pavilion, in the S of the park, was reconstructed after the original built during the Edo period. The garden boasts a gallery in which temporary exhibitions are held, an arts and crafts centre and shop, and a small zoo. It is open every day until sunset.

VICINITY

1 MEGI JIMA (2½mls/4km N; boat), or ONIGA SHIMA. Here you can visit the demon's cave which is associated with the legend of Momotaro. Lovely view over the Inland Sea.

Momotaro is a character well-known to Japanese children. Helped by his three companions, a monkey, a dog and pheasant, he is said to have overcome the demons which lived in the cave. The cave also used to serve as a meeting place for bandits.

2 *SHIRAMINE SAN (13mls/21km W; coach). It is reached by following a road for 7½mls (12km) which goes towards the coast, and then another (toll) road which heads S and takes you almost to the summit of this mountain. Wide views over Takamatsu to the E, the industrial towns of Sakaide and Marugame to the W, and of the Inland Sea. By taking a road down again in the direction of Sakaide, you come to the mausoleum of Emperor Sutoku (12 c.) (3mls/5km).

3 SHINOE ONSEN (19mls/31km S; coach). Pleasantly situated in the mountains, this spa is mainly frequented by the inhabitants of Takamatsu.

4 SHIDO (8mls/13km E, along the N11; trains JNR and Takamatsu-Kotohira ER; coach). Leave Takamatsu and travel E in the direction of Yashima.

3mls (5km): toll road providing access to Yashima dera; N of Kotoden-Yashima station (Takamatsu-Kotohira ER) you can reach the summit of *Yashima by funicular railway, between Yashima Tozanguchi and Yashima Sanjo.

THE PURSUIT OF THE TAIRA. Harassed by the Minamoto clan and their partisans, the Taira twice found refuge on this plateau. Taira Munemori withdrew here in 1182 after being chased out of Dazaifu (Kyushu). Having gained the support of the local lords, he tried to settle in Fukuhara (Kobe), but was expelled again by Minamoto Yoshitsune who pursued him as far as Yashima and from there to Danno ura (Shimonoseki), where the Taira clan perished (1185).

Yashima reaches its highest point at Hokurei (925ft/282m) and juts out into the sea at Naga saki point. Beautiful view over the Inland Sea at sunset. You can visit Yashima dera, where the museum records the events of the struggle between the Taira (Heike) and the Minamoto (Genji). Historical and archaeological objects and remains.

5mls (8km); Mure; access road to *Goken zan, another wooded

promontory jutting out into the Inland Sea. It consists of four separate summits, the highest of which is 1200ft (366m). This is one of the loveliest viewpoints over the Inland Sea, with a view to the N towards Shodo shima. This mountain is also called Yakuri, from Yakuri ji, the 8th-c. temple built on its slopes.

8mls (13km): Shido, at the head of an attractive bay, where you can visit the Shido ji. This interesting temple (7th c.) contains several statues from the Heian period (Kannon of the eleven heads, Fudo, Bishamon ten) and ancient paintings of Juichimen Kannon and Shidodera Engi zue (history of this temple in paintings).

6mls (10km) to the SE (JNR train as far as Sanuki Tsuda station): Tsuda is situated at the point where Sanuki plain begins to widen. Here you can visit Kinrin Park with its beautiful pinewood stretching for 2½mls (4km) along the edge of the sea. 2mls (3km) to the NW, Chofuku ji houses a large wooden statue of Yakushi Nyorai (Kamakura period).

5 KOTOHIRA SHODO SHIMA, ZENTSUJI, SETO NAIKAI NATIONAL PARK, see entries under these names.

Takaoka (Island of Honshu)

Railway map on inside front cover.

Tokyo, 276mls (444km) - Gifu, 148mls (238km) - Kanazawa, 28mls (45km) - Nagano, 140mls (226km) - Niigata, 160mls (257km) - Toyama, 12mls (19km).

Toyama ken - pop: 159,664 - industrial town (textiles).

To the W. of Sho gawa, Takaoka is one of the principal economic centres of the district of Toyama, for which the port of Fushiki at Shimminato, on Toyama Bay, serves as an outlet.

In the town you can visit Zuiryu ji, 1ml (1.5km) S of the station, where there are some beautiful old buildings.

This temple was built in the 17th c. by Maeda Toshitsune in honour of his father Toshinaga; it contains holograph letters of the Emperor Go Yozei (1571-1617), of Oda Nobunaga and of Toyotomi Hideyoshi.

To the N of the station, Sakurababa Park stands on the site of an old military exercise ground; from there an avenue of cherry trees leads to Takaoka park (1ml/1.5km N) where there used to be a castle, with moat and ancient ramparts. It was built in 1609 by Maeda Toshinaga, but was later abandoned by his son Toshitsune, who preferred the residence at Kanazawa (see entry under this name).

VICINITY

1 KOMAKI DAM (14mls/22km S; coach). From this dam on the Sho gawa you can go by boat upstream through the *Sho gawa gorges to the little spa of Omaki. Further upstream are other dams and the beautiful Shirakawago region (see Takayama).

2 KANAZAWA, TOYAMA, see entries under these names; NOTO PENINSULA, see Hakui, Nanao, Wajima.

Takarazuka (Island of Honshu)

Map of Kansai, pp. 500–1.

Tokyo, 328mls (528km) – Kobe, 21mls (34km) – Kyoto, 32mls (52km) – Okayama, 112mls (180km) – Osaka, 18mls (29km) – Tottori, 138mls (223km).

Hyogo ken – pop: 127,179 – spa.

Built on the banks of the Muko gawa, which carves a channel to the N of the Rokko range, Takarazuka is not merely a spa (radioactive springs, temperature 86°F/30°C), it is also a realm of amusement centres, children's playgrounds, pachinko (pinball) parlours and some American amusements at which the Japanese excel.

Since it was founded in 1919, the Takarazuka Theatre has become famous for its all-women revues, created as a reaction against the classical theatre in which all the parts were played by men.

VICINITY

1 TAKEDAO ONSEN (5½mls/9km NW; coach; JRN train). Another spa in the Muko gawa valley.

2 ARIMA ONSEN (7½mls/12km W; coach; see Kobe vicinity). Scenic route across the northern slopes of Rokko san, via the Horai gorge.

3 KOBE, OSAKA, see entries under these names.

Takasaki (Island of Honshu)

Railway map on inside front cover.

Tokyo, 74mls (119km) – Fukushima, 204mls (329km) – Maebashi, 7mls (11km) – Nagano, 73mls (117km) – Niigata, 158mls (254km) – Urawa, 55mls (89km) – Utsunomiya, 71mls (115km).

Gumma ken – pop: 221, 429 – food industry.

Takasaki is an important stop on the main Joetsu line, in the direction of Niigata; here a railway line branches off and heads for the Nagano basin, which it reaches after climbing up as high as Karuizawa. Takasaki is the second largest town in the prefecture.

The politician Nakasone Yasuhiro, who became prime minister in 1982, was born in Takasaki in 1918.

Not far from the station, Takasaki Park is on the site where the castle used to stand; today you can visit the Yorimasa shrine there.

Known in the past as Wada jo, Takasaki Castle was built in the 15th c. by the Wada clan. It was later owned by the Uesugi, and then by the Takeda; it fell into the hands of the Hojo in the 16th c. From 1717 to

1868 it belonged to the Okochi, who were connected by marriage with the Matsudaira.

It is interesting to note that the Gumma Music Centre was designed by the architect Antonin Raymond.

☞ **VICINITY**

1 KANNON YAMA (2mls/3km SW; coach). The giant statue of Kannon (138ft/42m high) rises above the slopes of this hill.

2 YOSHII (7mls/11km S; coach; Joshin ER train). The Tako monument is situated here; together with those of Yamanoue and Yamana at Kanaizawa (other stations on this private line) it is a rare historical example of lapidary art; all three are known as the Kozuke monuments, after the former name for the Gumma prefecture.

■ Takayama (Island of Honshu)**

Map of Places of Interest, p. 70.

Tokyo, 212mls (342km) – Fukui, 112mls (180km) – Gifu, 97mls (156km) – Kanazawa, 112mls (180km) – Nagano, 105mls (169km) – Nagoya, 102mls (165km) – Otsu, 175mls (282km) – Toyama, 57mls (92km) – Tsu, 142mls (229km).

Gifu ken – pop: 62,000 – alt. 1,903ft (580m).

After leaving the beautiful Hida valley and passing through a tunnel, the railway line curves gently down into the valley of the Miya gawa immediately upstream of which stands Takayama, the 'little Kyoto of the Alps', set like a jewel in a ring of high mountains. The name Takayama itself means 'high mountain'. Far from the main thoroughfares, this locality has plenty to offer the tourist. It is rich in history and traditions, and is also an excellent point of departure for visiting Chubu Sangaku National Park or the Shirakawago region.

IN THE HEART OF THE PROVINCE OF HIDA. The Hida region (of which Takayama is the capital) has been inhabited since ancient times, as testified by discoveries of remains from the Jomon period. Later, in feudal times, the inhabitants of this province earned for themselves the reputation of being skilful carpenters and joiners. They practised their skills in the capital and at the great religious centres of Japan which they supplied with wooden artefacts. In the 15th and 16th c. Takayama and its region were ruled by the Anenokoji; the last of their line, Koretsuna, was dispossessed in 1587 by Kanamori Nagachika, who took possession of the province of Hida at the request of Toyotomi Hideyoshi. In 1692, the town passed into the control of the Tokugawa shoguns, who appointed a governor.

The Miya gawa flows through the town from S to N. To the W it bounds a flat area which extends as far as the station and the Sunori gawa, and to the E lies a more undulating region which rises up to where the Higashi yama temples are situated.

☐ Takayama Jinya ato (660yds/600m SE of the station; open daily from

09.00 to 16.30), whose entrance gives onto a little square near the Miya gawa (lively market every morning), was the seat of government of the province of Hida at the time of the Tokugawa.

You can visit the former apartments, separated by movable partitions and looking out onto a garden to the W. To the S of the garden, the former granaries are now divided into a number of rooms in which are displayed various documents of historical and economic interest. The whole building was restored in 1974.

On crossing the Miya gawa by the Naka bashi, you find rising up in front of you Shiro yama (½ml/1km SE of the station), now a public park. A castle built by the Kanamori once stood here. Wide views over Takayama and the surrounding mountains.

Shoren ji, to the N of this strip of high ground, has some attractive buildings which were rebuilt in the 16th c., in the Momoyama style. The temple itself dates from the 13th c., and contains some interesting examples of calligraphy and some paintings from the Edo period by Kano Tanyu and Maruyama Okyo.

As you go down again towards the town, a street leads N towards Takayama town hall, after crossing Hirokouji dori. Running parallel to it to the W are the following streets: Ichinomachi, Ninomachi, and Sannomachi (the most interesting because of its old houses), in which you can visit several museums of varying degrees of interest, all in what used to be private houses. They are Kyodo Gangu kan (collection of traditional Japanese toys), Hirata museum, Hida Minzoku kokokan (archaeological collection), Fujii Bijutsu Mingei kan (arts and crafts), and Hachiga Minzoku Bijutsu kan (arts and crafts).

KYODO KAN (1,000yds/900m E of the station; Kami Ichinomachi; closed from 29 December to 1 January). This is the most interesting museum, essentially devoted to arts and crafts and folklore, with displays of all kinds of traditional objects from the Hida mountains, some of which are still used today: method of manufacturing *sake*, examples of ancient calligraphy and sculptures by the priest Enku (p. 151).

If you continue heading N, you come across Yasukawa dori, the main artery of the town, then Enako gawa, here restrained between canal banks before it flows into the Miya gawa a little further on.

In the street which is a continuation of Ninomachi, you can take *Ojin machi (880yds/800m NE of the station), one of the streets in this town which has retained its traditional appearance.

On a corner by Enako gawa, you can visit Kurakabe Minge kan and, a little further on, Yoshijima ke, houses where the rich families of those names used to live. Today they are interesting models of the interiors traditional to Takayama.

At the end of Ojin machi you come to Hachiman gu, in front of which is a modern building, Takayama yatai kaikan, where there is an exhibition of beautiful floats from the Takayama festival. Most of them were built in the 17th and 18th c., and have since been restored. The most beautiful, Kirin tai, is attributed to the sculptor Yoroku Tamiguchi.

From Hachiman gu, you can proceed SE to Tera machi or Higashi yama, where there are a number of temples (Daio ji, Soyu, ji, etc.). The return route back towards the station is via Yasukawa and Kokubun ji dori.

This second street passes in front of Kokubun ji (330yds/300m NE of the station) of the province of Hida, which was founded in the 8th c., and is the oldest temple in Takayama. Among the buildings (rebuilt in 1588), there still stands a beautiful three-storeyed pagoda where you can see two remarkable statues of Kannon and Yakushi Nyorai.

1ml (1.5km) SW of the station, you should not miss a visit to *Hida minzoku mura (Hida village museum; open daily from 09.00 to 17.00; closed from 29 December to 1 January), an exceptional group of houses typical of the Hida region. A number of them are in the *gassho zukuri* style, which is found in the Shirakawago region (see below), and indeed they come from that valley. The Tanaka house is one of the oldest (15th c.). One of the most beautiful, the Nishioka house, used to belong to a Buddhist priest. Inside there is an exhibition of ancient agricultural and sericultural implements, kitchen utensils, clothes, etc.

VICINITY

1 SHONYU DO (14mls/22km E, along the N158; coach). Natural grotto that can be visited.

2 KAMIOKA (25mls/41km N; coach). Situated on the upper reaches of the Takahara gawa before if flows down from the mountains and into Toyama Bay, Kamioka is a small mining town where deposits of zinc, silver, gold and cadmium have been mined since the Edo period. The vicinity is noted for the beautiful *Takahara gorges, which extend upstream to the S as far as the high summits of Chubu Sangaku (see entry under this name), and along which runs the railway to Toyama.

3 ''SHIRAKAWAGO (55mls/88km NW as far as Shirakawa; coach). This beautiful region on the upper reaches of the Sho gawa is now partly swallowed up by Shirakawago barrier lake behind Mihoro dam, situated at an alt. of 2,493ft (760m). Many traditional houses were transported as far as the Hida village museum (see above). Nevertheless, you can still see some in the distinctive *gassho zukuri* style, with their high, steeply-sloping thatched roofs and three or four storeys, where several families would live. Some of the Taira clan took refuge in these valleys when they were defeated by the Minamoto (12th c.). Today the inhabitants are moving away to the towns, and the houses must be turned into museums if they are to be conserved. Shokawa and Shirakawa, roughly 18mls (30km) from each other, are the two most interesting villages in the valley. Festival at Shirakawa shrine 14-19 October.

4 GERO, CHUBU SANGAKU NATIONAL PARK, see entries under these names.

Takeo (Island of Kyushu)

Map of Kyushu (North), pp. 388–9.

Tokyo, 768mls (1,236km) – Fukuoka, 53mls (86km) – Nagasaki, 55mls (88km) – Saga, 20mls (33km).

Saga ken – pop: 35,377.

Takeo and, about 7mls (11km) away, Ureshino, are the two main spas of the Saga prefecture. Pleasantly situated in the hills, this ancient posting town en route to Nagasaki retains the atmosphere of the old traditional districts. The springs, 73° to 126°F (23° to 52°C), contain a large percentage of radium.

VICINITY

1 URESHINO (8mls/13km S; coach). The various alkaline springs 97° to 208°F (36° to 98°C) make this one of the most popular spas on the island of Kyushu. There are tea plantations on the slopes near Ureshino, and at Fudoyama you can see a tea bush which is more than 10ft (3m) in circumference at the base and more than 250 years old.

2 KARATSU, SAIKAI NATIONAL PARK, see entries under these names; ARITA, see Imari.

Tamano (Island of Honshu)

Map of Shikoku (Inland Sea), pp. 536–7.

Tokyo, 455mls (732km) – Hiroshima, 116mls (187km) – Kobe, 104mls (167km) – Tottori, 100mls (161km).

Port with services to Shodo shima and Takamatsu.

Okayama ken – pop: 68,446 – naval dockyards.

Tamano is an important town on the shores of the Inland Sea, S of Okayama, with Uno harbour providing the main point of access by sea to Takamatsu and the island of Shikoku (JNR ferry).

VICINITY

1 SHIBUKAWA BEACH (5mls/8km SW of Uno station; coach). One of the most popular beaches of the Inland Sea, set against a backdrop of hills. The University of Okayama Maritime Laboratory is situated here (oceanographic museum and aquarium).

2 KURASHIKI, OKAYAMA, SHODO SHIMA, SETO NAIKAI NATIONAL PARK, see entries under these names.

Tateyama (Island of Honshu)

Map of the Vicinity of Tokyo, p. 565.

Tokyo, 80mls (129km) – Chiba, 57mls (92km) – Mito, 145mls (234km) – Urawa, 94mls (151km).

Chiba ken - pop: 56,257 - fishing port.

Situated at the head of an attractive bay, Tateyama is where the two railways meet which go right around the Boso peninsula. From here you can travel along either of this peninsula's beautiful coastlines (Uchibo or Sotobo), the contours of which are constantly being reshaped by the sea. Tateyama is a pleasant place to stay during any season.

☞ **VICINITY**

1 KISARAZU (35mls/56km N, along the N127; JNR train; coach). The road and railway line go N along the very beautiful *west coast (Uchibo) of Boso peninsula.

14mls (22km): Hota beach, with the nearby seaside resort of Katsuyama, is one of the most popular beaches of the peninsula. Pearl culture.

15mls (25km): Kanaya (boat to Yokosuka-Kurihama), from where you can get a cable-car to Nokogiri yama (1,079ft/329m). On the S side are Nihon ji and the caves where the *Five Hundred Disciples of Buddha* are carved. Other sculptures are to be found here and there on the slopes of the mountain.

25mls (41km): Sanuki; from here you can go E to Kano zan (see Kisarazu vicinity). The road, which now turns away from the coast, crosses the Koito gawa before reaching the industrial town of:

35mls (56km): Kisarazu, see entry under this name.

2 KAMOGAWA (43mls/69km NE, via Shirahama; coach, JNR train direct). Leave Tateyama and go along the S of Tateyama Bay to:

6mls (10km): Suno saki; to the S, a toll road skirts Mera Bay.

12mls (20km): Mera. The road follows the Sotobo coast, which is more undulating and even more beautiful than that of Uchibo.

17mls (28km): Shirahama; popular seaside resort, to the south of which is Nojima zaki, the southernmost tip of the Boso peninsula. Here you can watch women diving for shells and edible seaweed.

27mls (43km): Chikura, a pleasant place in the S of the Boso peninsula. To the N, a toll road takes you back to the N128 and on to:

43mls (69km): Kamogawa, see entry under this name.

■ Tenri (Island of Honshu)

Map of Kansai, pp. 500–1.

Tokyo, 301mls (484km) – Kyoto, 30mls (49km) – Nara, 7½mls (12km) – Osaka, 27mls (44km) – Tsu, 63mls (102km) – Wakayama, 59mls (95km).

Nara ken - pop: 57,020.

Tenri, in the centre of the Nara basin, has been the headquarters since

1838 of a dissident Shinto sect (Tenri kyo), which now has more than a million followers. Festivals on 26 January and 26 October. The local archaeological and ethnographical museum makes an interesting visit.

1ml (1.5km) E of Tenri, Isonokami shrine holds the sword which Emperor Jimmu is said to have received from Takemikazuchi no Mikoto, the principal deity venerated at the shrine at Kashima (see entry under this name).

2mls (3km) N, at Ichinomoto (JNR train), you can visit Kakinomoto ji, which contains the tomb of Kakinomoto Hitomaro, the famous 8th c. poet.

Tenryu (Island of Honshu)

Tokyo, 160mls (258km) – Kofu, 123mls (198km) – Nagano, 169mls (272km) – Nagoya, 141mls (227km) – Shizuoka, 50mls (81km) – Yokohama, 144mls (232km).

Shizuoka ken – pop: 27,716.

Tenryu is situated where the gorges of Tenryu gawa end as it flows out into the Hammatsu basin. From there you can make an interesting excursion upstream towards the Sakuma dam, or you can travel downstream by boat for 8½mls (14km).

VICINITY

1 SAKUMA (27mls/43km N along the N152; coach). The road follows the course of the Tenryu gawa northwards, with wooded mountain slopes on either side.

13mls (21km): Tatsuyama, downstream from Akiha dam on the Tenryu; from there it is possible to reach:

3mls (5km) E (2h. on foot): Akiha san (alt. 2,743ft/836m); lovely view over the valleys of the Tenryu and its tributary, the Keta gawa. Near the summit is Akiha shrine, founded in the 8th c., and dedicated to Kagutsuchi no Kami, the fire god. Festival on the night of 15–16 December.

22mls (35km): Leave the N152, which carries on upstream along a tributary of the Tenryu gawa, and continue due N.

27mls (43km): Sakuma, below Sakuma dam, at an alt. of 853ft (260m) of the Tenryu gawa. This dam was completed in 1956 and produces 350,000 kW of electricity.

2 HAMAMATSU, see entry under this name.

Tokorozawa (Island of Honshu)

Map of the Vicinity of Tokyo, p. 565.

Tokyo, 22mls (36km) – Chiba, 45mls (73km) – Kofu, 48mls (77km) – Maebashi, 84mls (136km) – Mito, 96mls (154km) – Nagano, 139mls (224km) – Urawa, 25mls (40km) – Utsunomiya, 78mls (125km).

Saitama ken - pop: 236,476 - textile industry - aeronautical research centre.

To the NW of Tokyo, Tokorozawa is one of the capital's main satellite towns. From here you can reach lakes Tama and Sayama. Plantations of green Sayama tea on the hills round about.

👉 **VICINITY**

SAYAMO KO (3mls/5km SW; Seibu ER train from Tokorozawa or Tokyo-Ikebukuro station to Sayamako; change at Nishi-Tokorozawa). 550yds (500m) NW of Sayamako station is Sayama lake (Yamaguchi reservoir), to the E of which lies the UNESCO village where various pavilions have been built in the style of the different countries represented in that organization. Artificial ski slope. Konjo in, or Yamaguchi Kannon, is reputed to have been erected by Kobo Daishi in the 9th c.; the temple was rebuilt in the 16th and then the 18th c.

Sayama lake is connected by a tramline to Tama lake and to Seibu en (amusement park). Tama ko or Murayama ko is an artificial lake which, together with Sayama lake, provides most of Tokyo's water supply. The undulating and wooded surroundings make this one of the most popular areas in the Tokyo vicinity. The return journey to Tokyo is via Seibuen or Tamako station (Seibu ER).

◾ Tokushima (Island of Shikoku)

Map of Shikoku (Inland Sea), pp. 536–7.

Tokyo, 495mls (796km) - Kochi, 120mls (194km) - Matsuyama, 124mls (199km) - Takamatsu, 48mls (77km).

Principal town of Tokushima ken (pop: 383,059) - pop: 223,451 - industrial town and port - national and private universities.

A fishing port at the mouth of the Yoshino gawa, the town looks out onto the Kii straits to the E. Tokushima is greatly influenced by its position next to the sea and has been named 'water city'. During World War II 80% of it was destroyed and it had to be completely rebuilt. It now occupies fourth place among the cities on the island of Shikoku.

The town, bordered to the N by Yoshino gawa, is crisscrossed by canals and branches of rivers, which in turn are intersected by wide main roads.

To the NE of the station, Tokushima Park covers the wooded hill of Shiro yama, where the ruins of Tokushima Castle still stand in a very pretty landscape garden in the Momoyama style. The castle was built in 1586 by Hachisuka Iemasa, and remained in the family until 1868.

From the station, a magnificent wide avenue with a central lane of palm trees leads via Shinmachi bridge to the foot of:

*Bi zan (660yds/600m SW of the station; can be reached by coach and cable-car); a 2½ml/4km toll road climbs to the summit of this wooded hill (alt. 919ft/280m). View across the city as far as the Inland Sea. A pagoda in the form of a stupa, dedicated to the victims of World War II, was erected here in 1958.

660yds (600m) S of the cable-car's departure point, at the foot of Bi zan, is the Iga machi quarter, where the Portuguese officer Wenceslao de Moraes (1854-1929) used to live. He was consul in Tokushima from 1893 onwards and wrote several books about the region. Married to a Japanese girl, he lived in the Iga machi quarter until his death.

VICINITY

1 NYORIN JI (10mls/17km S; coach). Leave Tokushima to the SE by the N55.

5mls (9km): take a right turn off the N55 which goes on to Komatsushima, an extension to the S of Tokushima's industrial area.

7mls (11km); Joroku ji. Founded in the 7th c., this temple houses the statue of Kannon attributed to the priest Gyoki. Elegant doorway with one floor above it.

10mls (17km): Nyorin ji is built on the slopes of Nakatsu mine (2,536ft/773m) in a forest setting of pines and maples and leaping waterfalls. This temple houses a listed wooden statue of Nyorin Kannon.

2 'TSURUGI SAN (54mls/88km SW by the route indicated; train as far as Anabuki then coach). Leave Tokushima to the W by the N192 which follows the course of the Yoshino gawa upstream.

19mls (31km): Yamakawa, or at 24mls (39km): Anabuki; from there you can go N to the Dochu site (2½mls/4km from each place). Here the processes of erosion have formed crevices and capped earth pillars, some of which are 50-65ft (15-20m) high. From Anabuki, the road winds more and more as it heads S along the course of Anabuki gawa, a tributary of Yoshino gawa (Tsurugi kyo gorges), then crosses an initial mountain barrier before arriving at Tsurugi san.

55mls (88km): Minokoshi, alt. 4,593ft (1,400m): Enfuku ji and Tsurugi shrine (festival 17 July). From here you can take a toll road and go W along the Iya gawa valley to Ikeda (see entry under this name). From Minokoshi, a chairlift will take you up Nishijima, leaving you to complete the last half mile to the summit on foot (30-40 min.).

*Tsurugi san (6,404ft/1,955m) is Shikoku's second highest mountain and one of the most beautiful on the island. In good weather, the view extends in all directions across mountains covered in dense vegetation, made up of a large number of different species. This area is now a protected regional park of 52,379 acres (21,197 ha).

3 NARUTO, SETO NAIKAI NATIONAL PARK, see entries under these names.

■ Tokuyama (Island of Honshu)

Railway map on inside front cover.

Tokyo, 601mls (968km) – Hiroshima, 59mls (95km) – Matsue, 178mls (286km) – Yamaguchi, 28mls (46km).

Yamaguchi ken – pop: 98,520 – petrochemical industry.

Tokuyama bay, with its string of islands protecting it from the sea, has now been given over to industry, making Tokuyama one of the busiest towns of the district of Chugoku. The Shinkansen (Bullet train) stops here. In complete contrast, traditional methods are still used here in the working of granite quarries.

General Kodama Gentaro (1852-1906) was born in Tokuyama.

 VICINITY

YASHIRO (10mls/17km NE; coach). This is a bird sanctuary where white-crested cranes arrive in October from Mongolia and eastern Siberia.

T Tokyo (Island of Honshu)***

Map of Tokyo and vicinity, p. 565 – Tokyo centre, pp. 570–1 – Bunkyo ku, pp. 602–3 – Shinjuku ku, pp. 598–9 – Minatu ku, pp. 588–9.

Chiba, 23mls (37km) – Kofu, 88mls (141km) – Urawa, 15mls (24km) –Yokohama, 15mls (24km).

Capital of Japan (pop: 117,060,396) – main city of Tokyo (pop: 11,471,892) – pop: 8,351,893 – industrial city and commercial port – national university with faculities in all disciplines, regional universities, numerous private universities – archdiocese – congress centre – average annual temperature 58.5F°/14.7°C (January 38.7°F/3.7°C; August 79.5°F/26.4°C) – annual rainfall 61in (1,563mm) – average humidity 80% from June to September – longitude 140°E, latitude 35°N, the same as Oran and Baghdad.

'Two and a half years had passed since my last visit to Japan, and Tokyo was unrecognizable ... as usual! It's a city in a perpetual state of change, and from one stay to the next I notice ever more rapid transformations' (Robert Guillain). This introduction to *Japon, Troisième Grand* gives an idea of the atmosphere of this extraordinary city. The biggest city in the world – if you don't count Shanghai which has the largest population – occupies an area of more than 656sq. mls (1,700km²). The city does in fact seem to be a number of cities grouped together, which don't necessarily correspond to the administrative divisions (23 *ku* or districts), but are cities within the City, each with its busy shopping area, its parks, its buildings of all shapes and sizes, and its little private houses – the latter gradually being forced back to the residential outskirts.

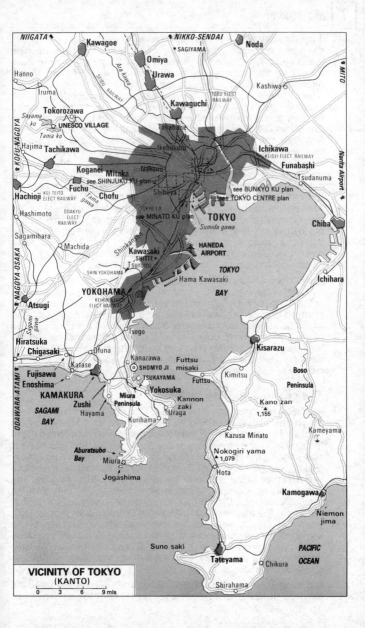

VICINITY OF TOKYO
(KANTO)

0   3   6   9 mls

Tokyo is a city unlike any other and, as with New York, you either like it or you don't. You can fall madly in love with Tokyo, or you can hate it, but you can't remain indifferent. If you become attached to it, it's usually for the rest of your life. This vibrant city, so full of life and offering a thousand things to do and see, is not as monstrous as some would have you believe. It's very easy to get around, using the underground or the urban trains, and the inhabitants are unrivalled for their politeness and willingness to help. The foreigner who has lost his way and stands consulting his map will soon be put back on the right route, and sometimes an obliging citizen will simply accompany him to make sure he finds his destination. Tokyo is also a city of contrasts with the old and the new side by side. It has kept its traditions and its old houses. Its young people like to dress even more outrageously than in the West, the women still wear their kimonos for festivals, and the taxi drivers sport white gloves. The elegance of Akasaka contrasts with the cosmopolitan character of Harajuku. By day, Shinjuku shops are bursting with gadgets and bargain goods, but by night, it is the Japanese Soho – the famous restaurant and night-club district of London's West End. Then there is sober downtown Manouchi with its hurrying businessmen. Tokyo is an exciting place where life seems to be lived to the full.

Tokyo doesn't stand still. The impression of it gained by those who have never been to Japan is no more than a pale reflection of the reality. From being a polluted and exhausting city, Tokyo's image has changed to that of a city where you can breathe without difficulty, and where parks and gardens provide havens of peace right in the centre of the immense metropolis. Tokyo is full of contradictions and the foreigner cannot but be fascinated by its extremes: take for example the high-rise buildings of Shinjuku at which you can gaze from the delicate Japanese garden in Shinjuku Gyoen Park.

The city in Japanese history

HISTORICAL SYNOPSIS UP TO THE 17TH C. Occupation of the site where Tokyo now stands goes back to ancient times, as evidenced by the discovery of the remains of prehistoric settlements in various parts of the capital. One of these was in the Yayoi quarter, and this name is now used as the term for a Neolithic period in Japanese prehistory (3rd c. BC to 3rd c. AD). At the end of the 6th c., Hashino Nakatamo was banished to the area near the estuary of the Sumida gawa. The foundation of Asakusa temple is attributed to him, and also the establishment of a fishing community which continued for several centuries. The true historical beginnings of Tokyo date back to 1457, when Ota Dokan built the first castle at Edo, around which the beginnings of the present city started to develop (end of 15th c.). After the assassination of Dokan by Uesugi Sadamasa, the town became the property of that family, then passed into the hands of the Hojo clan who controlled all of Kanto.

EDO, CAPITAL OF TOKUGAWA. In 1590, Toyotomi Hideyoshi entrusted the province of Kanto to Tokugawa Ieyasu (1542–1616), who had just subjugated Hojo Ujinao. Ieyasu chose as his residence Ota Dokan's former castle at Edo. When Hideyoshi died, he had under his control a large part of central Japan and, having assured his authority in the battle of Sekigahara (1600), he chose to make Edo the new seat of shogun government, with himself holding the newly re-established office of Shogun. In order to assert their political power, the Tokugawa shoguns forced the daimyo to live around Edo castle and made them leave their families behind as hostages if they went away. The construction of residences around the Shogunal palace thus established the plan of the present city. Tokyo rapidly acquired considerable importance, to the extent of gaining the upper hand over the Imperial capital of Kyoto and, during the following century, of outstripping Osaka in economic activity. The tradesmen grew richer and the daimyo ran into debt, the merchants became patrons of the arts, and Tokyo and Nipponese society were constructed. Despite a number of earthquakes, fires and revolts which reduced the town and its castle to ruins on several occasions between the 17th and 19th centuries, by 1840 Edo was already the second city in the world after London, with more than 500,000 inhabitants. A new era began in the middle of the 19th c., with the arrival of American ships in Tokyo Bay and the opening up of commercial and diplomatic relations with the United States. The pressures on the already weakened shogunate, the assassination in 1860 of minister Ii Naosuke (who signed the agreements with the Americans) and the nationalist movement in favour of the restoration of the Emperor all led in 1867-68 to the fall of the shogunate which its last supporters in Tokyo defended unsuccessfully at the battle of Ueno in 1868. The last of the shoguns had already fled in 1863 from Edo Castle, which was surrounded by the homes of the daimyo (but then the Tokugawa shoguns had compelled them to come and live there), and had withdrawn to Kyoto or Osaka.

TOKYO, CAPITAL OF JAPAN. Emperor Mutsuhito, Meiji tenno (1852-1912) made Edo the Eastern capital (which is what Tokyo literally means) and decided to transfer the Imperial residence from Kyoto to the Tokugawa Castle, the present site of the Imperial Palace. The houses of the daimyo were demolished to make way for new buildings for government, commercial and industrial use. 'The urban economy was based on the riches of the hinterland, the Kanto basin. The rapid development of manufacturing and of harbour traffic together with the concentration of manpower made the expansion of the city inevitable. Between 1890 and 1920 investments made by the *zaibatsu* (industrial trusts) enabled buildings to be constructed to the north. Tokyo expanded from a population of 596,000 in 1868 to 2,220,000 by 1923. This latter date is a sad one in the history of the city: the great earthquake in September of that year destroyed part of the northern and eastern districts and claimed more than 200,000 victims' (Maurince Moreau, *L'Economie du Japon*). Finally, in 1936, following elections, the results of which were judged to be unfavourable to the militarist regime of the time, a number of young officers made a series of political assassination attempts on the night of 25-26 February and tried to impose a military dictatorship. They were soon subdued, but the government persisted nonetheless in its Imperialist policies which led the country into war.

TOKYO SINCE THE WAR. The Japanese capital suffered very badly during World War II. Heavy bombing from March to May 1945 brought about more destruction and claimed more victims than the atomic bomb which was dropped on Hiroshima. The short speech by the reigning Emperor, Hiro Hito, broadcast on radio on 14 August 1945, led to numerous military men committing suicide because they could not accept Japan's surrender. This was officially signed on board U.S.S. *Missouri* in Tokyo Bay on 2 September 1945. The headquarters of the American occupation under MacArthur were situated in the Dai Ichi Seime Building until 1951. MacArthur introduced a series of reforms which, together with those of the Meiji era, contributed to the organization of contemporary Japan. As everywhere else in Japan, the Americans actively participated in rebuilding the capital and setting it to rights. Since then the city has regained its many functions as a political, industrial, economic and artistic centre. Since the Olympic Games in 1964, the face of the city has changed profoundly as it has been swept along on a tide of frenzied activity.

FAMOUS PEOPLE BORN IN TOKYO. Among the many famous personalities who first saw the light of day in Tokyo are the reigning Emperor Hiro Hito (born in 1901), his father the Emperor Yoshi Hito, Taisho tenno (1879-1926), and his son the Crown Prince Akihito (born in 1933); among the politicians are Yoshida Shigeru (1878-1967), Ishibashi Tanzan (born in 1884); the military men include Vice-Admiral Enomoto Buyo (1839-1908), General Nogi (1849-1912), Admiral Shimada Shigetaro (1883-1976), General Tojo Hideki (1884-1918), and the British General Sir Colin McVean Gubbins (1869-1976); scientists include Tomonaga Shin Ichiro (1906-79) and Yukawa Hideki (1907-81), both winners of the Nobel Prize for Physics; writers, Enomoto Kikaku (1661-1707), Kyoden (1761-1816), the painter and poet Sakai Hoitsu (1761-1828), Takizawa Kai, known as Kyokutei Bakin (1767-1848), Shikitei Samba (1776-1822), Kawatake Mokuami (1816-93), Hasegawa Tatsunoke, known as Futabatei Shimei (1864-1909), Natsume Soseki (1867-1912), Arishima Takeo (1878-1923), Higuchi Ichiyo (1872-96), Tanizaki Junichiro (born in 1886), Akutagawa Ryunosuke (1892-1927), Yoshida Kenichi (1912-77), Mishima Yukio (1925-70), the painter and lacquer artist Shibata Zeshin (1807-91); the composers Iamada Kosaku (born in 1886, also an orchestral conductor), Matsudaira Yoritsune (born in 1907) and Takemitsu Toru (born in 1930); producers and directors Kinugawa Teinosuke (born in 1896), Ozu Yasujiro (1903-63) and Kurosawa Akira (born in 1910); the *kabuki* actor Mitsugoro Bandao VIII (1906-75); the golf champion Higuchi Hisako (born in 1945), and the Olympic wrestler and restaurateur Aoki Hiroaki, known as Rocky Aoki (born in 1938).

THE PORT. Rebuilt after World War II, the port of Tokyo is one of the largest in Japan. It is designed for ships from 1,000 t to 2,000 t, and has facilities for oil storage and warehouses suitable for goods of all kinds. It is contantly being developed with new jetties being built out into the sea. Nevertheless, it cannot keep up with the stream of ships which have to wait in Tokyo Bay before coming alongside. This is the reason for the continuing extension of this huge port which is coming to encompass all the northern part of Tokyo Bay, on one side towards Kawasaki and Yokohama and on the other towards Chiba and Ichihara.

INDUSTRY AND DEVELOPMENT. Tokyo and its suburbs count as one of the main commercial and industrial centres in Japan. Although almost all the firms are small or medium-sized, Tokyo has several large complexes where efforts are combined to produce (in descending order of importance): electrical goods and machines, machines for textile manufacturing, food industry products, and products of the chemical and metallurgical industries. These firms employ 41.5% of Tokyo's working poplulation. The number of building sites springing up everywhere in the city is astounding. Public works and the setting up of industry are in fact the main concern of the industrial sector. The port area and transport infrastructures are another dynamic aspect of its activities. Located mainly in the centre of Tokyo, commercial companies ensure the exportation of goods manufactured in the city and elsewhere in Japan. Many foreign companies are also represented in the capital. All this activity is not without its problems.

Exploring the city

TWO DAYS IN TOKYO. This is the usual length of time devoted to Tokyo during a trip to Japan. Go on a tour of the city on the first morning, as suggested by the tourist agencies. This will give you a rapid and superficial impression of Tokyo, but will enable you to get your bearings. You will see the principal monuments and centres of interest: the Imperial Palace and its surroundings, the Diet, the Meiji Shrine, Tokyo Tower, Ginza, etc. Then spend the afternoon visiting the National Museum (and, if it's open, the Treasury of Horyu ji) and walking in Ueno Park.

The evening may be spent at the Kabuki-za theatre seeing a traditional show. During the interval, you can dine on grilled eel served in pretty lacquered boxes. However, it is best if the entire evening is organized by an agency to be sure of avoiding disappointment. After this, you are ready to finish off the evening in the Ginza bars.

On the second day, we suggest that you immerse yourself in Japanese life by going first to one of the big stores in the Nihonbashi quarter: Mitsukoshi (closed on Mondays) or Takashimaya (closed on Wednesdays). There is no need to buy anything. Explore the various floors, lingering in particular in the basement (reserved for food), and in the departments selling kimonos, toys, furniture and crockery. Note the stylishness of the shop assistants, and how calm, ordered and harmonious everything is. Such a visit, which could even include a lesson in the art of flower arranging, is truly one of the best

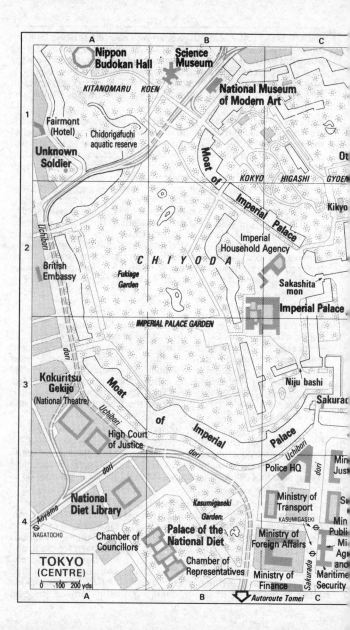

TOKYO (CENTRE)

0   100   200 yds

Autoroute Tomei

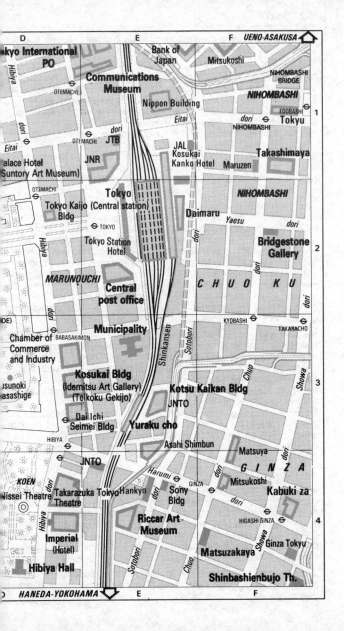

kyo International PO

Bank of Japan

Mitsukoshi

NIHOMBASHI BRIDGE

Communications Museum

NIHOMBASHI

OTEMACHI

Nippon Building

EDOBASHI

dori

dori

Eitai

dori ⊖

NIHOMBASHI

Tokyu

dori

Eitai

OTEMACHI

JTB

JAL Kosukai Kanko Hotel

Takashimaya

JNR

Maruzen

alace Hotel

Suntory Art Museum)

OTEMACHI

Tokyo

NIHOMBASHI

Tokyo Kaijo Bldg

(Central station)

Daimaru

Yaesu

dori

⊖ TOKYO

Hibiya

Tokyo Station Hotel

dori

Bridgestone Gallery

MARUNOUCHI

Central post office

C H U O   *K U*

dori

OE)

Municipality

BABASAKIMON

KYOBASHI ⊖

TAKARACHO

Chamber of Commerce and Industry

dori

Shinkansen

Satobori

Chuo

Showa

Kosukai Bldg (Idemitsu Art Gallery) (Teikoku Gekijo)

Kotsu Kaikan Bldg

JNTO

sunoki asashige

Dai Ichi Seimei Bldg

Yuraku cho

HIBIYA

Asahi Shimbun

Matsuya

JNTO

Harumi ⊖

GINZA

G I N Z A

KOEN

dori

Takarazuka Theatre

Tokyo Theatre

Hankyu

Sony Bldg

dori

Mitsukoshi

Kabuki za

Nissei Theatre

Hibiya

dori

dori

HIGASHI GINZA ⊖

Imperial (Hotel)

Riccar Art Museum

Satobori

Chuo

Showa

Ginza Tokyu

Matsuzakaya

Hibiya Hall

Shinbashienbujo Th.

introductions to daily life in modern Japan. You can of course do your shopping and then have lunch in the store, where the food can be very good.

Next, travel by taxi or underground (something you must experience) as far as Korakuen, the most beautiful garden in Tokyo, or, if you are an art lover, you can visit the collections in the Nezu Museum. End the afternoon in the delightful Asakusa quarter where you can dine in an atmosphere of 'old Japan'. Then move on to the nearby Ko-Kusai theatre (Kokusai Gekijo) for an incredible show of fountains and fire, or go to Shinjuku, Tokyo's equivalent of London's Soho. Finally, if you have time during the two days, have lunch or a drink in the restaurant on the tenth floor of the Palace Hotel where, recalling the writer Mishima, who was a regular visitor to these parts, you can admire the view looking down into the Imperial Palace grounds.

A WEEK IN TOKYO. It would be a pity to come to Japan and spend only one day in Tokyo, for you would have time only to join in the programmes organized by the agencies as suggested above. In fact, a minimum stay of a week is necessary if you really want to gain a proper impression of this incredible city – incredible in every sense of the word. You can then visit all the principal places of interest in turn, come back to those which particularly attracted you, explore the many parks and museums, learn to appreciate the animation of the people which seems to differ from one district to another, and experience all the repugnant and bewitching aspects of this city. But beware, lest you find that you cannot tear yourself away!

THE CITY ON FOOT. Tokyo is a very tiring city, with crowds almost everywhere, traffic jams, considerable distances between the main tourist attractions and consequently long journeys by public transport, with the constant blare of the train's loudspeakers in your ears. The Japanese have reconciled themselves to the situation and many fall asleep if they have been lucky enough to get a seat. Visitors on foot generally limit themselves to certain busy areas such as Marunouchi and Ginza, between 10.00 and 22.00, Asakusa and Shinjuku, full of life in the evenings, and the large parks and gardens which make up for the lack of greenery elsewhere. Ueno and its museums offer plenty to gratify your aesthetic sense, and will hold your interest for an entire day.

IF YOU LIKE...

Japanese temples and shrines. Tokyo's religious buildings, of recent construction or reconstruction, generally cannot equal those of Kyoto. To get an idea of the principal places where the people of Tokyo gather, visit Meiji jingu, Yasukuni jinja, Hie jinja and Tosho gu (Ueno), which are among the most famous shrines in the city. Among the temples we suggest Asakusa, Zojo ji, Gokoku ji, Sengaku ji, Hommon ji, Nishiarai Daishi, etc.

Japanese gardens. These are in fact parks, and there are a great many of them, all worth a visit. They do not call for contemplation and meditation as do those of the Kyoto temples, but are simply a pleasure to the eye: Koraku en, Rikugi en, Hama Rikyu koen, Shinjuku gyoen, Kiyosumi koen, the iris garden of Meiji jingu, Myoshuno Taki koen, Chizan so and Happo en (the last two mentioned are private gardens).

The Japanese arts. Tokyo's museums are the richest in Japan and house art collections of the first order (as with any other museum, not all the items are on display at any one time). The National Museum in Ueno Park comes at the top of the list, then there are Okura and Nezu Museums, Idemitsu Gallery, etc. The National Museum of Modern Art shows the direction contemporary Japanese artists are taking.

Western arts. The Japanese are avid collectors of anything Western and it is said that the museums do not skimp when it comes to the acquisition of Western works. Visit the National Museum of Western Art, the Bridgestone Gallery and the temporary exhibitions mounted by the other museums and the big stores.

Science and technology. Tokyo has several museums devoted to these areas: the National Science Museum, the Science Museum, the Transport Museum, the Tokyo Tower Museum, etc.

The pleasures of life. Names such as Asakusa, Ginza, Roppongi, Shibuya and Shinjuku, to foreign ears and to the ears of the Japanese alike, are sufficient to conjure up the epicurean atmosphere of these areas where you can 'live it up': restaurants, hostess bars, shows, shops and arcades offer plenty to occupy you in the evenings.

A Chiyoda ku

Street plan: pp. 570–1.

Tokyo, Yurakucho, Kanda, Akihabara, Ochanomizu, Suidobashi, Iidabashi, Ichigaya, Yotsuya, JNR stations.

Chiyoda ku is the centre, the very heart of Tokyo. Largely taken up by the Imperial Palace, whose grounds cover 249 acres (101 ha), this is the centre for most of the capital's political, economic and intellectual activity which overflows into the Kasumigaseki, Marunouchi and Kanda quarters. Proceeding in an anticlockwise direction around these, we will describe each in turn. However, this tour is not easily done on foot, so select beforehand the places you wish to visit.

► ***IMPERIAL PALACE** (plan: C2, ½ml/1km W of the JNR stations of Tokyo and Yurakucho; underground stations: Hibya, Nijubashimae, Takebashi). Residence of His Majesty Hiro Hito and not open to the public, except on 2 January (presentation of the good wishes to the Emperor) and 29 April (the Emperor's birthday). With its broad moats spanned by bridges and its ramparts crowned by pines, one is reminded of the presence, albeit discreet, of a royalty which used in the past to be considered divine.

Ota Dokan built the first castle at Edo in 1457. At that time, the buildings were surrounded by several miles of walls with 25 fortified gates, which could be reached only via the bridges across the moats.

An avenue of pines linked the castle to the sea, and from his residence Ota Dokan was able to see Mount Fuji. In the 16th c. the estate passed from the hands of Hojo clan to those of Tokugawa Ieyasu, who had part of the buildings razed. He built a formidable fortress which was later called the West Castle. He dug a triple line of moats, reinforced with steep slopes made with enormous blocks of granite which he had brought by sea from Hyogo. The new palace was of such large dimensions that it took 49 years to complete. Emperor Meiji came to live in it in 1869, but four years later it was destroyed by fire, and only the moats remained. However, the Emperor had it rebuilt according to the same plans. The palace was damaged again during World War II (fire in 1945), but reconstruction was completed in 1968.

In front of the Palace stretches the vast Imperial Palace Esplanade (plan: C2-D3 to D2-D3), separated to the S and E from Hibiya Park and from Marunouchi by the broad moats of Hibiyabori and Babasakibori (carp and swans), and crossed from N to S by the wide Uchibori dor.

In the SE part of this esplanade there is a bronze statue of Kusunoki Masashige on horseback (14th c.); he was instrumental in the restoration of the Emperor Go Daigo.

In the SW corner you can see Sakurada mon, the former gateway to the Imperial Palace, in front of which the minister Ii Naosuke was assassinated in 1860, after he had signed the Kanagawa trade agreement with Townsend Harris (see Yokohama).

Beyond Sakurada mon, the Palace is separated from the esplanade by a large moat full of water, crossed by Ishibashi (a stone bridge with two arches) a little to the N. This bridge is used by visitors to the Imperial Palace who then arrive at Nijubashi gateway (usually closed to the public).

Behind Ishi bashi rises Fushimi turret, a rare relic from the 17th c. At its base a metal bridge has replaced Niju bashi, which was a famous wooden bridge made of two superimposed roadways.

It was here that about 50 Japanese committed suicide in 1945 when the Emperor announced the country's surrender.

Inside the palace enclosure, Niju bashi leads out onto a broad terrace where 20,000 people gather to see the Emperor appear on the balcony of Chowda den. Behind the latter, the palace is built on an E-W axis, reconstructed by the architect Yoshimura Junzo in a modern style strongly influenced by buildings from the Nara and Heian periods. Contemporary artists helped in its decoration. The Emperor's private residence (Fukiage), a biology laboratory and the Imperial Household servants' quarters are also within the palace enclosure.

To the N of Nijubashi mon are Sakashita mon, then Kikyo mon, through which you can pass into the eastern part of the Imperial Palace gardens.

†HIGASHI GYOEN (plan: C1; underground stations: Otemachi and Takebashi; open daily except Mondays, Fridays and the days of official ceremonies, from 09.00 to 16.00; last admittance 15.00). The entrances to these gardens (52 acres/21 ha) are the Kikyo mon to the S, Hirakawa mon to the N, and Ote mon to the E, the latter being a reconstruction dating from 1967, of the original of 1620.

These gardens, on several levels, are on the former sites of Honu maru and Nino maru (see Himeji) of Edo Castle, Nino maru was the residence of the shogun's heirs. The pretty garden which Kobori Enshu is said to have created in 1630 was redesigned in 1961. The Shogunal palace, which was on the site of Hon maru, was destroyed by fire in 1863. The keep (Tenshudai), the foundations of which you can see to the NW, had already burned down in 1657. In its time it was the tallest in Japan. To the E of the foundations is Togaku do, a concert hall built in 1966.

To the S of Hon maru, Fujimi Yagura turret used to serve as a point from which to view Mount Fuji, now hidden by the smog which envelops Tokyo.

The broad moats which border the Imperial Palace Esplanade to the E are overlooked by the beautiful buildings of:

MARUNOUCHI (plan: D2-E2; underground stations: Hibiya, Nijubashimae). Opposite the Imperial Palace is the commercial district, the principal banks and head offices of Japanese and foreign companies (about 8,000).

When Tokyo became the capital of Japan, the government buildings were set up in this quarter, but they were destroyed by fire in 1872. The ground was bought back in 1893 by Mitsubishi on the Emperor's orders. Many buildings were then constructed of brick, and the quarter given the nickname of 'Little London'. The bombs in 1945 destroyed Marunouchi once again, and the beautiful buildings, which now form a harmonious group, were constructed after the war. However, the uniformity has been broken by the construction of the Tokyo Kaiji Building in red brick.

Between Hibiya dori to the W and the JNR railway lines to the E runs the main artery of this quarter, its pavements bordered by flowerbeds full of colour. The buildings tower upwards on both sides to about ten storeys, each forming an individual unit and consisting of its own little world of offices, shops and restaurants (the latter generally occupying the ground floor and the basement). Thousands of people work here. You will notice the Kokusai Building (plan: D3, fourth block on the l. after Harumi dori) which extends W as far as Hibiya dori. It houses the Imperial Theatre and:

IDEMITSU ART GALLERY (plan: D3; address 1-1, 3-chome, Marunouchi, Chiyoda ku; 330yds/300m NW from Yurakucho eki, JNR; underground station: Hibiya; entrance in the S side of Kokusai Bldg, take the lift up to 9th floor; open daily except Mondays from 10.00 to 17.00). This gallery was founded in order to house Idemitsu Sazo's collections and opened its doors for the first time in 1966. On display are a number of ink drawings, woodblock prints and examples of calligraphy, but most notable is the beautiful collection of pottery and ceramics from Japan, China, Persia, the Mediterranean and Europe.

One room is devoted to the Buddhist monk Sengai (1750–1837). His artistic works are full of humour and are greatly influenced by Zen. Among his examples of calligraphy, which are displayed in rotation, you will observe the association between a square, a triangle and a circle which together represent the Universe (not all critics agree with this symbolic interpretation).

The great traditional centres where Japanese pottery is made are represented here (Karatsu, Kutani, Kyoto, Seto, etc.). The collection of Chinese ceramics is one of the most important in the country because of its variety and the wide historical range represented. One room is arranged so that comparisons can be made between the different styles of pottery from the Ancient World (with an emphasis on 14th-c. Chinese influences on pottery discovered near Cairo). The *ukiyo-e* prints displayed in this museum represent the work of about 70 artists, among whom are famous names such as Moronobu, Utamaro, Hokusai and Hiroshige.

To the S of Kokusai Building, overlooking Hibiyabori moat, is the Dai ichi Seimei Building, one of the few buildings spared by the bombings in 1945. General MacArthur had his headquarters there until 1951.

YURAKU CHO (plan: E3; Yurakucho station, JNR; underground station: Hibiya). This area extends to the E and S of Marunouchi on both sides of the railway lines, bordered on the E by an expressway (with Sukiyabashi shopping arcade and International Arcade beneath it) and Sotobori dori. Less formal than Marunouchi although adjacent to it, this quarter is one of the liveliest and most cosmopolitan of the capital. To the E of the railway lines you will see the Tokyo Kotsu Kaikan Building (head office of the JNTO, revolving restaurant at the top), the Asahi press building, head office of the newspaper with the biggest circulation in the world, and the Nichigeki Theatre (variety shows, light revues, films).

To the S of Harumi dori, on the edge of Hibiya Park (p. 582), is the imposing Imperial Hotel, one of the most luxurious in the city. It was erected in 1968 to replace the old hotel, which was built for foreign visitors in 1916–22 on the Emperor's orders by the architect Frank Lloyd Wright. The building was specially designed to be resistant to earthquakes and suffered hardly at all during the great earthquake of 1923.

Opposite the Imperial Hotel are the Nissei, Takarazuka and Yarakuza theatres, and between the hotel and Harumi dori are several important cinemas (which usually show premières), as well as the cafés and little restaurants which abound on either side of the railway lines, the offices of numerous airline companies, and the information office of the JNTO, which opens onto Harumi dori. This quarter is sometimes compared to Broadway or Montparnasse and is an extension of Ginza (p. 582) to the E of the railway line.

To the N of Yuraku cho is the seat of metropolitan government, Tokyo Town Hall (arch. Tange Kenzo; decorated with frescoes and ceramics by Okamoto Taro). In front of the Town Hall is the statue of Ota Dokan (see The city in Japanese history), and to the W is the Tokyo Chamber of Commerce and Industry. The latter building also houses a branch of the American Chamber of Commerce, a number of foreign companies, and an important library.

TOKYO CENTRAL STATION (plan E2). To the N of Marunouchi and Yuraku cho is Tokyo's central station whence radiate most of the lines which serve Japan. It is also the terminus for the Bullet train, Shinkansen.

The old brick buildings in the neo-Renaissance style (1914) open to the W onto a broad square (Tokyoekimae) with Tokyo central post office to the S, the head office of Japan National Railway to the N, and the Marunouchi and Shin Marunouchi buildings to the W. On the other side, looking E onto Yaesuguchi, Tokyo station is a tall, modern building housing the great Daimaru store with an underground car park and several basement arcades with cafés and restaurants.

Every day, more than a million people pass through Tokyo station, and there are over 2,000 train departures. The Shinkansen lines will eventually extend from Tokyo to Ueno station, and there are plans to construct a new central station between these two.

To the N of Tokyo station and Marunouchi is the Ote machi quarter bounded to the N by Sotobori dori and crossed from E to W by Eitai dori. Several newspapers and advertising companies have set up their headquarters in this sector.

In the W, Eitai dori comes to an end in front of the Imperial Palace, opposite Otemon (p. 570). To the S, between this street and the Imperial Palace moats, is the Palace Building which contains the Palace Hotel and Suntory Museum of Art (address: 9th floor of Palace Bldg, 1-1-1, Marunouchi, Chiyoda ku; 660yds/600m NW of Tokyo eki; underground station: Otemachi; open daily except Mondays from 10.00 to 17.00). This museum was opened in 1961 and houses collections of Japanese *objets d'art* and arts and crafts from the 15th c. onwards.

Towards the N between Eitai dori and Sotobori dori you can see Otemachi Building (erected in 1958), which has the largest floor-space of any office building in Asia (1,198,022sq. ft/111,300m^2) and where about 10,000 people work, and also the Post and Telecommunications Museum (open daily except Mondays from 09.00 to 16.30; scientific objects and instruments, stamps and postcards, etc.).

Sotobori dori runs parallel to a former Edo canal overhung by a modern expressway. To the N of this road is the quarter of:

KANDA (plan of Bunkyo ku, pp. 602-3: B4; JNR Kanda station; underground stations: Awajicho, Kanda). This area lies to the NE of the Imperial Palace, and several private universities are situated here (Chuo, Hosei, Meiji and Nihon, all founded at the end of the 19th c.). Here too publishing companies and bookshops flourish, attracting students from all over the capital, so that Kanda could be said to resemble the Latin Quarter in Paris. The people in this quarter are young and cosmopolitan, making it a friendly place. It overflows into neighbouring Surugadai (to the NW) and Jimbo cho (to the W), where you can find all kinds of old books, both Japanese and Western. Two-thirds of all secondhand books are sold here.

If you go N along Chuo dori from Kanda station, just off this street and in a curve of the railway line you come to:

■ **THE TRANSPORT MUSEUM** (plan of Bunkyo ku, pp. 602–3: B4; address: 1-25, Suda cho, Chiyoda ku; 660yds/600m N of Kanda eki, JNR; 330yds/300m NE of the underground station of Awajicho; open daily except Mondays from 09.30 to 17.00). This museum, set up by the Japanese Travel Bureau, contains about 20,000 exhibits covering all the means of locomotion possible or imaginable. Among the most interesting exhibits are the first Japanese locomotive, which went into service in 1872 between Tokyo and Yokohama and was made in England, and the Benkei locomotive (made in America in 1880) which was used in Hokkaido.

The second important street heading W from Chuo dori is Hongo dori, which is a continuation of Hibiya dori. Before crossing the railway line (Chuo line), it goes past the apse of:

✝ **NICOLAI CATHEDRAL** (plan of Bunkyo ku, pp. 602–3: A4; 220yds/200m S of Ochanomizu station, JNR, and 220yds/200m N of the underground station of Shin Ochanomizu). This is the Greek Orthodox church which is named after its founder.

Built by Father Ioan Kasatkin Nikolai (1863-1912), a Russian, it had to be restored following the 1923 earthquake.

Half-way between Chuo dori and Hongo dori, Sotobori dori crosses the railway line (Chuo line) and a deep canal. Sotobori dori runs parallel to the latter for a time before a street off to the right brings you back to Hongo dori a little further up, but before you reach this street on the right you pass:

卍 **YUSHIMA SEDIO** (plan of Bunkyo ku, pp. 602–3: B4; 220yds/200 m NE of the JNR station and underground station of Ochanomizu). This is a shrine dedicated to Confucius and founded in 1690 by Tokugawa Tsunayoshi. Rebuilt in 1935, it contains statues of Confucius and of other Chinese sages.

Opposite, a little street leads to Kanda Myojin (plan: B3), a shrine dedicated in the 8th c. to Okuninushi no Mikoto, and rebuilt in 1934. Here Kanda or Taira Masakada is venerated; he tried to make Kanto into an independent state in the 10th c. (see Narita). Festival of Kanda Matsuri 14 to 16 May.

Kanda includes Akihabara to the N (JNR station of that name), which is the area of Tokyo specializing in audiovisual equipment.

The broad Kudan Yasukuni dori crosses Kanda and Surugadai and leads to the most northerly point of:

KITANOMARU PARK (Tokyo plan, pp. 570–1 A1; 1½ml/2km W of Kanda station; 330yds/300m S of Kudanshita underground station and 330yds/300m W of Takebashi underground station). The Park is now separated from the Imperial Palace of which it was once a part. Here you can visit:

NIPPON BUDOKAN (plan: A1). A hall of the Martial Arts, it was built for the Olympic Games in 1964 (judo contests). Yumedono at Horyu ji (see Ikaruga) was the inspiration for this polygonal building, which seats 1,500 and is still used for sports contests. Its other uses include that of a congress and concert hall.

SCIENCE MUSEUM (plan: B1; 330yds/300m SE of Nippon Budokan; address: 2-2, Kitanomaru Koen, Chiyoda ku; open daily except Mondays from 09.30 to 16.50). This museum was opened in 1964 and occupies a sizeable building. On display are a number of dioramas, diagrams, mock-ups and models which you can work yourself and are very popular with the parties of schoolchidren who visit the museum. We recommend that you start your visit on the 5th floor.

'NATIONAL MUSEUM OF MODERN ART (plan: B1; 330yds/300m S of the Science Museum; 330yds/300m W of Takebashi underground station; address 3, Kitanomaru koen, Chiyoda ku; open daily from 10.00 to 17.00). This museum, designed by the architect Taniguchi Yoshiro, houses a large number of Japanese works of art and examples of arts and crafts dating back to the beginning of the century.

The majority of works on display are very faithful to the aesthetic traditions of Japanese art, despite having assimilated the new national and foreign tendencies. Among the paintings worthy of a mention are works by Shimomura Kanzan (scroll of Ohara Goko after the Heike legend, 1908); Yorozu Tetsugoro (*Reclining Woman*, 1917; Yasuda Yukihiko (*Eclipse of the Sun*, 1925); Maeta Kani (*Nude*, 1928) Kondo Koichiro (*Dramatic Night Scene after the Rain*, 1929); Koide Narashige (*Seascape*, 1930); Uemura Shoen (*Mother and Child*, 1934); Kawabata Ryushi (*Fire at Kinkaku*, 1950); Kayama Matazo (*Winter*, 1957); Umehara Ryuzaburo (*Mount Asama*, 1959); Iwashashi Eien (*Erosion*, 1959); Maeda Seison (*Stone Sarcophagus*, 1962); Higashiyama Kaii (*Tree in Winter*, 1964). Watercolours, drawings and prints of Onchi Koshiro (*Spring Study*); Hagiwara Hideo; pottery by Imaizumi Yoshiaki; also an earthenware jar (1958) by Tomimoto Kenkichi and a bronze vase (1963) by Nishi Daiyu.

From Kitanomaru Park, Kudan Yasukuni dori runs W past:

YASUKUNI JINJA (880yds/800m NE of Ichigaya station and 880yds/800m SW of the underground station of Kudanshita). It was built on Kudan hill in memory of the soldiers who have died for their country since 1868. On the l., near the main entrance, is a statue of the statesman Shinagawa Yajiro (1843–1900).

Note the simplicity of the main building, built according to the orthodox Shinto style. The *torii* at the entrance to the shrine is the largest one made of marble in Japan and dates from 1933.

Festivals 21 to 25 April and from 18 to 21 October. Noh plays in the open air during the O bon festival (13-14 July).

The street which runs to the S along the moats forming the W border of Kitanomaru Park leads to the Monument to the Unknown Soldier (650yds/600m SE of Yasukuni jinja; built in 1959, before joining Uchibori dori to the W. Uchibori dori continues to the W of the Imperial Palace moats and to the S meets the start of Shinjuki dori, which goes W to:

YOTSUYA (plan of Shinkuku ju: pp. 598–9; F1; 1½ml/2km SW of Yasukuni jinja; JNR station and Yotsuya underground station). To the SE of the station you can see the Roman Catholic Church of Saint Ignatius, built in 1949. The altar was given by a Brooklyn church in New York. The stained-glass windows were made in Belgium.

Behind this church is the Catholic University of Saint Sophia (Sophia University, founded in 1914). The sports fields benefit from the old dried-out moats which extend below ground level to the W. To the SE of this university, you can easily spot the New Otani hotel (tall tower with 1,000 rooms and a pretty Japanese garden), which is one of Tokyo's largest hotels.

A small street skirting this hotel to the E brings you to Shimizudani koen (770yds/700m SE of Yotsuya; 440yds/400m N of Akasaka-Mitsuke underground station), a little public garden. There is a monument in memory of Okubo Toshimichi, one of the instigators of the Meiji Restoration, who was assassinated not far from here in 1878.

To the S of this garden you cross an ancient moat and a large crossroads, with the viaducts of the expressways crossing overhead. Beyond, you come to:

AKASAKA (½ml/1km SE of Yotsuya; Akasaka-Mitsuke underground station). It is a busy quarter crossed by Sotobori dori (hotels, restaurants and bars). Akasaka is the capital's fashionable night-life quarter. It borders on Shinjuku and Roppongi, which are more popular, and is frequented by well-to-do members of Tokyo society who can afford to patronize its expensive establishments.

Behind the Hilton Hotel you can climb the hillock of Hoshigaoka, on which stands the Hie shrine or Sanno sama (440yds/400m SE of Akasaka-Mitsuke underground station), transferred in the 17th c. by Ieyasu from Edo castle. This was the capital's most popular shrine during the Tokugawa period. The main building and outbuildings were destroyed during World War II and have been partly reconstructed since.

The shrine's main festival is on 15 June with a procession of palanquins.

Not far away, on another hill to the NE, is the Parliament building:

JAPANESE DIET BUILDING (Tokyo plan, pp. 570–1: B4; 660yds/600m NE of

Hie jinja; Kokkaigijidomae underground station. Sakurodamon, the seat of goverment, is made of reinforced concrete and granite from Yamaguchi and Hiroshima. It is decorated with marble from Yamaguchi and Okinawa.

It was started in 1918 and completed in 1936. Its huge tower (217ft/66m high) dominates the entire quarter and for a long time was the tallest building in Japan. The Diet consists of two chambers: the Chamber of Councillors, with 252 seats, which occupies the right-hand side of the building, and the Chamber of Representatives, 491 seats, which is situated on the left-hand side. The members are elected by universal suffrage. They appoint the Prime Minister whose office is confirmed by the Emperor.

The Diet's main façade is turned towards the Imperial Palace and overlooks Kasumigaseki garden. In the central hall you can see bronze statues of Prince Ito, Marquis Okuma and Count Itagaki, three great modern Japanese statesmen who worked in favour of constitutional government. Apply to the JNTO if you would like to visit the building.

The Prime Minister's official residence is a short distance to the S of the Diet.

To the N of Kasumigaseki garden is the museum dedicated to Ozaki Yukio (1859-1954), who was a member of the Chamber of Representatives from 1890 until his death. He was known as the father of the Japanese parliament.

To the N of the Parliament building you can visit the Diet Library (plan: A4; open daily from 09.30 to 17.00 except Sundays, festivals and the last day of each month), the equivalent of the British Library in London (architect Mayekawa Kunio). It now has a collection of more than 3 million books.

If you cross Aoyama dori (N of the library), near the Imperial Palace moats you can see the:

*HIGH COURT OF JUSTICE (plan: A3; 660yds/600m N of the Diet). It is a very handsome modern building, completed in 1974 (architect Okada Shinichi). It takes the form of several cubes of concrete and granite which make up massive balanced windowless shapes. A vast dome lets daylight into the main hall where the sessions are held.

Further N is the National Theatre (Kokuritsu Gekijo; plan: A3), which consists of two theatres (1,764 and 630 seats) where the different forms of Japanese theatre are shown periodically. The architect was Takenaka Komuten.

If you continue along the moats to the SW of the Imperial Palace, opposite Sakurada mon (p. 574) and beyond the Police Station, you arrive at:

KASUMIGASEKI (plan: C4; 770yds/700m SE of the Diet; Kasumigaseki underground station). This is the quarter where the main government buildings of the capital are situated.

To the S of this quarter, near the Ministry of Education, is the tall Kasumigaseki Building, which was the first skyscraper to be built in Tokyo (35 floors).

 HIBIYA KOEN (plan: D4; 550yds/500m E of Kasumigaseki; 550yds/500m SW of Yurakucho station, JNR; Hibiya underground station). This park, to the E of Kasumigaseki, covers 40 acres (16 ha) and is the best situated in Tokyo. It was laid out in 1904 and was the first Western style park in Japan, although Japanese influence is still evident. In olden times the daimyo had their residences here, then, after the Meiji Restoration, it was turned into a military exercise ground.

The park has two small lakes, beds of flowers, lawns and fountains with displays of azaleas in May and chrysanthemums in November.

To the S of the park are Hibiya municipal library and Hibiya hall where meetings, conferences and concerts are held.

Further S, and opening onto Hibiya dori, is the House of Japanese Radio and Television (Nihon Hoso Kaisha, NHK), whose main building was completed in 1939. There are 18 radio studios, television studios and an auditorium which seats 800 people.

To the NE of Hibiya garden is the Yuraku cho quarter (p. 576).

B Chuo ku

Street plan: p. 570–1.

Bakurocho and Shin Nihombashi JNR stations.

This district, E of Chiyoda ku, has been progressively reclaimed from the Sumida gawa estuary since the 17th c. Two main through roads (Chuo dori and Harumi dori) cross in the Ginza quarter, which is one of the centres of Tokyo nightlife and where some of the city's most beautiful shops are situated. The financial centre of the capital is to the N, near Nihombashi, and further S is Tokyo's central market, a number of important hospitals (Saint Luke's hospital and the National Cancer Centre) and the Tokyo International Trade Centre (Harumi).

GINZA (plan: F4; 550yds/500m SE of Yurakucho JNR station; Ginza and Higashi Ginza undergound stations, which are connected by a subway). This is one of Tokyo's most glittering quarters, with the two crossroads of Sukiyabashi and Harumi dori with Chuo dori marking the main centres. In fact, Ginza is a direct continuation of Yurako cho (see Chiyoda ku).

Ginza was drained on the orders of the shogun Tokugawa Ieyasu in 1603. The name 'Ginza' (*gin*, silver; *za*, seat) has its origins in the fact that Ieyasu is said to have had the mint moved from Shizuoka to this part of Tokyo. In 1873, Ginza, between Kyobashi and Shimbashi, became the first street in Tokyo to be paved (with bricks). The symbol of Ginza is the weeping willow, and an old Japanese song goes, 'the chestnut trees of Paris, the weeping willows of Ginza'. Unfortunately the latter only exist now in memory.

All day and all evening, people stroll about in Ginza, pausing in front of the beautiful shop window displays. The Japanese for this activity is *gin bura* (*bura*, a stroll). Chuo dori is closed to motor traffic on Sundays, when the big stores stay open. In Ginza you can find the finest bars, restaurants, tearooms and night clubs. At night the whole quarter glitters with neon advertisements, but after 22.00, when the cinemas close, Ginza empties while nightlife is still in full swing in Shinjuku.

To the SE of Chuo dori and Showa dori, Harumi dori goes past Kabuki za (plan: F4; 880yds/800m SE of Yurakucho eki, JNR; Higashi–Ginza underground station), one of the most popular theatres in Tokyo, where the principal Kabuki actors are trained. It was founded in 1624, and rebuilt in 1950 in a modern architectural style influenced by traditional building methods; it has 2,200 seats.

Parallel with Harumi dori, to the S, runs Miyuki dori, which is narrower and forms the continuation of a street running alongside the Imperial Hotel. If you follow it under the railway lines and expressway you come to the Riccar building.

RICCAR ART MUSEUM (plan: E4; 220yds/200m SW of Ginza underground station; address 2–3, Ginza 6-chome, 7th floor; open daily except Mondays from 11.00 to 18.00). The museum houses collections of old *ukiyo-e* woodcuts and the blocks from which they were made.

CHUO DORI (plan: F1, 2, 3, 4; underground stations: Ginza, Takaracho, Nihombashi). The broad 'high street' of Chuo ku connects Shimbashi in the S with Nihombashi (1½mls/2.5km to the N), crossing the Ginza quarter and Harumi dori in between. All along this street and in its immediate vicinity are the most attractive little shops, the buildings belonging to the great Japanese trade names and the most famous big stores in Tokyo. From S to N are, to name a few: Matsuzakaya, Wake, Matsuya, Takashimaya (without doubt the most luxurious), Maruzen, Tokyu, etc. Most of these big stores put on series of exhibitions well worth seeing.

Heading N along Chuo dori, beyond Matsuya store, you pass Ginza Boeki, which houses the Tokyo Central Museum of Arts (address: 2-7-18, Ginza, Chuo ku; open daily except Mondays from 10.00 to 18.00): Western and Japanese paintings. Beyond Kyobashi, Chuo dori crosses Yaesu dori, which runs at right-angles to Tokyo station with the latter's vast modern building towering at its W end. At the corner of Yaesu dori and Chuo dori is Bridgestone Building, which houses the:

*BRIDGESTONE GALLERY (plan: F2; 440yds/400m E of Tokyo eki; ½ml/1km N of Ginza-Harumi dori; 440yds/400m N of Kyobashi underground station; address: 1-1, Kyobashi, Chuo ku; entrance on Yaesu dori; open daily except Mondays from 10.00 to 17.30; closed from 23 December to 4 January). This museum, which was founded with the aid of funds donated by Ishibashi Shojiro, houses one of the richest private collections of Western art in Tokyo and in the whole of Japan. There are many European paintings dating from the 17th c. to modern times, including a large number of works by the French Impressionists. The museum also possesses engravings, sculptures from antiquity and by contemporary artists, works in copper; ancient pottery, etc. Various exhibitions are held here periodically.

Among the Western painters you will see works by Rubens (*Portrait of a Man*), Rembrandt (*St Paul and the Soldiers*, 1628), Guardi (*View of Venice*), and Gainsborough (*Portrait of a Lady*). Nineteenth-century painters and the Impressionists are represented by Corot (*The Italian Girl*, about 1826–28), Courbet (*Snow*), Pissaro (*The Kitchen Garden*, 1878), Manet (*Portraits of M. Brun*, 1879, and *Méry Laurent*, 1882), Degas (*After Bathing*, about 1900), Cézanne (*Self-Portrait* and *Mont Ste-Victoire*, c. 1898–1900), Monet (*Twilight in Venice* 1908), Renoir (*Bather*, 1914), Gauguin (*Portrait of a Young Woman*, 1886), Sisley (*St Mammès on a June Morning*, 1884), Van Gogh (*Still Life*), and Utrillo (*The St Denis Canal*, c. 1906–08. Among the painters closer to our time are Bonnard (*Landscape near Vernon*, 1929), Matisse (*Odalisque with Arms Raised*, 1921), Rouault (*Pierrot*, 1925), Dufy, Picasso (*Head of a Woman*, 1923), Modigliani, Bourdelle, etc.

Among the principal Japanese painters inspired or trained by Western artists are Asai Chu (1856–1907; *The Bridge over the Loing at Grez*, 1901); Kuroda Seiki (1866–1924; *Young Girl from Bréhat*, 1891); Fujishima Taheji (1867–1943; about 60 works, including *Ciociara*); Okada Saburosuke (1869–1939); Mitsutani Kunishiro (1874–1936); Aoki Shigeru (1882–1911; about 20 canvasses, including *Self-Portrait*, 1903, and *The Good Catch*, 1904); Fujita Tsuguji (1886–1968; about 15 works, including *Still Life with Inkpot and Pipe*, 1926); Koide Narashige (1887–1931, including *Roses*, 1931); Yasui Sotaro (1888–1955); Umehara Ryuzaburo (born in 1888, *View of Sorrento from Naples*, 1921); Kishida Ryusei (1891–1929, *Portrait of His Daughter Reiko*, 1920); Koga Harue (1895–1933); Saeki Yuzo (1898–1928); Sekine Shoji (1899–1919; *Boy*, 1919).

Sculpture is represented by interesting examples from the Mediterranean area dating from ancient and protohistoric times, notably the *Bust of a Sumerian Woman* (approx. 14th c. BC); a fragment of Egyptian *bas-relief* in limestone depicting a procession (15th c. BC) and a statue in black granite of *Sokhmit with the Face of a Lion* (approx. 14th c. BC); *Statue of a Young Girl* (Greek marble dating from 6th c. BC) and a pretty marble statue of *Aphrodite* (Hellenistic period). French sculpture is represented by a beautiful *Head of Christ* in wood from the north of France (14th c.) and modern works in bronze by Barye, Degas (*Head of a Woman*), Rodin (*Female Faun Standing*, stone, 1884), Bourdelle (*Penelope*, about 1907–12), Maillol (*Desire*, about 1905), and Despiau (*Head of a Great Reed Warbler*, 1919).

The museum also boasts engravings by Rembrandt and Manet, lithographs by Toulouse-Lautrec and etchings by Picasso. Finally, you can see examples of pottery from different periods and countries (Greece, 6th to 4th c. BC; Persia, 11th and 12th c. AD) and copper objects of Roman origin (1st and 2nd c. AD).

To the N, beyond Eitai dori, Chuo dori leads you to an old bridge.

NIHOMBASHI (plan: F1; 880yds/800m NE of Tokyo eki; Nihombashi underground station). This bridge is the central point from which all distances used to be measured. It was originally made of wood, but was reconstructed in granite in 1911. Today the bridge is completely overwhelmed by the motorway viaducts which straddle it.

Beyond Nihombashi is the Muro machi quarter, which Chuo dori also crosses. When you have gone as far as Mitsukoshimae station you will see the big Mitsukoshi store, and behind it the head office of the Bank of Japan (plan: E1). If you go E (Muromachi I-chome), opposite the big store you will see the monument to the memory of William Adams (see Yokosuka), which marks the site of his house at Edo.

A traditional quarter known for the number of artisans working there. Muro machi extends between the underground stations of Ningyocho and Higashi-Nihombashi. You can get pleasantly lost in the maze of little streets and houses which have a charm of their own.

KABUTO CHO. Immediately to the S of Nihombashi, two streets lead E to where Tokyo Stock Exchange is situated (Tokyo shoken torihiki sho; 440yds/400m E of Nihombashi; 440yds/400m NE of Edobashi underground station). It is now the most important in the world, and is the oldest in Japan, having been built in 1878. (If you wish to visit it, write in advance to: Chuo ku Nihombashi, Kabuto cho, 1-chome.)

In this quarter, to the S of the Stock Exchange, you can visit the :

YAMATANE MUSEUM OF ART (330yds/300m S of the stock exchange; Kayabacho underground station; address: 2-10, Kabuto cho, Nihombashi, Chuo ku; open daily except Mondays from 11.00 to 17.00). On display in the museum are a number of Japanese works painted since the Meiji period (1868).

If you go NE along Shin Ohashi dori from Kayaba cho you come to Suiten gu (770yds/700m NE of Kayabacho underground station), a popular shrine dedicated to Ameno Minakanushi no kami, protector of sailors and expectant mothers. Festivals on the 15th of each month, and on 5 May, 31 December and 1 January.

Shin Ohashi dori continues to the Sumida gawa and crosses it. Before you get to the bridge, you will see Hamacho Park to the N (2mls/3km NE of Harumi dori; 550yds/500m NE of Suiten gu; 550yds/500m SE of Higashinihombashi underground station), with its sports fields. Nearby is the Meiji za (1,770 seats) which, since its reconstruction in 1950, is one of the most modern theatres in the city.

From Ginza, Harumi dori continues SE in the direction of Tokyo Port. Beyond Kabuki za (p. 583), this street comes to:

TSUKIJI (880yds/800m SE of Ginza; Tsukiji underground station). This quarter is the centre of food supplies for Tokyo, and here you can find some of the best-known restaurants serving Japanese food.

To the N of Harumi dori you will see Tsuki ji Hongan ji. This temple (founded in 1521), belonging to the Nishin Honganji sect, was rebuilt in 1934 according to plans by the architect Ito Chuta. It is a mixture of Indian and modern styles. The bell comes from Ota Dokan's castle and the drum which beats the hours was brought back from Korea by Toyotomi Hideyoshi.

Beyond Tsukiji, Harumi dori crosses Kachidoki swing bridge (built between 1931 and 1940) and takes you to Harumi cho, where Urashima hotel is situated. SW of this hotel is Tokyo International Trade Centre (1½ml/2km S of Tsukiji; bus the length of Harumi dori) where 270,000 sq. ft (25,000m²) of floorspace is available for big trade fairs. One of the buildings (architect Murata Masachika) is built in the form of a half-circle and can accommodate 15,000 people.

TOKYO CENTRAL MARKET (¾ml/1.2km S of Ginza; ½ml/1km SW of Tsukiji underground station). The southern part of Tsukiji quarter is occupied by the market. It was built in 1934 and covers a surface area of 2,100,000sq. ft (195,000m²).

Originally, the market at Nihombashi was for fish (p. 585), and for over 300 years this was the most important market in Edo. Today the central market is the scene of all transactions, whether they deal with fish (there is a very busy fish market at about 05.00), meat, vegetables or fruit.

Ships of 3,000t can come alongside, and more than 30,000 people spend some time here each day. Nearby there are banks, post offices and alley after alley swarming with people where numerous stalls do a brisk trade in the mornings. Through Tsukiji pass the majority of the 1,850t of rice, 450t of fish, 100t of meat (...), 30t of seaweed, the 1½ million eggs, and the 1,000t of vegetables and fruit which Tokyo consumes each day. There are six branches of the central market in different parts of the city: Kanda, Sumida, Shinagawa, Toshima Shinjuku and Adachi. All this activity goes to make Tokyo one of the biggest food markets in the world.

A stay in Tokyo would not be complete without a visit to the fish market. Wandering about among the beautifully laid out stalls piled high with octopus, tuna, dried fish, and incredible varieties of shellfish and seafood is certainly an experience not to be missed. Try tasting the raw fish, as the buyers do: the fishmonger will cut off a little square of pink flesh from an enormous tuna so that you can find out just how fresh and tasty his wares are. The atmosphere is very relaxed and friendly, but is rather wet and slippery underfoot. Boots or strong shoes should be worn.

To the S, parallel to the central market, on a 62-acre (25-ha) site is:

*HAMA RIKYU ONSHI KOEN (plan, pp. 588–9; F1; 550yds/500m SW of the central market, ¾ml/1.2km S of Ginza; 880yds/800m SE of Shimbashi JNR station and underground station; open daily from 09.00 to 16.00, staying open until 17.00 in July and August; entrance at the northern corner of the park). This garden is a typical and very pure example of a daimyo garden of the Edo period, which should be visited in spring when the cherry trees are in blossom.

Originally there was a villa here belonging to the Matsudaira daimyo of Kofu, which became the property of the Imperial Household in 1871. The grounds were given to the city in 1945 and since then the garden has been open to the public.

The park boasts an ornamental lake whose level rises and falls with the tides. Three bridges shaded by wistaria provide access to a little island. From the esplanade bordered with pinetrees which runs along the SE part of the gardens you can see the Sumida estuary where the river empties into Tokyo Bay.

➤ If you walk round the garden you come to Takeshiba landing stage where you can board a motor launch for Asakusa. This excursion up the Sumida enables you to avoid the underground or the traffic jams and also shows you something of the river.

C Minato ku

Street plan: pp. 588–9.

Hamamatsucho, Shimbashi, Shinagawa, Tamachi JNR stations.

Minato ku, the 'port' district, situated to the S of the centre, is bordered on the E by Tokyo Bay and the port, and on the W by Azabu (Roppongi being the most lively part of this quarter) and Akasaka, both particularly elegant residential areas. This district formed the southern limit of the city before 1932. There are many hotels and embassies. A maze of little streets makes it difficult for the stroller to get his bearings throughout this sector, where the interesting places to see are further away from the main streets and railway and underground stations.

SHIMBASHI (plan: F1; railway and underground stations of this name). This busy quarter in the N of Minato ku forms the turning point between this district and Chiyoda ku.

The first railway line from Tokyo to Yokohama was opened at Shimbashi station in 1872.

To the N of Shimbashi, Sotobori dori turns W towards Kasumigaseki and Akasaka (see Chiyoda ku).

➤ From Shimbashi, go S along the continuation of Chuo dori (p. 582), Dai ichi Keihin Kokudo, an important main road which crosses all the southern quarters of Tokyo and finally becomes Tokai do (N1 major route). ½ml (1km) S of Shimbashi this street comes to:

HAMAMATSU CHO. This quarter is now dominated by the immense World Trade Centre Building (Sekai Boeki Center, plan: F2; ½ml/1km S of Shimbashi; Hamamatsucho JNR station). The 40-storey tower block (499ft/152m high) is one of the tallest in the capital (architect Nikken Sekkei Komu) and is occupied by a large number of trading companies. An observation platform provides a wonderful view over Tokyo port. The monorail begins at the base of this building; it connects Hamamatsu cho to Haneda airport (8mls/13km S).

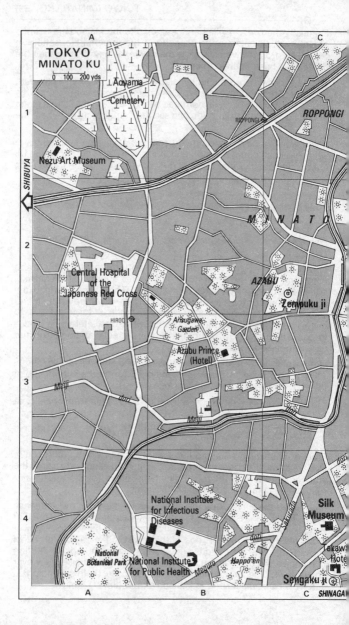

TOKYO
MINATO KU
0   100   200 yds

Aoyama
Cemetery

ROPPONGI

ROPPONGI

SHIBUYA

Nezu Art Museum

M I N A T O

AZABU

Central Hospital
of the
Japanese Red Cross

Zempuku ji

HIROO

Arisugawa
Garden

Azabu Prince
(Hotel)

Meiji

dori

Meiji

dori

National Institute
for Infectious
Diseases

Silk
Museum

National
Botanical Park

National Institute
for Public Health   Meguro

Happo en

Takawa
Hotel

Sengaku ji

A   B   C   SHINAGA

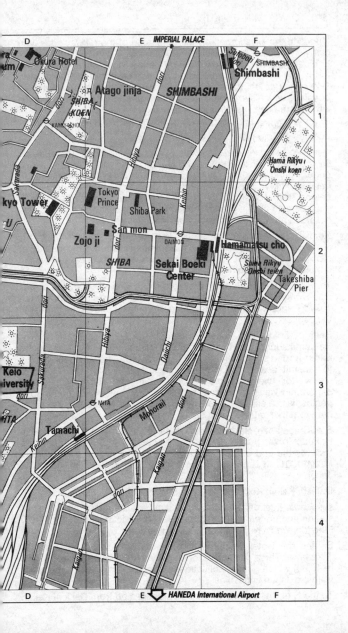

Opposite the skyscraper, on the other side of the railway lines, you can visit Shiba Rikyu Onshi teien (plan: F2), a garden typical of the Edo period. It was created in 1698 by Okubo Tadatomo and was given to the city by Emperor Hiro Hito on the occasion of his marriage in 1924. The garden is not quite so impressive now because of the tall buildings which surround it. Beyond the garden to the E is Takeshiba jetty where boats leave for Izu archipelago.

From Hamamatsu cho you can go W to Shiba Park, passing the porticos of Zojo ji and Tokyo tower en route.

 SHIBA KOEN (plan: D2-E2; 2mls/3km S of the Imperial Palace; 850yrds/800m W of Hamatsucho station; Onarimon and Shibakoen underground stations). This park covers an area of 64 acres (26 ha) between Hibiya dori to the E and Sakurada dori to the W and used to belong to the Buddhist temple of Zojo ji. There used to be several mausoleums here and also the temple of Benzaiten, but the garden has been reorganized considerably in recent years.

Zojo ji, the headquarters of the Jodo Buddhist sect in the Kanto region, used to be the temple of the Tokugawa family. The portal (San mon) with two red-lacquered storeys dates from 1605. Behind it is the temple's new main building.

To the S of this temple, the prehistoric site of Maruyama was discovered. To the N of Zojo ji, part of Shiba park is taken up by the Tokyo Prince Hotel (arch. Takenaka Komuten), one of the largest in the capital.

Behind Zojo ji is Tokyo tower (plan: D2; ¾ml/1.2km W of Hamamatsucho JNR station; 550yrds/500m S of Kamiyacho underground station). It is 1,093ft (333m) high and was built in 1958 to transmit local television programmes. It is the tallest metal tower in the world. Two platforms (at 387ft/118m and 768ft/234m) afford panoramic views over the city, Tokyo Bay, and the Izu and Boso peninsulas. A science museum occupies several floors in the lower part, together with souvenir shops and restaurants.

S of Shiba koen, Sakurada dori and Hibiya dori join Dai ichi Keihin Kokudo (p. 587). Sakurada dori goes past Keio University, founded towards the end of the Tokugawa shogunate by Fukuzawa Yukichi (1834-1901). It is one of the most important private universities in Japan.

Dai ichi Keihin Kokudo takes you S to the popular quarter of:

SHINAGAWA (just off plan: C4; 2mls/3km S of Shiba koen; Shinagawa station and underground station). Here there is an important railway junction, with several of Tokyo's big hotels nearby.

Behind the Hotel Pacific is the Takanawa Art Museum (4-10-30, Takanawa, Shiba, Minato ku; open daily except Mondays from 10.00 to 16.00) which houses collections of *objets d'art* and arts and crafts from old Japan and China.

To the N of Shinagawa, Shiba dori branches off from Dai ichi Keihin

Kokudo and heads W. Not far along it is:

SENGAKU JI (plan: C4; ½ml/1km N of Shinagawa; 1¾mls/2.8km S of Shiba koen; 220yds/200m W of Sengakuji underground station). This temple was founded by Tokugawa Ieyasu in 1612. On the l. you come to the graves of the 47 *ronin* who were condemned to *seppuku* (ritual suicide) for avenging their former master.

These *ronin* (or *samurai* who have lost their master) were vassals of Asano Naganori, lord of Ako (see entry under this name). In 1701, Asano drew his sword in the shogun's palace against Kira Yoshinaka, who had offended him, and for this crime he was ordered to kill himself. His *samurai* resolved to avenge him. They waited until public interest had died down and they had been forgotten, then in December 1702 they suddenly attacked Kira's residence (p. 620) and beheaded him. Their task accomplished, they placed their victim's head on Asano's grave and went to report their deed of valour. They calmly awaited the reaction of the authorities, who condemned them to *seppuku*. Their story has been made into a Kabuki theatre play called *Chushingura*, which always draws large audiences. The memory of these *ronin* is still cherished by the Japanese, and their number corresponds to that of the Nipponese prefectures.

The grave of their leader, Oishi Yoshino, is in a corner of the garden, covered by a roof. Next to it is the grave of Asano Nagamori. The name and age of each of the others is carved on their graves. The youngest, the leader's son, was only 15, and the eldest *ronin*, Horibe Kanamaru, was an old man of 77. In the courtyard you can still see the basin in which the *ronin* washed their enemy's head before placing it on Asano's grave. Inside one of the temple buildings are a number of relics which used to belong to the *ronin*, as well as their portraits on wood. Festivals on 4 February, 6 April, 5 May and 14 December.

In front of Sengaku ji, Shiba dori bends round and heads towards Sakurada dori. The first on the l. past Sengaku ji takes you to the Gallery of Silks (open daily from 10.00 to 17.00; shop, and display of silks from the past). Sakurada dori comes from the direction of Keio University (p. 590) and continues SW towards Gotanda. Meguro dori branches W of this street and leads to Meguro, passing by the National Institute for Infectious Diseases, an offshoot of Tokyo University and the centre for biological research into epidemic diseases. This building also houses the National Institute for Public Health, founded in 1939 with the aid of a donation from the Rockefeller Foundation. Almost opposite this Institute you can see Happo en (plan: B4), one of the prettiest private gardens in Tokyo (restaurant). Continuing along Meguro dori, you come to the:

*NATIONAL PARK FOR NATURE STUDY (plan: A4; 1ml/1.5km W of Sengaku ji; 1ml/1.5km NW of Shinagawa; 550yds/500m NE of the JNR station of Meguro; open daily except Mondays and the day following a national holiday from 09.00 to 16.00). This park covers an area of about 50 acres (20 ha) and is a centre for ecological studies of the life of insects, birds and plants. It used to belong to the estate of the Matsudaira of Takamatsu at Edo, and was opened to the public in 1955. The dense vegetation of this wooded park gives an impression of what the ancient Musashi forests that used to grow around Edo were like. Between the park and the Institute for Public Health is a fairly broad street which heads N and goes past the Kitazato Institute (research into infectious diseases). This institute was founded in 1914 by Dr Kitazato Shibasaburo (1852-1931), one of Japan's great bacteriologists. The street then passes beneath an expressway, crosses Ebisu dori, Furu gawa and, beyond Meiji dori, comes to Hiroo, whence it continues N in the direction of Aoyama cemetery (p 595). On the r., a little street leads from Hiroo to:

ARISUGAWA NO MIYA KINEN KOEN (plan: B3; 1ml/1.5km N of the National Park for Nature Study; 1ml/1.5km NE of the JNR station of Ebisu 220yds/200m E of Hiroo underground station). During the Edo period, this park belonged to Nambu, lord of Mino, then became the property of Prince Arisugawa in 1896. In 1934, Prince Takamatsu gave the garden to the city of Tokyo in memory of the Arisugawa family from whom he had inherited it.

The park is situated in the pleasant Azabu quarter, which is one of the city's main residential areas. Among the low houses surrounded by little gardens are many embassies. A small street runs along the S side of Arisugawa Park. Follow this E and take the fourth street on the l. (ask for directions) to:

ZEMPUKU JI (plan: C2; 880yds/800m NE of Arisugawa Park; 1ml/1.3km SW of Shiba koen; ½ml/1km S of that of Roppongi). This temple is said to have been founded in 832 by Kobo Daishi. It was destroyed several times by fire, and was last rebuilt after World War II.

Inside is a treasury which contains the sacred formula written by Kobo Daishi, as well as some Buddhist sculptures and paintings. A stone monument was erected in 1936 by the Americano-Japanese Society to recall that this temple housed the American legation for more than ten years. The monument bears a bronze medallion with the image of Townsend Harris, first envoy of the American delegation in 1859. In the park there is a very beautiful ginkgo tree, the largest and probably the oldest in Tokyo. According to legend, it sprang up from the walking stick of the famous priest Shinran (13th c.).

From Zempuku ji you can go NE to Shiba Park.

To the N of Shiba Park is Atago yama, with Sakurada dori running to the W of it. To the N of this hill you can visit:

ATAGO JINJA (plan: E1; ½ml/1km N of Shiba koen; 330yds/300m NE of Kamyyacho underground station). You reach this shrine by going up a winding road on the western side of the hill and then by ascending either of two flights of stone steps: the masculine way (*Otoko zaka*), which consists of 86 steps ending at the shrine; and the feminine way (*Onna zaka*), the steps of which are shallower.

The story goes that Otoko zaka was used by Magaki Heikuro in 1634 when, on the orders of the shogun Tokugawa Iemitsu, he climbed on horseback to the summit of the hill to pick some blossom from a plum tree. Men of fashion and poets are also said to have climbed this hill to gaze upon the snow and the moon.

To the S of Atago hill you can visit the Broadcasting Museum (1-10, Atago cho, Shiba, Minato ku; open daily except Mondays from 09.30 to 16.30): history of radio and television in Japan.

From Atago yama, if you cross Sakurada dori to the W, you can climb another hill dominated by Hotel Okura, which you can also reach by going S from Sotobori dori down a street opposite the Kasumigaseki Building (p. 576). Beside this important hotel you can visit:

*OKURA MUSEUM (plan: D1; 550yds/500m NW of Atago yama; 1ml/1.3km NW of Shiba koen; 660yds/600m SW of Toranomon underground station; address: 3, Aoi cho; Akasaka, Minato ku; open daily except Mondays from 10.00 to 16.00). It houses a collection of antiquities from Japan, China and India which once belonged to Baron Okura Kihachiro. This is one of the capital's most outstanding museums and has an important library attached to it. The following is a list of some of the works periodically on display.

Sculptures are to be found on the ground floor. Among the Indian and Chinese works are an interesting statue of Buddha in sandstone (5th c.) from the Chinese province of Hopei; a small gilded bronze of uncertain origin from the 11th c. representing Vishnu (either from Bengal or Nepal); and a wooden statue of Kuan Yin (Kannon), a beautiful piece from northern China dating from the Song (or Sung) period (12th-13th c.). Among the Japanese works are a beautiful *statue of Fugen seated on an elephant, a rare sculpture inspired by Hoke kyo (painted wood, from the Fujiwara period, 12th c.), and a statue of the priest Horen (13th c.).

The first floor is primarily reserved for *paintings*: there are a number of painted scrolls (*emakimono and kakemono*) from the 13th, 14th and 15th c., including the *zuishin teiki emaki* (13th c.), an illuminated scroll called 'cavalry *aides-de-camp*' which depicts nine members of the Imperial guard accompanying the retired Emperors Go Shirakawa and Go Saga; these *emakimono* are attributed to Fujiwara Nobuzane (1177-1265); a posthumous portrait of Prince Shotoku in the form of a scroll in the *yamato e* style, dating from the 13th c. Kamakura period; on the occasion of a reading from the *Simala sutra*; the Iwashimizu Hachiman mandala, from a shrine of that name at Kyoto and showing it as it was in the 13th c. (Kamakura period); a painting of Nirvana from the 14th c. which, although from a later period, is reminiscent of similar paintings in the Koya san Museum and the Nara National Museum (see entries under these names); and 16 painted scrolls of Buddha's disciples (Juroku Rakan; Kamakura period, 14th c.). Several paintings have been influenced by the Kano school: *Bird and Celosia cristata* by Maejima Soyu (16th c.), a pupil of Kano Motonobu: *Picking Tea at Uji* and *Horse Racing at Kamogawa Shrine* (Kyoto), folding screens (17th c.) by Kusumi Morikage, a pupil of Kano Tanyu; and another pair of folding screens depicting cormorant fishing (*ukai*) by Tanyu himself; the folding screens of fluttering fans are attributed to Sotatsu. Several traditional painters from the 19th and 20th c. are also represented in this museum: *Bamboo and Orchids*, folding screens by Tsubuki Chinzan (1801-54); *Waterfalls in the Mountains in Autumn*, painting on silk by Kawai Gyokudo (1873-1957), etc. You can also see Chinese documents printed on paper by using woodblocks (China, Song [or Sung] period), and an *Introduction to the Kokin shu Anthology*, a work of calligraphy attributed to Minamoto Toshiyori (1058-1129).

The museum also contains beautiful Noh and Kyogen costumes and masks from the Edo period; pottery, amongst which is a hexagonal dish made by Ogata Kenzan and decorated with a Juro by his brother Ogata Korin (1658-1716); lacquered objects, among them a casket of Korean origin (Koryo period, 918-1392) inlaid with mother-of-pearl, and a writing desk said to have been given by Tokugawa Tsunayoshi (1649-1709) to one of his vassals. Finally, there are a number of Chinese archaeological finds (Fu, Chou and Chin periods between the 17th and 3rd c. BC), with a particularly rare piece among them: a lacquered Chin bowl from the 3rd c. BC.

Okura museum is roughly half-way between Sakurada dori to the E and an avenue overhung by an expressway to the W. This avenue heads SW to:

ROPPONGI (plan: C1; ½ml/1km SW of Okura museum; 1ml/1.5km W of Shiba koen; Roppongi underground station). Here is a quarter overflowing with life and movement. As soon as the neon lights come on, everything comes to life. Hundreds of restaurants serve all kinds of specialities, and there are Japanese bars, English pubs, discothèques and cabarets. Trendy youngsters rub shoulders with the average Japanese. Elegance, dishevelled chic and Japanese punk all intermingle.

Beyond Roppongi, the avenue mentioned above crosses Zaimoku cho, then comes to Gaien Higashi dori. Before this street, to the SW of the expressway, is the Pentax Gallery (Kashumicho Corp., 3-21-20, Nishi Azabu, Minato ku; open daily except Mondays and national holidays from 10.00 to 17.00), the only museum of photography in Japan.

Beyond Gaien Higashi dori, next to the Fuji building, a street branches off the expressway and crosses Takagi cho, heading for Aoyama dori. A little further on you will find the entrance to the gardens of the former villa Nezu, where you can visit:

*NEZU ART MUSEUM (plan: A1; ¾ml/1.2km W of Roppongi; 770yds/700m SE of Omotesando underground station; address 6-5-36, Minami Aoyama, Minato ku; open daily except Mondays and the day following national holidays from 09.30 to 16.30). The building housing the museum (founded in 1941) is in the N corner of the park, where there are several pavilions reserved for the tea ceremony.

The museum possesses about 4,800 works of art collected by Nezu Kaichiro: extracts from the *Sutra on Cause and Effect* (Nara period); the *Pilgrimage of Zenzai Doji to the Fifty-five Saints* (Heian period, paints on silk); *Nachi Waterfall* (Kamakura period, 14th c.), a painting in the Chinese style, only on display for two months of the year; *Landscape*, attributed to Shubun (Muromachi period, ink and paints on paper); *Landscape* by Kenko Shokei (vertical scroll from the Muromachi period, ink and light paints on paper); *Gladioli* by Ogata Korin (folding screen, Edo period), and the *folding screen of Irises*, one of this painter's most famous works: on a gold background the flowers are depicted, parallel and upright painted in only two shades of blue which contrast with the green leaves. With only these three colours Korin suggests a 'truly bewitching rhythm'.

Notice also the three large Chinese tomb bronzes (Cheou period, 12th c. BC), the porcelain, lacquerware, examples of calligraphy, and metal utensils used in the ceremony.

On leaving the Nazu museum, go NE to the:

AOYAMA CEMETERY (plan: A1; 550yds/500m NE of Nezu museum; 1,000yds/900m W of Roppongi; Nogizaka underground station). It was set up in 1872. This and Tama cemetery in Tokyo's western outskirts, near Fucho, are the capital's largest.

In the cemetery you can see the tombs of many famous Japanese, a large number of whom participated in the Meiji Restoration, among them Okubu Toshimichi (1830-78). Also worthy of mention are three great kabuki actors; Ichikawa Danjuro (the first, ninth and tenth); the politicians Inukai Tsuyoshi (1855-1932), Ikeda Hayato (1899-1965), and Yoshida Shigeru (1899-1967); the novelists Ozaki Koyoo (1867-1903), and Shiga Naoya (1883-1971); Kitazato Shibasaburo (1852-1931), founder of the Institute which bears his name (p. 592); Mikimoto Kokichi (1858-1954), 'king of the Japanese pearl' (see Toba); and General Nogi Maresuke (1849-1912), victor of Port Arthur during the Russo-Japanese war (1904-5), who committed suicide because he did not want to survive his lord, Emperor Meiji (1854-1912).

To the N of Aoyama cemetery is Aoyama dori, which runs from the centre of Akasaka (p. 580) to Shibuya (p. 601). Near Akasaka, this street is bordered to the N by:

AOYAMA PALACE (plan of Shinjuku ku, pp. 598-9; F3). The Palace is surrounded by a huge park which includes the separate Palace of Akasaka and Togu Palace, the official residence of the Crown Prince. During the Edo period, this estate belonged to the lords of Kii and Sasayama. In 1874 it became the residence of the Dowager Empress (Omiya palace).

AKASAKA PALACE (plan: F2; 1½ml/2km N of Aoyama cemetery; 1½ml/2km W of the Imperial Palace, 660yds/600m S of JNR Yotsuya station; 880yds/800m NW of Akasaka-Mitsuke underground station). This palace is to the N of the park. It is built on the site of the former residence of the Kii branch of the Tokugawa clan, and Emperor Meiji lived there during the rebuilding of the Imperial Palace.

The new palace took ten years to build and was opened in 1909. It became the palace of the Crown Prince and also served as an annex to the Imperial Palace. The architect Katayama Toyu drew up the plans in the classical European style for a two-storey building in granite and marble of different colours from France, Italy, Greece and Norway. Many rooms were decorated by French and Japanese painters. Today, Akasaka Palace is placed at the disposal of the foreign guests of the Japanese government.

The traditional ceremony of 'contemplating the chrysanthemums' takes place in the park. Various kinds of these flowers are on show, and the Emperor (the chrysanthemum is his emblem), the Empress and everyone of importance comes to admire them.

D Shibuya ku and Shinjuku ku

Street plan: pp. 598–9.

Ebisu, Harajuku, Okubo, Sendagaya, Shibuya Shinjuku, Shin Okubo, Takadanobaba, Yoyogi JNR stations.

These two districts, which we will consider as a whole, extend to the W of Chiyoda ku (p. 573) and Minato ku (p. 587). The various quarters, some working-class, some residential, are dominated by two important centres, Shibuya and Shinjuku, which provide a large proportion of Tokyo's amusements with their big stores, theatres and cinemas. There are also some large parks in this sector: Shinjuku gyoen and the inner and outer Meiji jingu parks, with the Meiji shrine in the last, are of particular interest. The tallest buildings in Tokyo are found in these districts, as well as the capital's main sporting complexes built for the Olympic Games in 1964 (Yoyogi is an architectural triumph).

From Akasaka Palace (see above), a street running to the N of Aoyama Park takes you W towards Gaien Higashi dori. Just before you reach this street, on the l. is Meiji Kinen kan (plan: E2). This building was once part of Aoyama Palace where Prince Ito Hirobumi read the draft for the first national constitution in the presence of Emperor Meiji. Since the last war this pavilion has been used for marriage ceremonies and other gatherings.

Beyond Gaien Higashi dori you come to the:

OUTER GARDEN OF THE MEIJI SHRINE (plan: D2, D3–E2, E3, ½ml/1km N of Aoyama cemetery; to the S of the JNR stations of Sendagaya and Shinanomachi). This garden is on the site of the former Aoyama parade ground. In the NE of the park you can visit the Meiji Gallery (open daily from 09.00 to 16.30), dedicated to Emperor Mutsuhito and his wife. Inside the massive building, 80 paintings depict the lives of the sovereign and his wife.

The W part of the park is taken up by the sports facilities of the Meiji

Olympic Park, with a stadium seating 85,000, a baseball ground (seats 60,000) a football ground (Prince Chichibu's, seats 20,000), a swimming pool (13,000 spectators), and a boxing ring (seats 20,000). There is also a sports museum (Sendagaya Kokuritsu Kyogio, Shibuya ku; open daily except Mondays from 10.00 to 17.00), which houses souvenirs of Prince Chichibu, the sports enthusiast to whom this museum is dedicated, and photographs and documents on the Olympic Games in Japan and world-wide.

Leave the park at the NW corner, between the swimming pool and the stadium, and pass beneath the railway lines as you go N to Shinjuku dori, which heads W to the centre of Shinjuku. To the S of this street, another runs parallel to it and provides access to:

'SHINJUKU GYOEN (plan: C1, C2–D1, D2; ½ml/1km N of Meiji Olympic Park; 880yds/800m SE of the JNR stations of Shinjuku and Yoyogi). This 143-acre (58-ha) park, where the rarest varieties of cherry tree have been planted, is visited by large numbers of Tokyo residents at weekends. It is a haven of peace close to the hectic activity of Shinjuku, and provides a relaxing place to stop, before once again facing the turbulent metropolis. The Japanese gardens are particularly peaceful.

These gardens occupy almost the entire site of the former residence of the Naito, a daimyo family. The Imperial 'cherry bud' garden party was held here from 1917 to World War II, as was the chrysanthemum festival. In 1927 the funeral of Emperor Taisho, the father of the present Emperor, was held here. Since the war, the gardens have become the property of the state and are open to the public. There is a display of chrysanthemums for several weeks each year starting on 1 November.

A garden in the French style was created here in 1906 by Henri Martinet, the head gardener at Versailles. There is also an English garden with large expanses of lawn. Some of the greenhouses are open to the public and you can see tropical plants such as orchids, cacti, etc. In the Japanese garden is the Taiwan pavilion, made from materials which came from that island.

To the N of Shinjuku gyoen, Shinjuku dori arrives at the centre of:

SHINJUKU plan: B1; 880yds/800m NW of Shinjuku gyoen; 3mls/5km W of the Imperial Palace; JNR and underground stations of Shinjuku). Here is one of Toyko's busiest quarters, frequented in the evenings by a motley crowd of all social backgrounds out on the town. There are cinemas, all kinds of restaurants, bars, night clubs, noisy pachinko parlours, and fortune tellers in dimly lit rooms. By day, Shinjuku is the centre for every kind of gadget and electronic equipment; it has the largest choice and lowest prices for hi-fi, the latest Canon and Nikon models, Walkmans, calculators, etc.; in short, anything which might interest the tourist who can't wait to spend his yen.

To the W of the railway lines, Shinjuku station, one of the capital's busiest, is surmounted by the large stores of Keio and Okakyu which

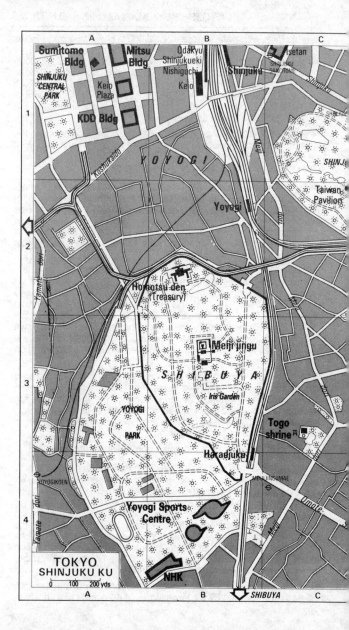

TOKYO
SHINJUKU KU
0   100   200 yds

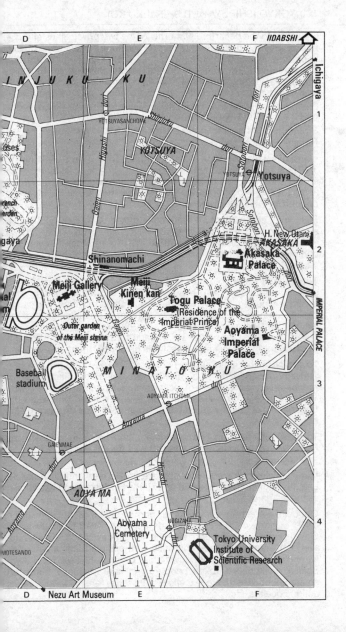

are linked to the departure platforms of the two private lines of those names. Beyond the station tower the capital's highest skyscrapers, impressive buildings between 560ft (170m) and 660ft (200m) tall. They are Keio Plaza hotel, the Shinjuku Mitsui Building, the Shinjuku Sumitomo Building and the KDD Building, all theoretically capable of resisting the strongest earthquake. Surrounded by small traditional houses, these buildings are an extraordinary sight. Between them, a broad main street heads W towards Shinjuku Central Park.

From Shinjuku you can take the train (JNR Yamanote line) to Harajuku station, and visit the:

*INNER GARDEN OF THE MEIJI SHRINE (plan: B3; 1ml/1.5km S of Shinjuku; JNR station Harajuku; Meiji-jingumae underground station). Meiji shrine is in the centre of these gardens which occupy an area of 178 acres (72 ha) and are planted with 130,000 trees given by Japanese people from all the provinces.

Meiji jingu and its gardens were constructed as a result of a public subscription in memory of Emperor Meiji (1854–1912), whose funeral was held in this place. Work started in 1915 and took ten years to complete. Today this is one of the main centres of pilgrimage in Japan.

The original shrine, of great simplicity, was built in the pure Shinto style. Unfortunately, on 1 August 1945, the main building was destroyed during an air raid together with the oratory and some smaller shrines. They were replaced by temporary buildings after the war and, in 1958, were all restored according to the initial plans. The broad *torii* at the entrances were made from hinoki wood brought from Mount Alisan in Taiwan. Festivals on 3 May, 1 and 3 November.

To the N of the main shrine (110yds/100m) is Homotsu den, the Treasury (open daily from 09.00 to 16.30), a building made of reinforced concrete where objects which belonged to Emperor Meiji are on display. You can see the coach in which he rode when the Imperial constitution was promulgated in 1889. It was drawn by six horses.

To the S of the main entrance is an *Imperial garden where the Emperor and his wife, whose health was delicate, used to stroll up and down.

Many species of iris and water lily are grown here and they make a beautiful sight in late June and early July. For this reason it is known as the iris garden.

Opposite the entrance to the inner park of the Meiji shrine, near the JNR station of Harajuku, and between Meiji-jingumae and Omotesando underground stations, is Omote sando, a beautiful avenue planted with trees and lined with splendid little shops. You should not miss strolling down this 'Champs-Elysées' of Tokyo. Stylish, westernized Tokyo people meet here in a very European environment. There are excellent patisseries and sidewalk cafés, antique dealers, etc.

'MUSEUM OF JAPANESE WOODBLOCK PRINTS (plan: C4; JNR Harajuku station; Meiji-jingumae underground station; 1-10-10, Jingu-mae, Shibuya ku; open from 10.30 to 17.00). The museum houses a private collection of 12,000 prints, 500 of which are originals including *Beauty in the Snow* by Koryusai, and *Mount Fuji* by Hokusai, two unique masterpieces. The collection also includes a library of 200 books on Japanese prints and 900 folding screens.

'YOYOGI SPORTS GROUND (plan: B4; 880yds/800m S of Meiji jingu; JNR Harajuku station; underground stations of Meiji-jingumae and Yoyogikoen). To the S of the inner park of the Meiji shrine is this park, which was laid out for the Olympic Games in 1964. Here you can see the remarkable national gymnasium designed by the architect Tange Kenzo, with its metal roof suspended on steel cables from two huge pillars. The adjoining annex is supported by a single pillar in the centre.

To the SW of this complex is the House of Radio (NHK), built by Yamashita Toshiro.

To the S of Yoyogi you come to the centre of:

SHIBUYA (just off plan: B4; ½ml/1km S of Yoyogi; 2mls/3km S of Shinjuku; JNR and underground stations of Shibuya). This very busy, popular quarter lies around Shibuya station, the departure point for several private railways. Shibuya station is renowned as a meeting place where people wait for each other in front of the famous statue of Hachiko the dog. It is a very lively place, mainly inhabited by students and very westernized young people. There are many restaurants and shops.

Shinjuku is bounded to the N by Edo gawa which skirts the modern part of this district between the JNR stations of Takadanobata and Iidabashi. Meiji dori heads N from Shibuya and Shinjuku and crosses this river shortly after crossing Waseda dori, which leads E to:

WASEDA UNIVERSITY (3½mls/6km N of Shibuya; 2mls/3km NE of Shinjuku; 550yds/500m NW of Waseda underground station; ask for directions). Founded in 1882 by Marquis Okuma Shigenobu, it is one of the most important private educational institutions in Japan.

To the N of the University you can visit the Museum of Theatre (I-chome, Totsuka, Shinjuku ku, open daily except Mondays and the day after national holidays from 09.00 to 16.00; closed from 1 August to the 2nd Monday in September), established in memory of Tsubouchi Shoyo (1859-1935), a great dramatist and translator of Shakespeare. This museum, the only one of its kind in Japan, is situated in the University grounds and houses a large number of exhibits; it also has a stage.

E Bunkyo ku

Street plan: pp. 602-3.

Ochanomizu and Suidobashi JNR stations.

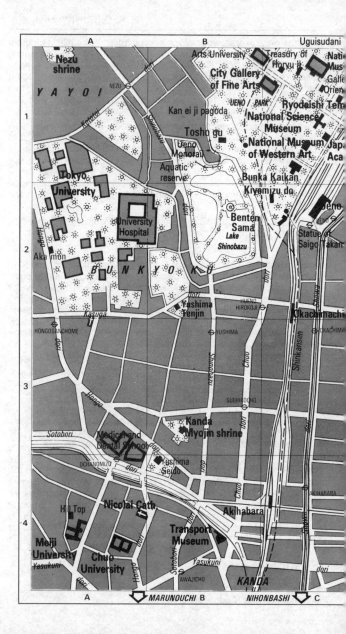

A B Uguisudani

Nezu shrine

Arts University
Treasury of Horyu ji
National Museum
Gallery
Orient

City Gallery of Fine Arts

YAYOI

NEZU

UENO PARK

Ryodaishi Tem

Kan ei ji pagoda

National Science Museum

1

Tosho gu

National Museum of Western Art

Japan Aca

Ueno Monorail

Aquatic reserve

Bunka Kaikan

Kiyomizu do

Tokyo University

University Hospital

Benten Sama

Lake Shinobazu

Ueno

Aka mon

Statue of Saigo Takam

2

BUNKYO KU

Yushima Tenjin

dori

UENO HIROKOJI

Okachimachi

HONGOSANCHOME

Kasuga

YUSHIMA

Chuo

OKACHIMA

Shinkansen

3

Hongo

SUEHIROCHO

Sotobori

Kanda Myojin shrine

Medical and Dental School

OCHANOMIZU

Yushima Seido

Chuo

AKIHABARA

HILTop

Nicolai Cath.

Akihabara

4

Meiji University

Transport Museum

Chuo University

Yasukuni

Yasukuni

Sotobori

AWAJICHO

KANDA

dori

A MARUNOUCHI B NIHONBASHI C

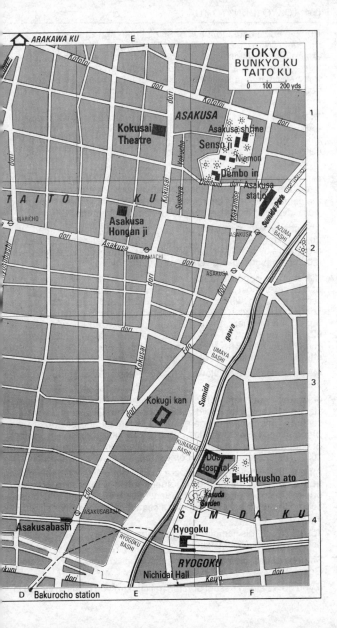

ARAKAWA KU

E

F

1

ASAKUSA

Kokusai Theatre

Asakusa shrine

Senso ji

Nigmon

Dembo in

Asakusa station

T A I T O

K U

NARICHO

Asakusa Hongan ji

Asakusa dori

TAWARAMACHI

ASAKUSA

ASAKUSA

SUMIDA Park

AZUMA BASHI

Kototoi dori

Kototoi

Yakucho

Suchiya

Kokusai

Makamisa

Benuzhi dori

2

gawa

UMAYA BASHI

Sumida

3

Kokugi kan

Kokusai

Edo

KURAMAE BASHI

Dos Hospital

Hifukusho ato

Yasuda Garden

S U M I D A   K U

4

Asakusabashi

ASAKUSABASHI

Edo

Ryogoku

RYOGOKU BASHI

RYOGOKU

kuni

dori

Nichidai Hall

Keiyo

dori

Bunkyo ku, situated to the N of Shinjuku ku and Chiyoda ku, makes up the NW part of old Tokyo. The large numbers of students attending the national and private universities live in this district. It is also a residential area of the capital, with a predominance of small, low houses in a criss-cross of peaceful little streets. Every so often you may come across one of the public gardens which are among the most pleasant in Tokyo.

To the N of Waseda University you can cross the Edo gawa and go up to Mejiro dori which, if you turn l. onto it, goes past Nihon Women's University (founded in 1901) and, if you turn r., takes you to Tokyo Cathedral. Find your way by looking for the bell tower or ask for directions.

SAINT MARY'S CATHEDRAL (880yds/800m NE of Waseda University; ½ml/1km N of Waseda underground station). Built by Tange Kenzo, the cathedral forms a Latin cross at the apex of its arches. The curved walls give the building an impressive feeling of lightness.

The chapel with baptismal fonts, in the form of an open hand, was designed by Seiji Shimizu. The altar is made of Italian marble and the organs are by the Dutchman Verschueren. The bells in the bell-tower (203ft/62m high) were given by West Germany.

*Chinzan so, opposite the cathedral and to the S of Mejiro dori, is one of the city's most beautiful private gardens. The restaurant of the same name, to which it belongs, unfortunately detracts from its charm. The garden used to belong to Prince Yamagata Aritomo during the Meiji era, then to Baron Fujita Denzaburo, who had the 9th-c. three storeyed pagoda transported there in 1925 from the Hiroshima area. The garden was restored and made even more attractive after the war. The lanterns come from Kyoto and Nara.

Mejiro dori leads E to Otawa dori, which leads NW to Shinobazu dori and to:

GOKOKU JI (½ml/1km N of Tokyo Cathedral; 1ml/1.5km SE of the JNR station of Ikebukuro; 550yds/500m SW of Shin Otsuka underground station). This temple is one of the city's largest and belongs to the Shingon sect. It was founded in 1681 in honour of Keisho in, mother of shogun Tokugawa Tsunayoshi, and the main building dates from 1697. The Gekko den (1600) comes from Mii dera (see Otsu vicinity).

Among the temple's treasures are a mandala which probably dates from the Kamakura period. A Kannon inlaid with amber, of Indian origin, is also the principal statue venerated here. The hill which rises behind the temple was made into a cemetery for the Imperial Family in 1873.

To the W of this temple, in Zoshigaga cemetery, is the grave of Lafcadio Hearn (see Matsue).

Shinobazu dori (see below) crosses Kasuga dori to the NE, beyond Gokoku ji.

If you go SE along Kasugi dori for 1ml (1.5km) you come to Denzu in, built in 1602 by Tokugawa Ieyasu in honour of his mother. This temple was rebuilt after the war, and houses a statue of Amida by the priest Eshin (11th c.) and a statue of Daikoku ten of Indian origin.

Shinobazu dori then crosses another street which leads SE to Hisakata cho where you can visit:

TOKYO UNIVERSITY BOTANICAL GARDEN (Koishikawa Sho-Kubutsu en; 1ml/1.5km E of Gokoku ji; 550yds/500m W of Hakusan underground station). The garden belongs to the science faculty. Six thousand different kinds of plants are grown on an area of 40 acres (16 ha). There are also some beautiful trees planted at the end of the 17th c. when these gardens were laid out by the Tokugawa for the purpose of growing medicinal plants.

Shinobazu dori continues NE and crosses Hakusan dori, then Hongo dori. Near this second crossroads, to the NW, you come to:

RIKUGI EN (1ml/1.5km N of the botanical garden; 1½mls/2.5km NE of Gokoku ji; 550yds/500m S of the JNR station of Komagome; 660yds/600m NE of Sengoku underground station; entrance at the E corner of the park). This is a garden designed in the 18th c. by Yanagisawa Yoshiyazu and given to the city in 1934 by Baron Iwasaki. A large proportion of it is taken up by a lake in the centre of which is an island supposed to symbolize Mount Fuji. The garden (25 acres/10 ha) is one of Tokyo's loveliest.

At the corner of Shinobazu and Hongo streets is the oriental library of Toyo Bunko, which specializes in China and the Far East. Today it is part of the Diet library (p. 580).

To the S of Rikugi en, Hakusen dori (see above) joins Kasuga dori, and near where these two main streets cross, to the SW, you will find:

KORAKU EN (2mls/3km S of Rikugi en; 1¾mls/2.8km SE of Gokoku ji; 660yds/600m NW of the JNR station of Suidobashi; Korakuen underground station). The garden extends over 17 acres (7 ha); it used to cover 62 acres (25 ha). It is one of Tokyo's most beautiful gardens, but the view is unfortunately marred by the surrounding buildings.

Koraku en marks the site of the former residence of Tokugawa Yorifusa, first lord of Mito. Its plan was influenced by Shu Shun Sui (1600–59), a Chinese scholar who had taken refuge in Japan and had been taken in by Tokugawa Mitsukuni, lord of Mito.

The lake was designed by Tokugawa Iemitsu and has a little island with a temple dedicated to Benten. The island is connected to the garden by the Bridge of the Full Moon, which is semi-circular and with its reflection in the water makes a complete circle, hence its name.

To the E of Koraku en is an amusement park, a swimming pool, ice rink, a stadium seating 3,800, and the velodrome of Koraku en. Kodo kan, a very famous school of judo and a national centre for the sport, is situated at the corner of Hakusan dori and Kasuga dori.

Beyond Koraku en, Kasuga dori crosses Hongo dori, which takes you N to Aka mon and:

NATIONAL UNIVERSITY OF TOKYO (plan: A2, ¾ml/1.2km NE of Koraku en; 1½mls/2.5km SE of Rikugi en; ¾ml/1.1km NW of the JNR station of Okachimachi; 550yds/500m NE of Hongosan chome underground station). The various faculties of the university are grouped about a landscape garden.

This, the most important university in Japan, occupies the former estate of the Maeda family, who were lords of Kanazawa. Only Aka mon (the Red Gate) remains, erected in 1827 to commemorate an alliance by marriage between the Maeda and the Tokugawa.

The State University was founded in 1869 and is the country's highest educational institution, directly controlled by the State. In its present form it includes faculties of arts, science, law, economics, agriculture, technology and medicine, together with a hospital, laboratories, study rooms, etc. The library was destroyed in 1923, but has been rebuilt and restocked with the aid of many personal bequests. The university also possesses rich archaeological collections (prehistoric collections in particular).

To the N of the university, an important archaeological site was discovered in the Yayoi quarter in 1889. The pottery found here made it possible to identify a stage in Japanese civilization which corresponds to a rapid transition from the Bronze to the Iron Age. This period was given the name of the quarter, Yayoi (3rd c. BC to 3rd c. AD).

To the S of the university, Kasuga dori bends round slightly to the NE. If you continue straight ahead down a side street you come to Yushima Tenjin (plan: B2), founded in the 14th c., then restored by Ota Dokan. It is dedicated to Sugawara Michizane (see Dazaifu, Fukuoka vicinity).

F Taito ku

Street plan: pp. 602–3.

Asakusabashi, Ueno, Uguisudani JNR stations.

Taito ku, bounded to the E by the Sumida gawa, is one of the best-known districts of Tokyo because of Ueno Park and its museums (National Museum), and also because of Asakusa quarter, one of the liveliest areas of the capital with its theatres, cabarets, all-night restaurants, etc. Senso ji is situated here, and it must be one of the few places in the world where the sacred and the secular are so closely intermingled.

Continuing E from Tokyo University, before it comes to the railway lines, Kasuga dori (see above) crosses Chuo dori (p. 583) which continues N to Ueno.

Lake Shinobazu (plan: B2), lying at the foot of the hill on which Ueno Park is situated, is about 1½ml (2km) in circumference.

About five centuries ago, Tokyo Bay came up as far as this lake in the middle of which is a temple dedicated to Benzai ten. There are many lotus plants and a collection of aquatic animals. A monorail connects the lake with Ueno Zoo.

To the E of Lake Shinobazu, Chuo dori comes to the flight of steps which lead to:

UENO PARK (plan: C1; ¾ml/1.2km NE of Tokyo University; 2½mls/4km N of the Imperial Palace; JNR station and Ueno underground station). The park is one of the city's largest parks. It is of special interest because of its monuments and museums.

This park belonged to several daimyo, notably Todo, Tsugaru and Hori. During the Kan ei period (1624–44), the shogun Iemitsu seized it and had all the houses of the daimyo moved. His counsellor, the monk Tenkai, then built Kanei ji for the Tokugawa family, but this temple was burnt down at the time of the Meiji Restoration during a battle between the partisans of the Emperor and those of the Tokugawa. After the Restoration, the whole park was converted into a public garden (1878), and given to the city in 1924.

At the top of the steps mentioned above, you come to Sanno dai or Sakuragaoka, a little platform planted with cherry trees and featuring the bronze statue of Saigo Takamori (1827–77), one of the leaders of the Meiji Restoration. Behind it there is a monument to the Shogitai; *shogitai* is the collective name for the partisans of the last shogun who were opposed to the Restoration.

To the NW of the statue, on the l., is the temple of Kiyomizu do, built in 1631 in imitation of Kiyomizu dera in Kyoto (see entry under that name). If you continue NW, you go past Seiyoken restaurant near which is Ueno belfry, often mentioned in Japanese poems. Next, head in the direction of the pagoda and you will come to Toshu gu which is nearby.

*TOSHU GU (plan: B1) was founded in 1626 in memory of Tokugawa Ieyasu (see Nikko). The present buildings are meticulously decorated and underwent alterations in 1651.

Inside, the treasures include holograph letters by Ieyasu and his descendants and collections of military weapons. The 50 bronze lanterns which surround the shrine were given by various daimyo.

The beautiful five-storey pagoda which towers up in front of this shrine is one of the few remains of Kanei ji. It was moved here in 1957.

To the N of Toshu gu is Ueno Zoo (open daily except the last three days of the year, from 09.00 to 16.30); established in 1882 and given to the city in 1924. This is Japan's most important zoo.

From Toshu gu or the zoo you can go E and rejoin the central path through Ueno Park, Takeno dai, which leads N to the National Museum. Before reaching it, you pass the Metropolitan Art Gallery

(1926) on your l., which houses a series of temporary exhibitions (contemporary Japanese artists in particular), the most interesting being held in autumn.

■ ***NATIONAL MUSEUM** (Tokyo Kokuritsu Hakubutsu kan; plan: C1; 660yds/600m NE of Tosho gu; 880yds/800m N of the JNR station of Ueno; address: Ueno koen, Taito ku; open daily except Mondays from 09.00 to 16.30). The museum was established in 1871 and is today indisputably the most comprehensive and most interesting museum in all Japan. However long you are staying in Tokyo it is well worth a visit.

The museum's main building was constructed between 1932 and 1937 as a replacement for the former Museum of the Imperial Household which had been badly damaged in the 1923 earthquake. The museum and its collections were deeded to the State in 1947.

THE COLLECTIONS AND HOW THEY ARE ARRANGED. The grounds of the National Museum extend over some 25 acres (10 ha.), with the various buildings in the centre. Opposite the entrance gate is the museum's main building (Hon kan) which covers 5 acres (2 ha.). It was built in 1937 and has displays on two floors of the main Japanese collections: sculpture, painting, costumes and fabrics from the past, pottery, lacquerware, armour, etc. To the l. of it is Hyokei kan, which dates from 1908 and is the museum's oldest building. It houses prehistoric and protohistoric archaeological collections from Japan. On the r. is Toyo kan, a gallery of oriental art, completed in 1968. This is the most modern building and contains works of oriental origin (mainly sculpture), from China to the Mediterranean, which have influenced Japanese art. Behind Hyokei kan, Horyuji Homotsu kan (built in 1962) houses the precious works from Horyu ji (see Ikaruga), given to the Imperial Household during the Meiji era (1868–1912). This last building is known as the Shoso in of Tokyo, an allusion to the Shoso in at Nara (see entry under this name). Offices, an auditorium and a restaurant complete the museum's facilities.

The museum is equipped with the latest technology. Apart from devices in case of fire or earthquake, it is supplied with the most advanced equipment for maintaining constant temperature and humidity, and for providing appropriate lighting and ventilation. The exhibits, which are changed from time to time, are displayed in such a way as to enhance their qualities. Not all can be on show at the same time since the museum possesses no fewer than 11,155 paintings, 3,392 examples of calligraphy 3,421 pieces of fabric, 5,162 pieces of pottery, 4,028 examples of lacquerware, 20,053 items of metalwork, and 1,521 sculptures.

We have taken much of our information from the book entitled *Tokyo, le Musée National* (Les Deux Coqs d'or, 1968), with a preface by Okada Jo, Director of the Arts and Sciences Department.

HON KAN

On the ground floor of the main building are displays of sculpture, kimonos and ancient fabrics, *objets d'art* in metal, swords and armour, pottery and architectural scale models. On the first floor you will find paintings, and examples of calligraphy, lacquerware and woodwork. Visitors circulate around the building in an ordered anticlockwise direction in relation to the main façade.

*_Sculpture_ (see Nara, Kyoto, Kamakura). Japanese works relating to Buddhism, some dating back to the Nara period. 'In the history of Japanese sculpture, Buddhist statuary occupies a prominent position. Almost all the sculptures on display in Tokyo Museum belong to different temples, and the collection of Japanese works which actually belongs to the museum itself is in fact very modest' (Okada Jo). Among the works most worthy of note are several statues from the Nara period (Nikko Bosatsu) and Heian (Juni shinsho), and also some works from the Kamakura period, including the famous seated, **Minamoto Yoritomo, in wood of various colours, with eyes inlaid with rock crystal.

The human individual becomes merged with the indefinable, homogeneous forms of the wood which, though worked by the sculptor, still retains its natural hardness, as if to indicate the steadfast unity of the model's character. The legs, folded at a pronounced angle, project with a power which makes this detail the dominant element of the figure. (...) The hands and feet are not prominent; only the head is expressive. It shows the calm and decided reflection of a man of action' (*Tokyo, Le Musée National,* Les Deux Coqs d'or). This statue resembles that of Uesugi Shigefusa, which is kept at Kamakura (see entry under this name).

*_Masks_. 'When speaking of Japanese sculpture, one should not forget the development of the art of mask-making, the oldest masks being those for *gigaku*. It is believed that *gigaku* was introduced into Japan in 612 (twentieth year of Empress Suiko's reign) by a man named Mimashi from Paekche. It was very popular from the Asuka period to the Nara period (...). *Gigaku* was superseded by *bugaku* during the Heian period, and other masks were made for this type of performance. However, from the Muromachi period onwards Noh flourished (...). Noh masks are small and stylized. The delicate face is able to express joy and pain by turns, depending on the actor's movements. There are also some masterpieces among the Kyogen masks, which are very elaborate and comic' (Okada Jo).

**_Costumes_. 'During the modern era, while the various craft activities declined, the art of weaving flourished and articles of the greatest luxury were produced' (Okada Jo). Designs, colours, dyeing processes and weaving techniques enabled very rich costumes to be made, as for example those worn by Noh actors.

*_Objets d'art in metal_. Since the Yayoi period the Japanese have excelled in this art. Tokyo Museum has collected many objects relating to Buddhist worship, as well as articles used in the tea ceremony, which represent a range from the Heian to the Muromachi periods (8th to 16th c.). You will also see mirrors, sword hilts, daggers, harness and Japanese armour of designs which are among the most original in the world: the *koto* are the old sabres from the beginning of the Heian period to the Momoyama period, and the *shinto* are more recent sabres from later periods.

**Ceramics (see Imari, Kaga, Karatsu, Seto). The exhibits are arranged in groups according to the period and place where they were produced, each group possessing its own individuality. Among the most beautiful pieces are a dish decorated with flowers and birds (Kutani pottery, end of 17th c.); a vase decorated with plum blossom by Ninsei Nonomura (Kyoto, 17th c.); a dish decorated with bamboo hedges and vine stems (Nabeshima porcelain, 18th c.). The museum also possesses the *collections of Hirota Matsushige, among which are some very beautiful pieces designed for the tea ceremony (from Bizen or Mino), including some superb Raku.

Architectural scale models. These models are of some of the most famous buildings in Japan: Byodo in at Uji, Yumedono of Horyu ji, etc.

The first floor of Hon kan is almost entirely taken up by paintings. These occupy the place of honour in the museum and make up one of the richest of Japanese collections. Also on display are beautiful examples of calligraphy, and wooden and lacquerware *objets d'art*.

***Paintings. All the Japanese schools up to the 20th c. are represented by outstanding works. Woodcut prints are also an important feature.

Heian period (797-1185): This is essentially distinguished by religious painters influenced by Buddhism, which played an important role in those days (new Tendai and Shingon sects). 'The end of the Heian period saw the emergence of a large number of secular paintings for the decoration of the lords' residences. Decorative paintings on sliding doors (*fusuma*) and folding screens (*byobu*) were much sought after for the houses of high society. The style of these paintings was typically Japanese and was called *yamato e* (Yamato painting) from an ancient name for Japan' (Okada Jo).

**Kujaku Myoo (beginning of the 12th c.) is the 'peacock king', the deified bird which devours snakes. It is one of the oldest and most beautiful paintings in the museum. 'The deity with four arms, symbol of his many powers, is seated with his legs crossed on a lotus flower placed on a peacock with outspread wings. In each of his hands he holds an emblem: a lotus flower, an orange, a pomegranate and a long peacock feather. The background consists of a double iridescent aureole and a wide green and gold nimbus which takes up the feather motif and represents the bird fanning out its tail. In the four corners are little liturgical vases on lotus-shaped pedestals. They contain a half-open lotus bud from which emerges a vajra, sacred symbol of lightning. The composition is strictly frontal and the delicate treatment of the golds and the garments is reminiscent of the miniature' (*Tokyo, le Musée National*).

**Fugen Bosatsu (beginning of the 12th c.) is a painted scroll representing the bodhisattva Samantabhadra, the 'merciful divinity' who is the central character in the popular *Sutra of the Lotus*. The artist has represented him seated on a white elephant in an attitude of quiet prayer, an essentially feminine figure with splendid jewels and rosy skin. The Fujiwara artist has blended the sensual and the spiritual here in a very striking manner.

**Kokuzo Bosatsu (mid 12th c.), 'who bestows wisdom on human beings, appears here in the disc of the moon supported by a rock (…). The lines of the deity's impassive features are extremely fine. The subtlety of this work is characteristic of the aristocratic, effeminate taste of the end of the Heian period' (Akiyama Terukazu, *Japanese Painting*).

**Semmen Hokke kyo are extracts from the *Sutra of the Lotus*, written in calligraphy on fans, with painted scenes from life which seem to be independent of the text. The fans in this collection are mostly kept in Shitenno ji at Osaka (see entry under this name).

You will also see the *Juroku Rakan*, the 'sixteen disciples of the Buddha' (end of 11th c.) which comes from Raijo ji (Shiga prefecture).

Kamakura period (1185–1333): Starting at the end of the Heian period and continuing throughout the Kamakura period, a form of painting developed which is peculiar to the Japanese: *emakimono*, which are scrolls of painted silk which unroll horizontally. Painting in the *yamato e* style found an excellent means of expression on these *emakimono*.

Among these scrolls are **Jigoku Zoshi* (Scroll of the Underworld) and **Gaki Zoshi* (Scroll of the Starving Spectres) which 'were no doubt composed with a view to proselytism between the end of the Heian period and the start of the Kamakura period' (Okada Jo). These scrolls, the most important elements of which are on display in the National Museum, are also exhibited in the museums at Kyoto and Nara.

The museum has in its possession the six scrolls of **Kegon shu*, which were made during the Kamakura period and come from Kozan ji at Kyoto. 'Their distinctive style shows an important change in ideas on drawing. The great freedom of line and the fluidity of colours set this work apart from all those which preceded it' (Théo Lésoualc'h).

From this same temple come the scrolls of **Choju giga*, which are a satirical caricature, using animals, of Buddhist life of the period. However, 'these black and white drawings do not reveal any unity of style or of subject matter. Moreover, in the complete absence of text, it is difficult to understand the significance of each scene or the link which unites the subjects represented on these four scrolls, and several different interpretations have already been put forward' (Akiyama Terukazu).

Heiji Monogatari Ekotoba (end of the 13th c.) is one of the great scrolls in the *yamato* style. Its subject matter is secular and retraces the political disturbances which took place at the end of the 12th c. 'These scrolls are characterized by a series of compositions full of movement and always well balanced. The artist was above all at pains to describe the beauty of the armour and harness which truly reached its highest degree of perfection at this time. Despite the characteristics which were common to work from the same studio, these scrolls exhibit slight differences in their manner of expression. This suggests that the whole series took half a century to complete' (Akiyama Terukazu).

Ippen Shonin Eden (1299) is a 'series of scrolls which recounts the life of pilgrimage of the monk Ippen (13th c.). Shortly after his death, his favourite disciple Shokai, who had always accompanied his master, wrote the story of his life. The painter En i, who had doubtless also accompanied the great monk on his pilgrimages, illustrated this story with forty-eight scenes mounted on twelve scrolls. Contrary to the usual practice of the period, when paper was used as the support for scrolls, this work was carefully executed on silk' (Akiyama Terukazu).

Muromachi period: 'Besides *yamato e*, tinged with lyricism in its harmony of lines and colours, black and white painting using Indian ink (*sumi e*) of the Muromachi period (1337–1573) expressed the spiritual severity of Zen Buddhism (...). The foundations of painting with Indian ink were laid by the monks Nyosetsu and Shubun (*Reading among the Reeds*). With the arrival of Sesshu (*Landscape, Autumn and Winter Landscapes*), Japanese landscapes in ink attained perfection' (Okada Jo). This period also saw the rise of the Kano school (see Kyoto).

The Monk Sien tzu, by the monk Kao Shunen, is one of the first works in Indian ink (beginning of the 14th c.). 'On this scroll, the artist has portrayed Sien tzu, the legendary figure of a hermit monk who together with his companion Chu tou, lived on the animals and above all the small crustaceans which they managed to catch (...) Kao Shunen has represented the monk here with his shrimping net beside a stream, beaming with joy at having caught a crayfish (...). The figure, amusingly caricatured, is sketched with the greatest economy. The style is sober and concise, but succeeds very well in its impressionist effects' (*Tokyo, Le Musée National*).

**Three *Landscapes* by Sesshu. 'The famous painter Sesshu Toyo (1420–1506) achieved the greatest artistry in painting with ink in Japan (...). Strengthened by a visit to China at the height of his creative powers, Sesshu painted with taut brush strokes powerful classical pictures such as *Landscape in Autumn* or *Landscape in Winter* in which one senses the calligrapher's touch. However, he also excelled in the impressionist style of the tachistes, who achieved their beautiful effects by economizing on ink and using marks made by loading the brush to a greater or lesser degree' (D. and V. Elisseeff, *La Civilisation Japonaise*).

Elsewhere you will see a very beautiful realistic portrait below a piece of calligraphy of the monk Ikkyu by Bokusai (16th c.).

Momoyama period (1586-1615): This period is relatively short but full of brilliance. It is partly influenced by the arrival of the Europeans who introduced new pictorial techniques (see Namban Museum at Kobe). In order to assert the prestige of the powerful lords of the period, 'painting was employed to decorate both large surfaces and furniture such as folding screens. *Yamato e*, already decorative in itself, merged with the *suiboku* technique to produce effects of uncommon splendour, with broad, vigorous and dazzling brush strokes. (...) The painters of the Kano school especially devoted themselves to this kind of work, but those of the Tosa school also joined them with great success. It is above all they who were responsible for merging *yamato e* and *kara e* in the Chinese style, of which only the "black and white" of the Song (Sung) and Yuan tradition remained at that time' (*Tokyo, Le Musée National*).

From the Tosa school: *Moonlit Landscape* attributed to Tosa Mitsuyoshi (end of 16th c.).

From the Kano school: **Stroll at Takao*, by Kano Hideyori (16th c.), **Tree, Clouds and Mountain* and *Ch'as fu and the Ox*, by Kano Eitoku (1543-1590); **Pinewood*: 'grace of movement, serenity of tones and freshness of expression characterize the mastery of Hasegawa Tohaku' (Akiyama Terukazu).

Also worthy of note is *A Scene from Country Life*, an anonymous work from the beginning of the 17th c.

Edo period (1615-1867): 'During this period, in addition to the Kano and Tosa schools which were already well established, other schools progressively appeared, among them those of Sotatsu and Korin, the *bunjinga* school ('literary men's painting'), the Maruyama Shijo school, the *ukiyo-e* school with Western leanings' (Okada Jo).

The bridge at Uji, a painted folding screen by an unknown artist, is from the beginning of this period, as is *The Kabuki*, attributed to Hishikawa Moronobu.

The **woodcut prints (ukiyo-e): 'The art of making woodcuts and colour printing belongs more to illustration than to true painting. However, some artists were able to develop a real talent for making the blocks and reproducing the prints. Their reputation was such that they were considered on a level with painters. (...) Some artists, among them Hishikawa Moronobu (1618-94), began to produce woodcuts representing the life of prostitutes from the "flower quarters", or the life of famous Kabuki actors. These works were then called *ukiyo-e*, or "images of a floating world" (Louis Frédéric, *Japon*). The greatest masters of *ukiyo-e* in the 18th and 19th c. were Harunobu Suzuki (1725-70), Kiyonaga Torii (1752-1815), Utamaro

Kitagawa (1753-1806), Hokusai (1760-1849), and Hiroshige Ando (1797-1858). Japanese prints, especially those depicting erotic subjects, enjoyed a great reputation in the West starting in the 19th century.

All the above-mentioned artists are represented in the Tokyo Museum.

You will see the series *Women in the Wind* by Kaigetsudo Ando; portraits of actors by Toshusai Sharaku; thirty-six views of Mount Fuji by Hokusai and fifty-three stages on the Tokai do road by Hiroshige.

****Lacquerware*. Very beautiful collections. The oldest exhibits in lacquered wood date from the Heian period and many of them were made using the '*maki e*' technique which is typically Japanese. The design is made using liquid lacquer mixed with vegetable or mineral colours, then gold or silver fittings are sprinkled over it' (*Tokyo, le Musée National*). The majority of these objects are inlaid with mother-of-pearl and some have been signed by the great artists of the Edo period: Honami Koetsu, Ogata Korin, etc.

****Calligraphy*. The National Museum allows one to follow the interesting development of calligraphy which, while keeping its original Chinese style during the Nara period, is transformed into graceful cursive script of a purely Japanese nature from the Heian period onwards. During the Kamakura and Muromachi period it took on a more vigorous character, while the Edo period saw the return to favour of the old style of writing. From the Heian period you will see some beautiful writings attributed to Ono no Michikaze, and some outstanding examples from the Edo period.

TOYO KAN

The rooms here are on several levels and you will find departments of art from the Mediterranean, South east Asia and the Pacific, from Korea and above all from China. The basement is generally reserved for temporary exhibitions. The arts from the Chinese mainland are particularly well presented, and you can follow their development in sculpture, painting and ceramics.

Among the sculptures is a limestone bas-relief, with scenes showing dancing and cooking, which comes from a Han sarcophagus (2nd c. AD), and a very beautiful head of the Buddha in stone Northern Wei dynasty, 4th c.).

Among the paintings are *Figures under a Tree* a painting on paper (8th c.) from Sin Kiang province; Bodhisattva Kshitigarbha (Tang dynasty, 8th or 9th c.), given by the Guimet Museum in Paris in 1957; *Two Patriarchs Purifying their Hearts*, by Che K'o (period of the Five Dynasties, 10th c.); works from the Southern Song (Sung) dynasty: *Imaginary Voyage in the Siao Siang region*, attributed to Li Long Mien (end of 11th c.); several *works by Liang K'ai (beginning of 13th c.: *Landscape in the Snow, Portrait of the Poet Li Po, The Sixth Patriarch Cutting a Piece of Bamboo*); *Solitary Fisherman on the River*, by Ma Yuan (beginning of 13th c.); *The Genies of Theory and Practice, Han*

Shan and Shi te, by Yen Houei (Yuan dynasty, 14th c.); *Fantastic Landscape* by Li Tsai (Ming dynasty, 15th c.); **Flowers and Birds of the Four Seasons* by Liu Ki (Ming dynasty, by beginning of the 16th c.); *Landscape in the Snow* by Kou Touan (Ming dynasty, 16th c.).

Among the pottery (very beautiful pieces from China and Korea): painted vase from the Yang Chao period (2,000 to 2,500 BC); *glazed pottery (Tang dynasty, 8th c.); pottery from the Song dynasties (11th and 12th c.); beautiful goblets in blue Ch'ao tan or celadon porcelain of the Kuan type (Southern Song or Sung dynasty, 12th c.); *blue and white ceramics from the Yuan and Ming dynasties (14th and 15th c.).

You will also see many lacquered and bronze objects, among them a beautiful Yu vase (Chang Yin period, 11th c. BC).

HYOKEI KAN

The ground floor of this building is devoted to Japanese prehistory since Palaeolithic times, and the first floor is reserved for the Kofun civilization (large sepulchres).

'Until the present era, Japan was at the very edge of the world. Each element in its civilization arrived late to a greater or lesser degree according to the historical circumstances and the geographical distances from the Chinese, Siberian, Indian or Southeast Asian points of origin. Japan's chronology always seems to be on the fringe, always somewhat behind that of the continent, and the cultures sometimes mingle regardless of their initial chronologies (...). The Jomon civilization was brought to light at the end of the last century by the American E.S. Morse, who was the first in Japan to unearth shells amassed by the Jomon people [p. 624] (...). If the Jomon period and the partly nomadic lifestyle of these hunters and fishermen is forgotten today, the same is not true of the strange Jomon pottery, which was decorated by pressing rope into the clay. Its existence enables all finds in Japan dating back before the Bronze Age to be determined (...). The nature of the decorations and the changes in form and volume which succeeded one another over the ages have enabled the Jomon era to be divided into five periods, according to whether the base of the pottery became more rounded or flatter, whether the belly was more or less ornate, or whether the neck widened out to the extent of forming bulky protuberances whose baroque curves are pleasing to the modern eye.

'Agricultural Japan – and one is tempted to say the eternal, unchanged Japan – began in about the 3rd c. BC with the birth or sudden appearance of a highly developed culture, that of Yayoi. This culture was characterized by dominant practice of agriculture, the wide use of the potter's wheel and a knowledge of metallurgy (...). The great quality of people of the Yayoi culture (Yayoi is the name of the pottery which is typical of them) was that they made exceptional progress and quickly learned how to develop the elements of a chalcolithic culture. To the techniques for making bronze were added a whole series of techniques which were to bring about the lightning birth of a complete Neolithic culture on the rich soil of Japan. The potter's wheel meant that pottery with very pure lines could be made, in imitation of the functional metal models.

'For reasons not fully understood as yet, the Yayoi civilization emerged suddenly, at the beginning of the 4th c. AD, into a fully developed Iron Age [the tumuli or *Kofun*, date back to this period] (...). Today, we only have the stylized silhouettes of the *haniwa* from which to gain an impression of these ancient warriors whose energy went into founding the first Japanese State' [see Miyazaki] (D. and V. Elisseeff, *La Civilisation japonaise*).

Among the objects from the periods described above, there are many examples of *ceramics and pottery. You will see figurines in terracotta of anthropomorphic appearance which date from the mid Jomon period. They are known as *dogu*, and their appearance seems to tie in with the time when funeral rites were first practised. Following on from them are the many *haniwa* figurines which the museum has in its possession. The bronze artefacts are represented by weapons, beautiful mirrors, symbolic images of Amaterasu, the Shinto deity *par excellence* (see Ise), and 'bells' in bronze (*dotaku*) whose ancient purpose is still in doubt.

HORYUJI HOMOTSUKKAN

Open only on Thursdays if the weather is suitable (humidity of the air).

The collections extend over two floors and include some of the most beautiful **objects which used to belong to Horyu ji, near Nara (see Ikaruga). Among the loveliest, in particular from the Asuka period, are a little statue of the Buddha, seated (copper covered with gold plate, Asuka period, 7th c.); a **bronze mirror from the 8th c., 18¼in (46.5cm) in diameter; a *Buddhist standard (chiselled and gilded bronze, 7th to 8th c.); *Shotoku Taishi Eden*, illustrated biography of Prince Shotoku (painted panels of folding screens, attributed to Hata no Chitei, 1069); a beautiful group of statuettes depicting *Lady Maya and her followers (gilded bronze, Asuka period). You can also see many examples of calligraphy, textiles, religious objects in bronze and wood, sacred mirrors, *lacquered objects, musical instruments, and *gigaku masks. Most of these objects are of Japanese or Chinese origin.

The garden which lies to the N of the National Museum contains a little lake, a storehouse from the Kamakura period (*azekura* style), Rokuso an (teahouse, 17th c.), Okyo kan (decorated by Maruyama Okyo, 1742), and Kyo kan.

☞ To the W of the National Museum's grounds are the Faculties of Fine Arts and Music of Tokyo University (p. 606). Skirting the National Museum gardens to the W, you can go N to:

 KANEI JI (440yds/400m NW of the JNR station of Uguisudani). It was a very important Buddhist centre under the Tokugawa regime. The temple was built on the site of the National Museum and was burnt down at the time of the Meiji Restoration. The present temple was built on the site of the Daiji in, the former main building of Choraku ji at Serata (Gumma district), and was moved here in 1875.

To the SE of Kanei ji, and to the N of the National Museum, are the tombs of the Tokugawa family (the public is not allowed into the enclosure). The monuments to the shogun Tokugawa Ietsuna (1639–80) and Tokugawa Tsunayoshi (1646–1709) are here. Unfortunately they were damaged during the war. However, a beautiful gate remains with the Emperor's cartouche.

If you continue skirting the National Museum, you will find to the E of it Jigen do or Ryodaishi temple (plan: C1). It contains the portrait of the Grand Master Jigen Tenkai sojo, the founder of Kanei ji (see above).

To the S of the temple is the Japan Academy (Gakushi in), of which there are 150 members divided between the two areas of literature and social sciences, and natural and applied sciences. To the W of this academy is:

NATIONAL SCIENCE MUSEUM (Kokuritsu Kagaku Hakubutsu kan; plan: C1; 550yds/500m N of Ueno station; address: Ueno koen, Taito ku; open daily except Monday from 09.00 to 16.30). The museum was established in 1928 by the Minister for National Education. It houses collections relating to zoology, botany, physical geography, physics, chemistry, astronomy, meteorology, oceanography, space, electricity, and mineralogy. It also contains experimental apparatus, laboratories, a library, and a conference room.

To the S of this museum is the:

**NATIONAL MUSEUM OF WESTERN ART (plan: C1; 550yds/500m S of the National Museum; 440yds/400m N of Ueno station; address: Ueno koen, Taito ku; open daily except Monday from 09.30 to 17.00). The three-storey building is made of reinforced concrete and was built in 1959 according to Le Corbusier's plans in order to house Matsukata Kojiro's collection (1865–1950). It contains masterpieces of Western painting and sculpture.

You can see *sculptures by Rodin, Bourdelle, Maillol and **paintings from the 19th and 20th c., which consist mainly of works by Cézanne (*The Flagon* and *The Tureen; Boating*); Cottet (*Women at the Moulin Rouge*) Courbet (*The Waves; Woman with Naked Breast*), Delacroix (studies); Gaugin (*Little Breton Girls on the Horizon; Brittany Landscape*); Monet (*Poplar in the Sun; Boating; White Waterlilies*); Pissarro (*The Conversation*); Renoir (*Woman with a Hat; Parisian Girls in Algerian Dress*); Signac (*Island of Groix*); etc.

To the S of this museum is the Tokyo Municipal Festival Hall (plan: C1). It is a large building, built for Tokyo's fifth centenary and designed by the architect Maekawa Kunio. The building contains two auditoriums seating 2,300 and 600 people respectively. The acoustics are particularly remarkable.

Nearby is the Japanese Academy of Fine Arts (dance, music, art), a building in the Heian style (architect Yoshida Isoya) used for concerts, conferences, slide shows, exhibitions, ceremonies and plays.

To the SE of Ueno Park is Ueno station (plan: C2), the point of departure for trains serving N, NE and NW Japan. The station was rebuilt in 1932 and is one of the largest in the country. From here, an underground line passing beneath Ueno Park serves the Shinkansen station of Omiya with departures for Morioka and Niigata.

On leaving Ueno station and heading away from Ueno Park, take Asakusa dori in the direction of Sumida gawa.

Just before you come to Tawaramachi underground station you can go N to Asakusa Hongan ji (plan: E2, ½ml/1km E of Ueno station), commonly called Monzeki. This temple was founded in 1657 and was used to receive envoys from Korea. During the war with China (1894–95) it housed prisoners of war. It was destroyed in the 1923 earthquake, and the building subsequently erected suffered during the air raids of 1945, but it has now been restored to its former splendour.

If you continue along Asakusa dori, beyond Kokusai dori and a little before Edo dori you will come to a street specializing in souvenir shops, Nakamise dori, which is lined with stalls. It takes you N to:

ASAKUSA PARK (plan: F1; 1ml/1.5km NE of Ueno station; 660yds/600m N of Asakusa underground station). This park is situated in the midst of one of Tokyo's liveliest districts. The enormous 'amusement quarter' runs parallel to Kokusai dori and you can find theatres, restaurants and 'love hotels' side by side. The dazzling neon signs of the bowling alleys and cinemas are switched on at dusk.

Asakusa Park contains several monuments, among them Senso ji (Asakusa dera) known by the name of Kannon of Asakusa, to whom this temple is dedicated.

The temple has always been famous and is said to have been founded in the 7th c. by three fishermen, Hashino Nakatomo, Hinokuma Hamanari and Takenari, who had caught a small gold statue of Kannon in their nets.

The imposing main building, Kannon do, which dated from 1651, was burnt down during the last war together with the main gate (Nio mon) and the five-tiered pagoda. A replica of Kannon do in reinforced concrete was completed in 1955, thanks to the generosity of the faithful. On the ceiling of the main hall are works by contemporary painters: *Dragons,* by Kawabata Rushi, and *Rain and flowers by the gods*, by Domoto Insho. Nio mon was rebuilt in 1964 and the pagoda was also reconstructed at the same time.

The east gate (Niten mon) and Asakusa shrine (commonly called Sanja sama), to the N of this gate, escaped destruction during the war. The shrine was built on the orders of the third shogun Iemitsu, in memory of the fishermen who founded Asakusa temple. Festival on 17 and 18 May.

 In Asakusa Park you will find Dembo in, with a *landscape garden (which can be viewed on written application), planned in the 17th c. by Kobori Enshu.

½ml (1km) NW of Asakusa Park, via Kokusai dori, you will come to Otori jinja, dedicated, among others, to Yamato Takeru (see Kameyama). In November there is a market here selling bamboo rakes decorated with lucky charms; it always attracts a large crowd.

1ml (1.5km) S of Asakusa Park, via Edo dori (see above) and Kuramae dori, you will come to Kokugi kan (plan: E3), built after World War II for the practice of Sumo wrestling. There are fights in January, May and September. Nearby is the Sumo Museum (2-1-9, Kuramae, Taito ku; open daily except Mondays from 09.00 to 17.00) which houses displays relating to the history of the sport, and objects which belonged to famous champions.

G Sumida ku and Koto ku

Kameido, Kinshicho, Ryogoku JNR stations.

These two districts between Sumida and Ara kawa suffered greatly as a result of the 1923 earthquake. They are criss-crossed by canals and are heavily industrialized, with the land to the S having been reclaimed progressively from the sea. The port of Tokyo is being developed in this area.

Heading E from Asakusa, Asakusa dori crosses the Sumida gawa at Komagata bridge and continues in this direction. When you come to Honjo Azumabashi underground station there is a crossroads with Mitsume dori, which leads N to:

SUMIDA PARK (plan: F2; 880yds/800m E of Asakusa Park; 550yds/500m N of Honjo Azumabashi underground station). The park extends on either side of Sumida gawa.

The part of the park on the l. bank of the Sumida is situated in Mukojima. This used to be one of the most sought-after areas of the capital. Unfortunately, many trees have been cut down and an expressway has been built along by the river, destroying much of its charm.

To the N of the park is Mimeguri jinja, and 440yds/400m N of this shrine is Chomyo ji, dedicated to Benzai ten. Festival the first week in January.

Mitsume dori (see above) leads into Mito kaido, which heads NE to a junction with another main road leading in the direction of Hyakka en and Shirahige bridge.

HYAKKA EN (1ml/1.5km NE of Sumida koen; 440yds/400m SW of Tamanoi station, Tobu Railway from Asakusa), or the garden of the 'hundred flowers'.

This garden was created between 1804 and 1817 by Sahara Kikuu and was restored following damage during the war. Many of the shogun used to come to the pavilion of flowers (also rebuilt), especially Tokugawa Ienari (1773-1841). There is a monument in this garden in memory of famous Japanese poets.

From Komagata bridge (see above), Kototoi dori crosses the districts of Sumida and Koto from N to S.

After the intersection with Kuramaebashi dori, Kototoi runs alongside:

TOKYO TO IREIDO (plan: F4; 1ml/1.5km SW of Sumida Park; 1ml/1.5km S of Asakusa; 550yds/500m NE of the JNR station of Ryogoku). Where you can see Hifukusho ato, the Earthquake Memorial.

On 1 September 1923, the day of the earthquake which claimed 58,000 lives, the inhabitants of Tokyo took refuge on this large, open piece of ground in order to avoid the fires which were springing up all round. However, sparks from the surrounding buildings set fire to the belongings which these helpless people were attempting to save. Surrounded by flames, they were unable to escape, and 35,000 of them were burned alive.

In the three-tiered pagoda, the calcined bones of the victims are contained in the huge urns. This monument is also the resting place for the ashes of the 100,000 civilian victims of World War II, and since 1951 it has been known as the Funeral Building of Tokyo Metropolis for earthquake and war victims (Tokyo to Ireido). The ossuary is below ground.

Behind the monument is the Memorial Hospital of the Fraternity (Doai Kinen Byoin), built with the money from a fund started in America to help the earthquake victims. To the S is Yasuda Garden, partly restored, which was given to the city in 1912 by the baron of that name. Kototoi dori continues S and, just beyond the railway lines, crosses Keiyo dori, which leads to the famous bridge of Ryogoku bashi. This used to be the capital's entertainment area during the Edo period, and Kira Yoshinaka, who was assassinated in 1702 by the 47 *ronin*, had his residence here (see Sengaku ji, p. 591).

For the most part straight as an arrow, Kototoi dori finally bends slightly to the SW as it skirts:

**KIYOSUMI KOEN (1½ml/2km S of Tokyo to Ireido; 1½mls/2.5km E of Nihombashi; 1ml/1.5km S of the JNR station of Ryogoku; ½ml/1km N of Monzennakacho underground station). Although not many people come here, it is one of the most beautiful of Tokyo's landscape gardens.

During the Edo period, Kuze Yamatono kami used to live here. In the 19th c. it became the property of Baron Iwasaki who gave it to the city in 1913. The garden was restored after the war and the beautiful rhododendrons for which it is famous, bloom here.

Kototoi dori continues its course and, before reaching Eitai dori, skirts the western edge of the Fukagawa Park, where you will see the temple of Fukagawa Fudoson and Tomioka Hachiman gu.

After Aioi bashi, Kototoi dori becomes Tsukishima dori, which connects with Harumi dori to the SW (p. 583).

H Additional places to visit

FROM ASAKUSA, take the Tobu Isesaki line (Tobu ER) to Daishimae (12th station). 440yds (400m) W of the station you can visit *Nishi Arai Daishi (Nishi Arai machi, Adachi ku), founded by Kobo Daishi. Here is venerated the statue of Zowo Gongen which dates back to the Fujiwara period (12th c.), and also the statue of Kannon attributed to Kobo Daishi. A third statue representing this priest is said to avert disaster. Festival on the 21st of each month. A beautiful garden wth peonies surrounds the temple.

- **FROM TOKYO** (p. 577) **OR UENO** (p. 618), take the Keihin-Tohoku line (JNR) to:

Nippori, from where you can take the Keisei ER to the Horikirishobuen (5th station). 1ml (1.5km) SW of the station you can visit the Iris Garden or Horikiri (Horikiri Shobu en; Horikiri machi, Katsushika ku), the first gardens where these flowers were cultivated during the Edo period. Today it is only 11 acres (4.5 ha) in size, but it attracts many visitors when the irises are in bloom in mid June.

It is usually necessary to change at Aoto to reach Shibamata (9th station from Nippori). 550yds (500m) NE of the station you can visit *Daikyo ji or Taishaku ten (Shibamata cho 1-chome, Katsushika ku), founded in 1644 by the priest Nitchu (Nichiren sect). In the temple's main hall is a small statue in pearwood of Taishaku ten, attributed to Nichiren. The door into the temple is decorated with beautifully sculpted dragons and tigers which are thought to be the oldest of their kind in existence. This temple attracts many visitors who patronize the little shops which line the long, narrow street leading from the station.

From Kaminakazato you can go 550yds (500m) S of the station to Kyu Furukawa tein (27-2-3, Nishigahara 1-chome, Kita ku), which originally belonged to Mutsu Munemitsu, a famous diplomat during the Meiji period. This garden contains pavilions in the English style and teahouses built of Japanese paulownia wood.

From Oji you can visit the Paper Museum, to the SE of the station (take the S exit from the platform; 1-1-18, Horifune, Kita ku; open daily except Mondays and holidays from 09.30 to 16.30). It contains educational displays on how paper is made, on its many uses, and on the different kinds of oriental and Western paper.

On a hill to the SW of the station is Asukayama Park (Oji machi, Kita ku), which covers 11 acres (4.5 ha). It was planted in the 18th c. by shogun Tokugawa Yoshimune, and is still famous for its cherry trees which flower in April.

½ml (1km) NW of the station is *Nanushi no taki garden (Kishi machi, Kita ku), or the garden of Narumi Waterfalls, famous since the Edo period for its fountains.

 - FROM IKEBUKURO, an important district and commercial centre which has developed since the beginning of the 20th c. Important station in the centre of a very busy quarter.

750yds (700m) S of the station, Kishimojin do, founded in 810 by the priest Jikaku.

850yds (800m) W of the station is Rikkyo University, known to foreigners as Saint Paul's University.

If you take the Seibu-Ikebukuro line (Seibu ER) you will come to:

 The terminus of Toshimaen (6th station), from where you can visit Toshima Park (Mukoyama machi, Nerima ku), 350yds (300m) NW of the station. This is a large amusement park equipped with sports grounds, children's play areas, open air theatres, a zoo, pleasure garden, etc.

Shakujiikoen (8th station), from where you can go to Shakujii Park (550yds/500m SW of the station), a large proportion of which is taken up by Lake Sampoji. Here you can get some idea of what the ancient plain of Musashi used to be like which once surrounded Edo. Nearby is Sampo ji, founded in the 14th c., and Kato Museum (Museum of the Cicadas; Shakujii 2-chome, Nerima ku; open daily from 09.00 to 16.00 except when it rains), which is a branch of the Kato Entomological Institute.

- FROM SEIBU SHINJUKU, where Takadanobaba station (JNR) is situated, you can take the Seibu Shinjuku line (Seibu ER) to:

Araiyakushimae (3rd station along from Takadanobaba), where you can visit:

Arai Yakushi temple (Arai machi, Nakano ku), 550yds (500m) SW of the station, a hermitage in honour of the healing Buddha, founded in 1586 by Umehara Shogen. Here a statue of Buddha attributed to Kobo Daishi is venerated. This temple, known by the name of Kosodate, is frequented by women who wish to have children, or who hope that their sick children may be cured. Festivals on the 8th and 12th of the months of January, May and September.

660yds (600m) N of the station is Tetsugak do (Ekoda 1-chome, Nakano ku), temple of philosophy founded in 1904 'for the education of the spirit' by Dr Inoue Enryo (1859–1919), an eminent philosopher and moralist. Among the buildings is the shrine dedicated to the 'Four Wise Men of the World': Buddha, Confucius, Socrates and Kant. In the garden there is the Pavilion of the Cosmos and the Reimei Kaku pavilion. The festival of philosophy is in November.

- FROM SHINJUKU STATION (p. 597), take the Keio line (Keio Teito ER) to:

Rokakoen (10th station), to visit Roka Park or Koshun en (Kasuya machi, Setagaya ku), ½ml (1km) S of the station, where the house of the novelist Roka Tokutomi (1868–1927) is situated: manuscripts and mementoes.

By changing at Shimotakaido (6th station from Shinjuku), you can go S (3rd station along) to Miyanosaka, where you can visit Gotoku ji (Setagaya 2-chome, Setagaya ku), 330yds (300m) NE of the station. This temple was founded in 1480 by Kira Sakyodayu Masatada, and Ii Naosuke (1814-60), who was assassinated in front of Edo Palace (p. 574), is buried here.

→ Near the station of Shoinjinjamae (3rd station beyond Miyanosaka) you can visit Shoin jinja (Wakabayashi machi, Setagaya ku), founded in honour of Yoshida Shoin (1830-59), a novelist and outstanding educator of the late Tokugawa period. Festival on 17 October. Setagaya road is almost a mile (1.5km) long, and on 15 and 16 December Setagaya Boroichi is held there (a sort of Tokyo flea market).

▬ - **FROM SHIBUYA STATION** (JNR), take the Inokashira line of the Keio Teito ER to:

Komaba Todaimae (2nd station) where, to the N of the station, Tokyo University's Faculty of Liberal Arts is situated. To the W of the precinct you can visit Mingei kan (3-30, 4-chome, Komaba, Meguro ku; open daily except Mondays from 10.00 to 17.00, closed from 1 January to 28 February). Here there is a very important collection of about 20,000 objects relating to Japanese folklore, as well as some from Korea. To the N you will find the Museum of Modern Japanese Literature (4-3-55, Komaba, Meguro ku; open daily except Sundays and holidays from 09.30 to 16.30).

Eifukucho (8th station), where you can go ½ml (1km) N of the station to Omiya Hachiman gu (Omiya koen, Omiya machi, Suginami ku), in the midst of a vast garden, part of which, down by the river Arai, is planted with rhododendrons. Festival on 19 September.

→ 1½mls (2.5km) to the N (or 660yds/600m SW of Higashikoenji underground station) is Myoho ji, rebuilt in 1771. A statue of Nichiren is venerated here, carved by one of his disciples, Nichiro, at the end of the 13th c. Big Oeshiki festival each year in October.

▬ Via the Tokyoko line (Tokyo ER) from Shibuya you can reach:

Yutenji (3rd station), where you can visit Yuten ji (Naka Meguro 3-chome, Meguro ku), 550yds (500m) E of the station. This temple was built in 1719 in memory of the priest Yuten, who is buried in the temple enclosure.

Toritsudaigaku (5th station), from where you can go 1ml (1.5km) NW to Komozawa Olympic Park, about 100 acres (40 ha) in size. Note the athletics stadium, the roof of which does not require supporting pillars.

▬ - **FROM MEGURO** (JNR station), in the centre of a very lively quarter, the outskirts of which are essentially residential.

660yds (600m) W, via Meguro dori, you will come to Otori shrine and can visit the nearby Meguro Kiseichu kan (Shimo Meguro, Meguro ku; open daily from 11.00 to 14.00 except Sundays and holidays). It houses a rare collection of about 4,000 specimens of parasites, the area in which this museum specializes.

Via the Mekawa line (Tokyo ER) you can go to:

Fudomae (1st station) where, 660yds (600m) to the NW, you can visit Ryusen ji or Meguro Fudo (Shimo Meguro, 3-chome, Meguro ku). This temple was founded in 808 by Ennin (Jikaku Daishi) who, following a dream, made the statue of Fudo which is venerated here. Hon do, of recent construction, has a painted ceiling (dragon) by Kawabata Ryushi. In the gardens to the NE of the temple, Rakan ji houses the statues of the 300 Rakan, sculpted by Matsuoka Genkei in the 17th c. Festival on the 28th of each month. On 28 October, sweet potatoes are given away. These were introduced into Japan by Aoki Konyo (1698-1769), who is buried nearby.

- **FROM THE JNR STATION OF SHINAGAWA** (p. 590), take the Keihin Tohoku line (JNR) to:

Oimachi, where you can take the Denen Toshi line (Tokyu ER) to:

Kohonbutsu (10th station) where, 110yds (110m) N of the station, you can visit *Joshin ji, the temple of the nine Buddhas (Okusawa 7-chome, Setagaya ku), founded in the 17th c. on the site of Okusawa Castle. Hon do dates from 1698, and Nio mon from 1793. Big festival of Bon matsuri 16-18 August.

Kaminoge (13th station) where, 550yds (500m) S of the station, you can visit Goto Bijutsu kan (3-9-25, Kaminoge, Setagaya ku; open daily except Monday from 09.30 to 16.30), in the style of the Heian period. It houses the collections of Goto Keita which include the famous *Genji Monogatari scrolls (ink and paintings on silk) from the Heian period (see Tokugawa Museum at Nagoya).

Omori, in the centre of a residential quarter frequented by the businessmen of Tokyo and Yokohama.

To the N of the station, a monument indicates the site where prehistoric remains were discovered during a dig carried out by the American professor E.S. Morse.

1½ml (2km) SW of the station (bus) the temple of Hommon ji (½ml/1km) S of Nishimagome underground station; Ikegami Hon machi, Ota ku), the main centre of the Nichiren sect, is situated on a wooded hill. Apart from the five-tiered pagoda, built in 1608, and the pavilion of the *sutra*, all the buildings were destroyed in April 1945 and have been gradually rebuilt since. In the temple you can see a wooden statue of Nichiren (1222-82; see Kamakura), who died near the ancient village of Ikegami. Big Oeshiki festival each year on 12 October.

Katamata, where (550yds/500m to the S) Umeyashiki is situated, a garden of age-old plum trees where, at the beginning of the Meiji period, the great men of government used to like to meet.

Via the Ikegami line (Tokyo ER), from Katamata station, you can go to:

Ikegami (2nd station), 880yds (800m) S of Hommon ji (see above).

Senzokuide (8th station), near Senzoku Pond. Here you can see a statue of Nichiren, who used to come here to perform his ablutions, and a monument to Saigo Takamori (1827-77, see Kagoshima).

Via the Keihin Kyuko line (Keihin Kyuko ER; direct services from Shimbashi) from Shinagawa (see above), you can go to:

Aomono Yokocho (4th station). 440yds (400m) to the W you can visit Kaian ji (Minami Shinagawa 3-chome, Shinagawa ku), founded by Hojo Tokiyori (13th c.). This temple owes its name (*kaian*, calm sea) to a legend which recounts that a statue of Kannon of the thousand hands was found in the stomach of a shark. At the moment of the animal's death the storm which was raging suddenly abated.

Anamori Inari (4th station, on the Haneda branch line), near the shrine of this name, which is approached up a long avenue of *torii* painted in red.

Hanedakuko (15th station), from where you can go 880yds (800m) E to Haneda airport (monorail from Hamamatsucho, p. 587), built near the, sea and put into service in 1931.

I Vicinity of Tokyo

CHIBA, CHOFU, FUCHU, HACHIOJI, KAMAKURA, KAWASAKI, NARITA, YOKOHAMA, NATIONAL PARKS OF CHIBU TAMA, FUJI-HAKONE-IZU AND NIKKO: see entries under these names. These destinations are suitable for full or half-day excursions from Tokyo. Ask for information at the tourist agencies.

Tomakomai (Island of Hokkaido)

Railway map on inside front cover.

Tokyo, 672mls (1082km) – Asahikawa, 114mls (184km) – Hakodate, 157mls (252km) – Otaru, 66mls (106km) – Sapporo, 42mls (67km).

Hokkaido – pop: 192,000 – industrial city (paper making, industries using wood, iron and steel industry) and port.

Tomakomai is one of the busiest cities in Hokkaido. Its population has almost doubled in ten years. It was a modest fishing port during the Edo period, but today it is the main centre for the making of newsprint and adjoins a vast artificial harbour completed in 1963. Together with the town of Muroran (see entry under this name), about 37mls (60km) to the W, Tomakomai constitutes one of the most advanced sectors of industrial activity in Hokkaido.

VICINITY

1 SHIRAOI (14mls/22km SW; JNR train; coach). 550yds (500m) NE of the station, on the edge of the little lake of Poroto, you can visit the Ainu village of Shiraoi, which is one of the best known in Hokkaido.

Here you can see half a dozen thatched dwellings, once you have made your way between the numerous souvenir shops. The chief's house is the most interesting, with a little museum displaying a number of objects and presenting scenes from Ainu life (see Hokkaido).

2 BIRATORI (62mls/100km E, partly via the N235; JNR train as far as Saru station, then coach for 8mls/13km), another Ainu village in the Saru valley, which is bordered by steep hills. Behind this village there used to be a fort where a shrine was built in 1799 in honour of Minamoto Yoshitsune, who is said to have found refuge in this region after escaping from the battle of Koromogawa (see Chuson ji, in the vicinity of Ichinoseki).

3 MURORAN, SHIKOTSU TOYA NATIONAL PARK, see entries under these names.

◼ Tomioka (Island of Honshu)

Tokyo, 80mls (128km) - Fukushima, 194mls (312km) - Maebashi, 19mls (31km) - Nagano, 75mls (121km) - Niigata, 190mls (306km) - Urawa, 63mls (102km) - Utsunomiya, 90mls (145km).

Gumma ken - pop: 48,000 - spinning.

Situated on a tributary of the Tone gawa, Tomioka was the first Japanese town to put into practice, from 1872 onwards, a modern method of weaving raw silk, called the Tomioka method.

VICINITY: MYOGI SAN (22mls/36km NW as far as Matsuida; Joshin Etsu ER train as far as Shimonita, then coach). Leave Tomioka to the W by the N254.

8mls (13km): Shimonita, terminus of the private line, from where you continue by the same road.

11mls (17km): side road to the r. towards Myogi san.

10mls (16km) to the W, via the N254, then another road (coach from Shimonita): Kozu pasture, cattle-rearing area with walks on the slopes of Arafune san (4,668ft/1,423m), which it is possible to climb.

13mls (21km): a *toll road branches off to the l. skirting the slopes of Myogi san.

*Myogi san consists of Mounts Haku un (3,547ft/1,081m), Kinkei (2,808ft/856m) and Kondo (3,740ft/1,140m). Kondo lies to the W and is the summit of this ancient volcano which erosion has sculpted into cliffs, steep slopes, and strangely shaped isolated rocks. From the summit (about half an hour's climb), there is a view over the Kanto basin and the neighbouring mountains which make up the *Myogi Arafune Saku kogen Regional Park.

At the foot of this mountain is the Myogi shrine, built in the shade of a magnificent wood of tall Japanese cedars.

22mls (36km): Matsuida, from where you can go by train (JNR) to Annaka and Takasaki (see entry under this name).

Tosa (Island of Shikoku)

Map of Shikoku (Inland Sea), pp. 536–7.

Tokyo, 552mls (889km) – Kochi, 10mls (16km) – Matsuyama, 75mls (121km) – Takamatsu, 171mls (276km) – Tokushima, 134mls (216km).

Kochi ken – pop: 32,000.

To the W of Niyodo gawa, Tosa bears the name of the ancient province in which it is situated, now known as Kochi prefecture. This region is famous for the magnificent breed of dog which bears its name.

VICINITY

*YOKONAMI SANRI** (17mls/27km as far as Susaki, coach). To the S of Tosa you come to Usa, and from there, after crossing the toll bridge over the narrow sound of Yokonami (which extends for about 7½mls/12km), you arrive at Shiraga hana and the south coast, with the Pacific Ocean beyond. A toll road follows the coast, which is beautiful here and has little islands dotted along it.

Tottori (Island of Honshu)

Railway map on inside front cover.

Tokyo, 428mls (689km) – Hiroshima, 186mls (300km) – Kobe, 119mls (191km) – Matsue, 83mls (133km) – Okayama, 85mls (137km).

Principal town of Tottori ken – pop: 118,000.

Near the mouth of the Sendai gawa, on the Sea of Japan, Tottori is situated in the midst of a plain blocked off to the N by a famous sand hill. The city has become one of the principal economic centres of San in, the northern façade of Chugoku.

From the station, one of Tottori's main streets heads NE through the city to the Prefecture.

220yds (200m) from the station it crosses a street down which, on the l., is situated the *Tottori Museum of Popular Art (Sakae cho, open daily except Monday). This museum occupies an old, restored granary similar to those at Kurashiki (see entry under this name). The most interesting collections are of local furniture, lacquerware and pottery from the past.

A circular building nearby houses a collection of statuettes of Jizo Bosatsu from the Tottori region.

To the NW of the Prefecture, Hisamatsu Park (1ml/1.5km N of the station) occupies the site of the former castle of Tottori. Today, only a few traces of the moats and ramparts remain.

This castle was built in the 16th c. by Yamana Masamichi. It then came under the control of the Mori clan and, in the 17th c., was entrusted by the Tokugawa to the Ikeda clan.

To the N of the castle is a cable-car to Hisamatsu yama, from where there is a view over the famous Tottori dunes and the sea.

1ml (1.5km) SE of the castle (1½ml/2km NE of the station; bus) you can visit the attractive shrine of Ochidani, built in 1650 in honour of Tokugawa Ieyasu. Behind it is Ochidani Park.

770yds (700m) SW of Ochidani jinja (ask for directions) is the little temple of Kannon which is surrounded by a pretty landscape garden. garden.

VICINITY

1 YOSHIOKA ONSEN (7mls/12km W; coach): spa (springs from 106° to 131°F/41° to 55°C) reached by skirting to the S the vast lagoon of Koyama, dotted with little islands.

2 AOYA (16mls/25km W, via the N9; JNR train; coach). As they leave Tottori, the road and the railway line cross the Sendai gawa and run along to the N of Koyama lagoon. Tottori's coastal strip of dunes separates the road from the Sea of Japan which can be reached from Hakuto beach.

11mls (17km): road to the l. to Ketaka and 1½ml/2km) the spa of Hamamura, where the springs spout up out of the sand.

16mls (25km): Aoya, from where you can go N to the attractive beach of Natsudomari, sheltered to the E by Nagao Point.

3 DAISEN OKI AND SAN IN KAIGAN NATIONAL PARKS, see entries under these names.

Towada Hachimantai (National Park; Island of Honshu)**

Map of Tohoku, pp. 232–3.

HOW TO GET THERE

- From Aomori, take the coach to Nenokuchi (38mls/61km) and Yasumiya on the shores of Towada Lake. You can also go by train (JNR) to Towada Minami station (72mls/116km in 1h. 50) from where you can get to Towada ko, or to Hachimantai station (81mls/130km in 2h. 15), from where you can cross Hachimantai Plateau.

- From Hirosaki (25mls/41km SW of Aomori) or Kuroishi (7mls/11km NE of Hirosaki), you can go by coach to Nenokuchi (39mls/63km SE of Hirosaki), to the NE of Towada ko.

- From Morioka, you can take the train (JNR) to Hachimantai (52mls/83km in 1h. 15) and Towada Minami (60mls/97km in 1h. 40), from where, as above, you can get to Lake Towada or Hachimantai Plateau. From Morioka it is also possible to go to Obuke station (17mls/28km N) in order to cross Hachimantai Plateau.

- From Towada, on the N4, between Aomori and Morioka, you can take the coach to Nenokuchi and Towada ko.

Towada Park and Hachimantai Plateau are the two main features of this national park (205,964 acres/83,351 ha), one of the most beautiful in northern Japan. The great Ou mountain chain, of volcanic origin, is the dominant geographical characteristic of this area. Iwate san (6,696ft/2,041m; see Morioka) is the highest point.

1 FROM TOWADA MINAMI TO AOMORI (6mls/10km N, partly by the N103; coach from Yasumiya station, boat from there to Nenokuchi, then coach to Aomori). From Towada Minami station, the N103 takes you NE to:

4mls (7km): Oyu spa.

1½ml (2km) SE: *Nonakado megalithic circle, which is said to be a prehistoric sun dial. This construction is unique, being in the form of a standing stone around which smaller stones are arranged lengthwise like the spokes of a wheel.

14mls (22km): the N104 branches off to the r., and you can take it to go and see (1ml/1.5km E) Choshi waterfall.

17mls (28km): *Hakka gote (alt. 2,123ft/647m), from where unexpectedly you see the whole of Lake Towada before you.

22mls (36km): Yasumiya, to the S of Lake Towada, and W of Nakayama promontory. From there we recommend continuing by boat (approx. 1h.) to Nenokuchi.

To the N of Yasumiya you can visit Towada shrine, dedicated to Yamato Takeru (see Kameyama), and go on to Ouranaiba, the furthest point on Nakayama promontory. On the shores of the lake are the statues of two young girls in gilded bronze, a memorial to Takeda Chiyosaburo, Ogasawara Koichi and the writer Omachi Keigetsu who popularized this place at the end of the 19th c.

**Towada ko (23sq.mls/59km^2; alt. 1,316ft/401m) is 1,240ft (378m) deep. The lake was formed in a crater and it is one of the largest and deepest in Japan. It is surrounded by wooded hills and dominated to the E by Herai dake (3,802ft/1,159m). To the S, two promontories jut out into the water: Nakayama and Ogura. They divide the southern part of the lake into three distinct bays, their steep rocks plunging sheer into the water. Excellent views from the top of these rocks. The boat skirts round each of the promontories in turn.

27mls (44km): Nenokuchi, from where you can climb Onko dake (3,458ft/1,054m): beautiful view over the whole of the lake.

39mls (63km) NW, along the N102 (coach), you come to Hirosaki (see entry under this name), after climbing once again above the level of the lake and, beyond Takinosawa toge, joining the valley of the Hiyakko gawa, on the banks of which are several spas, among them Kuroishi.

From Nenokuchi, the N102 runs along the beautiful valley of *Oirase keiryu, with its maplewoods and with the outflow from Towada ko to the NE. Several waterfalls cascade down the rocks which line the river's course.

36mls (58km): Yakeyama, small spa. You leave the Oirase gawa valley and the N102 and head NW towards Aomori.

39mls (62km): Tsuta Onsen, a spa whose location in the woods was praised by Omachi Keigetsu. There are several small lakes nearby.

48mls (78km): Sukaya Onsen, from where you can climb Hakkoda san (see below). Tohoku University has an institute for research into alpine plants at this spa.

53mls (85km): cable-car to Hakkoda san.

*Hakkoda san is an ancient volcano with eight summits, of which O dake (5,194ft/1,583m) is the highest. In clear weather there is a view over Mutsu Bay, the Sea of Japan and the Pacific Ocean. Beautiful forests cover the slopes and there is skiing in winter.

66mls (106km): Aomori, see entry under this name.

2 FROM HACHIMANTAI TO OBUKE, across Hachimantai plateau (39mls/63km SE; coach). From Hachimantai station you can go S to:

11mls (18km): Toroko; spa where the Hachimantai toll road branches off; very beautiful route.

34mls (54km) SW, along another road (coach): Tazawako (see vicinity of Omagari) is reached via the spa of Tamagawa (springs at 208°F/98°C), Yoroibata dam and the Tama valley, which lies between Tazawa lake and Komaga lake.

The **Hachimantai area of high mountain plateaux extends over about 101,313 acres (41,000 ha). It is a volcanic region, in which the main peaks are Iwate (6,696ft/2,041m; see Morioka), Komaga (5,371ft/1,637m, see Omagari), Hachimantai (5,295ft/1,614m), Chausu (5,177ft/1,578m) and Yake (4,482ft/1,366m). Paravolcanic phenomena still frequently occur in this region (bubbling mud, emissions of steam, patches of sulphur) and there are many hot springs; Fukenoyu, Goshogake and Tamagawa are among the most famous. The whole area is carpeted with alpine flowers and forests grace the mountain slopes.

28mls (45km): Goshogake Onsen, at the end of the toll road; spa at an altitude of 3,609ft (1,100m), with several volcanic phenomena in the vicinity. It is possible to climb Chausu yama (5,177ft/1,578m), from where there is a wide view. There is also a cable-car.

39mls (63km): Obuke, JNR station from where you can go by train to Morioka, see entry under this name.

Toyama (Island of Honshu)

Railway map on inside front cover.

Tokyo, 270mls (434km) – Gifu, 165mls (266km) – Kanazawa, 40mls (64km) – Nagano, 162mls (261km) – Niigata, 155mls (249km).

Principal town of Toyama ken – pop: 290,000 – textile, chemical and pharmaceutical industries.

Near the mouth of the Jinzu gawa, on Toyama Bay, this ancient feudal town has, from its earliest days, put to good use the paddyfields which extend over the surrounding plains. The Maeda clan were responsible for making it into an industrial town and, from the 17th c. onwards, its products were exported to China, Korea and Southeast Asia. Today, Toyama is still a busy commercial centre and an important railway destination; the harbour suburb of Higashi-Iwase provides the commercial outlet. It is also the centre of traditional herbal medicine in Japan.

In the city centre you can see the site of the former castle of the Maeda (1,000yds/900m S of the station), today a public garden.

The Jimbo built a castle on this site in the 16th c., and Sasa Narimasa seized it in 1581. He was ousted a few years later by Maeda Toshiie, who gave Toyama to his grandson Toshitsugu. The family lived there until the Restoration in 1868, and encouraged the economic development of the town.

VICINITY

1 KUREHA YAMA (2½mls/4km W; coach); public park laid out on a wooded hill with a view over the city and surrounding area, in particular the majestic Tate yama chain (see Chubu Sangaku National Park).

2 YATSUO (8½mls/14km S; JNR train; coach); spa and traditional centre of Japanese papermaking. Himpo ji makes an interesting visit, with its 20 or so listed Buddhist paintings.

3 KANAZAWA, TAKAOKA, TAKAYAMA, CHUBU SANGAKU NATIONAL PARK, see entries under these names; **NOTO PENINSULA,** see Hakui, Nanao, Wajima.

Toyohashi (Island of Honshu)

Railway map on inside front cover.

Tokyo, 170mls (274km) – Gifu, 66mls (107km) – Nagano, 197mls (317km) – Nagoya, 42mls (68km) – Shizuoka, 66mls (107km) – Tsu, 88mls (142km).

Aichi ken – pop: 275,000 – industrial city: textile factories, silk conditioning.

Situated in the bay at the mouth of the Toyo gawa, this ancient feudal town has become one of the busy centres around Tokai do, at the confluence of the great natural waterway drained by the Tenryu gawa. Today, the city is heavily industrialized and overflows into the bay itself where land has been reclaimed from the sea all along the eastern side.

½ml (1km) NE of the station, overlooking the city and in a loop of the Toyo gawa, a public garden has been laid out on the site of the former castle of Toyohashi.

The castle was built at the end of the 15th c. by Makino Naritoki. It had various owners, including the Imagawa, the Ikeda, the

Matsudaira and finally, from 1712 to 1868, the Okochi who were connected by marriage with the Matsudaira.

☞ **VICINITY**

1 IRAKO MISAKI (29mls/46km SW, via the N259; or Toyohashi Railway train to Mikawa Tahara, then coach). This point marks the tip of Atsumi peninsula, which closes off Mikawa Bay to the S. Near here you can see Irako shrine and the marine arch of Hii. From Irako misaki you can take a boat to Morozaki, Nishiura or Toba, or you can return along a road which follows the Pacific coast. Attractive seascapes on either side of the peninsula.

2 GAMAGORI, HAMAMATSU, see entries under these names.

■ Tsu (Island of Honshu)

Map of Places of Interest, p. 70.

Tokyo, 258mls (416km) – Gifu, 65mls (104km) – Kyoto, 61mls (98km) – Nagoya, 46mls (74km) – Nara, 65mls (104km) – Otsu, 53mls (86km) – Wakayama, 103mls (166km).

Principal town of Mie ken – pop: 132,000 – industrial town.

At the mouth of the Ano gawa, Tsu used to be called Anotsu, and was one of Japan's main ports for trade with China. The Taira had their naval base there, but a series of earthquakes at the end of the 15th c. put an end to the town's maritime activities.

330yds (300m) SW of Tsu station (JNR and Kintetsu) you can visit the attractive park of Kairaku, which is situated on the slopes of a hill to the W of the city. From here there are fine views over the city and Ise Bay.

This park used to belong to the Todo family who governed the town of Tsu. You can visit the regional museum where there are collections relating to art and archaeology.

If you leave the park and cross the railway lines to the S of the Prefecture, you come to Shitenno ji on your r. (770yds/700m S of the station). This is one of Tsu's most beautiful temples, established in the 7th c. by Prince Shotoku (see Ikaruga).

The temple's main building was reconstructed in 1615 and houses portraits of Prince Shotoku and a lord of Todo, as well as a wooden statue of Yakushi Nyorai.

To the SE of this temple you cross the Ano gawa. From here to the Iwada gawa runs a broad avenue, the most beautiful in the city, where Tsu town hall is situated.

To the E of this main street, via Higashi machi, you can reach Kannon ji (1ml/1.5km S of the station), one of the most famous temples dedicated to Kannon, the goddess of mercy. Like that of Asakusa in Tokyo (p. 618), it is situated in the midst of a boisterous amusement quarter.

To the W of the central street, level with the Town Hall, you come to Tsu Castle, now a public garden. The tower has been rebuilt.

The castle was given by Oda Nobunaga in 1575 to his son Nobuo. It was owned by the Todo from 1608 to 1868.

Immediately to the S of the Iwada gawa, 1ml (1.8km) SE of Tsu Castle, on the edge of Ise Bay, is the lovely beach of Aoki (1ml/1.8km E of the JNR station of Aoki).

Finally, to the S of the city, ½ml (1km) SE of Aoki station (2mls/4km S of Tsu station), you can visit Yuki shrine dedicated to Yuki Munehiro. He was a partisan of Emperor Go Daigo in the 14th c., and upheld his cause against Ashikaga Takauji. Festival on 1 and 2 May when there is a sumo contest.

VICINITY

1 ISJINDEN (2½mls/4km NW: JNR train; coach); near the station you can visit Senshu ji, founded in the 13th c. by the priest Shinran in the Tochigi prefecture and transferred to this site in the 17th c. Hon do houses a statue of Amida, donated in the 18th c. by Emperor Sakuramachi, and Miei do contains a statue of the priest Shinran, which dates from the 17th c. The temple also has several painted scrolls from the Kamakura period and a handwritten document by the priest Shinran.

2 SAKAKIBARA ONSEN (9mls/15km W; coach), among wooded hills where there are several hot springs. Near here the pile of Kaiichi shells was discovered.

3 AOYAMA KOGEN (26ml/42km W; via the N165 and a toll road; coach). This mountainous region which rises to an altitude of 2,772ft (845m) is part of the Akame Ichishikyo Regional Park from where you can see over Ise Bay and the Kizu gawa basin. To the SE is the outline of the Ise shima peninsula.

4 KAMEYAMA, ISE SHIMA NATIONAL PARK, see entries under these names.

Tsuchiura (Island of Honshu)

Tokyo, 41mls (66km) – Chiba, 47mls (75km) – Fukushima, 150mls (242km) – Mito, 30mls (49km) – Urawa, 62mls (100km) – Utsunomiya, 60mls (97km).

Ibaraki ken – pop: 112,000.

Near one of the arms of the vast lagoon of Kasumi, Tsuchiura is in the heart of the Suigo Tsukuba Regional Park, and is therefore a good point of departure for a number of excursions. Famous park of cherry trees on the banks of the Sakura gawa, 'river of the cherry trees'.

VICINITY

1 KASUMIGA URA (boats on the lake in summer), to the E of Tsuchiura, is set in a landscape typical of the S of Ibaraki prefecture, where water is the dominant feature. It is one of the biggest lakes in Japan (69sq.

mls/178km²) and has its outflow to the SE between Kashima and Sawara (see entries under these names) in the direction of Kita ura and the Tone gawa.

2 IWASE (26mls/42km N; Kanto Railway train). Take the N125 out of Tsuchiura.

11mls (17km): Hojo, where you leave the N125 and continue up the valley of the Sakura gawa.

12mls (20km): Tsukuba, from where you can go to:

→ 2½mls (4km) E (coach): Tsukuba shrine, from where you climb *Tsukuba san: wooded mountain with two peaks, Nantai (masculine 2,854ft/870m) and Nyotai (feminine, 2,874ft/876m), each of which has a little shrine on top and affords *beautiful views. Mount Fuji is visible in clear weather. A toll road runs S along the mountain ridge for about 6mls (10km).

19mls (31km): Makabe, at the foot of the N side of Tsukuba san.

→ 1ml (1.5km) SE you can visit Densho ji, founded in 1268 by the priest Hosshin, a native of Makabe. The temple, which once came under the estate of the Asano, contains statues of the 47 *ronin* (see Sengaku ji in Tokyo, p. 591). Surrounded by beautiful cherry trees.

26mls (42km): Iwase, where, 1½ml (2km) N of the station, you can visit the temple of Tomiya Kannon or Oyama ji. It has a beautiful three-storeyed pagoda dating from 1465.

→ 2½mls (4km) E (JNR train): Haguro where, 1ml (2km) NW of the station, you will find Isobe shrine, surrounded by Sakugarawa Cherry Tree Park. Cherry blossom in April.

■ Tsuruga (Island of Honshu)

Map of Places of Interest, p. 70.

Tokyo, 290mls (467km) – Fukui, 40mls (64km) – Gifu, 73mls (118km) – Kanazawa, 89mls (143km) – Kyoto, 62mls (100km) – Otsu, 55mls (88km).

Fukui ken – pop: 68,000 – port.

At the head of a narrow bay protected to the NW by Tateishi misaki, Tsuruga occupies a beautiful site on the Sea of Japan from where you can go N along the Echizen coast or explore the rugged shore of Wakasa Bay. The second Japanese nuclear power station was built in the Tsuruga region in 1969.

From early times, Tsuruga was the outlet on the Sea of Japan for Yamato and was the first port to have trading relations with Korea and even Eastern Siberia. The town was very prosperous in the Nara period but experienced a certain decline during the Kamakura period, when it served as a base for punitive expeditions against the populations in the N of the country. Near Tsuruga, Go Daigo's partisans put up a vain fight in 1337 against the armies of Ashikaga Takau ji.

Ⱥ In the town, ½ml (1km) N of the station, you can visit Kehi jingu, dedicated to Emperor Chuai and his wife the Empress Jingu. The high *torii* of this shrine was made with wood which is said to have drifted from Sado island. Festival from 2 to 5 September.

Ⱥ If you continue N from this shrine, 1½ml (2km) N of the station you will come to Kanagasaki gu, dedicated to Takanaga and Tsunenaga, sons of Emperor Go Daigo.

These princes, supported by General Nitta Yoshisada, entrenched themselves in the castle which used to stand on this site. They were attacked by Ashikaga Takau ji and met their death here.

An attractive park with cherry trees surrounds the shrine, and there is a view over the town and Tsuruga Bay.

1½mls (2.5km) NW of the station (bus), near the coast, is the vast park of Kehino Matsubara, which includes a beach bordered by pines. Motor launches in the bay. The shrine of Matsubara is here, dedicated to Takeda Kounsai (1803–65) and his partisans.

A native of Mito region, Kounsai had sided with the Imperialist movement and rebelled against the agreements made by the Tokugawa with the foreigners. He took refuge here and was forced to commit suicide.

⌐ **VICINITY**

1 TATEISHI MISAKI (10mls/16km N; coach as far as Jogu jinja).

5½mls (9km): Jogu jinja, founded in 703. This shrine is famous for Omu ishi (the parrot stone), which makes a noise when struck. The shrine's bell is said to have been brought back from Korea when Toyotomi Hideyoshi's expedition returned at the end of the 16th c.

10mls (16km): Tateishi misaki, on which there is a lighthouse. Wide view across the whole of Wakasa Bay and Tsuruga Bay to the SE.

2 MIKATA (26mls/42km W, via Baijoga take; JNR train). After cutting across the base of the Tateishi peninsula, the N27 heads W to the shore of Kugushi lake.

11mls (18km): Mihama, from where you can take the coach a toll road which climbs:

17mls (28km): *Baijo take: beautiful view over the *five lakes of Mikata (Kugushi, Suigetsu, Mikata, Suga and Hiruga) and Wakasa Bay.

19mls (31km): a coast road branches off and takes you to:

→ 5mls (8km) NW: *Tsunekami misaki, attractive seaside spot opposite the little island of Ogami.

26mls (42km): Mikata, from where you can take the train back to Tsuruga or continue to Obama.

3 OBAMA, see entry under this name; BIWA KO, see Otsu.

■ **Tsuruoka** (Island of Honshu)

Map of Tohoku, pp. 232-3.

Tokyo, 299mls (481km) - Akita, 75mls (120km) - Fukushima, 120mls (193km) – Niigata, 93mls (149km) – Sendai, 99mls (159km) - Yamagata, 63mls (101km).

Yamagaten ken - pop: 99,800 - industrial town: textiles, wood, canning industry.

Tsuruoka is situated to the W of Otori gawa, at the foot of a mountainous region of volcanic origin dominated by Mount Gassan. There are several spas in the surrounding area.

The novelist Chogyu Takayama (1871-1902) was born in Tsuruoka.

880yds (800m) S of the station you can visit the house where Chogyu Takayama was born.

▄▄ In the centre of the town, 1½ml (2km) SW of the station, Tsuruoka Park is situated on the site of the former castle which used to belong to the Sakai family. Shonai shrine is dedicated to their ancestors.

You can also visit Chido Museum (1½mls/2.5km SW of the station) which houses collections of local arts and crafts, archaeological finds and various objects collected by the Sakai.

☞ **VICINITY**

1 YUTAGAWA ONSEN (5mls/8km SW; coach), spa renowned since the 7th c. From here you can climb Kimbo zan (1,506ft/459m), which overlooks this spa to the E. At the summit there is a small shrine and views over Tsuruoka and the sea.

2 YUNOHAMA (9mls/15km NW; coach; private railway). To the W of Tsuruoka a road leaves the N7 and crosses the railway lines to the NW.

4mls (7km): Uzen Oyama, from where you can visit the wooded park of Oyama.

➡ 2mls (3km) N (private railway station): temple of Zempo ji, founded in the 10th c.

9mls (15km): Yunohama; spa and seaside resort, situated on the edge of a rocky coast which continues N in a straight line, following the alluvial basin of the Mogami gawa, which flows into the sea further N at Sakata.

3 ATSUMI (19mls/31km SW, via the N7; JNR train; coach). Leave Tsuruoka to the W by the N7.

10mls (16km): Yura, small spa. From here you continue S along the beautiful rocky coast of the Sea of Japan, passing the beauty spot of Yaotome ura.

19mls (31km): Atsumi, from where you can get to:

➡ 1½ml (2km) E (coach): Atsumi Onsen, one of the oldest known spas in

Japan. It is still very popular and is famous for its saline waters which change colour according to the seasons. The spa is situated in a little valley with several waterfalls and is overlooked to the NE by Atsumi dake (2,415ft/736m). It is possible to climb this mountain.

6mls (9km) S of Atsumi (JNR train; coach): Nezugaseki, which you can reach by following the beautiful *rocky coastline dotted with clumps of pines. Just off the coast is the little island of Benten jima.

4 **DEWA SANZAN** (27mls/44km SE as far as Yudono san, along the N112; coach). The 'three mountains of Dewa' form part of Bandai Asahi National Park (see entry under this name).

The sacred mountains of Dewa consist of Gassan (6,496ft/1,980m), Yudono san (4,934ft/1,504m) and Haguro san (1,430ft/436m). They form part of the great volcanic chain of Asahi, of which Asahi dake (5,840ft/1,780m), towering up to the S, is one of the dominant features. These mountains are especially venerated by the itinerant priests of the Shugendo sect and attract about 200,000 pilgrims each year. Festival on 15 July in honour of the gods of these peaks at Ideha shrine on Mount Haguro.

11mls (17km) E of Tsuruoka (coach): Haguro san (alt. 1,430ft/436m) is a piece of high ground jutting out to the N of Gassan. Ideha jinja is situated here and is dedicated to the god of the same name. It is the easiest of the Gassan shrines to reach from Tsuruoka.

26mls (42km): a toll road branches off in the direction of Yudono san.

27mls (44km): this road comes to an end and you have to continue on foot to Yudono san (4,934ft/1,504m) and *Gassan (6,496ft/1,980m), the main peak, which takes three hours to climb. Extensive views from the summit.

17mls (28km) S: Yudonosan jinja, from where you can climb *Asahi dake (6,135ft/1,870m), a large mountain well off the beaten track, characterized by inaccessibility, alpine landscape, wild animals (bears, monkeys, antelopes), alpine flowers and solitude.

Tsuyama (Island of Honshu)

Tokyo, 434mls (698km) – Hiroshima, 142mls (228km) – Kobe, 93mls (150km) – Matsue, 86mls (139km) – Okayama, 39mls (63km) – Tottori, 43mls (76km).

Okayama ken – Pop: 85,000 – alt. 302ft (92m).

Half-way between Okayama and Tottori, Tsuyama is an important crossroads and railway junction, now completed by the arrival of the new Trans-Chugoku Expressway. This ancient feudal town has taken on a new lease of life beside the Yoshi gawa.

1ml (1.5km) N of the station, Kakuzan Park is on the site of the former castle of Tsuyama, whose ramparts take the form of terraces one above the other. Beautiful cherry trees.

↔ 1½mls (2.5km) NE of the station is the prehistoric site of Numa. There are several Yayoi dwellings which have been reconstructed according to designs closely based on archaeological evidence.

☞ VICINITY

1 TANJO JI (10mls/16km S; JNR train). Situated 550yds (500m) NW of the station, Tanjo ji was built in 1193 to mark the birthplace of the priest Honen, founder of the Jodo sect (see Kyoto), by one of his disciples. The temple houses a statue of Honen Shonin by the priest himself.

2 YUNOGO ONSEN (13mls/21km SE; coach; JNR train as far as Mimasaka station, then coach). This spa, which has been in use since ancient times, is set in an attractive, verdant area. Hot springs at 99°F (37°C) which have dermatological healing properties.

3 OKUTSU ONSEN (20mls/32km NW; coach). A collection of several hot springs which are divided into three main groups: Okutsu, Otsuri and Kawanishi. The water is from 104° to 109°F (40° to 43°C) and has healing properties sought by those suffering from gastric and nervous disorders and asthma. Pretty gorges of Okutsu near Otsuri.

Ube (Island of Honshu)

Railway map on inside front cover.

Tokyo, 647mls (1,042km) – Hiroshima, 105mls (169km) – Matsue, 178mls (286km) – Yamaguchi, 22mls (36km).

Yamaguchi ken – pop: 165,000 – industrial town.

At the mouth of the Koto gawa, overlooking the Inland Sea, Ube is an important industrial centre where coal mining constitutes the principal activity. Some of the few coal deposits in the island of Honshu are to be found here and in the Joban region (see Iwaki). The port provides the commercial outlet for this region which also has a chemical industry.

To the E of Ube is Tokiwa Park (3mls/5km E; coach, JNR train), on the edge of Tokiwa lake. From here there is a view of the Inland Sea.

Ueno (Island of Honshu)

Tokyo, 276mls (444km) – Gifu, 86mls (138km) – Kyoto, 47mls (76km) – Nagoya, 63mls (102km) – Nara, 31mls (50km) – Otsu, 55mls (88km) – Wakayama, 88mls (141km).

Mie ken – pop: 64,000 – alt. 548ft (167m).

Established on the ancient road linking Nagoya and Osaka, Ueno became an important stopping place on this route and grew up around the castle. This belonged to the Todo clan, who were also the lords of Tsu.

The *haiku* poet Matsuo Munefusa, known as Basho (1644–94), was born in Tsuge near Ueno.

In the city centre, near Uenoshi station (Kintetsu ER), you can visit Ueno Park. The keep of Hakuko was reconstructed here in 1953 to the design of the original, built in 1611.

The castle was erected in the 16th c. by Takigawa Katsutoshi. It subsequently became the property of the Tsutsui clan, and then passed into the hands of the Todo family.

The park also contains the Basho museum. This houses a collection of writings and memorabilia of the poet, who was the greatest Japanese exponent of the *haiku* form (p. 92). The Minomushi teahouse is also dedicated to his memory.

Uji (Island of Honshu)

Map of Kansai, pp. 500–1.

Tokyo, 308mls (495km) – Fukui, 114mls (183km) – Kobe, 59mls (95km) – Kyoto, 12mls (19km) – Nara, 19mls (30km) – Osaka, 29mls (47km) – Otsu, 19mls (31km) – Tsu, 71mls (115km).

Kyoto fu – pop: 110,000 – production of green tea.

This important region lies at the foot of a range of hills which border the Kyoto basin to the E, and from which flows Uji gawa. Along with Kyoto and Nara, it forms a large tourist area and is particularly famous for Byodo in.

 ˙˙BYODO IN (550yds/500m SE of Uji station). It is near the Uji gawa. Hoo do is the principal building in this temple, which is one of the most harmonious examples of Japanese architecture from the Heian period.

At the end of the 9th c. there was a villa here belonging to Minamoto Toru. A century later the estate came under Fujiwara Michinaga (966–1027), one of the greatest Fujiwara ministers at the beginning of the Heian period. His son Yorimichi built Hoo do and lived there secluded from the world. Byodo in, with its dual function of temple and palace, continued to be occupied by different members of the Fujiwara family and miraculously escaped destruction, unlike the surrounding buildings.

˙˙Hoo do. 'The central pavilion (1053), called the Pavilion of the Phoenix (Hoo do), is flanked by two side buildings of lesser height each connected to it by a gallery. This is typical of the *shinden* architectural style which was employed in palaces of the Heian period (...). The palace is reflected in the waters of an artificial lake and, thus doubled, it resembles more than ever the image of a bird in flight that the architects of the Heian period strove to attain' (D. and V. Elisseeff, *La Civilisation Japonaise*). The central pavilion is crowned with a figure of a phoenix in gilt bronze from which it takes its name.

The **˙˙statue of Amida** is to be found in the pavilion. This marvellous 11th-c. statue, attributed to the priest Jocho, was constructed using a technique known as *yosegi* which involves the assembly of individually carved pieces of wood into the finished work. The statue, seated on a lotus-shaped pedestal, served as a model for later works.

Amida 'is seated, calm and impassive, in an attitude of meditation, with his gaze fixed in the distance. Behind him is a huge nimbus, and above is a richly decorated canopy. His smooth features and his simplicity contrast with the intricate sculptures surrounding the statue. The atmosphere emanating from Amida is characteristic of the transformation of the faith, benevolent now, welcoming and peaceful. The intricacy of the nimbus, with little figures on lotus flowers representing souls who have just arrived in paradise, reflects the taste of the Court for a flamboyant style' (Peter C. Swann, *Japan*).

The interior of Hoo do is lined with panels decorated with lacquer paintings representing the *Paradise of Amida which are attributed to Tamenari Takuna. 'On the leaves of the five doors and on the three inside walls are representations of the nine Descents of Amida (*raigo*), which correspond to the nine degrees of salvation according to the good or bad conduct of the deceased. The scenes on the two side doors and on the two doors in the front wall are better preserved and provide the most authentic examples of painting from this golden age' (Akiyama Terukazu, *La Peinture Japonaise*). In addition to these paintings there are some landscapes of equally outstanding execution illustrating the four seasons.

To the N of Hoo do, Kannon do contains a statue of the divinity of that name (from the end of the Heian period) and is also known as Tsuridono, the Hall of Fishing, since it was once possible to catch fish from the building itself in the Uji gawa which flowed past beneath it.

Nearby you will see a monument dedicated to the memory of Minamoto Yorimasa who, defeated by the Taira on Uji bridge in 1180, was forced to commit suicide on this spot.

The bell in the belfry at Byodo in is said to be of Indian origin.

Near Byodo in, Agata shrine is dedicated to Konohana Sakuyahime no Mikoto, wife of Ninigi no Mikoto and goddess of Mount Fuji, to whom the Sengen shrines are dedicated. Festival 5 June.

To the N of Byodo in, Uji gawa is crossed by the famous Uji bridge, which is said to have been built originally in the mid 7th c. by the priest Docho.

Situated on the road from Kyoto to Nara, this bridge was of great strategic importance, especially in the Heian and Kamakura periods, and was frequently at the centre of battles for its possession. One of the most famous took place in 1180 between Taira Tomomori and Minamoto Yorimasa, who was defeated. In 1184, Kiso Yoshinaka was also defeated there by his cousin Minamoto Yoshitsune. It is said that Toyotomi Hideyoshi stood on this bridge to draw water from the river for a tea ceremony in the 16th c. Since then, on the 1st of October each year, a ritual ceremony has been performed here.

On a little island to the S of the bridge you can see a stone pagoda with thirteen storeys. It was built in the 13th c. by the priest Eison and restored in 1908.

Hojo in, to the SE of the bridge, is also known as Hashi dera (Temple of the Bridge). Here you can see a monument commemorating the building of Uji bridge. It dates from 646 and is the oldest known monument in Japan.

A little futher on is Uji shrine, thought to have been founded in 313 on the site of a residence of Prince Uji Wakiiratsuko, son of Emperor Ojin. This religious place consists of a lower shrine, with buildings from the Kamakura period, and an *upper shrine, built in the 10th c., whose buildings are said to be the oldest belonging to the Shinto religion in Japan.

If you continue climbing Asahi hill which rises up behind the shrine you will come to Kosho ji, built on the wooded slopes. This temple was founded in 1233 by the priest Dogen, who introduced the Soto sect and was also the founder of Eihei ji (see the Vicinity of Fukui). Alterations were carried out on the buildings in 1649.

VICINITY

1 *MAMPUKU JI (2mls/3km N; JNR and Keihan ER trains as far as Obaku). This temple was built between 1661 and 1688 by the Chinese priest Ingen and is an example of the architectural style of the Ming period. Among its buildings, the following are of interest: Daiyu Ho den, built of teak imported from Thailand; and Hatto, where 60,000 wooden matrices are kept which were used in the 17th c. for printing the *sutra* of the Obaku sect, to which the temple belongs.

2 JORURI JI (16mls/25km SE; JNR train as far as Kamo - change at Kizu - then coach). Situated 2½mls (4km) S of Kamo station, this temple is famous for its statue of *Kichijo ten, made from cypress wood. The statue of the god was influenced by Chinese sculpture and is luxuriously apparelled. All its component parts have been carved individually and then assembled: 'the whole gives an impression of sumptuousness which befits the goddess of Good Fortune' (Peter C. Swann). You can also see a statue of Fudo Myo o, carved by Koen (1311). Hon do and the temple's pagoda (1178) date from the Fujiwara period.

3 KYOTO, NARA, see entries under these names; BIWA KO, see Otsu.

Unzen Amakusa (National Park of; Island of Kyushu)**

Map of Kyushu (North), pp. 388–9.

HOW TO GET THERE

– From Isahaya, Nagasaki and Sasebo. Isahaya is connected by JNR trains to Fukuoka, as well as to Nagasaki (20mls/32km in 20 min.) and Sasebo (38mls/61km in 50 min.); direct coach services from Nagasaki and Sasebo to Isahaya. From Isahaya you can continue (by coach) to Unzen and Shimabara, and from there to the Amakusa archipelago. Coaches form a direct link from Nagasaki to Kumamoto, and to Hondo via Unzen and Shimabara.

– From Hondo, Shimabara, Ushibuka; these places are actually within the park itself. Shimabara is connected to Kami Shima by boat and Ushibuka to Hondo by coach.

- From Kumamoto you can take the coach direct to Hondo via Amakusa's five bridges. It is also possible to get to Nagasaki via Misumi, Shimabara and Isahaya if you take the Kyushu Kokusai Kanko Bus which connects Beppu and Nagasaki.

The magnificent volcanic massif of Unzen and the Amakusa archipelago make up this national park, where sea and mountain form a harmonious whole. On the map, the shorelines are drawn as a complex network of islands and peninsulas so that it is sometimes difficult to tell which is which. This region was the setting for a bloody episode in the history of Japanese Catholicism. The National Park of Unzen Amakusa covers 63,258 acres (25,600 ha).

FROM ISAHAYA TO HONDO (85mls/136km SE along our route, coach from Isahaya; direct coach from Nagasaki taking the ferry from Shimabara to Misumi; from Kumamoto, coach in the direction of Hondo or from Shimabara and Nagaski via Misumi). Isahaya (pop. 72,000) is an ancient feudal town at the junction of the roads from Fukuoka, Nagasaki and Sasebo.

FROM ISAHAYA TO KUCHINOTSU, via the east coast of the Shimabara peninsula (48mls/78km SE; Shimabara Railway train). The private railway runs along the beautiful coastline of this peninsula, which is dominated by the Unzen massif.

18mls (29km): Taira, with the little harbour of Kunimi, from where you can take the boat to Nagasu on the other side of Shimabara bay.

26mls (42km): Shimabara, see the main itinerary below, at 37mls (60km).

28mls (45km): Shimabara Gaiko, from where you can take the boat to Hondo, Matsushima, Misuni, Nagasu or Omuta.

41mls (66km): Minami Arima (Harajo station) where, 550yds (500m) SE of the station and close to the sea, you will find the site of Hara Castle.

SHIMABARA REBELLION. In 1637, 35,000 peasants who had risen against the local lords of Shimabara and Amakusa withdrew here. Following the defeat of Matsukura Shigeharu, daimyo of Shimabara, Okochi Nobutsuna finally succeeded in April 1638, after several months of siege, in defeating the rebels who were by this time weak from lack of food. The majority of these unfortunate people were Christians, and they were massacred for having revolted against their lords and the religious persecution to which they had been subjected. Their leaders were Ashizuka Chuemon (1578-1638) and Masuda Shiro, who was only 16 years old. This revolt was a decisive factor in closing Japan to foreign influences. A monument has been erected in memory of the many victims.

48mls (78km): Kuchinotsu, a little harbour on the southern tip of the

Shimabara peninsula, from where you can take the boat to Oniike on Shima island.

 From Isahaya, follow the N57 E which, at Aino (7mls/12km), crosses the base of the Shimabara peninsula and takes you to:

10mls (16km): a wonderful *belvedere, overlooking Tachibana bay. There is a superb view to the E towards Mount Unzen.

12mls (19km): Chijiwa, a small fishing harbour at the head of Tachibana bay, which is dominated by Mount Unzen.

17mls (28km): Obama, a pleasant spa which has been in use since the 17th c. and is situated at the foot of Mount Unzen. The mountain affords protection from the weather, making Obama a popular seaside resort and place to stay. A spring gushes forth at Fukiage as a geyser.

14mls (22km) S (coach): Kuchinotsu (see below), which is reached via the E coast of the Shimabara peninsula.

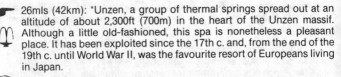 26mls (42km): *Unzen, a group of thermal springs spread out at an altitude of about 2,300ft (700m) in the heart of the Unzen massif. Although a little old-fashioned, this spa is nonetheless a pleasant place. It has been exploited since the 17th c. and, from the end of the 19th c. until World War II, was the favourite resort of Europeans living in Japan.

 There are three main groups of springs accompanied by strange volcanic phenomena: solfataras, sulphurous steam, hot mud, geysers, etc. The spa is situated in the *wooded park of Unzen where you can visit several 'hells' (*jigoku*, see Beppu).

1½ml (2km) S, along the Obama road, is Issaikyo waterfall.

From the centre of the resort, a **toll road (coach) weaves its way between the main peaks of the Unzen massif for about 7mls (11km). There are views on either side over Tachibana and Shimbara bays, and it is possible to see as far as Mount Aso (see entry under this name). Fugen dake (4,462ft/1,360m) is the highest peak and can be reached by cable-car. The entire massif offers excellent walks and climbs.

37mls (60km): Shimabara Gaiko (see above, second itinerary, 28mls/34km), S of the town Shimabara (pop: 51,000), is another spa at the foot of Mount Unzen on the E side.

 Near Shimabara station (Shimabara Railway; 2mls/3km N of Shimabara Gaiko) you can visit Moridake jo, where the keep, a proud five storeys high, has recently been rebuilt. In the 17th c. it was the residence of Matsukura Shigeharu, against whom the Christians of Shimabara revolted in 1637 and who died during the siege of Hara jo.

Today the castle houses an interesting museum with a collection of mementoes from this episode in Japan's history, evoking the clandestine Christianity of the Edo period. In a corner of the castle, the Seibo Museum has an exhibition of works by the contemporary sculptor Seibo Kitamura.

550yds (500m) W of the castle is Kamishin cho, a street very reminiscent of the ancient towns of the Edo period.

➨ 13mls (21km) SW: Hara jo (see above, second itinerary, at 41mls/66km).

🔌 From Shimabara, take the boat (Kyushu Shosen) to Misumi. Near Shimabara you will see the many islets of Tsukumo jima which rose up out of the sea in 1792 when Mount Bizan (2,687ft/819m) erupted, a mountain situated to the W of this area.

54mls (87km): Misumi is situated on the end of a peninsula which separates the bays of Shimabara and Yatsushiro. From there you can take the coach or train (JNR) to the town of Kumamoto (28mls/45km NE; see entry under this name). It would be preferable to continue (by coach) towards the S via the N266 and the Five Amakusa Bridges (*Amakusa Pearl line), which connect Misumi peninsula with Oyano shima and Kami shima. The largest of the bridges, Maejimi bashi, is 560yds (510m) in length. The bridges were completed in 1966.

65mls (104km): Matsushima, to the NE of the island of Kami shima, from where you can take the boat NE to Shimabara or E to Yatsushiro.

85mls (136km): Hondo (pop: 43,000), principal town of Amakusa shoto, in the NE of Shimo shima, itself the principal island of the archipelago. Hondo is separated from Kami shima by a narrow channel crossed by a bridge.

◾ In Hondo you can visit the Christian Museum, which houses a collection of objects and documents relating to the underground region. The Martyrs Park is on the site where Hondo Castle used to stand, and there is also a Christian cemetery.

*Amakusa shoto includes a total of more than a hundred islands, of which Shimo (220sq. mls/570km^2) and Kami (89sq. mls/231km^2) are the largest. These hilly islands (2,238ft/628m at Kura dake) form an attractive coastline of creeks and islets. Pearls are cultured here and good quality clay means that pottery is also made in the region. The islands are scattered with relics of the Christians who, despite persecution, attempted to continue practising their religion.

🔾 FROM HONDO TO USHIBUKA (65mls/104km SW via the N324 and the W coast of Shimo shima; coach via Tomioka and Amakusa). Leave Hondo and go N:

8½mls (14km): Oniike, in the N of Shimo shima, from where you can go to Kuchinotsu.

20mls (32km): Reihoku, separated by Shikizaki point from the little harbour of Tomioka, whose castle (1½ml/2km to the NW, near the point) was also besieged by the Shimabara rebels.

27mls (44km): Shimoda, Amakusa's only spa (springs from 108° to 120°F/42° to 49°C) and, a little further on, the rocks of Myoken ura.

34mls (54km): Amakusa. From here onwards the coastline becomes much more jagged and picturesque and forms the *Amakusa Maritime Park.

43mls (70km): Sakitsu, one of the most beautiful places in Amakusa, with a charming village clustered round a quaint church in the neo-Gothic style.

65mls (86km): you come to the N266 which connects Hondo directly with Ushibuka.

53mls (104km): Ushibuka (pop: 31,000), an important fishing port at the southern tip of Shimo shima. Off the E coast of Shimo shima is a cluster of islands of many shapes and sizes.

▨ Urawa (Island of Honshu)

Map of the Vicinity of Tokyo, p. 565.

Tokyo, 15mls (24km) – Chiba, 34mls (54km) – Kofu, 109mls (175km) – Maebashi, 62mls (100km) – Mito, 85mls (136km) – Nagano, 127mls (205km) – Utsunomiya, 58mls (93km).

Principal town of Saitama ken – pop: 358,000 – industrial and residential town.

To the NW of Tokyo, Urawa merges with the vast suburbs of the capital and its only claim to individuality is based on its role as an administrative centre and on the existence of some local industries.

☞ **VICINITY**

SAGI YAMA (8½mls/14km NE: coach). It is known as the hill of the Noda egrets. There is a bird sanctuary here, where large numbers of birds of the heron family gather in March and September.

▨ Usa (Island of Kyushu)

Map of Kyushu (North), pp. 388–9.

Tokyo, 718mls (1,155km) – Fukuoka, 70mls (113km) – Kumamoto, 114mls (184km) – Miyazaki, 163mls (262km) – Oita, 38mls (61km).

Oita ken – Pop: 59,000.

The vast shrine of Usa, outside the town, is the main attraction of this area.

卄 ****USA SHRINE** (3½mls/6km S of the JNR station; coach, excursion from Beppu). Near the N10, this shrine stands in a huge *park where vermilion buildings contrast with the intense green of the foliage. This, and the ones at Ise and Izumo, are the most important shrines in Japan. Main festival on 18 March.

Usa Hachiman gu is one of the most ancient Shinto foundations in Japan. Usa became legendary when Emperor Jimmu put in there on his voyage between the province of Hyuga and Yamato. Some say that the present shrine was founded in 570, and others in 725. It was dedicated to Emperor Ojin and his mother Empress Jingu. Wake Kiyomaro went there in 768 on the orders of Empress Shotoku, who wished to marry Dokyo the monk. She was refused permission, for members of the Imperial Family must not marry beneath their station. In 1556, Otomo Sorin, lord of Funai (Oita) and master of Kyushu, burnt Usa shrine to ashes because the monks were considered to be too unruly. Yoshimune, the son of Sorin, restored the shrine at the end of the 16th c., and it has been rebuilt several times since.

After crossing the Yorimo gawa, a broad avenue will take you through the shrine gardens from N to S. On reaching the little shrine of Togu, this avenue curves round to the E and then a flight of steps leads up to Kamimiya (the upper shrine), where the main buildings are situated. The Hon den is surrounded by a corridor with a beautiful tiered doorway opening onto it. In front of the doorway is a spacious courtyard.

To the E of this courtyard you can visit the shrine's interesting treasury which houses a number of ancient paintings, some mikoshi, swords and bronze artefacts, Noh costumes and masks, two wooden statues of the Deva kings, etc.

To the W of Kamimiya, you can continue along the central avenue to Shimo jinja, the lower shrine. N of these two shrines, Hishigata ike adds a charming touch to the landscape garden. In the middle of this lake is Emadono pavilion.

▪ Usuki (Island of Kyushu)

Map of Kyushu (North), pp. 388–9.

Tokyo, 788mls (1,268km) – Fukuoka, 136mls (219km) – Kumamoto, 121mls (194km) – Miyazaki, 117mls (188km) – Oita, 31mls (50km) – ferry service to Yawatahama.

Oita ken - pop: 44,500.

Usuki is a pleasant fishing port at the head of an inlet, where Otomo Sorin built a castle in 1564. The main tourist attractions of Usuki are the 60 rock carvings of Buddha, the town centre and the three-storeyed pagoda of Tshi-to (Heian period, Nara style).

VICINITY

1 ˙USUKI SEKIBUTSU (5mls/8km SW; coach; excursion from Beppu: JNR train from Beppu or Oita: Kamisuki stop). Here you will find an exceptional group of 60 statues of Buddha, carved in high relief in the rock itself. The *first (10ft/3.2m tall) is the most impressive. These carvings are of a grandeur and serenity influenced by Chinese art of the period, and are a rare example of Japanese sculpture in stone. They are the most beautiful cave carvings in Japan, and still bear traces of colour. It seems that these statues were sculpted in the 12th c. under the patronage of an influential monk or local lords. Although

the statues are not the only examples of such work in the area, they are the most important. Mangetsu ji used to stand nearby.

2 FUREN SHONYUDO (18mls/29km SW; coach). This consists of two natural caves in the mountainside, the larger one measuring 460yds (420m) in length. This spot is dominated by Yato kogen (2,349ft/716m), from where there is a view of the jagged coastline between Usuki and Saiki.

3 OITA, see entry under this name.

■ Utsunomiya (Island of Honshu)

Railway map on inside front cover.

Tokyo, 71mls (115km) – Fukushima, 106mls (171km) – Maebashi, 64mls (103km) – Mito, 47mls (75km) – Urawa, 58mls (93km).

Principal town of Tochigi ken (pop: 1,173,000) – pop: 377,800 – alt. 371ft (113m) – national university.

Situated on a tributary of the Kinu gawa, which flows to the E of the city. Utsunomiya was once an important trading stop at the junction of the Tohoku line and a road leading to Nikko. Today it is a busy place, the principal town and main economic centre of the Tochigi prefecture.

The historian and politician, Gamo Kumpei (1768–1813) was born in Utsunomiya.

Opposite the station (JNR) you will come upon a main road which crosses the city from E to W, and 770yds (700m) S of this you will see the park of the former castle of Utsunomiya (¾ml/1.2km SW of the JNR station; 660yds/600m SE of Tobu Utsunomiya station). Today, only the moats and ramparts remain.

This castle was built in the 11th c. by the Utsunomiya family.

To the N of the main road mentioned above, there is a hill on top of which stands Futarasan jinja (½ml/1km W of the JNR station; 550yds/500m NE of Tobu Utsunomiya station). Gamo Kumpei is buried in the enclosure.

Further N is the large park of Hachiman yama, where there are other religious buildings and sporting facilities. From here there are wide views of Utsunomiya and the surrounding area extending as far as the mountains of Nikko.

VICINITY

1 *OYA JI (5½mls/9km NW; coach). This temple was founded in the 9th c. by Kobo Daishi, near a rock shelter where several Buddhist statues had been carved out of the walls. These are the oldest of their kind in Japan.

The statue of Kannon of the thousand arms is 13ft (4m) high.

To the NW of the temple is Kogashi yama (1,913ft/583m; 4mls/7km up to the summit), whose wooded slopes offer pleasant walks. A huge statue of Kannon (89ft/27m high) was sculpted in 1956 in a clearing on the side of this mountain.

2 IMAICHI, NIKKO NATIONAL PARK, see entries under these names.

Uwajima (Island of Shikoku)

Map of Shikoku (Inland Sea), pp. 536–7.

Tokyo, 638mls (1,027m) – Kochi, 96mls (154km) – Matsuyama, 52mls (83km) – Takamatsu, 191mls (308km) – Tokushima, 216mls (348km).

Ehime ken – pop: 69,000 – fishing port.

At the head of one of the most indented bays in the island of Shikoku, Uwajima was a feudal trading town. It remains one of the main centres of activity in the southern part of the island, but has been outstripped by the industrialized cities in the N which border on the Inland Sea. The town makes a good stopping place en route to Ashizuri Uwakai National Park.

770yds (700m) SW of the station, on a hill overlooking the town, the port and the bay, is Uwajima Castle. The tower was built in 1665 and contains a museum with displays relating to the history of Uwajima and its castle.

The castle itself was built in 1600 by Toda Katsutaka. In 1614 it became the residence of Date Munezumi, grandson of Masamune (see Sendai), whose family remained in Uwajima until 1868.

Beyond the castle, 1½ml (2km) SW of the station (bus), you can visit the beautiful landscape garden of Tensha en, designed in the 18th c. at the behest of the Date family. 1½ml (2km) SE of the station is Uwasuhiko jinja, built at the lower end of Atago Park, from where the view extends as far as the island of Kyushu.

VICINITY

1 NAMETOKO KEIKOKU (4mls/7km SE as the crow flies; accessible from the village of Matsuno, 11mls/17km SE by JNR train). This waterfall cascades down an immense rock face in the midst of a beautiful mountain setting in Ashizuri Uwakai National Park.

2 ASHIZURI UWAKAI NATIONAL PARK, see entry under this name.

Wajima (Island of Honshu)

Railway map on inside front cover.

Tokyo, 393mls (632km) – Fukui, 130mls (209km) – Gifu, 221mls (355km) – Kanazawa, 81mls (130km) – Toyama, 134mls (216km).

Ishikawa ken – pop: 38,500 – fishing port.

In the N of the Noto peninsula, which projects into the Sea of Japan and curves round in the direction of Sado island. Wajima is a suitable point of departure for exploring this beautiful peninsula.

VICINITY

1 **HEGURA JIMA** (30mls/48km N; boat). This small island lies to the N of the Noto peninsula; a number of fishermen from Wajima spend the summer here. Ama divers.

 2 **MONZEN** (16mls/25km SW, via the N249; coach). Here you can visit *Soji ji which, before the fire of 1898, was one of the main temples of the Soto sect.

This temple, like Eihei ji (see Fukui), was founded by the priest Dogen or Shoyo Daishi. The majority of the temple buildings have been restored.

Before crossing the humpbacked bridge, you will see (on the l.) Kyo zo, a *sutra* library, with pigeon-holes on a revolving drum. It was made by the carpenter Gondo Yoshiharu (1743). After crossing the bridge you will come to San mon, a beautiful door in zelkowa wood with statues of Kannon and Jizo Bosatsu carved in it. This door opens onto a courtyard surrounded by handsome *buildings richly decorated with sculptures. On the r., Butsu den contains a statue of Shaka Nyorai. Opposite, in Hatto or Taiso do, homage is paid to the founder priest Shoyo Daishi, and on the l., So do or Zazen do is a building reserved for the practice of Zen. Outside the enclosure you will also see Danto in, built in the 14th c., and Kannon do, the temple's oldest building, said to have been founded by the priest Gyoki (8th c.).

➤ 3½mls (6km) W of Monzen (coach): the attractive little harbour of Kuroshima, which has retained its character from the past.

3 NOTO (65mls/105km SE, skirting round the peninsula to get there; organized excursions). Leave Wajima and head E along the N249.

3½mls (6km): road on the r. which takes you (2mls/3km S) to Konosu zan (alt. 1,860ft/567m), from where you can see the northern coast of Noto peninsula.

7mls (11km): Shirayone; on the hillsides around here you will see terraced paddyfields, looking as though they mark the contour lines of the slopes. This is very characteristic of rice-growing in the East.

12mls (20km): Machino, where you can see the farm of the Tokikuni, one of the largest in Japan, which is said to have always been occupied by the descendants of Taira Tokikuni, banished here by Minamoto Yoritomo in the 12th c. Further on, the road follows the coastline of *Oku Noto Kongo, a magnificent succession of rocky crags which plunge into the sea. The coast maintains this rugged character as far as Suzu misaki.

17mls (27km): *Sosogi kaigan, one of the most beautiful places along this rocky coast.

21mls (33km): Otani; turn l. off the N249 in order to continue along the coast road.

31mls (50km): Rokko zaki then (34mls/55km) Suzu misaki, which mark the northernmost tip of the Noto peninsula.

40mls (65km): Takojima, end station of JNR, from where you can take the train which runs along the S coast of Noto peninsula before heading off in the direction of Kanazawa.

44mls (71km): Suzu (pop: 33,500), important fishing port to the NE of Noto Hanto. Further on is the attractive coastline of Mitsukejima kaigan which is closed off to the S by Aka saki.

48mls (77km): Uchiura, where you have to leave the N249 once more to get to:

55mls (89km): *Tsukumo wan, a very jagged bay with numerous rocky inlets, given the name 'the ninety-nine coves'.

58mls (93km): Ogi, a little harbour and spa.

65mls (105km): Noto, another harbour from where you can take the boat to Nanao and the train to Kanazawa (see entries under these names).

V Wakayama (Island of Honshu)

Map of Places of Interest, p. 71.

Tokyo, 362mls (582km) – Nara, 63mls (101km) – Osaka, 44mls (71km) – Tsu, 103mls (166km).

Principal town of Wakayama ken – pop: 395,000 – industrial town and port – national and regional universities.

At the mouth of the Kino kawa, in the NW of the Kii peninsula, Wakayama was an important feudal town and still is the main economic centre of this peninsula today. For the tourist, Wakano ura is one of the most remarkable places in Japan.

From Wakayama station, one of the city's main roads goes W towards the Kino kawa. Near the town hall it crosses the wide Komatsubara dori, which cuts across the city from N to S.

 To the SE of this crossroads, Wakayama Park (1ml/1.5km W of Wakayama station; ½ml/1km SE of Wakayamashi station) is the setting for Wakayama Castle, which used to stand in the centre of the town.

After becoming master of Negoro Temple (see Vicinity) in 1585, Toyotomi Hideyoshi ceded Wakayama to his brother Hidenaga. The latter had a castle built, which he entrusted to Kuwayama Shigeharu. In 1600, Tokugawa Ieyasu placed Asano Yukinaga there, and then Yorinobu (1602–71), son of Ieyasu, took possession of it in 1619. He was the ancestor of the important Wakayama branch of the Tokugawa family.

The castle was completely rebuilt in 1850, and the present three-storeyed keep was built in 1958. It houses some historical relics and documents relating to the Tokugawa family and also has displays of local arts and crafts. From the castle there is a view over the city and the surrounding area.

Komatsubara dori runs alongside Wakayama Park and heads S to Akiba yama Park (2½mls/4km S of Wakayama eki; bus), where there is a shrine of the same name and several other religious buildings.

This street forks off to the l. (N42) in the direction of Waka gawa, while the r. fork passes the shrines of Tosho gu and Temman gu, leading to Mitara ike to the N of:

*Wakano ura (3mls/5km S of Wakayamashi and 3½mls/6km SW of Wakayama station; bus from these two stations), Wakayama's spa and one of the most beautiful spots in the Kii peninsula. From there you can take the cable-car to the viewpoint of Takatsushi yama, or continue W to Saiga zaki Park with its rocky promontory.

From the junction mentioned above, you can also reach the estuary of the Waka gawa and, if you continue straight ahead and go under the railway lines, you will come to:

KIMI DERA (3mls/5km S of Wakayama station and 660yds/600m SE of the JNR station of Kimiidera). Situated in a pleasant forest setting, this temple was founded in 770 by the Chinese priest Iko. A statue of Kannon of the eleven heads is venerated here. It is said to have been discovered at the foot of a tree. The Hondo was rebuilt in the 18th c.

and several of the temple buildings (Dai mon, belfry, pagoda) are designated. Large numbers of cherry trees blossom in the surrounding park at the end of March.

VICINITY

1 KADA (7mls/12km NW; Nankai ER train). This little harbour lies opposite the *islands of Tomoga which you can reach by boat. Lying between the Kii peninsula and Awaji shima (see under this name), these islands offer beautiful views together with opportunities for walks and camping.

2 KOKAWA (14mls/23km E along the N24; JNR train). Leave Wakayama and head E up the Kion kawa valley.

10mls (16km): Iwade; road on the l. to:

2½mls (4km) N (coach): *Negoro dera, a temple founded in 1126 by the priest Kokyo Daishi. Although it was partly destroyed by Toyotomi Hideyoshi at the end of the 16th c., this temple has some interesting buildings such as Daishi do, built in 1391 (statue of Kokyo Daishi), and Taho to, a pagoda in the form of a stupa, rebuilt c. 1515. There is a pretty wooded area around the temple with cherry trees in blossom at the beginning of April.

14mls (23km): Kokawa, a small town in the Kino gawa valley, dominated by the Kii mountains.

½ml (1km) N: Kokawa dera. This temple was erected in 770, destroyed in 1585 by Toyotomi Hideyoshi, and rebuilt in 1715. A beautiful statue of Kannon of the thousand hands is venerated here. The painter Reizei Tamechika lived at Mike Shoin, which belongs to this temple, during the 19th c. There is a painted scroll by him in the *yamato e* style depicting the history of the temple.

3 KOYA SAN, SETO NAIKAI NATIONAL PARK, see entries under these names.

■ Wakkanai (Island of Hokkaido)

Railway map on inside front cover.

Tokyo, 899mls (1,477km) - Abashiri, 216mls (347km) - Asahikawa 160mls (258km) - Rumoi, 119mls (192km) - Sapporo, 209mls (337km).

Hokkaido - pop: 54,000 - fishing port.

Wakkanai is the most northerly town in Japan. Tourists wishing to explore Rishiri Rebun Sarobetsu National Park will choose to stay here. It is also an important base for fishing in the area where the Sea of Japan meets the Sea of Okhotsk, and has the advantage of not being iced up in winter.

To the W of the town is Wakkanai Park, which contains several monuments, among them one dedicated to the victims of Sakhalin, known as the Door of Ice; another is in honour of Mamiya Rinzo, the first Japanese explorer to come to Hokkaido, in 1800; and another is in

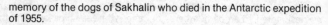

memory of the dogs of Sakhalin who died in the Antarctic expedition of 1955.

☞ **VICINITY**

1 NOSHAPPU MISAKI (3mls/5km NW; coach). This point, crowned by a lighthouse, marks the western end of Wakkanai Bay. Views across to Rishiri.

2 SOYA MISAKI (20mls/32km NE; coach). This point, at 45° 31' N, has the same latitude as Grenoble, in France. It is separated from Sakhalin island to the N by Soya Strait, also known as La Pérouse Strait after the famous navigator who passed through it in 1787. This is where Oya shio and Kuro shio merge, the two important currents which run on either side of Japan.

3 TOYOTOMI (25mls/40km S; JNR train). From here you can go to:

3½mls (6km) SE (coach): Toyotomi Onsen, saline springs at 109°F (43°C), said to be good for stomach disorders. A deposit of natural gas has been discovered nearby.

4 RISHIRI REBUN SAROBETSU NATIONAL PARK, see entry under this name.

Yaeyama shoto (Nansei shoto)**

Map of Nansei shoto, pp. 430–1.

Tokyo, 1,212mls (1,950km) - Okinawa, 261mls (420km).

Okinawa.

A group of about 20 islands, including three main ones, Iriomote, Ishigaki and Yonakuni, make up this archipelago which marks the end of Nantei shoto, before you come to the island of Taiwan. Lying between eastern China and the Pacific Ocean, these tropical islands offer dream holidays and are becoming more and more popular with young Japanese couples on their honeymoon. They are much wilder and more interesting than Okinawa or Miyako jima. They enjoy a delightful climate all year round (av. 61°F/16°C), but they can be affected by typhoons which cut off communications with the rest of Japan.

ISHIGAKI JIMA. On this mountainous island, which has a complex shoreline stretching N as far as Hirakubo zaki, the highest point is Omoto dake (1,726ft/526m).

Ishigaki (pop: 39,000) is the principal town of the island and also of the archipelago. You can visit Miyara Donchi, the former seignorial residence, built in the style typical of the archipelago with a large roof of brown tiles. This residence was put up in 1819 and is surrounded by a beautiful tropical garden. A little further N you will come across Torin ji (1614), which houses two statues of the Deva kings.

Between the town and the airport, in the village of Miyara on the E coast, you can visit a beautiful old house which has been turned into the local museum (pottery, *bingata*) and an interesting workshop where designs are printed on fabric using blocks of coral sawn in half.

On the inland road from Ishigaki to Nagura bay is an interesting pottery and weaving centre in a cluster of houses of traditional style (cotton: *kasuri*; silk; cloth made from banana fibres: *bashofu*).

If you go N along the W coast of Ishigaki (taxi), you come to the beautiful *bay of Kabira with its limpid water (9mls/15km; pearl culture) the dense tropical forest of Yonebara (12mls/20km), the little waterfall of Arakawa (14mls/23km), and Hirano (33mls/53km), near Hirakubo zaki (lighthouse), the most northerly point on the island.

➤ 3½mls (6km) W of the town of Ishigaki (hydroplane or boat), *Taketomi jima is of interest for its little streets bordered by walls of dry stone behind which shelter traditional houses and gardens. One of these houses has been converted into a little folklore museum. The beaches are famous for their sand with its star-shaped grains.

➤ *IRIOMOTE (17mls/27km W of Ishigaki jima; hydroplane or boat from Ishigaki harbour to Otomi and Ohara). Smaller and more mountainous than Ishigaki, the highest point of this island is Kami dake (1,542ft/470m). There is a single road in the N of the island and the rest is almost entirely made up of virgin forest, where it would be advisable to take a guide. By crossing the island via the valleys of the Nakama and the Urauchi gawa (about 14mls/22km) you will come to Otomi and Sonai. This island comes under the protection of the Iriomote National Park (30,092 acres/12,506ha), and is the home of a very rare species of cat, the Iriomote wildcat.

The recommended excursion is up the Urauchi gawa by boat (1h. through the jungle), then a 40-min. walk to the falls of Mariyudo and Kampira.

➤ *YONAKUNI JIMA (79mls/127km W of Ishigaki; plane; boat). Smaller than the other two, this island is also mountainous with Urabu dake its highest point at 758ft (231m). It is the most westerly of the islands of Japan (longitude 122°/56°E). Sonai, in the N of the island, is the main town.

☞ From there you can go (4mls/7km W; taxi) to Kubura Bay, one of the most interesting on the island. On the E coast (2½mls/4km on foot from Sonai) is the beautiful isolated rock of Saninu dai. In some places the thatched dwellings have been replaced by houses with tiled roofs. They are surrounded by bamboo fencing as a protection from the violent winds.

■ Yamagata (Island of Honshu)

Map of Tohoku, pp. 232–3.

Tokyo, 246mls (396km) – Akita, 133mls (214km) – Fukushima, 57mls (92km) – Niigata, 106mls (170km) – Sendai, 39mls (63km).

Principal town of Yamagata ken (pop: 875,000) – pop: 237,000 – alt. 420ft (128m) – production of raw silk – national university.

In one of the central valleys of Tohoku, which runs parallel to the Asahi and Ou chains on either side, Yamagata is a traditional centre of economic activity not far from other important towns (Nanyo, Kaminoyama, Tendo, Higashige, Murayama) that are situated along this valley. From Yamagata the Zao mountains are easily reached (see below, Vicinity), and you can also get to Asahi dake (see Tsuruoka).

Yamagata Park (550yd/500m N of the station, and W of the railway lines) is surrounded by the moats and ramparts of the former Yamagata Castle.

In 1335, this castle became the property of Shiba Kaneyori, whose descendants took the name of Mogami. This family was dispossessed in 1662 and the Torii clan became the owners. Several other daimyo succeeded one another as occupants of the castle during the Edo period, among them the Mizuno from 1845 to 1868.

½ml (1km) NE of the castle (1ml/1.5km NE of the station) is Chitose or Mamigasaki Park, near the river of that name. Here you will find Yakushi do, founded in the 8th c.

½ml (1km) S of the station (ask for directions) is the shrine of Hachiman. It was also founded in the 8th c. when Yamagata became an observation post in the struggle against the Ainu. It is famous for its beautiful evergreen oaks (*kunugi*) which can still be seen there.

VICINITY

1 YAMADERA (8mls/13km NE: JNR train; coach). To the N of the station, in a particularly attractive rocky and wooded spot, are situated the buildings of *Risshaku ji or Yama dera, some on top of the rocks themselves. This temple was founded in 860 by the priest Ennin, and most of the buildings have since been rebuilt. Nemoto Chu do is of particular interest. Beyond Nio mon, a long flight of steps takes you up to Okuno in, at the top of the hill.

Yamadera is dominated to the NE by *Omoshiro yama (4,147ft/ 1,264m), the 'strange mountain' whose slopes are an exceptional sight with their rocks, torrents and waterfalls. The rock with a hole, *Tennen Sekkyo, is one of the most famous natural phenomena of this area. You can take the coach to Okuyamadera (2mls/3km SE of the station) and explore this park where the waterfalls of Jizo and Nana taki are the most spectacular.

2 ZAO ONSEN (11mls/18km SE; coach). Situated on the NW slopes of Zao zan, this spa (springs from 104° to 117°F/40° to 47°C) makes a good base for walks or for skiing (December to April) on the mountain. There are numerous cable-cars, chair-lifts, ski-lifts, etc.

From Zao Onsen the recommended route is to take the **Zao Echo line (coach; 29mls/46km) to Togatta Onsen. The wooded landscape takes on a quite singular appearance in winter: the 'ghost trees', covered in frozen snow, assume the strangest forms. Along this route, a road branches off and leads N to Lake Dokko, from where you can climb *Kumano (6,040ft/1,841m), the main peak of Zao zan, a volcano which has been extinct since the 18th c.

Yamaguchi (Island of Honshu)

Map of Places of Interest, p. 71

Tokyo, 754mls (1,214km) - Hiroshima, 88mls (141km) - Matsue,

155mls (250km).

Principal town of Yamaguchi ken - pop: 105,000 - national university.

Today at some distance from the main southern through routes of Chugoku (San-Yo), Yamaguchi was once an important centre and is still the intellectual heart of the prefecture which bears its name.

SAINT FRANCIS XAVIER'S MISSION. The town was founded in 1350 by Ouchi Hiroyo and designed on the model of the Imperial capital Kyoto. The powerful Ouchi family and the town prospered together, welcoming the daimyo who fled from the political disturbances of the capital. Ouchi Yoshitaka (1507-51) also welcomed Saint Francis Xavier to Yamaguchi and gave him a disused temple where he succeeded in establishing a large Christian community. The following year (1551) Saint Francis left Yamaguchi for the Indies, but died in the Bay of Hong Kong. After his departure the Buddhist priests asserted their opposition to Christianity. The Jesuits were forced to leave Yamaguchi for Funai (Oita). Moreover, the power of the Ouchi had weakened considerably, and Yamaguchi passed into the hands of Otomo Yoshinaga in 1552 and Mori Motonari in 1557, in whose family it remained until the Restoration in 1868. After the battle of Sekigahara, the Mori clan chose to live in Hagi (see entry under this name), which brought about the decline of Yamagato. They returned in 1863.

The politician Kishi Nobusuke was born in Yamaguchi in 1896.

1ml (1.5km) NW of the station you come to Kameyama en which is on the site where a residence belonging to the Ouchi once stood. This 15-acre (6-ha) park is famous for its maples and azaleas. To the S of the hill is Yamaguchi Cathedral, built in 1952 in memory of Saint Francis Xavier. Its façade is reminiscent of the Château de Navarre where the saint was born.

Further N, Yamaguchi prefecture occupies what used to be the grounds of the castle of the Mori. There are traces of moats and ramparts. Still further N are two temples surrounded by gardens. That of Ruriko ji is said to have been designed originally by Sesshu (1420-1506). The pagoda of this temple dates from the 15th c.

1½mls (2.5km) NE of the station, on the site of Daido ji where Saint Francis Xavier established his religious community, a granite cross has been erected bearing a medallion with the bust of the famous missionary on it.

☞ **VICINITY**

1 ˙CHOMON KYO (12mls/20km NE; coach). Here are the attractive rocky gorges of the Abu gawa, with fantastically shaped rocks obstructing the watercourse; they are bordered by maples which should be seen in autumn. Takahaga dake (2,500ft/762m) towers over the scene.

2 ˙˙AKIYOSHI DAI (17mls/28km NW; coach). Leave Yamaguchi and head SW along the N9.

1½ml (2km): Yuda Onsen, springs from 140° to 158°F (60° to 70°C), beneficial to those suffering from rheumatism and skin diseases.

Festivals on 10 April and 10 October. Leave the N4 here and climb up to the W onto the heights overlooking Yamaguchi.

11mls (18km): take the road on the r. to Mito.

13mls (21km): continue along the road on the l. to Shuho.

16mls (26km): side road on the r., just before Shuho, to:

17mls (28km): *Akiyoshi do, one of the largest limestone caves in the world, 6mls (10km) in length (open from 08.30 to 16.30). An underground watercourse runs through the cave and, at its centre, a lift takes you up to the plateau of *Akiyoshi dai (toll road from the entrance to the cave; coach). This is a huge karst formation (3,420 acres/1,384 ha) with rocks of all shapes and sizes. The landscape is very unusual for Japan, and there is a science museum specializing in the study of this plateau which you can visit. About a hundred other caves are known to exist in this plateau.

Yamato Koriyama (Island of Honshu)

Map of Kansai, pp. 500–1.

Tokyo, 309mls (496km) – Kyoto, 29mls (47km) – Nara, 4mls (7km) –Osaka, 21mls (34km) – Tsu, 69mls (111km) – Wakayama, 67mls (108km).

Nara ken – pop: 63,000.

Today, Koriyama is an important little town in the Nara basin, not far from the capital of ancient times. The town is surrounded by numerous pools and specializes in the breeding of goldfish, mostly for export to gardens throughout the world.

To the N of Koriyama station (Kintetsu ER) you can see the ruins of the former castle, built in 1565 by Odagari Harutsuga.

VICINITY

1 JIKO IN (2mls/3km SW; 850yds/800m) N of the JNR station of Yamato Koizumi; coach) was founded in 1663 by the tea-master Katagiri Sekishu. There is a very attractive garden inspired by Zen and famous for its mosses, maples and azaleas.

2 NARA, see entry under this name.

3 HORYU JI, see Ikaruga.

Yamato Takada (Island of Honshu)

Map of Kansai, pp. 500–1.

Tokyo, 314mls (506km) – Kyoto, 39mls (63km) – Nara, 16mls (26km) – Osaka, 22mls (35km) – Tsu, 56mls (90km) – Wakayama, 48mls (78km).

Nara ken - pop: 59,500.

The main attraction of this place, situated in the S of the Nara basin, is a visit to Taima dera on the lower slopes of Nijo san (1,555ft/474m), which forms part of the Kongo chain.

*TAIMA DERA (3½mls/6km W; Coach; ½ml/1km W of Taima dera station, Kintetsu ER, which you can get to from Takadashi station in Yamato or Tenno ji station in Osaka). Founded in 612, this temple was moved here in 684. It was constructed originally on the plan of the first Buddhist temples of the Asuka period, but since then almost all of it has been rebuilt.

The visitor approaches Taima dera through Ro mon, a tiered doorway which opens to the E of the courtyards. To the W of these courtyards is Hon do or Mandara do, rebuilt in 1243. It contains a *painting of the Buddhist Paradise, executed in 763 by Chujo hima, daughter of Fujiwara Toyonari.

This painting, on a delicate support of woven fibres, is in poor condition. Only an old copy, which gives an idea of the work, is on show for the faithful to see. The mandala rests on a pedestal from the Nara period, inlaid with mother-of-pearl.

Before you come to Hon do, you will see Ko do (rebuilt at the beginning of the 14th c.) and (to the S of the latter) Kon do (rebuilt in the 13th c.), which contains several statues from the Heian, Fujiwara and Kamakura periods as well as a *Miroku Bosatsu, one of the oldest Japanese statues made of dried lacquer and dating from 685.

To the S of Kon do you will see the two Pagodas of the East and the West (To to and Sai to). This is the only Japanese temple which has retained pagodas, buildings which were once the pride of the great temples of Japan. They were built in the 8th and 9th c.

Taima dera also has a beautiful garden which was laid out during the Edo period. Festivals 14 and 15 May.

■ **Yanagawa** (Island of Kyushu)

Map of Kyushu (North), pp. 388-9.

Tokyo, 761mls (1,224km) - Fukuoka, 42mls (68km) - Kumamoto, 42mls (67km) - Oita, 103mls (165km) - Saga, 9mls (15km).

Fukuoka ken - pop: 51,000.

Near the estuary of the Chikugo gawa on Ariake bay, Yanagawa is an ancient feudal town where the Tachibana clan lived during the Edo period. It still has some old houses bordering on the *Yabe gawa which has been canalized. Trips by flat-bottomed boat down this river are particularly pleasant.

Boats depart from Taiko bashi, near Kaigetsuro, one of the most attractive houses of the old town whose praises were sung by the poet Hakushu. The trip ends near Suiten gu and Tachibanaka teien, a landscape garden created in 1697 for the Tachibana. The many little islands in the lake are meant to imitate the famous site of Matsushima (see Shiogama). A little further on you can visit the birthplace of the local poet Hakushu Kitahara (1885–1942), which was once a sake distillery.

Yawatahama (Island of Shikoku)

Map of Shikoku (Inland Sea), pp. 536–7.

Tokyo, 603mls (971km) – Kochi, 111mls (179km) – Matsuyama, 42mls (68km) – Takamatsu, 178mls (287km) – Tokushima, 231mls (372km).

Ehime ken – pop: 56,000 – ferries to Beppu, Usuki, Uwajima.

In the N of Uwa Bay, which shelters behind the long Sada peninsula, Yawatahama is an important fishing port on the island of Shikoku. It is also a centre of satsuma production.

VICINITY

1 KIN ZAN (10mls/16km; coach). You can visit Shusseki ji at the summit of this mountain which is also known by the name of Kana yama. *Wide views over Shikoku, the Inland Sea and Uwa Bay with Sada misaki jutting out between them.

2 MISAKI (34mls/54km W; coach), a little harbour from where you can take the boat to Saganoseki on the island of Kyushu.

11mls (18km) further on is *Sada misaki, at the tip of the longest and narrowest of the Japanese peninsulas (it is about 30mls/50km long). A series of rocky outcrops averaging 1,000 to 1,300ft (300 to 400m) outline attractive bays on either side. The extreme tip of Sada peninsula is only about 6mls (10km) from Seki zaki (island of Kyushu) and boasts a lighthouse and a plantation of ako trees, a kind of banyan.

Yokkaichi (Island of Honshu)

Map of Places of Interest, p. 70.

Tokyo, 237mls (382km) – Gifu, 43mls (70km) – Kyoto, 64mls (103km) – Nagoya, 25mls (40km) – Nara, 66mls (107km) – Otsu, 57mls (91km) – Tsu, 21mls (34km) – Wakayama, 124mls (200km).

Mie ken – pop: 255,000 – industrial town (textiles, glass, ceramics, iron and steel industry, petrochemicals) and port.

To the N of the estuary of the Suzuka gawa, on Ise Bay at the point where the railway line from Nagoya forks, with one line going to Ise and the other to Osaka. Yokkaichi is the centre of the industrial zone N of Ise. The town was razed during the 1945 bombings and has been completely rebuilt; it has now become one of the busiest towns in modern Japan. Its oil terminal and industrial developments have been built partly on land reclaimed from the sea.

☞ **VICINITY**

1 YUNOYAMA ONSEN (12mls/19km W; coach; Kintetsu ER train for 11mls/17km). This spa is located at an altitude of 1,043ft (318m) on the Mitaki gawa which flows into the sea at Tsu. View over the Ise Bay and Nagoya. From Yunoyama you can take the cable-car to Gozaisho yama (3,970ft/1,210m); extensive views from the summit, ski-slopes. This mountain is one of the highest in the beautiful **wooded park of Suzuka, which extends across the mountainous ridge between Ise Bay and Lake Biwa. A toll road (coach) crosses these mountains and heads towards Tsuchiyama.

2 KAMEYAMA, TSU, see entries under these names.

Y Yokohama (Island of Honshu)*

Map of Tokyo vicinity, p. 565 – plan of Yokohama area, p. 664 – plan of city centre, p. 665.

Tokyo, 15mls (24km) – Kofu, 87mls (140km) – Shizuoka, 86mls (142km).

Principal town of Kanagawa ken – pop: 2,774,000 – industrial city (shipyards, car industry, electrical goods, petrochemicals, textiles) and port – national, regional and private universities – cathedral city.

Lying to the S of Tokyo, Yokohama was until recently the main port of entry for visitors to Japan. The port lies in a sheltered position to the N of the promontory where the Westerners established themselves from 1859 onwards. Yokohama was also one of the first Japanese ports to open up for international trade. Despite the profound effect on the city of the 1923 earthquake and the bombings during World War II, Yokohama has remained one of the largest trading ports in Japan. It is a city in a state of flux, where the visitor is constantly amazed by the modern buildings, expressways on piles, land reclaimed from the sea, industrial developments and extension to the harbour, which is spanned by an immense bridge.

THE TREATY OF KANAGAWA. When, in 1853, Commodore Matthew C. Perry landed in Japan, bringing a message from President Fillmore to the 'Head of the Japanese State', Yokohoma was no more than a fishing village. In accordance with the clauses of the treaty signed at Kanagawa (29 July 1858) between Ii Naosuke and Townsend Harris, Japan was opened to the Western world. Part of the coastal lands of Yokohama was granted to the foreigners for use as a settlement, and steps were taken to ensure their safety.

URBAN DEVELOPMENT. In 1872 the first railway line was built from Tokyo to Yokohama. In 1887, a mains water supply was installed. By 1869 the town had a population of 121,000 and was established as a municipality. The harbour was extended in 1896 and gradually the city boundaries expanded as the population increased. After the 1923 earthquake, Yokohama had a population of 405,000. The 1938 census showed a spectacular increase to a population of 850,000. The city was rebuilt, made more attractive with wide streets and new public buildings, and the beach cleaned up. Until the start of war in the Pacific, the port of Yokohama continued to expand and the city enjoyed the most prosperous years in its history until it suffered the terrible bombardment of 29 May 1945. The Korean War again prompted the development of Yokohama.

The Composer Mayuzumi Toshiro was born in Yokohama in 1929.

THE PORT. Since 1951 the harbour facilities have been growing continuously. The main docks stretch northwards in the direction of Kawsaki. 22% of Japanese exports (cereals, food products, silk, manufactured goods) and 19% of Japanese imports (cereals, food products, fuel) are handled by the port which is also equipped to receive 1.5 billion m^3 of natural gas per year. Today it is congested, but the harbour is in the process of being extended and in future will stretch right round Tokyo Bay past Kawasaki and the city of Tokyo (see entry under this name).

From Yokohama station (JNR) it is possible to go straight to Sakuragicho station (Keihin Kyuko ER direct train from Shinagawa to Tokyo), N of Yokohama city centre which opens onto the harbour and is bordered to the S by Yamate hill, where the Westerners settled in the 19th c.

Kamonyama Park (plan of city centre: A1; 770yds/700m NW of Sakuragicho eki, JNR) is on a hill where stands a bronze statue of Ii Naosuke Kamon no kami (1815–50), who signed the Kanagawa agreements for Japan.

In the park there is a library and concert hall (architect Mayekawa Kunio) set among cherry trees. View over the harbour and city.

200yds (200m) S of this park is Iseyama Daijin gu (plan of city centre: A1), a dependency of the shrines at Ise. Festivals 14, 15 and 16 May. View over the harbour.

Further S still you will find Naritasan Emmei in or Nogeyama Fudo (plan of city centre: A2), dedicated to Fudo myo o. A fair is held here three times a month (on the 1st, 15th and 28th) in the temple enclosure, to the SW of which is:

Noge yama Park (plan of city centre: A2; 880yds/800m W of Sakuragicho eki, JNR; 330yds/300m NW of Hinodecho station, Keihin Kyuko ER). Two gardens belonging to two rich citizens of Yokohama, together with adjoining land, went to make up this park which is laid out in the Japanese style. There is also a swimming pool, an open-air and an indoor theatre, a playing field and a zoological garden. View over the city and harbour.

On leaving the park, make your way to Isezaki cho to the SE (plan of city centre: A3–B3; 660yds/600m S of Sakuragicho station and 220yds/200m NW of Kannai JNR station), a very busy area with large stores (Nozawaya and Matsukiya), cinemas and souvenir shops. The

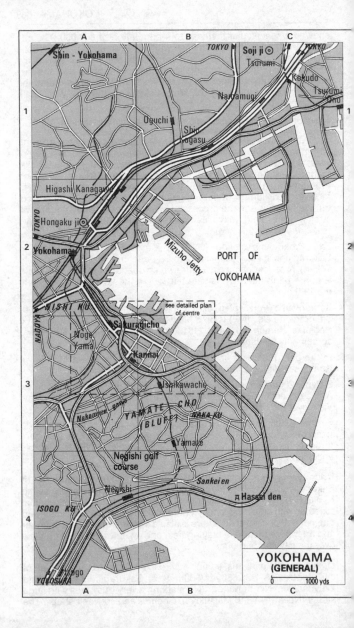

YOKOHAMA
(GENERAL)

0   1000 yds

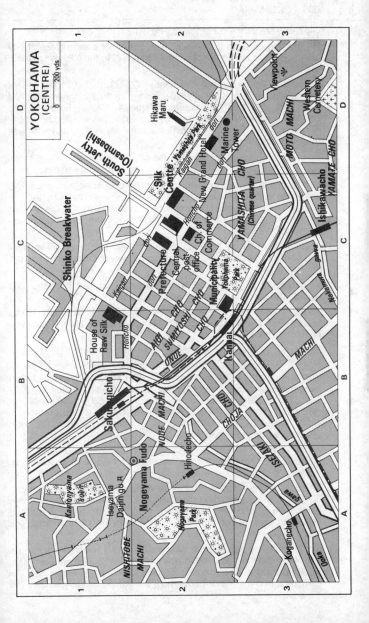

YOKOHAMA
(CENTRE)

0   200 yds

Shinko Breakwater

South Jetty
(Osambashi)

House of
Raw Silk

Silk
Centre

Hikawa
Maru

Yamashita Park

Prefecture

Central
post
office

City of
Commerce

New Grand Hotel

Taikan

Marine
Tower

Viewpoint

Western
Cemetery

MOTO
MACHI

YAMASHITA
CHO

YAMATE
CHO

Ishikawacho

dori

Honcho

dori

dori

dori

Kangai

tori

Honcho

AOI
CHO

SUMIYOSHI
CHO

ONOE
CHO

Municipality

Yoshidama

Yoshidama

Kanai

Nakamura

gawa

MACHI

Sakuragicho

NOGE
MACHI

Hinodecho

Iseyama
Dajin-gu

Nogeyama
Fudo

Nogeyama
Park

CHOJA
CHO

ISEZAKI

Koganecho

gawa

Ooka

Kamburayama
Beach

NISHTOBE
MACHI

A   B   C   D

1   2   3

Japanese are very fond of this quarter which they call *zaki*.

On passing beneath the railway lines at Kannai station (plan of city centre: B2), you will see Yokohama Town Hall to the NE, and to the E of that:

Yokohama Park (plan of city centre: C2-C3; 440yds/400m NE of Kannai eki, JNR), laid out in 1876 specially for the foreigners who had been allocated their own residential quarter. Within the park are a chapel, a baseball stadium, a gymnasium and an amphitheatre. Recently one of Baltard's pavilions from les Halles in Paris was reconstructed here.

To the E of the park runs one of the city's large streets which takes you N to Kaigan dori. Just before reaching it you will see the:

Silk centre (plan of city centre: C2; 880yds/800m NE of Kannai eki, JNR), the first and second floors of which are occupied by the silk museum (displays of silkworms, cocoons and silks). On the ground floor there is a tourist information office, and the upper floors are taken up by a hotel.

Just across the road is Osambashi, the main pier where passenger and cruise ships dock. You can get a good view of the whole port from the end of this pier.

Kaigan dori runs alongside Yamashita park (plan of city centre: D2) which borders on Yokohama harbour for about ½ml (1km).

There you can visit the steamship *Hikawa Maru* (11,625t) which was used on the trans-Pacific route between 1930 and 1960. It has now been converted into a youth hostel.

To the SE of the park is a tower (plan of city centre: D2) built to commemorate the port's centenary (348ft/106m high, good views).

Running parallel to Kaigan dori to the S is Honcho dori, which you have to cross to get to the Chinese quarter (plan of city centre: C3-D3; 880yds/800m SE of Kannai station and 880yds/800m NE of Ishikawacho station, JNR), designated as such by the government in 1863. Numerous little restaurants, bars, cabarets, pachinko parlours, etc., make this sector a lively place.

Each year on 10 October, 13 May (Kouan Yu) and 25 August (Confucius), typically Chinese festivals are held, with processions, masks and dragons.

To the S of the Chinese quarter is Yamata hill (plan of city centre: C3-D3), with several streets leading up it. The Westerners called this hill the 'Bluff', and they built several wooden residences on it in the European style of the period. Some of them are still standing. The water tower was built by the French.

On this hill you can see the Western Cemetery (plan of city centre: D3; 440yds/400m SE of Ishikawacho station, JNR) where 3,000 foreigners are buried (English, French, Dutch, etc.). To the E of the cemetery, in the grounds of Myoho ji, are some strangely-shaped old plum trees and there are some cherry trees on the hill behind the temple.

To the N of this quarter is a little garden with good views over Yokohama port.

From Kannai station a street runs beside the railway lines to the SW of the Chinese quarter, crosses Nakamura gawa, passes through a tunnel under Yamate hill, beyond the Kitagata and Hommoku quarters, comes to the Makado quarter where you can visit Sankei en. You can also reach this garden by taking a street which continues on from Kaigan dori at the foot of Yamate hill.

SANKEI EN (plan of the entire city: B4; 1ml/1.5km SE of Yamate station; 2½mls /4km SE of Sakuragicho station, bus from the latter). This park's name is the pseudonym of its first owner (Sankei, 'three little valleys'), Hara Tomitaro, a leading merchant who did much of his business with the foreigners. This garden was opened to the public in 1906 and is pleasant to visit all year round. The old buildings which have been reconstructed here are of particular interest.

On a hill to the S of the park's main lake is an exquisite three-storey pagoda dating from the Muromachi period. It originally stood in the grounds of Tomyo ji (Yamashiro province) and was moved here in 1914. On the S side of this hill is a terrace from which you can see Yokohama's new industrial area which has been built on land reclaimed from Negishi Bay, already partly filled in. At the foot of this hill, to the l., are the Batsu den of Tokei ji (Kamakura period), the beautiful Yanohara farmhouse (18th c.), which comes from the province of Hida, and the little teahouse of Yokobue.

To the W of the park is *Nai en, the inner garden, where you will see Rinshun kaku, near a little lake. It was wrongly thought to have been built by Toyotomi Hideyoshi; it was in fact the Kishu, lords of Iwate near Osaka, who were responsible for its construction. The following are also worthy of note: the pavilions of Gekka den (16th c.) originally from Fushimi Palace (see Kyoto) and of Choshu kaku (this one has a single storey and comes from Nijo Castle at Kyoto; 17th c.); the mausoleum of Tenzui ji, which comes from Daitoku ji in Kyoto (16th c.); Tenju in, which comes from Kamakura (16th c.); and several teahouses from the 16th and 17th c.

440yds (400m) SE of Sankei en (ask for directions) is Hassei den (plan of the entire city: B4), an octagonal two-storey building built in 1932 by the statesman Adachi Kenzo as a national centre of spiritual education. It contains statues of the Eight Wise Men of the World: Sakyamuni, Confucius, Socrates, Jesus, Prince Shotoku, and the priests Kobo Daishi, Shinran and Nichiren.

ADDITIONAL PLACES TO VISIT ...

From Yokohama station (JNR), the length of the Keihin Kyuko line (Keihin Kyuko ER):

- Going N towards Tokyo:

½ml (1km): Kanagawa (1st station). NW of the station is Hongaku ji (plan of the entire city: A2) on Shima yama hill. In 1856 this temple was the base of the provisional American legation and in 1858 the commercial treaty of Kanagawa (see section on history) was signed here.

3mls (5km): Namamugi (5th station). Its name recalls an incident of 1862: British merchants had refused to dismount before the procession of Shimazu Hisamitsu, lord of Kagoshima; for this one of them was killed by the daimyo's men. The British were unable to obtain prompt compensation, and bombarded Kagoshima.

5mls (8km): Keihin Tsurumi (7th station). 660yds (600m) W of the station you can visit *Soji ji (plan of the entire city: C1; Tsurumi JNR station is nearer), which is a particularly representative example of Kamakura architecture. Today it is one of the greatest monasteries of the Soto sect of Zen Buddhism, on a par with Eihei ji (see Fukui vicinity). Some of the buildings come from the former ruined temple of Monzen (see Wajima vicinity) and were transferred here in 1911. The temple contains a painting on silk representing Daibasatta, patriarch of Zen in India. The grounds surrounding the temple are very extensive. Not far from here is the big velodrome at Kagetsuen.

- Heading S towards Yokosuka:

3½mls (6km): Gumyo ji (6th station). To the SE of the station, Gumyo ji is situated in a busy quarter. It was spared during the war and is one of the oldest temples in Yokohama. Inside is a wooden statue of Kannon of the eleven heads, a work dating from the Fujiwara period. The temple also has a garden planted with apricot and cherry trees which are magnificent in spring.

11mls (18km): Kanazawabunko (12th station). 770yds/700m E of the station is Shomyo ji, founded in 1269 by Kanazawa Akitoki, son of Sanetoki (see below). Both of them are buried in the temple gardens. A modern building in the temple grounds now houses the famous Kanazawa library.

This library was started in 1275 by Kanazawa Sanetoki, who was related by marriage to the Hojo. Contributions to the collection were made by members of the Hojo family, who were enlightened booklovers, and by the scholarly monks of the neighbouring temple. At that period it included Buddhist, Confucian and Taoist works from all the Chinese schools, Japanese books, medical works, etc. However, after the destruction of the seignorial clan of Hojo, the library was abandoned and a large number of works were dispersed and lost. Tokugawa Ieyasu had the remaining books transferred to Edo Castle in 1602. The library was built up again in 1930 under the direction of Kanagawa prefecture.

Apart from rare books and documents, there are some treasures which belonged to the old library: *statues of Kannon of the eleven heads, of Shaka Nyorai, Aizen Myo o, and Miraku Bosatsu and a copy of *Issai kyo* (a complete collection of Buddhist sutrà) from the Song

(Sung) period, published in China (open daily from 09.30 to 16.30 except Mondays, the last day of the month and at the end of the year).

VICINITY

KAMAKURA, MIURA, TOKYO, YOKOSUKA, ZUSHI, see entries under these names.

Yokosuka (Island of Honshu)

Map of the Vicinity of Tokyo, p. 565.

Tokyo, 29mls (46km) – Kofu, 101mls (162km) – Shizuoka, 102mls (164km) – Yokohama, 14mls (22km).

Pop: 378,000 – industrial town and port.

On the N side of Miura peninsula, which juts out into the entrance to Tokyo Bay, Yokosuka enjoys a privileged position which meant that during World War II it was second only to Kure as a Japanese naval base. The French engineer Verny was involved in the construction of the naval base in the 19th c. The *Satsuma* was launched here in 1910 and was at the time the largest amoured vessel in the world. After the war, the American Fleet in the Far East was based here, and today the Japanese self-defence fleet uses it as a base. Japanese expeditions to the Antarctic Ocean also set out from here.

1ml (1.6km) SE of Yokosuka JNR station (880yds/800m NE of Yokosuka Chuo station, Keihin Kyuoko ER), in a public garden near the Inaka cho coast, you will find the *Mikasa*, the flagship which under the command of Admiral Togo participated in the battle of Tsushima strait (see Iki and Tsu shima) during the Russo-Japanese War (1904–05).

The ship was converted into a museum in 1949 (open from 09.00 to 16.00) and contains 7,000 different kind of shells, an aquarium, articles which belonged to Admiral Togo, etc.

1½ml (2km) SE by boat is the little island of Saru, which was once of strategic importance. Today it is a pleasant tropical garden where monkeys (*saru*) and deer run free.

VICINITY

1 TSUKAYAMA PARK (2mls/3.5km NW; coach; 1ml/1.5km NW of Yokosuka JNR station and ½ml/1km SW of Anjinzuka station, Keihin Kyuko ER).

William Adams and his wife are buried in this park, which is laid out on the slopes of Mount Hatakae (alt. 682ft/208m).

Adams was the first Briton to land in Japan, following a shipwreck in 1600. Shogun Tokugawa valued him for his knowledge of the sea and he was forced to remain. 'Despite numerous requests, Adams was never allowed to return to England to see his wife and children. He was given a Japanese wife, and even a title and some land. He was confined to the port of Ito and spent the rest of his life setting up a merchant navy for the *bakufu* (François Toussaint, *Histoire du Japon*). He died in 1620 after being transferred to the British trading post at Hirado. He took the Japanese name of Miura Anjin, and a commemorative ceremony is held on 14 April every year.

2 KINUGASA PARK (3mls/5km SW; ½ml/1km SW of Kinugasa JNR station; coach from Yokosuka station). This park is situated on a hill where the castle of the Miura once stood. They were dispossessed in 1180 by Hatakeyama Shigetada. There is a view over Miura peninsula, and cherry trees are the park's main feature.

3 URAGA (4mls/7km SE; Keihin Kyuko ER train). It is at the head of a narrow bay protected by Kannon zaki. During the Edo period this was a port of inspection for vessels entering Tokyo Bay.

In 1846 Commodore James Biddle anchored off Uraga and sought the conclusion of the trade agreements with Japan. He failed, but opened the way for Commodore Perry who, seven years later, was more successful.

3mls (5km) E of Uraga (coach): *Kannon zaki lies opposite Futtsu point on the Boso peninsula. The lighthouse dates from 1869 and there is a little nature museum. Good views.

4 KURIHAMA (5½mls/9km SE; JNR and Keihin Kyuoko ER trains) another inlet on the Miura peninsula, to the S of that of Uraga.

Admiral Perry, accompanied by 300 sailors and soldiers, came ashore here on 14 July 1853 to start negotiations with a view to opening Japanese ports to American trade. He obtained an understanding in 1854, which was confirmed in 1858 by the Kanagawa treaty (see Yokohama).

In 1901, in the presence of Rear-Admiral Rogers (Perry's grandson), a monument was erected commemorating this event. Nearby (1ml/1.5km S of the station), a museum traces the different episodes in the arrival of the 'black ships'. Festival 14 July. To the S of Kurihama is a large thermal power station which serves Tokyo and Yokohama.

■ Yonago (Island of Honshu)

Railway map on inside front cover.

Tokyo, 490mls (789km) – Hiroshima, 134mls (216km) – Kobe, 162mls (260km) – Matsue, 21mls (33km) – Okayama, 82mls (132km) – Tottori, 62mls (100km).

Tottori ken – pop: 121,000.

Yonago and the nearby thermal spa of Kaike are situated at the base, and on either side of the spit of sand called Sakaiminato, the northern end of which stops just short of Shimane peninsula. Yonago overlooks Naka umi lagoon to the W, and the spa overlooks Miho Bay to the E. To the SE towers the superb mountain of Dai sen.

The thermal spa of Kaike (3mls/5km NE of the station; bus) is situated on Miho Bay which has a beautiful beach bordered by a pinewood. Saline springs between 172° and 187°F (78° and 86°C).

VICINITY

MATSUE, OKI SHOTO, DAISEN OKI NATIONAL PARK, see entries under these names.

Yonezawa (Island of Honshu)

Map of the main railway lines on inside back cover.

Tokyo, 209mls (337km) – Akita, 229mls (369km) – Fukushima, 27mls (43km) – Niigata, 57mls (91km) – Sendai, 76mls (123km) – Yamagata, 34mls (55km).

Yamagata ken – pop: 93,000 – alt. 804ft (245m) – textile industries.

Just to the N of the Azuma mountains, and some distance from the peaks of Iimori yama (5,233ft/1,595m) and Iide san (6,906ft/2,105m), Yonezawa is basically a mountain town surrounded, amazingly, by a fertile basin, near which the Uesugi clan established their residence. Several spas in the surrounding area bear witness to the recent volcanic activity of these mountains.

MATSUGASAKI PARK (1½ml/2km W of Yonezawa station; bus). The park is on the site of the former castle of Yonezawa.

This castle was built at the end of the 12th c. by Nagai Tokihiro, a partisan of Minamoto Yoritomo. In the 16th c. it passed into the hands of Date Masamune, then of Gamo Ujisato. Finally, in 1601, it became the property of Uesugi Kagekatsu, in whose family it remained until the Restoration in 1868.

In the park you can see the shrines of Uesugi, dedicated to Uesugi Kenshin (16th c.) and of Matsugasaki, dedicated to Uesugi Harunori, who was also known by the name of Yosan. The latter introduced the silk industry to Yonezawa in the 18th c.

On a hill 1,600ft (500m) NW of the station is Sashien Park, which is said to be on the site of the former residence of Sato Masanobu, whose children sided with Minamoto Yoshitsune (see Chosun ji, p. 240). Pinewood.

VICINITY

1 ONOGAWA ONSEN (7mls/12km SW; coach). These are saline springs helpful for rheumatism sufferers. One of the springs (Amano yu, Spring of the Lady) is linked with the legend of a young girl who, while searching for her father, found him at the same time as she found this spring, thanks to the miraculous intervention of Yakushi Nyorai, the healing Buddha.

2 SHIRABU ONSEN (9mls/15km S; coach). It lies at an alt. of 3,000ft (900m) on the NW slopes of Nishi Azuma san (6,640ft/2,024m), which you can climb in 4½ hours. There is a cable-car to the ski slopes of Tengendai, near the thermal spring of Azuma Kokusai, at an alt. of

4,600ft (1,400m); skiing from December to April. Beyond Shirabu, a scenic *toll road twists and turns until it comes to Lake Hibara (22mls/35km as far as Urabandai; see Bandai Asahi National Park).

3 ITAYA (12mls/19km SE; JNR train). The station is at an alt. of 2,300ft (700m), and from there you can go SW to the thermal springs of Goshiki and Shin Goshiki (3mls/5km), and Namekawa (5mls/8km), at an alt. of 2,549ft (777m).

4 BANDAI ASAHI NATIONAL PARK, see entry under this name.

■ Yoshino (Island of Honshu)*

Map of Kansai, pp. 500–1.

Tokyo, 326mls (525km) – Kashihara, 16mls (25km) – Nara, 29mls (46km).

Nara ken.

Yoshino is the most famous place in Japan for cherry blossom in spring. There are about 100,000 cherry trees, divided into several groups. The town also has an important place in Japanese history during the civil wars of the 14th c. Many religious buildings still survive and this remarkable area now comes under the protection of Yoshino Kumano National Park (see entry under this name).

A SITE CHOSEN BY THE EMPERORS. A semi-legendary chronicle relates that in the Yoshino area Emperor Jimmu confronted Nagasane hiko, master of the region. Imperial victory led to Yamato opening its doors and to the establishment of the Japanese dynasty. Several centuries later, Ojin tenno made Yoshino his place of residence and other emperors visited this remarkable area. In 1185 Minamoto Yoshitsune, hounded by his intransigent brother Yoriromo (see Chuson ji, p. 240) took refuge at Yoshino for a time.

THE COURT AT YOSHINO. In 1333 Prince Morinaga made Kongobu ji, then the main temple of Yoshino, into a fortress in order to hold out against the Hojo clan from whom Emperor Go Daigo was trying to wrest power (see Kamakura, Kyoto). In 1336, Go Daigo himself took up residence in this temple after fleeing from Kyoto where Emperor Komyo had just acceded to the throne. Go Daigo thus became the representative of the Court of the South (or of Yoshino), which was opposed to that of the North (Kyoto), since nobody else succeeded in taking the lead. After several clashes, the courts of the South and the North (Nambokucho) were finally reunited in 1388, when Emperor Go Kameyama was able to return to Kyoto, where in 1392 he abdicated in favour of Go Komatsu, the representative of the older court of the North.

HITOME SEMBON (A 'thousand trees beneath one's gaze'). This is the name given to each of the main groups of cherry trees. The blossom is at the height of its glory between 10 and 15 April. The trees are said to have been planted at the end of the 7th c. by the Buddhist priest

Enno Ozunu, who placed the trees under the protection of Zao Gongen, a god representing strength and anger against the spirit of evil. Cutting them down was forbidden and their numbers multiplied. Today much careful attention is still lavished on these cherry trees.

NB: From Kyoto, Nara and Osaka, Yoshino station can be reached by Kintetsu ER trains, usually with a change at Saidaiji (or at Yagi if one leaves from Osaka-Namba). Alternatively, departing from the same towns you can take JNR trains to Yoshinoguchi station, continue by Kintetsu train to Yoshino and from there take the funicular railway to Yoshinoyama. Bus services are provided beyond this point.

The Yoshino funicular crosses the cherry tree plantation of Shimono sembon ('the thousand trees below') and emerges near the road which runs along the ridge of the Yoshino hills. This road is bordered by low houses (souvenir shops); the ground floor of these houses, opening onto the street, is in fact the upper floor, there being one or two floors below that at the back.

If you go N along this road, 1½ml (2km) further downhill you come to Yoshino shrine (1ml/1.5km SW of Yoshinojingu station, Kintetsu ER), which is dedicated to Emperor Go Daigo.

If you carry on up this road to the S, after 660yds (600m) you will see Kimpusen ji, of which *Zao do is the main building.

This temple, founded by the priest Gyoki (670–749), was rebuilt in the 15th c. after the fire of 1348. Its height of 112ft (34m) makes it one of the largest wooden buildings in Japan. The statues of the Deva kings of Nio mon are attributed to the famous sculptors Unkei and Tankei (12th-13th c.). The temple's treasury houses several precious objects from the Heian and Kamakura periods.

Nearby are the ruins of the former Kongobu ji, which was the main temple of Yoshino where the emperors of the Court of the South took up residence. You can see the remains of fortifications which they built.

440yds (400m) S of Zao do are the shrines of Yoshimizu and Katte (or Yamaguchi), and 990yds (900m) further along the same road you come to Chikurin in on the r., where the landscape garden is attributed to the master Senno Rikyu (16th c.). Nearby are the 'thousand trees in the middle' (Nakano sembon). Next take a winding road (not the toll road) heading S (see below), up to:

*Saruhiki zaka, from where there is a view of Kamino sembon ('the thousand trees at the top').

Further on, the road comes to an end (1ml/1.5km E of Chikurin in; 2mls/3km SE of Yoshinoyama funicular railway station) at Nyorin ji. In the temple enclosure is the tomb of Emperor Go Daigo (1287-1338; see section on history).

If you can take the toll road mentioned above, you will pass to the S the shrine of Yoshino Mikumari, which was built in 1604 by Toyotomi Hideyori, son of Hideyoshi. Finally you will come to the shrines of

Kimpu and Kokeshimizu (1,640ft/500m below). The priest and poet Saigyo (1118–90) set up a hermitage where the latter shrine now stands. This is also where you will find Okuno sembon, the last group of Yoshino's cherry trees (3½mls/6km SE of Yunoyama).

■ Yoshino Kumano** (National Park of; Island of Honshu)

Map of Natural Resources, p. 64.

HOW TO GET THERE

- From Matsusaka and Tsu, take the JNR train to Owase (55mls/89km; 1h. 10 from Matsusaka) and change to a train to Kushimoto.

- From Nara, Osaka or Wakayama, you can travel to Gojo station (25mls/40km in 1h. from each of these stations; sometimes it is necessary to change at Oji), from where you can continue by coach to Shingu (94mls/151km).

- From Tanabe and Wakayama you can take the JNR train to Kushimoto (99mls/159km from Wakayama in 2h. 45), and continue to Owase along the Kumano coast.

This mountainous coastal park (136,839 acres/55,378 ha) has some of the most beautiful landscapes in Japan. The Yoshino mountains are situated in the heart of the Kii peninsula, with the coast of Kumano forming the peninsula's eastern sea border. Kumano's shrines make this a place of pilgrimage and enhance its interest for the tourist.

FROM OWASE TO KUSHIMOTO (68mls/109km SW via the N42; JNR train). Owase (pop: 33,500), which means 'eagle tail' in Japanese, is situated at the head of one of the most beautiful **bays in Japan, surrounded by magnificent scenery. The hills plunge into the sea, and behind them tower the high mountains of Yoshino, Odaigahara san at 5,561ft (1,696m) being one of the main peaks. You can take a boat trip round the bay, which has unfortunately been marred by oil installations.

From Owase the railway line runs along fairly close to the coast and passes through tunnel after tunnel. The N311 also follows this beautiful *rugged coastline, and is well worth taking despite the detour of an additional 21mls (34km); if possible ask for directions all along this route.

The N42 heads further inland and passes through tunnels beneath the slopes of Takamine san:

15mls (24km): junction with the N169 which goes N up the *valley of the Kitayama gawa with the beautiful Yoshino mountains on either side.

Along this road you will come to Ikehara dam (16mls/25km; alt. 1,043ft/318m), and at 37mls (59km) to a toll road heading in the direction of Odaigahara san (10mls/16km), from where you will see some of the loveliest views of the Yoshino mountains. (A coach will take you up here from Yamato Kamiichi station, Kintetsu, near Yoshino.)

19mls (31km): junction with the N311 which comes from Owase along the coast (see above).

→ 1ml (1.5km) S: *Onigajo (Demons' Castle), a rocky formation eroded into a hollow shape by the sea. The waves come crashing into this place, which could have been used as a thieves' den.

21mls (33km): Kumano (pop: 31,200), a fishing port. Beyond the coastline becomes straighter. You will pass the site of Shichiri mihama on the way to:

37mls (60km): Shingu (pop: 42,500). Large quantities of undressed timber are stored in this town at the mouth of the Kumano gawa, which is also a fishing port.

Emperor Jimmu is said to have disembarked here after he was driven from Naniwa (see Osaka). From here he went up the valley, crossed the Yoshino mountains and then conquered the Yamato region.

550yds (500m) NW of the station, near the river, are the ruins of Shingu Castle, built about 1180 by Minamoto Yukiie, uncle of Yoritomo. The Horiuchi clan owned it during the 16th c., and in the following century it became part of the estate of the Tokugawa of Wakayama.

1ml (1.5km) NW of the station you can visit the shrine of Kumano Hayatama, one of the most important in the region, set among trees and with the river flowing nearby. Festival (Ofune matsuri) on 15 and 16 October commemorating the arrival of the Kumano gods from the province of Izumo.

Among the buildings (which have been recently reconstructed), Ro mon is of interest since it contains the carved wooden panels attributed to Hidari Jingoro (1594-1634). The treasury museum houses a large number of objects, most of them given to the shrine in 1390. There are cypress wood fans painted with landscapes, flowers and birds, among them Kumano hi ogi, and also lacquerware, pottery, objects used in religious ceremonies, and weapons. From the shrine a flight of steps (have a look at these) leads up to Kannokura jinja, which marks the spot where the three gods of Kumano 'landed'. Their names are Hayatama, Ketsu miko and Fusumi, and they are venerated at the shrines of Shingu, Hongu and Nachi.

To the S of Shingu stretches the beautiful beach of Sanomatsushima.

→ 31mls (50km) NW of Shingu (2h. by boat; landing stage on the N bank of the river, opposite the shrine, 2mls/3km NW of the station; bus), you can take a boat trip up the Kumano gawa and then the Kitayama gawa as far as the magnificent **Doro hatcho. The river is enclosed between high walls of rock covered in trees at Kami doro and Oku doro, which are among the most beautiful gorges in Japan.

FROM SHINGU TO HONGU (23mls/37km NW via the N168; coach). From

Shingu you follow the twisty, narrow valley of the Kumano gawa, also known as *Kuri kyo. Launches from Doro hatcho (see above) ply up and down the river.

15mls (24km): confluence of the Kitayama gawa from the N, with the Totsu kawa, beside the road continues, heading NW.

22mls (35km): Ukegawa, where there is a road on the l. to:

→ 2mls (3km) SW: Kawayu Onsen, whose spring is in the bed of the Daito gawa itself.

☞ 23mls (37km) Hongu, where you can visit *Nimasu jinja, or Kumano Hongu, the largest of the Kumano shrines. It is dedicated to Susano o Mikoto and is said to have been founded in the 1st c. BC. From the 10th c. onwards it was popular with the emperors and lords of Japan who went there on pilgrimages. The present buildings were put up in 1802 at the request of the shogun Tokugawa Ienari. In 1889, following a flood, the shrine was moved to its current site, at some distance from its original position. It contains a mandala painted on silk, representing the arrival of the gods of Kumano (Kamakura period). Festival 7 January.

→ 2mls (3km) W along the N311 (coach): Yunomine Onsen, an abundant spring (160° to 194°F/71° to 90°C) known since the Heian period. Legend has it that Terute Hime brought her lover, Oguri Hangan, to this spring when he was ill with the plague, and he was cured (see Fujisawa). Beyond Yunomine, the N311 continues towards Shirahama (see entry under this name) and Tanabe (39mls/63km).

From Hongu, the N168 continues N in the direction of Gojo (94mls/151km from Shingu).

☞ Beyond Shingu, the **Kumano coast once again becomes jagged and rough until you get to Kushimoto.

47mls (75km): Nii katsura (boats to Kochi and Tokyo) is one of the most pleasant places along the Kumano coast. It has a thermal spring, and the little Museum of the Whale makes an interesting visit. Across the entrance to the attractive *bay of Katsuura lie a little island and Noroshiyama promontory, from where there is a view of the area.

Boat trips around the bay and nearby islands, known by the name of Kino Matsushima.

→ 7mls (12km) NW (coach): Kumano Nachi. Here you can see the beautiful *Nachi waterfall (427ft/130m), one of the highest in Japan. A little further up the mountain is Kumano Nachi shrine, built in the 4th c. in the Kumano style. It contains a mandala painted in the 16th c. Festival of *hi matsuri (festival of fire) on 14 July (bearers of torches and fans). You will also see Seiganto ji, once a dependency of the shrine, which is dedicated to Nyorin Kannon. The main building of this temple was rebuilt in 1590. Beyond Nachi shrine you come to the summit of Myoho san (alt. 2,461ft/750m), from where there is a *view of the area and out to sea.

☞ 48mls (78km): Yukawa Onsen, in a narrow cove to the S of Katsuura

Bay. Springs from 104° to 108°F (40° to 42°C).

52mls (83km): road on the l. to Taiji (aquarium) and the rocky point of Kandori zaki (3mls/5km).

63mls (101km): Koza, at the mouth of the Koza gawa.

16mls (26km) NW (coach): Shichikawa dam (381ft/116m), which you can reach via the beautiful *gorge of Koza.

65mls (105km): on the l. you will see *Hashikui iwa, strange lines of rocks with a layout reminiscent of the piers of a bridge (*hashii*). Tradition has it that Kobo Daishi made them.

68mls (109km): Kushimoto, a little harbour and spa in the extreme S of the Kii peninsula.

From Kushimoto you can tour the *Shiono peninsula (7mls/12km round trip; coach). The Shiono misaki lighthouse marks the most southerly point of the island of Honshu.

1½ml (2km) E (boat): Oshima, an island with a jagged shoreline in the E of which is Kashino zaki, where there is a monument in memory of the Turkish sailors who ran aground there in 1890.

From Kushimoto, you can go NW to the spa of Shirahama (42mls/67km; JNR train; see entry under this name), along the attractive southern coast of the Kii peninsula with its numerous inlets and clusters of little islands.

Z

■ Zentsuji (Island of Shikoku)

Map of Shikoku (Inland Sea), pp. 536–7.

Tokyo, 491mls (790km) – Kochi, 73mls (118km) – Matsuyama, 81mls (130km) – Takamatsu, 24mls (39km) – Tokushima, 71mls (114km).

Kagawa ken - pop: 39,500.

At some distance from the Inland Sea, on the railway line which connects Takamatsu to Kochi, Zentsuji takes great pride in having been the home of one of the great priests of Japanese Buddhism, Kobo Daishi (774–834).

☼ Zentzu ji (1ml/1.5km W of the station) was founded in 813 by the priest Kukai (Kobo Daishi). The temple is named after Zentsu Saeki, father of Kukai, who had a house here. The majority of the buildings were reconstructed in the 17th c.

Among the buildings you will see Jogyo do, which contains a statue of Buddha Gautama accompanied by his assistants, and Kon do or Yakushi do (14th c.), where there is a large wooden statue of Yakushi Nyorai. The five-storeyed pagoda (151ft/46m high) was rebuilt in 1882. The temple treasury houses a number of objects of religious significance, mementoes of and works by Kobo Daishi, as well as two beautiful wooden statues of Jizo Bosatsu and Kishijo ten (Fujiwara period). The two magnificent camphor trees in the park date back to the time of the temple's foundation.

☞ VICINITY

1 BYOBUGA URA (5mls/8km NW; coach). This is an attractive beach situated in a bay on the Inland Sea, with Mi saki forming its western limit. View of the islands of the Inland Sea. Kukai is said to have been born at Byobuga ura.

2 KANNONJI, KOTOCHIRA, see entries under these names.

■ Zushi (Island of Honshu)

Map of the Vicinity of Tokyo, p. 565.

Tokyo, 32mls (52km) – Kofu, 98mls (157km) – Shizuoka, 87mls (140km) – Yokohama, 17mls (28km).

Kanagawa ken – pop: 53,400 – seaside resort.

To the E of Kamakura, on Sagami Bay, Zushi is a fashionable seaside resort and residential town. The Imperial family has a villa by the sea in neighbouring Hayama.

☞ VICINITY

1 HAYAMA (2½mls/4km S; coach). Along the coast to the S of Isshiki, where the Imperial villa is situated, lies Hayama public park (4¼ acres/1.7 ha), which at one time belonged to the villa.

2 FUJISAWA, KAMAKURA, MIURA, YOKOSUKA, see entries under these names.

Useful information

Key

rms.:	rooms	com.:	communal
Tel.:	telephone	conf. rms.:	conference rooms
V.:	see	fest.:	festival

Tourist and hotel symbols

This list of accepted symbols for tourist and hotel information is common to all the *Guides Bleus*; all the symbols do not, therefore, necessarily appear in this volume.

⒤	Tourist office, information	A/c	Air conditioning
✈	Airports, airlines	🛗	Lift elevator
⚓	Boat services	🛁	Bathroom or shower
🚆	Stations, reservations, information	☎	Telephone in rooms
🚋	Trams, streetcars, trolleybuses	TV	TV in rooms
🚌	Buses	🚍	Private bus service
🚗	Motoring information: Car hire, taxis, garages	❊	Garden
✉	Postal services, post codes	♣	Park
△	Camping	⛱	Swimming pool
	Hotel classification	≋	Private or public beach
		♀	Tennis
*****	De luxe	⌄/9	Golf – 9 holes
****	Very good	⌄/18	Golf – 18 holes
***	Good		
**	Simple	🏇	Riding
*	Modest	🅿	Hotel parking
¶	Restaurant	P	Parking
*	Exceptional cooking		
▥	Central heating		

ABASHIRI (Hokkaido), p. 117.
Tel. 01524; ✉ 099-24.

Youth hostels:
Abashiri, 208-2, Kitahama, Abashiri (Tel. 6-2630), 52 beds
Yuai-so, 34, Tento zan, Abashiri (Tel. 3-2697), 300 beds, 2½mls (4km) SW (bus).

Airport: Memanbetsu, 12mls (19km) S (coach); flights *TDA* to Sapporo and Hakodate.

Airline: *Toa Domestic Airlines*; reservations (Tel. 3-2851).

Rail: *JNR* to Asahikawa, Hakodate, Kushiro, Sapporo.

Coach: to Higashi Mohoto, Kawayu Onsen, Kitami, Saroma, Shari, Utoro.

Excursion: Abashiri Coastal Park (May–Oct.)

Events: Drift-ice festival at *Okhotsk*, mid-Feb, magical spectacle.

AIZU WAKAMATSU (Fukushima ken), p. 118

Tel. 02422; ✉ 965.

** Ryokan:**
Higashiyama Grand Hotel, Higashiyama Onsen (Tel. 2-3500), 46 rms.

Business hotel:
Green Hotel Aizu, opposite station (Tel. 4-5181).

Rail: *JNR*; stations: *Aizu-Wakamatsu, Kita-Wakamatsu* and *Nishi-Wakamatsu*, to Aizu Takinohara, Atsushio, Koide, Koriyama, Niigata, Sendai, Tokyo (Ueno).

Coach: *Aizu Bus* to Fukushima, Inawashiro, Yanaizu.

Excursions:
Bandai Asahi National Park (*Aizu Bus*).

Specialities: lacquered objects for the home.

Events: *Yanaizu Onsen* fest. 7 Jan., 13 Mar., 7/14 Jul., 31 Aug., and 1 Sept.

Sports: golf (Aizu Bandai Country-Club).

AKAN (Hokkaido National Park), p. 120.

Lodgings:
- At Akan Kohan Onsen (Tel. 015467; ✉ 085-04).

Ryokan:
* *Akankoso*, Akanko Onsen (Tel. 2231), 68 rms.
  New Akan Hotel, Akanko Onsen (Tel. 2121), 119 rms.

Youth hostel: *Akan Choritsu*, Akan Kohan (Tel. 2818), 60 beds.

– At Kawayu Onsen (Tel. 015483; ✉ 088-34).

Hotel:
** *Kawayu Plaza*, Teshikaga cho (Tel. 2211), 93 rms (83 Jap.) ♯ ▥ A/c 🛁 🔒 ☎ TV P bar, shops, conf. rms, Jap. com. bath.

Youth hostel: *Mashu ko*, 883 Genya, Teshikaga machi (Tel. 2-5318). 112 beds, bus.

[ℹ] **Department delegation for tourism**, 4-1-1, Sanno (Tel. 62-1111).

Hotels:
*** *Akita Dai ichi*, 1-3-5, Naka dori (Tel. 34-1141; telex 8422-11), 197 rms (3 Jap.) ♯ ▥ A/c 🛁 🔒 ☎ TV ♪/⁹ 🖼 bar.
** *Akita New Grand*, 5-2-1, Naka dori, Sue Cho, Dotenaga machi (Tel. 34-5211), 111 rms (2 Jap.), ♯ ▥ A/c 🛁 🔒 ☎ TV ☀ ♪/⁹ 🖼.

Ryokans:
* *Eitaro*, 6-15, Senshuyadome machi (Tel. 33-4151), 39 rms.
  Hotel Chiritei, 4-2-1,

Tsuchizaki minato Chuo (Tel. 45-0191), 12 rms.

Business hotel: *Hawaii Shin-honten*, 5-1-7, Naka dori (Tel. 33-1110).

Youth hostel: *Yabase Seinen no ie,* 86, Yabase (Tel. 23-0008), 92 beds.

Restaurants:
* *Akida Club* (sukiyaki), 5-2-30, Naka dori (Tel. 33-2101).
* *Kappo Soshu* (Jap. food), 5-1-11, Omachi (Tel. 23-7226).
  Suginoya (Jap. food), 4-1-15, Naka dori (Tel. 35-5111).

✈ **Airport:** Akita, 2mls (3km) W. (bus); flights *ANA* to Tokyo and Osaka: *TDA* to Sapporo.

Airlines: *All Nippon Airways*, reservations (Tel. 33-1470); – *Toa Domestic Airlines*, reservations (Tel. 23-2816).

🚂 **Rail:** *JNR*; stations: *Akita, Tsuchizaki*; Oga, Osaka, Tokyo.

Specialities: gold, silver and worked bronze jewellery; *Akita fuki* (giant rhubarb). sake, *kiritanyo* (local sukiyaki); Akita, Obako, pedigree dogs.

Events: *Bonten*, 17 Jan. at shrine of Miyoshi, Port fest. 20-21 Jul. at Tsuchizaki, *Kanto matsuri* (procession of lanterns) 6-7 Aug.

Amagi Yugashima (V. Fuji-Hakone-Izu), p. 174
Amakusa shoto, p. 645.
Amami O shima, p. 126

AMAMI SHOTO (Kagoshima ken), p. 126

Tel. Amami oshima Naze (09975); Kikai jima (099765); Okino erabu (09979); Tokuno shima (09978); Yoron jima (099794); – ⊠ : Naze (894).

🛈 **Tourist advice for the islands**, 2-5-8, Saiwai-che, Naze (Tel. 2-1111).

Hotel:
** *Amami Grand*, 18-1, Obama cho, Naze (Tel. 2-6411), 70 rms (34 Jap.) ⅋ ▥ A/c 🛆 ☎ TV ♦ ▨ ⊷ P bar, hairdresser, boutique.

Ryokan:
** *Amami Seaside Hotel*, Yagijima, Naze-shi (Tel. 2-5511), 72 rms.

Youth hostel:
Yoronto Takakuraso, 1025, Chabana, Yoron-machi, Oshimagun (Tel. 2273), 40 beds.

✈ **Airports:** Amami oshima (Akagina), 9mls (15km) NE of Naze (coach); flights *ANA* to Kagoshima and Naha; *TDA* to Fukuoka, Kagoshima, Kikai jima, Oita, Okino erabu jima, Osaka, Tokuno shima. Kikai jima (Kikai); flights *TDA* to Amami oshima.
Okino erabu jima (Kunigami), 9mls (15km) NE of China (coach); flights *TDA* to Amami oshima, Kagoshima.
Tokuno shima (Amagi); flights *TDA* to Amami oshima, Kagoshima.

Airlines: *All Nippon Airways*,

reservations at Naze (Tel. 2-7272); *Toa Domestic Airlines*: reservations at Naze (Tel. 2-5211), to Kikai jima (Tel. 73), to Okino erabu (Tel. 2-0221), to Tokuno shima (Tel. 2-0223).

🛳 **Sea travel:** from Amami oshima (Naze) to Tokyo, Kobe, Kagoshima, Tokuno shima, Okinawa; from Kika jima to Kagoshima, Tokunoshima (Amagi); from Okino erabu to Kagoshima, Kobe, Okinawa; from Yoron Jima to Kagoshima, Kobe, Okinawa; the islands are interlinked.

🚌 **Coaches:** several services on the islands of O shima, Tokuno shima, Okono erabu, as well as excursions.

Specialities: Amami no tsumugi (silk fabric).

Amano Hashidate, p. 405.
Amano san, p. 406.
Amihari Onsen, p. 406.
Anan, p. 127.
Anori zaki, p. 265.
Ao shima, p. 404.
Aobane, p. 174.

AOMORI (Aomori ken), p. 128.
Tel. 0177; ⊠ 030.

🛈 **Tourist Information Centre**, 1-1-1, Nagashima cho (Tel. 22-1111).

Hotel:
*** *Aomori*, 1-1-23, Tsutsumi machi (Tel. 75-4141; telex 8127-55), 53 rms (2 Jap.), 2 ⅋ ▥ A/c ♨ 🛆 ☎ TV 🖸, bar, hairdresser, boutique, bowling.

Ryokan:
** *Aomori Kokusai Hotel*, 1-6-

18, Shin machi (Tel. 22–4321), 69 rms (1 Jap.).

Business hotels:
Aomori Green, 1-1-22, Shin machi (Tel. 23–2001).
Sun Route Aomori, 1-9-10, Shin machi (Tel. 75–2321).

Youth hostels:
Youth Hostel, 13-9, Chaya machi (Tel. 41–7416), 160 beds.
Asamushi, 203-6, Yamashita, Asamushi (Tel. 52–2865), 160 beds.

✈ **Airport:** Aomori, 7mls (12km) S; flights *TDA* to Tokyo.

Airline: *Toa Domestic Airlines*, reservations (Tel. 23–1211).

⚓ **Sea travel:** *Seikan ferry (JNR)* to Hakodate; *Higashi Nihon car ferry* to Hakodate, Muroran; hydrofoil to Asamushi, Mutsu (Ominato).

🚆 **Rail:** *JNR* to Minmaya, Sendai, Osaka, Tokyo (Ueno).

🚌 **Coach:** to Morioka, Noheji, Towada Minami.

Excursions: to the Towada Hachimantai National Park.

Events: **Nebuta matsuri*, 3-7 Aug. with night procession of large decorated papier mâché figures.

Sports: Winter sports at the Hakkoda san 11mls (18km) SE.

Tel. 07378; ✉ 649–03.

Ryokan:
Arida Kanko Hotel, Miyazaki cho (Tel. 2–5201), 130 rms.

🚆 **Rail:** *JNR*, Minoshima station trains to Nagoya, Osaka; - *Arida Railway* from Fujinami to Kanayaguchi.

Specialities: Satsuma orange known as *Kishu mikan*.

Tel. 0166; ✉ 070.

Hotel:
*** *New Hokkai*, Shijo dori 6-chome, Gojo dori (Tel. 24–3111), 98 rms (3 Jap.) 5 🍴 ▥ A/c 🛏 🛁 ☎ 📺 ❀ ♪/¹⁸ 🔲 bar, hairdresser, boutique.

Business hotel:
Asahikawa Prince, Hiden 1 – 90, 7-chome, 1-jyodori (Tel. 22–5155).

Youth hostel: *Asahikawa*, Inosawa ski jo, Kamui cho (Tel. 61–2751), 60 beds.

Restaurant:
Kagetsu Kaikan (Jap. & Chin. food), 7-8, Sanjo-dori (Tel. 22–1101).

✈ **Airport:** Higashi Kagura, 9mls

(15km) SE (coach); flights *TDA* to Tokyo.

Airlines: *All Nippon Airways*, Toho Seimei Bldg, 9-chome, Gojo (Tel. 23–6261); – *Japan Air Lines*, Takugin Bldg, 9-chome, Shijo (Tel. 24–1234); – *Toa Domestic Airlines*, Migi Gojo 9-chome, Miyashita dori (Tel. 24–3291).

Rail: *JNR* to Abashiri, Hakodate, Kushiro, Otaru, Sapporo.

Coaches: to Soun kyo, Rubeshibe, Tennin kyo.

Events: winter fest, begin. Feb.

Specialities: fabrics (*Atsuhi*).

Asama Onsen (V. Matsumoto), p. 396.
Asamushi Onsen, p. 129.
Asarigawa Onsen, p. 504.
Ashibe, p. 253.
Ashikaga, p. 131.
Ashimori, p. 479.
Ashi no ko, p. 170.
Ashinoyu Onsen, p. 168.
Ashizuri misaki, p. 133.

ASHIZURI UWAKAI (Ehime and Kochi ken, National Park) p. 132.

Lodgings:
– At Tosa Shimizu
Tel. 08808; ✉ 787-03.

Ryokan:
Ashizuri Kokusai Hotel, Ashizuri misaki (Tel. 8–0201), 51 rms (11 West.)

Youth hostel:
Kongofukuji, Ashizuri misaki, 80 beds.

Aso (Bay), p. 253.

ASO (Kumamoto and Oita ken; National Park), p. 133.

Lodgings:
– At Beppu and Kumamoto V. under these place names.
– At Aso
Tel. 09673; ✉ 869–21 or 869–23.

Hotel:
** *Aso Kanko*, Yunotani, Choyo mura, Aso gun (Tel. 5–0311), 90 rms (60 Jap.) ¶¶ ▥ A/c 🏊 ☎ ❀ 🖾 ↙/¹⁸ 🔲 bar.

Ryokans:
Asonotsukasa, 1197 Matsunoki, Oaza Kurogawa, Aso machi, Aso-gun (Tel. 4–0811), 65 rms.
Aso Hotel, 99 Oaza Uchinomaki, Aso machi, Aso gun (Tel. 2–0525), 56 rms.
Kadoman, 1095–1, Oaza Uchinomaki, Aso machi, Aso gun (Tel. 2–0615), 92 rms.
Soyokaku, 385–1, Oaza Uchinomaki, Aso machi, Aso gun (Tel. 2–0621), 88 rms.

Minshuku:
Marufuku, 4377–1, Miyaji, Ichinomiya cho, Aso gun (Tel. 2–1130), 9 rms.

Youth hostel:
Aso, Bochu, Aso machi, Aso gun Tel. 4–0804, 60 beds.

– At Yufuin Onsen
Tel. 097784; ✉ 879–51.

Hotel:
** *Kuju Lakeside*, 21746–6, Kawanishi, Yufuin cho (Tel. 3151), 69 rms (35 Jap.). ¶¶ ▥ A/c 🍴 🏊 ☎ 📺 ♠ ↙/¹⁸ P hairdresser, boutique, Jap. com. bath, bowling, skating.

Ryokan:
* *Kinrinko*, Kawakami, Yufuin cho (Tel. 3011), 12 rms.

Aso Onsen (V. Aso), p. 133
Aso san, p. 133

Asozu Onsen (V. Kurayoshi),
p. 338.
Asuka, p. 305.
Atagawa Onsen (V. Fuji-
Hakone-Izu), p. 172.

ATAMI (Shizuoka ken), p. 137.
Tel. Atami, Ajiro Onsen, Izusan Onsen (0557); Yugawara
Onsen (0465);—✉ : Atami,
Ajiro Onsen, Izusan Onsen
(413); Yugawara Onsen
(259-03).

Lodgings:
- At Atami

Hotel:
**** *New Fujiya*, 1-16, Ginza cho
(Tel. 81-0111; telex 03927-
682), 318 rms (139 Jap.) 4 ¶
▥ A/c 🛁 🎣 ☎ TV 🖾 🛥 🚗
bars, boutique, Jap. com.
bath, bowling, conf. rm (2,000
seats).

Ryokans:
*** *Atami Fujiya*, 13-8, Ginza cho
(Tel. 81-7111), 162 rms.
*** *Atami Kinjokan*, 10-33,
Showa cho (Tel. 81-6261),
111 rms.
** *Happoen*, 12-1, Miniguchi
cho (Tel. 81-6125), 21 rms.
** *Kiunkakau Honkan*, 4-2,
Showa cho (Tel. 81-3623), 31
rms.
** *New Akao*, 1993-250, Atami
(Tel. 81-5151), 256 rms.
* *Onoya Ryokan*, 3-9, Wada-
hama-Minami cho
Tel. 82-1111), 206 rms.

- At Izusan Onsen, 1ml (2km)
N.

Ryokans:
*** *Miharukan* (Tel. 81-7131),
73 rms.
** *Fukiya* (Tel. 81-5195), 39 rms.

- At Yugawara Onsen, 4 mls
(7km) N.

Ryokans:
*** *Toyoko* (Tel. 62-4141),
43 rms.
** *Kanzan* (Tel. 63-2121), 49
rms.
** *Suimeikan* (Tel. 62-2511), 5
rms.
* *Amanoya* (Tel. 62-2121), 68
rms.

🛳 **Sea travel:** boats to Hatsu-
shima, O shima; hydrofoil to
Eno shima, Ito.

🚃 **Rail:** *JNR;* Shinkansen to
Tokyo, Osaka; trains to
Fukuoka, Hamada,
Kagoshima, Maibara, Nachi
Katsuura, Osaka,
Shimonoseki, Tamano, Toky

Cablecar: to Kuro dake.

🚌 **Coaches:** to Hakone
Odawara, Shimoda.

Excursions: to the Fuji-
Hakone-Izu National Park,
from Tokyo (in English).

Travel agency: *JTB*, New
Fujita Building (Tel. 81-7155

Specialities: camellia oil,
Satsuma oranges, umeyoka
(apricot-flavoured bean
sweetmeat), camphorwood
objects, handmade paper.

Sports: golf (*Atami Golf
Club*); beaches.

Atsumi (V. Tsuruoka), p. 63
Attoko, p. 451.
Awa Amatsu, p. 296.

AWAJI SHIMA (Hyogo ken)
p. 138.

Tel. Sumoto (07992); Fukura
(07995);—✉ : Sumoto (656)
Fukura (656-05).

Lodgings:
- At Sumoto

Ryokans:
* *Kaigetsukan*, Kaigan dori (Tel. 2-1100), 100 rms.
* *Hotel New Awaji*, Komoe (Tel. 2-2521), 48 rms.
* *Mikumakan*, Yamate (Tel. 2-0203), 82 rms.

– At Fukura

Youth hostel:
Awaji, Nandan cho (Tel. 2-0460) 52 beds.

Sea travel: *Kansai Kisen*, from Sumoto to Kobe and Fuke; from Yura to Kobe and Fuke; from Shizuki to Izumi-Otsu; – *Bantan Renraku Kisen*, from Iwaya to Akashi; other services from Ura to Kobe, from Tsuna to Sumiyoshi and Izumi-Otsu, from Fukura to Naruto.

Coaches: all round the island.

Excursions: *Awaji Kotsu*, from Sumoto and Fukura.

Sports: beaches; marina at Sumoto (Tel. 4-0401).

Awara (V. Fukui), p. 181.
Awazu Onsen (V. Komatsu), p. 326.
Ayukawa, p. 266.
Azuchi, p. 488.
Azuma Kofuji, p. 142

Baijoga take, p. 635.

BANDAI ASAHI (Fukushima, Niigata and Yamagata ken; National Park), p. 141.

Lodgings:
– At Tsuchiyu Onsen
Tel. 0245; ✉ 960-21.

Ryokans:
* *Sanuiso*, Tsuchiyu Onsen,

Fukushima-ken (Tel. 95-2141), 44 rms.

– At Urabandai
Tel. 02413; ✉ 969-27.

Ryokans:
*** *Banso*, Kitashiobara mura, Yama-gun (Tel. 2-2111), 21 rms.
  * *Urabandai Kogen Hotel*, Kitashiobara mura, Yama-gun (Tel. 2-2211), 53 rms.

– At Aizu Wakamatsu, Fukushima, Yonezawa V. under these place names.

Bandai Atami Onsen (V. Koriyama), p. 327.
Bandai san, p. 141.
Bando, p. 450.
Benten jima (V. Hamamatsu), p. 206.

BEPPU (Oita ken), p. 142. Tel. 0977; ✉ 874.

ⓘ **Tourism section:** Beppu-eki (Tel. 24-2838).

Hotels:
*** *Kamenoi*, 5-17 Chuo machi (Tel. 22-3301; telex 07734-75), 88 rms (36 Jap.) ‖ ▥ A/c ♨ ⌂ ☎ TV ✻ ⛱ boutique, Jap. com. bath.
*** *Nippaku*, 3-12-26, Kitahama (Tel. 23-22-91), 55 rms. (18 Jap.) ‖ ▥ A/c ♨ ⌂ ☎ TV ✻ ⛱ ▦
*** *Suginoi*, Kankaiji (Tel. 24-1141; telex 07734-67), 606 rms (49 Jap.) ‖ ▥ A/c ♨ ⌂ ☎ TV ✻ ⛱ ⁄¹⁸ P hairdresser, boutiques, Jap. com. bath (without doubt the most amazing in Japan), bowling.
  ** *Hinago*, 7-24, Akiba cho (Tel. 22-1111), 64 rms (8 Jap.) ‖ ▥ A/C ♨ ⌂ ☎ TV ▦

Ryokans:
*** *Hotel Kodama*, Tsurumi (Tel.

66–2211), 56 rms.
*** *Hotel New Showaen*, Kankaiji (Tel. 22–3211), 33 rms.
*** *Shiragikuso*, Kamitanoyu cho (Tel. 21–2111), 35 rms.
** *Bokaiso*, Kitahama (Tel. 22–1241), 42 rms.
** *Oniyama Hotel*, Kannawa (Tel. 66–1121), 62 rms.
* *Beppu Fujikan Hotel*, Mochigahama (Tel. 23–6111), 85 rms.
* *Nogami Hotel*, Kitahama (Tel. 23–2141), 31 rms.
Seifuso, Kitahama (Tel. 24–3939), 62 rms.

Business hotel:
Star, 10–29, Tanoyu cho (Tel. 25–1188).

Youth hostel:
Beppu, Kankaiji Onsen (Tel. 23–4116), 150 beds.

✈ **Airport:** Aki, 24mls (39km) NE (hovercraft and coach; V. Oita).

⚓ **Sea travel:** *Kansai Kisen* to Matsuyama, Imabari, Takamatsu, Shodo shima (Sakate), Kobe, Osaka; – *Seto Naikai Steamship Co.* and *Uwajima Transport Co.* to Itsukushima, Hiroshima, Kure; – hovercraft to Oita and airport.

Shipping line: *Kansai Kisen*, Minami Ishigaki (Tel. 22–1311).

🚃 **Rail:** *JNR* to Fukuoka, Hiroshima, Kagoshima, Kitakyushu Kumamoto, Kyoto, Misumi, Miyakonojo, Miyazaki, Okayama, Osaka, Tokyo.

Cablecar: to Tsurumi dake.

🚌 **Coaches:** to Fukuoka, Kagoshima, Miyazaki, Nagasaki, Saikai.

Taxis: you are advised to use this form of transport to see the springs (pre-arranged fee).

Excursions: to mounts. Aso, Utsuki, Yabakei.

Travel agency: *JTB*, Kokusai Kankokaikan Bldg, Kitahama (Tel. 22–1271).

Guided visit: from Mar. to Nov. afternoons (in English) – info. at hotel.

Specialities: lemons and limes.

Events: *Sakura matsuri* in Apr.

Sports: *Beppu Kokusai Golf Club*; marina.

C

CHIBA (Chiba Ken) p. 145. Tel. 0472; ✉ 280.

ℹ️ **Tourist Information Centre**, 1-1, Ichiban cho (Tel. 23–2730).

Hotels:
** *Chiba Grand*, 121–2, Chiba Minato (Tel. 41–2111), 82rms (4 Jap.) 🍴 ▥ A/c 🛁 🛋 ☎ 📺 ❄ 📻 hairdresser
** *Chiba Keisei*, 14–1, Chiba

cho (Tel. 22–2111), 59 rms (3 Jap.) ¶¶ ▥ A/c 🛏 🛋 ☎ TV hairdresser.

Business hotel:
Takane, 2-21-11, Kasuga (Tel. 41–8051).

Youth hostel:
Inage Kaihin, Inage kaigan (Tel. 43–9505), 60 beds.

✈ **Airport:** Narita, 16 mls (25km) NE.

Airline: *Japan Air Lines*, Chiba Central Plaza Bldg, 3–17-1, Chuo (Tel. 25–5211).

⚓ **Sea travel:** *Ocean Ferry* to Tokushima.

🚂 **Rail:** *JNR* to Tokyo, Chosi, Mitaka, Narita, Tateyama; – *Keisei Electric Railway* to Narita, Tokyo.

Travel agency: *JTB*, New Chiba Bldg, 2 Fujimi (Tel. 27– 9221).

Sports: golf (*Keiyo Kokusai Country Club, Sodegaura Country Club*).

Chiburi jima, p. 481.
Chichi jima (V. Ogasawara shoto), p. 475.
Chichibu, p. 145.
Chichibu Tama (National Park), p. 146.
Chihaya, p. 308.
Chijiwa, p. 644.
Chikabumi, p. 130.
Chikami yama, p. 254.
Chikubu jima, p. 410.
Chikura (V. Tateyama), p. 560.
Chinen, p. 484.

CHINO (Nagano ken), p. 147.
Tel. Tateshina Onsen (026667); Shirakaba ko (026668); ✉ 391–03.

Lodgings:
– At Tateshina Onsen

Hotel:
*** *Heidi*, 1-1, Tateshina Kogen (Tel. 2001), 20 rms ¶¶ ▥ A/c 🛏 🛋 ☎ TV ❄ ski, skating, fishing.

Ryokan:
* *Hotel Shinyu*, Tateshina, Chino machi (Tel. 2020), 55 rms.

Business hotel:
Noble, Chino, Chino-shi (Tel. 2-8585).

– At Shirakaba ko

Ryokan:
* *Shirakabako Kanko Hotel*, Kitayama, Chino machi (Tel. 2201), 70 rms.

Youth hostel:
Shirakabako, Shirakaba kohan, Chino machi (Tel. 2031), 70 beds.

🚂 **Rail:** *JNR* to Tokyo, Itolgawa, Matsumoto, Nagoya.

🚌 **Coaches:** to Komoro, Matsumoto.

Chishima retto, p. 451.
Chita (peninsula), p. 207.
Chofu, p. 148.
Chogosonshi ji, 448.
Chokai san, p. 518.
Chomei ji, p. 488.
Chomon kyo, p. 658.

CHOSHI (Chiba ken), p. 149.
Tel. 0479; ✉ 288.

Ryokan:
Hotel New Daishin, 10292, Inubo saki (Tel. 22-5024), 38 rms.

Youth hostel:
Inubo so, 10292-10, Inubo saki (Tel. 22-1252), 50 beds (Inubo station).

Rail: *JNR,* to Tokyo; – *Choshi Electric Railway* to Tokawa.

Coaches:to Chiba, Hokota, Kashima, Mito.

Choshi kei, p. 549.

CHUBU SANGAKU (Gifu, Nagano and Toyama ken; National Park, p. 150.

Lodgings:
– At Kamikochi
Tel. 026395.

Hotel:
** *Kamikochi Imperial*, Minami Azumi gun (Tel. 2001), 154 rms. ¶¶ 🏠 ☎ 📺 ♣ 📼 boutique; open in Jul. and Aug.

– At Tateyama
Tel. 0764.

Hotel:
** *Tateyama*, Murodo daira, Ashikuraji (Tel. 41-3333). 85 rms (10 Jap.) ¶¶ ▥ A/c ♨ 🏠 ☎ 📺 **P** boutiques, ski.

Youth hostel:
Sugita, Senjuga hara (Tel. 82-1754), 44 beds.

– At Matsumoto, Takayama, Toyama.
V. under these place names.

Chugushi, p. 463.
Chuson ji, p. 240.
Chuzenji ko (V. Nikko), p. 463.

D

Daikon jima, p. 395.
Daio, p. 265.
Dai sen, p. 154.
Daisen (V. Daisen Oki), p. 154.

DAISEN OKI (Shimane and Totori ken; National Park), p. 153.

Lodgings:
– At Daisen
Tel. 085952; ✉ 689-33:

Ryokan:
Hotel Daisen, Daisen cho, Saihaku gun (Tel. 2111), 56 rms.

Youth hostel:
Daisen, Daisen cho, Saihaku gun (Tel. 2501), 102 beds.

– At Yubara Onsen
Tel. 086762; ✉ 714-04:

Ryokans:
* *Yubara Kokusai Kanko Hotel*, Yuhara cho, Maniwa gun (Tel. 2111), 300 beds.
* *Horaiya*, Yuhara cho, Maniwa gun (Tel. 2321), 100 beds.
Aburaya Bekkan, Yuhara cho, Maniwa gun (Tel. 2006), 130 beds.

– At Kawakami
Tel. 086768; ✉ 714-04.

Youth hostel:
Hiruzen, Kami Fukuda, Kawakami mura, Maniwa gun (Tel. 30-62), 55 beds.

– At Izumo, Matsue, Kurayoshi, Yonago
V. under these place names.

DAISETSUZAN (Hokkaido; National Park), p. 154.

Lodgings:
– At Sounkyo Onsen
Tel. 01658; ✉ 078-17.

Ryokans:
** *Sounkaku Grand Hotel*, Kamikawa cho (Tel. 5-3111), 235 rms.
* *Hotel Soun*, Kamikawa cho (Tel. 5-3311), 201 rms.
Hotel Daisetsu, Kamikawa cho (Tel. 5-3211), 243 rms.

E

E

Lodgings:
– At Amagi Yugashima
Tel. 05588; ✉ 410-32.

Ryokan:
* *Shirakabeso*, 1594,
Yugashima cho, Tagata gun
(Tel. 5-0100), 24 rms.

– At Atagawa Onsen
Tel. 0557; ✉ 413-03.

Ryokans:
** *Atagawa View Hotel*, 1271,
Naramoto, Higashi Izu machi,
Kamo gun (Tel. 23–1211),
58 rms.
* *Atagawa Yamatokan*, 986-2,
Naramoto, Higashi Izu machi,
Kamo gun (Tel. 23–1126),
60 rms.

– At Dogashima Onsen
(Tel. 05585; ✉ 410-35).

Ryokan:
* *Dogashima Ginsuiso*, 2977-1,
Nishina, Nishi Izu machi,
Kamo gun (Tel. 2-1211).

– At Funabara Onsen
(Tel. 05588; ✉ 410-31).

Ryokan:
*** *Funabara Hotel*, Amagi
Yugashima cho, Tagata gun
(Tel. 7-0211), 92 rms.

– At Fuji Yoshida
Tel. 05555; ✉ 401-03.

Youth hostel:
Fuji Yoshida, 2-chome,
Shimo Yoshida Honcho
(Tel. 2-0533), 30 beds.

– At Hakone
Tel. 0460; ✉ 250-03/04/06.

Hotels:
*** *Fujiya*, 359, Miyanoshita,
Hakone machi (Tel. 2-2211;
telex 13892-718), 189 rms (7
Jap.) ⊮ ▥ ▥ ☎ TV ♣ ▨ ⌇/18
bar, hairdresser, boutiques,
Jap. com. bath, bowling, ski,

recept. and conf. rms.

*** *Hakone Kanko*, 1245, Sengokuhara, Hakone machi (Tel. 4-8501; telex 3892-601), 109 rms (8 Jap.) ‖ ▥ A/c ▤ ▥ ☎ TV ▨ ⏣/18 P hairdresser, boutique, Jap. com. bath, recept. and conf. rm.

*** *Kowaki en*, 1297 Ninotaira, Hakone machi (Tel. 2-4111; telex 3892-730), 245 rms (42 Jap.) ‖ ▥ A/c ▤ ▥ ☎ TV ✳ ▨ P hairdresser, boutiques, Jap. com. bath, bowling, recept. rm.

** *Hakone*, 65, Hakone machi (Tel. 3-6311; telex 3892-765), 34 rms (4 Jap.) ‖ ▥ ▤ ▥ ☎ TV ✳ ≈ ⏣/18 P boutiques.

** *Kagetsu en*, 1244, Itari, Sengo-kuhara, Hakone machi (Tel. 4-8621), 73 rms (17 Jap.) ‖ ▥ A/c ▤ ▥ ☎ TV ✳ ⏣/18 P Jap. com. bath.

Ryokans:
*** *Naraya*, 162, Miyanoshita, Hakone machi, Ashigarashimo gun (Tel. 2-2411), 25 rms.

*** *Senkyoro,* Hakone machi, Ashigarashimo gun (Tel. 4-8521), 61 rms.

** *Chokoku no mori Hotel*, Hakone machi, Ashigarashimo gun (Tel. 2-3375), 60 rms.

Youth hostel:
Hakone Sounzan, 1320 Gora, Hakone machi, Ashigarashimo gun (Tel. 2-3827), 27 beds.

– At Hokkawa Onsen
(Tel. 0557; ✉ 413-03.

Ryokan:
* *Hokkawa Tsuruya Hotel*, Higashi Izu machi, Kamo gun (Tel. 23-1212), 44 rms.

– At Imaihama Onsen

Tel. 05583; ✉ 413-05.

Ryokan:
* *Imaihama Tokyu Hotel*, Kawazu cho, Kamo gun (Tel. 2-0501), 70 rms.

– At Inatori Onsen
Tel. 0557; ✉ 413-04.

Ryokan:
* *Hotel Ginsuiso*, Higashi Izu machi, Kamo gun (Tel. 95-2211), 78 rms.

– At Izu Nagaoka Onsen
Tel. 05594; ✉ 410-21/22.

Ryokans:
*** *Izu Fujimi Hotel*, Nirayama cho, Tagata gun (Tel. 4-2121) 46 rms.

*** *Sakanaya*, Izu Nagaoka cho, Tagata gun (Tel. 8-1201), 22 rms.

** *Nanzanso*, Izu Nagaoka cho, Tagata gun (Tel. 8-0601), 37 rms.

* *Hakkeien*, Izu Nagaoka cho, Tagata gun (Tel. 8-1500), 49 rms.

* *Suihokaku*, Nirayama cho, Tagata gun (Tel. 8-1451), 36 rms.
Shiraishikan, Izu Nagaoka cho, Tagata gun (Tel. 8-0610), 45 rms.

– At Kawaguchiko
Tel. 05557; ✉ 401-03.

Hotel:
** *Fuji View*, 511 Katsuyama, Minami Tsuru gun (Tel. 055583-2511), 68 rms (8 Jap.) ‖ ▥ A/c ▥ ☎ TV ✳ ≈ ♀ ⏣/18 ▥ P boutique, ski.

Ryokan:
* *Kawaguchiko Hotel Shinkan*, Kawaguchiko machi, Minami Tsuru gun (Tel. 2-1313), 26 rms.

– At Osawa Onsen

Tel. 05584; ✉ 410–36.

Ryokan:

** *Osawa Onsen Hotel*,
Matsuzaki cho
(Tel. 3-0121), 26 rms.

– At Shimoda Onsen
Tel. 05582; ✉ 415.

Hotel:

** *Shimoda Tokyu*, 5-12-1,
Shimoda (Tel. 2-2411), 177
rms (16 Jap.) ¶ ▥ A/c 🛁 🏠
📞 📺 ❄ 🖼 🌊 ♨/¹⁸ **P**
boutique, Jap. com. bath,
recept. rm.

Ryokans:

* *Seiryuso*, Kouchi, Shimoda
(Tel. 2-1361), 25 rms.

* *Shimoda Onsen Hotel*,
Takegahama, Shimoda
(Tel. 2-311), 98 rms.

– At Shuzenji Onsen
Tel. 0558; ✉ 410–24.

Ryokans:

** *Kikuya*, Shuzenji machi,
Tagata gun (Tel. 72-2000),
57 rms.

* *Asaba*, Shuzenji machi,
Tagata gun (Tel. 72-0700),
26 rms.

– At Toi
Tel. 05589; ✉ 410–33.

Ryokan:

*** *Gyokushoen Arai*, 289-1, Toi,
Toicho, Tagata gun
(Tel. 8-100), 25 rms.

– At Yamanakako
Tel. 05556; ✉ 401–03.

Hotel:

*** *Mount Fuji*, 1360-83,
Yamanakako mura
(Tel. 2-2111), 111 rms (22
Jap.) ¶ ▥ A/c 🛁 🏠 📞 📺 🖼 �
♨/⁹ ♨/¹⁸ 🎿 **P** boutiques,
bowling, ski.

Ryokans:

New Yamanakako Hotel,

352-1, Yamanakako mura,
Minami Tsuru gun,
(Tel. 2-2311) 66 rms.

Fuyokaku Hotel Konaya,
Yamanakako mura
(Tel. 2-2520), 40 rms.

– At Atami, Gotemba, Ito, Izu
shoto, Kofu, Numazu
V. under these place names.

Fujiidera, p. 176.
Fujimishita, p. 467.
Fujinomiya, p. 176.
Fuji san, p. 164.

FUJISAWA (Kanagawa ken),
p. 177.
Tel. 0466; ✉ 251.

Ryokan:

* *Iwamotoro Bekkan Enoshima*,
2-16-6, Katase kaigan (Tel.
26–4111), 27 rms.

Restaurant:

Suekiro Shonan-ten (steaks),
4-13-6, Kugenuma kaigan
(Tel. 34-2225).

⚓ **Sea travel:** *Tokai Steamship
Co.,* from Enoshima to O
shima; hydrofoil from
Enoshima to Atami, Ito.

🚆 **Rail:** Fujisawa station: *JNR* to
Tokyo, Odawara; *Enoshima
Kamakura kanko Electric
Railway* to Kamakura;
*Odakyu Electric Railway to
Tokyo*; – Katase-Enoshima
station: *Odakyu ER* to Tokyo.

Monorail: Shonan-Enoshima
to Ofuna.

🚌 **Coaches:** to Kamakura,
Odawara, Tokyo, Yokosuka.

Sports: golf (*Fujisawa Public
Golf Course, Sagami Country
Club*); – Shonan marina, at
Enoshima (Tel. 25-2211).

Fuji Yoshida (V. Fuji-Hakone-Izu), p. 165.
Fukaura, p. 215.
Fukuda, p. 548.
Fukue, p. 194.

FUKUI (Fukui ken), p. 179.
Tel. 0776; ✉ Fukui (910);
Awara (910–41).

☐ **Tourist Information Centre**,
3-17-1, Ote machi
(Tel. 21–1111).

Lodgings:
– At Fukui

Hotel:
** *Fukui Palace*, 2-1-3, Junka cho (Tel. 23–3800), 37 rms (7 Jap.) ¶ ▥ A/c 🛁 🏦 ☎ TV boutique, Jap. com. bath, sauna.

Business hotel:
New Nawaya, 3-11-28, Chuo (Tel. 24–1182).

Youth hostel:
Fukui, 2-5-33, Nishiki, Mikuni cho (Tel. 82-5400), 80 beds.

18– At Awara, 12mls
19 km) N.

Ryokans
*** *Beniya*, 4-510, Onsen, Awara cho, Sakai gun
(Tel. 77-2333), 23 rms.
** *Yagi*, 4-418, Onsen, Awara cho, Sakai gun
(Tel. 77-2008), 75 rms.

Youth hostel:
Tojimbo, Takidani, Mikuni cho, Sakai gun (Tel. 82-5400), 66 beds.

– At Eikei ji 12mls (20km) E.

Youth hostel:
Eiheiji Monzen, 22-3, Shihi, Eiheiji machi, Yoshida gun (Tel. 63-3123), 44 beds.

✈ **Airport**: Harue, 4mls (7km) N (coach); flights *ANA* to Tokyo, Komatsu.

Airline: *All Nippon Airways*, reservations (Tel. 51–0596).

🚆 **Rail:** *JNR*, to Aomori, Kanazawa, Nagoya, Naoetsu, Niigata, Osaka, Toyama; – *Keifuku Electric Railway*, to Mikuni, Ono, Eiheiji; – private line to Ota, Takefu.

🚌 **Coaches:** to Echizen, Eiheiji, Kaga, Tojimbo, Yoshizaki, Onsen.

Events: *Great Festival of Fukui*, 1 Aug.

FUKUOKA (Fukuoka ken), p. 181.
Tel. Fukuoka (092);
Chikushino (09292); ✉ 815.

☐ **Tourist Information Centre**, Hakata station
(Tel. 431-3003).

Hotels:
**** *Nishitetsu Grand*, 2-6-60, Daimyo, Chou ku
(Tel. 771-7171; telex 0723-351), 308 rms. (4 Jap.) 5 ¶ ▥ A/c 🛁 🏦 ☎ TV ❋ ☒ ♉ **P** bars, hairdresser, bowling, conf. rm. (800 seats).
*** *Hakata Miyako*, 2-1-1, Hakata Eki Higashi, Hakata ku (Tel. 441-3111; telex 724-3111; telex 724-585), 269 rms (6 Jap.) ¶ ▥ A/c 🛁 🏦 ☎ TV **P** bar, hairdresser.
*** *Hakata Tokyu*, 1-16-1, Tenjin, Chuo ku (Tel. 781-7111; telex 0723-295), 266 rms (10 Jap.) 2 ¶ ▥ A/c 🛁 🏦 ☎ TV **P** hairdresser, boutique, bars, recept. and conf. rm (300 places).
*** *Station Plaza*, 2-1, Hakata Ekimae, Hakata Ku
(Tel. 431-1211;
telex 0723-536), 248 rms (3 Jap.), ¶ ▥ A/c 🛁 🏦 ☎ TV 🛗 bars, hairdresser, boutiques.

** *Hakata Shiroyama*, 5-3-4, Nakasu, Hakata ku (Tel. 281-2211), 126 rms (4 Jap.) ¶ ▬ A/c ♨ ♨ ☎ TV P bar.

** *New Hakata*, 1-1, Hakata Eki, Chuo gai, Hakata ku (Tel. 431-1111), 105 rms (2 Jap.) ¶ ▬ A/c ♨ ♨ ☎ TV P bar, hairdresser, boutique.

** *Takakura*, 2-7-21. Watanabe dori, Chuo ku (Tel. 731-1661), 81 rms (30 Jap.), ¶ ▬ A/c ¶ ♨ ☎ TV P bar, boutique.

Ryokans:

*** *Fukuoka Kanko Hotel*, Marumeikan, 5-6-1, Nakasu, Hakata ku (Tel. 29-0715), 31 rms.

*** *Fukuoka Yamanoue Hotel*, Tojin machi, Chuo ku (Tel. 77-2131), 34 rms.

** *Gekkoen*, 2-3-15, Kiyokawa, Chuo ku (Tel. 53-5531), 23 rms.

Business hotels:
Hakata Daiichi, 2-1-27, Hakatacki Higashi (Tel. 411-2501).
Lion's Hotel Hakata, 3-15-10, Hakata Ekimae (Tel. 451-7711).

Restaurants:
* *Royal* (West. food), 603, Nakasu, Hakata ku (Tel. 471-2479).
* *Fuyo Bekkan* (Jap. food), 2-5--22, Toko, Hakata ku (Tel. 471-6111).
* *Haginomiya-Sanso* (Jap. food), 1-18-1, Takamiya, Minami ku (Tel. 531-7131).
* *Shin Miura* (Mizutaki), 21-12, Sekijo machi, Hakata ku (Tel. 291-0821).

✈ **Airport:** Itazuke, 4mls (6km) SE (bus); *ANA* flights to Iki shima, Nagoya, Okinawa, Osaka, Tokyo; *JAL* flights to Okinawa, Osaka, Sapporo, Tokyo; *TDA* flights to Hiroshima, Kagoshima, Matsuyama, Miyazaki, Takamatsu, Tokyo.

Airlines: *Air France*, Nihon Seimei Fukuoka Bldg, 14-8, Tenjin 2-Chome, Chuo ku (Tel. 713-1565); – *All Nippon Airlines*, Fukuoka Asahi Bldg, 1-1, Hakata Elimae 2-chome, Hakata ku (Tel. 441-2211); – *Japan Air Lines*, 1, Kami Gofuku machi, Hakata ku (Tel. 271-4411); *Swissair*, Nishitetsu Grand Hotel, Room 308, 2-6-60, Daimyo, Chuo ku (Tel. 77-7171); – *Toa Domestic Airlines*, Fukuoka Mainichi Kaikan Bldg, 16-1, Tenjin 1-chome, Chuo ku (Tel. 76-1779).

⚓ **Sea travel:** from Hakata port to Shikano shima, Iki shima, Tsu shima; from Meinohama to Nokono shima.

🚆 **Rail:** Hakata station: *JNR*; *Shinkansen* to Osaka, Tokyo; other trains to Beppu, Kagoshima, Kitakyushu, Kumamoto, Kyoto, Nagasaki, Oita, Okayama, Osaka, Tokyo, Tosu; – Fukuoka station: *Nishi Nippon Railway (Nishitetsu)* to Omuta; – Kaizuka station: *Nishitetsu* to Tsuyazaki.

🚌 **Coaches:** stations at Hakata and Tenjin cho; *JNR* coaches to Iizuka, Nogata, Yamaguchi; – *Nishitetsu* coaches to Beppu, Kitakyushu, Kumamoto, Oita, Sasebo, Unzen.

Excursions: *Nishitetsu* coaches to Beppu, Kagoshima.

🚗 **Car hire:** *Nippon*, 2-8, Tenjin, Chuo ku (Tel. 781-5988); – *Nissan*, Nissan Rent a car

Bldg, 1–12–5, Hakata Eki Higashi (Tel. 431–8131).

Travel agency: *JTB*, 1 Tenjin, Chuo ku (Tel. 771–5931).

Shopping: at Tenjin, Kawabata, Nishijin.

Specialities: *Hakata nangyo (terracotta dolls), Hakata ori (silk fabrics), Hakata mizutaki (chicken dish).

Events: *Tamaseseri*, 3 Jan. at Hakozaki gu; – *Hakata Dontaku*, 3–4 May, procession in city streets; – *Hakata Yamagaser*, 1–15 Jul. at Kushida jinja.

Sports: golf (*Fukuoka Country Club, Koga Golf Club*); – Fukuoka sports centre, 2–2–43, Tenjin: *sumo* contests in Nov. (Tel: 74–1661); Kokusai sports centre, 2–2, Chikoku-Hommachi, Hakata ku, Fukuoka shi (Tel. 291–9311).

Places, sites and monuments:
Faculty of Medicine, p. 185.
Fukuoka, p. 185.
Hakata, p. 184.
Hakozaki, p. 185.
Hakozaki Hachiman gu, p. 185.
Higashi Koen, p. 185.
Kinryu ji, p. 185.
Kushida jinja, p. 185.
Maizuri koen, p. 185.
Nakasu, p. 185.
Nishi koen, p. 185.
Ohori koen, p. 185.
Shofuku ji, p. 185.
Sumiyoshi jinja, p. 184.

Fukura (Hyogo ken), p. 140.
Fukura (Yamagata ken), p. 518.

FUKUSHIMA (Fukushima ken), p. 188.
Tel. Fukushima (0245); Iizuka

(02454); ✉ : Fukushima (960); Iizuka (960–02).

□ **Tourist Information Centre**, 2–16, Sugitsuma cho (Tel. 21–1111).

Lodgings:
– At Fukushima

Hotel:
Tatsumiya, 5–1, Sakae machi (Tel. 22–5111), 60 rms ¶ ▥ A/c ▦ ⌂ ☎ TV ♪/9 ▣ ski, skating.

Ryokan:
* *Fumiya*, 2–29, Shin machi (Tel. 23–3577), 12 rms.

Business hotels:
Ebisu Grand Hotel, Soneda cho (Tel. 33–4166).
Fukushima, 6–1, Funaba cho (Tel. 21–3211).

– At Iizaka Onsen 6mls (10km) N.

Ryokans:
*** *Hotel Suikoen*, Iizaka Onsen (Tel. 2–3301), 60 rms.
*** *Hotel Takanoha*, Iizaka Onsen (Tel. 2–3241), 39 rms.
* *Ichirakuso*, Iizaka Onsen (Tel. 2–4111), 25 rms.
Akagawaya, Iizaka Onsen (Tel. 2–2221), 32 rms.

⚭ **Rail:** *JNR; Shinkansen* to Tokyo, Sendai, Morioka; other trains to Akita, Aomori, Morioka, Niigata, Sendai, Tokyo, Tamagata; – *Iizaka Line* (private) to Yunolizaka.

● **Coaches:** to Aizu Wakamatsu, Haramachi, Inawashiro, Sendai, Tokyo.

Specialities: bonsai trees, kokeshi dolls.

Fukuwata, p. 255.

FUKUYAMA (Hiroshima ken), p. 188.

Tel. Fukuyama (0849); Tomo (08498); ✉ Fukuyama (720); Tomo (720-02).

Lodgings:
- At Fukuyama

Hotel:
* *Fukuyama Grand*, 2-7-1, Nishi machi (Tel. 21-5511; telex 06-435-10), 90 rms (8 Jap.), ⊪ ▥ A/c ⛲ ⌂ ☎ TV ❋ P hairdresser, boutiques, bar.

Ryokan:
** *Matsunoya*, 2-20, Ebisu machi (Tel. 23-8222), 47 rms.

Business hotel:
Fukuyama Kokusai, 1-1-26, Shiro micho (Tel. 24-2411).

- At Tomo 9mls (14km) S.

Ryokan:
** *New Kinsui Kokusai*, Tomo cho (Tel. 2-2111), 45 rms.

⚓ **Sea travel:** from Fukuyama to Shiraishi jima and Marugame; from Tomo to Tadotsu; hydrofoil to Onomichi.

🚈 **Rail:** *JNR; Shinkansen* to Fukuoka, Osaka; other trains to Fukuoka, Hiroshima, Kagoshima, Kumamoto, Miyazaki, Miyoshi, Oita, Okayama, Osaka, Shimonoseki, Tokyo.

🚌 **Coaches:** to Okayama, Tomo, Yamano Onsen.

Funabara Onsen (V. Fuji-Hakone-Izu), p. 174.
Funakoshi, p. 510.
Furen shonyudo, p. 648.
Furubira, p. 504.

FURUKAWA (Miyagi ken), p. 189.
Tel. Naruko Onsen (02298); ✉ Naruko Onsen (989-68).

Lodgings:
- At Naruko Onsen, 19mls (31km) NW.

Ryokan:
*** *Naruko Hotel* (Tel. 3-2001), 125 rms.
* *Yokoyo Hotel* (Tel. 3-3155), 82 rms.

🚈 **Rails:** *JNR; Shinkansen* to Morioka, Tokyo; other trains to Sendai, Shinjo.

🚌 **Coaches:** to Ishinomaki, Naruko, Sendai.

Winter sports: at Naruko Onsen 19 mls (31km) NW: 6 chair lifts, 3 drag lifts; season from begin. Dec. to mid-Apr.

Specialities: wooden dolls (*Narugo kokeshi*).

Furumachi, p. 255.
Fuse, p. 480.
Futaba, p. 208.
Futami (Mie ken, V. Ise shima), p. 264.
Futami (Okinawa), p. 486.
Futomi, p. 295.
Fuyushima, p. 520.

G

GAMAGORI (Aichi ken), p. 191.
Tel. Gamagori (0533); Hazu (056362); ✉ : Gamagori (443); Hazu (44-07).

Lodgings:
- At Gamagori

Ryokans:
*** *Gimpaso*, Nishiura cho (Tel. 57-3101), 70 rms.
*** *Hotel Fukinuki*, Miya cho (Tel. 69-1211), 110 rms.
** *Nampuso*, Nishiura cho (Tel. 57-2101), 60 rms.
** *Shofuen*, Miya cho (Tel. 68-6611), 120 rms.

– At Hazu 6mls (9km) SW.

Ryokans:
* *Sangane Grand Hotel*, Higashi Hazu (Tel. 3121), 45 rms.
Sanshuen, Higashi Hazu (Tel. 2440), 64 rms.

🏛 **Sea travel:** *Meitetsu Kaijo Kanko Steamship*, hydrofoil to Nishiura and Shino jima; – *Kinki Nippon Tourist Co*, and *Shima Katsuura Kanko Steamship Co*, to Toba.

🚂 **Rail:** *JNR* to Tokyo, Nagoya; – *Nagoya Railroad Co. (Meitetsu)* to Nagoya.

🚌 **Coaches:** To Nagoya, Okazaki, Toyohashi.

Sports: marina, Wakamiya Jisaki (Tel. 68-6810).

Gassan, p. 637.
Geibi kei, p. 242.
Gembi kei, p. 242.
Gembu do, p. 521.
Genkai (coastal park), p. 187.
Gensei koen, p. 118.

GERO (Gifu ken), p. 192. Tel. 05762; ✉ 509-22.

Ryokans:
*** *Suimeikan*, Gero cho, Mashita gun (Tel. 5-2800), 129 rms.
Bosenkan, Gero cho, Mashita gun (Tel. 5-2048), 53 rms.

🚂 **Rail:** *JNR* to Gifu, Nagoya, Takayama, Toyama.

🚌 **Coaches:** to Gifu, Nakatsugawa, Takayama.

GIFU (Gifu ken), p. 192. Tel. 0582; ✉ 500.

ℹ️ **Tourist Information Centre**, Yabuta (Tel. 72-1111).

Hotels:
*** *Gifu Grand*, 648, Nagara (Tel. 33-1111), 153 rms (71 Jap.), ¶¶ ▥ A/c 🛏 🏨 ☎ TV ❋ ▦ ♪/18 P bar, hairdresser, Jap. com. bath, bowling.
*** *Nagaragawa*, 51, Ukaiya (Tel. 32-4111); 97 rms (47 Jap.), ¶¶ ▥ A/c 🏨 ☎ TV ❋ ♪/18 P bar, boutique, Jap. com. bath.

Ryokans:
** *Juhachiro*, 10, Minato machi (Tel. 65-1551), 78 rms.
** *Negarakan*, 20-1, Nagara, (Tel. 32-7117), 48 rms.
* *Sugiyama*, 73-1, Nagara (Tel. 31-0161), 49 rms.

Business hotel:
Gifu Washington, 8-20, Kogana machi (Tel. 65-4111).

Youth hostels:
Gifu, Kami Kanoyama (Tel. 63-6631).
Kodama so, Ken ei, Nagara Fukumitsu (Tel. 32-1922), 150 beds.

Restaurants:
* *Banshokan* (West. and Chinese food), 2-18, Omiya cho (Tel. 62-0039).
* *Gifu Kaikan* (West. and Jap. food), 39-1, Tsukasa machi (Tel. 64-2151).

🚂 **Rail:** Gifu Hashima station: *Shinkansen* trains, 8mls (13km) SW (bus); – Gifu station: *JNR* to Fukuoka, Kagoshima, Kanazawa, Kumamoto, Nachi-Katsuura, Nagano, Nagasaki, Nagoya, Osaka, Tokyo, Toyama; – Shin Gifu station: *Nagoya Railroad (Meitetsu)* to Nagoya, Osu, Toyohashi, Unuma; – Tetsumeicho station *(Meitetsu tramway)* to Ibigawa, Mino, Tanigumi.

Cablecar: from Gifu koen to Kinka zan.

Coaches: to Fukui Gero, Hikone, Nagoya, Yunoyama.

Specialities: * *Gifu jochin*, decorated lanterns; paper art; *ayu*, small trout.

Events:
Cormorant fishing from 11 May to 15 Oct. on the Nagara gawa; fest. of the naked pilgrims, 10 Dec.; fest. of the Nagara gawa, 16 Jul.

Ginowan, p. 484.
Godai san, p. 323.
Goishi misaki, p. 510.
Goka, p. 480.
Gokasho ura, p. 265.
Gonoura, p. 253.
Gora, p. 169.
Goshiki, p. 139.
Goshikiga hara, p. 156.
Goshogake Onsen, p. 630.

GOTEMBA (Shizuoka ken), p. 193.
Tel. 0550.

Youth hostel:
Gotemba, Higashiyama (Tel. 2–3045), 52 beds.

Restaurant:
Suehiro Gotemba-ten (steaks), 3406, Hakonedo, Higashi-Tanaka (Tel. 3–1178).

Rail: *JNR* to Kozu, Numazu, Tokyo.

Coaches: to Atami, Kofu, Numazu, Odawara.

Excursions: round Fuji via the lakes.

Goto retto, p. 194.
Goza, p. 265.
Gushikawa, p. 486.
Gyodo san, p. 131.
Gyokusen do, p. 483.

H

Habikino, p. 196.
Habomai shoto, p. 451.
Habuminato, p. 271.
Hachijo jima (V. Izu shoto), p. 271.
Hachimantai, p. 630.

HACHINOHE (Aomori ken), p. 196.
Tel. 0178.

Hotel:
* *Hachinohe Grand*, 14, Ban cho (Tel. 46–1234), 122 rms (5 Jap.) ¶ ▬▬ ▬▬ A/c ▦ ▣ ☏ TV ❊ ▨ ∫/18 P bar, hairdresser, boutique.

Business hotel:
Universe Hachinohe, 31–5, Baba machi (Tel. 43–7711).

Airport: Hachinohe, 3mls (5km) N (coach); *TDA* flights to Hanamaki, Sapporo, Tokyo.

Airline: *Toa Domestic Airlines*, reservations (Tel. 43–8311).

Sea travel: to Tomakomai.

Rail: *JNR* to Aomori, Kuji, Sendai, Tokyo.

Coaches: to Kuji.

Events: *Emburi matsuri*, at Shiragi jinja, 17–20 Feb.

Hachioji, p. 197.
Hachiro gata, p. 472.
Hagachi zaki, p. 176.

HAGI (Yamaguchi ken), p. 198.
Tel. 08382; ✉ 758.

Ryokans:
** *Hagi Kanko Hotel*, 1189, Oaza chinto (Tel. 5–0211), 86 rms.
** *Hagi Kokusai Kanko Hotel Rakutenchi*, 6–509, Oaza chinto (Tel. 5–0121), 88 rms.

Minshuku:
Senjuan, 351, Tsuchihara
(Tel. 2-2382), 15 rms.

Youth hostel: *Hagi Shizuki*,
Jonai, Horinouchi
(Tel. 2-0733), 100 beds.

Sea travel: to O shima, Ai
shima, Mi shima.

Rail: *JNR*, to Fukuchiyama,
Fukuoka, Osaka.

Coaches: to Akiyoshi, Hofu,
Ogori, Yamaguchi.

Specialities: Hagi pottery.

HAKODATE (Hokkaido), p.
199.
Tel. Hakodate (0138); Onuma
(013867); ✉: Hakodate (040);
Yunokawa Onsen (042);
Onuma (041-13).

Lodgings:
– At Hakodate

Hotels:
*** *Hakodate Kokusai*, 5-10, Ote
machi (Tel. 23-8751; telex
9926-04), 120 rms (11 Jap.),
❙❙ ▥ A/c ♨ ⌂ ☎ TV ♪/18 ⛟
P bar, hairdresser,
boutiques, bowling.
*** *Hakodate Royal*, 16-9, Omori
cho (Tel. 26-8181), 117 rms
(62 Jap.) 3 ❙❙ ▥ A/c ♨ ⌂ ☎
TV ♪/18 ▣ bar, hairdresser,
boutiques, recept. rms.

Ryokans:
*** *Yunokawa Kanko Hotel*, 2-4-
20, Yunokawa machi (Tel. 57-
1188), 151 rms (15 West.).
** *Meigetsuen Pacific Hotel*,
2-10-1, Yunokawa machi (Tel.
57-0181), 92 rms (4 West.).

* *Yunohama Hotel*, 1-2-30,
Yunokawa machi
(Tel. 59-2231), 115 rms (11
West.).

Business hotel:
Urban Hotel Katsura, 1-5-18,
Yonokawa cho
(Tel. 59-2020).

Minshuku:
Horaiso, 30-17, Horaicho
(Tel. 26-4855), 20 rms.

– At Onuma 17 mls (28km) N.

Ryokan:
** *Kowaki en*, Onuma koen,
Nanae machi, Kameda gun
(Tel. 2321), 55 rms.

Youth hostels:
Onuma, Nanae machi,
Kameda gun (Tel. 2172), 60
beds.
Ikusandar Onuma, 498-6-7,
Onuma cho, Nanae machi,
Kameda gun (Tel. 2845), 100
beds.

Airport: Hakodate, 4mls (7km
E (coach); *ANA* flights to
Tokyo, *TDA* to Sapporo.

Airlines: *All Nippon Airways,
Toa Domestic Airlines*, 14-12
Wakamatsu cho
(Tel. 23-8811).

Sea travel: *JNR, Seikan ferry*
to Aomori; – *Higashi Nihon
Ferry*, to Aomori, Noheji,
Oma.

Rail: *JNR* to Abashiri,
Asahikawa, Esashi, Kushiro,
Matsumae, Sapporo.

Coaches: to E-san Matsumae,
Onuma.

Events: Snow and ice fest. at
Hakodate and Onuma, end-
Jan; – Port festival, begin.
Aug.

Winter sports: at Onuma, 17
mls (28km) N from Dec. to

March (3 chairlifts, 2 drag lifts).

HAMAMATSU (Shizuokaken), p. 204.
Tel. Hamamatsu (0534); Arai, Benteniima, Kosai (05359); Hosoe, Kanzanji Onsen (05352); ✉: Hamamatsu (430); Bentenjima (431-02); Kanzanji Onsen (431-12).

Lodgings:
- At Hamamatsu

Hotel:
** *Hamamatsu Grand*, 1-3-1, Higashi Iba (Tel. 52-2111), 100 rms ⫪ ▥ A/c ⛨ 🛀☎ 📺 P bar, hairdresser, boutiques.

Ryokans:
*** *Hotel Sagano, 204*, Magome cho (Tel. 54-5501), 15 rms.
** *Chotokan*, 1-3-1, Higashi Iba (Tel. 54-6311), 20 rms.

Business hotels:
Yonekyu, 93, Denma cho (Tel. 55-3131).
Futami, 370, Haya machi (Tel. 52-7168).

- At Bentenjima, 9mls (14km) W.

Ryokans:
*** *Marubun*, Maisaka cho (Tel. 2-1611), 57 rms.
** *Hakusatei*, Maisaka cho (Tel. 2-0050), 39 rms.

* *Takasagoen*, Maisaka cho (Tel. 2-3131), 35 rms.

- At Kanzanji Onsen, 9mls (15km) NW.

Ryokans:
*** *Kanzanji Kokusai Kanko Hotel*, Kanzanji cho (Tel. 7-0085), 52 rms.
* *Kanzanji Lake Hotel*, Kanzanji cho (Tel. 7-0124), 57 rms.

- At Uchiyama, 11mls (18km) W.

Youth hostel:
Hamanako, Arai machi (Tel. 4-0670), 179 beds.

Restaurants:
** *Inamba* (Jap. food), 1-3-1, Higashi Inamba (Tel. 54-6311), at Hamamatsu
* *Benisuzume* (Jap. food), 287, Ta machi (Tel. 52-1590), at Hamamatsu.
* *Sazanamikan* (Jap. food), 2219, Kanzanji (Tel. 7-0070), at Kanzanji Onsen, 9mls (15km) NW.

🚆 **Rail:** *JNR (Shinkansen)* to Tokyo, Osaka; other trains to Fukuoka, Hamada, Kagoshima, Nachi-katsuura, Osaka, Tokyo; - *Enshu Railway* to Nishi Kajima.

🚌 **Coaches:** to Nagoya, Shizuoka, Tenryu.

Excursions: coaches (*Entetsu bus*) around Hamana ko.

Travel agency: *JTB*, Kaji cho (Tel. 53-2111).

Specialities: musical instruments.

Events: Kite fest. at Nakatajima, 3-5 May.

Sports: Hamana ko marina, 1380 Iride Aza Chojya, Kosai (Tel. 8-0711).

Hamamura (V. Tottori), p. 628.
Hamana ko, p. 205.
Hamasaka (V. San in Kaigan), p. 521.

HANAMAKI (Iwate ken), p. 206.
Tel. 0198; ✉ 025.

Ryokans:
- *** *Kashoen* (Tel. 27-2111), 41 rms, at Hanamaki Onsen 6mls (9km) NW.
- *** *New Shidodaira Hotel* (Tel. 24-2011), 24 rms, at Shidodaira Onsen 6mls (10km) NW.

✈ **Airport:** Hanamaki, 4mls (6km) N (coach); *TDA* flights to Hachinohe, Tokyo.

🚆 **Rail:** *JNR* to Aomori, Kamaishi, Morioka, Sendai, Tokyo.

🚌 **Coaches:** to Kamaishi, Morioka.

Hanamaki Onsen (V. Hanamaki), p. 206.
Hananuki keikoku, p. 552.
Handa, p. 206.
Happo Onsen, p. 276.
Harajo, p. 643.
Haramachi, p. 207.
Harazuru Onsen (V. Kurume), p. 341.
Haruna ko, p. 533.
Hase dera, p. 519.
Hashihama, p. 254.
Hatage Onsen, p. 401.
Hatano, p. 513.
Hatsu shima, p. 138.
Hattori Ryokuchi (park), p. 502.
Hayama, p. 679.
Hayashida, p. 310.
Hazu, p. 190.
Heda, p. 175.
Hedo misaki, p. 485.
Hegura jima, p. 650.
Hibara ko, p. 142.
Hida gawa, p. 192.

Hidaka, p. 470.
Hei zan, p. 384.
Higashi, p. 486.
Higashiyama Onsen, p. 119.
Hikawa, p. 147.
Hikimi, p. 393.

HIKONE (Shiga ken), p. 208.
Tel. 07492.

Hotel:
- ** *Omi Plaza*, 1911, Matsubara cho (Tel. 22-8101), 47 rms ¶¶ ▦ A/c ♨ 🅿 bar, boutique, bowling.

🚆 **Rail:** Maibara station 4mls (7km) N., *Shinkansen* stop. Hikone station: *JNR* to Kyoto, Maibara, Nagoya, Tsuruga; *Omi Railway* to Kibukawa, Taga.

🚌 **Coaches:** to Gifu, Otsu, Tsuruga.

HIMEJI (Hyogo ken), p. 209.
Tel. Himeji (0792); Shioda Onsen (079336); ✉ : Himeji (670); Shioda Onsen (671-21).

Lodgings:
- At Himeji

Hotel:
- ** *Himeji New Osaka*, 198-1, Ekimae cho (Tel. 23-1111), 38 rms (4 Jap.) ¶¶ ▦ A/c ♨ ▦ bar.

Ryokan:
- ** *Banryu*, Shimodera machi (Tel. 85-2112), 17 rms.

Business hotels:
Himeji Castle, 207, Hojyo (Tel. 84-3311), 222 rms.
Himeji Plaza, 78, Shimizu, Toyosawa cho (Tel. 81-9000).

- At Shioda Onsen 9mls (15km) N.

Ryokan:
- ** *Yumenoi*, Yumesaki cho (Tel. 135), 47 rms.

♨ **Sea travel:** from Shikama, Kansai Kisen to Shodo shima; other service to Ieshima shoto.

🚄 **Rail:** Himeji station: *JNR (Shinkansen)* to Fukuoka, Okayama, Osaka, Tokyo; other trains to Fukuoka, Hiroshima, Kagoshima, Kumamoto, Kurayoshi, Kyoto, Miyakonojo, Miyazaki, Nagasaki, Oita, Okayama Osaka, Shimonoseki, Tamano, Tokyo, Tottori, Toyooka, Tsuyama; *Sanyo Electric Railway* to Kobe; – Shikama station: *JNR* to Toyooka. – Shinmaiko station; *Sanyo ER* to Kobe.

🚌 **Coaches:** to Ako, Kobe, Toyooka.

Travel agency: *JTB,* Sanwa Bldg, Arami machi (Tel. 22-2141).

Specialities: toys, leatherware.

Events: Castle fest. 22 Jun. – *Kenka matsuri,* 14–15 Oct. at the Matsubara shrine.

Sports: Matogaba Marina (Tel. 54-0923).

Hinokage, p. 466.
Hirado, p. 212.
Hiradoguchi, p. 515.

HIRADO SHIMA (Nagasaki ken), p. 211.
Tel. 09502; ⊠ 575.

Ryokans
** *Hirado Kanko Hotel,* Okubo machi (Tel. 2101), 59 rms.
* *Hirado Kaijo Hotel,* Okubo machi (Tel. 2154), 44 rms.

♨ **Sea travel:** to Hiradoguchi, Ikitsuki shima, Oshima, Kashimae, Sasebo.

🚄 **Rail:** *JNR* from Hiradoguchi

to Fukuoka, Nagasaki, Sasebo.

🚌 **Coaches:** to Shijiki zaki; from Hiradoguchi to Karatsu, Kitakyushu, Sasebo.

Events: *Janguwara* Folk Dance.

Hiraizumi, p. 240.
Hiraoka, p. 499.
Hiratsuka, p. 213.
Hirayu Onsen, p. 151.
Hiromine yama, p. 211.
Hiroo, p. 520.
Hirosaki, p. 214.

HIROSHIMA (Hiroshima ken), p. 216.
Tel. Hiroshima (0822); Miyajima (08294); ⊠ : Hiroshima (730 to 733); Miyajima (739–05).

🗊 **Tourist Information Centre,** 10–52, Moto machi (Tel. 28–2111).

Lodgings:

– At Hiroshima

Hotels:
**** *Hiroshima Grand*, 4-4 Kami Hachobori cho (Tel. 27–1313; telex 652-666), 404 rms (6 Jap.) ⫪ ▥ A/c 🛏 🛆 ☎ 📺 ☀ 🍴 bar, hairdresser, boutique, recept. rms.
*** *Hiroshima Kokusai*, 3–13, Tate machi (Tel. 48–2323), 85 rms (17 Jap.) ⫪ ▥ A/c 🛏 🛆 ☎ 📺 🖼 🍴 bar, hairdresser, boutiques, Jap. com. bath, bowling.
*** *Hiroshima Station*, 2–37, Matsubara cho (Tel. 62–3201; telex 652-993), 156 rms (9 Jap.) ⫪ ▥ A/c ☎ 📺 🛆 ☎ 📺 P bar, boutiques.
** *Hiroshima River Side*, 7–14, Kaminobori cho (Tel. 28–1251), 92 rms (5 Jap.) ⫪ ▥ A/c 🛏 🛆 ☎ 📺 bar.

Ryokans:

Fuyo Besso, 2-5-7, Futaba no sato, Higashi ku (Tel. 61-3939), 23 rms.

Mitakiso, Mitaki cho (Tel. 37-1402), 21 rms.

Business hotels:

Hokke Club Hiroshimaten, 7-3, Naka machi (Tel. 48-3371).

Hiroshima Central, 1-8 Kanaya macho (Tel. 43-2222).

Minshuku:

Ikedaya, 6-36, Dobashi cho, Naka ku (Tel. 31-3329), 14 rms.

Youth hostel:

Hiroshima, 1-13-6, Ushida shin machi (Tel. 21-5343).

– At Miyajima 14mls (22km) SW.

Ryokans:

*** *Miyajima Royal Hotel*, Miyajima machi, Saeki gun (Tel. 4-2727), 40 rms.

** *Kamefuku*, Miyajima cho, Saeki gun (Tel. 4-2111), 48 rms.

Restaurants:

** *Amagi* (Jap. food), 10-10, Kami Nobori cho (Tel. 21-2375).

** *Hanbei* (Jap. & West. food), 8-12, Hon Ura cho, Minami ku (Tel. 82-7121).

** *Kinsui* (Jap. food), 6-16, Dobashi cho, Naka ku (Tel. 32-0143).

* *Hada Besso* (Jap. & West. food), 26, Funari cho (Tel. 37-2016).

* *Hyotei* (Jap. food), 6-16, Dobashi cho (Tel. 32-0143).

✈ **Airport:** at Kanonshin machi, 4mls (7km) SW of the station (bus); – flights: *ANA* to Tokyo; *TDA* to Fukuoka, Osaka.

Airlines: *All Nippon Airways*, Kyoya Bldg, 10-9 Teppo cho (Tel. 27-2201); – *Japan Air Lines*, Hachobori Bldg, 13-14, Hachobori cho (Tel. 227-95-11); – *Toa Domestic Airlines*, reservations (Tel. 33-3241).

⚓ **Sea travel:** from the port of Ujina 3mls (5km) S of station: *Hankyu Ferry* to Hyuga; *Seto Naikai Kisen* to Beppu, Imabari, Kure, Mitarai, Mitsuhama, Miyajima, Nagehama; *Uwajima Transport Co.* to Beppu, Kure, Miyajima; – from Dejima 4mls (6km) S of station: *Green Ferry* to Osaka.

🚄 **Rail:** Hiroshima station: *Shinkansen* to Fukuoka, Okayama, Osaka, Tokyo; other trains to Fukuoka, Iwakuni, Kagoshima, Kumamoto, Kyoto, Matsue, Miyakonojo, Miyazaki, Miyoshi, Nagasaki, Nagoya, Oita, Okayama, Osaka, Sandankyo, Shimonoseki, Tokyo. – Nishi-Hiroshima station: *JNR* to Hiroshima, Iwakuni; *Hiroden Electric Railway* to Miyajimaguchi.

🚌 **Coaches:** to Iwakuni, Kure, Masuda, Matsue, Yamaguchi.

Excursions: half day to Itsukushima (in English).

🚗 **Car hire:**

Nippon, 2-10-6, Higashi Senda cho (Tel. 43-3794); – *Nissan*, 9-15, Fujimi cho (Tel. 44-2310).

Taxis: *Private Corporation* (Tel. 92-3351).

Travel agency: *JTB*, Matsubara cho (Tel. 61-2241).

Guided tour: half-day, leaving 14.00 from Hiroshima Grand Hotel (in English).

Specialities: toys, pearl oysters, fruit.

Shopping: Hon dori.

Events: *Kangen sai* at Itsukushima shrine, mid-Jul.; – Peace fest., 6 Aug., at Peace Memorial Park.

Hirota (peninsula), p. 510.
Hiruzen kogen, p. 153.

HITA (Oita ken), p. 222.
Tel. 09732; ✉ 877.

Ryokans:
* *Kizantei Hotel*, Hita Onsen, Kuma cho (Tel. 3–2191), 44 rms.
Tower Hotel Sanyokan, Hita Onsen, Kuma cho (Tel. 2–2134), 24 rms.

Business hotel:
Hita Business Hotel Kanesen, 5–1, Nakahon machi (Tel. 4–1000).

Rail: *JNR*, to Beppu, Fukuoka, Kitakyushu, Nagasaki, Oguni, Tosu.

Coaches: to Aso, Fukuoka, Nakatsu, Oita.

Excursions: to Yaba kei.

Speciality: *Onda* pottery.

Events: Cormorant fishing, Jul.–Sept.

Hitachi, p. 224.
Hitoyoshi, p. 224.
Hiwasa, p. 128.
Hojo, p. 634.
Hokkaido, p. 225.
Hokki ji, p. 250.
Hondo (V. Unzen Amakusa), p. 645.
Hondo (V. Honshu), p. 230.
Hongu, p. 676.
Honshu, p. 230.

Hon Yabakei, p. 223.
Horin ji, p. 250.
Horoizumi, p. 520.
Horyu ji, p. 244.
Hoshino Onsen (V. Joshin Etsu kogen), p. 275.
Hota, p. 560.
Hotaka dake, p. 151.
Hozan ji, p. 448.
Hozu gawa, p. 294.
Hyakusawa Onsen, p. 215.
Hyuga, p. 237.
Hyuga jima, p. 264.

I

Ibuki yama, p. 473.
IBUSUKI (Kagoshima ken), p. 238.
Tel. 09932; ✉ 891-04.

☐ **Tourist information:** Ju cho (Tel. 2–2111).

Hotel:
*** *Ibusuki Kanko*, 3755, Juni cho (Tel. 2–213), 639 rms (172 Jap.) ⫙ ⫙ A/c ⫙ ⫙ ☎ TV ⫙ ⫙ ⫚ ⫛/¹⁸ P bar, hairdresser, boutiques, Jap. com. bath, bowling, conf. rm (3,000 seats).

Ryokans
*** *Ibusuki Kaijo Hotel*, Juni cho (Tel. 2–2221), 110 rms.
*** *Ibusuki Seaside*, Ju cho (Tel. 3–3111), 83 rms.
** *Ibusuki Hakusuikan*, Higashikata (Tel. 2–3131), 130 rms.

Youth hostel:
Ibusuki, 2–1–20, Yunohama (Tel. 2–2758).

⚓ **Sea travel:** from Ibusuki: to O-Nejime; *Kuko hovercraft* to Kagoshima, Kajiki, Sakurajima; – from Yamagawa 4mls (7km) SW: to Nejime,

Sata; *Kagoshima shosen* to Tanega shima, Yaku shima.

🚃 **Rail:** *JNR*, to Kagoshima, Kitakyushu, Makurazaki, Miyazaki.

🚌 **Coaches:** to Kagoshima.

Excursions: to Kaimon dake.

Tel. Ichinoseki (01912); Takinoue (019105); ✉ 021.

Lodgings:

– Ichinoseki

Business hotel:
** *Ichinoseki Green,* 1, Minami Shin machi (Tel. 3-8616), 26 rms. ¶ ▦ A/c ♨ ☎ 📺

– At Takinoue

Ryokan:
Ishibashi Hotel Itsukishien, 15, Minami, Takinoue (Tel. 29-2101), 32 rms.

🚃 **Rail:** *JNR, Shinkansen* to Morioka, Tokyo; other trains to Akita, Aomori, Kitakami, Morioka, Ofunato, Sendai, Tokyo.

🚌 **Coaches:** to Ishinomaki, Kesennuma, Mizusawa, Morioka, Sukawa.

Tel. 02696; ✉ 389.

Hotel:
** *Fujita Madarao Kogen*, Madarao kogen (Tel. 2-3571), 81rms. ¶ ▦ A/c ♨ ☎ 📺 🔔 🚽 ⚲ **P** bar, Jap. com. bath, boutique, hairdresser at Madarao 4mls (6km) W.

🚃 **Rail:** Iiyama station: *JNR* to Nagano, Nagaoka; – Kijima station: *Nagano Electric Railway* to Nagano.

🚌 **Coaches:** to Nagano Naoetsu, Yudanaka.

Sports: Winter sports at Madarao and Nozawa.

Tel. Imaichi, Kawaji Onsen, Kinugawa Onsen (0288); Shiobara Onsen (028732); ✉ : Kawaji Onsen (321-26); Kinugawa Onsen (321-25); Shiobara Onsen (329-29).

Lodgings:

– At Kawaji Onsen 14mls (23km) N.

Ryokan:
** *Ichiryukaku*, Fujiwara machi, Shioya gun (Tel. 78-1111), 132 rms.

– At Kinugawa Onsen 8mls (13km) N.

Ryokans:

** *Asaya Hotel*, Fujiwara machi, Shioya gun (Tel. 7-1111), 311 rms.

* *Kinugawakan Honten*, Fujiwara machi, Shioya gun (Tel. 7-1122), 81 rms.

– At Shiobara Onsen 34mls (54km) NE.

Ryokan:

* *Hotel Myogaya*, Shiobara machi, Shioya gun (Tel. 2-284), 43 rms.

Rail: Shimo-Imaichi station: *JNR* to Nikko, Tokyo, Utsunomiya; – Tobu Imaichi station: *Tobu Railway* to Nikko, Tokyo, Utsunomiyato Kinugawa, Nikko, Tokyo.

Coaches: to Kinugawa, Nikko, Tokyo, Utsunomiya, Yaita.

Imaihama Onsen (V. Fuji-Hakone-Izu), p. 172.
Imari, p. 256.
Imazu, p. 506.
Imbu, p. 484.
Inada, p. 303.
Inatori Onsen (V. Fuji-Hakone-Izu), p. 172.
Inawashiro, p. 257.
Inawashiro ko, p. 257.
Inland Sea, p. 536-7.
Inubo saki, p. 149.

INUYAMA (Aichi ken), p. 257. Tel. 0568; ✉ 484.

Hotels:

** *Meitetsu Inuyama*, 107, Kita (Tel. 61-2211), 120 rms (30 Jap.) ¶ ▥ A/c 🛏 🏠 ☎ TV ☀ 🔲 ♨/18 **P** bar, boutique, bowling.

Ryokan:

*** *Hakuteikaku*, 107-1, Aza Kita Koken, Oaza (Tel. 61-2211), 19 rms.

Youth hostel:
Inuyama, Tsugao (Tel. 61-1111), 96 beds.

Rail: *Nagoya Railroad (Meitetsu)* to Mitake, Nagoya, Unuma, Yaotsu.

Monorail: from Inuyama-Yuen to the zoo.

Coaches: to Gifu, Nagoya.

Events: Cormorant fishing on the Kiso gawa, Jun.-Sept.

Io jima, p. 475.
Irako misaki, p. 632.
Iriomote, p. 656.
Iro zaki, p. 176.
Isa, p. 484.
Isahaya (V. Unzen Amakusa), p. 643.
Ise, p. 258.

ISE SHIMA (Mie ken; National Park), p. 258.

Lodgings:

– At Futami
Tel. 059643; ✉ 519-06.

Ryokans:

** *Futami Urashima*, Futami cho, Watarai gun (Tel. 2-1011), 52 rms.

* *Ikenouraso*, Futami cho, watarai gun (Tel. 3-2525), 97 rms.

– At Hamajima
Tel. 05995; ✉ 517-04.

Ryokans:

*** *Hiraiso*, Hàmajima cho, Shima gun (Tel. 3-0053), 40 rms.

* *Okushima Kanko Hotel Nampuso*, 1416, Hamajima cho, Shima gun (Tel. 3-2111), 38 rms.

– At Kashikojima
Tel. 05994; ✉ 517-05.

Hotel:

*** *Shima Kanko*, 731, Shimmei,

Ago cho, Shima gun
(Tel. 3–1211; telex 4975–011),
200 rms (55 Jap.) ¶¶ ▦ A/c
♨ 🏛 ☎ TV ❀ 🔲 ⇌ ℚ ⌇/¹⁸ 🛢
P bar, hairdresser,
boutiques, bowling.

– At Toba
Tel. 05992; ✉ 517.

Hotel:
*** *Toba International*, 1–23–1,
Toba cho (Tel. 5–3121; telex
4973–789), 126 rms (25 Jap.)
¶¶ ▦ A/c ♨ 🏛 ☎ TV ⇌ ⌇/¹⁸
P bar, boutiques.

Ryokans:
*** *Fujita Toba Kowaki en*, 1061,
Arashima cho (Tel. 5–3251),
95 rms.
*** *Hotel Taiike*, Ohama cho
(Tel. 5–4111), 60 rms.
** *Kogaso*, 237–1, Ohama cho
(Tel. 5–2170), 39 rms.
** *New Mishimo*, 1069–201,
Sakade cho (Tel. 5–5111),
52 rms.
** *Sempokaku*, 2–12–24, Toba
cho (Tel. 5–3151), 46 rms.
* *Kimpokan*, 1–10–38, Toba cho
(Tel. 5–2001), 38 rms.
* *Toba Seaside Hotel*, Arashima
cho (Tel. 5–51–51), 69 rms.

ITO (Shizuoka ken), p. 267.
Tel. 0557; ✉ 414.

Hotel:
*** *Kawana*, 1459, Kawana
(Tel. 45–1111), 148 rms (8
Jap.) 4 ¶¶ ▦ A/c ♨ ☎ TV ♠

🔲 ⇌ ⌇/¹⁸ P bar, boutiques,
conf. rm.

Ryokans:
* *Hatoya Hotel*, Oka
(Tel. 36–4126), 237 rms.
*** *New Tokai*, 1–8, Takara cho
(Tel. 37–0114), 40 rms.
*** *Yonewakaso*, Hirono
(Tel. 37–5111), 16 rms.
** *Hotel Ebina*, Matsubara
(Tel. 37–3111), 82 rms.
** *Yokikan*, Suehiro cho
(Tel. 37–3101), 25 rms.

Youth hostel:
Ito, Komuroyama koen
(Tel. 45–0224), 96 beds.

⚓ **Sea travel:** to Atami, Eno
shima, Hatsu shima, O shima.

🚃 **Rail:** *JNR* to Tokyo Shimoda;
– *Izu Kyuko Railway* to
Shimoda.

🚌 **Coaches:** to Atami, Moto
Hakone, Shimoda, Shuzenji.

Sports: golf at Kawana.

ITOIGAWA (Niigata ken), p.
261.

Lodgings:

– At Hakuba 11mls (*18km*) S.
Tel. 025557; ✉ 949–04.

Ryokan:
Hotel Daietsu, Hakuba Onsen
(Tel. 2121), 28 rms.

🚃 **Rail:** *JNR* to Kanazawa,
Matsumoto, Naoetsu, Niigata,
Osaka, Tokyo, Toyama.

🚌 **Coaches:** to Hakuba,
Naoetsu, Toyama.

IWAKI (Fukushima ken) p.268.
Tel. 0246; ✉ 972.

Miyake jima to Hachijo jima, Kozu shima, Nii jima, O shima, Shimoda, Tokyo; – from Nii jima to Kozu shima, Miyake jima, O shima; – from O shima: Motomachi or Okada, to Shimoda, Tokyo; from Motomachi to Atami, Eno shima, Hachijo jima, Ito, Kozu shima, Miyake jima, Nii jima. – All these services are available once or more often per week through *Tokai Steamship Co.* or *Izu Hakone Railway's Steamer.*

🚌 **Coaches:** Reliable services on main islands.

Excursions: around island of O shima, from Motomachi or Okada, and at Hachijo jima.

Specialities: camellia oil at O shima; tropical plants and ornate weaving (*Kihachijo*) at Hachijo jima.

Events: Teko matsuri, 16 Jan. at Hachiman Okada shrine, at O shima.
– Folk dances from Hachijo jima.

J

JOSHIN ETSU KOGEN
(Gumma, Nagano and Niigata ken; National Park), p. 274.

Lodgings:
– At Hoshino Onsen
Tel. 02674; ✉ 389–01

Ryokan:
** *Hoshino Onsen Hotel*, Karuizawa machi, Kita Saku gun (Tel. 5-5121), 58 rms.

– At Karuizawa
Tel. 02674; ✉ 389–01

Hotels:
*** *Karuizawa Prince*, 1016-75, Karuizawa (Tel. 2-5211), 72 rms. ⫼ ▥ A/c ♨ ⌂ ☎ 📺 ♣ ⌇/18 ⛳ P bar, boutiques.
** *Kajima no Mori*, Hanareyama, Karuizawa (Tel. 2-3535), 35 rms (8 Jap.) ⫼ ▥ A/c ⌂ ☎ 📺 ♜ ⌇/18 ⛳ P bar, boutique.
** *Mampei*, Sakuranosawa, Karuizawa (Tel. 2-2771), 110 rms (14 Jap.) ⫼ ▥ A/c 📺 ❉ ⌇/18 ⛳ P bar, boutique.
** *Seizan*, 1016, Karuzawa (Tel. 2-2761), 82 rms (24 Jap.), bungalows ⫼ ▥ A/c ⌂ ☎ 📺 ♣ ♜ ⌇/18 ⛳ P bar, boutique.

Ryokans:
*** *Hotel New Hoshino*, Karuizawa machi, Kita Saku gun (Tel. 5-6081), 30 rms.
* *Shiotsubo Onsen Hotel*, Karuizawa machi, Kita Saku gun (Tel. 5-5441), 44 rms.

– At Kusatsu Onsen
Tel. 027988; ✉ 377–17

Ryokans:
*** *Hotel Ichii*, Kusatsu machi, Agatuma gun (Tel. 2511), 75 rms.
Nakazawa Village, Kusatsu

machic, Agatsuma gun
(Tel. 3232), 42 rms.

- At the Shiga Kogen
Tel. 02693; ✉ 381-04

Hotels:

** *Okushiga Kogen*, Okushiga
Kogen, Yamanouchi machi,
Shimotakai gun (Tel. 4-2034),
48 rms (14 Jap.) ⊮ ▥ A/c ⊮
♨ ☎ TV ☀ ▦ ✧ ⍰/¹⁸ P bar,
boutique.

** *Shiga Heights*, 7148, Hirao,
Yamanouchi machi,
Shimotakai gun (Tel. 4-2111),
142 rms (15 Jap.) ⊮ ▥ ⛩ ♨
☎ TV ♠ ⍰/¹⁸ P bar, boutique,
Jap. com. bath.

Ryokan:

*** *Hoppo Kokusai Hotel*,
Maruike Onsen, Yamanouchi
machi, Shimotakai gun
(Tel. 4-2845), 27 rms.

- At Yudanaka Onsen
Tel. 02693; ✉ 381-04.

Ryokans:

* *Kanaguya Hotel*, Shibu Onse,
Yamanouchi machi,
Shimotakai gun (Tel. 3-3131),
41 rms.

* *Kokuya Hotel*, 2200, Oaza
Hirao, Yamanouchi machi,
Shimotakai gun (Tel. 3-2511),
23 rms.

- At Myoko kogen
V. under this place name.

Jozankei (V. Shikotsu Toya),
p. 539.
Juni ko, p. 215.

K

Kabe shima, p. 302.
Kada, p. 653.

KAGA (Ishikawa ken), p. 277.
Tel. Kaga (07617); ✉ Kaga

(922); Katayamazu (922-04);
Yamanaka (922-01);
Yamashiro (922-02).

Lodgings:

- At Katayamazu

Ryokans:
Hokuriku Koganol Hotel, A-5,
Katayamazu (Tel. 4-1041),
72 rms.
Yataya, Se-1-1, Katayamazu
(Tel. 4-1181), 101 rms.

- At Yamanaka Onsen 6mls
(*km*) SE.

Ryokans:

*** *Shisuien*, Yamanaka machi,
Enuma gun (Tel. 8-0033),
51 rms.

** *Suimei*, Yamanaka machi,
Enuma gun (Tel. 8-1616),
61 rms.

* *Hotel Hassoen*, Yamanaka
machi, Enuma gun
(Tel. 1-1020), 38 rms.

- At Yamashiro Onsen 4mls
(*6km*) SE.

Ryokans:

*** *Yamashitaya*, Yamashiro
Onsen (Tel. 7-2222), 86 rms.

** *Yamaya Banshokaku*,
Yamashiro Onsen
(Tel. 7-1515), 58 rms.

* *Hyakumangoku*, Yamashiro
Onsen (Tel. 7-1111), 162 rms.

✈ **Airport:** Komatsu, 9mls
(15km) N (coach) V. under
this place name.

🚌 **Rail:** *JNR* to Aomori,
Kanazawa, Nagoya, Naoetsu,
Niigata, Osaka, Toyama.

🚍 **Coaches:** to Awara, Fukui,
Kanazawa.

Specialities: *habutae* weaving
and other silks; Kutani China.

Kaga (Shimane ken), p. 394.
Kagami yama, p. 302.

KAGOSHIMA (Kagoshima ken), p. 278.
Tel. Kagoshima (0992);
Sakurajima (099293); ⊠ :
Kagoshima (890 to 892);
Sakurajima (891–14).

[i] **Tourist Information Centre**,
14-50, Yamashita cho
(Tel. 26-8111); – Kagoshima
Tourist Association, 9–1,
Meizan cho (Tel. 23-9171); –
Tourist Office of Kagoshima
city, 11-1, Yamashitacho
(Tel. 23-1111).

Lodgings:

– At Kagoshima

Hotel:
*** *Shiroyama Kanko*, 95,
Shinshoin cho (Tel. 24-2211),
622 rms (37 Jap.) 4 ¶¶ ▥ A/c
🛗 🏦 ☎ TV ❀ 🖼 ♨/18 **P** bar,
hairdresser, boutiques,
bowling, sports rm, sauna.

Ryokans:
*** *Kagoshima Kokusai Hotel
Kakumei kan*, Shiroyama cho
(Tel. 23-2241), 54 rms.
* *Kagoshima Daiichiso*, 1-38-8,
Shimo arata (Tel. 57-2121) ¶¶
▥ A/c 🛗 🏦 ☎ TV
* *Fukiageso Hotel*, 18-15,
Terukuni cho (Tel. 24-3500),
70 rms.

Business hotels:
Kagoshima Gasthof, 7-3, Cho
cho (Tel. 52-1401).
Kagoshima Daiichi, 1-4-1,
Takashi (Tel. 55-0256).

Minshuku:
Hondaso, 15-23, Izumi cho
(Tel. 22-9090), 8 rms.

Youth hostel:
Fujin-Kaikan, 2-4-12,
Shimoarata (Tel. 51-1087), 45
beds.

– At Sakurajima 2mls (*3km*) E.

Ryokan:
*** *Sakurajima Kanko Hotel*,
Sakurajima cho, Kagoshima
gun (Tel. 2211), 60 rms.

Youth hostel:
Sakurajima, Hakamagoshi,
Nishi Sakurajima, Omura,
Kagoshima gun (Tel. 2150),
95 beds.

✈ **Airport:** Kagoshima 28mls
(*45km*) *N*; coach, hydrofoil to
Kajiki, then coach; – flights
ANA to Amami O shima,
Nagoya, Okinawa, Omura,
Osaka, Tokyo; *TDA* flights to
Amami O shima, Fukuoka,
Kikai jima, Oita, Okino Erabu
jima, Tanega shima, Tokuno
shima, Tokushima, Yaku
shima (obtain info.).

Airlines: *All Nippon Airways*,
Nagoku Nissei Bldg, 11-5,
Chuo cho (Tel. 55-5435); –
Japan Air Lines, New
Kagoshima Hotel, 6-5 Chuo
machi Kagoshimashi
(Tel. 58-2311); – *Toa
Domestic Airlines*, Sumitomo
Seimei Bldg, 3-22,
Yamanoguchi (Tel. 26-8132).

⚓ **Sea travel:** from the jetty of
Bosado: to Tarumizu; – from
the jetty of Meizan: *Kyushu
Shosen* to Tanega shima;
Orita Kisen to Yaku shima;
Kagoshima Shosen to Tanega
shima, Yuka shima; – from the
jetty of Sakurajima: hydrofoil
to Ibusuki, Kaijiki; Sakurajima
(quays near Kagoshima
station); – from the New
Harbour (1½ mls/*2.5km* E of
Nishi Kagoshima eki; coach);
Oshima Unyu or *Shokoku
Yusen* to Kikai jima, Amami O
shima, Tokuno shima, Okino
erabu jima, Yoronto shima,
Okinawa shima; – from
Taniyama (6mls/*10km* S;

coach): *Nihon Kosoku Ferry* to Kochi, Nagoya, Osaka; – from Sakurajima (2mls/3km E); hydrofoil to Ibusuki, Kajiki.

Rail: Nishi-Kagoshima main station or Kagoshima: *JNR* to Fukuoka, Hiroshima, Kitakyushu, Kumamoto, Kyoto, Makurazaki, Miyazaki, Okayama, Osaka, Tokyo, Yamakawa.

Coaches: to Ibusuki, Kirisshima, Miyazaki, Sendai; near Nishi Kagoshima eki.

Car hire: *Avis*, Nishi Kagoshima, 1–33, Terukuni cho (Tel. 24-1756); – *Nippon*, 16-7, Chuo cho (Tel. 58-3336); – *Nissan*, Nishi Kagoshima Eki mae (Tel. 52-0563).

Travel agency: *JTB, c/o Kagoshima Hayashida Hotel*, Sengoku cho (Tel. 22-8155).

Specialities: oranges, giant radishes from Sakurajima; Satsuma pottery.

Shopping: Tenmonkan dori, Naya dori.

KAMAKURA (Kanagawa ken), p. 281.
Tel. 0467; ✉ 248.

Hotel:
*** *Kamakura Park*, 33-6, Sakanoshita (Tel. 25-5121), 25 rms (14 Jap.) ‖ ▥ A/c ▦ ☎ TV ▨ P sauna.

Ryokan:
** *Kaihinso*, 8-14, Yuigahama 4-chome (Tel. 22-0960).

Minshuku:
Choboan, 3-14-9, Inamuragasaki (Tel. 23-1578), 4 rms.

Youth hostel:
Nihon Gakusei Kaikan, 293, Sakanoshita, Yuigahama kaigan (Tel. 25-1234), 400 beds.

Restaurant:
** *Royal Lobster Seafood* (West. food), 21-1, Sakanoshita (Tel. 24-8611).

Rail: Kamakura station: *JNR* to Tokyo, Yokosuka; *Enoshima Kamakura Kanko Electric Railway* to Fujisawa; – Ofuna station: *JNR* to Odawara, Omiya, Tokyo.

Monorail: from Ofuna to Fujisawa.

Coaches: to Odawara, Tokyo, Yokohama, Yokosuka.

Excursions: half-day tour of the town from the station; excursions with commentary in English from Tokyo to region of Hakone (visit to the Great Buddha only).

Events: *Kamakura* fest. 7–14 Apr., procession along Wakamiya Oji; – *Yasubame* (archers on horseback), 16 Sept. at Tsurugaoka Hachiman gu.

Specialities: pottery, wood carvings and lacquerware (*Kamakura bori*).

Kamoenai, p. 505.

KAMOGAWA (Chiba ken), p. 295.
Tel. 04749; ✉ 296.

Ryokan:
** *Kamogawa Grand Hotel*, 820, Hiroba (Tel. 2-2111), 150 rms.

🚂 **Rail:** Awa-Kamogawa station: *JNR* to Tateyama, Tokyo.

🚌 **Coaches:** to Katsuura, Kisarazu, Tateyama.

Kamuikotan, p. 130.
Kamui misaki, p. 504.
Kanaiwa, p. 299.
Kanaya (Chiba ken, V. Tateyama), p. 560.
Kanaya (Shizuoka ken), p. 541.

KANAZAWA (Ishikawa ken), p. 296.
Tel: 0762; ✉ : Kanazawa (920); Yuwaku Onsen (920-12).

ℹ️ **Tourist Information Centre**, 2-1-1, Hirosaka cho (Tel. 61-1111).

Lodgings:

- At Kanazawa

Hotels:
*** *Kanazawa Miyako*, 6-10, Konohana cho (Tel. 31-2202; telex 5122-203), 88 rms. (2 Jap.) 🍴 ▥ A/c ♨ 🛁 ☎ 📺 🔲 bar, boutiques.
*** *Kanazawa New Grand*, 1-50, Takaoka machi (Tel. 33-1311; telex 5122-357), 122 rms. (3 Jap.) 🍴 ▥ A/c ♨ 🛁 ☎ 📺 ▨ **P** bar, hairdresser, boutiques, bowling.
*** *Kanazawa Sky*, 15-1 Musashi machi (Tel. 33-2233; telex 5122-716), 120 rms (24 Jap.) 🍴 ▥ A/c ♨ ➖ 🛁 ☎ 📺 **P** bar, boutiques.

Ryokans:
* *Hotel Kinkaku*, 31, Higashi Mikage machi (Tel. 52-1265), 16 rms.
Chaya, 2-17-21, Hon machi (Tel. 31-2225), 24 rms.

Business hotel:
Kanazawa Central, 4-1, Horikawa cho (Tel. 63-5311), 39 rms 🍴 ▥ A/c ♨ 🛁 ☎ 📺.

Minshuku:
Nogi Ryokan, 4-16, Konohana cho (Tel. 21-8579), 20 rms.
Ginmatsu, 1-17-18, Higashiyama (Tel. 52-3577), 12 rms.

Youth hostel:
Kanazawa, 37, Suehiro cho (Tel. 52-3414) 120 beds.

- At Yuwaku Onsen 9 mls (*14km*) SE.

Hotel:
** *Hakuunro*, Yuwaku machi (Tel. 35-1111), 100 rms (67 Jap.) 🍴 ▥ 🛁 🛁 ☎ 📺 ▨ ⚲ ♨/18 **P** bar, boutique.

Restaurants:
** *Kaga Sekitei* (Jap. food), 1-9-23, Hirosaka (Tel. 31-2208).
** *Tsubajin Wako* (West. food), 5-1-8, Tera machi (Tel. 41-2181).
** *White House* (Chin. food), 1-38-30, Higashiyama (Tel. 52-2271).
** *Kappo Ogawa* (Jap. food), 2-7-15, Katamachi (Tel. 31-1908).
** *Kitamar* (Jap. food), 2-3-3, Katamachi (Tel. 61-7176).
* *Seifuso* (Jap. food), 1-19-1, Higashiyama (Tel. 52-2824).
* *Yamanoo* (Jap. food), 1-31-25, Higashiyama (Tel. 52-5171).

✈️ **Airport:** Komatsu, 22mls

(35km) SW (coach) V. this place name.

Airlines: *All Nippon Airways*, reservations (Tel. 31–3111); – *Japan Air Lines*, Tohoseimei Bldg, 1-10 Oyama cho (Tel. 64-3211).

Rail: Kanazawa station: *JNR* to Aomori, Nagoya, Naoetsu, Niigata, Osaka, Takojima, Tokyo, Toyama, Wajima; *Hokuriku Railway*, to Uchinada-Awagasaki. Nomachi station: *Hokuriku Railway* to Hakusanshita, Neagari.

Coaches: to Fukui, Fukumitsu, Hakui, Toyama.

Car hire: *Nippon*, 30–23, Horikawa cho (Tel. 25–6127); – *Nissan*, 1-4-8, Hon machi (Tel. 33-3217).

Travel agency: *JTB*, Fukuku Seimei Bldg, Shimozutsumi cho (Tel. 61–6171).

Events: *Hyakuman Goku* fest. in mid-June; costumed procession.

Specialities: *Kaga yuzen, painted fabric, Kutani pottery.

Shopping: Kata machi, Yokoyasue cho.

Sports: skiing at Jo zen; 9mls (*15km*) SE.

Kanka kei, p. 549.
Kannon ji, p. 188.
Kannonji, p. 300.
Kannon yama, p. 556.
Kannon zaki, p. 670.
Kannoura, p. 408.
Kano zan (V. Kisarazu), p. 303.
Kanoya, p. 300.
Kanzanji Onsen (V. Hamamatsu), p. 206.

KARATSU (Saga ken), p. 301. Tel. 09557; ✉ 847.

Hotel:
* *Karatsu Seaside*, 4–4019–198, Higashi Karatsu (Tel. 3–5185), 59 rms (27 Jap.) ⫿ ▬ A/c ⚓ ⌂ ☎ TV ☀ ⚲ ♪/18 **P** bar, boutique, bowling.

Rail: Karatsu or Nishi Karatsu station: *JNR* to Saga, Sasebo; Higashi Karatsu station: *JNR* to Fukuoka, Saga.

Coaches: to Fukuoka, Hiradoguchi, Saga, Yobuko.

Events: *Okunchi Matsuri* of Karatsu Shrine, 3 and 4 Nov. (street procession).

Karuizawa (V. Joshin Etsu kogen), p. 274.
Karurusu Onsen, p. 539.
Kasama, p. 303.
Kasa yama, p. 199.
Kashihara, p. 303.
Kashikojima (V. Ise shima), p. 265.

KASHIMA (Ibaraki ken), p. 306. Tel: Itako (02996); Kashima (02999); ✉ : Itako (311–24); Kashima (314).

Lodgings:

– At Kashima

Hotel:
*** *Kashima Central*, 182–38, Hiraizumi, Kamisu cho (Tel. 2–5511), 152 rms. ⫿ ▬ A/c ⚓ ⌂ ☎ TV ☀ ⚲ ♪/18 ⚲ **P** bar, hairdresser, boutiques, conference rm.

– Itako:

Ryokans:
* *Itako Hotel*, Itako machi, Name-gata gun (Tel. 2-3130), 51 rms.

Kinugasa, p. 670.
Kinugawa Onsen (V. Imaichi),
p. 255.
Kin zan, p. 661.
Kirishima (mountain chain)
p. 310.
Kirishima jingu, p. 311.

KIRISHIMA Yaku
(Kagoshima and Miyazaki
ken; National Park), p. 309.

Lodgings:

– At Ebino kogen
Tel. 09843; ✉ 889-43.

Ryokan:
** *Ebino Kogen Hotel Bekkan*,
Suenaga (Tel. 3-1155), 43
rms.

– At Kirishima Onsen
Tel. 09957; ✉ 899-66.

Hotel:
** *Hayashida Onse*, 3958,
Takachiho, Makizono cho,
Aira gun (Tel. 8-2911), 449
rms (179 Jap.). ⅋ ▭ A/c ♨
🛁 ☎ TV ♦ ▨ ⚲/18 🏌 P bar,
Jap. com. bath, gaming room,
night-club, open air theatre.

Ryokan:
** *Kirishima Hotel*, Makizono
cho, Aira gun (Tel. 8-2121),
107 rms.
– At Kagoshima and Miyazaki:
V. under these place names.

Kisakata, p. 518.

KISARAZU (Chiba ken), p.
311.
Tel. Futtsu (04788); Kano zan
(047862); Kisarazu (0438); ✉:
Futtsu (299-12); Kano zan
(292-11); Kisarazu (292).

Lodgings:
– At Kisarazu:

Ryokans:
* *Hotel Kangetsuso*, 2-2-1,

Shinden (Tel. 22-4141),
23 rms.
* *Kisarazu Onsen Hotel*, 2-3-5,
Fujimi (Tel. 22-2171), 38 rms.

Business hotel:
Kisarazu Park, 3-2-30,
Shinden (Tel. 23-3491).

– At Futtsu 9 mls (*15km*) SW.

Ryokan:
Futtsu Kanko Hotel, 2348,
Futtsu (Tel. 7-2111), 21 rms.

– At Kano zan 15mls (*24km*)
S.

Ryokan:
Hotel Kanozan, Kano zan,
Kimitsu (Tel. 23), 25 rms.

🛳 **Sea travel:** *Nippon Car Ferry*
to Kawasaki; – *Tokai
Steamship* to Tokyo; –
Tokyowan ferry, to
Yokohama.

🚝 **Rail:** *JNR* to Chiba, Kasuza-
Kameyama, Tateyama, Tokyo.

🚌 **Coaches:** to Kamogawa,
Kano zan, Mobara, Tateyama

Kiso Fukushima, p. 311.
Kiso gawa (gorges), p. 312.
Kiso gawa (rapids), p. 400.

KITAKYUSHU (Fukuoka ken),
p. 312.
Tel. 093; ✉ 800.

Hotels:
*** *Kokura*, 3-10, Semba cho,
Kokura ku (Tel. 531-1151;
telex 7127-57), 101 rms (4
Jap.) ⅋ ▭ A/c 🛁 🏠 ☎ TV ▨
bar, hairdresser, boutiques.
** *Kokura Station*, 1-1-1, Asano,
Kokura ku (Tel. 521-5031), 35
rms (9 Jap.) ⅋ ▭ A/c 🛁 🏠
☎ TV P bar, hairdresser,
boutique.
* *New Tagawa*, 3-46,
Furusenba cho, Kokurakita
ku (Tel. 521-3831), 94 rms (18
Jap.) ⅋ ▭ A/c 🛁 🏠 ☎ TV P

Business hotel:
Kitakyushu Daiichi, 11-20, Konya machi, Kokurakita ku (Tel. 551-7331).

Youth hostel:
Kita-kyushu, Hobashira koen, 1481, Hirahara, Ogura, Yahata ku (Tel. 681-8142).

✈ **Airport:** Kokura 4mls (6km) SE (coach); flights *ANA* to Osaka.

Airlines: *All Nippon Airways*, Marugen Bldg, 3-8, 4-chome, Uo machi, Kokura ku (Tel. 551-1836); – *Japan Air Lines*, Pasco Kokura Bldg, 2-1-1, Satai cho, Kokurakita ku (Tel. 551-5322).

⚓ **Sea travel:** from Kokura port: *Hankyu Ferry* to Kobe; *Iki-Tsushima Kisen* to Tsu shima; *Kansai Kisen* to Matsuyama; *Tokai Steamship* to Tokyo; – from Shin Moji port: *Meimon Car Ferry* to Nagoya, Yokkaichi; – from Kanda 8mls (13km) SE: *Nishi Nihon Ferry* to Kobe; *Taiyo Ferry* to Osaka.

Shipping line: *Kansai Kisen*, 77, 2-chome, Asano cho, Kokura ku (Tel. 531-4431).

🚉 **Rail:** Kokura station: *JNR; Shinkansen* to Fukuoka, Okayama, Osaka, Tokyo; other trains to Fukuoka, Hiroshima, Kagoshima, Kumamoto, Kyoto, Miyakonojo, Miyazaki, Moji, Mojiko, Nagasaki, Nagoya, Oita, Okayama, Osaka, Sasebo, Tagawa, Tokyo, Yatsushiro, Yunomae; – Moji station: *JNR* to Fukuoka, Hiroshima, Kagoshima, Kumamoto, Kyoto, Miyakonojo, Miyazaki, Moji, Mojiko, Nagasaki, Oita,

Osaka, Sasebo, Tokyo, Tosu, Yatsushiro, Yunomae; – Mojiko station: *JNR* to Kagoshima, Miyazaki, Yatsushiro, Yunomae; – Wakamatsu station: *JNR* to Iizuka, Tagawa; – Orio station: *JNR* to Iizuka, Kagoshima, Mojiko, Oita, Tagawa, Tokyo, Wakamatsu, Yatsushiro, Yunomar; *Nishi Nippon Railroad (Nishitetsu)* to Moji; – Uomachi station: *Nishitetsu* to Kitagata, Moji, Orio, Tobata; – Chuomachi station: *Nishitetsu* to Tobata; – Sadamoto station: *Nishitetsu* to Moji, Orio; *Chikuho Electric Railway* to Nogata.

Funicular: from Ogarakoen to Hobashirayama.

🚌 **Coaches:** to Beppu, Fukuoka, Hita, Iizuka, Yamaguchi.

Events: *Gion Daiko*, 10-12 Jul. at Yasaka shrine with a procession of floats.

Kitaura (Akita ken, V. Oga), p. 472.
Kitaura (Miyazaki ken), p. 466.
Kita ura, p. 306.
Kitayama gawa (valley), p. 674.
Kitayama zaki, p. 509.
Kiyosumi yama, p. 296.
Kiyotaki (Tochigi ken), p. 463.
Kiyotaki (Tokyo to), p. 197.

KOBE (Hyogo ken), p. 314. Tel. 078; ✉ 650 to 657.

ℹ️ **Tourist Information Centre,** Kobe Kotsu Center Bldg. (2nd floor), Sannomiya *JNR* station (Tel. 331-8181).

Hotels:
*** *Kobe Portopia*, Nakamachi 6-chome, Minatojima, Ikuta ku

(Tel. 302–1111) 560 rms ¶ ▦ A/c 🛏 ⬥ 🏛 ☎ TV P bar, conf. rms.

*** *New Port*, 3–13, Hamabe dori 6-chome, Chuo ku (Tel. 231–4171; telex 5623–058) 208 rms (1 Jap.) ¶ ▦ A/c 🛏 🏛 ☎ TV 🖥 bar, boutiques.

*** *Rokko Oriental*, 1878, Nishioaniyama, Rokkosan cho, Nada ku (Tel. 891–0333; telex 5623–028) 60 rms (12 Jap.) ¶ ▦ A/c 🛏 🏛 ☎ TV 🥢/¹⁸ 🏌 P bar, boutiques.

*** *Kobe International*, 8–9–1, Goko dori, Fukiai ku (Tel. 221–8051) 48 rms (3 Jap.) ¶ ▦ A/c 🛏 🏛 ☎ TV 🖥 bar, boutique.

** *Rokkosan*, 1034, Minami Rokko, Rokkosan cho, Nada ku (Tel. 891–0301) 72 rms (4-Jap.) ¶ ▦ A/c 🛏 🏛 ☎ TV 🥢/¹⁸ P bar, boutique.

Ryokan:

** *Hotel Kobe*, Kumochi cho, Fukiai ku (Tel. 221–5431) 47 rms.

Business hotels:

Suijo, 1–2–8, Mizuki dori, Hyogo ku (Tel. 575–5871). *Green Hill*, 2–18–63, Kano cho, Ikuta ku (Tel. 222–5489). *Kobe Union*, 2–5, Nunobiki cho, Fukiai ku (Tel. 222–6500). *Kobe Washington Hotel*, 2–8–2, Shimoyamate cho, Chuo ku (Tel. 331–6111).

Youth hostels:

Tarumi Kaigan, 5–58, Kaigan dori, Tarumi ku (Tel. 707–2133) 28 beds; – *YMCA*, Shimo Yamate dori, Ikuta ku (Tel. 331–0123); – *YMCA* Kamitsutsui dori, Fukiaj ku (Tel. 231–6201).

Restaurants:

** *Komon* (Jap. food; spec.: shobu-shabu), 1–4–11, Nakayamate dori, Chuo ku (Tel. 351–0673).

** *Fujiwara* (Jap. food; spec.: tempura) 14, Motomachi dori, Chuo Ku (Tel. 331-33–73).

** *Tensuke* (Jap. food; spec.: sushi), 7–16, Nakayamate dori, Chuo ku (Tel. 391–2073).

** *Doi* (Jap. food; spec.: yakitori), 1–4–22, Sannomiya cho, Chuo ku (Tel. 391–44–01).

** *Kobe Steak* (West. food), 4–3–3, Kano cho, Chuo ku (Tel. 391–2581).

** *Minsei* (Chin. food), 1–3–4, Motomachi dori, Chuo ku (Tel. 331–5435; reserve).

* *Aien* (Chin. food), 3–4–10, Kitanagasa dori, Chuo ku (Tel. 331–3354).

✈ **Airport:** *Osaka International*, at Ikeda 19mls (31km) NE; coach from Sannomiya station; V. Osaka.

Airlines: *Air France*, Kotsu Center Bldg, 101 Sannomiyo cho, Ikata ku (321–6003); – *All Nippon Airways*, Kobe Kotsu Center Bldg., 1, Sannomiya machi 1-chome, Ikuta ku (Tel. 391–3835); – *Japan Airlines*, Kobe Shimbun Kaikan, 7–1–1, Kumoi dori, Chuo Ku (Tel. 251–7511).

⚓ **Sea travel:**
– From Kobe (Naka jetty): *Kansai Kisen* to Awaji shima, Beppu, Imabari, Kannoura, Matsuyama, Miyazaki, Okinawa, Osaka, Shodo shima, Takamatsu; – services to Kawanoe.
– From Kobe (jetty 4): *Oshima Unyu Kisen* to Amami

Oshima, Tokuno shima, Okino erabu jima, Yoron jima, Okinawa; – international services.
– From Higashi Kobe (Fukae): *Kansai Kisen* to Hyuga; – *Nishi Nihon Ferry* to Kanda (Kitakyushu); – *Shikoku Ferry* to Takamatsu; – *Tukushima Hanshin Ferry* to Tokushima; – services to Matsuyama, Oita, Sakai.

Navigation company:
Kansai Kisen, Naka tottei, Hatoba cho, Ikuta ku (Tel. 391-6601).

Rail:
– Shin Kobe station; *JNR, Shinkansen* to Fukuoka, Okayama, Osaka, Tokyo.
– Sannomiya station (main): *JNR* to Fukuoka, Himeji, Hiroshima, Kagoshima, Kumamoto, Kurayoshi, Kyoto, Miyakonojo, Miyazaki, Nagasaki, Osaka, Sasebo, Shimonoseki, Tokyo, Tottori; – *Keihanshin Electric Railway* (Hankyu ER) to Kyoto, Osaka, Suma, Takarazuka; – *Hanshin Electric Railway* to Motomachi, Osaka; – *Sanyo Electric Railway* to Himeji, Rokko.
– Kobe station: *JNR* to Hiroshima, Kumamoto, Oita, Osaka, Shimonoseki; – *Hankyu ER* to Kyoto, Osaka Suma, Takarazuka; – *Hanshin ER* to Osaka, Suma; – *Sanyo ER* to Himeji, Rokko, Suma.
– Motomachi station: *JNR* to Himeji, Osaka; – *Hankyu ER* to Kyoto, Osaka, Suma, Takarazuka; – *Hanshin ER* to Osaka, Suma; – *Sanyo ER* to Himeji, Rokko.
– Suma station: *JNR* to Himeji, Osaka; – *Hankyu ER*

to Kyoto, Osaka, Takarazuka; – *Hanshin ER* to Osaka; – *Sanyo ER* to Himeji, Rokko.
– Rokko station: *Hankyu ER* to Kyoto, Osaka, Sannomiya, Suma, Takarazuka; – *Sanyo ER* to Himeji.
– Shinkaichi station: *Hankyu ER* to Kyoto, Osaka, Suma, Takarazuka; – *Hanshin ER* to Osaka, Suma; – *Kobe Electric Railway* (*Shintetsu ER*) to Ao, Arima, Sanda; – *Sanyo ER* to Hemeji, Kobe, Rokko.

Funicular: from Dobashi to Rokko san; – from Takao to Maya station.

Cablecars: from Rokko san to Arima; – from Maya station to Maya san; – from Sumaura to Sumaura belvedere.

Coaches: to Himeji, Nagoya, Osaka, Sanda, Tokyo.

Car hire: *Avis*, Kobe Takahama Station, c/o Mitsubishi Warehouse Co., 1-46, Higashi Kawasaki cho, Ikuta ku (Tel. 351-2027).

Travel agency: *JTB*, 5-1-305 Kotonoo cho, Chuo ku.

Banks: *Bank of Kobe*, 56, Naniwa cho, Ikuta ku; – *Bank of Tokyo*, 24 Kyo machi, Ikuta ku; – *Sumitomo*, 11, Sakaemachi dori 1-chome, Ikuta ku.

Central post office: 6-19, Sakaemachi dori, Ikuta ku.

Specialities: silk, bamboo goods.

Shopping:
Motomachi dori Sannomiya districts.
'Tax-free' shops (electronics, hi-fi): *Kobe Audio Center*, 2-

9–6, Sannomiya cho, Chuo ku (Tel. 391–4211); – *Kobe Sacom Co.*, 3-chome Motomachi dori, Chuo ku (Tel. 331–2431); – *Masani Electric Co.*, 1-chome 10–2, Motomachi dori, Chuo ku (Tel. 331–0212).

Events: *Irizomeshiki*, start of the Arima Onsen water-cure season, 2 Jan.; – *Port Festival* 21 and 22 Oct.; – *Arima Onsen Festival* 2 and 3 Nov.

Night life:
At Portopia hotel: 'Sky lounge' (30th floor; cabaret and jazz), 10–1, Minatojima, Nakamachi 6-chome, Chuo ku (Tel. 302–1111); – at the Oriental hotel: Cellar Bar 'La Lande' (bands), 25, Kyomachi, Chuo ku (Tel. 331–8111); – Washington hotel (jazz-piano and bar), 2–8–2, Shimoyamate cho, Chuo ku (Tel. 331–6111).

Nightclubs: *Club Cherry*, Ikuta Shinmachi, Sannomiya cho, Ikuta ku (Tel. 331–2345); – *The King's Arms Tavern*, 61, Isobe dori 4-chome, Fukiai ku (Tel. 221–3774).

Places, sites and monuments:
Botanical Gardens, Municipal, p. 320.
Dairyu ji, p. 320.
Fukai ku, p. 319.
Fukusho ji, p. 321.
Futatabi san, p. 320.
Hyogo ku, p. 321.
Ikuta jinja, p. 319.
Ikuta ku, p. 318.
Kaigan dori, p. 318.
Kobe Shoko Boeki Center, p. 319.
Maya san, p. 320.
Motomachi dori, p. 318.
Mount Hachibuse, p. 322.
Museums
– Museum of Ceramics, p. 319.
– Hyogo Museum of Modern Art, p. 320.
– Namban Municipal Art Museum, p. 319.
Nada ku, p. 320.
Naka Pier, p. 318.
Nofuku ji, p. 321.
Parks
– Minatogawa park, p. 321.
Suwayama Park, p. 319
– Oji park, p. 320.
Port of Kobe, p. 318.
Rokko san, p. 321.
Sakaemachi dori, p. 318.
Sannomiya, p. 318.
Santica Town, p. 318.
Shiogara Lake, p. 320.
Shrines
– Minatogawa shrine, p. 319.
– Nanko shrine, p. 319.
– Wadatsumi shrine, p. 322.
Soraku en, p. 319.
Suma dera, p. 321.
Suma ku, p. 321.
Sumano ura, p. 322.
Tarumi, p. 322.
Taisan ji, p. 322.
Toritenjo ji, p. 321.
Town Hall, p. 318.
US Consulate General, p. 318.
Zensho ji, p. 321.

KOCHI (Kochi ken), p. 322.
Tel. 0888; ✉ 780 and 781.

🚹 **Tourist Information Centre,**
5-1-45, Moto machi
(Tel. 22-8111).

Hotels:
★★★ *Dai ichi*, 2-2-12, Kitahon machi 2-chome (Tel. 83-1441; telex 5882-379) 120 rms 🍴 🎳 A/c 🛗 🎿 ☎ TV P bar, hairdresser, boutiques.

Ryokans:
★★★ *Joseikan*, Kami machi (Tel. 75-0111), 56 rms.

*** *Sansuien Hotel*, Masugata (Tel. 22-0131), 131 rms.

Business hotel:
Itcho, 3-11-12, Harimaya cho (Tel. 83-2166).

Youth hostel:
Kochi Hitsuzan, Koishiki cho (Tel. 33-2789), 50 beds.

✈ **Airport:** Kochi, 9mls (15km) E; coach; – flights *ANA* to Miyazaki, Osaka, Tokyo; – flights *TDA* to Osaka and Nagoya.

Airlines: *All Nippon Airways*, Mikuro Bldg., 2-30, 2-chome, Hon machi (Tel. 22-5385); – *Toa Domestic Airlines*, reservations (Tel. 83-9611).

⚓ **Sea travel:** *Kansai Kisen*, to Kannoura, Kobe, Osaka; – *Nihon Kosoku Ferry* to Kagoshima, Nachi Katsuura, Nagoya, Tokyo.

🚉 **Rail:** Kochi station: *JNR* to Komatsushima, Kubokawa, Nakamura, Susaki, Takamatsu, Tokushima, Uwaijimu; – *Private electric railway* from Aki to Ino, crossing the centre of Kochi.

Cablecar: to Godai san.

Coaches: to Matsuyama, Muroto, Tosa.

Specialities: *Katsubushi*, dried fish; *onagadori*, long-plumed cockerels; Tosa dogs; weapons and cutlery.

KOFU (Yamanashi ken), p. 323.
Tel. 0552; ✉ 400.

🛈 **Tourist Information Centre,** 1-6-1, Marunouchi (Tel. 37-1111).

Ryokans:
** *Tokiwa Hotel*, Yumura Onsen

(Tel. 52-1301) 43 rms.
* *Hotel Mitsui*, Yumura Onsen (Tel. 52-8891) 37 rms.
Dan rokan, 1-19-16, Marunouchi (Tel. 37-1331) 18 rms.

Business hotels:
Nissho, 5-11-18, Asahi (Tel. 52-0401).
Naito, 2-2-15, Aioi (Tel. 32-1611).

Youth hostel:
Kofu, Kami Obina machi (Tel. 22-2295) 80 beds.

🚉 **Rail:** *JNR* to Fuji, Itoigawa, Matsumoto, Nagano, Nagoya, Tokyo.

🚌 **Coaches:** to Fujinomiya, Fuji Yoshida.

Excursions: to the Five Lakes of Fuji.

Kojima (V. Kurashiki), p. 337.
Kokawa, p. 653.
Koko kei, p. 551.
Kokubun ji, p. 427.
Kokura (V. Kitakyushu), p. 313.
Komaga take, p. 201.
Komaki (dam), p. 554.

KOMATSU (Ishikawa ken), p. 325.
Tel. 0761; ✉ 923.

Lodgings:
At awazu Onsen 6mls (10km) S.

Ryokans:
** *Hoshi*, Awazu machi (Tel. 65-1111) 72 rms.
* *Kamiya*, Awazu machi (Tel. 65-2222) 52 rms.

✈ **Airport:** Komatsu 3mls (5km) W; coach; – flights *ANA* to Fukui, Nagoya, Niigata, Sapporo, Tokyo; this is also Kanazawa airport.

Airlines: V. Kanazawa.

KUMAMOTO (Kumamoto ken), p. 333.
Tel. 0963; ✉ 860.

[i] **Tourist Information Centre,**
6-18-1, Suizenji
(Tel. 66-1111).

Hotels:
** *Kumamoto Castle*, 4-2 Joto machi (Tel. 53-6111) 52 rms.
🍴 ▬ A/c 🛗 🛆 ☎ TV 🖥 bar, boutique.
** *New Sky*, 2 Higashi Amidaji machi (Tel. 52-2111) 201 rms.
(52 Jap.) 🍴 ▬ A/c 🛗 🛆 ☎ TV ❄ P bar, hairdresser, boutique.

Business hotels:
Kumamoto Daiichi, 356, Motoyama machi
(Tel. 25-5151).
Taiun, 2-7-10, Nihongi
(Tel. 22-3388).

Minshuku:
Komatsuso, 1-8-13 Kasuga
(Tel. 55-2634), 15 rms.

Youth hostel:
Kumamoto Shiritsu, 1320-1, Shimazaki machi
(Tel. 52-2441) 64 beds.

Restaurant:
* *Okumura* (Jap. food), 1-1-8, Shin machi (Tel. 52-8101).

✈ **Airport:** Takuma 12mls (20km) NE; coach; - flights *ANA* to Miyazaki, Nagoya, Osaka, Tokyo.

Airlines: *All Nippon Airways*, reservations (Tel. 54-2200); - *Japan Airlines*, Asahishimbun Daiichiseimei Bldg, 4-7 Hanabara machi
(Tel. 22-5211); - *Korean Airlines*, 10-3 Kamitori machi (Tel. 54-4716).

🚍 **Rail:** - Kumamoto station: *JNR* to Beppu, Kukuoka,

Kagoshima, Kitakyushu, Kyoto, Misumi, Miyazaki, Oita, Okayama, Osaka, Takamori, Tokyo, Yatsushiro, Yunomae.
- Kamikumamoto station: *JNR* to Fukuoka, Kurume, Kitakyushu; - *Kumamoto Electric Railway* to Kikuchi; - Fujisaki station: *Kumamoto ER* to Kikuchi.

🚌 **Coaches:** to Aso, Beppu, Fukuoka, Nagasaki, Omuta, Ushibuka.

Excursions: to Amakusa shoto, Aso san.

Travel agency: *JTB*, Kotsu Center, Shimo dori
(Tel. 53-2501).

Specialities: pottery, bamboo goods, inlaid metal.

Events: *Boshita festival* 11 to 15 Sept. at Fujisaki shrine.

Kumano (V. Yoshino Kumano), p. 675.
Kumano Nachi, p. 676.
Kumanoyu Onsen, p. 276.
Kume jima, p. 486.
Kunashiri, p. 451.
Kuniga kaigan, p. 480.
Kuno zan, p. 548.
Kurahashi, p. 340.
Kurama yama, p. 386.

KURASHIKI (Okayama ken), p. 335.
Tel. 0864; ✉ 711.

[i] **Town Hall tourist centre,**
2-6-14, Chuo (Tel. 22-4111).

Hotels:
** *Kurashiki Kokusai*, 1-1-44, Chuo (Tel. 22-5141), 70 rms.
(4 Jap.) 🍴 ▬ A/c 🛗 🛆 ☎ TV ❄ P bar, boutique.
** *Mizushima Kokusai*, 4-20, Mizushima, Aoba cho
(Tel. 44-4321), 74 rms. (1

Jap.) ‖ ▥ A/c 🛏 🏠 ☎ TV P
bar, boutique.

Ryokan:
*** *Shimoden Hotel*, Obatake
(Tel. 79-7111), 137 rms.

Business hotel:
Kurashiki Station, 2-8-1, Achi
(Tel. 25-2525).

Minshuku:
Kurashiki Tokusankan, 8-33,
Hon cho (Tel. 25-3056),
14 rms.

Youth hostel:
Kurashiki, Minamiura,
Sambonmatsu, Mukaiyama
(Tel. 22-7355), 80 beds.
Washuzan, Obatake
(Tel. 79-9280), 60 beds.

🛥 **Sea travel:** from Mizushima or
Shimotsui to Marugame; –
from Kojima to Sakaide.

� **Rail:** – Shin Kurashiki station:
JNR, Shinkansen to Fukuoka,
Hiroshima, Okayama, Osaka,
Tokyo; other trains to
Hiroshima, Okayama, Osaka.
– Kurashiki station: *JNR* to
Fukuoka, Hamada,
Hiroshima, Izumo,
Kagoshima, Kumamoto,
Kyoto, Masuda, Nagasaki,
Ogori, Oita, Okayama, Osaka,
Shomonoseki, Tokyo,
Yonago; – private line to
Mizushima.
– Chaya station: *JNR* to
Okayama, Tamano.
– Shomotsui station:
Shimotsui Electric Railway to
Kogawa.

🚌 **Coaches:** to Kasaoka,
Okayama, Soja.

Travel agency: *JTB*, 2-9-10
Achi (Tel. 22-5601).

Specialities: pottery, plaited
straw from Igusa.

KURAYOSHI (Tottori ken), p.
338.
Tel. Kurayoshi (0858); Asozu
Onsen (085835); Misasa
Onsen (08584). ✉ Kurayoshi
(682); Asozu Onsen (682-07);
Misasa Onsen (682-02).

Lodgings:
– At Asozu Onsen 5mls (9km)
NE.

Ryokan:
** *Bokoro*, Hawai cho, Tohaku
gun (Tel. 2221), 76 rms.

– At Misasa Onsen 6mls
(10km) SE.

Ryokan:
* *Izanro Iwasaki*, Misasa cho,
Tohaku gun (Tel. 3-0111),
102 rms.

Youth hostel:
Misasa, Mitoku, Misasa cho,
Tohaku gun (Tel. 3-2691),
48 beds.

� **Rail:** *JNR* to Yamamori,
Yonago.

🚌 **Coaches:** to Tottori, Yonago.

KURE (Hiroshima ken),
p. 339. Tel. 0823.

Hotel:
*** *Kure Hankyu*, 2-6-3, Hon dori
(Tel. 21-1281), 34 rms. (4
Jap.) ‖ ▥ A/c 🛏 🏠 ☎ TV ▣
bar, boutiques.

🛥 **Sea travel:** from Kure to
Hiroshima, Matsuyama; –
from Aga 3mls (5km) E, to
Horie.

� **Rail:** *JNR* to Hiroshima,
Iwakuni, Mihara, Okayama,
Osaka.

🚌 **Coaches:** to Hiroshima,
Takehara.

Kureha yama, p. 631.
Kurihama, p. 670.

Kurikoma yama, p. 242.
Kuro dake, p. 138.

KUROISO (Tochigi ken), p. 333.
Tel. Kuroiso 02877; Nasu 028776; ✉ Kuroiso 325; Nasu 325-04.

Lodgings:
- At Nasu Onsen 10mls (16km) N.

Hotel:
*** *Nasu Royal*, 3375-7, Takaku Otsu, Nasu machi (Tel. 8-2001), 77 rms. (18 Jap.) ⑪ ▥ A/c 🛎 🅿 ☎ TV ☀ 🏞 ♨/¹⁸ bar, hairdresser, boutiques, Jap. com. bath, bowling, skiing.

Ryokans:
*** *Nasu View Hotel*, Nasu machi (Tel. 3111), 111 rms.
** *Matsukawaya*, Nasu machi (Tel. 3131), 68 rms.

🚆 **Rail:** *JNR, Shinkansen* to Morioka, Sendai, Tokyo; other trains to Akita, Fukushima, Koriyama, Sendai, Tokyo, Yamagata.

🚌 **Coaches:** to Nasu, Nikko, Shirakawa.

Sports: skiing and golf at Nasu.

Kuroshima, p. 651.
Kuroyon (dam), p. 152.

KURUME (Fukuoka ken), p. 341.
Tel. Kurume (0946); Harazuru Onsen (09466); ✉ Kurume (838); Harazuru Onsen (838-15).

Lodgings:
- At Harazuru Onsen 19mls (30km) E.

Ryokan:
** *Roppokan*, Haki machi,

Asakura gun (Tel. 2-1047), 36 rms.
* *Taisenkaku*, Haki machi, Asakura gun (Tel. 2-1140), 100 rms.

🚆 **Rail:**
- Kurume station: *JNR* to Beppu, Fukuoka, Kagoshima, Kitakyushu, Kumamoto, Kyoto, Miyazaki, Nagasaki, Oita, Okayama, Osaka, Tokyo, Tossu, Yunomae, Yatsushiro.
- Nishitetsu-Kurume station: *Nishi Nippon Railroad (Nishitetsu)* to Amagi, Fukuoka, Omuta.

🚌 **Coaches:** to Fukuoka Kumamoto, Saga.

Specialities: lacquered goods *(rantai)*, oiled paper umbrellas.

Kusa, p. 223.
Kusambe, p. 549.
Kusatsu (V. Joshin Etsu kogen), p. 274.
Kushimoto (V. Yoshino Kumano), p. 677.

KUSHIRO (Hokkaido), p. 342.
Tel. 0154; ✉ 085.

Business hotel:
Sun Route Kushiro, 13-26, Kurogane cho (Tel. 4-7711).

Youth hostel:
Kushiro, Tsurugadai (Tel. 41-1676), 50 beds.

✈ **Airport:** Kushiro, 14mls (22km) W; coach; - flights *TDA* to Sapporo, Tokyo.

Airline: *Toa Domestic Airlines*, Iwata Bldg, Kita O dori (Tel. 23-9116).

⚓ **Sea travel:** *Kinkai Yussen* to Tokyo.

🚆 **Rail:** *JNR* to Abashiri, Asanikawa, Hakodate,

Kawayu, Kitami, Nemuro, Sapporo, Takikawa.

Coaches: to Akan kohan, Kawayu Onsen, Kitami, Nemuro, Rausu.

Events: *Ice Festival* begin. Feb.; – *Port Festival* begin. Aug.

Sports: golf (*Kushiro Golf Course*).

Kusuyaga take, p. 469.
Kutani, p. 277.
Kutchan, p. 539.

KYOTO (Kyoto fu), p. 342
Tel. 075; ✉ 600 to 606.

Japanese National Tourist Office (*JNTO*), Kyoto Tower Bldg, Higashi Shiokoki cho, Shimogyo ku (Tel. 371–0480); **Kyoto Regional Tourist Dept**., Kyoto Kaikan, Obazaki Park, Sakyo ku (Tel. 761–6051).

Lodgings:
– Higashiyama ku.

Hotels
** *Miyako*, Sanjo Keage, Higashiyama ku (Tel. 771–7111; telex 5422–132) 480 rms (27 Jap.) 4 ¶ ▥ A/c ♨ ▨ ☎ TV ☀ ▦ ♪/¹⁸ P bar, hairdresser, boutiques, sauna, conf. rm. (800 seats).
** *Kyoto Park*, 644–2, Sanjusan-gendo Mawari machi, Higashiyama ku (Tel. 525–3111; telex 5422–777) 61 rms. ¶ ▥ A/c ♨ ▨ ☎ TV ☀ P bar.

Ryokans:
* *Kyoyamato,* Minami, Masuya cho, 359, Higashiyama ku (Tel. 541–1126), 14 rms.
** *Seikoro*, Toiyamachi dori, Gojo-Sagaru, Higashiyama Ku (Tel. 561–0771), 24 rms.
** *Tozankaku*, 431 Myohoin,

Mackawa cho, Higashiyama ku (Tel. 561–4981), 134 rms.

Minshuku:
Ladies in Sakata, Masuya cho, Kodaji, Higashiyama ku (Tel. 541–2108), 6 rms.

Youth hostel:
Higashiyama, 112, Shirakawa bashi, Sanjo dori, Higashiyama ku (Tel. 771–5509) 64 beds.

– Kamigyo ku.

Hotels:
*** *New Kyoto,* Horikawa Maruta machi, Kamigyo ku (Tel. 801–2111) 246 rms. (8 Jap.) ¶ ▥ A/c ♨ ▨ ☎ TV ▦ bar, hairdresser, boutiques, conf. rm.
** *Palace Side Kyoto*, Shimotachiuri Aguru, Karasuma dori, Kamigyo ku (Tel. 431–8171) 120 rms ¶ ▥ A/c ♨ ▨ ☎ TV bar, boutique.

Minshuku:
Horikawa Umemura, Nakadachiuri Sagaru, Higashi, Horikawa, Kamigyo Ku (Tel. 441–8404), 8 rms.

– Nakagyo ku.

Hotels:
**** *International Kyoto*, 284, Nijo Aburanokoji, Nakagyo ku (Tel. 222–1111; telex 5422–158) 334 rms. (31 Jap.) ¶ ▥ A/c ♨ ▨ ☎ TV ☀ ▦ ♀ P bar, hairdresser, boutiques, conf. rm.
*** *Fujita*, Nishizume, Nijo Ohashi, Nakagyo ku (Tel. 222–1511; telex 5422–571) 195 rms. (18 Jap.) ¶ ▥ A/c ♨ ▨ ☎ TV ☀ ▦ bar, hairdresser, boutiques, conf. rm.

Ryokans:
** *Sumiya*, Fuyacho dori, Sanjo

Sagaru, Nakagyo ku
(Tel. 221-2188), 26 rms.
** *Hiiragiya*, Fuyacho Aneyakoji
Agaru, Nakagyo ku (Tel.
221-1136), 33 rms.
** *Ikumatsu*, Kiyamachi dori,
Oike Agaru, Nakagyo ku
(Tel. 231-4191), 24 rms.
** *Matsukichi*, Goko machi,
Sanjo Agaru, Nakagyo ku
(Tel. 221-7016), 15 rms.

Business hotels:
Kyoto, Ichinofunairi cho, Oike
Agaru, Kiyamachi dori,
Nakagyo ku (Tel. 222-1220).
Kyoto Garden, Oike, Minami
Iru, Muromachi dori, Nakagyo
ku (Tel. 255-2000).

- Sakyo ku.

Hotel:
*** *Holiday Inn*, 36, Nishihiraki
cho, Takano, Sakyo ku
(Tel. 721-3131; telex 05422-
251) 150 rms. ¶ ⅲ A/c 🛏 🛋
☎ TV ☀ 🖼 P bar,
hairdresser, boutiques,
bowling.

Ryokan:
* *Yachiyo*, 34 Nanzenji Fukuchi
cho, Sakyo ku (Tel.
771-4148), 26 rms.

- At Shimogyo ku.

Hotels:
**** *Kyoto Grand*, Horikawa
Shiokoji, Shimogyo ku
(Tel. 341-2311; telex
5422-551) 402 rms. (6 Jap.) 3
¶ ⅲ A/c 🛏 🛋 ☎ TV ☀ 🖼 P
bar, hairdresser, boutiques,
bowling, sauna, conf. rm.
(1,000 seats).
*** *Kyoto Century*, 680 Higashi
Shiojoki machi, Higashi Toin
dori, Shiokoji Sagaru
(Tel. 375-0111) 245 rms. ¶ ⅲ
A/c 🛏 🛋 ☎ TV 🖼 P bars,
boutiques.
*** *Kyoto Station*, Higashi Toin

dori, Shiokoji, Shimogyo ku
(Tel. 361-7151; telex
5422-456) 130 rms. ¶ ⅲ A/c
🛏 🛋 ☎ TV P bar,
hairdresser, boutiques.
** *Kyoto Tower*, Karasuma,
Shichijo Sagaru, Shimogyo
ku (Tel. 361-3211) 148 rms.
(2 Jap.) ¶ ⅲ A/c 🛏 🛋 ☎ TV
🖼 bar, hairdresser, boutiques

Ryokans:
*** *Kaneiwaro Bekkan*,
Kiyamachi dori, Shimogyo ku
(Tel. 351-5010) 23 rms.
** *Nabeshima Hizenya*, Nishi iru
Shimogyo ku (Tel. 361-8421)
38 rms.
** *Sanoya*, Higashinotoin dori,
Shichijo Sagaru, Shimogyo
ku (Tel. 371-2185), 42 rms.

Business hotels:
Kyoto Central Inn, Shijo
Kawaramachi, Shimogyo ku
(Tel. 211-1666).
New Ginkaku Inn, Shichijo
Sagaru, Higashinotoin dori,
Shimogyo ku (Tel. 341-2884)

- Ukyo ku.

Youth hostel:
Utano, Nakayama cho,
Uzumasa, Ukyo ku
(Tel. 462-2288) 160 beds.

Restaurants:
*** *Java* (Indon. food), Shijo
Agaru Higashi, Kawaramachi
Nakagyo ku (Tel. 221-7851).
*** *Manyoken* (French food),
364, Naramono cho, Higashi
iru, Fuya cho, Shimogyo ku
(Tel. 221-1022).
** *Jubei* (sushi), Shinbashi
Agaru, Nawate dori,
Higashiyama ku
(Tel. 561-2698).
** *Minokichi* (Jap. food; spec.:
sukiyaki, shabu-shabu), 65,
Torii machi, Awataguchi,
Sakyo ku (Tel. 771-4185).

** *Kyorinsen* (tempura), Masuya cho, Kodaiji, Higashiyama ku (Tel. 541-9111).

** *Dai ichi* (Jap. food), Shimo Chojamachi dori, Sembon Nishi iru, Kamigyo ku (Tel. 461-1775).

** *Doi* (Jap. food), 353, Kodaiji Masuya cho, Higashiyama ku (Tel. 561-0309).

** *Hiro ya* (Jap. food), 56, Kurama Kifune cho, Sakyo ku (Tel. 741-2401).

** *Kitcho* (Jap. food), 58, Susukinobaba cho, Saga Tenryuji, Ukyo ku (Tel. 881-1101).

** *Inn Tamahan* (kaiseki), Shimogawara Gion, Higashiyama ku (Tel. 561-3188; reserv.).

** *Minoko* (kaiseki), Gion Kiyoi cho, Higashiyama ku (Tel. 561-0328).

** *Otowa* (sushi), 565, Nakano machi, Shijo Agaru, Shinkyogoku, Nakagyo ku (Tel. 221-2412).

** *Yasaka* (sukiyaki), Yasata dori Nishi, Higashi oji, Higashiyama ku (Tel. 551-1121).

** *Izumoya* (sukiyaki), Shijo Ohasti, Ponto cho (Tel. 221-2501).

** *Karudan* (Chin. food), 11-2, Nishikujoin cho, Minami ku (Tel. 661-2464).

** *Le Relais d'Okazaki* (French food), Higashiyama Nijo Higashi, Okazaki, Sakyo ku (Tel. 761-1326).

* *Steak House Nanzen* (steak), Jingumichi Sanjo (Tel. 771-1823).

Airport: *Osaka International* at Itami 25mls (40km) SW; coach from Kyoto station; V. Osaka.

Airlines: *Air France*. International Hotel, Nijo Sagaru Abuna Koje, Nakagyo ku (Tel. 241-1771); – *All Nippon Airways*, International Hotel (Tel. 211-5471); – *Japan Air Lines*, Asahi Bldg, Yanagino Banba kado, Oike dori, Nakagyo ku (Tel. 222-0222); – *Korean Airlines*, 4th floor, Kuroda Bldg, 30 Fujimoto Yorimachi Shijo dori, Aburakoji Nishi, Shimogyo ku (Tel. 231-0191).

Sea travel: *Kansai Kisen*, Muromachi Shijo dori, Shimogyo ku (Tel. 221-1815).

Rail:
– *Kyoto station:* JNR, *Shinkansen* to Fukuoka, Okayama, Osaka, Tokyo; other trains to Aomori, Fukuoka, Kagoshima, Kanazawa, Kinosaki, Kumamoto, Kurayoshi, Nachi katsuura, Nagano, Nagasaki, Nagoya, Naoetsu, Nara, Niigata, Osaka, Sasebo, Shirahama, Tokyo, Toyama, Yonago; – *Kinki Nippon Electric Railway (Kintetsu)* to Kashikojima, Nara.
– *Chushojima station:* Keihan *Electric Railway* to Osaka, Uji.
– *Demachiyanagi station:* *Keifuku Electric Railway*, to Kurama, Yase Yuen.
– *Katsura station:* Keihanshin *Electric Railway (Hankyu)* to Arashiyama, Kawaramachi, Kobe, Osaka, Takarazuka.
– *Kawaramachi station:* Hankyu ER to Kobe, Osaka, Takarazuka.
– *Keihan Sanjo station:* Keihan ER to Osaka, Otsu, Uji.
– *Kitano Hakubaicho station:*

Keifuku ER to Arashiyama.
- Shijo Omiya station:
Hankyu ER to Kawaramachi,
Kobe, Osaka, Takarazuka;
Keifuku ER to Arashiyama.

Funicular: from Yase Yuen to
Hiei.

Coaches: to Kameoka, Kobe,
Nagoya, Nara, Osaka, Tokyo.

Excursions: to Nara (in
English).

Car hire: *Nippon*, 42-13,
Kitanouchi cho, Nishi Kujo,
Minami ku (Tel. 681-0311);
Nissan, 94 -3, Ikenouchi cho,
Nishi Kujo, Mihami ku
(Tel. 661-2161).

Travel agencies: *Fujita Travel
Service Co.,* International
Hotel, Nijo Sagaru Abura Koji
dori, Nakagyo Ku (Tel. 222-
0121); - *Hankyu Express
International*, Kawaramachi
Shijo, Shimogyo ku (Tel.
211-1053); - *JTB*, 856 Higashi
Shiokoji cho, Shimogyo ku
(opposite station,
Tel. 361-7241).

Tour of the city: half day
(morning and afternoon),
leaves main hotels at 08.30
and 13.00; in English.

Imperial Household Agency:
Kyoto Imperial Palace,
Kamigyo ku (Tel. 211-1211).

Bank: *Kyoto Bank*, Karasuma
dori, Matsubara (Tel.
361-2211).

Main post office: 843-12,
Higashi Shiokoji, Shimogyo
ku (Tel. 361-4151).

Shopping:
Commercial districts:
between Sanjo dori and Shijo
dori and Higashiyama district
(antiques only).

Large stores: *Daimaru*, Shijo
Takakura-nishi, Shimokyo ku
(Tel. 211-8111); -
Takashimaya, Shijo
Kawaramachi Nishi,
Shimokyo ku (Tel. 221-8811)

Selected addresses: *Kyoto
Handicraft Center* (all sorts o
crafts and tax-free shop),
Kumano Jinja Higashi, Sakyc
ku (Tel. 761-5080); -
Kitayama (pearls), Sanjo,
Kawaramachi, Nakakyo ku
(Tel. 221-0019); - *Itochu*
(kimonos and silk),
Kawaramachi Higashi,
Shimokyo ku (Tel. 221-0308);
- *Gion ISHI* (antiques), 555,
Gion machi, Minamigawa,
Higashiyama ku (Tel.
561-2458); - *Kaji's Antique*,
Shinmonzen dori,
Higashiyama ku
(Tel. 561- 4114);
- *Nakashin* (antiques),
Shinmonzen dori,
Higashiyama ku
(Tel. 561-2906); - *Kabukiya
Doll* (dolls), Kawaramchi dor
Takoyakushi Agaru
(Tel. 221-7781); - *Lacquer
Ware Asobe* (lacquered
goods), Takakura Shijo dori,
Shimokyo ku
(Tel. 221-5786); - *Sakuraiya*
(souvenirs), Sanjo
Shinkyogoku, Nakagyo ku
(Tel. 221-4652); - *Koshida
Satsumaya* (porcelain),
Furumonzen dori
(Tel. 561-2015).

Entertainment:
Noh theatres: *Kongo Hall*,
Muromachi, Shijo Agaru,
Nakagyo ku (Tel. 221-3049);
- *Kyoto kanze Kaikan*, 44,
Enshojimachi, Okazaki,
Sakyo ku (Tel. 771-6114); -
Oe Hall, Yanaginobamba,

Higashi iru, Oshikoji, Nakagyo ku (Tel. 231-7625).

Kabuki theatre: *Minamiza*, Shijo Ohashi lamoto, Higashiyama ku (Tel. 561-1155).

Music hall, Folk entertainments: *Kobu Kaburenjo (Miyako Odori* in Apr.), Gion Higashiyama ku (Tel. 541-3391); – *Pontocho Kaburenjo (Kamoga wa Odori* in May and Oct.), Pontocho Sagaru, Sanjo, Nakagyo ku (Tel. 221-2025).

Concerts: *Kyoto Kaikan Hall*, Saishoji cho, Okazaki, Sakyo ku (Tel. 771-6051).

Traditional arts: tea ceremony, ikebana, bunraku, gagaku, kyogen, etc.; *Yasaka Hall*, Gion Corner (Tel. 761-0019); reserve at hotels and travel agencies.

Night life: Throughout Pontocho district: bars, nightclubs, geisha houses.

Nightclubs: *Bel Ami*, 23, Gion machi Kitagawa, Higashiyama ku (Tel. 771-6191); – *Gion*, Ishidanshita Gion, Higashiyama ku (Tel. 561-9111).

Events: *Okera Mairi*, 1 Jan. at Yasakas shrine; – *Toshiya*, archery competition, 15 Jan., at Sanjusangen do; – **Miyako Odori*, cherry tree dance in Apr., at Kobu Kaburenjo; – *Mibu Kyogen*, from 21 to 29 Apr., at Mibu dera; – **Kamogawa Odori*, in May and Oct. at Pontocho Kaburenjo; – **Aoi matsuri*, 15 May, procession from Imperial Palace to shrines of

Shimogamo and Kamigamo; – **Mifune matsuri*, third Sun. in May, boat fest. at Arashiyama; – *Takigi No*, 1 and 2 June, performances of the various schools of Noh at Heian shrine; – **Cormorant fishing* in Jul. and Aug. at Arshiyama; – **Gion matsuri*, 16 and 17 Jul. procession of floats in streets of Kyoto; – *Daimonji* bonfire, 6 Aug. on Myoiga dake; – **Jidai matsuri*, 22 Oct., procession of about 2,000 people, in costumes representing various periods of Japanese history, at Heian shrine.

Cultural institutions: *British Council*, Nishi machi, Kitashirakawa, Sakyo ku (Tel. 791-7151); – *Centro culturale italo-giapponese*, Ushinomiya cho, Yoshida, Sakyo ku (Tel. 761-4356); – *Goethe Institut*, Ushinomiya cho, Yoshida, Sakyo ku (Tel. 761-2188); – *Institut franco-japonais*, Higashi Ichijo dori, Yoshida, Sakyo ku (Tel. 761-2105).

Place, sites and monuments:
Amida do, p. 365.
Amidaga mine, p. 364.
Arashiyama, p. 379.
Arashi yama, p. 379.
Atago yama, p. 379.
Botanical Garden, p. 373.
Chion in, p. 366.
Chion ji, p. 371.
Chishaka in, p. 363.
Chobo ji, p. 354.
Daigo, p. 383.
Daigo ji, p. 383.
Daigoku den, p. 360.
Daihoon ji, p. 360.
Daikaku ji, p. 379.
Daimonji yama, p. 370.
Daisen in, p. 374.

M

MATSUE (Shimane ken), p. 393
Tel. 0852; ✉ 690.

ℹ️ **Tourist Information Centre,**
1, Tono machi
(Tel. 22-5111; 21-4034).

Hotels:
** *Ichibata*, 30, Chidori cho
(Tel. 22-0188) 50 rms. (16 Jap.) ¶¶ ▥ A/c 🛗 🔔 ☎ 📺 ✳ ♨ bar, boutique, Jap. com. bath.

Ryokans:
** *Meirinkaku*, Kuniya cho
(Tel. 22-3225), 15 rms.
* *Horaiso*, Tono machi
(Tel. 21-4337), 14 rms.
* *Suimeiso*, 26 Nishchicha machi (Tel. 26-3311), 39 rms. (11 West.).
* *Minami Kan*, at *Kyomise*, on Shinji lake (Tel. 21-5131).

Business hotels:
Matsue Plaza (Tel. 26-6650).
Kita Matsue (Tel. 26-2910).

Youth hostel:
Matsue, 1546, Kososhi machi
(Tel. 36–8620), 82 beds.

Restaurant:
Minami (Jap. food) 19,
Suetsugu Honmachi
(Tel. 21–5131).

✈ **Airport:** at Izumo, 11mls
(18km) W. V. under this place
name.

⚓ **Sea travel:** to Daikon jima,
Mihonoseki.

🚂 **Rail:**
– Matsue station: *JNR* to
Fukuoka, Hamada, Izumo,
Okayama, Osaka, Tokyo.
– Kita Matsue station: *Ichibata
Electric Railway*, to Izumo,
Taisha.

🚌 **Coaches:** to Hiroshima,
Izumo, Mihonoseki.

Travel agency: *JTB*, Asahi
machi (Tel. 23–2020).

Speciality: Sodeshi porcelain.

Shopping:
Commercial district:
Higashihon with Kyomise
shopping arcade.

Matsuida, p. 626.
Matsukami, p. 215.
Matsumae, p. 395.

MATSUMOTO (Nagano ken),
p. 395.
Tel. 0263; ✉ Matsumoto 390;
Asama Onsen 390–03;
Usukushigahara Onsen
390–02.

Lodgings:
– At Matsumoto

Business hotels:
Matsumoto Tourist, 2-4-24,
Fukashi (Tel. 33–9000) 63 rms.
Matsumoto Town, 1–38, Chuo
2-chome (Tel. 32-3339) 47
rms.

Minshuku:
Gendai, 2-6-6, Ote
(Tel. 32–4825), 10 rms.

– At Asama Onsen 3mls
(15km) N.

Ryokans:
*** *Hotel Omoto*, Hongo mura,
Higashi Chikuma gun
(Tel. 46–2385), 42 rms.
** *Hotel Izutsu*, Hongo mura,
Higashi Chikuma gun
(Tel. 46–1120), 42 rms.
* *Higashiyama Kanko Hotel*,
Hongo mura, Higashi
Chikuma gun (Tel. 46-2200),
30 rms.

Youth hostel:
Asama Onsen, 237-3, Asama,
Hongo mura, Higashi
Chikuma gun (Tel. 46–1335),
50 beds.

– At Utsukushigahara Onsen
3mls (5km) E.

Ryokan:
* *Utsukushigahara Onsen
Hotel*, Satoyamabe
(Tel. 33–2141), 63 rms.

✈ **Airport:** Matsumoto, at 6mls
(10km) SW; (coach); – flights
TDA to Osaka.

Airline: *Toa Domestic Airlines*,
reservations (Tel. 58–5925).

🚂 **Rail:** *JNR* to Itoigawa,
Nagano, Nagoya, Niigata,
Osaka, Tokyo; – *Matsumoto
Electric Railway* to
Shimashima.

🚌 **Coaches:** to Kamikochi,
Nagano, Omachi, Takayama,
Suwa.

Matsushima (Kumamoto
ken), p. 645.
Matsushima (Miyagi ken),
p. 544.
Matsushiro, p. 412.

MATSUYAMA (Ehime ken), p. 397.
Tel. 0899; ✉ 790.

🛈 **Tourist Information Centre,** Masuyama station (Tel. 31-3914).

Hotels:
** *Oku Dogo*, 267, Sue machi (Tel. 77-1111), 266 rms. (94 Jap.) ❙❙ ▥ A/c 🛁 🏠 ☎ TV 🖃 bar, hairdresser, boutique, Jap. com. bath, bowling.

Ryokans:
** *Dogo Kokusai Hotel Yamatoya*, 20-8, Dogo Yuno machi (Tel. 41-1137), 97 rms. (11 West.).
** *Funaya*, 1-33, Dogo Yuno machi (Tel. 47-0278), 41 rms.
** *Juen*, 4-4, Dogo Sagidani machi (Tel. 41-0161), 76 rms.

Business hotel:
Taihei, 3-1-15, Heiwa dori (Tel. 43-3560), 85 rms.

Minshuku:
Matsuyama, 414-6, Yamagoe cho (Tel. 43-8386), 16 rms.

Youth hostel:
Shinsen en, 1-27, Dogo Imaichi (Tel. 24-7760), 35 beds.

✈ **Airport:** Yoshida, at 4mls (6km) W (coach); –*ANA* flights to Nagoya, Osaka, Tokyo; *TDA* flights to Fukuoka, Miyazaki, Okayama.

Airlines: *All Nippon Airways*, reservations (Tel. 48-3131); – *Toa Domestic Airlines*, reservations (Tel. 48-3281).

⚓ **Sea travel:**
– From Mitsuhama 5mls (8km) W; bus: *Ishizaki Kisen* or *Seto Naikai Kisen*, to Hiroshima, Kure; – other services to Iwakuni, Oita, Yanai.
– From Takahama 6mls (10km) NW; bus: *Ishizaki Kisen*, to Hiroshima, Ikuchi jima, Kure, Omi shima, Onomichi, Osaki Kami jima, Osaki Shimo jima; – *Kansai Kisen*, to Beppu, Imabari, Kitakyushu, Kobe, Osaka, Shodo shima, Takamatsu.
– From Horie 6mls (10km) N; coach: services to Kure.

🚂 **Rail:**
– Matsuyama station: *JNR* to Takamatsu, Uwajima.
– Matsuyamashi station: *Iyo Railway*, to Iyo, Kawauchi, Takahama.

Funicular: from Shinonome-guchi to Katsuyama.

🚌 **Coaches:** to Imabari, Kochi, Niihama, Uwajima.

Excursions: to Ishizuchi san.

Sports: golf (*Matsuyama Golf Club*); – marina: *Fuji Kanko Marina*, at Takahama (Tel. 52-1457).

Matsuzaki, p. 178.
Megi jima, p. 553.
Meiji mura, p. 258.
Mera, p. 560.
Mihama (Aichi ken), p. 207.
Mihama (Fukui ken), p. 635.
Mihara yama, p. 270.
Mihono Matsubara, p. 536.
Mihonoseki, p. 395.
Mikata, p. 635.
Mikatahara, p. 205.
Mikkabi, p. 205.

MINAKAMAI (Gumma ken), p. 398.
Tel. 02787; ✉ 379-16.

Ryokans:
*** *Fujiya Hotel*, Minakami machi, Tone gun (Tel. 2-3270), 78 rms.

** *Hotel Juraku*, Minakami machi, Tone gun (Tel. 2-2521), 109 rms.

* *Sokai Hotel*, Minakami machi, Tone gun (Tel. 2-2570), 71 rms.

Rail: *JNR* to Akita, Kanazawa, Niigata, Tokyo.

Coaches: to Numata.

Minami Arupusu (National Park), p. 399.
Minami Arima, p. 643.
Minami Ashigara, p. 471.
Minami Awaji, p. 140.
Minami Chita, p. 207.
Minami Yabakei, p. 223.
Minatogawa, p. 483.
Mine, p. 253.
Mine Onsen, p. 175.
Minmaya, p. 129.
Minobu san, p. 324.
Mino Kamo, p. 400.
Minokoshi, p. 251, 563.
Misaki, p. 661.
Misasa Onsen (V. Kurayoshi), p. 338.
Mi shima, p. 199.

MISHIMA (Shizuoka ken), p. 400.
Tel. 0559.

Business hotel:
Mishima, 9-17, Kotobuki cho (Tel. 72-0555), 60 rms.

Rail: *JNR, Shinkansen*, to Osaka, Tokyo; other trains to Shizuoka, Tokyo; – *Izu-Hakone Railway*, to Shuzenji.

Coaches: to Atami, Gotemba, Ito, Numazu, Odawara, Shimoda, Shuzenji.

Misumi (V. Unzen Amakusa), p. 645.
Mitake, p. 323.
Mitake jinja, p. 147.

MITO (Ibaraki ken), p. 401.
Tel. Mito (0292); Oarai (029267); ⊠ Mito (311); Oarai (311-13).

□ **Tourist Information Centre,** 5-38, Sannomaru 1-chome (Tel. 21-8111).

Ryokan:
Oarai Park Hotel, Oarai machi, Higashi Ibaraki gun (Tel. 2171), 21 rms. at Oarai 7mls (12km) SE; coach.

Rail: *JNR* to Aomori, Fukushima, Hitachi Ota, Iwaki, Kashima, Morioka, Sendai, Takasaki, Tokyo.

Coaches: to Choshi, Hitachi Kashima, Shimodate, Utsunomiya.

Sports: golf: *Oarai Golf Club.*

Mito hama, p. 175.
Mitsushima, p. 514.
Miura, p. 402.
Miyakejima (V. Hiroshima), p. 220.
Miyakejima, p. 271.
Miyako, p. 509.
Miyako shoto, p. 403.
Miyanoshita, p. 168.

MIYAZAKI (Miyazaki ken), p. 404.
Tel. Miyazaki 0985; Aoshima 09856; ⊠ Miyazaki 880; Aoshima 889—22.

□ **Tourist Information Centre,** 2-10-1, Higashi Tachibana dori (Tel. 24-1111).

Lodgings:

– At Miyazaki.

Hotels:
*** *Phoenix*, 2-1-1, Matsuyama (Tel. 23-6111), 118 rms. (22 Jap.) ¶¶ ▥ A/c 🏛 🏠 ☎ 📺 ❋ ▥ ◁ **P** bar, hairdresser, boutiques, bowling.
*** *Seaside Phoenix*, 3083, Hamayama, Shioji

(Tel. 39-1111), 194 rms. (96 Jap.) ⊞ ▥ A/c ♨ ⌂ ☎ TV ✳ ▦ ≈ ⚲ ⚲/18 P bar, hairdresser, boutiques, bowling.

** *Miyazaki Kanko*, 1-1-1, Matsuyama (Tel. 27-1212), 200 rms. (97 Jap.) ⊞ ▥ A/c ♨ ⌂ ☎ TV ✳ P bar, boutique.

** *Plaza Miyazaki*, 1-1, Kawahara cho (Tel. 27-1111; telex 77-7977), 155 rms. (28 Jap.) ⊞ ▥ A/c ♨ ⌂ ☎ TV ✳ ▦ P

Ryokans:

*** *Hotel Kandabashi*, Tachibana dori (Tel. 25-5511), 107 rms.
*** *Konanso*, Yodogawa cho (Tel. 51-5101), 65 rms.
*** *Miyazaki Grand Hotel*, Matsuyama (Tel. 22-2121), 31rms.
** *Hotel Nihombashi*, Hiroshima (Tel. 24-5566), 36 rms.

Business hotel: *Miyazaki Daiichi*, 5-4-14, Tachibanadori (Tel. 24-8501).

Youth hostel: *Miyazaki Ken Fujin Kaikan*, 3-10, Asahi, 1-chome (Tel. 24-5787), 50 beds.

- At Aoshima 10mls (16km) SE.

Ryokans:

*** *Aoshima Kanko Hotel*, Minami Aoshima cho (Tel. 65-1211), 81 rms.
*** *Aoshima Park Hotel*, Kaeda (Tel. 65-0111), 100 rms.

Minshuku: *Sasa*, 4-4-6, Aoshima cho (Tel. 65-1383), 7 rms.

✈ **Airport:** *Miyazaki*, 3mls (5km) SE; coach; - *ANA* flights to Kochi, Kimamoto, Nagoya Osaka, Tokyo; - *TDA* flights to Fukuoka, Matsuyama.

Airlines: *All Nippon Airways*, reservations (Tel. 51-7291); - *Toa Domestic Airlines*, reservations (Tel. 51-7295).

⚓ **Sea travel:** *Kansai Kisen*, 167, Higashi 1-chome, Tachibana dori (Tel. 25-3324).

🚆 **Rail:** *JNR* to Beppu, Fukuoka, Hiroshima, Kagoshima, Kanoya, Kitakyushu, Kyoto, Miyakonojo, Osaka, Tokyo.

Coaches: to Kirishima Onsen, Miyakonojo, Nichinan, Saito.

Travel agency: *JTB*, c/o Goto Shoji Bldg, Miyazaki eki (Tel. 22-7147).

Event: *Festival of Miyazaki shrine*, end Oct.

MIYAZU (Kyoto fu), p. 405 Tel. 07722; ✉ 626.

Ryokans:

*** *Gemmyoan*, Aza Monju (Tel. 2-2171), 32 rms.
** *Monjuso*, 510, Aza Monju (Tel. 2-7111), 38 rms.

Youth hostel: *Amanohashidate*, Manai, Nakano (Tel. 7-0121), 60 beds.

⚓ **Sea travel:** to Ichinomiya, Ine.

🚆 **Rail:** *JNR* to Fukui, Kanazawa, Kyoto, Maizuru, Osaka, Toyooka, Tsuruga.

🚌 **Coaches:** to Fukuchiyama, Maizuru, Tango, Toyooka.

Mizukue, p. 154.
Mizushima (see Kurashiki), p. 335.
Mogami gawa (rapids), p. 518.
Mogi, p. 419.
Moiwa yama, p. 526.
Moji (see Kitakyushu), p. 313.
Monobe, p. 428.
Monzen (Akita ken), p. 472.

Monzen (Ishikawa ken), p. 650.

Monzen (Tochigi ken), p. 255.

MORIOKA (Iwate ken), p. 406.
Tel. Morioka 0196; Tsunagi Onsen 019689; ✉ 020.

⛩ **Tourist Information Centre,** 10-1, Uchimaru (Tel. 51-3111).

Hotels:
Royal Morioka, 1-11-11, Saien (Tel. 53-1331), 98 rms. (2 Jap.) ⅋ ▬ A/c ✿ ⌂ ☎ TV ☀ ♪/9 ▣ P skiing, skating, canoeing.
** *Morioka Grand*, 1-10, Atagoshita (Tel. 25-2111), 50 rms. (15 Jap.) ⅋ ▬ A/c ✿ ⌂ ☎ TV P bar, hairdresser, boutique.

Ryokans:
** *Hotel Taikan*, 37-1, Aza Yunodate, Tsunagi (Tel. 89-2121), 102 rms.
* *Kadoya Hotel*, 1-13-14, Minami Odiri (Tel. 24-2632), 15 rms.

Business hotel:
Morioka Rifu, 18-5, Nasugawa cho (Tel. 54-4151).

Restaurant:
Wakana (West. food), 1-3-33, Osawa, Kawahara (Tel. 53-3333).

✈ **Airport:** at Hanamaki, 20mls (32km) S (coach); V. under this place name.

Airline: *Toa Domestic Airlines*, reservations (Tel. 23-4141).

🚆 **Rail:** *JNR, Shinansen* to Sendai, Tokyo; other trains to Akita, Aomori, Kamaishi, Kuji, Miyako, Sendai, Tokyo, Yamagata.

🚌 **Coaches:** to Kuji, Miyako, Sendai.

Excursions: to Towada Hachimantai National Park.

Travel agency: *JTB*, 2 Nakanohashi, Uchimaru (Tel. 51-3331).

Event: *Chagu Chagu Umakko*, equestrian display at Sozen shrine, 15 Jun.

Speciality: *Nembutetsu*: iron goods (kettles).

Morizane Onsen, p. 223.
Morozaki, p. 207.
Motobu (see Okinawa shoto), p. 485.
Moto Hakone, p. 169.
Motosu, p. 166.
Motosu ko, p. 166.
Motoura, p. 265.
Motsu ji, p. 240.
Mugi, p. 128.
Mukai jima, p. 489.
Mure, p. 553.
Muro, p. 519.
Murodo, p. 152.

MURORAN (Hokkaido), p. 407. Tel. 0143.

Business hotel:
Muroran Royal, 2-21-11. Nakashima machi (Tel. 44-8421), 61 rms.

Youth hostel: *Muroran*, 3-12-2, Miyaki cho (Tel. 44-3357), 96 beds.

⚓ **Sea travel:** *Higashi Nihon Ferry*, to Aomori, Oma.

🚆 **Rail:**
– Higashi-Muroran station: *JNR* to Abashiri, Asahikawa, Hakodate, Kushiro, Muroran, Sapporo.
– Muroran station: *JNR* to Hakodate, Higashi-Muroran, Sapporo.

▣ **Coaches:** to Noboribetsu, Sapporo, Sobetsu, Tomakomai.

Muroto, p. 408.
Mutsu, p. 408.
Myogi san, p. 626.
Myojo ji, p. 202.

MYOKO KOGEN (Niigata ken), p. 409.
Tel. 02558; ✉ 949-21.

Hotel:
** *Akakura Kanko*, Myoko Kogen, Nakakubiki gun (Tel. 7-2501), 53 rms. (23 Jap.) ⑪ ▥ A/c 🛁 🏛 ☎ 📺 ⚓/¹⁸ 🦌 **P** bar, Jap. com. bath, skiing.

Ryokan:
* *Akakura Hotel*, Akakura Onsen, Myoko Kogen machi (Tel. 7-2001), 80 rms.

▦ **Rail:** Taguchi station: *JNR* to Kanazawa, Niigata, Tokyo.

▣ **Coaches:** to Nagano, Naoetsu.

Sports: winter sports at Myoko Kokusai (skilifts) from mid Dec. to end Apr. (night skiing).

N

Naeba, p. 467.
Nagahama, p. 410.

NAGANO (Nagano ken), p. 405.
Tel. Nagano (0262); Shinano (02625); ✉ Nagano (380); Shinano (389-13).

ⓘ **Tourist Information Centre,** 692-2, Habashita, Minami Nagano (Tel. 32-0111).

Lodgings:
– At Nagano.

Hotels:
*** *Kikusai Kaikan*, 976, Agata machi (Tel. 34-1111), 70 rms. (1 Jap.) ⑪ ▥ A/c 🛁 🏛 ☎ 📺
** Hotel Saihokukan, 528-1 Agata machi (Tel. 35-3333). 82 rms: (20 Jap.) ⑪ ▥ A/c 🛁 🏛 ☎ 📺

Ryokan:
* *Saihokokukan*, 528, Agata machi (Tel. 32-3161), 24 rms.

Business hotels:
Aoki, 1356, Suehiro cho (Tel. 26-1271)
Nagano Palace, 1326, Ishico Minami (Tel. 26-2221).

– At Shinano 16 mls (25 km) N.

Ryokans:
* *Kurohime Grand Hotel*, Shinano machi, Kamiminochi gun (Tel. 5-3181), 34 rms.
* *Nodaya Hotel*, Shinano machi, Kamiminochi gun (Tel. 8-2331), 16 rms.

Restaurant:
* *Nakajima Kaikan* (Jap. and West. food), 1361, Suehiro cho, Minami Nagano (Tel. 26-0175).

▦ **Rail:** *JNR* to Itoigawa, Kanazawa, Nagoya, Naoetsu, Niigata, Osaka, Tokyo; – Nagano Electric Railway, to Kijima, Yudanaka.

▣ **Coaches:** to Iiyama, Matsumoto, Myoko Kogen, Omachi, Shiga Kogen, Tokyo.

Excursions: to Shiga Kogen.

Travel Agency: *JTB*, Ekimae dori, Suehiro cho (Tel. 26-0267).

NAGASAKI (Nagasaki ken), p. 412.
Tel. 0958; ✉ 850.

ⓘ **Tourist Information Centre,** 2-13, Edo machi (Tel. 24-1111).
Town Hall Tourism Dept, 2-22 Sakura machi (Tel. 25-5151).
Commercial and Tourist Centre Nagasaki, Nagasaki Sangyo Kotsu Kaikan (2nd floor), 3-1 Daikoku machi (Tel. 23-4041).
Tourist Office: at the station (Tel. 22-1954).

Hotels:
*** *Nagasaki Tokyu*, 18-1, Minami Yamate cho (Tel. 25-1510), 230 rms. ❙❙ ▥ A/c ♨ ▦ ☎ TV ▣ bar, boutiques.
*** *New Nagasaki*, 14-5, Daikoku machi (Tel. 26-6161), 60 rms. ❙❙ ▥ A/c ♨ ▦ ☎ TV bar, hairdresser, boutiques, Jap. com. bath, bowling.
** *Nagasaki Grand*, 5-3, Manzai machi (Tel. 23-1234), 70 rms. (3 Jap.) ❙❙ ▥ A/c ♨ ▦ ☎ TV ▣ bar, boutique.
** *New Oriental*, 5, Dekidaidu cho (Tel. 22-3171), 29 rms. ❙❙ ▥ A/c ♨ ▦ ☎ TV
** *New Tanda*, 2-24, Tokiwa machi (Tel. 27-6121), 161 rms. ❙❙ ▥ A/c ♨ ▦ ☎ TV
** *Parkside*, 14-1, Heiwa machi (Tel. 45-3191), 54 rms. (2 Jap.) ❙❙ ▥ A/c ♨ ▦ ☎ TV

Ryokans:
*** *Hakuunso*, Kajiya machi (Tel. 26-6307), 40 rms.
*** *Nagasaki Kanko Hotel Sumeikan*, Chikugo machi (Tel. 22-5121), 106 rms.
*** *New Hotel Chuoso*, Manzai machi (Tel. 22-2218), 25 rms.
*** *Yutaro*, Irabayashi machi (Tel. 22-8166), 58 rms.
** *Nagasaki Kokusai Hotel Nisshokan*, Nishizaka machi (Tel. 24-2151), 160 rms.

Business hotels:
Nishikyushu Daichi, 2-1, Daikoku machi (Tel. 21-1711).
Harbor Inn Nagasaki, 8-17, Kabajima cho (Tel. 27-1111).

Minshuku:
Matsushita, 6-36, Yayoi cho (Tel. 23-3500), 7 rms.

Youth hostel:
Nagasaki, Tateyama cho (Tel. 23-5032), 90 beds; – *Nagasaki Oranda zaka*, 6-14, Higashi Yamate cho (Tel. 22-2730), 55 beds.

Restaurants:
* *Chisan* (West. food), Manzai machi (Tel. 26-9277).
* *Fuukiro* (Jap. food), Kami Nishiyama machi (Tel. 22-0253).
* *Harpin* (West. food), Kozen machi (Tel. 22-7443).
* *Hashimoto* (Jap. food), Nakagawa machi (Tel. 25-2001).
* *Okano* (tempura), Moto Shikkui machi (Tel. 24-3048).
* *Shikairo* (Chin. food), Kago machi (Tel. 22-1296).
* *Toakaku* (Chin. food), Kajiya machi (Tel. 22-1251).

✈ **Airport:** at Omura, 25mls (40 km) N (coach); V. under this place name.

Airlines: *All Nippon Airways*, Matsumoto Bldg., 2-7, Tamae cho (Tel. 23-8294); – *Japan Air Lines*, Sumitomo Seimei Nagasaki Bldg., 7-1, Manzai machi (Tel. 22-4114).

⚓ **Sea travel:** from Nagasaki: *Kyushu Shosen* to Goto retto; – from Mogi 5 mls *(8km) SE: Kyushu Shosen*, to Shimo shima (Amakusa shoto).

🚂 **Rail:** *JNR* to Beppu, Fukuoka,

Kyoto, Oita, Osaka, Sasebo, Tokyo, Tosu.

🚋 **Tramway:** One-day free pass available from Tourist Office.

🚌 **Coaches:** to Beppu, Fukuoka, Kumamoto, Sasebo.

🚗 **Car hire:** *Nippon*, Nagasaki eki, Daikoku machi (Tel. 26–0480); – *Nissan*, Nagasaki ekimae, Daikoku machi (Tel. 25–1988).

Travel agency: *JTB*, 1–95, Oage-cho, Nagasaki eki (Tel. 23–1261).

Tour of the city: every morning, Mar. to Nov., leaving from the station (in English).

Specialities: cultured pearls, coral, tortoiseshell.

Shopping: Higashi Hamano dori, Hamaichi dori.

Events: Feast of the Twenty-six Martyrs, 5 Feb.; – Port Festival, 27–29 Apr.; – *Peiron*, water sports (festival of Chinese origin), 1st and 2nd Sun. of Jun.; – *Bon matsuri*, 13–15 Jul.; – Anniversary of atomic explosion, 9 Aug.; – *Abonchinou* at Sofukuji, 26–28 Aug.; – *Okunchi matsuri* at Suwa 7–9 Oct.

Nagasaki bana, p. 238.
Nagato, p. 419.
Nagatoro, p. 146.
Nago (V. Okinawa shoto), p. 484.
Nagoro, p. 251.

NAGOYA (Aichi ken), p. 419. Tel. 052; ✉ 450 to 466.

ℹ️ **Tourist Information Centre,** 3-1-2, Sannomaru. Naka ku (Tel. 961-2111).

Hotels:
*** *International*, 3-23-3. Nishiki, Naka ku (Tel. 961-3111; telex 0444-3720), 263 rms. (7 Jap.) 4 🍴 🍸 A/c 🛗 🛎️ 📺 bar, hairdresser, boutiques, travel agency, conf. rm. (500 seats).
**** *Nagoya Castle*, 1-15, Hinokuchi cho, Nishi ku (Tel. 521-2121; telex 0445-2988), 254 rms. (3 Jap.) 🍴 🍸 A/c 🛗 🛎️ ☎️ 📺 ☀️ 🖼️ 📻 bar, hairdresser, boutiques, conf. rm. (2,000 seats).
*** *Meitetsu Grand*, 1-223, Sasashima cho, Nakamura ku (Tel. 582-2211; telex 0442-2031), 242 rms. (2 Jap.) 4 🍴 🍸 A/c 🛗 🛎️ ☎️ 📺 ☀️ 📻 bar, hairdresser, boutique, bowling.

Ryokans:
*** *Maizurukan*, 8, Kitanegi cho, Nakamura ku (Tel. 541-1346), 24 rms.
** *Suihoen*, 4-1-20, Sakae, Naka ku (Tel. 241-3521), 25 rms.

Business hotels:
Nagoya Loren, 1-8-40, Nishiki, Naka ku (Tel. 211-4581).
Daiichi Washington, 3-18-28, Nishiki, Naka ku (Tel. 951-2111).
Nagoya Crown, 1-8-33, Sakae, Naka ku (Tel. 211-6633).

Youth hostels:
Kameiri, Tashiro cho, Chigusa ku (Tel. 781-9845), 100 beds; – *YMCA*, 33 Nishi Kawabata 5-chome, Naka ku (Tel. 31-3116); – *YWCA*, 1, Shin Sakae cho 2-chome, Naka ku (Tel. 961-7707).

Restaurants:
** *Hasshokan Nakamise* (Jap. food), 2-12-20, Sakae, Naka ku (Tel. 221-1801).
* *Kamome* (Jap. food), 2-7,

Shirakabe cho, Higashi ku
(Tel. 931-8506).

* *Kawabun* (Jap. food), 2-12-19, Marunouchi, Naka ku
(Tel. 231-1381).

* *Suihoen* (Jap. and Chin. food); 4-1-20, Sakae, Naka ku
(Tel. 241-3521).

* *Taimeshiro* (Jap. food), 2-18-32, Nishiki, Naka ku
(Tel. 211-6355).

✈ **Airport:** *Nagoya International*, at Komaki 8mls *(13km) N*; coach; - flights *ANA* to Fukuoka, Hachijo jima, Kagoshima, Komatsu, Kumamoto, Matsuyama, Miyazaki, Oita, Okinawa, Sapporo, Sendai, Shirahama, Tokyo; - flights *JAL* to Fukuoka and Tokyo (3 times per week); - flights *TDA* to Kochi.

Airlines: Air France, 16-22 Meieki 3-chome, Nakamura ku (Tel. 551-4141); - *All Nippon Airways*, 223, Sasashima cho 1-chome, Nakamura ku (Tel. 571-2301). - *Japan Air Lines*, Toyo Bldg. 14-16, 2-chome Meieki, Nakamura ku (Tel. 563-4141).; Sabena, Chubu Nippon Bldg., 1-1, Sakae 4-chome, Naka ku (Tel. 251-1733); - Swissair, Meitetsu Grand Hotel, Room 352, 223, Sasajima cho 1-chome, Nakamura ku (Tel. 582-6946) - *Toa Domestic Airlines*, 18-30, Nishiki 3-chome, Naka ku (Tel. 261-4616).

⚓ **Sea travel:** *Kinki Nippon Tourist Co.,* and *Shima Katsuura Kanko Steamship Co.,* to Toba; - *Meimon Car Ferry,* to Kitakyushu, Yokkaichi; - *Nippon Kosoku Ferry,* to Kagoshima, Kochi; -

Taiheiyo Enkai Ferry, to Sendai, Tomakomai; - other services to Oita; - international services.

🔭 **Rail:**
- Nagoya station: *JNR, Shinkansen,* to Fukuoka, Okayama, Osaka, Tokyo; other trains, to Fukuoka, Hamada, Ise, Kagoshima, Kameyama, Kimamoto, Kushimoto, Matsumoto, Nachi Katsuura, Nagano, Nagasaki, Niigata, Osaka, Sasebo, Shimonoseki, Shingu, Shirahama, Tamano, Tokyo; - *Kinki Nippon Railway (Kintetsu)* to Kashikojima, Osaka, Yunoyama Onsen; - *Nagoya Railroad (Meitetsu),* to Gifu, Inuyama, Kowa, Tokoname, Toyohashi, Toyota, Tsushima. - Horikawa station: *Meitetsu,* to Seto.
- Kami Iida station: *Meitetsu,* to Inuyama.

Metro: one line between Nakamura koen and Fujigaoka; one line between Ozone and Nagoyako or Aratama; they cross at Sakae.

🚌 **Coaches:** to Gifu, Hamamatsu, Ise, Kobe, Kyoto, Matsumoto, Osaka, Tokyo.

🚗 **Car hire:** *Avis*, Nayabashi Parking Lot, Sakae 1-1701-1, Naka ku (Tel. 221-8081); - *Hertz*, 1-12-19, Nishki, Naka ku (Tel. 231-6137); - *Nippon*, 2-44, Nagano cho, Nishiku (Tel. 551-1976); - *Nissan*, 1-13, 4, Sakae, Naka ku (Tel. 221-8195).

Excursion: to Ise (in English); information at hotels.

Travel Agency: *JTB*, 1-3-3, Naeki, Nakamuru ku.

Specialities: pottery (*Noritake*), lacquerware, paper goods, fans, musical instruments, toys.

Shopping: around the station, and districts of Hirokoji and Sakae machi.

Events: *Fest. of Naked Men*, 13 Jan., at Kanoyama shrine; – *Atsuta matsuri*, 5 Jun. at Atsuta jinja; – *Port Fest.* 20 and 21 Jul.; – *Nagoya Fest.* from 10 to 20 Oct., Higashi yama Park.

Sports: golf (*Nagoya Golf Club*); – sumo: *Aichi City gymnasium*, 1-1 Ninomaru, Naka ku (tournament from 1 to 15 Jul.).

Nagoya (Saga ken), p. 302.
Naha (V. Okinawa shoto) p. 475.
Nakadomari, p. 484.
Nakadori shima, p. 195.
Nakagusuku, p. 486.
Naka Karuizawa, p. 275.
Nakamura, p. 133.
Nakanojo, p. 533.
Nakano shima, p. 480.
Nakanoyu Onsen, p. 150.
Nakaoshi, p. 485.
Naka Shibetsu, p. 451.
Nakata, p. 269.
Nakatone, p. 503.
Nakayama, p. 396.
Nakoso (V. Iwaki), p. 269.
Namari Onsen, p. 206.
Nametoko keikoku, p. 649.
Nanao, p. 427.
Nango, p. 452.
Nankoku, p. 427.
Nansei shoto, p. 428.
Naoetsu, p. 432.

NARA (Nara ken), p. 432 Tel. 0742; ✉ 630.

☐ **Tourist Information Centre,** Nobori Oji cho (Tel. 22-1101).

Hotels:
*** *Nara*, 1096, Takabatake cho (Tel. 26-3300, telex 5522-108), 73 rms. (5 Jap.), ¶¶ ▥ A/c ☵ ⌂ ☎ 📺 ✱ ↙/¹⁸ **P** bar, boutiques.
** *Yamatosanso*, 27, Kawakami cho (Tel. 26-10-11), ¶¶ ▥ A/c ☵ ⌂ ☎ 📺

Ryokans:
*** *Nara Park*, Horai cho (Tel. 44-5255), 52 rms.
** *Kasuga Hotel*, Noborioji cho (Tel. 22-4031), 48 rms.

Business hotels:
Dai Gomon, 23, Minosho cho Yamato Koriyama shi (Tel. (07435) 3-7501).
Three Em, 2-257, Shibatsuji cho (Tel. 33-5656).

Youth hostel: Nara, Konoike Undokoen, Horen cho (Tel. 22-1334), 200 beds.

Restaurants:
* *Edosan* (Jap. food), 1167, Takahata cho (Tel. 26-2662).
* *Kusanoe* (Jap. food), 151, Rokujo Higashi cho (Tel. 33-1017).
* *Garden Yamato* (Jap. and West. food), 40-1, Noborioji cho (Tel. 26-2266).
* *Kikusui* (Jap. and West. food), 1130, Takahata Bodai cho (Tel. 23-2001).
* *Sushitsune Honten* (sushi), 15, Hashimoto cho (Tel. 22-2310).

🚄 **Rail:**
– Nara station: *JNR* to Kameyama, Kyoto, Nagoya, Oji, Osaka, Shingu, Shirahama, Tokyo, Yamato-Takada.
– Kintetsu-Nara station: *Kinki Nippon Railway (Kintetsu)* to

Kyoto, Osaka.
- Saidaiji station: *Kintetsu ER* to Kashikojima, Kyoto, Nara, Osaka, Tenri, Yoshino.

🚌 **Coaches:** to Ikaruga, Kyoto, Osaka, Shingu.

🚗 **Car hire:** *Nippon*, Kintetsu-Nara eki, 1-1, Nakasuji machi (Tel. 24-5701).

Travel agency: *JTB*, Kitagawa-Bldg., Nishi Gomon cho (Tel. 23-2525).

Tour of the city: One day in English; leaving from Kyoto.

Events: *Yamayaki Fest.* 15 Jan, burning of herbs, on the Wakakusa yama, commemorating the end of rivalry between two temples; - *Setsubun lantern fest.* 3 and 4 Feb. at Kasuga shrine; - *Omizutori*, 12 May at Nigatsu do; - *Emperor Shomu's fest. Shomu*, 2 May, at Todai ji; - *Bon matsuri* and *lantern fest.*, 15 Aug., at Kasuga shrine; - *cutting of stags' antlers* in mid Oct; - *Bon matsuri*, 17 Dec., at Kasuga Wakamiya shrine.

Specialities: lacquerware, dolls, fans, Noh masks, goods made from antlers, tea whisks.

Shopping: Sanjo dori.

Narita, p. 449.
Naruko Onsen (V. Furukawa), p. 189.

NARUTO (Tokushima ken). p. 450.
Tel. 08868; ✉ 772.

Ryokan:
** *Mizuno*, Muyacho Okazaki (Tel. 5-4131), 33 rms.

Youth hostel:
Hayashisaki, Muya cho (Tel. 6-4561), 50 beds.

⚓ **Sea travel:**
- From Naruto: *Atan Renraku Kisen*, to Awaji shima.
- From Oge jima 7 mls (12 km) *N*: services to Awaji shima, Kobe.

🚆 **Rail:** *JNR* to Tokushima.

🚌 **Coaches:** to Kamiita, Takamatsu, Tokushima.

Events: *Kite fest.* between Jun. and Aug. - *Awa Odori*, in mid Aug.

Naruto kaikyo, p. 450.
Nasu Yumoto, p. 340.
Natsuigawa, p. 269.
Naze (V. Amami shoto) p. 126.
Nejime, p. 301.
Nemuro, p. 451.
Nenokuchi, p. 629.
Nezamino toko, p. 312.
Nezugaseki, p. 637.
Nibukawa Onsen, p. 254.

NICHINAN (Miyazaki ken), p. 452.
Tel. 09872; ✉ 888.

🚆 **Rail:** *JNR* to Beppu, Kanoya, Miyakonojo, Miyazaki, Shibushi.

🚌 **Coaches:** to Kashima, Miyakonojo, Miyazaki.

Nichinan kaigan, p. 452.
Nihon dara, p. 547.
Niibo, p. 513.

NIIGATA (Niigata ken), p. 452.
Tel. 0252; ✉ 951.

ℹ️ **Tourist Information Centre,** 1602, Gakko cho (Tel. 23-5511).

Hotels:
*** *Niigata*, 5-11-20, Bandai (Tel. 45-3331) 112 rms. (14 Jap.) 🍴

▥ A/c ≜ ☎ TV ✳ ⚓ **P** bar, hairdresser, boutiques.

** *Okura Niigata*, 6-53, Kawabata cho (Tel. 24-6111), 303 rms. (2 Jap.) ¶¶ ▥ A/c ≜ ⚓ ☎ TV bar, hairdresser, boutiques.

** *Niigata Toei*, 2-1-6, Benten cho (Tel. 44-7101), 46 rms. (13 Jap.) ¶¶ ▥ A/c ≜ ⚓ ☎ TV bar, bowling.

Ryokan:

** *Onoya*, 981, Furumachi dori, Rokuban cho (Tel. 29-2951), 24 rms.

Business hotels:

Aster, Niban cho, Higashi Nada dori (Tel. 28-4033).
Niigata Station, 1-2-10, Benten cho (Tel. 43-51-51).

Restaurants:

* *Atarashiya* (Jap. food), Furumachi dori (Tel. 22-2712).
* *Ikinaritei* (Jap. food), 573, Nishi Ohata cho (Tel. 23-1188).
* *Kinshabu* (Shabu-Shabu), 620, Nishi Ohata cho (Tel. 23-4326).
* *Nabejaya* (Jap. food), Hachiban cho, Higashihori dori (Tel. 22-6131).

✈ **Airport:** Niigata at 5mls (9km) NE (coach); – *ANA* flights to Komatsu, Sapporo; – *TDA* flights to Osaka, Tokyo; – *JAL* international flights and *Aeroflot* to Khabarovsk (USSR).

Airlines: *All Nippon Airways*, reservations (Tel. 44-5812); – *Japan Air Lines*, Teiseki Bldg., 1-3-1, Higashi O dori (Tel. 41-4611); – *Toa Domestic Airlines*, reservations (Tel. 47-1600).

⚓ **Sea travel:** *Sado Kisen* to Sado.

🚆 **Rail:**
– Niigata station: *JNR, Shinkansen* to Tokyo; other trains to Akita, Aomori, Kanazawa, Kori-yama, Nagaoka, Naoetsu, Osaka, Sendai, Tokyo.
– Kencho station: *Niigata Kotsu* to Tsubame.

🚌 **Coaches:** to Kashiwazaki, Murakami, Nagaoka, Niitsu, Shibata.

Travel agency: *JTB*, 959 Rokuban cho, Kamachi dori (Tel. 22-4141).

Events: *Niigata Fest. 21 to 23 Aug., especially at Bandai Ohashi.*

Niijima, p. 271.
Nil Katsuura (V. Yoshino Kumano), p. 676.

NIKKO (Fukushima and Tochigi ken National Park of), p. 455.

Lodgings:

– At Chuzenji
Tel. 0288; ✉ 321-16.

Hotel:

** *Chuzenji Kanaya*, 2482 Chugushi (Tel. 55-0356), 33 rms. (1 Jap.) ¶¶ ▥ A/c ⚓ ☎ TV ⚲ **P** skiing.

Ryokans:

** *Chuzenji Hotel*, Chuzenji Onsen (Tel. 5-0333), 121 rms.
* *Izumiya*, Chuzenji Onsen (Tel. 5-0340), 38 rms.

– At Nasu Onsen
V. Imaichi.

– At Nikko
Tel. 0288; ✉ 321.

Hotel:

*** *Nikko Kanaya*, 1300, Kami

Hatsuishi cho (Tel. 54-0001; telex 3544-451), 91 rms. ¶| ▥▥ A/c 🛁 ☎ TV 📻 🖼 ✦/¹⁸ P bar.

Minshuku:
Rindo-No-Ie, Tokorono (Tel. 3-0131), 5 rms.

Youth hostel:
Nikko, Tokorono (Tel. 54-1013), 50 beds.

– At Shiobara Onsen V. Kuroiso.

– At Yumoto Onsen Tel. 028862; ✉ 321-16.

Ryokans:
** *Oku Nikko Onsen Hotel*, Yumoto Onsen (Tel. 2441), 24 rms.

Niko kyo, p. 339.
Nimoshiri, p. 130.
Nippara (cave), p. 147.
Nirayama Onsen, p. 174.
Nishibetsu, p. 451.
Nishi Chugoku Sanchi (nature park), p. 222.
Nishi Iyayama, p. 251.
Nishikiga ura, p. 138.
Nishi Mikawa, p. 514.
Nishinomote, p. 503.
Nishino shima (Shimane ken), p. 480.
Nishino shima (Tokyo to), p. 475.
Nishiumi, p. 132.
Nishiura Onsen, p. 191.

NOBEOKA (Miyazaki ken), p. 465.
Tel. Nobeoka (09823); Takachiho (09827); ✉ Nobeoka (882); Takachiho (882-11).

Lodgings:

– At Nobeoka

Ryokan:
*** *Hotel Kisetsuen*, Kitakoji (Tel. 3-6688), 30 rms.

– At Takachiho 35 mls (*56km*) *NW*.

Ryokan:
*** *Hotel Shinshu*, Takachiho cho, Nishi Usuki gun (Tel. 2-3232), 55 rms.

Youth hostel:
Takachiho, 5899-2, Tochimata, Mitai, Nishi Usuki gun (Tel. 2-3021), 60 beds.

🚃 **Rail:** *JNR*, to Beppu, Fukuoka, Hiroshima, Kagoshima, Kyoto, Miyakonojo, Miyazaki, Osaka, Takachiho, Tokyo.

🚌 **Coaches:** to Aso, Hyuga, Kitaura.

Noboribetsu (V. Shikotsu Toya), p. 538.
Noborito, p. 309.
Noda, p. 509.
Nojiri ko, p. 412.
Noma, p. 207.
Nonakado, p. 629.
Nonoichi, p. 203.
Nopporo (Regional Forest Park) p. 526.
Norikura dake, p. 151.
Noro san, p. 339.
Nosappu misaki, p. 451.
Noshappu misaki, p. 654.
Noto, p. 651.
Noto Kongo, p. 202.
Noto shima, p. 427.
Notoro misaki, p. 117.
Nozawa Onsen, p. 243.
Nukabira, p. 155.
Numata, p. 466.

NUMAZU (Shizuoka ken), p. 468.
Tel. 0559; ✉ 410.

Ryokan:
*** *Hakkoen*, 1838, Higashi Hongo cho, Kami kanuki (Tel. 31-1331), 11 rms.

Restaurant:
* *Chikuei* (Jap. food), 119,

Agetsuchi cho (Tel. 62–1521).

Sea travel: to Heda, Matsuzaki, Mito, Toi.

Rail: *JNR* to Kozu, Shizuoka, Tokyo.

Coaches: to Fujinomiya, Fuji, Yoshida, Hakone, Shimoda.

Sports: *Numazu Marina* (Tel. 39–0421).

Nyorin ji, p. 563.

Oami, p. 255.
Oarai (V. Mito); p. 402.

OBAMA (Fukui ken), p. 469. Tel. 07705; p. ⊠ 917.

Ryokan:
Seihinkan, 75, Hioshi (Tel. 2–0030), 21 rms.

Youth hostel:
Obama, Aoi (Tel. 2–2158), 60 beds.

Rail: *JNR* to Kanazawa, Osaka, Toyooka, Tsuruga.

Coaches: to Imazu, Miyazu, Tsuruga.

Specialities: Wakasa lacquered goods.

Obama (Nagasaki ken), p. 644.
Obe, p. 548.

OBIHIRO (Hokkaido), p. 470. Tel. Obihiro (01552); Tokachigawa Onsen (015546); ⊠ Obihiro (080); Tokachigawa Onsen (080–02).

Lodgings:

– At Obihiro

Hotel:
Grand Hotel, Minami 3-chome, Nishi Nijo (Tel. 22–4181), 78 rms (4 Jap.) ¶ ⅢⅢ A/c ⌾ ⌂ ☎ TV sauna.

Business hotel:
Green, 6, Miami 12-chome, Nishi Jyo (Tel. 26–1111).

Youth hostel:
Obihiro, 6, Minami 15-chome, Higasni Nijo (Tel. 22–7000), 85 beds.

– At Tokachigawa 7 mls (11km) *E*.

Ryokan:
Sasai Hotel, Tokachigawa Onsen, Otofuke cho (Tel. 2211), 72 rms.

Airport: Obihiro, at 4 mls (7km) SW *(Coach)*; – *TDA* flights to Sapporo, Tokyo.

Airline: *Toa Domestic Airlines*, Minami 12-chome, Nishi Ichijo (Tel. 3–8011).

Rail: *JNR* to Hakodate, Hiroo, Kushiro, Sapporo, Tokachi Mitsumata.

Coaches: to Akan ko, Hidaka, Hiroo, Kushiro, Shikaribetsu ko.

Oboke, p. 251.
Obuke, p. 630.
Oda, p. 470.
Odaito, p. 451.
Odawara, p. 471.
Odo kaigan, p. 132.
Ofuna, p. 294.
Ofunato (V. Rikuchu Kaigan), p. 510.

OGA (Akita ken), p. 472. Tel. Oga (01852); Kitaura (018533); ⊠ Oga (010) Kitaura (010–06).

Lodgings:

– At Kitaura 8 mls *(13km)* NW.

Ryokans:
*** *Oga Prince Hotel*, 70, Aza

Ichinomorishita, Kitaura Yumoto (Tel. 33-2161), 43 rms.

* *Oga Hotel*, 13-1, Aza Kusahihara, Kitaura Yumoto (Tel. 33-3101); 68 rms.

Youth hostel:
Oga, Nakazato, Kitaura Yumoto (Tel. 3125).

Rail: Funagawa station: *JNR*, to Akita.

Coaches: to Akita, Noshiro.

Excursions: Oga Bus, around Oga peninsula.

Events: *Seto fest.* at Shinzan shrine 13 to 15 Feb. – *Namahage fest.* 31 Dec. throughout the peninsula.

Oga Onsen, p. 472.
Ogaki, p. 473.

OGASAWARA SHOTO
(Tokyo, National Park of), p. 474.

Lodgings:
– At Chichi jima (Tel. 0106).

Ryokans:
** *Ogasawara Kanko Hotel*, Okumura, Ogasawara mura (Tel. 337-7541), 21 rms.

* *Ogasawara Kaikan*, Chichi jima, Ogasawara mura (Tel. 337-7541), 33 rms.

Tourist Information Centre: 3-1-1, Ote machi (Tel. 36-1111).

Hotels:
*** *Oita Dai ichi*, 1-1-1, Funai cho (Tel. 36-1388), 162 rms. ¶ ▥ A/c 🛁 🏧 ☎ TV 🖼 hairdresser, bar, boutiques.
*** *Oita Nishitetsu Grand*, 1-92, Maizuru machi (Tel. 36-1181; telex 07722-86), 221 rms. (5 Jap.) ¶ ▥ A/c 🛁 🏧 ☎ TV ♪/18 🔖 hairdresser, boutiques, conf. rm. (250 seats).
** *Central*, 1-4-28, Funai cho (Tel. 36-2777), 112 rms. ¶ ▥ A/c 🛁 🏧 ☎ TV ☀ ♪/9 P

Business hotel:
Oita Orient, 3-9-28, Funai cho (Tel. 32-8238), 107 rms.

✈ **Airport:** Aki, at 16 mls (26km) N; hovercraft and coach service; – *ANA* flights to Nagoya, Osaka; – *TDA* flights to Kagoshima, Tokyo.

Airlines: *All Nippon Airways*, Kowa Bldg., 4-20, 3-chome, Funai cho (Tel. 35-0727); – *Toa Domestic Airlines*, reservations (Tel. 35-2150).

⚓ **Sea travel:**
– From Oita (Nishi Oita station): to Kobe, Matsuyama, Nagoya.
– From Oaza 2mls (3km) NE of Oita eki; bus: hovercraft to Beppu and Oita airport. V. also Beppu

Shipping line: *Oita Hover ferry*, 1309-206, Oaza Imazura (Tel. 58-7180).

Rail: *JNR* to Beppu, Fukuoka, Hiroshima, Kagoshima, Kitakyushu, Kumamoto, Kyoto, Misumi, Miyakonojo, Miyazaki, Nagasaki, Osaka, Tokyo.

Coaches: to Aso, Beppu, Fukuoka, Hita, Usuki.

Events: *Tsurusaki Odori*, 18 and 19 Aug.; – *Kakuno ichi*, costumed procession between 1 and 11 Sept.

OKAYAMA (Okayama ken), p. 476.
Tel. 0862; ✉ 700.

[i] **Tourist Information Centre,** 2-4-6, Uchisange (Tel. 24-2111).

Hotels:
*** *New Okayama*, 1-1-25, Ekimae cho (Tel. 23-8211), 82 rms. (2 Jap.) ¶¶ ▥ A/c ♨ 🏠 TV hairdresser, boutique.
** *Okayama Grand*, 2-10, Funabashi (Tel. 33-7777), 31 rms. (3 Jap.) ¶¶ ▥ A/c ♨ 🏠 ☎ TV P
** *Okayama Plaza*, 116, Hama (Tel. 72-1201), 85 rms. (2 Jap.) ¶¶ ▥ A/c ♨ 🏠 ☎ TV ▣ bar, hairdresser, boutique.

Ryokans:
** *Shinmatsunoe*, Ifuku cho (Tel. 52-5131), 53 rms.
Ishiyama Kadan, Marunouchi (Tel. 25-4801), 40 rms.

Business hotels:
Okayama New Station, 18-9, Ekimoto cho (Tel. 53-6655).
Okayama Park, 2-5-12, Tomachi (Tel. 32-1101).

Restaurant:
Koraku (Jap. food), 2-1-25, Marunouchi (Tel. 22-6781).

✈ **Airport:** Okayama, at 5mls (8km) S *(bus);* – *ANA* flights to Tokyo; – *TDA* to Matsuyama.

Airlines: *All Nippon Airways*, reservations (Tel. 24-3381); – *Toa Domestic Airlines*, reservations (Tel. 63-2711).

Sea travel: *Nambi Marime Transport Co.,* to Shodo shima, Takamatsu; – *Ryobi Unyu Steamship Co.,* to Shodo shima.

Shipping line: *Ryobi Unyu Steamship Co.,* Okayama ko (Tel. 62-3155).

Rail
– Okayama station: *JNR Shinkansen* to Fukuoka, Osaka, Tokyo; other trains to Fukuoka, Hamada, Hiroshima, Izumo, Kagoshima, Kumamoto, Kyoto, Masuda, Miyakonojo, Miyazaki, Nagasaki, Ogori, Oita, Osaka, Sasebo, Shimonoseki, Tamano, Tokyo, Tottori, Yonago
– Omoto station: *JNR* to Okayama Tamano; – *Okayama Dentetsu*, to Okayama ko.

Coaches: to Kurashiki, Niimi, Soja, Tamano, Tsuyama.

Excursion: Kurashiki and Washu zan.

Travel agency: *JTB*, J.T.B. Bldg., 1-7-36 Omote machi (Tel. 32-9111).

Specialities: Bizen porcelain, hemp carpets, Muscat grapes.

Shopping: around the station, in the large stores (*Daimaru, Takashimaya*) and on Marunouchi.

Sports: *Daido Marina* (Tel. 62-2947).

Okazaki, p. 479.
Okinajima, p. 257.
Okinawa jima, p. 481.
Okinawa kaigan, p. 484.
Okinawa Senseki, p. 483.

OKINAWA SHOTO (Okinawa), p. 481.

Tel. Koza (0989); Motobu (09804); Nago (09805); Naha (0988); ⊠ Nago (905); Naha (902).

ⓘ **Tourist Information Centre:** Naha, 1-2-32, Izumizaki (Tel. 55-4209).

Lodgings:

– At Naha

Hotels:

*** *Okinawa Grand Castle*, 1-132-1, Yamakawa cho, Shuri (Tel. 86-5454), 304 rms. (1 Jap.) 5 ❙❙ ▥ A/c 🛏 🛋 ☎ TV 🖼 P bar, boutiques, bowling.

*** *Okinawa, Harbour View*, 2-46, Izumizaki (Tel. 53-2111); telex 79-5236), 341 rms (5 Jap.) ❙❙ ▥ A/c 🛏 🛋 ☎ TV P

*** *Okinawa Miyako*, 40, Asa Matsukawa (Tel. 87-1111), 334 rms. 4 ❙❙ ▥ A/c 🛏 🛋 ☎ TV 🖼 P bar, boutiques.

*** *Moon Beach* (Tel. 65-1020; telex 795.603), 475 rms. (67 Jap.) ❙❙ ▥ A/c 🛏 🛋 ☎ TV ☀ 🖼 ⚓ 🖼 bars, hairdresser, boutiques.

** *Seibu Orion*, 1-2-21, Asato (Tel. 66-5533), 219 rms. ❙❙ ▥ A/c 🛏 🛋 TV ☀ ⚓ ⚓/9 P sailing, fishing.

Youth hostels: *Naha*, 51, Onoyama-cho, Naha (Tel. 57-0073), 100 beds; *Tama – Tamazone-so*, 54, Asato, Naha (Tel. 33-5377), 30 beds.

– At Koza 15mls (24km) NE of Naha.

Hotels:

*** *Okinawa Hilton*, 1478 Kita Nagagusuku (Tel. 38-1566) 188 rms ❙❙ ▥ A/c 🛏 🛋 ☎ TV ☀ ⚓ P bar, hairdresser, boutiques.

** *Koza Kanko*, Moronizato (Tel. 37-1173), 75 rms. ❙❙ ▥ A/c 🛏 🛋 ☎ ⚓ bar.

** *Kyoto Kanko*, 285 Uechi (Tel. 37-1125), 94 rms. ❙❙ ▥ A/c 🛏 🛋 ☎ TV 🖼 bar.

– At Motobu 50 mls (81 km) N of Naha.

Hotels:

Okinawa Royal View, 938, Ishikawa, Motobu cho, Kunigami gun (Tel. 8-3631), 92 rms. ❙❙ ▥ A/c 🛏 🛋 ☎ TV ☀ 🖼 ⚓ ⚓/9 🖼 sailing, rowing, fishing.

– At Nago 40 mls (64km) NE of Naha.

Hotel:

** *Futabaso*, 297, Nago (Tel. 2-2828), 43 rms. ❙❙ ▥ A/c 🛋 ☎ TV

✈ **Airports:**

Okinawa: *Naha*, 2½ mls (4 km) S of Naha (bus); – *ANA* flights to Anami, Oshima, Fukuoka, Kagoshima, Nagoya, Osaka, Tokyo; *JAL* flights to Fukuoka, Osaka, Tokyo; *Swal* flights to Ishigaki jima, Kume jima, Miyako jima, Minami Daito jima; *international flights*. Kume jima: *Goshikawa*, – *Swal* flights to Okinawa. Minami Daito jima: *Minami Daito;* – *Swal* flights to Okinawa.

Airlines:

Koza: *Japan Air Lines*, Awase Meadows Shopping Center, 202, Aza Yamasato (Tel. 37-3401)
Naha: *All Nippon Airways*, Ryukyu Seimei Bldg., 3-1-1, Kumoji (Tel. 34-2620); – *Japan Airlines*, Kokuba Bldg., 3-21-1, Kumoji (Tel. 62-3311); – *Southwest Airlines*, Naha

Airport Terminal Bldg., 306–1, Aza Kagamizu (Tel. 57–2114).

🛱 **Sea travel:**
– Okinawa shoto:
From Naha: *Port of Naha:* – *Oshima Unyu* to Amami Oshima, Kagoshima, Kobe, Okino erabu jima, Tokuno shima, Tokyo, Yoron jima; – *Shokoku Yusen*, to Amami Oshima, Kagoshima, Okino erabu jima, Tokuno shima; – international services. – *Port of Naha-Tomari*: services to Ishigaki jima, Kume jima, Miyako jima, Tokashiki jima, Zamami shima; – hovercraft to the Expo '75 site.
From Motobu (*Toguchi*): services to Ie shima, Iheya jima, Izena jima.
From Sashiki: service to Kudaka jima.
From Yonagusuku (*Yakena*): services to Hamahiga jima, Henza jima, Ikei jima, Miyagasuku jima, Tsuken jima.
– Iheya-Izena shoto:
Services from Iheya and Izena to Okinawa (Motonobu).
– Kerama retto:
Services from Tokashiki and Zamami to Okinawa (Naha).
– Kume jima:
Service from Nakazato to Okinawa (Naha).
– Daito shoto:
Services between Kita Daito and Minami Daito jima.

🚌 **Coaches:** to Okinawa for whole island; coach station at Nishi Hon cho.

Excursions: *Nahakotsu and Ryukyu Bus* to Okinawa Senseki, Gyokusen do, Hedo misaki.

🚗 **Car hire:**
Naha: *Nippon*, 42–3, Asahi machi (Tel. 33–0913); – *Nissan*, 2–15–7 Kumoji (Tel. 33–2882).

Travel agency:
Naha: *JTB*, Asahi Seimei Okinawa Bldg., 2–1 Kumoji.

Specialities: ceramics, coral jewellery, lacquered goods, textiles (*kasuri and bingata*), glass, pork-based food.

Events: procession of geishas from Tsuji (Naha), in Dec. or Jan.; – *Harii fest.* (boat races) at Itoman, Naha, Yanbaru, in summer; *Eisa fest.* at Itoman, Naha, Yohahara, in summer; – bull fights; – numerous folk dances.

Sports: karate and other bare hand sports typical of Okinawa – sea-diving: *Naha Suien*, Naha (Tel. 55–0434).

Omura, p. 488.
Onagawa, p. 266.
Ondo, p. 339.
O Nejime, p. 301.
Onigajo, p. 675.
Oniike, p. 645.
Onioshidashi, p. 275.
Onneyu Onsen, p. 155.
Onoaida, p. 503.
Onogawa Onsen, p. 671.

ONOMICHI (Hiroshima ken), p. 489.
Tel. 0848; ✉ 722.

Ryokans:
** *Hotel Kinkaen*, Nishi Tsuchido cho (Tel. 22-7151), 12 rms.
Nishiyama Bekkan, Sanba cho (Tel. 22-3145), 13 rms.
Senkojisango, Nishi Tsuchido cho (Tel. 22-7168), 31 rms.
Takamisanso, Mukaishima cho (Tel. 44-1710), 21 rms.

Youth hostel: *Onomichi Yuai sanso*, Senkoji koen (Tel. 22-5554), 70 beds.

🏛 **Sea travel:** *Innoshima Steamship Co.,* to Habu, Imabari; – *Seto Naikai Steamship Co.,* to Ikuchi jima, Imabari, Matsuyama, Oni shima, Nichama, Tadotsu, Tomo.

🚃 **Rail:** *JNR*, to Fukuoka, Kagoshima, Kumamoto, Kyoto, Nagasaki, Oita, Okayama, Osaka, Sasebo, Shimonoseki, Tokyo.

🚌 **Coaches:** to Fukuyama, Hiroshima, Miyoshi, Mukai shima.

Event: Port fest. begin. Apr.

Antake san, p. 312.
Onuma koen (V. Hakodate), p. 201.
Onyu, p. 469.
Orofure toge, p. 539.

OSAKA (Osaka fu), p. 489.
Tel. 06; ✉ 530 to 556.

ℹ️ **Tourist Information Centre,** 2, Otemaeno cho, Higashi ku (Tel. 345-2189).

Lodgings:
– Abeno ku

Hotel:
** *Echo Osaka*, 1-4-7, Abeno suji, Abeno ku (Tel. 633-1141), 83 rms. (1 Jap.) 🍴 ▥ A/c 🛁 🛋 ☎ 📺 🖼 bar, boutique.

Ryokan:
Mikasa, Asahi machi, Abeno ku (Tel. 641-0293), 22 rms.

– Higashi ku

Hotels:
**** *International*, 58, Hashizume cho, Uchihon machi, Higashi ku (Tel. 941-2661; telex 529-3415), 394 rms. (3 Jap.) 7 🍴 ▥ A/c 🛁 🛋 ☎ 📺 ☀ 🖼 bar, hairdresser, boutiques, conf. rms. (1,300 seats).
*** *Osaka Castle*, 2-35, Kyobashi, Higashi ku (Tel. 942-2401; telex 529-8505), 90 rms. 🍴 ▥ A/c 🛁 🛋 ☎ 📺 🖼 bar, boutiques.

Ryokans:
*** *Hotel Hishitomi*, Hon machi Higashi ku (Tel. 261-1112), 23 rms.
** *Onoya*, 1-16, shima-machi, Higashi-ku (Tel. 942-37457).

– Higashi Sumiyoshi ku

Youth hostel:
Osaka Nagai, 450, Higashi Nagai cho, Higashi Sumiyoshi ku (Tel. 699-5631), 108 beds.

– Higashi Yodogawa ku

Ryokan:
** *Shin Osaka Biwako Hotel*,

Jyuso Higashino cho, Higashi Yodogawa ku (Tel. 301-8537), 29 rms.

Business hotel:
Shin-Osaka Sen-I City, 2-2-17, Nishimiyahara, Yodogawa ku (Tel. 363-1201).

– Kita ku

Hotels:
***** *Royal*, 2-1, Tamae cho, Kita ku (Tel. 448-1121; telex 563350), 1,600 rms. (15 Jap.) 9 ¶ ▥ A/c ▤ ▥ ☎ TV ❋ ▦ P bar, hairdresser, boutiques, hammam, conf. rm. (2,000 seats).

*** *Hanshin*, 8, Umeda cho (Tel. 344-1661; telex 523-4269), 241 rms. (2 Jap.) ¶ ▥ A/c ▤ ▥ ☎ TV ▣ bar, hairdresser, boutiques.

Ryokan:
*** *Osaka Dai ichi Hotel Bekkan*, Taiyuji cho (Tel. 312-8181), 15 rms. YMCA: 13, Nishi Ogi machi. Kita ku (Tel. 361-0838).

Business hotel:
Osaka Green, 3-11, Kita dori, Nishi Nagahori, Kita-ku (Tel. 532-1091).

– Minami ku.

Ryokans:
*** *New Naniwa Hotel*, Yamato cho, Minami ku (Tel. 213-1241), 25 rms.
** *Daikokyya Honten*, Soemon cho, Minami ku (Tel. 211-4819), 20 rms.
* *Kamenoi*, Uchiandoji dori, Minami ku (Tel. 761-2271). 19 rms.

– Miyakojima ku

Hotel:
** *Osaka Riverside*, 5-10-160, Nakano cho, Miyakojima ku

(Tel. 928-3251), 102 rms. (6 Jap.) ¶ ▥ A/c ▤ ▥ ☎ TV ❋ P bar, hairdresser, boutiques, Jap. com. bath.

– Naniwa ku

Ryokan:
*** *Hotel Ichiei*, Shinkawa, Naniwa ku (Tel. 641-2525), 20 rms.

– Nishi ku

Ryokan:
Gaen, Kitahorie Miike dori, Nishi ku (Tel. 541-0433), 20 rms.

Business hotel:
New Oriental, 2-6-10, Nishi Honmachi, Nishi ku (Tel. 538-7141).

Youth Hostel:
YMCA, 12, Tosabori 2-chome, Nishi ku (Tel. 441-0892).

– Oyodo ku

Hotels:
***** *The Plaza*, 2, Minami Oyodo, Oyodo ku (Tel. 453-1111; telex 524-5557), 581 rms. (5 Jap.) 3 ¶ ▥ A/c ▤ ▥ ☎ TV ❋ ▦ P bar, hairdresser, boutiques, bowling, conf. rm. (2,500 seats).

**** *Toyo*, 1-21, Toyosaki Nishi dori, Oyodo ku (Tel. 372-8181; telex 523-3886), 636 rms. (4 Jap.) 4 ¶ ▥ A/c ▤ ☎ TV ❋ P bar, hairdresser, boutique, bowling, sauna, conf. rm. (900 seats).

– Tennoji ku

Hotel:
*** *Osaka Miyako*, 110, Horikoshi cho, Tennoji ku (Tel. 779-1501; telex 527-8930), 151 rms. (8 Jap.) ¶ ▥ A/c ▤ ▥ ☎ TV bar, boutiques.

– Nanikawa ku

Business hotel:
Nankai, 2–680, Shinkawa cho, Nanikawa ku (Tel. 649–1521).

Restaurants:
**** *Kitcho* (Jap. food), 3–23, Koraibashi, Higashi ku (Tel. 231–1937).

*** *Taiko en* (Jap. and West. food) 9–10, Amijima machi, Miyakojima ku (Tel. 356–1111).

** *Honmorita* (suki-yaki), 7, Ichiban cho, Namba Shinchi, Minami ku (Tel. 211–3608).

** *Hon Musashi Kaikan* (suki-yaki, shabu-shabu), 2–15–24, Sonezaki, Kita ku (Tel. 311–5575).

** *Kagairo* (Jap. food), 1–29, Kitahama, Higashi ku (Tel. 231–0272).

** *Kikuya* (tempura), 3, Umegae cho, Kita ku (Tel. 312–3196).

** *Hachisaburo* (sushi), 3–23, Namba Shinchi, Minami ku (Tel. 211–3201).

** *Sakura Kadan* (Jap. food). 2–1–6, Higashi Kobashi (Tel. 981–0630).

** *Matsumoto* (kaiseki), 8–3, 1-chome, Dotonbori, Minami ku (Tel. 211–5652).

** *Minokichi* (suki-yaki, shabu-shobu), Yagi Bldg, B1, Minami, Kutaro cho 2-chome, Higashi ku (Tel. 262–4185).

** *Osaka Joe's* (West. food; spec.: crab, crayfish). IM Excellence Bldg. 2F, 1–11–20 Sonezakishinchi, Kita ku (Tel. 344–0124).

✈ **Airports:** *Osaka International*, at Itami 12 mls (19 km) N; coaches from Osaka and Shin Osaka stations; – *ANA* flights to Fukuoka, Kagoshima, Kitakyu-shu, Kochi, Kumamoto,

Matsuyama, Miyazaki, Oita, Okinawa, Omura, Sapporo, Takamatsu, Tokyo, Tottori; – *JAL* flights to Fukuoka, Okinawa, Sapporo, Tokyo; – *TDA* flights to Amami Oshima, Hiroshima, Izumo, Kochi, Matsumoto, Niigata, Shirahama, Tokushima, Ube, Yonago; – international flights.

Airlines: *Air France*, Kangin Yodoya – bushi Bldg., Okawa cho, Higashi ku (Tel. 201–8761). – *All Nippon Airways*, 2–6, Shibata cho, Kita ku (Tel. 374–5131). – *Japan Air Lines*, Asahi Shimbun Bldg., 3, Nakanoshima 3-chome, Kita ku (Tel. 201–1231); – *Korean Airlines*, 3–12, Hon machi, Higashi ku (Tel. 262–1110); – *Sabena*, Nishi Hanshin Bldg., (Tel. 341–8081). – *Toa Domestic Airlines*, 1–3, Umeda, Kita ku (Tel. 341–9431).

⚓ **Sea travel:**
From Osaka ko (*5 mls/8 km SW; metro*): Kansei Kisen to Beppu, Imabari, Kobe, Matsuyama, Shodo shima, Takamatsu; – *Nihon Kosoku Ferry*, to Kagoshima; – *Tokushima Hanshin Ferry* to Tokushima; – other services to Kochi.
From Osaka Nanko (8 mls/13 km SW; bus): *Green Ferry* to Hiroshima; – *Kansai Kisen*, to Tokushima; – *Muroto Steamship*, to Muroto; – *Nippon Car Ferry*, to Hyuga, Kobe; – *Taiyoo Ferry*, to Kanda (Kitakyushu).

🚃 **Rail:**
Abenosbashi station: *Kinki Nippon Electric Railway*

(Kintetsu) to Kawachi Nagano, Ebisucho station: *Nankai Electric Railway* to Hirano. Katamachi station: *JNR* to Kizu.

Minatomachi station: *JNR* to Kameyama, Nagoya. Namba station: *JNR* to Shingu; – *Kintetsu ER* to Kashikojima, Nagoya, Nara, Shigisanguchi, Yoshino; – *Nankai ER* to Fuke, Koya san, Wakayama.

Nishi Kujo station: *JNR* Loop Line to Osaka and Tennoji; – *Hanshin Electric Railway*, to Kobe, Sakurajima.

Osaka station (main): *JNR* to Aomori, Hiroshima, Kagoshima, Kumamoto, Kurayoshi, Kyoto, Miyakonojo, Miyazaki, Nagano, Nagasaki, Niigata, Oita, Sasebo, Shimonoseki, Tokyo, Toyama; – *Loop Line* to Tennoji.

Shin Osaka station: *JNR Shinkansen* to Fukuoka, Okayama, Tokyo; other trains to Aomori, Hiroshima, Kagoshima, Kanazawa, Kumamoto, Miyakonojo, Nagasaki, Niigata, Sasebo, Tokyo, Toyama.

Tenjinbashisuji station: *Keihanshin Kyuko Electric Railway (Hankyu)* to Kita Senri.

Tennoji station: *JNR* to Kameyama, Kyoto, Minatomachi, Nagoya, Nara, Shingu, Shirahama.

Umeda station: *Hankyu ER* to Kobe, Kyoto, Minoo, Takarazuka; – *Hanshin ER* to Kobe.

Metro: *Chuo line* from Fukaebashi to Osakako; – *Midosuji line*, from Esaka to Abiko; – *Sakaisuji line* from Tenjin Bashisuji to Dobutsuenmae; – *Sennichimae line* from Noda Hanshin to Minami Tatsumi – *Tanimachi line* from Yao Minami to Dainichi. – *Yotsubashi line* from Yao Minami to Dainichi. – *Yotsubashi line* from Nishi Umeda to Nakafuto.

🚌 **Coaches:** from Osaka to Kobe, Kyoto, Nagoya, Nara, Takarazuka, Tokyo.

🚗 **Car hire:** *Nippon*, 1-1-3, Shibata cho, Kita ku (Tel. 373-2652); – *Nissan*, 19-22, Chaya machi, Kita ku (Tel. 372-0289).

Tour of the city: half-day (afternoon) from Mar. to Nov.; leaves from main hotels; in English. City tour organized by *Osaka Municipal Tour Bus Information Bureau*, leaves from Osaka station; reservations and information from following stations: Umeda (Tel. 361-7504), Namba (Tel. 641-6910) and Tennoji (Tel. 622-5230).

Industrial Tourism: a tour organized by the Tourist Office (Tel. 345-2189) to visit the large companies in the Osaka region: Kirin Brewery, NHK, Matsushita, Daihatsu, Suntory, Fuji color and many others (in Mar.–Apr., Jul., Aug., and Oct.).

Meet the Japanese: 'Home visit system', information from Osaka Tourism Association. (Tel. 261-3948).

Excursions: in English, to Ise, Kyoto; leaves from main hotels.

Travel Agency: *JTB*, Asahi Bldg., Nakanoshima 3-

chome, Kita ku
(Tel. 771–6971).

✉ **Main post office:** Nada machi, Kita ku (Tel. 235–1321).

Banks: *Bank of Japan*, 23, Nakanoshima 1-chome, Kita ku; – *Banque Nationale de Paris*, Okbayashi Bldg, 37 Kyobashi 3-chome, Higashi ku (Tel. 944–1351). – *Bank of Indo-China and Suez*, Kintetsu Honmachi Bldg., 28–1, 4-chome, Higashi ku (Tel. 251–4491); – *Fuji*, 25–1, Imabashi 5-chome, Higashi ku; – *Mitsubishi*, 15–1, Dojima Hama dori, 1-chome, Kita ku; – *Mitsui*, 1, Koraibashi 2-chome, Higashi ku; – *Sumitomo*, 22, Kitahama 5-chome, Higashi ku.

Shopping:
Shinsaibashi commercial street; most of the large stores, and a multitude of smaller shops, are to be found here: *Daimaru*, Shinsaibashi suji, Minami ku (Tel. 271–1231); *Sogo*, Shinsaibashi suji, Minami ku (Tel. 203–1331). Nippon-bashi district for all types of hi-fi equipment, gadgets, etc.; 7 mins. on foot from Namba, the greatest no. of shops with 'discount' prices: *Toa-onkyo*, 3–6–1–chome, Nippon bashi, Naniwa ku (Tel. 631–1081); *Kawaguchi Musen Co*, 4–8–12, Nippon bashi, Naniwa ku (Tel. 631–0321). Underground shopping arcades below Namba and Umeda stations: futurist decor, lots of shops.

Entertainments:
Noh theatre: *Otsuki Seiinkai*, 2 Uahom machi, Higashi ku

(Tel. 768–9478).
– **Kabuku Theatre:** *Shin Kabukiza*, 59, Namba 5-chome, Minami ku (Tel. 631–2121).
– **Bunraku:** *Asahi za*, 1, Higashi Yagura cho, Minami ku (Tel. 211–6431).

Night life: Dotonbori district: one of the most important centres of Osaka with its theatres, bars, cinemas and restaurants. Sennichimae: another entertainment district, also enlivened by cabarets, bars and cinemas (near Namba station).

Selected addresses: *Cabaret Metro*, 6, Soemon cho, Minami ku (Tel. 211–9131); – *Cabaret Universe*, 1525, Kawahara cho 1-chome, Minami ku (Tel. 641–8731); – *Club Arrow*, 100, Doyama cho, Kita Ku (Tel. 361–3535).

Events: *Toa Ebisu*, 9 to 11 Jan. at Imamiya Ebisu shrine (Naniwa ku); – *Doyadoya*, 14 Jan. at Shitenno ji, Shoyo e or Oshorai, 22 Apr. at Shitennoji (court dances); – *Osaka International Fair*, every two years, in Apr. or May: – *Tenjin matsuri*, 24 and 25 Jul. at Temman gu with decorated boats on the Dojima gawa; – *Summer fest*. 9 Jul. at Ikutama shrine; – Port fest. 15 Jul.; – *Sumiyoshi matsuri*, 31 Aug. at Sumiyoshi shrine.

Sports: golf (*Ibaraki Country Club, Takatsuki Golf Club*); – sumo, 3–4–36, Namba, Naka, Naniwa ku (Tel. 631–0120); martial arts; – judo, 4–15–11, Nagato, Joto ku (Tel. 961–0640); – aikido, Tenshin Dojo, 1–10–8, Juso Higashi

Yadogawa ku (Tel. 304–8710).

Consulates: Belgian, Uchi-hommachi, Higashi ku (Tel. 941–5881); French, Minamihommachi, Higashi ku. (Tel. 252–5995); Swiss, Dojima, Kita ku, (Tel. 344–7671).

Places, sites and monuments:
Osake Caste, p. 495
Dotombori, p. 497.
Higashi ku, p. 494.
Homyo ji, p. 498.
Imperial Palace of Naniwa, p. 496.
Kita ku, p. 494.
Minami ku, p. 497.
Mint, the p. 494.
Museums:
– Electrical Science Museum, p. 497.
– Fujita Museum, p. 499.
– Japanese Craft Museum, p. 499.
– Municipal Fine Art Museum p. 498.
Municipal Natural Science Museum, p. 496.
Nakanoshima, p. 494.
Namba, p. 497.
Naniwa ku, p. 498.
Nishi ku, p. 494.
Osaka Castle, p. 494.
Osaka Merchandise Bldg., p. 496.
Osaka Tower, p. 499.
Parks
– Sakuranomiya Park, p. 499.
– Tennoji Park, p. 498.
Shrines
– Sumiyoshi shrine p. 499.
– Imamiya Ebisu shrine, p. 498.
Shinsekai, p. 498.
Shitenno ji, p. 497.
Temma gu, p. 494.
Tennoji ku, p. 496.
Tsutenkaku Tower, p. 498.
Utsubo koen, p. 496.

Osawa (gorge), p. 165.
Ose zaki, p. 195.
Oshika, p. 266.
Oshika (gorge), p. 339.
O shima (Miyagi ken), p. 510.
O shima (Miyazaki ken), p. 452.
O shima (Tokyo to, V. Izu shoto), p. 270.
O shima (Wakayama ken), p. 677.
Oshimizu, p. 467.
Oshoro, p. 504.
Osore zan, p. 408.
Osugi, p. 428.

OSUMI SHOTO (Kagoshima ken), p. 502.
Tel. Tanega shima (09973); Yaku shima (09974).

Lodgings:

–At Tanega shima.

Ryokan:
** *Tanegashima Kanko Hotel*, Nishinoomote (Tel. 2–100), 30 rms.

– At Yaku shima

Ryokan:
** *Tashirokan*, Miyanoura (Tel. 2–0018), 22 rms.

✈ **Airports:** Tanega shima, at *Nakatane* 15 mls (25 km) S of Nishinoomote; coach; *TDA* flights to Kagoshima; – Yaku shima 7 mls (11 km) SE of Miyanoura and 7 mls (10 km) NW of Ambo, coach; *TDA* flights to Kagoshima, Tanega shima.

Airlines: *Toa Domestic Airlines*; reservations: Tanega shima (Tel. 2–1155); Yaku shima (Tel. 2–9183).

⚓ **Sea travel:** From Tanega shima: *Kagoshima shosen* from Nishinoomote to Kagoshima, and from

Shinama to Yamakawa and Yaku shima. From Yaku shima: *Kagoshima shosen* from Ambo to Tanega shima and Yamakawa; from Miyanoura to Kagoshima; – other services from Miyanoura to Kuchi erabu jima.

🚌 **Coaches:** Tanega shima: from Nishinoomote to Shimama; – Yaku shima: from Ambo or Miyanoura to Kurio and Nagata.

Otaguchi, p. 428.
Otaka, p. 208.
Otaki, p. 312.
Otani, p. 651.
Otanoshike, p. 342.

OTARU (Hokkaido), p. 503.
Tel. 0134; ✉ 047.

Hotel:
** *Hokkai*, 1-5-11, Inaho (Tel. 25-1511), 42 rms. (15 Jap.) ¶ ▥ A/c 🛁 🏧 ☎ TV ❋ P bar, hairdresser, boutique.

Business hotel:
Otaru Green, 3-3-1, Inaho (Tel. 33-0333).

⚓ **Sea travel:** to Maizuru, Tsuruga, Rishiri to.

🚆 **Rail:** *JNR*, to Asahikawa, Hakodate, Sapporo, Wakkanai.

🚌 **Coaches:** to Bikoku, Iwanai, Sapporo.

Otetsuji, p. 386.
Otomi (cliffs), p. 469.

OTSU (Shiga ken), p. 505.
Tel. 0775; ✉ 520.

ℹ **Tourist Information Centre,** 4-1-1, Kyo machi (Tel. 24-1121).

Hotel:
*** *Biwako*, 5-35, Yanagasaki

(Tel. 24-1255; telex 05464-868), 116 rms. (82 Jap.) ¶ ▥ A/c 🛁 🏧 ☎ TV 🎛 ♨ P bar, hairdresser, boutiques.

Ryokans:
*** *Hakkeikan*, Hama Otsu (Tel. 23-1633), 38 rms.
** *Hotel Koyo*, Chagasaki (Tel. 24-0176), 232 rms.

🚆 **Rail:** Otsu station: *JNR* to Kyoto, Nagoya, Osaka, Tokyo, Tsuruga.
Hama Otsu station: *Keihin Electric Railway* to Ishiyama, Kyoto, Sakamoto.
Shiga station; *JNR* to Kyoto, Osaka, Tsuruga.

Funicular: from Sakamoto to Hiei zan.

🚌 **Coaches:** to Kusatsui, Kyoto, Tsuruga.

Events: *Lake Biwa Festival*, end Jul.

Sports: several marinas on Lake Biwa, esp. *Shiga*, 1-2, Yanagasaki (Tel. 24-1781).

Otsuka, p. 244.
Oura, p. 215.
Owa, p. 146.
Owakidani, p. 170.
Owani Onsen, p. 214.
Owase (V. Yoshino Kumano), p. 674.
Oyadomari, p. 485.
Oya ji, p. 648.
Oyashirazu, p. 268.
Oyu, p. 629.
Ozega hara, p. 467.
Oze numa, p. 467.

R

Raiden kaigen, p. 505.
Ranshima, p. 504.
Rausu (V. Shiretoko), p. 546.
Rebun, p. 511.

Lodgings:

– At Kesennuma
Tel. 02262; ✉ 988.

Hotel:
Hotel Boyo, 3-1-25, Sakana machi (Tel. 2–4500), 46 rms.

– At Ofunato
Tel. 01922; ✉ 022.

Hotel:
Ofunato Frang Hotel, Ofunato cho (Tel. 6–6101), 39 rms.

– At Rikuzen Takata
Tel. 01925.

Youth hostel:
Rikuzen Takata, Sunamori, Kesen machi (Tel. 4246), 96 beds.

S

SADO (Niigata ken), p. 512.
Tel. Aikawa (02597); Ogi (025986); Ryotsu (02592); Sawata (025952); ✉ Akiawa (952–15); Ogi (952–06); Ryotsu (952); Sawata (952–13).

Lodgings:
– At Aikawa

Ryokan:
Yamaki Hotel, Kabuse, Aikawa machi, Sado gun (Tel. 4–3366), 42 rms.

– At Ogi.

Ryokan:
* *Hotel New Kihachiya*, Ogi machi, Sado gun (Tel. 330), 16 rms.

Minshuku:
Shimizuso, 85, Oazako Washimizu, Ogi cho, Sado-gun (Tel. 6–2538), 7 rms.

Youth hostel:
Senkaku so, 369-4, Himezu, Aikawa machi, Sado gun (Tel. 5–2011), 20 beds.

– At Ryotsu

Ryokans:
** *Sado Green Hotel Kiraku*, Shizaki Onsen (Tel. 3032), 28 rms.
* *Lake View Hotel Yamago*, Shizaki Onsen (Tel. 3171), 36 rms.

– At Sawata

Ryokan:
* *Kokusai Sado Kanko Hotel*, 2043, Yawata, Sawatas machi, Sado gun (Tel. 2141), 64 rms.

🛆 **Sea travel:** *Sado Kisen*: from Ryotsu to Niigata; from Akadomari to Kashiwazaki; from Ogi to Naoetsu; – other service from Ryotsu to Ogura.

Events: folk dances: Sado Okesa.

SAGA (Saga ken), p. 514.
Tel. 09526; ✉ Saga (840); Yamato (840–04).

Lodgings:

– At Yamato 5mls (8km) N.

Ryokan:
*** *Hotel Ryutoen*, Kawakamikyo

Onsen, Yamato cho
(Tel. 2-3111), 77 rms.

🚌 Rail: *JNR* to Fukuoka
Kitakyushu, Kure, Kyoto,
Nagasaki, Osaka, Sasebo,
Tokyo.

🚌 Coaches: to Fukuoka,
Karatsu, Kashima, Sasebo,
Yanagawa.

Events: *Menfuryu dances* at
Sega shrine in Oct.

Saganoseki, p. 476.
Sagara, p. 540.
Sagi yama, p. 646.
Saidaiji, p. 477.
Saikai (National Park), p. 515.
Saikai bashi, p. 526.
Sai ko, p. 166.
Sai Ojima, p. 486.
Saito, p. 515.
Sakai, p. 516.
Sakakibara Onsen, p. 633.
Sakamoto, p. 507.
Sakata, p. 517.
Sakihama, p. 408.
Sakitsu, p. 646.
Sakuma, p. 561.
Sakunami Onsen, p. 530.
Sakurai, p. 518.
Sakurajima (V. Kagoshima),
p. 281.
Samani, p. 520.
Sambe Onsen, p. 470.
Sandan (gorges), p. 222.

SAN IN KAIGAN (Hyogo,
Kyoto and Tottori ken;
national park) p. 520.

Lodgings:
– At Hamasaka
Tel. 07968.

Youth hostel: *Hamasaka
Shiroyama enchi*, Hamasaka
cho, Mikata gun (Tel. 2-1282),
80 beds.

– At Kinosaki
Tel. 079632; ✉ 669-61.

Ryokans:
*** *Ryokufukaku*, Yushma, Kino
saki cho (Tel. 2834), 27 rms.
** *Blue Kinosaki*, Asahi machi,
Kinosaki cho (Tel. 3131),
92 rms.
** *Nishimuraya*, Yushima,
kinosaki cho (Tel. 2211),
43 rms.
* *Mancaraya*, Yushima, Kinotaki
cho (Tel. 2321), 34 rms.
* *Josenkaku*, Yushima,
Kinosaki cho (Tel. 2821),
37 rms.

– At Toyooka
Tel. 079628; ✉ 669-61.

Ryokan:
Kimparo, Seto (Tel. 2500),
47 rms.

– At Yumura Onsen
Tel. 07969; ✉ 669-68.

Ryokans:
*** *Izutsuya*, Onsen cho, Mikata
gun (Tel. 2-1111), 102 rms.
* *New Tomiya*, Onsen cho,
Mikata gun (Tel. 2-0001),
44 rms.

– At Tottori
V. under this place name.

Sanriku, p. 510.
Sanuki, p. 560.

SAPPORO (Hokkaido), p.
522.
Tel. 011; ✉ 060.

🛈 **Tourist Information Centre,**
6, Kita Sanjo Nishi, Chuo ku
(Tel. 211-3341).

Hotels:
**** *Sapporo Grand*, 4-2, Nishi,
Kita Ichijo, Chuo ku
(Tel. 261-3311); telex 0932-
613), 196 rms. (16 Jap.) 5 🍴
▥ A/c 🛏 🛁 ☎ TV ❋ 🖼 bar,
hairdresser, boutiques, conf.
rm. (1,000 seats).

**** *Sapporo Prince*, 11, Nishi, Minami Nijo, Chuo ku (Tel. 231-5310; telex 0933-949), 228 rms. (2 Jap.) 3 ¶¶ ▥ A/c 🛏 ⊭ 🛋 ☎ TV 🔲 bar, hairdresser, boutiques, bowling, conf. rm. (1,000 seats).

*** *Century Royal*, Nishi, 5-chome, Kita Gojo, Chuo ku (Tel. 231-2121; telex, 0932-330), 340 rms. ¶¶ ▥ A/c 🛏 🛋 ☎ TV P bar, boutiques, sauna.

** *Sapporo Royal*, 1, Higashi, Minami Shichijo, Chuo ku (Tel. 511-2121), 88 rms. (7 Jap.) ¶¶ ▥ A/c 🛏 🛋 ☎ TV ❋ 🔲 bar, hairdresser, boutique.

Ryokans:
* *Hotel Maruso*, 3-3, Nishi Kita Ichijo, Chuo ku (Tel. 221-0111), 38 rms.
* *Sapporo Daijchi Hotel*, 10, Odori Nishi, Chuo Ku (Tel. 221-1101), 70 rms.

Business hotels:
Soen Green, Nishi 14-chome, Kita Ichijo, Chuo ku (Tel. 231-1661).
Sapporo Washington, 1, Nishi 4-chome, Kita Ichijo, Chuo ku (Tel. 251-3211).

Minshuku:
Yoshizumi Ryokan, Nishi 9-chome, Minami Nijo Chuo ku (Tel. 231-3853), 8 rms.

Youth hostels:
Nakanoshima, 2-chome, Ichijo, Nakanoshima, Toyohira ku (Tel. 831-8752), 70 beds; – *Sapporo Shiritsu Lions*, 1277, Miyanomori, Kotoni machi, Chuo ku (Tel. 611-4709), 100 beds.

Restaurants:
** *Bobaitei* (Jap. food), Nishi 3-chome, Minami Schichijo Chuo ku (Tel. 511-1161).

** *Hyosetsu Nomon Shinkan* (Jap. food), Nishi 2-chome Minami Gojo, Chuo ku (Tel. 521-2161).

* *Kaiyotei* (Jap. food), Nishi 1-chome, Ninami Juichijo, Chuo ku (Tel. 511-3361).

* *Otemon* (suki-yaki), Nishi 1-chome, Minami Juichijo, Chuo ku (Tel. 531-2875).

* *Sentozasho* (Jap. food), Nishi 3-chome, Minami Schichijo, Chuo ku (Tel. 511-4171).

✈ **Airports:** *Chitose*, at 26 mls (42 km) SE; coaches from *ANA* and *JAL* terminals: – *ANA* flights to Nagoya, Niigata, Osaka, Sendai, Tokyo; *JAL* flights to Osaka, Tokyo; *TDA* flights to Tokyo. *Okadama*, at 4 mls (7 km) N (coach); – *TDA* flights to Abashiri, Akita, Hachinone, Hakodate, Kushiro, Obihiro, Wakkanai.

Airlines: *All Nippon Airways*, Ita and Kato Bldg., 1, Kita Shijo Nishi 4-chome, Chuo ku (Tel. 231-4411); – *Toa Domestic Airlines*, Mitsui Bldg., 251-4231.

🚆 **Rail:** *JNR* to Abashiri, Asahikawa, Hakodate, Kushiro, Nayoro, Nemuro, Otaru, Takikawa, Wakkani.

Metro: from Azabu cho to Makomanai and from Kotoni to Shiraishi; the two lines cross at Odori.

🚌 **Coaches:** to Bikuni Chitose, Jozan kei, Otaru, Shikutsu ko, Tomakomai, Toya ko; – bus stations: *Shakotan Bus*, at the corner of Ishikari kaido and Kita Ichijo; *Donan Bus*, Kita Shijo, Nishi 4, also at Sapporo eki.

Car hire: *Nippon*, 3-2-9, Kita Rokujo Nishi, Kita ku (Tel. 741-7645); – *Nissan*, Kita Gojo, Nishishi 7-chome, Kita ku (Tel. 281-3951); – *Ryowa*, Minami Jujo, Nishi 10-chome, Chuo ku (Tel. 511-3111).

Travel agency: *JTB*, c/o Nippon Seimei Bldg., 4 Kita Sanjo Nishi, Chuo ku (Tel. 241-6201).

Specialities: wooden crafts; Ainu fabrics.

Night life: Susukino district: about 3,500 restaurants and bars; numerous cabarets.

Shopping: *Minami Ichijo dori*, Nishisan chome, around Sapporo eki. *Tanukikoji*: commercial district with about 300 boutiques, shops and cinemas. *Odori koen promenade*: underground shopping arcade.

Events: *Snow Festival* on the Odori (ends on 1st Sun. in Feb.).

Sports: golf (*Makomamai Golf Club, Sapporo Golf Club*); – Skiing: *Moiwa yama*, from Dec. to Mar.; *Teine Olympia skiing ground*, from Nov. to Mar.

Sarome ko, p. 118.

SASEBO (Nagasaki ken), p. 526.
Tel. 0956; ✉ 857 and 858.

Hotel:
** *Matsukura*, 5-15, Shirahae cho (Tel. 23-5271), 48 rms. (9 Jap.) ¶¶ ▥ A/c 🛏 🄰 ☎ 📺 bar, boutique.

Ryokan:
** *Yumihari Kanko Hotel*, Udogoe cho (Tel. 23-9221), 58 rms.

Business hotel:
Sasebo Green, 4-1, Miura cho (Tel. 24-6261).

Restaurant:
* *Grill Mon* (Chin. food), 6-2, Shirohae cho (Tel. 23-5111).

🏛 **Sea travel:** from Sasebo to Goto retto; – from Kashimae 2 mls (3 km) W, at Hirado.

🚃 **Rail:** *JNR* to Fukuoka, Karatsu, Kyoto, Nagasaki, Osaka, Tokyo, Tosu.

🚌 **Coaches:** to Fukuoka, Hiradoguchi, Karatsu, Nagasaki, Takeo.

Specialities: Mikawachi pottery.

SENDAI (Miyagi ken), p. 527.
Tel. 0222; ✉ 980

□ **Tourist Information Centre:** 3-8-1, Hon cho (Tel. 63-2111).

Hotels:
*** *Koyo*, 4-1-7, Ichiban cho (Tel. 62-6311; telex 852-820), 63 rms. ¶¶ ▥ A/c 🛏 🄰 ☎ 📺
** *Sendai City*, 2-2-10, Chuo (Tel. 23-5131), 56 rms. (2 Jap.) ¶¶ ▥ A/c 🛏 🄰 ☎ 📺
** *Sendai*, 1-10-25, Chuo (Tel. 25-5171), 89 rms. (4 Jap.) ¶¶ ▥ A/c 🛏 🄰 ☎ 📺 ✻ bar, hairdresser, boutique.
** *Sendai Grand*, 3-7-1, Ichiban cho (Tel. 25-2101), 74 rms. (1

Jap.) ¶ ▥ A/c 🛁 🛋 ☎ TV 🖼
bar, hairdresser.

Ryokan:
* *Miyako Hotel*, 2-9-14, Hon cho (Tel. 22-4647), 37 rms.

Business hotels:
Sendai Royal, 4-10-11, Chuo (Tel. 27-5131).
Sendai Washington, 2-3-1, O machi (Tel. 62-1171).
Green, 2-5-6, Nishiki cho (Tel. 21-4191).

Youth hostel:
Sendai Akamon, 61, Kawauchi Kawamae cho (Tel. 64-1405), 100 beds.

Restaurants:
* *Sendai Seiyoken* (West. food), Shin Sendai Bldg, 1-1-30 O machi (Tel. 22-7834).
* *Yogorosushi* (sushi), Kokubun cho 2-chome, 15-20 (Tel. 23-3874).

✈ **Airport:** at 12 mls (19 km) SE; coach; – *ANA* flights to Nagoya, Sapporo and Tokyo.

Airlines: *All Nippon Airways*, Nittsu Bldg., Higashi Goban cho (Tel. 66-3355); – *Japan Air Lines*, Tohoku Denryoku Bldg, 3-7-1, Ichiban cho (Tel. 61-2241).

Sea travel: from the port of Sendai 9 mls (14 km) E; coach to Nagoya, Tomakomai.

🚆 **Rail:** *JNR, Shinkansen* to Morioka, Tokyo; other trains to Akita, Aomori, Fukushima, Ishinomaki, Morioka, Tokyo, Yamagata.

🚌 **Coaches:** to Fukushima, Matsushima, Naruko, Yamagata.

Travel agency: *JTB*, 3-6-1 Ichiban cho (Tel. 21-3611).

Shopping: Higashi Ichiban cho, O machi, Shintemma cho, Nakake cho.

Specialities: wooden dolls (kokeshi).

Events: * *Tanabata*, 6–Aug.

Sengokujara, p. 169.
Senjoga hara, p. 465.
Senri, p. 506.
Senzu (Shizuoka ken), p. 541.
Senzu (Tokyo to), p. 264.
Sesso kyo, p. 541.
Seto (Aichi ken), p. 531.
Seto (Nagasaki ken), p. 253.
Seto (Shizuoka ken), p. 205.
Seto Naikai (National Park), p. 531.
Setouchi (bay), p. 126.
Shakotan (peninsula), p. 505.
Shazen (gorge), p. 147.
Shibetsu, p. 451.
Shibu, p. 148.

SHIBUKAWA (Gumma ken), p. 533.
Tel. Agatsuma (027964); Ikaho (027972); ✉ : Agatsuma (377-06); Ikaho (377-01).

Lodgings:
– At Ikako 5 mls (9 km) W.

Hotel:
** *Hashimoto*, 586, Ikaho Onsen (Tel. 2035), 25 rms. (10 Jap.) ¶ ▥ A/c 🛁 🛋 TV ♦ ♨/18 🐾 P boutique, Jap. com. bath.

– At Agatsuma 16 mls (26 km) NW.

Ryokan:
* *Shima Grand Hotel*, Shima Onsen (Tel. 2211), 43 rms.

– At Ikaho 5 mls (9 km) W.

Ryokans:
** *Moriaki*, Ikaho machi, Kita Gumma gun (Tel. 2601), 63 rms.

* *Ikahokan*, Ikaho machi, Kita Gumma gun (Tel. 3131), 63 rms.

Rail: *JNR*, to Manza-Kajikazawa guchi, Niigata, Tokyo.

Coaches: to Haruna ko, Maebashi, Numata, Takasaki.

Shibukawa (Okayama ken), p. 559.
Shibushi (bay), p. 301.
Shichiriga hama, p. 294.
Shido, p. 554.
Shiga kogen (V. Joshin Etsu kogen) p. 276.
Shigina Onsen, p. 223.
Shiiba, p. 237.
Shikabe Onsen, p. 201.
Shikano shima, p. 187.
Shikaribetsu ko, p. 156.
Shikaribetsu Onsen, p. 156.
Shikine jima, p. 271.
Shikoku, p. 534.
Shikotsu ko, p. 538.

SHIKOTSU TOYA (Hokkaido National Park), p. 538.

Lodgings:
- At Jozankei
Tel. 011365; ✉ 061-23.

Ryokan:

* *Hotel Shikanoyu*, Jozankei Onsen, Minami ku, Sapporo (Tel. 598-2311), 197 rms.
Jozankei Hotel, Jozankei Onsen, Minami ku, Sapporo (Tel. 598-2111), 180 rms.

Youth hostel:

* *Jozankei*, 310, Jozankei Onsen, Minami ku, Sapporo (Tel. 2858), 56 beds.

- At Noboribetsu Onsen
Tel. 01438; ✉ 059-05.

Ryokans:

* *Noboribetsu Prince Hotel*, Noboribetsu Onsen (Tel. 4-2255), 209 rms.

* *Dai ichi Takimoto kan*, Noboribetsu Onsen (Tel. 4-2111), 360 rms.

Youth hostel:
Akashiya so, Noboribetsu Onsen (Tel. 4-2616), 55 beds.

- At Shikotsu kohan
Tel. 012325; ✉ 066-02.

Ryokan:

** *Shikotsuko Grand Hotel*, Okotan, Shikotsuko, Chitose (Tel. 5-2636).

- At Toyako Onsen
Tel. 01427; ✉ 049-57.

Hotel:

*** *Manseikaku*, 21, Aza Toyako Onsen machi, Abuta cho, Abuta gun (Tel. 5-2171), 200 rms. A/c TV /18 **P** bar, hairdresser, boutique, Jap. com. bath.

Ryokans:

*** *Toya Park Hotel*, 29 Aza Toyako Onsen machi, Abuta cho, Abuta gun (Tel. 5-2445), 167 rms.

* *Toya Kanko Hotel*, 33 Aza Toyako Onsen machi, Abuta cho, Abuta gun, 134 rms.

Youth hostel:
Showa Shinzan, 79, Sobetsu Onsen, Sobetsu cho (Tel. 5-2776), 285 beds.

Shimabara (V. Unzen amakusa). p. 644.
Shimada, p. 540.
Shimama, p. 503.
Shimanokoshi, p. 509.
Shimizu (Hokkaido), p. 470.

SHIMIZU (Shizuoka ken), p. 541.
Tel. 0543; ✉ 424.

Ryokan:

*** *Hagoromo Hotel*, 1282-1, Miho (Tel. 34-1234), 22 rms.

Youth hostel:
Miho, Masaki, Miho
(Tel. 34-0826), 100 beds;
– *Nihondaira Lodge*, 1482,
Mabase, Nihondaira
(Tel. 34-2738), 60 beds.

Rail: *JNR*, to Kagoshima,
Nachi-Katsuura, Osaka,
Shimonoseki, Shizuoka,
Tokyo, Toyama; – private line
to Shizuoka.

Coaches: to Fuji, Kofu,
Shizuoka.

Shimobe, p. 324.
Shimoda (Kumamoto ken),
p. 645.
Shimoda (Shizuoka ken, V.
Fuji-Hakone-Izu), p. 172.
Shimokamo, p. 176.
Shimokita Hanto (Regional
Park) p. 409.
Shimonita, p. 626.

SHIMONOSEKI (Yamaguchi
ken), p. 542.
Tel. 0832.

Hotels:
** *Sanyo*, 2-9, Mimosusakawa
machi (Tel. 23-5291), 36 rms.
(7 Jap.) ¶¶ ▥ A/c ♨ 🅿 bar, Jap. com. bath,
bowling.
** *Shimonoseki Grand*, 31-2,
Nabe cho (Tel. 31-5000), 45
rms. (4 Jap.) ¶¶ ▥ A/c ♨ 📺 bar, boutique.

Business hotel:
Shimonosheki Station, 2-8-1,
Takezakichi (Tel. 32-3511).

Youth hostel:
Hinoyama, Mimosusokawa
machi (Tel. 22-2753), 52 beds.

Restaurants:
* *Tsukihi* (Jap. food), 62,
Ginnankai, Tokuyama
(Tel. 21-3737).
* *Shizuka* (Jap. food and
steaks), 582-1, Enoue, Oaza

Maeda (Tel. 23-6251).

Sea travel: to Pusan (Korea).

Rail:
– Shin Shimonoseki station:
JNR, Shinkansen to Fukuoka,
Okayama, Osaka, Tokyo,
other trains to Fukuoka,
Hiroshima, Shimonoseki,
Yamaguchi.
– Shimonoseki station: *JNR*
to Fukuoka, Kagoshima,
Kumamoto, Kyoto, Masuda,
Miyakonojo, Miyazaki,
Nagasaki, Nagato, Nagoya,
Oita, Okayama, Osaka,
Sasebo, Tokyo, Yamaguchi.

Coaches: to Fukuoka,
Nagato, Yamaguchi.

Shimotane, p. 503.
Shimotsu, p. 129.
Shimotsu kaigan, p. 306.
Shinano (V. Nagano), p. 412.
Shingu (V. Yoshino Kumano),
p. 675.
Shin Hirayu Onsen, p. 151.
Shin Hotaka, p. 151.
Shinju to, p. 265.
Shin Kazawa Onsen, p. 275.
Shinoe Onsen, p. 553.
Shino jima, p. 207.
Shintoku, p. 150.
Shin Yaba kei, pl. 223.
Shin yu, p. 310.
Shiobara Onsen (V. Imaichi),
p. 255.
Shioda, p. 211.

SHIOGAMA (Miyagi ken), p.
543.
Tel. 02235; ✉ 981-02.

Lodgings:

– At Matsushima 6 mls,
(10 km) N.

Ryokans:
** *Hotel Taikanso*, 10-76, Aza
Inuta, Matsushima cho,
Miyagi gun (Tel. 4-2161),
119 rms.

* *Matsushima Dai ichi Hotel*, 9, Aza Senzui, Matsushima cho, Miyagi gun (Tel. 4-2151), 32 rms.

🛥 **Sea travel:** to Kinka zan, Matsushima wan (excursion).

🚃 **Rail:**
– Shizuoka station: *JNR* to Aomori, Sendai, Tokyo.
– Nishi-Shiogama, Hon-Shiogama, Higashi-Shiogama, Hamada and Matsushima Kaigan stations: *JNR* to Ishinoma ki, Sendai.

🚌 **Coaches:** to Furukawa, Ishinomaki, Sendai, Tokyo.

Events: **Grand maritime festival* from 9 to 11 Jul.

Shino (peninsula), p. 677.
Shirabu Onsen, p. 671.
Shirahama (Chiba ken), p. 560.

SHIRAHAMA (Wakayama ken), p. 545.
Tel. 07394; ✉ 649-22.

Hotel:
*** *Pacific*, 2018, Shirahama cho (Tel. 2-2733), 70 rms. (34 Jap.) 🍴 ▦ A/c 🛁 📺 ⛩ ❋ ▨ ⚓ ⚲/¹⁸ **P** bar, boutiques, Jap. com. bath.

Ryokans:
*** *Gampuso*, Shirahama cho, Nishi Muro gun (Tel. 2-3423), 79 rms.
** *Hotel Koganoi*, 3753, Shirahama cho, Nishi Muro gun (Tel. 2-2922), 123 rms.
* *Shiraraso Grand Hotel*, 868, Shirahama cho, Nishi Muro gun (Tel. 2-2566), 125 rms.

✈ **Airport:** Nanki Shirahama, at 3 mls (5km) S (coach); – *ANA* flights to Nagoya; *TDA* flights to Osaka, Tokyo.

Airlines: *All Nippon Airways*, reservations at the airport (Tel. 2-4600); – *Toa Domestic Airlines*, reservations at the airport (Tel. 3-4328).

🛥 **Sea travel:** hydrofoil to Kainan, Kobe; other service to Tanabe.

🚃 **Rail:** Shirahama station, 3 mls (5 km) E; coach: *JNR* to Nagoya, Osaqka, Shingu, Tokyo.

🚌 **Coaches:** to Hongu, Kushimoto, Ryujin Onsen, Wakayama.

Excursions: around the peninsula.

Shirahone Onsen, p. 150.
Shiraito (waterfall), p. 166.
Shirakaba ko (V. Chino), p. 149.
Shirakawago, p. 558.
Shiramine, p. 197.
Shiramine san, p. 553.
Shirane san, p. 276.
Shiraoi, p. 625.
Shirayone, p. 651.

SHIRETOKO (Hokkaido National Park), p. 546.

Lodgings:
– At Rausu Onsen
Tel. 01538; p. ✉ 086-18.

Ryokan:
Shiretoko Kanko Hotel, Rausu Onsen, Yunosawa (Tel. 7-2181), 51 rms.

– At Utoro
Tel. 015224

Minshuku:
Chikoso, Aza Utoro, Shari cho, Shari gun (Tel. 4-2058), 17 rms.

Youth hostel:
Shiretoko, Utoro, Shari machi (Tel. 4-2034), 326 beds.

Shirikishinai, p. 202.

Shizuga take, p. 410.

SHIZUOKA (Sizuoka ken),
p. 546.
Tel. 0542; ✉ 420.

☐ **Tourist Information Centre,**
9–6, Ote machi (Tel. 21-2111).

Hotel:
** *Shizuoka Grand Hotel
Nakazimaya*, 3–10, Koya
machi (Tel. 53-1151), 109 rms.
(10 Jap.) ¶ ▥ A/c 🛁 🏧 ☎
TV P bar, boutiques, sauna.

Ryokan:
* *Yashimaen*, 4–13, Higashi
Takajo machi (Tel. 45-2131),
17 rms.

Business hotel:
Shizuoka Green, 5–6, Denma
cho (Tel. 52-2101), 72 rms.

✈ **Airline:** *Japan Air Lines*,
Nakazimaya Bldg., 3–10,
Konya machi (Tel. 55-5295).

🚂 **Rail:**
– Shizuoka station: *JNR,
Shinkansen* to Fukuoka,
Osaka, Tokyo; other trains to
Fukuoka, Kagoshima, Kofu,
Kumamoto, Nachi-Katsuura,
Nagasaki, Osaka, Sasebo,
Shimonoseki, Tamano, Tokyo.

– Shin Shizuoka station:
private line to Shimizu.

🚌 **Coaches:** to Hamamatsu,
Shimizu.

SHODO SHIMA (Kagawa
ken), p. 548.
Tel. Tonosho (08796);
Uchinomi (08798):
✉ Tonosho (761-41),
Uchinomi (761-44).

Lodgings:

– At Tonosho

Hotel:
*** *Shodoshima International*,
24–67, Tonosho cho, Shozu
gun (Tel. 2-1441), 106 rms.
(10 Jap.) ¶ ▥ A/c 🛁 🏧 ☎
TV ❋ ▦ ⚓ P bar, boutique.

Ryokans:
*** *Hotel New kankai*, Tonosho
cho, Shozu gun (Tel. 2-1430),
47 rms.
*** *Toyoso*, Tonosho cho, Shozu
gun (Tel. 2-1166), 57 rms.

Minshuku:
Tsurumi, 1963, Naeba, Utsmi
cho, Shozu gun (Tel. 2-2449),
9 rms.

Youth hostel:
Shodoshima, Tonosho cho,
Shozu gun (Tel. 62-1627), 50
beds.

⚓ **Sea travel:**
– From Fukuda: *Kansai Kisen*
to Himeji.
– From Ikeda: services to
Takamatsu, Tonosho.
– From Obe: service to
Hinase.
– From Sakate: *Kansai Kisen*
to Beppu, Kobe, Osaka,
Takamatsu.
– From Tonosho: *Kansai
Kisen* to Himeji, Ie shima,
Takamatsu, Tomano; – *Nambi
Marine Transport Co.* and
Ryobi Unyu, to Okayama; –
Shikoku Ferry to Takamatsu;
– *Shodoshima Kyuko Ferry* to
Tamano.
– From Uchinomi-Kusambe:
service to Takamatsu.

🚌 **Coaches:** several services
around the island.

Excursions: *Shodoshima Bus*
from Sakate or Tonosho.

Specialities: truffles, pearls,
olive oil.

Sho gawa (gorges), p. 554.
Shoji ko, p. 166.
Shomyo (waterfall), p. 152.

Shonyu do (cave), p. 558.
Shosen (narrow pass), p. 324.
Shosha zan, p. 211.
Shuri, p. 482.
Site of Expo '75, p. 485.
Sobetsu Onsen, p. 539.
Soja, p. 477.
Soto kaifu kaigan, p. 513.
Soun (gorges), p. 155.
Sounkyo (V. Daisetsuzan), p. 155.
Souzan, p. 170.
Soya misaki, p. 654.
Subashiri, p. 164.
Suga jima, p. 265.
Suge numa, p. 465.
Suishei shokobutsu en, p. 527.
Sukawa Onsen, p. 242.
Sukumo, p. 132.
Sumatakyo Onsen, p. 541.
Sumoto (V. Awaji shima), p. 139.
Susa wan, p. 199

SUWA (Nagano ken), p. 549.

Tel. Shimo Suwa (02662); Suwa (02665); ⊠ Shimo Suwa (393); Suwa (392).

Lodgings:

- At Suwa

Ryokans:
Nunohan, 3-2-9, Kogan dori, Suwa (Tel. 2-5500), 32 rms.
Suwako Royal Hotel, 3-2-2, Kogan dori Suwa (Tel. 2-2660), 46 rms.

- At Shimo Suwa, 2½ mls (4 km) NW.

Ryokan:
*** *Suwa Prince Hotel*, Shimo Suwa machi (Tel. 7-2100), 36 rms.

Youth hostel:
Suwako, 9209, Takagi, Shimo Suwa machi (Tel. 7-7075), 40 beds.

🚌 **Rail:** *JNR* to Itiogawa, Matsumoto, Nagoya, Tokyo.

🚌 **Coaches:** to Chino, Lida, Matsumoto, Shirakaba ko.

Suwa ko, p. 549.
Suzaki, p. 173.
Suzu, p. 651.
Suzuka (wooded park), p. 662.

T

Tabayama, p. 147.
Tachibana, p. 127.
Tachikue kyo, p. 273.
Tada, p. 513.
Tadami gawa, p. 120.
Taga, p. 209.
Taihei zan, p. 124.
Taira, p. 643.
Taira (W. Iwaki), p. 269.
Taisekiji, p. 177.
Tajima Mihonoura, p. 521.
Tajimi, p. 551.
Takachiho (V. Nobeoka), p. 466.
Takachiho kyo, p. 466.
Takachihono mine, p. 310.
Takahagi, p. 551.
Takahama, p. 469.
Takahara (gorges), p. 558.

TAKAMATSU (Kagawa ken), p. 552.
Tel. 0878; ⊠ 760.

ⓘ **Tourist Information Centre:** 4-1-10, Ban cho (Tel. 31-1111).

Hotels:
*** *Takamatsu Grand*, 10-5-1, Kotobuki cho (Tel. 51-5757; telex 05822-557), 136 rms. ⅏ ▥ A/c ♨ ⌂ ☎ TV ✳ P bar, boutiques.
*** *Takamatsu International*, 2191-1, Kita cho (Tel. 31-1511), 108 rms. (5

Jap.) ¶¶ ▥ A/c ▨ ▧ ☎ TV ☀ ▦ **P** bar, hairdresser, boutique, bowling, skating rink.

Ryokans:
** *Tokiwa Honkan*, Tikiwa cho (Tel. 61-5577), 22 rms.
* *Hotel Kawaroku*, Hyakken machi (Tel. 21-5666), 30 rms.

Business hotels:
Tokoju, 3-5-5, Hanazono cho (Tel. 31-0201).
Takamatsu City, 8-13, Kamai cho (Tel. 34-3345).
Takamatsu Station, 1-1³⁄₁₆ Kotobuki cho (Tel. 21-6989).

Youth hostels:
Takamatsu City, Okamoto cho (Tel. 85-2024), 52 beds; – *Kagawa ku*, Yashima, 34, Yashima Higashi machi (Tel. 41-9813), 96 beds.

Restaurant:
Kawaro ku (Jap. and West. food), 1-2, Hyakken machi (Tel. 21-5666).

✈ **Airport:** at 3 mls (5 km) SE (coach); – *ANA* flights to Osaka, Tokyo; *TDA* flights to Fukuoka, Tokyo.

Airlines: *All Nippon Airways*, Kansai Kisen Bldg., Tamamo cho (Tel. 22-2323); – *Japan Air Lines*, Fukoku Seimei Bldg., 1-5-1, Kotobuki cho (Tel. 22-7511); – *Toa Domestic Airlines*, reservations (Tel. 21-8021).

⚓ **Sea travel:** *Kansai Kisen* to Beppu, Imabari, Kobe, Matsuyama, Nihama, Osaka, Shodo shima; – *Shikoku Ferry* to Kobe, Shodo shima, Tamano; – *JNR*, Uko Kokudo Ferry to Tamano.

Shipping lines: *Kansai Kisen*, 1-10 Tamamo cho

(Tel. 51-5661); – *Shikoku Ferry*, 10-32 Tamamo cho (Tel. 51-0131).

🚆 **Rail:**
– Kawaramachi station: *Takamatsu-Kotohira Electric Railway*, to Kotohira, Shido, Nagao, Takamatsu.
– Takamatsu station: *JNR* to Kochi, Matsuyama, Mugi, Nakamura, Tokushima, Uwajima; – *Takamatsu-Kotohira ER* to Kotohira.

🚌 **Coaches:** to Anabuki, Kochi, Kotohira, Matsuyama.

Tour of the city: half-day (morning) in English.

Travel Agency: *JTB*, JTB Bldg., 7-6, Kajiya cho (Tel. 51-2111).

Shopping: Marugame cho, Hyogo cho, Minami Shin machi, Katahara cho.

Specialities: Japanese paper, lacquerware, fans, sunshades.

Sports: marina at *Hamano cho* (Tel. 22-1668).

Takamatsu (Okayama ken), p. 478.
Takano zaki, p. 129.

TAKAOKA (Toyama ken), p. 554.

Tel. 0766; ✉ 933-01.

Business hotel:
** *Takaoka Miyako*, 1023 Suehiro cho (Tel. 21-0385), 50 rms.

Youth hostel:
Zuiryuji, 35, Seki Hon machi (Tel. 22-0179), 30 beds.

🚆 **Rail:** *JNR*, to Aomori, Himi, Johana, Kanazawa, Nagoya, Niigata, Osaka, Tokyo, Toyama; – *Toyama Chiho Railway* to Shimminato.

🚌 **Coaches:** to Himi, Kanazawa, Toyama.

Takao san, p. 197.

TAKARAZUKA (Hyogo ken), p. 555.
Tel. 0797; ✉ 665.

Hotel:
*** *Takarazuka*, 1-46, Umeno cho (Tel. 87-1151); telex 5645-698), 165 rms. (6 Jap.) ❚❚ ▥ A/c 🛁 🅿 📞 📺 ☀ ☀ P bar, hairdresser, boutiques, conf. rm. (150 seats).

Ryokans:
** *Shofukaku*, Mefu (Tel. 87-2331), 28 rms.
* *Shimaya*, Sakae machi (Tel. 87-1771), 26 rms.

🚆 **Rail:** *JNR*, to Amagasaki, Fukuchiyama, Osaka, Tokyo; – *Keihanshin Electric Railway (Hankyu)* to Kobe, Osaka; – *Hanshin Electric Railway* to Osaka.

Takasaki, p. 555.
Takasaki yama, p. 143.
Takasu, p. 301.
Takakeru jinja, p. 215.
Takawashi, p. 177.

TAKAYAMA (Gifu ken), p. 556.
Tel. 0577; ✉ 506.

Hotel:
** *Hida*, 2-60, Hanaoka cho (Tel. 33-46-00), 29 rms. (19 Jap.) ❚❚ ▥ A/c 🛁 🅿 📞 📺 boutiques.

Ryokans:
** *Seiryu*, 6, Hachiman machi (Tel. 32-0448), 22 rms.
* *Hishuya*, 2581, Kamioka Motomachi (Tel. 33-4001), 16 rms.

Minshuku:
Iwatakan, 4-166-3, Ojin machi (Tel. 33-4917), 16 rms.

Matsuyama Ryokan, 5-11, Hanasoto cho (Tel. 32-1608), 25 rms.

Youth hostel:
Tenshoji, 83, Tenshoji machi (Tel. 32-6345), 150 beds.

Restaurants:
*** *Susaki* (Jap. food), 4-14, Shinmei machi (Tel. 32-0023)
* *Arisu* (Jap. and West. food), 87, Shimoichino machi (Tel. 32-2000).
* *Suzume* (West. food), 24 Aioi cho (Tel. 32-0300).
* *Hida no Jizakeya* (Jap. food), 54, Suehiro cho (Tel. 34-5000).

🚆 **Rail:** *JNR*, to Gifu, Nagoya, Toyama.

🚌 **Coaches:** to Gero, Matsumoto, Toyama.

Events: *Nijuyokka ichi*, fleamarket, 24 Jan. at Hon machi and Yasugawa; – *Haru matsuri*, 14 and 15 Apr. at Hie shrine, with procession of floats; – Sosha matsuri, 5 May at the shrine of the same name; – Aki matsuri, 9 and 10 Oct. at Hachiman shrine.

Takayu Onsen, p. 142.
Takedao Onsen, p. 555.
Takeo (Niigata ken), p. 453.

TAKEO (Saga ken) p. 559.
Tel. *Takeo* (09542); Ureshino (09544); ✉ : Takeo (843); Ureshino (843-03).

Lodgings:

– At Takeo

Ryokans:
*** *Mifuneyama Kanko Hotel*, Takeo machi (Tel. 3-3131), 75 rms.

– At Ureshino, 8 mls (13 km) S.

Ryokans:

*** *Wataya Besso*, Ureshino cho, Fujitsu gun (Tel. 2-0210), 180 rms.

** *Shinsenkaku*, Ureshino cho, Fujitsu gun (Tel. 3-1100), 91 rms.

* *Ureshino Onsen Hotel*, Ureshino cho, Fujitsu gun (Tel. 3-0140), 38 rms.

🚋 **Rail:** *JNR*, to Karatsu, Kyoto, Osaka, Sasebo.

🚌 **Coaches:** to Imari, Kashima, Saga, Sasebo.

Lodgings:

– At Tateyama

Ryokan:

* *Hotel Tateyama Garden*, 2292-10, Hojo (Tel. 2-0140), 23 rms.

– At Chikura, 6 mls (10 km) E.

Ryokan:

** *Hotel Chikura*, Chikura machi, Awa gun (Tel. 4-3111), 28 rms.

– At Kanaya, 15 mls (25 km) N.

Ryokan:

* *Nokogiriyama Kanko Hotel*, 2178, Kanaya (Tel. 9-2211), 28 rms.

⚓ **Sea travel:** *Tokyowan Ferry* from Kanaya to Yokosuka.

🚋 **Rail:** *JNR* to Chiba, Tokyo.

🚌 **Coaches:** to Kamogawa, Kisarazu.

Toga, p. 472.
Togatta Onsen, p. 657.
Togendai, p. 170.
Togi, p. 202.
Toguchi, p. 485.
Toi (Miyazaki ken), p. 452.
Toi (Shizuoka ken), p. 175.
Toi misaki, p. 452.
Tojimbo, p. 181.
Tokachigawa Onsen (V. Obihiro), p. 470.
Tokachi Mitsumata, p. 155.
Tokai, p. 224.
Tokawa, p. 149.
Tokoname, p. 207.
Tokoro, p. 118.
Tokorozawa, p. 561.
Tokuno shima, p. 127.
Tokura, p. 467.

TOKUSHIMA (Tokushima ken), p. 562.
Tel. 0886; ✉ 770.

🛈 **Tourist Information Centre:**
1, Mandai cho (Tel. 21-2335).

Hotels:
** *Astoria*, 2-20, Kamiya cho (Tel. 53-6151), 25 rms (1 Jap.) ¶| ▥ A/c ♨ ▨ ☎ TV
** *Tokushima Park*, 8-3, Tokushima cho (Tel. 25-3311), 82 rms. (7 Jap.) ¶| ▥ ☎ ♨ ▨ TV ✳ ▣ bar.

Ryokans:
*** *Kanko Hotel Bizan Honkan*, Higashi Yamate cho (Tel. 22-7781), 21 rms.
** *Sumiya*, 2-8, Nakatori machi (Tel. 52-9161), 10 rms.

Business hotel:
Tokushima, 1-15, Shin kura machi (Tel. 52-6131), 40 rms.

Youth hostel:
Tokushima, 7-1, hama, Ohara machi (Tel. 62-1505), 80 beds.

✈ **Airport:**
Matsushige, 13km N.-E (car);

– *T.D.A.* to Kagoshima, Osaka, Tokyo.

Toa Domestic Airlines, reservations (Tel. 25-2533).

⚓ **Sea Travel:**
Kansai Kisen and Tokushima Hanshin Ferry Kobe, Osaka; – *Ocean Ferry* Chiba; – other service Fuke.

🚆 **Rail:**
JNR to Ikeda, Kochi, Mugi, Takamatsu, Naruto.

🚌 **Coaches:**
Events to Anabuki, Anan, Naruto, Takamatsu.

*Awa Odori same festival in Tokushima between 15-18 August

TOKUYAMA (Yamaguchi ken), p. 564
Tel. 0834; ✉ 745.

Ryokans:
*** *Marufuku Hotel*, 3 Sakurababa dori (Tel. 21-5113), 30 rms.
*** *Yuno Kanko Hotel*, Yno (Tel. 83-2300), 17 rms.

Restaurant:
* *Marufuku* (cuis. occ Western and Chinese), 3, Sakurababa dori (Tel. 21-5113).

⚓ **Sea Travel:**
to Taketazu

🚆 **Rail:**
JNR Fukuoka, Okayama, Osaka, Tokyo, other trains to Fukuoka, Kagoshima, Kumamoto, Kyoto, Miyazaki, Nagasaki, Oita, Okayama, Osaka, Sasebo, Tokyo.

🚌 **Coaches:**
to Iwakuni, Yamaguchi.

TOKYO (Tokyo to), p. 564.
Tel. 03; ✉ 100 to 180.

Ministry of Transport:
(Tourism Department), 1
Kasumigaseki 2-chome,
Chiyoda ku (Tel. 580-3111);
– JNTO (Japan National
Tourist Office): headquarters,
Tokyo Kotsu Kaikan Bldg.,
2-13 Yuraku cho, Chiyoda ku
(Tel. 216-1901); information
centres, Kotani Bldg., 1-6-6,
Yuraku cho, Chiyoda ku
(Tel. 502-1461) or at Narita
airport, (Tel. 0476/24-3198);
information in English
(Tel. 503-2911) or French
(Tel. 503-2926).

ⅰ **Tourist Information Centre,**
3-5-1, Marunouchi, Chiyoda
ku (Tel. 212-5111).

Lodgings:

– Bunkyo ku

Hotel:
*** *Daiei*, 1-15, Koishikawa,
Bunkyo ku (Tel. 813-6271;
telex 272-2266), 82 rms. (24
Jap.) ¶ ▥ A/c 🛗 🛆 ☎ TV 🖻
bar.

Business hotels:
Kizakan, 4-37-20, Hongo,
Bunkyo ku (Tel. 812-1211).
Suidobashi Grand Hotel,
1-33-2, Hongo, Bunkyo ku
(Tel. 816-2101).

– Chiyoda ku

Hotels:
**** *Grand Palace*, 1-1-1,
Iidabashi, Chiyoda ku
(Tel. 264-1111); telex 232-
2981), 500 rms. ¶ ▥ A/c 🛗
🛆 ☎ TV P bar, hairdresser,
boutiques, conf. rm (1,500
seats).
**** *Imperial*, 1-1-1, Uchisaiwai
cho, Chiyoda ku

(Tel. 504-1111; telex
222-2346), 1,300 rms. 9 ¶ ▥
A/c 🛗 🛆 TV 🖻 5 bars,
hairdresser, shopping arcade,
travel agency, conf. rm. (2,400
seats).
***** *New Otani*, 4, Kioi cho.
Chiyoda ku (Tel. 265-1111;
telex 232-2275), 2,044 rms. (2
Jap.) 5 ¶ ▥ A/c 🛗 🛆 ☎ TV
✳ 🖾 ℚ P bar, hairdresser,
boutiques, travel agency,
conf. rm (3,000 seats).
***** *Palace*, 1-1-1, Marunouchi,
Chiyoda ku (Tel. 211-5211;
telex 222-2580), 407 rms. ¶
▥ A/c 🛗 🛆 ☎ TV ✳ 🖻 bar,
hairdresser, boutiques, conf.
rm. (1,500 seats).
**** *Diamond*, 25, Ichiban cho,
Chiyodo ku (Tel. 263-2211;
telex 232-2764), 162 rms. ¶
▥ A/c 🛗 🛆 ☎ TV ✳ 🖾 🖻
bar, boutiques, conf. rm. (400
seats).
**** *Tokyo Hilton*, 2-10-3, Nagata
cho, Chiyoda ku
(Tel. 581-4511; telex
222-3605), 476 rms. (3 Jap.)
¶ ▥ A/c 🛗 🛆 ☎ TV ✳ 🖾 P
bar, hairdresser, boutiques,
night club, conf. rm. (1,650
seats).
*** *Akasaka Prince*, 1, Kioi cho,
Chiyoda ku (Tel. 234-1111),
42 rms. (1 Jap.) ¶ ▥ A/c 🛗
🛆 ☎ TV ✳ 🖾 🖻 bar,
hairdresser, boutiques, conf.
rm. (1,900 seats).
*** *Akasaka Tokyu*, 2-14-3,
Nagato cho, Chiyoda ku
(Tel. 580-2311; telex 222-
4310), 566 rms. ¶ ▥ A/c 🛗
🛆 ☎ TV 🖻 bar, hairdresser,
boutiques.
*** *Fairmont*, Kudan Minami,
Chiyoda ku (Tel. 262-1151;
telex 232-2883), 243 rms. ¶
▥ A/c 🛗 🛆 ☎ TV ✳ 🖻 bar,
hairdresser, boutiques.

*** *Marunouchi*, 1-6-3, Marunouchi, Chiyoda ku (Tel. 215-2151; telex 222-4655), 210 rms. (2 Jap.) ❘❘ ▥ A/c ♨ ⌂ ☎ TV ❄ bar, hairdresser, boutiques.

*** *Toshi Center*, 2-4-1, Hirakawa cho (Tel. 265-8211), 55 rms. (14 Jap.) ❘❘ ▥ A/c ♨ ⌂ ☎ TV ▣ bar, hairdresser, conf. rm. (1,000 seats).

* *Hill Top*, 1-1, Kanda Surugadai, Chiyoda ku (Tel. 293-2311), 87 rms. ❘❘ ▥ A/c ♨ ⌂ ☎ TV

** *Kokusai Kanko*, 1-8-3, Marunouchi, Chiyoda ku (Tel. 215-3281), 95 rms. ❘❘ ▥ A/c ♨ ⌂ ☎ TV ▣ bar, hairdresser.

Ryokan:

* *Fukudaya*, 6, Kioi cho, Chiyoda ku (Tel. 261-8577), 14 rms.

Business hotels:
Akihabara Pearl, 2-13, Sakuma cho, Chiyoda ku (Tel. 861-6171).
Tokyo Green Hotel Suidobashi, Kanda Misaki cho, Chiyoda ku (Tel. 295-4161).

Youth hostels:
Ichigaya, Goban cho, Chiyoda ku (Tel. 262-5950), 132 beds; – *YMCA*, 7, Kanda, Mitoshiro cho, Chiyoda ku (Tel. 293-1911); – *YWCA*, 8-8 Kudan Minami 4-chome, Chiyoda ku (Tel. 293-5421).

– Chuo ku

Hotels:

*** *Ginza Dai ichi*, 8-13-1, Ginza, Chuo ku (Tel. 542-5311; telex 252-3714), 806 rms. ❘❘ ▥ A/c ♨ ⌂ ☎ TV ▣ bar, hairdresser, boutiques.

*** *Urashima*, 2-5-23, Harumi,

Chuo ku (Tel. 533-3111; telex 252-4297), 1,001 rms. ❘❘ ▥ A/c ♨ ⌂ ☎ TV ❄ ▦ bar, hairdresser, boutiques, bowling, gym, sauna.

Ryokans:

*** *Shinkomatsu*, 1-9-13, Tsukiji, Chuo ku (Tel. 541-2225), 10 rms.

* *Hotel Yaesu Ryumeikan*, Yaesu, Chuo ku (Tel. 271-0971), 34 rms.

Business hotel:
Center Hotel Tokyo, 2-52, Kabuto cho, Chuo ku (Tel. 667-2711).

– Meguro ku

Hotels:

*** *Gajoen*, 1-8-1, Shimo Meguro, Meguro ku (Tel. 491-0111; telex 246-6006), 110 rms. (4 Jap.) ❘❘ ▥ A/c ♨ ⌂ ☎ TV ❄ P bar, hairdresser.

** *New Meguro*, 1-3-18, Chuo cho, Meguro ku (Tel. 719-8121), 31 rms. (1 Jap.) ❘❘ ▥ A/c ♨ ⌂ ☎ TV ❄ ▦ bar, hairdresser.

– Minato ku

Hotels:

***** *Okura*, 3, Aoi cho, Akasaka, Minato ku (Tel. 582-0111; telex J22-790), 980 rms. (11 Jap.) 7 ❘❘ ▥ A/c ♨ ⌂ ☎ TV ❄ 2 ▦ P 5 bars, hairdresser, shopping arcade, travel agency, gym, Turk. bath, massages, conf. rm. (2,600 seats).

***** *Takanawa Prince*, 3-13-1, Takanawa, Minato ku (Tel. 447-1111; telex 242-3232), 458 rms. 9 ❘❘ ▥ A/c ♨ ⌂ ☎ TV ❄ ▦ P bar, hairdresser, boutiques, nightclub, conf. rm. (4,000 seats).

*** *Tokyo Prince*, 3-3-1, Shiba Park, Minato ku (Tel. 432-1111; telex 242-2488), 510 rms. 7 ¶ ▥ A/c 🛏 🏛 ☎ TV ☀ 🖼 P 2 bars, hairdresser, shopping arcade, travel agency, bowling, conf. rm. (2,760 seats).

*** *Shiba Park*, 1-5-10, Shiba Park, Minato ku (Tel. 443-4131; telex 242-2917), 330 rms. ¶ ▥ A/c 🛏 🏛 ☎ TV 🖼 bar, hairdresser, boutiques.

*** *Azabu Prince*, 3-5-40, Minami Azabu, Minato ku (Tel. 473-1111), 32 rms. ¶ ▥ A/c 🏛 ☎ TV ☀ 🖼 bar, hairdresser, boutiques, conf. rm. (200 seats).

** *Takanawa*, 2-1-17, Takanawa, Minato ku (Tel. 443-9251), 217 rms. ¶ ▥ A/c 🛏 🏛 ☎ TV 🖼 bar, hairdresser, boutique.

** *Tokyu kanko*, 2-21-6, Akasaka, Minato ku (Tel. 582-0451), 48 rms. ¶ ▥ A/c 🛏 🏛 ☎ TV

Business hotels:
Akasaka Shandia, 7-6-13, Akasaka, Minato ku (Tel. 586-0811).
Sun Hotel Shimbashi, 3-5-2, Shimbashi, Minato ku (Tel. 591-3351).

– Nerima ku

Ryokan:
* *Kin Eikaku*, 2-26, Toyotamakami, Nerima ku (Tel. 991-1186), 15 rms.

– Ota ku

Hotels:
*** *Haneda Tokyu*, 2-8-6, Haneda kuko, Ota ku (Tel. 747-0311; telex 246-6560). 297 rms. (4 Jap.) ¶ ▥ A/c 🛏 🏛 ☎ TV 🐟 ☀ 🖼

P bar, hairdresser, boutiques.

** *Tokyo Air Terminal*, 2-3-1, Haneda kuku, Ota ku (Tel. 747-0111), 50 rms. ¶ ▥ A/c 🛏 🏛 ☎ TV P bar, hairdresser, boutique.

– Shibuya ku

Hotel:
*** *Sun Route Tokyo*, 2-3-1, Yoyogi, Shibuya ku (Tel. 375-3211; telex 232-2288), 562 rms. ¶ ▥ A/c 🛏 🏛 ☎ TV P

Youth hostel:
Tokyo Yoyogi, Olympic Memorial Youth Center, Yoyogi Kamizono cho, Shibuya ku (Tel. 467-9163), 150 beds.

– Shinjuku ku

Hotel:
***** *Keio Plaza*, 2-2-1, Nishi Shinjuku, Shinjuku ku (Tel. 344-0111; telex 232-2544), 1,057 rms. (4 Jap.) ¶ ▥ A/c 🛏 🏛 ☎ TV ☀ 🖼 P bar, hairdresser, shopping arcade, travel agency, conf. rm. (2,000 seats).

Ryokan:
*** *Tokiwa*, 2-328, Nishi Okubo, Shinjuku ku (Tel. 202-4321), 27 rms.

– Sumida ku

Business hotel:
Ryogoku Pearl, 1-24-24, Yokoami, Sumida ku (Tel. 626-3211).

– Taito ku

Hotel:
*** *Takara*, 2-16-5, Higashi Ueno, Taito ku (Tel. 831-0101; telex 265-5001), 100 rms. (4 Jap.) ¶ ▥ A/c 🛏 🏛 ☎ TV 🖼 🖼 bar, hairdresser.

Business hotel:

Hokke Club Ueno Ikenohataten, 2-1-48, Ikenohata, Taito ku (Tel. 822-3111).

Eating out:

Tokyo's restaurants may be counted in the hundreds. The districts of Roppongi and Akasaka are most notable.

– Bunkyo ku.

Restaurants:

*** *Chinzanso* (Jap. and West. food), 2-10-8, Sekiguchi, Bunkyo ku (Tel. 943-1111).

** *Goeimon* (tofu), 1-1-26, Hon Komagome, Bunkyo-ku (Tel. 811-2015).

– Chiyoda ku

Restaurants:

*** *Totenko Hibiya ten* (Chin. food), Toho Twin Bldg., 1-2-3, Yuraku cho, Chiyoda ku (Tel. 504-2751).

** *Tonta* (yakitori), 1-7-19, Uchisaiwai cho, Chiyoda ku (Tel. 580-5982).

** *Otemachi Fukudaya* (Jap. food), Asahitokai Bldg., 2-6-1, Okmachicho, Chiyoda ku (Tel. 242-3646).

** *Nadaman* (Jap. food), Hotel Imperial, 1-1-1, Uchisaiwai cho, Chiyoda ku (Tel. 503-7981).

– Chuo ku

Restaurants:

*** *Inagiku* (tempura), 2-6, Kayaba cho, Nihombashi, Chuo ku (Tel. 669-5501).

**** *Kanetanaka* (Jap. food), 7-18-17, Ginza, Chuo ku (Tel. 541-2556).

**** *Shin Kiraku* (Jap. food), 4-6-7, Tsukiji, Chuo ku (Tel. 541-5511).

*** *Benihana* (French food), 4, Nihombashi dori 1-chome, Chuo ku (Tel. 241-0600).

*** *Jisaku* (Jap. food), 14-19, Akashi cho, Chuo ku (Tel. 541-2391).

** *Chikuyotei* (unagi), 8-14-7, Ginza, Chuo ku (Tel. 542-0789).

** *Konjaku-Tei* (okonomi-yaki). 2-8-15, Ginza, Chuo ku (Tel. 564-1258).

** *Okahan Honten* (suki-yaki), 7-6-16, Ginza, Chuo ku (Tel. 571-1417).

* *Hamadaya* (Jap. food), 3-12, Ningyo cho, Nihombashi, Chuo ku (Tel. 661-5435).

* *Kinsen* (Jap. food), 5th fl. of Kintetsu Bldg., 4-4-10, Ginza, Chuo ku (Tel. 561-8708).

* *Zakuro* (Jap. food), 2-7-19, Kyobashi, Chuo ku (Tel. 564-0825).

Wakatsuki (oden), 4-13-16, Ginza, Chuo ku (Tel. 541-6730).

– Meguro ku

Restaurant:

*** *Furusato* (Jap. food), 4-1, Aobadai 3-chome, Meguro ku (Tel. 463-2310).

– Minato ku

Restaurants:

** *Seryna* (shabu-shabu), 3-12-2, Roppongi, Minato ku (Tel. 402-1051).

** *Hasejin Azabu ten* (suki-yaki) 3-3-15, Azabudai, Minato ku (Tel. 582-7811).

** *Akasaka Asada* (Jap. food), 3-6-4, Akasaka, Minato ku (Tel. 585-6606).

** *Shiruyoshi* (tempura), 6-2-12 Akasaka, Minato ku (Tel. 587-1876).

** *Kushihachi* (yakitori), Seishi-do Bldg., 3-10-9, Roppongi, Minato ku (Tel. 403-3060).

** *Matsuri* (yakitori), Toda Bldg., 7-16-5, Roppongi, Minato ku (Tel. 402-2570).

* *Umeko* (sushi), 3-13-21, Nishi-Azabu, Minato ku (Tel. 401-0376).

* *Brasserie Bernard* (French food), Kajimaya Bldg., 7-14-3, Roppongi, Minato ku (Tel. 405-7877).

- Shibuya ku

Restaurants:

** *Isshin* (Jap. food), 1-13-8, Jingu mae, Shibuya ku (Tel. 401-7991).

** *Tiffany* (French food), 6-35, Jingu mae, Shibuya ku (Tel. 409-7777).

- Shinjuku ku

Restaurants:

*** *Minokichi* (Jap. food), 48th fl. of Shinjuku Sumimoto Bldg., 2-6-1, Nishi Shinjuku, Shinjuku ku (Tel. 346-2531).

*** *Kurumaya* (Jap. food), 2-37-1, Kabuki cho, Shinjuku ku (Tel. 209-5411).

*** *Keio Plaza Okahan* (suki-yaki), 7th fl. of Keio Plaza Hotel, 2-2-1, Nishi shinjuku, Shinjuku ku (Tel. 344-0596).

** *Saint-Claire* (steaks, suki-yaki), Tokyo Josho Bldg., 1-13-8, Nishi Shinjuku, Shinjuku ku (Tel. 343-0440).

** *Tonkichi* (oden), Kinokuniya Bldg., 3, Shinjuku, Shinjuku ku (Tel. 352-6639).

** *Kakiden* (Jap. food), Yasuyo Bldg., 1-1, Tsunohazu, Shinjuku ku (Tel. 352-5121).

- Suginami ku

Restaurant:

** *Kokeshiya* (West. food), 3-14-6, Nishi Ogi Minami, Suginami ku (Tel. 334-5111).

- Taito ku

Restaurants:

** *Sushi-Hatsu* (sushi), 2-11-4, Asakusa, Taito ku (Tel. 844-3293).

** *Iidaya* (Jap. food; spec. dojo), 3-3-2, Nishi Asakusa, Taito ku (Tel. 843-0881).

** *Komagata Dojo* (dojo), 1-7-12, Komagata, Taito ku (Tel. 842-4001).

** *Maruta Goshi* (oden), 2-32-11, Asakusa, Taito ku (Tel. 841-3192).

** *Totenko* (Chin. food), 1-4-33, Ikenohata, Taito ku (Tel. 828-5111).

* *Ichinao* (Jap. food), 3-8-6, Asakusa, Taito ku (Tel. 874-3032).

* *Kameseiro* (Jap. food), 1-1-1, Yanagibashi, Taito ku (Tel. 851-3101).

✈ **Airports:**

- *Narita International Airport*, distant from city centre (41 mls/65km E). Various means of transport link Tokyo to Narita: *JNR* trains from Tokyo station to Narita, then bus (75 mins by fast service, 63 mins by express); direct express train from *Keisei Skyliner*, Uneo-Keisei station (75 mins journey to Narita terminus, then 6 mins bus to the airport); *Airport Limousine Bus*, from Tokyo Air Terminal (Hakozaki, Nihonbashi) to the airport (70 mins journey); avoid taxis - they are very expensive (c. 1 hr. journey). Narita airport is reserved for international flights.

- *Haneda airport* (Ota ku). Access: *Monorail* from Hamamatsucho and coaches from the major hotels; - *ANA*, flights to Akita, Fukui, Fukuoka, Hachijo jima,

Hakodata, Hiroshima, Kagoshima, Kochi, Komatsu, Kumamoto, Matsuyama, Miyazaki, Nagoya, Okayama, Okinawa, Omura, Osaka, Oshima, Sapporo, Sendai, Takamatsu, Ube, Yamagata, Yonago; – *JAL*, flights to Fukuoka, Okinawa, Osaka, Sapporo; – *TDA*, flights to Aomori, Asahikawa, Fukuoka, Hachinohe, Hanamaki, Kushiro, Niigata, Obihiro, Oita, Sapporo, Shirahama, Takamatsu, Tokushima. *Coach* from Narita to Haneda and vice-versa (every 30 mins).

Airlines: *Aeroflot* (Tel. 272-8351); – *Air France* (head office) New Aoyama Bldg., West 15F, 1-1, Minami Aoyama, 1-chrome, Minato ku (Tel. 584-1171); (agencies) Hibiya Mitsui Bldg., 1-12, Yuraku cho 1-chrome. Chiyoda ku (Tel. 508-05-51) and at Narita Airport (Tel. 047/632-7710); – *All Nippon Airways* (head office), Kasumigaseki Bldg., 2-5, Kasumigaseki 3-chome, Chiyoda ku (Tel. 552-6311); – *Japan Air Lines* (head office) 1-2, Marunouchi, Chiyoda ku (Tel. 747-1111); – *Korean Airlines* (Tel. 211-3311); – *Sabena*, 2-19, Akasaka 2-chome, Minato ku (Tel. 585-6551); – *Swissair*, Hibiya Park Bldg., 1, Yuraku cho 1-chrome, Chiyoda ku (Tel. 212-1016); – *Toa Domestic Airlines*, n° 18 Mori Bldg., 20, Shiba Nishikubo Akefune cho, Minato ku (Tel. 747-8111); – *UTA*, Room 412, Hibiya Park Bldg., Yurakucho 1-chrome, Chiyoda ku (Tel. 593-0773).

🏛 **Sea Travel:**
– From Ariake, 5mls (8km) *S* of Tokyo eki; bus): *Kinkai Yusen Ferry* to Nachi-Katsuura Kochi; – *Nihon Enkai Ferry* to Tomakomai. – From Takeshiba jetty, 2 mls (3 km) S, of Tokyo eki; 500 yds (500m) E of Hamamatsucho station: *Ogasawara Kisen* to Ogasawara (once a week); – *Oshima Unyu* to Amami Oshima, Okinawa; – *Tokai Steamship* to Oshima, Hachijo jima, Miyake jima, Shimoda.

Shipping lines: information at the Tourist Office. V. also Journey to Japan section.

🚆 **Rail:** headquarters of the national rail network (*Japanese National Railways*), Kokutetsu Bldg., 6-5, Marunouchi 1-chome, Chiyoda ku (Tel. 212-6311). – V. *Colour map inside back cover.* Among the many stations in Tokyo, the two largest are:
– *Tokyo station* (City centre; pl. E2, p. 571). *JNR*, Shinkansen to Fukuoka, Hiroshima, Kyoto, Osaka, etc.; other trains to Aomori, Atami, Chiba, Fukuoka, Fukushima, Hamada, Ito, Kagoshima, Kamogawa, Kumamoto, Nachi-Katsuura, Nagasaki, Narita, Niigata, Odawara, Ofuna, Ome, Omiya, Sasebo, Sendai, Shimoda, Shimonoseki, Shizuoka, Takao, Tamano, Tateyame, Yokosuka.
– *Ueno station* (Taito ku; pl. C2, p. 598): *JNR*, Shinkansen to Morioka, Sendai (via Omiya); other trains to Aizu Wakamatsu, Akita, Aomori,

Fukushima, Kanazawa, Karuizawa, Manza-Kajikazawaguchi, Morioka, Mito, Naoetsu, Niigata, Ome, Omiya, Sendai, Shibukawa, Takasaki, Tokyo, Toride, Utsunomiya, Yamagata.

Metro: it is essential to get a map from the Tourist Office. The 10 lines are easily recognized by colour and serve the whole city.
A few railway lines (JNR or private) complete the metropolitan network.

🚌 **Coaches:**
– From Seibu Shinjuku: to Karuizawa.
– From Shibuya: to Fujisawa, Nagano.
– From Shimbashi: to Hitachi.
– From Tokyo *(Tobu Center)*: to Aizu-Wakamatsu, Fukushima, Ikaho, Maebashi, Matsushima, Sendai.
– From Tokyo (*Yaesuguschi*): to Fujisawa, Hakone, Kobe, Kyoto, Miura, Nagoya, Osaka.

Taxis: radio-taxis (only in Japanese): *Nihon Kotsu* (Tel. 586–2151), *Kokusai* (Tel. 491–6001), *Daiwa* (Tel. 563–5151), *Hinomaru* (Tel. 814–1111).

🚗 **Car hire:** turn to Journey to Japan section (p. 30) for the addresses of hire companies.

Excursions: *Fujita* or *JTB* (in English), for one or several days to Nikko, Hakone, Kyoto, Inland Sea, Hiroshima, Beppu, Kyushu.

Tour of the city: half-days (morning or afternoon); commentary in English: leaves from major hotels; several tours at night.

Industrial tourism: a tour of businesses in Tokyo can be arranged by the *JTB* agency (Tues., Thurs., Fri.), V. address below.

Travel agencies: *American Express*, Toranomon, Mitsui Bldg., Kasumigaseki, Chiyoda ku (Tel. 502–4671); – *Fujita Travel Service*, Godo Bldg., 2–10, Ginza 6-chome, Chuo ku (Tel. 573–1011); – *Hankyu Express*, Express, 3rd Floor, Hankyu Kotsusha Bldg., 3–9, 3-chome, Shimbashi, Minato ku (Tel. 503–0211); *Imperial Household Agency,* Imperial Palace (Tel. 213–1111); – *JTB,* 6–4, Marunouchi 1-chome, Chiyoda ku (Tel. 284–7026); – *Kinki Nippon Tourist,* 19–2, Kanda Matsunago cho, Chiyoda ku (Tel. 255–7111); – *Nippon Travel Agency*, Shimbashi Ekimae Bldg., 20–15, Shimbashi 2-chome, Minato ku (Tel. 572–8181).

✉ **Post offices:** Main PO, 7–2, Marunouchi 2-chome, Chiyoda ku (Tel. 201–1561); – International PO, 3–3, Ote machi 2-chome, Chiyoda ku (Tel. 241–4877); – Telephone and telegram office (*Kokusai Denshin Denwa, KDD*), 5, 1-chome, Ote machi, Chiyoda ku (Tel. 270–5111).

Banks: *Bank of Indo-China*, 1–2, Akasaka 1-chome, Minato-ku (Tel. 582–0271); – Bank of Japan, 2–4, Nihombashi Hongoku cho 2-chome, Chuo ku (Tel. 279–1111); – *Bank of Tokyo*, 6–3, Nihombashi Hongoku cho 1-chome, Chuo ku (Tel. 245–1111); – *First*

National, 2-1, Ote machi 2-chome, Chiyoda ku (Tel. 279-5411). *Société Générale,* Hibiya, Chunichi Bldg., 1-3, Uchisaiwai cho 2-chome, Chiyoda ku (Tel. 503-9781).

Shopping:
The boutiques and large stores are open 6 days a week. They are grouped in the main commercial districts, each with its own speciality: *Haraijuku*: Japanese fashion; haute couture, ready-to-wear, antiques, accessories, etc.; – *Ginza*: luxury boutiques/pearls, silk; – *Shinjuku*: electrical, electronic and photographic goods; – *Akihabara*: cut-rate electronics.
There are also underground shopping precincts, notably the most interesting one under Tokyo station. The large stores have the advantage of having everything under one roof, thus avoiding any waste of time: crafts, ceramics (tea or sake services), clothes, kimonos, hi-fis, etc. Five stores are particularly well stocked: *Daimaru*, Tokyo Eki Bldg. (Tel. 212-8011; closed Weds.); – *Matsuya*, 3-6-1, Ginza, Chuo ku (Tel. 567-1211; closed Thurs.); – *Mitsukoshi*, 1-7-4, Nihombashi Muromachi (Tel. 241-3311; closed Monday); – *Odakyu*, 1-13, Nishi Shinjuku, Shinjuku ku (Tel. 342-1111; closed Thurs.); – *Takashimaya*, 2-4-1, Nihombashi, Chuo ku (Tel. 211-4111; closed Weds.) From the numerous speciality shops we give the following addresses: electrical or electronic goods: *Hirose Musen*, 1-10-5, Soto Kanda, Chiyoda ku (Tel. 255-2211); – *Laox*, 1-2-9, Soto Kanda, Chiyoda ku (Tel. 255-9041); – *Nishi Ginza Electric Center*, 2-1-1, Yuraku cho, Chiyoda ku (Tel. 501-5905); – *Yamagiwa Electric Co.*, 4-1-1, Soto Kanda, Chiyoda ku (Tel. 252-2111); cameras: *Doi Camera Co.*, 1-15-4, Nishi Shinjuku, Shinjuku ku (Tel. 344-23-10); – *Sakuraya*, 3-26-10, Shinjuku, Shinjuku ku (Tel. 352-4711); – *Yodobashi Camera Co.*, 3-26-8, Shinjuku, Shinjuku ku (Tel. 346-1511); crafts: *Bingoya*, 69 Wakamatsu cho, Shinjuku ku (Tel. 202-8778); – *Takumi craft shop*, 8-4-2, Ginza, Chuo ku (Tel. 571-2017); kimonos: *Erien*, 4-6-10, Ginza, Chuo-ku (Tel. 561-0860); – *Hayashi kimono store*, International Arcade, 2-1, Yuraku cho, Chiyoda ku (Tel. 501-4014). To take advantage of discount prices, go to the *Japan Taxfree Center* (kimonos, toys, photographic goods, pearls etc.), Toranomon 5-8-6, Minato ku (Tel. 432-4351).

Shows:
Noh theatre: *Ginza Hall*, 6-5-15, Ginza, Chuo ku (Tel. 571-0197); – *Kanze*, 1-16-4, Shoto, Shibuya ku (Tel. 469-5241); – *Kita*, 4-6-9, Kami Osaki, Shinagawa ku (Tel. 491-7773); – *Umewaka*, 2-6-14, Higashi Nakano, Nakano ku (Tel. 363-7748); – *Yarai*, 60, Yarai cho, Shinjuku ku (Tel. 268-7311); – *National Theatre*, 13, Hayabusa cho,

Chiyoda ku (Tel. 265–7411).
Kabuki theatre: *Kubuki za,*
4-3, Ginza Higashi, Chuo ku
(Tel. 541–3131); – *National
Theatre* (above).
Bunraku: *National Theatre.*
Western theatre: *Tokyo
Metropolitan Festival Hall,*
5-45, Ueno Koen
(Tel. 828–2111); *NHK Hall,* 2-
2-1 Jinna, Shibuya (Tel. 465–
1111); – *Hibiya Public Hall,*
1-1, Udagawa cho
(Tel. 463–5001); – *Yamaha
Hall,* 7-9-14, Ginza
(Tel. 572–3111); – *Bunkyo
Ward Hall,* 1-16-21, Kasuga
(Tel. 811–4076).

Night life:
The districts of Roppongi and
Shinjuku compete with those
of Ginza and Akasaka. If the
youth of Tokyo prefer the
bars and clubs of Shinjuku
and Roppongi, Ginza and
Akasaka have the smarter
establishments, often
frequented by business men
or Tokyo high society.

Music-hall, revues: *Tokyo
Takarazuka Theater,* 1-1-3,
Yuraku cho, Chiyoda ku
(Tel. 591–1211); – *Nichigeki
Music Hall,* 5th fl. Takarazuka
Theater, Yuraku cho, Chiyoda
ku (Tel. 501–6331).

Bars and pubs: *Kikansha*
(bar), 8-3-12, Ginza, Chuo ku
(Tel. 571–1345); – *Berni Inn*
(pub), KT Bldg., 3-16,
Akasaka Minato ku
(Tel. 580–3006); – *Nawanoren*
(pub), 7-22, Uchisaiwai cho,
1-chome, Chiyoda ku
(Tel. 508–9660); – *Lefty* (jazz-
bar), 3-35, Shinjuku, Shinjuku
ku (Tel. 354–2148); – *Lion*
(beer hall), 3-28, Shinjuku,
Shinjuku ku (Tel. 352–6606); –

Pub Chaya, 1st fl. Riccar
Bldg., Ginza (Tel. 571–3494).

Cabarets, night-clubs: *Club
Maiko* (geisha and maiko
show), 4th fl., Aster Plaza
Bldg., Ginza, Suzuran dori
(Tel. 574–7745); – *Mikado* (600
hostesses, several orchestras,
the largest cabaret in the
world), 2-14-6, Akasaka,
Minato ku (Tel. 583–1101); –
Copacabana (hostesses),
3-6-4, Akasaka, Minato ku
(Tel. 585–5811); – *Cordon
Bleu* (restaurant-cabaret;
French food), 6-6-4, Akasaka,
Minato ku (Tel. 582–7800); –
Club Misty (jazz), Roppongi,
4-chome (Tel. 402–7887); –
Monte-Carlo, 7-3, Ginza
Nishi, Chuo ku (Tel.
571–5671).

Discotheques: *Byblos* (the 'in'
disco of Tokyo), 3-8,
Akasaka, Minato ku
(Tel. 584–4484); *Chakras
Mandala* (young jet-set),
Square Bldg., 3-3, Roppongi,
Minato ku (Tel. 403–7655); –
Blue Shell (Caribbean style
for clientele 30–40 yrs.), 6th
fl., Roppongi Plaza Bldg.
(Tel. 479–1511); – *Galaxy,*
Social Bldg, 3-12-7, Akasaka,
Minato ku (Tel. 585–9871); –
Mugen, 3-8, Akasaka, Minato
ku (Tel. 584–4481); – *Mugen,*
18, Kabuki cho, Shinjuku ku
(Tel. 200–5642); – *Last Twenty
Cents,* 3-8-20, Roppongi,
Minatu ku (Tel. 403–0091); –
Zucchero, 1-1-5, Nishi
Azabu, Roppongi, Minato ku
(Tel. 403–6007).

Events: *Dezome shiki,* Fire
brigade parade, 6 Jan. at
Ginza; – *Kanda matsuri* from
14 to 16 May at Kanda
Myojin; – *Sanja matsuri,* 17

and 18 May, at Asakusa shrine; – *Sanno Festival*, 15 June, at Hie shrine; – *Oeshiki Festival*, 12 Oct. at Hommon ji.

Japanese Arts:

The **tea ceremony** is shown to foreigners, with lesson and demonstration, in the following places: *Sakura-kai* Shimo Ochiai 3-chome 2-25, Shinjuku ku (Tel. 951-9043); – *Tokyo an* (Imperial Hotel), 1-1-1, Uchisaiwai cho, Chiyoda ku (Tel. 504-1111); – *Chosho an* (Okura Hotel), 2-10-4, Toranomon, Minato ku Tel. 582-0111; – *Seisei an*, New Otani Hotel, 7th fl., Kioi cho 4-chome, Chiyoda ku (Tel. 265-1111).

Ikebana, a technique of flower arranging, is also the subject of demonstrations and courses by: *Ikenobo Ochanomizu Gakuin*, 2-3, Kanda Surugadai, Chiyoda ku (Tel. 291-9321); – *Sogetsuryu Ikebana School*, 7-2-21, Akasaka, Minato ku.

Sports:

sumo: *Kuramae Kokugikan*, 2-1-9, Kuramae, Taito ku (competitions in Jan., May and Sept.); – judo: *Kodo kan*, 1-16-30, Kasuga cho, Bunkyo ku; – kendo: *Metropolitan Police Board P.R. Center*, 3-5, Kyobashi, Chuo ku, – karate: *Nihon Karate Remmei So Hombu*, 4-14-12, Meguro, Meguro ku; – aikido: *Aikikai*, Shinjuku ku.

Cultural institutions:

Goethe Institut 5-56, Akasaka 7-chome Minato ku (Tel. 583-6369); – *Foreign Correspondent's Club*, Chiyoda Bldg. 1-2,

Marunouchi 2-chome, Chiyoda ku (Tel. 211-3161).

Embassies: *Belgium*, 5, Nibar cho, Chiyoda ku (Tel. 262-0191); – *Canada*, 3-38, Akasaka 7-chome, Minato ku (Tel. 408-2101); – *China*, 5-30, Minami Azabu 4-chome Minato ku (Tel. 403-3380); – *France* (embassy and consulate), 11-44, Minami Azabu 4-chome, Minato ku (Tel. 473-0171); – *Korea (South)*, 2-5, Minami Azabu 4-chome, Minato ku (Tel. 455-2601); – *Monaco* (consulate), Shin Kokusai Bldg., c/o Nihon Shokuhin Kako, 4-1, Marunouchi 3-chome, Chiyoda ku (Tel. 211-4994); – *Philippines* 6-15, Roppongi, 5-chome, Minato ku (Tel. 496-2731); – *Switzerland*, 9-12, Minami Azabu 5-chome, Minato ku (Tel. 473-0121); – *Thailand*, 14-6, Kamiosaki 3-chome, Shinagawa ku (Tel. 441-7352); – *USA*, 10-5, Akasaka 1-chome, Minato ku (Tel. 583-7141); – *USSR*, 1, Azabu Mamiana cho, Minato ku (Tel. 583-4224).

Places, sites and monuments
Akasaka, p. 580.
Akasaka Palace, p. 595.
Akihabara, p. 578.
Aoyama cemetery, p. 595.
Aoyama Palace, p. 595.
Arisugawa no miya Kinen koen, p. 592.
Asakusa Hongan ji, p. 618.
Atago jinja, p. 592.
Atago yama, p. 592.
Azabu, p. 592.
Bank of Japan, p. 580.
Bunko, p. 578.
Bunkyo ku, p. 601.
Catholic Church of Saint

TOMOKOMAI (Hokkaido),
p. 625.
Tel. 01442; ✉ 053.

Hotels:
** *Tomakomai*, 18, Omote machi
(Tel. 33-6121), 42 rms. (12
Jap.) ⑪ ▥ A/c ♨ 🏤 ☎ TV 📺
bar, hairdresser, boutique.
** *Tomakai Central*, 49, Futaba
cho (Tel. 2-9221), 19 rms. (1
Jap.), ⑪ ▥ A/c ♨ 🏤 ☎ TV

Business Hotel:
Okuni, 1-9-3, Shin Nakano
(Tel. 34-6441).

Youth hostel:
Utonaiko, Uenae
(Tel. 58-2153), 50 beds.

✈ **Airport:** Chitose, at 18 mls (29
km) NE. (V. Sapporo.)

⚓ **Sea travel:** *Nihon Enkai Ferry*,
to Tokyo; - *Taiheiyo enkai
Ferry*, to Nagoya, Sendai; -
other services to Hachnohe,
Oma.

🚂 **Rail:** *JNR* to Abashiri,
Asahikawa, Hakodate,
Kushiro, Muroran,
Oshamambe, Samani,
Sapporo. Toya.

☒ **Coaches:** to Chitose, Muroran, Noboribetsu, Sapporo, Shikotsu ko.

Tomioka (Gumma ken), p. 626.
Tomioka (Kumamoto ken), p. 645.
Tomo (V. Fukuyama), p. 189.
Tomoga shima, p. 653.
Tomuraushi Onsen, p. 156.
Tonosawa Onsen, p. 169.
Tonosho (V. Shodo shima), p. 549.
Tori jima, p. 475.
Toroko, p. 630.
Tosa, p. 627.
Tosa Shimizu (V. Ashizuri Uwakai), p. 133.
To shima, p. 271.
Toshita Onsen, p. 137.

TOTTORI (Tottori ken), p. 627.
Tel. Hamamura, (08578); Tottori (0857); ☒ Hamamura (689); Tottori (680).

[i] **Tourist Information Centre:** 1-220, Higashi machi (Tel. 26-7111).

Lodgings:

– At Tottori

Ryokan:
** *Kozeniya*, Eirakuonsen cho (Tel. 23-3311), 28 rms.

Business hotel:
Ohira, opposite JNR station, (Tel. 29-1111).

– At Hamamura Onsen, 12 mls (19 km) W.

Ryokans:
* *Tabakoya Bekkan*, Ketaka cho (Tel. 2-0211), 44 rms.
Hamanoya, Ketaka cho (Tel. 2-0321), 65 rms.

Restaurant:
National Kaikan (Jap. and West. food), 252, Eirakuonsen machi (Tel. 23-4141).

✈ **Airport:** (4 mls/7 km) NW (coach); *ANA* flights to Osaka.

₩ **Rail:** *JNR* to Fukuoka, Hamada, Kurayoshi, Okayama, Osaka, Tokyo, Wakasa, Yonago.

☒ **Coaches:** to Kurayoshi, Toyooka, Tsuyama.

TOWADA HACHIMANTAI (Akita, Aomori and Iwate ken; national park), p. 628.

Lodgings:

– At Yasumiya
Tel. 01765; ☒ 018-55.

Ryokan:
Miyago Kanko Hotel Bekkan, Towadako Yasumiya, Kosaka machi (Tel. 2101), 29 rms.

– At Yuze Onsen
Tel. 018624; ☒ 018-51.

Ryokans:
* *Himenoyu Hotel*, Yuze Onsen, Kazuno (Tel. 3-2011), 98 rms.
Yuze Hotel, Yuze Onsen, Kazuno (Tel. 3-2311), 80 rms.

– At Aomori and Morioka, V. under these place names.

Towada Minami, p. 629.
Towakda ko, p. 629.
Toya ko, p. 539.
Toyako Onsen (V. Shikotsu Toya), p. 539.

TOYAMA (Toyama ken), p. 630.
Tel. 0764; ☒ 930.

[i] **Tourist Information Centre:** 1-7, Shin Sogawa (Tel. 31-4111).

Hotels:
** *Meitetsu Toyama*, 1-18, Sakurabashi dori

(Tel. 31–8241), 42 rms (6 Jap.)
⊓ ▥ A/c 🛁 🛋 ☎ bar,
hairdresser, boutique,
bowling.

Ryokans:
*** *Kincharyo*, 3–19, Sakuragi
cho (Tel. 31–1108), 14 rms.
** *Ebitei Bekkan*, 9–21, Sakuragi
cho (Tel. 32–3181), 19 rms.
** *Sakasute*, 1–5–8, Marunouchi
(Tel. 41–4811), 19 rms.
** *Yoshihara*, 4–2, Uchisaiwai
cho (Tel. 32–0147), 30 rms.
* *Kawai Honkan*, 1–4–23, Chuo
dori (Tel. 21–8555), 21 rms.
* *Okudaya*, 3–11, Sakuragi cho
(Tel. 41–3601), 14 rms.

Business hotel:
Toyama Station, 1–4–1,
Takara cho (Tel. 32–4311),
61 rms.

Youth hostel:
Matsushita, Hamakurosaki
(Tel. 37–9010), 50 beds.

Restaurant:
Toichi (Jap. food), 10–2,
Shinsakura machi
(Tel. 41–7954).

✈ **Airport:** 4 mls (6 km) S
(coach): *ANA* flights to
Tokyo.

Airline: *All Nippon Airways*,
reservations (Tel. 32–2233).

🚄 **Rail:** *JNR* to Aomori,
Kanazawa, Nagoya, Niigata,
Osaka, Tokyo; – *Toyama
Chiho Railway*, to Kamiichi,
Sasazu, Senjugahara.

🚌 **Coaches:** to Himi, Kanazawa,
Kurobe, Yatsuo.

Toyohama, p. 207.

TOYOHASHI (Aichi ken),
p. 631.
Tel. Irako (05313); Toyohashi
(0532); ✉ Irako (441–36);
Toyohashi (441).

Lodgings:
– At Toyoshashi

Hotel:
*** *Toyohashi Grand*, 2–48,
Ekimae Odori (Tel. 55–6221;
telex 04322–117), 39 rms. ⊓
▥ A/c 🛁 🛋 ☎ 📺 📻 bar,
hairdresser, boutique.

Business hotel:
Toyohashi, 12, Hanazono cho
(Tel. 55–9222).

– At Irako, 29 mls (46 km)
SW.

Ryokan:
*** *Irako View*, Irako, Atsumi cho
(Tel. 5–6111), 159 rms.

🚄 **Rail:** *JNR, Shinkansen* to
Fukuoka, Okayama, Osaka,
Tokyo; other trains to Iida,
Matsumoto, Nachi Katsuura,
Nagasaki, Osaka, Sasebo,
Shizuoka, Tokyo; – *Nagoya
Railroad (Meitetsu),* to Gifu,
Nagoya; – *Toyohashi Railway*,
to Mikawa Tahara.

🚌 **Coaches:** to Atsumi, Gamagori, Hamamatsu, Toyokawa.

Toyooka (V. San in Kaigan),
p. 522.
Toyotomi, p. 654.
Toyotomi Onsen, p. 654.

TSU (Mie ken), p. 632.

ℹ️ **Tourist Information Centre:**
13, Komei cho (Tel. 26–111).

Business hotel:
Tsu, 2087–7, Nishiura Tose
(Tel. 26–4141), 50 rms.

Restaurants:
** *Uchikitei* (sukiyaki), 6–18,
Chuo (Tel. 28–7135).
* *Seigetsu* (Jap. food), 16–10,
Otobe (Tel. 28–0151).

🚄 **Rail:** *JNR* to Kii Tanabe,
Kyoto, Nachi, Katsuura,

Nagoya, Osaka, Toba, Tokyo; – *Kinki Nippon Railway (Kintetsu)*, to Kashikojima, Nagoya.

🚌 **Coaches:** to Ise, Kameyama, Ueno, Yokkaichi.

TSURUGA (Fukui ken), p. 634.
Tel. 07702; ✉ 914.

Ryokans:
*** *Kanko Hotel*, 2-8, Kawasaki cho (Tel. 2-0063), 34 rms.
** *Kitaguni Grand Hotel*, 80-1-3, Naka, Tsuruga shi (Tel. 2-4551), 38 rms.

⚓ **Sea travel:** to Otaru.

🚄 **Rail:** *JNR* to Aomori, Kanazawa, Nagoya, Niigata, Osaka, Toyama, Toyooka.

🚌 **Coaches:** to Fukui, Imazu, Nagahama, Obama.

TSURUOKA (Yamagata ken), p. 636.
Tel: Atsumi (023542); Tsuruoka (0235); Yunohama, (023572); ✉ Atsumin (999–72); Tsuruoka (997); Yunohama (997–12).

Lodgings:

– At Tsuruoka

Business hotel:
Sanno Plaza, 6-8, Sanno cho

(Tel. 22–6501), 109 rms.

– At Atsumi, 19 mls (31 km) SW.

Ryokan:
* *Bankokuya Banraikaku*, Atsumi Onsen (Tel. 3333), 85 rms.

– At Yunohama, 6 mls (15 km) NW.

Ryokans:
** *Takeya Hotel*, Yunohama Onsen (Tel. 2031), 53 rms.
* *Miyakoya Hotel*, Yunohama Onsen (Tel. 2101), 42 rms.
New Yunohama Hotel, Yunohama Onsen (Tel. 2021), 19 rms.

Restaurants:
** *Palace Kakuryo* (Jap. food), 1, Aza Hirono, Oaza Hondashi (Tel. 24–8800).
* *El Sun* (Jap. food), 11–63, Baba machi (Tel. 22–1400).

🚄 **Rail:** *JNR* to Aomori, Niigata, Osaka; – private line to Yunohama.

🚌 **Coaches:** to Atsumi, Sakata, Yamagata.

TSUYAMA (Okayama ken), p. 637.
Tel. Okutsu (08685); Tsuyama (0868); ✉ Okutsu (708–05); Tsuyama (706).

Lodgings:

– At Okutsu Onsen, 20 mls (32 km) NW.

Ryokans:
* *Okutsu Kanko Hotel*, Okutsu cho, Tomada gun (Tel. 2-0221), 26 rms.
Kajikaen, Okutsu cho,

Tomada gun (Tel. 2–0121), 29 rms.

🚆 **Rail:** *JNR* to Himeji, Niimi, Okayama, Tottori.

🚌 **Coaches:** to Kurayoshi, Okayama.

U

Ubako, p. 170.

UBE (Yamaguchi ken), p. 639. Tel. 0386; ✉ 755.

Ryokan:
Kawacho, Chuo cho (Tel. 31–1212), 21 rms.

Youth hostel:
Ube, Takahata, Kami Ube (Tel. 21–3613), 80 beds.

✈ **Airport:** at 2 mls (3 km) S (coach); – *ANA* flights to Tokyo, *TDA* flights to Osaka.

Airlines: *All Nippon Airways*, reservations (Tel. 31–8131); – *Toa Domestic Airlines*, reservations (Tel. 31–7331).

🚆 **Rail:** *JNR* to Fukuoka, Hiroshima, Kitakyushu Yamaguchi.

🚌 **Coaches:** to Shimonoseki, Yamaguchi.

Uchi (bay), p. 132.
Uchinada, p. 300.
Uchinami, p. 549.
Uchino, p. 453.
Uchinoura, p. 301.
Uchiura, p. 651.
Ueno, p. 639.
Uenohara kogen, p. 399.
Ugata, p. 265.

UJI (Kyoto fu), p. 640. Tel 0774; ✉ 611.

Ryokans:
*** *Seizanso Hotel*, Uji (Tel. 21–2181), 28 rms.

** *Hanayashiki Ukufuneen*, Uji (Tel. 21–2126), 39 rms.

🚆 **Rail:**
Uji station: *JNR* to Kyoto, Nara, Oji, Osaka, Shirahama. Keihan Uji station: *Keihan Electric Railway*, to Chushojima, Kyoto.

🚌 **Coaches:** to Kyoto, Nara, Osaka.

Events: Cormorant fishing, on Uji gawa, in summer.

Ukegawa, p. 676.
Umagaeshi, p. 463.
Uno, p. 559.
Uno ike, p. 207.
Unzen (V. Unzen Amakusa), p. 644.

UNZEN AMAKUSA (Kumamoto and Nagasaki ken; national park), p. 642.

Lodgings:

– At Hondo
Tel. 09692; ✉ 863.

Youth hostel:
Amakusa, 180, Hondo cho (Tel. 2–3085), 60 beds.

– At Isahaya
Tel. 09572; ✉ 854.

Ryokan:
* *Isahaya Kanko Hotel,* Kanaya machi (Tel. 2–3360), 49 rms.

– At Misumi
Tel. 096452; ✉ 869-32

Ryokan:
*** *Amakusa Pearl Line Hotel*, Misumi machi, Uto gun (Tel. 2605) 32 rms.

– At Shimabara
Tel. 09576; ✉ 855.

Youth hostel:
7938, Shimo Kawashiri machi (Tel. 2–4451), 60 beds.

– At Unzen
Tel. 095773; ⊠ 854-06

Hotel:
** *Unzen Kanko Hotel*, Obama cho, Minami Takaki gun (Tel. 3263), 65 rms. (11 Jap.) ¶ ▥ A/c ⌸ ☎ TV ♠ ♨/18 ⚓ P bar, Jap. com. bath.

Ryokans:
*** *Fukiya*, Obama machi, Minami Takaki gun (Tel. 3211), 90 rms.
** *Yumoto Hotel*, 316, Obama machi, Minami Takaki gun (Tel. 3255), 72 rms.
** *Hotel Toyokan*, 128, Obama machi, Minami Takaki gun (Tel. 3243), 130 rms.
* *Kyushu Hotel*, 320, Obama machi, Minami Takaki gun (Tel. 3234), 106 rms.

Youth hostel:
Seiun so, 500-1, Obama cho, Minami Takaki gun (Tel. 3273), 300 beds.

Tel. 0286.

Ⓘ **Tourist Information Centre,** 504, Hanawada machi (Tel. 23-3209).

Hotel:
** *Utsunomiya Royal*, 11-16, Eno machi (Tel. 34-2401), 139 rms. ¶ ▥ A/c ⌸ ⌸ ☎ TV P boutiques.

Business hotel:
Maruji, 1-22, Izumi cho (Tel. 21-2211).

�}🚃 **Rail:**
Utsunomiya station: *JNR, Shinkansen* to Morioka, Tokyo; other trains to Aizu-Wakamatsu, Akita, Aomori, Morioka, Nikko, Sendai, Tokyo, Yamagata.
Tobu Utsunomiya station: *Tobu Railway*, to Tokyo.

🚍 **Coaches:** to Mito, Nikko, Tochigi.

UWAJIMA (Ehime ken), p. 649.
Tel. 0985; ⊠ 798.

Ryokan:
* *Jonanso*, 1-12, Hirokoji (Tel. 22-4888), 20 rms.

Business hotel:
Uwajima Daichi, 1-3-9, Chuo cho (Tel. 25-0001).

Youth hostel:
Uwajima, Atago koen (Tel. 22-7177), 80 beds.

⚓ **Sea travel:** to Beppu, Yawatahama.

🚃 **Rail:** *JNR* to Ekawasaki, Takamatsu.

🚍 **Coaches:** to Matsuyama, Ozu, Sukumo, Yawatahama.

Events: *Fisherman's festival* 23 and 24 Jul.; – procession of 'giant ox' (*Ushi doni*) 28 and 29 Oct.; – *bullfights (togyu)* in summer.

Uzen Oyama, p. 636.

W

WAJIMA (Ishikawa ken),
p. 650.
Tel. 07682; ⊠ 928.

Minshuku:
Hakutoen, Kawai cho, Wajima
shi (Tel. 22-2178), 11 rms.
Shintani, Shinbashi dori,
Wajima shi (Tel. 22-0807),
7 rms.

Rail: *JNR* to Kanazawa.

Coaches: to Hakui, Nanao,
Suzu.

Excursions: around Noto
peninsula.

Specialities: *wajima nuri*,
lacquerware, shells.

Wakamatsu, p. 314.
Wakamiya Onsen, p. 428.
Wakasa sotomo, p. 469.

WAKAYAMA (Wakayama
ken), p. 651.
Tel. 0734; ⊠ 640 and 641.

 Tourist Information Centre:
1-1, Komatsubara dori
(Tel. 23-6111).

Ryokans:
*** *Kitamuraso*, 80, Tano
(Tel. 44-0101), 86 rms.
** *Aoikan*, 13, Juniban cho
(Tel. 31-3231), 25 rms.
** *Futagojimaso*, 599, Saikazaki
(Tel. 44-1145), 54 rms.
** *Seaside Hotel Kancho*, 82,
Tano (Tel. 44-0111), 31 rms.
** *Shinwakanoura Kanko Hotel*,
1482, Wakaura (Tel. 44-1121),
57 rms.
* *Azumaya Seaside Hotel*, 141,
Kada (Tel. 59-0015), 33 rms.
* *Okatokuro*, 1482, Wakaura
(Tel. 44-0151), 54 rms.

Bokairo, 1482, Wakaura
(Tel. 44-0114), 30 rms.
Furokan, 1679, Furoen,
Wakaura (Tel. 44-0141),
12 rms.
Nampu Hotel, 1817, Saikazaki
(Tel. 44-1504), 28 rms.

Restaurants:
** *Daiyoshi* (Jap. food), 7, Urata
machi, Kitano Shinchi
(Tel. 31-1888).
** *Hontorimatsu* (Jap. food),
2-17, Tomoda cho
(Tel. 22-0089).
* *Fuji* (Jap. and West. food),
Nokyo Bldg., 5-1, Misono cho
(Tel. 23-1238).
* *Suiyoken* (Jap. food), 5-12-1,
Misono machi (Tel. 24-3141).

 Sea travel: to Komatsushima.

 Rail:
Wakayama station (main):
JNR to Nagoya, Osaka,
Shingu, Shirahama, Toba; -
private line to Kishigawa.
Wakayamishi station: *JNR* to
Oji, Osaka, Toba; - *Nankai
Electric Railway*, to Lada,
Mizunoki, Osaka.

 Coaches: to Hashimoto,
Kainan.

WAKKANAI (Hokkaido),
p. 653.
Tel. 01622; ⊠ 097.

Business hotel:
Sun Hotel, 710, Chuo
3-chome (Tel. 2-5311),
53 rms.

Minshuku:
Noshappu, 2, Noshappu,
Wakkanai shi (Tel. 3-2203),
10 rms.

Youth hostel:
5-8-18, Hourai (Tel. 23-7333),
40 beds.

✈ **Airport:** Koetoi, at 7 mls (12

km) E (coach); *TDA* flights to Sapporo.

Airline: *Toa Domestic Airlines*, reservations (Tel. 2-4524).

🛇 **Sea travel:** to Rebun and Rishiri.

🚌 **Rail:** *JNR* to Asahikawa, Esashi, Hakodata, Sapporo.

🚌 **Coaches:** to Esashi.

Wakura Onsen, p. 427.
Washisaki, p. 512.

Y

Yabi Hita Hikosan (regional park), p. 223.
Yaba kei, p. 223.
Yaegaki jinja, p. 394.

YAEYAMA SHOTO (Okinawa), p. 655.
Tel. Ishigaki (09808); ✉ Ishigaki (907).

Hotels:
***   *Cavilla*, 934-4, Kawahira, Ishigaki (Tel. 2229), 12 rms., ¶ ▦ A/c ▦ ▦ ▦ P bar.
***   *Sun Coast*, 1-354, Maeri Ishigaki shi, 117 rms. ¶ ▦ A/c ▦ ☎ TV ▦ ▪/⁹ P bar, boutiques.

Ryokan:
**   *Hotel Miyahira*, 4-9, Misaki cho, Ishigaki (Tel. 2-6111), 92 rms.

Youth hostel:
Ishigaki Shi Tei, 287, Shinkawa, Ishigaki (Tel. 2720), 13 beds.

✈ **Airports:** Ishigaki; *Swal* flights to Miyako, Okinawa, Yonakuni; – Yonakuni; *Swal* flights to Ishigaki.

🛇 **Sea travel:**
– From Ishigaki: to Tarama jima, Miyako jima, Okinawa Iriomote jima, Yonakuni jima.
– From Iriomote: to Ishigaki.
– From Yonakuni: to Ishigaki jima.

Specialities: pineapple, coral, weaving, pottery, bingata.

Events: *Mamidoma* dances at Taketomi jima.

Yagen Onsen, p. 409.
Yahata, p. 313.
Yahiko, p. 453.
Yakeyama, p. 630.
Yaku shima (V. Osumi shoto), p. 503.
Yamada (Iwate ken), p. 510.
Yamada (Okinawa), p. 484.
Yamada Onsen, p. 510.
Yamadera, p. 657.

YAMAGATA (Yamagata ken), p. 656.
Tel. Yamagata (0236); Zao Onsen (023694); ✉ Yamagata (990); Zao Onsen (990-23).

ℹ **Tourist Information Centre,** 3-4-51, Hagato machi (Tel. 31-1111).

Lodgings:

– At Yamagata

Hotels:
***   *Onuma*, 2-1-10, Kojirakawa machi (Tel. 23-4143), 72 rms. ¶ ▦ A/c ▦ ▦ ☎ TV ❀ P bar, hairdresser, boutiques, conf. rm. (300 seats).
***   *Yamagata Grand*, 1-7-42, Hon cho (Tel. 41-2611), 79 rms. (3 Jap.) ¶ ▦ A/c ▦ ▦ ☎ TV ❀ ▦ bar, hairdresser, boutiques, conf. rm. (300 seats).

Business hotels:
Sakaiya, 1-4-10, Kasumi cho (Tel. 32-2311).
Green, 1-3-12, Kasumi cho (Tel. 22-2636).

Youth hostel:
Yamagata ken, Kyoiku kaikan, 12-37, Kinomi machi (Tel. 31-2953), 60 beds.

- At Zao Onsen, 11 mls (18 km) SE.

Ryokans:
** *Hotel Zao*, 963, Yuiri (Tel. 94-9191), 55 rms.
** *Hotel Jurin*, 814, Uwanodai (Tel. 94-9511), 30 rms.

Minshuku:
Ohira Sanso, 1118-1, Sando gawa (Tel. 94-9137), 14 rms.

Restaurants:
** *Kishokaku* (Jap. food), 2-8-81, Yakushi machi (Tel. 31-3644).
* *Mimasu* (Jap. and West. food), 2-3-7, Nanoka machi (Tel. 32-1252).

✈ **Airport:** Higashime, 14 mls (22 km) N; coach; *ANA* flights to Tokyo.

Airlines: *All Nippon Airways*, reservations (Tel. 32-0702).

🚄 **Rail:** *JNR* to Akita, Aomori, Oe, Sendai, Tokyo.

🚌 **Coaches:** to Fukushima, Sendai, Tsuruoka, Yonezawa.

Travel agency: *JTB*, c/o Yamagata Grand Hotel, 1 Hon machi (Tel. 23-6633).

Winter sports: at Zao zan, 11 mls (18 km) SE.

Yamagawa, p. 238.

YAMAGUCHI (Yamaguchi ken), p. 657.
Tel. Shuho (08376); Yamaguchi (0839); ✉ 753.

ⓘ **Tourist Information Centre**, 1-1, Taki machi (Tel. 2-3111).

Lodgings:

- At Yamaguchi

Ryokans:
*** *Matsudaya Hotel*, 3-6-7, Yuda Onsen (Tel. 22-0125), 40 rms.
** *Mizuno*, 4-1-5, Yuda Onsen (Tel. 22-0044), 83 rms.
* *Kamefuku Bekkan*, 4-7-1, Yuda Onsen (Tel. 22-2090), 33 rms.
Sansuien, 4-60, Midori cho (Tel. 22-0560), 15 rms.

- At Shuho, 17 mls (27 km) NW.

Youth hostel:
Akiyoshidai, Akiyoshi, Shuho cho, Mine gun (Tel. 2-0341), 150 beds.

🚄 **Rail:** *JNR*, Shinkansen station at Ogori, 7 mls (11 km) SW. Yamaguchi station: *JNR* to Masuda, Onoda.

🚌 **Coaches:** to Fukuoka, Hagi, Hofu, Mine, Ube.

Yofuke, p. 484.
Yoichi, p. 504.
Yokawa, p. 385.

YOKKAICHI (Mie ken),
p. 661.
Tel: Yokkaichi (0593);
Yunoyama (059392); ✉
Yokkaichi (510); Yunoyama
(510–12).

Lodgings:

– At Yokkaichai

Hotel:
** *Yokkaichi Miyako*, 7-3, Nishi
Shinchi (Tel. 52-4131), 177
rms. (4 Jap.) ¶ ▥ A/c ♨ ⌂
☎ TV P.

Business hotel:
Shin Yokkaichi, 5-3, Hamada
cho (Tel. 52-6181).

– At Yunoyama Onsen, 12 mls
(19 km) W.

Ryokans:
*** *Kotobukitei*, Yunoyama Onse,
Komono cho (Tel. 2-2131),
47 rms.
* *Grand Hotel Koyo*, Yunoyama
Onsen, Komono cho
(Tel. 2-3135), 33 rms.

♨ **Sea travel:** *Meimon Car Ferry*,
to Kitakyushu, Nagoya.

🚂 **Rail:** *JNR* to Kushimoto,
Katsuura, Osaka, Shingu,
Tanabe, Tokyo; – *Kinki
Nippon Electric Railway
(Kintetsu),* to Fujiwara,
Himaga, Kashikojima,
Nagoya, Yunoyama.

🚌 **Coaches:** to Nagoya,
Kameyama.

Yokogoshi, p. 453.

YOKOHAMA (Kanagawa
ken), p. 662.
Tel. 045; ✉ 231.

ℹ **Tourist Information Centre,**
1, Yamashita cho, Naka ku
(Tel. 681-0007).

Hotels:
*** *New Grand*, 10, Yamashita
cho, Naka ku (Tel. 681-1841),
197 rms. ¶ ▥ A/c ♨ ⌂ ☎ TV
≈ 🖼 bar, hairdresser,
boutiques.
*** *Yokohama Prince*, 3-13-1,
Isogo, Isogo ku
(Tel. 753-221), 37 rms. (1
Jap.) ¶ ▥ A/c ♨ ⌂ ☎ TV ☀
≈ ⚓/¹⁸ P bar, boutiques.
*** *Yokohama Tokyo*, 1-1-12,
Minami Saiwai cho, Nishi ku
(Tel. 311-1682; telex
3882-264), 219 rms. ¶ ▥ A/c
♨ ⌂ ☎ TV P bar, boutiques.
** *Aster*, 87, Yamashita cho,
Naka ku (Tel. 651-0141), 74
rms. (10 Jap.) ¶ ▥ A/c ♨ ⌂
☎ TV bar, hairdresser.
** *Empire*, 700, Matano cho,
Totsuka ku (Tel. 851-1431), 63
rms. ¶ ▥ A/c ♨ ⌂ ☎ TV ☀
≈ P boutiques, bowling.
** *Shin Yokohama*, 3672,
Shinohara cho, Kohoku ku
(Tel. 471-6011), 51 rms. (12
Jap.) ¶ ▥ A/c ♨ ⌂ ☎ TV 🖼
hairdresser.

Business hotels:
New Otani Inn Yokohama,
4-81, Sueyoshi cho, Naku ku
(Tel. 252-1311).
Central Inn Yokohama, 4-117,
Isezaki cho, Naka ku
(Tel. 251-1010).

Youth hostel: *Kanagawa*,
1, Momijigaoka, Nishi ku
(Tel. 241-6503), 60 beds.

Restaurants:
** *Kaori* (West. food), 70,
Yamashita cho, Naka ku
(Tel. 681-4401).
* *Kokonotsuido* (Jap. food),
1319, Taya machi, Totsuka ku
(Tel. 851-6121).
* *Kawara Golden* (shabu-

shabu, yakitori), Sakuragi cho, Golden Center 6 F (Tel. 201-4184).

✈ **Airport:** Narita international airport (V. Tokyo): – A bus service (*Limousine Bus Service*) supplies a direct link from Yokohama to Narita leaving from YCAT (Yokohama City Air Terminal) near the east exit of the main station, 2h journey.

Airlines: *All Nippon Airways*, 39, Tokiwa machi 4-chome, Naka ku (Tel. 641-2051); – *Japan Air Lines*, Sotetsu Bldg, 1-3-23, Kitasaiwai 1-chome, Nishi ku (Tel. 311-5522).

⚓ **Sea travel:** from Takashima jetty to Kisarazu; – from Yamashita jetty to Futtsu; – from south jetty (*Osambashi*), international service to Nakhodka (USSR).

Shipping lines: information at tourist office.

🚄 **Rail:**
– Shin Yokohama station: *JNR*, Shinkansen to Fukuoka, Osaka, Tokyo; other trains to Hachioji, Isogo.
– Yokohama station: *JNR* to Fukuoka, Hachioji, Hamada, Isogo, Kagoshima, Kumamoto, Nachi Katsuura, Nagasaki, Odawara, Ofuna, Omiya, Shimoda, Shimonoseki, Shizuoka, Tamano, Tokyo; – *Keihin Kyuko Electric Railway*, to Miura, Tokyo, Yokosuka, Zushi; – *Sagami Railroad*, to Atsugi; – *Tokyo Kyuko Electric Railway (Tokyu)*, to Sakuragicho, Tokyo.
– Isogo station: *JNR* to

Hachioji, Ofuna, Omiya.
– Sakuragicho station: *JNR* to Hachioji, Isogo, Ofuna, Omiya; – *Tokyu ER*, to Tokyo and Kamioka.
– Tsurumi station: *JNR* to Ofuna, Ogimachi, Okawa, Omiya, Umi-Shibaura.

Metro: from Chojamachi to Kamioka.

🚌 **Coaches:** to Fujisawa. Kamakura, Yokosuka, Narita.

🚗 **Car hire:** *Nippon*, Hama Bowl, 2-2-14, Kita, Nishi Ku (Tel. 311-0921).

Travel agency: *JTB*, 75, Aioi cho, 4-chome, Naka ku (Tel. 681-7541).

Banks: *Bank of Japan*, 20-1, Nihon Odori, Naka ku (Tel. 651-2601); – *Bank of Tokyo*, 27-1, Hon cho, 3-chome, Naka ku (Tel. 201-6971); – *Mitsubishi*, 41, Moto machi 4-chome, Naka ku (Tel. 211-2231); – *Mitsui*, 20, Moto machi 2-chome, Naka ku (Tel. 211-0031); – *Sumimoto*, 3-10 Hagoromo cho, 1-chome, Naka ku (Tel. 251-5541).

Specialities: silk, lacquerware, ivory goods, tortoiseshell.

Shopping:
There are three main commercial districts. Around Yokohama station are large stores (*Takashimaya Mitsukoshi*) and shopping centres: *Soketsu Joinus* and especially *Lumine* (8 floors full of shops and restaurants; one can buy everything in the same building). Motomachi district near Ishikawacho station is a smart area for shopping, a commercial

street with fashionable shops (objets d'art, antiques, clothes). Kannai station district has about 500 shops, used more by the local population than by the tourist (*Isezakicho* commercial centre).

Night life: cabarets and bars, Chin. restaurants in China Town.

Events: *Port festival*, in mid-May; – *Festival of the 'Black Boats'* 14 Jul.

Japanese arts: *Ikebana* and *chanoyu (tea ceremony) lessons at Yokohama Academy*, 3–32, Tsuruya cho, 4 Kanagawa ku (Tel. 311–5361).

Yokonami sanri, p. 627.

YOKOSUKA (Kanagawa ken), p. 669.
Tel. 0468.

Hotel:
** *Yokosuka*, 2–7, Yonegahama dori (Tel. 25–1111), 66 rms. ¶¶ ▥ A/c 🛁 ☎ TV P .

Youth hostel:
Kannonzaki, 1320, Kamoi (Tel. 41–1345), 50 beds.

⚓ **Sea travel:**
– From Yokosuka: to Osawa.
– From Kurihama, 6 mls (9 km) SE; coach: to Kanaya.
– From Uraga, 4 mls (7 km) SE; train: Keihin Kyuko ER; *Tokyowan Ferry*, to Kanaya.

🚃 **Rail:**
– Yokosuka station: *JNR* to Kurihama, Tokyo.
– Yokosuka Chuo station: *Keihin Kyuko Electric Railway*, to Kurihama, Tokyo, Uraga.

🚌 **Coaches:** to Fujisawa, Miura, Yokohama.

Specialities: seaweed growing.

Yonabara, p. 484.

YONAGO (Tottori ken), p. 670.
Tel. 0859; ✉ 683.

Hotel:
** *Yonago Kokusai*, 2–11, Kamo cho (Tel. 33–6611), 74 rms. (3 Jap.) ¶¶ ▥ A/c 🛁 🅰 ☎ TV ▱ 🖼 bar, boutiques, Jap. com. bath.

Ryokans:
*** *Kaike Gyoen*, Kaike Onsen (Tel. 33–3531), 106 rms.
** *Shofukaku*, Kaike Onsen (Tel. 22–4126), 51 rms.
* *Hisagoya*, Kaike Onsen (Tel. 22–2248), 31 rms.

Restaurant:
* *Victoria* (Jap. and Chin. food), 1–168, Kakuban cho (Tel. 22–6450).

✈ **Airport:** Yonago 6 mls (10 km) NW; coach: – *ANA* flights to Tokyo; *TDA* flights to Oki shoto, Osaka.

Airlines: *All Nippon Airways*, reservations (Tel. 22–9671); – *Toa Domestic Airlines*, reservations (Tel. 28–7161).

🚃 **Rail:** *JNR* to Fukuoka, Hamada, Izumo, Kyoto, Masuda, Okayama, Osaka, Sakaiminato, Tokyo.

Coaches: to Kurayoshi, Matsue, Sakaiminato, Tottori.

🚌 **Excursions:** to Mount Daisen.

Yonagusuku, p. 486.
Yonakuni jima, p. 656.

YONEZAWA (Yamagata ken), p. 671.

Tel. 0238; ✉ 992–14.

Ryokans:
* *Azuma Kanko Hotel*, Shirabu Onsen (Tel. 55-3141), 21 rms.
* *Hotel Yamakawa*, Onogawa machi (Tel. 32-2811), 27 rms.
Tengendai Hotel, Sumomoyama (Tel. 55-2231), 26 rms.

Business hotel:
Yonezawa Green, 1-13-23, Chuo (Tel. 23-3690).

Rail: *JNR* to Akita, Arato, Niigata, Tokyo, Tamagata.

Coaches: to Fukushima, Inawashiro, Kitakata, Nagai, Yamagata.

YOSHINO KUMANO (Mie, Nara and Wakayama ken; national park), p. 674.

Lodgings:
– At Kumano
Tel. 05978; ✉ 519–51

Ryokans:
*** *Grand Hotel Kumano Orange*, Kushiya cho (Tel. 9-2821), 69 rms.

– At Kushimoto
Tel. 07356, ✉ 649–35.

Hotel:
** *Kushimoto Urashima*, 2300-1, Hon cho, Nishi Muro gun (Tel. 2-1011), 138 rms. ⚏ ▥ A/c ⚎ ⚌ ☎ TV ☀ ▨ ⚬ P bar, bowling, Jap. com. bath.

Youth hostel:
Shionomisaki, 2843-1, Shionomisaki, Kushimoto cho, Nishi Muro gun (Tel. 2-0570), 56 beds.

– At Nii Katsuura
Tel. 0735; ✉ 649–53.

Ryokans:
*** *Koshinoyu*, 1108, Yukawa, higashi Muro gun (Tel. 2-1414) 105 rms.
** *Nakanoshima*, 1179-9, Katsuura cho, Higashi Muro gun (Tel. 2-1111), 161 rms.

Youth hostel:
Nachi, Hamanomiya (Tel. 2-0584), 50 beds.

– At Owase Tel. 05972; ✉ 519–36.

Business hotel:
Phoenix, 5-25, Sakae cho (Tel. 2-8111).

– At Shingu
Tel. 0735; ✉ 647.

Business hotel:
Station Hotel, 7031-1, Ekimae (Tel. 21-2200).

Youth hostel:
Shin gu, 1-9, 1-chome Kami Hon machi (Tel. 2-2309), 30 beds.

ZUSHI (Kanagawa ken), p. 679.
Tel. 0468

Hotel:
** *Zushi Nagisa*, 2-10-18, Shinjuku (Tel. 71-4260), 25 rms. (5 Jap.) ¶ ▥ A/c ▨ ☎ TV ⚓ P .

Ryokan:
** *Shindo Tei*, 2-10-3, Zushi (Tel. 71-2012) *exceptional food (spec.: wild boar).

🚆 **Rail:** Zushi station: *JNR* to Tokyo, Yokosuka. Zushikaigan station: *Keihin Kyuko Electric Railway*, to Tokyo.

🚌 **Coaches:** to Fujisawa, Kamakura, Miura, Yokohama, Yokosuka.